LET'S GO
Austria
Switzerland

"Lighthearted and sophisticated, informative and fun to read. *[Let's Go]* helps the novice traveler navigate like a knowledgeable old hand."
—*Atlanta Journal-Constitution*

"The guides are aimed not only at young budget travelers but at the independent traveler, a sort of streetwise cookbook for traveling alone."
—*The New York Times*

■ Let's Go writers travel on your budget.

"Retains the spirit of the student-written publication it is: candid, opinionated, resourceful, amusing info for the traveler of limited means but broad curiosity."
—*Mademoiselle*

"The writers seem to have experienced every rooster-packed bus and lunar-surfaced mattress about which they write."
—*The New York Times*

"All the dirt, dirt cheap."
—*People*

■ Great for independent travelers.

"A world-wise traveling companion—always ready with friendly advice and helpful hints, all sprinkled with a bit of wit."
—*The Philadelphia Inquirer*

"Lots of valuable information for any independent traveler."
—*The Chicago Tribune*

■ Let's Go is completely revised each year.

"Unbeatable: good sight-seeing advice; up-to-date info on restaurants, hotels, and inns; a commitment to money-saving travel; and a wry style that brightens nearly every page."
—*The Washington Post*

"Its yearly revision by a new crop of Harvard students makes it as valuable as ever."
—*The New York Times*

■ All the important information you need.

"Enough information to satisfy even the most demanding of budget travelers...*Let's Go* follows the creed that you don't have to toss your life's savings to the wind to travel—unless you want to."
—*The Salt Lake Tribune*

"Value-packed, unbeatable, accurate, and comprehensive."
—*The Los Angeles Times*

Let's Go Publications

Let's Go: Alaska & the Pacific Northwest 1998
Let's Go: Australia 1998 **New title!**
Let's Go: Austria & Switzerland 1998
Let's Go: Britain & Ireland 1998
Let's Go: California 1998
Let's Go: Central America 1998
Let's Go: Eastern Europe 1998
Let's Go: Ecuador & the Galápagos Islands 1998
Let's Go: Europe 1998
Let's Go: France 1998
Let's Go: Germany 1998
Let's Go: Greece & Turkey 1998
Let's Go: India & Nepal 1998
Let's Go: Ireland 1998
Let's Go: Israel & Egypt 1998
Let's Go: Italy 1998
Let's Go: London 1998
Let's Go: Mexico 1998
Let's Go: New York City 1998
Let's Go: New Zealand 1998 **New title!**
Let's Go: Paris 1998
Let's Go: Rome 1998
Let's Go: Southeast Asia 1998
Let's Go: Spain & Portugal 1998
Let's Go: USA 1998
Let's Go: Washington, D.C. 1998

Let's Go Map Guides

Berlin	New Orleans
Boston	New York City
Chicago	Paris
London	Rome
Los Angeles	San Francisco
Madrid	Washington, D.C.

Coming Soon: Amsterdam, Florence

**Let's Go
Publications**

Let's Go
Austria
& Switzerland
1998

Lisa M. Nosal
Editor

Nicolas R. Rapold
Associate Editor

Macmillan

HELPING LET'S GO

If you want to share your discoveries, suggestions, or corrections, please drop us a line. We read every piece of correspondence, whether a postcard, a 10-page email, or a coconut. Please note that mail received after May 1998 may be too late for the 1999 book, but will be kept for future editions. **Address mail to:**

**Let's Go: Austria & Switzerland
67 Mount Auburn Street
Cambridge, MA 02138
USA**

Visit Let's Go at **http://www.letsgo.com,** or send email to:

**fanmail@letsgo.com
Subject: "Let's Go: Austria & Switzerland"**

In addition to the invaluable travel advice our readers share with us, many are kind enough to offer their services as researchers or editors. Unfortunately, our charter enables us to employ only currently enrolled Harvard-Radcliffe students.

Published in Great Britain 1998 by Macmillan, an imprint of Macmillan General Books, 25 Eccleston Place, London SW1W 9NF and Basingstoke.

Maps by David Lindroth copyright © 1998, 1997, 1996, 1995, 1994, 1993, 1992, 1991, 1990, 1989, 1988 by St. Martin's Press, Inc.

Map revisions pp. xiv, xv, xvi, xvii, 78, 79, 80, 81, 82, 83, 122, 123, 125, 137, 138, 139, 149, 169, 171, 183, 195, 203, 205, 207, 224, 225, 245, 263, 265, 267, 299, 303, 333, 349, 357, 361, 371, 385, 391, 397, 419, 421, 425, 435 by Let's Go, Inc.

Published in the United States of America by St. Martin's Press, Inc.

Let's Go: Austria & Switzerland. Copyright © 1998 by Let's Go, Inc. All rights reserved. Printed in the United States of America. No part of this book may be used or reproduced in any manner whatsoever without written permission except in the case of brief quotations embodied in critical articles or reviews. For information, address St. Martin's Press, 175 Fifth Avenue, New York, NY 10010, USA.

ISBN: 0 333 71178 5

First edition

10 9 8 7 6 5 4 3 2 1

Let's Go: Austria & Switzerland is written by Let's Go Publications, 67 Mount Auburn Street, Cambridge, MA 02138, USA.

Let's Go® and the thumb logo are trademarks of Let's Go, Inc.

Printed in the USA on recycled paper with biodegradable soy ink.

ADVERTISING DISCLAIMER

All advertisements appearing in Let's Go publications are sold by an independent agency not affiliated with the production of the guides. Advertisers are never given preferential treatment, and the guides are researched, written, and published independent of advertising. Advertisements do not imply endorsement of products or services by Let's Go. If you are interested in purchasing advertising space in a Let's Go publication, contact: Let's Go Advertising Sales, 67 Mount Auburn St., Cambridge, MA 02138, USA.

About Let's Go

THIRTY-EIGHT YEARS OF WISDOM

Back in 1960, a few students at Harvard University banded together to produce a 20-page pamphlet offering a collection of tips on budget travel in Europe. This modest, mimeographed packet, offered as an extra to passengers on student charter flights to Europe, met with instant popularity. The following year, students traveling to Europe researched the first, full-fledged edition of *Let's Go: Europe,* a pocket-sized book featuring honest, irreverent writing and a decidedly youthful outlook on the world. Throughout the 60s, our guides reflected the times; the 1969 guide to America led off by inviting travelers to "dig the scene" at San Francisco's Haight-Ashbury. During the 70s and 80s, we gradually added regional guides and expanded coverage into the Middle East and Central America. With the addition of our in-depth city guides, handy map guides, and extensive coverage of Asia and Australia, the 90s are also proving to be a time of explosive growth for Let's Go, and there's certainly no end in sight. The first editions of *Let's Go: Australia* and *Let's Go: New Zealand* hit the shelves this year, expanding our coverage to six continents, and research for next year's series has already begun.

We've seen a lot in 38 years. *Let's Go: Europe* is now the world's bestselling international guide, translated into seven languages. And our new guides bring Let's Go's total number of titles, with their spirit of adventure and their reputation for honesty, accuracy, and editorial integrity, to 40. But some things never change: our guides are still researched, written, and produced entirely by students who know first-hand how to see the world on the cheap.

HOW WE DO IT

Each guide is completely revised and thoroughly updated every year by a well-traveled set of over 200 students. Every winter, we recruit over 140 researchers and 60 editors to write the books anew. After several months of training, Researcher-Writers hit the road for seven weeks of exploration, from Anchorage to Adelaide, Estonia to El Salvador, Iceland to Indonesia. Hired for their rare combination of budget travel sense, writing ability, stamina, and courage, these adventurous travelers know that train strikes, stolen luggage, food poisoning, and marriage proposals are all part of a day's work. Back at our offices, editors work from spring to fall, massaging copy written on Himalayan bus rides into witty yet informative prose. A student staff of typesetters, cartographers, publicists, and managers keeps our lively team together. In September, the collected efforts of the summer are delivered to our printer, who turns them into books in record time, so that you have the most up-to-date information available for your vacation. And even as you read this, work on next year's editions is well underway.

WHY WE DO IT

We don't think of budget travel as the last recourse of the destitute; we believe that it's the only way to travel. Living cheaply and simply brings you closer to the people and places you've been saving up to visit. Our books will ease your anxieties and answer your questions about the basics—so you can get off the beaten track and explore. Once you learn the ropes, we encourage you to put *Let's Go* down now and then to strike out on your own. As any seasoned traveler will tell you, the best discoveries are often those you make yourself. When you find something worth sharing, drop us a line. We're Let's Go Publications, 67 Mount Auburn St., Cambridge, MA 02138, USA (email: fanmail@letsgo.com).

HAPPY TRAVELS!

Contents

About Let's Go v
Maps ix
Acknowledgments x
Researcher-Writers xi
Let's Go Picks xiii
How to Use This Book xviii

ESSENTIALS 1

Planning Your Trip 1
Getting There 30
Once There 37

AUSTRIA 59

Vienna (Wien)   77
Weekend Excursions 121
    Prague (Praha) 121
    Budapest 136

Lower Austria   149
Approaching Burgenland 154
Neusiedler See 159
The Danube (Donau) 164

Northwest Austria   171
The Mühlviertel 179

Southeast Austria   182
The Drautal 188
The Murtal 190

Salzburger Land   203
Salzburg 204
Munich (München) 222
The Salzkammergut 233

Central Tirol   245
The Zillertal Alps 249
The Hohe Tauern National Park 252

Western Austria   263
The Lechtaler Alps 276
The Arlberg 278
Vorarlberg 283

SWITZERLAND 289

Western Switzerland — 299
- Lake Geneva (Lac Léman) 299
  - Geneva (Genève, Genf) 299
- Valais (Wallis) 333
- Lake Neuchâtel Region 347

Central Switzerland — 369
- Zurich (Zürich) 369
- Bern (Berne) 390
- The Berner Oberland 397

Eastern Switzerland — 418
- Italian Switzerland (Ticino) 418
- Graubünden (Grisons) 433
- The Bodensee 451

LIECHTENSTEIN 464

APPENDIX 467

INDEX 481

Maps

Austria (Österreich)	xiv
Austrian Rail Lines	xv
Switzerland (with Liechtenstein)	xvi
Swiss Rail Lines	xvii
Vienna	78-79
Central Vienna	80-81
Vienna Transportation	82-83
Prague	122-123
Central Prague	125
Central Budapest	137
Budapest	138-139
Lower Austria	149
Melk	169
Northwest Austria	171
Southeast Austria	183
Graz	195
Salzburger Land	203
Salzburg	205
Central Salzburg	207
Munich (München)	224-225
Central Tirol	245
Western Austria	263
Innsbruck	265
Central Innsbruck	267
Lake Geneva	299
Geneva	303
Valais Region	333
Lake Neuchâtel Region	349
Fribourg (Freiburg)	357
Basel (Bâle)	361
Zurich	371
Lucerne	385
Bern	391
The Berner Oberland	397
Ticino Region	419
Lugano	421
Locarno	425
Graubünden (Grisons)	435

Acknowledgments

A&S thanks everyone in the office who went out of their way to help at the last minute, especially Andrew, Ian, Caroline, Catharine, Alex, Måns, Kate, Allison, Dave, and Melanie—the grayboxes, moral support, and editing assistance were greatly appreciated; Sara, Luke, and Jed over in map-land; our outstanding R-Ws; Jake for correcting our math before it was too late; Anne; Emily, Lori, and Chuck; and Andrew—so nice we thanked him twice.

Lisa thanks Nic, for the late nights; Andrew, for being an unbelievable ME; Ian, for reminding me that people are more important than paper; Corey, for big bands, gelato gorging, and piazza pachangas; Mei-Mei, for charming me through another summer; Amy, for proving that there is life outside of Let's Go; (and while I'm at it) Steve, for boosting my ego early on; Måns and Alex for putting up with everything; the Romance Room, for letting me sneek in sometimes; Caroline and Catharine, for keeping me calm and cosmopolitan; Judy, for all the bagels; Caitlin, for putting up with my absences—they make the heart grow fonder, you know; Derek, for inspiring my overuse of "defenestration"; Mom, for decorating my apartment from afar; and Dad, for hauling up everything so that Mom could slipcover, hang, or frame it.

Nic thinks life's a pretty sweet fruit, but some people make it just a little bit sweeter: Lisa for being a dedicated comrade; Andrew for taking my mind on a daily constitutional; Måns and Alex for endless *joie de vivre*; Whitney for wickabee, rocko, wheewhonk, upholstering the furniture of this decrepit world, and Mr. Whiskers (like a… like a…; apologies; of course it doesn't); Oedipus and Hernando for the professionalism under demanding conditions (I can't believe it either!); Rinnthwaip Voorhees for giving me an antediluvian (proper!); Moss for the nocturnal visitation, *Wanderlust*, the perils of citrus and milk, and all the damned clams (soooo many!); Mum, Seb, and Rick for *alles*. If your name is not on this list and should be, come see me. Please to understand: I'm just the type of guy who likes to get comfy.

Editor	Lisa M. Nosal
Associate Editor	Nicolas R. Rapold
Managing Editor	Andrew E. Nieland
Publishing Director	John R. Brooks
Production Manager	Melanie Quintana Kansil
Associate Production Manager	David Collins
Cartography Manager	Sara K. Smith
Editorial Manager	Melissa M. Reyen
Editorial Manager	Emily J. Stebbins
Financial Manager	Krzysztof Owerkowicz
Personnel Manager	Andrew E. Nieland
Publicity Manager	Nicholas Corman
Publicity Manager	Kate Galbraith
New Media Manager	Daniel O. Williams
Associate Cartographer	Joseph E. Reagan
Associate Cartographer	Luke Z. Fenchel
Office Coordinators	Emily Bowen, Charles Kapelke
	Laurie Santos
Director of Advertising Sales	Todd L. Glaskin
Senior Sales Executives	Matthew R. Hillery, Joseph W. Lind
	Peter J. Zakowich, Jr.
President	Amit Tiwari
General Manager	Richard Olken
Assistant General Manager	Anne E. Chisholm

Researcher-Writers

Heidi Barrett *Zurich, Central Switzerland, Interlaken, Italian Switzerland, Graubünden*

Heidi was convinced that we only sent her to Switzerland because of her name. While we admit that we delighted in her recipe for *Heidi Schnapps*, snickered when she received free movie paraphernalia, and outright guffawed when she became the mascot at several *Pensionen*, we found that her true value lay in her color-coded copy, her inappropriate marginalia, and her gleeful descriptions of German bikers. The chocolate samples that she sent us didn't hurt, either. From baling hay to hiking through the mountains in the fog, Heidi truly experienced Switzerland.

Shalimar Abigail Fojas *Geneva, Lausanne, Western Switzerland, Basel*

Abigail's one of the most put-together people we know. From our first meetings to her farewell copybatch, she wowed us with her cultural sensitivity and complete confidence. Abigail glided through Switzerland, dodging questionable suitors and red geranium petals, in order to write remarkable prose and in-depth cultural analyses of every city she visited. Her itinerary included everything from major metropoli to two-horse towns, and she wrote up each place in calligraphic, rose-scented copy that made us the envy of the office.

Sara Kimberlin *Western Austria, Innsbruck, Salzburg, Liechtenstein*

Sara found the hills of Salzburg alive with the sound of...cows. Lots of 'em. Undaunted, Sara pressed on through the throngs of bovine and non-bovine tourists. Though her (non-bovine) traveling companions may have had less-than-stellar navigataional abilities, Sara sailed through her itinerary with aplomb. She traipsed through Western Austria (and Liechtenstein), sending back enough notes, brochures, and information for us to start our own tourist office. She even got a free passport stamp in Liechtenstein. What more could a girl want?

Jasmine Vasavada *Eastern Austria, Vienna, Southern Austria*

Jasmine heard the call of the beautiful blue Danube as she waltzed her way through the operas, palaces, and galleries of Baroque Austria. She survived Gay Pride Week while researching Vienna's clubs. She learned about Austrian customs while sharing a bottle of wine on the Neusiedler See. She reminded a charming older woman of her sister and brought her a few minutes of joy. In short, she brightened up the eastern half of Austria with her cheerful disposition and her overwhelming enthusiasm—Austria is a nicer place when Jasmine's there. Don't forget to write!

Kathleen McCarthy *Munich, Bavarian Alps, German Danube*
Christopher Brooke *Prague*
Bojan Žagrović *Budapest*
Douglas Muller *Black Forest*

Let's Go Picks

As our researchers scoured Austria, Switzerland, and Liechtenstein, they were amazed, astounded, charmed, and beguiled by a number of establishments (and sometimes even the cities themselves). We hope you will be, too.

Best Hostels Gorgeous balconies and hotel-like amenities await the ovine in you at the **Hiking Sheep Guesthouse** in Leysin (p. 329). Though you might not want to leave **Jugendherberge "Am Land"** in Solothurn (p. 353), check out the wrought-iron staircase on the way out if you can pry yourself from your room. Lugano's **Ostello della Gioventù** (p. 420) lets travelers experience life in an Italian villa. A paradise for travelers in need of forty winks, **Pensione Sinilill (Andi's Inn)** in Zell am See (p. 256) provides comfy beds after a day at the beach. Only a place worth saving could survive the Black Plague: the endlessly comfortable **Jugendherberge "Altes Siechenhaus"** in Feldkirch (p. 284). **Gasthaus Naturfreundehaus/Bürgerwehr** in Salzburg (p. 209) has the best view ever. Period.

Best Restaurants and Cafés (and we'll even throw in a *Biergarten* since we like you so much) **Giardino Café** in St. Moritz (p. 444). **Philippine Vegetarische Küche** in Innsbruck (p. 269). **Augustiner Bräu** in Salzburg (p. 214).

Best Museums The **Kunstmuseum** in Basel (p. 364) will take you through rooms of Picasso, van Gogh, the family Holbein, and more. Sober up as you witness evidence of man's brutality at **International Red Cross and Red Crescent Museum** in Geneva (p. 311). Do the Dance of Death at the **Bernisches Historisches Museum** in Bern (p. 396). Bookish? Want to be? Try the **Stiftsbibliotek** (Abbey library) in St. Gallen (p. 457). Morbidity lives at **Alpine Museum** in Zermatt (p. 342). Chilled chamois, dinosaur footprints, and the Last Bear of Valois all await you at the **Natural History Museum** in Sion (p. 338). Free beer (who could resist?) awaits at **Stiegl Brauwelt** in Salzburg (p. 219). The future is now at **Ars Electronica** in Linz, featuring virtual-flying-things and a 3-D room (p. 175). Medieval life is magnificently preserved in the rooms at the **Feldkirch Heimatsmuseum** (p. 284).

Best Hiking Take your pick from the wonderland of **Grindelwald** (p. 410), or stroll along the Aare in **Solothurn** as the Jura mountains keep watch (p. 353). After pounding the trails in **Zell am See**, take a dip in the lake (p. 255). If it's the most beautiful lakeside village in the world, why miss **Hallstatt** (p. 241)?

Best Skiing Ski in the summertime at **Zermatt** (p. 339), **Saas Fee** (p. 345), or **Les Diablerets** (p. 330), or try **St. Anton am Arlberg** (p. 279), **Lech** (p. 282), or **Kitzbühel** (p. 246). Cross-country trails call from **Seefeld in Tirol** (p. 273).

Our Researchers' Favorite Cities
Austria: Salzburg (p. 204), Zell am See (p. 255), and Hallstatt (p. 241).
Switzerland: Leysin (p. 329), Grindelwald (p. 410), and St. Gallen (p. 455).

The Best of the Rest
Best Nightlife: Treibhaus in Innsbruck (p. 273); 2 Stein in Salzburg (p. 215).
Best-Looking Cows (two-time winners): Upper Liechtenstein (p. 465).
Best Bathroom: Hotel Goldener Löwe in Mariazell (p. 153).
Best Gnome Gardens: Mürren (p. 416).
Best Nose: Maximilian in Innsbruck (p. 270).
Big Bell: Stephansdom in Vienna (p. 99).

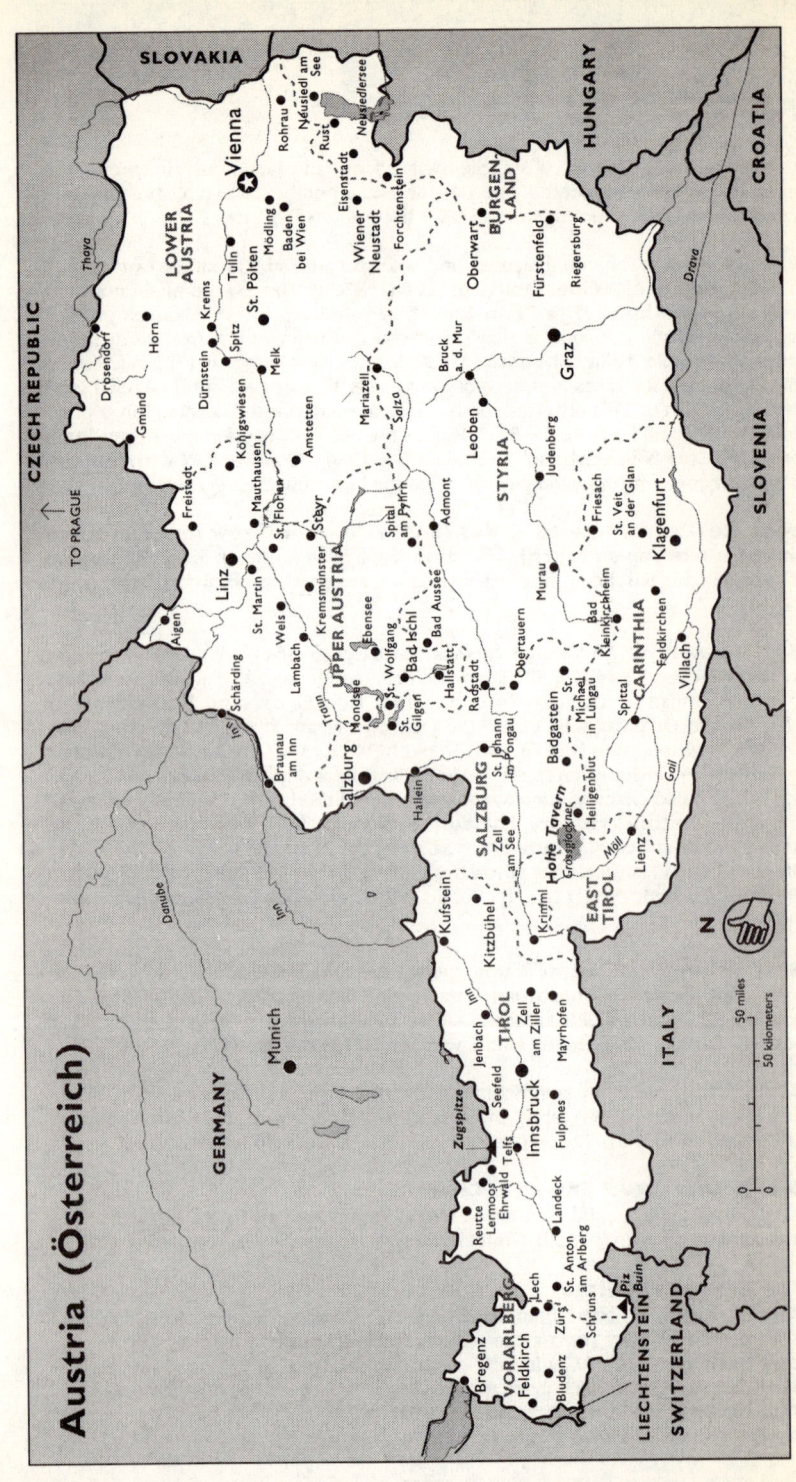

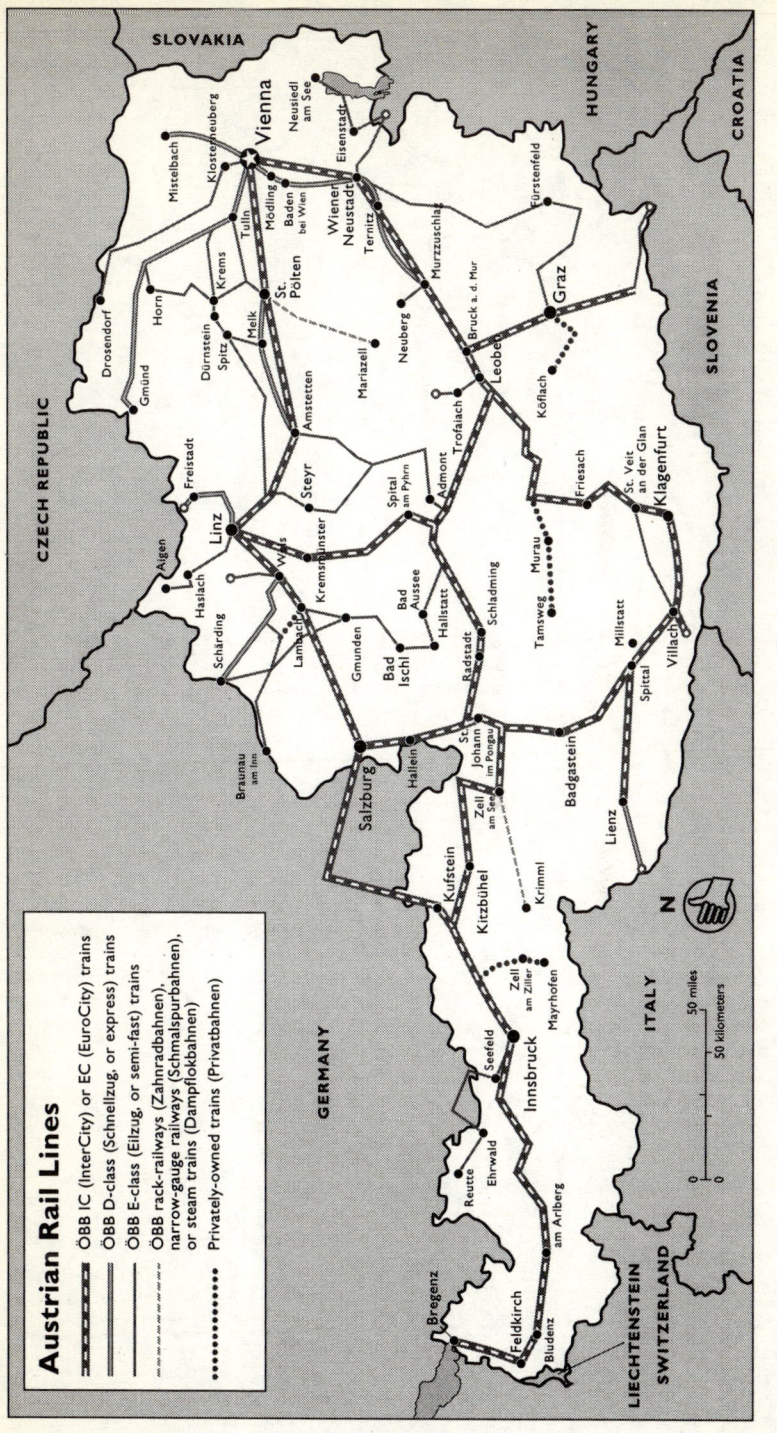

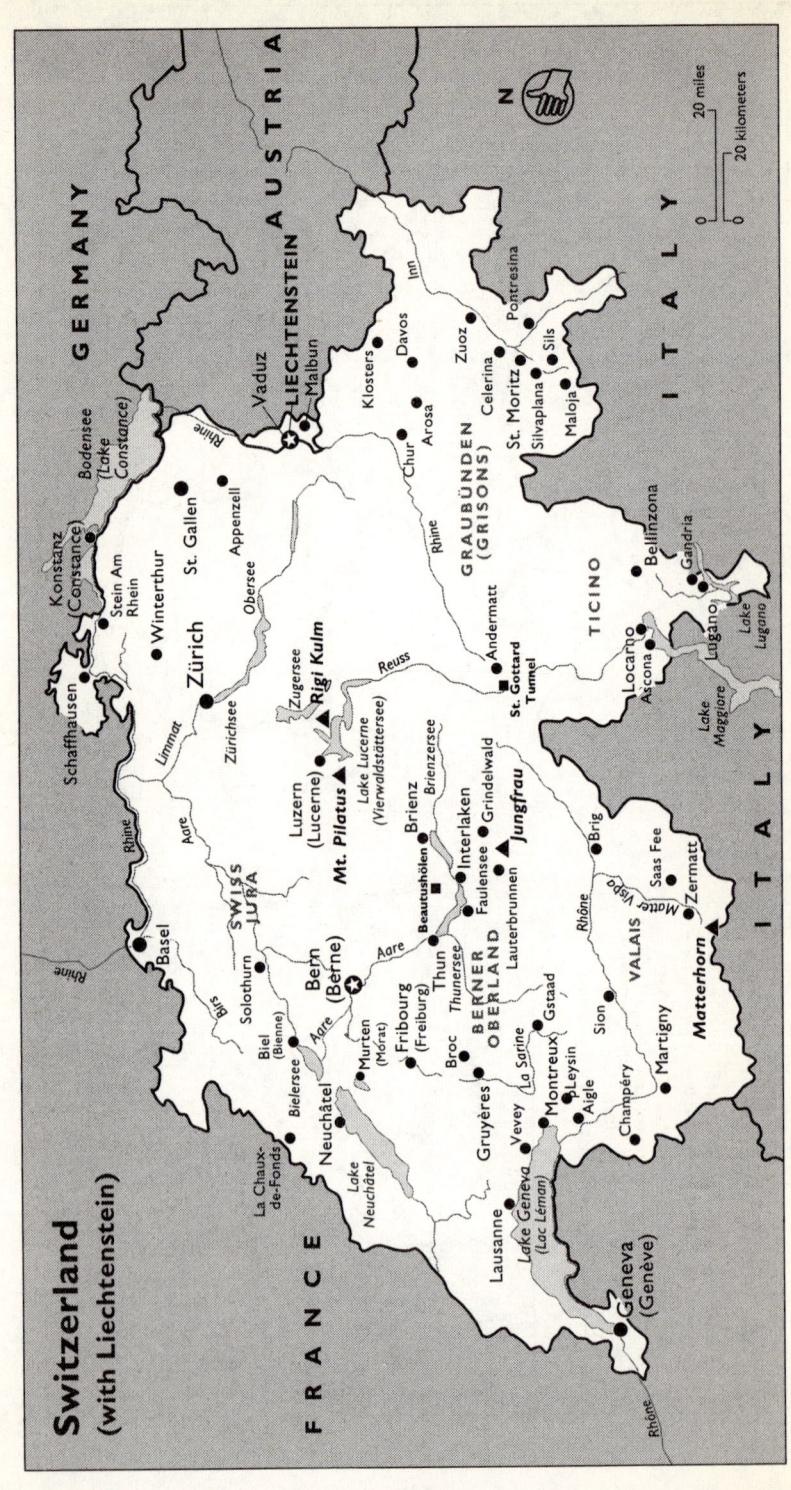

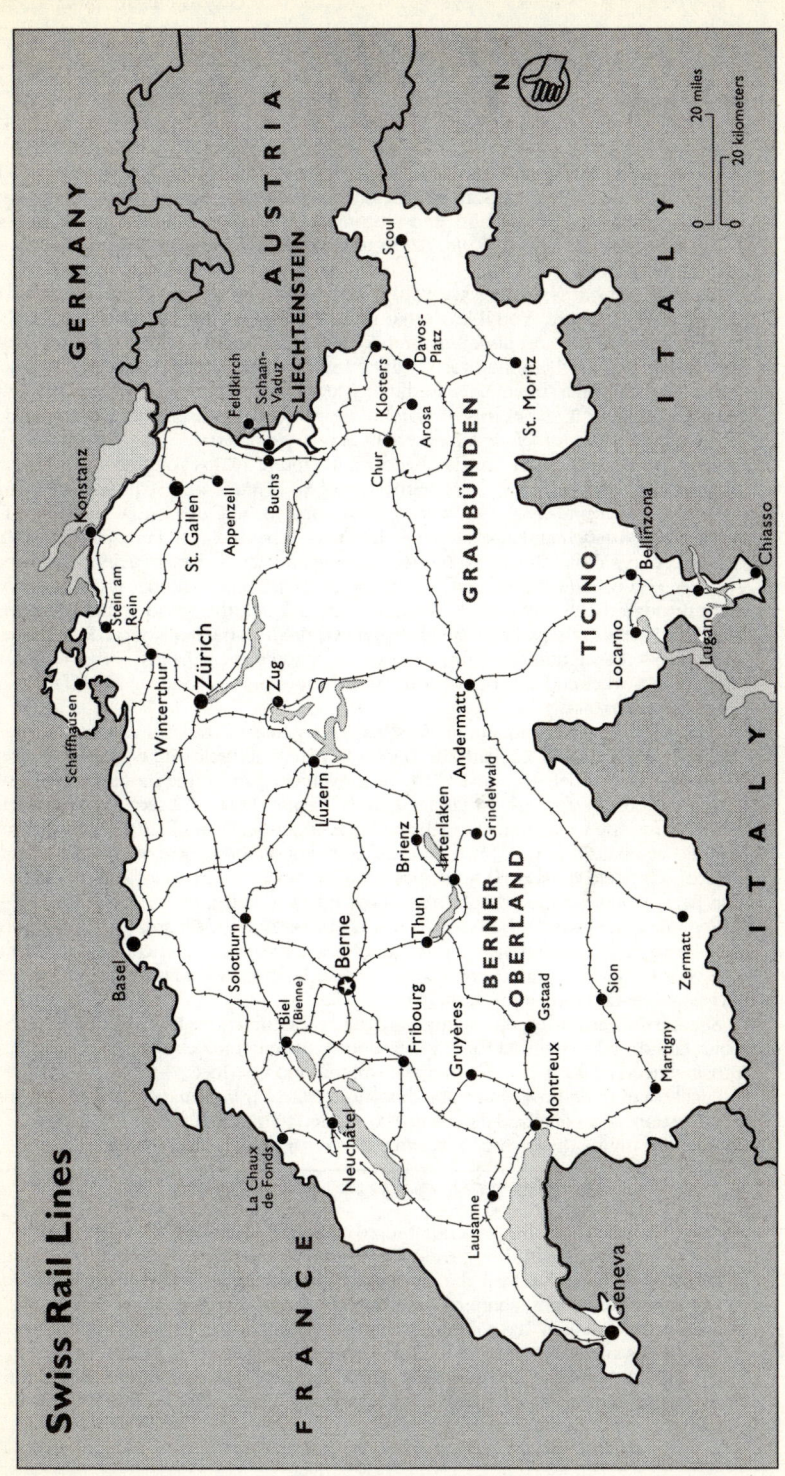

How to Use This Book

We've compiled this guide so that all travelers, from museum-hopping city mice to Alp-climbing country mice, can effortlessly navigate the peaks, valleys, castles, and galleries of Austria, Switzerland, and Liechtenstein—we even stole copy from *Let's Go: Eastern Europe* and *Let's Go: Germany* in order to bring you Prague, Budapest, and Munich. Enjoy.

We start you out with the **Essentials:** when to go, how to get there, and what to do once you're there. You'll learn that tipping is not required in Switzerland, that train tickets can get you discounts on bike rentals in Austria, and other such useful miscellany scattered among more general information on plane tickets, railpasses, hiking and camping, traveling solo, finding kosher and vegetarian restaurants—the list goes on and on. Read this section before you depart (or on the plane/train/bus ride over) and leap into your Alpine vacation well prepared.

Next, a crash course in Austrian history and culture whips you through 600 years of Habsburgs, two centuries of Mozarts, Klimts, and Freuds, and 30 pounds of *Schnitzel* with noodles and crisp *Apfelstrudel*, depositing you at Café Central in **Vienna** for *Kaffee und Kuchen* and a reflective look at your surroundings. Perhaps you'll do as the Habsburgs did and venture out to conquer new lands; **Prague** and **Budapest** make nice weekend destinations. From the beautiful blue Danube, waltz your way west through the rest of Austria. We guide you through the wooded hills of **Lower Austria,** the bicycle paths of the **Northwest,** the Italian flavors of the **Southeast,** the silver-screen giddiness of **Salzburg** (descending the hills just long enough to indulge in a weekend jaunt to **Munich**), and the Alpine wonderlands of **Tirol** and **Western Austria.**

Perched atop the mountainous Voralberg, we pause to consider Austria's western neighbor, Switzerland. Beneath the veneer of placid neutrality lurks a history of religious brawls, frenzied nonsensical artistic movements, and apple-shooting rebels. We start your journey through Switzerland on the gentle shores of **Lake Geneva** in the French-speaking west, then climb through the linguistically jumbled, French/German **Valais** region and set you down on the mainly francophone beaches of **Lake Neuchâtel. Central Switzerland** settles into German as it showcases Zurich, Lucerne, and Bern. Don't get too complacent—**Ticino** (a.k.a. Italian Switzerland) is next. *La Dolce Vita* gives way to the Germanic peaks of **Graubünden** and the international crossroads of the **Bodensee.** At this juncture, we whisk you into **Liechtenstein.** Get your passport stamped, send some postcards, and survey Europe from the only German-speaking monarchy in the world.

At each of these stops, we list not only the major attractions but also hotels, restaurants, laundromats, internet cafés, postal codes, and anything else we think you could possibly need or want in order to make your vacation perfect.

Finally, a note on **how *not* to use this book.** Take our information and coverage as a suggestion, not a finalized itinerary. We've tried to hit the highlights, but please set off on your own—then write to us and tell us what to include next year.

A NOTE TO OUR READERS

The information for this book is gathered by *Let's Go*'s researchers from late May through August. Each listing is derived from the assigned researcher's opinion based upon his or her visit at a particular time. The opinions are expressed in a candid and forthright manner. Other travelers might disagree. Those traveling at a different time may have different experiences since prices, dates, hours, and conditions are always subject to change. You are urged to check beforehand to avoid inconvenience and surprises. Travel always involves a certain degree of risk, especially in low-cost areas. When traveling, especially on a budget, always take particular care to ensure your safety.

ESSENTIALS

PLANNING YOUR TRIP

In the world of budget travel, better planning means a cheaper, more satisfying, and more hassle-free trip. If you don't know what you're doing when preparing for a trip and when actually abroad, you'll spend too much time, money, and aggravation fixing things along the way. If you don't anticipate your specific personal needs, you'll be even more miserable. Nasty surprises are always lurking around the corner for the uninformed traveler: this section of the book seeks to prevent both little annoyances and disasters and to help you get the most out of your stay.

When planning which towns to visit, read through *Let's Go*'s listings for those towns. These days, even some hostels require reservations, so you can't always do everything last-minute. Just remember: the more knowledge you have, the more prepared you'll be for fly-by-the-seat-of-your-pants travel.

■ When to Go

Because Austria and Switzerland are a mountain lover's paradise, tourism is a year-round industry. For small towns, especially in western Austria and eastern Switzerland, prices double and sometimes triple during the winter ski months (generally Nov.-March). Travelers should make reservations months in advance. Much of the flatter, eastern half of Austria, however, including Vienna and Salzburg, sees significantly fewer vacationers than normal during this time. In the summer, locals in both countries flock to tourist spots *en masse* for school vacations, usually in the last week of June. Although sights and hotels tend to be cheaper in May and June, rowdy and annoying school groups can thwart your plans by booking up even the most rural hostels years in advance. The cities tend to be especially busy then, as families and college students from everywhere whiz through on whirlwind summer vacations. In addition, almost every city has a gala music festival of some type during these months (see **Holidays and Festivals**, p. 468). Finally, small Swiss or Austrian ski playgrounds often become desolate ghost towns when the tourists pack up; some completely close down during the inter-seasonal periods (mid-April to late-May and mid-Oct. to late-Nov.). In general, April is always a good time to go, since tourists are not pouring from every hotel and museum and activities are still buzzing.

■ Useful Information

NATIONAL TOURIST OFFICES

Austria and particularly Switzerland are old pros at tourism, and any trip to either country begins at home with a visit to the tourist office. These offices can provide copious information for planning your trip, from helping you with a specific itinerary to providing personalized information for travelers with specific concerns. Order any brochures well before you leave.

Austrian National Tourist Offices
   Canada: 1010 Ouest rue Sherbourne #1410, **Montreal**, Que. H3A 2R7 (tel. (514) 849-3709; fax 849-9577); Granville Sq. #1380, 200 Granville St., **Vancouver**, BC V6C 1S4 (tel. (604) 683-8695; fax 662-8528).
   United Kingdom: 30 St. George St., London W1R 0AL (tel. (0171) 629 04 61; fax 499 60 38).
   U.S.: P.O. Box 1142, **New York**, NY 10108-1142 (tel. (212) 944-6880; fax 730-4568).

Swiss National Tourist Offices

Canada: 926 East Mall, **Etobicoke,** Ont. M9B 6K1 (tel. (416) 695-2090; fax 695-2774).
United Kingdom: Swiss Centre, Swiss Court, **London** W1V 8EE (tel. (0171) 734 19 21; fax 437 45 77).
U.S.: 608 Fifth Ave., **New York,** NY 10020 (tel. (212) 757-5944; fax 262-6116); 150 N. Michigan Ave. #2930, **Chicago,** IL 60601 (tel. (312) 630-5840; fax 630-5848).

TRAVEL ORGANIZATIONS

These organizations hunt down cheap airfares, rail passes, and accommodations. Students and everyone under 26 should inquire about further discounts.

Council on International Educational Exchange (CIEE), 205 East 42nd St., New York, NY 10017-5706 (tel. (888)-COUNCIL (268-6245); fax (212) 822-2699; http://www.ciee.org). A private, non-profit organization. Work, volunteer, academic, internship, and professional programs around the world. They also offer identity cards (including the ISIC and the GO25) and a range of publications, among them the useful free magazine *Student Travels*. Call or write for further information.

Federation of International Youth Travel Organizations (FIYTO), Bredgade 25H, DK-1260 Copenhagen K, Denmark (tel. (45) 33 33 96 00; fax 33 93 96 76; email mailbox@fiyto.org; http://www.fiyto.org), is an international organization promoting educational, cultural, and social travel for young people. Member organizations include language schools, educational travel companies, national tourist boards, accommodation centers, and other youth and student travel services. FIYTO sponsors the GO25 card (http://www.go25.org).

International Student Travel Confederation, Herengracht 479, 1017 BS Amsterdam, The Netherlands (tel. (31) 20 421 2800; fax 20 421 2810; email istcinfo@istc.org; http://www.istc.org). The ISTC is a non-profit confederation of student travel organizations that coordinate travel for young people and students. Member organizations include Student Air Travel Association (SATA), IASIS Travel Insurance, the International Student Identity Card Association (ISIC), and the International Association for Educational and Work Exchange Programs (IAEWEP).

TRAVEL PUBLICATIONS

Adventurous Traveler Bookstore, P.O. Box 1468, Williston, VT 05495 (tel. (801) 282-3963; fax 677-1821; email books@atbook.com; http://www.AdventurousTraveler.com). Free 40-page catalogue available upon request and online. Specializes in outdoors maps for the U.S. but has a small, good selection of maps and guides for Austria and Switzerland, both city and regional. You can order directly from their well-organized World Wide Web site.

Blue Guides: Published in Britain by A&C Black Limited, 35 Bedford Row, London WC1R 4JH; in the U.S. by W.W. Norton & Co. Inc., 500 Fifth Ave., New York, NY 10110; and in Canada by Penguin Books Canada Ltd., 10 Alcorn Ave., #300, Toronto, Ontario N4V 3B2. Invaluable and unmatched historical and cultural information as well as sightseeing routes, maps, tourist information, and hotel listings.

Bon Voyage!, 2069 W. Bullard Ave., Fresno, CA 93711-1200 (tel. (800) 995-9716, from abroad (209) 447-8441; fax (209) 266-6460; email 70754.3511@compuserve.com). Annual mail-order catalogue offers a range of products: books, travel accessories, luggage, electrical converters, maps, and videos. All merchandise may be returned for exchange or refund within 30 days of purchase, and prices are guaranteed. Will match competitors' prices.

The College Connection, Inc., 1295 Prospect St. Suite B, La Jolla, CA 92037 (tel. (619) 551-9770; fax 551-9987; email eurailnow@aol.com; http://www.eurailpass.com). Publishes *The Passport,* a booklet listing hints about every aspect of traveling and studying abroad. This booklet is free to *Let's Go* readers; send your request by email or fax only. The College Rail Connection, a division of the College Connection, sells railpasses with student discounts.

European Festivals Association, 120B rue de Lausanne, CH-1202 Geneva, Switzerland (tel. (22) 732 28 03; fax 738 40 12; email aef@vtx.ch). Publishes the free booklet *Festivals,* which lists dates and programs of many major European festivals,

USEFUL INFORMATION ■ 3

including music, ballet, and theater events. To receive the booklet, enclose 5 International Reply Coupons (see **Mail**, p. 55) for postage and write to Dailey-Thorp Travel, Inc., 330 West 58th Street, New York, NY 10019-1817.

Forsyth Travel Library, Inc., 1750 East 131st Street, P.O. Box 480800, Kansas City, MO 64148 (tel. (800) 367-7984; fax (816) 942-6969; email forsyth@avi.net; http://www.forsyth.com). A mail-order service that stocks a wide range of maps and guides for rail and ferry travel in Europe, sells rail tickets and passes, and offers reservation services. Sells the *Thomas Cook European Timetable* for trains (US$28, with full map of European train routes US$39; postage US$4.50 for Priority shipping). Call or write for a free catalogue, or visit their web site.

Hunter Publishing, P.O. Box 7816, Edison, NJ 08818 (tel. (908) 225-1900; fax 417-0482; email hunterpub@emi.net; http://www.hunterpublishing.com). Has an extensive catalogue of travel books, guides, language tapes, and quality maps, among them the *Charming Small Hotel Guide* (US$15) for Switzerland.

Michelin Travel Publications, Michelin North America, P.O. Box 19008, Greenville, SC 29602-9008 (tel. (800) 223-0987; fax 378-7471; http://www.michelin-travel.com). Publishes 4 major lines of superb travel-related material: *Green Guides*, for sight-seeing, maps, and driving itineraries; *Red Guides*, which rate hotels and restaurants; *In-Your-Pocket Guides;* and detailed, reliable road maps and atlases. All 4 available at bookstores worldwide.

John Muir Publications, P.O. Box 613, Sante Fe, NM 87504 (tel. (800) 888-7504; fax (505) 988-1680). In addition to many travel guides, John Muir publication puts out an excellent series of books by veteran traveler Rick Steves, including *Europe though the Back Door* (US$20), which features dos and don'ts of budget travel, and *Mona Winks: Self-Guided Tours of Europe's Top Museums* (US$19).

INTERNET RESOURCES

Like everything else in the 90s, budget travel is moving rapidly into the information age. With increasingly user-friendly personal computers and Internet technology, you can make airline, hotel, hostel, or car rental reservations and personally connect with others abroad, becoming your own budget-travel planner. **NetTravel: How Travelers Use the Internet,** by Michael Shapiro, is a thorough and informative guide to this process (US$25). There are a number of ways to access the **Internet.** Most popular are commercial Internet services like **America Online** (8615 Westwood Center Dr., Vienna, VA 22070; tel. (800) 827-6364) and **CompuServe** (tel. (800) 433-0389). Most universities and many employers also offer gateways to the Internet, often at no cost (unlike their commerical cousins above).

The World Wide Web

Increasingly the Internet forum of choice, the **World Wide Web** provides its users with not only text but also graphics and sound. These features plus the huge proliferation of web pages (individual sites within the World Wide Web) have made the Web the most active, exciting, and advertising-prone destination on the Internet, albeit still prey to corporate advertising. The Web's lack of hierarchy makes it difficult to distinguish between good information, bad information, and marketing. **Search engines** (services that search for web pages under specific subjects) can significantly aid the search process. **Lycos** (http://a2z.lycos.com), **HotBot** (http://www.hotbot.com) and **Infoseek** (http://guide.infoseek.com) are a few of the most popular. **Yahoo!** is a slightly more organized search engine; check out its travel links at http://www.yahoo.com/Recreation/Travel. Another way to explore is to find a site and navigate the Web through links from one site to another. Check out *Let's Go*'s own site (http://www.letsgo.com) for an always-current list of links. Or try these sites:

Austrian National Tourist Office (http://www.austria-info.at; North American edition, http://anto.com) has most of what you need to know about Austria: historical and cultural information on cities, train schedules, hiking tips, and links.

Switzerland Tourism (http://www.switzerlandtourism.ch) has everything you need to know about Switzerland, in a slightly more organized and thorough fashion that its Austrian counterpart. Numerous links cover anything the page proper misses, although they may require some hunting around the site.

Big World Magazine (http://www.paonline.com/bigworld), a budget travel 'zine, has a web page with a great collection of links to travel pages.

The CIA World Factbook (http://www.odci.gov/cia/publications/nsolo/wfb-all.htm) gives a great overview of a country's economy or an explanation of its system of government, as well as all the statistics an alamanac entry would have.

City.Net (http://www.city.net) is a very impressive collection of regional- and city-specific web pages. Just select a geographical area and you're golden.

Shoestring Travel (http://www.stratpub.com) is a budget travel e-zine, with feature articles, links, user exchange, and accommodation information.

The Student and Budget Travel Guide (http://asa.ugl.lib.umich.edu/chdocs/travel/travel-guide.html). Information on hotels, transportation, and more.

TravelHUB (http://www.travelhub.com) is a great site for cheap travel deals.

Foreign Language for Travelers (http://www.travlang.com) can help you brush up on your German, French, or any other language of your choice.

Let's Go also lists relevant web sites throughout different sections of the **Essentials** chapter. Web sites come and go very rapidly, and this week's top pick may disappear next week in favor of a brand-new site just waiting to be explored. So, explore.

■ Documents & Formalities

Be sure to file all passport applications several weeks or months in advance of your departure date. Demand for passports is highest between January and August, so try to apply as early as possible. Remember that you're relying on government agencies to complete these transactions, and a backlog in processing will have your best-laid plane ganging aglay faster than you can say "red tape."

When you travel, always carry on your person two or more forms of identification, including at least one photo ID. A passport combined with a driver's license or birth certificate usually serves as adequate proof of your identity and citizenship. Many establishments, especially banks, require several IDs before cashing traveler's checks. Never carry your passport, travel ticket, identification documents, money, traveler's checks, insurance, and credit cards all together—you risk being left entirely without ID or funds in case of theft or loss. Also carry several extra passport-size photos that you can attach to the sundry IDs or railpasses you will eventually acquire. If you're planning an extended stay, you might want to register your passport with the nearest embassy, consulate, or consular agent.

EMBASSIES AND CONSULATES

If you are seriously ill or in trouble, your embassy can provide a list of local lawyers or doctors; it can also contact your relatives. If you are arrested, consular officials can visit you in custody but can do little else to assist you. In extreme cases, they can offer emergency financial assistance, including transferring money.

Austrian Embassies and Consulates

Australia: Embassy, 12 Talbot St., Forrest ACT 2603, Canberra (tel. (02) 6295 1376; fax 6239 6751).

Canada: Embassy, 445 Wilborn St., Ottawa, Ont. K1N 6M7 (tel. (613) 789-144; fax 789-3431).

Ireland: Embassy, 15 Ailesbury Court Apartments, 93 Ailesbury Rd., Dublin 4 (tel. (01) 269 45 77; fax 283 08 60).

New Zealand: Consulate, P.O. Box 31219, Auckland 10 (tel. (09) 489 82 49).

South Africa: Embassy, 1109 Duncan St., Brooklyn, Pretoria 1045 (tel. (012) 46 24 83; fax 46 11 51).

U.K.: Embassy, 18 Belgrave Mews West, London, SW1X 8HU (tel. (0171) 235 37 31; fax 232 80 25).

DOCUMENTS & FORMALITIES ■ 5

U.S.: Embassy, 3524 International Court NW, Washington, D.C. 20008 (tel. (202) 895-6700; fax 895-6772). **Consulate,** 31 E. 69th St., New York, NY 10021 (tel. (212) 737-6400).

Swiss Embassies and Consulates

Australia: Embassy, 7 Melbourne Ave., Forrest ACT 2603 Canberra (tel. (02) 6273 3977; fax 6273 3428). **Consulate,** 420 St. Kilda Rd., 7th Floor, Melbourne VIC 3004; mailing address: Consulate General, P.O. Box 7026, Melbourne VIC 3004 (tel. (03) 9867 2266; fax 9866 4907).

Canada: Embassy, 5 Marlborough Ave., Ottawa Ont. K1N 8E6 (tel. (613) 235-1837; fax 563-1394). **Consulate,** 1572 av. Dr. Penfield, Montreal Que. H3G 1C4 (tel. (514) 932-7181; fax 932-9028); others in Toronto and Vancouver.

Ireland: Embassy, 6 Alesbury Rd., Bolsbridge, Dublin 4 (tel. (01) 269 25 15 or 269 15 66; fax 283 03 44; email 100634.3625@compuserve.com).

New Zealand: Embassy, 22 Panama St., Wellington (tel. (04) 472 15 93; fax 499 63 02).

South Africa: Embassy, 818 George Ave., Arcadia 0083; mailing address: P.O. 2289, 0001 Pretoria (tel. (012) 43 67 07; fax 43 67 71).

U.K.: Embassy, 16-18 Montague Pl., London W18 2BQ (tel. (017) 723 07 01; fax 723 70 01; email 100634.3637@compuserve.com; http://www.swissembassy.org.uk).

U.S.: Embassy, 2900 Cathedral Ave. NW, Washington, D.C. 20008 (tel. (202) 745-7900; fax 387-2564). **Consulate,** 665 5th Ave., 8th Fl., New York, NY 10022 (tel. (212) 758-2560; fax 207-8024); other consulates in Atlanta, Chicago, Houston, Los Angeles, and San Francisco.

PASSPORTS

Before you leave, photocopy the page of your passport that contains your photograph, passport number, and other identifying information. Carry one copy in a safe place apart from your passport, and leave another copy at home. These measures will help prove your citizenship and facilitate the issuing of a new passport if you lose the original document. Consulates also recommend carrying an expired passport or an official copy of your birth certificate in a separate part of your baggage.

If you do lose your passport in Austria or Switzerland, *immediately* notify the local police and the embassies in Vienna or Bern. You'll need to know all information previously recorded and show identification and proof of citizenship. A replacement may take weeks to process and may be valid only for a limited time. Some consulates can issue new passports within 24 hours upon proof of citizenship. Any visas stamped in your old passport will be irretrievably lost; in an emergency, ask for immediate temporary traveling papers that will permit you to reenter your home country.

Your passport is a public document belonging to your nation's government. You may have to surrender it to a foreign government official, but if you don't get it back in a reasonable amount of time, inform your local home government.

Australia: Citizens must apply for a passport in person at a post office, a passport office, or an Australian diplomatic mission overseas. An appointment may be necessary. Passport offices are located in Adelaide, Brisbane, Canberra City, Darwin, Hobart, Melbourne, Newcastle, Perth, and Sydney. A parent may file an application for a child who is under 18 and unmarried. Application fees are adjusted frequently. For more information, call toll-free (in Australia) 13 12 32.

Canada: Application forms in English and French are available at all **passport offices, post offices,** and most **travel agencies.** Citizens may apply in person at any one of 28 regional Passport Offices across Canada. Travel agents can direct the applicant to the nearest location. Canadian citizens residing abroad should contact the nearest Canadian embassy or consulate. For additional information, call (800) 567-6868 (24hr.; from Canada only) or call the Passport Office at (819) 994-3500. In Metro Toronto, call (416) 973-3251. Montréalers should dial (514) 283-2152. Refer to the booklet *Bon Voyage, But...* for further help and a list of Canadian embassies and consulates abroad (free from any passport office).

Ireland: Citizens can apply for a passport by mail to either the Department of Foreign Affairs, Passport Office, Setanta Centre, Molesworth St., Dublin 2 (tel. (01) 671

16 33); or the Passport Office, 1A South Mall, Cork (tel. (021) 627 25 25). Obtain an application at a local Garda station or request one from a passport office. The new Passport Express Service offers a 2 week turn-around and is available through post offices for an extra IR£3.

New Zealand: Application forms for passports are available in New Zealand from travel agents and Department of Internal Affairs Link Centres, and overseas from New Zealand embassies, high commissions, and consulates. Applicants may lodge completed applications at Link Centres and at overseas posts or forward them to the Passport Office, P.O. Box 10-526, Wellington, New Zealand. Processing time is 10 working days from receipt of a correctly completed application.

South Africa: Citizens can apply for a passport at any Home Affairs Office. For further information, contact the nearest Department of Home Affairs Office.

U.K.: British citizens, British Dependent Territories citizens, British Nationals (overseas), and British Overseas citizens may apply for a **full passport.** For a full passport, valid for 10 years (5 years if the applicant is under 16), apply in person or by mail to a passport office. Offices in London, Liverpool, Newport, Peterborough, Glasgow, and Belfast.

U.S.: Citizens may apply for a passport, valid for 10 years (5 years if applicant is under 18) at any authorized federal or state **courthouse** or **post office,** or at a **U.S. Passport Agency,** located in Boston, Chicago, Honolulu, Houston, Los Angeles, Miami, New Orleans, New York, Philadelphia, San Francisco, Seattle, Stamford, CT., or Washington D.C. Refer to the "U.S. Government, State Department" section of the telephone directory or call your local post office for addresses. If your passport is lost or stolen in the U.S., report it in writing to Passport Services, U.S. Department of State, 111 19th St. NW, Washington, D.C. 20522-1705 or to the nearest passport agency. For more information, contact the U.S. Passport Information's **24hr. recorded message** (tel. (202) 647-0518).

ENTRANCE REQUIREMENTS

Citizens of Australia, Canada, Ireland, New Zealand, the U.K., and the U.S. do not need visas for stays of up to three months in Austria and Switzerland (Brits can stay for six months in Austria). South Africans need visas for Austria but not Switzerland. Citizens of all these countries need valid passports to enter Austria and Switzerland and to re-enter their own country. Be advised that you may be denied entrance if your passport expires in fewer than six months and that returning to your home country with an expired passport may result in a hefty fine. Australians, New Zealanders, South Africans, and Canadians traveling on to Prague must acquire a visa. Australians and New Zealanders require visas to get to Budapest. Admission to Austria or Switzerland as a visitor does not include the right to work, which is authorized only by the Austrian or Swiss governments (see **Work,** p. 20). Citizens of these countries who wish to stay longer than the allotted time must carry a visa as well as a passport.

CUSTOMS: ENTERING

Unless you plan to import a BMW or an ebola-infected cow, you will probably pass right over the customs barrier with minimal ado. Austria and Switzerland prohibit or restrict the importation of firearms, explosives, ammunition, fireworks, controlled drugs, most plants and animals, lottery tickets, and porn. To avoid hassles about prescription drugs, ensure that your bottles are clearly marked, and carry a copy of the prescription to show to the customs officer. Officials may also seize articles manufactured from protected species, like certain reptiles.

CUSTOMS: GOING HOME

Upon returning home, you must declare all articles you acquired abroad and pay a **duty** on the value of those articles that exceed the allowance established by your country's customs service. Goods and gifts purchased at **duty-free** shops abroad are not exempt from duty or sales tax at your point of return; "duty-free" merely means non-taxable in the country of purchase.

DOCUMENTS & FORMALITIES ■ 7

Australia: Citizens may import AUS$400 (under 18 AUS$200) of goods duty-free, in addition to 1.125L alcohol and 250 cigarettes or 250g tobacco. Citizens must be over 18 to import alcohol or tobacco. There is no limit to the amount of Australian and/or foreign cash that may be brought into or taken out of the country, but travelers must report amounts of AUS$10,000 or more, or the equivalent in foreign currency. All foodstuffs and animal products must be declared on arrival. For information, contact the Regional Director, Australian Customs Service, GPO Box 8, Sydney NSW 2001 (tel. (02) 9213 2000; fax 9213 4000).

Canada: Citizens who remain abroad for at least 1 week may bring back up to CDN$500 worth of goods (including tobacco and alcohol) duty-free any time. Travelers can ship these goods (with the exception of tobacco and alcohol) home at any time, as long as they declare their value upon arrival. Citizens or residents who travel for a period between 48 hours and 6 days can bring back up to CDN$200 (including tobacco and alcohol). Goods under the CDN$200 exemption, as well as all alcohol and tobacco, must be in hand or in checked luggage. Citizens of legal age (which varies by province) may import up to 200 cigarettes, 50 cigars, 400g loose tobacco, 400 tobacco sticks, 1.14L wine or alcohol, and 24 355mL cans/bottles of beer; the value of these products is included in the CDN$200 or CDN$500. For more information, write to Canadian Customs, 2265 St. Laurent Blvd., Ottawa, Ontario K1G 4K3 (tel. (613) 993-0534), call the 24hr. Automated Customs Information Service at (800) 461-9999, or visit Revenue Canada at http://www.revcan.ca.

Ireland: Citizens must declare everything in excess of IR£142 (IR£73 per traveler under 15 years of age) obtained outside the EU or duty- and tax-free in the EU above the following allowances: 200 cigarettes, 100 cigarillos, 50 cigars, or 250g tobacco; 1L liquor or 2L wine; 2L still wine; 50g perfume; and 250mL toilet water. Goods obtained duty- and tax-paid up to a value of IR£460 (IR£115 per traveler under 15) in another EU country will not be subject to additional customs duties. Travelers under 17 may not import tobacco or alcohol. For more information, contact The Revenue Commissioners, Dublin Castle (tel. (01) 679 27 77; fax 671 20 21; email taxes@iol.ie; http://www.revenue.ie), or The Collector of Customs and Excise, The Custom House, Dublin 1.

New Zealand: Citizens may import up to NZ$700 worth of goods duty-free if intended for personal use or are unsolicited gifts. The concession is 200 cigarettes (1 carton), 250g tobacco, 50 cigars, or a combination of all 3 not to exceed 250g. Travelers may bring in 4.5L of beer or wine and 1.125L of liquor. Only travelers over 17 may import tobacco or alcohol. For information, contact New Zealand Customs, 50 Anzac Ave., Box 29, Auckland (tel. (09) 377 35 20; fax 309 29 78).

South Africa: Citizens may import duty-free: 400 cigarettes, 50 cigars, 250g tobacco, 2L wine, 1L of spirits, 250mL toilet water, 50mL perfume, and other consumable items up to a value of SAR500. Goods up to a value of SAR10,000 over and above this duty-free allowance are dutiable at 20%; such goods are also exempted from payment of VAT. Items acquired abroad and sent to the Republic as unaccompanied baggage do not qualify for any allowances. You may not export or import South African bank notes in excess of SAR2000. For more information, consult the free pamphlet *South African Customs Information*, available in airports or from the Commissioner for Customs and Excise, Private Bag X47, Pretoria 0001 (tel. (12) 314 99 11; fax 328 64 78).

United Kingdom: Citizens or visitors arriving from outside the EU must declare goods in excess of the following: 200 cigarettes, 100 cigarillos, 50 cigars, or 250g tobacco; still table wine (2L); strong liqueurs over 22% volume (1L), other liqueurs (2L), or fortified or sparkling wine; perfume (60 cc/mL); toilet water (250 cc/mL); and UK£136 worth of all other goods including gifts and souvenirs. You must be over 17 to import liquor or tobacco. These allowances also apply to duty-free purchases within the EU, but "other goods" then has a UK£71 allowance. Goods obtained duty- and tax-paid for personal use (regulated according to set guide levels) within the EU do not require any further customs duty. For information, contact Her Majesty's Customs and Excise, Custom House, Nettleton Road, Heathrow Airport, Hounslow, Middlesex TW6 2LA (tel. (0181) 910-3744; fax 910-3765).

United States: Citizens may import US$400 worth of accompanying goods duty-free and must pay a 10% tax on the next US$1000. Travelers must declare all purchases and should have sales slips ready. The US$400 personal exemption covers

8 ■ PLANNING YOUR TRIP

goods purchased for personal or household use (this exemption includes gifts) and cannot include more than 100 cigars, 200 cigarettes (1 carton), and 1L of wine or liquor. You must be over 21 to bring liquor into the U.S. If you mail home personal goods of U.S. origin, you can avoid duty charges by marking the package "American goods returned." For more information, consult the brochure *Know Before You Go,* available from the U.S. Customs Service, Box 7407, Washington, D.C. 20044 (tel. (202) 927-6724), or visit the Web (http://www.customs.ustreas.gov).

YOUTH, STUDENT, & TEACHER IDENTIFICATION

The **International Student Identity Card (ISIC)** is the most widely accepted form of student identification. Flashing this card can procure you discounts for sights, theaters, museums, accommodations, meals, trains, ferries, buses, airplanes, and other services. Ask about discounts even when none are advertised. The card also provides insurance benefits (see **Insurance,** p. 17). In addition, cardholders have access to a toll-free 24-hour ISIC helpline whose multilingual staff can provide assistance in medical, legal, and financial emergencies overseas (tel. (800) 626-2427 in the U.S. and Canada; elsewhere call the U.S. collect (713) 267-2525).

Many student travel agencies around the world issue ISICs, including STA Travel in Australia and New Zealand; Travel CUTS in Canada; USIT in Ireland and Northern Ireland; SASTS in South Africa; Campus Travel and STA Travel in the U.K.; Council Travel, Let's Go Travel, and STA Travel in the U.S.; and any of the other organizations under the auspices of the International Student Travel Confederation (ISTC). When you apply for the card, request a copy of the *International Student Identity Card Handbook,* which lists some of the available discounts. You can also write to Council for a copy. The card is valid from September to December of the following year and costs US$19 or CDN$15. Applicants must be at least 12 years old and degree-seeking students of a secondary or post-secondary school. Because of the proliferation of phony ISICs, many airlines and some other services require other proof of student identity, such as your school ID or a signed letter from the registrar attesting to your student status and stamped with the school seal. The US$20 **International Teacher Identity Card (ITIC)** offers the same insurance coverage and similar but limited discounts. For more information on these cards, consult the organization's web site (http://www.istc.org; email isicinfo@istc.org).

The Federation of International Youth Travel Organizations (FIYTO) issues a discount card to travelers who are under 26 but not students. Known as the **GO25 Card,** this one-year card offers many of the same benefits as the ISIC, and most organizations that sell the ISIC also sell the GO25 Card. A brochure that lists discounts is free when you purchase the card. To apply, you will need a passport, valid driver's license, or copy of a birth certificate; and a passport-sized photo with your name printed on the back. The fee is US$19, CDN$15, or UK£5. Information is available on the web at http://www.fiyto.org or http://www.go25.org, or by contacting Travel CUTS in Canada, STA Travel in the U.K., Council Travel in the U.S., or FIYTO headquaters in Denmark (see **Budget Travel Agencies,** p. 30).

DRIVING PERMITS AND CAR INSURANCE

If you plan to drive a car in Austria, you must have an **International Driving Permit (IDP)** with your driver's license. Most car rental agencies in Switzerland don't require the permit, but you should probably pick one up anyway, in case you cross any borders or get into a position (such as an accident or stranded in a smaller town) where the police may not read or speak English.

Your IDP, valid for one year, must be issued in your own country before you depart. A valid driver's license from your home country must always accompany the IDP. The application usually requires one or two photos, a current local license, an additional form of identification, and a fee. **Australians** can obtain an IDP (AUS$12) by contacting their local Royal Automobile Club (RAC), or the National Royal Motorist Association (NRMA) if in NSW or the ACT. **Canadian** license-holders can obtain an IDP (CDN$10) through any Canadian Automobile Association (CAA) branch office or by writing to CAA Central Ont., 60 Commerce Valley Drive East, Thornhill, Ontario L3T 7P9 (tel. (416) 221-4300). Citizens of **Ireland** should drop into their nearest Automobile Association (AA) for an IDP (IR£4), or phone (1) 283 3555 for a postal application form. In **New Zealand,** contact your local Automobile Association (AA) or their main office at 99 Albert Street, P.O. Box 5, Auckland (tel. (09) 377 4660; fax 309 4564; IDP NZ$8, postage NZ$2). In **South Africa,** local Automobile Association of South Africa offices have IDPs (SAR25). For more information call (011) 466 6641 or write to P.O. Box 596, 2000 Johannesburg. In the **U.K.,** IDPs (UK£4) wait at your local AA Shop. You can also call (01256) 49 39 32 and order a postal application form (allow 2-3 weeks). **U.S.** license-holders can obtain an IDP (US$10) at any American Automobile Association (AAA) office or by contacting AAA Florida, Travel Agency Services Department, 1000 AAA Drive (mail stop 28), Heathrow, FL 32746-5080 (tel. (407) 444-4245; fax 444-4247).

Most credit cards cover standard **insurance.** If you rent, lease, or borrow a car, you will need a **green card,** or **International Insurance Certificate,** to prove that you have liability insurance, whether or not your own insurance applies abroad (although that helps). Obtain it through the car rental agency; most include coverage in their prices. If you lease a car, you can obtain a green card from the dealer. Some travel agents offer the card; it's also available at border crossings, which usually have long lines. If you have a collision abroad, the accident will show up on your domestic records if you report it to your insurance company.

■ Money

> Prices in *Let's Go* and the exchange rates at the beginning of each country were compiled in the summer of 1997, when *Let's Go* researcher-writers for this edition were in the field. Prices and exchange rates may well change.

Travelers will find Switzerland expensive—believe us, writing this guide wasn't easy—but not unmanageable; Austria's a bit better. If you stay in hostels and prepare your own food, expect to spend anywhere from US$30-60 per day in Switzerland, depending on your needs. In Austria, costs run US$20-40. Transportation, especially through (and up) the mountains, will greatly increase these figures. Plan to keep a larger amount of cash than you do at home. Carrying it around with you, however, even in a money belt, is risky, and checks from home will probably not be acceptable. Inevitably you will have to rely on some combination of the innovations of the modern financial world, but keep their shortcomings in mind.

CURRENCY AND EXCHANGE

Currency exchange (*Geldwechsel* in German, *bureau de change* in French) commissions are scary. If you were to go through every country in Europe and exchange US$100, you would be left with less than a quarter of your original sum at the end. To minimize your losses, convert fairly large sums at one time. Better yet, convert large amounts in small towns, since they usually offer more generous commissions than heavily touristed city offices. Post offices generally offer good exchange rates and charge the best commissions. Although it is more expensive to buy Austrian or Swiss currency in other countries, convert enough money to cover the first 24 to 72 hours of your trip before heading out—you'll be able to zip through the airport and start your vacation without languishing in exchange lines.

The unit of currency in Austria is the **Schilling,** abbreviated as **AS, ÖS,** or, within Austria, simply **S.** Each *Schilling* is subdivided into 100 **Groschen (g).** Coins come in 2, 5, 10, and 50g, and 1, 5, 10, and 20AS denominations. Bills come in 20, 50, 100, 500, 1000, and 5000AS amounts. Exchange rates are standard among banks and exchange counters, while stores, hotels, and restaurants that accept payment in U.S. dollars apply a slightly lower exchange rate. Every establishment that exchanges currency charges at least 14AS. The primary Swiss monetary unit is the **Swiss Franc**

(SFr). A *franc* is divided into 100 *centimes* (called *Rappen* in German Switzerland). Coins are issued in 5, 10, 20, and 50 *centimes* and 1, 2, and 5SFr; bills in 10, 20, 50, 100, 500, and 1000SFr denominations. Currency exchange is easiest (and most convenient) at train stations and post offices, where rates are the same as or very close to bank rates with a much lower commission than banks. American Express services are usually tied to a travel agency. There are AmEx offices in Basel, Bern, Geneva, Lausanne, Lucerne, Lugano, Sion, and Zurich.

TRAVELER'S CHECKS

Traveler's checks are one of the safest and least troublesome means of carrying funds, as they can be refunded if stolen. Several agencies and many banks sell them, usually for face value plus a small percentage commission. (Members of the American Automobile Association, and some banks and credit unions can get American Express checks commission-free.) **American Express** and **Visa** are the most widely recognized, but other major checks are sold, exchanged, cashed, and refunded with almost equal ease. Keep in mind that in small towns, traveler's checks are less readily accepted than in cities with large tourist industries. Nonetheless, there will probably be at least one place in every town where you can exchange them for local currency. Order checks well in advance, especially when requesting large sums.

Each agency provides refunds **if your checks are lost or stolen,** and many provide additional services. (You may need a police report verifying the loss or theft.) Inquire about toll-free refund hotlines (in the countries you're visiting), emergency message relay services, and stolen credit card assistance when you purchase your checks.

You should expect a fair amount of red tape and delay in the event of theft or loss. To expedite the refund process, keep your check receipts separate from your checks and store them in a safe place, record check numbers when you cash them and leave a list of check numbers with someone at home, and ask for a list of refund centers when you buy your checks (American Express and Bank of America have over 40,000 centers worldwide). Keep a separate supply of cash or traveler's checks for emergencies. Never countersign your checks until you're prepared to cash them.

American Express: Call (800) 25 19 02 in Australia; in New Zealand (0800) 44 10 68; in the U.K. (0800) 52 13 13; in the U.S. and Canada (800) 221-7282). Elsewhere, call the U.S. collect (801) 964-6665. American Express traveler's checks are available for Swiss francs. They are the most widely recognized worldwide and the easiest to replace if lost or stolen. You can purchase checks for a small fee (1-4%) at American Express Travel Service Offices, banks, and American Automobile Association offices (AAA members can buy the checks commission-free). Card members can also purchase checks at American Express Dispensers in Travel Service Offices at airports and by ordering them by phone (tel. (800) ORDER-TC (673-3782)). American Express offices cash their checks commission-free (except where prohibited by national governments), although they often offer slightly lower rates than banks. You can also buy Cheques for Two, which can be signed by either of two people travelling together. Request the American Express booklet *Traveler's Companion,* which lists travel office addresses and stolen check hotlines for each European country. Online travel offices at http://www.aexp.com.

Thomas Cook MasterCard: For 24hr. cashing or refund assistance, call (800) 223-9920 in the U.S. and Canada; elsewhere call U.S. collect (609) 987-7300; from the U.K. call toll-free (0800) 622 101 or collect (01733) 502 995 or (01733) 318 950. Offers checks in Swiss francs. Commission 1-2% for purchases. Thomas Cook offices may sell checks for lower commissions and will cash checks commission-free. Thomas Cook MasterCard Traveler's Checks are also available from **Capital Foreign Exchange** (see **Currency and Exchange,** p. 9) in U.S. or Canadian dollars, French and Swiss francs, British pounds, and German marks.

Visa: Call (800) 227-6811 in the U.S.; in the U.K. (0800) 895 492; from anywhere else in the world call (01733) 318 949 and reverse the charges. The staff at any of the above numbers can tell you the location of their nearest office. You can report any type of Visa traveler's checks lost at the Visa number.

CREDIT CARDS

You can use major credit cards—especially **MasterCard** and **Visa**—to extract cash advances from associated banks and teller machines throughout Austria and Switzerland in local currency. Credit card companies get the wholesale exchange rate, which is generally 5% better than the retail rate used by banks and even better than the rate used by other currency exchange establishments. You will, however, be charged ruinous interest rates if you don't pay off the bill quickly, so be careful when using this service. **American Express** cards work in some ATMs and at AmEx offices and major airports. All such machines require a **Personal Identification Number (PIN)**, which credit cards in the United States do not usually carry. You must ask your credit card company to assign you a PIN before you leave; without it, you will be unable to withdraw cash with your credit card outside the U.S. Keep in mind that MasterCard and Visa have different names elsewhere ("EuroCard" or "Access" for MasterCard and "Carte Bleue" or "Barclaycard" for Visa).

Credit cards are also invaluable in an emergency that may leave you temporarily without other resources. Furthermore, credit cards offer an array of other services, from insurance to emergency assistance, which depend completely on the issuer.

American Express (tel. (800) 843-2273) has a hefty annual fee (US$55) but offers a number of services. AmEx cardholders can cash personal checks at AmEx offices outside the U.S. and can use U.S. Assist (tel. in U.S. and Canada (800) 554-2639; from abroad call U.S. collect (301) 214-8328), a 24-hour hotline offering medical and legal assistance in emergencies. Cardholders can take advantage of the American Express Travel Service; benefits include assistance with airline, hotel, and car rental reservations, baggage loss and flight insurance, sending mailgrams and international cables. Members can also partake of mail services at any one of the more than 1700 AmEx offices around the world. **MasterCard** (tel. (800) 999-0454) and **Visa** (tel. (800) 336-8472) are issued in cooperation with individual banks and some other organizations; ask the issuer about services that go along with the cards.

CASH CARDS

Cash cards—usually called ATM or bank cards—are widespread in Europe and elsewhere. In Austria and Switzerland, ATMs (sometimes labeled "Bankomat," with a green and blue "B") are widespread in most banks in major cities. Depending on the system that your bank at home uses, you will probably be able to access your own personal bank account. An ATM card offers great flexibility and is probably the most effective way to carry cash. Use your ATM card whenever possible, because, like credit cards, ATM cards get the wholesale exchange rate, generally 5% better than the retail rate most banks use. Beware: there is often a limit on the amount of money you can withdraw per day (usually about US$500—100SFR in Switzerland—depending on the type of card and account), and computer network failures are not uncommon. Keep all receipts—even if an ATM won't give you your cash, it may register a withdrawal on your next statement. Memorize your PIN code in numeral form since machines outside the U.S. and Canada often don't have letters on the keys. If your PIN is longer than four digits (some ATMs prevent you from entering PINs longer than four digits), ask your bank at home whether just the first four digits will work or if you'll need a new number. Be careful when using ATMs, which tend to be outdoors. Since almost all banks charge a fee for using the ATMs of other banks, you may be better off going inside to (gasp!) a human teller, when withdrawing large sums.

The two major international money networks are **Cirrus** (U.S. tel. (800) 4-CIRRUS (424-7787)) and **PLUS** (U.S. tel. (800) THE-PLUS (843-7587)). Almost all machines in Austria and Switzerland accept Cirrus, and PLUS covers 100 countries. The network charges US$3-5 to withdraw money abroad. If you can do it, carry two cards, one linked to each network—you'll be covered no matter where you are. Even so, as a backup, keep extra cash or a few traveler's checks in a secure place to help stave off unwanted money droughts.

12 ■ PLANNING YOUR TRIP

MONEY FROM HOME

One of the easiest ways to get money from home is to bring an **American Express** card. AmEx allows green-card holders to draw cash abroad from their checking accounts (up to US$1000 every 21 days, no service charge, no interest) at any of its major offices and many of its representatives' offices. To enroll in Express Cash, cardmembers may call (800) CASH NOW (227-4669). Outside the U.S., call collect (904) 565-7875. Unless you're using the AmEx service, avoid cashing checks in foreign currencies; they usually take weeks and a US$30 fee to clear.

Money can also be wired abroad through international money transfer services operated by **Western Union** (tel. (800) 325-6000). In the U.S., call Western Union any time at (800) CALL-CASH (225-5227) to cable money with your Visa, Discover, or MasterCard within the domestic United States and the U.K. The rates for sending cash are generally US$10 cheaper than with a credit card, and the money is usually available in the receiving within an hour or so.

In emergencies, U.S. citizens can have money sent via the State Department's **Overseas Citizens Service, American Citizens Services,** Consular Affairs, Room 4811, U.S. Department of State, Washington, D.C. 20520 (tel. (202) 647-5225; nights, Sun., and holidays (202) 647-4000; fax by request (202) 647-3000; http://travel.state.gov). For a fee of US$15, the State Department will forward money within hours to the nearest consular office, which will then disburse it according to instructions. The office serves only Americans in the direst of straits abroad; non-American travelers should contact their embassies for information on wiring cash.

TIPPING AND BARGAINING

The procedure for **tipping in Switzerland** is simple: you don't. Gratuities are already automatically factored into the prices. **In Austria,** menus will say whether service is included (*Preise inclusiv* or *Bedienung inclusive*); if it is, you really don't have to tip. If it's not, just round up the price for the tip (for a 162AS bill, tip 8AS), up to about 10 percent. Austrian restaurants expect you to seat yourself, and servers will not bring the bill until you ask them to do so. Say *"Zahlen bitte"* (TSAHL-en BIT-uh) to settle your accounts and don't leave tips on the table. Be aware that you will be charged for each piece of bread that you eat during your meal.

■ Safety and Security

Austria and Switzerland are both relatively free of violent crime, especially when compared to the U.S., but this fact should not be cause to let your guard down. Women travelers should also see **Specific Concerns,** p. 22.

EMERGENCY NUMBERS
AUSTRIA
Police: tel. 133. **Fire:** tel. 122. **Ambulance:** tel. 144.
SWITZERLAND
Police: tel. 117. **Fire:** tel. 118. **Ambulance:** tel. 144.

PERSONAL SAFETY

Tourists are particularly vulnerable to crime for two reasons: they often carry large amounts of cash and they lack local street savvy. To avoid unwanted attention, try to blend in. The gawking camera-toter is a more obvious target than the low-profile traveler. Walking directly into a café or shop to check a map beats checking it on a street corner. Better yet, look over your map before setting out. Muggings are more often impromptu than planned; nervous, over-the-shoulder glances can be a tip that you

SAFETY AND SECURITY

have something valuable to protect. When exploring a new city, extra vigilance is wise, but don't panic. Find out about unsafe areas from tourist information or the manager of your hotel or hostel. Especially if you travel alone, be sure that someone at home knows your itinerary and never tell anyone that you're traveling alone. You may want to carry a small whistle to scare off attackers or attract attention, and you should memorize the emergency number of the city or area.

When walking at night, stick to busy, well-lit streets and avoid dark alleyways. Don't cross through parks, parking lots, or other large, deserted areas. Whenever possible, *Let's Go* warns of unsavory neighborhoods, but you should exercise your own judgment about the safety of your environs. The flow of people reveals a great deal about the safety of an area; look for children playing, women walking in the open, and other signs of an active community. If you feel uncomfortable, leave as quickly and directly as you can, but don't let reasonable caution become paranoia.

If you are using a **car**, be sure to park your vehicle in a garage or well-traveled area. Wearing a seatbelt is the law in many areas. Children under 40lb. should ride only in a specially designed carseat, available for a small fee from most car rental agencies. The convenience or comfort of riding unbelted will count for little if someone you care about is injured or killed in an accident. Study route maps before you hit the road; mountain roads might have poor (or nonexistent) shoulders and few gas stations. Twisty Alpine roads may be closed in winter and, when open, require particular caution. Learn the **Alpine honk:** when going blind around an abrupt turn on such roads, stop and give the horn a toot before proceeding. Shift your car to low gear, drive slowly, brake occasionally, and *never* pass anyone, no matter how slow.

Let's Go does not recommend **hitchhiking,** particularly for women; see **Getting There,** p. 30 for more information. **Sleeping in your own car** is one of the most dangerous ways to get your 40 winks. If your car breaks down, wait for the police to assist you. If you must sleep in your car, do so close to a police station or a 24-hour service station. Sleeping out in the open is even more dangerous—stick to campsites.

No set of precautions will guarantee your protection from all of the situations you might encounter when you travel. A good self-defense course will give you more concrete ways to react to different types of aggression. **Impact, Prepare, and Model Mugging** can refer you to local self-defense courses in the United States (tel. (800) 345-KICK). Course prices vary from $50-400, and women's and men's courses are offered. Community colleges frequently offer inexpensive self-defense courses.

FINANCIAL SECURITY

Though not particularly prevalent in Austria and Switzerland, **con artists** are among the more colorful aspects of a city. Hucksters possess an innumerable range of ruses. Be aware of certain classics: sob stories that require money or distractions that allow enough time to snatch your bag. Be especially alert in these situations. Do not respond or make eye contact, walk away quickly, and keep a solid grip on your belongings. Contact the police if a hustler is particularly insistent or aggressive.

Don't put a wallet containing money in your back pocket. Never count your money in public and carry as little as possible. If you carry a purse, buy a sturdy one with a secure clasp and carry it crosswise on the side away from the street with the clasp against you. Secure packs with small combination padlocks that slip through the two zippers. (Even these precautions do not always suffice: moped riders who snatch purses and backpacks sometimes tote knives to cut the straps). A **money belt** is the best way to carry cash; you can buy one at most camping supply stores or through the Forsyth Travel Library (see **Useful Publications,** p. 50). A nylon zippered pouch with belt that sits inside the waist of your pants or skirt combines convenience and security. A **neck pouch** is equally safe, though less accessbile. Don't keep anything precious in a fanny-pack (even if it's worn on your stomach): your valuables will be highly visible and easy to steal.

In city crowds and especially on public transportation, pick-pockets are amazingly deft at their craft. Rush hour is no excuse for strangers to press up against you on the metro. If someone stands uncomfortably close, hold your bags tightly and move to another car. Be alert in public telephone booths: make sure no one's watching your calling card number. **Photocopies** of important documents allow you to recover them in case they are lost or filched. Carry one copy separate from the documents and leave another copy at home. Keep some money separate from the rest to use in an emergency or in case of theft. Label every piece of luggage both inside and out.

Be particularly careful on **buses** (for example, carry your backpack in front of you where you can see it), don't check baggage on trains, and don't trust anyone to "watch your bag for a second." Thieves thrive on **trains;** professionals wait for tourists to fall asleep and then carry off everything they can. When traveling in pairs, sleep in alternating shifts; when alone, use good judgement in selecting a train compartment: never stay in an empty one and use a lock to secure your pack to the luggage rack. Keep important documents and other valuables on your person and try to sleep on top bunks with your luggage stored above you (if not in bed with you).

Let's Go lists locker availability in hostels and train stations, but you'll need your own padlock. Lockers are useful if you plan on sleeping outdoors or don't want to lug everything with you, but don't store valuables in them. Never leave your belongings unattended—crime occurs in even the most demure-looking hostel or hotel. If you feel unsafe, look for places with either a curfew or a night attendant. When possible, keep valuables or anything you couldn't bear to lose at home.

If you travel by **car,** try not to leave valuable possessions like radios or luggage inside while you're off rambling. Radios are especially tempting. If your tape deck or radio is removable, hide it in the trunk or take it with you. If it isn't, at least conceal it under a lot of junk. Similarly, hide baggage in the trunk—although savvy thieves can tell if a car is heavily loaded by the way it sits on its tires.

Travel Assistance International by Worldwide Assistance Services, Inc. provides its members with a 24-hour hotline. Their year-long frequent traveler package ($235-295) includes medical and travel insurance, financial assistance, and help in replacing lost documents. Call (800) 821-2828 or (202) 828-5894, fax 828-5896, or write to 1133 15th St. NW, Ste. 400, Washington, D.C. 20005-2710. The **American Society of Travel Agents** provides extensive information and resources, both at their web-site (http://www.astanet.com) and in their free brochure, *Travel Safety.* You can obtain a copy by sending a request and self-addressed, stamped envelope to them at 1101 King St., Alexandria, VA 22313.

DRUGS AND ALCOHOL

Police officers, members of the *Polizei* or *Gendarmerie,* typically speak little English and tend to be very businesslike. Treat the police with the utmost respect at all times. Imbibing **alcohol** in Austria and Switzerland is generally trouble-free—beer is more common than soda, and a lunch without wine or beer would be unusual. In Switzerland, you must be 16 to drink legally. Each Austrian province sets a legal minimum drinking age; typically, anyone over 18 can drink whatever he or she wishes, and drinking beer is often legal at younger ages.

Drugs could easily ruin a trip. Every year thousands of travelers are arrested for trafficking or possession of drugs or for simply being in the company of a suspected user. Marijuana, hashish, cocaine, and narcotics are illegal in Austria and Switzerland, and the penalties for illegal possession of drugs range from severe to horrific. It is not uncommon for a dealer to increase profits by first selling drugs to tourists and then turning them in to the authorities for a reward. Even such reputedly liberal cities as Vienna, Salzburg, and Zurich take an officially dim view of strung-out tourists. The worst thing you can possibly do is carry drugs across an international border—you could not only end up in prison but also be hounded by a "Drug Trafficker" stamp on your passport for the rest of your life. If you are arrested, all your home country's consulate can do is visit you, provide a list of attorneys, and inform family and friends.

Make sure you get a statement and prescription from your doctor if you'll be carrying insulin, syringes, or any narcotic medications. Leave all medicines in their original labeled containers. What is legal at home may not be legal abroad; check with your doctor or the appropriate foreign consulate to avoid nasty surprises.

■ Health

Common sense is the simplest prescription for good health while you travel. If a **medical emergency** does crop up, call the country's **emergency number:** 144 in both Austria and Switzerland. Many of the first-aid centers and hospitals in major cities that *Let's Go* lists can provide you with medical care from an English-speaking doctor, and your consulate in major foreign cities should also have a list of English-speaking doctors in town. In most large towns, a rotating pharmacy is open 24 hours—consult the door of the nearest pharmacy to find out which one is open for the night. *Let's Go* lists hospitals within individual city listings.

BEFORE YOU GO

Always go prepared with any **medication** you may need while away, as well as a copy of the prescription and/or a statement from your doctor. Travelers with chronic medical conditions should consult their physicians before leaving. While **Cortisone** is available over the counter in the U.S., a prescription is required in Switzerland. Consult your doctor before you leave for information about these situations and other drugs in both Austria and Switzerland. Be aware that matching prescriptions with foreign equivalents may be hard; bring an extra week's supply. Remember that a *Drogerie* sells only toilet articles like soap and tampons; to purchase any health products (including aspirin, cough drops, contact lens solution, and condoms) or to get prescriptions filled you must go to an *Apotheke*. Austrian and Swiss **pharmacists** often speak English and can suggest proper treatment if you describe your symptoms.

In your passport, write the names of any people you wish to be contacted in case of a medical emergency and list any allergies or medical conditions you would want doctors to know about. If you wear glasses or contact lenses, carry an extra prescription and pair of glasses or arrange to have your doctor or a family member send a replacement pair in an emergency. Allergy sufferers should find out if their conditions are likely to be aggravated in the regions they plan to visit, and they should obtain a full supply of any necessary medication before the trip.

For general health information, contact the **American Red Cross.** The ARC publishes a *First-Aid and Safety Handbook* (US$5) available though the American Red Cross, 285 Columbus Ave., Boston, MA 02116-5114 (tel. (800) 564-1234).

Travelers with medical conditions (*e.g.* diabetes, allergies to antibiotics, epilepsy, heart conditions) may want to obtain a stainless steel **Medic Alert** identification tag (US$35 for first year, then $15 annually), which identifies the disease and lists a 24-hour collect-call information number. Contact Medic Alert Foundation, 2323 Colorado Ave., Turlock, CA 95382 (tel. (800) 825-3785). Diabetics can contact the **American Diabetes Association**, 1660 Duke St., Alexandria, VA 22314 (tel. (800) 232-3472), to receive copies of the article "Travel and Diabetes" and a diabetic ID card, which carries messages in 18 languages explaining the carrier's diabetic status.

ON THE ROAD AILMENTS

Eat well, drink enough, get enough sleep, and don't overexert yourself. If you're going to be doing a lot of walking, take along some quick-energy foods to keep your strength up. You'll need plenty of protein, carbohydrates, and fluids. The heat, though not Saharan, can be quite oppressive during the summer, especially in flat eastern Austria. Be warned that non-carbonated plastic **water bottles** (like Evian) are impossible to come by in Austria, even in grocery stores. Take a flask, and fill it with **tap water.** Drink water frequently to avoid dehydration.

Extreme cold is just as dangerous as heat. Warning signs of **hypothermia** are easy to detect: falling body temperature, shivering, poor coordination, exhaustion, slurred speech, sleepiness, hallucinations, or amnesia. Do not let hypothermia victims fall asleep if they are in the advanced stages—their body temperature will drop more, and they may die if they lose consciousness. Seek medical help as soon as possible. To avoid hypothermia, keep dry and stay out of the wind. In wet weather, wool and most synthetics, such as pile, will keep you warm, but most other fabric, especially cotton, will make you colder. Dress in layers, and watch for **frostbite** when the temperature is below freezing—look for skin that has turned white, waxy, and cold. If you find frostbite, do not rub the skin. Drink warm beverages, get dry, and slowly warm the area with dry fabric or steady body contact. Take serious cases to a doctor as soon as possible. Travelers to **high altitudes** must also allow their bodies a few days to adjust to lower oxygen levels in the air before exerting themselves.

If you plan to romp in the forest, try to learn any regional hazards. Know that any three-leafed plant might be poison ivy, poison oak, or poison sumac—pernicious plants whose oily surface causes insufferable itchiness if touched. **Ticks** are especially nasty, and can cause tick-borne encephalitis, a viral infection of the central nervous system transmitted by tick bites or by eating unpasteurized dairy products. The virus occurs most often in wooded areas. Austrians often refer to the disease as *Gehirnhautentzündung* (literally, inflammation of the brain; it's similar to meningitis). Be extremely careful when walking through the woods: cover as much skin on your lower body as you can (however unpleasant and unfashionable long pants tucked into high socks may be in the summer, this slight inconvenience is preferable to a hospital stay) and consider using a good tick repellent. Do not attempt to remove ticks by burning them or coating them with nail polish remover or petroleum jelly.

Remember to lavish your **feet** with attention. Make sure your shoes are appropriate for extended walking, change your socks often, use talcum powder to combat excess moisture, use lotion when they become too dry, and have some moleskin on hand to pad painful spots before they become excruciating blisters. Do *not* pick at your corns and callouses—the hardened skin offers good protection.

CONTRACEPTION AND STDS

Reliable contraceptive devices may be difficult to find while traveling. Women on the pill should bring enough to allow for possible loss or extended stays. Bring a prescription, since forms of the pill vary a good deal. The availablity and quality of condoms and contraceptive jelly vary in Austria and Switzerland—you may want to bring supplies from home. For information on contraception, condoms, and abortion worldwide, contact the **International Planned Parenthood Federation,** European Regional Office, Regent's College Inner Circle, Regent's Park, London NW1 4NS (tel. (0171) 487 7900; fax 487 7950).

Acquired Immune Deficiency Syndrome (AIDS) is a growing problem around the world. The World Health Organization estimates that there are around 13 million people infected with the HIV virus. Well over 90% of adults newly infected with HIV acquired their infection through heterosexual sex, and women now represent 50% of all new HIV infections. HIV is transmitted through direct blood-to-blood contact with an HIV-positive person—*never* share intravenous drug, tattooing, or other needles—and, more commonly, through sexual intercourse. Health professionals recommend the use of latex condoms; follow the instructions on the packet. Experts do not believe that casual contact (including drinking from the same glass or using the same eating utensils as an infected person) poses a risk. For more information on AIDS, call the **U.S. Center for Disease Control's** 24-hour hotline at (800) 342-2437. In Europe, write to the **World Health Organization,** attn: Global Program on AIDS, 20 Avenue Appia, 1211 Geneva 27, Switzerland (tel. (22) 791-2111), for international statistical material on AIDS. Or write to the **Bureau of Consular Affairs,** #6831, Department of State, Washington, D.C. 20520. Council Travel's brochure, *Travel Safe: AIDS and International Travel,* is available at all Council Travel offices.

Some countries do screen incoming travelers, primarily those planning extended visits for work or study, and deny entrance to HIV-positive people. Contact the consulate for information about this policy.

Sexually transmitted diseases (STDs) like gonorrhea, chlamydia, genital warts, syphilis, and herpes are a lot easier to catch than HIV and can be just as deadly. It's a wise idea to *look* at your partner's genitals before you have sex. Warning signs for

STDs include: swelling, sores, bumps, or blisters on sex organs, rectum, or mouth; burning and pain during urination and bowel movements; itching around sex organs; swelling or redness in the throat; flu-like symptoms with fever, chills, and aches. If these symptoms develop, see a doctor immediately. Condoms may protect you from certain STDs, but oral or even tactile contact can lead to their transmission.

■ Insurance

Beware of buying unnecessary travel coverage—your regular insurance policies may well extend to many travel-related accidents. **Medical insurance** (especially university policies) often cover costs incurred abroad; check with your provider. **Medicare's** "foreign travel" coverage is valid only in Canada and Mexico. Canadians are protected by their home province's health insurance plan for up to 90 days after leaving the country; check with the provincial Ministry of Health or Health Plan Headquarters for details. Australia has Reciprocal Health Care Agreements (RHCAs) with several countries—when traveling in these nations Australians are entitled to many of the services that they would receive at home. The Commonwealth Department of Human Services and Health can provide more information. Your **homeowners' insurance** often covers theft during travel. Homeowners are generally insured against loss of travel documents (passport, plane ticket, railpass, etc.) up to US$500.

ISIC and **ITIC** provide basic insurance benefits, including US$100 per day of in-hospital sickness for a maximum of 60 days and US$3000 of accident-related medical reimbursement (see **Youth, Student, & Teacher Identification,** p. 8). Cardholders have access to a toll-free 24-hour helpline whose multilingual staff can provide assistance in medical, legal, and financial emergencies overseas (tel. (800) 626-2427 in the U.S. and Canada; elsewhere call the U.S. collect (713) 267-2525). **Council** and **STA** offer a range of plans that can supplement your basic insurance coverage, with options covering medical treatment and hospitalization, accidents, baggage loss, and even charter flights missed due to illness. Most **American Express** cardholders receive automatic car rental (collision and theft, but not liability) insurance and travel accident coverage (US$100,000 in life insurance) on airline tickets purchased with the card. Contact Customer Service (tel. (800) 528-4800) for more information.

Remember that insurance companies usually require a copy of the police report for thefts or evidence of having paid medical expenses (doctor's statements, receipts) before they will honor a claim, and they may have time limits on filing for reimbursement. Always carry policy numbers and proof of insurance. Check with each insurance carrier for specific restrictions and policies.

Access America, 6600 West Broad St., P.O. Box 11188, Richmond, VA 23230 (tel. (800) 284-8300; fax (804) 673-1491). Covers trip cancellation/interruption, on-the-spot hospital admittance costs, emergency medical evacuation, sickness, and baggage loss. 24hr. hotline (if abroad, call collect (804) 673-1159 or (800) 654-1908).

Avi International, 90 Rue de la Victoire, 75009 Paris, France (tel. (1) 44 63 51 07; fax 40 82 90 35). Caters primarily to international youth travelers, covering emergency travel expenses, medical/accident and dental costs, and baggage loss.

The Berkely Group/Carefree Travel Insurance, 100 Garden City Plaza, P.O. Box 9366, Garden City, NY 11530-9366 (tel. (800) 323-3149 or (516) 294-0220; fax 294-1096). Offers 2 comprehensive packages that include coverage for trip cancellation/interruption/delay, accident and sickness, medical, baggage loss, bag delay, accidental death and dismemberment, and travel supplier insolvency. Trip cancellation/interruption available separately at US$5.50 per US$100 of coverage.

Globalcare Travel Insurance, 220 Broadway, Lynnfield, MA 01940 (tel. (800) 821-2488; fax (617) 592-7720); email global@nebc.mv.com; http://www.nebc.mv.com/globalcare. Complete medical, legal, emergency, and travel-related services. On-the-spot payments and special student programs, including benefits for trip cancellation and interruption. GTI waives pre-existing medical conditions and provides coverage for bankruptcy or default of cruise lines, airlines, or tour operators. Also included is a Worldwide Collision Damage Provision.

Travel Guard International, 1145 Clark St., Stevens Point, WI 54481 (tel. (800) 826-1300; fax (715) 345-0525; http://www.travel-guard.com). Comprehensive insurance programs from US$40. Programs cover trip cancellation/interruption, medical coverage abroad, emergency assistance, and lost baggage. 24-hr. hotline.

Wallach and Company, Inc., 107 West Federal St., P.O. Box 480, Middleburg, VA 20118-0480 (tel. (800) 237-6615; fax (540) 687-3172; email wallach.r@mediasoft.net). Comprehensive medical insurance including evacuation and repatriation of remains and direct payment of claims to service providers. Other optional coverages available. 24-hr. toll-free international assistance.

Alternatives to Tourism

PERMITS

To study in Switzerland for longer than three months, you need to fill out a residency permit and receive authorization from the Swiss authorities. To study in Austria, citizens of non-EU countries must have visas. Because of Austria's new EU status, citizens of member countries do not need visas to work or study in Austria. All foreigners, however, must have valid work permits. Most U.S. university programs will arrange all the permits for students. To work in either country, you must file residency forms from your country of current residence. When you submit your residency application, you must prove that you have been hired and that you have a place to live. While it's possible to go as a tourist and look for work, it's a catch-22: very few companies will hire you without a residency permit, but getting one requires a job.

STUDY

Foreign study programs vary tremendously in expense, academic quality, living conditions, degree of contact with local students, and exposure to local culture and languages. Exchange programs for high school students abound. Most American undergraduates enroll in programs sponsored by U.S. universities, and many colleges

- Vienna, the city of art, music and culture.
- Earn U.S. College Credit for your course!
- Well appointed modern school in the heart of Vienna.
- Lively neighbourhood of cafés, shops, Castle Belvedere and Operahouse.
- Welcome parties, Viennese waltzing, cycling, swimming.
- Trips to Budapest, Salzburg, Prague, Venice.
- Close to Alpine ski resorts.

Learn GERMAN
experience VIENNA

ACTILINGUA Academy
Gloriettegasse 8
A-1130 Vienna, Austria
Tel. +43-1-877 67 01
Fax +43-1-877 67 03
e-mail: actilingua@via.at
Internet: www.actilingua.com

ALTERNATIVES TO TOURISM

have offices that give advice and information on study abroad. Ask for the names of recent participants in these programs and get in touch with them in order to judge which program is best for you. The Internet has a study abroad website at www.studyabroad.com/liteimage.html.

American Field Service (AFS), 198 Madison Ave., 8th Fl., New York, NY 10016 (student information tel. (800) AFS-INFO (237-4636), administration 876-2376; fax (503) 241-1653; email afsinfo@afs.org; http://www.afs.org/usa). AFS offers summer, semester, and year-long homestay international exchange programs (including Austria and Switzerland) for high school students and recent high school graduates. Financial aid available.

Beaver College Center for Education Abroad, 450 S. Easton Rd., Glenside, PA 19038-3295 (tel. (888) BEAVER 9 (232-8379); fax (215) 572-2174; email cea@beaver.edu; http://www.beaver.edu/cea/). Operates study-abroad programs in Austria as well as a Peace Studies program. Summer and graduate programs also available. Applicants must have completed 3 full semesters at an accredited university.

College Semester Abroad, School for International Training, Kipling Rd., P.O. Box 676, Brattleboro, VT 05302 (tel. (800) 336-1616; fax (802) 258-3500). Offers extensive semester-long Study Abroad programs (US$9300-11500, including tuition, room and board, and airfare). Scholarships are available and federal financial aid is usually transferable from the student's home college or university.

Council on International Education Exchange, 205 E. 42nd St., New York, NY 10017 (tel. (888) COUNCIL (268-6245); fax (212) 822-2699; email info@ciee.org; http://www.ciee.org). Sponsors over 40 study abroad programs throughout the world. Contact them for more information.

Eurocentres, 101 N. Union St. #300, Alexandria, VA 22314 (tel. (800) 648-4809 (recorded info.), (888) 387-6236, or (703) 684-1494; fax (703) 684-1495; http://www.clark.net/pub/eurocent/home.htm). Head Office, Seestr. 247, CH-8038 Zurich, Switzerland (tel. (01) 485 50 40; fax 481 61 24). Language programs and homestays (US$500-5000) of 2 weeks to a year. Some financial aid available.

Institute of International Education (IIE), 809 United Nations Plaza, New York, NY 10017-3580 (tel. (212) 984-5413; fax 984-5358). For book orders: IIE Books, Institute of International Education, P.O. Box 371, Annapolis Junction, MD 20701 (tel. (800) 445-0443; fax (301) 206-9789; email iiebooks@pmds.com). A nonprofit, international and cultural exchange agency, IIE's library of study abroad resources is open to the public Tues.-Thurs. 11am-3:45pm. Publishes *Academic Year Abroad* (US$43, postage US$5) and *Vacation Study Abroad* (US$37, postage US$5). Write for a complete list of publications.

International Schools Services, Educational Staffing Program, 15 Roszel Rd., P.O. Box 5910, Princeton, NJ 08543 (tel. (609) 452-0990; fax 452-2690; email edustaffing@iss.edu; http://www.iss.edu). Recruits teachers and administrators for schools in Europe. All instruction in English. Applicants must have a bachelor's degree and two years of relevant experience. Nonrefundable US$100 application fee. The *ISS Directory of Overseas Schools* (US$35) is also helpful.

Language Immersion Institute, State University of New York at New Paltz, 75 South Manheim Blvd., New Paltz, NY 12561 (tel. (914) 257-3500; fax 257-3569; email lii@newpaltz.edu; http://www.eelab.newpaltz.edu/lii). Provides language instruction at all levels in French, German, and Italian. They also conduct 2-week summer courses, overseas learning vacations, and customized corporate instruction. Program fees are about US$295 for a weekend and US$625 for a 2-week course. College credit is available.

Language Partners International, White Birch Rd., Putnam Valley, NY 10579 (tel. (800) 444-3924 or (914) 526-2299; fax 528-9187). Reciprocal language-learning program for those over 18. One- to 4-week homestay programs during which the American language partner stays with a host family and learns a foreign language while helping one member of the family with their English. US$950-1150 includes room and board, teaching materials, and organizational assistance.

Peterson's Guides, P.O. Box 2123, Princeton, NJ 08543-2123 (tel. (800) 338-3282; fax (609) 243-9150; http://www.petersons.com). Their comprehensive Study Abroad (US$30) annual guide lists programs in countries all over the world and provides essential information on the study abroad experience in general. Their new *Learning Adventures Around the World* (US$25) lists volunteer, museum-hopping, study, and travel programs.

Youth For Understanding International Exchange (YFU), 3501 Newark St. NW, Washington, D.C. 20016 (tel. (800) TEENAGE (833-6243) or (202) 966-6800; fax 895-1104; http://www.yfu.org). Places U.S. high school students worldwide for year, semester, summer, and sport homestays.

WORK

There's no better way to submerge yourself in a foreign culture than to become part of its economy. Officially, you can hold a job only with a **work permit** (see **Alternatives to Tourism: Permits**). Your employer must obtain this document from the local government, usually by demonstrating that you have skills that locals lack—not the easiest of tasks. There are, however, ways to make it easier. Friends abroad can help expedite work permits or arrange work-for-accommodations swaps. Be an au pair; advertise to teach English. You might consider doing the rounds of resort hotels; these places employ many foreigners during the winter and often need English speakers. European Union citizens can work in any EU country, and if your parents were born in an EU country you may be able to claim dual citizenship or at least the right to a work permit. (Beware that citizenship in Switzerland involves military service.) Students can check with their universities' foreign language departments, which may have inside information concerning job openings abroad. Call the Austrian or Swiss Consulate or Embassy for more information about work permits.

If you are a **U.S. citizen** and a full-time student at a U.S. university, the simplest way to get a job abroad is through work permit programs run by **Council on International Educational Exchange (Council)** and its member organizations. Contact Council for more information (see **Study, p. 18**). Vacation Work Publications publishes *Work Your Way Around the World* (UK£11; postage UK£ 2.50, within U.K. UK£1.50) to help you along the way (see below).

Live & Learn
FRENCH or GERMAN !

● Lausanne ● Neuchâtel ● Lucerne

Whether beginning or advanced, our 2-12 week language & culture immersion programs will give you the opportunity to explore Switzerland as a local.

Students of all ages from around the world study 20-30 hours per week.

Optional excursions, and afternoon modules in history, art or business language

Host Family stays available

College Credit available

EUROCENTRES (800) 648-4809

ALTERNATIVES TO TOURISM ■ 21

InterExchange, 161 Sixth Ave., New York, NY 10013 (tel. (212) 924-0446; fax 924-0575; email interex@earthlink.net; http://www.interexchange.org). Au pair and teaching opportunities. 2- to 18-month placements in Austria and Switzerland (US$250-450 placement fee). Teaching programs in Czech Republic, Hungary, Finland, and Poland; must have a B.A. and some previous teaching experience (US$400 application fee).

Office of Overseas Schools, A/OS Room 245, SA-29, Dept. of State, Washington, D.C. 20522-2902 (tel. (703) 875-7800; http://www.state.gov/www/about_state/schools/). Keeps a list of schools abroad and agencies that arrange placement for Americans to teach abroad.

Useful Publications

Surrey Books, Ste. 120, 230 E. Ohio St., Chicago, IL 60611 (tel. (800) 326-4430; fax (312) 751-7330; email surreybks@aol.com). Publishes *How to Get a Job in Europe: The Insider's Guide* (1995 edition US$18).

Transitions Abroad Publishing, Inc., 18 Hulst Rd., P.O. Box 1300, Amherst, MA 01004-1300 (tel. (800) 293-0373; fax (413) 256-0373; email trabroad@aol.com; http://www.transabroad.com). Publishes *Transitions Abroad*, a bi-monthly magazine listing opportunities and printed resources for those seeking to study, work, or travel abroad, and *The Alternative Travel Directory*, a truly exhaustive listing of information for the "active international traveler." For subscriptions (U.S. US$25 for 6 issues, Canada US$30, other countries US$38), contact them at *Transitions Abroad*, Dept. TRA, Box 3000, Denville, NJ 07834 (tel. (800) 293-0373).

Vacation Work Publications, 9 Park End St., Oxford OX1 1HJ, U.K. (tel. (01865) 24 19 78; fax 79 08 85). Publishes a wide variety of guides and directories with job listings and info for the working traveler, including *Teaching English Abroad* (UK£10; postage UK£2.50, within U.K. UK£1.50) and *The Au Pair and Nanny's Guide to Working Abroad* (UK£9; postage UK£2.50, 1.50). Opportunities for summer or full-time work in numerous countries. Write for a catalogue.

Uniworld Business Publications, Inc., 257 Central Park West, 10A, New York, NY 10024-4110 (tel. (212) 496-2448; fax 769-0413; email uniworld@aol.com; http://www.uniworldbp.com). Check your local library for their *The Directory of American Firms Operating in Foreign Countries* (1996; US$220) and *The Directory of Foreign Firms Operating in the United States* (1995; US$200). They also publish regional and country editions of the 2 directories (US$29 and up).

VOLUNTEER

Volunteer jobs are available almost everywhere. You may receive room and board in exchange for your labor; the work can be fascinating (or stultifying). You can sometimes avoid the high application fees charged by the organizations that arrange placement by contacting the individual workcamps directly; check with the organizations. Listings in Vacation Work Publications's *International Directory of Voluntary Work* (UK£10; postage UK£2.50, within U.K.£1.50) can be helpful (see above).

Council Voluntary Services, 205 E. 42nd St., New York, NY 10017 (tel. (888) COUNCIL (268-6245); fax (212) 822-2699; email info@ciee.org; http://www.ciee.org). 2- to 4-week environmental or community service projects in over 30 countries. Participants must be at least 18 years old. Min. US$295 placement fee; additional fees may also apply for various countries.

Service Civil International Voluntary Service (SCI-VS), 5474 Walnut Level Rd., Crozet, VA 22932 (tel. (804) 823-1826; fax 823-5027; email scivsusa@igc.apc.org; http://wworks_com/~sciivs/). Arranges placement in workcamps in Europe (ages 18 and over). Local organizations sponsor groups for physical or social work. Registration fees US$50-250, depending on the camp location.

Specific Concerns

WOMEN TRAVELERS

Women travelers will likely feel safer and more secure in Austria and Switzerland than in other parts of Europe (like Budapest and Prague)—violent crime is generally rare. Socially defined gender roles are much more clearly demarcated in Austria and Switzerland than in the U.S. or Canada, although women's incomes are catching up with men's. Austria's feminist community thrives in Salzburg and Vienna, where a number of establishments cater to a liberated clientele. Unlike some parts of southern Europe, catcalls and whistling are not acceptable behavior in Austria and Switzerland.

Trust your instincts: if you'd feel better somewhere else, move on. Always carry extra money for a phone call, bus, or taxi. You might consider staying in hostels which offer single rooms that lock from the inside or in religious organizations that offer rooms for women only. Communal showers in some hostels are safer than others; check them before settling in. Stick to centrally located accommodations and avoid solitary late-night treks or metro rides. **Hitching** is never safe for lone women, or even for two women traveling together. Choose train compartments occupied by other women or couples; ask the conductor to put together a women-only compartment if he or she doesn't offer to do so first.

Look confident and as if you know where you're going (even when you're not and you don't), and consider approaching women or couples for directions if you are lost or feel uncomfortable. Your best answer to verbal harassment is no answer at all (a reaction is what the harasser wants). Wearing a conspicuous **wedding band** may help prevent attention, and claiming that you're off to meet your boyfriend/fiancé/husband often deters particularly aggressive suitors.

Don't hesitate to seek out a police officer or a passerby if you are being harassed. *Let's Go* lists emergency numbers (including rape crisis lines) in the Practical Information listings of most cities. Memorize the emergency numbers in the countries you visit (144 in both Austria and Switzerland). Carry a **whistle** or an airhorn on your keychain, and don't hesitate to use it in an emergency. A **Model Mugging** course will not only prepare you for a potential mugging but will also increase your confidence and your awareness of your surroundings (see **Personal Safety**, p. 12). If you want more information, try these publications:

Directory of Women's Media is available from the National Council for Research on Women, 530 Broadway, 10th Fl., New York, NY 10012 (tel. (212) 274-0730; fax 274-0821). The publication lists women's publishers, bookstores, theaters, and news organizations (mail orders, US$30).

A Foxy Old Woman's Guide to Traveling Alone, by Jay Ben-Lesser (Crossing Press, US $11). Information, informal advice, and a resource list on solo travel on a low-to-medium budget.

Handbook For Women Travellers, by Maggie and Gemma Moss (UK£9). Encyclopedic and well-written. Available from Piatkus Books, 5 Windmill St., London W1P 1HF (tel. (0171) 631 07 10).

A Journey of One's Own, by Thalia Zepatos (US$17). Interesting and very helpful, with a bibliography of books and resources. **Adventures in Good Company,** on group travel by the same author (US$17). Both available from The Eighth Mountain Press, 624 Southeast 29th Ave., Portland, OR 97214 (tel. (503) 233-3936; fax 233-0774; email eightmt@aol.com).

Women Going Places is a women's travel and resource guide geared towards lesbians that focuses on women-owned enterprises. Advice appropriate for all women. US$15 from Inland Book Company, 1436 W. Randolph St. Chicago, IL 60607 (tel. (800) 243-0138; fax (800) 334-3892) or a local bookstore.

Women Travel: Adventures, Advice & Experience by Miranda Davies and Natania Jansz (Penguin, US$13). Information on several foreign countries plus a decent bibliography and resource index. The sequel, *More Women Travel*, costs US$15. Both from Rough Guides, 375 Hudson St. 3rd Fl., New York, NY 10014.

SPECIFIC CONCERNS ■ 23

Women's Travel in Your Pocket, Ferrari Guides, P.O. Box 37887, Phoenix, AZ 85069 (tel. (602) 863-2408). Annual guide for women (especially lesbians) traveling in the U.S., Canada, the Caribbean, and Mexico (US$14, plus shipping).

OLDER TRAVELERS

Austria and especially Switzerland have among the highest mean life spans in the world. Travelers from the world over will only be heartened by the sight of frail older men pounding the trails at *Müesli*-fuelled teenybopper speeds. Seniors often qualify for hotel and restaurant discounts as well as discounted admission to many tourist attractions. If you don't see a senior citizen price listed, ask and ye may receive. In **Switzerland,** women over 62 and men over 65 qualify as seniors, and women over 60 and men over 65 make the cut for senior status in **Austria.** A **Seniorenausweiß** (senior identification card) entitles holders to a 50% discount on all Austrian federal trains, Postbuses, and BundesBuses, and the card works as an ID for discounted museum admissions. The card costs about 350AS, requires a passport photo and proof of age, and is valid for one calendar year. It is available in Austria at railroad stations and major post offices. Both National Tourist Offices offer guides for senior citizens. Many discounts require proof of senior status; prepare to be carded. In addition, agencies for senior group travel—like **Eldertreks,** 597 Markham St., Toronto, Ont., Canada, M6G 2L7 (tel. (416) 588-5000; fax 588-9839; email passages@inforamp.net); and **Walking the World,** P.O. Box 1186, Fort Collins, CO 80522 (tel. (970) 225-0500; fax 225-9100; email walktworld@aol.com)—are growing in popularity.

- **AARP** (American Association of Retired Persons), 601 E. St. NW, Washington, D.C. 20049 (tel. (202) 434-2277). Members 50 and over receive benefits and services, including the AARP Motoring Plan from AMOCO (tel. (800) 334-3300) and discounts on lodging, car rental, cruises, and sight-seeing. Annual fee US$8 per couple; $20 for three years; lifetime membership US$75.
- **Elderhostel,** 75 Federal St., 3rd Fl., Boston, MA 02110-1941 (tel. (617) 426-7788; fax 426-8351; email Cadyg@elderhostel.org; http://www.elderhostel.org).For those 55 or over (spouse of any age). One- to 4-week programs at colleges, universities, and other learning centers in over 70 countries on varied subjects.
- **Gateway Books,** 2023 Clemens Rd., Oakland, CA 94602 (tel. (510) 530-0299, credit card orders (800) 669-0773; fax (510) 530-0497; email donmerwin@aol.com; http://www.discoverypress.com/gateway.html). Publishes *Europe the European Way: A Traveler's Guide to Living Affordably in the World's Great Cities* (US $14), which has general hints for seniors considering long stays or retirement abroad.
- **National Council of Senior Citizens,** 8403 Colesville Rd., Silver Spring, MD 20910 (tel. (301) 578-8800; fax 578-8999). Memberships cost US$13 per year, US$33 for 3 years, or US$175 for a lifetime. Individuals or couples receive hotel and auto rental discounts, a senior citizen newspaper, and use of a discount travel agency.
- **Pilot Books,** 127 Sterling Ave., P.O. Box 2102, Greenport, NY 11944 (tel. (516) 477-1094 or (800) 79PILOT (797-4568); fax (516) 477-0978; email feedback@pilot-books.com; http://www.pilotbooks.com). Publishes a large number of helpful guides, including *Doctor's Guide to Protecting Your Health Before, During, and After International Travel* (US$10, postage US$2) and *Senior Citizens' Guide to Budget Travel in Europe* (US$6, postage US$2, new edition next year). Call or write for a complete list of titles.
- **No Problem! Worldwise Tips for Mature Adventurers,** by Janice Kenyon. Advice and information on insurance, finances, security, health, and packing. US$16 from Orca Book Publishers, P.O. Box 468, Custer, WA 98240-0468.
- **Unbelievably Good Deals and Great Adventures That You Absolutely Can't Get Unless You're Over 50,** by Joan Rattner Heilman. After you finish reading the title page, check inside for some great tips on senior discounts. US$10 from Contemporary Books.

DISABLED TRAVELERS

By and large, Austria and Switzerland are two of the more accessible countries for travelers with disabilities (*Behinderung*). Tourist offices can usually offer some information about which sights, services, etc. are accessible. Disabled visitors to **Austria** may want to contact the **Vienna Tourist Board,** Obere Augartenstr. 40, A-1025 Vienna (tel. (1) 211 14; fax 216 84 92), which offers booklets on accessible Vienna hotels and a general guide to the city for the disabled. The Austrian National Tourist Office in New York and Vienna offers many pages of listings for wheelchair-accessible sights, museums, and lodgings in Vienna—ask for the booklet *Wien für Gäste mit Handicaps (Vienna for Guests with Handicaps).* With three days' notice, the Austrian railways will provide a wheelchair that makes it easier to maneuver on a train. The international wheelchair icon or a large letter "B" indicates access. In **Switzerland,** disabled travelers can contact **Mobility International Schweiz,** Hard 4, CH-8408 Winterthur (tel. (052) 22 26 825; fax 22 26 838). Most Swiss buildings and restrooms have ramps. The Swiss Federal Railways have adapted most of their train cars for wheelchair access, and InterCity and long-distance express train have wheelchair compartments. The Swiss National Tourist Office publishes a fact sheet detailing *Travel Tips for the Disabled.*

Cities, especially Vienna, Zurich, and Geneva, publish mounds of information for handicapped visitors. *Let's Go* attempts to indicate which youth hostels have full or partial wheelchair access. All Hilton, InterContinental, and Marriott hotels have wheelchair access, but these accommodations aren't cheap.

- **Access Project (PHSP),** 39 Bradley Gardens, West Ealing, London W13 8HE, U.K. Distributes access guides to London and Paris for a donation of UK£5. Researched by persons with disabilities. The guides cover traveling, accommodations, sights, and entertainment. Includes "Loo Guide," which lists wheelchair-accessible toilets.
- **American Foundation for the Blind,** 11 Penn Plaza #300, New York, NY 10011 (tel. (212) 502-7600). Open Mon.-Fri. 8:30am-4:30pm. Information and services for the visually impaired. For a catalogue of products, contact Lighthouse Enterprises, 36-20 Northern Boulevard, Long Island City, NY 10011 (tel. (800) 829-0500).
- **Facts on File,** 11 Penn Plaza, 15th Fl., New York, NY 10001 (tel. (212) 967-8800). Publishes *Disability Resource,* a reference guide for travelers with disabilities (US$45 plus shipping). Available at bookstores or by mail order.
- **Graphic Language Press,** P.O. Box 270, Cardiff by the Sea, CA 92007 (tel. (760) 944-9594; email niteowl@cts.com; http://www.geocities.com/Paris/1502). Comprehensive advice for wheelchair travelers including accessible accommodations, transportation, and sights for various European cities. Their web site features worldwide trip reports from disabled travelers, tips, resources, and networking.
- **Mobility International, USA (MIUSA),** P.O. Box 10767, Eugene, OR 97440 (tel. (514) 343-1284 voice and TDD; fax 343-6812; email info@miusa.org; http://miusa.org). International Headquarters at rue de Manchester 25, Bruxelles, Belgium, B-1070 (tel. (322) 410-6297; fax 410 6874). Contacts in 30 countries. Information on travel programs, international work camps, accommodations, access guides, and organized tours for those with physical disabilities. Membership US$30 per year. Sells the 3rd Edition of *A World of Options: A Guide to International Educational Exchange, Community Service, and Travel for Persons with Disabilities* (US$30, nonmembers US$35, organizations US$40).
- **Moss Rehab Hospital Travel Information Service** (tel. (215) 456-9700, TDD (215) 456-9602). A telephone information resource center on international travel accessibility and other travel-related concerns for those with disabilities.
- **Society for the Advancement of Travel for the Handicapped (SATH),** 347 Fifth Ave. #610, New York, NY 10016 (tel. (212) 447-1928; fax 725-8253; email sathtravel@aol.com; http://www.sath.org). Publishes a quarterly color travel magazine *OPEN WORLD* (free for members or upon subscribing, non-members US$13). Also publishes a wide range of information sheets on facilitating travel and accessible destinations. Annual membership US$45, students and seniors US$30.

Twin Peaks Press, P.O. Box 129, Vancouver, WA 98666-0129 (tel. (360) 694-2462, MC and Visa orders (800) 637-2256; fax (360) 696-3210; email 73743.2634@compuserve.com; http://netm.com/mall/infoprod/twinpeak/helen.htm). Publishers of *Travel for the Disabled,* which provides travel tips, lists of accessible tourist attractions, and advice on other resources for disabled travelers (US$20). Also publishes *Directory for Travel Agencies of the Disabled* (US$20), *Wheelchair Vagabond* (US$15), and *Directory of Accessible Van Rentals* (US$10). Postage US$3.50 for first book, US$1.50 for each additional book.

The following organizations conduct tours or make other travel arrangements for those with disabilities:

Directions Unlimited, 720 N. Bedford Rd., Bedford Hills, NY 10507 (tel. (800) 533-5343; in NY (914) 241-1700; fax 241-0243). Specializes in arranging individual and group vacations, tours, and cruises for the physically disabled.

Flying Wheels Travel Service, 143 W. Bridge St., Owatonne, MN 55060 (tel. (800) 535-6790; fax 451-1685). Arranges trips for groups and individuals in wheelchairs or with other sorts of limited mobility.

The Guided Tour Inc., Elkins Park House, 114B, 7900 Old York Rd., Elkins Park, PA 19027-2339 (tel. (800) 783-5841 or (215) 782-1370; fax 635-2637). Organizes travel programs for persons with developmental and physical challenges and those requiring renal dialysis. Call, fax, or write for a free brochure.

BISEXUAL, GAY, AND LESBIAN TRAVELERS

Austria and Switzerland are less tolerant of homosexuals than many other nations; this intolerance is especially pronounced in the more conservative western Austria, where open discussion of homosexuality is mostly taboo. Few establishments will turn away homosexual couples, but public displays of affection are a cultural no-no and could attract unfriendly attention in some rural areas. In contrast, places like Geneva, Zurich, and Vienna have just about every variety of homosexual organization and establishment, from biker and Christian groups to bars and barber shops, but these services can be difficult to find. The German word for gay is *schwule;* for lesbian, *lesben* (LES-ben) or *lesbische* (LEZ-bisch-uh). Bisexual is *bisexual* or simply *bi* (bee). In French, *homosexuelle* can be used for both men and women, but the preferred terms are *gai* (GEH) and *lesbienne* (les-bee-YENN).

Austria's inhabitants generally consider homosexuality taboo, except in larger cities. The age of consent in Austria is 14. **Homosexuelle Initiative (HOSI)** is a nationwide organization with offices in most cities that provides information on gay and lesbian establishments, resources, and support and publishes warnings about aggressively intolerant areas and establishments. HOSI Wien, II, Novarag. 40, Vienna (tel. 216 66 04), publishes Austria's leading gay and lesbian magazine, the *Lambda-Nachrichten,* quarterly. A number of smaller and alternative organizations operate throughout the country. **Switzerland** does not officially recognize gay couples (even though homosexual prostitution has been legal since 1992 and is now on par with heterosexual prostitution). The age of consent in Switzerland is 16. There are several gay working groups in the larger cities. **Homosexuelle Arbeitsgruppe** is a national organization with offices in most cities. **Dialogai,** headquartered in Geneva (av. Wendt 57; mailing address: Case Postale 27, CH-1211, Geneva 7; tel. (022) 340 00 00; fax 340 03 98), formed a partnership with **l'Aide Suisse contre le Sida (ASS),** an organization that works against AIDS. Several gay publications are available in gay centers and bookshops; *Dialogai Info* provides information on French Switzerland, articles, interviews, and more. For information on organizations, centers, and other resources in specific cities, consult the city's **Practical Information** section; for information on bars and nightclubs, see the individual **Sights and Entertainment** sections.

Are You Two...Together? A Gay and Lesbian Travel Guide to Europe (Random House, US$18). Anecdotes and tips, overviews of regional laws relating to gays and

26 ■ PLANNING YOUR TRIP

lesbians, lists of gay/lesbian organizations and establishments catering to, friendly to, or indifferent to gays and lesbians. Available in bookstores.

Damron Travel Guides, P.O. Box 422458, San Francisco, CA 94142 (tel. (415) 255-0404 or (800) 462-6654; fax (415) 703-9049; email damronco@ud.com; http://www.damron.co). The *Damron Road Atlas* (US$16) contains color maps of major European cities with gay and lesbian resorts and listings of bars and accommodations. *Damron's Accommodations* lists gay and lesbian hotels around the world (US$19). Mail order is available for an extra US$5 shipping.

Ferrari Guides, P.O. Box 37887, Phoenix, AZ 85069 (tel. (602) 863-2408; fax 439-3952; email ferrari@q-net.com; http://www.q-net.com). Gay and lesbian travel guides: *Ferrari Guides' Gay Travel A to Z* (US$16), *Ferrari Guides' Men's Travel in Your Pocket* (US$16), *Ferrari Guides' Women's Travel in Your Pocket* (US$14), and *Ferrari Guides' Inn Places* (US$16). Available in bookstores or by mail order (postage/handling US$4.50 for the first item, US$1 for each additional item mailed within the U.S. Call or write for overseas shipping costs.)

Gay Europe (Perigee Books, US$14). A quick look at European gay life in countries, including restaurants, clubs, and beaches. Introductions to each country cover laws and gay-friendliness. Available in bookstores.

Gay's the Word, 66 Marchmont St., London WC1N 1AB (tel. (0171) 278 7654). The largest gay and lesbian bookshop in the U.K. Mail order service available. The organization has no catalogue of their publications, but they will provide a list of titles on a given subject. Open Mon.-Sat. 10am-6pm, Thurs. 10am-7pm, Sun. 2-6pm.

International Gay and LesbianTravel Association, P.O. Box 4974, Key West, FL 33041 (tel. (800) 448-8550; fax (305) 296-6633; email IGTA@aol.com; http://www.rainbow-mall.com/igta). An organization of over 1300 companies worldwide. Call for lists of travel agents, accommodations, and events.

International Lesbian and Gay Association (ILGA), 81 rue Marché-au-Charbon, B-1000 Bruxelles, Belgium (tel./fax 32 25 02 24 71; email ilga@ilga.org). Political information, such as the homosexuality laws of individual countries.

Spartacus International Gay Guides (US$33), published by Bruno Gmunder, Postfach 61 01 04, D-10921 Berlin, Germany (tel. (30) 615 00 342; fax (30) 615 91 34). Lists bars, restaurants, hotels, and bookstores around the world catering to gays. Also lists hotlines in various countries and homosexuality laws for each country. Available in bookstores and in the U.S. by mail from Lambda Rising, 1625 Connecticut Ave. NW, Washington, D.C. 20009-1013 (tel. (202) 462-6969).

Women Going Places (Inland Book Company, US$14). An international women's travel and resource guide emphasizing women-owned enterprises geared toward lesbians. Available in bookstores.

DIETARY CONCERNS

Kosher and vegetarian travelers will very likely run into problems in Austria and Switzerland. The two countries are devoutly carnivorous, although vegetarian restaurants have proliferated along with the blooming alternative scene in larger cities. Dairy products are by and large excellent and fish is common in lakeside resorts, but vegetarians who eat no animal products will have their work cut out for them. Vienna, the center of Austria's minute Jewish population, is the only city in Austria where it is remotely easy to keep kosher. The Swiss National Tourist Office distributes the pamphlet *The Jewish City Guide of Switzerland* (published by Spectrumpress International, Spectrum-House, Tanegg., 8055 Zurich), which lists synagogues, rabbis, butchers, kosher hotels and restaurants, and other useful information and phone numbers for kosher and Jewish travelers. They also publish a fact sheet listing hotels and restaurants that serve vegetarian, organically grown, or whole food. The Austrian National Tourist Office offers similar publications.

The International Vegetarian Travel Guide (UK£2) was last published in 1991. Order back copies from the Vegetarian Society of the UK (VSUK), Parkdale, Dunham Rd., Altringham, Cheshire WA14 4QG (tel. (0161) 928 07 93). VSUK also publishes *The European Vegetarian Guide to Hotels and Restaurants*. Call or send a self-addressed, stamped envelope to receive a list of publications.

SPECIFIC CONCERNS ■ 27

The Jewish Travel Guide lists synagogues, kosher restaurants, and Jewish institutions in over 80 countries, including Austria and Switzerland. Available from Ballantine-Mitchell Publishers, Newbury House 890-900, Eastern Ave., Newbury Park, Ilford, Essex, U.K. IG2 7HH (tel. (0181) 599 88 66; fax 599 09 84). The guide is available in the U.S. from Sepher-Hermon Press, 1265 46th St., Brooklyn, NY 11219 (tel. (718) 972-9010; US$15, shipping US$2.50).

North American Vegetarian Society, P.O. Box 72, Dolgeville, NY 13329 (tel. (518) 568-7970) publishes *Transformative Adventures,* a guide to vacations and retreats (US$15). Membership to the Society costs US$20, families US$26. Members receive a 10% discount on all publications.

MINORITY TRAVELERS

It is difficult to generalize and say that either Switzerland or Austria discriminates against any minorities, but minority travelers will undoubtedly encounter odd stares in smaller villages. The majority of travelers may never really notice anything but will merely feel a prickly vibe from annoying once-overs. In Switzerland, a growing population of foreign workers (Turks, for example) have received an especially bad image in these recessionary times; minority travelers may feel some of this resentment. The French Swiss maintain that intolerance is particularly prevalent in German Switzerland. Austria is overwhelmingly ethnically and racially homogeneous, which might make some travelers feel uncomfortable. Actual run-ins, however, are rare—Austrians and Swiss tend to be much too mild-mannered to hurl crude insults or provoke physical violence. *Let's Go* asks that its researchers exclude from the guides establishments that discriminate. If in your travels, you encounter discriminatory treatment, you should firmly but calmly state your disapproval and leave it at that. Please mail a letter to *Let's Go* if the establishment is listed in the guide so that we can investigate the matter next year (see **Helping Let's Go** in the very front of this guide).

TRAVELING WITH CHILDREN

Family vacations just require a little extra planning than most. When deciding where to stay, remember the special needs of young children; if you pick a pension, call ahead and make sure it's child-friendly. Breastfeeding is often a problem while traveling—pack accordingly or search for mother-friendly spots wherever you end up. Consider using a papoose-style device to carry your baby on walking trips. If you rent a car, make sure the rental company provides a car seat for younger children. Be sure that your child carries some sort of ID in case of an emergency or he or she gets lost, and arrange a meeting spot in case of separation when sight-seeing.

Restaurants often have children's menus and discounts, and virtually all museums and tourist attractions have a children's rate. Children under two generally fly for 10% of the adult airfare on international flights (this does not necessarily include a seat). Airlines usually discount international fares 25% for children ages two to 11.

Both National Tourist Offices publish books on traveling with children and families; write to them for more information. Many, but not all, Austrian and Swiss railways, airplanes, restaurants, hotels, and tours offer children's discounts or rates. Large cities and beach-type resorts like Lugano and Neusiedl am See are most amenable to families with small children. Ski villages have numerous guesthouses run by doting grandmother figures, which also bodes well for kids.

Some of the following publications offer tips for adults traveling with children or distractions for the kids themselves. You can also contact the publishers for information on related publications.

Backpacking with Babies and Small Children (US$10). Published by Wilderness Press, 2440 Bancroft Way, Berkeley, CA 94704 (tel. (800) 443-7227 or (510) 843-8080; fax 548-1355; email wpress@ix.netcom.com).

Take Your Kids to Europe by Cynthia W. Harriman (US$17). Published by Globe-Pequot Press, 6 Business Park Rd., Old Saybrook, CT 06475 (tel. (800) 285-4078; fax (860) 395-1418; email charriman@masongrant.com).

Travel with Children by Maureen Wheeler (US$12, postage US$1.50). Published by Lonely Planet Publications, Embarcadero West, 155 Filbert St. #251, Oakland, CA 94607 (tel. (800) 275-8555 or (510) 893-8555; fax 893-8563; email info@lonelyplanet.com; http://www.lonelyplanet.com). Also at P.O. Box 617, Hawthorn, Victoria 3122, Australia.

TRAVELING ALONE

There are many benefits to traveling alone, among them greater independence and challenge. Without distraction, you can write a great travel log in the grand tradition of Mark Twain, John Steinbeck, and Charles Kuralt, and as a lone traveler you have greater opportunity to meet and interact with natives. On the other hand, you may also be a more visible target for robbery and harassment. Lone travelers need to be well organized and look confident at all times—no wandering around back alleys looking confused. Try not to stand out as a tourist, and never admit that you are traveling alone. Maintain regular contact with someone at home who knows your itinerary. Still, a number of organizations can find travel companions for solo travelers who so desire.

Solo travel in Austria and Switzerland, even for women, is generally safe. Consider indoor accommodations when on your own—lone campers make easy targets for thefts and nocturnal sickos. The biggest disadvantage to traveling alone is the cost. It is much cheaper, especially in obscenely expensive Switzerland, to rent rooms in pairs or even triples if possible.

American International Homestays, P.O. Box 1754, Nederland, CO 80466 (tel. (303) 642-3088 or (800) 876-2048). Lodgings with English-speaking host families all over the world.

Connecting: News for Solo Travelers, P.O. Box 29088, 1996 W. Broadway, Vancouver, BC V6J 5C2, Canada (tel. (604) 737-7791 or (800) 557-1757). Bimonthly newsletter. Annual directory lists tours and lodgings with reduced or no single supplement. Subscription US$25.

Roadrunner Hostelling Treks, 6762 A Centinela Ave., Culver City, CA 90230 (tel. (310) 390-7495 or (800) 873-5872). Inexpensive guided trips (13 travelers max.) in Europe. Hostelling International accommodations.

The Single Traveler Newsletter, P.O. Box 682, Ross, CA 94957 (tel. (415) 389-0227). Bimonthly newsletter with tips on avoiding single-supplement fees. Subscription US$29.

Travel Companions, P.O. Box 833, Amityville, NY 11701 (tel. (516) 454-0880). Monthly newsletter with listings and helpful tips. Subscription US$48.

Traveling On Your Own, by Eleanor Berman (US$13). Lists information resources for "singles" (old and young) and single parents. Crown Publishers, Inc., 201 East 50th St., New York, NY 10022.

▨ Packing

If you don't pack carefully, you will pay—either with back problems or in postage to mail stuff home. The more stuff you have, the more stuff you have to lose, and the larger your pack, the more cumbersome it is to store safely. Before you leave, pack your bag, strap it on, and imagine yourself walking uphill for the next three hours. At the slightest sign of heaviness, unpack something. A good general rule is to lay out only what you absolutely need, then take half the clothes and twice the money.

LUGGAGE

If you plan to cover most of your itinerary by foot, a sturdy **backpack** is unbeatable. If you carry a **suitcase** or **trunk,** make sure it has wheels and check how heavy its is when empty. Hard-sided luggage is more durable but also heavier. Soft-sided luggage should have a PVC frame, a strong lining to resist bad weather and rough handling, and triple-stitched seams. If you are not backpacking, an empty, lightweight **duffel**

bag packed inside your luggage will be useful for storing dirty clothes, although a plastic bag does just as well. A smaller bag like a **daypack, rucksack,** or **courier bag** in addition to your pack or suitcase allows you to leave your big bag behind while sightseeing and also works an airplane carry-on. Lastly, guard your money, passport, railpass, and other important articles in **moneybelt** or **neck pouch,** available at any good camping store, and keep it with you *at all times.* The moneybelt should tuck inside the waist of your pants or skirt. See **Safety and Security** for more information.

CLOTHING AND FOOTWEAR

When choosing your travel wardrobe, aim for versatility and comfort. No matter what time of year you are visiting Austria and Switzerland, be prepared for cold weather and shifting mountain climates. In winter, bring warm clothing: polypropylene long underwear, pile or wool clothing, hat and mittens, and wind-proof layers. Summer in these countries brings rain—our researchers are still wringing out their clothes. Appropriate **rain gear** includes a waterproof jacket and a backpack cover. Gore-Tex® is a miracle fabric that's both waterproof and breathable; it's all but mandatory if you plan on hiking. Avoid cotton as outerwear, especially if you'll be outdoors a great deal. Even casual hikers should bring water-proofed **hiking boots;** pavement-pounding city-types should wear well-cushioned **sneakers.** In either case, break in your shoes before you leave. A double pair of socks—light silk or polypropylene inside and thick wool outside—will cushion feet, keep them dry, and help prevent blisters. Bring a pair of flip-flops for protection against the foliage and fungi that inhabit some hostel showers. Talcum powder in your shoes and on your feet can prevent sores, and moleskin is great for cushioning blisters.

> ### Packing Light, the Austrian Way
> Back in the summer of 1870, when the air was clean and all snow came from clouds, Austrian climbing legend Hermann von Barth took to the hills of the Karwendel Range in the Tirol and climbed no fewer than 88 peaks, 12 of which were first-ever ascents. His luggage: a drinking cup, binoculars, smelling salts, a lighter, a paintbrush to paint his name on each peak, and a bottle of poison in case he fell and wasn't able to rescue himself. He never fell.

MISCELLANEOUS

Note that some items may not always be readily available or affordable on the road: deodorant, razors, condoms, tampons, and contact lens solution. A **first-aid kit** (see **Health,** p. 15) can prove invaluable. Most **youth hostels** in Austria and Switzerland provide **sleepsacks.** If not, don't pay the linen charge—make the thing yourself. Fold a full-size sheet in half the long way and then sew it closed along the open long side and one of the short sides. Those less textilely-inclined can buy sleepsacks at any HI outlet store. *Let's Go* attempts to provide information on **laundromats** in the **Practical Information** for each city, but it may be easiest to use a sink. Bring a small bar or tube of detergent soap, a rubber squash ball to stop up the sink, and a travel clothesline. In Austria and Switzedrland, electricity is 220 volts AC, enough to fry any 110V North American appliance. Visit a hardware store for an adapter (which changes the shape of the plug) and a converter (which changes the voltage). Get both or a two-in-one adapter-converter. Don't mistake an adaptor for an adaptor-convertor or you'll melt your radio. Machines that heat-disinfect **contact lenses** will require a small converter (about US$20); consider switching temporarily to a chemical disinfection system (check with your lens dispenser to see if it's safe to switch, as a chemical system may damage some lenses). Contact lens supplies are sometimes rare or expensive in Austria and Switzerland. Bring enough saline and cleaner for your entire vacation, or wear glasses. In any case, bring a backup pair of glasses.

   Film is expensive just about everywhere. Bring rolls from home and develop them at home. If you're not a serious photographer, you might want to consider bringing a **disposable camera** or two rather than an expensive permanent one. Despite disclaimers, airport security X-rays *can* fog film, so either buy a lead-lined pouch from a camera store or ask the security to inspect it by hand. Always pack film in your carry-on luggage, since airports use higher-intensity X-rays on checked luggage.

Other useful items include: umbrella, resealable plastic bags (for damp clothes, soap, food, pens), alarm clock, waterproof matches, sun hat, needle and thread, safety pins, sunglasses, a personal stereo (Walkman) with headphones, pocketknife, notebook and pens, plastic water bottle, compass, string (makeshift clothesline and lashing material), towel, padlock, whistle, rubber bands, toilet paper, flashlight, cold-water soap, earplugs, insect repellant, electrical tape (for patching tears), clothespins, maps and phrasebooks, tweezers, garbage bags, and sunscreen.

GETTING THERE

The first challenge in European budget travel is getting there. Zurich is Switzerland's primary travel hub, but it's often cheaper to fly into Paris and take the TGV to your destination. Vienna is the cheapest destination in Austria, but it may be cheaper to fly into Munich and take a train to your destination. Budget travelers generally can't afford tickets with flexible return dates; traveling with an "open return" ticket can be pricier than fixing a return date and paying to change it. If you show up at the airport before your ticketed date of departure, the airline just might rewrite your ticket, even if it is supposedly precluded by company restrictions. Avoid one-way tickets—the flight to Europe may be economical, but the return fares can be outrageous.

■ Budget Travel Agencies

Students and people under 26 with proper identification need never pay full price for a ticket. They qualify for startlingly reduced airfares, available from student travel agencies like **Council** and **STA**. These agencies negotiate special reduced-rate bulk purchases with the airlines then resell the tickets. Seniors can also garner mint deals; many airlines offer discounts or passes for seniors and their companions.

Campus Travel, 52 Grosvenor Gardens, London SW1W 0AG (http://www.campus-travel.co.uk). 46 branches in the U.K. Student and youth fares on plane, train, boat, and bus travel. Discount and ID cards for students and youths, travel insurance for students and those under 35, and maps and guides. Telephone booking service: worldwide call (0171) 730 81 11, in North America (0171) 730 21 01, in Europe (0171) 730 34 02, in Scotland (0131) 668 33 03, in Manchester (0161) 273 17 21.

Council Travel (http://www.ciee.org/travel/index.htm), the travel division of Council, is a full-service travel agency specializing in youth and budget travel. Discount airfares on scheduled airlines, railpasses, hosteling cards, low-cost accommodations, guidebooks, budget tours, travel gear, and international student (ISIC), youth (GO25), and teacher (ITIC) IDs. U.S. offices include: Emory Village, 1561 N. Decatur Rd., **Atlanta,** GA 30307 (tel. (404) 377-9997); 2000 Guadalupe, **Austin,** TX 78705 (tel. (512) 472-4931); 273 Newbury St., **Boston,** MA 02116 (tel. (617) 266-1926); 1138 13th St., **Boulder,** CO 80302 (tel. (303) 447-8101); 1153 N. Dearborn, **Chicago,** IL 60610 (tel. (312) 951-0585); 10904 Lindbrook Dr., **Los Angeles,** CA 90024 (tel. (310) 208-3551); 1501 University Ave. SE #300, **Minneapolis,** MN 55414 (tel. (612) 379-2323); 205 E. 42nd St., **New York,** NY 10017 (tel. (212) 822-2700); 953 Garnet Ave., **San Diego,** CA 92109 (tel. (619) 270-6401); 530 Bush St., **San Francisco,** CA 94108 (tel. (415) 421-3473); 1314 NE 43rd St. #210, **Seattle,** WA 98105 (tel. (206) 632-2448); 3300 M St. NW, **Washington, D.C.** 20007 (tel. (202) 337-6464). **For U.S. cities not listed,** call 800-2-COUNCIL (226-8624). Also 28A Poland St. (Oxford Circus), **London,** W1V 3DB (tel. (0171) 287 33 37); **Paris** (tel. (01) 146 55 55 65); and **Munich** (tel. (089) 39 50 22).

Educational Travel Centre (ETC), 438 North Frances St., Madison, WI 53703 (tel. (800) 747-5551; fax (608) 256-2042; email edtrav@execpc.com; http://

www.edtrav.com). Flight information, HI-AYH cards, Eurail, and regional rail passes. Write for their free pamphlet *Taking Off*. Student and budget airfares.

Students Flights Inc., 5010 East Shea Blvd. #A104, Scottsdale, AZ 85254 (tel. (800) 255-8000 or (602) 951-1177; fax 951-1216; email jost@isecard.com; http://isecard.com). Also sells Eurail and Europasses and international student exchange IDs.

CTS Travel, 220 Kensington High St., W8 (tel. (0171) 937 33 66 for travel in Europe, 937 33 88 for travel world-wide; fax 937 90 27). Also at 44 Goodge St., W1. Specializes in student/youth travel and discount flights.

Let's Go Travel, Harvard Student Agencies, 17 Holyoke St., Cambridge, MA 02138 (tel. (617) 495-9649; fax 495-7956; email travel@hsa.net; http://hsa.net/travel). Railpasses, HI-AYH memberships, ISICs, ITICs, FIYTO cards, guidebooks (including *Let's Go*), maps, bargain flights, and budget travel gear. All items available by mail; call or write for a catalogue (or see the catalogue in center of this book).

Rail Europe Inc., 226 Westchester Ave., White Plains, NY 10604 (tel. (800) 438-7245; fax 432-1329; http://www.raileurope.com). Sells Eurail products and passes and point-to-point tickets. Up-to-date information on all rail travel in Europe.

STA Travel, 6560 Scottsdale Rd. #F100, Scottsdale, AZ 85253 (tel. (800) 777-0112; fax (602) 922-0793; http://sta-travel.com). Student and youth travel organization with over 150 offices worldwide offering discount airfares, railpasses, accommodations, tours, insurance, and ISICs. 16 offices in the U.S., including: 297 Newbury Street, **Boston,** MA 02115 (tel. (617) 266-6014); 429 S. Dearborn St., **Chicago,** IL 60605 (tel. (312) 786-9050); 7202 Melrose Ave., **Los Angeles,** CA 90046 (tel. (213) 934-8722); 10 Downing St., Ste. G, **New York,** NY 10003 (tel. (212) 627-3111); 4341 University Way NE, **Seattle,** WA 98105 (tel. (206) 633-5000); 2401 Pennsylvania Ave., **Washington, D.C.** 20037 (tel. (202) 887-0912); 51 Grant Ave., **San Francisco,** CA 94108 (tel. (415) 391-8407), **Miami,** FL 33133 (tel. (305) 284-1044). In the U.K., 6 Wrights Ln., **London** W8 6TA (tel. (0171) 938 47 11 for North American travel). In New Zealand, 10 High St., **Auckland** (tel. (09) 309 97 23). In Australia, 222 Faraday St., **Melbourne** VIC 3050 (tel. (03) 9349 6911).

Travel CUTS (Canadian Universities Travel Services Limited), 187 College St., Toronto, Ont. M5T 1P7 (tel. (416) 979-2406; fax 979-8167; email mail@travelcuts). Canada's national student travel bureau, with 40 offices across Canada. Also in the U.K., 295-A Regent St., **London** W1R 7YA (tel. (0171) 637 31 61). Discounted domestic and international airfares open to all; special student fares to all destinations. Issues ISIC, FIYTO, GO25, HI cards, and railpasses. Free *Student Traveller* magazine and information on the Student Work Abroad Program (SWAP).

Travel Management International (TMI), 1129 East Wayzata, Wayzata, MN 55391 (tel. (612) 404-7164 or (800) 245-3672). Diligent, prompt, and very helpful travel service offering student fares and discounts.

Usit Youth and Student Travel, 19-21 Aston Quay, O'Connell Bridge, Dublin 2 (tel. (01) 677-8117; fax 679-8833). In the U.S.: New York Student Center, 895 Amsterdam Ave., New York, NY 10025 (tel. (212) 663-5435; email usitny@aol.com). Additional offices in Cork, Galway, Limerick, Waterford, Maynooth, Coleraine, Derry, Athlone, Jordanstown, Belfast, and Greece. Specializes in youth and student travel. Offers low-cost tickets and flexible travel arrangements all over the world. Supplies ISIC and FIYTO-GO 25 cards in Ireland only.

Wasteels, 7041 Grand National Dr. #207, Orlando, FL 32819 (tel. (407) 351-2537; in London (0171) 834 70 66). A huge chain in Europe, with 200,000 locations. Request information in English from the London office (tel. (0171) 834 70 66; fax 630 76 28). Sells the Wasteels BIJ tickets, which are discounted (30-45% off regular fare) 2nd-class international point-to-point train tickets with unlimited stopovers (must be under 26 on the first day of travel); sold only in Europe.

■ By Plane

The **airline industry** attempts to squeeze every dollar from customers; finding a cheap airfare will be easier if you understand the airlines' systems. Call every toll-free number and don't be afraid to ask about discounts; if you don't ask, it's unlikely the staff will volunteer the information. Have knowledgeable **travel agents** (see above) guide you; better yet, have an agent who specializes in the region(s) you will be visiting to guide you. An agent whose clients fly mostly to Nassau or Miami will not be the best person to hunt down a bargain flight to Geneva. Travel agents may not want to spend time finding the cheapest fares (for which they receive the lowest commissions), but if you travel often, you should definitely find an agent who will cater to you and your needs and track down deals in exchange for your frequent business.

Students and seniors always qualify for some discounts (see **Budget Travel Agencies,** p. 30). Sunday newspapers often have travel sections that list bargain fares from the local airport. Outsmart airline reps with the phone-book-sized *Official Airline Guide* (check your local library; at US$359 per year, with fares US$479, the tome costs as much as some flights), a monthly guide listing nearly every scheduled flight in the world and toll-free phone numbers that allow you to call in reservations directly. *The Airlines Passenger's Guerilla Handbook* (US$15; last published in 1990) is a more renegade resource. More accessible is Michael McColl's *The Worldwide Guide to Cheap Airfare* (US$15), an incredibly useful guide for finding...cheap airfare.

The Internet is steadily becoming a very valuable resource for travel information. The *Official Airline Guide* has a website (http://www.oag.com) that allows users to access flight schedules. (One-time hook-up fee US$25, user's fee US$0.17-0.47 per min.). The site also provides information on hotels, cruises, and rail and ferry schedules. **TravelHUB** (http://www.travelhub.com) will help you search for travel agencies on the web. The **Air Traveler's Handbook** (http://www.cis.ohio-state.edu/hypertext/faq/usenet/travel/air/handbook/top.html) is an excellent source of general information on air travel—provided you can slog your way through typing in the address. Marc-David Seidel's **Airlines of the Web** (http://www.itn.net/airlines) provides links to pages and 800 numbers for most of the world's airlines. The newsgroup **rec.travel.air** is a good source for current bargains. A few airlines have even begun holding auctions on their websites, including **Icelandair** (http://www.centrum.is/icelandair) and **Finnair** (http://www.us.finnair.com).

The day of the week that you fly can dramatically affect the price of your ticket (see **Days of the Week** below). Most airfares peak between mid-June and early September. Traveling from hub to hub will win a more competitive fare than flying from smaller cities. Return-date flexibility is usually not an option for the budget traveler; traveling with an "open return" ticket can be more expensive than fixing a return date and subsequently paying to change it. Airlines practice "yield management," meaning the number of budget-priced seats on any flight is small and constantly subject to change. Call around. Flights to London are usually the cheapest way to cross the Atlantic. Whenever flying internationally, pick up your ticket well in advance of the departure date, have the flight confirmed within 72 hours of departure, and arrive at the airport at least three hours before your flight.

Days of the Week

While round-trip tickets may be cheaper during the week than on weekends, they also mean crowded flights, which in turn means competition for frequent-flier upgrades. Scheduling weekend flights is more expensive, but less crowded, and proves the best bet for using frequent-flier upgrades. Most business travelers travel on Thursdays, which makes stiff competition for upgrade hunters. Saturdays and Sundays present the best opportunities for frequent fliers.

COMMERCIAL AIRLINES

The commercial airlines' lowest regular offer is the **Advance Purchase Excursion Fare (APEX);** specials advertised in newspapers may be cheaper, but have more restrictions and fewer available seats. APEX fares provide you with confirmed reservations and allow "open-jaw" tickets (landing in and returning from different cities). Generally, travelers must make reservations seven to 21 days in advance, the tickets have seven- to 14-day minimum and up to 90-day maximum stay limits, and hefty cancellation and change penalties may apply. Book APEX fares early during peak season; by May you will have a hard time getting the departure date you want.

Look into flights to less-popular destinations or on smaller carriers. **Icelandair** (tel. (800) 223-5500) has last-minute offers and a stand-by fare from New York to Luxembourg (April-June 1 and Sept.-Oct. US$410; June-Aug. US$610). You must make reservations within three days of departure. **Martinair** (tel. (800) 627-8462 or (800) MARTINAIR) offers one-way only standby fares (US$210) from New York to Amsterdam (you're responsible for the ticket home).

Swissair (tel. (800) 221-4750), the national airline of Switzerland, serves most Swiss cities, though their fares tend to be high. They also offer car rental in conjunction with **Kemwel** and vouchers for over 1500 hotels starting at US$47. **Swisspak**, essentially their travel service, puts together customized tours "for all budgets," including packages with a 10% discount for senior citizens over the age of 62 of up to US$100. Further, they have forged a partnership with **Delta, USAir,** and **Singapore Airlines** that allows travelers to accumulate frequent-flier miles and to travel to numerous destinations. Contact the above Swissair number for more information.

Austrian Airlines, 608 Fifth Ave., New York, NY 10020 (tel. (800) 937-8181 or (212) 265-6350; fax 581-0695), the national airline of Austria, has the most non-stop flights and serves the most cities in Austria, but its fares tend to be high. Austrian Airlines flies daily non-stop from New York to Vienna and has flights from Chicago, London, and Johannesburg to Vienna. Austrian Airlines is associated with **OnePass**, Continental Airlines' frequent-flier program. Members can accrue and redeem their miles on Austrian Airlines flights, with some restrictions. If you are not a member of OnePass (tel. (800) 525-0280), join before you depart on Austrian Airlines. As with any airline's program, you'll earn thousands of miles just on this one round-trip flight. Austrian Airlines also has a partnership with **Delta** and has moved its operation at JFK International Airport in New York to Delta's Terminal 1A, making domestic-international connections easier. Call Delta for more information (tel. (800) 241-4141 in the U.S and most of Canada, in Nova Scotia (800) 361-6770). Dozens of carriers fly to Vienna, albeit often with changes and layovers.

Even if you think you have an airline's cheapest airfare for your destination, you may still be spending hundreds too much. Shop around.

TICKET CONSOLIDATORS

Ticket consolidators resell unsold tickets on commercial and charter airlines at unpublished fares. Consolidator flights are the best deals if you are travelling on short notice (you bypass advance purchase requirements since you aren't tangled in airline bureaucracy), on a high-priced trip, to an offbeat destination, or in the peak season when published fares are jacked way up. Consolidators generally reduce fares up to 30-40%. There are rarely age constraints or stay limitations, but unlike tickets bought through an airline, you won't be able to use your tickets on another flight if you miss yours, and you will have to go back to the consolidator rather than the airline to get a refund. Keep in mind that these tickets are often for coach seats on connecting (not direct) flights on foreign airlines, and that frequent-flier miles may not be credited. Decide what you can and can't live with before shopping.

Not all consolidators deal with the general public; many only sell tickets through travel agents. **Bucket shops** are retail agencies that specialize in getting cheap tickets. Although ticket prices are slightly marked up, bucket shops generally have access to a larger market, including wholesale consolidators, than would be available to the public. Look for bucket shops' tiny ads in the travel section of weekend papers; in the U.S., the Sunday *New York Times* is a good source. In London, a call to the **Air Travel Advisory Bureau** (tel. (0171) 636 50 00) can provide names of reliable consolidators and discount flight specialists. Kelly Monaghan's *Consolidators: Air Travel's Bargain Basement* (US$7, shipping US$2) from The Intrepid Traveler, P.O. Box 438, New York, NY 10034 (email intreptrav@aol.com), is an invaluable source.

Be a smart shopper; check out the competition. Among the many reputable and trustworthy companies are, unfortunately, some shady wheeler-dealers. Contact the local Better Business Bureau to find out how long the company has been in business and its track record. It's preferable, though not necessary, to deal with local consolidators so that you can visit in person, if necessary. Ask to receive your tickets as quickly as possible so you have time to fix any problems. Get the company's policy in writing: insist on a **receipt** with full details about the tickets, refund policies, and restrictions, and record the name of the person to whom you talked and when. You may want to pay with a credit card (despite the 2-5% fee); you'll be able to stop payment if you don't receive your tickets. Beware the "bait and switch" gag: shyster firms will advertise a super-low fare and then tell a caller that it has been sold. If the company can't offer you a price near the advertised fare on *any* date, the ad is a scam to lure in customers—report them to the Better Business Bureau. Also ask about accommodations and car rental discounts; some consolidators have fingers in many pies.

Try **Airfare Busters** (in Washington, D.C. (tel. (202) 776-0478), Boca Raton, FL (tel. (561) 994-9590), and Houston, TX (tel. (800) 232-8783); **Pennsylvania Travel,** Paoli, PA (tel. (800) 331-0947); **Cheap Tickets** (offices in Los Angeles, San Francisco, Honolulu, Seattle, and New York; tel. (800) 377-1000); or **Discount Travel International,** New York, NY (tel. (212) 362-3636; fax 362-3236). **Moment's Notice,** New York, NY (tel. (718) 234-6295; fax 234-6450; http://www.moments-notice.com), offers air tickets, tours, and hotels for a US$25 annual fee. **NOW Voyager,** 74 Varick St. #307, New York, NY 10013 (tel. (212) 431-1616; fax (212) 334-5243; email info@nowvoyagertravel.com; http://www.nowvoyagertravel.com), acts as a consolidator and books discounted international flights, mostly from New York, as well as courier flights (see **Courier Companies and Freighters** below), for a registration fee of US$50. For a processing fee that depends on the number of travelers and the itinerary, **Travel Avenue,** Chicago, IL (tel. (800) 333-3335; fax (312) 876-1254; http://www.travelavenue.com), will search for the lowest international airfare available, including consolidated prices, and rebates fares over US$300. You can also try **Rebel,** Valencia, CA (tel. (800) 227-3235; fax (805) 294-0981; email travel@rebeltours.com; http://www.rebeltours.com) or Orlando, FL (tel. (800) 732-3588).

Fly to Europe for 80% off
London $159. Paris $228. Rome $199.

We've got the lowest *roundtrip* airfares to Europe. Africa, $480. South America, $167. Asia, $335. China, $450. And more. (For less.) *What's the catch?* Join the Air Courier Association and fly as a courier for "big name" international freight companies.

AIR COURIER ASSOCIATION®
Fly to more of the world for less.

You'll go as a coach passenger on major scheduled airlines to handcarry time sensitive business documents. For your service you get dirt cheap airfares.

Hurry because we have limited seasonal enrollment. Visit us on the Internet, www.aircourier.org

For your Free Info Kit call
Call 8-5 MT
1-800-822-0888
1-303-215-9000 Denver, Colorado

STAND-BY FLIGHTS

Airhitch, 2641 Broadway, 3rd Fl., New York, NY 10025 (tel. (800) 326-2009 or (212) 864-2000; fax 864-5489) and Los Angeles, CA (tel. (310) 726-5000), will add a certain thrilling uncertainty to your departure date and destination—you'll need a completely flexible schedule on both sides of the Atlantic. Flights cost US$175 each way when departing from the Northeast, $269 from the West Coast or Northwest, $229 from the Midwest, and $209 from the Southeast. Travel within Europe is also possible, with rates ranging from $79 to $129. Here's the rub: you buy not a ticket but a promise that you will get to a destination near where you're intending to go within a window of time (usually 5 days) from a location in a region you've specified. You call in before your date-range to hear all of your flight options for the next seven days and your probability of boarding one of these flights. You then decide which flights you want to try to make and present the airline with a voucher that grants you the right to board a flight on a space-available basis. You must follow this procedure again for the return trip. Be aware that you may receive a monetary refund only if all available flights that departed within your date-range from the specified region are full, but future travel credit is always available. There are several offices in Europe, so you can wait to register for your return. The main office is in Paris (tel. (1) 47 00 16 30).

Air-Tech, Ltd., 588 Broadway #204, New York, NY 10012 (tel. (212) 219-7000, fax 219-0066), offers a very similar service. Their Travel Window is one to four days. Rates to and from Europe (continually updated; call and verify) are: Northeast US$169; West Coast US$239; Midwest/Southeast US$199. Upon registration and payment, Air-Tech sends you a FlightPass with a contact date, when you are to call them for flight instructions. You must go through the same procedure to return. The company grants no refunds unless it fails to get you a seat before your Travel Window expires. Air-Tech also arranges courier flights and regular disocunted flights.

Be sure to read all the fine print in your agreements with either company—a call to The Better Business Bureau of New York City may be worthwhile. Be warned that refunds are difficult to get and that clients' vouchers will not be honored if an airline fails to receive payment in time.

CHARTER FLIGHTS

Charters are flights that a tour operator contracts with an airline (usually one specializing in charters) to fly extra loads of passengers to peak-season destinations. Charters are often cheaper than flights on scheduled airlines, especially during peak seasons, although fare wars, consolidator tickets, and small airlines can beat charter prices. Some charters operate nonstop, and restrictions on advance-purchase deadlines and minimum stays are relatively lenient. However, charter flights fly less frequently than major airlines, make refunds particularly difficult, and are almost always fully booked. Schedules and itineraries may also change or be cancelled at the last moment (as late as 48 hours before the trip, and without a full refund), and check-in, boarding, and baggage claim are often much slower. As always, pay with a credit card if you can and consider traveler's insurance against trip interruption.

Try **Interworld** (tel. (305) 443-4929; fax 443-0351), **Travac** (tel. (800) 872-8800; fax (212) 714-9063; email mail@travac.com; http://www.travac.com), or **Rebel,** Valencia, CA (tel. (800) 227-3235; fax (805) 294-0981; email travel@rebeltours.com; http://rebeltours.com) or Orlando, FL (tel. (800) 732-3588). Don't be afraid to call every number and hunt for the best deal.

Eleventh-hour **discount clubs** and **fare brokers** offer their members savings on flights, including charter flights and tour packages. Research your options carefully. **Last Minute Travel Club,** 100 Sylvan Rd., Woburn, MA 01801 (tel. (800) 527-8646 or (617) 267-9800), and **Discount Travel International,** New York, NY (tel. (212) 362-3636; fax 362-3236; see **Ticket Consolidators** above), are among the few travel clubs that don't charge a membership fee. Others include **Moment's Notice** (see **Ticket Consolidators** above), **Travelers Advantage,** Stamford, CT (tel. (800) 548-1116; http://www.travelersadvantage.com; US$49 annual fee), and **Travel Avenue** (see

Ticket Consolidators above). Study contracts closely—you don't want to book yourself into an unwanted overnight layover.

COURIER COMPANIES AND FREIGHTERS

Those who travel light should consider flying internationally as a **courier**. The company hiring you will use your checked luggage space for freight; you're only allowed to bring carry-ons. You are responsible for the safe delivery of the baggage-claim slips (given to you by a courier company representative) to the representative waiting for you when you arrive—don't screw up or you'll be blacklisted among courier companies. You will probably never see the cargo you are transporting—the company handles it all—and airport officials know that couriers are not responsible for the baggage checked for them. Restrictions to watch for: you must be over 21 (in some cases 18), have a valid passport, and procure your own visa (if necessary); most flights are round-trip only with short fixed-length stays (usually one week); companies only issue single tickets (but a companion may be able to get a next-day flight); and most flights are from New York. Round-trip fares range from US$250-400 off-season to US$400-550 in summer. For an annual fee of US$45, the **International Association of Air Travel Couriers,** 8 South J St., P.O. Box 1349, Lake Worth, FL 33460 (tel. (561) 582-8320), informs travelers (via computer, fax, and mail) of courier opportunities worldwide. Steve Lantos publishes a monthly update of courier options in **Travel Unlimited** as well as general information on low-budget travel (write P.O. Box 1058A, Allston, MA 02134 for a free sample newsletter; subscription US$25 per year). Most flights originate from New York or London. **NOW Voyager** (see **Ticket Consolidators** above) acts as an agent for many courier flights worldwide, primarily from New York, and offers special last-minute deals. Other agents to try are **Halbart Express,** 147-05 176th St., Jamaica, NY 11434 (tel. (718) 656-5000; fax 917-0708; offices in Chicago, Los Angeles, and London), and **Discount Travel International** (tel. (212) 362-3636; see **Ticket Consolidators** above).

You can contact courier companies directly in New York, or check your bookstore or library for such handbooks as *Air Courier Bargains* (US$15, shipping $2.50; from The Intrepid Traveler, P.O. Box 438, New York, NY 10034; email intreptrav@aol.com). *The Courier Air Travel Handbook* (US$10, shipping $3.50) explains how to travel as an air courier and contains names, phone numbers, and contact points of courier companies. You can order the book directly from Bookmasters, Inc., P.O. Box 2039, Mansfield, OH 44905 (tel. (800) 507-2665).

Better Safe than Sorry

Everyone who flies should be concerned with airline safety. The type and age of the aircraft used often indicate the airline's safety level–aircraft not produced by Boeing, Airbus, McDonnell Douglas, or Fokker sometimes fall below acceptable standards, and aircraft over 20 years old require increased levels of maintenance. If you're flying a foreign airline, especially to Third World countries, consult one of the following organizations. Travel agencies can tell you the type and age of aircraft on a particular route, as can the *Official Airline Guide* (http://www.oag.com); this can be especially useful in Eastern Europe, where airlines often use less reliable equipment for inter-city travel. The **International Airline Passengers Association** (tel. (972) 404-9980) publishes a survey of accident rates on foreign airlines and provides safety information on carriers worldwide. The **Federal Aviation Administration** (http://www.faa.gov) reviews the airline authorities for countries whose airlines enter the U.S. and divides the countries into three categories: stick with carriers in category 1. Call the **U.S. State Department** (tel. (202) 647-5225; http://travel.state.gov/travel_warnings.html) for posted travel advisories that sometimes involve foreign carriers.

ONCE THERE

■ Tourist Information and Town Layouts

The **Swiss National Tourist Office** and the **Austrian National Tourist Office** both publish a wealth of information about tours and vacations; every town of any touristic importance whatsoever—and some of no importance at all—have local tourist offices. To simplify things, all offices are marked by a standard green "i" sign (blue in Switzerland). *Let's Go* lists tourist offices in the Practical Information section of each city. The staff may or may not speak English—the skill is not a requirement in smaller towns. In Swiss cities, look for the excellent **Union Bank of Switzerland maps,** which have very detailed streets and sites.

One thing to keep in mind is that the Austrian and Swiss creative palate for small-town names is rather dry. Many towns, even within the same state or province, have the same names (Gmünd or Stein, for instance). Before boarding any trains or buses, verify that the vehicle is heading for your intended destination. Once there, pick up a map from the tourist office. Most Austrian and Swiss train stations have luggage storage, currency exchange, and bike rentals (at a discount if you have a train ticket for that day or a valid railpass). The **post office** is often next door to the train station, even in larger cities. Most towns are small enough that all sights are within walking distance. If distances do prove daunting, local transportation generally covers any unmanageable trek. Buy local public transport tickets from *Tabak* stands, which sell them for reduced rates. Most ticket validation is based on the honor system, and many tourists interpret that as a free ride. Though certainly a tempting budget option, **Schwarzfahren** (black riding, i.e., riding without a ticket) can result in very unbudget-like fines, and playing "Dumb American" will probably only work once.

■ Getting Around

BY TRAIN

European trains retain the charm and romance that their North American counterparts lost generations ago. Second-class travel is pleasant, and compartments, which seat from two to six, are excellent places to meet fellow itinerants of all ages and nationalities. Train trips tend to be short since both Austria and Switzerland are relatively small. Gather your bags together a few stops before your own, since trains stop only for two to three minutes before zipping off. For longer trips, make sure that you are on the correct car, as trains sometimes split at crossroads. In large cities, make sure that you are at the correct train station. Towns in parentheses on schedules require switching trains at the town listed immediately before the parenthesis. For example, "Salzburg-Attnang-Puchheim-(Bad Ischl-Hallstatt)" means that in order to get to Bad Ischl or Hallstatt, you have to disembark at Puchheim and pick up a different train. You might want to ask if your route requires a change of trains, as the schedules are sometimes about as decipherable as ancient runes.

Trains are in no way theft-proof; lock the door of your compartment when you nap and keep your valuables on your person at all times. Non-smokers should not delude themselves into thinking that they'll be able to rest comfortably in smoking compartments. For overnight travel, a tight, open bunk called a *couchette* is an affordable luxury (about US$20; reserve at the station at least several days in advance).

The **Österreichische Bundesbahn (ÖBB),** Austria's federal railroad, operates one of Europe's most thorough and efficient rail networks—a 5760km system whose trains are frequent, fast, clean, comfortable, and always on or close to schedule. The ÖBB prints the yearly *Fahrpläne Kursbuch Bahn-Inland*, a 5cm-thick compilation of all rail, ferry, and cable-car transportation schedules in Austria. The massive compendium (100AS) is available at any large train station, along with its companion tomes, the *Kursbuch Bahn-Ausland* for international trains, and the *Internationales Schlafwagenkursbuch* for sleeping cars.

Getting around Switzerland is also a snap. Federal **(SBB, CFF)** and private railways connect most towns and villages, with trains running in each direction on an hourly basis. **Schnellzüge** (express trains) speed between metropoli, while **Regionalzüge** chug into each cowtown on the route. Each city has booklets listing train schedules, including a free booklet listing all major fares within the country. The national telephone number for rail information is 157 22 22 and has English operators.

Be aware that only private train lines may go to remote tourist spots, and therefore Eurail and Swisspasses might not be valid. Reservations can only be made on scenic, and not on regular, trains. Yellow signs announce departure times *(Ausfahrt)* and platforms *(Gleis, quai, binario)*. White signs are for arrivals *(Ankunft)*. On major Austrian lines, make reservations at least a few hours in advance.

International Passes

Ideally conceived, a railpass allows you to jump on any train in Europe, go wherever you want whenever you want, and change your plans at will. The handbook that comes with your railpass tells you everything you need to know and includes a timetable for major routes, a map, and details on ferries, steamers, buses, car rental, and hotels. In practice, it's not so simple. You still must stand in line to pay for seat reservations, supplements, couchette reservations, and initial pass validation. More importantly, railpasses don't always pay off. For ballpark estimates on point-to-point tickets, consult Rick Steve's **Europe Through the Back Door** newsletter or the **DERTravel** or **RailEurope** railpass brochure. Add the individual costs up and compare the total to the railpass price. If you're under age 26, the BIJ tickets are probably a viable option (see **Rail Tickets,** p. 39).

Eurailpass, P.O. Box 10383, Stamford, CT 06904, remains the best option for non-EU travelers. Eurailpasses are valid in most of Western Europe (with the notable exception of Britain). The EU designed Eurailpasses and Europasses for non-Europeans, and they distribute them almost exclusively outside of Europe. The EU sets the prices, so no one travel agent is better than any other for buying a Eurailpass.

Travelers under age 26 can buy a **Eurail Youthpass,** good for 15 days (US$365), 21 days (US$475), one month (US$587), two months (US$832), or three months (US$1028) of second-class travel. The two-month pass is the most economical. If you are traveling in a group, you might prefer the **Eurail Saverpass,** which allows unlimited first-class travel for 15 days (US$444), 21 days (US$576), one month (US$712), two months (US$1010), or three months (US$1248) per person in groups of two or more. **Eurail Flexipasses** allow limited first-class travel within a two-month period: 10 days (US$616), 15 days (US$812). **Youth Flexipasses,** for those under 26 who wish to travel second-class, are available for US$431 or US$568, respectively.

The **Europass** combines France, Germany, Italy, Spain, and Switzerland in one plan. With a Europass you can travel in any of these five countires from five to 15 days within a two-month window. First-class adult prices begin at US$316 and increase US$42 for each extra day of travel. With the purchase of a first-class ticket, you can buy an identical ticket for your traveling partner for 40% off. Second-class youth tickets begin at US$210 and increase US$29 for each extra day of travel. Children between the ages of four and 11 travel for half the price of a first-class ticket. You can also add associate countries (*e.g.* Austria/Hungary) for a nominal fee. The Europass introduces planning complications: you must plan your routes so that they only make use of countries you've "purchased." The train lines are serious about this restriction: if you cut through a country you haven't purchased, you will be fined.

You should plan your itinerary before buying a Europass. It will save you money if your travels are confined to between three and five adjacent Western European countries or if you know that you want to go only to large cities. Europasses are not appropriate if you like to take lots of side trips—you'll waste rail days. If you're tempted to add lots of rail days and associate countries, consider the Eurailpass.

You'll find it easiest to buy a Eurailpass before you arrive in Europe; contact Council Travel, Travel CUTS, Let's Go Travel (see **Budget Travel Agencies,** p. 27), **Rail Europe, Inc.,** 226-230 Westchester Ave., White Plains, NY 10604 (in U.S. tel. (800) 438-7245, fax 432-1329; in Canada tel. (800) 361-7245; fax (905) 602-4198; http://www.raileurope.com), **DERTravel Services,** 9501 W. Devon Ave. #400, Rosemont, IL 60018 (tel. (800) 421-2929; fax 282-7474; http://www.dertravel.com), or almost any other travel agent. If you're stuck in Europe and no one will sell you a Eurailpass, call an American railpass agent, who should be able to send a pass by express mail. Eurailpasses are not refundable once validated; you can get a replacement for a lost pass only if you have purchased insurance under the Pass Protection Plan (US$10).

People who've resided in Europe for at least six months can buy **InterRail Passes.** The Under 26 InterRail Card (from UK£189) allows either 15 days or one month of unlimited travel within one, two, three or all of the seven zones into which InterRail divides Europe; the cost is determined by the number of zones the pass covers. The Over 26 InterRail Card offers unlimited second-class travel in 19 countries in Europe for 15 days (UK£215) or one month (UK£275). For information and tickets in Europe, contact **Student Travel Center,** 1st Fl. 24 Rupert St., London, W1V 7FN (tel. (0171) 437 01 21, 437 63 70, or 434 13 06; fax 734 38 36; http://www.hols.com/studentt/). Tickets are also available from travel agents or large train stations.

Austria

Children under six in Austria travel free. Fares are 50% off for children ages six to 14. The **Austrian Rail Pass** is valid for four days of travel within a 10-day period on all rail lines, including Wolfgangsee ferries and private rail lines (2nd-class US$111, 1st-class US$165). **Austrian Rail Pass Junior,** for travelers under 15, provides the same discounts as its parent, but for less (2nd-class US$64, 1st-class US$95). Children under the age of 7 ride free. The card itself has no photo, so you must carry a valid ID in case of inspections. Keep in mind that the Rail Pass Junior is cheaper than many round-trip fares, so it may be an economical option even for short stays. The pass also entitles its holders to a 50% discount on bicycle rental in over 160 railway stations as well as the steamers of Erste Donau Dampfschiffahrts Gesellschaft (EDDG) operating between Passau, Linz and Vienna. The pass is sold in the U.S. by Rail Europe. **Bundesnetzkarte** are valid for unlimited travel through Austria, including Wolfgangsee ferries and private rail lines. The cards win half-price tickets for Bodensee and Danube ferries, and there's no surcharge on EC and SC first-class trains. (1- month of 2nd-class 3800AS, 1st-class 5700AS. Picture necessary.) The passes are sold only in Austria.

Switzerland

In Switzerland, children under 16 can travel free when accompanied by an adult with the **Swiss Family Card** (20SFr, no expiration date), which is not connected with the Swiss Family Robinson gift package. A **Swisspass** grants unlimited free travel on government-operated trains, ferries, buses in 30 Swiss cities, and private railways, and a 25-50% discount on many mountain railways and cable cars. Second-class prices are as follows: a four-day pass costs US$176; eight-day US$220; 15-day US$256; 1-month US$350 (ages 6-16 half-price, free if traveling with parents and the Swiss Family Card). The pass is sold abroad through Rail Europe or any major U.S. travel agency. Depending on exchange rates, it may be cheaper to buy the pass at train stations in Switzerland. The pass also has a very strict no-replacement policy. A **Swiss Flexipass** (US$176) is valid for any three days of second-class travel within 15 days. Unless you're planning to speed through all of Switzerland at warp speeds, the pass may not pay for itself. **Regional Passes** are available in major tourist offices for holders of Eurailpasses (50-175SFr). The **Swiss Card,** sold only abroad, works as a one-month Half-Fare Card and provides one free round-trip from an airport or border station (US$96). Travelers who plan on driving might consider the **Swiss Rail'n'Drive Pass.** It works like a Swiss Flexipass but adds three days of car rental with unlimited mileage and unlimited travel on the some of the private railways, such as the Glacier Express near Zermatt and the Panoramic Express. If you're traveling with three or four people, only two will have to buy the pass and the others need only buy the Swiss Flexipass. The pass includes car rental with manual transmission only, and rates vary depending on the car category you choose (2nd-class runs US$325-415).

Rail Tickets

You can **purchase tickets** at every train station, at Bahn-Total service stations, at the occasional automat, or from the conductor for a small surcharge. You can pay by check, up to a limit. Over 130 stations accept the major credit cards as well as American Express Traveler's Cheques and Eurocheques.

For travelers under 26, **BIJ** tickets (Billets Internationals de Jeunesse, sold under the names **Wasteels, Eurotrain,** and **Route 26**) are a great alternative to railpasses. Available for international trips within Europe and for travel within France as well as most ferry services, they knock 25-40% off regular second-class fares. Tickets are good for two months after purchase and allow a number of stopovers along the normal direct route of the train journey. The tickets are issued in Europe for a specific international route between two points, and travelers must use them in the direction and order of the designated route. BIJ tickets are available from European travel agents, at Wasteels or Eurotrain offices (usually in or near train stations), or directly at the ticket counter in some nations. Contact Wasteels in Victoria Station, adjacent to Platform 2, London SW1V 1JT (tel. (0171) 834 70 66; fax 630 76 28).

British and Irish citizens **over the age of 60** can buy their national senior pass and receive a 30% discount on first- and second-class travel in Austria and Switzerland. Restrictions on travel time may apply.

Useful Resources

The ultimate reference for planning rail trips is the **Thomas Cook European Timetable** (US$28, including a map of Europe with all train and ferry routes US$39; postage US$4.50). This timetable, updated regularly, covers all major and most minor train routes in Europe. Find it at any European **Thomas Cook Exchange Center.** Forsyth's **Traveling Europe's Trains** (US$15), by Jay Burnoose, includes maps and sightseeing suggestions. Available in most bookstores or from **Houghton Mifflin Co.,** 222 Berkeley St., Boston, MA 02116 (tel. (800) 225-3362; fax 634-7568), is the annual **Eurail Guide to Train Travel in the New Europe** (US$15), giving timetables, instructions, and prices for international train trips, day trips, and excursions in Europe. The annual railpass edition of Rick Steves' **Europe Through the Back Door** travel newsletter and catalogue, 120 Fourth Ave. N., P.O. Box 2009, Edmonds, WA 98020 (tel. (425) 771-8303; fax 771-0833; email ricksteves@aol.com; http://www.ricksteves.com), compares European railpasses with regional passes and point-to-point tickets. **Hunter Publishing,** P.O. Box 7816, Edison, NJ 08818 (tel. (908) 225-1900; fax 417-0482; email hunterpub@emi.net; http://www.hunterpublishing.com), offers a catalogue of rail atlases and travel guides. Titles include **Britain on the Backroads** and **The Trans-Siberian Rail Guide.**

BY BUS

Trains cost a pretty penny. Fortunately, Austria and Switzerland have a fair range of bus services. For Europe-wide service, **Eurolines,** 4 Cardiff Rd., Luton LU1 1PP, U.K. (tel. (01582) 40 45 11; fax 40 06 94) or 52 Grosvenor Gdns, Victoria Station in London (tel. (0171) 730 82 35), is Europe's largest operator of Europe-wide coach services. A Eurolines Pass offers unlimited 30-day (under 26 and over 60 UK£159; 26-60 UK£199) or 60-day (UK£199, UK£249) travel between 20 major tourist destinations. **Eurobus,** P.O. Box 3016, Workingham, Berkshire RG40 2YP (tel. (0118) 936 23 21; fax 936 23 22; http://www.eurobus.uk.com), offers cheap bus trips for those between ages 16 and 38. The buses, with English-speaking guides and drivers, stop at the doors of one hostel or budget hotel per city and let you hop on and off. Tickets are sold by zone (any 1 zone US$225; 2 zones US$400; 3 zones US$525). Travelers under 26 are eligible for discounts on all tickets.

GETTING AROUND ■ 41

Austria

The efficient Austrian bus system consists mainly of orange **BundesBuses.** Buses are generally complement the train system; they serve mountain areas inaccessible by train but do not duplicate long-distance, intercity routes covered by rail. Bus stations are usually adjacent to the train station. Buses cost about as much as trains, but no railpasses are valid. Always purchase round-trip tickets if you plan to return to your starting point. Buy tickets at a ticket office at the station or from the driver. For buses in heavily touristed areas during high season (such as the Großglockner Straße in summer), you should probably make reservations. All public buses are non-smoking.

Anyone can buy discounted tickets, valid for one week, for any particular route. A **Mehrfahrtenkarten** gives you six tickets for the price of five. A **Seniorenausweiß** for women over 60 and men over 65 entitles senior citizens to half-price bus and train fares for a year (350AS). **Children under six** ride free as long as they don't take up a full seat. **Children ages 6-15** and **large pets** (other than seeing-eye dogs ride) for half-price within Austria. Trips can be interrupted under certain conditions, depending on your ticket—be sure to ask. Small, regional bus schedules are available for free at most post offices. For more **bus information,** call (0222) 711 01 within Austria (outside Austria dial (1) instead of (0222)).

Switzerland

PTT **postal buses,** a barrage of banana-colored, three-brake-system coaches delivered to you expressly by the Swiss government, connect rural villages and towns, picking up the slack where trains fail to go. Swisspasses are valid on many buses, Eurailpasses are not. Even with the Swisspass, you might have to pay a bit extra (5-10SFr) if you're riding one of the direct, faster buses. In cities, public buses transport commuters and shoppers alike to outlying areas. Buy tickets in advance at automatic machines, found at most bus stops. The system works on an honor code and inspections are infrequent, but expect to be hit for 30-50SFr if you're caught riding without a valid ticket. *Tageskarte,* valid for 24 hours of free travel, run 2-7.50SFr, but Swiss cities are so small that you might as well travel by foot.

BY AIRPLANE

If you ever need to travel by plane during your visit, look around: you probably got confused and went to Australia. Austria and Switzerland are train and bus countries. Many youth discounts, however, can make airfare comparable to train tickets for longer distances (Geneva to Prague, for instance), but even these discounts can't touch railpass deals. These special fares require you to purchase tickets either the day before or the day of departure. Look to student travel agencies in Europe (SSR, especially) for cheap tickets. The **Air Travel Advisory Bureau** (see **Charter Flights,** p. 35) can put you in touch with international discount flights.

BY CAR AND VAN

Cars offer great speed, great freedom, access to the countryside, and an escape from the humdrum town-to-town mentality of trains. While a single traveler will probably lose money by renting a car, groups of two or three can make renting a viable option and groups of four or more will definitely travel more cheaply by car than by train. Rail and car packages offered by Avis and Hertz are often best for two or more people travelling together; contact the National Tourist Offices for country-specific plans.

To rent a car in **Austria,** you must be over 21 (older in some cases) and must carry an International Driver's Permit and a valid driver's license that you have had for at least one year (see **Driving Permits and Car Insurance,** p. 8). Most Austrian companies restrict travel into Hungary, the Czech Republic, and Slovakia, and rental taxes are high (21%). In **Switzerland,** the minimum rental age varies by company but is rarely below 21, and you must possess a valid driver's license that you have had for at least one year (foreign licenses are valid). Rates for all cars rented in Switzerland include an obligatory 40SFr annual **road toll,** called a *vignette.*

You can **rent** from a U.S.-based firm (Alamo, Avis, Budget, or Hertz) with European offices, from a European-based company with local representatives (Europcar), or from a tour operator (Auto Europe, Bon Voyage By Car, Europe By Car, and Kemwel Holiday Autos), which will arrange a rental from a European company at its own rates. Multinational companies offer greater flexibility, but tour operators often strike better deals. Rentals vary by company, season, and pick-up point. Expect to pay US$80-400 per week, plus tax (5-25%), for a teensy car. Airlines often offer special packages; you may get up to a week of free rental. Reserve well before leaving and pay in advance if you can—it's always much less expensive to reserve from the U.S. Always check if prices quoted include tax and collision insurance; some credit card companies will cover these costs automatically. Ask about discounts and check the terms of insurance, particularly the size of the deductible.

Rental agencies include: **Alamo** (tel. (800) 522-9696; http://www.goalamo.com); **Auto Europe,** 39 Commercial St., P.O. Box 7006, Portland, ME (tel. (800) 223-5555; fax 235-6321; http://www.auto-europe.com); **Avis Rent a Car** (tel. (800) 331-1084; http://www.avis.com); **Bon Voyage By Car** (tel. (800) 272-3299, in Canada (800) 253-3876); **Budget Rent a Car** (tel. (800) 472-3325); **Europe by Car,** One Rockefeller Plaza, New York, NY 10020 (tel. (800) 223-1516 or (212) 581-3040, in California (800) 252-9401; fax (212) 246-1458; http://www.europebycar.com); **Europcar,** 145 av. Malekoff, 75016 Paris (tel. (800) 227-3876, in Canada (800) 227-7368); **France Auto Vacances** (tel. (800) 234-1426); **Hertz Rent a Car** (tel. (800) 654-3001; http://www.hertz.com); **Kemwel Holiday Autos** (tel. (800) 678-0678; http://www.kemwel.com); **Payless Car Rental** (tel. (800) 729-5377).

Leasing or even buying and reselling a car is another option. Eric Bredesen's **Moto-Europa** (US$16; shipping US$3, overseas US$7), available from Seren Publishing, 2935 Saint Anne Dr., Dubuque, IA 52001 (tel. (800) 387-6728; fax (319) 583-7853), is a thorough guide to rental alternatives. The book includes itinerary suggestions, a motorists' phrasebook, and chapters on leasing and buying vehicles. More general information is available from the **American Automobile Association (AAA),** Travel Agency Services Dept., 1000 AAA Dr., Heathrow, FL 32746-5080 (tel. (800) 222-4357 or (417) 444-7380; http://www.aaa.com). For regional numbers of the **Canadian Automobile Association (CAA),** call (800) 222-4357.

Caravanning, usually involving a camper or motor-home, offers the advantages of car rental without the hassle of finding lodgings or cramming six friends into a leaky Citroën. You'll need those six buddies to split the gasoline bills, however. Prices vary even more than those for cars, but for the outdoor-oriented group trip, caravanning can be a dream. Contact the car rental firms listed above for more information.

On the Road

Austrian and Swiss highways are excellent. With armies of mechanized road crews ready to remove snow at moment's notice, roads at altitudes of up to 1500m generally remain open throughout winter. (Mountain driving does present special challenges, however; see **Personal Safety,** p. 12.) Cars drive on the right side of the road in both countries. The **speed limit** is 50km per hour (31mph) within cities unless otherwise indicated; outside towns, the limit is 130km per hour (81mph) on highways and 100km per hour (62mph) on all other roads. Driving under the influence of alcohol is a serious offense—fines begin at 700SFr (5000AS) and rise rapidly from there. Violators may also lose their licenses. The legal blood-alcohol limit is *very low.*

Many small Austrian and Swiss towns forbid cars to enter; some forbid only visitors' cars, require special permits, or restrict driving hours. Parking poses further problems: it's unavailable or restricted in some small cities, and while parking garages exist in larger cities, you'll have to battle the tourist hordes for a spot. Blue lines on the sidewalks mark short-term parking areas; purchase tickets for these spots from the machine nearby. **Gasoline stations** are self-service and open around the clock. To use them, first insert money into the pump. U.S. gasoline credit cards (or regular credit cards) are accepted only at American gas stations, including Exxon, Mobil, Shell, and Texaco. Consult local tourist offices for further information on driving.

EU citizens driving in Austria and Switzerland don't need any special documentation—registration and license will suffice. All cars must carry a first-aid kit and a red emergency triangle. All passengers in both countries must wear seatbelts, and children under 12 may not sit in the front passenger seat unless a child's seatbelt or a special seat is installed. Emergency phones are located along all major highways. The **Austrian Automobile, Motorcycle, and Touring Club (ÖAMTC)** (tel. (1) 71 19 97, in emergencies 120) provides an English-language service and sells a set of eight detailed road maps, far superior to the tourist office's map. (Open daily 6am-8pm.) The **Swiss Touring Club,** rue Pierre-Fatio 9, CH-1211 Geneva 3 (tel. (022) 737 12 12) operates road patrols that assist motorists in need; call 140 for help.

BY BICYCLE

Today, biking is one of the key elements of the classic budget Eurovoyage, and the proliferation of mountain bikes allows you to do some serious natural sight-seeing. The eastern part Austria is level and bicycle-friendly, but the Salzkammergut and Tirol reward effort the extra effort with more dramatic scenery. Remember that touring involves pedaling both yourself and whatever you store in the **panniers** (bags which strap to your bike). Take some reasonably challenging day-long rides at home to prepare yourself before you leave, and have a reputable shop tune up your bike. Wear visible clothing, drink plenty of water (even if you're not thirsty), and ride on the same side as the traffic. Know how to fix a modern derailleur-equipped mount and how to change a tire, and practice on your own bike. A few simple tools and a good bike manual will be invaluable. Be sure to buy a suitable **bike helmet**—at about US$25-50, they're a much better buy than head injury or death. U-shaped **Citadel** or **Kryptonite locks** are expensive (starting at US$30), but the companies insure their locks against the theft of your bike for one to two years. **Bike Nashbar,** 4111 Simon Rd., Youngstown, OH 44512 (tel. (800) 627-4227; fax 456-1223; http://www.nashbar.com), has excellent prices and beats advertised competitors' offers by US$.05.

Many airlines count bicycles as your second free piece of luggage, but a few airlines charge extra. The additional or automatic fee runs about US$60-110 each way. You must detach the pedals and the front wheel and pack the bike in a cardboard box, available at airports (US$10). Most ferries let you take your bike for a nominal fee.

Renting a bike beats bringing your own if you tour just one or two regions. Train stations rent your little two-wheeled friends and typically allow you to return the bike to any other station, and Austrian train stations generally reduce rental rates for travelers holding train tickets or valid Eurailpasses. Some stations also rent racing, mountain, and tandem bikes. Reservations are recommended, and you should bring photo ID. A standard seven-gear city bike goes for 150AS or 22-23SFr per day. Rock-conquering **mountain bikes** cost a bit more, children's bikes less. Trains often charge for bike transport (you must load and unload yourself). *Let's Go* lists other bike rental shops for most larger cities and towns, and some youth hostels rent bicycles for low prices.

For information on touring routes, consult the National Tourist Offices or any of the numerous books available. The **Touring Club Suisse,** Cyclo Tourisme, chemin Riantbosson 11-13, CH-1217 Meyrin (tel. (022) 785 12 22; fax 785 12 62), will send you information, maps, brochures, route descriptions, and mileage charts. May, June, and September are prime biking months. **The Mountaineers Books,** 1001 S.W. Klickitat Way #201, Seattle, WA 98134 (tel. (800) 553-4453 or (206) 223-6303; fax 223-6306; mbooks@mountaineers.org), offers tour books and **Europe By Bike,** by Karen and Terry Whitehill (US$15, shipping US$3), a great source of specific area tours in 11 countries. **Cycling Europe: Budget Bike Touring in the Old World** (US$13), by N. Slavinski from National Book Network, 15200 NBN Way, P.O. Box 190, Blue Ridge Summit, PA 17214-0190 (tel. (800) 462-6420), can help your planning.

If you are nervous about striking out on your own, **Blue Marble Travel** (in U.S. tel. (800) 258-8689 or (201) 326-9533; fax 326-8939; in Paris (01) 42 36 02 34; fax 42 21 14 77; http://www.blumarbl.com), offers bike tours designed for adults aged 20 to 50. Pedal with or without your 10 to 15 companions through the Alps. Grad students can get 15% discounts, and anyone can get "stand-by" fares in Europe. **CBT Bicycle**

Tours offers one- to seven-week tours, priced around US$95 per day. The price includes all lodging and breakfasts, one-third of all dinners, complete van support, airport transfers, three staff members, and extensive route notes and maps each day. Tours run May through August, with departures every seven to 10 days. In 1998, CBT will visit Belgium, England, France, Germany, Holland, Italy, Ireland, Luxembourg, and Switzerland. Contact CBT Bicycle Tours, 415 W. Fullerton #1003, Chicago, IL 60614 (tel. (800) 736-BIKE (2453) or (773) 404-1710; fax (773) 404-1833).

BY THUMB

Let's Go strongly urges you to consider seriously the risks before you choose to hitch. We do not recommend hitching as a safe means of transportation, and none of the information presented here is intended to do so.

Not everyone can be an airplane pilot, but any bloodthirsty bozo can drive a car. Hitching means entrusting your life to a random person who happens to stop beside you on the road and risking theft, assault, and sexual harassment. In spite of these risks, there are things to be gained—you can meet locals and get where you're going.

Men and women traveling in groups and men traveling alone might consider hitching (called "Autostop") beyond the range of bus or train routes. If you're a woman traveling alone, don't hitch. It's just too dangerous. A man and a woman are a safer combination, two men will have a harder time, and three will go nowhere. Avoid getting in the back of a two-door car, and never let go of your backpack. Don't get into a car that you can't exit again in a hurry. If you ever feel threatened, insist on getting out. Acting as if you are going to open the car door or vomit on the upholstery will usually get a driver to stop. Nocturnal hitching is particularly risky.

Still there? As for the actual process itself, where one stands is vital. Experienced hitchers pick a spot (well-lit, if at night) outside of built-up areas, where drivers can stop, have time to look over potential passengers as they approach, and return to the road without causing an accident. Hitching (or even standing) on super-highways is usually illegal: one may only thumb at rest stops or at the entrance ramps to highways. In the **Practical Information** section of many cities, *Let's Go* lists the tram or bus lines that take travelers to strategic points for hitching out. Finally, success will depend on appearance. Successful hitchers travel light and stack their belongings in a compact but visible cluster. Most Europeans signal with an open hand rather than a thumb; many write their destination on a sign in large, bold letters. Drivers prefer hitchers who are neat and wholesome—no one stops for anyone wearing sunglasses or carrying weapons, so leave your international terrorist costume at home.

BY FOOT

Much of Europe's grandest scenery is accessible only by foot. *Let's Go* describes many daytrips for those who want to hoof it, but native inhabitants (Europeans are fervent, almost obsessive hikers), hostel proprietors, and fellow travelers are the best source of information. See **Camping, Hiking, and the Outdoors** for extensive listings and information on exercising your right to bipedal locomotion.

■ Accommodations

Like most things Austrian and Swiss, accommodations in these countries are usually clean, orderly, and expensive. Wherever you stay, be sure to ask for a **guest card**. Normally, the "card" is merely a copy of your receipt for the night's lodging, sometimes available only after staying three nights or more. Guest cards generally grant discounts to local sports facilities, hiking excursions, town museums, and public transportation. In Austria, the 10AS tax that most accommodations slap on bills fund these discounts—take advantage of them to get your money's worth.

Let's Go is not an exhaustive guide to budget accommodations. Most local tourist offices distribute extensive listings (the *Gastgeberverzeichnis*), and many will reserve a room for a small fee. National tourist offices (see **National Tourist Offices,** p. 1) and travel agencies (**Travel Organizations,** p. 2) will also supply more complete lists of campsites and hotels. Be aware that *Privatzimmer* and *Pensionen* may close their doors without notice; it's always wise to call ahead.

HOSTELS

> **A Hosteler's Bill of Rights**
> There are certain standard features that we do not include in our hostel listings. Unless we state otherwise, you can expect that every hostel has: no lockout, no curfew, free hot showers, secure luggage storage, and no key deposit.

For tight budgets and those lonesome traveling blues, hostels can't be beat. Hostels (*Jugendherbergen* in German, *Auberges de Jeunesse* in French, *Albergi della Gioventù* in Italian) are the hubs of the gigantic backpacker subculture that rumbles through Europe every summer, providing innumerable opportunities to meet travelers from all over the world. Hostels are generally dorm-style accommodations, often in single-sex large rooms with bunk beds (although some hostels do offer private rooms for families and couples). They sometimes have guest kitchen facilities, bike or moped rentals, storage areas, and laundry facilities. Most guests are 17-25. Hosteling does have its drawbacks: some hostels close during certain daytime "lock-out" hours, have a curfew, impose a maximum stay, are sometimes spartan and cramped, have little privacy, or, less frequently, require that you do chores. Perhaps worst of all, you may run into **more mercilessly screaming prepubescent school groups than you care to remember.** Summer is an especially attractive season for the bubblegum set to invade hostels; try to arrive at a hostel before 5pm to insure that the hordes of children don't deprive you of a room. Fees range from US$5 to $25 per night; hostels associated with one of the large hostel associations often have lower rates for members. If you have Internet access, check out the **Internet Guide to Hostelling** (http://hostels.com), listing hostels from around the world and has oodles of information about hosteling and backpacking worldwide. **Eurotrip** (http://www.eurotrip.com/accommodation/accommodation.html) has information on budget hostels and several international hostel associations. For a nominal fee, you can make reservations in advance for over 300 **Hostelling International (HI)** hostels (see listing below) via the computerized International Booking Network (IBN; tel. (202) 783-6161).

HOSTEL MEMBERSHIP

Prospective hostel-goers should become members of the official youth hostel association in their country. All national organizations are members of **Hostelling International (HI).** A one-year HI membership permits you to stay at youth hostels all over the world at unbeatable prices. Despite the name, you need not be a youth; travelers over 26 may have to pay only an occasional surcharge for a bed. Save yourself trouble by procuring a membership card at home—some hostels don't sell them on the spot. It is possible to join once you're on the road, though. Show up at an HI hostel, and ask for a blank membership card with space for six validation stamps. Each night you'll pay a non-member supplement (equal to one-sixth the membership fee) and earn one Guest Stamp; get six stamps and you're a member.

An Óige (Irish Youth Hostel Association), 61 Mountjoy St., Dublin 7 (tel. (01) 830 45 55; fax 830 58 08; anoige@iol.ie). One-year membership is IR£7.50, under 18 IR£4, family IR£7.50 for each adult (children under 16 free). Prices from IR£4.50-9.50 a night. 37 locations.

Are You Ready to Choose Exciting Moments?

For Example: The lovely olympic city of Innsbruck within the heart of the European Alps. We offer the budget accomodation for skiing and sightseeing. It's young, it's trendy, it's open to the world. It's THE solution for groups, families and individuals. It's one out of more than hundred modern youth hostels in Austria. Be ready to choose: pure nature, crystal-clear lakes, historic cities, thrilling adventures in the heart of Europe.

ÖSTERREICHISCHES JUGENDHERBERGSWERK

Austria is ready for you!

For more information contact the Austrian Youth Hostelling Association: call ++431-533 18 33, email: oejhw@oejhw.or.at, www.oejhw.or.at/oejhw/

ACCOMMODATIONS ■ 47

Australian Youth Hostels Association (AYHA), Level 3, 10 Mallett St., Camperdown NSW 2050 (tel. (02) 9565 1699; fax 9565 1325; e-mail YHA@zeta.org.au). Memberships AUS$42, renewal AUS$26; under 18 AUS$12.

Hostelling International-American Youth Hostels (HI-AYH), 733 15th St. NW, Ste. 840, Washington, D.C. 20005 (tel. (202) 783-6161; fax 783-6171; email hiayhserv@hiayh.org; http://www.hiayh.org). Maintains 35 offices and over 150 hostels in the U.S. Memberships available at many travel agencies or the national office. One year membership US$25, under 18 US$10, over 54 US$15, family US$35. Reserve by letter, phone, fax, or through the International Booking Network (IBN), a computerized reservation system. Basic rules (with much local variation): check-in 5-8pm, check-out 9:30am (most urban hostels have 24hr. access), 3-night max. stay, no pets or alcohol allowed on the premises. Dorms US$5-22 per night.

Hostelling International-Canada (HI-C), 400-205 Catherine St., Ottawa, Ont. K2P 1C3 (tel. (613) 237 7884; fax 237 7868). Maintains 73 hostels throughout Canada. IBN booking centers in Edmonton, Montreal, Ottawa, and Vancouver; expect CDN$9-22.50 per night. Membership packages: One-year CDN$25, under 18 CDN$12; 2-year CDN$35; lifetime CDN$175.

Scottish Youth Hostels Association (SYHA), 7 Glebe Crescent, Stirling FK8 2JA (tel. (01786) 891400; fax 891333; email syha@syha.org.uk; http://www.syha.org.uk). Membership UK£6, under 18 UK£2.50.

Youth Hostels Association of England and Wales (YHA), Trevelyan House, 8 St. Stephen's Hill, St. Albans, Hertfordshire AL1 2DY, England (tel. (01727) 85 52 15; fax 84 41 26). Enrollment UK£9.50, under 18 UK£3.50; family UK£19; lifetime UK£130. Dorms UK£6.25-20.50, under 18 UK£4.25-17.20.

Youth Hostels Association of Northern Ireland (YHANI), 22 Donegall Rd., Belfast BT12 5JN (tel. (01232) 32 47 33 or 31 54 35; fax 43 96 99). One-year UK£7, under 18 UK£3; family UK£14 for up to 6 children. Dorms UK£8-12.

Youth Hostels Association of New Zealand (YHANZ), P.O. Box 436, 173 Gloucester St., Christchurch 1 (tel. (643) 379 9970; fax 365 4476; email info@yha.org.nz; http://www.yha.org.nz). Annual membership fee NZ$24.

Hostel Association of South Africa, P.O. Box 4402, Cape Town 8000 (tel. (021) 24 2511; fax 24 4119; email hisa@gem.co.za; http://www.gen.com/hisa). Membership SAR45; students SAR30; group SAR120; family SAR90; lifetime SAR225.

DORMS

Many **colleges and universities** open their residence halls to travelers when school is not in session; some do so even during term-time. These dorms are often close to student areas—good sources for information on things to do, places to stay, and possible rides out of town—and are usually very clean. No one policy covers all these institutions. Getting a room may be difficult, but rates tend to be low and many establishments offer free local calls. *Let's Go* lists colleges that rent dorm rooms among the accommodations for appropriate cities. College dorms are popular with many travelers, especially those looking for long-term lodging, so reserve ahead.

HOTELS

Hotels are expensive in Austria (singles 200-350AS; doubles 400-800AS) and ridiculously exorbitant in Switzerland (50-75SFr; 80-150SFr). Switzerland has set the international standard for hotels; even one-, two- and three-star accommodations may be much nicer than their counterparts in other countries. The cheapest hotel-style accommodations are places with **Gasthof** or **Gästehaus** ("inn") in the name; **Hotel-Garni** also indicates an inexpensive hotel. Continental breakfast *(Frühstuck)* is almost always included. Unmarried couples over 21 will generally have no trouble getting a room together.

PRIVATE ROOMS AND PENSIONS

Renting a **private room** *(Privatzimmer)* in a family home is an inexpensive and friendly way to house yourself. Such rooms generally include a sink with hot and cold running water and use of a toilet and shower. Many places rent private rooms only for

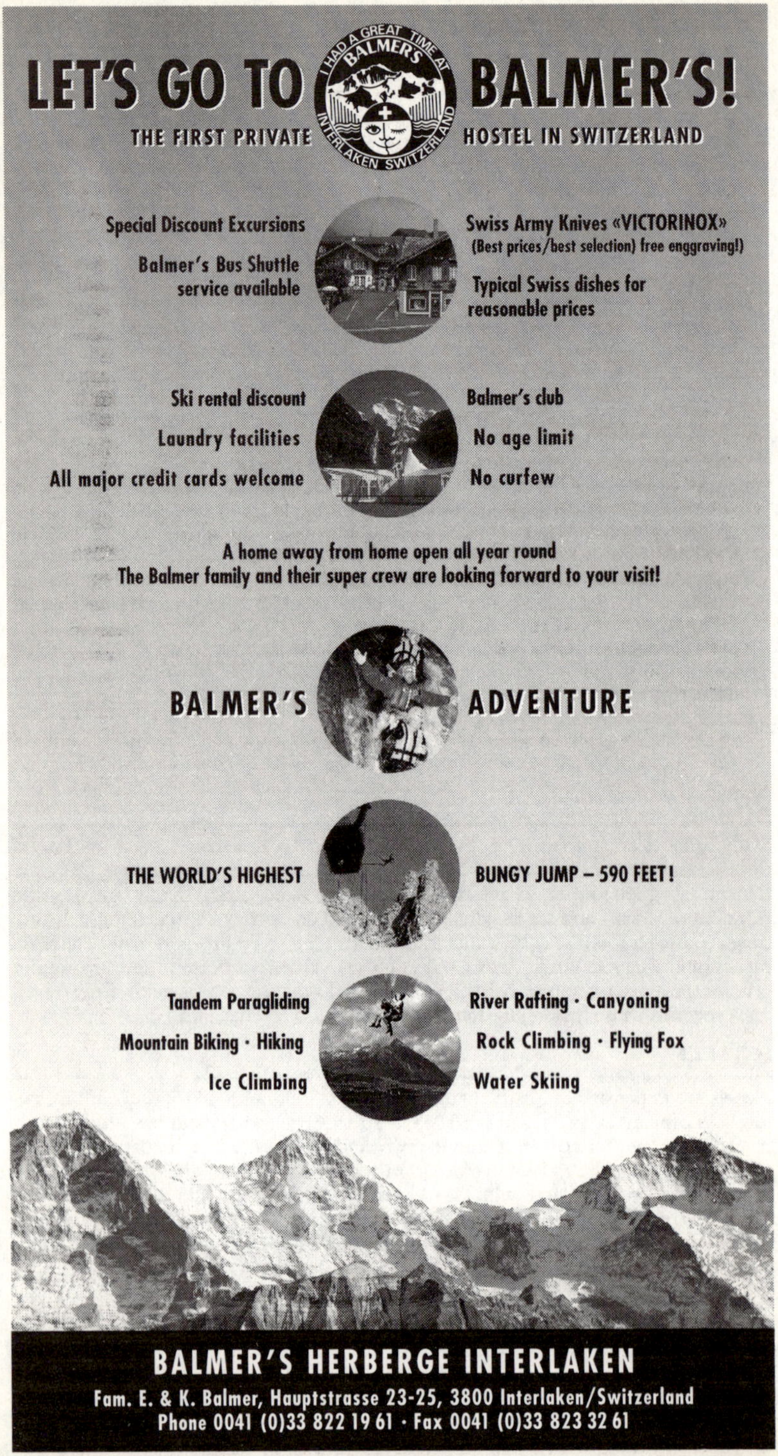

LET'S GO TO BALMER'S!
THE FIRST PRIVATE HOSTEL IN SWITZERLAND

I HAD A GREAT TIME AT BALMER'S INTERLAKEN SWITZERLAND

Special Discount Excursions

Balmer's Bus Shuttle service available

Swiss Army Knives «VICTORINOX»
(Best prices/best selection) free enggraving!)

Typical Swiss dishes for reasonable prices

Ski rental discount

Laundry facilities

All major credit cards welcome

Balmer's club

No age limit

No curfew

A home away from home open all year round
The Balmer family and their super crew are looking forward to your visit!

BALMER'S ADVENTURE

THE WORLD'S HIGHEST BUNGY JUMP – 590 FEET!

Tandem Paragliding

Mountain Biking · Hiking

Ice Climbing

River Rafting · Canyoning

Rock Climbing · Flying Fox

Water Skiing

BALMER'S HERBERGE INTERLAKEN
Fam. E. & K. Balmer, Hauptstrasse 23-25, 3800 Interlaken/Switzerland
Phone 0041 (0)33 822 19 61 · Fax 0041 (0)33 823 32 61

longer stays, or they may levy a surcharge (10-20%) for stays of less than three nights. *Privatzimmer* start at 25-60SFr per person in Switzerland. In Austria, rooms range from 150-200AS a night. Slightly more expensive, pensions *(Pensionen)* are somewhat similar to the American and British notion of a bed and breakfast and to the private rooms described above. Generally, finding rooms for only one person might be difficult, especially for one-night stays—many places will claim to be full. Most places have room with double beds *(Doppelzimmer)*; if the rooms have two beds, single travelers will have to pay more. You may have a private bathroom; you'll almost never have to share with more than four or five people. Continental breakfast is *de rigeur;* in classier places, meat, cheese, and an egg will grace your plate and palate. Since pensions are people's homes, be sure to treat them kindly. Always remember to shut doors behind you when you leave rooms—Austrians tend to keep doors to even empty rooms closed. These popular lodgings fill quickly; reserve ahead.

■ Long-term Stays

Home exchange is tourism's symbiosis—thousands of travelers pay a for-profit company to include their house or apartment on a list, and the company in turn unites two parties who plan a mutually thrilling switcheroo. For less than US$80 you can get a list of many thousands of residences owned by people who want to trade their homes. The benefits are manifold: you'll feel like a resident, circumvent hostels, transportation, and restaurant costs, and avoid leaving your own home empty. Discounts are available for customers over 62. A great site listing many exchange companies await at http://www.aitec.edu.au/~bwechner/Documents/Travel/Lists/HomeExchangeClubs.html. Renting a house or apartment may also be a good deal for some: the cost-effectiveness will depend on the length of stay and the desired amenities.

Europa-Let/Tropical Inn-Let, 92 North Main St., Ashland, OR 97520 (tel. (800) 462-4486 or (541) 482-5806; fax 482-0660; email Europa-Let@WaveNet), offers over 100,000 private rental properties with kitchens in 29 countries, including Austria and Switzerland. Customized computer searches allow clients to choose properties according to specific needs and budget. Especially advantageous for families, business people, large groups, or those planning to stay more than one week. Europa-Let is also the U.S. agent for Auto Europe car rental.

fair tours, Postbox 615, CH-9001 St. Gallen, Switzerland (email fairtours@gn.apc.org; http://www.gn.apc.org/fairtours), is a home exchange program for environmentally conscious travelers that provides an opportunity to avoid large-scale commercial tourism. Personal matching service. Send two international reply coupons to the address above for further information.

Hometours International, Inc., P.O. Box 11503, Knoxville, TN 37939 (tel. (800) 367-4668; email hometours@aol.com; http://thor.he.net/Ihometour/). Lodging in apartments, houses, villas, and castles. Brochures are US$5 for each country.

The Invented City: International Home Exchange, 41 Sutter St., Ste. 1090, San Francisco, CA 94104 (tel. in the U.S (800) 788-CITY, outside the U.S. (415) 252-1141; fax (415) 252-1171; email invented@aol.com). Listing of 1700 homes worldwide. For US$50, you get your offer listed in 1 and receive 3 catalogues. Members arranges all details of the swap themselves.

■ Camping, Hiking, and the Outdoors

With over 1200 campgrounds in Switzerland and more than 400 throughout Austria, **camping** is a popular option. In Switzerland, prices average 6-9SFr per person, 4-10SFr per tent—a joy to behold in such an expensive country. In Austria, prices run 50-70AS per person and 25-60AS per tent (plus 8-9.50AS tax if you're over 15), seldom making camping substantially cheaper than hosteling. You must obtain permission from landowners to camp on private property. Don't hold your breath—the traditionally conservative Austrians and Swiss are often very protective of their private property. The Swiss Tourist Office also gives information about sites. Most sites are open in the summer only, but some are year-round and 80 sites are specifically set aside for winter camping. Camping along roads and in public areas is forbidden.

USEFUL PUBLICATIONS

A variety of publishing companies offer hiking guidebooks to meet the educational needs of novice or expert. For information about camping, hiking, and biking, write or call the publishers listed below to receive a free catalogue.

- **Automobile Association,** AA Publishing. Orders and enquiries to P.O. Box 194, Rochester, Kent, ME2 4QG, U.K. (tel. (01634) 29 71 23; fax 29 80 00 or 29 80 02). Wide range of maps and guides, including *Camping and Caravanning: Europe*.
- **The Caravan Club,** East Grinstead House, East Grinstead, West Sussex, RH19 1UA, U.K. (tel. (0342) 32 69 44; fax 41 02 58), produces one of the most detailed English-language guides to campsites in Europe.
- **Family Campers and RVers/National Campers and Hikers Association, Inc.,** 4804 Transit Rd., Bldg. #2, Depew, NY 14043 (tel./fax (716) 668-6242). Membership fee (US$25) includes their publication *Camping Today*. For US$35, you can also get the International Camping Carnet, which is required by some European campgrounds but can usually be bought on the spot.
- **Recreational Equipment, Inc. (REI),** P.O. Box 1700, Sumner, WA 98352–0001 (tel. (800) 426-4840), publishes *Europa Camping and Caravanning* (US$20), an annually updated catalogue of European campsites. Few of their books are offered via mail-order, so check their retail stores.
- **Stanfords,** 12-14 Long Acre, London, WC2E 9LP, U.K. (tel (01718) 36 13 21; fax 36 01 89), supplies maps of just about anywhere, especially continental Europe.
- **The Mountaineers Books,** 1001 SW Klickitat Way #201, Seattle, WA 98134 (tel. (800) 553-4453 or (206) 223-6303; fax 223-6306; email mbooks@mountaineers.org). Many titles on hiking (including the *100 Hikes* series), biking, mountaineering, natural history, and conservation.

Affordable comfort at the foot of the Eiger

MOUNTAIN HOSTEL
Grindelwald
Switzerland
CH-3818 Grindelwald-Grund

Phone 41 33 853 3900 / Fax 41 33 853 4730

Rooms with bunk beds for 2, 4, and 6 people • Individual lockers • Washbasin in every room • Individual showers • TV • Games room with pool table and table tennis • Washer / Dryer • Covered outdoor self-cooking area • Mini shop • Locked storage for sports equipment • Next to train, bus, cablecar • Parking • Credit cards accepted

CAMPING AND HIKING EQUIPMENT

Purchase **equipment** before you leave—you'll know exactly what you have and how much it weighs. Spend some time examining catalogues and talking to knowledgeable salespeople. Whether you're buying or renting equipment, you should go out of your way to find sturdy, light, and inexpensive equipment.

Most good **sleeping bags** are rated by "season," or the lowest outdoor temperature at which they will keep you warm ("summer" means 30-40°F, "three-season" means 20°F, and "four-season" or "winter" means below 0°F). Sleeping bags are made either of down (warmer and lighter, but expensive and miserable when wet) or of synthetic material (heavier, more durable, and warmer when wet). Prices vary but might range from US$65-100 for a summer synthetic to US$250-550 for a good down winter bag. **Sleeping bag pads,** including foam pads (from US$15) and air mattresses (US$25-50), cushion your back and neck and insulate you from the ground. Another good alternative is the **Therm-A-Rest,** which is part foam and part air-mattress and inflates to full padding when you unroll it. The best **tents** are free-standing, with their own frames and suspension systems; they set up quickly and require no staking (except in high winds). Low-profile dome tents are the best all-around. Tent sizes can be somewhat misleading: two people *can* fit in a two-person tent but will find life more pleasant and remain on speaking terms for a longer period of time in a four-person tent. If you're traveling by car, go for the bigger tent. If you're hiking, stick with a smaller, 3-4lb. tent. Good two-person tents start at US$150, four-person tents at US$400, but you can sometimes find last year's model for half the price. Be sure to seal the seams of your tent with waterproofer, and make sure the tent has a rain fly.

If you intend to do a lot of hiking, you should have a **frame backpack. Internal-frame packs** mold better to your back, keep a lower center of gravity, and are flexible enough to allow you to hike difficult trails that require a lot of bending and maneuvering. **External-frame packs** are more comfortable for long hikes over even terrain; they keep the weight higher and distribute it more evenly. Whichever you choose, make sure your pack has a strong, padded hip belt, which transfers the weight from the shoulders to the legs. Any serious backpacking requires a pack of at least 4000 cubic inches. Allow an additional run US$125-500; cheaper packs may be less comfortable, and the straps are more likely to fray or rip. Before you buy any pack, try it on and imagine carrying it, full, a few miles up a rocky incline. Wear **hiking boots** with good ankle support appropriate for the terrain you'll be hiking. Your boots should fit snugly and comfortably over one or two wool socks and a thin liner sock. Be sure that the boots are broken in—a bad blister will ruin your hiking for days.

Rain gear should come in two pieces, a top and pants, rather than a poncho. **Synthetics,** like polypropylene tops, socks, and long underwear under a pile jacket, will keep you warm even when wet. When camping in autumn, winter, or spring, bring along a **"space blanket,"** which helps you to retain body heat and doubles as a groundcloth (US$5-15). Plastic **canteens** or water bottles keep water cooler than metal ones do and are virtually shatter- and leak-proof. Large, collapsible **water sacks** will significantly improve your lot in primitive campgrounds and weigh practically nothing when empty. They can get bulky, though. Bring **water-purification tablets** for those times when you can't boil water. Most campgrounds provide campfire sites, but you may want to bring a small **metal grate** or **grill** of your own. For those places that forbid fires or the gathering of firewood (virtually every organized campground in Europe), you'll need a **camp stove.** The classic Coleman starts at about US$30, and you can purchase the little blue cylinders for the "GAZ" butane/propane stove anywhere—just don't try to take them onto a plane. Campers should also look into buying an **International Camping Carnet,** similar to a hostel membership card. The card is required at a few campgrounds and provides discounts at others (available in North America from the **Family Campers and RVers Association;** in the U.K. from **The Caravan Club;** see **Useful Publications,** above). A **first aid kit, Swiss Army knife,** and **waterproof matches** or a **lighter** are essential camping items. Other useful items include: a **battery-operated lantern,** a **plastic groundcloth,** a **nylon tarp,** a **water-**

proof cover (although you can also store your belongings in plastic bags inside your backpack), and a **"stuff sack"** or plastic bag to keep your sleeping bag dry.

The mail-order firms listed below offer lower prices than those you'll find in many stores, but shop around locally in order to determine what items actually look like and weigh. Keep in mind that camping equipment is generally more expensive in Australia, New Zealand, and the U.K. than in North America.

Campmor, P.O. Box 700, Saddle River, NJ 07458-0700 (tel. (800) CAMPMOR (526-4784), outside the U.S. (201) 825-8300; email customer-service@campmor.com; http://www.campmor.com), has a wide selection of name-brand equipment at low prices. One-year guarantee for unused or defective merchandise.

Eastern Mountain Sports (EMS), One Vose Farm Rd., Peterborough, NH 03458 (tel. (603) 924-9591), has stores throughout the U.S. Though slightly expensive, they provide excellent service and guarantee customer satisfaction on most items. They don't have a catalogue, and they generally don't take mail or phone orders—call the above number for the branch nearest you.

Recreational Equipment, Inc. (REI), 1700 45th St. E, Sumner, WA 98390 (tel. (800) 426-4840; http://www.rei.com). Wide range of camping gear; great seasonal sales. Many items guaranteed for life (excluding normal wear and tear).

L.L. Bean, Freeport, ME 04033-0001 (tel. in Canada or the U.S. (800) 441-5713, in the U.K. (0800) 962 954, elsewhere (207) 552-6878; fax (207) 552-3080; http://www.llbean.com). This monolithic equipment and outdoor clothing supplier offers high quality and loads of information. Call or write for their free catalogue. Satisfaction guaranteed on all purchases.

Mountain Designs, P.O. Box 1472, Fortitude Valley, Queensland 4006, Australia (tel. (07) 3252 8894; fax (07) 3252 4569), is a leading Australian manufacturer and mail-order retailer of camping and climbing gear.

Sierra Designs, 1255 Powell St., Emeryville, CA 94608 (tel. (510) 450-9555; fax 654-0705), carries all types of tents, especially small and lightweight models.

Sierra Trading Post, 5025 Campstool Rd., Cheyenne, WY 82007-1802 (tel. (307) 775-8000; fax 775-8088; http://www.sierra-trading.com). Savings on name-brand outdoor clothing and equipment.

YHA Adventure Shop, 14 Southampton St., London, WC2E 7HA, U.K. (tel. (01718) 36 85 41). Main branch of one of Britain's largest outdoor-equipment suppliers.

CAMPERS AND RVS

Many North American campers harbor a suspicion that travelling with a **camper** or **recreational vehicle (RV)** is not "real camping." No such stigma exists in Europe, where RV camping, or "caravanning," is both popular and common. European RVs are smaller and more economical than the 40-foot Winnebagos of the American road. Renting an RV will always be more expensive than tenting or hostelling, but the costs compare favorably with the price of renting a car and staying in hotels, and the convenience of bringing along your own bedroom, bathroom, and kitchen makes it an attractive option for some, especially older travellers and families with small children.

It is not difficult to arrange an RV rental from overseas, although you will want to begin gathering information several months before your departure. Rates vary widely by region, season (July and Aug. are the most expensive), and type of RV. It always pays to contact several different companies to compare vehicles and prices. **Avis** and **Hertz** can arrange RV rentals overseas; **Auto Europe** and **Europcar** have branches in North America (see **By Car and Van,** p. 41). New Zealand's **Maui Rentals** (tel. 9275 3013; fax 9275 9690) rents RVs in Australia, New Zealand, and South Africa.

Camping Your Way through Europe by Carol Mickelsen (Affordable Press, US$15) and *Exploring Europe by RV* by Dennis and Tina Jaffe (Globe Pequot, US$15) are both good resources for planning this type of trip.

WILDERNESS AND SAFETY CONCERNS

Stay warm, stay dry, and **stay hydrated.** The vast majority of life-threatening wilderness problems stem from a failure to follow these rules. On any hike, however brief,

CAMPING, HIKING, AND THE OUTDOORS

you should pack enough equipment to keep you alive should disaster strike. Include **rain gear,** a **hat** and **mittens,** a **first-aid kit, high energy food,** and **water** in your pack. Dress in warm layers of **wool** or **synthetic materials** designed for the outdoors. Pile fleece jackets and Gore-Tex® raingear are excellent choices (see **Camping and Hiking Equipment**). Summer or winter, there are no exceptions to this list.

All hikers appreciate the beauty of the environment, but many do not recognize its potential dangers. Always check weather forecasts and pay attention to the skies when hiking. Weather patterns in mountainous regions can change instantly. A bright blue sky can turn to rain—or even snow—before you can say "hypothermia." If you're on a day-hike and the weather turns nasty, turn back. If you're on an overnight hike, start looking immediately for shelter. Never rely on cotton for warmth—this "death cloth" will be absolutely useless should it get wet. It retains water, holding it close to your skin and chilling your body. Wool and synthetic materials designed for the outdoors dry faster and pull water away from your body, allowing you to stay warm even when wet.

If possible, you should let someone know that you are going hiking, either a friend, your hostel, a park ranger, or some local hiking organization. If you get into serious trouble, use the Alpine Distress Signal—six audible or visible signals spaced evenly over one minute and followed by a break of one minute before repetition. Listen for a response of signals at 20-second intervals. Whether in a densely populated campground ten minutes from a major city or alone in the middle of the wilderness, you should follow basic camping safety rules. A good guide to outdoor survival is *How to Stay Alive in the Woods*, by Bradford Angier (Macmillan, US$8). See **Health** (p. 15) for information about basic medical concerns and first-aid. The most important thing is to protect yourself from the environment. This protection includes a proper tent with rain-fly, warm sleeping bag, and proper clothing (see **camping and hiking equipment,** p. 51). Bringing your water to a rolling boil or purifying it with iodine tablets generally affords the best protection.

Mountain safety experts often say that you can minimize the risks by following five golden rules. First, sudden mists can reduce visibility quickly, so always know where you are, carry appropriate maps and do not rely on the public signs posted. Second, wintry weather can blow into an area in minute; be well dressed. Third, leave marked paths only if you are experienced and have reliable advice from locals—there can be hidden dangers like mudslides, loose scree (gravel), ice-cored moraine (glacial refuse), unhikable vegetation, or steep snow patches on a seemingly innocuous fellside. Fourth, under no circumstances whatsoever walk on a snow-covered glacier without ropes, ice-axes, and a practical knowledge of how to use them. Snow may cover crevasses, and there is a hell of a lot more involved to pulling someone out than waggling a rope in front of them and tugging hard. Finally, watch where you step!

ENVIRONMENTALLY RESPONSIBLE TOURISM

While protecting yourself from the elements, take a moment to consider protecting the wilderness from you. At the very least, a responsible traveller practices **"minimum-impact camping"** techniques. Keep in mind that nothing left above the snowline ever decays. In order to keep the mountains beautiful, do not throw anything away, not even food refuse or paper towels. Save all of your trash and dispose of it when you get back to civilization. Don't cut vegetation or clear new campsites. Never build fires in the Alps, as grass fires start easily and the mountains do not recover from the ravages of fire. A campstove is the safer (and more efficient) way to cook. Make sure your campsite is at least 150 feet from water supplies or bodies of water. If there are no toilet facilities, bury human waste (but not paper) at least four inches deep, above the high-water line, and at least 150ft. from any water supplies and campsites.

HIKING

Austria and Switzerland are renowned for their hiking, with paths ranging from simple hikes in the foothills of the Swiss Jura to ice-ax-wielding expeditions through the glaciers of the Berner Oberland. Free **hiking** maps are available from even the most rinky-dink of tourist offices. Hiking trails are clearly marked by bright yellow signs indicating the time to nearby destinations, which may or may not bear any relation to your own expertise and endurance. ("Std." is short for *Stunden,* or hours.) Paths marked *"Für Geübte"* require special mountain-climbing equipment and are for experienced climbers only. For lengthy hikes, consider taking along a detailed map of the region you will be hiking. The best maps are the **Freytag-Berndt** maps (around US$10), available in bookstores all over Austria and Switzerland and from **Pacific Travellers Supply,** 12 W. Anapamu St., Santa Barbara, CA 93101 (tel. (805) 963-4438). Check these books out, too:

- **100 Hikes in the Alps.** Details various trails in Austria and Switzerland (US$15). Write to The Mountaineers Books, 1001 Klickitat Way, Ste. 201, Seattle, WA 98134 (tel. (800) 553-4453; fax 223-6306).
- **Walking Austria's Alps,** by Jonathan Hurdle. The Mountaineers Books (US$11).
- **Walking Switzerland the Swiss Way,** by Marcia and Philip Lieberman. The "Swiss Way" refers to hiking hut-to-hut. The Mountaineers Books (US$13).
- **Downhill Walking in Switzerland,** (US$12). Old World Travel Books Inc., P.O. Box 700863, Tulsa, OK 74170 (tel. (918) 493-2642).
- **Swiss-Bernese Oberland,** by Philip and Loretta Alspach. (US$17, handling US$2.50). Intercon Publishing, P.O. Box 18500-L, Irvine, CA 92623 (tel. (714) 955-2344; fax 833-3156).
- **Walking Easy in the Austrian Alps** and **Walking Easy in the Swiss Alps,** by Chet and Carolee Lipton (US$11). Gateway Books, 2023 Clemens Rd., Oakland, CA 94602 (tel. (510) 530-0299, orders only (800) 669-0773; fax 530-0497).

Austria

The most scenic way to see Austria is on foot. A membership in the **Österreichischer Alpenverein** provides an in-depth experience with the Tirolean Alps. The group provides a series of **huts** across the Tirol and throughout Austria, all located a day's hike from each other. This hut-to-hut option is provided to members at half price and a place in any of the huts is always assured. Third-party insurance, accident provision, travel discounts, and a wealth of maps and mountain information are also included with membership. For information, contact Österreichischer Alpenverein, Willhelm-Greil-Str. 15, A-6010 Innsbruck (tel. 587 828; fax 588 842). Membership (US$55, students under 25 US$40; one-time fee US$10) also includes use of some of the huts that the **Deutscher Alpenverein** (German Alpine Club) operates, all of which have beds. Sleeping in one of Austria's refuges is safer for the environment and generally safer for you—when you leave, you are expected to list your next destination in the hut book, thus alerting search-and-rescue teams if a problem should occur. Prices for an overnight stay without membership in the Alpenverein are 50-150AS, and no reservations are necessary.

The Austrian National Tourist Office publishes the pamphlet *Hiking and Backpacking in Austria,* with a complete list of Freytag-Berndt maps and additional tips. The **Touristenverein "Die Naturfreunde,"** Viktoriag. 6, A-1150 Vienna (tel. (1) 892 35 34), also operates a network of cottages in rural and mountain areas.

Switzerland

"A pocket knife with a corkscrew, a leathern drinking cup, a spirit flask, stout gloves, and a piece of green crepe or coloured spectacles to protect the eyes from the glare of the snow, should not be forgotten," wrote Karl Baedeker in his 1907 guide to Switzerland. The Swiss National Tourist Office still suggests ski glasses to avoid **snow blindness,** but somehow the spirit flask has dropped out of the picture.

Hiking offers the most rewarding views of Switzerland. 30,000 miles of **hiking trails** lace the entire country; yellow signs give directions and traveling times to nearby destinations. Bands of white-red-white mark trails; if there are no markings, you're on an "unofficial" trail, which is not always a problem—most trails are well maintained. Blue-white-blue markings indicate that the trail requires special equipment, either for difficult rock climbs or glacier climbing. Lowland **meandering** at its best awaits in the Engadin valley near St. Moritz; for steeper climbs, head to Zermatt or Interlaken. **Swiss Alpine Club (SAC) huts** are modest and extremely practical for those interested in trekking in higher, more remote areas of the Alps. Bunk rooms sleep 10 to 20 weary hikers side by side, with blankets (no electricity or running water) provided. SAC huts are open to all, but SAC members get discounts. The average rate for one night's stay without food is 30SFr, members 20-25SFr. Membership costs 126SFr, as a bonus you'll receive the titillating publication *Die Alpen*. Contact the SAC, Sektion Zermatt, Haus Dolomite, CH-3920 Zermatt, Switzerland (tel. (028) 672 610).

SKIING

Western **Austria** is one of the world's best skiing regions. The areas around Innsbruck and Kitzbühel in the Tirol are saturated with lifts and runs. Skiers swoosh year-round down some glaciers, including the Stubaital near Innsbruck and the Dachstein in the Salzkammergut. High season normally runs from mid-December to mid-January and from February to March. Local tourist offices provide information on regional skiing and can point you to budget travel agencies that offer ski packages.

Contrary to popular belief, **skiing in Switzerland** is often less expensive than in the U.S., if you avoid the pricey resorts. Ski passes (valid for transportation to, from, and on lifts) run 30-50SFr per day and 100-300SFr per week. A week of lift tickets, equipment rental, lessons, lodging, and *demi-pension* (half-pension, breakfast plus one other meal, usually dinner) averages 475SFr. Summer skiing is no longer as prevalent as it once was, but it's still available in Zermatt, Saas Fee, Les Diablerets, and on the Diavolezza in Pontresina.

With peaks between 3000m and 30,000m, the Alpine vertical drop is ample— 1000 to 2000m at all major resorts. For mountain country, winter **weather** in the Austrian Alps is moderate, thanks to lower elevation and distance from the ocean. Daytime temperatures in the coldest months (Jan. and Feb.) measure around -7°C (20°F), even when the nights are colder. Humidity is low, so snow on the ground stays powdery longer, and ice largely hibernates until spring.

You'll find various and sundry ways to enjoy the winter wonderland. Some cross-country ski centers charge trail fees to day users but exempt guests spending their holiday in the area. **Ski schools** throughout Austria can teach anyone to ski—based on decades of research and racing experience, the **Austrian Ski Method** is a unified teaching concept taught throughout the country. You can **rent skis** at the base of most mountains and at stores in ski villages.

■ Keeping in Touch

MAIL

Austria and Switzerland maintain rapid, efficient postal systems. Letters take between one and three days for delivery within Switzerland and one to two days within Austria. Airmail to North America takes four to five days from Austria and Switzerland. Mark all letters and packages *"Mit Flugpost"* or *"Par Avion."* In all cases, include the *postal code* if you know it; those of Swiss cities begin with "CH," Austrian with "A."

Generally, letters specifically marked "air mail" travel faster than postcards. Airmail from the U.S. to Europe averages four to five days. Allow two weeks from Australia and New Zealand; most of Africa takes upwards of two weeks. Major cities in southeast Asia take one to two weeks; as with most areas worldwide, times are more unpredictable from smaller towns. **Aerogrammes,** printed sheets that fold into envelopes and travel via airmail, are available at post offices. Most post offices charge exorbitant fees or simply refuse to send Aerogrammes with enclosures. If possible, send mail express or registered. Many U.S. post offices offer **International Express Mail** service, which sends packages under 8oz. to major overseas cities in 48 to 72 hours for US$11.50-14. Faster airmail costs too damn much. If you must, try **Federal Express** (U.S. tel. (800) 463-3339).

Surface mail is by far the cheapest and slowest way to send mail. It takes one to three months to cross the Atlantic and two to four for the Pacific—appropriate for sending large quantities of items you won't need to see for a while. When ordering books and materials from abroad, always include one or two **International Reply Coupons (IRCs)**—a way of providing the postage to cover delivery. IRCs should be available from your local post office as well as abroad (US$1.05).

You can send mail internationally through **Poste Restante** (the international phrase for General Delivery) to any city or town. It's well worth using—there are generally no surcharges, and it's much more reliable than you might think. Mark the envelope "HOLD" and address it, for example, "Gerald MOTHERSBAUGH, *Poste Restante*, City, Country." The last name should be capitalized and underlined. The mail will go to a special desk in the central post office, unless you specify a post office by street address or postal code. As a rule, it is best to use the largest post office in the area; sometimes, mail will be sent there regardless of what you write on the envelope. (*Let's Go* lists post offices in the **Practical Information** for each city and most towns.) It's helpful but not imperative to use the appropriate translation of *Poste Restante* (*Lista de Correos* in Spanish, *Fermo Posta* in Italian, *Postlagernde Briefe* in German) and mark the envelope *Bitte Halten* ("please hold"). When picking up your mail, bring your passport or other ID. If the clerks insist that there is nothing for you, have them check under your first name as well.

American Express travel offices throughout the world will act as a mail service for cardholders if you contact them in advance. Under this free **"Client Letter Service,"** they will hold mail for 30 days, forward it upon request, and accept telegrams. Just like *Poste Restante*, the last name of the person to whom the mail is addressed should be capitalized and underlined. Some offices will offer these services to non-cardholders (especially those who have purchased American Express Travellers' Cheques), but call ahead to verify. Check the **Practical Information** section of the countries you plan to visit; *Let's Go* lists AmEx office locations for most large cities. A complete list is available free from AmEx (tel. (800) 528-4800) in the booklet *Traveler's Companion* or online at http://www.americanexpress.com/shared/cgi-bin/tsoserve.cgi/travel/index.

YOU MAKE THE CALL

International direct dialing is a gas. First dial the **international dialing prefix** from the country you are in (011 in the United States), then the **country code** for the country you are calling. Next punch in the **area code** or **city code** (in the Practical Information listings for large cities). Finally, dial the **local number**. In most countries (excluding the U.S. and Canada), the first digit of the city code is the **domestic long-distance prefix** (usually 0, 1, or 9); omit it when calling from abroad but use it when dialing another region in the same country.

The quickest (and cheapest) way to **call abroad collect** is to go to a post office—almost all have pay phones—and ask for a *Zurückrufen*, or return call. You will receive a card with a number on it. Call your party and tell them to call you back at that number. At the end of the conversation, you pay for the original call.

Some companies, seizing upon this "call-me-back" concept, have created callback phone services. Under these plans, you call a specified number, ring once, and hang up. The company's computer calls back and gives you a dial tone. You can then make as many calls as you want at rates about 20-60% lower than you'd pay using credit cards or pay phones. This option is most economical for loquacious travelers, as services may include a US$10-25 minimum billing per month. For information, call **America Tele-Fone** (tel. (800) 321-5817), **Globaltel** (tel. (770) 449-1295), **International Telephone** (tel. (800) 638-5558), and **Telegroup** (tel. (800) 338-0225).

A **calling card** is probably your best and cheapest bet; your local long-distance service provider will have a number for you to dial while traveling (either toll-free or charged as a local call) to connect instantly to an operator in your home country. The

KEEPING IN TOUCH ■ 57

calls (plus a small surcharge) are then billed either collect or to the calling card. For more information, call **AT&T** about its **USADirect** and **World Connect** services (tel. (888) 288-4685; from abroad call (810) 262-6644 collect), **Sprint** (tel. (800) 877-4646, from abroad, call (913) 624-5335 collect), or **MCI WorldPhone** and **World Reach** (tel. (800) 444-4141, from abroad dial the country's MCI access number). In Canada, contact Bell Canada **Canada Direct** (tel. (800) 565 4708); in the U.K., British Telecom **BT Direct** (tel. (800) 34 51 44); in Ireland, Telecom Éireann **Ireland Direct** (tel. (800) 250 250); in Australia, Telstra **Australia Direct** (tel. 13 22 00); in New Zealand, **Telecom New Zealand** (tel. 123); and in South Africa, **Telkom South Africa** (tel. 09 03). Be careful: many pay phones in Switzerland will cut you off after a minute even if you are using a calling card.

MCI's WorldPhone also provides access to MCI's **Traveler's Assist,** which gives legal and medical advice, exchange rate information, and translation services. Many other long distance carriers and phone companies provide such travel infromation; contact your phone service provider for information.

Internal Calls: Switzerland

> Switzerland is in the process of updating its phone system. Some of the numbers that *Let's Go* lists have not yet been updated and may be incorrect.

Local calls cost 60 centimes. Phones take 10, 20, and 50 centime and 1 and 5SFr coins. Phones do not return change—press the red button to make additional calls before the money runs out. City codes are three digits long, numbers themselves six or seven. You can buy **phone cards (Taxcards)** at any post office, change bureau, or kiosk. In all areas, dial 111 for **information** (including directory assistance, train schedules, and other minutiae) and 191 or 114 for an **English-speaking international operator.** The **Anglo-phone** number is 157 50 14. It provides information ranging from weather reports to English-speaking doctor referrals (1.40SFr per minute).

Internal Calls: Austria

> The Austrian telephone network is becoming digitized, and phone numbers may change without notice after this book goes to press.

The Austrian telephone and postal system proves that the term "efficient state monopoly" is not an oxymoron. **Wertkarten (telephone cards),** available in post offices, train stations, and at *Tabak Trafik,* come in 50AS and 100AS denominations sold for 48AS and 95AS, respectively. The rate for local telephone calls is 0.84AS per minute from a pay phone. Phones that take cards are found in even remote villages—they announce themselves with blue stickers on the telephone booth. Green stickers mean that a phone accepts incoming calls. All others simply accept coins. When calling from a **post office,** take a number, run up a tab while talking, and pay the cashier when you're done. To make **local calls** without a phone card, deposit 2AS to start (less than 3min.) and 1AS for each additional 90 seconds. **Long distance** charges vary—drop in 5AS to start. The display next to the receiver indicates how much money has been deposited and shows the deductions made during the course of the call. Even when calling collect or using a phone card, you must pay for the local cost of the call. You also pay even if the call doesn't go through. On weekdays between 6pm and 8am and from 1pm Saturday to 8pm Monday, all phone calls within the country are one-third cheaper. This rate does not apply to international calls.

OTHER COMMUNICATION

Domestic and international **telegrams** offer an option slower than phone but faster than post. Fill out a form at any post or telephone office; cables arrive in one or two days. Telegrams can be quite expensive. **Western Union** (tel. (800) 325-6000; call collect from abroad), for example, adds to the per-word rate a country-specific surcharge. You may wish to consider **faxes** for more immediate, personal, and cheaper communiques. Cities have bureaus where you can pay to send and receive faxes.

Between May 2 and Octoberfest, **EurAide,** P.O. Box 2375, Naperville, IL 60567 (tel. (630) 420-2343; fax 420-2369; http://www.cube.net/kmu/euraide.html), offers **Overseas Access,** a service useful to travelers without a set itinerary. The cost is US$15 per week, US$40 per month, plus a US$15 registration fee. To reach you, people call, fax, or use the internet to leave a message; you receive it by calling Munich whenever you wish, which is cheaper than calling overseas. You may also leave messages for callers to pick up by phone.

If you're spending a year abroad and want to keep in touch with friends or colleagues in a college or research institution, **electronic mail (email)** is an attractive option. With minimal computer knowledge and a little planning, you can beam messages anywhere for no per-message charges. One option is to befriend college students as you go and ask if you can use their email accounts. If you're not the finagling type, **Traveltales.com** (http://traveltales.com) provides free, web-based email for travelers and maintains a list of cybercafés, travel links, and a travelers' chat room. **Katchup** (http://www.katchup.co.nz) offers a similar service for NZ$50 per year. Other free, web-based email providers include **Hotmail** (http://www.hotmail.com), **RocketMail** (http://www.rocketmail.com), and **USANET** (http://www.usa.net). Many free email providers are funded by advertising and may require subscribers to fill out a questionnaire. Search the Web (see **The World Wide Web, p. 3**) for a list of **cybercafés** around the world from which you can drink a cup of joe and email him too.

If you're already riding the infobahn at home, you should be able to find access numbers for your destination country—check with your internet provider before leaving. **America Online** (see **Internet Resources,** p. 3) now offers **"GLOBALnet,"** making it possible for American net-junkies to access the internet, chat rooms, and email through their home accounts while travelling in 70 countries. The only hurdles for budget travellers are the US$6-12 per hour surcharge and the fact that GLOBALnet only works on computers with AOL software already installed; in other words, to use the service you must travel with your own portable computer or install the software on computers as you go and log on as a guest.

Travelers who have the luxury of a laptop with them can use a **modem** to call an internet service provider. Long-distance phone cards specifically intended for such calls can defray normally high phone charges. Check with your long-distance phone provider to see if they offer this option; otherwise, try a **C.COM Internet PhoneCard** (tel. (888) 464-2266), which offers Internet connection calls for 15¢ per minute, minimum initial purchase US$5.

AUSTRIA

US$1= 13.14 Schillings (AS) 10AS = US$0.76
CDN$1= 9.58AS 10AS = CDN$1.04
UK£1= 21.38AS 10AS = UK£0.47
IR£1= 19.13AS 10AS = IR£0.52
AUS$1= 9.79AS 10AS = AUS$1.02
NZ$1= 8.53AS 10AS = NZ$1.17
SAR1= 2.86AS 10AS = SAR3.50
1SFr = 8.59AS 10AS = 1.16SFr
1 DM = 7.037AS 10AS = DM1.42
1kč = 0.38AS 10AS = 26.05kč
1Ft = 0.007AS 10AS = 151.87Ft

Country Code: 43
International Dialing Prefix: 900 from Vienna, 00 from elsewhere

At 32,276 square miles, Austria is almost exactly the size of Maine and lies at the same latitude as Maine's northern tip. Austria comprises nine semi-autonomous provinces, or *Bundesländer*. Counterclockwise from the northeast they are: Vienna (Wien), Lower Austria (Niederösterreich), Upper Austria (Oberösterreich), Salzburg, Tyrol (Tirol), Vorarlberg, Carinthia (Kärnten), Styria (Steiermark), and Burgenland. The concern for these provincial divisions varies according to region, but the history and identity of these smaller regions has been accumulating for centuries, while Austria the nation is relatively young. Many inhabitants therefore identify themselves more with their regional than their national home. The Tirolers are fervently Tirolean; the province nearly seceded from Austria after WWI to stay united with Südtirol. The Styrians are also extremely micro-patriotic (possibly because no one else can understand their dialect). While its internal borders delineate rigidly defined cultures, Austria's national borders tend to encompass fluid groups. Austria's population of 7.8 million is 99 percent German-speaking, but that statistic belies the presence of significant ethnic minorities. Many of the country's inhabitants were once on the other side of what is in many cases an arbitrary line. The Burgenlanders, for example, maintain their distinct Hungarian heritage, and the Slovenes of southern Carinthia and the Croats in Burgenland are guaranteed rights by the terms of Article Seven of the Austrian State Treaty of Vienna of 1955. A Hungarian minority inhabits a number of Burgenland towns and villages, and there is a small Slovak community in Vienna. Eighty percent of the Austrian population is Roman Catholic; a further 4.9 percent is Protestant, most ascribing to the Augsburg Confession.

For all its political transformations, Austria maintains an overpowering physical beauty. Onion-domed churches set against snow-capped Alpine peaks, lush meadows blanketed with edelweiss, pristine mountain lakes, dark cool forests, and mighty castles towering over the majestic Danube—Austria is a true dreamland. In the eastern portion of the European Alps, more than half of the country is covered by mountains. Western Austria, in particular, is dominated almost entirely by them, rising to the Großglockner, the highest peak in Austria at 3,797m (12,457ft.). Humans clearly play a lesser role in these areas; the two largest cities contain barely 300,000 people between them. The mountains generate year-round tourism: Alpine sports dominate the winter scene, while lakeside frolicking draws visitors in the warmer months. The Danube, Europe's longest river, has been central to Austrian industry and aristocracy since the country's beginning; both the Babenburgs and the Habsburgs set up residences on its shores. Vienna, once the imperial residence and now the country's capital, stands on the river's banks. To cap off all this scenery, forests and meadows cover two thirds of the total area of Austria, making it the most densely forested nation in Europe.

History and Politics

Perhaps the most remarkable aspect of Austrian history is the absence of a consistently Austrian identity. For centuries the locus of an empire that stretched throughout Europe, Austria was consistently ruled by ethnic Germans but always included a substantial ethnic mix—Magyars, Slovenes, Flemings, Slavs, and Italians were all part of the empire. Not until the 19th century did anything resembling a transcendent nationalism arise. Austria moved through governments like some people go through clothes: from centuries of imperial rule to the Austrian Republic to Hitler's mad barbarism to the 20th century's sedate and sanguine Second Republic. Austria has cultivated this unique identity—internationally neutral, democratic, Western-oriented, and a newly admitted member of the European Union. The Second Republic has fashioned a progressive social democratic welfare state as stable as any other in the hemisphere.

EARLY YEARS (10,000BC–AD800)

Though humans have inhabited Austria since Paleolithic times (80,000-10,000BC), little evidence of these early inhabitants remains. Around 5000BC, hunter-gatherers began to settle the highlands, where they farmed their food, raised stock animals, mined **salt** in the salt mines, and periodically froze in the Alpine passes. Archaeologists discovered one of these unfortunate creatures in 1991, his body preserved in the glacial ice of the Ötztal Alps.

Around 400BC, the **Celts** took control of the salt mines and established the kingdom of **Noricum**, which developed a successful culture and economy based on a far-ranging salt and iron trade. The **Romans** to the south appreciated the trade-link but conquered their Austrian neighbors anyway in 30-15BC to secure the Danube frontier against the marauding Germans. During the two-century *Pax Romana*, Noricum thrived and an urban economy developed, giving rise to such cities as **Vindobona** (Vienna), **Juvavum** (Salzburg), **Aguntum** (Lienz), and **Brigantium** (Bregenz). **Marcus Aurelius** wrote his famous *Meditations* and then died in Vindobona, starting a long tradition of Viennese emigré artists. Roman roads along the Danube and through the Alps allowed legions, traders, and missionaries (both pagan and Christian) free access until the end of the second century, when the frontier weakened. Germanic raids finally forced Romans to abandon the province in the 5th century.

Over the next three centuries, Huns, Ostrogoths, Lombards, and others occasionally rampaged through the Austrian territories, but they failed to establish any lasting settlement. Three primary groups occupied the region: the **Alemanni** in the south, the **Slavs** in the southwest, and the **Bavarians** in the north. Modern placenames ending in *-itz* indicate Slavic origins, while *-heim* and *-ing(en)* reveal Germanic settlement. The few Celts left in the highlands retained both Celtic place names and **Christianity**, though the new lowland settlers did not convert until Irish missionaries arrived in the early 7th century. The dukes of Bavaria further converted the population in an attempt to bring a semblance of law and order to the area and to create a power-base free of Frankish influence. The missionaries' successes created an archbishopric of **Salzburg** in 798. The city remained Austria's ecclesiastical capital well into the modern era.

Despite converting so many to the same religion, the Bavarian dukes, most notably **Duke Tassilo III** (740-788), were unable to secure Austria as a personal power base. **Charlemagne**, crowned Holy Roman Emperor, claimed eastern Austria as a border province of his Carolingian empire and began to develop a distinct concept

> After 5000BC, hunter-gatherers began to settle the highlands, farming, mining salt, and periodically freezing in the Alpine passes.

of Austria in an attempt to prevent war with the Bavarians' ever-expanding rule. The name *Österreich* means "Eastern Empire," referring to the easternmost lands that Charlemagne conquered.

THE HOUSE OF BABENBERG

The **Magyar** invasion ended with their defeat at Lechfeld at the hand of **Otto I,** the first magnate elected in Germany to continue the Holy Roman Empire. He installed **Leopold of Babenberg** as ruler of Austrian territories in 976, and Babenbergs ruled *Ostarrichi* (eastern Austria) from 976 to 1246. The Babenbergs stabilized the frontiers, extending their protectorate north of the Danube and east and south into Magyar (later Hungarian) lands. The Babenbergs' monasteries and abbeys played an important role in the recolonization of the depopulated country, as **German settlers** cleared the land for farming and increased the Germanic hold over the developing Austrian consciousness. Although the Babenbergs supported the pope against Henry IV during the **Investiture Conflict,** they were otherwise very loyal to the Holy Roman Emperors, including **Leopold III** (1095-1136), later Austria's patron saint.

The Babenberg territories benefited economically from traffic with the east during the Crusades. The family also secured a large part of the ransom that England paid to rescue **Richard the Lionheart,** who was detained in Austria by **Leopold V** on his way home from the Third Crusade. Leopold used the ransom to fortify the towns of Wiener Neustadt and Vienna. In that same year, 1192, Leopold V obtained the Duchy of **Styria** (today southeast Austria) through a contract of inheritance. In the first half of the 13th century, cultural life at the court of the Babenbergs was in full bloom. **Minnesingers** (minstrels) wrote epic ballads (including the **Nibelungenlied**) and **Romanesque architecture** came to a late fruition.

THE RISE OF THE HABSBURGS

The last Babenburg, **Friedrich II** "the Quarrelsome," was confronted with an angry emperor to the west, rebellious nobles to the north, and nervous Hungarians (threatened by Mongol invasion) to the east. The Hungarians were the first to get to him, and he died childless at their hands in 1246, leaving a fragmented and unruly Austria. The Bohemian King **Ottokar II,** who married Friedrich's sister, restored order, reconquered Styria, and attached the Duchy of **Carinthia** (now south-central Austria) to his holdings.

Meanwhile, after the 19-year *Interregnum,* a new emperor had emerged in the Holy Roman Empire—the Swiss **Rudolf of Habsburg,** who demanded the Slavic Ottokar's allegiance. When Ottokar refused, Rudolf attacked with support from the Austrian nobility and defeated Ottokar at Marchfeld in 1278. In 1282, Rudolf granted his two sons the Duchies of *Ostarrichi* and Styria, thus laying the foundations for Habsburg dynastic rule in the region. The Habsburgs would retain power in Austria almost continuously until 1918, through 19 Habsburg emperors and one empress.

At the inception of Habsburg rule, the family's dominance was far from secure, weakened by the lack of primogeniture (full inheritance by the first son). The territory was therefore divided among all the sons and created temporary instability. There were incessant revolts, even by the Swiss who had earlier belonged to one of the most loyal Habsburg territories. During the late Middle Ages, the Habsburgs expanded their holdings and defended their inflating borders. Rudolf the Founder's short rule (1358-1365) was marked by the acquisition of the Earldom of **Tirol.** He also founded the **University of Vienna** and commissioned improvements to St. Stephen's Cathedral. When Rudolf felt that his family had been passed over by the Luxembourg Emperor Karl IV, he forged several documents, later called the **Privilegium maius,** to demonstrate his dynasty's higher rank. Rudolf's descendant, Emperor **Friedrich III,** affirmed the claims made in these documents and strategically arranged the marriage of his son, **Maximilian I,** to the heiress of the powerful Burgundian kingdom. This union gave Austria control of the Low Countries. In response to incursions by the imperial Turkish forces along the Danube and Drau Rivers, Maximilian consolidated his regime through various **centralizing reforms.** During his rule, Vienna became a center of humanistic culture. In 1493, Maximilian became the first Habsburg to claim the title of Holy Roman Emperor without papal coronation, which gave the family hereditary rights to the imperial throne. Through prudent marital alliances, he ensured the hereditary succession of lands far and wide and laid the foundations for the vast territory to come under Habsburg rule during the pinnacle of the empire. Maximilian not only married well—his wife was heiress to the duchies of Burgundy as well as territories in western France—but also deftly arranged the marriage of his son Philip. Philip was joined to the daughter of Spain's royal duo, Ferdinand and Isabella, heirs to the combined **Kingdom of Spain.** The resulting child, Karl V, combined the inheritance of his four grandparents—Austria, the Netherlands, Aragon and its Italian and Mediterranean possessions, Castile, and the Spanish Americas—and was elected Holy Roman Emperor in 1519, which added Germany to the list. Dwarfing any other political entity in Europe, the Habsburg empire became the first on which the sun never set.

Under Karl V, the Habsburgs came the closest to their prophetic motto **"A.E.I.O.U.,"** meaning *"Alles Erdreich ist Österreich untertan"* (Austria is destined to rule the world). A less boastful and probably more accurate motto might have been the popular couplet written by the shrewd organizer of this whole affair, Maximilian, which stated: *"Bella gerant alii, tu felix Austria nube."* (Let other nations go to war; you, lucky Austria, marry—an early riff on "Make love, not war," that turned Austria into the Haight-Ashbury of the free-lovin' 1500s.)

OH, NO! THE HABSBURG EMPIRE

The massive territory and majestic imperial sheen concealed anxieties among the Habsburgs. The **Ottoman Empire,** which had been encroaching on Europe since the 14th century, began to threaten the continent more and more in the 1500s and 1600s. After the conquest of Constantinople, the Turks consistently undertook expeditions farther west, becoming a permanent threat to the Habsburg patrimonial lands. In 1529, their armies reached the gates of Vienna, but the city beat them back.

This victory was not sufficient to quell the disturbances, however. The Ottoman threat strained the stagnant Austrian economy; the emperors required a monstrous army to defend the territories and spent lavish amounts on construction and art to divert cultural attention from their French counterparts. Social unrest, fomented by the **Reformation,** further threatened stability. Burghers and nobles were drawn to Protestantism because it affirmed rationality, and peasants found the doctrine attractive because it freed them from onerous tithes to the Church. Social hierarchies, though, kept the two groups from forming a united front against the emperor and Church, but the peasants rebelled. The Austrian rulers hired mercenaries who crushed the rebels in the **Peasants' Wars** of 1525-6. Several leaders tolerant of Protestantism followed, but the Protestant Bohemians felt that the Habsburg emperor **Matthias** (1612-1619) was infringing on their religious liberties, especially when he sent two emissaries to sort things out. The Bohemians took matters into their own hands, throwing the emissaries out the window in the **defenstration of Prague** (1618) and then overthrowing Matthias. His successor, Archduke **Ferdinand II** (1619-1637), was not so easy to handle. His early victories over Protestant forces during the **Thirty Years War** (1618-1648) won the Habsburgs hereditary control of Bohemia and led to the forcible reconversion of most of the peasants to Catholicism and the consolidation of the Catholic church. But the **Peace of Westphalia,** ending the war in 1648, liberated the German states that the Habsburgs had been trying to consolidate.

In 1683, the Ottoman Turks sat on Vienna's doorstep once again. Austria's brilliant military response was largely the handiwork of **Prince Eugene of Savoy.** Not content to rest at home, Prince Eugene pressed his forces into Turkish lands and captured Hungary, Transylvania, and Croatia. Victory over the Turks generated an era of celebration; to honor Austrian prowess, magnificent buildings were constructed and wounded castles, churches, and monasteries were finally repaired. Opera flourished. This patriotic exuberance, tempered by a deep religious conviction, was the prevailing trademark of the Austrian **Baroque**. After Eugene of Savoy rescued Vienna from this second Turkish siege, **Leopold I** gave him control of the army. Eugene also successfully led the Habsburg troops against the French during the **War of Spanish Succession** from 1701 to 1714. **Louis XIV** fought to defend his newly inherited Spanish empire, passed to him by **Charles II**, ruler of Spain. When the war ended with the **Treaty of Utrecht** in 1713, France kept Spain, but the Habsburgs gained Belgium, Sardinia, and parts of Italy. By 1718, the Habsburg emperors had direct control of Bohemia, Moravia, Silesia, Hungary, Croatia, Transylvania, Belgium, Lombardy, Naples, Sicily, and, of course, Austria.

By the 1730s, however, the empire was extremely decentralized and poorly run. The nobles maintained great power over the large serf population. The minuscule middle class and guild artisans were held in check by Austria's location, inconvenient to most major trading routes. Though a benevolent and loyal man, Emperor **Karl VI** did not know how to run his empire. His diplomatic and military failures in life were matched by his failure at his death to leave a male heir. He was, however, able to pass the **Pragmatic Sanction** of 1713, in which most of the powers in Europe agreed to recognize succession of the Habsburgs through the female line if the male line fell extinct. This sanction allowed Charles' daughter **Maria Theresa** to become empress in 1740. Maria Theresa married Franz Stephan of Lorraine in 1736, who, though elected Emperor of the Holy Roman Empire in 1745, was overshadowed throughout his life by his wife's personality and intelligence.

Meanwhile, King of Prussia **Friedrich the Great** was beginning the military expansions that would one day lead to a powerful German state. One of his many successful campaigns snatched away Silesia (now southwest Poland), one of the empire's most prosperous provinces; Maria Theresa spent the rest of her life unsuccessfully maneuvering to reclaim it. The empress was, however, able to maintain her rule during the **Wars of Austrian Succession** from 1740 to 1748 with help from the Hungarians, but she lost the Italian lands of Lombardy. Diplomatic warfare ensued, waged by her wily foreign minister **Count Kaunitz**, who reconsidered the age-old rift between France and Austria and proposed an alliance between the two. The marriage of Maria Theresa's daughter to the future Louis XVI was one such outcome of what came to be known as the **Diplomatic Revolution** of 1756. Kaunitz's new alliance was not as successful as he planned, and the stalemate that resulted from the **Seven Years War** (1756-1763) underscored Austria's waning influence and the rise of Prussia as a great power. Maria Theresa and her son **Josef II** undertook a series of enlightened reforms to stimulate the economy, including improving tax collection, increasing settlements, encouraging religious freedom, aiding industry, and decreasing feudal burdens. A new state system transformed the agglomeration of lands that had hitherto been only loosely connected into a tightly administered central state. The empire, and Vienna in particular, became a center of culture and commerce. **Christoph Willibald Gluck, Josef Haydn,** and **Wolfgang Amadeus Mozart** composed their main works in the Theresian court of imperial Vienna. When Josef took over after Maria Theresa's death in 1780, Austria's movement toward a centralized and "rational" government accelerated. In 1781 Josef issued the **Toleration Patent**, granting numerous Protestant sects religious freedom, and liberated the serfs everywhere except Hungary (their emancipation soon followed). Though Josef initially encouraged public political consciousness and expression, his centralized bureaucracy relied on the Ministry of Police, which he used to censor the media and repress political dissidents.

> Franz Stephan, sometime Emperor of the Holy Roman Empire, was overshadowed throughout his life by his wife Maria Theresa.

THE END OF THE HOLY ROMAN EMPIRE

The doctrines behind the **French Revolution** gained ground in 18th-century Austria and represented a serious threat to Austrian absolutism. **Emperor Franz II**, grandson of Maria Theresa and nephew of the newly headless French Queen Marie Antoinette, joined the coalition against revolutionary France. The French Revolutionary National Assembly declared war on Austria in 1792, a war that would continue through France's Second Revolution and showcase the military genius of a young commander General **Napoleon Bonaparte**. The defeat of the Austrians in Northern Italy and the ensuing **Treaty of Campo Formio** in 1797, in which Austria recognized French possession of Belgium and parts of Italy, became the first in a long series of his victories. The treaty's reorganization of Germany heralded the final demise of the Holy Roman Empire. Facing the inevitable, Franz II renounced his claim to the now-defunct Holy Roman crown in 1804 and proclaimed himself Franz I, Emperor of Austria—only at this point was an Austrian empire as such founded. At the **Congress of Vienna** in 1815, which redrew the map of Europe after Napoleon's defeat, Austrian Chancellor of State **Clemens Wenzel Lothar Metternich**, "the Coachman of Europe," restored the old order in Europe while masterfully orchestrating the re-consolidation of Austrian power. Metternich preached the gospel of "legitimacy" and stability—in other words, the perpetuation of conservative government—to achieve a European balance of power. His machinations ushered in a long period of peace in Europe, during which commerce and industry flourished.

1848 AND THE REIGN OF FRANZ JOSEF

The first half of the 19th century was marked by immense technological progress. **Industrialization** took over, accompanied by rapid population growth and urbanization, and the working and middle classes were born. The French philosophy of a **middle-class revolution** reached Austria in the spring of 1848. Working together, students and workers built barricades, took control of the imperial palace, and demanded a constitution and freedom of the press. Metternich's government was so stunned that Metternich himself resigned and fled to England. A constituent assembly abolished feudalism in all non-Hungarian lands. Ethnic rivalries and political differences divided the revolutionary forces, however, and the Habsburgs were able to suppress the revolution in October of 1848. That year also marked the brutal suppression of a Hungarian rebellion (with help from Russia), the forced abdication of the weakened emperor **Ferdinand I**, and the coronation of **Kaiser Franz-Josef I**, whose reign (1848-1916) stands as one of the longest of any monarch in history. The new leader created a highly centralized state.

Losses to France and Italy were overshadowed by **Otto von Bismarck's** victory over the Austrian armies in 1866, which dislodged Austria from its leadership position in Germany and established Prussia in its place. Franz-Josef was forced to assent to what passed as a constitutional monarchy, but he remained firmly in control; the Austrian state actually became more centralized and autocratic than it was before. Under the terms of the **Ausgleich** (compromise) of 1867, a dual monarchy was established. **Hungary** gained theoretically equal status as a kingdom alongside Austria. In reality, German speakers still dominated the so-called **Austro-Hungarian Empire**. This construction was additionally flawed in its lack of concern for the countless other nationalities represented in the dual empire; Czechs, Poles, Slovenes, and Croats remained essentially powerless. By 1907 the Austrian Kingdom had ceded basic civil rights to the population and accepted universal male suffrage.

Along with liberalism and socialism, a new movement began to take hold in Austria during this period. **Pan-Germanism**, the desire to abandon the eastern empire and unite with the German Reich, flourished under the leadership of **Georg von Schönerer**, whose doctrines were to have a profound influence on Adolf Hitler. By the turn of the century, Vienna was in political turmoil; the anti-Semitic **Christian Socialists**, under **Karl Lueger**, were on the rise. *Ruhe und Ordnung* (peace and order) was the Kaiser's motto, but his policies amounted to trying to stop the irreversible tide of modernity. (He was known to eschew even indoor plumbing.)

The long period of peace that lasted until World War I was safeguarded by a complicated system of European **alliances** in which minor disputes could easily escalate into a conflict involving dozens of nations. In 1879 Austria-Hungary joined the German Empire, which, with the addition of Italy in 1882, formed the **Triple Alliance,** balancing the **Triple Entente** of France, Britain, and Russia (and later, the U.S.). Meanwhile, burgeoning nationalist sentiments, especially among the Serbia-inspired South Slavs, led to severe divisions within the multinational Austro-Hungarian Empire, complicated by tensions within the working-class.

WORLD WAR I AND THE FIRST REPUBLIC

Brimming with ethnic tension and locked into the rigid system of alliances, the Austro-Hungarian Empire was a disaster waiting to happen. The spark that set off the explosion was the assassination of **Franz Ferdinand,** the heir to the imperial throne, by a Serbian nationalist named **Gavrillo Prinzip** on June 28, 1914. Austria's declaration of war against Serbia set off a chain reaction that pulled most of Europe into the conflict: Russia ran to support Serbia, Germany to support Austria, and France to support its Entente partner, Russia. The technologically and organizationally backward Austrian army performed with spectacular ineptitude on the battlefield and was defeated every time it faced serious competition. Only the subordination of the Austrian forces to German command saved the empire from immediate collapse. Austria's wartime fortunes rose and finally fell with Germany's.

Franz Josef died in 1916, leaving the throne to his grandnephew **Karl I,** who tried to extricate Austria from the war with its empire intact. The Entente powers, recognizing that the Habsburg goose was already cooked, rebuffed Karl's advances and proclaimed a goal of self-determination for the Habsburg nationalities. On November 11, 1918, a week after signing an armistice with the Entente, Karl abdicated, bringing the 640-year-old dynasty to a close.

Worry over the country's economic viability following World War I caused revolution in the streets of Vienna and brought about the proclamation of the **Republic of Deutsch-Österreich** (German Austria), a constituent component of the Greater German Republic. The Entente was, however, leery of a powerful pan-German nation and forbade the merger. The new **Austrian republic,** or the **First Republic,** consisted of the German-speaking lands of the former Habsburg empire minus those granted to Italy, Czechoslovakia, and Hungary—or, in the famous words of French Premier Georges Clemençeau, "what's left over." The old empire had sprawled over 676,615 sq. km and encompassed some 51.4 million people. After WWI, the new republic covered only 83,850 sq. km and 6.4 million inhabitants.

The new Austria experienced an unhappy **interwar period.** The break-up of the empire undermined economic life as former markets became independent sovereign states and closed their borders to Austrian goods. Vienna's population was on the verge of famine. By the middle of the 1920s, however, the Austrian government had stabilized the currency and established economic relations with neighboring states. As in Germany, **Communists** attempted to revolt, but the Social Democrats suppressed the rebellion without relying on the right. Political divisions were sharp, especially between "Red Vienna" and the staunchly Catholic provinces; Social Democrats (Reds) and Christian Socialists (Blacks) regarded each other not merely as opposing parties but as opposing *Lager* (camps). The parties set up paramilitary organizations, and political violence became a fact of life. On this shaky democratic foundation, the authoritarian **Engelbert Dollfuss** created a government in 1932 on a one-vote majority in the National Assembly.

> On November 11, 1918, a week after signing an armistice with the Entente, Karl abdicated, bringing the 640-year dynasty to a close.

THE ANSCHLUß

The minority **Austrian Nazis** had been agitating for unification with Germany since Hitler took power, but their demands became more menacing after his stunning success facing down the Western powers. Four months after the establishment of the authoritarian Federal State of Austria, Nazi sympathizers attempted a coup in which they murdered Dollfuss. Dollfuss's successor, **Kurt Schuschnigg**, put down the insurgents but faced a stepped-up campaign by Hitler's agents. Schuschnigg sought to maintain Austria's sovereignty by allying with Italy and Hungary. In 1938, however, Hitler met with Schuschnigg in Berchtesgaden (see p. 232) and threatened to invade Austria if **Arthur Seyss-Inquart**, a Nazi, was not named Interior Minister. With the Austrian police thus under their control, the Nazis brought Austria to near chaos. On March 9, 1938, hoping to stave off a Nazi invasion, Schuschnigg called a referendum four days hence on unity with Germany. One day before the plebiscite was to take place, Nazi troops crossed the frontier, completing the *Anchluß* (unification). Although Josef Goebbels' propaganda wildly exaggerated the enthusiasm of Austrians for Hitler (as did a phony referendum in April, in which 99 percent of Austrians approved of the *Anschluß*), the myth that Austria was merely a prostrate victim is equally fallacious. When German troops marched into Vienna on March 14, thousands of Austrians turned out to cheer them on. The German Nazi **Racial Purity Laws** were subsequently extended to Austria, a disaster for Austrian Jews. Many managed to emigrate, but few were allowed to flee after March, 1938. Those left in Austria perished later in Nazi extermination camps. Today, less than 0.05% of Austria's population is Jewish.

THE SECOND REPUBLIC

After the German defeat in WWII, a coalition of Christian Socialists and Social Democrats declared a Republic with **Karl Renner** as president. The Allies did not impose reparations payments on Austria as they did on Germany, but they did occupy the country and withhold recognition of sovereignty for the decade following the war. The country was divided into four occupation zones: Britain, France, and the U.S. held the west, while the eastern portions, including Vienna, came under **Soviet** control. When Stalin assented to free elections, the Soviet-occupied zone voted overwhelmingly to rejoin their western compatriots in a united, democratic Austrian nation. The 1945 Austrian **Declaration of Independence** proclaimed the existence of an Austrian nation that, unlike the First Republic, claimed no fraternity with Greater Germany. Under the **Constitution Act** and the **State Treaty** of 1955, signed in Vienna's Belvedere Palace, Austria declared its absolute neutrality and earned national sovereignty. Austrian nationalism, which under the First Republic had been almost a contradiction in terms, has blossomed in the post-war period.

CURRENT GOVERNMENT

The foundation for the Second Republic rests upon the federal constitution of 1920 and its 1929 amendment. The constitution provides for a bicameral parliament, consisting of a popularly elected lower house, or **Nationalrat**, headed by a **Chancellor**; and an upper house, or **Bundesrat**, whose delegates are appointed by the provincial parliaments. The constitution also created the office of **Federal President**, a largely ceremonial (the president lacks executive power in peacetime) post.

Politics in the Second Republic have since been dominated by the **Socialist Party of Austria** (*Sozialistische Partei Österreichs*—SPÖ), renamed the **Social Democratic Party of Austria** (*Österreichische Sozialdemokratische Partei*, same abbreviation) in 1991. Though the majority, though, the party has often been compelled to govern in coalition with the second-largest party, the **People's Party of Austria** (*Österreichische Volkspartei*—ÖVP), the descendant of the Christian Socialists. In 1949, the fascist League of Independents tallied a surprising 10 percent of the vote. The League later renamed itself first the **Freedom Party** (*Freiheitliche Partei Österreichs*—FPÖ) and then the **Freedom Movement** (*Die Freiheitlichen*—F). The party continues to maintain strength, and it controls the legislature in the federal state of Carinthia.

While bitter struggle and confrontation characterized prewar politics, postwar politics have seen mainly cooperation, accommodation, and consensus. Under the SPÖ's stewardship, Austria built up one of the world's most successful **industrial economies**—Austria's unemployment and inflation rates are enviably low, even as Austrians enjoy the security of a generous, comprehensive **welfare state.** In 1983, the SPÖ lost ground and had to form the **Small Coalition** with the FPÖ (then under the control of its liberal wing). When the FPÖ fell back under the sway of the far Right, the SPÖ abandoned the Small Coalition and returned to the **Grand Coalition** with the ÖVP, an alliance that, though shaken by internal disputes, has persisted until today.

Disturbingly, the Freedom Movement, under the leadership of far-rightist **Jörg Haider,** often labeled a Nazi apologist, continued to do well among younger voters, especially as anxiety about immigration from Eastern Europe grew. Even worse, Austrians elected **Kurt Waldheim** to the largely ceremonial Austrian presidency in 1986 despite his having served as an officer in a Nazi-era German Army unit that committed heinous war crimes. As an international pariah, barred from making state visits to most places and forbidden even to enter the U.S., Waldheim was a serious embarrassment for Austria. The current president, **Thomas Klestil,** is more widely accepted.

RECENT YEARS

After several years of the status quo, the Grand Coalition of the SPÖ and ÖVP now faces competition for votes from the FPÖ, the right-wing Freedom Party skeptical of pro-EU policies and of the parties' pervasive role. In January 1997, Viktor Klima succeeded Franz Vranitzky as Chancellor, and Thomas Klestil, after a year of illness, seems likely to stand for re-election for President in 1998. Austria's application to the **European Union (EU)** was accepted in early 1995, and soon after the Austrian Schilling joined the European **Exchange Rate Mechanism**. Now, after being shut out for a while from the forthcoming **European Monetary Union (EMU)** because of a budget deficit, the Austrian economy seems strong enough to participate by 1999. The government hopes to maintain economic stability by streamlining subsidies, cutting welfare benefits and public expenditures, and beginning a more thorough privatization program. Participation in **NATO** has kindled much recent discussion, with Foreign Minister Wolfgang Schüssel advocating a more limited neutrality, and recent popular referenda have addressed issues of gender equality and genetically altered food.

A remarkable investor for its size and a large contributor of public funds, Austria has so far blessed citizens with a generous welfare state, although fears of exchanging a strong currency for the possibly weaker euro of the EU have arisen. Austria's forecasted inclusion in the EMU and its role as a gateway to Eastern Europe should mean sunny skies ahead.

■ Music

European culture may have found its most characteristic expression in the wealth of music it inspired, and Austrian music undoubtedly occupies the central position in Western Classical music tradition. The historical embryo for this phenomenon is the unique constellation of musical geniuses who created the **Viennese Classics.** the Austrian greats, including Haydn, Mozart, and Schubert, molded "Classical music" as we know it today. The composers who lived and worked in Vienna from 1780 to about 1828 (the year Schubert died) invested their music with a power transcending all frontiers and generations. They were followed by luminaries of the modern period, like Gustav Mahler and Arnold Schönberg, who consistently broke new ground.

THE CLASSICAL ERA

Toward the end of the 18th century, Vienna became the nexus of Europe's musical tradition, with a heady cultural atmosphere.

Franz Josef Haydn

Haydn is the first master musician wholly identified with Viennese Classicism. Born of humble lineage in Rohrau (in Lower Austria) in 1732, Haydn began his career as a boy chorister in the cathedral of St. Stephen in Vienna before working for the princes of Eszterházy (see **Eisenstadt**, p. 157). Conducting the orchestra of the royal court, he became the most celebrated composer in Europe.

Haydn created a variety of new musical forms that led to the shaping of the sonata and the symphony, structures that dominated musical doctrines of the entire 19th century. Fifty-two piano sonatas, 24 piano and organ concertos, 104 symphonies, and 83 string quartets provide rich and abundant proof of his pioneering productivity. Haydn even churned out the imperial anthem, *Gott erhalte Franz den Kaiser*, which he composed to rouse patriotic feeling during the Napoleonic wars. After WWI, when the new Austrian republic abandoned its anthem, Germany adopted *Gott erhalte* as its own national hymn, usually remembered as *Deutschland über Alles*.

Wolfgang Amadeus Mozart

Mozart's works may be the peak of Viennese Classicism. The study and interpretation of the approximately 600 works he wrote in the 35 years of his tragically short life have busied great musicians and more than a few hacks ever since. Mozart was born in Salzburg in 1756 to a father who quickly realized (and exploited) his son's musical genius. He was playing violin and piano by age four and composing simple pieces by five, all before formally learning the art of composition. When he was six, his father took him and his similarly talented sister Nannerl on their first concert tour of Europe, where they played the piano for the royal courts of Munich and Pressburg and the imperial court in Vienna. At 13, Mozart became *Konzertmeister* of the Salzburg court and returned to Salzburg periodically throughout his life.

His Viennese period produced his first mature concerti, his best-known operas, and the shamefully overwhistled "Eine kleine Nachtmusik."

During his Viennese period, the twenty-something *Wunderkind* produced his first mature concerti, his best-known Italian operas, *Don Giovanni* and *La Nozze di Figaro (The Marriage of Figaro)*, and his beloved and shamefully overwhistled string showpiece, *Eine kleine Nachtmusik*. By this time, Mozart was living in the style of the courtly society in which he moved, a stratum quite beyond his means. He was in constant debt and changed patrons frequently in attempts to boost his income.

As Thrasybulos Georgiades remarked, Mozart had "neither precursors nor successors" as an operatic composer. In his final years Mozart moved into a more Germanic style, creating works with reserved dramatic impact like *Die Zauberflöte (The Magic Flute)*—a *Singspiel* (comic opera) very different from the flamboyant *opera buffa* of his early years. Mozart's overwhelming emotional power found full expression in the *Requiem*, one of his last works before his early death in 1791.

Ludwig van Beethoven

Beethoven is considered the most remarkable representative of the new genre of artists working after Mozart. He was born into a family of Flemish musicians in Bonn in 1770 but lived in Vienna all his adult life. Beethoven approached the archetypal ideal of the artist as an individual responsible entirely to himself; he looked upon his work as the expression of his own intimate humanity.

Beethoven created a furor as a formal innovator in an epoch devoted to the fashionable cult of tradition. His gifts were manifest in his 32 piano sonatas, string quartets, overtures, and concertos, but shone most intensely in his nine epoch-shattering symphonies. The cultural and musical impact of his *Ninth Symphony* rivals that of any other piece from this time period. Among its innovations was the introduction of a human voice to the symphonic form—the chorus sings the text to Friedrich Schiller's *Ode to Joy.* Beethoven's *Fidelio,* which premiered May 23, 1814 at the Kärntnertortheater in Vienna after two failures in 1805 and 1806, is to this day regarded as one of greatest German operas.

Cut off at an early age by increasing deafness, the composer could maintain contact with the world only through a series of conversational notebooks, which provide an extremely thorough, though one-sided, record of his conversations. Whether perceived as the avatar of Viennese Classicism or as the prototype of the individualistic Romantic movement, Beethoven exercised a decisive, enduring, and undeniable influence on music and musical development, inspiring almost supernatural fear and admiration in his musical successors.

THE ROMANTIC ERA

Franz Schubert

Schubert was born in the Viennese suburb of Lichtenthal in 1797. He began his career as a boy chorister in the royal imperial Hofkapelle and later made his living teaching music. He finally became a composer, seeking and finding his "own way to great symphonic works." Adopting Beethoven, Haydn, and Mozart as his models, Schubert swept classical forms into the Romantic era. Mainly self-taught, he composed (almost) the *Unfinished Symphony* and the *Symphony in C Major,* now considered masterpieces but virtually unknown during his lifetime. His lyrical genius found a more popular outlet in a series of *Lieder,* poems set to music; works by Goethe, Schiller, and Heine were his favorites. Through his compositions, the *Lied* became a serious work in the tradition of Viennese Classicism.

Schubert's refreshingly new form was ideally suited to a new type of social and artistic activity—musical evenings. Reading and drinking became an event (the **Schubertiade**), still practiced today in Vorarlberg and Vienna. The great song cycles—*Die schöne Müllerin* and the tragically resigned *Winterreise*—frame Schubert's greatest and most mature creative period, derailed by his death in 1828. Schubert's genius for pure melody blazed a trail later built up by Schumann, the Strausses, and Mahler.

The Strauss Family

Beginning with Johann Strauss the Elder (1804-1849), the Strauss dynasty whirled the heels of Vienna for much of the 19th century. Largely responsible for what is known the world over as the "Viennese Waltz," Johann Strauss the Younger (1825-1899) shined in his youth as not only a brilliant violinist but also a savvy cultural entrepreneur. The insipid waltz, which first caught on in the Congress of Vienna in 1815, offered a new exhilaration that broke free from the older, stiffer forms of dancing then in vogue in Europe. The quick step allowed for more intimate physical contact as partners whirled about the room, arm in arm, constantly on the verge of falling down or getting intoxicatingly dizzy. Sensing the trend, Johann became its master, eventually writing the *Blue Danube* and *Tales from the Vienna Woods,* two of the most recognized waltzes of all time, and earning the title, the "King of the Waltz." In his spare time he managed to knock off some pretty popular opera as well; *Die Fledermaus* is his most celebrated. His brothers, Josef (1827-1870) and Eduard (1835-1916), though unable to eclipse his zenith, worked as conductors and composers.

Gustav Mahler

Gustav Mahler worked within the late Romantic tradition, but his melding of Romantic emotionalism and modern musical techniques brought his music fully into the 20th century. A tragic, turbulent life gave Mahler an acute sense of life's agonies, yet he realized the beauties of the world—his music is ultimately concerned with voicing the full range of emotions. In service of this goal, Mahler allowed himself new freedoms in composition, employing unusual instrumentations and startling harmonic juxtapositions. His Eighth Symphony, often called *Symphony of Thousand*, requires an orchestra and two full choruses. Mahler's works formed an integral part of the *fin de siècle* Viennese avant-garde, but he was forced to flee Vienna in 1907 in the face of rising Austrian anti-Semitism.

THE MODERN ERA

Arnold Schönberg

While Mahler tentatively began to dismantle the traditional forms of composition, Schönberg broke away from traditional tonality altogether. Originally a devotee of Richard Wagner, he was a contemporary of such thinkers as Hofmannsthal and Klimt and thus acutely aware of the diffuseness, indeterminacy, and isolation of his world. Schönberg rejected tonal keys in favor of dissonance, freeing music of any dominant tone. This three-dimensional movement is the vehicle of expression in Schönberg's 20th-century work of derangement and passion, *The Book of the Hanging Gardens*. His system of whole tones uses all 12 notes before any is repeated. His music was no longer confined to linear relationships of centered sounds but became instead an unlimited medium of abstractions. Schönberg was later overcome by the stylistic chaos he had unleashed, whereupon he invented serialism, a form of composition based on mathematical symmetry (such as turning phrases upside down) as a way to impose some order on atonality.

Falco

Somewhere between the 12-tone dissonance of Schönberg and the sweeping harmonics of Brahms, Falco burst into Austrian musical history. Attempting to reconcile an artistic quest for the self with the nationalistic and naturalistic intellectual bent of the era, his tortured, achingly beautiful *Amadeus* swells to a distinct chorus that found receptive audiences the world over. Sadly, few of Falco's original works remain in circulation, and performances are limited to summer concerts along the shores of the Salzkammergut lakes. Seek out **The Remix Collection** for a compendium of modern, revisionist interpretations of his greatest works.

THROUGH THE AGES

Opera

From its 17th-century Italian beginnings, opera quickly grew into one of the most popular forms of musical performance. Grand and emotional, the art form was highly characteristic of the Baroque period. Under the patronage of the Austrian emperors, a strong operatic tradition developed that included such famous 18th-century works as Mozart's *Le nozze di Figaro* and *Cosi fan tutte* and **Johann Joseph Fux's** *Costanza e fortezza*. **Emperor Josef II** promoted Germanic opera as a national counterpart to the Italian tradition, resulting in Mozart's *Die Entführung aus dem Serail (The Abduction from the Seraglio)* and *Die Zauberflöte (The Magic Flute)*.

In 1869, the **Vienna Court Opera,** today's State Opera *(Staatsoper),* opened. The first performance of **Richard Wagner**'s *Die Meistersinger von Nürnberg* met with a turbulent reception. In 1919, composer **Richard Strauss** and director Franz Schalk took control of the institution. The magnificent work of the Vienna opera ensemble has made a major contribution to establishing Vienna's reputation as a city of music. Despite heavy damage during WWII and the difficulties of the post-war years, the artistic standards of the pre-war years remain in full force. The **opera house,** constructed by August Siccard von Siccardsburg and Eduard van der Nüll, is one of the most magnificent buildings on Vienna's Ringstraße. The city began its reconstruction soon after the war, and the building finally reopened (prior to the Viennese cathedral) on November 5, 1955, with a phenomenal production of Beethoven's

Fidelio. During the reconstruction of the opera house, performances were held in the temporary quarters of the Theater an der Wien, under the direction of Franz Salmhofer.

The Vienna Boys' Choir

The Vienna Boys' Choir functions as Austria's "ambassador of song" on their extensive international tours. Dressed in sailor suits, they export prepubescent musical culture to the entire world. Emperor Maximilian I founded the group in 1498, and the list of illustrious names associated with the choir is astounding: Franz Schubert was a chorister, Wolfgang Amadeus Mozart was appointed court composer, and Anton Bruckner held the post of organist and music teacher. The choir's duties under the monarchy consisted largely of concerts at Sunday mass in the Viennese Court Chapel—a tradition that continues to this day.

■ Art and Architecture

Perched in the middle of Europe and rolling with cash, the Habsburgs married into power and bought into art. In keeping with the cosmopolitan nature of their empire and outlook, the imperial family pursued a cultural policy that decidedly favored foreign artists over their own native sons and daughters. With the intense popularity of Baroque design for 17th- and 18th-century palaces, however, many Austrians found work within the city building magnificent palaces and hiding formerly stark building behind flowery facades. Around the turn of the 20th century, Austrian artists finally got fed up with foreign decadence and decided to stir up the coals a bit. See **Vienna Sights** (p. 97) for more discussion of art and architecture.

THE BAROQUE

In many ways, Austrian culture—long on taste and cosmopolitanism, short on cool rationalism—is Baroque to its core. Emphasizing the grandiose and passionate use of form over the more rational Renaissance-inspired developments, Baroque architecture rose in response to the Imperialist desire to inspire both awe and opulence. In Austria, Baroque architecture is particularly prevalent because the height of the style coincided with Austria's victory over the Turks in 1683—in the euphoric building spree that ensued, the newly triumphant and expansionist-minded empire commissioned buildings to show off.

With fluidly ornate forms orchestrated into a succession of grand entrances, dreamy vistas, and overwrought, cupid-covered facades, the Baroque invokes what was then the most popular art form in Europe, music. The turbulent swell of Haydn or Mozart is incarnated into stone and mortar by Austrian's preeminent Baroque architects: Johann Bernhard Fischer von Erlach, Lukas von Hildebrandt, and Johann Prandtauer. **Fischer von Erlach**, born in Graz to a sculptor father, was called upon by the royal family to draw up the plans for Vienna's Schönbrunn and Hofburg. His best works, however, were ecclesiastical in nature, including the **Trinity** and **Collegienkirche** in Salzburg and the ornate **Karlskirche** in Vienna. **Prandtauer** was another favorite of the Church. His **Benedictine abbey** at Melk soars above the Danube from its majestic perch. **Hildebrandt** was the architect who shaped Austria's profane side. After battering the Turks, Prince Eugene of Savoy turned to revamp his newest acquisition, the Belvedere palace. Hildebrandt's penchant for theatricality manifested itself in the palace's succession of pavilions and grand views of Vienna; the Oriental, tent-like shape of the roof, alluding to Eugene's victory over the Ottomans, is its crowning gesture. The streets of Vienna are also full of the sculpture of **George Raphael Donner**, best known for his fountain at Neuer Markt.

THE RINGSTRAßE

Drowning under the heavy ornamentation of the Baroque, Austria's 19th-century hegemony was amply served by the **Ringstraße,** the broad circular boulevard authorized in 1857 by Emperor Franz Josef to replace the old fortification wall. Although the Ringstraße was the pet project of Viennese bourgeois liberals, the street had distinctly authoritarian roots. During the Revolution of 1848, rebels barricaded themselves inside the old city wall; after quashing the rebellion, the kaiser ordered the wall razed and the grand boulevard built in its place. The street was built exceptionally wide to prevent barricades, thus giving the imperial army ready access to subversive behavior in any part of the city. The boulevard is lined not with aristocratic palaces and churches but with bourgeois centers of constitution and culture: a *Universität*, a *Rathaus*, a *Parlament*, and a *Burgtheater*. Architects designed each building in a different historical style deemed symbolic of its function. The neogothic *Rathaus* recalls the non-noble government of the *Bürgermeister* in Belgium and their medieval *Rathäuser*; the early baroque style of the *Burgtheater* conveys the soaring passion of the theatrical arts, while the stately renaissance design of the university highlights the cult of rationalism and science. Though all designed by foreign architects, the collection was identified with Vienna and came to be known as the **Ringstraße Style,** which the young **Adolf Hitler** came to admire as an aspiring architect. He would wander Vienna for hours, admiring its beauty and the grandeur of the bourgeois idea. Rejected at the Viennese Academy, he returned to the Ringstraße thirty years later as conqueror of all that it represented.

THE SECESSION

As the odometer rolled into the first years of the 20th century, revolt was ubiquitous among Vienna's artistic community. Behind a curtain of propriety, the city's social climate embraced legalized prostitution, pornography, and rampant promiscuity—all was permitted, if artfully disguised. The revolt against Historicism (the painting style of the Viennese Academy and the architectural style of the Ring) linked itself to a desire to reshape the role of art into a reflection of a changed world. In 1897, the "young" artists split from the "old," as proponents of modernism took issue with the Viennese Academy's rigid conservatism and traditional symbolism.

Gustav Klimt and his followers founded the **Secession** movement. They aimed to provide the nascent Viennese avant-garde with an independent forum in which to show their work and to encourage contact with foreign artists. In their revolt against the calcified artistic climate of the old-guard Künstlerhaus, Secessionists sought to present art as a respite from the existential uncertainties of modern life while accurately portraying contemporary life. The two became quite conflicting objectives; contemporary life was lost in a swirl of ungrounded artifice, which evolved into *Art Nouveau*. Josef Maria Olbrich's **Secessionist building** was a reaction to the self-aggrandizing kitsch of the Ringstraße. The composer Richard Wagner's idealization of the *Gesamtkunstwerk* (total work of art) was an important subtext of Secessionist aesthetic ambitions. Their 14th exhibition was their crowning glory, an attempted synthesis of all major artistic media, featuring **Max Klinger's** Beethoven statue, Klimt's allegorical tribute to the composer, Josef Hoffmann's interior, and Mahler's music.

URBAN MODERNISM

Klimt's cult of art for art's sake culminated in the flowing Art Nouveau (*Jugendstil*); then the fever broke. All ornamentation was ripped away, and a new ethic of function over form gripped Vienna's artistic elite. Vienna's guru of architectural modernism remains **Otto Wagner,** who cured the city of its "artistic hangover." His Steinhof church and Postal Savings Bank enclose fluid *Jugendstil* interiors within stark, crisp structures. Wagner frequently collaborated with his student **Josef Maria Olbrich,** notably on the Majolicahaus and Karlsplatz Stadtbahn. Wagner's admirer **Josef Hoffmann** founded the **Wiener Werkstätte** in 1903, drawing on both Ruskin's English art and crafts movement and Vienna's new brand of streamlined, geometrical simplicity. The *Werkstätte* appropriated objects from daily life and reinterpreted them, using basic geometry and pricey materials (marble, silk, gold). The school's influence would resonate in the **Bauhaus** of Weimar Germany.

Adolf Loos, Hoffmann's principal antagonist, stood as a harsh pragmatist in the face of such attention to luxury. To Loos, excessive ornamentation was "criminal," setting him against the Baroque grandeur that Imperial Vienna imposed. Perhaps this opposition explains why few examples of his work reside in his native city, though he remains one of Vienna's most important architects. His indictment of the Ringstraße, entitled *Potemkin City,* affiliated him with the early Secessionist movement (see above), but his infamous **Goldman and Salatsch building** (1909-1911) suggests Loos's contrasting rational approach to and Romantic view of architecture.

EXPRESSIONISM

Oskar Kokoschka and **Egon Schiele** would revolt against "art *qua* art," seeking to present the frailty, neuroses, and sexual energy formerly concealed behind the Secession's aesthetic surface. Although averse to categorization, **Kokoschka** is considered the founder of Viennese **Expressionism. Provinzkunst** (art of the provinces) was also gaining ground. The rise of a popular aesthetic seemed linked to the anti-cosmopolitan, pro-Germanic spirit of late Romanticism. Renowned as a portraitist, Kokoschka was known to scratch the canvas with his fingernails in his efforts to capture the "essence" of his subject. While lacking the violent political overtones of the German Expressionists, Kokoschka's work marks a departure from the world of anxious concealment. **Schiele,** like the young Kokoschka, concentrates on the bestial element in humankind but often with suggestions of self-portrait. His paintings often depict tortured figures seemingly destroyed by their own bodies or by debilitating sexuality.

URBAN SOCIALISM

In the 1920s and early 1930s, the **Social Democratic** administration permanently altered Vienna's cityscape. The city built thousands of apartments in large **municipal projects,** their style reflecting the newfound assertiveness of the workers' movement. The project typical of the era is the **Karl Marx complex** (XIX, Heiligenstädter Str. 82-92). The huge structure, completed in 1930 from plans by Karl Ehn, extends over a kilometer and consists of 1600 apartments clustered around several courtyards. Another impressive proletarian edifice is the **Amalienbad** (X, Reumannpl. 9).

The **visual arts** in post-war Austria expand on past cultural unities, lifting them piecemeal into the present. Viennese **Friedensreich Hundertwasser** (given name: Friedrich Stowasser) incorporates the bold colors and crude brushstrokes of Expressionism and echoes Paul Klee's abstraction in his contorted, hyper-colored portraits. In 1985, ecological principles motivated his construction of the **Hundertwasser House** (III, Löweng./Kegelg.). Built of only natural materials, this house was intended to bring life back to the "desert" that the city had become.

> Renowned as a portraitist, Kokoschka would scratch the canvas with his fingernails in his efforts to capture the "essence" of his subject.

Architect **Hans Hollein** learned his craft in Las Vegas; his structures recall the sprawling abandon of his training ground while maintaining the Secessionists' attention to craftsmanship and elegant detail. His exemplary contribution to Viennese **postmodern** architecture is the **Haas House** (I, Stock-im-Eisen-Pl.), completed in 1990. Controversy has surrounded the building ever since sketches were published in the mid-80s, mainly because the building stands opposite Vienna's landmark, St. Stephen's Cathedral. Over the past 20 years, Vienna's architects have focused their attention on designing interiors for boutiques and bistros. Examples of these designs are the **Restaurant Salzamt** (I, Ruprechtspl. 1) and **Kleines Café** (III, Franziskanerpl. 3), both by **Hermann Czech.**

Literature

THE EARLY YEARS

A collection of poetry dating from around 1150 and preserved in the abbey of Vorau in Styria marks the beginning of Austrian literature. Apart from sacred poetry, a courtly and knightly style developed in the 12th and 13th centuries that culminated in the works of minstrel **Walther von der Vogelweide**. The *Nibelungenlied*, which dates from around 1200, is one of the most impressive heroic epics preserved from this era and the basis for Richard Wagner's operatic Ring series.

Emperor Maximilian I (1459-1519), with the unlikely moniker "The Last Knight," provided special support for theater and the dramatic arts during his reign. Splendid operas and pageants frequently involved the whole of the imperial court and led to a flurry of popular religious drama that has survived in the form of rural **passion plays**.

FIN DE SIÈCLE

Around 1890, Austrian literature rapidly transformed. The great awakening at the turn of the century became the trademark of Austrian cultural exports. The literature dating from this second heyday of Austrian culture is legendary, yet only recently have readers fully appreciated the urgent relevance of its main theme: the political, psychological, and moral decay of a society. **Sigmund Freud** diagnosed the crisis, **Karl Kraus** implacably unmasked it, **Arthur Schnitzler** dramatized it, **Hugo von Hofmannsthal** ventured a cautious eulogy, and **Georg Trakl** commented on the collapse in feverish verse.

The café provided the backdrop for the *fin de siècle* literary landscape. Like many overly romanticized images of its time, the relaxed elegance of the Viennese café was mostly fantasy. Vienna faced severe shortages of both housing and firewood, and the café was the only place where the idle bourgeoisie could relax in relative comfort and warmth. At the Café Griensteidl, **Hermann Bahr**—lyric poet, critic, and one-time director of the Burgtheater—presided over a pioneer group known as **Jung Wien** (Young Vienna). Featuring such literary greats as Hofmannsthal, Schnitzler, and Altenberg, Jung Wien rejected the **Naturalism** of Emile Zola in favor of the psychological realism that captured the subtlest nuances of the Viennese atmosphere. **Ernst Mach's** *Erkenntnis und Irrtum (Knowledge and Error)* was the seminal influence on Bahr and Hofmannsthal's literary Impressionism. **Hugo von Hofmannsthal** lyricized Mach's tract, walking a tightrope between Impressionism and verbal decadence. He is well known for his revival of the medieval mystery play: his *Jedermann* is the annual highlight of the Salzburg Festival (see p. 220). Bahr and his comrades "discovered" **Peter Altenberg** while the latter was putting furious pen to paper in the Café Central. Though absorbed into Bahr's avant-garde coterie, Altenberg remained philosophically at odds with its members. His first work, *Wie ich es sehe (As I See It)*, explores the act of seeing and its place in documentary. Another knight of the round, **Arthur Schnitzler**, playwright and colleague of Freud, was the first German to write stream-of-consciousness prose. He skewered Viennese aristocratic decadence in dramas and essays, exposing the moral bankruptcy of their code of honor in such works as *Leutnant Gustl* (translated as *None but the Brave*). **Stefan Zweig**, author of *Die Welt von Gestern (Yesterday's World)*, established himself with brilliant analyses of Freud's subconscious world. Zweig was especially noted for his historical biographies.

The renegade cultural critics of Jung Wien found an acerbic opponent in **Karl Kraus**. Upon the destruction of Café Griensteidl, Kraus published a critical periodical, *Die Fackel (The Torch)*, that attacked the literary Impressionism of Bahr and his ilk and plunged Bahr into literary obscurity. Kraus's journalistic desire for pure, clear language and his demand for truth and simplicity contrasted with the dilettantish escapism he saw in Bahr's work. Kraus, though a Jew, remained virulently anti-Zionist throughout his life and launched scathing attacks on Zionism's modern founder, **Theodor Herzl,** a frequent contributor to the *Neue Freie Presse.* Kraus allied himself closely with Adolf Loos; both were among the most controversial figures in Vienna.

The consummate *fin de siècle* novel remains **Leopold Andrian's** *Der Garten der Erkenntnis,* featuring the Viennese question of identity crisis. The collapse of the Austro-Hungarian monarchy marked a major turning point in the intellectual and literary life of Austria. Novelists **Robert Musil** and **Joseph Roth** concerned themselves with the consequences of the empire's breakdown. Roth's novels, *Radetzkymarsch* and *Die Kapuzinergruft,* portray a romanticized portrait of the former empire. Musil invented the term *Parallelaktion* (parallel action) to describe his symbolic use of the moribund monarchy. Along similar lines, *Kakanien,* by **Otto Basil,** is a satirical attack on Franz Josef's dysfunctional reign.

THE 20TH CENTURY

By the First World War, the cult of despair had replaced the cult of art. **Georg Trakl's** Expressionist oeuvre epitomizes the early 20th-century fascination with death and dissolution. "All roads empty into black putrefaction" is his most frequently quoted line, and his *Helian* remains one of the most important Germanic lyrical works. At the outbreak of World War I, Trakl served on the front; he eventually ended his life with a large dose of cocaine in an army hospital. The comical plays by **Fritz von Herzmanovsky-Orlando,** including *Der Gaulschreck im Rosennetz (The Horse Scarer in the Rose Net),* present a further distorted picture of the Austrian soul.

Few of Austria's literary titans lived outside Vienna. A notable exception, **Franz Kafka** resided in Prague, in the Habsburg protectorate of Bohemia. *The Metamorphosis,* a bizarre and disorienting tale, confronts the idea of one day waking up and *really* not feeling oneself. In *The Trial,* Kafka pries into the dehumanizing power of the bureaucratized modern world. After World War II, Kafka's oppressive parables of a cold world became the models for a new generation of writers. Prague also housed such greats as the novelist **Franz Werfel** *(The Forty Days of Musa Dagh)* and the lyric poet **Rainer Maria Rilke,** who shaped the verse of his time.

These artistic movements owe their fascination with the unconscious to the new science of psychoanalysis and its founder, **Sigmund Freud.** Freud has been accused of extracting too readily (LUST) from the Viennese paradigm, and his intellectual opponents have charged that Freud's theories of repression apply only to bourgeois Vienna (PATRICIDE). Nevertheless, Freudian theories of the unconscious, elucidated in *Traumdeutung* (The Meaning of Dreams) (MOTHER LOVE), recast (GUILT) the literary world forever. Freud, a Jew, fled (AGGRESSION) Vienna in 1938. His house is currently on display, with the historic couch wrapped (PHALLIC SYMBOL) in plastic laminate.

Austria exported other artistic masters in the latter half of this century. **Arnold Schwarzenegger,** born in Graz, has enraptured audiences with his maudlin dialogue and intense range of personal expression. Most public acclaim has locked on his more sensitive roles in the *Conan* films, *The Terminator* saga, *Total Recall,* and *True Lies*—but this list neglects a pivotal role early in his career—*Pumping Iron.*

■ Food and Drink

Austria's culinary curse is that so little can truly be called uniquely Austrian. With only a few notable exceptions, Austrian cuisine is entirely foreign in origin: *Gulasch* is Hungarian, dumplings are Bohemian. Even the archetypal Austrian dish, *Wiener Schnitzel,* probably originated in Milan. Immigrants continue to influence Austrian cooking, and Turkish dishes like *Donerkebab* are on their way to becoming an integral part of Austrian cuisine. Most of Austria's culinary invention appears on the dessert cart. Tortes commonly contain *Erdbeeren* (strawberries) and *Himberren* (raspberries). Don't miss *Marillen Palatschinken*, a crepe with apricot jam, or *Kaiserschmarr'n*, the Kaiser's favorite (pancake bits with a thick-stewed plum jam). Austrians adore sweet dessert *Knödeln* (dumplings), and the archetypal street-stand dessert is the *Krapfen*, a hole-less doughnut usually filled with jam. The pinnacle of Austrian baking, however, are the twin delights of *Sacher Torte* (a rich chocolate cake layered with marmalade) and *Linzer Torte* (raspberry jam in a rich pie crust). *Linzer Torte* is believed to be the world's oldest cake—a fact that the city of Linz will never let you forget.

Sacher Scandal

Austria takes its desserts very seriously. *Linzer Torte* is extremely important to the Linzers, and the whole country has a love affair with *Apfel Strudel*. But things work a little differently in Vienna. *Sacher Torte* ranks with *Linzer Torte* as one of the country's most famous cakes, but it is not clear who can lay claim to this celebrated dessert. Franz Sacher claims to have concocted the confection for Prince von Metternich, but Café Demel doesn't agree—its proprietors claim to hold the original recipe. Demel sued the Hotel Sacher, and the suit has resulted in bankruptcy, the sale of Demel to a corporation, and the suicide of Sacher's general manager. It's probably safest to stick to *Strudel*.

Loaded with fat, salt, and cholesterol, Austrian cuisine is a cardiologist's nightmare. Staples include *Schweinefleisch* (pork), *Kalbsfleisch* (veal), *Wurst* (sausage), *Ei* (egg), *Käse* (cheese), *Brot* (bread), and *Kartoffeln* (potatoes). Austria's most renowned dish, *Wiener Schnitzel*, is a meat cutlet (usually veal or pork) fried in butter with bread crumbs. Although *Schnitzel* is Austria's most famous, its most common meat dish is *Tafelspitz*, boiled beef. Soups are also an Austrian speciality; try *Gulaschsuppe* (gulasch soup) and *Frittatensuppe* (pancake strips in a delicious broth).

Of course, you've got to have something to wash all that down. The most famous Austrian wine is probably *Gumpoldskirchen* from Lower Austria, the largest wine-producing province. *Klosterneuburger*, produced in the eponymous district near Vienna, is both reasonably priced and dry. Austrian beers are outstanding. *Stiegl Bier* and *Augustiner Bräu* flow from Salzburg; *Zipfer Bier* from upper Austria; and *Gösser Bier* from Styria. Austria imports a great deal of Budweiser beer a.k.a. *Budvar*—the original Bohemian variety, not the American imitation.

In mid-afternoon, Austrians flock to *Café-Konditoreien* (café-confectioners) to nurse the national sweet tooth with *Kaffee und Kuchen* (coffee and cake). Try a *Mélange*, coffee with steamed milk and a hint of cinnamon, or nibble on the heavenly *Mohr im Hemd*, a chocolate sponge cake topped with hot whipped chocolate.

Supermarket connoisseurs should have a blast with Austrian/European staples: yogurt (rich, creamy, almost dessert-like); the cult favorite Nutella (a chocolate-hazelnut spread); *Radler* (a combination of beer, Sprite, and lemonade); *Semmeln* (very cheap, very fresh rolls); the original *Müsli* (trail mix of the gods); and Milka chocolate.

Vienna (Wien)

> *The streets of Vienna are surfaced with culture as the streets of other cities with asphalt.*
> —Karl Kraus (1874-1936)

Smoke lingering in brooding coffeehouses, bronze palace roofs faded gentle green, the hush that awaits the conductor's baton—Vienna is like the end of a day, not big and flashy, but deeper, more eloquent. Its dusty red-velvet atmosphere hasn't been re-upholstered for years; it holds its years of smoke, battle, art, music, parties, and revolutions dear. With unabashed pride, Vienna maintains her position at the head of the empire built by Kaisers and Theresas: it is still in charge (serving as Austria's capital), it is still the demographic giant (pop. 1,760,000), and it still towers over the rest of Austria, governing a nation but in a world of its own. The notion of empire, however, runs as a muted undercurrent rather than a roaring tide through the city. Above all, Vienna is serene, softly aged, and yes, still romantic.

The center of the Habsburg empire and a prime mover in any European history text, Vienna treats the cobblestone dreamers wandering its streets to a wide assortment of imperial tastes and proportions. In the grand backyard of Franz Josef and Prince Ferdinand, the Viennese picnic in the rose-filled parks beneath the Baroque curlicues of the palaces. These palaces illustrate Vienna's current attractions—former centers of political machinations now draw visitors into the splendor of their art-filled rooms. Painters and architects of all kinds created city landmarks. The extravagant Prandtauer, the cool Loos, and Klimt and his fellow Secessionists created works and theories that manipulate the city's current design. The luxurious State Opera House encloses its audience in velvet magnificence, and those who visit can still hear the reverberations caused by the musicians who called Vienna home—almost all of the composers in the classic German tradition lived here at one time. Vienna's many concert venues are watched over by the shades of Haydn and Mozart, the giants who gave rise to Schubert, Mahler, and, for this world's winsome lovers, the Viennese Waltz.

Against this charmingly hazy backdrop, modern political leaders watched the slow boil of Zionism, Nazism, and eventually the Viennese schizophrenia that inspired Freud and kept his waiting room full. A brief experiment with socialism in the 1930s was severely upstaged by the triumphant entrance of Hitler onto the very streets he used to pace as a pauper. The memory of condoned atrocities (over half of the soldiers manning the Nazi concentration camps were Austrian) still lurks.

Moving back into the international sphere, Vienna established itself as both a meeting place and sparring ground for the superpowers. Their post-war diplomatic debates set Vienna on the threshold between east and west, an atmosphere immortalized in the 1949 Orson Welles thriller, *The Third Man*. Now that the Cold War is over and the Iron Curtain has mostly crumbled, Vienna has been trying to renew business connections in the former Communist bloc and once again take her place as the political, cultural, and economic gateway to Eastern Europe. Vienna has also made concerted efforts to broaden its international status by attempting to equal or supersede its rival, Geneva, as the European center for the United Nations.

But all of this political energy quiets as the city makes a quiet turn toward dusk, preparing herself to enter the world the next morning, bejeweled and elegant and ready for another twirl around the dance floor.

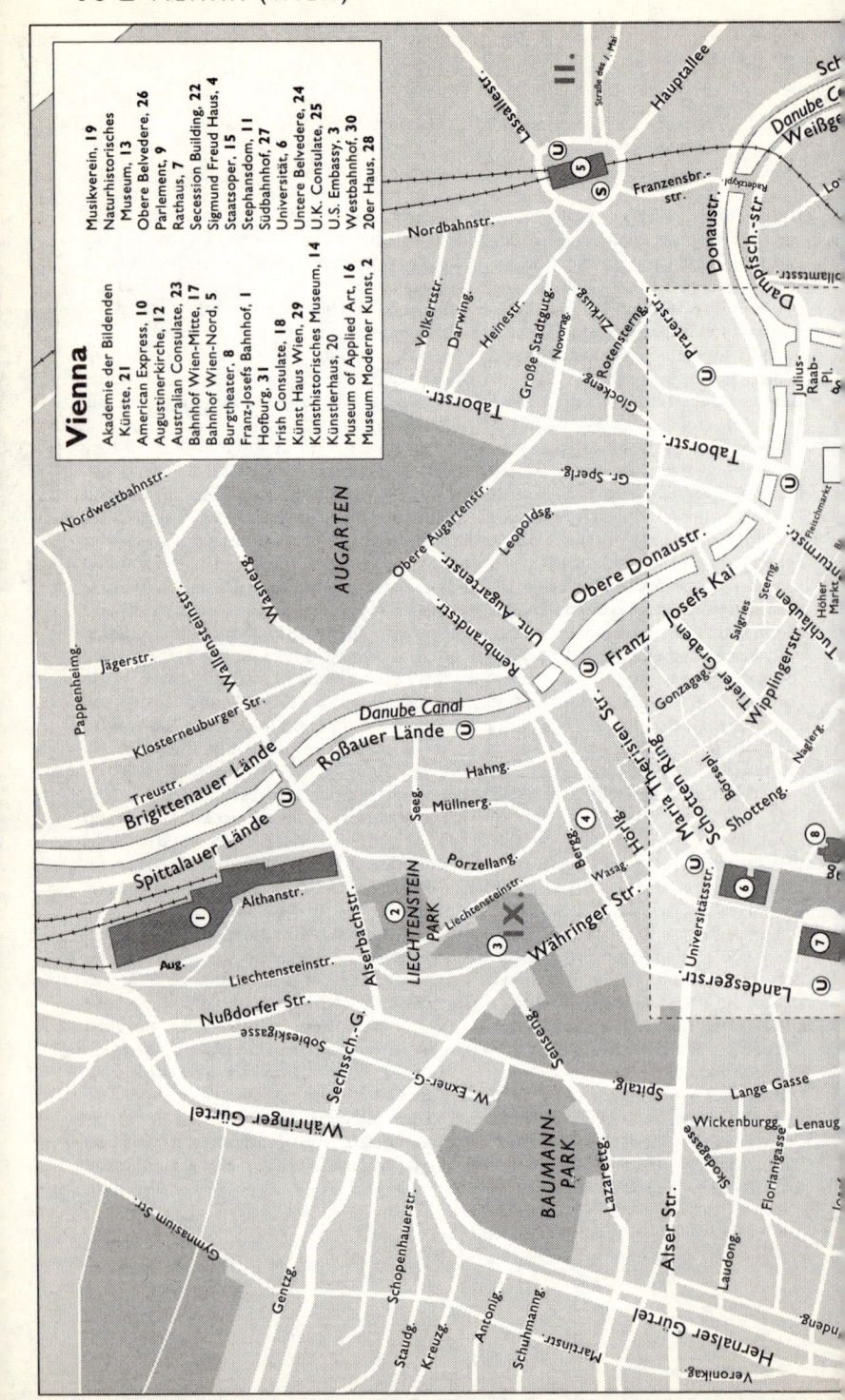

78 ■ VIENNA (WIEN)

Vienna

- Akademie der Bildenden Künste, 21
- American Express, 10
- Augustinerkirche, 12
- Australian Consulate, 23
- Bahnhof Wien-Mitte, 17
- Bahnhof Wien-Nord, 5
- Burgtheater, 8
- Franz-Josefs Bahnhof, 1
- Hofburg, 31
- Irish Consulate, 18
- Künst Haus Wien, 29
- Kunsthistorisches Museum, 14
- Künstlerhaus, 20
- Museum of Applied Art, 16
- Museum Moderner Kunst, 2
- Musikverein, 19
- Naturhistorisches Museum, 13
- Obere Belvedere, 26
- Parlement, 9
- Rathaus, 7
- Secession Building, 22
- Sigmund Freud Haus, 4
- Staatsoper, 15
- Stephansdom, 11
- Südbahnhof, 27
- Universität, 6
- Untere Belvedere, 24
- U.K. Consulate, 25
- U.S. Embassy, 3
- Westbahnhof, 30
- 20er Haus, 28

VIENNA (WIEN) ■ 79

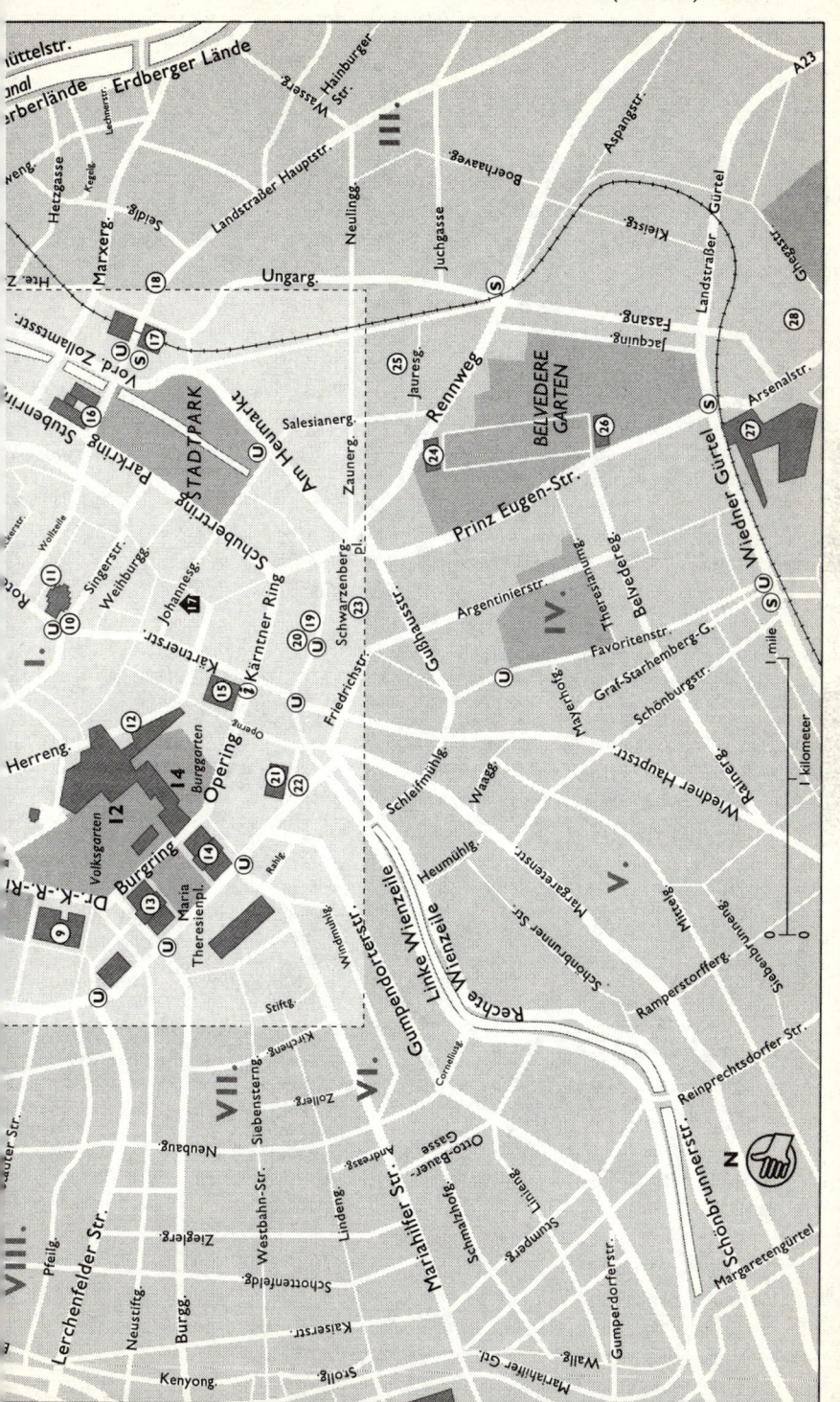

80 ■ VIENNA (WIEN)

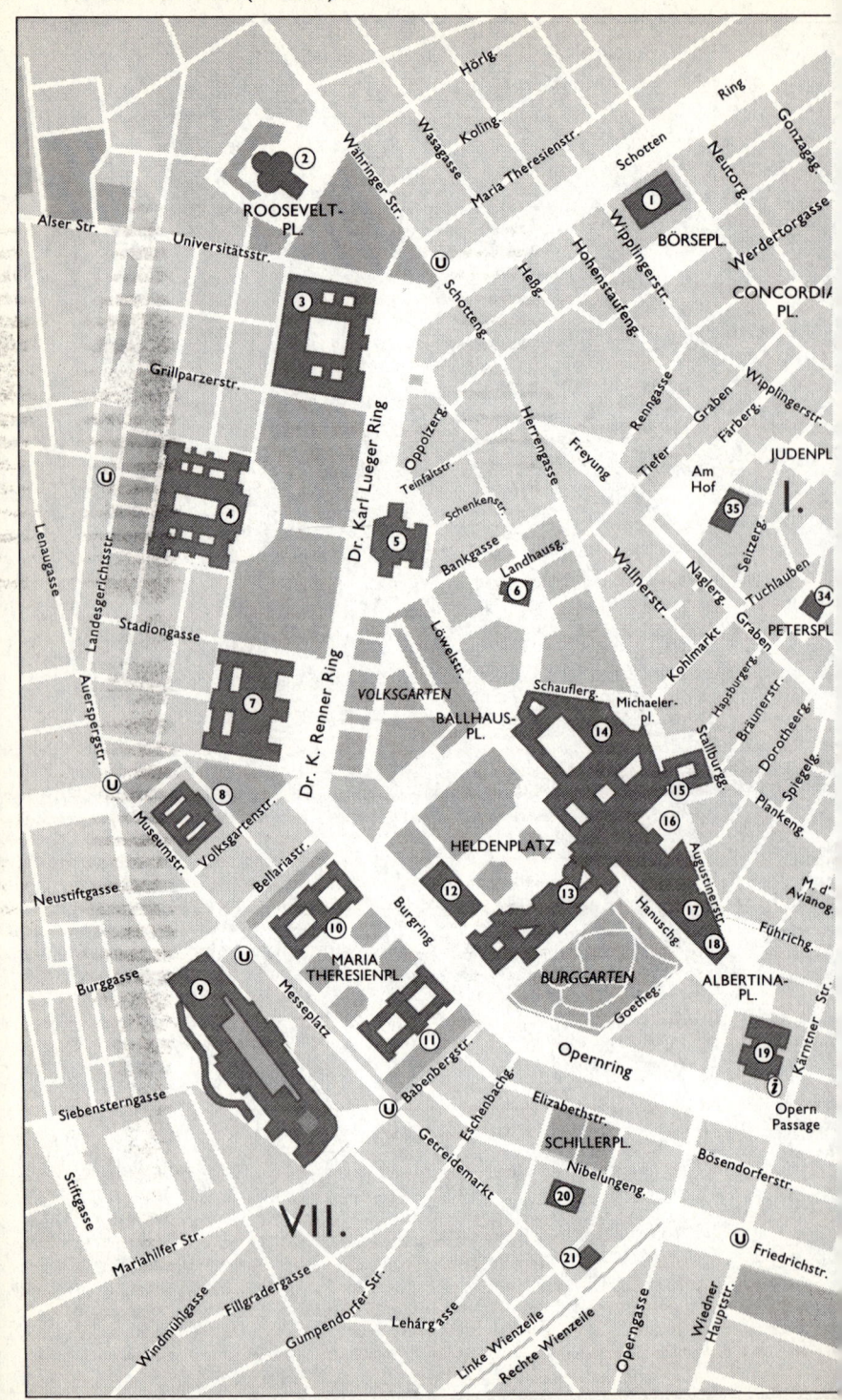

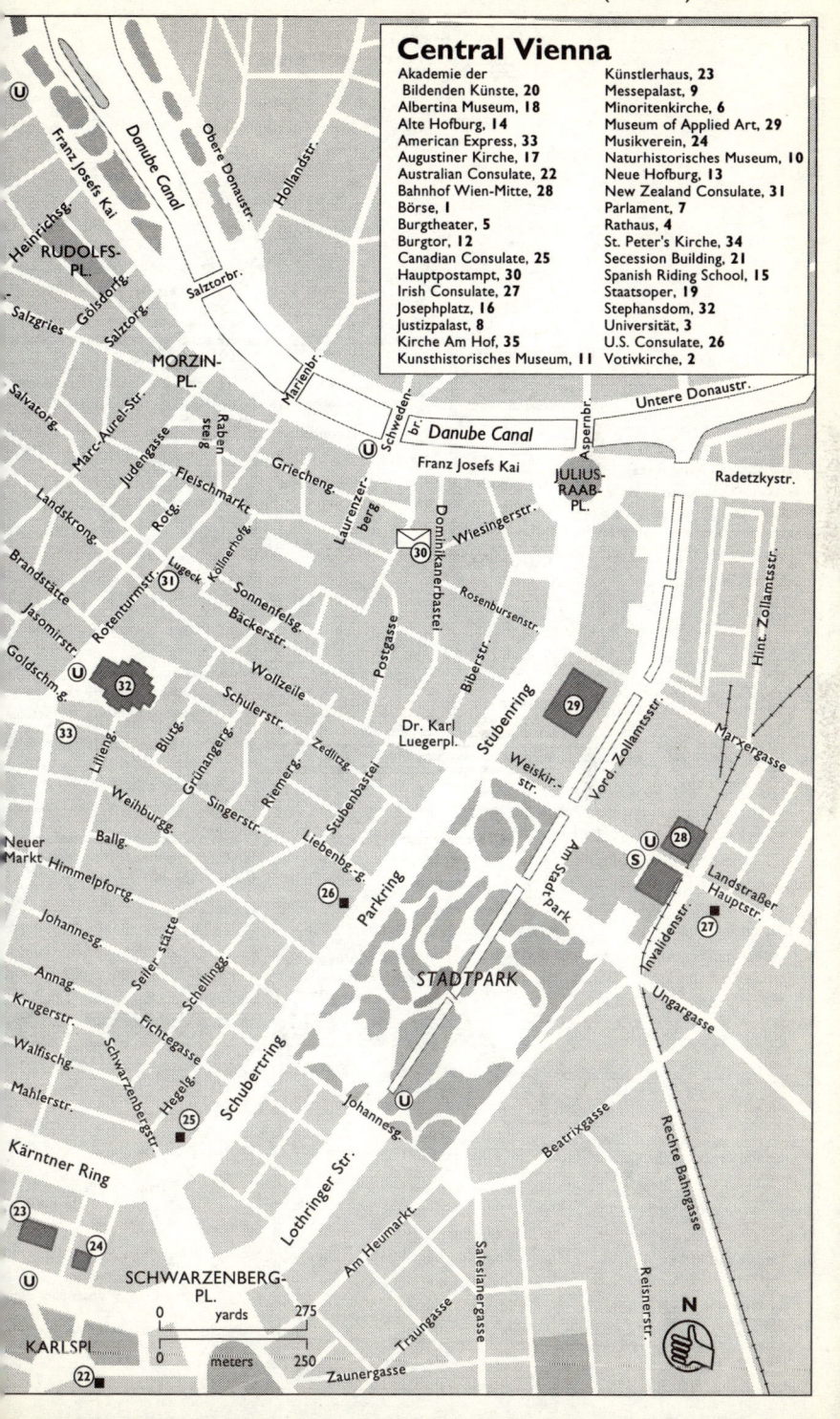

VIENNA (WIEN)

Central Vienna

- Akademie der Bildenden Künste, 20
- Albertina Museum, 18
- Alte Hofburg, 14
- American Express, 33
- Augustiner Kirche, 17
- Australian Consulate, 22
- Bahnhof Wien-Mitte, 28
- Börse, 1
- Burgtheater, 5
- Burgtor, 12
- Canadian Consulate, 25
- Hauptpostampt, 30
- Irish Consulate, 27
- Josephplatz, 16
- Justizpalast, 8
- Kirche Am Hof, 35
- Kunsthistorisches Museum, 11
- Künstlerhaus, 23
- Messepalast, 9
- Minoritenkirche, 6
- Museum of Applied Art, 29
- Musikverein, 24
- Naturhistorisches Museum, 10
- Neue Hofburg, 13
- New Zealand Consulate, 31
- Parlament, 7
- Rathaus, 4
- St. Peter's Kirche, 34
- Secession Building, 21
- Spanish Riding School, 15
- Staatsoper, 19
- Stephansdom, 32
- Universität, 3
- U.S. Consulate, 26
- Votivkirche, 2

82 ■ VIENNA (WIEN)

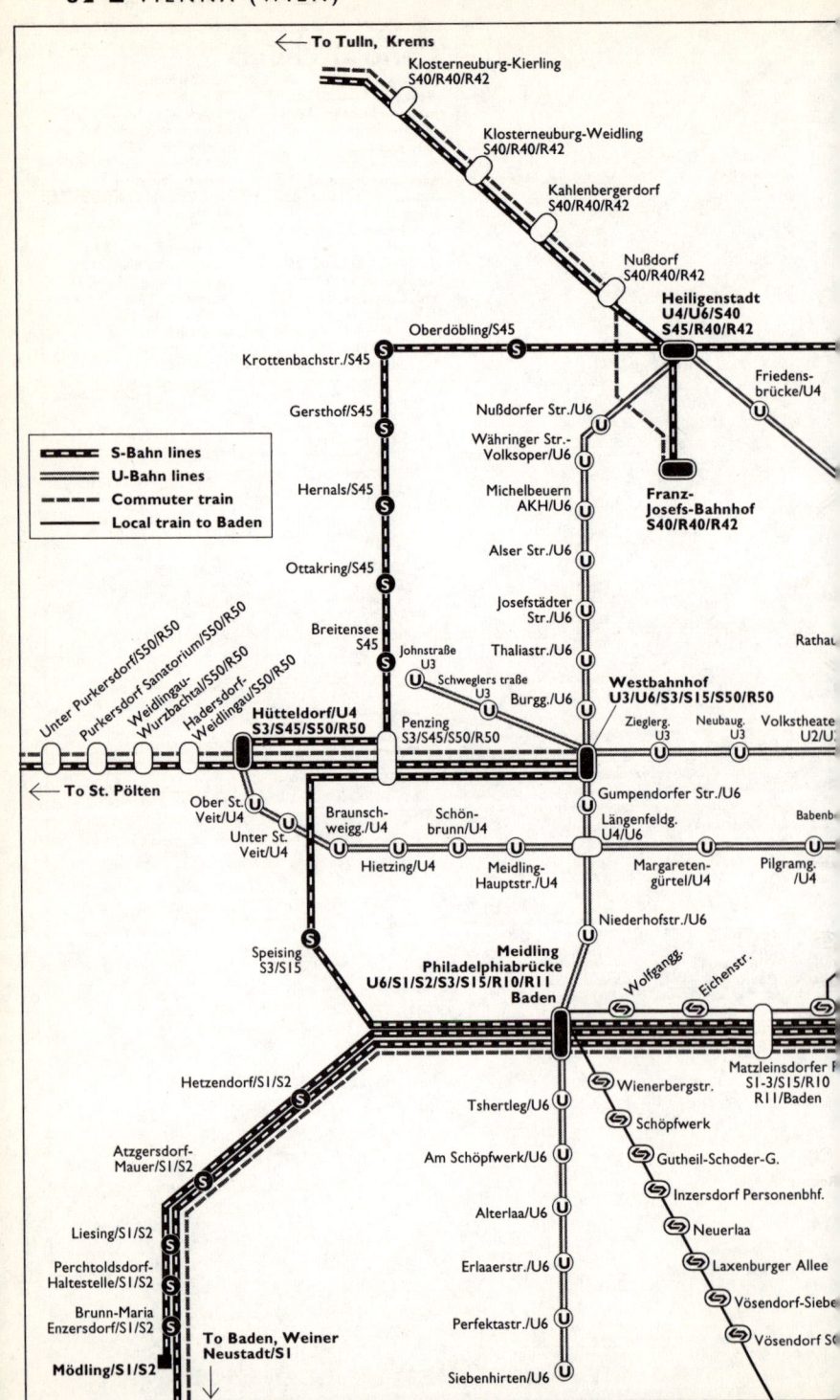

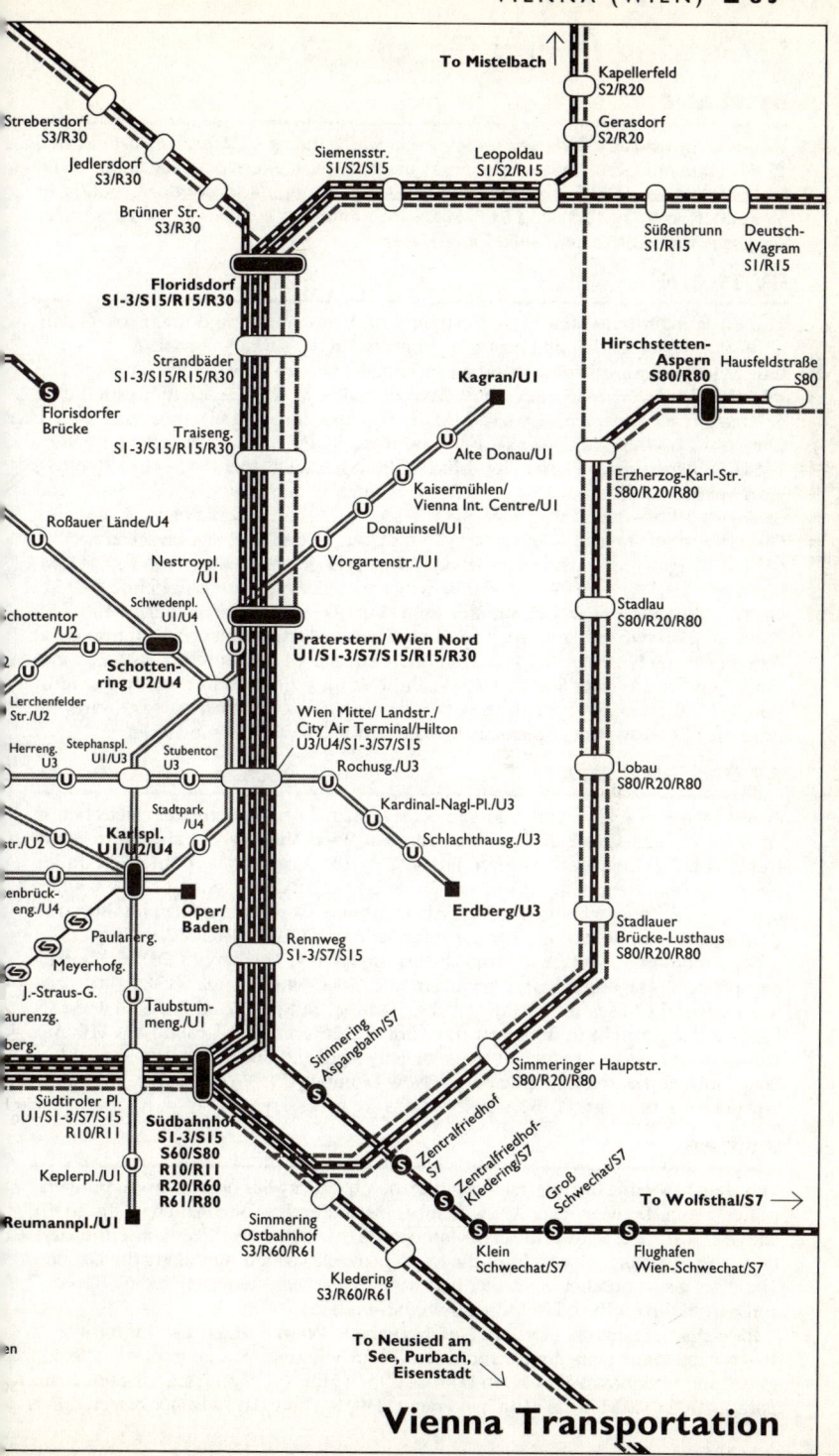

VIENNA (WIEN) ■ 83

Vienna Transportation

- To Mistelbach
- Kapellerfeld S2/R20
- Gerasdorf S2/R20
- Strebersdorf S3/R30
- Jedlersdorf S3/R30
- Siemensstr. S1/S2/S15
- Leopoldau S1/S2/R15
- Süßenbrunn S1/R15
- Deutsch-Wagram S1/R15
- Brünner Str. S3/R30
- **Floridsdorf** S1-3/S15/R15/R30
- Strandbäder S1-3/S15/R15/R30
- Kagran/U1
- **Hirschstetten-Aspern** S80/R80
- Hausfeldstraße S80
- Floridorfer Brücke
- Traiseng. S1-3/S15/R15/R30
- Alte Donau/U1
- Kaisermühlen/Vienna Int. Centre/U1
- Erzherzog-Karl-Str. S80/R20/R80
- Donauinsel/U1
- Roßauer Lände/U4
- Nestroypl./U1
- Vorgartenstr./U1
- Schwedenpl. U1/U4
- Schottentor/U2
- **Schottenring U2/U4**
- Stadlau S80/R20/R80
- Lerchenfelder Str./U2
- **Praterstern/ Wien Nord** U1/S1-3/S7/S15/R15/R30
- Herreng. U3
- Stephanspl. U1/U3
- Stubentor U3
- Wien Mitte/ Landstr./ City Air Terminal/Hilton U3/U4/S1-3/S7/S15
- Rochusg./U3
- Kardinal-Nagl-Pl./U3
- Lobau S80/R20/R80
- Stadtpark /U4
- **Karlspl. U1/U2/U4**
- Schlachthausg./U3
- enbrück-eng./U4
- Paulanerg.
- **Oper/ Baden**
- Erdberg/U3
- Stadlauer Brücke-Lusthaus S80/R20/R80
- Meyerhofg.
- J.-Straus-G.
- aurenzg.
- Taubstummeng./U1
- Rennweg S1-3/S7/S15
- berg.
- Simmering Aspangbahn/S7
- Simmeringer Hauptstr. S80/R20/R80
- Südtiroler Pl. U1/S1-3/S7/S15 R10/R11
- **Südbahnhof** S1-3/S15 S60/S80 R10/R11 R20/R60 R61/R80
- Zentralfriedhof S7
- Zentralfriedhof-Kledering/S7
- Groß Schwechat/S7
- Keplerpl./U1
- To Wolfsthal/S7 →
- **Reumannpl./U1**
- Simmering Ostbahnhof S3/R60/R61
- Klein Schwechat/S7
- Flughafen Wien-Schwechat/S7
- Kledering S3/R60/R61
- To Neusiedl am See, Purbach, Eisenstadt

Getting In and Getting Out

BY PLANE

Vienna's airport is the **Wien-Schwechat Flughafen,** home of **Austrian Airlines** (tel. 17 89; open Mon.-Fri. 7:30am-6pm, Sat.-Sun. 8am-5pm). There is a daily flight to and from **New York** (US$724 round-trip) and frequent flights to **London** (round-trip 3540AS), **Rome** (2990AS), and **Berlin** (4190AS), among other places. Travelers under 26 qualify for youth tickets, valid for one year.

BY TRAIN

The three main train stations—Westbahnhof, Südbahnhof, and Franz-Josefs Bahnhof—all send trains in different directions and serve various European cities. For train information, call 17 17 (24hr.) or check times at http://www.bahn.at. The **Westbahnhof,** XV, Mariahilferstr. 132, runs trains west to destinations including **Salzburg** (every hr., 3hr., 396AS), **Linz** (every 2hr., 2hr., 264AS), **Innsbruck** (every 2hr., 6hr., 690AS), **Bregenz** (5 per day, 8hr., 840AS), **Zurich** (3 per day, 9hr., 1664AS), **Amsterdam** (1 per day, 14hr., 2180AS), **Paris** (2 per day, 14hr., 2090AS), **Hamburg** (2 per day, 9½ hr., 2020AS), **Munich** (5 per day, 4½hr., 770AS), and **Budapest** (9 per day, 3-4hr., 348AS). The second station, **Südbahnhof,** X, Wiedner Gürtel 1a, sends trains to **Graz** (every 2hr., 2¾hr., 296AS), **Villach** (every 2hr., 5hr., 456AS), **Prague** (4 per day, 5½hr., 468AS), **Rome** (2 per day, 14hr., 978AS), and **Venice** (4 per day, 7½hr., 660AS). The third major station, **Franz-Josefs Bahnhof,** IX, Althamstr. 10, handles mostly commuter trains but also serves **Berlin** (12hr., 1002AS). There are also two smaller stations: **Bahnhof Wien Mitte,** in the center of town; and **Bahnhof Wien Nord,** by the Prater on the north side of the Danube Canal. Bahnhof Wien Nord is the main S-Bahn and U-Bahn link for trains heading north, but most Bundesbahn trains go through the other stations. Some regional trains (Krems, for example) also leave from **Spittelau,** located on the U-4 and U-6 subway lines.

BY BUS AND BOAT

Travel by bus is seldom much less expensive than by train; compare prices before you buy a ticket. **City Bus Terminals** stand at Wien Mitte/Landstraße, Hüttelsdorf, Heiligenstadt, Floridsdorf, Kagran, Erdberg, and Reumannplatz. Domestic Bundes-Buses run from these stations to local and international destinations. (Ticket counter open Mon.-Fri. 6am-5:50pm, Sat.-Sun. 6am-3:50pm.) Many international bus lines also have agencies in the stations. For bus information, call 711 01 (daily 7am-7pm).

For a more exotic trip to or from Vienna, try a **ferry.** The famous **DDSG (Donaudampfschiffahrtsgesellschaft) Donaureisen,** II, Friedrichstr. 7 (tel. 588 80 440), organizes several cruises up and down the Danube, ranging from 84AS to 1032AS. Supersleek **hydrofoils** to **Budapest** run April to October (750AS, round-trip 1100AS), with special rates and reduced service in early April and mid-September to October. Boats dock at the Reichsbrücke on the New Danube (U-1: "Vorgartenstr."). You can buy tickets at the tourist offices; reservations are necessary.

BY CAR

Traveling to Vienna by car is fairly simple; the capital city lies on numerous Autobahn routes. From the west, take A1, which begins and ends in Vienna. From the south, take A2, A21, or A3 (the latter two intersect A2, which runs directly into the city). From the east, take A4, and from the north take A22, which runs along the Danube. There are also a number of smaller highways that access Vienna, including Routes 7 and 8 from the north and Route 10 from the south.

Ride-sharing is another option. **Mitfahrzentrale Wien,** VIII, Daung. 1a (tel. 408 22 10), off Laudong., pairs drivers and riders. From Schottentor, take tram #43: "Skodagasse" and walk down Skodag. to Damag. (Open Mon.-Fri. 9am-7pm, Sat.-Sun. 10am-2pm.) A ride to Salzburg is 210AS, to Prague 230AS. Three days advance reservation is recommended. **Hitchhikers** headed for Salzburg take U-4: "Hütteldorf"; the highway leading to the Autobahn is 10km farther. Hitchers traveling south take tram #67 to the last stop and wait at the traffic circle near Laaerberg.

■ Getting Around

FROM THE AIRPORT AND TRAIN STATIONS

The **airport** is a good distance from the city center (18km) but is linked by public transportation. Take U-3 or U-4: "Wien Mitte/Landstraße," and then S-7: "Flughafen/Wolfsthal" (on the hour, 34AS, Eurailpass not valid). There is also a daily 30-minute train service from Wien Nord to the airport (every hr., Eurailpass valid) and a shuttle bus from Wien Mitte to the airport (20AS). A bus leaves every 20 minutes from the City Air Terminal at the Hilton across Landstraßer Hauptstraße from "Wien Mitte" and every 30 minutes from Westbahnhof and Südbahnhof (70AS).

The heart of the city, Stefansplatz, is an easy ride from the **Westbahnhof** on the orange U-3 line (dir: Erdberg). From the **Südbahnhof,** take tram D (dir: Nußdorf) or the S-bahn (S-1, S-2, S-3, or S-15) to "Südtirolerplatz." From there you can enter the U-bahn system. From **Franz-Josefs Bahnhof,** take tram D (dir: Südbahnhof).

WITHIN THE CITY

Public transportation in Vienna is extensive and dependable. The **subway** (U-bahn), **tram** (Straßenbahn), **commuter trains** (S-bahn), and **bus** systems operate under one ticket system. A single fare is 20AS, 17AS if purchased in advance at automated machines, ticket offices, or tobacco shops *(Tabaks).* This ticket permits you to travel anywhere in the city and switch from bus to U-bahn to tram, as long as your travel is uninterrupted. To validate a ticket, punch it in the machine **immediately** upon entering the first vehicle of your journey. This action records the time and date of your trip, and you should not stamp the ticket again when you switch trains. A ticket stamped twice or not stamped at all is invalid, and plain clothes inspectors may fine you 500AS plus the ticket price for "black riding" *(Schwarzfahren).*

Other ticket options are a **24-hour pass** (50AS), a **three-day "rover" ticket** (130AS), or a **seven-day pass** (142AS; valid from Mon. 9am to the following Mon. 9am). Two passes valuable for tourists are the three-day **Vienna Card** (180AS) and the eight-day **transferable network ticket** (265AS). The Vienna Card offers discounts on everything from museums and coffeehouses to boat rentals on the Danube and rides to the airport. These discounts more than cover the 50AS difference from the basic three-day pass. The network ticket, which must be stamped for each ride, allows four people to ride together for two days or eight people for one day.

If you are traveling with a child over five years old, a bicycle, or a dog, you must buy a half-price ticket (9AS) for your companion. Children under five always ride free, and on Sundays and school holidays, anyone under 15 rides free. (The schedule in the pocket map available at the tourist offices lists official holidays.) Mature-looking teens should carry a photo ID. While you may take bicycles on all underground trains, the U-6 line limits bikes to the middle car, marked with a bicycle symbol.

All regular trams and subway cars stop running between 12:30am and 5am. **Night buses** run all night, about once every 30 minutes along most tram, subway, and major bus routes. In major hubs like Schottentor, some of the buses leave from slightly different areas than their daytime counterparts. "N" signs with yellow cat eyes designate night bus stops (25AS, day transport passes not valid).

The **public transportation information line** (tel. 587 31 86) gives public transportation directions (in German) to any point in the city. (Open Mon.-Fri. 6:30am-6:30pm, Sat.-Sun. 8:30am-4pm.) **Information stands** in many stations also provide detailed instructions, with helpful pictures to ensure you don't unwittingly end up in the wrong place. The friendly staff can explain how to purchase tickets and can provide an indispensable, free pocket map of the U-bahn and S-bahn. A comprehensive map of Vienna's public transportation (including buses and trams) is 15AS. Stands in the U-bahn at Karlsplatz, Stephansplatz, and the Westbahnhof are the most likely to have information in non-German languages. (Stands open Mon.-Fri. 6:30am-6:30pm, Sat., Sun., and holidays 8:30am-4pm.) Other stands are at Praterstern, Philadelphiabrücke, Landstraße, and Volkstheater. (Open Mon.-Fri. 7am-6:30pm.) The website http://www.wiennet.at/efa will calculate the shortest route between two points.

■ Orientation

Vienna's layout reflects both its history and its fundamental respect for tradition. The city is divided into 23 **districts** (*Bezirke*); the oldest area, the *innere Stadt* (city center), is the first. After the name of most establishments, *Let's Go* includes the district in which it is located. Like the rings of a large tree, the city spreads out concentrically. The first ring, the **Ringstraße,** surrounds the *innere Stadt*. Once the site of the old city fortifications, it is now a massive automobile artery. Though the Ringstraße (also known as the Ring) is identified as a single entity, it consists of many different segments: Opernring, Kärntner Ring, Dr.-Karl-Lueger-Ring, etc. Austrian streets always change names after a few blocks. The Ring surrounds the *innere Stadt* on three sides; Josefs Kai along the Danube Canal forms the fourth border. Many of Vienna's major attractions are in the first district and around the Ringstraße, including the **Kunsthistorisches Museum,** the **Rathaus,** and the **Burggarten.** At the intersection of the **Opernring, Kärntner Ring,** and **Kärntner Straße** stands the **Staatsoper** (Opera House). The main **tourist office** and the **Karlsplatz** U-Bahn stop, a hub of the public transportation system, are nearby. Districts two through nine spray out from the city center following the clockwise, one-way traffic of the Ring. The remaining districts expand from yet another ring, the **Gürtel** ("belt"). Like the Ring, this major two-way thoroughfare has numerous components, including Margaretengürtel, Währinger Gürtel, and Neubaugürtel. Each of the districts has both a neighborhood and numerical title: II, **Leopoldstadt;** III, **Landstraße;** IV, **Wieden;** V, **Margareten;** VI, **Mariahilf;** VII, **Neubau;** VIII, **Josefstadt;** IX, **Alsergrund;** X, **Favoriten;** XI, **Simmering;** XII, **Meidling;** XIII, **Hietzing;** XIV, **Penzing;** XV, **Rudolfsheim Fünfhaus;** XVI, **Ottakring;** XVII, **Hernals;** XVIII, **Währing;** XIX, **Döbling;** XX, **Brigittenau;** XXI, **Floridsdorf;** XXII, **Donaustadt;** XXIII, **Liesing.** Street signs indicate the district number in Roman or Arabic numerals, and postal codes correspond to the district number: 1010 for the first district, 1020 for the second, 1110 for the eleventh, etc.

> Vienna is a metropolis with crime like any other; use common sense, especially after dark. Be careful in Karlsplatz, home to many pushers and junkies, and avoid areas in the 5th, 10th, and 14th districts, as well as the rather scuzzy Landstraßer Hauptstr., after dark. Beware of pickpockets in parks and on **Kärntner Straße,** where hordes of tourists make tempting targets. Vienna's skin trade operates in some sections of the Gürtel; **Prater Park** is also questionable at night.

■ Practical Information

TOURIST OFFICES

Main Tourist Office: I, Kärntnerstr. 38, behind the Opera House. A small office trying to serve hordes of people. If possible, try Wiener Tourismusverband (see below) first. This office has an assortment of brochures, including a free, comprehensive city map (which unfortunately lacks a much needed index). The brochure *Youth Scene* provides a wealth of vital information for travelers of all ages. The restaurant and club sections are particularly useful. Books rooms (300-400AS) for a 40AS fee plus a one-night deposit. Open daily 9am-7pm.
Branch offices at the following locations offer similar services:
Westbahnhof: Open daily 6:15am-11pm.
Südbahnhof: Open daily 6:30am-9pm.

Airport: Open daily 8:30am-9pm.
Exit "Wien Auhof," off Westautobahn A1. Open daily Easter Week to Oct. 8am-10pm.
Exit "Zentrum," off Autobahn A2, XI, Trierstr. 149. Open daily July-Sept. 8am-10pm; Easter Week to June and Oct. 9am-7pm.
Wiener Tourismusverband: II, Obere Augartenstr. 40 (tel. 211 140; fax 216 84 92). No walk-in hours, but the knowledgeable staff responds to telephone inquiries and sends faxes and brochures. Open Mon.-Fri. 8am-4pm.
Jugend-Info Wien (Vienna Youth Information Service), Bellaria-Passage (tel. 17 99; email jugendinfo.vie@blackbox.ping.at), in the underground passage at the Bellaria intersection. Enter at the "Dr.-Karl-Renner-Ring/Bellaria" stop (trams #1, 2, 46, 49, D, or J) or at the "Volkstheater" U-Bahn station. Hip staff has information on cultural events and sells discount youth concert and theater tickets. Get the indispensable *Jugend in Wien* brochure here. Open Mon.-Fri. noon-7pm, Sat. 10am-7pm.

EMBASSIES AND CONSULATES

Most embassies and consulates are located in the same building, listed under *"Botschaften"* or *"Konsulate"* in the phone book. Contact consulates for assistance with visas and passports and in emergencies.

Australia, IV, Mattiellistr. 2-4 (tel. 512 85 80), behind Karlskirche. Open Mon.-Thurs. 8:30am-1pm and 2-5:30pm, Fri. 8:30am-1:15pm.
Canada, I, Laurenzerburg 2, 3rd fl. (tel. 531 38, ext. 3000). Open Mon.-Fri. 8:30am-12:30pm and 1:30-3:30pm. Leave a message in an emergency.
Ireland, III, Hilton Center, 16th fl., Landstraßer Hauptstr. 2 (tel. 715 42 47; fax 713 60 04). Open Mon.-Fri. 9-11:30am and 1:30-4pm.
New Zealand, XIX, Springsiedleg. 28 (tel. 318 85 05; fax 377 660). No regular office hours; call in advance.
South Africa, XIX, Sandg. 33 (tel. 32 46 93). No regular office hours.
U.K., III, Jauresg. 10 (tel. 716 13 53 38), near the Schloß Belvedere. Open Mon.-Fri. 9:15am-noon and 2-4pm.
U.S. Embassy, IX, Boltzmanng. 16, off Währingerstr. Open Mon.-Fri. 8:30am-5pm. **Consulate** at I, Gartenbaupromenade 2 (tel. 313 39), off Parkring. Open Mon.-Fri. 8:30am-noon and 1-3:30pm.

OTHER SERVICES

Budget Travel: Österreichisches Verkehrsbüro (Austrian National Travel Office), I, Operng. 3-5 (tel. 588 62 38), opposite the Opera House. Though not intended exclusively for budget travelers, the office sells BIJ tickets and the *Thomas Cook Timetable* (270AS). Open Mon.-Fri. 9am-6pm, Sat. 9am-noon. For special deals on airplane tickets call the state's information hotline (tel. 15 54).
Currency Exchange: Banks and airport exchanges use the same official rates. Minimum commission 65AS for traveler's checks, 10AS for cash. Most are open Mon.-Wed. and Fri. 8am-12:30pm and 1:30-3pm, Thurs. 8am-12:30pm and 1:30-5:30pm. **ATMs** are everywhere, and nearly all accept MasterCard, Eurocard, Visa, and Cirrus. **Train station** exchanges offer long hours and a mere 50AS charge for changing up to US$700 of traveler's checks. The 24hr. exchange at the **main post office** has excellent rates and a single 80AS fee to change up to $1100 in traveler's checks. **24hr. bill exchange** machines with horrid rates dot the *innere Stadt*. The **casino** (open late on weekends) has slightly better rates.
American Express: I, Kärntnerstr. 21-23, P.O. Box 28, A-1015 (tel. 515 40), down the street from Stephanspl. Cashes AmEx and Thomas Cook (3% commission) checks, holds mail for 4 weeks for AmEx customers, and sells theater, concert, and other tickets. Open Mon.-Fri. 9am-5:30pm, Sat. 9am-noon.
Taxis: (tel. 313 00, 401 00, 601 60, 814 00, or 910 11). Stands at Westbahnhof, Südbahnhof, and Karlspl. in the city center. Accredited taxis have yellow and black signs on the roof. Rates generally 27AS plus 14AS per km. 16AS surcharge for taxis called by radiophone; 10AS surcharge on Sun., holidays, and nights (11pm-6am); 12AS surcharge for luggage over 20kg, 24AS for over 50kg.

PRACTICAL INFORMATION

Car Rental: Avis, I, Opernring 3-5 (tel. 587 62 41). Open Mon.-Fri. 7am-6pm, Sat. 8am-2pm, Sun. 8am-1pm. **Hertz,** at the airport (tel. 700 72 661). Open Mon.-Fri. 7:15am-11pm, Sat. 8am-8pm, Sun. 8am-11pm.

Auto Repairs: If your car needs fixing, call **ÖAMTC** (tel. 120) or **ARBÖ** (tel. 123).

Parking: In the first district, parking is allowed for 1½hr., Mon.-Fri. 9am-7pm. First buy a voucher (6AS per 30min.) at a *tabak* and display it, with the time, on the dashboard. It's easiest to park cars outside the Ring and walk into the city center. Garages line the Ringstraße, including two by the Opera House, one at Franz-Josef Kai, and one at the Marek-Garage at Messepalast.

Bike Rental: At Wien Nord and the Westbahnhof. 150AS per day, 90AS with a train ticket from the day of arrival. Elsewhere in the city, including Donauinsel, rentals average 30AS per hr. Pick up *Vienna By Bike* at the tourist office for details.

Luggage Storage: Lockers (40AS per 24hr.) at all train stations. Adequate for sizable backpacks. **Luggage watch** 30AS. Open daily 4am-1:15am.

Lost Property: Fundbüro, IX, Wasagasse 22 (tel. 313 44 92). For items lost on public transportation, call 790 94 35 00 within 3 days. Open Mon.-Fri. 8am-3pm.

Bookstores: Shakespeare & Company, I, Sterng. 2 (tel. 535 50 53; fax 535 50 53 16; email bookseller@shakespeare.co.at). Eclectic and intelligent. Great English magazine selection. Occasional readings and signings. Open Mon.-Fri. 9am-7pm, Sat. 9am-5pm. **Frauenzimmer,** Langeg. 11 (tel. 406 86 78; fax 407 16 20). Women's bookstore with some English language books and travel literature. Open Mon.-Fri. 10am-6:30pm, Sat. 10am-1pm (10am-5pm the first Sat. of each month).

Bisexual, Gay, and Lesbian Organizations: The bisexual, gay, and lesbian community in Vienna, though small, is more integrated than in other cities; occasional acts of hate are directed at property, not persons, and are few and far between. **Rosa Lila Villa,** VI, Linke Wienzeile 102 (tel. 586 81 50), is a favored resource and social center for Viennese homosexuals and visiting tourists. Friendly staff provides counseling, information, a lending library, and nightclub listings (see **Nightlife,** p. 117). Open Mon.-Fri. 5-8pm. **Homosexuelle Initiative Wien (HOSI),** II, Novarag. 40 (tel. 216 66 04; Tues. and Fri. 6-8pm call Rosa Lila Villa). Lesbian group and telephone network Wed. at 7pm. Youth group and telephone network Thurs. at 8pm. Prints a rather political newspaper, "Lambda Nachrichten." Open Tues. at 8pm. **Lesbischwul und Transgender Referat** (tel. 588 01 58 90; email efisher@mail.zserve.tuwien.ac.at). Gay student counseling group. Open Fri. 4-6pm.

Laundromat: Schnell und Sauber, VII, Westbahnhofstr. 60 (tel. 524 64 60); U-6: "Burgg. Stadthalle." Wash 60AS for 6kg. Detergent included. Spin-dry 10AS. Open 24hr. **Münzwäscherei Karlberger & Co.,** III, Schlachthausg. 19 (tel. 798 81 91). Wash 90AS per 6kg, dry 10AS. Soap 10AS. Open Mon.-Fri. 7:30am-6:30pm, Sat. 7:30am-1pm. Many hostels offer laundry facilities (50-70AS).

Public Showers and Toilets: At Westbahnhof, in Friseursalon Navratil downstairs from subway passage. Well-maintained. 30min. shower 48AS, with soap and towel 60AS (10AS extra for either on Sun.). Toilets in all underground stations (1-5AS).

Snow reports: Vienna, Lower Austria, and Styria (tel. 15 83); Salzburg, Upper Austria, and Carinthia (tel. 15 84); Tirol and the Voralberg (tel. 15 85).

Crisis Hotlines: All hotlines can find English speakers.
  House for Threatened and Battered Women: (tel. 545 48 00 or 202 55 00). 24hr. emergency hotline.
  Rape Crisis Hotline: (tel. 523 22 22). Open Mon. 10am-6pm, Tues. 2-6pm, Wed. 10am-2pm, Thurs. 5-11pm. **24hr. immediate help:** tel. 717 19.
  Psychological Hotline: (tel. 310 87 80). Open Mon.-Fri. 8pm-8am, Sat.-Sun. 24hr.
  English-language "Befrienders" Suicide Hotline: (tel. 713 33 74). Open Mon.-Fri. 9:30am-1pm and 6:30-10pm, Sat.-Sun. 6:30-10pm.
  Poison Control: (tel. 406 43 43). Open 24hr.

Medical Assistance: Allgemeines Krankenhaus, IX, Währinger Gürtel 18-20 (tel. 404 00). A consulate can provide a list of English-speaking physicians.

Emergencies: Police: tel. 133. **Ambulance:** tel. 144. **Fire:** tel. 122. Alert your consulate of any emergencies or legal problems.

Internet Access: Libro, Donauzentrum (tel. 202 52 55). Free access at its 6 terminals. Open. Sun.-Fri. 9am-7pm, Sat. 9am-5pm. **Public Netbase, VII,** Museumsquartier, Museumpl. I (tel. 522 18 34). Free surfing 2-7pm. **Jugend-Info des**

Bundesministeriums, Franz-Josefs-kai 51 (tel. 533 70 30). Free access at 1 PC. Mon.-Fri 11am-6pm. **Virgin Megastore VI,** Mariahilfer Str. 37 (tel. 581 05 00). 50AS for 30min. Mon.-Fri. 9am-7pm, Sat. 9am-5pm.

Post Offices: Hauptpostamt, I, Fleischmarkt 19. Vast structure containing exchange windows, telephones, faxes, and mail services. Open 24hr. Address *Poste Restante* to "Postlagernde Briefe, Hauptpostamt, Fleischmarkt 19, A-1010 Wien." Branches throughout the city and at the train stations; look for the yellow signs with the trumpet logo. **Postal Codes:** In the 1st district A-1010, in the 2nd A-1020, in the 3rd A-1030, and so on, to the 23rd A-1230.

Telephone Code: 0222 from within Austria, 1 from outside the country.

■Accommodations and Camping

One of the few unpleasant aspects of Vienna is the hunt for cheap rooms during peak season (June-Sept.). Don't leave your shelter to the vagaries of chance; write or call for reservations at least five days in advance. Otherwise, plan on calling from the train station between 6 and 9am during the summer to put your name down for a reservation. If your choice is full, ask to be put on a waiting list, or ask for suggestions—don't waste time tramping around. The list of budget accommodations in Vienna is available at almost every tourist office. Those unable to find a hostel bed should consider a *Pension*. One-star establishments are generally adequate and are most common in the seventh, eighth, and ninth districts. Singles start around 350AS, doubles 500AS. The summer crunch for budget rooms is slightly alleviated in July, when university dorms are converted into makeshift hostels. Bear in mind that these "dorms" are singles and doubles, not dormitories, and are priced accordingly.

If you're looking for a place to stay for a longer period of time, try **Odyssee Reisen and Mitwohnzentrale,** VIII, Laudong. 7 (tel. 402 60 61). They find apartments for 225-350AS per person per night. A week runs about 1200AS and a month starts at 2000AS. They charge 20% commission on each month's rent (120% limit). Bring your passport to register. (Open Mon.-Fri. 10am-2pm and 3-6pm.) Otherwise, visit either *Österreichische Hochschülerschaft* at Rooseveltpl. 5 or the bulletin boards on the first floor of the NIG building on Universitätstr. near the *Votivkirche*.

HOSTELS AND DORMITORIES

Myrthengasse (HI), VII, Myrtheng. 7 and **Neustiftgasse (HI),** VII, Neustiftg. 85 (for reservations at either: tel. 523 63 16 or 523 94 29; fax 523 58 49) The hostels, under the same management, are around the corner from each other. From Westbahnhof, U-6 (dir: Heiligenstadt): "Burggasse-Stadthalle" then bus #48A (dir: Ring): "Neubaug." Walk back on Burgg. one block and take the first right on Myrtheng. (15min.). From Südbahnhof, bus #13A (dir: Skodag./Alerstr.): "Kellermanng." Walk 2 blocks to your left on Neustiftg. and turn left on Myrtheng. A peaceful, leafy courtyard for your bread-and-cheese feast and comfortable, modern rooms with pine furniture. Reception at Myrthengasse daily 7am-11:30pm. 4- to 6-bed dorms with shower 160, 2-bed dorms with shower 190AS. Non-member surcharge 40AS. Sheets and breakfast included. Lockout 9am-3:45pm. Curfew 1am. Lunch or dinner 60AS. Laundry 50AS. Reservations recommended.

Believe It Or Not, VII, Myrtheng. 10, apt. #14 (tel. 526 46 58), across the street from the Myrthengasse hostel. Ring the bell; if no one answers noon-11pm try the caretaker's home phone (tel. 526 10 88). Funky and extremely social, the place offers 2 bedrooms, bunks rising to spacious ceilings, and a working kitchen. All this space to groove in comes complete with a gonzo caretaker who kicks you out 10:30am-noon to clean and then leaves you alone for the rest of the day. Her personal crash-course on Vienna is a must. Reception 8am until early afternoon—call if in doubt. 160AS; Nov.-Easter 110AS. Reservations recommended.

Gästehaus Ruthensteiner (HI), XV, Robert-Hamerlingg. 24 (tel. 893 42 02; fax 893 27 96). 3min. from the Westbahnhof and about 15min. from the city center. Exit on Äußere Mariahilferstr. (beyond the Gürtel), turn right from the station, turn left on Palmg., and take Robert-Hammerlingg. to the middle of the second block.

Bright, spotless rooms and a beautiful sun-filled oasis of ivy for a courtyard—with a barbecue and oversized chess set. Reception 24hr. Flexible 4-night max. stay. Summer dorm (sleeping bag required) 120AS; 10-bed dorms 139AS; 3- to 5-bed dorms 159AS; singles 239AS; doubles 225AS. Sheets (except for 10-bed rooms) and showers included. Breakfast 25AS. Lockers and kitchen available. Bicycle rental 89AS per day. Reservations recommended. Open July-Sept.

Jugendgästehaus Wien Brigittenau (HI), XX, Friedrich-Engels-Pl. 24 (tel. 332 82 940 or 330 05 98; fax 330 83 79), 25min. from city center. U-1 or U-4: "Schwedenpl." then tram N: "Floridsdorferbrücke/Friedrich-Engels-Pl." and follow the signs. It's the large green building behind the tram stop across the street and to the left of the tracks. Roomy, with exceptional facilities for the disabled. 6-night max. stay. Reception 24hr. Lockout 9am-1pm. Dorms 160AS; 2-bed dorms with bath 190AS. Lockers and breakfast included. Hearty lunch and dinner 60AS.

Kolpingfamilie Wien-Meidling (HI), XIII, Bendlg. 10-12 (tel. 813 54 87; fax 812 21 30). U-4 or U-6: "Niederhofstr." Head right on Niederhofstr. and take the fourth right onto Bendlg. This well-lit, modern hostel has 190 beds and stores valuables at the reception. Kind of boring, but then you didn't come to sit in the youth hostel, did you? Flexible reception times, but always open 6am-midnight. Check-out 9am. Lockout midnight-4am. Curfew midnight. 10-, 6-, and 4-bed dorms 100-155AS; doubles 435AS. Non-members add 20AS. Breakfast 45AS. Linen 65AS.

Schloßherberge am Wilhelminenberg (HI), XVI, Savoyenstr. 2 (tel. 485 85 03, ext. 700; fax 485 85 037, ext. 02). U-6: "Thaliastr." then tram #46 (dir: Joachimsthalerpl.): "Maroltingerg." From Schottentor, tram #44: "Wilhelminenstr." then bus #146B (#46 in Vienna): "Schloß Wilhelminenberg." The bus will pull up to the palace and you will think *Let's Go* is pulling your leg. Accommodations are actually to the left of the palace, and, though not as opulent, are still beautiful. Near the Vienna woods, the hostel has a fantastic—repeat, fantastic—view of the city. 164 impeccable rooms. Curfew 11:45pm; keycard 25AS. 4-bed dorms with bathroom 220AS. Group discounts. Reserve by phone, fax, or letter at least 2 days in advance.

Hostel Zöhrer, VIII, Skodag. 26 (tel. 406 07 30; fax 408 04 09), about 10min. from the city center. From Westbahnhof, U-6 (dir: Heiligenstadt): "Alserstr." then streetcar #43 (dir: Schottentor): "Skodag." From Südbahnhof, bus #13A: "Alserstr./Skodag." Crowded but comfortable and well located. Rose garden adjacent to a courtyard and furnished kitchen. 36 beds. Reception 7:30am-10pm. Check-out 9am. Lockout 11am-2pm. No curfew. 5- to 7-bed dorms with showers 170AS; 2-bed dorms 230AS. Breakfast (7:30-9:30am) and sheets included. Laundry 60AS. Front door/locker key deposit 100AS, with ID deposit 50AS.

Jugendgästehaus Hütteldorf-Hacking (HI), XIII, Schloßbergg. 8 (tel. 877 15 01 or 877 02 63; fax 877 02 632). From Karlspl., U-4: "Hütteldorf," take the Hadikg. exit, cross the footbridge, and follow signs to the hostel (10min.). Weary backpackers take bus #53B from the side of the footbridge opposite the station to the hostel. From Westbahnhof, S-50: "Hütteldorf." 35min. from the city center, this secluded hostel sits in one of Vienna's most affluent districts with great views of northwest Vienna. Often packed with high school groups. 271 beds in 2-, 4-, 6-, and 8-bed rooms, some doubles with showers. Reception 6:30am-11:45pm. Lockout 9am-4pm. Curfew 11:45pm; keycard 25AS. Dorms 153AS, with shower 183AS. Breakfast included. 2-course *menu* 62AS, 3-course 71AS. Lunch 71AS. Laundry 70AS.

Hostel Panda, VII, Kaiserstr. 77, 3rd Fl. (tel. 524 78 88). From Westbahnhof, tram #5: "Burgg." From Sudbahnhof, tram #18: "Westbahnhof" then tram #5: "Burgg." Fun and eclectic—a Hawaiian, ethno-Elvis feel in an old-fashioned, semi-*Jugendstil* Austrian apartment building. 35 mattresses packed into a pleasant co-ed dorm with huge ceilings. No curfew. Dorms 160AS, Nov.-Easter 110AS. 50AS surcharge for 1-night stays. Kitchen and TV. Bring lock for lockers. A few apartments available at **Apartments Lauria** in the same building, but the comfort and quality vary greatly. Reservations strongly recommended but require a 2-day min. stay. Visa, MC.

UNIVERSITY DORMITORIES

From July through September, the following university dorms become hotels, usually with singles, doubles, and a few triples and quads. These rooms don't have much in the way of character, but showers and sheets are standard, and their cleanliness and relatively low cost suffice for most budget travelers, particularly for longer stays.

Porzellaneum der Wiener Universität, IX, Porzellang. 30 (tel. 31 77 28 20; fax 31 77 28 30). From Südbahnhof, tram D (dir: Nußdorf): "Fürsteng." From Westbahnhof, tram #5: "Franz-Josefs Bahnhof" then tram D (dir: Südbahnhof): "Fürsteng." Entryway with a flag display worthy of the U.N. 10min. north of the Ring. Reception 24hr. Singles 175AS; doubles 350AS. Reservations recommended.

Ruddfinum, IV, Mayerhofg. 3 (tel. 505 53 84). U-1: "Taubstummeng." Rock on, dude! Buy a beer at the reception and veg in front of MTV. Why should your vacation differ from your college days? More intense guests watch CNN. Large rooms in a well-managed facility. Great location. Reception 24hr. Singles 270AS; doubles 480AS; triples 600AS. Breakfast included.

Gästehaus Pfeilgasse, VIII, Pfeilg. 6 (tel. 401 74; fax 401 76 20). U-2: "Lerchenfelderstr." Right on Lerchenfelderstr., right on Lange Gasse, and left on Pfeilg. The homesick will be reminded not of home but of their freshman dorm (except with clean sheets and no *Reservoir Dogs* posters). Reception 24hr. Singles 270AS; doubles 480AS; triples 600AS. Breakfast included.

Katholisches Studentenhaus, XIX, Peter-Jordanstr. 29 (tel./fax 34 92 64). From Westbahnhof, U-6 (dir: Heiligenstadt): "Nußdorferstr." then tram #38: "Hardtg." and turn left. From Südbahnhof, tram D: "Schottentor" then tram #38: "Hardtg." Laid-back atmosphere in the leafy 19th district. Unexciting, but the price is right. Singles 230AS; doubles 340AS. Showers and sheets included. Call ahead.

Studentenwohnheim der Hochschule für Musik, I, Johannesg. 8 (tel. 514 84 48; fax 514 84 49). Walk 3 blocks down Kärntnerstr. away from the Stephansdom, and turn left onto Johannesg. Fabulous location. Scrumptious, inexpensive meals. Reception 24hr. Singles 410AS, with bath 480AS; doubles 740AS; triples 780AS; quads 960AS; quints 1200AS. Breakfast and showers included.

Albertina Hotels Austria, I, Fürichg. 10 (tel. 512 74 93; fax 572 19 68), also commandeers dorms during the summer months, including **Albertina Auersperg,** VIII, Auerspergstr. 9 (tel. 406 25 40). Modern rooms practically on the Ring and a hop, skip, and jump from U-2: "Lerchenfelderstr." up Alserstr. Singles with sink 355AS, with shower 500AS; doubles 580AS, 820AS; triples with shower 1200AS. Breakfast and sheets included. Call central number first.

HOTELS AND PENSIONS

Check the hostels section for good singles deals as well. The prices are higher here, but you pay for convenient reception hours, no curfews, and no lockouts.

F. Kaled and Tina, VII, Lindeng. 42 (tel. 523 90 13). U-3: "Ziederg." Follow Ziederg. 2 blocks to Lindeng.; the hotel is on the right. Lovely private rooms with cable TV (CNN!). Singles 400AS, with bath 450AS; doubles 550AS, 650AS; triples 800AS.

Hotel Quisisana, VI, Windmühlg. 6 (tel. 587 71 55; fax 587 71 56). U-2: "Babenbergerstr.," turn right on Mariahilferstr., go 3 blocks, and bear left on Windmühlg. An old-fashioned hotel run by a charming older couple—it's difficult to feel uncomfortable here. Singles 330AS, with shower 380AS; doubles 540AS, 640AS; triples 900AS; quads 1200AS. Breakfast 40AS.

Pension Hargita, VII, Andreasg. (tel. 526 19 28). U-3: "Zieglerg." then head down Mariahilferstr. to Andreasg. The sun shines brightly through the windows on the carved wood of this comfortable *Pension*. Prime location. Singles 400AS, with shower 450AS; doubles 550AS, 650AS, with bath 800AS. Breakfast 40AS.

Pension Wild, VIII, Lange Gasse 10 (tel. 435 174; fax 526 04 92). U-3: "Volkstheater" then U-2: "Lerchenfelderstr." and take the first right. From Südbahnhof, bus #13A (dir: Alserstr./Skodag.): "Piaristeng." Turn left onto Lerchenfelderstr. and left again onto Lange Gasse. 30 beds. Reception daily 7am-10pm. No curfew, but grab a key for late nights. Singles 460-550AS; doubles 590-690AS; triples 860-960AS. Breakfast and shower included. Kitchen access. Reservations recommended.

Pension Falstaff, IX, Müllnerg. 5 (tel. 317 91 27; fax 317 91 864). U-4: "Roßauer Lände," cross Roßauer Lände, head down Grünentorg., and take the third left onto

Müllnerg. This small *Pension* is much quieter than its namesake, with a campy, linoleum flavor all its own. Singles 360AS, with shower 470AS; doubles 600AS, 720AS, with toilet 820AS. Extra bed 220AS. Breakfast included.

CAMPING

Wien-West, Hüttelbergstr. 80 (tel. 914 23 14 or 911 35 94). U-4: "Hütteldorf" then bus #14B or 152 (dir: Campingpl."): "Wien West." The most convenient campground, about 8km from the city center. 63AS, children 35AS; caravans 65AS; tents 40AS; 4-person bungalows from 415AS. Laundry machines, grocery stores, and cooking facilities available. Closed Feb.

Wien-Süd, Breifenfarterstr. 269 (tel. 865 92 18). From Westbahnhof, tram #60: "Wien-Süd." This site has laundry machines, grocery stores, cooking facilities. Same rates as Wien-West above. Open July-Aug.

Aktiv Camping Neue Donau, XXII, Am Kleehäufel 119 (tel. 220 93 10). U-1: "Kaisermühlen." Tents 40AS per person, electricity 48AS; large tents or trailers 64AS per person, electricity 68AS. Open May to mid-Sept.

Campingplatz Schloß Laxenburg (tel. (02236) 713 33), at Münchendorfer Str., Laxenburg. 15km from Vienna, but extremely popular and beautifully situated. Facilities include a restaurant, boat rental, heated pool, and supermarket. 69AS, children 36AS; caravans 65AS; tents 40AS. Open April-Oct.

■ Food and Coffee

"Here the people think only of sensual gratifications."
—Washington Irving, 1822

In a world full of uncertainty, the Viennese believe that the least you can do is face it with a full stomach. Food is not mere fuel for the body; it is an aesthetic and even philosophical experience that begins when you wish someone *"Mahlzeit"* (enjoy). Food and drink are in endless harmony here, and the city consumes both in great quantities. Cafés, *Beisln* (pubs), and *Heurigen* (wine gardens) all maintain their own particular balances between consumption and entertainment.

Viennese culinary offerings reflect the crazy patchwork empire of the Habsburgs. *Serbische Bohnensuppe* (Serbian bean soup) and *Ungarische Gulaschsuppe* (Hungarian spicy beef stew) exemplify Eastern European influences. *Knödel*, bread dumplings found in most side dishes, originated in the former Czechoslovakia. Even the famed *Wiener Schnitzel* (fried and breaded veal cutlets) probably first appeared in Milan. The culinary exchange worked both ways—as any Austrian schoolchild can tell you, crescent-shaped bread and pastries, *Kipferln*, were first made by Viennese bakers to celebrate the end of the Turkish sieges. It was only later that the French co-opted the design to make croissants. Boiled beef *(Tafelspitz)* is one of the few original hearty national treasures. Vienna is most renowned for its sublime desserts and chocolates—unbelievably rich, and priced for patrons who are likewise blessed. Most residents, however, maintain that the sumptuous treats are worth every *Groschen.* Unless you buy your sin wholesale at a local bakery, *Sacher Torte, Imperial Torte,* and even *Apfel Strudel* cost up to 40AS.

Vienna's restaurants are as varied as its cuisine. *Gästehäuser* and *Beisln* serve inexpensive meals that really stick to your ribs and are best washed down with much beer. *Würstelstände,* found on almost every corner, provide a quick, cheap lunch (a sausage runs 25AS or so). The restaurants near **Kärntnerstraße** are generally expensive—a better bet is the neighborhood north of the university and near the Votivkirche (U-2: "Schottentor"), where **Universitätsstraße** and **Währingerstraße** meet and reasonably priced *Gaststätten, Beisln,* and restaurants abound. The area radiating from the **Rechte** and **Linke Wienzeile** near Naschmarkt (U-4: "Kettenbrücke.") houses a range of cheap restaurants, and **Naschmarkt** itself contains open-air stands where you can purchase aromatic delicacies (bread and a variety of ethnic food) to sample while shopping at Vienna's premier flea market. Naschmarkt is an especially filling option for vegetarians in this carnivorous city. Come before 11am and walk to the far end of the square to find the cheapest prices from local farmers. (Open Mon.-Fri. 7am-6pm, Sat. 7am-1pm.) Most of the nearby 7th district **(Neuban)** is funky and pleasant. Almost all year long, **Rathausplatz** hosts inexpensive food stands tied into whatever the current festival happens to be. At Christmastime, **Christkindlmarkt** offers hot food and spiked punch amid vendors of Christmas charms, ornaments, and candles, and residents flock to the excellent and inventive **Bäckerei Schwarz**, XIII, Anhofstr. 138 (tel. 877 24 75; U-4: "Hütteldorf"). From the end of June through July, the **Festwochen** celebration brings international foodstuffs to the stands behind the seats of the various art and music films. (Stands open daily 11am-11pm.) The open-air **Brunnenmarkt** (U-6: "Josefstädterstr." then walk up Veronikag. 1 block and turn right) is extremely colorful and, as it's in a traditional workers' district, tends to be relatively inexpensive. **Weinerwald** has several branches for chicken-lovers in the first district. (Annag. 3, Freyung 6, Bellariastr. 12, and Schotteng. All open daily 7am-midnight.)

As always, supermarkets provide building blocks for cheap, solid meals, but prices vary tremendously. The lowest prices goods can be found on the shelves of **Billa, Konsum, Hofer,** and **Sparmarkt.** Slightly less common chains are **Ledi, Mondo, Renner,** and **Zielpunkt.** Travelers can buy kosher groceries at the **Kosher Supermarket,** Hollandstr. 10 (tel. 216 96 75). Be warned that most places, including restaurants, close Saturday afternoons and all of Sunday (on the first Sat. of every month, most shops close at 5 or 6pm.) In general, restaurants stop serving after 11pm. To join the legions of Viennese conquering the summer heat, seek out the **Italeis** or **Tichy** ice cream vendors or visit the delicious **Gelateria Hoher Markt,** I, Hoher Markt, just off Rotenturmstr. Expatriate Italians flock here to sample all 23 mouth-watering ice-cream flavors. (Open daily March-Oct. 9am-11pm.)

RESTAURANTS

The Innere Stadt

Trzesniewski, I, Dorotheerg. 1 (tel. 512 32 91), 3 blocks down the Graben from the Stephansdom. A famous stand-up restaurant, this unpronounceable establishment has been serving petite open-faced sandwiches for over 80 years. Favorite toppings include salmon, onion, paprika, and egg. The preferred locale of Franz Kafka, among others. 19 varieties of spreads on bread. 10AS per *Brötchen* (roll). Ideal place to grab a snack while touring the city center. Open Mon.-Fri. 9am-7pm, Sat. 9am-1pm. **Branch** at VII, Mariahilferstr. 26-30, in the Hermansky department store.

Levante, I, Wallnerstr. 2 (tel. 533 23 26). Walk down the Graben away from the Stephansdom, bear left on Kohlmarkt, and turn right on Wallnerstr. Greek-Turkish restaurant featuring stunning street-side dining and heaps of affordable dishes, including vegetarian delights. Student hotspot. Entrees 80-150AS. **Branches** at I, Wollzeile 19 (off Rotenturm, U-3 or U-1: "Stephanspl."); Mariahilferstr. 88a; and VIII, Josefstädterstr. 14 (U-2: "Rathaus"). All open daily 11am-11pm.

Brezelgwölb, I, Lederhof 9 (tel./fax 533 88 11). Excellent hearty cuisine even the Viennese call *"Altwiener"* (old Viennese). Cobblestones and classical music enhance the atmosphere of this old-fashioned *Backstube.* Don't leave without glancing at the rare intact piece of the medieval city wall in the courtyard—the rest was torn down to build the Ringstraße. Reservations recommended in the evening. Open daily 11:30am-1am, heated food until midnight.

Bizi Pizza, I, Rotenturmstr. 4 (tel. 513 37 05), on the corner of Stephanspl. Good food and a great deal in the heart of the city. This self-service restaurant, now an institution among the young and cashless, boasts a deliciously fresh salad bar (small 35AS, large 60AS) and huge individual pizzas (65-80AS, slices 30AS). Open daily 11am-11pm. **Branch** with the same hours at Franz-Josefs-Kai (tel. 535 79 13).

La Crêperie, I, Grünangerg. 10 (tel. 512 56 87), off Singerstr. near Stephanspl. A very enthusiastic decorator gave the interior a sweetly kitschy patchwork of Versailles and Louis XIV: Baroque wallpaper with gilded *fleur-de-lis* and metallic tassels alternate with indoor sculpted bushes and a bar disguised as a rustic, paint-peeling outdoor gazebo. Scrumptious crepes, both sweet and savory, 40-250AS. Open daily 11:30am-midnight.

Café Ball, I, Ballg. 5 (tel. 513 17 54), near Stephanspl. off Weihburgg. On a narrow cobblestone lane, the black and white stone floor, dark wood, and brass bar create an elegant, Bohemian atmosphere. Falafel 50AS. Open Mon.-Thurs. 10:30am-midnight, Fri.-Sat. 10:30am-2pm, Sun. 6pm-midnight.

Margaritaville, I, Bartensteing. 3 (tel. 405 47 86). Serves interesting Mexican food, most notably the *Fajita Lupita*. *Fajitas* aren't the only things sizzling as the night wears on. Tiny outdoor garden. Entrees 90-250AS. Open Mon.-Sat. 6pm-2am (heated food until 1am), Sun. 6pm-midnight.

Naschmarkt, I, Schwarzenbergpl. 16 (tel. 505 31 15). Like its outdoor namesake, this cafeteria-style restaurant features a tremendous selections of vegetables, meats, and desserts, along with a salad buffet (30AS) and daily *menus* from 50AS. Open Mon.-Fri. 6:30am-10:30pm, Sat.-Sun. 9am-10:30pm.

Outside the Ring

Tunnel, VIII, Florianig. 39 (tel. 42 34 65). U-2: "Rathaus," then with your back to the Rathaus head right on Landesgerichtstr. then left on Florianig. Pronounced "Toonehl" by the locals. Dark and smoky, with funky paintings, thick, heavy tables to gather around, and the occasional divan instead of chairs. The Tunnel is an extremely popular place prized for its dilapidated hipness, live music downstairs every night, and really affordable food. Daily lunch *menus* 45AS. Italian, Austrian, and Middle Eastern dishes, with many vegetarian options (45-125AS). Some of the cheapest beer in Vienna (0.50L *Gösser* 27AS), good pizza (55-85AS), and a breakfast menu (35AS) until 11:30am. Open daily 10am-2am.

Blue Box, VII, Richterg. 8 (tel. 523 26 82). U-3: "Neubaug." then turn onto Neubaug. and take your first right onto Richterg. You absolutely can't come to Vienna and miss this place. Although the interior looks more like a nightclub than a restaurant—jaundiced orange chandelier, blue leather couches, and not much light—the emphasis is on the food. Dishes are fresh, flamboyant, and above all, original. They often center around themes, whether regional (Russia, Louisiana, Tuscany) or general (sailors' fare, "color lessons," picnics, garlic). DJs pick the music to juxtapose with the meals. It's even a great place to come for a late (or really late) breakfast (until 5pm). Choose from Viennese, French, English, vegetarian—you name it. Open Tues.-Thurs. and Sun. 10am-2am, Fri.-Sat. 10am-4am, Mon. 6pm-2am.

Fischerbräu, XIX, Billrothstr. 17 (tel. 319 62 64). U-6: "Nußdorfer Str." then walk up Währinger Gürtel, tun left on Döblinger Hauptstr., and turn left onto Billrothstr. Popular spot for young locals. The leafy courtyard and jazz music make this restaurant an ideal spot to consume the home-brewed beer (large 40AS) and delicious food. The veal sausage (60AS) and the chicken salad (87AS) are excellent. Open Mon.-Sat. 4pm-1am, Sun. 11am-1am. Jazz brunch Sun. noon-3pm.

Amerlingbeisl, VII, Stiftg. 8 (tel. 526 16 60). U-2: "Babenberger" or U-3: "Neubang." Halfway between the stops on Mariahilferstr., turn onto Stiftg. After a couple of blocks you'll hit a cluster of outdoor restaurants. Walk past the first to Amerlingbeisl, a gem with live music and excellent Viennese pub food. Entrees 80-110AS, breakfast 55-90AS. Open daily 10am-2am (heated food served until 1am).

Restaurant am Radetzkyplatz, III, Radetzkypl. 1 (tel. 712 57 50). An old, mellowed, grand Austrian pub. At least 150 years of beer (0.50L 30AS) and food (60-160AS) have given the place worn bar railings and faded green walls. Sit outside under the striped awning and enjoy some of the cheapest food and drink in Vienna. Robust servings and veggie options. Open daily 10am-11pm.

Elsäßer Bistro, IX, Währingerstr. 30 (tel. 319 76 89). U-2: "Schottentor." Within the palace now housing the French Cultural Institute—walk in the garden and follow your nose. Wonderful food that even French expatriates call authentic. Most dishes hover at or below 120AS. Open Mon.-Thurs. 10am-9:30pm, Fri. 10am-4:30pm.

Nells, XVII, Alseggerstr. 26 (tel. 479 13 77). U-2: "Schottentor" then tram #40: "Alseggerstr." The garden tables, warm wooden interior, and original interpretations of traditional Viennese food draw a hip twentysomething crowd. Lots of different beers and *heuriger* wines. Open Mon.-Sat. 4pm-2am, Sun. 11am-2am.

COFFEEHOUSES AND KONDITOREIEN ■ 95

Hatam, IX, Währingerstr. 64 (tel. 310 94 50). Tram #40, 41, or 38: "Spitalg." Persian food at decent prices. Try their unbeatable *gorme sabse,* or grab a *Döner* to go (40-60AS). Entrees 75-165AS. Open daily 11am-11pm.

Schnitzelwirt Schmidt, VII, Neubaug. 52 (tel. 523 37 71). U-2 or U-3: "Volkstheater," then bus #49: "Neubaug." Every kind of *Schnitzel* (60-110AS) imaginable. Huge portions and low prices for the most carnivorous of desires and frugal of budgets. Open Mon.-Sat. 11am-11pm.

Stomach, IX, Seeg. 26 (tel. 310 20 99). Tram D: "Fürsteng." then walk down Porzellang. to Seeg. and turn right. First-class Austrian cooking with a Styrian kick; lots and lots of vegetarian food (100-210AS). Drop-dead gorgeous inner courtyard. Come early to get a table. Open Wed.-Sat. 4pm-midnight, Sun. 10am-10pm.

University Mensa, IX, Universitätsstr. 7, on the 7th floor of the university building, between U-2: "Rathaus" and "Schottentor." Open to all. Visitors can ride the old-fashioned elevator (no doors and it never stops; you have to jump in and out) to the 6th floor and take the stairs up. Typical university meals 25-60AS. Open Mon.-Fri. 8am-3pm. Other inexpensive student cafeterias serve their constituencies at:

Music Academy, I, Johannesg. 8 (tel. 512 94 70). Open Mon.-Fri. 8am-2pm. Food served 11am-2pm.

Academy of Applied Art, I, Oskar-Kokoschka-Pl. 2 (tel. 718 66 95). Open Mon.-Thurs. 9am-6pm, Fri. 9am-3pm.

Academy of Fine Arts, I, Schillerpl. 3 (tel. 58 81 61 38). Open Mon.-Fri. 9am-5pm. Closed June to early Sept.

Vienna Technical University, IV, Wiedner Hauptstr. 8-10 (tel. 586 65 02). Open Mon.-Fri. 11am-2pm.

Catholic University Student's Community, I, Ebendorferstr. 8 (tel. 408 35 87 39). *Menu* 33-40AS. Open Mon.-Fri. 11am-2pm.

Economics University, IX, Aug. 2-6 (tel. 310 57 18). Open Mon-Fri. 8am-7pm, holidays only until 3pm.

COFFEEHOUSES AND KONDITOREIEN

> *"Who's going to start a revolution? Herr Trotsky from Café Central?"*
> —anonymously quoted on the eve of the Russian Revolution

There is a steadfast rule for the Vienna coffeehouse—the drink matters, but the atmosphere in which it is consumed *really* matters. The 19th-century coffeehouse was a haven for artists, writers, and thinkers who flocked to its soft, brooding interior to flee unheated apartments that lacked telephones. In the coffeehouses, they surrounded themselves with dark wood and dusty velvet, ordered a cup of coffee, and stayed long into the night composing operettas, writing books, and cutting into each other's work. The bourgeoisie followed suit, and the coffeehouse became the living room of the city and an important piece of its history. At its tables gathered the intellectual world of Vienna and, in many cases, Europe. A grand coffeehouse culture arose. Peter Altenberg, "the café writer," scribbled lines, Kokoschka sallied forth, and Leon Trotsky played chess. Adolf Loos, prophet of 20th-century minimalist architecture, designed the interior of the Museum Café in smooth, spacious lines. Now no longer electric under the passionate sway of bristling artists, the coffeehouses rest in their illustrious pasts. The best places resist massive decorative overhauls, succumbing to a noble, comfortable decrepitude.

Viennese coffee is distinct, not quite as strong as an espresso, but with more kick than your average Coffeemate Dripmaster. One orders a *Kleiner* (small) or *Grosser* (large) and of various potencies: *Brauner* (brown, with a little milk) or *Schwarzer* (black, enough said). There is also a *Melange* (coffee with steamed milk), not unlike a *caffè latte,* and *Mazagron,* which is iced and laced with rum. Another Viennese quintessential is *Mokka mit Sclagrahm,* a mocha coffee with whipped cream. Be traditional and order an *Einspänner* (coffee and a glass filled with whipped cream beside it), or wow the whole café by drinking a *Kaisermélange*—a regular *Melange* with the yolk of an egg mixed in. Opulent pastries complete the picture. *Apfel Stru-*

del, cheesecakes, tortes, *Buchteln* (warm cake with jam in the middle—diabolical), *Palatschinken, Krapfen,* and *Mohr im Hemd* have all helped place Vienna on the culinary map. In some cafés, patrons must go to the counter to select and pay for a pastry and then give the receipt to the waiter, who will bring the pastry to the table.

In these living rooms of Vienna, time effectively stops. Coffeehouse etiquette dictates lingering in the dim hush. The waiter (often outfitted with black bow tie) will serve you as soon as you sit down but will then leave you alone for the rest of your stay. (If the server continually fills your water glass hours after you've finished your coffee, however, then you should probably take the hint and order something else.) Signal to the waiter that you are ready to leave by asking to pay: *"Zahlen bitte!"* A waiter will never approach without a summons—it is considered rude to rush patrons. Before you settle up, however, do as the Viennese do and the starving artists did—relax with your coffee and linger over a newspaper. Daily newspapers and magazines, many in English, are neatly racked and provided free of charge for patrons. The *Konditoreien* are no less traditional, but they focus their attention onto delectable creations rather than coffee. These pastries are something of a national institution—Switzerland may have its gold reserves, but Austria could back its currency with its world-renowned *Sacher Torte*.

The Innere Stadt

Café Hawelka, I, Dorotheerg. 6 (tel. 512 82 30), 3 blocks down Graben from the Stephansdom. Dusty wallpaper, dark wood, and red-striped velvet lounges that haven't been reupholstered in years—the Hawelka is shabby and glorious. Josephine and Leopold Hawelka put this legendary café on the map when they opened it in 1937—Leopold received an award from the Austrian government and Josephine a visit from Falco (see the picture on the wall). *Buchteln* (served only at 10pm) 35AS. Coffee 30-50AS. Open Mon. and Wed.-Sat. 8am-2am, Sun. 4pm-2am.

Café Museum, I, Friedrichstr. 6 (tel. 565 201), near the Opera. Head away from the *Innere Stadt* to the corner of Operng. and Friedrichstr. Built in 1899 by Adolf Loos, with striking curves, red leather, and lots of space. Simple and elegant, this spacious and comfortable meeting place attracts a mixed bag of artists, lawyers, students, and chess players. Open daily 7am-11pm.

Kleines Café, I, Franziskanerpl. 3. Turn off Kärntnerstr. onto Weihburg. and follow it to the Franziskanerkirche. Whimsical mix of the traditional and the funky. Brown leather and wood, a low vaulted ceiling, floor tiles, art exhibits, and nightclub posters coexist harmoniously. The salads here are minor works of art. Yes, it's *klein* (small). Open Mon.-Sat. 10am-2am, Sun. 1pm-2am.

Café Alt Wien, I, Bäckerg. 9 (tel. 512 52 22). Dimly lit place on a street behind the Stephansdom, amid ancient restaurants and cobblestone passages. Smoky red sofas and layers of avant-garde posters on the wall. At night the place buzzes but remains comfortably conversational. Open Mon.-Thurs. 10am-2am, Fri.-Sun. 10am-4am.

Café Haag, I, Schotteng. 2. U-2: "Schottenring" then head left. Gracefully classic, old-Vienna atmosphere without the formaldehyde stasis of museum-feeling preservation. Cool garden (the former Scottish cloister) for hot feet. Great pastries. Open Mon.-Fri. 8am-8pm, Sat. 10am-6pm.

Café Central, I (tel. 533 37 63), at the corner of Herreng. and Strauchg. inside Palais Ferstel. An opulent café steeped in history. Theodor Herzl and Sigmund Freud top a guest list that reads like the later chapters of your high school European history text. It was also the reknowned hangout of satirist Karl Kraus, Vladimir Ilych Ulianov (better known by his pen name, Lenin), and Leon Trotsky, who played chess at Central, fingering imperialist miniatures with cool anticipation. Alfred Polgar used the café's name to skewer the intellectual pretensions of the Viennese bourgeoisie in his essay *Theorie de Café Central*. Oh, they serve coffee, too, which comes with a little chocolate. Open Mon.-Sat. 9am-8pm. Live piano music 4-7pm.

Demel, I, Kohlmarkt 14, 5min. from the Stephansdom down Graben. *The* Viennese *Konditorei*. The atmosphere is near-worshipful in this legendary cathedral of sweets. A fantasy of mirrored rooms and cream walls, topped by the display case of magical desserts. Waitresses in convent-black serve the divine confections (40-50AS). Don't miss the *crème-du-jour*. Open daily 10am-6pm.

COFFEEHOUSES AND KONDITOREIEN ■ 97

> **Taster's choice**
> Legend dates Vienna's love affair with coffee back to the second Turkish invasion of 1683. Two months into the siege, Vienna was on the verge of falling to the Turks, until a Polish-born citizen named Kolschitzky volunteered his services. A dashing adventurer who had spent time within the Sultan's territories, Kolschitzky used his knowledge of Turkish language and customs to slip through the enemy camp and deliver a vital message to Vienna's relief forces, led by the Duke of Lorraine. The Duke then engaged the Turks in a bitter battle that sent them fleeing, leaving most of their camp behind. Kolschitzky claimed as his only compensation the many sacks of greenish beans left by the routed armies of the Sultan. The grateful city readily granted this reward, and Kolschitzky opened the first Viennese coffeehouse, Zur Blauen Flasche, became a huge success, and died a wealthy, revered, and caffeinated man.

Hotel Sacher, I, Philharmonikerstr. 4 (tel. 512 14 87), around the corner from the main tourist information office. This historic sight has served the world-famous **Sacher Torte** (50AS) in red velvet opulence for years. During the reign of Franz Josef, elites invited to the Hofburg would make late reservations at the Sacher—the emperor ate quickly, Elisabeth was always dieting, and as nobody dared eat after the imperial family had finished, all the guests left hungry and had a real dinner later at Hotel Sacher. Exceedingly elegant; most of the clientele is bedecked and bejeweled. Open daily 7am-11:30pm.

Cafe MAK, I, Stubeuring 3-5 (tel. 714 01 21), in the MAK museum. See **Bars,** p. 118.

Outside the Ring

Café Sperl, VI, Gumpendorferstr. 11 (tel. 586 41 58), 15min. from the *Westbahnhof.* Built in 1880, Sperl is one of Vienna's oldest and most beautiful cafés. Although some of the original trappings were removed during renovations, the *fin de siècle* atmosphere remains. Franz Lehár was a regular here; he composed operettas at a table by the entrance. Also the former home for Vienna's Hagenbund, an Art Nouveau coterie excluded from the Secession. Coffee 30-50AS; cake 30AS. Open Mon.-Sat. 7am-11pm, Sun. 5-11pm; July-Aug. closed Sun.

Café Drechsler, VI, Linke Wienzeile 22 (tel. 587 85 80), near Karlspl. Head down Operng. and continue on Linke Wienzeile. *The* place to be the morning after the night before. Early birds and night owls roost here over pungent cups of *Mokka.* Great lunch menu—try the *Spinatz.* Open Mon.-Fri. 4am-8pm, Sat. 4am-6pm.

Café Stein, IX, Währingerstr. 6 (tel. 319 72 41), near Schottentor. Chrome seats outside to see and be seen, and clustered tables indoors in the smoky red-brown and metallic interior. Intimate and lively, it slides into night as "Stein's Diner," when DJs appear. Billiards and Internet access (55AS per 30min 5-11pm; reserve your slot in advance). Open Mon.-Sat. 7am-1am, Sun. 9am-1am. Stein's Diner in the basement open Mon.-Sat. 7pm-2am.

Café Bauernfeld, IX, Liechtensteinstr. 42 (tel. 317 83 65). Tram D: "Fürstg." Silly, good-humored place with a Christmas-light-wreathed fish tank alongside bizarre fresco pieces that look as if they date from the 1940s. Be careful—the patched brown leather couches are so big you might lose your date. Open Mon.-Fri. 9am-2am, Sat. 2pm-2am, Sun. 2pm-midnight.

Café Prückel, I, Stubenring 24 (tel. 512 61 15). Spacious, with high ceilings. A 50s renovation added lime-green tablecloths, now faded, and time has conferred a noble slouch. Patronized by art students from the MAK (Museum of Applied Arts), which is down the street. Open daily 9am-10pm.

■ Sights

Viennese streets are laden with memories of glorious people and times past. You can gain an appreciation for the city by simply wandering the paths once trod by the likes of Klimt, Freud, and Mozart. *Vienna from A to Z* (with Vienna Card discount 60AS; available at the tourist office) provides all the information you need for a self-guided tour. Vienna's array of cultural offerings can boggle the mind; the tourist office's free *Museums* brochure lists all opening hours and admission prices. Individual museum tickets usually cost 20-80AS, discounted with the Vienna Card. Whatever you do, don't miss the **Hofburg**, the **Schloß Schönbrunn**, the **Kunsthistorisches Museum**, and the **Schloß Belvedere**. The range of available **tours** is equally overwhelming—walking tours, ship tours, bike and tram tours, bus tours, tours in a cup, tours over easy. Call the tourist office in advance to verify that the tours are operating on schedule. All of Vienna's tours are worthwhile, but the "Vienna in the Footsteps of the Third Man" tour, which takes you into the sewers and the graffiti-covered catacomb world of the Wien River's underground canals, is simply outstanding (bring your own flashlight). Tours on turn-of-the-century "old-timer" **trams** (tel. 790 944 026) run from May to October. (1½hr. 200AS. Departs from Karlspl. near the Otto Wagner Pavilion Sat. 11:30am and 1:30pm, Sun. 9:30, 11:30am, and 1:30pm.) The legendary drivers of **Fiakers**, or horse-drawn carriages, are happy to taxi you wherever your heart desires, but be sure to agree on the price before you set out. **Cycling tours** occur every day; contact **Vienna-Bike**, IX, Wasag. (tel. 319 12 58), for bike rental (60AS) or a two- to three-hour tour (280AS). Early booking is advised. **Bus tours** operate through various companies: **Vienna Sight-seeing Tours**, III, Stelzhamerg. 4/11 (tel. 712 46 83); **Cityrama**, I, Börgeg. 1, (tel. 534 13); and **Vienna Line**, I, Johannesg. 14 (tel. 512 49 350). Tours start at 200AS. Or create your own tour—buy a tram ticket, ride around the Ringstraße, and gawk to your heart's content.

THE INNERE STADT

The **First District** (*die Innere Stadt*), Vienna's social and geographical epicenter, is enclosed on three sides by the massive **Ringstraße** and on the northern end by the **Danube Canal**. Though *"die Innere Stadt"* literally translates as "the inner city," we're not talking American-style inner-city. Wealthy monarchs and 20th-century nation builders have maintained Vienna's perfectly preserved *Altstadt* (old town), the gallery that the artists of Austria, and in some cases all of Europe, rushed to fill. With the mark of master architects on everything from palaces and theaters to tenement housing and toilet bowls, the *Innere Stadt* is a testament to the genius that flowed through Vienna's veins. The historic transformations of the Austrian aesthetic are evident, as smooth *Jugendstil* designs peep out amid Rococo ornamentation—strange yet strangely harmonious bedfellows.

From Staatsoper to Stephansplatz

Apart from St. Stephan's Cathedral, no other building is as close to the hearts of the Viennese as the **Staatsoper** (State Opera House). Its construction had first priority in the massive Ringstraße project (see p. 104), and the grand building was completed in 1869. Due to a construction mistake, however, the builders dug the foundation and had to cut a full story of the building's grandeur. Upon viewing the building, Franz Josef agreed with the general consensus that it was "a little low." The two architects so badly wanted to create a worthy edifice that the lukewarm reactions at its opening drove one to suicide and caused the other to die two months later "of a broken heart." The emperor was so shocked that for the rest of his life, whenever he was presented with something he responded, *"Es ist sehr schön, es hat mich sehr erfreut"* (It's very beautiful, I enjoyed it very much). Opinions about the opera house changed over the years, and Vienna's collective heart broke when Allied bombing destroyed the building in 1945. Vienna meticulously restored the exterior and re-opened the building in 1955. The list of its former directors is formidable, including Gustav Mahler, Richard Strauss, and Lorin Maazel. If you can't make it to a performance, at least tour the gold, crystal, and red velvet interior. (Tours July-Aug. daily 10, 11am, 1, 2, and 3pm; Sept.-Oct. and May-June 1, 2, and 3pm; Nov.-April 2 and 3pm. 40AS, students 25AS.) Seeing an Opera is cheaper, though—ground-floor standing room tickets with an excellent view are only 20AS, and standing room anywhere else costs 15AS. Every February, the crystal and champagne **Opernball** waltzes its way, white-tied and well-heeled, into the Viennese social calendar.

Just across from the Opera lies another reminder of top hats and white gloves—the flag-bedecked **Hotel Sacher**. Even today a hotel and restaurant of prestige, this legendary institution once run by the formidable, cigar-smoking Anna Sacher served magnificent dinners over which the elite discussed affairs of state. The hotel's *separées* provided discreet locations where the elite conducted affairs of another sort.

Behind the Sacher in Albertinapl. lies a memorial to a more disturbing time in Viennese history: Alfred Hrdlicka's painful 1988 sculpture **Monument Gegen Krieg und Faschismus** (Memorial Against War and Fascism). This work commemorates the suffering of Austria's people during World War II. The twisted figures, especially the man on hands and knees, are a reminder of the horror of the Nazi period, in particular, the shameful events after the German *Anschluß*, when Viennese Jews of all ages were forced to scrub the streets clean of the anti-Nazi posters that had been posted by the Social Democrats.

From Albertinapl., Tegetthoffstr. leads to the spectacular **Neuer Markt**. In the middle stands the **Donnerbrunnen**, a fountain by George Raphael Donner, who surrounded a figure of the graceful Danube by four gods representing her tributaries. The 17th-century **Kapuzinerkirche** springs from the southwest corner of the square. Inside is the **Imperial Vault** *(Gruft)*, securing the remains (minus heart and entrails) of all the Habsburg rulers since 1633. Empress Maria Theresa rests next to her beloved husband Franz Stephan of Lorraine in an ornate Rococo sepulcher surrounded by delicate cherubim and a dome of wedding-cake proportions. Maria Theresa was crushed by the death of her husband and visited his tomb frequently. As she grew old and became unable to overcome gravity, the Empress had an elevator built to make her visits easier. On her last trip, the elevator stalled three times, prompting the empress to exclaim that the dead did not want her to leave. She was entombed there a week later. (Open daily 9:30am-4pm. 30AS, children 20AS.)

Just a quick step down Donnerg. lies **Kärntner Straße**, a grand boulevard lined with chic-but-*cher* cafés and boutiques, as well as street musicians playing everything from Peruvian folk to Neil Diamond ballads. Heading left brings wanderers back to Vienna's heart and an image of the **Stephansdom** reflected in the glass and aluminum of the **Haas Haus**. The view is even better inside the Haus, which has a café on the top floor. The Haus, considered something of an eyesore by most Viennese (much to the dismay of architect Hans Hollein), opened in 1990.

Stephansplatz to Michaelerplatz

From Stephanspl., walk down Rotenturmstr., cross Fleischmarkt to Rabensteig, and then turn left onto Seitenstettneg. to reach Ruprechtsplatz, adorned with a slew of street cafés and the Romanesque **Ruprechtskirche**, the oldest church in Vienna. The north side of the square looks out onto the **Danube Canal**, the waterway that defines the northern boundary of the *Innere Stadt*. Once you've taken in the quay, walk back down Ruprechtsstiege, onto Seitenstetteng., to find the **Synagogue**, Seitenstetteng. 2-4. This building, one of over 94 temples maintained by Vienna's 180,000 Jews until 1938, escaped Nazi destruction only because it stood on a residential block; the Nazis destroyed most of Vienna's other synagogues on November 9-10, 1938, during **Kristallnacht** (Crystal Night). The event received the almost inappropriately beautiful title because the glass shards that littering the streets the next day glittered like crystal. Fifty-odd years later, an armed guard patrols the synagogue.

Back at the top of Seitenstetteng. runs **Judengasse** ("Lane of the Jew"), a remnant of Vienna's old Jewish ghetto. **Hoher Markt** lies down the street; this square stands on the site of the Roman encampment **Vindobona** and served as the town's center during the Middle Ages. The square's most remarkable piece of architecture is much more recent—glance up at the **Ankeruhr clock** at noon to see this *Jugendstil* diversion in its full glory. Built in 1911, the mechanical timepiece has twelve historical figures that rotate past the old Viennese coat of arms, accompanied by music of their period. The figures depict the city's history from the era of Roman encampment up to Joseph Haydn's stint in the Boys' Choir. (One figure per hr. At noon, all the figures appear in succession.)

Wipplingerstraße heads west (right) from Hoher Markt past the impressive Baroque facade of the **Bohemian Court Chancellery**, now the seat of Austria's Constitutional Court. The **Altes Rathaus**, Friedrich-Schmidt-Pl. (tel. 525 50), stands directly across from here. Occupied from 1316 until 1885, when the government moved to the Ringstraße, the building stands behind a fountain by George Raphael Donner depicting the legend of Andromeda and Perseus. (Open Mon.-Thurs. 9am-5pm. Tours Mon., Wed., and Fri. 1pm). **Judenplatz**, on the opposite side of the Chancellery, presents a statue of Jewish playwright Ephraim Lessing. Originally erected in 1935, the statue was torn down by Nazis and only returned to Judenplatz in 1982.

A quick right off of Wipplingstr. down Stoss im Himmel rewards tourists with **Maria am Gestade,** a gem of a Gothic church with an extraordinarily graceful spire of delicately carved stone. The stained glass above the altar is one of the few remarkable examples of the art in Vienna. Past Judenpl., Drahtg. opens into the grand courtyard **Am Hof.** The Babenbergs used this square as the ducal seat when they moved the palace in 1155 from atop **Leopoldsberg** (in the Wienerwald) to the present site of Am Hof 2. The square where medieval jousters once collided now houses the **Church of the Nine Chairs of Angels** (built 1386-1662). Pope Pius VI gave the papal blessing here at the request of Baron von Hirsch on Easter in 1782, and Emperor Franz II proclaimed his abdication as Holy Roman Emperor in 1806 from the terrace. Am Hof was in use long before the Babenbergs, as evidenced by the **Roman ruins.** (Open Sat.-Sun. 11am-1pm.) In the middle of the square stands the **Mariensaüle**, erected to fulfill a vow sworn by Emperor Ferdinand III when the Swedes threatened Vienna during the Thirty Years War. A rather intimidating Mary crowns the pillar, while cherubim daintily dispatch the evils of hunger, plague, and war.

A jaunt down Steindlg. from Am Hof onto Milchg. leads to Petersplatz, home of the **Peterskirche.** Charlemagne, legend says, founded the first version of St. Peter's on this site in the 8th century, but town architects just couldn't resist tinkering with the structure throughout the ages. The present Baroque ornamentation was completed in 1733, with Rottmayer on fresco duty. Head out Jungferng. to the **Graben,** one of Vienna's main shopping drags; this pedestrian zone offers *Glühwein* (spiked hot punch) during the Christmas season. The Graben illustrates Viennese architectural evolution—Historicist and Secessionist facades stare warily at each other from across the promenade. One of the most interesting sights is the underground *Jugendstil* public toilets, designed by Adolf Loos. The **Pestsaüle** (Plague Column) in the square's center was built in 1693 in gratitude for the passing of the Black Death. According to the inscription, the monument is "a reminder of the divine chastisement of plagues richly deserved by this city," proving that the Viennese had ways of dealing with guilt complexes (and phallic symbols) long before Freud.

At the western end of the Graben, away from the Stephansdom, Kohlmarkt leads off to the left past **Demel Café**—though few sweet teeth can pass by Demel—and the **Looshaus** (1910). Contemptuous contemporaries branded the latter architectural wonder "the house without eyebrows." Admirers of both Classical and *Jugendstil* styles were scandalized by the elegant simplicity of this building. The bottom two floors stand behind green marble, and the top four floors are of pale green stucco with (gasp!) no facade decoration. Franz Josef was reportedly so disgusted with the atrocity built outside his bedroom window that he refused to use the Hofburg gate that faced it. The Looshaus sits on **Michaelerplatz**, named for the **Michaelerkirche** on its eastern flank. Leopold "the Glorious" of Babenberg purportedly founded the church as an expression of gratitude for his safe return from the Crusades. The church's Romanesque foundation dates back to the early 13th century, but construction continued until 1792 (note the Baroque embellishment over the doorway). In the middle of Michaelerplatz lie the **excavated foundations** of Old Vienna.

Ecclesiastical Vienna: The Stephansdom

Vienna's most treasured symbol, the **Stephansdom** (known affectionately as "Der Steffl" to locals), fascinates viewers with its Gothic intensity and smoothly tapered and highly photographed **South Tower**. The **North Tower** was originally intended

THE INNERE STADT ■ 101

> ### Dumb, Bad Luck
>
> Years ago, during the construction of the North Tower of the Stephansdom, a young builder named Hans Puchsbaum wished to marry his master's daughter. The master, rather jealous of Hans's skill, agreed on one condition: Hans had to finish the entire North Tower on his own within a year. Faced with this impossible task, Hans despaired until a stranger offered to help him. The good Samaritan required only that Hans abstain from saying the name of God or any other holy name. Hans agreed, and the tower grew by leaps and bounds. One day during construction the young mason spotted his love in the midst of his labor, and, wishing to call attention to his progress, he called out her name: "Maria." With this invocation of the Blessed Virgin, the scaffolding collapsed, and Hans plummeted 500ft. to his death. Rumors of a devilish pact spread, and work on the tower ceased, leaving it in its present condition.

to be equally high and graceful, but construction ceased after a spooky tragedy. Less-supernatural forces almost leveled the entire church—Nazi artillery at the end of World War II did massive damage. A series of photographs inside the church chronicles the painstaking reconstruction. The exterior of Stephansdom boasts some remarkable sculpture and monuments, and it deserves a lap around before you enter the building. The oldest sections, the Romanesque **Riesentor** (Giant Gate) and **Heidentürme** (Towers of the Heathens), were built during the reign of King Ottokar II, when Vienna was a Bohemian protectorate. Habsburg Duke Rudolf IV later ordered a complete Gothic retooling and thus earned the sobriquet "the Founder." (Tours of the cathedral in English Mon.-Sat. at 10:30am and 3pm, Sun. and holidays 3pm; 30AS. Spectacular evening tour July-Sept. Sat. 7pm; 100AS.) Inside, some of the important pieces include the Albertine Choir built in the early 14th century and the pulpit and organ loft by **Anton Pilgram**. Both works by this master are exquisite examples of late Gothic sculpture, so delicate that Pilgram's contemporaries warned him that the fragile organ pedestal would never bear the organ's weight. Pilgram replied that he would hold it up himself and carved a self-portrait at the bottom, bearing the entire burden of the structure on its back. The high altar piece of the **Stoning of St. Stephen** is just as stunning. Take the elevator up the **Nordturm** (North Tower; open daily April-Sept. 9am-6pm; Oct.-March 8am-5pm; elevator ride 50AS) for a view of the Viennese sprawl, or dare to climb the 343 steps of the South Tower for a better 360-degree view (open daily 9am-5:30pm; 25AS). Aspiring tightrope-walkers can saunter along the (fenced) walk on the outer side of the tower. Downstairs in the **Catacombs,** thousands of plague-victim skeletons line the walls. Look for the lovely **Gruft** (vault), which stores all of the Habsburg innards. Everyone wanted a piece of the rulers—the Stephansdom got the entrails, the Augustinerkirche got the hearts, and the Kapuzinergruft, apparently drawing the short straw, got the leftovers. (Tours Mon.-Sat. 10, 11, 11:30am, 2, 2:30, 3:30, 4, and 4:30pm; Sun. and holidays 2, 2:30, 3:30, 4, and 4:30pm. 50AS.) The **bell** of the Stephansdom is the world's heaviest free-ringing bell (the whole bell and not just the clapper moves)—its weight is not unrelated to the fact that the bell rings only on high church holidays.

Imperial Vienna: The Hofburg

The sprawling **Hofburg** (Imperial Palace; tel. 533 75 70) is a chronicle of the Habsburg family. Its construction began in 1279, and additions and renovations continued virtually until the end of the family's reign in 1918, when the structure had become a mini-city. On the whole, the palace is not particularly unified nor exceptionally beautiful, but it does provide an appropriate testimony to the peculiar splendor of the Habsburg Empire. Today, the complex houses the Austrian President's offices and the performance halls of the Lipizzaner stallions and the Vienna Boys' Choir. The hours fly as visitors lose themselves amid the pomp and circumstance. (Enter at Michaelerpl. 1; Imperial apartments open daily 9am-4:30pm.)

A stroll along the perimeter is the best way to start a tour. From Michaelerpl. and facing the palace, start your journey to the left to find the **Stallburg** (Palace Stables) right inside the passage, home to the Royal Lipizzaner stallions of the **Spanische Reitschule** (Spanish Riding School; tel. 533 90 32; fax 53 50 186). This renowned example of equine breeding is a relic of the Habsburg marriage to Spanish royalty. The Reitschule performances (April-June and Sept. Sun. 10:45am, Wed. 7pm; March Sun. 10:45am; 1½hr.) are always sold out; you must reserve tickets six months in advance. (Write to "Spanische Reitschule, Hofburg, A-1010 Wien." If you reserve through a travel agency, expect at least a 22% surcharge. Reservations only; no money accepted by mail. Tickets 250-900AS, standing room 200AS.) Watching the horses train is much cheaper. (Mid-Feb. to June and Nov. to mid-Dec. Tues.-Sat. 10am-noon; Feb. Mon.-Sat. 10am-noon, except when the horses tour. Tickets sold at the door at Josefspl., Gate 2, from about 8:30am. 100AS, children 30AS. No reservations.)

Keep walking around the Hofburg, away from the Michaelerkirche, to wander through the Baroque **Josefsplatz,** with an equestrian monument to Emperor Josef II. The modest emperor would no doubt be appalled at his statue's Roman garb, but the sculptor probably couldn't bring himself to depict the decrepit hat and patched-up frock coat favored by Josef. The stunning **Augustinerkirche** also sits on this square. 18th-century renovation restored the interior of this 14th-century Gothic church. The church is the proud possessor of the hearts of the Habsburgs, enshrined in the crypt below. Augustinerstr. leads right past the **Albertina,** the palatial wing once inhabited by Maria Christina (Maria Theresa's favorite daughter) and her hubby Albert. The Albertina now contains a film museum and the celebrated **Collection of Graphic Art**s (tel. 534 83; open Tues.-Fri. 10am-4pm, Sat. 10am-6pm).

Upon rounding the tip of the Albertina, cut around the monument to Erzherzog Albrecht and stroll through the exquisite **Burggarten** (Imperial Palace Gardens). The gorgeous, gently sloping lawn makes a perfect picnic spot. The opposite end of the garden opens onto the Ring and the main entrance into the Hofburg, just a few meters to he right. Enter through the enormous stone gate into the sweeping

---

Sisi, the Austrian Sensation

One hundred years ago in Switzerland, an anti-royalist terrorist killed the Empress of Austria. Today, Austria remembers Empress Elisabeth (better known everywhere as Sisi) not for her untimely death, her accomplishments, or even her life—the country has instead immortalized her beauty. When she married Franz Josef in 1854, the 16-year-old Bavarian princess was widely considered to be the most gorgeous woman in the world. Love, however, did not flourish—even in the hundreds of rooms of the Hofburg and Schönbrunn palaces, the imperial couple could not get far enough away from each other. Franz Josef therefore built the Hermes Villa in the Vienna Woods for his wife's private residence. There, she wrote such immortal and grumpy verse as (in translation): "Love is not for me. Wine is not for me. The first makes me ill. The second makes me sick." In other poems, she complained about her minimal duties as Empress, disparaged her husband, and labeled her children bristle-haired pigs. Always vain, she spent most of her time on starvation diets, to the chagrin of her servants and dinner guests who were not allowed to eat as long as she refused food. Sisi believed that her teeth were ugly, and she always kept her mouth closed in portraits. She avoided public appearances and accomplished literally nothing of note. Despite these flaws, Austrians never got over their love affair with Sisi's good looks. Over a century later, this melancholy, inconsequential, tight-lipped, beautiful woman is plastered on postcards and in guide books all over Austria. As recently as 1996, three separate "Elisabeth" plays and musicals were running in Vienna. She inspired a famous movie trilogy and even a Barbie doll. On April 4, 1998, a triple exhibit entitled, appropriately, "Elisabeth—Beauty for Eternity" opens at the Imperial Palace, at Schönbrunn, and at the Hermes Villa. The exhibit will run until February 16, 1999, as a monument to the power of an unhappy woman's pretty face.

Heldenplatz (Heroes' Square). The equestrian statues (both done by Anton Fernkorn) depict two of Austria's greatest military commanders. Archduke Karl's statue portrays him on a charger triumphantly reared on its hind legs with no other support, a feat of sculpting never again duplicated—even by Fernkorn. The poor man went insane, supposedly due to his inability to achieve the same effect in the second statue, portraying Prince Eugene of Savoy. To the right is the grandest part of the Hofburg, the **Neue Hofburg** (New Palace), built between 1881 and 1913. The double-headed golden eagle crowning the roof symbolizes the double empire of Austria-Hungary. The building, even in all its splendid majesty, is only a part of what the Habsburgs intended. Planned in 1869, the Neue Hofburg's design called for a twin across the Heldenplatz, and both buildings were to be connected to the Kunsthistorisches and Naturhistorisches Museums by arches spanning the Ringstraße. World War I put an end to the Empire and its grand designs. In 1938 following the *Anschluß*, Hitler spoke from the Neue Hofburg balcony to an appreciative crowd in Heldenpl. By 1945, the length of the entire square was covered with potato plants to feed the starving surviving citizens of the city. Today, the Neue Hofburg houses branches of the **Kuntshistorisches Museum,** including an extensive weapons collection and an assortment of antique instruments. Among the harps and violins are Beethoven's harpsichord and Mozart's piano, which has a double keyboard—the top for the right hand, the bottom for the left. The **Ephesus Museum** contains the massive findings of an Austrian excavation of Roman ruins in Turkey (see **Art Museums,** p. 111). Also within the Neue Hofburg is the exquisite **Nationalbibliothek** (National Library; tel. 53 41 03 97), which boasts an outstanding collection of papyrus, scriptures, and musical manuscripts. The library's **Prunksaal** (Gala Hall) is an awesome display of High Baroque. (Open Jan.-Feb. Mon.-Sat. 10am-2pm; March to mid-May and Nov.-Dec. Mon.-Sat. 10am-noon, mid-May to Oct. Mon.-Sat. 10am-4pm, Sun. 10am-1pm. 40AS.) The Hofburg continues an association with the Austrian government; the building attached to the Neue Hofburg is the **Reichskanzleitrakt** (State Chancellery Wing), most notable for the labors of Hercules, a group of buff statues said to have inspired the eleven-year-old Arnold Schwarzenegger, then on his first visit to Vienna, to begin his journey towards perfect pumpitude.

The arched stone passageway at the rear of Heldenplatz leads into the courtyard called **In der Burg,** surrounded by the wings of the **Alte Hofburg** (Old Palace). In the center is a monument to Emperor Franz II. Turn left under the arch of red and black stones crowned by a black eagle on a gilded shield to arrive at the **Schweizerhof** (Swiss Courtyard), named for the Swiss mercenaries who formed the Emperor's personal guard. This section is the oldest part of the Hofburg. Although the building's architecture is now mostly Renaissance, some pieces remain of the medieval fortress so necessary for the upwardly mobile aristocratic dynasty—the Habsburg stronghold was frequently under attack, twice by the Viennese themselves. On the right side of the courtyard stands the **Schatzkammer** (treasury), which contains such famous wonders as the crowns of the Holy Roman and Austrian Empires. The **Holy Lance** is, legend states, the one that pierced Christ's side during the Crucifixion. In front of this lance, the young Hitler was purportedly inspired to return to Germany and found the Nazi party. Just ahead is the Gothic **Burgkapelle** where the **Wiener Sängerknabenchor** (Vienna Boys' Choir) performs (see **Music,** p. 113).

Back at In der Burg, turn right to find yourself under the intricately carved ceiling of the **Michaeler Küppel.** The solid wooden door on the right leads to the **Schauräume,** the former private rooms of Emperor Franz Josef and Empress Elisabeth. Amid all the Baroque trappings, the two most personal items seem painfully out of place: Emperor Franz Josef's military field bed and Empress Elisabeth's personal wooden gym bear mute testimony to two lonely lives. The door on the left opens to reveal the **Hofsilber und Tafelkammer,** a display of outrageously ornate cutlery, trays, and pitchers that once adorned the imperial dinner table.

Monumental Vienna: The Ringstraße

The Hofburg's Heldenplatz gate presides over the northeastern side of the Burgring segment of the **Ringstraße.** In 1857, Emperor Franz Josef commissioned this 57m-wide and 4km-long boulevard to replace the city walls that separated Vienna's center from the suburban districts. The military, still uneasy in the wake of the revolution attempted nine years earlier, demanded that the first district be surrounded by fortifications; the erupting bureaucratic bourgeoisie, however, protested for the removal of all formal barriers and for open space within the city. Imperial designers struck a unique compromise: the walls would be razed to make way for the Ringstraße, a sweeping circle of traffic efficient for the large-scale transport of forces yet visually unobtrusive and therefore non-threatening. The mass traffic of the Ringstraße, a pathway around the inner city with no specific destination, creates a psychological "edge" or border, isolating life within from that without. This massive architectural commitment attracted participants from all over Europe. Urban planners put together a grand scheme of monuments dedicated to staples of Western culture: scholarship, theater, politics, and fine art. The collected Historicist result became known as the **Ringstraße Style.**

The Hofburg, the nexus of Vienna's imperial glory, extends from the right side of the Burgring. On the left is **Maria-Theresien-Platz,** flanked by two of the monumental foci of culture: the **Kunsthistorisches Museum** (Museum of Art History) and, on the opposite side of the square, the **Naturhistorisches Museum** (Museum of Natural History). When construction was completed on the museums, the builders stepped back and gasped in horror; they had put Apollo, patron deity of art, atop the Naturhistorisches Museum, and Athena, goddess of science, at the crown of the Kunsthistorisches Museum. Their horror abated when they realized that all could be mended—tour guides claim that each muse is situated intentionally to *look upon* the appropriate museum (see **Art Museums,** p. 111). A large statue immortalizes the throned Empress Maria Theresa, surrounded by her key statesmen and advisers, in the center of the square. The statue purportedly faces the Ring so that the Empress may extend her hand to the people.

As you continue clockwise around the Ring, the stunning rose display of the **Volksgarten** is on your right (see **Gardens and Parks,** p. 108), across the Ring from the **Parlament** building. This gilded lily of Neoclassical architecture, built from 1873 to 1883, is the first of the four principal structures designed to fulfill the program of bourgeois cultural symbolism. Now the seat of the Austrian National and Federal Councils, the building was once the meeting place for elected representatives to the Austro-Hungarian Empire. Before the artistic revolution at the turn of the century, mid-19th-century architects consistently turned to historical reference when designing buildings of important political and social position. All of the architectural forms in this edifice were supposed to evoke the great democracies of ancient Greece. (Tours mid-Sept. to mid-July Mon.-Fri. at 11am and 3pm; mid-July to mid-Sept. Mon.-Fri. 9, 10, 11am, 1, 2, and 3pm; Easter holidays 11am and 3pm.)

Just up the Dr.-Karl-Renner-Ring is the **Rathaus,** another masterpiece of historical symbolism. The building is an intriguing remnant of the late 19th-century neo-Gothic style, with Victorian mansard roofs and red geraniums in the windows. The Gothic reference is meant to recall the favored style of the *Freistädte* (free cities) of old; the first grants of trade-based municipal autonomy appeared at the height of the Gothic period in the early 12th-century. The Viennese, emerging from imperial constraints through the strength of the growing bureaucratic middle class, sought to imbue their city hall with the same sense of budding freedom. There are numerous art exhibits inside, and the city holds outdoor festivals in the square outside.

The Baroque and Rococo flourishes of the **Burgtheater,** across the Rathauspark and the Ring, capture the soaring spirit of the theatrical arts. Inside, frescoes by Gustav Klimt, his brother, and his partner Matsch depict the interaction between drama and history through the ages. Apparently, Klimt used contemporary faces as models for the audience members; notables of the day sent gifts to the artist in the hope that he would immortalize them in one of the murals. (Tours July-Aug. Mon, Wed., and Fri. 1, 2, and 3pm; Sept.-June on request.)

Immediately to the north, on Karl-Lueger-Ring, is the **Universität**. This secular cradle of rationalism is decidedly Renaissance in style. The university was the source of the failed 1848 bourgeois uprising and thereby received the most careful architectural attention; above all, the symbolism had to be *safe*. The planners sought to dispel all of the ghosts of dissatisfaction and revolt in the building's design, taking as their model the cradle of state-sponsored liberal learning—Renaissance Italy, which generated intellectual pursuits in the name of, not in confrontation with, the state. Inside the university (also known as the **Schottentor**) is a tranquil courtyard with busts of famous departed professors in the archways.

The surrounding side streets gush the typical assortment of university-bred cafés, bookstores, and bars. To the north, across Universitätsstr., the twin spires of the **Votivkirche** come into view. This neo-Gothic wonder and home of a number of expatriate religious communities is surrounded by rose gardens where students study and sunbathe in warm weather. Frequent classical music concerts afford opportunities to see the chapel's interior; look for posters announcing the dates throughout the year. Franz Josef's brother Maximilian commissioned the church as a gesture of gratitude after the Kaiser survived an assassination attempt in 1853 (see **Collaring the Suspect**).

Collaring the Suspect

The Habsburgs habitually strolled around Vienna with a full retinue of bodyguards. These casual jaunts were supposedly incognito—the emperor *demanded* that his subjects pretend to not recognize the imperial family. On one of these constitutionals in 1853, a Hungarian insurrectionist leapt from nearby bushes and attempted to stab the emperor. Franz Josef's collar was so heavily starched, however, that the knife drew no blue blood, and the crew of bodyguards dispatched the would-be assailant before he could strike again.

OUTSIDE THE RING

Operngasse cuts through Opernring, leading to the Ringstraße nemesis, the **Secession Building** (tel. 587 53 07), perhaps the greatest monument of turn-of-the-century Vienna. The cream walls, restrained decoration, and gilded dome clash strongly with the Historicist style of the Ringstraße. This cacophony was exactly the point. Otto Wagner's pupil Josef Olbrich built this *fin de siècle* Viennese monument to accommodate artists who scorned historical style and broke with the rigid, state-sponsored Künstlerhaus. Note the inscription above the door: *"Der Zeit, ihre Kunst; der Kunst, ihre Freiheit"* (To the age, its art; to art, its freedom). The Secession exhibitions of 1898-1903, which attracted cutting-edge European artists, were led by Gustav Klimt. His painting, *Nuda Veritas* (Naked Truth) became the icon of a new aesthetic ideal. Wilde's *Salomé* and paintings by Gauguin, Vuillard, van Gogh, and others created an island of modernity amid an ocean of Habsburgs and Historicism. The exhibition hall remains firmly dedicated to the display of cutting-edge art (see **Art Museums**, p. 111). Those ensnared by the flowing tendrils of *Jugendstil* can find plenty of other turn-of-the-century works in Vienna—ask the tourist office for the *Art Nouveau in Vienna* pamphlet, which contains photos and addresses in town.

The **Künstlerhaus**, Karlspl. 5, from which the Secession seceded, is just to the east, down Friedrichstr. This exhibition hall, attacked for its stodgy taste by Klimt and company, continues to display quite worthwhile collections. Next door the acoustically miraculous **Musikverein** houses the **Vienna Philharmonic Orchestra** (see **Music**, p. 113). The **Karlskirche** lies on the other side of Friedrichstr., across the gardens of Karlsplatz. Completed in 1793, this stunning church was built to fulfill a vow Emperor Karl VI made during a plague epidemic in 1713. In a curious amalgam of architectural styles, Byzantine wings flank minaret-like Roman columns, and a Baroque dome towers atop a classical portico. This unique blend continues in front of the church, with a reflecting pool and modern sculpture designed by 20th-century sculptor **Henry Moore**.

Modern Architecture: Wagner and his Disciples

Moore's additions to the Karlsplatz area and the Resselpark complemented the genius of Otto Wagner, the architect responsible for the massive **Karlsplatz Stadtbahn Pavilion**. This enclosure is one of many that he produced for the city's rail system when the structure was redesigned at the turn of the century. All of the U-6 stations between Längenfeldgasse and Heiligenstadt are other examples of Wagner's work. His attention to the most minute detail on station buildings, bridges, and even lamp-posts gave the city's public transportation an elegant coherence. Wagner's two arcades in Karlsplatz are still in use: one functions as an entrance to the U-Bahn station, the other as a café. Wagner diehards should also visit the acclaimed **Majolicahaus**, at Wienzeile 40, a collaborative effort by Wagner and Olbrich. Olbrich's *Jugendstil* ornamentation complements Wagner's penchant for geometric simplicity. The wrought-iron spiral staircase is by Josef Hoffmann, founder of the *Wiener Werkstätte*, an arts-and-crafts workshop that was as vital a part of *Jugendstil* as was Art Nouveau. The Majolicahaus' golden neighbor, the palm-leafy **Goldammer** building, is another Wagnerian mecca. In order to see the finest examples of Wagner's work and *Jugendstil* architecture, however, one must journey outside the city center.

Wagner's **Kirche am Steinhof**, XIV, Baumgartner Höhe 1 (tel. 910 60 23 91; U-2 or 3: "Volkstheater" then bus #48), stares down from high on a hill in northwest Vienna. The church combines streamlined symmetry and Wagner's signature functionalism with a decidedly Byzantine influence. The church has, at 27 seconds, the longest reverberation in the world. Koloman Moser, vanguard member of the Secession, designed the stained-glass windows, while *Jugendstil* sculptor Luksch fashioned the statues of Leopold and Severin poised upon each of the building's twin towers. The floor is sloped to facilitate cleaning, and holy water runs through pipes to keep it pure. Even the pews are functionally designed; they give nurses easy access to the worshipers, a relic of the days when Steinhof served as the provincial lunatic asylum. (Open Sat. 3-4pm. Free. Guided tours in German only.)

Postsparkasse (Post Office Savings Bank) is technically inside the Ring at George-Coch-Pl. 2. A bulwark of modernist architecture, the building raises formerly concealed elements of the building, like the thousands of symmetrically placed metallic bolts on the rear wall, to a position of exaggerated significance. This building was Wagner's greatest triumph of function over form; don't miss—you can't miss—the heating ducts. The distinctly Art Nouveau interior is open during banking hours free of charge. (Open Mon.-Wed. and Fri. 8am-3pm, Thurs. 8am-5:30pm.)

Modern Architecture: Hundertwasser and Public Housing

After constructing massively opulent palaces and public edifices before the war, post-WWI Vienna turned its architectural enthusiasm to the mundane but desperately necessary task of building public housing. The Austrian Social Democratic Republic set about building "palaces for the people." Though lovely in the eyes of certain theorists, these buildings testify to a largely discredited system in both politics and art. Whatever your political opinions, however, the sheer scale of these apartment complexes impresses. The most famous and massive is the appropriately christened **Karl-Marx-Hof**, XIX, Heiligenstadterstr. 82-92 (U-4 or 6: "Heiligenstadt"). This single building stretches out for a full kilometer and encompasses over 1600 apartments, with common space and interior courtyards to garnish the urban-commune atmosphere. The Social Democrats used this structure as their stronghold during the civil war of 1934, until army artillery shelled the place and broke down the resistance.

Breaking with the ideology of *"Rot Wien"* (Red Vienna, the socialist republic from 1918 until the *Anschluß*) that had resulted in sterile housing complexes like Karl-Marx-Hof, Fantastic Realist and environmental activist **Friedensreich Hundertwasser** designed **Hundertwasser Haus**, III, a 50-apartment building at the corner of Löweng. and Kegelg. Completed in 1985, the building makes both an artistic and a political statement. The trees and grass in the undulating balconies were to bring life back to the "desert" that the city had become; irregular windows, oblique tile columns, and free-form color patterns all contribute to the eccentricity of this blunt rejection of architectural orthodoxy. Architectural politics aside, this place is fun, bordering on the ridiculous—Hundertwasser's design team must have included droves of finger-painting toddlers.

Kunst Haus Wien, another Hundertwasser project, is just three blocks away at Untere Weißgerberstr. 13. The house is a museum devoted to the architect's graphic art (see **Art Museums,** p. 111). It's worth a visit just for a walk on the uneven floors (straight lines were "too mechanical, inhuman") and a drink of *Melange* in the café (open 10am-midnight; enter on Weißgerberlände after museum hours). Hundertwasser fanatics may also want to check out the **Müllbrennerei** (garbage incinerator) visible from the U-4 and U-6 lines to "Heiligenstadt." This huge jack-in-the-box of a trash dump has a high smokestack topped by a golden disco ball.

Palatial Vienna: Schwarzenberg, Belvedere, and Schönbrunn

The elongated **Schwarzenbergplatz** is a quick jaunt from Karlspl. along Friedrichstr., which becomes Lothringerstr. During the Nazi era, the city renamed the square "Hitlerplatz," and other evidence of unsavory military history dots the square. At the far end, a patch of landscaped greenery surrounds a fountain and a statue left to the city as a "gift" from Russia. The Viennese have attempted to destroy the monstrosity three times, but this product of sturdy Soviet engineering refuses to be demolished. Vienna's disgust with their Soviet occupiers is further evident in their nickname for an anonymous Soviet soldier's grave: "Tomb of the Unknown Plunderer." Behind the fountain is Hildebrandt's **Schwarzenberg Palace.** The 1697 building is now a swank hotel. Rumor has it that daughters of the super-rich travel here annually to meet young Austrian noblemen at the annual grand debutante ball.

While grand, the palace is but a warm-up for the striking **Schloß Belvedere,** IV, whose landscaped gardens begin just behind the Schwarzenberg. The Belvedere was once the summer residence of Prince Eugene of Savoy, Austria's greatest military hero. His distinguished career began when he routed the Ottomans in the late 17th century. Though publicly lionized, his appearance was most unpopular at Court—Eugene was a short, ugly, impetuous man. The Belvedere summer palace (originally only the **Untere** (Lower) **Belvedere**), ostensibly a gift from the emperor in recognition of Eugene's military prowess, was more likely intended to get Eugene out of the imperial hair. Eugene's military exploits, however, had left him with a larger bank account than his Habsburg neighbors (a fact that certainly didn't improve their relationship), and he decided to improve upon his new home. The result is the **Obere** (Upper) **Belvedere,** a masterpiece of the great Baroque architect Hildebrandt, designed not as a residence but as a place to throw parties to opulent and bacchanalian excesses. The building impresses with its Baroque flourishes, enhanced by one of the best views of Vienna—higher than the one from the Hofburg. This bit of architectural bombast did not settle well with the Habsburgs; the symbolism of Eugene looking down on the Emperor and the rest of the city was a bit unsettling to the royal family. Eugene's *pièce de resistance* was a rooftop facsimile of an Ottoman tent, which called undue attention to Eugene's martial glory. After Eugene's death, the Habsburgs snatched up the building (he never married or had children), and Archduke Franz Ferdinand lived there until his 1914 assassination. The grounds of the Belvedere, stretching from the Schwarzenberg Palace to the Südbahnhof, now contain three spectacular gardens (see **Gardens and Parks,** p. 108) and an equal number of comprehensive museums (see **Art Museums,** p. 111). The nearest U-Bahn stops to both palaces are "Stadtpark" or "Karlsplatz."

In truth, the Habsburgs need not have fretted over being outshown by Prince Eugene; **Schloß Schönbrunn,** XIII (U-4: "Schönbrunn"), the imperial summer residence, makes Belvedere appear waifish in comparison. The original plans for the palace were intended to make Versailles look like a gilded outhouse. The cost, however, was so prohibitive that construction on the original main building never even began.

Building finally commenced in 1695, but Maria Theresa's 1743 expansion created the most obvious architectural embellishments.

The view of the palace's Baroque symmetry from the main gate impresses, but this image is only a preparation for the spectacle that stretches out behind the palace. The view is a rigid orchestration of various elements, including a **palm house**, a **zoo**, a massive stone **fountain of Neptune**, and bogus **Roman ruins**, all set among geometric flower beds and handsomely coiffed shrubbery. Walk past the **flower sculptures** to reach Schönbrunn's most frivolous pleasure, the *Schmetterlinghaus* (Butterfly House), where soft-winged beauties fly free in the tropical environment. The compendium is crowned by the **Gloriette**, an ornamental temple serenely perched upon a hill with a beautiful view of the park and much of Vienna. Drink a somewhat pricey *Melange* in the temple's new café and survey your prospects. (Park open daily 6am-dusk. Free.) Tours of some of the palace's 1500 rooms reveal the elaborate taste of Maria Theresa's era. The frescoes lining the **Great Gallery** once looked upon the giddy Congress of Vienna, which loved a good party after a long day of divying up the continent. The six-year-old Mozart played in the **Hall of Mirrors** at the whim of the Empress and to the financial advantage of the boy's father. The **Million Gulden Room** wins the prize for excess: Indian miniatures cover the chamber's walls. In summer, concerts and festivals abound in the Hof. (Apartments open daily April-Oct. 8:30am-5pm; Nov.-March 8:30am-4:30pm. 100AS. Guided tours in English. 40AS.)

Built for Maria Theresa's husband in 1752, the **Schönbrunn Zoo** (Tiergarten) is the world's oldest menagerie. The style is allegedly Baroque, but the conditions border on the Gothic. The zookeepers, to be fair, are aware of this fact and are trying to remedy the situation. (Zoo open daily May-Sept. 9am-6:30pm; Feb. and Oct. 9am-5pm; Nov.-Jan. 9am-4:30pm; March 9am-5:30pm; April 9am-6pm. 70AS.)

Former Vienna: The Zentralfriedhof

The Viennese like to describe the **Zentralfriedhof** (Central Cemetery), XI, Simmeringer Hauptstr. 234, as half the size of Geneva but twice as lively. The phrase is meant not only to poke fun at Vienna's rival but also to illustrate Vienna's healthy attitude toward death. In the capital city, the phrase "a beautiful corpse" is a proud compliment, and the event of one's death is treated as a celebration. And death doesn't get any better than at the Zentralfriedhof. The tombs in this massive park (2 sq. km with its own bus service) memorialize the truly great as well as those who wished to be so considered after their demise. The cemetery is the place to pay respects to your favorite Viennese decomposer: the second gate (**Tor II**) leads to the graves of Beethoven, Wolf, Strauss, Schönberg, Moser, and an honorary monument to Mozart. Amadeus' true resting place is an unmarked mass paupers' grave in the **Cemetery of St. Mark**, III, Leberstr. 6-8. Zentralfriedhof's Gate T or I leads to the **Jewish Cemetery** and Arthur Schnitzler's burial plot. The state of Jewish Cemetery mirrors the fate of Vienna's Jewish population—many of the headstones are cracked, broken, lying prone, or neglected because the families of most of the dead are no longer in Austria to tend the graves. Various structures throughout this portion of the burial grounds memorialize the millions slaughtered in Nazi death camps. To reach the cemetery, take streetcar #71 from "Schwarzenbergplatz." (Open May-Aug. 7am-7pm; March-April and Sept.-Oct. 7am-6pm; Nov.-Feb. 8am-5pm.)

GARDENS AND PARKS

Gardens, parks, and forests are common Viennese attractions, brightening the urban landscape with scattered patches of green. During food shortages after WWII, the city distributed plots of land in sections of the 14th, 16th, and 19th districts to citizens to let them grow their own vegetables. These community *Gärten* still exist, full of roses and garden gnomes and marked by the huts of the original caretakers. The Habsburg's opened and maintained the city's primary public gardens throughout the last four centuries, and the areas only recently become public property. Especially noteworthy are the gardens of **Schloß Schönbrunn, Palais Belvedere**, and the **Augarten**.

GARDENS AND PARKS ■ 109

These meticulously groomed Baroque wonders have admirably upheld the intentions of their 18th-century landscapers.

The **Augarten,** Obere Augartenstr., is the oldest extant Baroque garden in Austria; Kaiser Josef II commissioned the garden in the 17th century for Vienna's citizens. Children play soccer between flowers and the various athletic facilities (including a swimming pool and tennis courts) that opened in 1940. Standing in the Augarten is the **Vienna China Factory,** founded in 1718, and the **Augarten Palace,** home to the Vienna Boys' Choir. The daunting concrete tower is the **Flakturm,** constructed as a Nazi anti-aircraft defense tower during WW II. This structure and similar creations in parks around the city were so sturdily constructed that an attempted explosive demolition failed (the walls of reinforced concrete are up to 5m thick). They stand as sad memorials to the country's intimate relationship with the Third Reich. To reach the park, take streetcar N: "Obere Augartenstr." and walk to the left down Taborstr.

By the Danube

The **Danube** provides a number of recreational possibilities northeast of the city. The recurrent floods became problematic once settlers moved outside the city walls, so the Viennese stretch of the Danube was restructured from 1870 to 1875 and again from 1972 to 1987. These renovations generated recreational areas, like new tributaries (including the **Alte Donau** and t

naukanal) and the **Donauinsel,** a thin slab of island stretching for kilometers. The Donauinsel is devoted to bicycle paths, swimming areas, barbecue plots, boat rental, and summer restaurants. Several bathing areas line the northern shore of the island, along the Alte Donau. (Open May-Sept. Mon.-Fri. 9am-8pm, Sat.-Sun. 8am-8pm. Admission from 50AS.) Take U-1 (dir: Kagran): "Donauinsel" or "Alte Donau." You can experience one of the most **spectacular views** of Vienna from the Donaupark: take the elevator up to the revolving restaurant in the **Donauturm** (Danube Tower), near the United Nations complex (U-1: "Kaisermühlen/Vienna International Center"). Also of note is the **Donau Insel Fest,** which will bring various stages for jazz or stadium rock June 20 to 22, 1998. Previous performers have included Erasure, Joe Cocker, and Sheryl Crow (see **Festivals,** p. 115).

The **Prater,** extending southeast from the Wien Nord Bahnhof, is a notoriously touristed amusement park. The park functioned as a private game reserve for the Imperial Family until 1766 and as the site of the World Expo in 1873. Squeezed into a riverside woodland between the Donaukanal and the river proper, it boasts ponds, meadows, and stretches of lovely virgin woods. The area near U1: "Praterstern" is the actual amusement park, offering various rides, arcades, restaurants, and casinos. Entry to the complex is free, but each attraction charges admission (generally 20AS). Rides range from garish thrill machines and wonderfully campy spook-house rides to the stately 65m **Riesenrad** (Giant Ferris Wheel). The wheel, which provides one of the prettiest views of Vienna, is best known for its cameo role in Orson Welles' postwar thriller, *The Third Man.* Locals cherish this wheel of fortune *extraordinaire* as one of the city's more obscure symbols. When it was destroyed in World War II, the city promptly built an exact replica. (Open May-Sept. 9am-midnight, Oct.-Nov. 3 10am-10pm, Nov. 4-Dec. 1 10am-6pm. 50AS. Ride lasts 20min.) Beloved by children during the day, the Prater becomes less wholesome after sundown.

The Danube Canal branches into the tiny **Wien River** near the Ring; this sliver extends to the southwest, past the *innere Stadt* and Schloß Schönbrunn. First, however, the Wien, replete with ducks and lilies, bisects the **Stadtpark** (City Park; U-4: "Stadtpark"), off the Park Ring. Built in 1862, this area was the first municipal park outside the former city walls. The sculpted vegetation provides a soothing counterpoint to the central bus station and Bahnhof Wien-Mitte, just yards away. One of Vienna's most photogenic monuments, the **Johann-Strauss-Denkmal,** sits there.

Along the Ring

Stroll clockwise around the Ring to reach the **Burggarten** (Gardens of the Imperial Palace), a well-kept park with monuments to such Austrian notables as Emperor

Hot to trot

White, royal, dancing, and one of the biggest tourist attractions in Vienna? No, it is not the Royal Ballet's performance of *Swan Lake*. In Vienna, these three traits classify horses—more specifically, the Lipizzaner stallions of the *Spanische Reitschule* (Spanish Riding School). The Royal Stables, some of the most architecturally important Renaissance buildings in Vienna, were built as a residence for the Archduke Maximilian in the mid-16th century and were later converted to the stables of the royal stud. The choice of Lipizzaner horses, known for their snowy-white coats and immense physical strength and grace, was a circumstantial one for the royal (now federal) breed. The Austrian Emperor in Lipizza, near Trieste, ordered a "celebration" equine breed upon the Habsburg's annexation of the Spanish realms in the late 16th century. Breeders mixed Arab and Berber genes, and once the stud line had been established, the Lipizzaners were imported to Austria proper to dance in the spotlight of the Renaissance heyday of *haute école* horsemanship. Despite their fame, the Lipizzaners have held on tenuously to their survival over the centuries. Aficionados of horsemanship can recount the several times the breed almost ended. The horses ran from the French in the Napoleonic wars, and they barely survived the poverty that ensued after World War I and the breakup of the Empire. During World War II, they escaped destruction in a safe haven in Czechoslovakia. In 1945, U.S. General Patton flagrantly violated his own orders to stay put by leading a madcap Eastern push to prevent the plundering Russians, who confiscated just about everything in their path, from reaching the four-legged treasures first. In the early 1980s, an epidemic of virus in the stud killed upwards of thirty of the brood mares, and today, stud farmers worry that the decreasing number of Lipizzaners may lead to health problems resultant from inbreeding. It seems that memorizing intricate prancing steps is not the only thing the magnificent horses need to worry about.

Franz Josef and Emperor Franz I. The **Babenberger Passage** leads from the Ring to the bubble-gum-sweet **Mozart Memorial** (1896), which features Amadeus on a pedestal surrounded by instrument-toting cherubim. In front of the statue is a lawn with a treble clef crafted of red flowers. Reserved for the imperial family and members of the court until 1918, the Burggarten is now a favorite for young lovers and lamentably hyperactive dogs. Walk behind the Hofburg to the area near the vaulted greenhouse/café to find students sunbathing in this prime hangout for the twenty-something set.

Heldenplatz, farther up the Ring, abuts the **Volksgarten,** once the site of the Bastion Palace destroyed by Napoleon's order. Be sure to seek out the **"Temple of Theseus,"** the monument to Austrian playwright Franz Grillparzer, and the **Dolphin Fountain,** a masterful bit of sculpture by Fenkhorn. The Volksgarten's monument to Empress Elisabeth, assassinated in 1898 by an Italian anarchist, was designed by Hans Bitterlich. The throned empress casts a stony glance upon Friedrich Ohmann's goldfish pond. The most striking feature of this space, though, is the **Rose Garden,** populated by thousands of different rose species.

West of the 13th *Bezirk* is the **Lainzer Tiergarten** (Lainz Game Preserve). Once an exclusive hunting preserve for the Habsburgs, this enclosed space has been a protected nature park and reserve since 1941. Along with paths, restaurants, and spectacular vistas, the park encloses the **Hermes Villa.** This erstwhile retreat for Empress Elisabeth houses exhibitions by the Historical Museum of the City of Vienna. Take U-4 (dir: Hütteldorf): "Hietzing," change to streetcar #60: "Hermesstr.," and then take bus #60B: "Lainzer Tor." (Open Wed.-Sun. and holidays 9am-4:30pm. 50AS.)

The **Türkenschanz Park,** in the 18th *Bezirk*, attracts a plethora of leashed dachshunds bristling at the peacocks. The long-haired garden is a wonderful stop on the way to the *Heurigen* of the 19th district. In summer, feed ducks or gaze in Monet-like rapture at the water lilies. In winter, come for sledding or ice-skating. Whenever you visit, don't miss the beloved Turkish fountain with its graceful arabesques. Enter the park anywhere along Gregor-Mendel-Str., Hasenauerstr., or Max-Emmanuelstr.

When in 172-1011, do as the 172-1011's do.

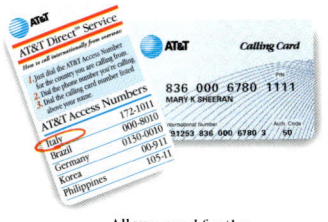

All you need for the clearest connections home.

Every country has its own AT&T Access Number which makes calling from overseas really easy. Just dial the AT&T Access Number for the country you're calling from and we'll take it from there. And be sure to charge your calls on your AT&T Calling Card. It'll help you avoid outrageous phone charges on your hotel bill and save you up to 60%.* For a free wallet card listing AT&T Access Numbers, call 1 800 446-8399.

It's all within your reach.

AT&T

http://www.att.com/traveler

Clearest connections from countries with voice prompts, compared to major U.S. carriers on calls to the U.S. Clearest based on customer preference testing. *Compared to certain hotel telephone charges based on calls to the U.S. in November 1996. Actual savings may be higher or lower depending upon your billing method, time of day, length of call, fees charged by hotel and the country from which you are calling. ©1997 AT&T

Photo: R. Olken

Greetings from Let's Go Publications

The book in your hand is the work of hundreds of student researcher-writers, editors, cartographers, and designers. Each summer we brave monsoons, revolutions, and marriage proposals to bring you a fully updated, completely revised travel guide series, as we've done every year for the past 38 years.

This is a collection of our best finds, our cheapest deals, our most evocative description, and, as always, our wit, humor, and irreverence. Let's Go is filled with all the information on anything you could possibly need to know to have a successful trip, and we try to make it as much a companion as a guide.

We believe that budget travel is not the last recourse of the destitute, but rather the only way to travel; living simply and cheaply brings you closer to the people and places you've been saving up to visit. We also believe that the best adventures and discoveries are the ones you find yourself. So put us down every once in while and head out on your own. And when you find something to share, drop us a line. We're **Let's Go Publications,** 67 Mount Auburn St., Cambridge, MA 02138, USA (email: fanmail@letsgo.com; http://www.letsgo.com). And let us know if you want a free subscription to **The Yellowjacket,** the new Let's Go Newsletter.

The **Pötzleindorfer Park,** at the end of tram line #41 (dir: Pötzleinsdorfer Höhe) from Schottentor, feeds into the lower end of the Vienna Woods. Wild deer roam through the overgrown Alpine meadows and woodland. Far to the north and west of Vienna sprawls the illustrious **Wienerwald,** made famous by Strauss' celebrated waltz, "Tales of a Vienna Woods." The woods, jealously conserved by the Viennese, extend up to the slopes of the first foothills of the Alps. Take U-4 or U-6:"Heiligenstadt" then bus #38A: "Kahlenberg." For more information about walks in Viennese woods, call 859 751 or contact Jahrfreunde, Landesgruppe Wien, 36 Diefenbachstr., A-1150. The area around Kahlenberg, Cobenzl, and Leopoldstadt is criss-crossed with hiking paths (*Wanderwege*) marked by colored bars painted on tree trunks. When they besieged Vienna in 1683, the Turks camped in this area, now overflowing with the elderly residents hobbling through the woods (the #38A isn't nicknamed "the Granny-mover" for nothing). Stride alongside them, through the incredible natural beauty of the hills as the countless German Romantics did before you. Or, follow in the Pope's footsteps and visit the **Leopoldskirche,** a renowned pilgrimage site.

■ Museums

Vienna owes its vast selection of masterpieces to two distinct factors: the acquisitive Habsburgs and Vienna's own crop of unique art schools and world-class artists (see p. 71 for the complete story of Vienna's artistic heritage). Works representing all of the distinctly Viennese movements, as well as countless other works culled from myriad nations and epochs, await in Vienna's world-class assortment of exceptional museums. Though painting and architecture may dominate, Vienna's treasures are as diverse as the Habsburg possessions. The Ephesus Museum and the Museum für Völkerkunde, with its collection of Benin bronzes, exemplify the Habsburg collecting prowess; other subjects range from "Horseshoeing, Harnessing, and Saddling" to "Heating Technology." An exhaustive list is impossible to include here; check the *Museums* brochure at the tourist office for other listings.

ART MUSEUMS

Kunsthistorisches Museum (Museum of Fine Arts; tel. 525 240), across from the Burgring and Heldenpl. on Maria Theresa's right. The world's fourth-largest art collection. The works by Brueghel are unrivaled, and the museum possesses entire rooms of Rembrandt, Rubens, Titian, and Velazquez. Ancient and classical art, including an Egyptian burial chamber, are also well-represented. The lobby is pre-Secession Klimt—a mural depicting artistic progress from the classical era to the 19th century—painted in the Historicist style he would later attack. Open Tues.-Sun. 10am-6pm. Picture gallery also open Thurs. until 9pm. Another **branch** of the museum resides in the Neue Burg (Hofburg) and contains the Arms and Armor Collection (the 2nd-largest collection in the world), and Ancient Musical Instruments Collections. Same hours as picture gallery. 100AS, students and seniors 50AS.

Austrian Gallery (in the Belvedere Palace; tel. 795 570), III, Prinz-Eugen-Str. 27, behind Schwarzenbergpl. The collection is split into two parts. The **Upper Belvedere** (built in 1721-22 by Hildebrandt) houses Austrian Art of the 19th and 20th centuries. Most of the famous Secessionist works reside here; especially well-represented are Waldmüller, Makart, Schiele, Kokoschka, and Klimt, whose gilded masterpiece, *The Kiss,* has enthralled visitors for nearly a century. As you wander among the works, pause to take in the breathtaking views of the city from the upper floors. Use the same ticket to enter the **Lower Belvedere,** where the **Baroque Museum** has an extensive collection of sculptures by Donner, Maulbertsch, and Messerschmidt and David's famous portrayal of Napoleon, gallantly reared on his horse as he rides into battle. The **Museum of Medieval Austrian Art** is also here. Romanesque and Gothic sculptures and altarpieces by *Süddentisch* masters abound. Both Belvederes open Tues.-Sun. 10am-5pm. 60AS, students 30AS.

Akademie der Bildende Kunst (Academy of Fine Arts), I, Schillerpl. 3 (tel. 588 16 225), near Karlpl. Designed in 1876 by Hansen of Parlament, Musikverein, and Börse fame. The collection that contains Hieronymus Bosch's *Last Judgment* and works by a score of Dutch painters, including Rubens. Open Tues. and Thurs.-Fri. 10am-2pm, Wed. 10am-1pm and 3-6pm, Sat.-Sun. and holidays 9am-1pm.

Secession Building, I, Friedrichstr. 12 (tel. 587 53 07), on the western side of Karlspl. Originally built to house artwork that didn't conform to the Kunsthaus' standards, the Secession building gave the break-out prophets of modern art space to hang their work; Klimt, Kokoschka, and the "barbarian" Gauguin were featured early on. Rather than canonize these early pioneers, the museum continually seeks to exhibit that which is new and fresh. Substantial contemporary works are exhibited here, but most major Secessionist works are housed in the Belvedere. Klimt's *Beethoven Frieze* is the major exception—this 30m-long work is Klimt's visual interpretation of Beethoven's *Ninth Symphony*. A series of serpentine scenes depict humanity's weaknesses and desires. Open Tues.-Sat. 10am-6pm, Sun. 10am-4pm. 30AS, students 15AS. Special exhibition 60AS, 30AS.

Museum Moderner Kunst (Museum of Modern Art; tel. 317 69 00). Two locations. The first is in the Liechtenstein Palace, IX, Fürsteng. 1. Tram D (dir: Nußdorf): "Fürsteng." Yes, these *are* the same Liechtensteiners who own that tiny country between Switzerland and Austria (see p. 464). They still hold the deed to this palace, and others throughout the country. The *Schloß*, surrounded by a manicured garden, boasts a collection of 20th-century masters from Magritte to Motherwell. The second location is at the **20er Haus** (tel. 799 69 00), III, Schweizer Garten, down Arsenalstr. and opposite the Südbahnhof. Its large, open Bauhaus interior provides the perfect setting for the substantial collection of ground-breaking 60s and 70s work—Keith Arnnat and Larry Poons among them—alongside contemporary artists. Open Tues.-Sun. 10am-6pm. Admission to one of the two 45AS, students 25AS; for both 60AS; children 30AS. Wheelchair facilities.

Österreichisches Museum für Angewandte Kunst (MAK) (Austrian Museum of Applied Art), I, Stubenring 5 (tel. 711 360). U-3: "Stubentor." The oldest museum of applied arts in Europe. Otto Wagner furniture and Klimt sketches sit amid crystal, china, furniture, and rugs dating from the Middle Ages to the present. Open Tues.-Wed. and Fri.-Sun. 10am-6pm, Thurs. 10am-9pm. 90AS, students 45AS.

Kunst Haus Wien, III, Untere Weißgerberstr. 13 (tel. 712 04 91). U-1 or 4: "Schwedenpl." then bus N: "Radetzkypl." Built by Hundertwasser for Hundertwasser. One of his greatest achievements, the crazily pastiched building hosts international contemporary exhibits. Ya gotta love what he does with the floor. Open daily 10am-7pm. 90AS, students 50AS.

Kunsthalle Wien, IV, Treitlstr. 2 (tel. 521 890), in Karlspl. Stellar international exhibits. Open Wed. and Fri.-Mon. 10am-6pm, Thurs. 10am-8pm.

Museum für Völkerkunde, I, Neue Burg 1 (tel. 534 300), in Heldenpl. The Habsburg agents brought back a surprisingly good collection of African and South American art. Visit Benin bronzes and West African Dan heads, or Montezuma's feathered headdress. Open Wed.-Mon. 10am-4pm. Tours Sun. 11am.

OTHER COLLECTIONS

Historisches Museum der Stadt Wien (Historical Museum of the City of Vienna), IV, Karlspl. 5 (tel. 505 87 47), to the left of the Karlskirche. A collection of historical artifacts and paintings document the city's evolution from the Roman encampment through 640 years of Habsburg rule. Memorial rooms to Loos and Grillparzer, plus temporary exhibitions on all things Viennese. Open Tues.-Sun. 9am-4:30pm. Free on Fri. 9am-noon. 50AS, students 20AS, seniors 25AS.

Sigmund Freud Haus, IX, Bergg. 19 (tel. 319 15 96), near the Votivkirche. U-2: "Schottentor" then walk up Wahringerstr. to Berggasse. This meager museum, where a cigar is just a cigar, was Freud's home from 1891 until the *Anschluß*. Almost all of Freud's original belongings moved with him out of the country, including the leather divan. Lots of photos and documents, including the young Freud's report cards. Open daily July-Sept. 9am-6pm; Oct.-June 9am-4pm. 60AS, students 40AS.

Naturhistorisches Museum (Natural History Museum; tel. 521 770), across from the Kunsthistorisches Museum. Displays the usual animalia and decidedly unusual giant South American beetles and dinosaur skeletons. Two of its star attractions are man-made: a spectacular floral bouquet comprised of gemstones and the Stone-Age

MUSIC ■ 113

beauty *Venus of Willendorf*. Open Mon. and Wed.-Sun. 9am-6pm; in winter, first floor only 9am-3pm. 30AS, students 15AS.

Bestattungsmuseum (Undertaker's Museum), IV, Goldeg. 19 (tel. 501 95 227). The Viennese take their funerals very seriously, giving rise to a morbidly fascinating exhibit that is, in its own way, as typically Viennese as *Heurigen* and waltzes. Contains coffins with alarms (should the body decide to rejoin the living) and Josef II's proposed reusable coffin. Open Mon.-Fri. noon-3pm by prior arrangement only.

Jewish Museum, I, Dorotheerg. 11 (tel. 535 04 31). This museum focuses on the history and contributions of Austria's Jewish community. Exhibits on Freud and psychoanalysis as well as works by Arnold Schönberg and Bronica Killer-Pinell. Open Sun.-Wed. and Fri. 10am-6pm, Thurs. 10am-9pm.

Künstlerhaus, Karlspl. 5 (tel. 587 96 63). Temporary exhibits, usually contemporary and non-European art. Open Mon.-Wed. and Fri.-Sun. 10am-6pm, Thurs. 10am-9pm. 90AS, students 40AS.

■ Entertainment

MUSIC

> The State Opera and the Philharmonic Orchestra are closed in July and August. The Vienna Boys' Choir is on tour in August. The Lippizaner Stallions do not dance in July and August. Many an unsuspecting tourist has carefully planned a trip, only to be disappointed by these most inconvenient facts of Viennese life.

Like Vienna's architecture and art, the city's music always teeters on the cutting edge. Mozart, Beethoven, and Haydn created their most stunning masterpieces in Vienna, comprising the First Viennese School. A century later, *fin de siècle* Expressionist composers Schönberg, Webern, and Berg teamed up to form the Second Viennese School. Every Austrian child must learn to play an instrument during schooling, and the **Konservatorium** and **Hochschule** are world-renowned conservatories. Even pampered Habsburg heirs became instrumentally deft enough for private performances. All year, Vienna presents performances ranging from the above-average to the sublime, with much surprisingly accessible to the budget traveler.

"Too many notes, dear Mozart," observed Josef II after the premiere of *Abduction from the Seraglio*. "Only as many as are necessary, Your Majesty," was the genius's reply. The Habsburgs may be forgiven this critical slip, for they have provided invaluable support of opera: the **Staatsoper** remains one of the top five companies in the world and performs about 300 times from September through June. **Standing-room tickets** provide a glimpse of world-class opera for a pittance. Those with the desire (and the stamina) to say "been there" should start lining up on the western side of the Opera (by Operng.) half an hour before curtain (2-3hr. in tourist season) in order to get tickets for the center—the side views are rather limited. Find a space on the rail and tie a scarf around it to reserve your spot if you wish to grab a coffee or *Wurst*. (Balcony 20AS, orchestra 30AS. Formal dress not necessary, but dress as well as you can.) Students feeling lucky should try the box office a half-hour before curtain; unclaimed tickets go for 50AS (ISIC *not* valid—bring a university ID). Advance tickets range from 100 to 850AS and go on sale a week before the performance at the **Bundestheaterkasse,** I, Hanuschg. 3 (tel. 514 44 22 60), next to the opera along the Burggarten. Get there at 6-7am of the first day for a good seat; some Viennese camp overnight for major performances. Bundestheaterkasse also sells tickets for the three other public theaters: the **Volksoper, Burgtheater,** and **Akademietheater.** (Open Mon.-Fri. 8am-6pm, Sun. 9am-noon. ISIC *not* valid for student discounts, university ID required). The Volksoper shows operas and operettas in German, sometimes translated; the other two venues feature classic dramas in German. Discount tickets go on sale a half-hour before curtain at the individual box offices (50-400AS). Nearby, classy **fiakers** (horse and carriage rides) get you home before the clock strikes twelve; agree on a price with the driver beforehand. A 40-minute ride can cost as much as 800AS.

The world-famous, top-notch **Wiener Philharmoniker** (Vienna Philharmonic Orchestra) included Gustav Mahler among its directors; a bust in his honor stands in the concert hall. Regular performances take place in the **Musikverein,** I, Dumbastr. 3 (tel. 505 81 90), on the northeast side of Karlspl. The Philharmoniker also play at every Staatsoper production. Tickets to Philharmoniker concerts are mostly on a subscription basis, with few tickets at the Musikverein box office. Call ahead for availability. (Box office open Sept.-June Mon.-Fri. 9am-6pm, Sat. 9am-noon. Write Gesellschaft der Musikfreunde, Dumbastr. 20, A-1010 Wien for more information.) The Philharmoniker **New Year's concert,** a tradition since the 18th century, is broadcast the following morning by the ÖRF (Austrian Broadcasting Corporation). Vienna's second fiddle, the **Vienna Symphony Orchestra,** is frequently on tour but plays some concerts at the Konzerthaus, III, Lothingerstr. 20 (tel. 72 12 11).

The 500-year-old **Wiener Sängerknabenchor (Vienna Boys' Choir)** is another famous and beloved musical attraction. The pre-pubescent prodigies perform Sundays at 9:15am (mid-Sept. to June) in the **Burgkapelle** (Royal Chapel), the oldest section of the Hofburg. Reserve tickets (60-280AS) at least two months in advance; write to Hofmusikkapelle, Hofburg, A-1010 Wien, but do not enclose money. Pick up tickets at the Burgkapelle on the Friday before mass from 11am to noon or on the Sunday of the mass by 9am. Unreserved seats go on sale from 5pm on the preceding Friday, maximum two per person. Standing room is free, but arrive before 8am to make it into the *Burgkapelle.* The lads also perform every Friday at 3:30pm at the Konzerthaus in May, June, September, and October. For tickets (370-420AS), contact Reisebüro Mondial, Faulmanng. 4, A-1040 Wien (tel. 588 04 141; fax 587 12 68). Or have awe-inspiring—and free—musical experiences at the **Sunday High Masses** at 10 or 11am in the major churches (Augustinerkirche, Michaelerkirche, Stephansdom). The music resonates in its proper context and atmosphere.

THEATER AND CINEMA

In the past few years, Vienna has made a name for itself as a city of musicals, with productions of such Broadway and West End favorites as *Phantom of the Opera* and *Les Misérables,* or the long-running home-grown favorite *Elisabeth,* a very creative interpretation of the late empress's life. The **Theater an der Wien,** VI, Linke Wienzeile 6 (tel. 588 30), once produced musicals of a different sort, hosting in its 18th-century edifice the premieres of Beethoven's *Fidelio* and Mozart's *Die Zauberflöte* (The Magic Flute). The nobility found that Mozart had crossed the line of good taste by composing an opera in German (such an *ugly* language), so they blocked the scheduled premiere at the Staatsoper. The masterpiece was finally performed here, thrilling the peasants, who could finally understand the plot. For the sake of tradition, the Staatsoper still occasionally sends productions of Mozart opera to be performed here.

Vienna's English Theatre, VIII, Josefsg. 12 (tel. 402 12 60), presents English-language drama. (Box office open Mon.-Fri. 10am-6pm, Sat.-Sun. 10am-4pm. Tickets 150-420AS, student rush 100AS). The **International Theater,** IX, Porzellang. 8 (tel. 319 62 72; tickets 220AS, under 26 120AS), is another English-language venue. **Films** in English usually play at **Burg Kino,** I, Opernring 19 (tel. 587 84 06; last show usually around 8:30pm, Sat. around 11pm); **Top Kino,** VI, Rahlgassel 1 (tel. 587 55 57; open daily 3pm-10:30pm), at the intersection of Gumpendorferstr.; and **Hadynkino** (last show usually around 9:30pm), on Mariahilferstr. near U-3: "Neubang." As the language becomes fashionable, more theaters show movies in English or with subtitles—look in the newspaper for films with OF, OV, EOV, or OmU after the title. **Votivkino,** Währingerstr. 12 (tel. 317 35 71), near Bergg. and Schottentor, is an arthouse popular with the university crowd and shows all films with German subtitles. **Artis Kino, Filmcasino,** and **Stöberkino** also show subtitled art and foreign films. Be warned—you pay for the row you sit in, and seats are assigned. On Monday, however, all seats are discounted to 70AS. In summer, there is an **open-air cinema** in the Augarten park (all shows at 9:30pm; 70AS). From Schottenring, take tram #31: "Gaußpl." While Vienna hosts a full-sized film festival in August (see **Festivals**), the rest of the year the Austrian **Filmmuseum,** Augustinerstr. 1 (tel. 53 37 05 40), shows a rotating program of classic and avant-garde films.

FESTIVALS

Vienna hosts an array of important annual festivals, mostly musical. Look for the tourist office's monthly calendar for dozens of concerts and performances. The **Vienna Festival** (mid-May to mid-June) has a diverse program of exhibitions, plays, and concerts. Of particular interest are the celebrated orchestras and conductors joining the party. The Staatsoper and Volkstheater host the annual **Jazzfest Wien** during the first weeks of July, featuring many famous acts. For information, contact Jazzfest Wien, Estepl. 3/13, A-1030 Wien (tel. 712 34 34). While other big guns take summer siesta, Vienna has held the **Klangbogen** every summer since 1952, featuring **Wiener Kammeroper** (Chamber Opera) performances of Mozart's operas in an open-air theater set among the ruins of Schönbrunner Schloßpark. Pick up a brochure at the tourist office. From the end of July to the beginning of August, the **Im-Puls Dance Festival** (tel. 93 55 58) attracts some of the world's great dance troupes and offers seminars to enthusiasts. Some of Vienna's best parties are thrown by the parties (political, that is). The Social Democrats host a late-June **Danube Island Festival,** which drew over 2 million politically active booty-shakers in 1997, and the Communist Party holds a **Volkstimme Festival** in mid-August. Both cater to impressionable youngsters with free rock, jazz, and folk concerts. In mid-October, the annual city-wide film festival, the **V'iennale,** kicks off. In past years, the program has featured over 150 movies from 25 countries. One final free treat not to be missed is the **nightly film festival** in July and August, in the Rathauspl. at dusk. Taped operas, ballets, operettas, and concerts enrapture the diverse audience.

HEURIGEN (WINE GARDENS)

Created by imperial edict in the early 18th century, *Heurigen* are one of Vienna's most beloved institutions. Citizens have collectively met, discussed, and celebrated life in these pastoral settings for generations, with no signs of letting up. To this day, the *Heurigen,* marked by a hanging evergreen at the door, continue to sell their new wine, mineral water, and rustic snacks. Beer, coffee, and all but the most Austrian of sodas are forbidden, and the *Heuriger* owners would not have it any other way.

The wine called *Heuriger* is young wine from the most recent harvest and has typically been grown and pressed by the *Heuriger* owner himself. Good *Heuriger* is generally white (*Grüner Veltliner* or *Riesling* are best), fruity, and full of body. *Heuriger* is ordered by the *Achtel* or *Viertel* (eighth or quarter liter respectively). In local parlance, one doesn't drink the wine, one "bites" it, mixing it with air inside the mouth to better taste its youth and freshness. *G'spritzer* (wine and tonic water) is a popular drink, and patrons frequently order a bottle of wine and water to mix themselves.

Half of the pleasure of visiting a *Heuriger,* however, comes not from the wine but from the atmosphere. The worn picnic benches and old shade trees provide an ideal spot to contemplate, converse, or listen to *Schrammelmusik,* sentimental, wine-lubricated folk songs played by aged musicians who inhabit the *Heuriger.* Drunken patrons often take the matter into their own hands and begin to belt out verses praising the *Bäckchen* (cheeks) of girls in the Wachau. A *Heuriger* generally serves simple buffets (grilled chicken, salads, pretzels) that make for enjoyable and inexpensive meals. Those looking for some down-home fare should order *Brattfett* or *Liptauer,* a spicy paprika and cream cheese spread for your bread.

At the end of the summer, *Sturm* (sweet, cloudy, unpasteurized wine) is available at the *Heurigen.* At the end of August or the beginning of September in **Neustift am Wald,** now part of Vienna's 19th district, the *Neustifter Kirtag mit Winzerumzug* rampages through the wine gardens: local vintners march in a mile-long procession through town, carrying a large crown adorned with gilt nuts. After the **Feast of the Martins** on November 11, the wine from last year's crop becomes "old wine," no longer proper to serve in the *Heurigen.* The Viennese do their best to spare it this fate by consuming the beverage in Herculean quantities before the time's up. Grab a liter of wine to help the locals in their monumental task.

Heurigen cluster together in the northern, western, and southern Viennese suburbs, where the grapes grow. The most famous region, **Grinzing**, produces strong wine, perhaps to distract patrons from the high prices. Better atmosphere and prices abound in **Sievering, Neustift am Wald, Stammersdorf,** and **Neuwaldegg**. The least expensive and least touristed *Heurigen* operate in Stammersdorf and **Strebersdorf** (from Schottentor, bus #31 and 32, respectively). True *Heuriger* devotés should make the trip to **Gumpoldskirchen**, a celebrated vineyard village with decent bus and train connections to Vienna and Mödling. Most vineyard taverns are open 4pm to midnight. *Heuriger* costs about 25AS per *Viertel*. Casual dress is fine.

Buschenschank Heinrich Niersche, XIX, Strehlg. 21 (tel. 440 21 46). U-1: "Währingerstr./Volksoper" then bus #41A: "Pötzleindorfer Höhe." Walk uphill one block and turn right on Strehlg. Hidden from tourists and beloved by locals, the beautiful garden overlooks the fields of Grinzing—an oasis of green grass, cheerful voices, and relaxation. *Weiße G'spritzer* (white wine with tonic water) 18AS. Open Wed.-Mon. 3pm-midnight.

Heuriger Josef Lier, XIX, Wildgrubeng. 44 (tel. 320 23 19). Tram #38 from Schottentor to the end of the line. Walk up the Grinzigersteig to the Heiligenstädter Friedhof (cemetery), and leave the asphalt for Stadtwanderweg 1 along Schreiberbach onto Mukental and then finally Wildgrub (10min. after the cemetery). Set right into the vineyards, this *Ur-Heuriger* recalls the times before the tour bus. The place boasts a panoramic view of Vienna from the natural beauty of the Vienna Woods. Only one white and one red wine here—Josef Lier's own, from the vineyards you're sitting in. The dishes are equally *Alt-Wiener* and equally excellent—boiled eggs, pickles, *Liptauer,* and *Wurst,* to name just a few.

Zum Krottenbach'l, XIX, Krottenbachstr. 148 (tel. 440 12 40). U-6: "Nußdorfstr." then bus #35A (dir: Salmannsdorf): "Kleingartenverein/Hackenberg." With a terraced garden on the fertile slopes of Untersievering, the *Heuriger* offers a lush perch for savoring the fruit of the vine. An underground spring flows through the terraces, gurgling into fountains and running past tables in the rustic tavern with thick wooden beams. Hot and cold buffet. Open daily 3pm-midnight.

Weingut Helm, XXI, Stammersdorferstr. 121 (tel. 292 12 44). Tram #31 to the last stop; turn right by the *Würstelstand*, then turn left. The family who owns and staffs this establishment generates a friendly atmosphere. The garden itself is quite attractive with great old trees. Open Tues.-Sat. 3pm-midnight.

Franz Mayer am Pfarrplatz Beethovenhaus, XIX, Pfarrpl. 2 (tel. 37 12 87). U-4 or U-6: "Heiligenstadt" then bus #38A: "Fernspechamt/Heiligenstadt." Walk up the hill and head right onto Nestelbachg. Beethoven used to stay in the *Heuriger* when it offered guest quarters. Festive and cool patios. Open Mon.-Fri. 4pm-midnight, Sun. and holidays 11am-midnight. Live music 7pm-midnight.

Weingut Heuriger Reinprecht, XIX, Cobenzlg. 22 (tel. 32 14 71). U-4 or U-6: "Heiligenstadt" then bus #38A: "Grinzing." This *Heuriger* is a fairy-tale stereotype—pic-

---

Thicker than blood

The Viennese connection to wine is a strong one, so strong that the stuff played a vital role in the Habsburg's rise to power. In 1273 Ottokar II of Bohemia, Rudolf of Habsburg's one rival to the throne of the Holy Roman Empire, holed himself up in Vienna, where he enjoyed strong support. Rudolf marched to the town walls and told the Viennese in no uncertain terms that if Ottokar did not go, the surrounding vineyards would. The Viennese got their priorities straight. The *Heurigen* also owe their existence to another Habsburg. In 1784 Josef II, the man who gave Vienna the Edict of Tolerance and the reusable coffin, promulgated another enlightened edict allowing wine growers to sell their most recent vintage, as well as food and fruit juices. Farmers soon sold their crops, pork, and poultry out of the rooms where customers used to sample their wines. Those rooms evolved into the buffets that now serve the patrons.

nic tables as far as the eye can see under an ivy-laden trellis, with *Schrammel* musicians strolling from table to table. One of the more touristed establishments, but don't be surprised to hear whole tables of nostalgic Austrians break into song with the accordion. Note the incredible bottle opener collection as you walk in. *Viertel* 30AS. Open March-Nov. daily 3:30pm-midnight.

WINTER IN VIENNA

The Viennese don't let those long winter nights go to waste. Christmas festivities begin in November with *Krampus* (Black Peter) parties. *Krampus* is a hairy devil that accompanies St. Nicholas on his rounds and gives bad children coal and sticks. On November 5th, people in Krampus suits lurk everywhere from nightclubs to supermarkets, rattling their chains and chasing passersby.

As the weather gets sharper, all the summertime *Würstel* huts turn their coats and begin roasting *Maroni* (chestnuts) and *Bratkartoffeln* (potato pancakes) on charcoal grills. Cider, punch, and *Glühwein* (a hot, spiced wine that warms you to the tips of your toes with the first sip) also appear at streetside stands. **Christmas markets** *(Christkindlmärkte)* open around the city. The somewhat tacky **Rathausplatz Christkindlmärkte** is probably the best known of the yule marketplaces, usually offering excellent *Lebkuchen* (similar to gingerbread—try the *Heidelberger* variety) and beeswax candles. (Open daily 9am-8pm.) **Schloß Schönbrunn's** *Weihnachtsmarkt* also offers exquisite traditional wares, at a price. (Open Mon.-Fri. noon-7pm, Sat.-Sun. and holidays 10am-7pm.) For offbeat gifts, visit the Spittelberg market, where artists and university students offer their creations. (Open Mon.-Fri. 2-8pm, Sat.-Sun. and holidays 10am-8pm.) Most of the theaters, opera houses, and concert halls have Christmas programs (see **Music,** p. 113 or **Theater and Cinema,** p. 114).

Before Christmas festivities have even died down, the Viennese gear up for New Year's Day. The twin highlights of the New Year's season are the **Silvester concert** (New Year's concert) by the Viennese Philharmonic, broadcast worldwide, and the flashy **Imperial Ball** in the Hofburg (for tickets, contact Kongresszentrum Hofburg, A-1014 Wien; tel. 587 36 66, ext. 23; fax 535 64 26). For those lacking seven-digit incomes, the City of Vienna organizes a huge chain of parties in the Inner City. Follow the **Silvesterpfad,** marked by lights hung over the street, to hit outdoor karaoke, street waltzing, and more. Every year rumors circulate that the great bell of St. Stephen's tower will ring on New Year's. The powerful bell has remained silent for over 100 years because experts fear the foundations of the church might crack.

New Year's is barely over before Lent arrives in February, and the **Fasching** (Carnival) spins the city into a bubbly daze of bedlam. These are the weeks of the Viennese waltzing balls. The most famous is the **Weiner Opernball** (Viennese Opera Ball), which draws the Princess Stephanies and Donald Trumps the world over. Tickets must be reserved years in advance (international celebrities can contact Opernball-Büro, A-1010 Wien, Goetheg. 1; tel. 514 44 26 06). You don't have to sit out if you can't make the Opernball—*Fasching* is a democratic season and there are balls for all tastes, the well-padded and the out-at-the-elbows. Even the kindergarteners in public pre-schools have *Fasching Krapfen* parties, and McDonald's puts up carnival crepe banners. For an absolutely cost-free *Fasching* celebration, come to the **carnival parade** that winds its way around the Ring, merrily stopping traffic the day before Lent begins. For the more temperately minded, the city sets up an enormous outdoor skating rink in Rathauspl. in January and February.

■ Nightlife

In its dark, soothing bars and on its groovy, kinetic dance floors, Vienna parties until dawn. From the dilapidated and crawling college pub to the swank and stylish watering hole, you can find the right place for every kind of thirst and wallet. Certain areas contain a high bar to cobblestone ratio, making a night of bacchanalian wandering deliriously easy. One such area, recommended to the loud, crowd-loving, and smoky type, is the **Bermuda Dreieck (Triangle),** named after its frequenters who, listing to port like overstuffed Spanish treasure galleons, lose their wind and their way and slowly sink. The area comprises about ten bars down Rotenturmstr., away from the Stephansdom. Follow Rotenturm to Fleischmarkt and then take Rabensteig to Seitenstetteng. on your left. If your vision isn't foggy and your compass is still oriented, continue on to Ruprechtspl., where pub tables line up against the walls of Ruprecht's church. The church sternly overlooks some of the best summer outdoor seating in Vienna, with cobblestones, stained glass, and the nearby Danube. Revelry moves inside from 11pm until 2 or even 4am. For more relaxed, less seasick action, head to the smooth **Bäckerstraße**—cool, ancient grottos where the lights are dim and the beer is perfect. Though not as packed with bars, the **Eighth District,** behind the University, and the area around **U-3: "Stubentor"** have been known to help needy souls down a few. Bars are known by the moniker *Beisl* or *Lokal*—use these words when asking the inebriated local where he has come from and where you should go.

The club scene whirls and rages every night of the week, later than bars. DJs spin wax until at least 4 or even 6am. A fact of Viennese dance life: it starts late. If you arrive at some place at 11pm, it will be a scene from your junior high school dance. As usual, the best nights are Friday and Saturday. The cover charges are reasonable and the theme nights frenetic and varied enough to please everyone. While techno still rears its digitalized head, house and soul enjoy a strong following as well.

A couple of other hints about nightlife: First, pick up a copy of the indispensible *Falter* (28AS) at a newsstand. It offers a complete guide to nocturnal events, from Opera schedules to club listings. Second, regular public transportation stops operating at around midnight. Find a night bus schedule and plan accordingly.

BARS

The term "bar" has a loose definition in Vienna. Many restaurants (see **Restaurants,** p. 93) live a Dr. Jekyll-Mr. Hyde dual existence as a place both to eat and to party.

The Innere Stadt

Benjamin, I, Salzgries 11-13 (tel. 533 33 49). Just outside of the Triangle area. Go down the steps from Ruprecht's church, left onto Josefs Kai, and left again on Salzgries. Dark and quintessentially groovy. Persian rugs hang on the walls; candles shine from wine bottles covered with wax. Filled with old, eclectic furniture. Can get rowdy on weekends, but the place designates a separate area for the cool and mellow. Student crowd and great beer—*Budvar* (37AS) and *Kapsreiter* (43AS). Open Sun.-Thurs. 7pm-2am, Fri.-Sat. 7pm-4am.

Krah Krah, I, Rabensteig 8 (tel. 533 81 93). From Stephanspl., head down Rotenturmstr. and continue straight and slightly to your left on Rabensteig. Consummate "Triangle" spot. Long bar serves 50 kinds of beer on tap. Popular outdoor seating until 10pm. Open Sun.-Wed. 11am-2am, Thurs.-Sat. 11am-3am.

Zwölf Apostellenkeller, I, Sonnenfelsg. 3 (tel. 512 67 77), behind the Stephansdom. To reach this underground tavern, walk into the archway, take a right, go down the long staircase, and discover grottos that date back to 1561. One of the best *Weinkeller* (wine cellars) in Vienna and a definite must for catacomb fans. Beer 37AS. *Viertel* of wine from 25AS. Open Aug.-June daily 4:30pm-midnight.

Esterházykeller, I, Haarhof 1 (tel. 533 34 82), off Naglerg. Vienna's least expensive *Weinkeller.* Try the Burgenlander *Grüner Veltliner* wine (26AS). Open in summer Mon.-Fri. 11am-11pm; in winter Mon.-Fri. 11am-11pm and Sat.-Sun. 4-11pm.

Kaktus, I, Seitenstettung. 5 (tel. 533 19 38), in the heart of the triangle. Packed with the bombed and the beautiful. Candles and atmospheric slouch. Open Sun.-Thurs. 6pm-2am, Fri.-Sat. 6pm-4am.

Roter Engel, I, Rabensteig 5 (tel. 535 41 05), across from Krah Krah. Artsily-decorated bar with live music nightly ranging from bubble-gum pop to electrifying blues. Some of us would like to know where they manage to dig up so many good Austrian and German bands. Cover 50-100AS. Open Mon.-Wed. 3pm-2am, Thurs.-Sat. 3pm-4am, Sun. 3pm-2am (5pm-2am in winter).

DISCOS AND DANCE CLUBS ■ 119

Bierleutgeb, I, Bäckerstr. 12 (tel. 512 26 37). One of Bäckerstr.'s cool subterranean grottos. Excellent beer bar, mainly Ottakring on tap. Also a restaurant with lots of Styrian specialties. Open Mon.-Thurs. 5pm-1am, Fri. 5pm-2am.

Jazzland, I, Franz-Josefs-Kai 29 (tel. 533 25 75). U-1 or U-4: "Schwedenpl." Jazz music of all styles and regions—check the schedule first. Excellent live music filters through the soothing brick environs. Hefty 120-250AS cover is often worth it. Open Tues.-Sat. 7pm-2am. Music 9pm-1am.

Café MAK, I, Stubenring 3-5 (tel. 714 01 21), in the museum. Tram #1 or 2: "Stubenring." Light, bright, white, and very tight at night. Peak through glass walls into the museum, or dine outside among the sunflowers. Very lively with a student crowd after 10pm. Open Tues.-Sun. 10am-2am (heated food until midnight).

Santo Spirito, I, Kampfg. 7 (tel. 512 99 98). From Stephanspl., walk down Singerstr. and turn left onto Kumpfg. (5min.). This bar will change your idea of classical music forever. The stereo here pumps out Rachmaninoff's second piano concerto while excited patrons co-conduct. Little busts on the wall pay homage to famous baton-wavers. Heats up in the winter, when the volume soars behind closed doors. Owner vacations in July, otherwise open daily from 6pm until people leave.

Club Berlin, I, Gonzag. 12 (tel. 533 04 79). Spiffy men and black-clad women wind their way around the partitions in this former wine cellar—a simultaneously intimate and expansive atmosphere. Open Sun.-Tues. 6pm-2am, Fri.-Sat. 6pm-4am.

Outside the Ring

Alsergrunder Kulturpark, IX, Alserstr. 4 (tel. 407 82 14). On the old grounds of a turn-of-the-18th-century hospital, Kulturpark is not one bar but many. A favorite outdoor hangout for the Viennese who flock here to the beer garden, *Heurige,* champagne bar—the list goes on. All sorts of people and all sorts of nightlife—just about anything you might want for a happening night out. Open daily April.-Oct. 4pm-2am. Call about the frequent concerts here.

Chelsea, VIII, Lerchenfelder Gürtel 29-31. The best place in Vienna for live "alternative" music. Period. Open daily 4pm-4am.

Miles Smiles, VIII, Langeg. 51 (tel. 405 95 17). U-2: "Lerchenfelderstr." Head down Lerchenfelderstr. and take the first right. Cool as "Sketches of Spain." The music is post-1955 jazz. Open Sun.-Thurs. 8pm-2am, Fri.-Sat. 8pm-4am.

Europa, VII, Zollerg. 8 (tel. 526 33 83). Buy a drink, scope the scene, and just vogue. Surrounded by concert posters and funky light fixtures, the hip twentysomething crowd hangs out late *en route* to further intoxication. Open daily 9am-4am.

Känguruh, VI, Bürgerspitalg. 20 (tel. 597 38 24). Decent little bar with over 70 brands of beer. Snacks available. Open daily 6pm-2am.

Plutzer Bräu, VII, Stiftg. 6 (tel. 526 12 15). U-3: "Neubaug." Follow signs for Stiftg., on the right-hand side. Spacious, popular brewhouse makes beer hounds out of even the stuffiest non-believers.

DISCOS AND DANCE CLUBS

U-4, XII, Schönbrunnerstr. 222 (tel. 85 83 18). U-4: "Meidling Hauptstr." Formerly *the* disco in Vienna and still crowded. A behemoth with all the trappings, including 2 separate dance areas, a dancer's cage, and slide shows. Five floors and rotating theme nights please a varied clientele. Cover 50-100AS. Open daily 11pm-5am.

Titanic, VI, Theobaldg. 11 (tel. 587 47 58). U-2: "Babenbergerstr." Walk up Mariahilferstr. and take the third left. No pretensions, just deep, sweaty grooves in the cavernous rooms. Two dance floors, concrete and crowded, with lots of soul. Occasional older music. No cover. Open Sun.-Thurs. 7pm-2am, Fri.-Sat. 7pm-4am.

B.A.C.H., Bachg. 21 (tel. 450 18 58). Lots of live funky concerts and theater acts as well as straight-up dancing in this subterranean nightclub. Definitely left of center. Open Sun.-Thurs. 8pm-2am, Fri.-Sat. 8pm-4am.

Volksgarten, I, Burgring/Heldenpl. (tel. 63 05 18). Nestled on the edge of the Volksgarten Park near the Hofburg. Zip up the leisure suit and strap on the platform soles. Definite 70s vibe. Comfy red couches provide the perfect spot for wallflowers to mellow. In good weather, the place rolls back the roof so clubbers can pulse under the stars. Mon. "Vibrazone" kicks out the funk and groove while the Sun.

morning breakfast club (6am-2pm) is the place to prolong the buzz of Saturday's uproarious "Kinky Disco." Cover 70-100AS. Open daily 10pm-5am.

BISEXUAL, GAY, AND LESBIAN CAFÉS AND CLUBS

For recommendations, support, seasonal parties, or contacts, call or stop by the **Rosa Lila Villa** (see **Practical Information,** p. 86). The helpful staff can give you lists of events, clubs, cafés, and discos (available in English). They also sponsor **Frauenfeste** (women's festivals) four times per year. Pick up a copy of *Connect,* a Viennese gay magazine available at most newsstands, for up-to-date information.

- **Café Willendorf,** VI, Linke Wienzeile 102 (tel. 587 17 89), in the Rosa Lila Villa. A café, bar, and restaurant with an outdoor terrace and excellent, creative vegetarian fare. Open daily 7pm-2am; meals until midnight.
- **Berg das Café,** IX, Bergg. 8 (tel. 319 57 20). A mixed café/bar by night, casual hang-out by day. Open daily 10am-1am.
- **Why Not,** I, Tiefer Graben 22 (tel. 535 11 58). A relaxed bar/disco for women and men. Open Fri.-Sat. 11pm-4am, Sun. 9pm-2am. Women-only one Thurs. per month.
- **Eagle Bar,** VI, Blümelg. 1 (tel. 587 26 61). A bar for men. Diverse clientele derived from the leather and/or denim set. Open daily 9pm-4am.
- **Nightshift,** VI, Corneliusg. 8 (tel. 586 23 37). A bar for men, preferably in black leather. Sun.-Thurs. 10pm-4am, Fri.-Sat. 10pm-5am.
- **U-4,** (see p. 119.) Thurs. is "Gay Heavens Night," 11pm-5am.
- **Café Savoy,** VI, Linke Wienzeile 36. A café/bar for gay men and women of mixed ages. Open Tues.-Fri. 5pm-2am, Sat. 9am-6pm and 9pm-2am.

■ Daytrips from Vienna

For other possible daytrips, see **Eisenstadt** (p. 157) and **Baden bei Wien** (p. 154).

MÖDLING

"Poor I am, and miserable," Beethoven wrote before his arrival in Mödling. Seeking physical and psychological rehabilitation, he schlepped all this way for that *je ne sais quoi* only a mineral spring could offer. He wrote *Missa Solemnis* within Mödling's embrace, and his spirits thoroughly improved. About 20 minutes from Vienna by S-Bahn (Eurailpass valid), Mödling maintains the charm that has drawn nobility and artists to this "cradle of ideas" since the Babenberg era. Minstrel Walther von der Vogelweide performed his epics in town, and later musical geniuses, including Schubert, Wagner, and Strauss, made their way here to glean inspiration from the stunning scenery. Many turn-of-the-century artists (like musician Hugo Wolf, poet Peter Altenberg, and painters Egon Schiele and Gustav Klimt) planted at least temporary roots at the spa. In his house on Bernhardgasse, Arnold Schönberg developed his 12-tone chromatic music and posed for a renowned Kokoschka portrait. To this day, Mödling remains a favorite recreational destination; the **Stadtbad** (city bath) down Badstr. has huge outdoor and indoor swimming pools, a sauna, sunbathing, massage therapy, and zillions of screaming children climbing on a funky orange octopus thing—go in the morning when everything is much more sane. There are also facilities for golf, tennis, horseback-riding, and fishing. In the evening, summer clientele flock to the *Heurigen,* enjoying the cool night breeze and the healthy grapes.

This elegant and serene town of 20,000 permanent inhabitants hides within the Wienerwald. Marked hiking trails cut through the town, leading to the ruins of the **Babenbergs' Castle,** the Neoclassical **Liechtenstein Palace,** and the Romanesque **Liechtenstein Castle** (both in Maria Enzersdorf, a neighboring town). The well-preserved *Altstadt* presents two Romanesque churches (check out the amazing stained glass in the **Pfarrkirche St. Othman** and the huge black onion dome atop the majestic **Karner** tower) and a charming Renaissance **Rathaus.** Mödling's **City Museum,** Josef Deutsch Pl., displays archaeological finds that trace the town's history back to 6000BC. (Open April-Dec. Sat.-Sun. 10am-noon and 2-6pm.)

Buses from Mödling (dir: Hinterbrühl) run through **Heiligenkreuz,** a beautifully pink Baroque Cistercian monastery on a hillside. Founded by Leopold V, the man who imprisoned Richard the Lionhearted for ransom, the church was originally intended as a "school of love" and a reformation of the pre-existing Benedictine order. Life at Heiligenkreuz was never particularly austere. You can visit the Weinkeller where the monks pressed their own grapes or walk through the chapel that still has ornamentation and beautiful stained-glass windows despite several medieval missives—church elders threatened that if the decoration was not removed within 2 years, the abbot, prior, and cellarer would have to fast on bread and water every sixth day until it was removed. Visitors can enter the abbey itself only by taking a tour. (Open 9am-6pm. 45AS, children 25AS.) The same bus that goes to Heiligenkreuz halts one stop later at **Mayerling,** the hunting lodge where heir to the throne Archduke Rudolf shot his bourgeois lover, Marie Vetsera, whom court protocol forbid him to marry, and then killed himself. In Hinterbrühl, the last stop, you find the largest underground lake in Europe. This former mineral mine was flooded in 1912, but the Nazis drained it and assembled the fuselage of the first jet fighter in the grotto.

For information and *Privatzimmer* lists, head to the **tourist office** *(Gästedienst),* Elisabethstr. 2 (tel. (02236) 267 27), next to the Rathaus. From the train station, walk up the hill and left down Hauptstr. all the way to the end at the Rathaus. (Open Mon.-Fri. 8am-noon and 1-4pm.) Trains and *Schnellbahn* leave from Vienna's Südbahnhof and arrive in Mödling all day long (30AS), and a bus leaves every hour from Südtiroler-Pl. in Vienna. The bus from the Vienna Kennedybrücke also runs into town.

KLOSTERNEUBURG

Easily accessible via the buses from Heiligenstadt (every 30min., 27AS), Klosterneuburg is a **monastery** founded by Leopold III in 1114. The church contains the renowned high Gothic masterpiece, the Verduner Altar. (Museum open May-Sept. 15 Sat.-Sun. and holidays 10am-5pm.) In 1730, Karl IV moved into Klosterneuburg and began a **palace** that was to match the enormity of the monastery—thus symbolizing the equal importance of *Gottesreich* (God's kingdom) and the *Kaiserreich* (Emperor's kingdom). The wildly extravagant Baroque palace will keep the crowds from the tour bus oohing and aahing. Note especially the crown of the Holy Roman Emperor at the crest of the palace. The library is also stupendous, with over 200,000 ancient tomes. Call the abbey (tel. (02243) 62 10) early to arrange a tour.

Klosterneuburg has a **Jugendherberge,** Hüttersteig 8 (tel. (02243) 83 501), to which the forlorn traveler unable to find a bed in Vienna could easily commute. The hostel offers 65 beds at 120AS each. As with every other hostel in the area, groups of screaming kids occasionally descend. (Open Jan. 5 to mid-Sept.)

WEEKEND EXCURSIONS

Travel often introduces visitors to a culture fashioned long before the advent of 20th century political boundaries. Such is certainly the case in Austria, whose imperial flourish once covered a much larger part of Europe than what is now circumscribed by its national borders. Though now no longer a part of the Austrian nation, cities like Prague (the erstwhile capital of the Holy Roman Empire) and Budapest were extremely close to the Habsburgs' heart. Both cities make excellent and highly recommended weekend destinations from Vienna.

■ Prague (Praha)

According to legend, Princess Libuše stood on Vyšehrad above the Vltava and declared, "I see a city whose glory will touch the stars; it shall be called Praha (threshold)." Medieval kings, benefactors, and architects fulfilled the prophecy, as soaring

122 ■ WEEKEND EXCURSIONS: PRAGUE (PRAHA)

HOSTELS
1. Hostel Sokol
2. CKM
3. Junior Hotel Praha
4. Hotel Juventus

Prague
1. Canadian Embassy
2. Palace Belvedere
3. National Gallery
4. St. Vitus Cathedral
5. Royal Palace
6. Basilica of St. George
7. Lobkovic Palace
8. U.K. Embassy
9. Wallenstein Palace
10. St. Nicholas Church
11. U.S. Embassy
12. Church of Our Lady Victorious
13. Charles Bridge
14. National Theater
15. New Town Hall
16. National Museum
17. Smetana Theater
18. Praha hlavní nádraží
19. Church of Our Lady of the Snows
20. Bethlehem Chapel
21. Kafka's Birthplace
22. Maislova Synagóga
23. Vysoká Synagóga
24. Staronová Synagóga
25. Old Town Hall
26. Týn Church
27. Church of St James
28. Powder Tower
29. Masarykovo nádraží
30. Florenc Bus Station
31. Pražská Informační Sluzba (PIS)
32. Čedak Office
33. Main Post Office
34. Anešský klášter (St. Agnes Convent)
35. American Express Office
36. Kafka's Grave

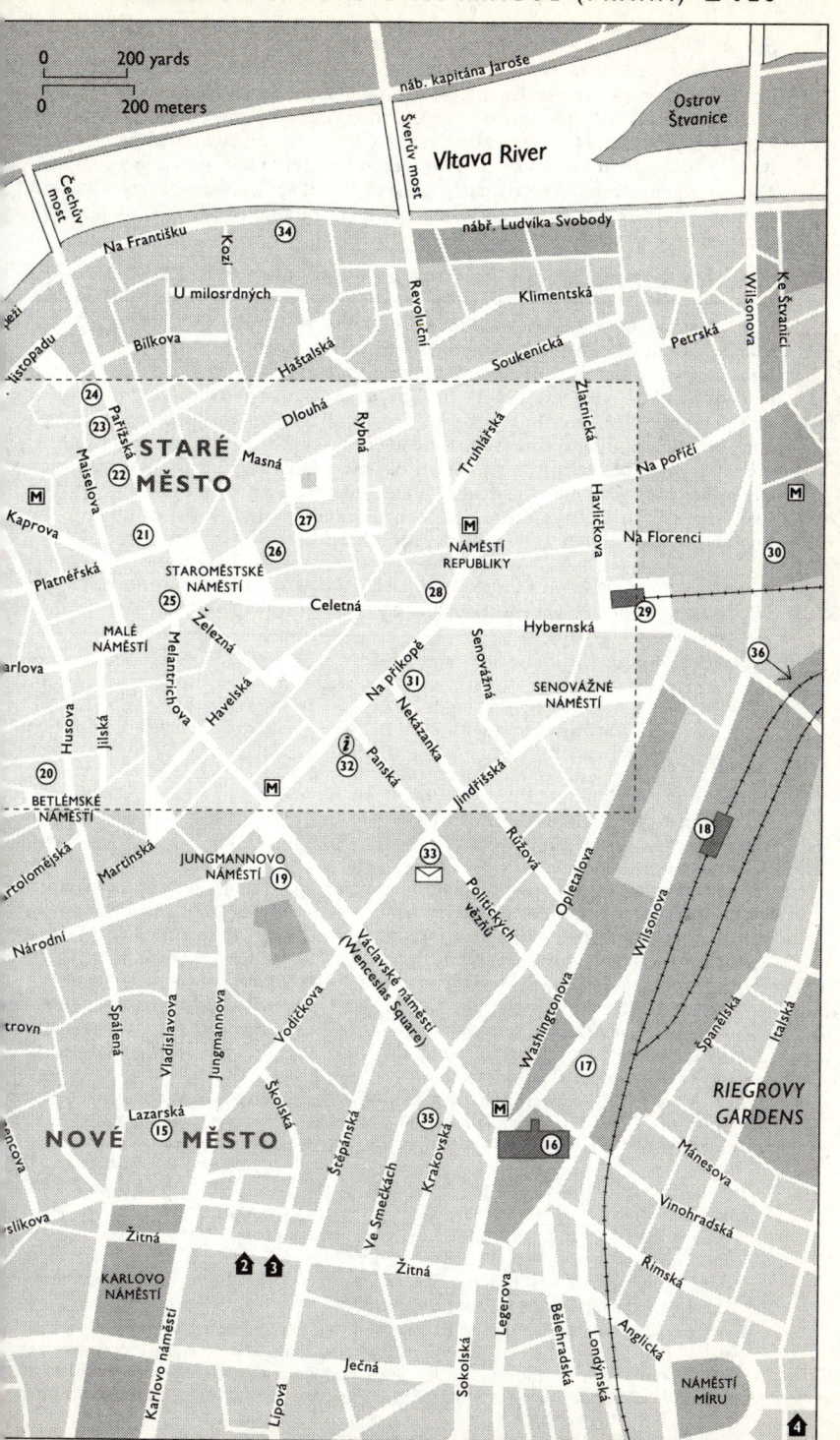

WEEKEND EXCURSIONS: PRAGUE (PRAHA) ■ 123

cathedrals and lavish palaces announced Prague's status as the capital of the Holy Roman Empire. But the city's character differed sharply from the holy splendor of Rome and Constantinople: legends of demons, occult forces, and mazes of shady alleys thrust this "city of dreams" into the shadows and provided fodder for Franz Kafka's tales of paranoia. Only this century has the spell been broken, as the fall of the Berlin Wall brought hordes of euro-trotting foreigners to the once-isolated capital. Tourists and entrepreneurs have long since explored and exploited every nook and cranny of the city, but these same visitors give Prague a festive air that few places in the world can match.

ORIENTATION AND PRACTICAL INFORMATION

Straddling a bend in the Vltava, Prague is a mess of suburbs and winding streets. **Staré Město** (Old Town) lies along the southeast riverbank; across the Vltava sits the **Hradčany** castle with **Malá Strana** at its south base. Southeast of the Old Town spreads **Nové Město** (New Town), and farther east across **Wilsonova** lie the **Žižkov** and **Vinohrady** districts. **Holešovice** in the north has an international train terminal; **Smíchov**, the southwest end, is the student-dorm suburb. All train and bus terminals are on or near the Metro system. **Metro B: "nám. Republiky"** is the closest stop to the principal tourist offices and accommodations agencies. Don't just refer to your map: study it. *Tabak* stands and bookstores vend indexed *plán města* (maps). The English-language weekly *The Prague Post* provides news and tips for visitors.

> Prague is in the process of carrying out a telephone-system overhaul; throughout 1998 many numbers will change (though the eight-digit ones are less likely to).

Tourist Offices: An "i" sign indicates a tourist agency that books rooms, arranges tours, and sells maps and guidebooks. Be wary: these private firms didn't just appear in a burst of benevolence. **Prague Information Service** (*Pražská Informační Služba*), Staromwstske nám. 1 (tel. 24 48 25 62, English information 54 44 44), happily sells maps (40kč), arranges tours, and books musical extravaganzas. Open Mon.-Fri. 9am-7pm, Sat.-Sun. 9am-6pm. **Čedok**, Na příkopě 18 (tel. 24 19 71 11), has a formidable institutional memory from 40 years of socialist monopoly but isn't yet fully user-friendly. Open Mon.-Fri. 8:30am-6pm, Sat. 9am-1pm.

Budget Travel: CKM, Jindřišská 28 (tel. 24 23 02 18; fax 26 86 23), sells budget air tickets and discount cards for students and those under 26 (ISICs and Go25 150kč; Euro26 350kč). The office also books rooms in Prague (300kč and up). Open Mon.-Fri. 9am-6pm. A **branch** at Žitná 12 (tel. 24 91 57 67) handles bus, rail, and train tickets. Open Mon.-Fri. 9am-6pm. **KMC**, Karoliny Světlé 30 (tel. 24 23 06 33), sells HI cards (300kč) and can book HI hostels almost anywhere. Open Mon.-Thurs. 9am-noon and 2:30-5pm, Fri. 9am-noon and 2:30-5:30pm.

Passport Office: Foreigner police, Olšanská 2 (tel. 683 17 39). Metro A: "Flora." Walk down Jičínská and turn right onto Olšanská, or take tram 9. Visa extensions. Open Mon.-Tues. and Thurs. 7:30-11:45am and 12:30-2:30pm, Wed. 7:30-11:30am and 12:30-5pm, Fri. 7:30am-noon.

Embassies: Travelers from **Australia** and **New Zealand** have honorary consuls (tel. 24 31 00 71 and 25 41 98 respectively) but should contact the U.K. embassy in an emergency. **Canada**, Mickiewiczova 6 (tel. 24 31 11 08). Metro A: "Hradčanská." Open Mon.-Fri. 8am-noon and 2-4pm. **Ireland**, Tržiště 13 (tel. 53 09 02). Metro A: "Malostranská." Open Mon.-Fri. 9:30am-12:30pm and 2:30-4:30pm. **South Africa**, Ruská 65 (tel. 67 31 11 14). Metro A: "Flora." Open Mon.-Fri. 9am-noon. **U.K.**, Thunovská 14 (tel. 57 32 03 55). Metro A: "Malostranská." Open Mon.-Fri. 9am-noon. **U.S.**, Tržiště 15 (tel. 57 32 06 63, after hours 53 12 00). Metro A: "Malostranská." From Malostranské nám., head down Karmelitská and take a right onto Tržiště. Open Mon.-Fri. 8am-1pm and 2-4:30pm.

Currency Exchange: The best rates for American Express and Thomas Cook's traveler's checks are at their respective offices. Exchange counters are everywhere—hotel lobbies, tourist information agencies, and along the street—with wildly varying rates. **Chequepoints** are mushrooming around town and may be the only

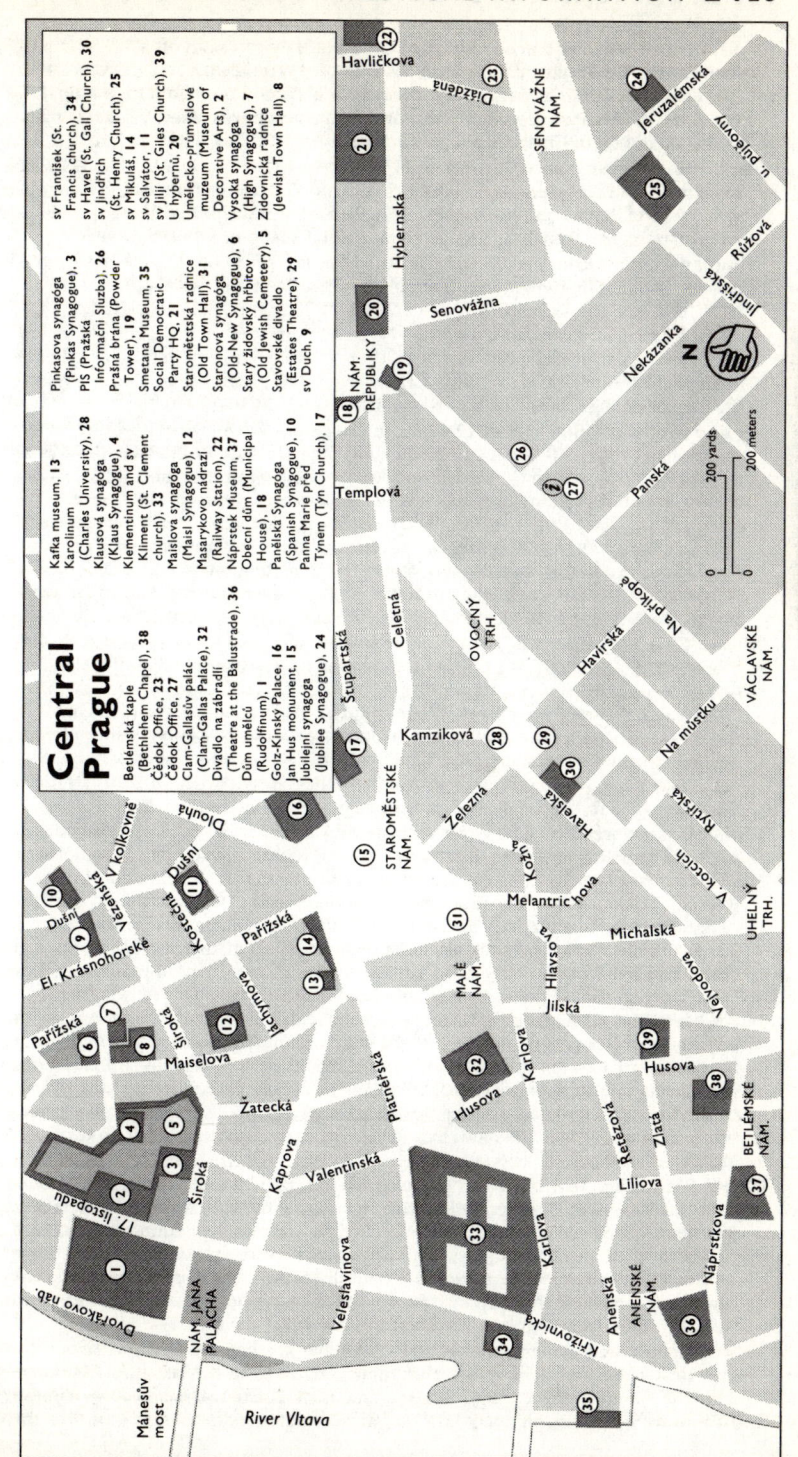

ORIENTATION AND PRACTICAL INFORMATION ■ 125

Central Prague

Betlémská kaple (Bethlehem Chapel), 38
Čedok Office, 23
Čedok Office, 27
Clam-Gallasův palác (Clam-Gallas Palace), 32
Divadlo na zábradlí (Theatre at the Balustrade), 36
Dům umělců (Rudolfinum), 1
Golz-Kinský Palace, 16
Jan Hus monument, 15
Jubilejní synagóga (Jubilee Synagogue), 24
Kafka museum, 13
Karolinum (Charles University), 28
Klausová synagóga (Klaus Synagogue), 4
Klementinum and sv Kliment (St. Clement church), 33
Maislova synagóga (Maisl Synagogue), 12
Masarykovo nádraží (Railway Station), 22
Náprstek Museum, 37
Obecní dům (Municipal House), 18
Panělská synagóga (Spanish Synagogue), 10
Panna Marie před Týnem (Týn Church), 17
Pinkasova synagóga (Pinkas Synagogue), 3
PIS (Pražská Informační Služba), 26
Prašná brána (Powder Tower), 19
Smetana Museum, 35
Social Democratic Party HQ, 21
Staroměstská radnice (Old Town Hall), 31
Staronová synagóga (Old-New Synagogue), 6
Starý židovský hřbitov (Old Jewish Cemetery), 5
Stavovské divadlo (Estates Theatre), 29
sv Duch, 9
sv František (St. Francis church), 34
sv Havel (St. Gall Church), 30
sv Jindřich (St. Henry Church), 25
sv Mikuláš, 14
sv Salvátor, 11
sv Jiljí (St. Giles Church), 39
Uměleckoprůmyslové muzeum (Museum of Decorative Arts), 2
U hyberrnů, 20
Vysoká synagóga (High Synagogue), 7
Židovnická radnice (Jewish Town Hall), 8

places open when you need to change cash, but they can skim off a 10% commission. **Komerční Banka,** main branch Na příkopě 33 (tel. 24 02 11 11; fax 24 24 30 20), exchanges cash and traveler's checks for a 2% commission. Open Mon.-Fri. 8am-5pm. **ATMs** are everywhere. The one at **Krone supermarket,** Václavské nám. 21, is hooked up to Cirrus, EuroCard, Eurocheque, MC, Plus, and Visa.

American Express: Václavské nám. 5, 113 26 Praha 1 (tel. 24 21 99 92; fax 24 22 11 31). Metro A or C: "Muzeum." Mail held. MC and Visa cash advances (3% commission). **ATMs.** Exchange office open daily 9am-7pm; travel office May-Sept. Mon.-Fri. 9am-6pm, Sat. 9am-2pm; Oct.-April Mon.-Fri. 9am-5pm, Sat. 9am-noon.

Thomas Cook: Národní tř. 28 (tel. 21 10 52 76; fax 24 23 60 77). Cashes Cook's checks commission-free. MC cash advances. Open Mon.-Sat. 9am-7pm, Sun. 10am-6pm. Also Staroměské nám. 5/934 (tel. 24 81 71 73). Open daily 9am-7pm.

Flights: Ruzyně Airport (tel. 20 11 11 11), 20km northwest of city center. Bus 119 from Dejvická or the **airport bus** (tel. 20 11 42 96) from nám. Republicky (90kč) or Dejvická (60kč). Taxis to the airport are exorbitant. Many major carriers fly into Prague, including **ČSA** (Czech National Airlines; tel. 20 10 43 10).

Trains: For information, call 24 22 42 00, international fare information 24 61 52 49. Prague has 4 terminals—make sure you go to the right one. **Praha Hlavní Nádraží** (tel. 24 61 72 50; Metro C: "Hlavní Nádraží") is the biggest, but most international trains run out of **Holešovice** (tel. 24 61 72 65; Metro C: "Nádraží Holešovice"). To: **Berlin** (5 per day, 5hr., 1342kč), **Budapest** (6 per day, 8hr., 1018kč), **Vienna** (4 per day, 5hr., 709kč), and **Warsaw** (3 per day, 10hr., 722kč). Domestic trains go from **Masarykovo** (tel. 24 61 72 60; Metro B: "nám. Republiky"), on the corner of Hybernská and Havlíčkova, or from **Smíchov** (tel. 24 61 72 55; Metro B: "Smíchovské Nádraží"), opposite Vyšehrad.

Buses: ČSAD has three *autobusové nádraží* (bus terminals). The biggest is **Praha-Florenc,** Křižíkova (tel. 24 21 49 90, information 24 21 10 60), behind the Masarykovo Nádraží train station. Metro B or C: "Florenc." To **Berlin** (1 per day, 6hr., 750kč) and **Vienna** (6 per week, 8½hr., 330kč). The staff speaks little English and the timetables are a little tricky; start by looking for the bus-stop number of your destination. Buy tickets at least a day in advance—they sometimes sell out. Students may get a 10% discount. The Tourbus office upstairs (tel. 24 21 02 21) sells **Eurolines** tickets. Open Mon.-Fri. 8am-8pm, Sat.-Sun. 9am-8pm.

Public Transportation: The **metro, tram,** and **bus** services are pretty good and share the same ticket system. Buy tickets from newsstands, machines in stations, or **DP** (*Dopravní Podnik;* transport authority) kiosks. Punch tickets upon first use. Basic 6kč ticket good for one short ride; more useful 10kč ticket valid for 1hr. (90min. 8pm-5am and all day Sat., Sun, and holidays), allowing you to switch from bus to tram to metro and back again. Large bags 5kč each, as are bikes and prams without babies in them (free *with* babies, so don't forget the baby). Plainclothes DP inspectors roam Prague issuing 200kč spot fines. Make sure you see their official badge and get a receipt. The metro's 3 lines run daily 5am-midnight: A is green on the maps, B is yellow, C is red. **Night trams** 51-58 and **buses** run all night after the last metro; look for the dark blue signs at bus stops. DP also sells **tourist passes** valid for the entire network (24hr. 50kč, 3 days 130kč, 1 week 190kč). **DP offices** by the Jungmannovo nám. exit of Můstek station (tel. 24 22 51 35; open daily 7am-9pm) or by the Palackého nám. exit of Karlovo nám. station (tel. 29 46 82; open Mon.-Fri. 7am-6pm).

Taxis: Taxi Praha (tel. 24 91 66 66) and **AAA** (tel. 24 32 24 32) operate 24hr. Generally 20-30kč plus 15-20kč per km. Before entering the cab, make sure the meter has been reset. On shorter trips, check that the meter is running by saying *"Zapněte taximetr";* for longer trips set a price beforehand. Always ask for a receipt *("Prosím, dejte mi paragon")* with distance traveled, price paid, and the driver's signature; if the driver doesn't write the receipt, you aren't obligated to pay. As you may have guessed, locals strongly distrust cab drivers.

Hitchhiking: Hitchhiking in and around Prague has become increasingly dangerous. Don't do it. Those hitching east take tram 1, 9, or 16 to the last stop. To points south, they take Metro C: "Pražskeho povstání," walk left 100m, and cross náměstí Hrdinů to 5 Května (highway D1). To Munich, hitchers take tram 4 or 9 to the

ACCOMMODATIONS AND CAMPING ■ 127

intersection of Plzeňská at Kukulova/Bucharova. Those going north take a tram or bus to "Kobyliské nám." then bus 175 up Horňátecká.

Luggage Storage: Lockers in all **train and bus stations** take two 5kč coins. If these are full, or if you need to store your pack for longer than 24hr., use the left luggage offices in the basement of **Hlavní nádraží** (15kč per day for first 15kg) and halfway up the stairs at **Florenc** (10kč per day up to 15kg; open daily 5am-11pm). Watch your bags as you set your locker code.

English-Language Bookstore: The Globe Bookstore, Janovského 14 (tel. 66 71 26 10). Metro C: "Vltavská." Many used books, a big noticeboard, and a coffeehouse. A legendary (pick-up) center of Anglophone Prague. Open daily 9am-5pm.

Laundromat: Laundry Kings, Dejvická 16 (tel. 312 37 43), 1 block from Metro A: "Hradčanská." Cross the tram *and* railroad tracks then turn left onto Dejvická. Wash 60kč. Dry 15kč per 8min. Soap 10-20kč. Beer 11kč (ah, Prague). The noticeboard aids apartment hunters, English teachers, and friend-seekers. Use the spinner to save on drying. Open Mon.-Fri. 6am-10pm, Sat.-Sun. 8am-10pm. Travelers can sometimes informally arrange laundry services in private flats.

Pharmacies: Koněvova 210 (tel. 644 18 95) and Štefánikova 6 (tel. 24 51 11 12). Open 24hr. You may need to ask for *kontrcepční prostředky* (contraceptives), *náplast* (bandages), or *dámské vložky* (tampons).

Emergencies: Na Homolce (hospital for foreigners), Roentgenova 2 (tel. 52 92 21 46, after hours 57 21 11 11). Open Mon.-Fri. 8am-4pm. **American Medical Center** (tel. 80 77 56). **Canadian Medical Centre** (tel. 316 55 19).

Post Office: Jindřišská 14. Metro A or B: "Můstek." Address *Poste Restante* to Jindřišská 14, 110 00 Praha 1, Czech Republic. Pick-up at window 28; open Mon.-Fri. until 8pm. For stamps go to window 16, letters and parcels under 2kg windows 12-14. Office open 24hr. You can mail parcels over 2kg only at **Celní stanice** (customs office), Plzeňská 139. Metro B: "Anděl" then tram 4, 7, or 9: "Klamovka."

Postal Code: 110 00.
Telephone Code: 02.

ACCOMMODATIONS AND CAMPING

While hotel prices rise, the hostel market is glutted. Prices have now stabilized around 200-300kč per night. The smaller hostels are friendly and often full—the Strahov complex and other student dorms bear the brunt of the summer's backpacking crowds. A few bare-bones hotels are still cheap, and growing numbers of residents are renting rooms. Sleeping on Prague's streets is too dangerous to consider.

Accommodations Agencies

Hawkers and agents besiege visitors at the train station with offers of rooms for around US$15-30 (500-1000kč). These arrangements are generally safe, but if you're wary of bargaining on the street, call around or try one of the agencies listed below. Make sure any room you accept is close to public transportation and that you understand what you're paying for; if you're at all confused, have the staff write it down. Payment is usually accepted in Czech, German, or U.S. currency.

Konvex 91, Ve Smečkách 29 (tel. 96 22 44 44; fax 22 21 15 02). Specializes in apartment rental: 440-590kč per person per night near the TV tower or 590-720kč in Staré Město. Hostels from 340kč per night. English and French spoken.

Ave., Hlavní Nádraží (tel. 24 22 32 26; fax 24 23 07 83), left from the main hall of the train station. The growing firm offers hundreds of rooms (shared and private) from 440kč per person and hostel beds from 170kč. Open daily 6am-10pm.

Hello Travel Ltd., Senovážné nám. 3 (tel. 24 21 26 47), between Na příkopě and Hlavní Nádraží. Arranges every sort of housing imaginable. Hostel beds 10-13$US. Singles in pensions from US$35; doubles US$56. Low-season: US$23; US$56. Pay in kč, DM, or by credit card (AmEx, Diners, MC, V). Open daily 10am-9pm.

Hostels

In the Strahov neighborhood west of the river next to the Olympic stadium, an enormous cluster of dorms/hostels opens up in July and August. These rooms cater to those who arrive in the middle of the night *sans* clue, but many prefer the smaller, more personable hostels. It's best to phone the night before you arrive or at checkout time (around 10am) to snag a bed. Staffs generally speak English well.

The Clown and Bard, Bořivojova 102 (tel. 27 24 36). Metro A: "Jiřího z Poděbrad" then walk down Slavíkova and turn right onto Ježkova; continue until the intersection with Bořivojova. Prague's newest hostel, in a converted 19th-century Žižkov building, provides beds in the roomy attic dorm for 200kč. Private rooms 250-350kč per person. Apartments from 300kč per person. Wildly popular in summer '97, owing much to the cellar bar, featuring beer and Leonard Cohen. Open daily 8am-1am.

Slavoj Wesico (a.k.a. **Hostel Boathouse**), V náklích 1a (tel. 402 10 76). From Holešovice station or Metro A: "Staroměstská," tram 17 (south): "Černý Kůň." Descend by the balustrade on the river side and walk to the Vltava. Strikingly clean rooms above a working boathouse. 3- to 5-bed dorms 250kč. 50kč surcharge for one-night stays. Breakfast 50kč. Laundry 80kč. Key deposit 50kč. Call ahead.

V podzámčí, V podzámčí 27 (tel. 472 27 59). Metro C: "Budějovická" then bus 192 to the third stop—ask the driver to stop at "Nad Rybníky." Talking with Eva, the Czech in charge, is a delight. Kitchen, satellite TV, laundry service (100kč), and 2 cats. 2- to 4-person dorms 240kč.

Libra-Q, Senovážné nám. 21 (tel. 24 23 17 54; fax 24 22 15 79). Metro B: "nám." Republiky or C: "Hlavní Nádraží." Great location, just above the *Elle* and *Bohemian Model* offices, near Staré Město. 8-bed dorms 280kč; triples 1200kč; quads 1500kč.

Domov Mládeže, Dykova 20 (tel. 25 06 88; fax 25 14 29). From Metro A: "nám. Jiřího z Poděbrad" then follow Nitranská and turn left on Dykova. Possibly the most enjoyable hostel trek ever. 60 beds in the peaceful, tree-lined Vinohrady district. Clean but not sterile 2- to 7-person dorms 300kč. Breakfast included.

ESTEC Hostel, Vaníčkova 5, blok 5 (tel. 57 21 04 10; fax 57 21 52 63). Metro A: "Dejvická" then bus 217 or 143: "Koleje Strahov." Hundreds of beds. Try for a double (280kč per person) in the refurbished basement of blok 5. 24hr. reception. Check-in 2pm. Crowded basement dorms 180kč; singles 400kč; triples 750kč. Breakfast 50kč. MC, V, AmEx, Eurocard.

Traveller's Hostels, in 8 dorms throughout the city center. The one at **Husova 3** (tel. 24 21 53 26), smack dab in Staré Město, is the classiest. Metro A: "Národní třída" then turn right onto Spálená, which turns into Na Perštýně after Národní, and then into Husova. Dorms 400kč. Brand new outfit at **Dlovhá 33** (tel. 231 13 18), in Staré Město in the same building as the Roxy club. 6-bed dorms 250kč; doubles 900kč; triples 1170kč. **Neklanova 32** (tel. 24 91 55 32) is also new. Metro C: "Vyšehrad" then head down Slavojova and it's on the left. Dorms 270kč. **Střelecký ostrov** (tel. 24 91 01 88), on the island off most Legii. Metro B: "Národní třída." Dorms 300kč. **Mikulandská 5** (tel. 24 91 07 39). Metro B: "Národní třída." Dorms 270kč. **Křížovnická 7** (tel. 232 09 87). Metro A: "Staroměstská." Dorms 230kč. **Růžova 5** (tel. 26 01 11). Metro C: "Hlavní nádraží." Dorms 220kč.

Welcome Hostel, Zikova 13 (tel. 24 32 02 02; fax 24 32 34 89). Metro A: "Dejvická"; from escalators, follow Šolinova to Zikova. Check-in 2:30pm. Check-out 9:30am. Singles 350kč; doubles 480kč. They also run a Strahov dorm, Vaníčková 5, blok 3 (tel. 52 71 90; see directions for ESTEC, above). Singles 300kč; doubles 440kč.

Hotels and Pensions

With so many tourists infiltrating Prague, hotels are upgrading their service and appearance, and budget hotels are now scarce. Beware that hotels may try to bill you for a more expensive room than the one you in which you stayed. The better budget hotels require reservations up to a month in advance. Call, then confirm by fax.

Hotel Standart, Přístavní 2 (tel. 87 52 58 or 66 71 04 71; fax 80 67 52). Metro C: "Vltavská" then tram 1, 3, 14, or 25: "Dělnická." Continue along the street, then make a left. Very quiet neighborhood that gets very dark at night. Spotless hall showers and bathrooms. Singles 595kč; doubles 750kč; triples 995kč; quads 1090kč. All rooms 350kč per person for HI members. Breakfast included.

Pension Unitas, Bartolomějská 9 (tel. 232 77 00; fax 232 77 09), in Staré Město. Metro B: "Národní." Formerly a monastery where Beethoven once performed, then a Communist jail where Václav Havel was incarcerated. Havel's basement room (P6) is now a quad outfitted with bunk beds, small windows, and heavy iron doors (1900kč). Singles 1000kč; doubles 1200kč; triples 1650kč. The Convent of the Gray Sisters still owns the place, so no smoking or drinking in the rooms.

Hotel Unitour, Senovážné nám. 21 (tel. 24 10 25 36; fax 24 22 15 79). The budget hotel arm of Libra-Q (above). Singles 750kč, with shower 890kč; doubles 810kč, 1250kč; triples 1200kč, 1480kč; quads 1400kč.

B&B U Oty (Ota's House), Radlická 188 (tel./fax 57 21 53 23). 400m from Metro B: "Radlická," up the slope. Kitchen facilities and free laundry services available after 3 nights. Singles 450kč; doubles 700kč; triples 900kč; quads 1200kč. 100kč per person surcharge for one-night stays.

Camping

Tourist offices sell a guide of campsites near the city (15kč).

- **Caravan Park** (tel. 54 09 25; fax 54 33 05) and **Caravan Camping** (tel. 54 56 82), on Císařská Louka, a tranquil peninsula on the Vltava. Metro B: "Smíchovské nádraží" then tram 12: "Lihovar" and walk toward the river and onto the shaded path. 95kč; tents 90-140kč. Caravan Park bungalows: 2-person 480kč; 4-person 720kč. Caravan Camping rooms 310-365kč per person. Reserve bungalows and rooms by fax.

- **Sokol Troja,** Trojská 171 (tel./fax 688 11 77), north of the center in the Troja district. Metro C: "Nádraží Holešovice" then bus 112: "Kazanka," the fourth stop, and walk 100m. 90kč; tent 70-150kč. Dorm, bungalow, and flat accommodations 155kč, 165kč, 135kč. Other grounds line the same road.

- **Na Vlachovce,** Zenklova 217 (tel./fax 688 02 14). From Nádraží Holešovice, bus 175 or 102 toward Okrouhlická; get off and continue in the same direction. 2-person barrels (220kč per bed) for those who've always wanted to crawl into a barrel of *Budvar*. Great view of Prague. Reserve a week ahead.

FOOD

The general rule is that the nearer you are to the tourist throngs on Staroměstské nám., Karlův most, and Václavské nám., the more you'll spend. Check your bill carefully—restaurants charge for everything the waiter brings, including ketchup and bread. In Czech lunch spots, *hotová jídla* (prepared meals) are cheapest. Vegetarian eateries are opening up, but in many restaurants limit veggie options to fried cheese. Outlying Metro stops become marketplaces in summer. Look for the daily **vegetable market** at the intersection of Havelská and Melantrichova in the Old Town. For a real bargain, go to the basement in the **Krone department store,** on Wenceslas Square at the intersection with Jindřišská (open Mon.-Fri. 8am-7pm, Sat. 8am-6pm, Sun. 10am-6pm), or the **Kotva department store** (tel. 24 21 54 62) on the corner of Revoluční and nám (open Mon. 7am-7pm, Tues.-Fri. 7am-8pm, Sat. 8am-6pm).

Restaurants

- **Lotos,** Platnéřská 13 (tel. 232 23 90). Metro A: "Staroměstská." Veggie Czech food with lotsa leeks. Leek soup 15kč. Soy cubes with dumplings 52kč. Wheat-yeast *Pilsner* 22kč for 0.5L. 7-herb tea 19kč. Open daily 11am-10pm.

- **Klub Architektů,** Betlémské nám. 169 (tel. 24 40 12 14). Walk through the gates and descend to the right. A 12th-century cellar thrust into the 20th century with sleek table settings and copper pulley lamps. Veggie options 60-70kč. Meat dishes around 100kč. Chinese cabbage soup 20kč. Open daily 11am-midnight.

- **U Medvídků,** Na Perštýně 7 (tel. 24 22 09 30), on the outskirts of Staré Město. Metro B: "Národní tř." There's a *restaurace* and a *pivnice* (pub), but the latter is cheaper and more fun. Patrons have consumed pretty good Czech food at very good prices here since 1466. "Bear's Foot toast" 35kč. Beef sirloin with cranberries 71kč. Open Mon.-Sat. 11:30am-11pm, Sun. 11:30am-10pm.

- **Restaurace U Pravdů,** Žitná 15 (tel. 29 95 92). Metro B: "Karlovo nám." A deservedly popular Czech lunch spot. Fish dishes 61-76kč. Pork dishes 77kč. Potato *knedlíky* 15kč. Big glass of *Staropramen* beer 16kč; *Radegast* beer 19kč. Open Mon.-Fri. 10am-11pm, Sat.-Sun. 11am-11pm.

Jáma (The Hollow), V Jámě 7 (tel. 90 00 04 13), off Vodičkova. Metro A and C: "Muzeum." Attracts a diverse but largely non-Czech crowd. Weekend brunch (89-119kč) comes with free coffee refills. Other options include a "super veggie burro" (124kč) and burgers (99-116kč). Open daily 11am-1am.

Bar bar, Všehrdova 17 (tel. 53 29 41). Metro A: "Malostranská." Left off Karmelitská from Malostranské nám. A jungle jungle of salads salads with meat meat, fish fish, cheese cheese, or just veggies veggies (all 54-89kč). A good vibe, good music, and 40 varieties of good whiskey from 41kč. *Velkopopovický kozel* on tap 15kč per 0.5L. Open Mon.-Fri. 11am-midnight, Sat.-Sun. noon-midnight.

Malostranská Hospoda, Karmelitská 25 (tel. 53 20 76), by Malostranské nám. Metro A: "Malostranská." Chairs spill out onto the square from the pub's vaulted interior. Good *guláš* 58kč. Draft *Staropramen* 13kč per 0.5L. English menu. Open Mon.-Sat. 10am-midnight, Sun. 11am-midnight.

Penzion David, Holubova 5. Tram 14 (catch it by the main post office): "Laurová" then turn left off the main street and then a right on Holubova. Caters to gay men, with some of the best food in town. Entrees mostly 45-125kč. Lunch *menu* a dirt-cheap 45kč. Open Mon.-Fri. 11am-11pm, Sat.-Sun. noon-midnight.

Cafés

When Prague journalists are bored, they churn out another "Whatever happened to café life?" feature. Ignore their pessimism as you gaze soulfully into your coffee at one of the places listed below.

U malého Glena, Karmelitská 23 (tel. 535 81 15 or 90 00 39 67), just south off Malostranské nám. Metro A: "Malostranská." The "light entree" menu has veggie plates from 70kč. Czechs and foreigners here; some descend to the **Maker's Mark bar** for jazz or blues at 9pm (cover 50-70kč). Open daily 7:30am-2am.

U Knihomola, Mánesova 79 (tel. 627 77 68). Metro A: "Jiřího z Poděbrad." A living room with comfy couches and coffee-table literature. Coffee 20kč. Carrot cake 75kč. Open Mon.-Thurs. 10am-11pm, Fri.-Sat. 10am-midnight, Sun. 11am-8pm.

The Globe Coffeehouse, Janovského 14 (tel. 66 71 26 10). Metro C: "Vltavská." Tasty, bitter black coffee (20kč per cup), a slightly pricey weekend brunch menu (omelette 120kč), and all the expat gossip. Open daily 10am-midnight.

U červeného páva, Kamzíková 6 (tel. 24 23 31 68). Metro A: "Staroměstská." Wander down Celetná from the square. Proof that not everything around Staroměstské nám. is over-touristed. Quiet cafe-bar for gays and straights. Espresso 28kč.

SIGHTS

Orient yourself before tackling the city's many scattered sights. Central Prague is structured by three streets that form a leaning *"T."* The long stem of the *T* is the boulevard **Václavské nám.** (Wenceslas Sq.). The **National Museum** sits at the bottom of this street. Busy and pedestrian **Na příkopě** forms the right arm of the *T* and leads to **nám. Republiky** at its far end. The left arm, **28. října** becomes **Národní** after a block and leads to the **National Theater** on the river. A maze of small streets leads to Staroměstské nám., two blocks above the *T*. There are two prominent **St. Nicholas churches**—in Malá Strana near the castle and on Staromětské nám.

Václavské náměstí (Wenceslas Square) Not so much a square as a broad boulevard, **Václavské nám.** owes its name to the equestrian statue of the Czech ruler and saint **Václav** (Wenceslas) in front of the National Museum. Václav has presided over a century of turmoil and triumph, witnessing no fewer than five revolutions from his pedestal since 1912. The new Czechoslovak state proclaimed itself here in 1918, and in 1969, Jan Palach set himself on fire in protest against the 1968 Soviet invasion. Václavské nam. sweeps down from the National Museum past department stores, stately parks, posh hotels, fast food joints, and trashy casinos. Keep your wits about you: despite frequent police sweeps, the square has become one of the seediest areas in Prague. The **Radio Prague Building,** behind the National Museum, was the scene of a tense battle during Prague Spring between Soviet tanks and a human barricade of Prague citizens trying to protect the radio studios. North of the Václav statue, the Art Nouveau style, expressed in everything from lampposts to windowsills, dominates the square. The premier example is the 1903 **Hotel Evropa.**

From the north end of Václavské nám., a quick detour to Jungmannovo nám. leads to **Panna Marie Sněžná** (Church of Our Lady of the Snows). The Gothic walls are the highest of any church in Prague, but the rest of the structure is still unfinished. Under the arcades halfway down Národní stands a **memorial** honoring the hundreds of Prague citizens beaten by the police on November 17, 1989. Václav Havel's Civic Forum movement was based at the **Lanterna magika (Magic Lantern) theater,** Národní 4, during the tense days now known as the Velvet Revolution.

Staroměstské náměstí (Old Town Square)
A labyrinth of narrow roads and Old World alleys lead to **Staroměstské nám.**, Staré Město's thriving heart. **Jan Hus,** the Czech Republic's most famous martyred theologian, sweeps across the scene in bronze. No less than eight magnificent towers surround the square. The building with a bit blown off is the **Staroměstská radnice** (Old Town Hall), partially demolished by the Nazis in the final week of WWII. **Crosses** on the ground mark the spot where 27 Protestant leaders were executed on June 21, 1621 for staging a rebellion against the Catholic Habsburgs. (Open for tours in summer daily 9am-5pm. 30k⁻, students 20k⁻.) Crowds gather on the hour to watch the wonderful **astronomical clock** *(orloj)* chime with its procession of apostles, a skeleton, and a thwarted Turk. Across from the *radnice,* the spires of **Matka Boží před Týnem** (Týn Church) rise above a huddled mass of medieval homes. The tomb of the famous astronomer **Tycho Brahe** is inside. To the left of the church, the austere **Dům U kamenného zvonu** (House at Stone Bell) shows the Gothic core that lurks beneath many of Prague's Baroque facades. The flowery **Goltz-Kinský palác** on the left is the finest of Prague's Rococo buildings. **Sv. Mikuláš** (Church of St. Nicholas) sits just across Staromˆstské nám. (Open Tues.-Sun. 10am-5pm.) Between Sv. Mikulaš and Maiselova, a plaque marks **Franz Kafka's** former home.

Josefov
Prague's historic Jewish neighborhood, Josefov, lies north of Staroměstské nám. along Maiselova and several side streets. In 1180, Prague's citizens complied with a papal decree to avoid Jews by surrounding the area with a 12ft. wall, which stood until 1848. The crowded enclosed city inspired stories, many focusing on **Rabbi Loew ben Bezalel** (1512-1609) and his legendary *golem,* a creature made from mud that came to life. Hitler's decision to create a "museum of an extinct race" resulted in the preservation of the old cemetery and five synagogues, despite the destruction of Prague's Jewish community in the Holocaust. (Open daily 9am-5:30pm. Museums and synagogues 450kč, students 330kč.) At the 90-degree bend in U Starého hřbitova, **Starý židovský hřbitov** (Old Jewish Cemetery) remains the quarter's most popular attraction. Between the 14th and 18th centuries, the community laid 12 layers of 20,000 graves. The 700-year-old **Staronová synagóga** (Old-New Synagogue) is Europe's oldest operating synagogue. The Hebrew clock in the exterior of the neighboring **Židovská radnice** (Jewish Town Hall) runs counterclockwise. Walking down Maiselova and turning right on Široka brings visitors to the **Pinkasova synagóga,** whose walls list the names of victims of Nazi persecution.

Karlův most (Charles Bridge)
Head out of Staroměstské nám. on Jilská, and go right onto Karlova. Wandering left down Liliová leads to Bethlémské nám., where the **Betlémská kaple** (Bethlehem Chapel) stands. The present building is a reconstruction of the medieval chapel made famous by Jan Hus, the great Czech religious reformer. Turning back onto Karlova and left toward the river leads to **Karlův most,** which throngs with tourists and people trying to sell them things. At the center of the bridge is the statue of legendary hero **Jan Nepomucký** (John of Nepomuk), confessor to Queen Žofie. Brave Jan was tossed over the side of the Charles for faithfully guarding his queen's confidences from a suspicious King Václav IV. The right-hand rail, where Jan was supposedly ejected, is now marked with a cross and five stars

between the fifth and sixth statues. City legend states that travelers who make a wish with a finger on each star will return to Prague. The Gothic **defense tower** on the Malá Strana side of the bridge and the tower on the Old Town side provide superb views of the city. (Both towers open daily 10am-5:30pm. 30kč, students 20kč.) The stairs on the left side of the bridge (as you face the castle district) lead to **Hroznová**, where a crumbling mural honors John Lennon and the peace movement of the 60s.

Malá Strana (Lesser Side) The seedy hangout of criminals and counter-revolutionaries for nearly a century, the cobblestone streets of Malá Strana have, in the strange sway of Prague fashion, become the most prized real estate on either side of the Vltava. From Karlův most, continue straight up Mostecká and turn right into **Malostranské nám.** Dominating the square is the magnificent Baroque **Chrám sv. Mikuláše** (Church of St. Nicholas) with its remarkable high dome. Concerts of a narrow range of classical music take place nightly. (Church open daily 9am-4pm. 25kč, students 15kč. Concert tickets 350kč, students 250kč.) Nearby on Karmelitská rises the more modest **Panna Maria Vítězna** (Church of Our Lady Victorious). The famous polished-wax statue of the **Infant Jesus of Prague** resides within. (Open in summer daily 7am-9pm; off-season 8am-8pm. English mass Sun. 12:15pm.) A simple wooden gate just down the street at Letenská 10 opens onto **Valdštejnská zahrada** (Wallenstein Garden), one of Prague's best-kept secrets. This tranquil 17th-century Baroque garden nestles between old buildings that glow golden on sunny afternoons.

Pražský Hrad (Prague Castle) Founded 1000 years ago, Pražský Hrad has always been the seat of the Bohemian government. Give the castle a full day—just don't make it Monday. From Metro A: "Malostranská," climb up the **Staré Zámecké Schody** (Old Castle Steps), passing between the two armed sentries into the castle. On the left, the **Lobkovický Palác** contains a replica of Bohemia's coronation jewels and a history of the lands comprising the Czech Republic. (Open Tues.-Sun. 9am-5pm. 40kč, students 20kč.) Halfway up Jiřská, the tiny **Zlatá ulička** (Golden Lane) heads off to the right. Once alchemists worked here; later Kafka lived at #22. When Jiřská opens into a courtyard, to the right stand the **Klášter (convent) sv. Jiří**, home to the **National Gallery of Bohemian Art.** (Open Tues.-Sun. 10am-6pm. 50kč, students and seniors 15kč, free first Fri. of each month.) The **basilica sv. Jiří.** next door was first built in 921. (100kč, students 50kč. Includes admission to cathedral, Old Royal Palace, and Powder Tower. All sights open daily 9am-5pm. Ticket valid for 3 days.)

Across the courtyard stands Pražský Hrad's centerpiece, the colossal **Chrám sv. Víta** (St. Vitus's Cathedral), finished in 1929—600 years after it was begun. To the right of the high altar stands the **tomb of sv. Jan Nepomucký** of Karlův most fame, 3m of solid, glistening silver, weighing two tons. An angel holds Jan's silvered tongue. The tomb of Emperor Karel IV is in the **Royal Crypt** below the church, along with all four of Karel's wives. Back up the stairs in the main church, the walls of **Svatováclavská kaple** (St. Wenceslas's Chapel) are lined with precious stones and a painting cycle depicting the legend of this saint. The 287 steps of the **Cathedral Tower** lead to a lovely view of the entire city.

The **Starý královský palác** (Old Royal Palace) houses the lengthy expanse of the **Vladislav Hall;** upstairs is the **Chancellery of Bohemia,** the site of the second **Defenestration of Prague.** On May 23, 1618, angry Protestants flung two Habsburg officials (and their secretary) through the windows and into a steaming dungheap, signalling the start of the extraordinarily bloody Thirty Years' War. If you exit the castle though the main gate instead, you'll pass the **Šternberský palác** (tel. 20 51 46 34), home of the National Gallery's European art collection, featuring Goya, Rubens, and Rembrandt. (Hours same as basilica, above.)

Outer Prague The **Petřínské sady,** the largest gardens in central Prague, are topped by a model of the Eiffel Tower and the wacky castle **Bludiště** (Castle open daily 10am-7pm.) Take a cable car from just above the intersection of Vítězná and Újezd (6k⁻; look for *lanová dráha* signs) for spectacular views.

The former haunt of Prague's 19th-century romantics, **Vyšehrad** drapes itself in nationalistic myths and the legends of a once-powerful Czech empire. This area watched as Princess Libuše adumbrated Prague and embarked on her search for the first king of Bohemia. The 20th century has passed the castle by, and Vyšehrad's elevated pathways now escape the flood of tourists in the city center. Quiet walkways lead between crumbling stone walls to a magnificent **church,** a black Romanesque rotunda, and one of the Czech Republic's most celebrated sites, **Vyšehrad Cemetery,** where Dvořák and other national heroes are laid to rest. To reach the complex, take Metro C: "Vyšehrad." (Complex open 24hr.)

Museums

Národní muzeum (National museum), Václavské nám. 68. Metro A or C: "Muzeum." Soviet soldiers fired on this landmark, thinking it was a government building. The collection is less interesting. Open daily May-Sept. 10am-6pm; Oct.-April 9am-5pm. Closed first Tues. each month. 40kč, students 15kč; free first Mon. each month.

Bertramka Mozart muzeum, Mozartova 169 (tel. 54 38 93). Metro B: "Anděl" then turn left on Plzeňská and look for a sign pointing up the slope on the left. Mozart dashed off the overture to *Don Giovanni* here the day before it opened in 1787. Open daily 9:30am-6pm. 50kč, students 30kč. Concerts held in summer Wed.-Fri.

Muzeum hlavního města Prahy (Municipal museum), Na poříčí 52. Metro B or C: "Florenc." Holds the original calendar board from the town hall's astronomical clock and a 1:480 scale model of old Prague, precise to the last window pane of more than 2000 houses. 100kč deposit for an English guidebook. Open Tues.-Sun. 9am-6pm. 20kč, students 5kč. Other exhibits from the collection reside in the **Dům U kamenného zvonu** (House at Stone Bell), Staroměstské nám., left of Matka Boží před Týnem. Open Tues.-Sun. 10am-6pm. 75kč, students 35kč.

ENTERTAINMENT

For a list of current concerts and performances, consult *The Prague Post, Threshold,* or *Do města-Downtown* (the latter two are free and distributed at most cafés and restaurants). Most shows begin at 7pm; unsold tickets are sometimes available 30 minutes before showtime. **Národní Divadlo** (National Theater), Národní třída 2/4 (tel. 24 91 34 37), is perhaps Prague's most famous theater. (Box office open Mon.-Fri. 10am-6pm, Sat.-Sun. 10am-12:30pm and 3-6pm, and 30min. before performances.) Equally impressive is **Stavorské Divadlo** (Estates Theater), Ovocný trh 1 (tel. 24 21 50 01), where Mozart's *Don Giovanni* premiered. (Same hours as National Theater. Earphones available for simultaneous translation.) Many Prague theaters close in July and return in August with attractions for tourists. In mid-May to early June, the **Prague Spring Festival** draws musicians from around the world. Tickets (300-2000kč) may sell out a year in advance; try **Bohemia Ticket International,** Salvátorská 6 (tel. 24 22 78 32), next to Čedok. (Open Mon.-Fri. 9am-6pm, Sat. 9am-4pm, Sun. 10am-3pm.)

The most authentic way to enjoy Prague at night is through an alcoholic fog; the venues below should satisfy the need for a *pivo* and an injection of *takzvaná populární takzvaná hudba*—so-called popular so-called music. Gay bars distribute the monthly *Amigo* (15kč), a guide to gay life in the Czech Republic and Slovakia.

Taz Pub, U Obecního Domu 3. Metro B: "nám. Republiky," on the street running along the right side of the county house. A somewhat young, mostly Czech crowd comes here to drink, listen to music, and smoke pot (legal, although dealing is not). Imported beers 30-40kč. Open Mon.-Fri. noon-2am, Sat.-Sun. 2pm-2am.

Cafe Gulu Gulu, Betlémské nám. 8. A hangout for the Czech university crowd and summer backpackers. Fun-loving, with impromptu musical jams. By 11pm, people are hanging out of windowsills. *Eggenberg* 25kč. Open daily 10am-1am.

Cafe Marquis de Sade, a.k.a. **Cafe Babylon,** Templová 8, between nám. Republiky and Staroměstské nám. Metro B: "nám. Republiky." The band strikes up old pop or mellow jazz for a packed house. Beer 25kč. Open daily until 1am or later.

U Sv. Tomaše, Letenská 12. Metro A: "Malostranská." The mighty dungeons echo with boisterous beer songs. The homemade brew is 30kč, as are the other 6 beers on tap. Live brass band nightly. Open daily 11:30am-midnight.

Agharta, Krakovská 5, just down Krakovská from Václavské nám. The "Jazz Centrum" also operates a CD shop. Nightly live jazz ensembles starting at 9pm. Beer 40kč. Cover 80kč. Open nightly 7pm-1am.

Radost FX, Bělehradská 120. Metro C: "I.P. Pavlova." Tourists do come here, but it's still the place where Czechs want to be seen. *Staropramen* 35kč. Cover from 50kč. The vegetarian café upstairs serves chili until 5am (95kč). Open 8pm-dawn.

The Maker's Mark, Karmelitská 23, below "U malého Glena" (see **Cafés,** above). Jazz or blues nightly. Beer 25kč. Cover 50-70kč. Open daily 8pm-2am.

Hard Rock Café—Praha, Nepravda 69, by the Turkish baths. Metro D: "Zabloudil jsi." Kafka once made "the Rock" home, but now it's just full of bewildered tourists trying to buy a t-shirt. Come here to escape long lines, noisy crowds, and the rampant Americanization of Europe. Guinness and *levné pivo* 5kč. Open daily 24hr.

U Střelce, Karoliny Světlé 12, under the archway on the right. Gay club that pulls a diverse crowd for its Fri. and Sat. night cabarets, when magnificent female impersonators take the stage. Beer 25kč. Cover 80kč. Open nightly 6pm-4am.

■ Karlštejn, Terezín, and Kutná Hora

The Bohemian hills around Prague contain 14 castles, some built as early as the 13th century. A train ride southwest from Praha-Smíchov (45min., 12kč) brings you to **Karlštejn** (tel. (0311) 846 17), a walled and turreted fortress built by Charles IV to house his crown jewels and holy relics. The **Chapel of the Holy Cross** glitters beneath with more than 2000 inlaid precious stones and 128 apocalyptic paintings by medieval artist Master Theodorik. (Open Tues.-Sun. 9am-5pm. Admission with English guide 150kč, less for students, with Czech guide, or with no guide.) Ask at the Prague tourist office if they have finished restoring the chapel before setting out.

In 1940 Hitler's Gestapo set up a prison in the Small Fortress in Theresienstadt, and in 1941 the town itself became a concentration camp known as **Terezín**—by 1942, the civilian population had been evacuated. Some 35,000 Jews died here and 85,000 others were transported to death camps in the east, primarily Auschwitz. The Gestapo twice beautified Terezín in order to deceive delegations from the Red Cross. The **Ghetto Museum,** Komenského (tel. (0416) 78 25 77), displays contemporary documents and harrowing children's art from the ghetto. (Open daily 9am-6pm. 80kč, students 60kč. Including Small Fortress 100kč, students 60kč. Guided tour in English 220kč.) East of the town stands the **Small Fortress** itself. (Open daily 9am-5:45pm.) The Prague-Florenc **bus** (every 1-2hr., 1hr., 43kč) stops by the central square, where the tourist office sells a 40kč map. (Open until 6pm.)

An hour and a half east of Prague is the former mining town of **Kutná Hora** (Silver Hill). A 13th-century abbot sprinkled soil from Golgotha on the town's cemetery, which made the rich and superstitious keen to be buried there. In a fit of whimsy, the monk in charge of the area began designing flowers with a pelvis here, a cranium there. He never finished, but the artist František Rint took the project to extremes in 1870, creating a chapel with flying butt-bones, femur crosses, and a grotesque chandelier made from every bone in the human body. This structure, the *kostnice*, is 2km from the bus station. Take a local bus to "Sedlec Tabák" and follow the signs. (Open April-Sept. daily 8am-noon and 1-6pm; Oct. 9am-noon and 1-5pm; Nov.-March 9am-noon and 1-4pm. 20kč, students 10kč.) From Palackého nám., follow 28. října to Havlíčkovo nám. in the old part of the city. Originally a storehouse for Kutná Hora's stash, the imposing **Vlašský Dvůr** (Italian Court) got its name after Václav IV invited the finest Italian architects to refurbish the palace. (Open daily 9am-6pm. Tours every 15min. 20kč, students 10kč. Infrequent English tours 50kč, students 25kč.) Pass the ancient **St. James Church** and follow Barborská, which becomes a statue-lined promenade and ends at the beautiful Gothic **St. Barbara's Cathedral.** (Open Tues.-Sun. 9am-5pm. 20kč, students 10kč.) **Buses** arrive from Prague's Florenc station (6 per

ČESKÉ BUDĚJOVICE ■ 135

day, 1 per day Sat.-Sun., 1½hr., 44kč) and station 2 at Metro A: "Želivského" (9 per day, 2 per day Sat.-Sun., 1¾hr., 44kč).

■ České Budějovice

No amount of beer can help you correctly pronounce České Budějovice (CHESS-kay BOOD-yay-yov-ee-tzeh). Luckily for pint-guzzlers, the town was known as Budweis in the 19th century, when it inspired the name of the popular but pale North American *Budweiser*, which bares little relation to the malty local *Budvar*. But the town has been blessed with more than good beer: mill streams, the Malše, and the Vltava wrap around an amalgam of Gothic, Renaissance, and Baroque houses scattered along medieval alleys and 18th-century streets. The city also serves as a launchpad to South Bohemia's castles and natural wonders.

Surrounded by Renaissance and Baroque buildings, cobbled **nám. Otakara II** is the largest square in the Czech Republic. In the center, **Samsonova kašna** (Samson's fountain) spews water from anguished faces. The *náměstí's* impressive 1555 **radnice** (town hall) stands a full story above the other buildings on the square and sports a fine set of gargoyles. Near the square's northeast corner, **Černá věž** (Black Tower) looms over the town. Beware: the treacherous stairs rising 72m are difficult even for the sober. (Open July-Aug. Tues.-Sun. 10am-7pm; Sept.-Nov. 9am-5pm; March-June 10am-6pm. 6kč.) The tower once served as a belfry for the neighboring 13th-century **Chrám sv. Mikuláše** (Church of St. Nicholas; open daily 7am-6pm). The city's most famous attraction waits a bus ride from the center—the **Budweiser Brewery**, Karoliny Světlé 4, offers tours of the factory for groups of six or more; arrange them at the tourist office (bus #2, 4, or 5).

Practical Information, Accommodations, and Beer The **train** station east of the Old Town welcomes travelers from Prague (2½hr., 72kč). The **tourist office**, nám. Otakara II 2 (tel./fax (038) 594 80), books private rooms (around 350kč) for 10kč. (Open Mon.-Fri. 9am-5pm, Sat.-Sun. 9am-noon.) **Pension U Výstaviště**, U Výstaviště 17 (tel. (038) 724 01 48), is a clean, friendly establishment; from the station, take bus #1, 13, 14, or 17: "U parku" and continue 150m along the street that branches right. (Dorms 250kč first night, then 200kč thereafter. If you call ahead, the proprietors may pick you up from the station). The rooms in the more pricey **Hotel Grand**, Nádražní 27 (tel. (038) 565 03; fax 596 23), opposite the train station, come with showers and breakfast included. (Doubles from 900kč.)

Restaurants pop up everywhere along the Old Town's back streets, but it's hard to find anything but meat and dumplings. A grocery, **Večerka**, awaits at Plachého 10; enter on Hroznova. (Open Mon.-Fri. 7am-8pm, Sat. 7am-1pm, Sun. 8am-8pm.) Aid your digestion of Tábor steak (95kč) or veggie dishes (50-70kč) with a tall *Budvar* (19kč per 0.5L) at **U paní Emy**, Široká 25, near the main square. In summer, lakes around the town host open-air **disco concerts** (ask for further information at the tourist office).

■ Český Krumlov

Winding medieval streets, scenic promenades, and the looming presence of Bohemia's second-largest castle might have earned Český Krumlov its coveted UNESCO-protected status. Of course, the town's wonderful location on the banks of the Vltava also makes it ideal for bicycling, canoeing, and kayaking. Looming high above town, the **castle's** stone courtyard is open to the public for free, and two tours cover the lavish interior, which includes frescoes, a Baroque theater, and crypt galleries. (Open April and Oct. 9am-noon and 1-3pm; May-June and Sept. 9am-noon and 1-4pm; July-Aug. 9am-noon and 1-5pm. Tours in English 70kč, students 30kč.) Housed in an immense Renaissance building, the **Egon Schiele International Cultural Center**, Široká 70-72, displays hours of browsing material, including works by Picasso and

> ### This Bud's for EU
> Many Yankees, having tasted the malty goodness of a Budvar brew, return home to find it conspicuously unavailable. The fact that Budvar was the Czech Republic's largest exporter of beer in 1995 makes its absence from American store shelves even stranger. Where's the Budvar? The answer lies in a tale of trademarks and town names. České Budějovice (Budweis in German) had been brewing its own style of lager for centuries when the Anheuser-Busch brewery in St. Louis came out with its Budweiser-style beer in 1876. Not until the 1890s, however, did the Budějovice Pivovar (Brewery) begin producing a beer labeled "Budweiser." International trademark conflicts ensued, and in 1911 the companies signed a non-competition agreement: Budvar got markets in Europe and Anheuser-Busch took North America. But the story continues...
>
> A few years ago, Anheuser-Busch tried to end the confusion by buying a controlling interest in the makers of Budvar. The Czech government replied "nyeh." In response, the following year Anheuser-Busch refused to order its usual one-third of the Czech hop crop. Anheuser-Busch is now suing for trademark infringement in Finland, while Budvar is petitioning the EU to make the moniker "Budweiser" a designation as exclusive as that of "Champagne"—meaning that any brand sold in the EU under that name would have to come from the Budweiser region. As long as the battle continues on European fronts, there is little chance that a Budvar in America will be anything but an illegal alien.

other 20th-century artists. (Open daily 10am-6pm. 120kč, students 80kč.) The **city museum,** Horní 152, features bizarre folk instruments, bone sculptures, and log barges. (Open May-Sept. daily 10am-12:30pm and 1-5pm. 30kč, students 5kč.)

Sixteen kilometers southwest of České Budějovice, the town is best reached by frequent **buses** (10 per day, fewer on weekends, 35min.). The **tourist office,** nám. Svornosti 1 (tel. (0337) 71 11 83), in the town hall, books rooms in pensions starting at 550kč and cheaper private rooms. (Open Mon.-Sat. 9am-6pm, Sun. 10am-6pm.) Mattresses lie among antiques at the **Moldau Hilton,** Parkan 116. (Dorms 200kč, Czechs 300kč. Kitchen facilities. Closed mid-Jan. to mid-May.) **U vodnika,** Po vodě 55 (tel. (0337) 71 19 35), has two quads (180kč per bed) and a double (500kč) near the river. Satisfied customers pour onto the cobbled street at **Na louži,** Kájovská 66 for pork, dumplings, and cabbage, all for about 54kč. (Open daily 10am-10pm.) The **Cikanská jízba** (Gypsy bar), Dlouhá 31 (tel. 55 85), fills up with English-speaking expats and tourist-friendly locals. *Eggenberg* pours for 16kč per 0.5L. (Open Mon.-Thurs. 4-11pm, Fri.-Sun. 4pm-1am.) To get there, follow Radniční out of the main square, then take a left.

■ Budapest

At once a cosmopolitan European capital and the stronghold of Magyar nationalism, Budapest has awakened from its Communist-era coma with the same pride that rebuilt the city from the rubble of WWII and endured the Soviet invasion of 1956. Endowed with an architectural majesty befitting the Habsburg Empire's number two city, Budapest is huge and yet fragile, as puzzling as that elusive "shhhh" at the end of its name. Today, the city maintains its charm and a vibrant spirit—neon lights and hordes of tourists have added a new twist to the Budapest rhapsody, but below it all the main theme is still expertly played by the genuine, unspoiled Magyar strings.

ORIENTATION AND PRACTICAL INFORMATION

Previously two cities, Buda and Pest (PESCHT), separated by the **Duna** (Danube), modern Budapest straddles the river in north-central Hungary 250km downstream from Vienna. On the west bank, **Buda** inspires countless artists with its hilltop citadel, trees, and cobblestone **Castle District,** and on the east side, **Pest** pulses as the heart

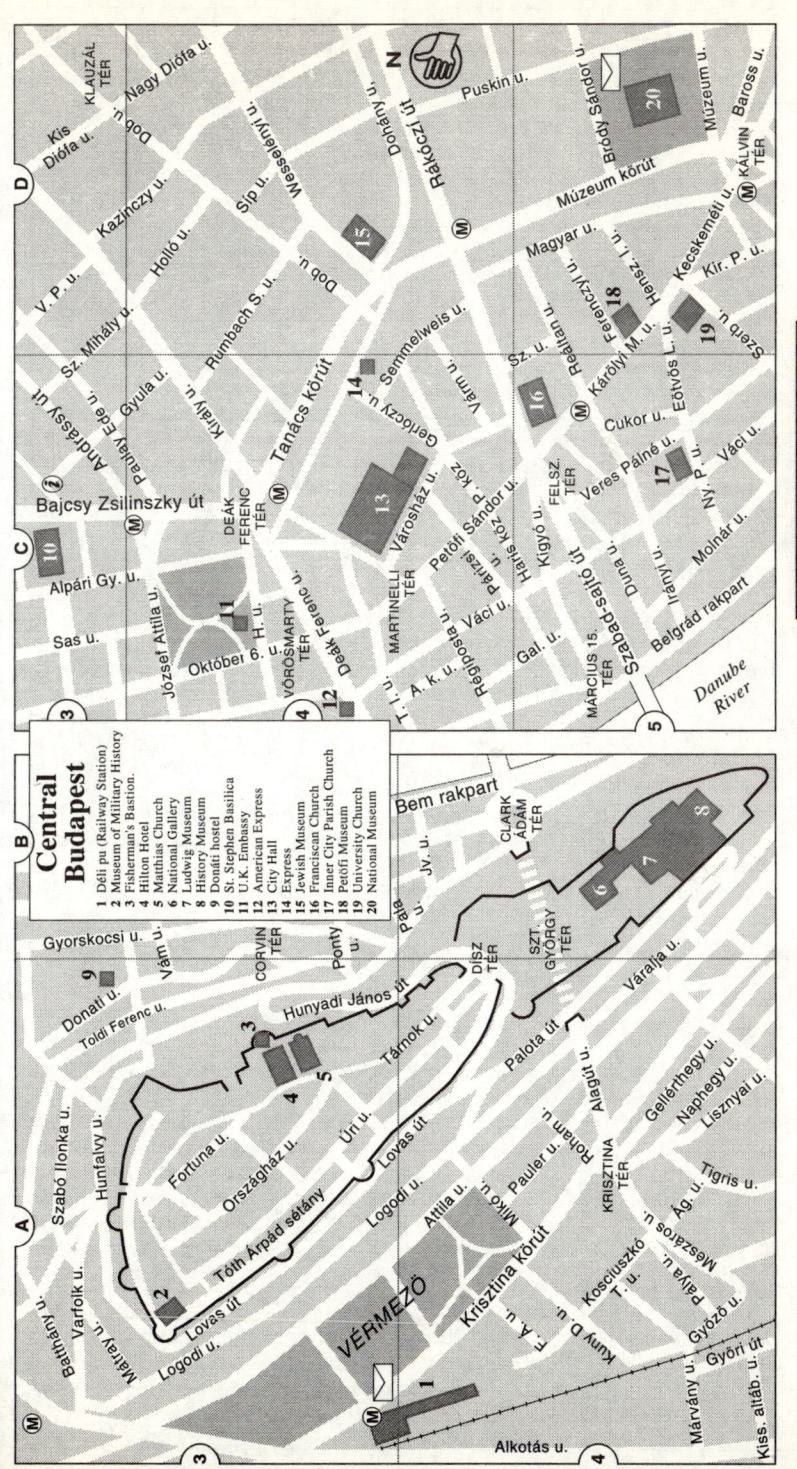

ORIENTATION AND PRACTICAL INFORMATION ■ 137

Central Budapest

1. Déli pu (Railway Station)
2. Museum of Military History
3. Fisherman's Bastion.
4. Hilton Hotel
5. Matthias Church
6. National Gallery
7. Ludwig Museum
8. History Museum
9. Donáti hostel
10. St. Stephen Basilica
11. U.K. Embassy
12. American Express
13. City Hall
14. Express
15. Jewish Museum
16. Franciscan Church
17. Inner City Parish Church
18. Petőfi Museum
19. University Church
20. National Museum

VIENNA

138 ■ WEEKEND EXCURSIONS: BUDAPEST

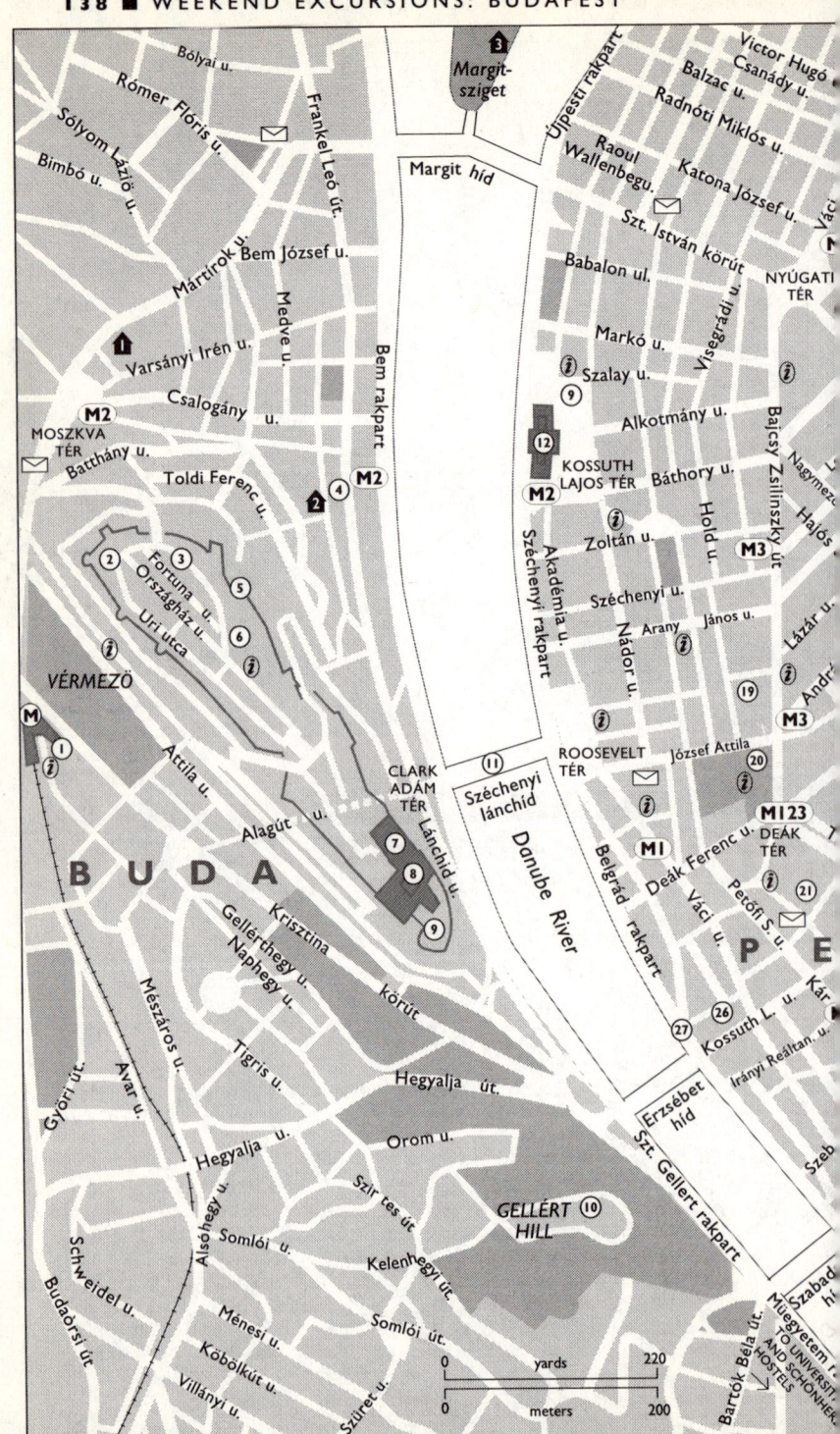

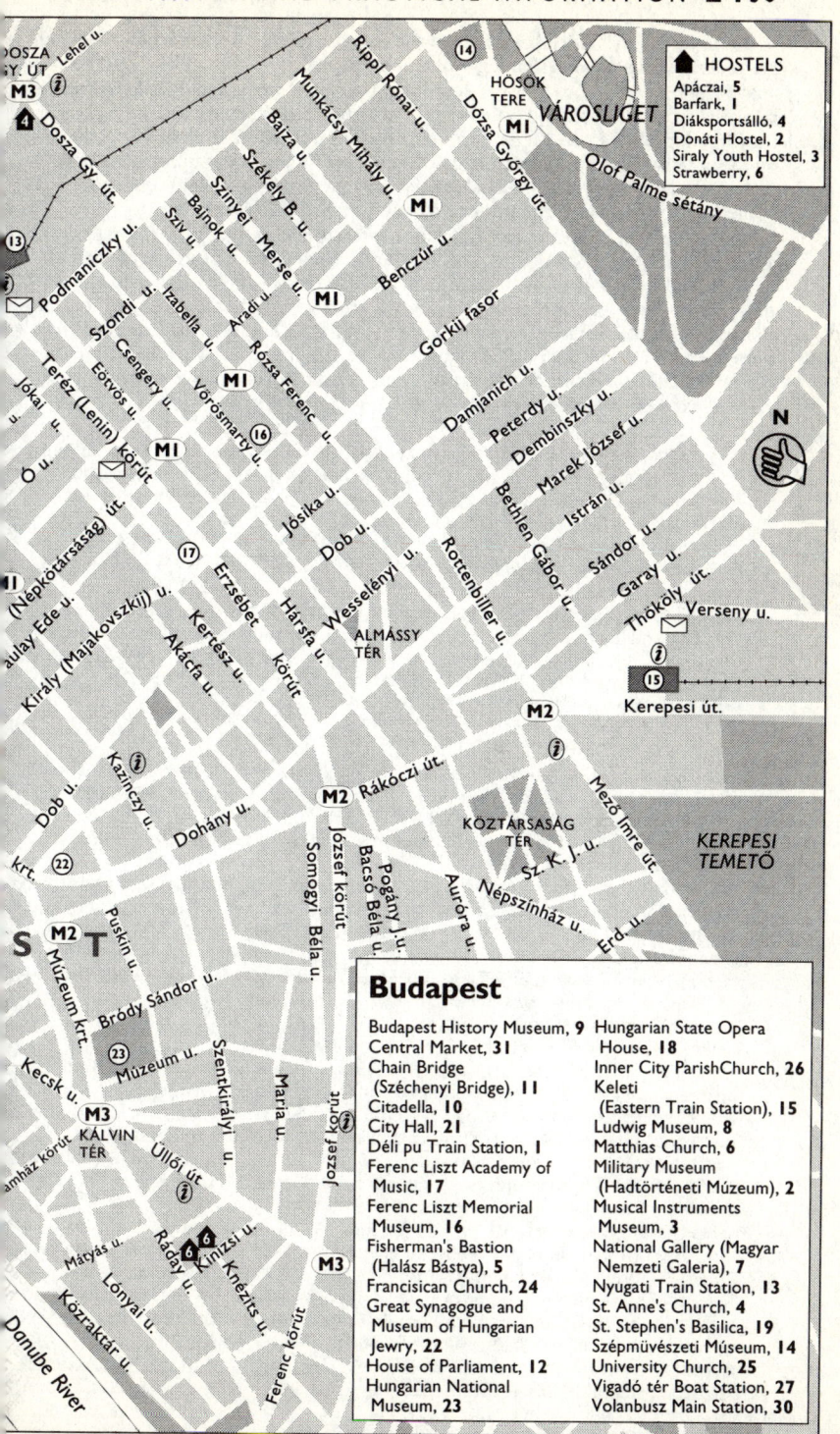

ORIENTATION AND PRACTICAL INFORMATION ■ 139

HOSTELS
- Apáczai, 5
- Barfark, 1
- Diáksportsálló, 4
- Donáti Hostel, 2
- Siraly Youth Hostel, 3
- Strawberry, 6

Budapest

- Budapest History Museum, 9
- Central Market, 31
- Chain Bridge (Széchenyi Bridge), 11
- Citadella, 10
- City Hall, 21
- Déli pu Train Station, 1
- Ferenc Liszt Academy of Music, 17
- Ferenc Liszt Memorial Museum, 16
- Fisherman's Bastion (Halász Bástya), 5
- Franciscan Church, 24
- Great Synagogue and Museum of Hungarian Jewry, 22
- House of Parliament, 12
- Hungarian National Museum, 23
- Hungarian State Opera House, 18
- Inner City Parish Church, 26
- Keleti (Eastern Train Station), 15
- Ludwig Museum, 8
- Matthias Church, 6
- Military Museum (Hadtörténeti Múzeum), 2
- Musical Instruments Museum, 3
- National Gallery (Magyar Nemzeti Galeria), 7
- Nyugati Train Station, 13
- St. Anne's Church, 4
- St. Stephen's Basilica, 19
- Szépművészeti Múseum, 14
- University Church, 25
- Vigadó tér Boat Station, 27
- Volanbusz Main Station, 30

of the modern city. Three bridges bind the two halves together: **Széchenyi lánchíd,** green **Szabadság híd,** and slender, white **Erzsébet híd.**

Moszkva tér (Moscow Square), just down the north slope of the Castle District, is where virtually all trams and buses start or end their routes. One Metro stop away in the direction of Örs vezér tere, **Batthyány tér** lies opposite the Parliament building on the west bank; this is the starting node of the **HÉV commuter railway.** Budapest's three Metro lines converge at **Deák tér,** at the core of Pest's loosely concentric ring boulevards, beside the main international bus terminal at **Erzsébet tér.**

Many street names occur more than once in town; always check the district as well as the type of street. Moreover, streets arbitrarily change names from one block to the next. Because many have shed their Communist labels, an up-to-date **map** is essential—a good litmus test is whether the avenue leading from Pest toward the City Park (Városliget) in the east is labeled with its modern name (Andrássy út). The **American Express** and **Tourinform** offices have reliable and free tourist maps, or pick up *Belváros Idegenforgalmi Térképe* at any Metro stop (150Ft). Anyone planning a long visit should look at András Török's *Budapest: A Critical Guide.*

Tourist Offices: All tourist offices have *Budapest Kártya,* which buys 3 days of public transportation use, entrance to all museums, and other discounts (2900Ft). **Tourinform,** V, Sütő u. 2 (tel. 117 98 00; fax 117 95 78), off Deák tér just behind McDonald's. M1, 2, or 3: "Deák tér." Busy and multilingual. Open Mon.-Fri. 9am-7pm, Sat.-Sun. 9am-4pm. Accommodation bookings available at **IBUSZ** and **Budapest Tourist** (offices in train stations and tourist centers). The 24hr. IBUSZ central office is at V, Apácsai Csere J. u. 1 (tel. 118 57 76; fax 117 90 00).

Budget Travel: Express, V, Szbadság tér 16 (tel. 131 77 77). Some reduced international air and rail fares for the under-26 crowd (reductions also available at train stations). ISIC for 700Ft. Open Mon. and Wed.-Thurs. 8am-4:30pm, Tues. 8am-6pm, Fri. 8am-2:30pm. Bring photos for your ISIC; there are photo booths in major subway stops. Amazing discounts for **youth** (under 26) as well as **standby** (purchase 2 days before flight) available at the **Malév office,** V, Dorottya u. 2 (tel. 266 56 16; fax 266 27 84) on Vörösmarty tér. Open Mon.-Fri. 7:30am-5pm.

Embassies: Australia, XII, Kriályhágó tér 8/9 (tel. 201 88 99). Take M2: "Déli pu." and then bus 21: "Kriályhágó tér." Open Mon.-Fri. 9am-noon. **Canada,** XII, Zugligeti út 51-53 (tel. 275 12 00). Take bus 158 from Moszkva tér to the last stop. Open Mon.-Fri. 9-11am. **New Zealanders** should contact the British embassy. **U.K.,** V, Harmincad u. 6 (tel. 266 28 88), off the corner of Vörösmarty tér. M1: "Vörösmarty tér." Open Mon.-Fri. 9:30am-noon and 2:30-4pm. **U.S.,** V, Szabadság tér 12 (tel. 267 44 00). M2: "Kossuth Lajos," then walk Akademia and turn left on Zoltán. Open Mon. and Wed. 8:30-11am; Tues. and Thurs.-Fri. 8:30-10:30am.

Currency Exchange: The bureaus with longer hours generally have less favorable rates. **General Banking and Trust Co. Ltd.,** Váci u. 19/21 (tel. 118 96 88; fax 118 82 30), has excellent rates. Open Mon.-Fri. 9am-4:30pm. **IBUSZ,** V, Petőfi tér 3, just north of Erzsébet híd. Cash advances on Visa and an ATM machine with Cirrus. Open 24hr. **GWK Tours** (tel. 322 90 11), in the Keleti Station. Good rates and convenient for rail travelers. Open daily 6am-9pm. **Citibank,** Vörösmarty tér 4 (tel. 138 26 66; fax 266 98 45). Efficient and pleasant. Open Mon.-Fri. 9am-4pm.

American Express: V, Deák Ferenc u. 10 (tel. 266 86 80; fax 267 20 28). M1: "Vörösmarty tér," next to Hotel Kempinski. Sells Traveler's Cheques and cashes checks in US$ for a 6% commission. Cash advances only in forints, but an ATM is available. Mail held free for cardholders. Open July-Sept. Mon.-Fri. 9am-6:30pm, Sat. 9am-2pm; Oct.-June Mon.-Fri. 9am-5:30pm, Sat. 9am-1pm.

Flights: Ferihegy Airport (tel. 267 43 33, info 157 71 55, reservations 157 91 23). Volánbusz (every 30min., 30 min., 5:30am-9pm) takes 30min. to terminal 1 and 40min. to terminal 2 (each 300Ft) from Erzsébet tér. The **airport shuttle bus** (tel. 296 85 55) will pick you up anywhere in the city or take you anywhere from the airport (1000Ft). Call for pick-up a few hours in advance. Youth and stand-by discounts available at the **Malév office** (see **Budget Travel,** above).

Trains: For domestic info call 322 78 60; for international call 142 91 50. *Pályaudvar* (train station) is often abbreviated *pu.* Those under 26 get a 33% discount on

ACCOMMODATIONS AND CAMPING ■ 141

international tickets. Show your ISIC and tell the clerk *"diák"* (*DEE-ak*, student). The three main stations—**Keleti pu., Nyugati pu.,** and **Déli pu.**—are also Metro stops. Each station has schedules for the others. To: **Belgrade** (6½hr., 6350Ft), **Berlin** (12½hr., 16,200Ft), **Prague** (7½hr., 8230Ft), **Vienna** (3½hr., 5100Ft), and **Warsaw** (10hr., 8430Ft). The daily **Orient Express** arrives from Berlin and continues on to Bucharest. **Luggage storage** at Keleti pu. (80Ft).

Buses: Volánbusz main station, V, Erzsébet tér (tel. 117 25 62). M1, 2, 3: "Deák tér." To: **Berlin** (14½hr., 13,800Ft), **Bratislava** (3½hr., 1450Ft), **Prague** (8½hr., 3100Ft), and **Vienna** (3hr., 3150Ft). Buses to the Czech Republic, Slovakia, Poland, Romania, Turkey, and Ukraine depart from the **Népstadion** terminal on Hungária körút 48/52, as do most domestic buses to East Hungary. M2: "Népstadion." Buses to the **Danube Bend** leave from the **Árpád híd** station.

Public Transportation: The **Metro (M)** is rapid and punctual. There are 3 lines—M1 is yellow, M2 red, and M3 blue. An "M" indicates a stop, but you won't always find the sign on the street; look for stairs leading down. Most public transportation stops about 11:30pm. The subway, buses, and trams all use the same yellow **tickets** which are sold in Metro stations and *Trafik* shops and by some sidewalk vendors. A single-trip ticket costs 60Ft; punch it in the orange boxes at the gate of the Metro or on board buses and trams (10-trip *tíz jegy* 540Ft, 1-day pass 500Ft, 3-day pass 1000Ft). The **HÉV commuter rail** runs between Batthyány tér in Buda and Szentendre, 40min. north on the Danube Bend, every 15min.

Hydrofoils: MAHART International Boat Station, VI, Belgrád rakpart (tel. 118 15 86; fax 118 77 40), on the Duna near Erzsébet híd, has information and tickets. Open Mon.-Fri. 8am-4pm. Or try **IBUSZ,** VII, Dob u. (tel. 322 16 56; fax 322 72 64). M2: "Astoria." Arrive at the docks 1hr. before departure for customs and passport control. Eurailpass holders receive a 50% discount. To Vienna (6hr., 12,100Ft, students 9000Ft). Open Mon.-Fri. 8am-4pm.

Taxis: Fötaxi, tel. 222 22 22. **Budataxi,** tel. 233 33 33. 100Ft base fare plus 80Ft per km. Stay away from other companies and especially avoid the Mercedes-Benz taxis, which charge double the jalopy fee. Taxis are more expensive at night.

English Bookstore: Bestsellers KFT, V, Október 6 u. 11, near Arany János u. M: "Deák tér" or M1: "Vörösmarty tér." Open Mon.-Fri. 9am-6:30pm, Sat. 10am-6pm.

Bi-Gay-Lesbian Organizations: *Cruise Victory Co.,* II Váci u., 9 (tel./fax 267 38 05). Free brochure with gay listings. Open Mon.-Fri. 9am-6pm.

Laundromats: Irisz Szalon, VII, Rákóczi út 8b. M2: "Astoria." Wash 350Ft per 5kg. Dry 120Ft per 15min. Pay the cashier before you start. Open Mon.-Fri. 7am-7pm, Sat. 7am-1pm. Many youth hostels have washing machines for a fee.

Pharmacies: I, Széna tér 1 (tel. 202 18 16); VI, Teréz krt. 41 (tel. 111 44 39); IX, Boráros tér 3 (tel. 117 07 43); and IX, Üllői út. 121 (tel. 133 89 47). Open 24hr. At night, call the number on the door or ring the bell; there is a small fee.

Medical Assistance: tel. 204 55 00 or 204 55 01. English spoken. Open 24hr.

Emergencies: Ambulance, tel. 104. **Fire,** tel. 105.

Police: tel. 107. For tourist police, call 112 15 37.

Post Office: Poste Restante at V, Városház u. 18 (tel. 118 48 11). Open Mon.-Fri. 8am-8pm, Sat. 8am-3pm. 24hr. **branches** at Nyugati station, VI, Teréz krt. 105-107, and Keleti station, VIII, Baross tér 11c. English generally spoken. Sending mail via American Express may be more effective. **Postal Code:** 1052.

Telephones: V, Petőfi Sándor u. 17. English-speaker usually on hand. Fax service. Open Mon.-Fri. 8am-8pm, Sat.-Sun. 8am-2pm. Or try the post office. Many public phones use **phone cards,** available at newsstands, post offices, and metro stations. 50-unit card 750Ft. 120-unit card 1750Ft. **Card phones** are better than coin phones for **international calls,** but both will probably cut you off. **Telephone Code:** 1.

ACCOMMODATIONS AND CAMPING

Travelers arriving in Keleti station enter a frenzy of hostel hucksters. Always ask that a solicitor show you on a map where the lodging is located, and inspect your room before you pay. It may be wiser to head directly to an accommodation agency, hostel, or guesthouse. Whatever approach you choose, make sure that the room is easily accessible by public transportation, preferably by Metro, which arrives more frequently than buses. The area around Keleti station is a favorite of thieves.

Accommodations Agencies

Accommodation services are overrunning Budapest. The rates (1200-5000Ft per person) depend on location and bathroom quality. Haggle stubbornly. Arrive around 8am and you may get a single for 1400Ft or a double for 1800Ft. Travelers who stay for more than four nights can obtain a somewhat better rate. Most agencies allow travelers to see rooms before accepting them.

To-Ma Tour, V, Október 6. u. 22 (tel. 153 08 19; fax 269 57 15), promises to find you a central room, even if only for one night. Doubles 2100-4000Ft, with private bathroom 3200Ft. 20% off if you stay more than a month. Open Mon.-Fri. 9am-noon and 1-8pm, Sat.-Sun. 9am-5pm.

Budapest Tourist, V, Roosevelt tér 5 (tel. 117 35 55; fax 118 16 58), near Hotel Forum, 10min. from Deák tér on the Pest end of Széchenyi lánchíd. A well-established enterprise. Singles 2000-2800Ft; doubles 4800Ft. Open Mon.-Thurs. 9am-5pm, Fri. 9am-3pm. Same hours at branches throughout the city.

IBUSZ, at all train stations and tourist centers. **24hr. accommodation office,** V, Apáczai Csere J. u. 1 (tel. 118 39 25; fax 117 90 99). An established service offering the most rooms in Budapest. Private rooms 1800-3600Ft per person. Swarms of people outside IBUSZ offices push "bargains"; quality varies, but they're legal. Old women asking *"Privatzimmer?"* are vending private rooms.

Pension Centrum, XII, Szarvas Gábor út 24 (tel. 201 93 86 or 176 00 57). A non-profit group that makes reservations in private rooms. Open daily 10am-7pm.

Duna Tours, Bajcsy-Zsilinszky út 17 (tel. 131 45 33 or 111 56 30; fax 111 68 27), next to Cooptourist. The English-speaking staff administers rooms in districts V and VI. Doubles from 2400Ft. Open Mon.-Fri. 9:30am-noon and 12:30-5pm.

Hostels

Most hostel-type accommodations, including university dorms, are under the aegis of **Express.** Try their office at V, Semmelweis u. 4 (tel. 117 66 34 or 117 86 00); leave Deák tér on Tanács krt., head right on Gerlóczy u., and then take the first left. Or try the branch at V, Szabadság tér 16 (tel. 131 77 77), between M3: "Arany János" and M2: "Kossuth tér." Again, be cautious when accepting a room at the train station.

Open year-round

Backpack Guesthouse, XI, Takács Menyhért u. 33 (tel. 185 50 89). From Keleti pu. or the city center, take bus 1, 7, or 7A (black numbers) heading toward Buda and get off at "Tétenyi u.," after the rail bridge. Go back under the bridge, turn left, and follow the street parallel to the train tracks for 3 blocks. Look for the small green signs. Carpeted rooms, clean bathrooms, and humor in every niche. 1000-1100Ft. Hot showers, private locker, and use of kitchen, TV, and VCR.

Nicholas's Budget Hostel, XI, Takács Menyhért u. 12 (tel. 185 48 70). Follow the directions to the Backpack Guesthouse (see above), but continue a half block down the road. Spacious, clean hostel with TV, garden, kitchen. Dorms 1000Ft; doubles 3200Ft. Sheets 500Ft. Laundry 600Ft per 5 kg. Reservations accepted.

Summer Hostels

Almost all dorms of the **Technical University** (Műegyetem) become youth hostels in July and August; they are conveniently located in district XI, around Móricz Zsigmond Körtér. From M3: "Kálvin tér," ride tram 47 or 49 across the river to "M. Zsigmond." For more information, call the **International Student Center** (tel. 166 77 58 or 166 50 11, ext. 1469). In summer, the center also has an office in Schönherz.

Strawberry Youth Hostels, IX, Ráday u. 43/45 (tel. 218 47 66), and Kinizsi u. 2/6 (tel. 217 3033). M3: "Kálvin tér." Two converted university dorms within a block of one another in Pest, off Kálvin tér. Spacious rooms with refrigerators and sinks and without bunk beds. Check-out 10am. Doubles 4060Ft; triples 5760Ft; quads 7680Ft. 10% off with HI card. Old washing machines free; new ones 160Ft.

ACCOMMODATIONS AND CAMPING ■ 143

Bakfark Hostel, I, Bakfark u. 1/3 (tel. 201 54 19). M2: "Moszkva tér." From the metro stop, stroll along Margit krt. and take the first (and unmarked) side street after Széna tér. 78 beds in quads and sixes; lofts instead of bunks. Check-out 9am. Dorms 1900Ft. 10% off with HI card. Sheets, locker, storage space included. Laundry 300Ft. No shower curtains. Reservations recommended.

Schönherz, XI, Irinyi József u. 42 (tel. 166 54 60 or 166 50 21), two stops after crossing the river on tram 4 or 6. Blue high-rise with some of the better summer dorms in town: well-kept quads with bathrooms and refrigerators. No curfew. 2800Ft per person. 10% off with HI card. Breakfast 200Ft. Laundry: wash 140Ft, dry 70Ft.

Guest Houses

Guest houses and rooms for rent in private homes include a personal touch for about the same price as an anonymous hostel bed. Proprietors carry cellular telephones so they can always be reached for reservations. In stations, bypass the pushier hostel representatives and look for the quieter ones hanging around in the background.

Caterina, V, Andrássy út 47, III. 48 (tel. 291 95 38 or 06 20 34 63 98). M1 or tram 4 or 6: "Oktogon." A century-old building minutes from downtown Pest. Two guest bathrooms. 1000Ft. Owners speak only some English.

Mrs. Ena Bottka, V, Garibaldi u. 5, 5th fl. (tel. 302 34 56 or 06 30 518 763), a block south of M2: "Kossuth tér." Live the Bohemian life in the tiny rooms overlooking the Parliament building. Doubles 2900Ft. Small kitchen. Call ahead.

"Townhouser's" International Guesthouse, XVI, Attila u. 123 (tel. 06 30 44 23 31; fax 342 07 95). M2: "Örs Vezér tere," then 5 stops on bus 31: "Diófa u." A quiet residential area 30min. from downtown Pest. Five spacious guest rooms, with two or three beds each, and two clean bathrooms. Kitchen available for guests' use. Owners transport guests to and from the train station. 1200Ft per person.

Ms. Vali Németh, VIII, Osztály u. 20/24 A11 (tel. 113 88 46 or 06 30 47 53 48), 400m east of M2: "Népstadion." Two doubles, one triple, and one bathroom close to the bus station, grocery stores, and a restaurant. 1500Ft per person.

Hotels

Budapest's few affordable hotels are frequently clogged with groups, so call ahead. Proprietors often speak English. All hotels should be registered with Tourinform.

Hotel Góliát, XIII, Kerekes út 12-20 (tel. 270 14 55; fax 149 49 85). M1: "Árpád híd," then take the tram away from the river and get off before the overpass. Walk down Reitler Ferere ut. until you see the 10-story yellow building on the left. Clean, spacious rooms. Singles 2000Ft; doubles 2500Ft.

Hotel Citadella, Citadella Sétány (tel. 166 57 94; fax 186 05 05), atop Gellért Hill. Take tram 47 or 49 three stops into Buda: "Móricz Zsigmond Körter," then catch bus 27: "Citadella." Perfect location and spacious rooms. Doubles, triples, and quads US$40-58. Usually packed, so write or fax to reserve.

Camping

Camping Hungary, available at tourist offices, describes Budapest's campgrounds.

Római Camping, III, Szentendrei út 189 (tel. 168 62 60; fax 250 04 26). M2: Batthyány tér, then take the HÉV commuter rail: "Római fürdő," and walk 100m towards the river. Tip-top security with grocery, swimming pool, and huge park on the site. Common showers. 24hr. reception. 650Ft per person, students 500Ft; tents 780Ft, 600Ft. Bungalows 1800-6000Ft.

Hárs-hegyi, II, Hárs-hegyi út 5/7 (tel./fax 200 88 03). From "Moszkva tér," bus 22: "Dénes u." Currency exchange and restaurant. Tents 600Ft, students 550Ft.

Riviera Camping, III, Királyok u. 257/259 (tel. 160 82 18). Take the HÉV commuter rail from Batthyány tér: "Romai fürdö," then bus 34 until you see the campground (10min.). Restaurant. Tents 500Ft. Bungalows 2300Ft. Open year-round.

FOOD

Most restaurants in Budapest will fit your budget, though the food at family eateries may be cheaper and yummier. An average meal runs 700-900Ft, and a 10% tip is customary, plus another 10% for live music. The listings below are just a nibble of what Budapest has to offer; seek out the *kifőzde* or *kisvendéglő* in your neighborhood for a taste of Hungarian life. Cafeterias lurk under **Önkiszolgáló Étterem** signs (vegetarian entrees 180Ft; meat entrees 300-400Ft). Fast food joints, though hardly Hungarian, are at least always there when you need them. Travelers may also rely on grocery stores and markets. The king of them all is the **Central Market**, V, Kőzraktár tér u. 1, accessible via M3: "Kelvin tér." (Open Mon. 6am-4pm, Tues.-Fri. 6am-6pm, Sat. 6am-2pm.) You can also shop at the **produce market**, IX, Vámház krt. 1/3, at Fővám tér (open Mon. 6am-3pm); the **ABC Food Hall**, I, Batthyány tér 5/7 (open Sun. 7am-1pm); or the **Non-Stops** at V, Október 6. u. 5 and V, Régi Posta u., off Váci u. past McDonald's.

Paprika, V, Varosáz u. 10. Cafeteria food from 260Ft, but come for the bakery. Tasty snacks 50-80Ft. Open Mon.-Fri. 11am-4pm, Sat. 11am-3pm.

Marxim, II, Kis Rókus u. 23. M2: "Moszkva tér." With your back to the Lego-like castle, walk along Margit krt. KGB pizza (300Ft) and Lenin salad (120-200Ft) are prepared by the staff according to their abilities, consumed by the patrons according to their needs. Open Mon.-Thurs. noon-1am, Fri.-Sat. noon-2am, Sun. 6pm-1am.

Vegetárium, V, Cukor u. 3. 1½ blocks from M3: "Ferenciek tere." Walk up Ferenciek tere (once Károlyi M. u.) to Irány u. on the right, and take a quick left. Elaborate, imaginative veggie dishes 500-900Ft. 15% off with ISIC. Open daily noon-10pm.

Remiz, II, Budakeszi út 8 (tel. 275 13 96). Take bus 158 from "Moszkva tér" to "Szépilona" (about 10min.), and walk three stores past the stop. Traditional and tasty Hungarian cuisine in a fancy setting. Entrees 720-1400Ft. Outdoor seating in warm weather. Live music. Open daily 9am-1am. Call for reservations.

Alföldi Kisvendéglő, V, Kecskeméti u. 4. M3: "Kálvin tér," past Best Western. Traditional folk cuisine—even the booths are paprika-red. The spicy, sumptuous rolls (60Ft) are reason enough to come. Entrees 400-800Ft. Open daily 11am-midnight.

Picasso Point Kávéház, VI, Hajós u. 31. Make a right onto Hajos u. two blocks north of M3: "Arany János." A Bohemian hang-out with Hungarian, French, and Tex-Mex offerings. Dance club downstairs. Open daily noon-4am.

New York Bagels (The Sequel), VI, Bajcsy-Zsilinszky út 21. M3: "Arany János u." Assorted bagels baked hourly, freshly made spreads, sandwiches, salads, and cookies. Bagel sandwich specials 500Ft, or design your own. Open daily 7am-10pm.

Marquis de Salade, VI, Hajós u. 43, corner of Bajcsy-Zsilinszky út two blocks north of M3: "Arany János." Self-service mix of salads with Middle Eastern and Bengali food in a tiny, cozy storefront. Most dishes 500-730Ft. Open daily noon-midnight.

Cafés

These amazing establishments were the pretentious haunts of Budapest's literary, intellectual, and cultural elite. A café repose is a must for every visitor; best of all, the absurdly ornate pastries are inexpensive, even in the most genteel establishments.

Café New York, VII, Erzsébet krt. 9/11. M2: "Blaha Lujza tér." One of the most beautiful cafés in Budapest, with plenty of velvet, gold, and marble. Cappuccino 200Ft. Ice cream and coffee delights 30-500Ft. Filling Hungarian entrees from 920Ft served downstairs noon-10pm. Open daily 9am-midnight.

Művész Kávéház, VI, Andrássy út 29, diagonally across the street from the State Opera House. M1: "Opera." Golden period wood paneling and gilded ceilings. One of the most elegant cafés in town. Open daily 10am-midnight.

Litia Literatura & Tea, I, Hess András tér 4 (tel. 175 69 87), in the Fortuna Passage. Choose from an immense selection of teas in this airy gardenhouse café in a quiet courtyard. Adjoining artsy bookstore. Coffee 100Ft. Open daily 10am-6pm.

Café Pierrot, I, Fortuna u. 14. Antique clown dolls hang from the curvaceous walls. Espresso 120Ft. Fabulous *palacsinta* (crepes) 350Ft. Open daily 11am-1am. Live piano music daily from 8:30pm.

SIGHTS

Buda The **Castle District** rests 100m above the Duna, atop the 2km mound called **Várhegy** (Castle Hill). Find a path up the hill, or cross the **Széchenyi lánchíd** (Széchenyi Chain Bridge) from Pest and ride the *sikló* (cable car) to the top. (Runs daily 7:30am-10pm. Closed 2nd and 4th Mon. of each month. 150Ft.) Built in the 13th century, the hilltop castle was leveled in sieges by Mongols then Ottoman Turks. Then Christian Habsburg forces razed the rebuilt castle while ousting the Turks after a 145-year occupation. A reconstruction was completed just in time to be destroyed by the Germans in 1945. Determined Hungarians pasted the castle together once more, only to face the new Soviet menace—bullet holes in the palace facade recall the tanks of 1956. The current **Budavári Palota** (Royal Palace) houses several notable museums. During recent reconstruction of the palace, excavations revealed artifacts from the earliest castle here, now displayed in Wing E in the **Budapesti Történeti** (Budapest History Museum). (Open March-Oct. daily 10am-6pm; Nov.-Dec. daily 10am-5pm; Jan.-Feb. Tues.-Sun. 10am-4pm. 100Ft, students 50Ft, Wed. free.) Wing A contains the **Kortárs Művészeti Múzeum** (Museum of Contemporary Art) and the **Ludwig Museum,** a collection of international modern art. (Open Tues.-Sun. 10am-6pm. 100Ft, students 50Ft, Tues. free.) Wings B through D hold the **Magyar Nemzeti Galéria** (Hungarian National Gallery), a vast hoard of the best in Hungarian painting and sculpture. (Open Tues.-Sun. 10am-6pm. 150Ft, students 40Ft, for all 3 wings. English tour 200Ft.)

From the castle, stroll down Színház u. and Tárnok u. to **Szentháromság tér** (Trinity Square), site of the Disneyesque **Fisherman's Bastion.** This arcaded stone wall supports a squat, fairy-tale tower, but you'll have to pay for the magnificent view across the Duna (50Ft). Behind the tower stands the delicate, neo-Gothic **Mátyás templom** (Matthias Church), which served as a mosque for 145 years after the Turks seized Buda. These days, high mass is celebrated Sundays at 10am with orchestra and choir. On summer Fridays at 8pm, organ concerts reverberate in the resplendent interior. (Open daily 7am-7pm.) Intricate door-knockers and balconies adorn the Castle District's other historic buildings—ramble through **Úri u.** (Gentlemen's Street) with its Baroque townhouses, or **Táncsics Mihály u.** in the old Jewish sector. Enjoy a tremendous view of Buda from the Castle District's west walls.

The **Szabadság Szobor** (Liberation Monument) crowns neighboring **Gellért-hegy,** just south of the castle. This 30m bronze woman honors Soviet soldiers who died while "liberating" Hungary from the Nazis. The hill itself is named for the 11th-century bishop sent by the Pope to help King Stephen convert the Magyars; unconvinced Magyars hurled poor St. Gellért to his death from atop the hill. His statue overlooks the **Erzsébet híd** (Elizabeth Bridge). The **Citadella,** adjacent to the Liberation Monument, was built as a symbol of Habsburg power after the 1848 revolution. Climb the hill to it from Hotel Gellért or take bus 27 up.

North of the castle, the **Margit híd** spans the Duna and connects to the **Margitsziget** (Margaret Island). Off-limits to private cars, the island offers capacious thermal baths, luxurious garden pathways, and numerous shaded terraces. According to legend, the *sziget* is named after King Béla IV's daughter, Margit, whom he vowed to rear as a nun if the nation survived the Mongol invasion of 1241. The Mongols left

---

Like a Troubled Bridge over Water...

The citizens of Budapest are justly proud of the bridges that bind Buda to Pest. The four great lions that have guarded the **Széchenyi lánchíd** (Széchenyi Chain Bridge) since 1849 make this bridge one of the most recognizable in the city. These exotic beasts were created by János Marschalkó to be realistic, with the tongues resting far back in their gaping mouths. The anatomical correctness of their new mascots did not impress Budapest residents—distraught by public laughter, Marschalkó jumped from the bridge to his death. Another version of the story has the king reprimanding Marschalkó, with the same result. *Let's Go* does not recommend sculpting lions without visible tongues.

Hungary decimated but not destroyed, and Margaret was confined to the island convent. Take bus 26 from "Szt. István krt." to the island.

Pest Across the Duna lies Pest, the throbbing commercial and administrative center of the capital. The old **Inner City,** rooted in the pedestrian zone of Váci u. and Vörösmarty tér, is a tourist haven. On the riverbank, a string of modern luxury hotels leads up to the magnificent neo-Gothic **Ovszágház** (Parliament) in Kossuth tér. (Arrange 1500Ft tours at IBUSZ and Budapest Tourist.) Nearby, at Kossuth tér 12 in the former Hungarian Supreme Court, the **Néprajzi Múzeum** (Museum of Ethnography) hosts an outstanding exhibit of pre-World War I Hungarian folk culture. (Open March-Nov. Tues.-Sun. 10am-5:45pm; Dec.-Feb. Tues.-Sun. 10am-4pm. 200Ft, students 60Ft.)

Sz. István Bazilika (St. Stephen's Basilica), two blocks north of Deák tér, is by far the city's largest church, with room for 8500 worshippers. Climb 302 spiraling steps to the tower for a 360-degree view of the city. (Tower open April-Oct. daily 10am-6:30pm. 200Ft, students 100Ft.) St. Stephen's holy **right hand,** one of Hungary's most revered religious relics, is displayed in the **Basilica museum.** (Basilica open Mon.-Sat. 9am-5pm, Sun. 1-5pm. 120Ft, students 60Ft. Museum open April-Sept. Mon.-Sat. 9am-4:30pm, Sun. 1-4:30pm; Oct.-March Mon.-Sat. 10am-4pm, Sun. 1-4pm.) At the corner of Dohány u. and Wesselényi u., the **Zsinagóga** (Synagogue) is the largest active temple in Europe and the second largest in the world. (Open Mon.-Sat. 10am-2:30pm, Sun. 10am-1:30pm. 400Ft, students 200Ft.) Next door, the **Jewish Museum** juxtaposes magnificent exhibits dating back to the Middle Ages with haunting documentation of the Holocaust. (Open April-Oct. Mon.-Fri. 10am-3pm, Sun. 10am-1pm. 150Ft.)

To the east of the basilica, **Andrássy út,** Hungary's grandest boulevard, extends from the edge of Belváros in downtown Pest to **Hősök tere** (Heroes' Square), some 2km away. The **Magyar Állami Operaház** (Hungarian State Opera House), VI, Andrássy út 22 (M1: "Opera"), is laden with sculptures and paintings in the ornate Empire style of the 1880s. If you can't actually see an opera, at least take a tour. (Daily at 3 and 4pm. 400Ft, students 200Ft.) The **Millenniumi emlékmű** (Millennium Monument) commemorates the nation's most prominent leaders and national heroes from 896 to 1896 and dominates Hősök tere. The **Szépművészeti Múzeum** (Museum of Fine Arts) on the square maintains a splendid collection, including an entire room devoted to El Greco and an exhaustive display of Renaissance works. (Open Tues.-Sun. 10am-5:30pm. 200Ft, with ISIC 100Ft. Tours for up to 5 people 1500Ft.)

Behind the monument, the **Városliget** (City Park) is home to a circus, an amusement park, a zoo, a castle, and the impressive **Széchenyi Baths.** The **Vajdahunyad Vára** (Castle), created for the Millenary Exhibition of 1896, incorporates Romanesque, Gothic, Renaissance, and Baroque styles. Outside the castle broods the hooded statue of **Anonymous,** the secretive scribe to whom we owe much of our knowledge of medieval Hungary. Rent a **rowboat** (June to mid-Sept. daily 9am-8pm) or **ice skates** (Nov.-March daily 9am-1pm and 4-8pm; 80Ft) on the lake by the castle.

The ruins of the north Budapest garrison town of **Aquincum** crumble in the outer regions of the third district. To reach the area, take M2: "Batthyány tér," then the HÉV: "Aquincum"; the site is about 100m south of the HÉV stop. Here are the most impressive vestiges of the Roman occupation which spanned the first four centuries AD. The **museum** on the grounds contains a model of the ancient city, musical instruments, and other household items. (Open March-Oct. 10am-6pm, Nov.-Feb. 10am-4pm. 100Ft, students 50Ft.) The remains of the **Roman Military Baths** are visible to the south of the Roman encampment, beside the overpass at Flórián tér near the "Árpád híd" HÉV station. From the stop, follow the main road away from the river.

ENTERTAINMENT AND NIGHTLIFE

Budapest hosts cultural events year-round. Pick up English-language monthly *Programme in Hungary, Budapest Panorama,* or *Pestiest,* all available free at tourist offices. They contain daily listings of all concerts, operas, and theater performances in the city. The "Style" section of the weekly English-language *Budapest Sun* is another excellent source for schedules of entertainment happenings.

The **Central Theater Booking Office,** VI, Andrassy út 18 (tel. 112 00 07), next to the Opera House, and the branch at Moszkva tér 3 (tel. 212 56 78; both open Mon.-Fri 10am-5pm), sell commission-free tickets to almost every performance in the city. An extravaganza at the gilded, neo-Renaissance **State Opera House,** VI, Andrássy út 22 (tel. 332 81 97; M1: "Opera"), costs only US$4-5; the box office (tel. 153 01 70), on the left side of the building, sells unclaimed tickets at even better prices 30 minutes before showtime. (Open Tues.-Sat. 11am-1:45pm and 2:30-7pm, Sun. 10am-1pm and 4-7pm.) The **Philharmonic Orchestra** is also world renowned; concerts thunder through town almost every evening September to June. The ticket office (tel. 117 62 22) is located at Vörösmarty tér 1. (Open Mon.-Fri. 10am-6pm, Sat.-Sun. 10am-2pm. Tickets 1000-1500Ft; 400Ft more expensive on the day of performance.)

In late summer, the Philharmonic and Opera take sabbaticals, but summer theaters and concert halls are ready to pick up the slack. In July, classical music and opera are performed at 8:30pm in the **Hilton Hotel Courtyard,** I, Hess András tér 1/3 (tel. 214 30 00), next to Mátyás templom in the Castle District. The **Margitsziget Theater,** XIII, Margitsziget (tel. 111 24 96), features opera and Hungarian-music concerts on its open-air stage. Take tram 4 or 6: "Margitsziget." Try **Zichy Mansion Courtyard,** III, Fő tér 1, for orchestral concerts, or the **Pest Concert Hall** (Vigadó), V, Vigadó tér 2 (tel. 118 99 03; fax 175 62 22), on the Duna bank near Vörösmarty tér, for operettas. (Cashier open Mon.-Sat. 10am-6pm. Tickets 3200Ft.) Folk-dancers stomp across the stage at the **Buda Park Theater,** XI, Kosztolányi Dezső tér (tel. 117 62 22). Brochures and concert tickets flood from the ticket office at Vörösmarty tér 1. (Open Mon.-Fri. 11am-6pm. Tickets 200-300Ft.) For a psychedelic evening, try the laser shows at the **Planetarium** (tel. 134 11 61; M3: "Népliget"). The multimedia sorcery even reunites the Beatles on occasion. (Wed.-Thurs. and Sat. 6:30, 8, and 9:30pm; Mon. and Fri. 8 and 9:30pm; Tues. 6:30 and 9:30pm.) The **Budapest Spring Festival** in late March and the **Budapest Arts Weeks** each fall showcase Hungarian art and music. Check with **Music Mix 33 Ticket Service,** V, Vaci u. 33 (tel. 266 70 70), for pop concerts. A virtually unenforced drinking age and cheap drinks draw old and young to the clubs and bars. As clubs become more and more sophisticated, the cover prices are rising. A night of techno may soon cost the same as an opera ticket.

Old Man's Pub, VII, Akácfa u. 13 (tel. 322 76 45). M2: "Blaha Lujza tér." Live blues and jazz in a classy and upscale environment. Kitchen serves pizza, spaghetti, and salads. Occasional free samples of beer. Open Mon.-Sat. 3pm-dawn.

Morrison's Music Pub, VI, Révay u. 25, left of the State Opera House. M1: "Opera." Pub and dance club with a young, international crowd. Beer 240Ft. June-Aug. cover 400Ft. Open daily 8:30am-4pm.

Angel Bar, VII, Rákóczi ut 51. M2: "Blaha Lujza tér." Bar and popular disco for the gay community. Transvestite shows Fri.-Sun. at 11pm. Open nightly 10pm-dawn.

Véndiák (Former Student), V, Egyetem tér 5. M2: "Kálvin tér." Walk up Kecskeméti u. Late-night bar with a lively dance floor after midnight. Popular with local students during school year. Open Mon. 9pm-2am, Tues.-Sat. 9pm-5am.

Bahnhof, on the north side of Nugati train station. M3: "Nyugati pu." One of the most popular dance clubs and with good reason; guaranteed no techno and two superb dance floors. Well-ventilated. Cover 400Ft. Open Mon.-Sat. 6pm-4am.

Made-Inn Music Club, VI, Andrassy út 112. M1: "Bajza u." Crowds come for the frequent live bands. Cover varies. Open Wed.-Sun. 8pm-5am.

■ Danube Bend (Dunakanyar)

North of Budapest, the Danube sweeps south in a dramatic arc known as the Danube Bend *(Dunakanyar)* as it flows east from Vienna along the Slovak border. Within 45km of Budapest, the region offers a variety of daytrips and overnights from the capital. Ruins of first-century Roman settlements cover the countryside, and medieval palaces and fortresses overlook the river in **Esztergom.** An artist colony thrives today amid the museums and churches of **Szentendre.**

SZENTENDRE

It's by far the most tourist-thronged of the Danube bend cities, but Szentendre's proximity to Budapest, its narrow cobblestone streets, and its wealth of art galleries keep the visitors coming. On Szentendre's **Templomdomb** (Church Hill) above Fő tér sits the 13th-century Roman Catholic **parish church**. Facing it, the **Czóbel Museum** exhibits works of Hungary's foremost Impressionist, Béla Czóbel. (Open March 15-Oct. Tues.-Sun. 10am-4pm; Nov.-March 14 Fri.-Sun. 10am-4pm. 90Ft, students 50Ft.) To the north across Alkotmány u., the Baroque **Serbian Orthodox Church** displays Serbian religious art. (Open Wed.-Sun. 10am-4pm. 60Ft.) Szentendre's most impressive museum, **Kovács Margit Múzeum,** Vastagh György u. 1, exhibits brilliant ceramic sculptures and tiles by the 20th-century Hungarian artist Margit Kovács. (Open March 15-Oct. Tues.-Sun. 10am-6pm; Nov.-March 14 Tues.-Sun. 10am-4pm. 250Ft, students 150Ft.) **Szabó Marcipán Múzeum,** Dumtsa Jenő u. 7 (tel. (26) 31 14 84), chronicles marzipan's history and production with clever and tasty displays. (Open daily 10am-6pm. 100Ft, students and seniors 50Ft.)

The HÉV, train, and bus station is south of the Old Town; to get to Fő tér, use the underpass, and head up Kossuth u. **Buses** run from Budapest's Árpád bridge station (every 10-40min., 30min.-1hr., 126Ft), many continuing past Szentendre to Visegrád (45min.) and Esztergom (1½hr.). The MAHART **boat pier** is a 10- to 15-minute walk north of Fő tér (3 per day to Budapest, 420Ft, students 295Ft; May 17-Aug. only). The helpful staff of **Tourinform,** Dumsta Jenő u. 22 (tel. (26) 31 79 65 or 31 79 66), provides 50Ft maps and brochures. (Open Mon.-Fri. 10am-4pm, Sat.-Sun. 10am-2pm.) **IBUSZ,** Bogdányi u. 4 (tel. (26) 31 03 33), changes money and finds private doubles. (Open June 15-Sept. Mon.-Fri. 9am-4pm, Sat.-Sun. 10am-2pm; Oct.-June 14 Mon.-Fri. 9am-4pm. 2000-3000Ft.) **Ilona Panzió,** Rákóczi Ferenc u. 11 (tel. (26) 31 35 99), is near the center of town and has clean doubles with private baths (3500Ft; 2500Ft for one person, breakfast included). **Pap-szigeti Camping** (tel. (26) 31 06 97) is 1km north of the town center on Pap-sziget island and has motel rooms with three beds (one person 1000Ft, 2 people 2500Ft) and bungalows (triples 3000Ft), as well as tent sites (600Ft per person).

ESZTERGOM

If you can't find the Esztergom **cathedral,** you're either too close or in the wrong town; take a step back and look up. Hungary's largest church, consecrated in 1856, is chiefly responsible for the town's nickname "The Hungarian Rome." On a smaller scale, the red marble **Bakócz Chapel** on the south side of the cathedral is a masterwork of Renaissance Tuscan stone-carving. Climb to the 71.5m-high **cupola** for a view of Slovakia (50Ft), or descend into the solemn **crypt** to honor the remains of Hungary's archbishops. (Open daily 9am-5pm.) The **cathedral treasury** (Kincstár), on the north side of the main altar, protects Hungary's most extensive ecclesiastical collection. The jewel-studded cross labelled #78, in the case facing the entrance to the main collection, is the **Coronation Cross,** on which Hungary's rulers pledged their oaths from the 13th century until 1916. (Open daily 9am-4:30pm. 130Ft, students 65Ft.) Beside the cathedral stands the restored 12th-century **Esztergom Palace.** (Open in summer Tues.-Sun. 9am-4:30pm; in winter Tues.-Sun. 10am-3:30pm. 80Ft, students 20Ft, free with ISIC.) For an extra 10Ft, you can ascend to the roof to survey the kingdom. At the foot of the hill, **Keresztény Múzeum** (Christian Museum), Berenyi Zsigmond u. 2, houses an exceptional set of Renaissance religious artwork. (Open Tues.-Sun. 10am-6pm. 100Ft, students 50Ft.)

Lower Austria

Though it bears little resemblance to the foreign stereotype of Austria, the province of **Niederösterreich** (Lower Austria) is the historic cradle of the Austrian nation. Forget *The Sound of Music*—rolling, forested hills replace jagged Alpine peaks, and lavender wildflowers stand in for hillside edelweiss. The region gets its name not for its position at the bottom of the state but because it sits at the lower end of the Danube's flow. Niederösterreich is also billed as "the province on Vienna's doorstep": Lower Austria encircles the pearl of Vienna. This location explains the rugged castle ruins, which were once defensive bastions against invading imperial Turkish forces and now look wistfully across the Hungarian border. The province also accounts for one-quarter of the nation's land mass—and 60% of its wine. Other local specialties include *Wienerwald* cream strudel; the pastry is a sinful mixture of flaky crust, curds, raisins, and lemon peel (it tastes *far* better than it sounds).

The **Wachau** region of Lower Austria, between the northwestern foothills of the Bohemian Forest and the southeast Dunkelsteiner Wald, is a magnificent river valley. Today, you can savor the celebrated Wachau wines at the wine cellar of any local vintner. Off the beaten tourist route, the **Waldviertel** region is a vast tract of mountains and trees stretching between the Danube and the Czech Republic. Though the regional villages and hamlets are treasure troves of history, the chief attractions are the densely forested woodlands interspersed with lakes and pools where hiking paths meander hundreds of miles over hill and dale. Enjoy the forest, but beware—dangerous ticks here carry a virus that results in *Gehirnentzündung* (inflammation of the brain), a disease similar to meningitis (for more information, see **Essentials: Health,** p. 15).

■ St. Pölten

St. Pölten (pop. 50,000) is like the old optical illusion of two faces in one: at one moment, the face of a wizened old woman; at another, that of a pretty young maid, turned away. Bishop von Passau granted a charter to St. Pölten, then the Roman town Aelium Cetium, in 1159, making St. Pölten the oldest city in Austria. It is, however, the youngest capital—St. Pölten became the capital of Lower Austria in 1986. Both ancient and modern, St. Pölten watches travelers trip through the town's active shopping district, museums, and theaters. The zeal of the famous Baroque architect Jacob Prandtauer, Joseph Munggenast, and their contemporaries add flair to the pretty pastel town.

Orientation and Practical Information Kremsergasse divides the town in two. As you leave the train station and cross Bahnhofpl., Kremserg. is at ten o'clock. Follow it until you hit the Rathausg. and then turn right to reach St. Pölten's heart, **Rathausplatz.** The **train station** rumbles at Bahnhofpl., abutting the pedestrian zone, and sends direct trains to **Hütteldorf** and the **Vienna Westbahnhof** two or three times every hour. Right in front of the train station, the **bus** depot runs buses to **Melk** and **Krems.** A free complete schedule is available at the bus stop ticket counter (tel. 343 466; open Mon.-Fri. 7:30am-12:30pm). The **tourist office** (tel. 353 354; fax 28 19), is in the Rathauspassage, the tunnel under the cotton-candy Rathaus. The staff provides oodles of information about St. Pölten, regional events, and the wonders of the surrounding Lower Austrian lands. They'll also give you a room list, suggest a madcap night on the town (ask for the *IN Szene* brochure), lead you on a one-hour **tour** of the inner city (call up to a week in advance), or distribute a **cassette tour** (20AS) in any one of several languages. (Open Mon.-Fri. 8am-6pm; May-Oct. Mon.-Fri. 8am-6pm, Sat. 9:30am-5pm, Sun. and holidays 10am-5pm.) They won't make room reservations; look next door on the wall of the Reisebüro for a free reservations phone. The best place to **exchange money** is the **Postsparkasse Österreichischer Bank (PSK),** Rathausg. 2 (tel. 354 571; fax 354 575), across the street from the post office. **Lockers** are available 24 hours a day (small 30AS, large 40AS). You can **rent bikes** (tel. 528 60) at the train station. (150AS, with train ticket 90AS. Open daily 5:45am-10pm.) The main **post office,** Bahnhofpl. 1a, is right by the train station. (Open Mon.-Fri. 7am-8pm, Sat. 7am-1pm.) The **postal code** is A-3100. The **telephone code** is 02742.

Accommodations and Food St. Pölten works well as a day trip. Since the town lost its only youth hostel a few years ago, you might consider staying in the hostels in **Krems** (tel. (02732) 834 52; see p. 165), **Melk** (tel. (02752) 26 81; see p. 167), or **Vienna** (see p. 89). The tourist office maintains a list of *Privatzimmer,* most of which are outside the city limits.
   St. Pölten's local specialties include oysters, fried black pudding, and savory Wachau wine. Many shops and cafés flourish in the *Fußgängerzone* surrounding the Dom and the Rathaus. **B&B (Bier & Brötchen),** Schreing. 7 (tel. 520 72), has soup and sandwiches, good beer, a salad bar (36AS), and outside seating. (Open Mon.-Fri. 10:30am-11pm, Sat. 9:30am-2pm. Live music first Sun. of the month, 10am-2pm.) A comfortable Viennese café with newspapers and lingering guests, **Café Melange,** Kremserg. 11, on the second floor, tends to draw a younger crowd. (Open Mon.-Fri. 7:30am-6:30pm, Sat. 7:30am-5pm.) **Café Punschkrapfel,** Domg. 8, is named for its specialty—a small chocolate rum cake covered with pink icing. Other offerings include fruit frappes (34AS) and a salad buffet (35AS), which taste best in the popular outdoor seating area. Cheap and healthy fixings await at the St. Pölten **Julius Meinl** supermarket, Kremserg. 21. (Open Mon.-Fri. 7:30am-6pm, Sat. 7:30am-12:30pm.)

Sights and Entertainment As in many other Austrian towns, St. Pölten's architecture suffered heavy damages during WWII. The city fixed the broken Baroques, restoring many of the structures to their original grandeur. Their overriding flourishes and facades makes the city an architectural bonanza—just take a stroll and see for yourself. Joseph Maria Olbrich's masterful turn-of-the-century *Jugendstil* (art nouveau) buildings set off Prandtauer's florid Baroque confections.

The **Rathausplatz** at St. Pölten's core was erected in the 13th century, though recent archeological excavations reveal that a Roman settlement had sprouted there in the first millennium. The building to the left of the city hall, at Rathauspl. 2, earned the name **Schubert Haus** due to Franz's frequent visits to the owners, Baron von Münk and his family. A neo-Grecian Schubert (bare-chested, no less) conducts above the window at the portal's axis. The **Institut der Englischer Fräulein** (Institute of Mary Ward), Linzer Str. 9-11, was founded in 1706 for the instruction of girls from noble families. The expansive front sports a magnificent white-on-pink facade with Corinthian columns and vaguely religious life-sized reliefs.

St. Pölten's **Wiener Straße** has been a thoroughfare since the Romans rolled through. After 1100, the street became the central axis of the bourgeois-trader settlement established by the Bishop of Passau. At the corner of Wiener Str. and Kremserg. stands the oldest pharmacy in St. Pölten, the **Hassack-Apotheke,** happily curing headaches and hemorrhoids since 1595. What beautifully painted shutters! **Herrenplatz** has withstood the haggling of St. Pölten's daily market for centuries. A narrow alley just after Wiener Str. 31 leads to **Domplatz,** which retains its charm despite its new-found parking-lot status. The remains of the Roman settlement of Aelium were discovered here when some clumsy sewer installers tripped over Roman hypocausts (an ancient floor heating system). Be sure to stop by the actual **Dom** (cathedral) to see its pleasant salmon tones and gilded Baroque encrustations, added by Prandtauer when he transformed the original Roman basilica.

St. Pölten maintains a few good museums. The encyclopedic **Stadt Museum,** Prandtauerstr. 2, near the Rathaus, often has special exhibits on cultural and historical themes in addition to its very thorough permanent collection on St. Pölten from pre-Roman times to the present, containing artifacts ranging from transplanted church pews to Roman coins to 18th-century cloth samples. (Open daily 9am-5pm. 50AS, students 20AS.) Part of the exhibit is located in **Schloß Pottenbrunn** outside of St. Pölten. Buses run from the train station to the palace every hour.

The town maintains two **theaters.** "**Die Bühne im Hof**" (the stage in the courtyard), Linzerstr. 18 (tel. 352 291; fax 522 94), has mostly modern theater and dance pieces. The original open-air theater was so popular that the courtyard was enclosed and additional seating added. Theatergoers still couldn't get enough, so another, larger theater has opened. The tourist office offers a program detailing the productions. Prices range from 70 to 350AS, depending on what's showing (students and seniors 50% off). **Landeshauptstadt Theater,** Rathauspl. 11 (tel. 352 02 619), stages traditional opera and ballet. Tickets run 160-290AS, but the box office sells less-expensive standing room tickets on the evenings of performances. Seasonal festivities include the **St. Pöltner Festwoche,** which brings all kinds of cultural events to the local theaters and museums at the end of May. From the end of September to early October, the **Sacred Music Festival** features free concerts in the churches of St. Pölten.

For more earthly pleasures, check out the **flea market** that comes to the Einkaufszentrum Traisenpark from 8am to 3pm every Sunday. Crafts, toys, art, antiques, books, furniture—everything you could dream of and more awaits haggling.

■ Mariazell

The local Benedictine superior's motto for Mariazell is *"Gnadenzentrum Europas"* (Europe's Center of Mercy). While this moniker may be something of an exaggeration, time spent here does feel blessed. Tilting precariously on the side of the Alps, the little town is both an unabashed resort town and the most important pilgrimage site in Central Europe. The faithful come here to pay homage to a miraculous Madonna of linden wood. The hand-carved statue was once owned by the traveling monk Magnus, who in 1157 established a chapel in Mariazell (see **Mary, Mary, Quite Contrary**, p. 153). Travelers with less spiritually lofty goals come to Mariazell to ski in the Bürgeralpe or bake by the waters of the Erlausee.

Orientation and Practical Information To reach Mariazell **by car** from **Vienna,** take Autobahn A-1 west to St. Pölten, and exit onto Rte. 20 south to Mariazell (1hr.). From **Leoben** or **Bruck an der Mur,** take Rte. S-6 to Kapfenberg and then Rte. 20 north to Mariazell. From **Graz,** take Rte. S-35 north to Bruck an der Mur then Rte. S-6 to Rte. 20 north.

Mariazell is difficult to access by train; bus trips are easier. Twenty minutes from Mariazell, the **train station,** Erlaufseestr. 19 (tel. 22 30), is most useful for **renting bikes** (90AS per day) and **storing luggage** (30AS per day; open daily in summer 5am-7:10pm, in winter 5am-6:30pm). If you must travel by train in the summer, you might consider a **Mariazellerland-Erlebnis ticket,** which includes round-trip fare to Mariazell, a pass for the Bürgeralpe-Seilbahn, and discounts at selected restaurants in Mariazell (from Vienna's Westbahnhof 365AS; from St. Pölten 255AS). **Buses** leave Mariazell for **Bruck an der Mur** (5:45, 6:25, 7:50am, 3:30, and 6:10pm; 94AS), **Graz** (5:45am and 3:30pm), and **Vienna** (5:25am and 6:10pm, 3hr., 170AS). The **bus station** is directly behind the post office, near Hauptpl. (Open Mon.-Fri. 8am-noon and 2-4pm, Sat. 8-11am. Information desk open Mon.-Fri. 9:30-11:30am and 2:30-4:30pm, Sat.-Sun. 9:40-10:10am and 3:15-3:55pm.)

The **tourist office,** Hauptpl. 13 (tel. 23 66; fax 39 45), has information on skiing, boating, fishing, and hiking as well as bus, train, and accommodations listings. The multilingual staff also makes free room reservations. From the train station, turn right on St. Sebastian and walk till the fork in the road. Take the left fork up the hill to Wienerstr., turn right, and walk to Hauptpl. The office is straight ahead. (Open May-Sept. Mon.-Sat. 9am-12:30pm and 2-5:30pm, Sat. 9am-noon and 2-4pm, Sun. 10am-noon; Oct.-April Mon.-Fri. 9am-12:30pm and 2-5:30pm, Sat. 9am-noon and 2-4pm.) For **currency exchange** or a 24-hour **ATM,** stop by **Sparkasse,** Grazerstr. 6 (tel. 23 03), just behind the post office. (Open Mon.-Fri. 8am-noon and 2-4pm, Sat. 8-11am.) In medical **emergencies,** call the St. Sebastian Hospital, Spitalg. 4 (tel. 22 22). Travelers and locals alike head to **Zur Gaudenmutter,** Hauptpl. 4 (tel. 21 02), to fulfill their pharmaceutical needs. (Open Mon.-Fri. 8am-noon and 2-6pm, Sat. 8am-noon, Sun. 9am-noon.) The **post office** is upstairs. (Open Mon.-Fri. 8am-noon and 2-5pm, Sat. 8-10am.) The **postal code** is A-8630. The **telephone code** is 03882.

Accommodations and Food Mariazell's **Jugendherberge (HI),** Fischer-von-Erlach-Weg 2 (tel. 26 69; fax 266 988), is both immaculate and lively. Designed for large groups, the hostel is equipped with a huge breakfast room, activity rooms, a basketball court, a ping-pong table, and a huge, grassy hill with cows out back. The dorms are a bit tight; lockers and showers are on the hall. More luxurious doubles and family rooms (some with balcony) have private bathrooms with shower. From Hauptpl., follow Wiener Neustädterstr. (left of the church, just past the *Lebkuchen* stands), and turn left on Fischer-von-Erlach-Weg. The hostel is on the left across from the Hallenbad. (Reception 8am-1pm and 5-10pm. Curfew 10pm; key available. No lockout. Dorms 150AS; doubles 360AS; quads 720AS. Winter: 150AS; 380AS; 760AS. 20AS surcharge for one-night stays. Family discounts available. Breakfast included. Members only. Reservations recommended. Owners may close for vacation around Oct. or Nov. Visa, MC.) Enjoy the comforts of home at **Haus Wechselberger,** Bilderiweg 8 (tel. 23 15). The Wechselberger family rents out a few rooms in their house, complete with antique beds with high, ornate head- and footboards. Several rooms have balconies with views of the surrounding hills. (200AS. Winter: 10AS surcharge. Hall showers and toilets. Breakfast included.) Though crowded, **Camping Erlaufsee** (tel. 21 48 or 21 16), behind Hotel Herrenhaus near the west dock, is in a lovely spot just by the lake on Erlaufseestr. It's equipped with showers, toilets, a refrigerator, and

Mary, Mary, Quite Contrary

In 1157, Magnus the Good Monk set out on a mission in the mountains. Ever prepared, he brought a servant, a horse, and his precious hand-carved statue of the Holy Mary. One night, Magnus and his companion had the bad fortune to encounter a robber who, seeing how fiercely Magnus defended the statue, drew his dagger and demanded that Magnus hand over the treasure. Fearless Magnus rose and held the statue at arm's length in front of him. The mesmerized robber dropped his dagger and muttered "Maria," giving the monk and his companion time to flee. They set up camp a safe distance away and went to bed. Shortly after midnight, Magnus heard a woman's voice pleading with him to wake up. The monk opened his eyes to a shimmering vision of Mary, insisting that he take the statue and run. The monk woke his companion, and they took off into the night—with a pack of robbers in hot pursuit. Thanks to Mary, the two had a head start, but they were brought to a sudden standstill: a huge stony cliff gaped before them. Without hesitation, Magnus held the statue aloft and said a heartfelt prayer. With a great rumble and creak, a passage opened in the stone, just wide enough for the two travelers. They walked into a lush green valley, where slightly bewildered lumberjacks made them feel at home. At Magnus' request the locals built a little wooded chapel, or "Zell," for the miraculous Mary statue. The valley became known as "Maria in der Zell," or "Mariazell."

an activity room. (50AS, children under 15 25AS; tents 40AS.) For a quiet stay on the mountainside, try the lovely **Alpenhaus Ganser,** Brünnerweg 4 (tel. 46 85). On the way to town from the train station, turn left from Wienerstr. at the tennis courts. Around the bend, stairs built into the mountain provide a shortcut. Uphill and indoors you'll find homemade furniture, hand-carved wood, a delightful breakfast room, and rooms with fantastic views and southern light. Other amenities include a parking garage and sleds in the winter that you can ride directly to the cable car. A ski trail leads straight to the front door. (2-night min. stay. 160AS per person in summer, 180AS in winter. Hall showers. Breakfast included.)

Cheap food and occasional live music can be found at **Stüberl Goldener Stiefel** (tel. 27 31) at the corner of Wiender Neustädtstr. and Dr.-Karl-Lueger-Str. (Pizza 45-80AS. Open Mon.-Sun. 8:30am-midnight.) For some history with your supper, stop by the **Wirsthaus Brauerei,** Wiener Str. 5 (tel. 25 23). Made with a warmer fermentation process than industrial lagers, the unfiltered Altbier is best when fresh (27AS). Grab a handful of sweet malt or a homemade pretzel (17AS) to accompany the beer. The restaurant proudly displays four generations of family portraits and a photo of Kaiser Franz Josef's 1910 visit to Mariazell. (Open Mon.-Wed. 10am-11pm, Fri.-Sat. 10am-midnight, Sun. 10am-7pm.) There is a **Julius Meinl** supermarket on Wiener Str. (open Mon.-Fri. 5am-6pm, Sat. 8am-5pm), and many wonderful *Lebkuchen* stands operate outside the town church. Specializing in bee products, **Hotel Goldener Löwe,** Hauptpl. 1a, across from the church, lets you sit on the terrace overlooking Hauptpl. while sipping homemade mead (the drink of the gods). The hotel also lets the young at heart try candlemaking (Sat. and Sun. 3pm) or gingerbread baking (by appointment; 35AS, plus a fee for materials). But the real reason to visit is the **first-floor bathroom**—as you enter, the holy chamber lights up by itself. A waterfall runs on the wall, and a map of constellations in the stall helps you ponder your fate. Each stall is also equipped with a 15-minute hourglass. Says a vendor across the street: "I have been to Paris; I have been in the grand hotels of New York City. But never have I seen such a bathroom."

Sights and Entertainment This pilgrimage town—Mariazell means "Mary's chapel"—has received hundreds of thousands of pious wanderers over the centuries, all journeying to visit the **Madonna** within the **Basilica** (tel. 25 95). Black Baroque spires visible from any spot in town cap the Basilica, in the middle of Hauptpl. Crowds file in, one after another; German, Czech, Hungarian, and other tongues fill the air. Mass quantities of gold and silver adorn the High Altar, which depicts a huge silver globe encircled by a snake. On the **Gnadenaltar** (Mercy Altar) in the middle of the church the miraculous Madonna rests. Empress Maria Theresa, who had her first holy communion in Mariazell, donated the silver and gold grille that encloses the Gnadenaltar. (Basilica open daily 6am-7pm. Free guided tours by appointment through the Superiorat, Kardinal-Tisserant-Pl. 1.) The church's amazing **Schatzkammer** (treasure chamber) contains gifts from scores of pious Europeans. (Open Tues.-Sat. 10am-3pm, Sun. 11am-3pm. 40AS, students 20AS.)

With a range of activities, Mariazell caters to throngs of bronzed, ultra-healthy (rhymes with wealthy...) outdoor types. Located just under the Bürgeralpe and a short jaunt away from the Gemeindealpe, the area's ideal for **skiing**. A six-minute walk away from Hauptpl. at Wienerstr. 28, a **cable car** (tel. 25 55) zips to the top of the Bürgeralpe. (Runs every 20min. July-Aug. 8:30am-5:30pm; April-June and Oct.-Nov. 9am-5pm; Sept. 8:30am-5pm. Ascent 60AS, descent 40AS, round-trip 90AS; with guest card or student ID 55AS, 40AS, 75AS.) Ski lifts and trails line the top (one-day pass 260AS, 2-day 470AS). For ski information on the Bürgeralpe, Gemeindealpe, Gußwerk, Tribein, and Köcken-Sattel Mountains (no lifts here), contact the Mariazell tourist office. In the summer, **hiking** prevails in these areas, but it might also be fun to rent a **mountain bike** from **Sport Zefferer** on Wiener Neustädterstr., up the street from the tourist office. (Open Mon.-Sat. 8am-noon and 2-6pm. 100AS per day.)

All of Mariazell's water sports revolve around the **Erlaufsee,** a wondrous Alpine oasis six kilometers outside the city limits. Bunches of lakeside beaches allow for some of the best sunbathing in central Austria. **Buses** (tel. 21 66) run from Mariazell to the lake at 9:10am, 1:10, 3, and 3:15pm (20AS). **Steam train engines** (tel. 30 14), proclaimed by the tourist office to be "the oldest in the world," also whiz around the lake. (Runs July-Sept. on weekends and holidays. 50AS, round-trip 80AS.) Once at the water's edge, try renting an **electric boat** (100AS for 30min.) or a **paddle** or **row boat** (70AS for 30min.) from **Restaurant Herrenhaus** (tel. 22 50). Those interested in **scuba diving** in the Erlaufsee can contact **Harry's Tauchschule,** Traismauer 5 (tel. (02783) 77 47), for information about lessons and equipment rental.

APPROACHING BURGENLAND

South and southeast of Vienna, from the easternmost portion of the Wienerwald to northwest Burgenland, lies a region of rolling hills and dense woodlands. The Leitha River runs along the Burgenland border north of Wiesen to Wiener Neustadt and to nations east, while the peaks of the Rosaliengebirge glower at the borderlands near Hungary. The Burgenland gets its name not because the region has a plethora of castles (*Burg* means "castle"), but because there are so many towns that end in "burg"—Piesburg, Wieselburg, Eisenburg, etc. These villages are primarily grape towns, with vineyards producing world-famous wines and friendly taverns proudly serving the fruits of their labor. Textile and foodstuff factories along with major chemical and iron plants abound in this industrial center, driving the tourist-independent economy.

■ Baden bei Wien

Baden is the favorite weekend spot for Viennese trying to get away from it all. All day, every day, a supply of water with a natural temperature of 36°C (96°F) springs from the ground. Since the age of Roman rule, bathers have cherished the spa for the therapeutic effects of its sulfur springs. The Holy Roman Emperors used Baden as a summer retreat, and the honor became official in 1803 when Emperor Franz I moved the summer court here. The Emperor gave Baden an imperial reputation, and many big names have relaxed at its baths: Mozart, Schubert, Strauss, Beethoven, and, of course, Falco. Under imperial patronage in the 19th century, Biedermeier culture flourished. City notables generated magnificent specimens of architecture and art and encouraged the burgeoning science of horticulture. As a tribute to the Emperor's presence, Baden created a rosarium extending from the center of town to the Wienerwald (90,000 sq. m) and containing over 20,000 roses. In one step, you can leave behind the carefully tended roses and enter the enormous, trail-laced tract of woodland.

Orientation and Practical Information Baden's prices are the snakes slithering through this paradise. Resist temptation and make Baden a daytrip from Vienna, only 27km away. **By car** from the west, take the West Autobahn to "Alland-Baden-Mödling (Bundesstr. 20)." From Vienna, take the Süd Autobahn and exit at "Baden." The Vienna local railway runs a direct **train** from Vienna to Josefpl., just outside the Baden *Fußgängerzone*. (Leaves Vienna's Westbahnhof at 10am and 4:15pm. 30min. Return trips leave Josefpl. at 8:40am and 3:05pm.) Better yet, take the **Badner Bahn**, a tram that runs every 15 minutes between Josefpl. and the Opera House in Vienna. Still another option is the **Wiener-Lokal Bahn**, which runs every 30 minutes to an hour from Baden's main station on Waltersdorferstr. to Wien Meidling in Vienna. Trains also stop in Baden en route to and from Vienna every 15 minutes (34AS). The main Baden **bus** stops are Wiener-Lokal Bahn and Josefpl. Approximately 50 buses run per day between Baden and Vienna (stop: "Heinrichshof/Opera"; last bus from Vienna 3:10am, last bus from Josefpl. 2:21am; 58AS).

Baden's **tourist office**, Brusattipl. 3 (tel. 868 00; fax 441 47), is accessible from the Josefpl. bus and tram stop. Walk toward the fountain and follow Erzherzog-Rainer-Ring to the second left (Grüner Markt). The tourist office is in the left corner. The patient, English-speaking staff provides all the necessary brochures and information. They offer free **tours** of the *Altstadt* (Mon. at 2pm and Thurs. at 10am, 1½hr.) and the wine region (Wed. 3pm, 2hr.), as well as **wine tastings** (Thurs. 4-7pm or by appointment) and free guided **hiking** or **biking** tours. (Open May-Oct. Mon.-Sat. 9am-12:30pm and 2-6pm, Sun. 9am-12:30pm.) The train station offers **bike rental** (50AS) and **luggage storage** (30AS). **Public toilets** are at Grüner Markt and the train station. The **postal code** is A-2500. The **telephone code** is 02252.

Accommodations and Food If you want to spend the night in Baden despite admonishments from the budget fairy, the tourist office will apprise you of your limited budget options. **Haus Taschler**, Schlosserg. 11 (tel. 484 41), is a beautiful house set on an ivy-laden alley off Gutenbrunner Park, halfway between Josefpl. and the Strandbad. Well-furnished rooms with kitchen facilities are 180AS, including a private shower. Call in advance; the place fills quickly and prefers long-term guests. **Pension Steinkellner**, Am Hang 1 (tel. 862 26), offers decent rooms at reasonable prices (for Baden). It's a bit of a walk from the center of town, but the friendly proprietors will pick you up if you need a short ride. (Singles 290AS, with shower 300AS.)

Food options are plentiful but not cheap. **Café Damals**, Rathausg. 3 (tel. 426 86), in a cool, ivy-hung courtyard facing the Hauptpl., is a relaxing place to lunch and linger, despite the un-nostalgic Austrian Top 40 tunes. Try a delicate salad for 40AS. (Open Mon.-Fri. 9:30am-11pm, Sat. 9:30am-5pm, Sun. 11am-5pm.) **Zum Vogelhändler**, Vöslauerstr. 48 (tel. 852 25), is a pub where the Baden youth flock to imbibe the local wine and snack on small, hot dishes. Try the specialty, *nockerl* (60-87AS). For a little history with your *Tafelspitz*, visit the **Gasthaus zum Reichsapfel**, Spielg. 2, the oldest guesthouse in Baden. Follow Antong. one block from Theaterpl.; the restaurant is on the corner. Since the 13th century, Gasthaus zum Reichsapfel has served as a tavern for hungry wayfarers. Those less interested in the history may still be entertained by the chess, checkers, and huge collection of *Hagar the Horrible* comic books and *Mad* magazines—in German, of course. (Open Wed.-Mon. 11am-2pm and 5-11pm.) **Bier-Pub Einhorn**, Josefpl. 3, is where Baden "nightlife" happens. Go for snacks (38-120AS), drinks, and the saloon-like decor. (Open Mon.-Thurs. 10:30am-2am, Fri. 10:30am-4am, Sat. 9:30am-4am, Sun. 4pm-2am.) For a meal on the run, **Billa**, Wasserg. 14, lies on the way from the train station to the *Fußgängerzone*. (Open Mon.-Thurs. 7:30am-6:30pm, Fri. 7:30am-8pm, Sat. 7am-5pm.) A fresh **farmer's market** beckons at Grüner Markt. (Open Mon.-Fri. 8am-7pm, Sat. 8am-1pm.)

Sights and Entertainment The baths were the biggest attraction in the days of Mozart and Beethoven (and Augustus), and they remain the bait that draws guests today. Although they smell like sulfur (i.e., bad), they're warm, relaxing, and good for you. The largest one, the **Strandbad,** Helenenstr. 19-21, lets you simmer in the hot sulfur thermal pool and then cool off in normal chlorinated pools. Kids will get hysterical over the huge water slide and pool—questionably Roman, but definitely fun. (Mon.-Fri. 79AS, Sat.-Sun. 92AS; after 1pm, 66AS and 79AS. Swimming pool only, 25AS.) From May until September 28, visit the smaller (but just as toasty) pool at Marchetstr. 13, behind the *Kurdirektion* (49AS). The **Kurdirektion** itself, Brusattipl. 4 (tel. 445 31), is the center of all curative spa treatments, housing an indoor thermal pool mainly for patients but open to visitors (72AS). The spa has underwater massage therapy (295AS), sulfur mud baths (305AS), and regular or "sport" massages (310AS).

Centered around Hauptpl., Baden's lovely *Fußgängerzone* features the **Dreifaltigkeitsäule** (Trinity Column), erected in 1718 to thank God for keeping the plague from Baden; the **Rathaus;** and Franz Josef I's summer residence at #17. At Rathausg. 10 is the **Beethovenhaus,** where the composer spent his summers from 1804 to 1825. Beethoven banged out part of *Missa Solemnis* and much of his *Ninth Symphony* here. The reverent museum features such relics as the composer's death mask and locks of hair. (Open Tues.-Fri. 4-6pm, Sat.-Sun. and holidays 9-11am and 4-6pm.)

North of Hauptpl. via Maria-Theresa-G. lies the glory of Baden, the **Kurpark.** Set into the southeast edge of the Wienerwald, this meticulously landscaped, shady garden boasts monuments to Mozart and Beethoven. The park became an important frolic zone in Europe when the Congress of Vienna met in the early 19th century. Bigshot European political figures could escort the Imperial Court here, and after Sunday mass throngs of townsfolk would gather to watch the dignitaries strut through the park. The delightful **Theresiengarten** was laid out in 1792, when the Kurpark was still called "Theresienbad," and the **flower clock** in the middle of the Kurpark grass began ticking in 1929. If you're overloaded with money, visit the park's **Casino.** (Free entrance. Must be 19 or older. Semi-formal dress required.) The **Emperor Franz-Josef Museum,** Hochstr. 51 (tel. 411 00), perches atop the Badener Berg at the end of the park (follow signs through the *Sommerarena* along Zöllner and Suckfüllweg) and holds exhibitions of folk art, weapons, religious pieces, and photography. (Open April-Oct. Tues.-Sun. 1-7pm; Nov.-March Tues.-Sun. 11am-5pm.) A **Doll and Toy Museum,** Erzherzog-Rainer-Ring 23 (tel. 410 20), displays over 300 dolls from different countries, including a 12mm Tirolean doll from the early 1800s. The collection's other little people include teddy bears, Japanese ceremonial dolls, and marionettes from Prague. (Open Tues.-Fri. 4-6pm, Sat.-Sun. and holidays 9-11am and 4-6pm.)

Baden's **Beethoven Festival** takes place from mid-September to early October, with performances by famous Austrian artists and film screenings at the Stadttheater. For tickets, contact Kulturamt der Stadtgemeinde Baden, Hauptpl. 1, A-2500 Baden (tel. 868 00 231; fax 868 00 210). From late June to mid-September, the **Sommerarena** in the Kurpark offers a magnificent, open-air setting for performances of classic Viennese operettas, including works by Fall and Lehár. (Tickets 90-420AS, standing room 30AS.) For tickets, call 485 47, write to Stadttheater Baden Kartenbüro, Theaterpl. 7, A-2500 Baden, or stop by the box office in the Stadttheater on Kaiser-Franz-Ring-Str. (Open Tues.-Sat. 10am-noon and 5-6pm, Sun. and holidays 10am-noon.) Last-minute tickets go on sale at the door 30 minutes before the concert.

In the blooming days of June, Baden holds the **Badener Rosentage,** a multi-week celebration of local roses at the height of the season. The wide range of activities are generally free. World-class **horse racing** also occurs near the Casino from May to September. Call 887 73 or 886 97 for details. In September, Baden hosts **Grape Cure Week,** a Bacchanalian gathering of stands from local wineries in Hauptpl. selling fresh grapes and grape juice. The theory behind the event is that periodically one needs to irrigate one's system, and the best way to do so is by gobbling grapes (1kg of grapes per day). Some take the medicinal philosophy to heart, but for most, it's an excuse to party. For details, stop by one of the *Buschenschanken.* (Stands open daily

8am-6pm. First 500 guests get free grape juice.) Baden rules state that the *Lokalen,* or pubs, can only open for two weeks at a time—the rotating schedule is available at the tourist office. Gathered branches outside a store's doors will tell you it's open.

■ Eisenstadt

Where I wish to live and die.

—Josef Haydn

Haydn, *Heurigen,* and Huns are three Hs that pushed Eisenstadt into cultural significance. **Josef Haydn** composed the melodies that inspired Mozart here, and his wish to live and die in Eisenstadt was happily met by his patrons, the **Esterházys,** powerful Hungarian landholders claiming descent from Attila the Hun. To this day one of the wealthiest families in Europe, they were instrumental in helping the Habsburgs maintain their power. They first lived in Eisenstadt when it was part of Hungary and decided to keep their palace even when borders changed. Today they own many of the region's famed vineyards, whose divine *Heurige* (new wine, or a place selling new wine) is often compared to wine produced in Bordeaux.

Orientation and Practical Information Only 50km from Vienna, Eisenstadt is centered around Hauptstraße, a big chunk of the city's *Fußgängerzone.* From the train station, follow Bahnstr. (which becomes St. Martinstr. and Fanny Eißlerg.) to its middle. At Hauptstr., the Schloß Esterházy is on your left at the end of the street, and the **tourist office** (tel. 673 90; fax 673 91; email tue.info@bnet.co.at) is nestled in the right wing of the Schloß Esterházy. The wonderful English-speaking staff has information on accommodations, musical events, tours, and *Heurigen* in Eisenstadt and throughout the region. For countryside immersion, ask for *Beim Bauern Zu Gast,* which lists winegrowers who rent rooms in their houses. The office organizes several **guided tours** of the city, including one focusing on Josef Haydn, one on the "Trail of the Esterházy Princes," and one on Judaism in the Burgenland. The tours last up to 2½ hours and cost 600AS for as many as 20 people. Tailor-made tours are available with advance notice. (Open May-Oct. Mon.-Sat. 9am-5pm, Sun. 9am-1pm.)

To get to Eisenstadt by **car,** take Bundestr. 16 south from Vienna. From Wiener Neustadt, take Bundestr. 153 east. There is an underground parking garage (25AS per hr.) just outside the Esterházy Palace in the *Zentrum.* The train station is a bit of a walk from the city center at the end of Bahnstr. **Trains** leave for Eisenstadt from **Wien Meidling** in Vienna (about 2 or 3 per hr., 1hr., 69AS) with a possible switch at Wulkaprodersdorf. Another option is to take the S-bahn from Vienna Südbahnof (every hr., 1½hr., 68AS) and switch trains in Neusiedl am See. You may find it more convenient to take a **bus** from Wien Mitte directly to Eisenstadt (70AS). Buses run from Eisenstadt to **Rust, Mörbisch,** and **Wiener Neustadt.** The **bus station** (tel. 23 50) is on Dompl. next to the cathedral. A bus information office (tel. 623 50) is there to answer questions about bus schedules and prices. (Open Mon.-Fri. 9am-noon and 2-3pm). The train station (tel. 626 37) **rents bikes** (100AS per day, with train ticket 50AS; mountain bikes 150-200AS; reservations advised). **Store luggage** (30AS) there or at the bus station (10AS) during its business hours only. (Station open Mon.-Fri.7:30am-8:15pm, Sat.-Sun. 8:40am-8:15pm.) **Exchange currency** at **Creditanstalt Bankverein** on the corner of St. Martin and Dompl. (Open Mon.-Thurs. 8am-1pm and 2-4pm, Fri. 8am-3pm.) Public **bathrooms** are at Dompl., the Esterházy Palace, and the parking lot behind Colmanpl. near the tourist office. The **post office** (tel. 651 71), on the corner of Pfarrg. and Semmelweise near the other end of Hauptstr., has package services and the best rates for traveler's checks. (Open Mon.-Fri. 7am-7pm, Sat. 7am-1pm.) The **postal code** is A-7000. The **telephone code** is 02682.

Accommodations and Food Consider Eisenstadt as a daytrip—with no youth hostel in the vicinity, *Privatzimmer* are the only budget option. Most are on the outer city limits and rent only during July and Aug. The youth hostels in **Vienna**

(tel. 523 63 16 or 523 94 29; see p. 89), **Neusiedl am See** (tel. 22 52; see p. 160), and **Wiener Neustadt** (tel. 296 95) are cheaper and only an hour away. During July and August, migrant hordes descend and reservations are a must. A friendly manager tends bar at **Hotel Franz Mayr,** Kalvarienbergpl. 1 (tel. 627 51), directly across from the Bergkirche. All rooms have shower and toilet. (Singles 400AS; doubles 700AS; triples 850AS; quads 900AS. Breakfast included. Reservations recommended.) At **Wirtshaus zum Eder,** Hauptstr. 25 (tel. 626 45), in Hauptpl., you can engage in deep conversation over wine in an airy courtyard with oil paintings and pristine, white awnings. (Singles 440-590AS; doubles 590AS; triples 790AS. Breakfast included.)

Gasthaus Kiss, Neusiedlerstr. 34 (tel. 61 182), cooks up huge servings of hearty Austrian food in a snug inn. Borrowing its name from the famed Viennese haunt, **Café Central,** Hauptstr. 40 (tel. 645 08), is a pleasant, unassuming little café in a shady courtyard off the main street. A mainly student crowd consumes offerings like hot milk and rum (31AS) and filling tuna salads (42AS). Near the palace and across from the hospital, **Stüberl zum "alten Gewölbe,"** Esterházystr. 21 (tel. 738 13), features a daily *menu* of homemade soup, entree, and dessert for 58AS. Sit down at a rustic pine table and quench your thirst with fresh-pressed carrot or apple juice for 15AS. (Open Mon.-Fri. 6:30am-6pm.) The many **Heurigen** offer modest, generally affordable meals with their wines. Eisenstadt also has a few grocery stores: **Spar Markt,** Esterházystr. 38 and Bahnstr. 16-18 (both open Mon.-Fri. 7am-12:30pm and 2:30-6pm, Sat. 7am-noon), and **Julius Meinl,** Hauptstr. 13 (open Mon.-Fri. 8am-6pm, Sat. 7:30-noon).

Sights and Entertainment In a fit of largesse, the fabulously wealthy Esterházys, who still own **Schloß Esterházy,** leased the family home to the provincial government, giving the public access to some of its magnificent rooms. The government occupies 40% of the castle, some rooms for office space, others for public viewing. The family lives in the remaining 60% of the castle. When they bought their portion for 125,000AS, the government apparently overlooked the Esterházys's clause that made the government responsible for the cost of renovating and maintaining their part of the house. Rumor has it the government has spent more than 40 million shillings on the upkeep of the Red Salon's silk tapestry alone. Built on the footings of the Kanizsai family's 14th-century fortress, the castle-turned-palace acquired its cheerful hue when the Esterházy family showed allegiance to the great Austrian Empress in the 18th century by painting the building *Maria Theresien gelb* (Maria Theresian yellow). In the magnificent **Haydnsaal** (Haydn Hall), the hard-working composer conducted the court orchestra almost every night from 1761 to 1790. Classical musicians consider Haydnsaal *the* acoustic mecca. When the government took over the room, they removed the marble floor and replaced it with a wooden one. Now the room is so acoustically perfect that seats for concerts in the room are not numbered—supposedly every seat provides the same magnificent sound. Guest artists are invited to sing, but more often than not Haydn fills the hall. Even when the music stops, the room is a Baroque symphony of red velvet, gold, monumental oil paintings, and intricate woodwork. (Tours Easter-Oct. daily every hr. 9am-4:30pm; Oct.-Easter Mon.-Fri. 40min. 50AS, students and seniors 30AS.) Extending the town's Haydn obsession, **Haydnmatinees** (tel. 633 84 15; fax 633 84 20) from May to October feature four fine fellows, bewigged and bejeweled in Baroque costumes of imperial splendor, playing a half-hour of impeccable Haydn. (Tues. and Fri. 11am in the palace. 80AS.) The palace also hosts **Haydnkonzerte.** (July-Aug. Thurs. at 8pm; May-June and Sept.-Oct. Sat. at 7:30pm. 160-250AS.) True Haydn enthusiasts can wait for The Big One: the **International Haydntage 1998,** September 11 to 20 (200-10000AS).

The *Kapellmeister* had a short commute to the concert hall each day: he lived just around the corner. His modest residence is now the **Haydn-Haus,** Haydng. 21 (tel. 626 52), exhibiting original manuscripts and other memorabilia. (Open Easter-Oct. daily 9am-noon and 1-5pm. Guided tours by appointment. 20AS, students 10AS. Combination ticket for Haydn-Haus and Landesmuseum 40AS, students 20AS.) After composing in Eisenstadt, Haydn now decomposes here. The *maestro* lies buried in the **Bergkirche** (tel. 626 38), placed there in 1932 after phrenologists removed his head to search for signs of musical genius on the skull's surface. Displayed at the Vienna Music Museum for years, the head was reunited with its body in 1954. (Open Easter-Oct. daily 9am-noon and 1-5pm. 25AS, students 10AS.) Entrance to the Bergkirche includes admission to the **Kalvarienberg,** an annex housing the 14 Stations of the Cross. The fixed, passionate expressions on the hand-carved biblical figures' faces give this extended shrine a peculiarly disturbing impact. Stand in the central nave and try to distinguish the real Doric columns from the *trompe l'oeil* paintings.

The **Jüdisches Museum,** Unterbergstr. 6 (tel. 651 45; email info@oejudmus.or.at; http://www.oejudmus.or.at/oejudmus), celebrates Austrian Jewish heritage, especially religious holidays. The Esterházys were known for their hospitality toward Jews, who played a major part in their rise to power: by settling Jews in Eisenstadt, they circumvented the law preventing Christians from lending money with interest. A small synagogue and a disturbing black room with a Nazi banner cap the museum experience. (Open May-Sept. Tues.-Sun. 10am-5pm; Oct.-May Mon.-Thurs. 8am-4pm, Fri. 8am-1pm. 50AS, students 40AS.) Around the corner on Wertheimer-Str., near the hospital, is a small **Jewish cemetery** with headstones dating back several decades.

Eisenstadt's Jewish Community

The history of Jews in Eisenstadt is an extraordinary tale of rise, cruel fall, and vanishing. As early as 1675, Prince Paul Esterházy was touched by the plight of the persecuted Jews and decided to shelter them as "Schutzjuden" (protected Jews) on his estates. From 1732 on, the Jewish quarter of Eisenstadt formed the independent community of "Unterberg-Eisenstadt," which remained unique in Europe until 1938. In that year, the Jews of the Burgenland were among the first to be affected by the deportation orders of the Nazis. Today only two Jewish families remain in Eisenstadt.

For a more frivolous afternoon, stop by the **Burgenländische Feuerwehrmuseum,** Leithabergstr. 41 (tel. 62 105). Austria's first fire-fighting museum displays cute fire-buggies—cross-breeds between a steam engine and a circus wagon. Also on hand are spectacular fire helmets worthy of Greek heroes. (Open Mon.-Thurs. 8am-noon and 1-4pm, Fri. 9am-1pm. 10AS, students 5AS.)

Of course, leaving Eisenstadt without wine is like leaving Linz without the *torte*. In early July the **Winzerkirtag Kleinhöflein** floods Hauptpl. with kegs, flasks, and bottles as local wineries attempt to sell their goods. Mid-August brings the **Festival of 1000 Wines,** when wineries from all over Burgenland crowd the palace's Orangerie with their Dionysian delicacies. If you like music with your wine, visit in June when the **Eisen Stadt Fest** provides all kinds of sounds, from *schrammelmusik* to rock. At any other time of the year, fresh wine is available straight from the source in the wineries themselves. Most are small and aren't allowed to open for more than three weeks per year to sell their wine. Fear not—the wineries stagger their opening times so that wine is always available. To find out which *Buschenschank,* or *Schenkhaus,* is open, ask the tourist office for the schedule or look in the local newspaper. Most of the *Buschenschanken* are clustered in Kleinhöfler Hauptstr.

NEUSIEDLER SEE

Covering 320 sq. km, the Neusiedler See is a vestige of the water that once blanketed the entire Pannenian Plain. With no outlets or inlets save underground springs, this steppe lake is only two meters at its deepest, receding periodically to expose thousands of square meters of dry land. Indeed, in the mid-19th century, the lake dried up entirely. Warm and salty, the lake is a haven for birds and humans alike. More than 250 species of waterfowl dwell in the thickets formed by its reeds, and every summer thousands of sun-hungry vacationers flock to its various resorts for swimming, sailing, fishing, and cycling. **Cruises** on the Neusiedler See allow you to travel between Rust,

Illmitz, and Mörbisch with your bike for about 60AS one way and 100AS round-trip. **Gangl** (tel. (02175) 21 58 or 27 94) runs boats every hour from Illmitz to Mörbisch (April-Oct. 10am-5pm; May-Sept. 9am-6pm). **Holiday Lines** (tel. (02683) 55 38) in Purbach has cruises from Rust to Illmitz (Tues. and Fri.-Sat. 10am and 4pm) and back again (Sun. 11am and 5pm). In Mörbisch, **Schiffahrt Weiss** (tel. (02685) 83 24) cruises to Illmitz (May-Sept. daily 8:30am-6pm, every 30min.).

■ Neusiedl am See

Less than an hour from Vienna by express train, Neusiedl am See is the gateway to the Neusiedler region. The principal attraction is the lake, not the town, so consider Neusiedl a day at the beach. There are two **train stations** in Neusiedl. The **Hauptbahnhof** is 15 minutes by foot from the center of town. (Information and ticket window open daily 5am-9pm. Eisenstadt round-trip 17AS; Vienna 68AS, round-trip 98AS.) To get to town, take a right onto Bahnstr. and follow the slope of the road right onto Eisenstädterstr. (which becomes Obere Hauptstr.) and into Hauptpl. The other train station, **Neusiedl Bad,** is centrally located on Seestr., a right at the end of Untere Hauptstr. The adjacent bus station, Seestr. 15a (tel. 24 06), offers a **Fahrradbus** (#1813) that carries bikers and bikes to and from Mörbisch, Neusiedl, and Illmitz. There's also service every hour to Vienna (85AS) and Bruck an der Leitha (34AS).

The **tourist office** (tel. 22 29; fax 26 37), in the *Rathaus* on Hauptpl., distributes pamphlets about the resort town, helps with accommodations, and offers advice on boat and bike rental. (Open July-Aug. Mon.-Fri. 8am-7pm, Sat. 10am-noon and 2-6pm, Sun. 4-7pm; May-June and Sept. Mon.-Fri. 8am-4:30pm; Oct.-April Mon.-Thurs. 8am-noon and 1-4:30pm, Fri. 8am-1pm.) **Raiffeisbank,** Untere Hauptstr. 3 (tel. 25 64), has the best rates for your ducats. Given the town layout, it may make your day easier to **rent a bike** at Seestr.-Schilfweg 3, by Pension "La Paloma." Don't let the giant white Hungarian herd dog scare you away—that's just his way of saying *"Grüß Gott."* (200AS per day, students and additional days 100AS, 40AS per hr.) **Store luggage** at the train station (30AS). Dial 133 in case of **emergency**. The **post office** is on the corner of Untere Hauptstr. and Lisztg. (Open Mon.-Fri. 8am-noon and 2-6pm, Sat. 8-10am.) The **postal code** is A-7100, and the **telephone code** is 02167.

Heavy tourist activity, partly assured by Neusiedl's proximity to Vienna, makes finding accommodations tough. To reach the newly renovated **Jugendherberge Neusiedl am See (HI),** Herbergg. 1 (tel./fax 22 52), find Wienerstr. and then take a left onto Goldbergg. The hostel is on the corner at Herbergg. It's an uphill walk, but don't get discouraged—the renovations have equipped the hostel with a sauna and winter greenhouse in which to unlace your steaming boots and stretch out your tired toes. The hostel sports 86 beds in 20 quads and three doubles. There are showers in every room, but the bathrooms are on the hall. (Reception daily 8am-2pm and 5-8pm. 161AS, under 19 145AS. Breakfast included. Sheets 15AS. Key deposit 100AS. Reservations recommended. Open March-Oct.) **Gasthof zur Traube,** Hauptpl. 9 (tel. 24 23), has a cordial staff and pretty, pink rooms, each with shower and toilet. (Singles 390AS; doubles 630AS. Prices drop after 4 nights. Add 10AS in high season. Breakfast included.) **Rathausstüberl** (tel. 28 83; fax 288 307), around the corner from the Rathaus on Kircheng., has a lovely shaded courtyard, great wine, and plenty of fresh fish and vegetarian dishes. (Entrees 70-150AS. Open March-Dec. daily 10am-midnight.) Rathausstüberl doubles as a sunny *Pension*. (315-355AS per person with breakfast buffet. Reservations recommended.) On your way to the beach grab a picnic at the **Billa** grocery store on Seestr. (Open Mon.-Thurs. 7:30am-6:30pm, Fri. 7:30am-8pm, Sat. 7am-5pm.) Stop by **Rauchkuchl,** Obere Hauptstr. 67 (tel. 25 85), to try *Blaufränker* red wine or other homemade specialties and hear Neusiedl's *mundart* dialect spoken by the friendliest people around. (Open Mon.-Sat. 5-11pm.)

You're here, you've got your bathing suit and towel, now where's the **beach?** Head to the end of Seestr. (1km), or catch the bus from the Hauptbahnhof or Hauptpl. (every hr. until 6pm). The beach is a bit rocky but pleasant (12AS, children 4AS). The **Segelschule Neusiedl am See** (tel. 87 60) at the docks on the far right will get you on the water on a sailboard (1hr. 140-340AS, half- or full-day 345-1730AS), dinghy (3- to 4-person boat 140 per hr.), or standard surfboard (300AS for the weekend). (Open daily 8:30am-6pm.) Close by on Seestr. rest **motorboats** (140-200AS per hr.), **paddleboats** (80AS per hr.), and **rowboats** (40AS per hr.) at **Bootsvermietung Leban.**

▩ Rust

During the summer, tourists inundate this tiny, self-appointed wine capital of Austria to partake of the fruit of the vine. Ever since 1524, when the Emperor granted the wine-growers of Rust the exclusive right to mark the letter "R" on their wine barrels, Rust has been synonymous with good—nay, really good—wine. The town is particularly known for its production of sweet dessert wines, called *Ausbruch* (literally "break out"). These high-quality wines come from grapes allowed to dry up and sweeten a bit more than regular wine-grapes (on their way to raisinhood) before the farmer "breaks out" the center and presses the juice. The quantity of dessicated grapes needed for a bottle is astounding, and so, consequently, is the price. The income from the wine (or maybe its inebriating qualities) enabled the town to purchase its independence from Kaiser Leopold I in 1861. The price? 60,000 gold guilders and 36,000 liters of the priceless *Ausbruch* wine. Wine isn't Rust's only attraction, however. The unspoiled town center, with its medieval houses and nesting storks, and Rust's location on the *Neusiedlersee* make this town one of the most irresistibly beautiful places of the Austrian countryside.

Orientation and Practical Information Rust is 10km east of Eisenstadt on the Neusiedler See. By **car** from Eisenstadt, take Bundesstr. 52 straight into Rust. From Vienna, take Autobahn A4 to Neusiedl am See, Bundesstr. 50 south until Seehof, and then follow signs. **Buses** run between Eisenstadt and Rust several times per day (34AS), between Rust and Vienna (Wien Mitte/Landstr.) four times a day (120AS), and to and from Neusiedl am See once per day (30min., 52AS). Rust does not have a train station. The **bus station** is located just behind the post office at Franz-Josef-Pl. 14. To reach the award-winning *Fußgängerzone*, leave the post office and turn left. You will almost immediately come to the intersection of Oggauerstr. and Conradpl. Take a left onto Conradpl. until you come to a triangular plaza. In front of you will be the *Rathaus*. Inside, the **tourist office** (tel. 502; fax 502 10) hands out maps, plans bicycle tours, and gives information on wine tastings, the beach, and *Privatzimmer*. (Open Mon.-Fri. 8am-noon and 2-6pm, Sat. 9am-noon, Sun. 10am-noon; Oct.-April Mon.-Fri. 8am-noon and 1-4pm.) The hyper-bionic display board outside the tourist office displays all the best accomodations; green lights indicate vacancies and a convenient phone allows you to call the hotels for free. The **Raiffeisenkasse Rust,** Rathauspl. 5 (tel. 285), is the best place to **exchange money.** (Open Mon.-Fri. 8am-noon and 1:30-4pm.) The Raiffeisenkasse also has a **24-hour ATM. Reisebüro Blaguss** in the *Rathaus* and **Ruster Freizeitcenter** (tel. 595) by the beach are open late and provide currency exchange in an emergency. The **post office** will exchange money but not traveler's checks. (Open Mon.-Fri. 8am-noon and 2-6pm.) The **postal code** is A-7071, and the **telephone code** is 02685.

Accommodations and Food Tourists pack Rust in July and August, but one of Rust's 1200 beds is usually available. If not, try the **Jugendherberge** in **Neusiedl am See** (tel. (02167) 22 52; 145AS; see p. 160). Since Rust's hostel recently closed, a reservation at one of the many *Privatzimmer* is strongly recommended during festival times. Some *Privatzimmer* will not accept telephone reservations for a one-night stay, but most will not turn you away at the door if there's a free room. Be warned: prices in the high season are bound to rise. **Haus Rennhofer,** Am Hafen 9 (tel. 316), has small, clean, and airy rooms, most with balconies, on the street closest to the shore. There's also a yard for sunbathing. (Singles 160AS; doubles 320AS; triples 480AS. Breakfast and showers included.) From April through October, there's always room for tent-dwellers at **Ruster Freizeitcenter** (tel. 595), which offers showers, washing machines, a game room, a playground, and a grocery store. (Reception 7:30am-10pm. 44-55AS, children 16-27AS; tent 38-44AS. Showers included.) The grounds are only five minutes from the beach, to which guests receive free entrance.

For the truly hungry, **Zum Alten Haus** (tel. 230), on the corner of Raiffenstr. and Franz Josefpl., serves up gargantuan portions (we're not kidding!) of *Schnitzel* and salad for only 80AS. (Open Tues.-Sun. 9am-10pm.) Since they're not selling wine to Kaiser Leopold anymore, the local vineyards have opted to open the ubiquitous restaurants called *Buschenschanken*, offering inexpensive snacks with superb wine. To avoid a restaurant tax, *Buschenschanken* stay open only six months per year; the calendar of openings is available at the tourist office. For the ultimate in elegance, allow yourself to be seated at **Peter Schandl**, Hauptstr. 20 (tel. 265). Outdoor seating. Beautiful salads. Heavenly wine. The restaurant is a bit on the expensive end (wine from 16AS; 70AS for the classic *Ausbruch*), but it's a wonderful experience. Hung with corn-cobs, **Alte Schmiede** (tel. 467), Seestr. 24, has a courtyard roofed with grape vines and a stone-and-wood interior. Listen to the daily (often live) gypsy music while feasting on traditional Austrian food with a Hungarian twist or on a variety of vegetarian dishes. **A & O Markt Dreyseitel** (tel. 238) on Weinbergg. between Mitterg. and Schubertg. sells the raw materials for a meal. (Open Mon.-Fri. 7am-noon and 3-6pm.)

Sights and Entertainment By day, Rust's visitors enjoy any one of a number of outdoor activities. Sun bunnies can lounge and splash on the south shore of the **Neusiedler See**. There is a **public beach** (tel. 591) complete with showers, lockers, rest rooms, telephones, water slide, and snack bar (30AS per person, after 4pm 70AS). Though the murky waters of the lake daunt some swimmers, the water is actually of drinking quality. The muddy color comes from the shallow, easily disturbed clay bottom (the deepest section is 2m). For those who remain unconvinced, the beach also has a chlorine pool. Be sure to keep the entrance card—you'll need it to exit the park again. To reach the beach, walk down the Hauptstr. and take a left onto Am Seekanal and then a right onto Seepromenade, which cuts through all of the marsh lands (about 7km) surrounding the perimeter of the lake. These marsh reeds (sometimes almost 2m high) create a bug-infested beach inconvenient for bathing anywhere other than at the designated areas. **Storks**, however, thrive on this vegetation. These large, white, majestic birds have been nesting atop the chimneys for years; signs on the corner of Seezeile and Hauptstr. indicate their rooftop hang-outs. The storks come to Rust at the end of March, and from the end of May you can see the babies in the nests. The chicks stay home for two months before flying away and beginning their adult lives. The storks have also hatched a second post office, the **Storks' Post Office**, A-7073 Rust, at the *Rathaus*. Its stork postmark provides funds to support the birds. (Mail stamped with it, however, *must* be sent from Rust.)

If lounging at the beach strikes you as too inactive, try **renting a boat** from **Family Gmeiner** (tel. 493 or (62683) 55 38), next to the beach on the water's edge. **Sailboats** are 90AS per hour or 270AS for five hours. **Paddleboats** are 70AS per hour and 270AS for five hours. **Electric boats** are 110AS per hour and 330AS for five hours. The same company also runs **Schiffsrundfahrten** (boat tours) which will tour the lake or transport you to Illmitz on the opposite shore. (Boats leave Rust April 30-Sept. 25 Tues., Fri.-Sun., and holidays at 10am and 4pm and return from Illmitz at 11am and 5pm.) Besides swimming, boating, and bird-watching, tourists flock to the Neusiedler See area to **bike**. The lake area is criss-crossed with bicycle routes, many along the lake shore or winding in and out of the little towns of both Austria and Hungary. The route is about 170km long, but those out for less intense biking can do a section and then take the bus back, or take the Illwitz boat to the opposite shore and then bicycle back. Buses to Neusiedl am See on Sundays in the summer (around 9am and 4pm) have bike racks and big *"FAHRRADBUS"* ("bikebus") signs on the windshield. For more bus information, call (02167) 24 18 or 240 65 40.

Early-morning strollers down the 16th-century elm-lined streets of the *Altstadt* are rewarded with chiming church bells and crowing roosters. The *Altstadt* is one of the three in Austria to have won the title of *"Modelstadt"* from the Europa-Rat committee

NEAR RUST: MÖRBISCH ■ 163

> ### Birds of a Feather
> Since 1910, Rust's storks have been attracted to the high chimneys of the Burger houses, and at one point in 1960 nearly 40 pairs were nesting in the old city. Soon, however, locals noticed a decline and began to voice their concern over the dwindling number of these endangered birds. In 1987 Rust and the World Wildlife Federation initiated a special joint program to protect and re-establish the birds. The storks eat mainly frogs, fish, snakes, and beetles—critters found among Neusiedler See's reedy marshes. When the reeds grew too tall, the storks had difficulty finding food. The city of Rust therefore borrowed cattle from another part of Austria and plunked them down in the marshes to act as natural lawnmowers. The program seems to be working; 9 pairs of storks came to roost in 1996, hatching 20 little storklings. The only remaining concern is, who's bringing the storks *their* babies?

in Strasbourg (the other two cities are Salzburg and Krems). The award praises the preservation of traditional Austrian buildings. To learn more, participate in one of the hour-long **tours**, featuring discussions of Rust's history, culture, wine, and storks. (May-Sept. Wed. and Sat. 10am from the tourist office. 25AS, with guest card 20AS.) Tours are ordinarily only offered in German, but groups of 10 or more can arrange English tours. Wine garden tours are offered Thursdays at 6pm at **Weingut Marienhof** and Fridays at 5pm at **Familie Beilschmidt's**.

Rust's **Fischerkirche,** around the corner from the tourist office, was built between the 12th and 16th centuries and is the oldest church in Burgenland. In the 13th century, the church gained buildings when Queen Mary of Hungary attempted to escape the Mongols. She stranded herself on the Neusiedl See, and a fisherman saved her. Grateful to live, she donated the Nikolausbeneficium and Marienkapelle, parts of the Fischerkirche. Because Rust is such a small town, the Romanesque and Gothic sections have survived untouched by the ravages of Baroque remodeling. Check out the beautiful medieval frescoes and the brick floor. (Open May-Sept. Mon.-Sat. 10am-noon and 2:30-6pm, Sun. 11am-noon and 2-4pm; Oct.-April Mon.-Fri. 11am-noon and 2-3pm, Sun. 11am-noon and 2-4pm. Tours by appointment. Call Frau Kummer at 550. 10AS, students 5AS.) Rust also houses the only **Weinakademie** (tel. 64 51 or 453; fax 64 31) in Austria. The institution offers courses in everything from wine cultivation to basic bartending and legal points. They also hold wine tours and tastings in the region. The offices are at Hauptstr. 31. (Open July to mid-Sept. daily 2-4pm; Oct.-June Sat.-Sun. and holidays 2-4pm. 60-80AS for 5-10 tastes.) Many town vintners *(Weinbauern)* offer wine tastings and tours of their cellars and vineyards: **Rudolf Beilschmidt,** Weinbergg. 1 (tel. 326) has tours May through September every Friday at 5pm, and **Weingut Marienhof,** Weinbergg. 16 (tel. 251), also offers vineyard tours and tastings every Tuesday April through September at 6pm for 60AS.

■ Near Rust: Mörbisch

The tiny village of Mörbisch lies 5km along the Neusiedler See to the south, easily within cycling distance of Rust. **Buses** from Eisenstadt to Mörbisch leave every two hours (18AS), and buses from Neusiedl am See to Mörbisch leave twice per day (22AS). Many buses also go through the Rust-Mörbisch stretch (17AS) on their way to other places. However, a walk from Rust along the 6km country lane to Mörbisch is manageable (about 1½hr.) and provides a fantastic foray into the countryside. Small vineyard tractors and the worn-out country bikes of the vineyard wives pass on the road, which runs through the fertile vines that have brought such fame to the region. Notice the *Hütterhütte* (stone huts) where young men would spend weeks in solitude, guarding grapes from man and bird. Whitewashed houses, brightly painted doors, and dried corn hanging from the walls mark the village, the last settlement on the western shore of the lake before the Hungarian border. The village is centered around Hauptstraße, where the **tourist office** lies, at #23 (tel. (02685) 88 56; fax 840 39). Pick up very helpful brochures on Mörbisch and the surrounding Burgenland, as

LOWER AUSTRIA

well as a list of accommodations. (Open July-Aug. daily 9am-6pm; May-June and Sept. Mon.-Sat. 9am-6pm; March-April and Oct. Mon.-Fri. 9am-5pm; Nov.-Feb. Mon.-Thurs. 9am-3pm.) The town has its own beach, whose biggest draw is the floating theater that hosts an operetta festival each summer—the **Mörbisch Seefestspiele.** The operetta slated for 1998 is *Der Vogelhändler* (The Birdseller) by Karl Zeller. Performances float atop the lake most Thursdays and every Friday, Saturday, and Sunday from mid-July to the end of August. Tickets are 200AS to 700AS, available through the tourist office or the Burgenland information center at Schloß Esterházy in Eisenstadt (see p. 157). **Blaguss Reisen** (tel. (02682) 662 10; fax 662 10 14) in Vienna arranges a shuttle bus to Mörbisch at 6pm from Wiedner Hauptstr. 15 in Vienna. It returns after the fat lady has sung (round-trip 180AS). Reserve a seat when ordering tickets.

There are many *Pensionen* and *Privatzimmer* in Mörbisch, but for a sunny room and cheerful surroundings less than five minutes from downtown stay at **Winzerhof Schindler,** Kinog. 9 (tel./fax 83 18). Taste their homegrown wine and grape juice on a seaside terrace. (300AS per person. Wheelchair accessible with advance notice.)

Mörbisch is truly a wine town, and never is this more evident than during the **Weinfesttage** during the first weekend of July—the main street becomes one large *Heurige* and thousands of Viennese flock to the little town. During the last weekend of June's **Weinblutenfest,** visitors can ride a horse-drawn carriage from one vineyard to the other, stopping to sample the wine, for 100AS per person.

THE DANUBE (DONAU)

The "Blue Danube" may largely be the invention of Johann Strauss's imagination, but this mighty, muddy-green river still merits a look. You can glide between its banks on a ferry or pedal furiously along its shores on a bike—either way, you'll experience the calming, misty beauty of Austria's most famous river.

The legendary **Erste Donau Dampfschiffahrts-Gesellschaft (DDSG)** runs ships every day from May to late October. The firm operates an office in **Vienna,** II, Friedrichstr. 7 (tel. 588 80 440); elsewhere, tickets are available at tourist offices. The **ferries** run from Vienna to Krems (4-5hr., round-trip 318AS) and beyond (84AS-1032AS). Express boats will take you to Bratislava (1¾hr., 330AS) or Budapest (5-6hr., 750AS, round-trip 1100AS). **Hydrofoils** zip from Vienna to Krems (2hr., 180AS, round-trip 340AS) and venture as far as Budapest (reduced service early April to mid-Sept.; 750AS, round-trip 1100AS). Fortunately, Eurailpasses are valid, and families may travel for half-price (min. one parent and one child ages 6-15; under 6 travel free with a parent; pets half fare, muzzle required). Contact the DDSG or local tourist offices for special ship/bus and ship/train ticket combinations. Specialty tours include the "Nibelungen," which goes through the areas described in the saga, a summer solstice cruise (Sonnendfahrt), which steams by the solstice bonfires in the Wachau valley, and a Henrigen Ride with a live *Liederabend* trio. To bury yourself fully in Austrian culture, strap on your blue suede shoes for "The King Lives" tour with a crew of Elvis impersonators. Discover the melodious lilt that German accents impart on the phrase "hunk a' hunk a' burnin' love."

Cyclists should take advantage of the **Lower Danube Cycle Track,** a velocipede's Valhalla. This riverside bike trail between Vienna and Naarn links several Danube villages, including Melk and Dürnstein. The ride offers captivating views of crumbling castles, latticed vineyards, and medieval towns, but your attention is inevitably drawn back to the majestic current of the river. Area tourist offices carry the route map and bike rental information—you can **rent bikes** at the Melk, Spitz, and Krems docks (with that day's ferry ticket 35AS, with another day's ticket 70AS; without a cruise 150AS). The ferries charge 35AS to transport private bikes or those rented from other places.

Between Krems and Melk along the Vienna-Grein bike route, numerous ruined castles testify to the magnitude of Austria's glorious past. One of the most dramatic fortresses is the 13th-century **Burg Aggstein-Gastein,** which commands the Danube. The castle was formerly inhabited by Scheck von Wald, a robber-baron known to fearful sailors as **Schreckenwalder** (terrible forest man). The lord was wont to impede the passage of ships with ropes stretched across the Danube and then demand tribute from his ensnared victims.

■ Krems and Stein

Located in the Danube valley at the head of the Wachau region, a region known particularly for its rich wine heritage, Krems and Stein are surrounded by lush, green hills filled with terraced vineyards. Historically, Krems and Stein shared a mayor to coordinate trade and military strategy on the critical Danube trading route. Much of the region's wealth came from the tolls on traders—no wonder the Kremser Penny was the first coin minted by the Habsburgs.

Stein, the medieval half of this urban binarism, seems still to live in the first millennium—its crooked, narrow, cobblestone passages twist and wind back on themselves. Bordered by high stuccoed walls that lean with age, this venerable labyrinth has daunted many a would-be conqueror. A few steps to the east, **Krems** lives and breathes, accepting invading shoppers to a modern *Fußgängerzone* (when medieval Stein's your neighbor, Baroque *is* modern).

In the same valley, vineyards give rise to 120 different wines and, in years past, were the stomping-ground of French wine legend **Hans Moser.** Moser developed the now-standard **"raised vine" technique,** raising the poor things from whence they had lain, technologically impaired, for centuries. Head for **Kellergasse,** the high street in Stein that lies next to those hills of plenty, where *Heurigen* offer the fruit of these vines as well as great views of the **Stift Göttweig** (abbey) across the Danube.

Orientation and Practical Information Most visitors arrive on bicycles, but the **train station** is a five-minute walk to the *Fußgängerzone*. Exit out the front door of the Bahnhof, cross Ringstr., and continue straight on Dinstlstr. which leads to the *Fußgängerzone*. The station has **lockers** for 30AS, **luggage storage,** and **bike rental** (tel. 825 36 44; open daily 5:30am-6:45pm). Regional trains connects Krems to **Vienna** (Spittelau station; 136AS) through Tulln. Travelers to other big cities must change trains in St. Pölten. Directly in front of the station is a **bus depot,** with routes to Melk and St Pölten.

Krems lies along the popular **DDSG ferry** route from **Passau** through **Linz** to **Vienna** (for information, see p. 164). The ferry station is on the riverbank close to Stein and the hostel, near the intersection of Donaulände and Dr.-Karl-Dorreck-Str. To reach Krems from the landing, walk down Donaulände until it becomes Ringstr. and then take a left onto Utzstr. To reach Stein, follow Dr.-Karl-Dorreck-Str. and then take a left onto Steiner Landstr.

The **tourist office** is housed in the Kloster Und at Undstr. 6 (tel. 826 76; fax 700 11; http://www.krems.gv.at). From the train station, take a left on Ringstr. and continue (10min.) until Martin-Schmidt-Str. Turn right and follow the street to the end; the office is across the street and to the right. The excellent staff has amassed tons of information on accommodations, sports, and entertainment, as well as the indispensable *Heurigen Kalendar*, which lists the opening times of regional wine taverns. Guided walking tours in several languages leave for Krems or Stein (1½hr., 35AS per person, min. 20 people). The office doubles as an official travel agency and can book flights and hotel rooms anywhere in Austria—and beyond. (Open Easter-Oct. Mon.-Fri. 9am-6pm, Sat.-Sun. 10am-noon and 1-6pm.) **ATMs** dot the shopping streets, but the **post office** also offers **currency exchange** (tel. 826 06) and is right off Ringstr. on Brandströmstr. (Open Mon.-Fri. 8am-noon and 2-6pm, Sat. 8-11am.) You can **rent bikes** at the Donau Campground (half-day 40AS, full-day 60AS), the ferry landing (90AS per day, with ship ticket 40AS), and the train station (90AS per day, with ticket 40AS). The town **postal code** is A-3500. The **telephone code** is 02732.

Accommodations and Food No matter where you stay, ask your hosts for a **guest card** that grants a number of discounts. The **Jugendherberge Radfahrer (HI)**, Ringstr. 77 (tel. 834 52; for advance bookings, call the central office in Vienna at 586 41 45 or fax them at 586 41 453), is a clean hostel accommodating 52 in comfortable four- and six-bed rooms. The garage accommodates the bicycles that traverse the nearby Passau-Vienna bike path. (Members only. Reception 7-9:30am and 5-8pm. Dorms 135AS. 20AS surcharge on stays less than 3 nights. Tax, and sheets included. Breakfast 15-20AS. Lockers 10AS. Open April-Oct.) Karl and Ingred Hietzgern's **Baroque Burgerhaus,** Untere Landstr. 53 (tel. 761 84 or 740 36; fax 761 84), lies in the *Altstadt* of Krems. The building was three small houses in the Middle Ages, joined with one facade in the Baroque period. The Hietzgerns have filled the house with *jugendstil* furniture and hand-painted wood and will happily tell you about anything and everything Krems. (2- and 3-bed dorms with shower 280AS, with Welcome card (mid-June to mid-Sept.) 210AS.) **Gästehaus Stasny,** Steiner Landstr. 22 (tel. 828 43), offers nine comfortable beds in rooms with showers and cable TV, around a pleasant courtyard. (250-280AS per person. 20AS surcharge on stays less than 3 nights.) *Privatzimmer* abound on Steiner Landstr. **ÖAMTC Donau Camping,** Wiedeng. 7 (tel. 844 55), rests on the Danube, right by the marina. (Reception 7:30-10am and 4:30-8:30pm. 50AS per person plus 10.50AS tax, children 35AS; tents 30-60AS (bring your own); cars 40AS. Showers included. Electrical hookup 25AS. Facilities for disabled guests. English spoken. Open Easter to mid-Oct.)

The area around the pedestrian zone overflows with restaurants and streetside cafés. **Schwarze Kuchl,** Untere Landstr. 8 (tel. 831 28), offers a salad buffet (small 38AS, large 48AS), soup (20-30AS), and bread. (Open Mon.-Fri. 8am-7pm, Sat. 8am-1pm, first Sat. of the month until 5pm.) Right next door is the famous **Konditorei Hagmann** (tel. 83 167), known throughout Krems for its outstanding pastries and chocolates. Try the *Marillenstrudel* (28AS), but beware—you may find yourself returning for breakfast, lunch and dinner. Grab a *Wachauer Kugel* (ball of chocolate and nougat) for the road. (Open Mon.-Fri. 7am-7pm, Sat. 7am-1pm, first Sat. of the month until 6pm.) **Haus Hamböck,** Kellerg. 31 (tel. 845 68), in Stein, has a charming leafy terrace with a view of the town's spires and a restaurant bedecked with old *Faß* (kegs), presses, and other vineyard tools. The jolly proprietor gives free tours of the cellar, with a free tasting. (Wine 22AS a glass, snacks 30-50AS. Open daily 3pm till people leave.) The cheapest eats in town are available at the **Julius Meinl** supermarket, on the corner of Gaheisstr. and Obere Landstr. (Open Mon.-Fri. 7:30am-6:30pm, Sat. 7:30am-5pm.)

Sights and Entertainment In Stein, almost every building is on **Steiner Landstraße,** a stunningly preserved vestige of the Middle Ages. Don't stop here, however—climb the hills. Above Krems and Stein, the lovely terraced vineyards, with the vines photosynthesizing in neat little rows, immediately command attention. The **Heurigen** (wine cellars) are not to be missed. Plan carefully, however—the cellars can stay open only three weeks every two months from April to October. Better-safe-than-sorry types pick up a schedule from the tourist office; press-your-luck gamblers just stroll down Kellergasse in Stein and hope to happen upon on an open cellar. If you don't have time for *Heurigen,* stop by the city-owned **Weingut Stadt Krems,** Stadtgraben 11 (tel. 801 440; fax 801 442), on the edge of the pedestrian zone. This winery lacks the attached restaurant, but it does offer free tours of the cellar and bottling center. The free tastings that follow the tour usually seduce one or two visitors into buying a bottle of wine, which runs 40-100AS. (Open for tours Mon.-Fri. 8am-noon and 1-4pm, Sat. 8am-noon.) Those who can still walk straight should lunch down to the historic abbey cellar of **Kloster Und,** Undstr. 6 (tel. 73 073; fax 832 23 78), by the tourist office. The cellar has all of Austria's regional wines—for 140AS, you get a basket of bread, mineral water to cleanse the palate, and two hours to weave through the selection of more than 100 wines, from the noble Riesling of Wachau to the nutty Neuburger of Burgenland. Bring a sweater—dry white wines complain if not kept at 10 to 11 degrees Celsius.

Built in the Dominekanerkloster, the lovely **Weinstadt Museum,** Kornermarkt 14 (tel. 801 441), features the curious combination of paintings by the world-renowned Baroque artist Marten Johann Schmidt and, in the cloister cellars, archaeological treasures from the Paleolithic Era through the Middle Ages. Most charming are the many exhibits about the history, practice, and religious symbolism of viticulture. (Hours vary; call ahead and check before heading out.)

The *Fußgängerzone,* the center of mercantile activity, runs down Obere and Untere Landstr. The entrance to the pedestrian area is marked by the **Steiner Tor,** one of four medieval city gates flanked by two Gothic towers. Various market places line Obere Landstr. The first is Dominikanerpl., which houses the **Dominikaner Kirche,** now the Weinstadt Museum. Farther down the pedestrian zone is **Pfarrkirche Platz,** home of the Renaissance **Rathaus** and the **Pfarrkirche** with its piecemeal Romanesque, Gothic, and Baroque architecture. While there, walk up the hill to the **Piaristen-Kirche,** where newly renovated life-sized statues depict Jesus' crucifixion. Finally, at the end of the pedestrian zone is the **Simandlbrunnen,** a fountain depicting a husband kneeling in front of his domineering wife, begging for the house keys so he can stay out late with the boys.

Culturally, the double city enjoys a number of theater and music events and other rotating exhibits. The **Kunsthalle Krems** (tel. 86 69) has recently opened a new building on the corner of Steiner Landstr. and Dr.-Karl-Dorreck-Str., near Stein. The large exhibition hall always has a large cultural or historical exhibit, usually on postmodern and non-European art. (Open daily 10am-6pm. 40-90AS, discounts for students and seniors.) The **Motorrad-Museum Krems-Egelsee,** idling at Ziegelofeng. 1 (tel. 413 013), will keep the moto-maniac in you entranced for an afternoon. The museum features an extraordinary collection of exhibits on the history of motorcycles and motor technology. (Open daily 9am-5pm. 40AS, students 20AS.) Each year the one-day **Donaufestival** brings open-air music and dancing at the end of June and kicks off a summer of cultural activities that include theater, circus, symposia, *Lieder,* folk music, and even flamenco. From mid-July to the beginning of August, Krems hosts a **Musikfest,** featuring a number of organ, piano, and quartet concerts that take place in the Kunsthalle and various churches. Tickets are available at the Kunsthalle, Minoritenpl. 4, A-3504 Krems (tel. 826 69). Throughout the year, many **churches** have sacred music and organ concerts, which are overwhelmingly beautiful and usually free.

■ Melk

On March 24, 1089, Austrian Margrave Leopold II turned over the church and castle atop the Melk cliff to Benedictine Abbot Sigibod. This act begat the **Benedictine Monastery** and, subsequently, the village of Melk. Each year over 400,000 folks visit Melk, a lovely daytrip from Vienna or Krems and a stop on the Passau-Vienna cycling route.

Floating majestically over the town, the enormous white and yellow monastery is a treasure trove for Baroque enthusiasts and an important site in the history of the Austrian Catholic Church. Indeed, Austria invested heavily to restore this wedding cake of a building; the restoration project, begun in 1978, finished in 1996, just in time to celebrate Austria's 1000th birthday, "Ostarrichi-Österreich 996-1996." Melk is still a living monastery, home to 25 active monks who toil away inside—praying, brewing drinks, and teaching the youth of Austria at the monastery school. Below the abbey, life putters along by the Renaissance houses in narrow pedestrian zones, cobblestone streets, old towers, and remnants of the medieval city wall.

Orientation and Practical Information Trains link Melk to Amstetten and St. Pölten. **Bike rental** (150AS, with rail ticket 90AS), **currency exchange,** and **luggage storage** (30AS) are all available at the station. Just outside the station's main entrance is the **bus depot.** Bus #1451 chugs from Melk to Krems (64AS) and #1538 from Melk to St. Pölten (46AS). Melk lies on the **DDSG ferry** route between Vienna and Passau (from Vienna 530AS; from Krems 238AS; for information, see p. 164).

Melk's **tourist office** (tel. 230 732 or 230 733; fax 230 737), on the corner of Babenbergerstr. and Abbe-Stadler-G. next to the Rathauspl., has maps and pamphlets on town history and athletic activities in the Wachau region. The office has large **lockers** (10AS) and bike racks and makes room reservations for free. From the train station, walk down Bahnhofstr. and then straight on Bahng. Turn right at Rathauspl. and cross it, staying to the right side until you hit Abbe-Stadler-G. (Open July-Aug. daily 9am-7pm; Sept.-Oct. and April-June Mon.-Fri. 9am-noon and 2-6pm, Sat. 10am-2pm.) The **post office** is at Bahnhofstr. 3. (Open Mon.-Fri. 8am-noon and 2-6pm, Sat. 8-10am.) The **postal code** is A-3390. The **telephone code** is 02752.

Accommodations and Food Head back to Krems if everything is full in Melk. The recently renovated **Jugendherberge,** Abt-Karl-Str. 42 (tel. 26 81; fax 42 57), is about a 10-minute walk from the train station (turn right as you exit and follow the green signs). The friendly hostel offers 104 beds with picnicky checkered sheets in quads with private showers and hall toilets. In summer, guests can eat outside in an ivy-hung yard or make use of the ping-pong tables, volleyball net, and soccer area. (Reception daily 8-10am and 5-9pm. Dorms 147AS first 2 night, then 123AS; under 19 120AS, 107AS. Tax 10.50AS. Breakfast included. Open April-Oct.) *Privatzimmer* are another option—the tourist office has a list. **Camping Kolomaniau** (tel. 32 91) overlooks the Danube next to the ferry landing. (Reception 8am-midnight. 35AS, children 20AS; tents 35AS; cars 25AS. Tax 10.50AS. Showers 15AS.) **Gasthof Goldener Stern,** Sterng. 17 (tel. 22 14), has respectable rooms and hearty Austrian fare at its downstairs restaurant. Try a vegetable *pfannegerichte,* brought to the table in the pan—a whole month's supply of vitamins and cheese for only 85AS. (Reception daily 7am-midnight. Singles 260-300AS; doubles 400-500AS. Discounts on long stays. Hall showers and toilets. Breakfast included.)

Restaurants abound on Rathauspl., but look elsewhere for the less tourist-oriented joints. A five-minute walk west through Hauptpl. brings you to **Restaurant zum "Alten Brauhof,"** Linzerstr. 25 (tel. 22 96), with charming outdoor seating that almost looks out on the Danube. Try the buttery *Schnitzel* with fries or rice (90AS). Synthetic palm trees and oh-so-chic decor greet you at **Il Palio,** Wiener Str. 3 (tel. 47 32), but you'll be there to drink beer and taste some of the best ice cream in Austria. (Open daily 9am-midnight.) At night, the streets may seem empty, but **"Nostalgiebers I" Alt Melk,** Wienestr. 10 (tel. 44 58), certainly won't be. Step into the intimate warmth of deep red velvet curtains, cream-colored walls, and old black-and-white photo portraits and enjoy a *cabernet sauvignon* (28AS) or a milkshake with the genial, mixed-age crowd. (Open Sun.-Thurs. 4pm-2am, Fri.-Sat. 4pm-4am. Live music 1st and 3rd Thurs. of the month.) During the day, **SPAR Markt,** Rathauspl. 9, has bread to spread, pears to share, apples to grapple, oranges to…well, um…never mind. (Open Mon. and Wed.-Fri. 7am-6pm, Sat. 7am-noon.)

Clemens and Friedrich: Holier than Wood?

In the fourth century AD, the bodies of early Christian martyrs persecuted by the Romans would be hidden in the catacombs, their graves marked by urns of blood. When people found urns of blood found by a tomb (as by Clemens and Friedrich, the two housed in the side altar of Melk's abbey church), they knew they'd found a saint. By the 18th century, a major relic cult was flourishing, helped by the stipulation that a church could not be consecrated without a saint's remains. Traffic in relics of every conceivable body part raged. Not that Melk needed skeletons: the Melker Kreuz contains something that suffices quite nicely—a highly polished, thumbnail-sized piece of wood believed to be from the Holy Cross itself.

MELK ■ 169

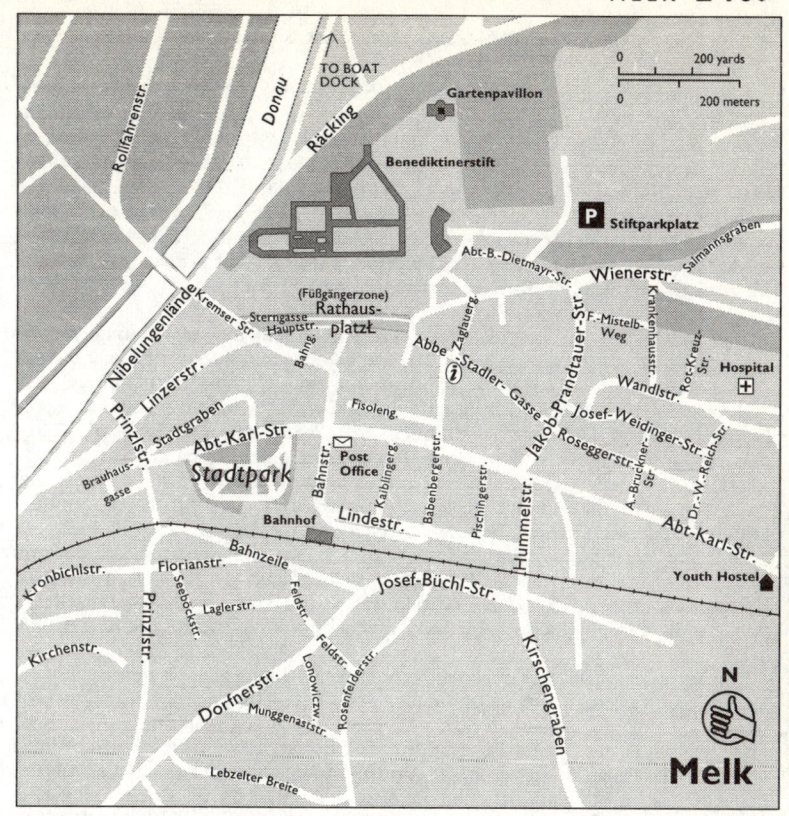

Sights and Entertainment To visit Melk is to visit the **Benediktinerstift** (Benedictine abbey), which commands marvelous views of the city and the surrounding Danube countryside. The "profane" wing is open to the damn public and includes the friggin' imperial chambers where such *%#!*@! notables as Emperor Karl VI, Pope Pius VI, and Napoleon took shelter. You won't find "Napoleon wuz here" scribbled anywhere, but the great and informative exhibits more than compensate. Stroll through the cool, marble halls and gaze at the Habsburg portraits lining the wall: in an act of political deference, Franz I points to his wife, the ever dominant Maria Theresa. The stunning **abbey library** is brimming with sacred and secular texts that were painstakingly hand-copied by monks. The two highest shelves in the gallery are fake—in typical Baroque fashion, the monks sketched book spines onto the wood to make the collection appear more formidable. The **church** itself, maintained by 25 monks, is a Baroque masterpiece. Maria Theresa donated the two skeletons that adorn the side altars—unknown holy men from the catacombs of Rome. But the centerpiece of the monastery is the **Melker Kreuz** (Melk Cross)—gold, jewels, the works, all circa 1363. Stolen twice, the Cross always exposed its thief and returned home to Melk through supernatural movement, perhaps inspiring the monastery's aggressive slogan *"Non coronabitur nisi legitime certaverit"* ("Without a legitimate battle, there is no victory"). The monks keep up with the times, allowing temporary exhibits of contemporary art and even commissioning modernist artist Peter Bischof to create new, harmonious paintings over the irreparable frescoes in the interior of the main courtyard. (Abbey open daily April-Oct. 9am-5pm; May-Sept. 9am-6pm. Last entry 1hr. before closing. Fantastic guided tours Nov.-March at 11am, 2, and (in

THE DANUBE (DONAU)

English) 3pm, or by arrangement. 55AS, students 30AS, tour 15AS. Call 231 22 32 for more information.)

Five kilometers out of town is **Schloß Schallaburg** (tel. (02754) 63 17), one of the most magnificent Renaissance castles in central Europe. The castle's architecture is reason enough to visit: Romanesque, Gothic, Renaissance, and Mannerist influences converge in the terra cotta arcades of the main courtyard. The floor explodes with a 1600-piece **mosaic.** The place doubles as the **International Exhibition Center of Lower Austria** (tel. 63 17), a center that goes out of its way to bring foreign cultures to life. Buses leave Melk's train station every day 10:30am and 3:10pm and leave the castle 15 minutes later (10min., 30AS, students 15AS). Or you can hike up to the complex; ask the tourist office for a map from Melk to the palace. (Open May-Sept. Mon.-Fri. 9am-5pm, Sat.-Sun. 9am-6pm. 60AS, students 20AS.)

Hikers can enjoy the network of trails surrounding Melk that wind through tiny villages, farmland, and wooded groves. The tourist office provides a great map, which lists area sights and hiking paths, and handouts on the 10km Leo Böck trail, 6km Seniorenweg, and 15km Schallaburggrundweg. **Cyclists** might enjoy a tour along the Danube toward Willendorf on the former canal-towing path. The **Venus of Willendorf,** an 11cm voluptuous stone figure and one of the world's most famous fertility symbols, was discovered there in 1908. Thought to be 30,000 years old, she is now on display in Vienna. A more sedate option, **ferries** travel to the other side of the Danube to **Arnsdorf,** where the local *jause* (an Austrian version of British high tea), here called *Hauerganse* (vintner's special), will load enough carbos to send you through the vineyards and apricot orchards back to Melk. The ferry returns past the **Heiratswald** (Marriage Woods). Romantic Melk awards couples who marry in Melk a young sapling tree, which the happy couple plants and tends for the rest of their lives.

The **Sommerspiele Melk** (Melk Summer Festival) comes to town in early July. An intimate open-air stage in front of the monastery's pavilion provides the perfect setting for creative staging and world-class theater. The acting is so fine and the ambience so special that even those with little knowledge of German can enjoy a wonderful evening. Tickets (from 105AS) are available at the Melk city hall, theater ticket offices, travel agencies throughout Austria, and the box office next to the monastery after 7:15pm before performances. (Performances early July to mid-Aug. Fri.-Sat. 8:30pm. For more information, call 23 07.)

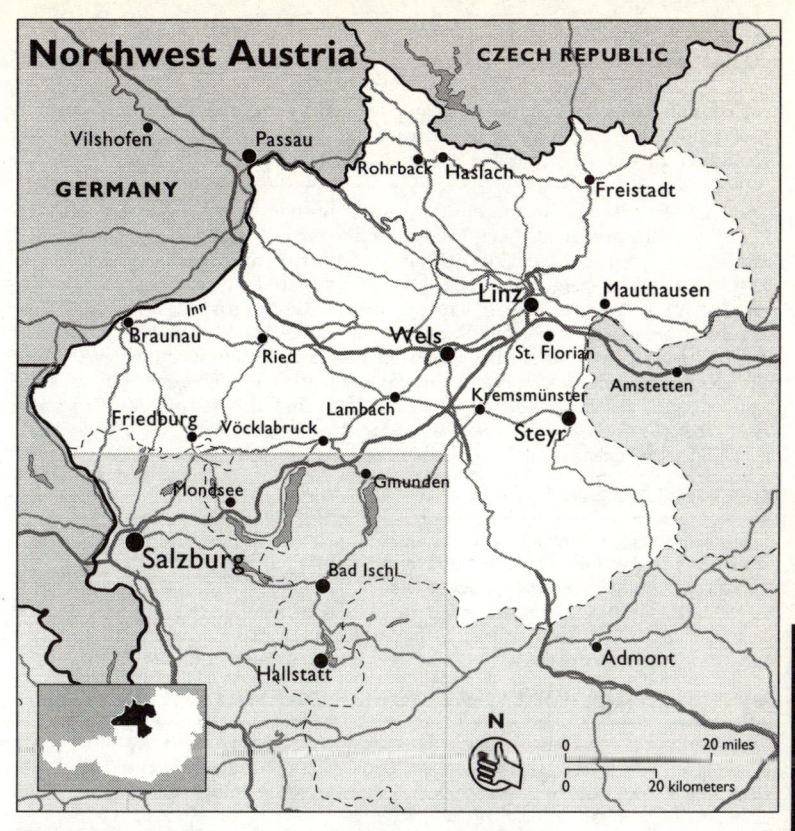

Northwest Austria

Oberösterreich (Upper Austria) derives its name not from its northern position but from the flow of the Danube in Austria; sister province Niederösterreich (Lower Austria) is where the river flows down into Hungary. The province encompasses everything north of Salzburg but not quite north of Vienna (that's Niederösterreich) and comprises three distinct regions: the **Mühlviertel** in the north; the **Innviertel** to the west of Linz in the Danube valley; and the **Pyhrn-Eisenwurz** in the south. The provincial capital is **Linz,** a major center of iron, steel, and chemical production and home to many modern Danube port installations. The area is Austria's second most productive source of oil and natural gas since World War II, and several large-scale hydroelectric power stations have been built along the Danube and its tributary, the Enns.

While the mountains here are less rugged, the relatively flat terrain makes for wonderful **bicycling tours,** heavily covered by the region's tourist offices and popular with vacationing locals. Well-paved paths, suitable for cyclers of any age and ability, wind their way through the entire province. A popular "cultural tour" of Upper Austria makes a circuit from Linz, through **Steyr,** and on to **Wels,** and several hotels in these towns offer special discounts for travelers on wheels. Four tours start from Wels and lead to the surrounding *Möst* country, where the local apple cider, unique for its pungent vinegar flavor, is brewed. Bike paths also follow the Danube southeast toward Vienna, bisecting the province.

Linz

> Linz is not Lienz, a small Italo-Austrian city in East Tirol. Many a tourist has inadvertently ended up in the wrong town. When asking for information, you can always state the city's complete name, Linz an der Donau.

The third largest city in the country and one-time home to Kepler, Mozart, Beethoven, Bruckner, and Hitler, Linz sits on the banks of the blue(ish) Danube and magisterially rules over the industrial sector of Austria. Sandwiched between Vienna to the east and Salzburg to the west, Linz suffers from the typical middle-child syndrome—not as cosmopolitan as Vienna yet not as quaintly provincial as Salzburg, Linz expends a great deal of effort to differentiate itself. It seems more rooted in the 20th century than many other Austrian cities, inviting tourists into its modern-art gallery and electronics museum. Its citizens are unusually friendly (unburdened by the tourist overload of Vienna and Salzburg), and its annual festivals—the orgiastic **Brucknerfest** (music festival) and the vibrant, pulsing **Pflasterspektakel** (street performer's fair)—draw artists and crowds from all over the world.

GETTING TO LINZ

Midway between Salzburg and Vienna and on the line between Prague and Graz, Linz is a transportation hub for both Austria and Eastern Europe. Transport to Linz is thus very simple. Frequent **trains** connect to major Austrian and European cities. All **buses** arrive and depart from the **Hauptbahnhof**, where schedules are available. Purchase tickets from the bus driver rather than attempting to plan around a sporadically open ticket window. **Motorists** can arrive on the main West Autobahn (A1 or E16).

ORIENTATION AND PRACTICAL INFORMATION

Linz straddles the **Danube**, which curves west to east through the city. Most of the *Altstadt* sights crowd along the southern bank, near **Nibelungenbrücke**. This pedestrian area includes the huge **Hauptplatz**, just south of the bridge, and extends down **Landstraße**, which ends near the train station.

Tourist Office: Hauptpl. 1 (tel. 707 01 777; fax 772 873; email tourist.infolinz@jk.uni-linz.ac.at), in the Altes Rathaus. The multilingual staff helps find rooms at no charge. Pick up *A Walk Through the Old Quarter* for a summary of the *Altstadt*'s main attractions. Open May-Sept. Mon.-Fri. 7am-7pm, Sat. 9am-7pm, Sun. 10am-7pm; Oct.-April Mon.-Fri. 8am-6pm, Sat. 9am-6pm, Sun. 10am-6pm.

Currency Exchange: At most **banks**, nearly all of which have **ATMs**. Banks are open Mon.-Wed. 8am-4:30pm, Thurs. 8am-5:30pm, Fri. 8am-2pm. Change larger amounts of cash at the **post office**, which offers better rates. Exchange open Mon.-Fri. 7am-5pm, Sat. 8am-1pm. 60AS commission.

American Express: Bürgerstr. 14, A-4021 Linz (tel. 669 013). All traveler's checks cashed, but no currency exchanged. Open Mon.-Fri. 9am-5:30pm, Sat. 9am-noon.

Trains: Hauptbahnhof, Bahnhofpl. (tel. 17 17). To: **Vienna** (every 30min., 2hr., 264AS); **Salzburg** (every 30min., 1½hr., 192AS); **Innsbruck** (every hr., 3½hr., 516AS); **Munich** (every hr., 3hr., 400AS); and **Prague** (4 per day, 4hr., 265AS).

Ferries: Wurm & Köck floats between **Passau** (tel. (0851) 929 292, fax 355 18) and **Linz** (tel. (0732) 783 607; fax 783 60 79). 5-7hr., depending on current. One-way 242AS. Boats reach and leave Linz at the Donau Schiffstation, on the south side of the river, and stop at a number of Austrian and Bavarian towns along the way. Discounts for seniors and children under 15. Ferries run late April-Oct.

Public Transportation: Linz's public transport system runs to all corners of the city. Two trams (#1 and 3) start near the *Hauptbahnhof* and run north through the city along Landstr. and Hauptpl. and across Nibelungenbrücke. Several buses crisscross Linz as well. Nearly all vehicles pass through **Blumauerpl.**, down the block and to the right from the train station. The hub closer to the city center is **Taubenmarkt**, south of Hauptpl. on Landstr. A ticket for 4 stops or less ("Mini") costs 9AS;

ACCOMMODATIONS AND CAMPING ■ 173

more than 4 ("Midi") 18AS; and a 24hr. ticket ("Maxi") 36AS. Buy tickets from any machine at all bus or streetcar stops and stamp them before boarding; those caught *Schwarzfahren* (riding without a ticket) fork over 400AS. Weekly passes valid Mon.-Sun. Multiple-day passes available at *Tabaks* and the tourist office—stamp them as well before you board the first time.

Taxis: At the **Hauptbahnhof**, Blumauerpl., and Hauptpl., or call 69 69.
Parking: Free parking at **Urfahrmarkt.**
Bi-Gay-Lesbian Organizations: Homosexuelle Initiative Linz (HOSI), Schubertstr. 36 (tel. 600 898). Discussion tables Thurs. 8pm at Gasthaus Agathon, Kapuzinerstr. 46. **Frauenfropenbüro,** Klosterstr. 7 (tel. 177 20 18 50).
Bike Rental: At the train station. 150AS per day, with train ticket 90AS. **Neues Amtsgebäude,** Urfahrmarkt 1. 100AS per day. Open daily 10am-6pm.
Luggage Storage: At the train station. 30AS. Lockers 20-30AS.
Pharmacies: Central Linz has *Apotheke* everywhere. Try **Central Apotheke,** Mozartstr. 1 (tel. 771 783). Open Mon.-Fri. 8am-noon and 2-6pm, Sat. 8am-noon.
Post Office: Bahnhofpl. 11, next to the train and bus stations. Open Mon.-Fri. 7am-8pm, Sat. 7:30am-8pm. Information open Mon.-Fri. 8am-5pm, Sat. 8am-4pm.
Postal Code: A-4020.
Telephone Code: 0732.

ACCOMMODATIONS AND CAMPING

Linz suffers from a lack of cheap rooms. The city is just urban enough that locals aren't allowed to rent rooms privately, so it's usually best to stick to the youth hostels. Wherever you stay, call ahead to ensure a room; vacant rooms never remain so for long. You may also consider taking the train to the nearby town of Steyr (every hr., 45min., change trains in St. Valentin). See **Steyr,** p. 177, for complete information.

Jugendherberge Linz (HI), Kapuzinerstr. 14 (tel. 782 720 or 778 777), near Hauptpl., offers the cheapest beds in town in an excellent location. From the train station, tram #3: "Taubenmarkt" then cross Landstr., walk down Promenade, continue on Klammstr., and turn left on Kapuzinerstr. The hostel's on the right. Airy, quiet rooms. Cats roam the picnic-tabled courtyard. 36 beds in 4- to 6-bed rooms. Reception daily 8-10am and 5-8pm or so. The friendly young proprietress speaks perfect English with an American-English-Australian accent. No curfew; the key to your free locker opens the front door. Dorms 150AS, under 19 125AS. Non-members add 40AS. Private showers. Breakfast 25AS. Sheets included. Laundry available. Reservations recommended.

Jugendgästehaus (HI), Stanglhofweg 3 (tel. 66 44 34). From Blumauerpl. (near the train station), bus #27 (dir: Schiffswerft): "Froschberg." Walk straight on Ziegeleistr., turn right on Roseggerstr., and continue on to Stanglhofweg. Bland exterior conceals a livable interior. Clean and spacious with lots of closet space. Private showers and hall toilets. Reception daily 8am-4pm and 6-11pm. Singles 303AS; doubles 406AS; quads 612AS. Guest tax 8AS. Breakfast included. Call ahead.

Goldenes Dachl, Hafnerstr. 27 (tel. 67 54 80). From the train station, bus #21: "Auerspergpl." Continue in the same direction along Herrenstr. for half a block, then turn left onto Wurmstr. Hafnerstr. is the first right. Or turn right on Bahnhofstr. and bear left onto Volksgartenstr. before Blumauerpl. Continue until it hits Herrenstr. then turn left on Wurmstr. Narrow corridors and staircases allow for large rooms. Run by a motherly woman with an eye for comfort. Singles 260AS; doubles 460AS, with shower 490AS. This little *Pension* has only 15 beds—call ahead.

Gasthof Wilder Mann, Goethestr. 14 (tel. 65 60 78). From the station, go down Bahnhofstr., turn left on Landestr. at Blumauerpl., then turn right on Goethestr. (7min.). 2min. from Blumauerpl., the main transportation hub. Large, impeccable rooms, many with sofa and chairs. Restaurant downstairs. Reception daily 8am-9pm. Singles 300AS, with shower 370AS; doubles 520AS, 620AS. Breakfast 50AS.

Camping Pleschinger See (tel. 24 78 70). On the Linz-Vienna biking path on Pleschinger Lake. 45AS; tents 45AS. Tents only. Open May to late Sept.

FOOD

Duck into the alleyway restaurants off Hauptpl. and Landstr. to avoid ridiculously inflated menu prices. Linz's namesake dessert, the **Linzer Torte,** is unique for its deceptively dry ingredients—very little flour and absolutely no cream. The secret is in the red-currant jam filling, which slowly seeps through and moisturizes the dry, crumbly crust. Not all *Linzer Tortes* are the same; the best *tortes* sit out for at least two days after baking for maximum jam saturation.

Café Traxlmeyer, Promenadestr. 16. Make Trax for a delicious breakfast! (It had to be said. We apologize for any harm caused to you or your loved ones.) Giant orange awnings shade the garden tables of this Viennese-style café. For 50AS you can nibble on rolls and jam, sip coffee from your own little pot, flip through newspapers, and dream up your own horrid puns until the afternoon. *Tortes* 24AS. Open Mon.-Sat. 8am-10pm.

Mangolds, Hauptpl. 3. Vegetarian Valhalla. This cafeteria-style restaurant in screaming primary colors offers only the fresh stuff. Nearly all the vegetables and eggs are 100% organic. Extravagant salad bar and freshly-squeezed fruit drinks. Entrees 43-68AS. Open Mon.-Fri. 11am-8pm, Sat. 11am-5pm.

Etagen Beisl Weinstube, Domg. 8 (tel. 771 346), on the 2nd floor. Mingle with locals and wash down the *Oma's Pfandl* (granny's frying pan) special with beer until the wee hours. Hot entrees 77-97AS. Open Tues.-Sat. 6pm-2am.

Jindrak Konditorei, Herrenstr. 22, though other branches dot Linz. Rumored to serve the best *Linzer Torte* (17.50AS) in Linz. Other mouth-watering sweets line up behind the counters. Open Mon.-Sat. 8am-6pm.

Levante, Hauptpl. 13 (tel. 793 430). Real Turkish and Greek food at real prices. Open daily 11:30am-11:30pm.

Gasthaus Goldenes Schiff, Ottensheimerstr. 74 (tel. 239 879). On the scenic banks of the Danube. From Hauptpl., cross the bridge, turn left, go around the Neues Rathaus, and walk upstream along the river for 7min. Well worth the walk. Locals pile in the *Gastgarten* for 100AS dinners. Open Wed.-Sun. 9am-10pm.

Markets

Julius Meinl, Landstr. 50. Open Mon.-Fri. 7:30am-6:30pm, Sat. 7:30am-5pm.

SPAR Market, Steing. at Walterg., near the hostels. Open Mon.-Fri. 7:30am-1pm.

SIGHTS AND ENTERTAINMENT

Start your exploration of Linz at **Hauptplatz,** which hugs the Danube's south bank. The city constructed the enormous plaza in the 14th and 15th centuries when it gained new wealth from the taxation of all the salt and iron passing through the town. The focus of the square is the marble **trinity column,** symbolizing the city's escape from the horrors of war, famine, and the plague in the 18th century. An octagonal tower and an astronomical clock crown the Baroque **Altes Rathaus.** To date, only two people have ever addressed the public from the its balcony: Adolf Hitler and Pope John Paul II. Free-spirited star-gazer Johannes Kepler (the fellow who formulated the elliptical geometry of planetary orbit) wrote his major work, *Harmonices Mundi,* while living around the corner at Rathausg. 5. The building now houses Uncle Dagobert's Dart Den—a few beers may inspire you to rethink the geometry of the dartboard. On nearby Domgasse stands Linz's glorious twin-towered **Alter Dom** (Old Cathedral). The 19th-century symphonic composer and organist extraordinaire Anton Bruckner played here during his stint as church organist. (Open daily 8am-noon and 3-6:30pm.) To the south, the neo-Gothic **Neuer Dom** (New Cathedral) impresses visitors with its 19th-century, Godzilla-scale edifice (the largest in Austria). For sheer olfactory ecstasy, visit the **Botansicher Garten's** world-famous cactus and orchid collections. (Open daily May-Aug. 7:30am-7:30pm; Sept. and April 8am-7pm; Oct. and March 8am-6pm; Nov.-Feb. 8am-5pm. 10AS, under 18 free.)

Cross Nibelungenbrücke to reach the left bank of the Danube. This area of Linz, known as **Urfahr,** was a separate city until Linz swallowed it up in the early decades of this century. This section boasts some of the oldest buildings in the city and a captivating view of Linz from the apex of the **Pöstlingberg** (537m). To reach the base of the summit, take tram #3: "Bergbahnhof Urfahr." From there, either hike 0.5km up Hagenstr. (off Rudolphstr., which is off Hauptstr. near the bridge) or hop aboard the **Pöstlingbergbahn** (tel. 780 17 545), a San Francisco-style trolley car that ascends the summit in a scenic 20 minutes (every 20min. daily 5:20am-8pm, 25AS, round-trip 40AS, children half-price). The twin-towered **Pöstlingbergkirche** (Parish Church), the city symbol, stands guard over the city from the hill's crest. To indulge your nascent romanticism, take the Grottenbahn into the fairy-tale **caves** of Pöstlingberg, outfitted with dwarves, dragons, and Princes Charming. (Open April -Nov. Mon.-Fri. 9am-6pm, Sat.-Sun. 10am-5pm; Dec. daily 10am-5pm. 45AS, under 15 20AS.)

Linz is also equipped with many intriguing museums. The **Neue Galerie,** Blütenstr. 15 (tel. 23 93 36 00), on the second floor of the Lentia 2000 shopping center across the river, boasts one of Austria's best modern and contemporary art collections. Works by Klimt, Kokoschka, Lieberman, and others line the walls. (Open June-Sept. Mon.-Wed. and Fri. 10am-6pm, Thurs. 10am-10pm, Sat. 10am-1pm; Oct.-May Mon.-Wed. and Fri.-Sun. 10am-6pm, Thurs. 10am-10pm. 60AS, students 30AS.) The new **Ars Electronica,** Hauptstr. 2 (tel. 712 12 10; fax 712 12 12; email info@aec.at; http://www.aec.at), just over the bridge from Hauptpl., bills itself as the "museum of the future." It's a bird, it's a plane, it's *you* strapped to the ceiling in a full-body flight simulator that sends you soaring over Upper Austria. After this not-so-natural high, head downstairs to the CAVE, an amazing interactive 3-D room, for an experience guaranteed not to leave you flat. The museum hopes to offer email access for visitors soon. (Open Wed.-Sun. 11am-7pm. 80AS, students and seniors 40AS.) The **Linzer Schloßmuseum,** Tummelpl. 10 (tel. 774 419), presents the city's history. (Open Tues.-Fri. 9am-5pm, Sat.-Sun. 10am-4pm. 50AS, students 30AS. English brochure available.)

From mid-September to mid-October, the month-long **Brucknerfest** rages on as the city stages the works of Linz's native son Anton Bruckner at the Brucknerhaus concert hall, an acoustically perfect venue (220-1100AS, standing room 40-50AS). Contact Brucknerhauskasse, Untere Donaulände 7, A-4010 Linz (tel. 775 230; fax 761 22 01; http://www.brucknerhaus.linz.at) for tickets. (Open daily 10am-6pm.) The opening concert (the end of the first week in Sept.), billed as *Klangwolke* (Sound Cloud), includes a spectacular open-air laser show accompanied by Bruckner's Seventh Symphony broadcast live into the surrounding Donaupark to the thrill of 50,000 fans. During the third weekend of July, the city hosts **Pflasterspektakel,** a free, two- to three-day international street performers' festival. Every few steps down Landstr. and Hauptpl., different performers from as far away as Australia perform Houdini acts, fire-eating, outdoor theater, bongo concerts, and other such feats before the young, funky, social crowd that converges on Linz to cheer them on.

Linzer nightlife is sleepy but does have a pulse. Prod it awake at the **Bermuda Dreieck** (Bermuda Triangle), behind the west side of Hauptpl. (head down Hofg. or just follow the crowds of decked-out pub crawlers. Frequented by *Linzers* as well as tourists, this area has the highest bar- and nightclub-to-square-meter ratio in the city. In Hauptplatz itself, try **Alte Welt Weinkeller,** Hauptpl. 4, a popular hangout for a mixed crowd of Linzers. Soak up wine and spirits in this arcaded, Renaissance-era "wine and culture cellar." (Open Mon.-Sat. 5pm-2am, food served 6-11pm.) **17er Keller,** Hauptpl. 17 (duck through the archway and enter the steel door on your right), will serve you an apple-juice-and-cinnamon tequila while you listen to their mix of jazz, funk, blues, and rock. (Open Mon.-Sat. 7pm-2am, Sun. 7pm-1am.) For reggae and a mellow, mixed-ages crowd, drop by **Café Say,** Klammstr. 6 (tel. 774 521), off Promenadeg. and around the corner from the youth hostel. (Open 6pm until whenever everyone leaves.) Gay bar-hoppers hop to the subdued **C+C Café,** Bethlehemstr. 30 (tel. 770 862), managed by a grandmotherly hostess who may be the nicest *Linzerin* in all the city. (Open Mon.-Sat. 6pm to whenever people go home.) *Linzers* also flock to the other side of the Danube for after-hours entertainment. Grab a bench at **Fischergartl,** Flußg. 3 (tel. 710 123), the beer garden on the left as you cross the bridge. (Open Mon.-Thurs. 11:30am-2pm and 5pm-1am, Fri.-Sat. 6pm-1am.)

Near Linz

MAUTHAUSEN

About half an hour down the Danube from Linz stand the remains of a Nazi concentration camp (*Konzentrationslager*, abbreviated KZ). Unlike other camps in south Germany and Austria, Mauthausen remains very much intact. The barracks in which 200,000 prisoners, mainly Russian and Polish, toiled, suffered, and perished are clearly visible, rising bleakly from the landscape. The chilling sight renders the memorials that enjoin the world to "Never Forget" almost superfluous. The **Todessteige** (Staircase of Death) leads to the stone quarry where inmates were forced to work until exhaustion. The steep but even steps currently in place were added for tourists' safety—when the inmates worked here, there was nothing but a twisted, stony path dotted with boulders and jagged rocks. As the prisoners descended, the guards often violently pushed the last in line so that the entire group tumbled down the path. Occasionally the SS simply pushed prisoners off the heights onto the rocks and into the deep murky pond below—the surrounding cliff was known as **Parachuter's Wall.** The inner part of the camp is now a museum (tel. (07238) 22 69). Also accessible are the roll call grounds, gas chambers, torture rooms, and barracks (inmates polished the floors and walls every single day and were only allowed to enter barefoot). A free brochure or audio-tape tour (in English) walks you though the central part of the camp. (Open April-Sept. 8am-5pm; Oct. to mid-Dec. and Feb.-March 8am-4pm. Last entrance 1hr. before closing. 20AS, students and seniors 10AS.) To reach the camp from **Linz,** take a **train** to Mauthausen (transfer at St. Valentin). A special **Oberösterreichischer Verkehrsverbund day pass** (102AS) pays for the round-trip train ticket from Linz plus all city transportation in Linz and Mauthausen. Beware—the Mauthausen train station is 6km away from the camp, and a bus stops 2km from the camp only twice a day during the week and not at all on weekends. A better option is to store luggage (30AS) at the Mauthausen **train station** (tel. (67238) 22 07) and rent a **bicycle** (70AS with train ticket). Pick up a map from the train station. If traveling **by car,** exit Autobahn A1 (Vienna-Linz) at Enns.

ST. FLORIAN ABBEY

Seventeen kilometers from Linz lies the abbey of St. Florian, Austria's oldest Augustinian monastery. According to legend, the martyr Florian was bound to a millstone and thrown in the Enns river. Although he perished, the stone miraculously floated and is today the abbey's cornerstone. The complex owes much of its fame to composer Anton Bruckner, who began his career here first as choirboy, then as teacher, and finally as organist. His body is interred beneath the organ, allowing him to groove to the vibrations of his well-loved pipes for eternity. The abbey (tel. (07224) 890 210; fax 890 260) contains the **Altdorfer Gallery,** filled with altarpieces by 15th-century artist Albrecht Altdorfer of Regensburg, master of the Danube school. The fourteen **Kaiserzimmer** (imperial rooms), built in case of an imperial visit, virtually rumble with Baroque splendor. Inside the spectacular, recently renovated church (the only part of the abbey accessible without a tour) sits the enormous **Bruckner Organ.** Twenty-minute concerts on the monster instrument play every day at 2:30pm (30AS, students 20AS). A tour of the abbey minus the *Kaiserzimmer* leaves daily. (Abbey open April-Oct. 70AS, students 60AS, children 20AS. Tours every hr. 10-11am and 2-4pm). To reach the abbey from Linz, take bus #2040 or 2042: "St. Florian Stift," but pick up the bus again at "St. Florian Markt" in downtown St. Florian or "Lagerhaus." Both are a 15-minute walk from the abbey (30min., round-trip 48AS).

KREMSMÜNSTER

The fabulous **Kremsmünster Abbey** (tel. (07583) 527 52 16; fax 527 52 88), 32km south of Linz, belongs to Austria's oldest order and dates from AD 777 (an auspicious year for an abbey). Some 75 monks still call the abbey home, and it administers parish churches as far-flung as Brazil. The abbey owns most of the land in the area, including 3800 hectares of woods and a wine-producing vineyard (the monks' wine is sold at the ticket office). The **library,** which has two rows of books on every shelf and hidden doors in the bookcases, is Austria's third largest and boasts many medieval tomes. Visitors are not allowed to handle the books, but guides will take out any volume and page through it for you on request. The **Kaisersaal,** built in case of an imperial visit, is a rich Baroque gallery with marble columns and somewhat cartoonish ceiling frescoes that make the rooms seem much higher than they actually are. The abbey's **Kunstsammlung** (art collection) tour covers the library, the Kaisersaal, several art galleries, and the **Schatzkammer** (treasury), which shelters a beautifully engraved golden chalice dating from the time of Charlemagne. The monks' collection of minerals and semi-exotic animal specimens is on display in the seven-story **Sternwarte.** Also open to visitors is the **Fischkalter,** five fantastic fish fens for feeding fasting friars' friends fresh flounder. Actually, the Fischkalter is a series of arcaded pools set with pastoral statues spouting water. Wooden stag heads adorned with real antlers adorn the room—see if you can find the two with radishes in their mouths. (Open daily 9am-noon and 1-6pm. Central chapel free. Fischkalter 10AS—entrance through the ticket office. Kunstsammlung tours April-Oct. at 10, 11am, 2, 3, and 4pm; Nov.-March at 11am and 2pm. 1hr. 45AS, students 30AS. Sternwarte tour May-Oct. 10am, 2, and 4pm. 1½hr. 50AS, students 20AS. Both tours include the Fischkalter.)

The town of Kremsmünster itself boasts twisty medieval streets and daunting, steep stairway paths overgrown with moss and wildflowers. Fresh fruit sprouts up at the **open-air market** in Marktpl. (Open Fri. 1-6pm.) **Café Schlair** (tel. (07583) 777 217), on Haupstr. kitty-corner from the tourist office, serves pastries and fresh-fruit drinks for 25-40AS. (Open Mon.-Tues. and Thurs. 8am-7pm, Wed. 8am-noon, Fri. 8am-5pm, Sat.-Sun. 8am-6:30pm.) If you decide to stay the night, try the **Bauernhof Gossenhub,** Schürzendorf 1 (tel. (07583) 77 52), a lovely farmhouse with clean, simple rooms for 160AS (40AS surcharge for stays of less than 3 days).

Trains go to Kremsmünster from **Linz** (every hr., 45min., 128AS). From the station, follow Bahnhofstr. as it curves left, then right, then left again, and continue on to Marktpl. The path to the abbey starts at the **tourist office,** Rathauspl. 1 (tel. (07583) 72 12; open Tues. and Fri. 9am-noon and 3-6pm, Wed.-Thurs. 9am-noon).

STEYR

Steyr is famous as a jewel of medieval city planning. Much of the city looks as it has for the past 500 years, with winding, narrow cobbled alleyways, carved arches, and high stone walls. Two mountain rivers, the **Steyr** and the **Enns,** intersect in the middle of the town, dicing Steyr into 3 distinct parts. Steyr's comely surface hides the city's industrial identity. The city is well-known for its iron trade and holds a unique position in the annals of modern technology—in 1884, Steyr was the first town in Europe to use electric street lighting. Who would have guessed?

Stadtplatz, packed with 15th-century buildings, is the *Altstadt*'s focal point. The 16th-century **Leopoldibrunnen** (Leopold fountain), with its ornamental, wrought-iron spigots and bright flowers, vies with the Rococo **Rathaus** across the square for the title of ornamental heavyweight champion. Gotthard Hayberger, Steyr's famous mayor, architect, and Renaissance man-about-town, designed the town hall. The former **Dominican Church** (*Marienkirche*), also crammed into Stadtpl., was born a Gothic building but grew into a Baroque facade in the early 17th century. Unfortunately, most of Steyr's beautiful residences have been transformed into banks or shops, with modern interiors hidden behind ornate facades. The major exception is the **Innerberger Stadel,** Grünmarkt 26. Now the local **Heimatmuseum,** it contains a plethora of puppets, an extensive stuffed bird collection, and the three Cs of medieval weaponry: crossbows, cannons, and cutlery. (Open Tues.-Sun. 10am-4pm. Free.) Berggasse, one of the numerous narrow lanes typical of Steyr, leads from Stadtpl. up to the pink **Lamberg Schloß,** where the **Schloß Galerie** showcases temporary art exhibits. (Open Tues.-Sun. 10am-noon and 2-5pm. 25AS, students and children free.) If you're not in the museum mood, wander in the palace's cool green courtyards.

Trains connect Steyr to Linz (approx. every hr., 45min., 69AS, round-trip 138AS). To reach the city center from the train station, exit the station right and take the first left onto Bahnofstr. After crossing the river, turn left immediately down Engeg., which leads straight to Stadtpl. The **tourist office,** Stadtpl. 27 (tel. 532 29; fax 532 29 15, email steyr-info@ris.at; http://www.upper.austria.org/regionen/steyr), in the *Rathaus,* offers **guided tours** of the town (May-Oct. Sat. 2pm) and **headset tours** anytime the office is open. Either tour is 45AS. (Open Jan.-Nov. Mon.-Fri. 8:30am-6pm, Sat. 9am-noon; Dec. Mon.-Fri. 8:30am-6pm, Sat. 9am-4pm, Sun. 10am-3pm.)

■ Admont

The tiny town of Admont, the gateway to the Gesäuse Alpine region, lies just over the Styrian border on the Enns River. Benedictine monks first built an abbey here in the 11th century, and although fire has repeatedly ravaged the complex, the stubborn friars have refused to let the church go up in smoke. The current **Benediktinerstift** (Benedictine abbey) was completed in 1776. Its domed ceiling, supported by thick brick walls, saved the library from yet another fire in 1865; the abbey was the sole unharmed building. The frescoed **library,** the largest monastery collection in the world, contains over 150,000 volumes, including 9th-century illuminated manuscripts on display. Four Joseph Stemmel statues dominate the central gallery. *Death* portrays a human skeleton (look closely—the wings are actually hanging folds of skin). The virtues of *Heaven* are tame next to the vices of *Hell,* Stemmel's most famous work. Seven figures represent the seven deadly sins, including wrath (the crazed main figure) and intemperance (with bottle and sausages). But most unusual is *The Last Judgement,* in which a small devil (whose glasses and beard supposedly cast him in the image of the abbey treasurer of Stemmel's time) crouches at the young man's feet. From the walls, sixty-eight gilded busts of philosophers, poets, and historians glare disdainfully at the intellectually inferior below. Hidden stairways lead to the upper balconies—the guides happily direct wayward wanderers. The same building holds the **Schatzkammermuseum** (tel. 23 12), which contains Admont artifacts, and the **natural history museum,** full of bottled snakes, insects, and other assorted animalia. (Library and museums open April-Oct. daily 10am-1pm and 2-5pm; Nov.-March by appointment. Combined admission 60AS, students 30AS. English information sheets 5AS.) The **Heimatmuseum,** which displays local historical paraphernalia, is also in the abbey complex. (Open May-Oct. daily 9:30am-noon and 1-4:30pm. 20AS, children 10AS.) The abbey isn't entirely secular, however—a huge neo-Gothic **church** stands in the middle of the grounds (free).

The other reason to come to Admont is—honestly—the youth hostel, **Schloß Röthelstein** (tel. 24 32; fax 279 583), reputedly the most beautiful hostel in Europe. Housed in a restored 330-year-old castle, the hostel presides over the town and boasts ski lifts, winter ice skating, a sauna (costs extra), a tennis court, a soccer field, and even a small track. Indoors, a huge stone hall with draped ivy, chandeliers, and two floors of arches serves as the main dining area, and an exquisite *Rittersaal* (knights' hall) functions as a concert venue. You'll forget you're in a hostel when you see the large rooms and windows, brass fixtures, wood furniture, private telephones, and elegant lamps. The only challenge is getting here—yes, it *is* that lone castle sitting very high on the very big hill. Store heavy bags at the train station (30AS overnight) and prepare for a 45-minute walk. From the train station, turn left down Bahnhofstr. and left again at the post office. Cross the tracks and continue straight down that road for 25 minutes (don't turn right at the "Fußweg" sign pointing to the castle, unless you feel mountain-goatish), past the lumberyard. Turn right at the "Schloßherberge Röthelstein" sign and follow the paved road as it curves up and up. Morning buses run from the station only to the base of the uphill path. Taxis (tel. 28 01 or 23 23) from the station run about 60AS. Dorm-style rooms are usually reserved for groups. (3- to 4-bed dorms 145-185AS; 4- to 8-bed dorms 130-155AS; 2-bed dorms 215-260AS. 40AS surcharge for stays of less than 3 nights. Open Jan.-Oct. Hearty meals 50AS. Parking.) If the trek is too intimidating, you might try a *Privatzimmer.* Several line

Paradiesstr. along the route to the hostel and generally run about 180-250AS. Closer to the town center, **Frühstückspension Mafalda,** Bachpromenade 75 (tel. 21 88), awaits travelers who just couldn't face the uphill climb to the hostel. At the post office, turn left and cross over the rail tracks and then take the next two rights and cross over the tracks again. Mafalda is right under the tracks—a fact all too evident come sleepy-time. (Singles 240AS; doubles 420AS. Hall showers included. 40AS surcharge for one-night stays.) The **ADEG supermarket** is on the way to the tourist office. (Open Mon.-Thurs. and Sat. 7:30am-noon, Fri. 7:30am-noon and 3-6pm.)

The Admont **tourist office** (*Fremdenverkehrsbüro;* tel. 21 64; fax 36 48) tracks down rooms for free. To reach the tourist office from the train station, turn left down Bahnhofstr. and take the second right at the conspicuous post office; the tourist office is five minutes away on the left. (Open Mon.-Fri. 8am-noon and 2-6pm, Sat. 9am-noon; Sept.-May Mon. 8am-noon, Tues.-Fri. 8am-5pm.) **Trains** run to **Selzthal,** the regional hub (every 1-2hr., 34AS). Get to Selzthal from Linz (2hr., 168AS; see **Linz,** p. 172) or via Bruck an der Mur (every 2hr., 1¼hr.) **Buses** depart from the front of the tourist office. The **postal code** is A-8911. Admont's **telephone code** is 03613.

THE MÜHLVIERTEL

Far north of the smoggy environs of Linz, the Mühlviertel offers shaded woodland paths, quiet agricultural fields, and pastures populated only by the occasional cow. The region was once the stomping grounds of pagan Celts. The Christians stormed in during the Middle Ages and decided to civilize, decorating the terrain with churches constructed out of the supposedly Celt-proof local granite. When not saving the world from pagans, this granite filters the famed mineral-rich waters of the region, considered curative in homeopathic circles.

Although the Mühlviertel is still considered part of industrial Austria, the region's industry is really of the arts-and-crafts variety. Along the popular centuries-old **Mühlviertel Weberstraße** (Fabric Trail), analogous on a country-lane scale to the Middle Eastern Silk Road, various textile-oriented towns display their unique methods of linen preparation. Other vacation trails include the **Gotische Straße,** which winds past multitudes of High Gothic architectural wonders, and the **Museum Straße,** which boasts more **Freilichtmuseums** (open-air museums) than you can shake a loom at. These museum villages typically recreate the 15th- and 16th-century peasant lifestyle in a functional hamlet. Iron from Steiermark (Styria) flowed through the Mühlviertel on its way to Bohemia along the **Pferdeisenbahn,** an ancient trade route once traversed by horse-drawn caravans and now a favorite hiking route. All through this pastoral countryside, *Bauernhöfe* (farm houses) open their doors to world-weary vacationers in search of a little rural R&R. For nifty tourist brochures about trails, *Bauernhöfe,* area hiking, or the Mühlviertel in general, contact the **Mühlviertel Tourist Office,** Blütenstr. 8, A-4040 Linz, Postfach 57 (tel. (0732) 235 020 or 238 155).

■ Freistadt

Due to its strategic location on the *Pferdeeisenbahn,* **Freistadt** was a stronghold of the medieval salt and iron trade and remains the main city in industrial Mühlviertel. Unlike most industrial cities, however, Freistadt basks in fresh air and lush, verdant crop fields; coming up from Linz, you'll be surprised by the sudden shift from brick walls to rolling pastures. In 1985, Freistadt received the International Europa Nostra Prize for the finest restoration of a medieval *Altstadt.* Visitors can journey around its well-preserved inner and outer wall fortifications, scan the horizon from its watch tower, feast inside its castle, and swim in the surrounding moat. Come sit in one of the many Gastgärten perched on the city's inner wall overlooking the moat and enjoy the locally brewed **Freistädter Bier.** Many liken Freistadt to Germany's Rothenburg, another town seemingly untouched for the past, oh, five or six centuries.

Orientation and Practical Information Freistadt, at the juncture of the Jaunitz and Feldiast Rivers, is easily accessible from **Linz. Buses** are the most convenient option. Buses #2232 and 2084 leave from Linz's main train station every hour (round-trip 100AS) and arrives at Böhmertor in Freistadt, which lies just outside the old city walls, a two-minute walk to Hauptpl. **Trains** from Linz run every two hours (round-trip 78AS) and arrive at the *Hauptbahnhof,* 3km outside of town. You can catch the city **shuttle bus** from the back of the station to Hauptpl. (10AS). The shuttle, however, only runs weekdays, leaving the train station twice daily at 8:25 and 11:25am. To hoof it to the city center, turn right, walk down the street (it will merge with Leonfeldnerstr.), turn left onto Bahnhofstr. (which becomes Brauhausstr.), and follow it until the end at Promenade/Linzerstr. At this intersection, the main gate to the town, the Linzertor, will be visible; **Hauptplatz** lies within. **Taxis** (tel. 723 54) to the old town cost 70-100AS. The tiny **tourist office,** Hauptpl. 12 (tel. 729 74; fax 732 07), has a free reservations service and provides information about the surrounding Mühlviertel villages. (Open May-Sept. Mon.-Fri. 9am-noon and 3-7pm, Sat. 9am-noon; Oct.-April Mon.-Fri. 9am-noon and 2-5pm.) **Store luggage** (30AS) and **rent bikes** (150AS, with train ticket or Eurailpass 90AS) at the station. The **post office,** Promenade 11 at St. Peterstr., exchanges only hard cash. (Open Mon.-Fri. 8am-noon and 2-5:30pm, Sat. 8-10:30am.) The **postal code** is A-4240. The **telephone code** is 07942.

Accommodations and Food Freistadt has a few reasonably priced accommodations. Its castle looms ominously behind Freistadt's **Jugendherberge (HI),** Schloßhof 3 (tel. 43 65). From the tourist office, walk around the corner to the red building right off Hauptpl. next to Café Lubinger. The hostel is busy with students from April to July and during the early fall, but it's so empty during the rest of the year that the owner is rarely in. Hand-painted stripes, silly cartoons, trees, and homemade paintings decorate the walls, and the rooms are very comfortable and clean. Call ahead and leave a message. The accommodating proprietor, Margarete Howel, will wait from 6 to 8pm to give you a key; if no one is there or you don't arrive in time, call her at home at 32 68. (Dorms 70AS, non-members 90AS. Hall showers and toilets. Breakfast 30AS. Sheets 30AS. Kitchen facilities in the youth center below.) For a perfectly positioned place, pick **Pension Pirklbauer,** Höllg. 2/4 (tel. 24 40), in the *Altstadt* right next to the Linzertor. All rooms have shower, toilet, telephone, and TV. If you ask in advance, you can have breakfast in the *Gästegarten* overlooking the old moat. (Singles 230AS; doubles 400AS. Breakfast included.)

There are a variety of cheap eats at cozy *Gästehäuser;* prowl around for different offerings. Enjoy a *tête-à-tête* at **Café Vis à Vis,** Salzg. 13 (tel. 42 93). It offers such local fare as *Mühlviertel Bauernsalat mit Suppe* (farmer's salad with soup, 60AS) and *Freistädter* beer in a garden crowded with young people. Midday *menus* run 63-90AS. (Open Mon.-Fri. 9:30am-1am, Sat. 5pm-1am.) **Foxi's Schloßtaverne,** Hauptpl. 11 (tel. 39 30), right next to the tourist information center, caters to an older but no less raucous crowd. Weekday *menus* (70-88AS) offer a soup, main course, and side order. The Greek salad (75AS) is humongous, and pizza is available for sit-in and take-out. They, too, serve *Freistädter* beer. (Open 11am-1am, kitchen open until 11pm.) The best ice cream in all of Mühlviertel (we're not sure how dubious an honor that may be) awaits at **Café Lubiner,** Hauptpl. 10 (soft-serve 12AS, scoops of the hard stuff 7AS each). Pastries (25AS) and a great breakfast selection round out the menu. (Open Sun.-Mon. and Wed.-Fri. 8am-7pm, Sat. 8am-6pm.) The most convenient grocery store is **Uni Markt,** Pragerstr. 2, at Froschau behind the Böhmertor side of the *Innere Stadt.* The market is a one-stop bargain shop for a half a dozen varieties of *Freistädter* beer. (Open Mon.-Fri. 8am-7pm, Sat. 7:30am-12:30pm.)

Sights and Entertainment The tower of Freistadt's remarkable 14th-century castle, the **Bergfried** (50m from the hostel), houses the **Mühlviertler Heimathaus** (tel. 22 74). This regional museum displays traditional tools, clothing, and other period pieces. (Obligatory tour May-Oct. Tues.-Sat. 10am and 2pm, Sun. 10am; Nov.-

FREISTADT ■ 181

> ### Hooked on Pfonics
> Ach, German, the musical language—every sound just rolls off the tongue and caresses the ears. A few German sounds are particularly charming to non-native speakers, such as the lovely "pf" combination, found at the beginning of many German words and pronounced with two distinct consonants: "p-f." Try these few sentences to practice sounding like a native: *"Ein pfan in der Pfalz freßt einen pfirsichen Pfarrkuchen. Ein Pflaume-farber Pferrd fahrt pfeilschnell durch eine Pforte und freßt den Pfau. Das Pferd ein Pflanzenfresser war, aber er hat gedacht, der Pfau ein Pflanze oder vielleicht eine Pfingrose war."* (Translation: "A peacock at the imperial palace ate a peach pancake. Quick as an arrow a plum-colored horse burst through a gate and ate the peacock. The horse was an herbivore, but he mistook the peacock for a plant, perhaps a peony.")

April Tues.-Fri. 2pm. 10AS.) Descend through an archway down through Ölberggasse's cobbled, shoulder-width twistings and its lovely hidden garden, or walk around the old moat that circumscribes the old city, now a stretch of gardens and mossy duck ponds. Numerous **hiking trails** branch out to amazing Mühlviertel destinations; consider hiking out of town and catching a bus back. Freistadt lies on the Mühlviertel **Museumstrasse,** a path linking many of the region's museums, and on the **Pferdeisenbahnwanderweg,** a 237km hiking trail along the former medieval trade route (see **Hooked on Pfonics** above). A mildly strenuous one-hour hike zigzags up Kreuzweg to **St. Peter's Church.** A large map on the Promenade illustrates other local hiking paths, but there are no organized tours of the area. Stop by **Wolfsgruber Bookstore,** Pfarrgg. 16 (tel. 305 61), for help in planning your excursion. (Open Mon.-Fri. 7:30am-noon and 2:30-6pm, Sat. 7:30am-noon.) The tourist office also provides hiking maps (10-35AS), free bus schedules, and biking maps (25AS).

Freistadt's pride and joy is the **Freistädter Brauerei,** a community-owned brewery in operation since 1777. Don't be surprised to see "I only drink Freistadt beer" stickers plastered on the steering wheels of most of the area's buses. In the 13th century, Freistadt granted every male citizen the right to brew and sell his own beer. Herzog Rudolph IV revoked the right in 1363, realizing that he could make a profit by controlling production of the popular froth. The issue was finally resolved in 1737 when the city dissolved all small breweries and established a commonly held community brewery, still in operation outside the town walls at Promenade 7. The brewery conducts free tours that conclude with equally **free beer** every Wednesday at 2pm from September to May. To join a tour, ask at a local *Gästehaus* that serves *Freistädter* beer (they almost all do) or call the brewery for more info (tel. 57 77). Each July and August, Freistadt holds a two-month festival of food and international music, the **Wirthausmusi,** with daily events scattered throughout town. Multicultural meets medieval—or just another excuse to drink *Freistädter* beer? You make the call.

Southeast Austria

Austria's harshest peaks guard the Italian and Slovenian borders from within the southern regions of **Carinthia** (Kärnten) and **East Tirol** (Osttirol). Italian architecture, a sunny climate, and a distinctly laid-back atmosphere give Carinthia a Mediterranean feel not unlike Switzerland's Ticino region. The palpable warmth of the local population, however, can be deceiving. Four percent of the state's inhabitants are ethnic Slovenes (Austria's only significant national minority), and the xenophobic Carinthian Homeland Movement makes no secret of its desire to send them packing. In the "Town-Sign War" of the 1970s, for example, the Slovenes lobbied for bilingual street signs (in both German and Slovene); the Austrian majority soundly defeated the measure. Unrest in the former Yugoslavia has only exacerbated the situation.

Also encompassing the provinces of **Styria** (Steiermark) and **Burgenland**, southeastern Austria's rolling Alpine foothills and gentle valleys are topographically unexciting by Austrian standards—which explains the relative dearth of tourists. Styria's rich deposits of iron ore made it very exciting to some, however, and Styria became one of Europe's first centers of primitive industry. The region also cashes in on the gold and precious stones of Graz, its burgeoning provincial capital. Like many Mediterranean regions, the Burgenland is drenched with endless fields of sunflowers, rows of yellow faces all oriented like solar panels. The vineyard-covered land belonged to Hungary until 1918, and the Magyar influence is still evident in the region's food, architecture, and dress.

If you'll be in Carinthia for an extended period, consider investing in a **Kärnten Card**, good for up to three weeks of unlimited local transportation, free admission to most area sights and museums, and discounts on many cable cars, boat cruises, toll roads, stores, and restaurants. The card is great deal at 345AS (ages 6-14 170AS) and is available at area tourist offices.

■ Klagenfurt

At the crossroads of north-south and east-west trade routes, Klagenfurt has burgeoned into a major summertime destination. Playfully dubbed "the Austrian Riviera," the easygoing, southernmost provincial capital of Austria attracts thousands of work-weary Austrians who unwind in its beachfront suburbs. Only 60km north of Italy, this Carinthian capital leads a lifestyle like its southern counterparts; locals enjoy casual strolls around a palette of outdoor cafés, Italian Renaissance courtyards, wrought iron tracery, and tree-lined avenues framed by Alpine peaks.

GETTING TO KLAGENFURT

Planes arrive at the **Klagenfurt-Wörthersee Airport** (tel. 415 000). Flights from Vienna are budget-hostile (every 2hr., round-trip 2560AS). To get to the airport from the train station, take bus #40, 41, or 42: "Heiligenpl." then switch to bus #45: "Flughafen." **By car,** Klagenfurt lies on Autobahn A2 from the west, Rte. 91 from the south, Rte. 70 from the east, and Rte. 83 from the north. From **Vienna** or **Graz,** take Autobahn A2 south to Rte. 70 west. **Trains** chug to the **Hauptbahnhof** at the intersection of Südbahngürtel and Bahnhofstr. To reach the town center from the station, follow Bahnhofstr. to Paradieserstr and turn left. Neuerpl. is two blocks down on the right. The **Ostbahnhof,** at the intersection of Meißtalerstr. and Rudolfsbahngürtel, is for shipping only. **Buses** depart across the street from the main train station.

ORIENTATION AND PRACTICAL INFORMATION

Alterplatz, Neuerplatz, and **Heiligengeistplatz,** the town's bus centers, comprise the three-ring circus of the city's center. They lie within the **Ring,** the inner district of Klagenfurt, which bustles with social and commercial activity. St. Veiter Ring, Völker-

ORIENTATION AND PRACTICAL INFORMATION ■ 183

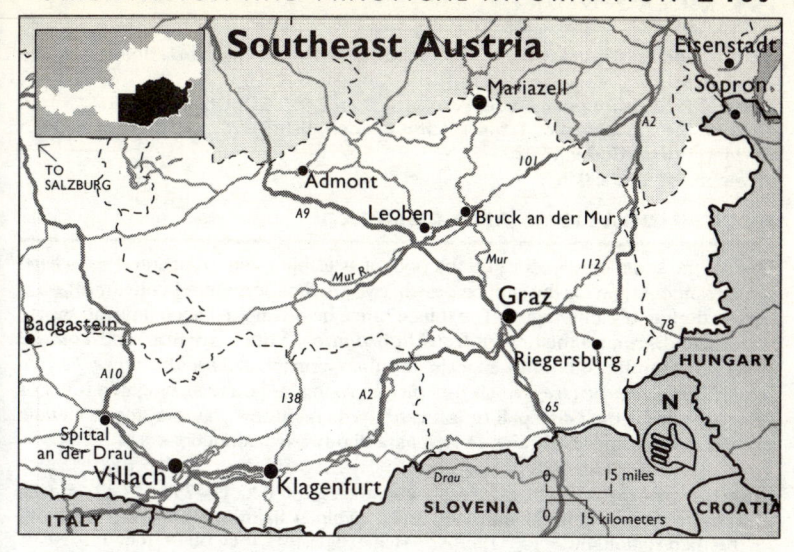

markter Ring, Viktringer Ring, and Villacher Ring border this area. Streets within the Ring generally run in a north-south/east-west grid. The **Lendkanal**, a narrow waterway, and **Villacherstr.** go from the city's center 3km to the Wörthersee.

- **Tourist Office: Gäste Information** (tel. 537 223; fax 537 295; email klagenfurt-info@w-see.or.at; http://www.w-see.or.at/Klagenfurt) is on the first floor of the Rathaus in Neuerpl. From the station, go down Bahnhofstr. and turn left on Paradieserg., which opens into Neuerpl. The well-staffed, English-speaking office supplies colorful brochures and helps find rooms for no fee. Daily tours of the *Altstadt* July-Aug. 10am (call 2 weeks in advance to arrange a tour in English). Open May-Sept. Mon.-Fri. 8am-8pm, Sat.-Sun. 10am-5pm; Oct.-April Mon.-Fri. 8am-5pm.
- **Currency Exchange:** Best rates at the main post office (exchange open Mon.-Fri. 7:30am-5pm) and its train station branch.
- **Trains: Hauptbahnhof** (tel. 17 17). To: **Lienz** (2 per day, 1¾hr., 216AS), **Salzburg** (9 per day, 3hr., 316AS), the **Vienna Südbahnhof** (12 per day, 4¼hr., 416AS), and **Villach** (30min., 64AS). Make other connections in Salzburg or Vienna. Open 24hr.
- **Buses: BundesBuses** reach most destinations in Carinthia. To: **Villach** (68AS), **Pörtschach** (34AS), **St. Veit** (48AS), **Friesach** (82AS), and **Graz** (176AS). Ticket window (tel. 581 10) open Mon.-Fri. 6am-6pm, Sat.-Sun. 7am-6pm.
- **Public Transportation:** Klagenfurt boasts a punctual and comprehensive bus system. The tourist office can provide a *Fahrplan* (bus schedule). The central bus station is at Heiligengeistpl. Single-fare rides 20AS. Buy individual tickets or a 24hr. pass (40AS) from the driver. *Tabak* kiosks sell cut-rate blocks of tickets. Illegal riders pay a 400AS fine.
- **Car Rental: Hertz,** Villacherstr. 4 (tel. 561 47). **Avis,** Villacherstr. 1c (tel. 559 38).
- **Bike Rental:** At the *Hauptbahnhof.* 150AS, with that day's train ticket 90AS. **Fahrradies** has 9 stations all over town—including the tourist office, across from the train station, and the campground—that rent bikes for 20AS for 1hr., 40AS for 3hr., 80AS for 1 day (students 50AS), 300AS for 1 week. The tourist office distributes the pamphlet *Radwandern*, detailing local bike paths and bike-accessible sights.
- **Luggage Storage:** At the train station. 20AS per piece. Lockers 20AS. Open 24hr.
- **Bi-Gay-Lesbian Organizations: Gay Hot-Line Klagenfurt,** Postfach 193 (tel. 504 690). Hotline open Wed. 6-8pm. **Bella Donna Frauenzentrum** (Women's Center), Villacherring 21/2 (tel. 514 201). Open Mon.-Fri. 9am-1pm.
- **Pharmacy:** Pharmacies abound. **Landschafts-Apotheke,** Alterpl. 32, and **Obir-Apotheke,** Baumbachpl. 21, provide two distinguished options.
- **Hospital: Klagenfurt Krankenhaus,** St.-Veiter-Str. 47 (tel. 538).

■ KLAGENFURT

Emergencies: Ambulance, tel. 144. **Medical Assistance,** tel. 141. **Police,** tel. 133 or 53 33.
Post Office: Main post office, Pernhartg. 7 (tel. 556 55). Open Mon.-Fri. 7:30am-8pm, Sat. 7:30am-1pm. **Train station branch,** Bahnhofpl. 5. (tel. 58 10). Open 24hr. **Postal Code:** A-9020.
Telephone Code: 0463.

ACCOMMODATIONS AND CAMPING

Though the summer heat dries up the pool of available rooms, Klagenfurt does have some compensation for the sudden dearth: two student dormitories convert to youth hostels during July and August. The tourist office helps sniff out accommodations for no fee and distributes the helpful *Hotel Information* (with a city map) and *You are Welcome* pamphlets, both in English, and the German *Ferienwohnunger, Ferienhäuser, Privatequartiere*, which lists private rooms. If you're staying in a hotel or *Pension*, ask for the **Gästepaß** (guest card), which entitles you to a free city guide and discounts at specified cafés, museums, and other area attractions.

Jugendherberge Klagenfurt, Neckheimg. 6 (tel. 230 020; fax 230 02 020), at Universitätstr., is close to the university and a 20min. walk from the Wörthersee. From the train station, bus #40, 41, or 42: "Heiligengeistpl." then bus #10 or 11: "Neckheimgasse" from stand 2. This immaculate hostel, seemingly designed for the Jetsons, features a bubblegum-pink and baby-blue color scheme and assorted foliage. All rooms are quads with bunk beds, private showers, and toilets. Reception daily 7-9am and 5-10pm. 175AS. Non-members 215AS. Curfew 10pm. Breakfast (7-8am) and sheets included. Dinner 80AS. Key deposit 200AS, a passport, or a student ID. Reservations recommended.

Jugendgästehaus Kolping, Enzenbergstr. 26 (tel. 569 65; fax 569 65 32). From the station, head down Bahnhofstr. and turn right at Viktringer Ring, left at Völkermarkter Ring, right at Feldmarschall-Conrad-pl. (which becomes Völkermarkterstr.), and right on Enzenbergstr. (20min.). The friendly family Kolping provides simple rooms decorated by a single cross. 24hr. reception. Dorms 150AS, with private shower 190AS, under 18 170AS; singles 190AS. Surcharge for one-night stay 20AS. Breakfast included. Open early July to early Sept.

Pension Klepp, Platzg. 4 (tel. 322 78). The closest accommodation to the train station, Klepp is a 10min. walk from both the station and the city center. From the station, follow Bahnhofstr., take the third right onto Viktringer Ring, then take the second right onto Platzg. Comfortable rooms with large windows. Hall toilets and showers. Singles 250AS; doubles 415AS.

Jugendheim Mladinski Dom, Mikschallee 4 (tel. 356 51; fax 356 51 11). Follow the directions to Jugendgästehaus Kolping, but instead of turning down Enzenbergstr., continue down Völkermarkterstr. and turn right on Mikschallee (25min.). Another option is to take bus #40, 41, or 42: "Heiligergeistpl." then bus #70 or 71 (dir: Ebental): "Windischkaserne" from stand 13, and then continue in the same direction (bus runs Mon.-Sat. until 6:50pm). Mladinski Dom serves as a student dorm during the school year and converts into a pleasant bed-and-breakfast from early July to early Sept. Private toilets and showers. Reception Mon.-Fri. 6am-midnight, Sat.-Sun. 24hr. Curfew 10pm; key available. Singles 255AS; doubles 410AS; triples 435AS. Children under 12 130AS, under 6 90AS. Discount after 3 nights 20AS. Breakfast 25AS. Gym and parking.

Klagenfurt-Wörthersee Camping-Strandbad (tel. 211 69; fax 211 69 93), at the Metnitzstrand off Universitätsstr. From the train station, bus #40, 41, or 42: "Heiligengeistpl." then bus #12: "Strandbad Klagenfurter See." Turn left immediately upon disembarking and walk for 2min. The campsite will be to the left, on the edge of the Wörthersee. On-site grocery store, miniature golf, and beach. Mid-June to late Aug. 80AS per person, ages 3-14 40AS; large site 100AS; small site 20AS. May to mid-June and late Aug. to Sept. 50AS, ages 3-14 25AS. Year-round tax for persons over 18 12AS. Showers and beach entry included. Open May-Sept.

FOOD

Like its Italian counterparts, Klagenfurt finds gastronomical and cultural sustenance in the myriad cafés that freckle the old city's squares and streets. You don't have to walk far or look hard to find an inexpensive place to eat, especially in Neuerplatz and Kardinalplatz and along Burggasse. The tourist office prints *Sonntagsbraten*, a pamphlet listing the addresses and operating hours of cafés, restaurants, clubs, and bars.

Rote Lasche (Red Tongue), Villacherstr. 21, on the corner of Villachstr. and Villacher Ring. File under: "Eatery of the Absurd." This ultracool, vegetarian-specialty restaurant was inspired and decorated by Klagenfurter absurdist artist Victor Rogy. The diner-like restaurant is upholstered tip-to-tail with his artwork, from the 4m red rubber tongue that greets you at the door and lends its name to the restaurant to the racks of postcards displaying some of his tamer works. The impeccably tuxedoed waiters help complete the sensory overload by delivering what could be the most delicious vegetarian dishes in Austria. Banana curry rice 69AS; peppers stuffed with potato purée 88AS. Open Mon.-Fri. 11am-midnight, Sat. 11am-3pm.

Café Musil, at Neuerpl., is the city's most famous cookie, cake, and coffee connection. Open Mon.-Sat. 8:15am-7:30pm, Sun. 9am-7:30pm. A fairly dressy, larger bistro version awaits at 10 Oktoberstr. 14, open until 10pm.

Zuckerbäckerei-Café-Konditorei-Imbiße D. Todor, Feldmarschall-Conrad-Pl. 6 (tel. 511 835). Now *that's* a mouthful. This everything-in-one café is a quick and inexpensive haven for any meal. Chow down on *Salatschüssel* (a salad concoction, 35-50AS) and *Schinken-Käse Toast* (ham and cheese on toast, 30AS) in the sun-drenched, ivy-enclosed *Gastgarten* out back. Also serves ice cream (7AS), candy, and freshly baked goods (12-28AS). Open Mon.-Fri. 7am-9pm, Sat. 7am-2pm.

Rathausstüberl, Pfarrpl. 35 (tel. 579 47), on a hidden cobblestone street right by the *Pfarrkirche*. Freshly prepared Carinthian specialties at attractively low prices. *Käsenudel mit grünem Salat* (cheese and potato dumplings with green salad) and other daily specials 75AS. Italian entrees 65-78AS. People-watch on the outdoor terrace on balmy summer evenings. English menus available. Open Mon.-Fri. 8:30am-midnight, Sat. 8:30am-2pm and 7pm-2am.

Seerestaurant-Strandbad, Strandbad Klagenfurt See (tel. 261 396). Large salad buffet, snacks, and, from 5pm in summer, scrumptious fish, flesh, or fowl grilled before your eyes. Try the *Grillhendl* (grilled chicken, 58AS) and enjoy the open air. Open daily 8am-midnight.

Markets

Every Thursday and Saturday from 8am to noon, the compact **Benediktinerplatz** on the lower west side of the *Altstadt* welcomes a barrage of rickety, wooden stands showcasing fresh fruits and vegetables.

SPAR Markt, Hermang. just off Heiligengeistpl. Open Mon.-Fri. 8am-6:30pm, Sat. 8am-1pm. Another on Bahnhofstr. with a small, cheap restaurant inside. After 3pm, breads and sweets in the *Konditorei* are half-price. Open Mon.-Fri. 7:30am-6:30pm, Sat. 7:30am-5pm.

Konsum, Bahnhofpl. 1, next to the main bus terminal. Open Mon.-Fri. 8am-6pm, Sat. 8am-noon. Another branch directly behind the hostel, on Universitätsstr. Open Mon.-Fri. 8am-12:30pm and 2:30-6pm, Sat. 8am-noon.

Biokost, Wiesbadener-Str. 3, is a health-food market right off of Neuerpl. Open Mon.-Fri. 7:30am-6:30pm, Sat. 7am-12:30pm.

SIGHTS AND ENTERTAINMENT

A tour of Klagenfurt should begin with a walk through the city's *Altstadt*. The tourist office's pamphlet, *A Walk Round Klagenfurt's Old Town*, or one of the free guided tours leaving from the front of the Rathaus (July-Aug. Mon.-Sat. 10am; usually in German) lead Klagenfurt's visitors through the city's main sights. Buildings in this part of town display a strange amalgam of architectural styles: Biedermeier, Italian Renaissance, Mannerist, Baroque, and *Jugendstil* facades all attempt to upstage each other.

At the edge of Alterpl. stands the 16th-century **Landhaus,** originally an arsenal and later the seat of the provincial diet. The symmetrical towers, staircases, and flanking projections create an elegant courtyard sprinkled with the banana-yellow umbrellas of numerous outdoor cafés. The flourishes of the interior truly deserve accolades—665 brilliant coats of arms blanket the walls. Artist Johann Ferdinand Fromiller took nearly 20 years to complete these pieces. Don't let the ceiling's "rounded" edges fool you—the room is perfectly rectangular. (Open April-Sept. Mon.-Fri. 9am-noon and 12:30-5pm. 10AS, students 5AS.)

A brisk stroll through Kramergasse, one of the oldest streets in Klagenfurt, leads directly to **Neuerplatz.** Here, merry-go-rounds for the young, cafés for the caffeinated, and soapboxes for the cantankerous are all readily available amid the torrent of motion and activity. Standing proudly over the eastern end, a (rather large) statue of (rather large) Maria Theresa glares regally at the skateboarders launching themselves off her pedestal. Confounding her indignity, a 60-ton half-lizard/half-serpent copper creature with an overbite spits water in her direction. This fountain depicts the **Lindwurm,** Klagenfurt's heraldic beast. This virgin-consuming monster once terrorized the Wörthersee area and prevented the settlers from draining the marshes. Enter Hercules, monster-slayer and all-around *Übermensch.* He quickly dispatched the beast—craftily lodging a barbed hook in the throat of a sacrificial cow—and saved the village. Today, the Lindwurm still terrorizes Klagenfurt, albeit more subtly—Puff the Magic Dragon-esque stuffed animals turn up *everywhere.*

One of Klagenfurt's largest museums was Franz Josef's favorite, the **Landesmuseum,** Museumg. 2 (tel. 536 30 552). The museum houses the *Lindwurmschädel,* the fossilized rhinoceros skull discovered in 1335 that, three centuries later, inspired the Lindwurm statue at Neuerpl. Other pieces include 18th-century musical instruments, a giant Großglockner Strasse relief map, and ancient Celtic and Roman artifacts. The Medusas at the corners of the miraculously intact 3rd-century Dionysus mosaics could take on a Lindwurm any day. (Open Tues.-Sat. 9am-4pm, Sun. 10am-1pm. 30AS, children 15AS.) The **Kärntner Landesgalerie,** Burgg. 8 (tel. 536 30 542), two blocks east of Neuerpl., is home to an eccentric collection of 19th- and 20th-century artwork, with a focus on Carinthian Expressionism and well-endowed papier-mâché turkeys. (Open Mon.-Fri. 9am-6pm, Sat.-Sun. 10am-noon. 20AS, students 5AS.) The **Robert Musil Museum,** Bahnhofstr. 50 (tel. 501 429), honors the work of its namesake, Austria's most famous modern bard, with an archive of his writings. (Open Mon.-Fri. 10am-noon and 2-4pm, Sat. 10am-noon. Ring the bell to be let in. Free.)

Two blocks south of Neuerpl. off Karfreitstr. is Klagenfurt's **Domplatz** and **Kathedrale.** Rebuilt after Allied bombing in 1944, the nondescript modern exterior of the building and surrounding square render the church almost indistinguishable from Klagenfurt's other buildings. The cathedral's interior, however, is gloriously awash in high arches, crystal chandeliers, pink and white floral stucco, and a brilliant gold altar. Other ecclesiastical paraphernalia are on display in the tiny **Diözesanmuseum** (tel. 502 498), next door at Lidmanskyg. 10, including the oldest extant stained-glass window in all of Austria—a humble, 800-year-old sliver portraying Mary Magdalene. (Open daily mid-June to mid-Sept. 10am-noon and 3-5pm; mid-Sept. to mid-Oct. and May to early June 10am-noon. 30AS, students 10AS, children 5AS.)

Klagenfurt and its suburbs are home to no fewer than 23 castles and mansions; the tourist office's English brochure *From Castle to Castle* suggests a path to view them all and gives details on architecture and operating hours. Another tourist office brochure, the German *Museumswandern,* gives addresses and opening hours for the city's 15 museums and 22 art galleries.

Homesick or eager to see more of the world? Don't miss Klagenfurt's most shameless concession to tourist kitsch, the **Minimundus** park, Villacherstr. 241 (tel. 21 94), minutes from the Wörther See. Artists have created intricately detailed models of over 160 world-famous buildings and sights—all on a 1:25 scale. You'll be on eye level with the Parthenon, Big Ben, the Taj Mahal, and numerous more obscure buildings. For a taste of home, depending on where home is, check out the Sydney Opera House, a Maori Communal House, Buckingham Palace, or the Statue of Liberty. So

SIGHTS AND ENTERTAINMENT ■ 187

this is what Godzilla feels like. At night, an outstanding lighting system illuminates the models. From the train station, take bus #40, 41, or 42: "Heiligengeistpl." then switch to bus #10, 11, 20, 21, or 22 (dir: Strandbad): "Minimundus." (Open July-Aug. Sun.-Tues. and Thurs.-Fri. 8am-7pm, Wed. and Sat. 8am-9pm; May-June and Sept. daily 9am-6pm; April and Oct. daily 9am-5pm. 90AS, children 6-15 30AS, seniors 65AS, groups of 10 or more 60AS per person. Extensive and necessary English guidebooks 30AS.) All profits go to the Austrian "Save the Child" society, a fact you can use to soothe your stinging wallet.

Next door to Minimundus is **Happ's Reptilien Zoo,** founded to educate the public about snakes. To prevent the senseless persecution of the Lindwurm's descendents, the zoo presents varied exhibits on snakes' environments and histories. Evidently Herr Happ has a rather loose definition of "reptile"—along with the puff adders, tortoises, and iguanas, the reptile zoo features spiders, scorpions, rabbits, guinea pigs, and local Wörther See fish. The accident-prone should avoid Saturday's weekly piranha and crocodile feeding. (Open daily May-Sept. 8am-6pm; Oct.-April 8am-5pm. 75AS, students 65AS, children 35AS.) The **planetarium** (tel. 217 00), behind the zoo, has several shows daily (75AS, under 18 45AS) and stargazing at 9pm on clear Wednesday nights (50AS, children 30AS). Elton John croons beneath the German narration—you'll never view the stars in quite the same way again.

To maximize your entertainment *Schilling,* read the tourist office's *Veranstaltung-Kalender* (calendar of events), available in English. The tourist office also distributes brochures listing concerts, gallery shows, museum exhibits, and plays, including the cabaret performances in the **Theater im Landhauskeller** throughout July and August. Tickets are available through **Reisebüro Springer** (tel. 387 05 55; 120AS, students 80AS; performances in German). The **Stadttheater,** built in 1910, is Klagenfurt's main venue for major operas, plays, and dance. For tickets, call the tourist office or the theater's box office (tel. 540 64; 40-520AS; students and seniors half-price; open mid-Sept. to mid-June Tues.-Sat. 9am-noon and 4-6pm). The best of Klagenfurt's sizzling nightlife rages in the pubs of **Pfarrplatz.** The **Disco Bus** (tel. 505 311) often runs from 9:30pm to 3:15am, picking up and dropping off party-goers at various area discos and bars (July-Aug. only; bus leaves from Heiligengeistpl.; round-trip 20AS).

On humid spring and summer days, crowds bask in the sun and loll in the clear water of the nearby **Wörther See.** This water sport haven is Carinthia's warmest, largest, and most popular lake. The two closest beaches to Klagenfurt are the **Strandbad Klagenfurt See** and the **Strandbad Maiernigg.** (Both open daily 8am-8pm. 35AS, children 15AS; after 3pm 20AS, children 7AS. Family card with 1 adult and up to 5 children 50AS, with 2 adults 80AS. Locker key deposit 50AS.) The former is crowded but near the hostel and easily accessible by public transportation. From the train station, take bus #40, 41, or 42: "Heiligengeistpl." then bus #10, 11, or 12: "Strandbad Klagenfurter See." To enjoy the water without getting wet, rent a **rowboat** (30min. 24AS), **paddle boat** (42AS), or **electric boat** (66AS). Strandbad Maiernigg is far from the noise and fuss of its busier counterpart, but you'll need a car or a bicycle to get there. From downtown, ride along Villacherstr. until it intersects Wörther See Süduferstr., and then follow signs to "Wörther See Süd." **Stadtwerke Klagenfurt Wörthersee-und-Lendkanal-Schiffahrt** (tel. 211 55; fax 211 55 15) offers scenic cruises on the lake and short rides down the canal. The two-hour cruise (round-trip 170AS) goes as far as **Velden,** on the opposite shore, and allows stops at designated docks along the way. The Stadtwerke Klagenfurt information center in Heiligengeistpl. sells advance tickets. A *Radwandern* brochure, free at the tourist office, suggests seven one-and-a-half-hour tours, 20 two-hour tours, and 12 four-and-a-half-hour tours. One of these tours winds through a 20km, two-hour circuit of castles and churches.

SOUTHEAST AUSTRIA

THE DRAUTAL

Bordered by Italy to the south and Slovenia to the southeast, central Carinthia's **Drautal** (Drau Valley), with its moderate climate, well-endowed watering holes, and proximity to southern Europe, evokes locales decidedly un-Teutonic. The region gingerly combines skiing and water sports in high- and lowlands carved by the **Drau**, between the Höhe Tauern and the Villacher Alps. At a mere 2000m (a baby-step above the timberline), the mountains are favored not just with lumber and the white stuff but with valuable minerals: iron ore, lead, tungsten, zinc, and manganese. Nestled among these lazy peaks are numerous popular lakes, streams, and warm-water springs, where curative spas toast visitors even in the coldest months.

Although the Drautal contains the transportation hub of **Villach** and an electronic components industry at its core, a variety of lakeside resorts exist. These resorts include the Millstätter See, the Ossiacher See, and the baths of smaller towns and villages like the Broßer-Mühldorger See near Gmünd and the Faaker See near Villach. Fitness buffs can enjoy hiking, water sports, and mountain biking. When the frost arrives, ice-skaters twirl on the lakes in which swimmers backstroked months ago.

■ Villach

Awe-inspiring mountain backdrops and an intriguing, multicultural atmosphere make Villach (pop. 55,000) a more interesting transportation hub than most. Just north of the border between Austria, Italy, and Slovenia, Villach has a split personality; even the street musicians betray the influence of cultural neighbors with their lilting traditional Carinthian, German, and Italian. The **Villach Kirchtag** celebrates these three heritages simultaneously with food, song, and dance (see below). Nevertheless, Villach shifts uneasily under its cultural burden. Although Carinthia declared allegiance to Austria in 1920, the strife in the former Yugoslavia has subtly but painfully refocused attention on ethnic differences here.

Orientation and Practical Information Villach sprawls on both sides of the Drau River. Bahnhofstr. leads from the train station, over a 9th-century bridge, to the economic and social heart of Villach, **Hauptplatz.** Narrow cobblestone paths weave through this central area, revealing hidden restaurants and cafés on every new corner. Two sweeping arcs of stores flank Hauptplatz, closed off at one end by a towering church and by the Drau at another.

Villach's **tourist office,** Europapl. 2 (tel. 244 44; fax 244 44 17), gives advice on local attractions and area skiing and also helps find accommodations for free. From the train station, walk out to Bahnhofstr., take a left onto Nikolaig. after the church, and walk 50m. The ivy-covered office is on your right. (Open July 21-Aug. and late Dec. to March Mon.-Fri. 8am-6pm, Sat. 9am-noon; April-July 20 and Sept.-Nov. Mon.-Fri. 8am-noon and 1:30-6pm, Sat. 9am-noon.) An **ATM** operates on Hauptpl. under the **Bank fur Kärnten und Steiermark. Trains** go to **Vienna Südbahnhof** (456AS), **Innsbruck** (436AS), **Klagenfurt** (64AS), **Salzburg** (264AS), and **Graz** (356AS). A free city **bus** travels a circuit every 20 minutes (Mon.-Fri. 8:40am-6:20pm, Sat. 8:40am-12:20pm). **Ferries** cruise the Drau, departing from the dock beneath the north end of the main bridge (mid-June to mid-Sept. 9:30, 11:40am, 2, and 4pm; May to early-June and late Sept. 2pm; 2hr.; 105AS, ages 6-15 52.50AS). A **taxi** stand is located at the Bahnhof, or call 288 88, 310 10, or 322 22. **Hertz,** inside the **Springer Reisebüro** at Hans-Gasser-Pl. 1 (tel. 269 70), rents cars. (Open Mon.-Fri. 8am-noon and 2-5pm.) You can **rent bikes** at the **train station** (150AS per day, with train ticket or Eurailpass 90AS) or at **Das Radl,** Italienstr. 22b (tel. 269 54). The station also has 24-hour electronic **lockers** fit for a cyber-king (20-40AS). The local **hospital** is at Nikolaig. 43 (tel. 208). Dial 20 30 to reach the **police** headquarters. The mailman cometh to the main **post office** (tel. 267 710), at the right of the train station, and **exchanges** his **currency.** (Open Mon.-Fri. 7am-5pm.) The **postal code** is A-9500. The **telephone code** is 04242.

VILLACH ■ 189

Accommodations and Food Budget accommodations accessible by foot in Villach are rare. You might consider spending the night in nearby Klagenfurt (20min. by train; see above). Travelers with cars should check out the tourist office's *Pension* list, which details many outlying bargains accessible only by car. The most reasonably priced establishment in town is **Jugendgästehaus Villach (HI)**, Dinzlweg 34 (tel. 563 68). From the train station, walk up Bahnhofstr. and go over the bridge and through Hauptpl. Turn right on Postg., walk through Hans-Gasser-Pl., which merges into Tirolerstr., and bear right at St. Martinstr. Dinzlweg is the first street on the left (20-30min.). The hostel is tucked away past all of the tennis courts. This pleasant facility, plastered with neon yellow and orange à la 1976, houses 150 in spacious five-bed dorms, each with its own shower. Make reservations—the hostel is often filled with school groups. (Reception daily 7-10am and 5-10pm. Curfew 10pm. Dorms 160AS. Breakfast and sheets included. Lunch or dinner 80AS each. Bike rental 15AS per hr., 80AS per day. Keys available with passport or ID deposit.)

Finding a place to eat in Villach is easier than finding lodging. **Lederergasse** overflows with small, cheap eateries, while **Hauptplatz** and the sprawling **Kaiser-Josef-Platz** seat swankier Raybanned patrons. **Pizzeria Trieste**, Weißbriachg. 14 (tel. 250 058), bakes up its popular pies for 65-100AS. (Open daily 10am-11pm.) Overlooking the Drau at Nikolaipl. 2, **Konditerei Bernhold** (tel. 254 42) tempts with colorful pastries (12-29AS), devilish ice cream concoctions, and refreshing mixed drinks. Patrons sip nonchalantly on cappuccino (28AS) as they watch ships pass in the night. (Open Mon.-Fri. 7:30am-7pm, Sat. 8am-7pm, Sun. 9:30am-7pm.) Picnic supplies wait at the **SPAR Markts**, in Hans-Grasser-Pl. and at 10 Octoberstr. 6. (Open Mon.-Fri. 7:30am-6:15pm, Sat. 7:30am-5pm.)

Sights and Entertainment Any tour of Villach traverses the bustling **Hauptplatz**, the commercial heart of the city for 800 years. The southern end of the square lives in the mighty Gothic shadow of the **St. Jakob-Kirche**, one of Villach's 12 lovely churches. Slightly raised on a stone terrace, this 12th-century church was converted during the Reformation in 1526 and thereby became Austria's first Protestant chapel. In the Counter-Reformation, however, it switched back, regrouped, and now stands as a gorgeous Catholic church. The high altar's gilt Baroque canopy dazzles the most jaded eyes and almost obscures the staid Gothic crucifix suspended just in front. An ascent up the tallest steeple in Carinthia (94m), the church's **Stadtpfarrturm** (tel. 205 475), provides your daily exercise and a view of Villach and its environs. (Open July-Aug. Mon.-Thurs. and Sat. 10am-6pm, Fri. 10am-9pm; June-Sept. Mon.-Sat. 10am-6pm; Oct. and May Mon.-Sat. 10am-4pm. 20AS, students and children 10AS.)

Villach's **Stadtmuseum,** Widmanng. 38 (tel. 20 53 49), exhibits archaeological and mineral displays from six millennia, clocks, hats, 18th-century portraits, and the original gold-on-black Villach coat of arms from 1240—an eagle talon clutching a mountain top. The 90kg soldered statue of Eisner Leonhard, patron saint of prisoners, formerly stood in St. Leonhardskirche outside of Villach. A local tradition required that anyone who wanted to marry must first be able to carry the statue around the church—before trading it for a new ball and chain. (Open May-Oct. daily 10am-4:30pm; Nov.-April Mon.-Fri. 10am-6pm, Sat. 10am-noon and 2-5pm. 30AS, students 20AS, children under 15 free.)

Five minutes from the congested streets of Hauptpl. is the small **Schillerpark,** home of the Relief von Kärnten, an enormous topographic model of Carinthia. The park has made molehills out of mountains—all the better to see them, my dear. Walk up Hauptpl. until it turns into 10 Oktoberstr. and turn left on Peraustr. The park is one block in on your right. (Open May-Oct. Mon.-Sat. 10am-4:30pm. 20AS, students 10AS, under 15 free.) Two blocks farther down Peraustr. looms the Baroque **Heilig-Kreuz-Kirche,** the dual-towered pink edifice visible from the city bridge. A colorful mural adorns the high, newly renovated dome. On the other side of the Drau, the **Villacher Fahrzeugmuseum** (tel. 255 30 or 224 40) is parked at Draupromenade 12. Hundreds of antique automobiles present a rubber-burning ride into the history of

SOUTHEAST AUSTRIA

transportation. (Open Mon.-Sat. 9am-5pm, Sun. 10am-5pm; Oct.-May daily 10am-noon and 2-4pm. 50AS, ages 6-14 25AS, family pass 100AS.)

Less crowded than the Wörther See, the **Faaker See** is a small but no less beautiful lake at the foot of a mountain between Villach and its suburb **Maria Gail.** The sleek peaks around Villach also make for excellent **skiing,** with a plethora of resorts to woo the winter traveler. A one-day regional lift ticket valid for four areas costs about 300AS (children 180AS); other combinations are also available. Come summer, the **Villach Kirchtag** (church day), held since 1225 on the first Saturday of August, rolls in, far from holy. The town celebrates its "birthday" with raucous revelry (entrance into the *Altstadt* during the day 60AS, in the evening 70AS).

THE MURTAL

Eons ago, before the mining of iron ore and manganese became *de rigueur* in south Austria, the **Mur River** in central and southern Styria carved a valley among the Gleinalpen to the west, Seetaler Alpen to the south, and Seckauer and Niedere Tauern to the north. Long, upland, pastured ridges flank the valley. Half of the region is covered by forests, and another quarter by grasslands and vineyards.

The Mur begins in the Salzburger Land and eventually joins the Drau in the former Yugoslavia. Low, rolling hills (2000m high at most) make the region golden for cyclists and hikers. Sprinkled among the ups and downs are small towns, old fortresses, and farms, surrounded by the vineyards that produce some of Austria's finest wines. Even cosmopolitan Graz, the jewel in the provincial crown, remains intimately connected to the land: a half hour's walk can take one out of the city and deep into hill and dale. The mostly rural countryside retains the charm of an earlier age, and the industry depends upon the mineral resources buried within the rounded mountains. The old commercial iron trade route, the **Steirische Eisenstraße** (Styrian Iron Road), winds through valleys and waterfalls from Leoben to Styria's pride and joy, the Erzberg (Iron Mountain), and on through the Enns Valley.

With its two main towns—Leoben and Graz—the Murtal represents yesterday's Austria. Almost every house in the valley proudly displays an *Alte Bauernkalender* (Old Farmer's Calendar), a tradition for some 250 years. The calendar is a small, colorfully illustrated booklet, the equivalent of an American *Farmer's Almanac;* many visitors consider it the superlative Styrian souvenir.

■ Leoben

Cloistered in the heartland of Austria's "Iron Belt," Leoben (pop. 35,000) lies cradled between a ring of mountains and the Mur River, which borders all but its southern edge. Although 1000-year-old Leoben is the largest city in Styria next to Graz, it still maintains a pastoral, even rustic, atmosphere. At the southernmost point on the Steirische Eisenstraße, Leoben is the proud home of a rather competitive **Mining University,** as well as seven other research institutions. Iron-ically, the world of heavy labor and industry doesn't mar the natural beauty of Leoben. Three-quarters of the town's area is woodland, crowned by the idyllic city park "Am Glacis," visited by, among other notables, **Emperor Napoleon Bonaparte.** Its floral splendors have several times won Leoben the title of "most beautiful town in Styria" in the **Provincial Flower Competition,** and nearly all residents boast kaleidoscopic backyard gardens brimming with tiger lilies and marigolds that would make Martha Stewart jealous. Leoben makes a nice change of pace from the more hectic, bustling, tourist-oriented sites in Austria. You have the time to enjoy the local specialties, including mushroom goulash, "Shepherd's Spit," and the excellent (and cheap) local *Gösser* beer.

Orientation and Practical Information The Mur River surrounds the town; from the train station, you must cross it to reach the heart of Leoben. **Franz-Josef-Strasse** (the main town artery) and **Peter-Tunner-Strasse** run parallel for the length of the town, leading to Hauptplatz and beyond. Leoben is just minutes from Autobahn A9, which runs south to Graz and northwest to Steyr and Linz.

The **train information counter** (tel. 425 45) at the station can help decipher the snarl of rail lines. (Open Mon.-Fri. 9am-noon and 2-4pm.) Several major routes pour into the transit hub at **Bruck an der Mur** (every 20min., 15min., 34AS). Direct trains run to **Graz** (every 2hr., 110AS) and **Vienna** (every 90min., 276AS); trains to **Salzburg** (316AS) and **Klagenfurt** (every 2hr., 228AS) usually go through Bruck an der Mur. The train station also has **lockers** (20AS), and **luggage storage** (30AS; open Mon.-Sat. 5am-10pm, Sun. 6am-10pm). The main **bus station** is a 10-minute walk from the train station, at the corner of Franz-Josef-Str. and Parkstr. Buses run from Leoben to the rest of Styria. Pick up bus schedules from the train station.

Leoben's **tourist office**, Hauptpl. 12 (tel. 440 18; fax 482 18), will help you plan your visit to the Murtal and cheerfully dispense a hotel list and a complimentary map. (Open Mon.-Thurs. 7am-noon and 1:30-5pm, Fri. 7am-1pm.) Walk straight out of the train station, cross the river, and take your second right onto Franz-Josef-Str. Follow the road past the bus terminal to the main square. The tourist office is on the right. A new underground **parking garage** is under Hauptpl.; the old one stands on Kärtnerstr. (5AS per 30min.). **Taxi stands** are at Hauptpl. and the train station. Drop a postcard at the Otto Wagner-esque **post office** at Erzherzog-Johann-Str. 17. (Open Mon.-Fri. 8am-7pm, Sat. 8-10am.) The **postal code** is A-8700. The **telephone code** is 03842.

Accommodations and Food Leoben has few—make that no—budget accommodations and only nine establishments total. The closest thing to a good deal is **Hotel Altman**, Südbahnstr. 32 (tel. 422 16), with 22 beds and a small bowling alley in a convenient, albeit busy, location. The three-lane bowling alley tends to fill with local folks joyfully and copiously partaking in the beverage that has been linked to the sport since the time of Adam—beer. To reach the hotel, walk out of the train station and immediately turn left on Südbahnhofstr. Walk alongside the rail tracks for 10 minutes; the hotel is on the right. Private TV sets, showers, and hardwood floors help make Altman more luxurious than most hotels in this price range. (Singles 330AS; doubles 550AS. Breakfast included. Other meals 55-155AS. Bowling alley open Tues.-Sun. 10am-midnight; 10AS for 10min. English spoken. Free parking. Visa, MC.) Cheaper hostels await in neighboring towns from May to September, like the **Jugendherberge (HI)** in Bruck an der Mur, Theodor-Körner-Str. 37 (tel. (03862) 534 65; fax 560 89), 16km to the east, with 50 beds in quads and larger dorms. The owner will even pick you up from the station if you call in advance.

Fans of Italian or typical Austrian cooking will have no trouble in Leoben. Try **Gasthof Familie Hölzl**, Kärtnerstr. 218 (tel. 421 07), across from the Stadttheater, which seems caught between two worlds, with Italian flags on the walls and *Wiener Schnitzel* on the menu. Pasta (60-76AS), salads drenched in olive oil (42-54AS), and fish (95-98AS) also appear. (Open Mon.-Fri. 8am-8pm, Sat. 8am-2pm.) Or explore Kirchgasse, home to a number of cheap restaurants. Another alternative is **La Pizza**, Langg. 1 (tel. 453 47), which has large pizzas for two (59-94AS) but nowhere to sit—take out a pie to enjoy by the river. (Open Mon.-Fri. 11am-2pm and 5-10pm, Sat.-Sun. 11am-10pm.) Potential picnickers pack perishables at the **private markets** along Franz-Josef-Str. or at **Billa**, Langg. 5. (Open Mon.-Thurs. 7:30am-6:30pm, Fri. 7:30am-8pm, Sat. 7am-1pm.) A **farmer's market** sets up in Kirchpl. (Tues. and Fri. 7am-1pm.)

Sights and Entertainment Most of Leoben's attractions cluster around **Hauptplatz**, 10 minutes from the train station (cross the bridge and bear right onto Franz-Josef-Str.). Sights are designated by a square with a bizarre imprint of an ostrich eating iron horseshoes, one held daintily between its toes and the other protruding from its beak. This city symbol alludes to Leoben's dependence on the iron trade—in the Middle Ages, ostriches were thought capable of eating and digesting iron. That's a goose, you say? When it was designed, no one knew what an ostrich looked like.

Most of the buildings on Hauptplatz are former homes of the **Hammerherren** (Hammer men), another reminder of the iron trade. The most ornate of the bunch is the 1680 **Hacklhaus,** bearing a dozen statues on its pink facade. The top six figures represent half of the 12 Christian virtues. Justice holds a sword and a balance, Hope brandishes an anchor, and Wisdom views the world through the mirror in his hand. The bottom figures depict the four seasons, including Old Man Winter on the bottom row, warming his icy fingers over a roaring fire. Standing guard at the entrance to Hauptpl. are the **Denkmäler und Monumente** (memorial statues and monuments), beautifully crafted works erected to ward off the fires and plague that devastated much of Styria in the early 18th century. Look for Florian, the fire-proof saint, and the reclining, plague-resistant St. Rosalia.

Just outside Hauptpl. is the **Pfarrkirche Franz Xavier,** a rust-colored church with twin towers built from 1660 to 1665 by the Jesuits. The simple facade belies an elaborate interior and a high altar bedecked with remarkable Solomonic columns. Next door is the **Museum der Stadt Leoben,** Kirchg. 6, a rich collection of portraits and documents that traces the city's historical development. (Open Mon.-Thurs. 10am-noon and 2-5pm, Fri. 10am-1pm. 20AS, students 5AS.) An ever-vigilant fungus, the **Schwammerlturm** (Mushroom Tower) guards the bridge over the Mur.

You'd be hard-pressed to find any mushrooms sprouting in Leoben's meticulously manicured gardens. Stroll through the **Stadtpark "Am Glacis"** one block past Hauptpl. There, you can visit the **Friedensgedenkstätte** (Peace Memorial), which commemorates the peace treaty with Napoleon signed here in 1797. The small museum showcases an exhibit detailing the political and military events surrounding the treaty—see the very feather pen that Napoleon used to inscribe his signature. (Open May-Sept. daily 9am-1pm and 2-5pm. Free.)

A scenic 30-minute walk along the Mur rewards you with the chance to inspect the **Gösser brewery.** Examine antique brewing machinery, wander around inside the **Göss Abbey** (the oldest abbey in Styria), and then guzzle down a free stein of fresh brew. Regardless of whether you make a tour (the free beer is worth it), try visiting the **beer museum,** with exhibits on the brewery's history and revolutionary changes in brewing techniques. (For 1½hr. tours, call 226 21. Museum open Mon.-Fri. 8am-noon and 2-4pm.) There's more than beer brewing in Leoben, though. The **Stadttheater,** Kärntnerstr. 224 (tel. 406 23 02), is the oldest functioning theater in all of Austria. (Theater on vacation June-Sept. Box office open Mon.-Sat. 9:30am-12:30pm and Thurs.-Fri. 4pm-6:30pm). The city fills the summer void with the **Leobener Kultursommer,** a program of theater, classical and pop concerts, literary readings, and treasure hunts for children. Pick up a free program from the tourist office.

■ Riegersburg

Perched atop an extinct volcano, the majestic Riegersburg castle stands watch over the diminutive valley town that bears its name. Riegersburg the town has known little peace since its founding in the 9th century BC—Roman domination and Hungarian invasions periodically forced the citizens to seek solace and safety on the remarkably rocky hill. Baroness Katharina Elisabeth Freifrau von Galler completed the castle in a flurry of construction, making it one of the largest and most impregnable fortresses in Austria—108 rooms surrounded by two miles of walls with five gates and two trenches. The fearsome castle withstood the 1664 Ottoman onslaught, with Riegersburg and the surrounding villages driving the Turks back in the great Battle of Mogersdorf. Despite the cheerful vineyards at the foot of the castle, Riegersburg's daunting appearance and the **Witch Museum** that it houses evoke a fairy-tale era.

Orientation and Practical Information If you've got a **car,** Riegersburg makes an excellent day trip from Graz. Take A-2 and exit at Ilz. Otherwise, poor train-bus connections necessitate careful planning. Ride the **bus** directly from Graz (Andreas-Hofer-Pl.; Mon.-Sat. 12:35pm, Mon.-Fri. 5:30pm, Sun. 10:45am; 100AS), or take the **train** from Graz to Feldbach (every hr., 1hr., 100AS) and switch to the bus into Riegersburg (5 per day on weekdays, 0-2 per day on weekends, 30 min.; 20AS). Buses to Graz from Riegersburg generally leave at ungodly hours (Mon.-Sat. 5:40am and 6:05am, Sun. a more pious 5:35pm); those to nearby Feldbach (10km) leave frequently but never on Sunday. Riegersburg serves as a fine stopover on the route from Graz into **Hungary:** a one-way ticket from Feldbach to the border town Szentgottard costs 60AS (6 per day, 30min.). If necessary, you can always call a **taxi** (tel. (03152) 25 35) to take you back to Feldbach (170-210AS). Otherwise, the small **tourist office** (tel. 86 70), actually a corner of a craft shop across from Saurugg on the way up to the castle, can help you find a room. (Open April to mid-Oct. daily 10am-6pm, mid-Oct. to March 10am-noon and 2-6pm.) The **post office** stands at Riegersburgstr. 26. (Open Mon.-Fri. 8am-noon and 2-6pm.) You can **change money** there, or stroll to **Raiffeisen Bank,** down the street at Riegersburgstr. 30. (Open Mon.-Fri. 8am-noon and 2-4:30pm.) The town **postal code** is A-8333. The **telephone code** is 03153.

Accommodations and Food The **Jugendherberge im Cillitor (HI)** (tel. 82 17), is on the path up to the castle and is actually incorporated into the fortress walls. Walk up Riegersburgstr. toward the castle, take a right at the tourist office, and struggle up the last, extremely steep 100m. Little short of the end of feudalism (it's still going strong, right?) would change the medieval atmosphere created by the small windows, large keys, noisy locks, and spears. Iron bars traverse the few geranium-filled windows of the large dorm rooms. (Curfew 10pm. Dorms 135AS, under 19 115AS. Non-members add 30AS. Breakfast included; other meals 50-60AS. Sheets 30AS. Hall showers and toilets. Generally open May-Sept., depending on demand.) At the bottom of Riegersburg's hill is **Lasslhof,** Riegersburgstr. 20 (tel. 201 or 202), a yellow hotel with a popular bar/restaurant. The proprietor collects "art"—loosely defined—and the common areas overflow with an eclectic mix of framed works. (Reception 8am-10pm. Dorms 170-240AS. July 15-Sept.15 surcharge for singles 30AS. Breakfast included. English spoken.) At the restaurant downstairs, wolf down *Wiener Schnitzel* with potatoes and salad (75AS), or snack on the *Frankfurter mit Gulaschsaft* (38AS). Hikers stock up on groceries at **Saurugg,** right across the street from the tourist office. (Open Mon.-Fri. 7am-noon and 2:45-6:15pm, Sat. 7:15am-12:15pm.)

Sights and Entertainment Riegersburg relies heavily on the revenue from tourists who gawk at the well-preserved remains of the huge **medieval fortress,** the town's only man-made attraction. But like the foreign invaders of the past, sightseers must also tackle the treacherously steep, stone-paved path leading up to the castle. Bring sturdy shoes and bottled water, lest you share the fate of many a young 17th-century Turk. The path itself is arguably the best part of the castle: sweeping views of the surrounding farms and rolling hills reward visitors at every turn, and benches, vineyards, stone arches, and monuments provide good excuses to catch your breath. Ask a local to point out the prince and princess's current residence—note the swimming pool instead of a moat. You might circle the castle and climb up the Eiselstieg (donkey stairs) instead. Legend claims that this back entrance was built in the 17th century when two feuding brothers owned the place—one closed off the way to the top. Actually, the stairs were laid in the 15th century as a food transportation route before the two quarrelsome brothers were even a glint in their aristocratic father's eye. The ruts in the stone path near the top were carved by the thousands of horse-drawn carts in the centuries before Goodyear. On your way up, look for an inconspicuous crescent moon carved into the stone wall to mark the highest point reached by invading Turks. The castle itself houses several well-displayed exhibits and museums. The **Burgmuseum** showcases 16 of the castle's 108 rooms, packed with art and historical notes on the Liechtenstein family (yes, like the country), who own this and other Austrian castles. The **Weiße Saal** (White Hall), with its wedding-cake ceiling flourishes and crystal chandeliers, lacks only elegantly dressed couples waltzing around the floor. The **Witches' Room** contains an eerie collection of portraits of alleged witches (including Katharina "Green Thumb" Pardauff, executed in 1675 for causing flowers to bloom in the middle of winter) and a real iron maiden. (Insert your own 80s thrash-metal band joke here.) The **Hexenmuseum** (Witch Museum) spreads over 12 more rooms, with an exhibit on the most expansive witch trial in Styrian history (1673-1675). Filled with torture devices, funeral pyres, and other ghastly exhibits, the museum testifies to the power of superstitious hysteria. (Open April-Oct. daily 9am-5pm. 1hr. tours in German on the hr. 10AS. Self-guided English tour available. Admission 85AS, students 50AS; combination ticket with Burgmuseum 120AS, 80AS.)

You can best appreciate the castle's ageless beauty from among the surrounding web of gravel **paths** and stone staircases. Study the elaborate iron pattern covering the well in the castle's second courtyard carefully—it's said that any woman who can spot the horseshoe within the complex design will find her knight in shining armor within a year. In the shadow of the castle whimpers the rather meager **Greifvogelwarte Riegersburg**, which showcases caged birds of prey. (Open Easter-Oct. 50AS, students 30AS. Shows with trainers dressed in castle finery Mon.-Sat. 11am and 3pm, Sun. 11am and 2 and 4pm. 60AS, students 40AS.) At one of the many *Buschenschank* on the hills surrounding the castle, try the Schilcher wine, a rosé grown from hearty native grapes. After a long, hot day of castle conquering and hiking, take a plunge in the **Seebad Riegersburg**, a small swimming lake created by nature and nurture together (30AS, under 16 15AS).

■ Graz

As Austria's second largest city, with a thriving arts community drawn from 45,000 university students, Graz just can't understand why it doesn't attract more tourists. For centuries this capital of Styria (pop. 250,000) has been a center of arts and sciences to rival any other in the Teutonic world. Graz's prosperity and international renown brought Emperor Friedrich III here in the mid-15th century. Astronomer Johannes Kepler was similarly lured to the Karl-Franzens-Universität, founded in 1585 as a Jesuit College. Further testifying to the power of this cultural citadel, **Arnold Schwarzenegger** was reared in Graz before he left his family and trainer (who still live here) to become Conan, the Terminator, and, in the biggest leap of Hollywood imagination, pregnant. The small pond where he proposed to Maria Shriver is now a pilgrimage site for die-hard fans, despite the bemused protestations of tourist officials that it's "nothing special."

Since Charlemagne claimed this strategic crossroads for the Carolingian empire, Graz (now 60km from the Slovenian and Hungarian borders) has witnessed over a thousand years of European-Asian hostility. The ruins of the fortress perched upon the **Schloßberg** commemorate the turmoil; the stronghold withstood battering at the hands of the Ottoman Turks, Napoleon's armies (three times), and most recently the Soviet Union during WWII. Despite its turbulent history, however, the city and its red-tiled roofs, refreshing parks, museums, and monuments provides a welcome respite from the throngs of tourists in Austria's Big Three (Vienna, Salzburg, and Innsbruck). Innumerable theaters, the **Forum Stadtpark**, the renowned **Steirischer Herbst** (an avant-garde festival founded in 1968 and held every October), and the summer music festival **Styriarte**, have contributed to the culture you'd expect of a university town, in many ways challenging elite big sister Vienna. Graz's *fin de siècle* period is occurring now, and with its artistic offerings—Stravinsky instead of Strauss, Mamet instead of Mahler—Graz is fast becoming a cultural epicenter for Austria.

GETTING TO AND FROM GRAZ

Flights arrive at the **Flughafen Graz**, Flughafenstr. 51, 9km from the city center. All trans-continental flights are routed through Vienna. **Trains** depart from the **Hauptbahnhof**, on Europapl., where you can get a free *Bahneurbindungen* (train timetable). Further connections can be made through Vienna. (The *Ostbahnhof* on Conrad-von-Hötzendorf-Str. is mainly a freight station; don't get off here unless you came in a crate.) The **Graz-Köflach Bus (GKB)** departs from Griespl. for West Styria. For the remainder of Austria, the **BundesBus** departs from Europapl. 6 (next to the train station) or, more often, from Andreas-Hofer-Pl.

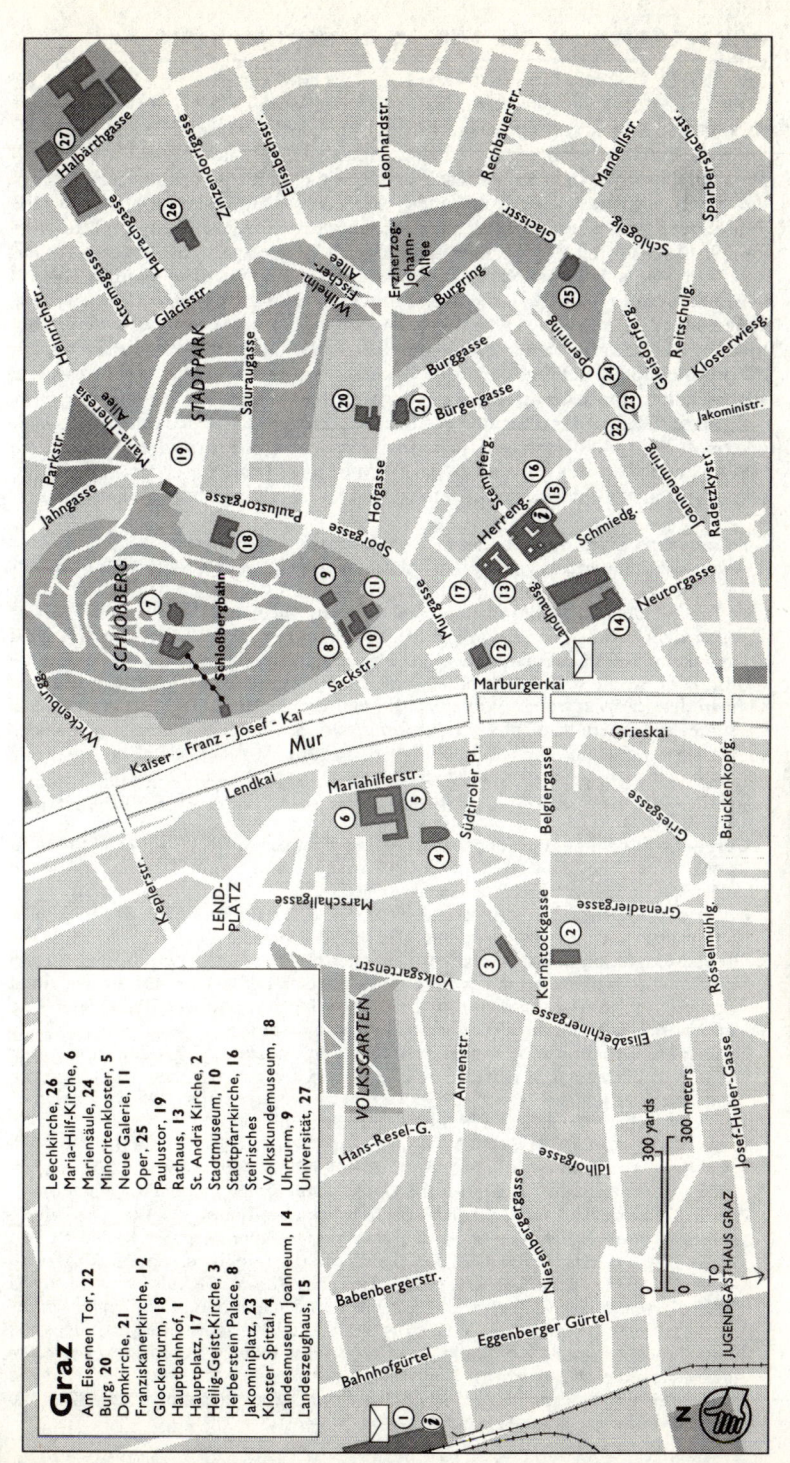

GRAZ ■ 195

Graz

Am Eisernen Tor, 22
Burg, 20
Domkirche, 21
Franziskanerkirche, 12
Glockenturm, 18
Hauptbahnhof, 1
Hauptplatz, 17
Heilig-Geist-Kirche, 3
Herberstein Palace, 8
Jakominiplatz, 23
Kloster Spittal, 4
Landesmuseum Joanneum, 14
Landeszeughaus, 15
Leechkirche, 26
Maria-Hilf-Kirche, 6
Mariensäule, 24
Minoritenkloster, 5
Neue Galerie, 11
Oper, 25
Paulustor, 19
Rathaus, 13
St. Andrä Kirche, 2
Stadtmuseum, 10
Stadtpfarrkirche, 16
Steirisches Volkskundemuseum, 18
Uhrturm, 9
Universität, 27

ORIENTATION AND PRACTICAL INFORMATION

Graz straddles the Mur River in the southeast corner of Austria, on the northern edge of the Graz plain. The city serves as a gateway to Slovenia (50km south) and Hungary (70km east). Fully two-thirds of Graz's five sq. km consist of beautiful parklands, earning it the extraordinarily pithy nicknames "Garden City" and "Green City." **Hauptplatz**, on the corner of Murg. and Sackstr., forms the social and commercial center of the city. Hauptplatz is directly in front of the *Rathaus* and lies in the shadow of the **Schloßberg** fortress ruins. **Herrengasse**, which runs from the Hauptpl. to Jakominipl., forms the heart of the pedestrian zone and is lined with cafés, boutiques, and ice cream shops. **Jakominiplatz** (Yah-ko-MEE-nee-plahtz) near the Eisernes Tor and five minutes from Hauptpl., is the hub of the city's bus and streetcar system. The Graz **Universität** is tucked away in the northeast part of Graz, near the posh residential district of St. Leonhard. The **Hauptbahnhof** lies on the other side of the river, a short ride from Hauptpl. on tram #1, 3, or 6. To get to the city center by foot from the train station, follow Annenstr. up and over Hauptbrücke (15min.).

If you're staying in Graz for at least three days and are eligible for student or senior discounts, you might consider purchasing a **Graz Card** form the tourist office (180AS), which entitles you to three days of free bus and tram travel, 10 to 60 percent reductions on most museums, and 5 to 10 percent off at some shops and restaurants.

Tourist Office: Main office, Herreng. 16 (tel. 807 50; fax 807 55 55; email graz.tourismus@computerhaus.at; http://www.sime.com/congress/gtg.htm). Cordial staff gives away one city map and sells a more detailed version (25AS), books rooms (30AS), and supplies information on all of Styria, including the location of Arnold Schwarzenegger's former home in nearby Thal. The office is littered with posters and pamphlets of cultural events. Procure a brochure of area hotels and a separate listing of private rooms. The office leads **tours** of the *Altstadt* in English and German that start out front (every day 2:30pm; Nov.-March Sat. only; 75AS). Open in summer Mon.-Fri. 9am-7pm, Sat. 9am-6pm, Sun. and holidays 10am-3pm; in winter Mon.-Sat. 9am-6pm, Sun. and holidays 10am-3pm. **Branch** (tel. 91 68 37) at the main train station. Open Mon.-Sat. 9am-6pm, Sun. and holidays 10am-3pm.

Consulates: South Africa, Villefortg. 13 (tel. 322 548). **U.K.,** Schmiedg. 10 (tel. 826 105).

Currency Exchange: Best rates at **American Express** (40AS charge) and the main **post office.** Most banks open Mon.-Fri. 8am-noon and 2-4pm. On Sun., exchange offices at both post office branches are open.

American Express: Hamerling. 6, A-8010 (tel. 817 010; fax 817 008). Holds mail and exchanges currency. Open Mon.-Fri. 9am-5:30pm.

Flights: Flughafen Graz, Flughafenstr. 51 (tel. 29 02). Shuttles (20AS) leave the airport to Graz 6 times per day, with the last bus at 6:45pm. They also stop at Hotel Daniel, Hotel Weitzer, and Griespl. before arriving at the airport 30min. later. The information office at the airport is open daily 6am-8pm.

Trains: Hauptbahnhof, Europapl. (tel. 98 48, information 17 17; lines open 7am-9pm). To: **Salzburg** (6 per day, 4¼hr., 396AS), **Linz** (5 per day, 3½hr., 336AS), **Innsbruck** (4 per day, 6hr., 540AS), **Vienna** (9 per day, 2½hr., 296AS), **Zurich** (1 per day, 10hr., 1052AS), and **Munich** (1 per day, 6hr., 690AS).

Buses: Graz-Köflach Bus (GKB), Köflneherg. 35-41 (tel. 59 87), is open Mon.-Fri. 8am-5pm. The BundesBus office, Andreas-Hofer-Pl. 17 (tel. (0660) 80 20), is open Mon.-Fri. 6am-6:30pm. **Branch** at the *Hauptbahnhof* open Mon.-Fri. 9am-noon.

Public Transportation: Grazer Verkehrsbetriebe, Hauptpl. 14 (tel. 887 408), offers a thorough *Netzplan* of bus and tram routes. Open Mon.-Fri. 8am-5pm. Purchase single tickets (20AS) and 24hr. tickets (40AS) from the driver, booklets of 10 tickets (150AS) or week-tickets (92AS) from any *Tabak*. Tickets are valid for all trams, buses, and the cable car that ascends to the Schloßberg. Children half-price. Be sure to stamp your ticket, or face the wrath of a 500AS fine. Most tram lines run until 11pm, most bus lines until 9pm. Check the schedules posted at every *Haltestelle* (marked with a green "H") for details.

Taxi: Funktaxi, Griespl. 28 (tel. 983). **City-Funk,** Glockenspielpl. 6 (tel. 878). We want da noise, we want da funk!

Car Rental: Avis, airport and Schlögelg. 10 (tel. 812 920; fax 841 178). **Budget,** Bahnhofgürtel 73 (tel. 916 966; fax 916 68 34), and airport (tel. 291 54 13 42). **Hertz,** Andreas-Hofer-Pl. (tel. 825 007; fax 810 288). **Europcar,** airport (tel. 296 757; fax 242 547).

Automobile Clubs: ÖAMTC, Giradig. (tel. 50 42 61) and **ARBÖ,** Kappellenstr. 45 (tel. 271 60 00).

Bike Rental: At the train station. 150AS per day, 90AS with Eurailpass or valid ticket.

Luggage Storage: At the train station. 30AS per day, 4am-10pm. Lockers 20-30AS.

English-Language Bookstores: Englische Buchhandlung, Tummelpl. 7 (tel. 82 62 66), sells virtually every book you might ever want, in English. Hardcovers are sometimes cheaper than paperbacks, but then you have to carry them. Open Mon.-Fri. 9am-6pm, Sat 9am-noon. Experience reverse culture shock at **American Discount,** Jakoministr. 12 (tel. 832 324), a warehouse of every imaginable American magazine, comic book, and basketball jersey. Open Mon.-Fri. 9am-12:30pm and 2:30-6pm, Sat. 9am-12:30pm.

Bi-Gay-Lesbian Organizations: Rosarote Panther/Schwul-lesbische Arbeitsgemeinschaft Steiermark, Postfach 34 (tel. 471 119). **Frauenberatungstelle** (Women's Information Center), Marienpl. 5/2 (tel. 916 022).

Laundromat: Putzeri Rupp, Jakominstr. 34 (tel. 821 183), has do-it-yourself (5kg load 65AS) and professional handling. Open Mon.-Fri. 8am-4pm, Sat. 7am-noon.

Crisis Hotline: Steirische AIDS-Hilfe, Schmiedg. 38 (tel. 815 050). Drop-in hours Mon. and Wed. 11am-1pm, Tues. and Thurs.-Fri. 5-7pm.

Pharmacy: Bärenapotheker, Herreng. 11 (tel. 83 02 67), opposite the tourist office. Open Mon.-Fri. 8am-12:30pm and 2:30-6pm, Sat. 8am-noon.

Hospital: Krankenhaus der Elisabethinen, Elisabethinerg. 14 (tel. 90 63), near the hostel.

Emergencies: Police, tel. 133. **Ambulance,** tel. 144.

Police: (tel. 888 27 75), at the main train station. Open 24hr. Outside doors open 8am-5pm; ring the doorbell at other times.

Post Office: Main office, Neutorg. 46. Open Mon.-Fri. 7am-11pm, Sat. 7am-2pm, Sun. 8am-noon. A **branch office,** Europapl. 10, is next to the main train station. Open 24hr. Postal code: A-8010; branch office A-8020.

Internet Access: Internet Café, Andreas-Hoger-Pl. 9. Well, you're not here for the bar. 40AS for 30min. The **hostel** also has internet access (see below).

Telephone Code: 0316.

ACCOMMODATIONS

Sniffing out a cheap bed in Graz may require a bit of detective work, as most budget hotels, guest houses, and pensions run 300-450AS per person, and several are located in the boondocks. Luckily, the web of local transport provides a reliable and easy commute to and from the city center. Ask the tourist office about *Privatzimmer* (most 150-300AS per night), especially in the tourist-bloated summer months.

Jugendgästehaus Graz (HI), Idlhofg. 74 (tel. 914 876; fax 914 87 688), 15min. from the train station. Note: The walk is through a bit of a red-light district; *Let's Go* advises taking particular caution at night. Exit the station and cross the street, head right on Eggenberger Gürtel, take a left at Josef-Huber-G. (after the Nissan dealership), and then take the first right at Idlhofg. The hostel is hidden behind the parking lot on your right. Or, from Jakominipl., take bus #31 (dir: Webling), 32 (dir: Seiersburg), or 33 (dir: Gemeindeamte): "Lissag." (last bus around midnight) and walk 2min. back to the hostel. Clean, spacious rooms with large lockers and private toilet and shower. Omnipresent insomniac undead school groups, but the congenial management goes out of its way to fit in backpackers. No real curfew; security system lets you in 11pm-2:30am. Key also available. Reception daily 7am-11pm. No lockout. 6- or 8-bed dorms 135AS; doubles 400AS; quads 540AS. Surcharge for first night 20AS. Non-members add 40AS. Breakfast and sheets included. Hearty dinner 65AS. Laundry 45AS. Internet access 15AS for 15min.

Hotel Strasser, Eggenberger Gürtel 11 (tel. 913 977; fax 916 856), 5min. from the train station. Exit the station, cross the street, and head right on Bahnhofgürtel; the hotel is on the left, across from a huge sign for *Kaiser Bier*. Thick glass windows keep the large, wood-paneled rooms relatively insulated from the busy street. Singles 340AS, with shower 440AS; doubles 560AS, with shower 660AS; triples 840AS; quads 1000AS. Breakfast included. English spoken. Free parking.

Hotel Zur Stadt Feldbach, Conrad-von-Hötzendorf-Str. 58 (tel. 829 468; fax 847 371), 20min. south of Jakominipl. From Hauptpl. or Jakominipl., take tram #4 (dir: Liebnau) or 5 (dir: Puntigam): "Jakominigürtel." The hotel is on the corner to the right. This modest, 30-bed hotel with simple, no-nonsense furnishings earns points for colorful comforter covers. 24hr. reception on the 2nd floor. Singles 350AS; doubles 500AS, with shower 650AS; triples with shower 750AS. Breakfast 50AS.

Gasthof Schmid Greiner, Grabenstr. 64 (tel. 681 482). From the bus station, bus #58 (dir: Mariagrün): "Grabenstr.," turn right, walk 30m, and head right on Grabenstr. for 10min. Peaceful establishment imbued with old-world charm. Snow-white comforters, antique wood furnishings, and delicate lace curtains grace the tidy rooms. Ring the bell to be let in; if at first you don't succeed, try, try, again on the other side of the building. Singles 340AS; doubles 460AS, with toilet 480AS.

FOOD

Graz's 45,000 students sustain a bonanza of cheap eateries. Inexpensive meals await at Hauptplatz and Lendplatz, off Keplerstr. and Lendkai, where concession stands sell *Wurst,* ice cream, beer, and other fast food until about 8pm. Numerous markets stand along Rösselmühlgasse, an extension of Josef-Huber-G., and on Jakoministrasse directly off Jakominipl. Low-priced student hangouts line Zinzendorfgasse near the university. Note that most salads come dressed in the local dark pumpkin-seed oil.

University Mensa, Sonnenfelspl. 1 (tel. 32 33 62), just east of the Stadtpark at the intersection of Zinzendorfg. and Leechg. Bus #39: "Uni./Mensa." The best deal in town in a bright, spacious, new building. Simple and satisfying *menus,* vegetarian *(Vollwert)* or with meat, for 47-51AS. Large à la carte selection includes salads and grilled meats. Blue tickets, distributed only to university students, shave 8AS off the price of a meal. Open Mon.-Fri. 11am-2:30pm.

Gastwirtschaft Wartburgasse, Halbärthg. 4. Trendy posters and loud music make this indoor/outdoor café/bar Graz's premier student hangout. Tasty food compensates for the wait. Lunch specials 50-60AS. Pasta, vegetarian, and meat dishes 42-120AS. Open Mon.-Thurs. 9am-1am, Fri. 9am-4am, Sat. 6pm-1am.

Calafati, Lissag. 2 (tel. 916 889), a 3min. walk from the hostel. Lunch combinations (main course, soup or spring roll, and dessert 42-55AS) make this slightly out-of-the-way Chinese restaurant quite a bargain. Several vegetarian and take-out options 65-78AS. Lunch bargain daily 11:30am-3pm; dinner daily 5:30-11:30pm.

Café-Pizzeria Catherina, Sporg. 32 (tel. 827 263). This popular pizzeria even serves breakfast (ham and 2 eggs, American style 32AS). Play Connect Four while you wait for the super-solicitous staff. Take-out pizza slices (21AS) are the perfect size to combat late-night munchies. Whole pies 55-82AS. Salads 28AS. Open Mon.-Sat. 7:30am-midnight, Sun. 9:30am-midnight.

Markets

Graz is blessed with seemingly countless small grocery stores that sell all the necessary ingredients for a picnic lunch; pick up a few bites and sup under a tree in the relaxing, quiet **Volksgarten** located right off Lendpl. There are also **outdoor markets** at Kaiser-Josef-Pl. and Lendpl., where vendors hawk their fruits and vegetables amid a dazzling splash of reds, greens, and yellows. (Open Mon.-Sat. 7am-12:30pm.) Other markets line Hauptpl. and Jakominipl. (Open Mon.-Fri. 7am-6pm, Sat. 7am-12:30pm.)

Feinkost, Bahnhofgürtel 89, near the train station. A small fruit, vegetable, and essential food shop. Open Mon.-Fri. 8am-6pm, Sat. 8am-12:30pm. **Feinkost Exler** is a quick jaunt to the left from the youth hostel. Open Mon.-Fri. 7am-1pm and 3-6pm, Sat. 7am-noon. **Feinkost Muhrer** borders closely on Hauptpl. in Franziskanerpl. Open Mon.-Fri. 6:30am-7:30pm, Sat. 6:30am-noon.

Merkar, Europapl., to the right of the *Bahnhof.* Free parking in underground garage for customers. Open Mon.-Thurs. 8am-7pm, Fri. 7:30am-7:30pm, Sat. 7am-5pm.

Interspar, at the intersection of Lazarettg. and Lazarett-Gürtel in the enormous City Park shopping mall. Open Mon.-Wed. and Fri. 9am-7:30pm, Thurs. 9am-8pm, Sat. 8am-1pm. A **branch** is next door to the *Mensa.* Open Mon.-Fri. 8am-1pm and 4-6:30pm, Sat. 7:30am-12:30pm.

SIGHTS

"Tastes, architecture, and slaps in the face are all different" is an old Styrian saying, and the buildings of Graz prove at least the first two. The central *Altstadt* packs dozens of classical arches, domes, and red-tiled roofs into a twisting maze of cobblestone streets, while the stark modern buildings of Technical University a few blocks away, are just one example of the influence of Graz's well-known modern School of Architecture. A fun and systematic way to explore diverse Graz is through the tourist office's guide, *A Walk through the Old City* (10AS). The tourist office itself is a sight; situated in the **Landhaus,** which is still the seat of the provincial government, the building was remodeled by architect Domenico dell'Allio in 1557 in masterful Lombard style. Through the arch to the right is an arcaded stone courtyard, overflowing with geraniums in summer, a glorious reminder of the Italian Renaissance.

On the other side of the tourist office, you'll find the most bizarre yet fascinating attraction in Graz, the **Landeszeughaus** (Provincial Arsenal), Herreng. 16 (tel. 877 36 39 or 877 27 78), built from 1642 to 1645 by Anton Solar. In the 17th century when Ottoman invasions rivaled death and taxes in regularity, Graz's rulers assessed the need for an on-premises weapons stash. The result of their efforts, after some political haranguing, is this gargantuan armory—the world's largest and the only one preserved in its entirety, with 30,000 harnesses and weapons dating from the late Middle Ages to the early 19th century. In the early 18th century, when the Turkish threat had dissipated, the government foolishly resolved to dispose permanently of the antiquated weapons. This action upset locals, who wanted the arsenal to stand as a monument to the soldiers' bravery and faithfulness in the fight against the "sworn enemy of Christendom." Empress Maria Theresa consented to maintain this unique historical monument in its original condition. Today, the eerie four-story collection includes enough scintillating spears, muskets, and armor to outfit 28,000 burly mercenaries, as well as a full set of armor for a horse—too heavy for battle and so reserved for martial ceremonies. (Open April-Oct. Mon.-Fri. 9am-5pm, Sat.-Sun. 9am-1pm. 25AS, seniors 10AS, students free. Free English information sheet.)

The arsenal is just a tiny part of the collection of the **Landesmuseum Joanneum,** the oldest public museum in Austria. The assembled holdings are so vast and eclectic that officials have been forced to categorize the legacy and to house portions in separate museums scattered throughout the city. Admission to each museum is 25AS, seniors 10AS, students free. The **Neue Galerie,** Sackstr. 16 (tel. 829 155), off Hauptpl., showcases off-beat, avant-garde contemporary works and a collection of 19th- and 20th-century paintings in the gorgeous Palais Herberstein. Be sure to catch a glimpse of the mountains from the palace's weatherbeaten courtyard. (Open Tues.-Sun. 10am-6pm, Thurs. 10am-8pm. Free.) For an even more impressive collection of works from the medieval Baroque periods, check out the **Alte Galerie,** Neutorg. 45 (tel. 801 74 770). Especially awe-inspiring are the larger-than-life statues that comprise Veit Königer's *Group of Annunciation* and Brueghel's graphic and grotesque *Triumph of Death,* in which an army of skeletons slaughters archduke and peasant alike. (Open Tues.-Fri. 10am-5pm, Sat.-Sun. 10am-1pm.) The **Natural History Museum,** encompassing geology, paleontology, mineralogy, zoology, and other -ologies, is at Rauberg. 10. The museum boasts a specimen of the largest beetle in the world and real stuffed animals with some striking expressions: startled deer, preying vultures, mating birds, and others. (Open Mon.-Fri. 9am-4pm, Sat.-Sun. 9am-noon.)

Another worthy collection awaits at the **Stadtmuseum,** Sackstr. 18 (tel. 82 25 80), with exhibits on area history. (Open June-Oct. Tues. 10am-9pm, Wed.-Sat. 10am-6pm, Sun. 10am-1pm.) The **Hans-Mauracher-Museum,** Hans-Mauracher-Str. 29 (tel. 392 394), is dedicated to the eminent Graz sculptor. (Open Tues.-Thurs. and Sun. 10am-5pm.) The **Abteilung für Volkskunde,** Paulustorg. 13 (tel. 830 416), showcases ethnic and social history. (Open April-Oct. Mon.-Fri. 9am-4pm, Sat.-Sun. 9am-noon.) The **Robert Stolz Museum,** Mehlpl. 1 (tel. 815 951), offers exhibits and concerts honoring the native baton-waver. (Open April-Sept. Tues.-Fri. 2-5pm, Sat.-Sun. 10am-1pm; Oct.-March Tues.-Thurs. 2-5pm, Sun. 10am-1pm.)

Dominating the inner city of Graz is the towering **Schloßberg** (castle hill), the onetime site of a fortress built in the Middle Ages. Rising 473m, the steep Dolomite peak has had a long, colorful history. The strategic location helped defend the site against the Turks in the 16th and 17th centuries and the French 100 years later. The 16thcentury **Glockenturm** (bell tower) and the 13th-century **Uhrturm** (clock tower) perched atop the peak are visible from almost any spot in Graz. The Uhrturm acquired its present appearance—the circular wooden gallery with oriels and the four huge clockfaces 5.4m in diameter—when the castle was reconstructed in 1556. But remember when setting your watch by the Uhrturm's faces that the clocks' hands are reversed: the big hand indicates the hour, not the minute. Originally, the clock only had one big hand, visible from town, set to show the hour. The huge bell in the Glockerturm, called the "Lisl," has sounded since 1578.

Napoleon never did manage to defeat the Schloßberg fortress until *after* he conquered the rest of Austria—he then he razed the fortress in an infantile, jealous rage. The town, however, managed to rescue the bell and clock towers by paying the little Emperor a sizeable ransom. You can see the fortress-turned-park by ascending the **Felsenstieg,** a beautiful, dramatic stone staircase snaking up the mountain from Schloßbergpl., or by taking the cable car. Almost obscured by the great views, a small **Garnisons museum** showcases cannons and military equipment. (Open daily 10am-5pm. 20AS, students and children 10AS.)

Descend the hill on the eastern side near the Uhrturm via Dr.-Karl-Böhm-Allee, pass through the Paulustor arch, and you'll arrive at the lovely floral **Stadtpark** (city park). Separating the old city from the lively university quarter, the carefully tended gardens provide a large island of calm right in the heart of the city, attracting walkers, sunbathers, and frisbee players. Graz acquired the ornate central fountain, which has eight figures holding huge spitting fish, at the 1873 Vienna World's Fair. Paris snatched up the two complementary side pieces, now in Pl. de la Concorde. The **Künstlerhaus,** a museum nestled in the Stadtpark, showcases eclectically themed exhibitions ranging from Tibetan artifacts to Secessionist paintings. (Open Mon.-Fri. 10am-5pm, Sat.-Sun. 10am-1pm. 40AS, students 20AS.) The 13th-century Gothic **Leechkirche,** Zinzendorfg. 5, between the Stadtpark and the university, is the city's oldest structure. Inside the chapel, a wooden altar with white, three-dimensional figures contrasts sharply with the glittery gold of most Austrian churches.

South of the fountain, the Stadtpark blends into the **Burggarten,** a bit of carefully pruned greenery complementing what remains of Emperor Friedrich III's 15th-century **Burg.** Freddie had "A.E.I.O.U." inscribed on his namesake wing of the palace. This cryptic inscription is varyingly interpreted as *"Austria Est Imperare Orbi Universo," "Austria Erit In Orbe Ultima,"* or *"Alles Erdreich Ist Österreich Untertan"*—all three involve Austria's domination of the world. Friedrich's son, Maximilian I, enlarged the building and in 1499 commissioned the unique Gothic double spiral staircase, thus predating Watson and Crick by almost 500 years. He also inserted the **Burgtor** (Castle Gate) into the city walls.

Stroll through the Burg's courtyard and out through the giant gate to find Hofg. and the **Dom** (cathedral). In 1174, Friedrich III had the existing Romanesque chapel retooled to transform the three-bayed cathedral into late-Gothic style, but the simple exterior hides the interior's exquisite Baroque embellishments. In 1485, the church mounted a picture of the "Scourges of God" on the south side of the building to remind Christians of the most palpable trinity of the time: the Black Death, Ottoman invasions, and the locusts—a combination that had wiped out 80% of the population five years earlier. Inside the cathedral, a beautiful silver and gold organ and thick marble pillars await visitors. The huge fresco over the lintel, ostensibly Christ, actually bears the features of Emperor Friedrich III—worshippers believed that if they caught a glimpse of his eyes, they would pass without harm. Originally, a thick wooden gate covered the front of the church, since the commoners were only supposed to hear the priests and never see them. The Emperor got a choice seat high above the left side and was able to watch. The priest controlled the hands of the clock under the organ from the pulpit and could stop them if he felt the need to pray longer.

Next door, the solemn 17th-century Habsburg **Mausoleum**, one of the finest examples of Austrian Mannerism, stands atop a grey stone staircase. Look to the right for the golden eagle, the world's largest weather vane. The domed tomb was intended for the Emperor Ferdinand II but actually holds the remains of his mother, Archduchess Maria. Master architect Johann Bernard Fischer von Erlach designed the frescoes inside. (Open Mon.-Thurs. and Sat. 11am-noon and 2-3pm. Free.) The **Opernhaus** (opera house), at Opernring and Burggasse, was built in under two years by Viennese theater architects Fellner and Helmer. The two drank their cup of inspiration from the masterful bottle of Fischer von Erlach. The Graz **Glockenspiel**, located just off Engeg. in Glockenspielpl., opens its wooden doors every day at 11am, 3, and 6pm to reveal life-size wooden figures spinning to a slightly out-of-tune folk song. The black and gold ball underneath turns to show the phases of the moon.

To the west of Graz proper, **Schloß Eggenberg**, Eggenberger Allee (tel. 583 264), stands as an artifact of past grandeur. Built under the auspices of the Imperial Prince Ulrich of Eggenberg, this grandiose palace holds the regional hunting museum, coin museum, and an exhibition of Roman artifacts. The city wasted no modesty on the elegant **Prunkräume,** designed around the theme of cosmology and astronomy. Count the palace windows—all 365 of them. To see the apartments of state, renowned for their 17th-century frescoes and ornate chandeliers, you must join one of the free tours (in German; every hr. 10am-noon and 2-4pm). The frescoes are, you know, standard stuff—scenes of war and violence, a son's head being served on a dinner plate, and the like. The macabre trend continues with the hunting museum, which features a roomful of perennially popular freaks: ill-conceived Bambis with crazy growths where horns should be and even a four-legged duckling. The enchanting **game preserve** that envelops the palace proves nature's handicraft is every bit as magnificent as the work of bishops or princes. Royal blue peacocks wander and squawk freely. Take tram #1 (dir: Eggenberg): "Schloß Eggenberg." (*Prunkräume* open April-Oct. daily 10am-1pm and 2-5pm. Hunting museum open March-Nov. daily 9am-noon and 1-5pm. Game preserve open daily May-Aug. 8am-7pm; March-April and Sept.-Oct. 8am-6pm; Jan.-Feb. and Nov.-Dec. 8am-5pm. Entire complex 80AS, students 40AS; gardens only 2AS.) Classical concerts are given in the **Planetensaal** (Planet Hall; tel. 825 000) in the palace. (Aug.-Sept. Mon. at 8pm. Tickets from 130AS.)

Across Herreng. from the Landzeughaus is the lemon yellow **Stadtpfarrkirche**, originally the Abbey Church of the Dominicans in the 16th century. Done up in late Gothic style, the church suffered severe damage from WWII air raids. When Salzburger artist Albert Birkle designed new stained-glass windows for the church in 1953, one made worldwide news: the left panel behind the high altar portrays the scourging of Christ, silently watched over by two figures bearing an uncanny resemblance to Hitler and Mussolini. The church is surprisingly unfrequented—you'll have ample solitude for introspection. The church holds organ concerts early July to early September on Thursdays at 8pm (70AS, students 40AS).

ENTERTAINMENT

Graz's vibrant, dynamic population prides itself on being able to cultivate high art while simultaneously letting it all hang out. Entertainment in Graz has something to suit even the most curmudgeonly vacationer. Students can check the **student administration office** of the university, which has billboards papered with concert notices, student activity flyers, and carpool advertisements for all of Austria. For progressive, envelope-pushing drama, Graz's remarkable neo-Baroque **Opernhaus** (opera house), at Opernring and Burgg. (tel. 80 08), sells standing-room tickets at the door an hour before curtain call. The yearly program includes operas and ballets of worldwide repute; for many young hopefuls, Graz is considered a stepping stone to an international career. One big show comes each July while the regular companies are on vacation—1996 and 1997 brought the Bolshoi Ballet. Tickets cost a pretty penny (490-1750AS), but standing-room slots start at 100AS and student rush tickets at 150AS. The **Schauspielhaus,** a theater at Freiheitspl. off Hofg. (tel. 80 05), also sells bargain seats just before showtime. All tickets and performance schedules are available at the **Theaterkasse,** Kaiser-Josef-Pl. 10 (tel. 80 00; fax 800 85 65; open Mon.-Fri. 8am-6:30pm, Sat. 8am-1pm), and the Zentralkartenbüro, Herreng. 7 (tel. 830 255).

In late September and October, the **Steierischer Herbst** (Styrian Autumn) festival celebrates avant-garde art with a month of modern abstraction. Contact the director of the festival, Sackstr. 17 (tel. 823 007; fax 835 788; email stherbst@ping.at; http://www.ping.at/members/stherbst), for details. Since 1985, the city has hosted its own summer festival, **Styriarte,** as well. Mostly classical concerts are held daily from late June to early July in the gardens of the Schloß Eggenberg, the large halls of Graz Convention Center, and the squares of the old city. The renowned Graz conductor, Nikolaus Harnoncourt, sets the tone. (Tickets for most events start at 200AS. For information, email styriarte@mail.styria.co.at or surf http://www.styria.co.at/styriarte.) The award-winning movie theater **Rechbauerkino,** Rechbauerstr. 6 (tel. 830 508), occasionally screens undubbed American flicks (80AS, 60AS on Mon.). Tuesday is English Film Night at the **Royal Kino,** on Conrad-von-Hötzendorfstr., a few blocks south of Jakominipl. (80AS, 60AS on Mon.). Keep your eye out for the summer film festival, **Classics in the City,** when the courtyard at the tourist office fills with chairs and happy people watching operas like *The Barber of Seville* on a giant screen. (July-Aug. daily 8:30pm in good weather. In bad weather, they still play music. Everybody wins!) Of course, the best things in life are free—stroll down **Sporgasse,** a narrow cobblestone path squeezed between two rows of brightly lit shops, or meander down **Herrengasse** to hear the trumpets and violins echoing against the facades of the *Altstadt*. Every summer the **American Institute of Musical Studies** transfers to Graz. Vocal and instrumental students perform constantly on the streets and in concert halls—ask for a schedule of works ranging from Broadway to Schönberg at the tourist office. Also be sure to pick up the cultural magazine *Graz Derzeit*, free at the tourist office, for a daily, mind-boggling list of events with details on prices and locations (on-line at http://www.iic.wifi.at/graz/veranstaltungen/derzeit).

NIGHTLIFE

Each day when the sun sets on Graz, the quarter of a million inhabitants change into their party threads and collectively paint the town red. The hub of after-hours activity can be found in the ubiquitous **"Bermuda Triangle,"** an area of the old city behind Hauptpl. and bordered by Mehlpl., Färberg., and Prokopiag. Like the one in Vienna, the Triangle's dozens of beer gardens and bars are packed with people all night, every night; sitting in an outdoor café is *de rigueur*, at least until 11pm, when local ordinance requires that festivities move indoors. The area is patronized by as many Graz students as Armani-clad business-mongers, but more scholars sip their beers in the pubs lining Zinzendorfg. and Halbärthg. near the university.

Kulturhauskeller, Elisabethstr. 30, underneath the Kulturhaus. Young crowd and cool locale dictate the loud, sometimes overwhelming music in this bar. The partying doesn't really get started until 11pm on weekends. Tall glass of *Weißbier* 34AS. No shorts or military duds. IDs checked. Obligatory coat check and security fee 20AS. Open Mon.-Sat. 8pm-3:30am.

Café Harrach, Harrachg. 26 (tel. 322 671). Quaff a beverage at this local student haunt, which serves a more sophisticated clientele in its quiet, outdoor seating. A half-liter of *Gösser* goes for 29AS, but most everybody's throwing back white wine spritzers (26AS). Open Mon.-Fri. 5pm-midnight, Sat.-Sun. 7pm-midnight.

Tom's Bierklinik, Färberg. 1 (tel. 845 174), has the largest stock of international beers in Austria. Go ahead and try prescriptions from Hawaii, Trinidad, or India (all 75AS), or just get a local fix with a glass of *Murauer Pils* (32AS). Walk-in hours daily 8pm-4am. No appointment necessary.

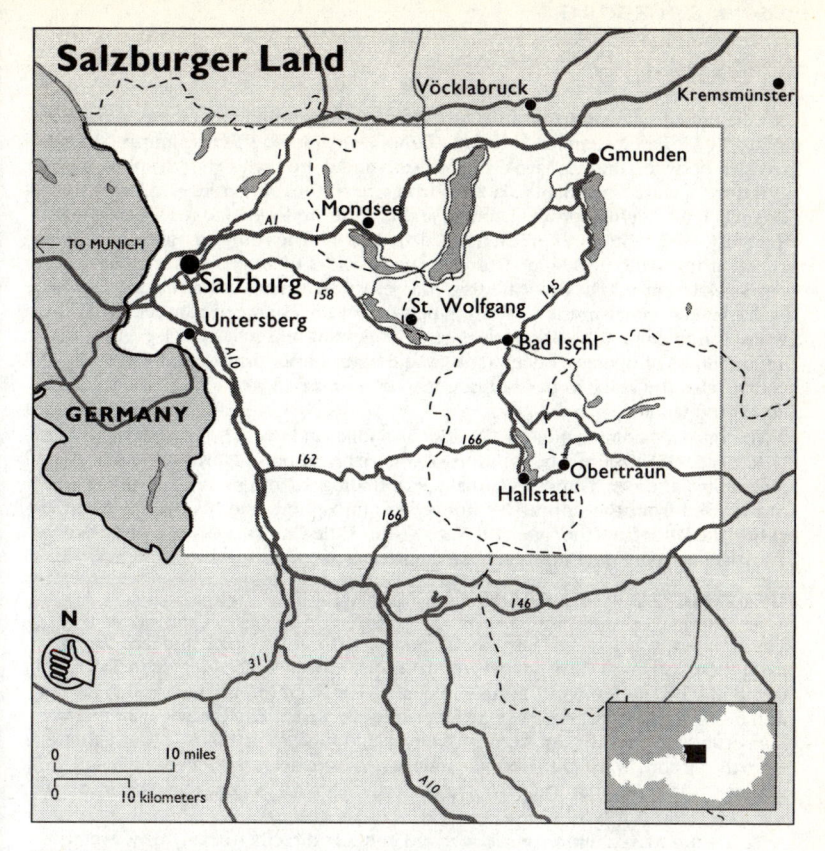

Salzburger Land

Once one of Europe's most powerful archbishoprics, the province of Salzburg remained an autonomous entity until 1815, when that crazy Congress of Vienna up and gave it to Austria. The region built up its tremendous wealth with "white gold"—salt, not cocaine—in an industry that flourished from the Iron Age onward. The name "Salzburg" comes from *Salz* (German for salt), and several localities in the region also have some derivative of *Hall* (an archaic Celtic term for salt) in their name. Although tourism displaced the salt trade long ago, figures of St. Barbara, the patron saint of miners, linger everywhere. The major attraction of Salzburger Land is the Baroque magnificence of its capital city, Salzburg. The dramatic natural scenery and placid lakes of the Salzkammergut, which straddles the provincial boundaries of Salzburg, Styria, and Upper Austria, make for one of Austria's favorite vacation spots.

Though all this mineral mining may seem soporific, when the Salzburger Land lets down its hair, it does so in style. Every three years on the last Sunday in July, an historic **Pirates' Battle** is held on the Salzach River at **Oberndorf**. The pirates' camp is situated below the State Bridge. According to the ritual plot, the brigands attack and rob a saltboat and then fire on the town of **Laufen,** on the opposite (Bavarian) side of the river. Eventually, the defeated pirates try to escape. They are arrested and condemned to death, but their sentence is quickly modified to "death by drowning in beer," which signifies the beginning of a lavish feast.

Salzburg

For the city of Salzburg (pop. 150,000), the three most important factors about real estate are Mozart, Mozart, and Mozart. *The Sound of Music* is a close fourth. Though wedged between three foliage-covered peaks and dotted with church spires, medieval turrets, and resplendent palaces, Salzburg nevertheless considers as its forte not its spectacular sights but its historical and current performance relationship with the music of favorite son Wolfgang Amadeus Mozart. The composer makes his presence felt throughout the city, from its narrow alleys to its grand music halls. The city's adulation reaches a deafening roar every summer during the **Salzburger Festspiele** (summer music festival), when financially endowed admirers from the world round come to pay their respects. The Festspiele is a five-week event featuring hundreds of operas, concerts, plays, and open-air performances. Salzburg is, of course, also the place to pay homage to *The Sound of Music*'s saccharine, trilling von Trapp family.

The one-two combination of "Wolfie" and Julie Andrews *et al* makes the otherwise peaceful Salzburg a beacon for tourists rich and poor. Never mind that both Mozart and the von Trapps eventually left, finding Salzburg a bit too stifling (the former fled from the oppressive bourgeois atmosphere and his over-managerial father, the latter from the tone-deaf Nazis)—this Little City That Could couldn't keep away its onslaught of visitors even if it wanted to.

GETTING TO AND FROM SALZBURG

The cheapest way to reach Salzburg by plane is to fly into Munich and take the train from there. Salzburg does have its own airport, however, the **Flughafen Salzburg** (tel. 858 02 51), 4km west of the city center. For flight information, call **Austrian Airlines/Swissair** (tel. 854 511). Several airlines jet each day between such major European cities as Paris, Amsterdam, Vienna, and Innsbruck. Bus #77 (dir: Bahnhof from the airport, Walserfeld from the train station) connects the train station and the airport (every 15-30min. daily 5:55am-11:26pm, 15min.). A taxi from the airport to the train station costs 90-120AS.

Trains run to Salzburg from all over and connect directly to many major international and domestic cities. There are two train stations: the **Hauptbahnhof** on Südtirolerpl. is the first depot for trains coming from Vienna; the Rangier Bahnhof is the first stop when coming from Innsbruck but serves mainly as a cargo station—don't get off here. The **regional bus depot** (tel. (0660) 51 88) is 100m in front of the main train station. BundesBuses chug throughout the Salzkammergut region.

Motorists coming from Vienna can exit at any of the numerous Salzburg-West exits on Autobahn A1. Among these exits, the Flughafen exit is near the airport; the Salzburg Nord exit is near Itzling and Kasern; and the Salzburg Süd exit lies south of the city near Schloß Hellbrunn and Untersberg. Rte. A8 and E52 lead from the west into Rosenheim and then branch off to Munich and Innsbruck. Autoroute A10 heads north from Hallein to Salzburg. To reach the Salzkammergut area and the scenic road that leads to the top of Gaisberg, take Grazer Bundesstr. (Rte. 158) from Gnigl behind Kapuzinerberg. Since public transportation is efficient within the city limits, consider the **"Park and Ride"** parking lots—park for free when you get off the highway and take the bus into town. The most convenient lot is **Alpensiedlung Süd** on Alpenstr. (exit: Salzburg Süd), but a bigger lot is open in July and August at the **Salzburger Ausstellungszentrum** (exit: Salzburg-Mitte).

ORIENTATION AND PRACTICAL INFORMATION

Salzburg, the capital of the province of the same name, lies at the midpoint of Austria's length, 470m above sea level. Three wooded hills surround the town, which hugs the banks of the **Salzach River** a few kilometers from the German border. The *Hauptbahnhof* is on the northern edge of downtown, and buses connect it to downtown proper: #1, 5, 6, 51, and 55. The river divides downtown Salzburg. On

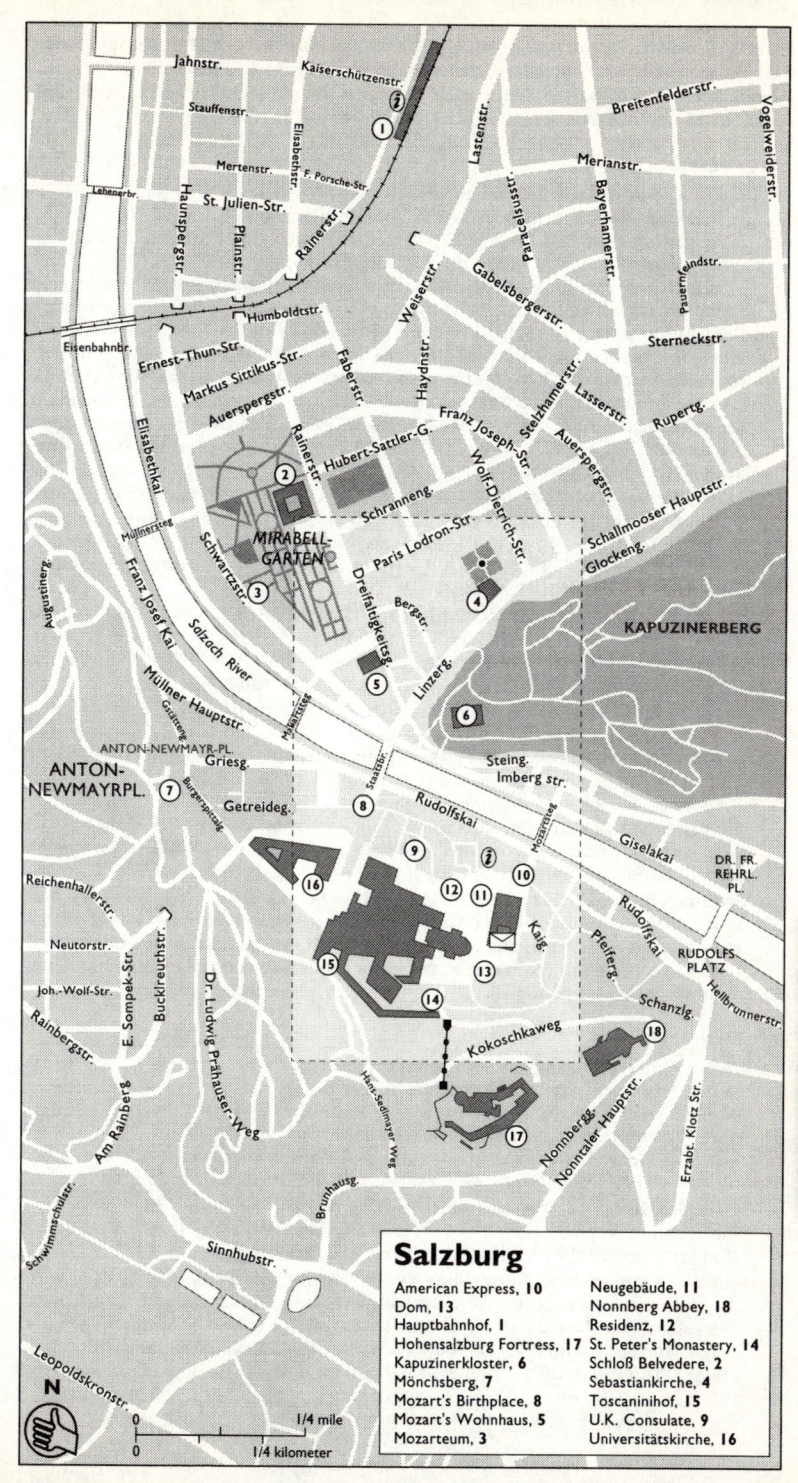

ORIENTATION AND PRACTICAL INFORMATION ■ 205

Salzburg

- American Express, 10
- Dom, 13
- Hauptbahnhof, 1
- Hohensalzburg Fortress, 17
- Kapuzinerkloster, 6
- Mönchsberg, 7
- Mozart's Birthplace, 8
- Mozart's Wohnhaus, 5
- Mozarteum, 3
- Neugebäude, 11
- Nonnberg Abbey, 18
- Residenz, 12
- St. Peter's Monastery, 14
- Schloß Belvedere, 2
- Sebastiankirche, 4
- Toscaninihof, 15
- U.K. Consulate, 9
- Universitätskirche, 16

SALZBURGER LAND

the west bank is the *Altstadt,* crouching below the **Mönchsberg** (Monk's Mountain); on the east side is the *Neustadt,* centered around **Mirabellplatz.** From the bus, disembark at "Mirabellpl." or "Mozartsteg" to access the city sights. By foot, Mirabellpl. is 10 to 15 minutes from the train station, left down Rainerstr.

Agencies

Tourist Office, Mozartpl. 5 (tel. 847 568 or 889 87 330; fax 889 87 342; email tourist@salzburginfo.or.at; http://www.salzburginfo.or.at), in the *Altstadt.* From the train station, bus #5, 6, 51, or 55: "Mozartsteg" then curve around the building into Mozartpl. On foot, make a left on Rainerstr., go to the end, cross Staatsbrücke, then continue along the river's west bank upstream to Mozartsteg (20min.). The office has free hotel maps (exactly the same as the 10AS city map). Reservation service 30AS, for 3 or more people 60AS, plus a 7.2% deposit deductible from the first night's stay. The overworked staff will tell you which hostels have available rooms. The office is your source for the Salzburg Card (see p. 215). Open daily July-Aug. 9am-8pm; Sept.-June 9am-6pm. There are other **branches** at the **train station platform #2a** (tel. 889 87 340), open Mon.-Sat. 8:45am-8pm; the **airport** (tel. 851 211 or 852 091), open daily 9am-9pm; and the **Alpensiedlung Süd "Park and Ride"** lot (tel. 889 87 360).

Budget Travel: ÖKISTA, Wolf-Dietrich-Str. 31 (tel. 883 252; fax 881 819; email info@oekista.co.at; http://www.oekista.co.at/oekista), near the International Youth Hotel. Open Mon.-Fri. 9am-5:30pm. **Young Austria,** Alpenstr. 108a (tel. 625 75 80; fax 625 75 821), part of *Österreichisches Jugendferienwerk.* Open Mon.-Fri. 9am-5pm, Sat. 9am-noon.

Consulates: South Africa, Erzabt-Klotz-Str. 4 (tel. 843 328; fax 843 77 880). Open Mon.-Fri. 8am-1pm and 2-5pm. **U.K.,** Alter Markt 4 (tel. 843 133). Open Mon.-Fri. 9am-noon. **U.S. Consulate Agency,** Herbert-von-Karajan-Pl. 1 (tel. 848 776; fax 849 777), in the *Altstadt.* Open Mon., Wed., and Fri. 9am-noon.

Currency Exchange: Banks offer better rates for cash than AmEx offices but often charge higher commissions. Banking hours are Mon.-Fri. 8am-12:30pm and 2-4:30pm. **Rieger Bank** at Alter Markt and Getriedeg. has extended currency exchange hours: July-Aug. Mon.-Fri. 9am-8pm, Sat. 9am-6pm, Sun. 10am-6pm; Sept.-June Mon.-Fri. 9am-7pm, Sat. 9am-5pm, Sun. 10am-5pm. The currency exchange at the train station is open daily 7am-9pm. **Panorama Tours** offers cash currency exchange at bank rates with no commission; available only to guests taking their tour (see *Sights,* p. 215).

American Express: Mozartpl. 5, A-5020 (tel. 80 80; fax 808 01 78). The office provides all banking services and charges no commission on their own checks. Better rates than banks for cash and other checks. Holds mail for check- or card-holders, books sightseeing tours, and reserves music festival tickets. Open Mon.-Fri. 9am-5:30pm, Sat. 9am-noon.

Transportation

Trains: Hauptbahnhof, on Südtirolerpl. (tel. 17 17 for information). To: **Innsbruck** (every hr., 2hr., 336AS); **Graz** (every hr., 4½hr., 396AS); **Vienna** (every 30min., 3½hr., 396AS); **Munich** (every 30min., 2hr., 294AS); **Zurich** (6 per day, 6hr., last connection at 4pm, 866AS); **Budapest** (9 per day, 7½hr., 736AS); **Prague** (4 per day, 544AS, connect in Linz); and **Venice** (7 per day, 7½hr., last connection at 10:15pm, 470AS). The reservation office is open daily 7am-8:15pm.

Buses: Regional bus depot (tel. (0660) 51 88). BundesBuses zip all over. To: **Mondsee** (every hr., 1hr., 57AS); **St. Wolfgang** (every hr., 1½hr., 86AS); and **Bad Ischl** (every 2hr., 1½hr., 95AS). For schedule information, call 167.

Public Transportation: Information at the **Lokalbahnhof** (tel. 872 145), next to the train station. An extensive network of 18 buses cuts through the city, with central hubs at Hanusch-Pl. by Makartsteg, "Äußerer Stein" by Mozartsteg, Mirabellpl., and the *Bahnhof.* Tickets are cheapest from *Tabaks* (day pass 32AS, week 100AS). You can purchase single-ride tickets from vending machines at bus stops (15AS) or on the bus (21AS). You must punch your ticket when you board in order to validate it—failure to do so can result in heavy fines. Buses usually make

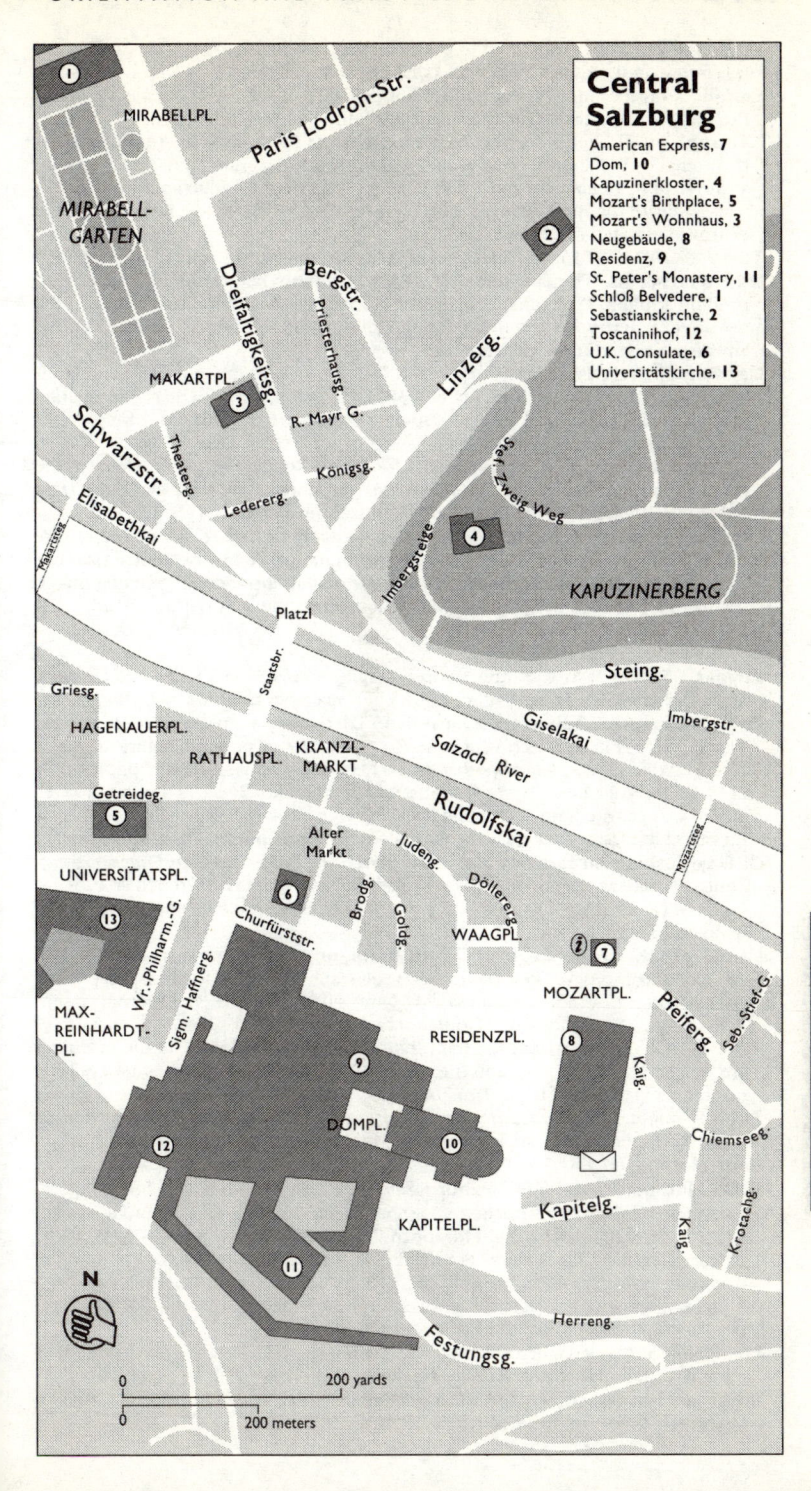

ORIENTATION AND PRACTICAL INFORMATION ■ 207

Central Salzburg

- American Express, 7
- Dom, 10
- Kapuzinerkloster, 4
- Mozart's Birthplace, 5
- Mozart's Wohnhaus, 3
- Neugebäude, 8
- Residenz, 9
- St. Peter's Monastery, 11
- Schloß Belvedere, 1
- Sebastianskirche, 2
- Toscaninihof, 12
- U.K. Consulate, 6
- Universitätskirche, 13

their last run from downtown to outer destinations at 10:30-11:30pm, earlier for less-frequented routes. Check the schedule posted at stops.

Parking: Consider the "Park and Ride" option (see p. 204). If you *must* park within the city, try **Altstadt-Garage** inside the Mönchsberg, open 24hr.; **Mirabell-Garage** in Mirabellpl., open 7am-midnight; or **Parkgarage Linzergasse** at Glockeng. (off Linzerg.), open Mon.-Fri. 7am-11pm, Sat. 7am-2pm. Other lots are at the airport, Hellbrunn, and Akademiestr. (15AS per hr.). Blue lines on the sidewalk indicate that parking's available; buy a ticket for the space from one of the nearby automated machines.

Taxis: tel. 81 11, 17 15, or 17 16. Stands at Hanuschpl., Residenzpl., Makartpl., and the train station. The city runs a **BusTaxi** to fill in when the public buses stop running at night. Pick the bus up at the stop at Hanuschpl. or Theaterg. and tell the driver where you need to go. Every 30min. nightly 11:30pm-1:30am. 30AS for any distance within the city limits.

Car Rental: Avis, Ferdinand-Porsche-Str. 7 (tel. 877 278; fax 880 235), and **Budget,** Rainerstr. 17 (tel. 873 45; fax 882 387), are in the airport. The cheapest automobile rental place is **Kalal,** Alpenstr. 2 (tel./fax 620 006). All offices offer insurance and unlimited mileage.

Bike Rental: Climb every mountain and ford every stream with a bicycle from the train station counter #3 (tel. 888 73 163). 150AS per day, with that day's train ticket 90AS; 1 week 670AS. Bike paths wind all through the city.

Hitchhiking: Hitchers headed to Innsbruck, Munich, or Italy (except Venice) take bus #77 to the German border. Thumbers bound for Vienna or Venice take bus #29 (dir: Forellenwegsiedlung) until the Autobahn entrance at "Schmiedlingerstr." or bus #15 (dir: Bergheim) to the Autobahn entrance at "Grüner Wald."

Other Practical Information

Luggage Storage: At the train station. Large lockers 30AS for 2 calendar days. Small lockers 20AS. Luggage check 30AS per piece per calendar day. Open 24hr.

English-Language Bookstores: American Discount, in a passage in Alter Markt 1 (tel. 757 541). Those craving American culture can pick up American magazines, boxing gloves, and paperbacks. To help you plan your next trip, pick up a *Let's Go* for your next trip at **Buchhandlung Motzko Reise,** Rainerstr. 24 (tel. 883 311), near the train station. English-language books at their main store across the street at Elisabethstr. 1. Both open Mon.-Fri. 9am-6pm, Sat. 9am-5pm.

Bi-Gay-Lesbian Organizations: HUK-Salzburg (Gay Christian Organization), Philharmonikerg. 2 (tel. 841 327). **Frauenkulturzentrum** (Women's/Lesbians' Center), Elisabethstr. 11 (tel./fax 871 639). Office and hotlines open Mon. 10am-noon and Thurs. 3-5pm.

Laundromat: Norge Exquisit Textil Reinigung, Paris-Lodronstr. 16 (tel. 876 381), on the corner of Wolf-Dietrich-Str. Self-serve wash and dry 82AS, soap 28AS. Open Mon.-Fri. 7:30am-4pm, Sat. 8-10am. Full-serve 185AS. Open Mon.-Fri. 7:30am-6pm, Sat. 8am-noon. **Constructa Wasch Salon,** Kaiserschützenstr. 10 (tel. 876 253), across from the train station. Self-serve 135AS. If all the machines are full, leave your clothes and the proprietor will put them in the first available machine. Open Mon.-Fri. 7:30am-7pm, Sat. 7:30am-1pm.

Public Toilets: In the *Altstadt* under the archway between Kapitelpl. and Dompl. (7AS). Cheaper ones in the Festungsbahn lobby (3AS).

Rape Hotline: tel. 881 100.

AIDS Hotline: AIDS-Hilfe Salzburg, Saint-Julienstr. 31, 4th fl. (tel. 881 488).

Pharmacies: Elisabeth-Apotheke, Elisabethstr. 1 (tel. 871 484), a few blocks left of the train station. **Alte f.e. Hofapotheke,** Alter Markt 6 (tel. 843 623), is the oldest pharmacy in Salzburg. Pharmacies in the city center are open Mon.-Fri. 8am-6pm, Sat. 8am-noon; outside the center Mon.-Fri. 8am-12:30pm and 2:30-6pm, Sat. 8am-noon. There are always three pharmacies available for emergencies; check the list on the door of any closed pharmacy.

Medical Assistance: When the dog bites, when the bee stings, when you're feeling sad, call the **Hospital,** Müllner Hauptstr. 48 (tel. 448 20).

Emergencies: Police, tel. 133. Headquarters at Alpenstr. 90 (tel. 63 83). **Ambulance,** tel. 144. **Fire,** tel. 122.

ACCOMMODATIONS AND CAMPING ■ 209

Post Office: At the *Hauptbahnhof* (tel. 889 70). Mail your brown paper packages tied up with string at the main office next to the train station. The office has a self-serve photocopiers and currency exchange. Address *Poste Restante* to Postlagernde Briefe, Bahnhofspostamt, A-5020 Salzburg. Open daily 6am-11pm.
Branch at Residenzpl. 9 (tel. 844 121). Open Mon.-Fri. 7am-7pm, Sat. 8-10am.
Postal Code: A-5020.
Telephone Code: 0662.

ACCOMMODATIONS AND CAMPING

Salzburg has no shortage of hostels—but, then again, the city has no shortage of tourists either. Real estate in Salzburg is even more expensive than in Vienna; most affordable accommodations are on the outskirts of town, easily accessible by local transportation. Ask for the tourist office's list of private rooms (separate from the hotel map) or the *Hotel Plan* for information on hostels. The tourist office charges 30AS plus 7.2% fee of your room to make reservations. An under-utilized resource is the **HI booking network** (see **Hostel Membership,** p. 45). From mid-May through mid-September, hostels fill by mid-afternoon—call ahead. During the festival, never show up without reservations or later than noon. Hotels fill months in advance, and most youth hostels and *Gästehäuser* are full days before. Hostels have long abandoned the practice of letting late stragglers crash on the floor.

Hostels and Dormitories

Gästehaus Naturfreundehaus/Bürgerwehr, Mönchsberg 19c (tel. 841 729), towers over the old town from the top of the Mönchsberg. The easy way (by elevator): bus #1 (dir: Maxglan): "Mönchsbergaufzug" then walk down the street a few steps and through the stone arch on the left to the Mönchsberglift (elevator). The elevator takes you to the top of the mountain (runs daily 9am-11pm, round-trip 27AS). At its summit, turn right, climb the steps, and go down the paved path to the left, following signs for "Gästehaus Naturfreundehaus"—watch for the sign at the 180-degree left turn uphill along the stone wall. The hostel is on the right, through the arch labeled "Bürgerwehr." With all the red umbrellas, it may look like a restaurant, but it's the hostel. By foot (for those with strong legs and light backpacks): bus #1 (dir: Maxglan): "Karajanpl." then continue straight ahead, across the street and along the front of the Festspielhaus. Go through the arch on the right into Toscaninihof. Hike up the 332 stairs that start in the back right corner, bearing right the whole time on the top paths up to the red-umbrella-bedecked hostel. Get a princely view on a pauper's budget. Genial proprietors have their hands full running the terrific restaurant downstairs as well. Only holds 28 in 2- to 6-bed rooms, so reservations are recommended. Reception daily 8am-10pm. Curfew 1am—start hustling up those stairs at quarter till. Dorms 120AS. Showers 10AS per 4min. Breakfast (on the terrace with a magnificent view of Salzburg) 30AS. Sheets 10AS. Open May to mid-Oct.

International Youth Hotel (YoHo), Paracelsusstr. 9 (tel. 879 649 or 834 60; fax 878 810), off Franz-Josef-Str. Exit the train station to the left and turn left onto Gabelsbergerstr. through the tunnel. Take the second right onto Paracelsusstr. (7min.). A rollicking pitstop for homesick Americans and Canadians—you may even forget you're in a German-speaking country. Filled with beer-sipping postcard writers in the afternoon and a frat-party atmosphere in the evening. Despite the raucous inhabitants, the hostel is remarkably clean and well run. *The Sound of Music* screened daily at 1:30pm. The hostel restaurant's perpetual happy hour makes it more popular than most local bars. Reception daily 8am-10pm. "Curfew" 1am (not very strict); theoretical quiet time starts at 10pm, but the party generally rages on until 2-3am. Dorms 140AS; doubles 360AS; quads 640AS. Showers 10AS per 6min. Breakfast 30-55AS. Dinner entrees 30-75AS. Lockers 10AS. Stylish sleepsacks 20AS. The new YoHo membership card grants holders discounts at some of Salzburg's attraction.

Institut St. Sebastian, Linzerg. 41 (tel. 871 386; fax 871 38 685). From the station, turn left on Rainerstr., go past Mirabellpl., turn left onto Bergstr., and turn left at the end onto Linzerg. The hostel is through the arch on the left just before the

SALZBURGER LAND

church. This privately owned hostel-like accommodation, built right on the St. Sebastian church grounds, recently received a complete facelift, and the entire complex is now clean and modern. Located smack-dab in the middle of the historic *Neustadt*, the institute is a women-only university student dorm, but the proprietors welcome travelers of either gender. The cemetery of the St. Sebastian church, which abuts the dormitory, makes for a very quiet and peaceful neighborhood. The hotel-like singles, doubles, and triples are gorgeous. Great rooftop terrace open in summer. 24hr. reception, but call ahead. No curfew. Only 90 beds, so reservations are strongly recommended. Only dorms available Oct.-June. Dorms 170AS; singles 300AS, with shower and toilet 360AS; doubles 600AS, 630AS; triples 690-780AS. Dorm sheets 30AS. Free lockers. Kitchen facilities available, including refrigerators with little lockable cupboards—ask for a key at the reception. Pots and bowls for rent. Laundry 40AS.

Jugendgästehaus Salzburg (HI), Josef-Preis-Allee 18 (tel. 842 670 or 846 857; fax 841 101), southeast of the *Altstadt*. Bus #5, 51, or 55: "Justizgebäude," or walk from the tourist office southeast (upstream, with traffic) along the river, bear right onto Hellbrunnerstr., turn right onto Nonntaler Hauptstr., and then take the first left. Sunny, spacious rooms off brightly colored corridors. Omnipresent school groups make frequent use of the on-site video-game room, café, and disco. Clean and well-run despite the somewhat chaotic atmosphere—the YoHo for Europeans. Ridiculous reception hours. Here it goes: Mon.-Fri. 7-9am, 11-11:30am, noon-1pm, 3:30-5:30pm, 6-9:30pm, and 10pm-midnight; Sat.-Sun. 7-9am, 11-11:30am, noon-1pm, 4:30-7:30pm, and 10pm-midnight. No lockout. Curfew midnight. Dorms 160-164AS; doubles with shower 520-528AS; quads with shower 840-856AS. Non-members add 40AS first night. Shower, breakfast, and sheets included. Lunch or dinner 68AS. Kitchen, laundry facilities, and lockers available. Bike rental 90AS. Reservations recommended. Outstanding wheelchair facilities.

Eduard-Heinrich-Haus (HI), Eduard-Heinrich-Str. 2 (tel. 625 976; fax 627 980). It's a bit *fa* (a long, long way to run), *so* (a needle pulling thread) take bus #51 (dir: Salzburg Süd): "Polizeidirektion." Cross the street, continue down Billrothstr., and turn left on the Robert-Stolz-Promenade footpath. Walk 200m and take the first right; the hostel is large building up the driveway on the left. Young people swarm to this quiet area near university housing. Enormous 6- to 7-bed rooms with lockers to match. Significantly more beds July-Aug. Reception daily 7-9am and 5pm-midnight. Lockout 9am-5pm. Summer curfew midnight, winter 11pm; key available. Dorms 160AS, non-members 200AS. Showers and breakfast (7-9am) included.

Haunspergstraße (HI), Haunspergstr. 27 (tel. 875 030; fax 883 477), just minutes from the train station. Walk straight out Kaiserschützenstr. (past the Forum department store), which becomes Jahnstr. Take the third left onto Haunspergstr. A student dorm that becomes a hostel July-Aug. No groups allowed—die-hard backpackers, rejoice! Houses 125 in spacious 2- to 4-bed rooms. Staff occasionally disappears from the office; just wait. Reception daily 7am-2pm and 5pm-midnight, but the hostel fills by late afternoon. Curfew midnight. Dorms 160AS. Non-members add 40AS first night. Sheets, shower, and breakfast included. Laundry 80AS. Open July-Aug.

Aigen (HI), Aignerstr. 34 (tel. 623 248; fax 232 48 13). From the station, bus #5: "Mozartsteg" then bus #49 (dir: Josef-Käut-Str.): "Finanzamt," and walk 5min. along the road. It's the yellow, estate-like building on your right. If you've missed the bus, walk from the tourist office over the river on Mozartsteg, turn right on Imbergstr., follow the street around the rotary as it becomes Bürglsteinstr., and then bear right onto Aignerstr. (30min.). Jungle-like potted plants in the reception and hallways. lead to huge, bare 6-bed rooms with wooden floors. TV and weight machines downstairs. Accommodates 135 in rooms with 2-6 beds. Reception daily 7-9am and 5pm-midnight. Curfew midnight. Dorms 180AS, non-members 220AS. Breakfast, showers, and sheets included. Large cupboards but no lockers in rooms.

ACCOMMODATIONS AND CAMPING ■ 211

Hotels and Pensions

Pensionen within the city are scarce and expensive, and service is a crapshoot. Better quality and lower prices await on the outskirts of town, and public transportation puts these establishments within minutes of downtown Salzburg. Rooms on **Kasern Berg** are officially out of Salzburg, which means the tourist office can't officially recommend them, but the charming hosts and bargain prices make these pensions little-known steals. All northbound regional train runs to Kasern Berg (generally every 30min. daily 6:17am-11:17pm, 4min., 17AS, Eurailpass valid). Get off at the first stop, "Salzburg-Maria Plain," and take the only road up the hill. All the Kasern Berg pensions are along this road. If you call in advance, many of the hotel proprietors will pick you up at the Kasern station. Or, from Mirabellpl., take bus #15 (dir: Bergheim): "Kasern" then hike up the mountain (15min.). By car, exit Autobahn A1 on "Salzburg Nord." The Kasern Berg pensions Haus Linden, Haus Christine, Haus Seigmann, and Germana Kapella work together to find rooms for guests. Another emergency option is camping, a possibility even for domestic souls who have never spent a night under the stars. Some of Salzburg's campsites have beds in pre-assembled tents.

Whatever you decide, **never trust proprietors who accost you at the train station**—they often charge outlandish prices with additional hidden costs for sparse rooms in La-La Land. This advice goes for the train station at Kasern Berg as well as the *Hauptbahnhof* in Salzburg.

Haus Lindner, Panoramaweg 5, formerly Kasern Berg 64 (tel. 456 681). Frau Lindner's house is on a gravel road set 15m back from the main Kasern Berg street. Spacious rooms have hardwood floors and the occasional balcony. Throw rugs give the place a "Mom-I'm-home" feel. Families with children are welcome—there's even a playground around back. Doubles 320-400AS; triples 480-600AS; quads 640-800AS. Shower and breakfast included. Reservations recommended.

Haus Christine, Panoramaweg 3 (tel. 456 773), next to Haus Lindner and run by Frau Lindner's sister. Comfortable, newly renovated rooms. Breakfast room features huge windows with a stunning view of Salzburg. Doubles 320AS-400AS; triples 480-600AS; quads 640-800AS. Shower and breakfast included. Call ahead.

Haus Rosemarie Seigmann, Kasern Berg 66 (tel. 450 001). English-speaking Rosemarie welcomes guests to rooms with hand-painted cupboards, flowered curtains, and stuffed animals. Listen to birds singing from the stone terrace overlooking the Alps. Bright rooms with fluffy comforters. Doubles 340-400AS; triples 510-600AS. Breakfast and showers included. One-night stays welcome.

Germana Kapeller, Kasern Berg 64 (tel. 456 671), below Haus Lindner. English-speaking hostess oversees enchantingly traditional rooms and screens *The Sound of Music* upon group demand (guests only). 170-200AS per person. Showers and complete breakfast included. Call ahead.

Haus Ballwein, Moostr. 69 (tel./fax 824 029). Bus #1: "Hanuschpl." then the southbound bus #60 and ask the driver to stop at Gsengerweg. Enormous, spotless rooms decorated with pastels and beautiful new furniture. The country farmhouse has wonderful farmland for hiking and offers a relaxing rural reprieve from the bustle of city tourism. Amazing breakfast includes eggs from the *Pension*'s own chickens. 200AS per person, with shower 240AS. Rooms with shower in the newly-built house with gorgeous pastoral views 250AS. Breakfast included.

Haus Kernstock, Karolingerstr. 29 (tel. 827 469; fax 827 469). Bus #77 (dir: Flughafen): "Karolingerstr." and follow signs for the street number, as the road twists strangely (15min. from rail station). Three-star pension has huge rooms with balcony, private bath, and hand-painted cupboards. Amiable hostess screens *The Sound of Music* and has 4 bikes to lend. Doubles 440-500AS; triples 660-750AS; quads 880-1000AS. All-you-can-eat breakfast included. Laundry 80AS. Visa, MC.

Pension Sandwirt, Lastenstr. 6a (tel./fax 874 351). Exit the station from the platform #13 staircase, turn right on the footbridge, turn right at the bottom onto Lastenstr., and go behind the building with the post sign (3min.). Its close proximity

SALZBURGER LAND

SALZBURG

to the *Hauptbahnhof* is its only distinguishing feature. Singles 280-300AS; doubles 440-460AS, with shower 500-550AS; triples 600AS. Large breakfast included.

Haus Elisabeth, Rauchenbichlerstr. 18 (tel./fax 450 703). Bus #51: "Itzling-Pflanzmann" (last stop) then walk up Rauchenbichlerstr. over the footbridge and continue right along the gravel path. Amazing rooms with balconies and sweeping views of the city. Hostess stuffs her guests with a huge, free breakfast of corn flakes, yogurt, bread, and jam. Singles with shower 300-330AS; doubles 500-550AS.

Haus Moser, Turnebuhel 1 (tel. 456 676), above Haus Rosemarie Seigmann; climb up the hidden stairs on the right side of Kasern Berg road across from #64. A mountainside, dark-timbered home with spacious rooms filled with fur rugs and deer heads. Singles 170-200AS; doubles 340-400AS; triples 510-600AS; quads 700-800AS. "Welcome drink," all-you-can-eat breakfast, and shower included.

Camping

Camping Stadtblick, Rauchenbichlerstr. 21 (tel. 450 652; fax 458 018), next to Haus Elisabeth. By car, take exit "Salzburg-Nord" off A1. Behind a copse of trees, with a sweeping view of the city. 65AS, *Let's Go*-toting students 60AS; tent 15AS; bed in a tent 80AS; car 25AS. 4-person mobile home, TV, and showers included, 125AS per person. Laundry 70AS. On-site store. Open March 20-Oct. 31.

Camping Nord-Sam, Samstr. 22-A (tel. 660 494). Bus #33 (dir: Obergnigl): "Langmoosweg." Shady, flower-bedecked campground with a small swimming pool to boot. 53AS; site 99AS. April to mid-June and Sept.-Oct. 40AS; 76AS. Laundry 75AS. Electricity 25AS. Open April-Oct.

FOOD

Blessed with fantastic beer gardens and countless pastry-shop patios, Salzburg begs its guests to eat outdoors. The local specialty is *Salzburger Nockerl*, a large soufflé of eggs, sugar, and raspberry filling baked into three mounds that represent the three hills of Salzburg. Another regional favorite is *Knoblauchsuppe* (garlic soup), a rich cream soup loaded with croutons and pungent garlic—a potent weapon, use it only as a last resort against irritating bunkmates. During the first two weeks of September, local cafés dispense *Sturm*, a delicious, cloudy cider (appropriately reminiscent of a storm) that hasn't quite finished fermenting.

There are more of the world-famous **Mozartkugeln** (chocolate "Mozart balls") lining café windows than notes in all of Mozart's works combined. A Salzburg confectioner invented the treats in 1890, but mass-production inevitably took over. Although the mass-produced *Kugeln* wrapped in gold and red are technically *echt* (authentic), try to sniff out the rarer, handmade ones wrapped in blue and silver, impossible to find outside of Salzburg. Reasonably priced samples are sold individually at the **Holzmayr** confectioners in the Alter Markt (5AS each, 7AS for the real, handmade McCoy). Confectioners make the *Kugeln* by covering a hazelnut-marzipan with nougat and then dipping it in chocolate; the blue and silver variety have more marzipan than the mass-produced ones.

Bars, restaurants, and cafés are difficult to classify because, more often than not, they become each of those things at different times during the day. A *beisl*, for example, serves coffee in the morning, tea in the afternoon, and beer in the evenings.

Restaurant Zur Bürgerwehr-Einkehr, Mönchsberg 19c (tel. 841 729). Follow the directions to the Naturfreundehaus/Bürgerwehr. The mom-and-pop owners of the Naturfreundehaus (see **Hostels and Dormitories,** p. 209) operate this restaurant at the top of the Mönchsberg. On sunny days, escape the tourist throng below as you repose beneath the terrace's red umbrellas and enjoy the best view in town of the *Altstadt*, Festung, Kapuzinerberg, and Salzach. This restaurant has one of the most reasonably priced *menus* around. Schwarzenegger-sized full meals from 68-108AS. Mmmm, these are a few of our favorite things. Kitchen open May-Oct. Sat.-Thurs. 10am-9pm.

Humboldt-Stuben, Gstätteng. 6 (tel. 843 171), across the street from the Mönchsberg elevator. Affordable traditional Salzburger specialities, including *Pinzgauer Kasnock'n* (98AS) and *Salzburger Nockerl* for two (92AS). Bacon-and-egg hamburger 59AS. Over 20 vegetarian salad offerings. Super-crowded at night. Open daily 10am-1:30am.

Zum Fidelen Affen, Priesterhausg. 8 (tel. 877 361), off Linzerg. Phenomenal food in a dark-wood pub, pleasantly crowded with locals, tourists, and everyone else. Drinks 30AS. Full meal of salad and main course 87-110AS. Try the spinach *Spätzle* (potato-based noodles, 88AS) or the beef with onion gravy (89AS). English menu available. Open Mon.-Sat. 5pm-1am.

Der Wilde Mann, Getreideg. 20 (tel. 841 787), in the passage. Huge portions of *Wiener Schnitzel*, potatoes, and *Stiegl Bier* for the wild man (or woman) in all of us. Sit at lovely carved wooden furniture for a traditional Austrian meal, cooked in an incredible tiled oven. Entrees run 70-120AS and are worth every *Groschen*. Pleasantly less touristed than nearby bistros but locals crowd the place at lunch. Open Mon.-Sat. 9am-9pm.

Vegy, Schwarzstr. 21 (tel. 875 746). Vegetarian restaurant with a domestic, relaxing atmosphere. Have a seat at a table or buy a quick meal to go. Very filling food. Daily *menu* with entree and soup 78AS. Open Mon.-Fri. 10:30am-6pm.

University Mensa (tel. 844 96 09), across from Sigmund Haffnerg. 16 and through the iron fence. A good deal for penny-pinchers. 2 hot entrees, one for carnivores (49AS) and one for veggie-hounds (37AS), and soup available every day. Desserts and drinks are not included. Valid student ID required (ISICs accepted). Open Mon.-Thurs. 9am-4pm, Fri. 9am-3pm. Get there early—ravenous students sometimes deplete the food supply.

Fischmarkt, at Hanuschpl. in the *Altstadt*. Mammoth trees reach through the roof of this Danish seafood restaurant. A local favorite. Very casual and very packed—the crowds may force you to eat outside. Fish sandwiches are 22-35AS; glasses of beer are 21AS. The restaurant also sells fresh seafood by the kg. Open Mon.-Fri. 8:30am-6:30pm, Sat. 8:30am-1pm.

Trześniewski, Getreideg. 9 (tel. 840 769), behind the chocolate counter and butcher shop. Kafka's favorite hangout in Vienna now has a new franchise on the ground floor of Mozart's *Geburtshaus* (birthplace). While indulging in their wonderful open-faced sandwiches, you can ponder who would roll over in his grave first. Sandwiches only 9AS, but you'll probably need about 4 to make a good lunch. Open Mon.-Fri. 8:30am-6pm, Sat. 8:30am-1pm.

Pizza Casanova, Linzerg. 23 (tel. 875 031). Don't be put off by the burlesque joint with the same name next door—Pizza Casanova knows that the way to a man's heart is through his stomach. Large pies 66-105AS. Healthy selection of veggie and whole-grain pizza. Open daily 11am-3pm and 6-11pm.

Shakespeare, Hubert Sattlerg. 3 (tel. 879 106), off Mirabellpl. Culturally schizophrenic: wonton soup, Greek salad, *Wiener Schnitzel*, and just about anything else 23-90AS. Doubles as a bar(d)—great music. Open daily 10am-1am, but the Chinese cook takes Sundays off. Visa, MC.

Cafés

Café im Kunstlerhaus, Hellbrunnerstr. 3 (tel 845 601). Low-key café popular with students, artists, and their fans. Wide variety of drinks—treat yourself to a café amaretto or a shot of tequila. Local bands play Tues. and Thurs. nights. Sat. is lesbian night. Open Mon.-Fri. 11am-11pm.

Café Tomaselli, Alter Markt 9 (tel. 844 488). A favorite haunt for wealthier Salzburger clientele since 1705. In 1820, Mozart's widow and her second husband came here to write the dead man's bio. Today it's one of the most famous cafés in Austria. Have some tea (a drink) with jam and bread. Pay the drink server and dessert server separately. Open Mon.-Sat. 7am-9pm, Sun. 8am-9pm.

Café Fürst, Brodg. 13 (tel. 843 759), near Alter Markt. Faces off with the equally haughty Café Tomaselli across Alter Markt. Specializes in the original *Mozartkugeln* (10AS a pop—savor slowly). Vast selection of candies, chocolates, pastries, *tortes*, strudels, and cakes. Catch one of the splendiferous tables outside if you can. Branch in Mirabellpl. Open daily in summer 8am-9pm; in winter 8am-8pm.

Café Bazar, Schwarzstr. 3 (tel 874 278). Affordable drinks and small meals in a tree-lined garden along the banks of the Salzach. Yogurt with raspberry juice 38AS. *The* place to go for Turkish coffee (37AS). Open mid-July to Aug. Mon.-Sat. 7:30am-11pm, Sun. 9am-11pm; Sept. to mid-July Mon-Sat. 9:30am-11pm.

Kaffeehäferl, Getreideg. 25 (tel. 844 349), in the passage across from McDonald's. Unpretentious courtyard café provides a needed respite from the tourist rush of G-street. The neighboring flower shop adds to the olfactory pleasure. Quiche Lorraine 45AS; strawberry milkshake 35AS. Open Mon.-Sat. 9am-7pm, Sun. noon-7pm.

Markets

In most cases, markets are open weekdays 8am to 6pm, Saturday 8am to noon. Salzburg has many supermarkets on the Mirabellpl. side of the river but very few in the *Altstadt*. **SPAR** is widespread, and the giant **EuroSpar** sprawls next to the train station bus terminal. **Open-air markets** occur at Universitätpl. (Mon.-Fri. 6am-7pm, Sat. 6am-1pm) and Mirabellpl. down into Hubert-Sattlerg. (Thurs. 6am-2pm). If you're in town on Saturday morning, you can pick up your organic tomatoes and sausage lard at Max Rheinhardtpl. in the *Altstadt*.

BEER GARDENS AND BARS

Munich may be the beer capital of the world, but a good deal of it flows south to Austria's beer gardens *(Biergärten)*. Beyond Mozart and *The Sound of Music*, beer gardens are an essential part of Salzburg's charm and an absolute must-visit for travelers. Many of the gardens also serve moderately priced meals, but like everything else in Salzburg, they tend to close early. These lager oases cluster in the center of the city, especially around the Salzach River. Nightclubs in the *Altstadt* (especially along Gstätteng. and near Chiemseeg.) generally attract younger folk and tourists. For a less juvenile atmosphere, hit the other side of the river—especially along Giselakai and Steing.

Augustiner Bräu, Augustinerg. 4 (tel. 431 246). From the *Altstadt*, pick up the footpath at Hanuschpl. and follow it alongside the river, walking with the current. Go left up the flight of stairs past the Riverside Café, cross Müllner Hauptstr., and walk uphill. Augustinerg. is the first left. The brewery, inside the *Kloster* with the big tower, is a Salzburg legend. The great beer brewed by the Müllner Kloster is poured into massive steins from even more massive wooden kegs. The outdoor garden provides room for 1300, and the indoor salons seat an additional 1200. Numerous sausage, salad, and bread concession-stands inside placate grumbling stomachs. Liters 56AS (be nice and tip the tap-*meister* 4AS), half-liter 28AS. Open Mon.-Fri. 3-11pm, Sat.-Sun. 2:30-11pm.

Sternbräu, Getreideg. 34 (tel. 842 140), in the *Altstadt*—duck into any number of passages at the end of Getreideg. Formerly a brewery, now just a place to drink and eat in mass quantities. 2 beer gardens, self-service snack bar with sausages and smaller meals, and sit-down restaurant. Open daily 9am-11pm.

K&K Stieglkeller, Festungsg. 10 (tel. 842 681), off Kapitelpl. near the Festungsbahn. Perched halfway up the mountainside on the way to the *Festung*, this garden has a fantastic view of all the roofs and spires of the *Altstadt*. *Stiegl* beer on tap and reasonably priced food. Don't wander in accidentally around 7:30pm, when the pub hosts a *Sound of Music* live dinner show. Open May-Sept. daily 10am-10pm.

Pub Passage, Rudolfskai 22-26, under the Radisson Hotel by the Mozartsteg bridge. A shopping promenade for youthful bar-hopping. All these bars are located in the corridors of the "mall" and are open until 2-4am. Though all remarkably similar, each has its own "unique" gimmick: **Tom's Bierklinik** brags beers from all over the world; **The Black Lemon** offers Latino night every Wed.; **Bräu zum Frommen Hell** burns with 80s music; and **Hell** sells itself as a TV sports bar.

SIGHTS: THE ALTSTADT ■ 215

2 Stein, Giselakai 9 (tel. 880 201). Or not to Stein. Possibly the coolest bar in town. Previously a gay bar, now a favorite spot for a mixed clientele of all genders and orientations. Happy hour with 2-for-1 drinks daily 6-8pm. Open daily 5pm-4am.
Felsenkeller, in a cave in Toscaninihof next to the Festspielhaus. Tavern atmosphere and a relaxed crowd. Open Sun.-Fri. 3:30pm-midnight, Sat. 4pm-midnight.
Flip, Gstätteng. 17 (tel. 843 643). Young crowd, packed bar. Open daily until 3am.
Disco Seven, Gstätteng. 7 (tel. 844 181). 2 floors of dancing. Young clientele. Open daily till 4am.
Frauen Café, Sittikusstr. 17 (tel. 871 639). A relaxed lesbian hangout where women convene to drink and chat. Open Wed.-Sat. 8pm-midnight.
Schwarze Katze, Fruhdiele, Auerspergstr. 45 (tel 875 405). For those who miraculously found a late-night scene in Salzburg and/or got locked out of their hostels, the Black Cat magnanimously opens its doors. Dark, low-key atmosphere guaranteed not to grate on early morning nerves. Open Tues.-Sun. 4am-noon.

Bovine Befuddlement

Salzburg's clever archbishop once saved the city's pride, the **Hohensalzburg** fortress, from imminent destruction. During the **Peasant Wars** (see **Oh, No! The Habsburg Empire,** p. 62), the peasants surrounded the fortress in an attempt to starve the archbishop out. When the archbishop had only one cow left, he painted the remaining beast with different spots on both sides and paraded him back and forth along the castle wall in distinct view of the peasants below. Since the peasants, as the saying goes, were simple-minded folk, they believed that the archbishop had a great reserve of food and promptly cancelled their embargo attempts. Talk about a tanning.

SIGHTS

The tourist office sells a **Salzburg Card,** which grants admission to most museums and sights and access to all public transportation. The card is a great deal if you plan to cram a great deal of sight-seeing into a short period of time (24hr. card 190AS; 48hr. 270AS, 72hr. 360AS; children ages 7-15 half-price).

The Altstadt

Salzburg sprang up under the protective watch of the **Hohensalzburg** castle and fortress (tel. 804 22 123), which tower atop the imposing Mönchsberg. Built between 1077 and 1681 by the ruling archbishops, the structure is now the largest completely preserved castle in Europe. To view the splendid rooms inside, visitors must take one of the castle's first-rate tours, which wind through torture chambers, formidable Gothic state rooms, the fortress organ, and the impregnable watchtower that affords an unmatched view of the city. The tours also include the archbishop's medieval indoor toilet—a technological marvel in its day. The Rainer Museum (see p. 219) inside the fortress displays medieval instruments of torture. (Fortress open daily July-Sept. 8am-7pm; Nov.-March 9am-5pm; April-June 9am-6pm. 35AS, children 20AS. 1hr. castle tours, in English and German, daily July-Aug. 9:30am-5:30pm, April-June and Sept.-Oct. 9:30am-5pm, Nov.-March 10am-4:30pm. Castle tour, museum, and fortress 65AS, children 35AS.) To reach the castle, walk up the hill or take the overpriced **Festungsbahn** (cable car; tel. 842 682) from Festungsg. (every 10min. April-Oct. 9am-9:30pm, Nov.-March 9am-5pm; ascent 59AS, children 32AS; round-trip 69AS, 37AS). Since the ride terminates inside the castle, cable-car tickets include the castle's entrance fee. The myriad footpaths atop the Mönchsberg give a bird's-eye view of the city; hikers meander down the leafy trails to the *Altstadt* below or descend via the **Mönchsberglift** (elevator) built into the mountain at Gstätteng. 13, near Café Winkler. (Elevator operates daily 9am-11pm. 16AS, round-trip 27AS.)

At the bottom of the Festungsbahn is **Kapitelplatz,** home of a giant chess grid, a fountain depicting Poseidon wielding his scepter, and tradespeople bartering their wares. If you stand at the chess grid and face the mountain, you'll see the entrance to **St. Peter's Monastery** at the back right corner through the cemetery. The lovely cemetery, **Petersfriedhof**, is one of the most peaceful places in Salzburg—possibly because guided tours are forbidden to enter. The various headstones are works of art, some dating back to the 1600s. Though a popular subject for romantic painters, this secluded spot is best known as the site where Liesl's Nazi boyfriend Rolf blew the whistle on the von Trapp family in *The Sound of Music*. (Open daily April-Sept. 6:30am-7pm; Oct.-March 6:30am-6pm.) Near the far end of the cemetery, against the mountains, is the entrance to the **Katakomben** (catacombs; tel. 844 57 80), where Christians allegedly worshipped in secret as early as AD 250. (Tours every hr. in English and German May-Sept. 10am-5pm; Oct.-April 11am-noon and 1:30-3:30pm. 12AS, students 8AS.) Past the arch near the catacombs stands **Stiftskirche St. Peter.** The church began as a Romanesque basilica and still boasts a marble portal from 1244. In the 18th century, the building received a Rococo face-lift, and now green and pink moldings curl delicately across the graceful ceiling and gilded cherubim blow golden trumpets to herald the stunningly decorated organ. The steeple tower and clock are also new(er) additions. (Open daily 9am-12:15pm and 2:30-6:30pm.) The courtyard on the other side of the gate facing St. Peter's entrance leads to the monastery at **Toscaninihof.** One wall of the complex is part of the Felsenreitenschule, formerly the Rock Riding School for the archbishops' horses and now the **Festspielehaus** (Opera House), which houses many of the events of the Festspiele. Because the opera house is not open to the public, a poster has been affixed to the wall depicting the stone arches that comprise the rear wall of the stage. These arches are best known for their appearance in *The Sound of Music*'s penultimate scene.

The distinctive dome of the **Universitätskirche** (University Church) stands watch over Universitätspl. near the Festspielhaus and daily farmer's market. Generally considered Fischer von Erlach's masterpiece, this massive chapel (one of the largest Baroque chapels on the continent) is quite celebrated in European Baroque circles (see **The Baroque,** p. 71). The pale interior and enormous dome create a vast open space pierced only by the natural light radiating from the apse and accented by Baroque cherubim lounging on sculpted clouds all over the immense nave.

From Universitätspl., several passages lead through tiny courtyards filled with geraniums and creeping ivy and eventually give way to the stampede of **Getreidegasse.** This labyrinth of winding pathways and 17th- and 18th-century facades is one of the best-preserved (and well-touristed) streets in Salzburg. Many of Getreidegasse's shops have wrought-iron signs dating (they claim) from the Middle Ages when the illiterate needed pictorial aids to understand which store sold what. Some suspect a few of these signs are modern tourist revivals…golden arches, for example, don't objectively suggest hamburgers. Maybe Pavlov could explain.

Wolfgang Amadeus Mozart was unleashed upon the world from the imaginatively dubbed **Mozart's Geburtshaus** (birthplace), on the second floor of Getreideg. 9 (tel. 844 313; fax 840 693), one of Salzburg's most touristed attractions. The long red and white flag suspended from the roof serves as a beacon for music pilgrims worldwide. Although he eventually settled in Vienna, his birthplace holds the most impressive collection of the child genius's belongings: his first viola and violin, a pair of keyboard instruments, and even a lock of hair purportedly from his noggin. An incredible set of dioramas chronicle previous *Festspiele* productions of Mozart's operas. (Open July-Aug. daily 9am-6:25pm; Sept.-June 9am-5:25pm. In summer show up before 11am to beat the crowds. 65AS, students and seniors 50AS, children 20AS.)

The **Neugebäude,** opposite the AmEx office, supports both the city government's bureaucracy and a 35-bell **Glockenspiel.** Every day at 7, 11am, and 6pm, the delightful, slightly off-key carillon rings out a Mozart tune (specified on a notice posted on the corner of the Residenz), and the tremendous pipe organ atop the Hohensalzburg fortress bellows a response.

Long before the Mozart era, Archbishop Wolf Dietrich dominated the town's cultural patronage. The clergyman's image still inspires masterful music at the annual

Salzburger Festspiele, when opera comes to the courtyard of the archbishop's magnificent **Residenz** (tel. 840 42), opposite the Glockenspiel. The ecclesiastical elite of Salzburger Land have resided here, in the heart of the *Altstadt*, for the last 700 years. Tours lead through the imposing Baroque staterooms *(Prunkräume)* and an astonishing three-dimensional ceiling fresco by Rottmayr. (Tours in German July-Aug. daily every 30min. 10am-4:30pm; Sept.-June Mon.-Fri. every hr. 10am-3pm; 40min.; 50AS, students and seniors 40AS.) The Residenz also houses a gallery (see p. 220).

Dead-center in Residenzplatz is the immense and hard-to-miss 15m horse fountain—the largest Baroque fountain in the world—with amphibious horses charging through the water (observe the webbed hooves). Appropriately, **fiakers** (horse-drawn carriages) congregate around the fountain, which explains the barnyard odor. (Carriage rides 380AS for 25min. Be sure to ask if the driver speaks English.) The immense Baroque **Dom** (cathedral) forms the third wall of Residenzplatz. Wolf Dietrich's successor, Markus Sittikus, commissioned the cathedral from Italian architect Santino Solari in 1628. The three dates above the archways list the years of the cathedral's renovations. The statue in front of Domplatz depicts the Virgin Mary—around her swarm four lead figures representing Wisdom, Faith, the Church, and the Devil. Mozart was christened here in 1756 and later worked at the cathedral as *Konzertmeister* and court organist.

The Neustadt

Staatsbrücke, the only bridge from the *Altstadt* over the Salzach open to motorized traffic, leads into the new city along **Linzergasse**, a medieval-esque shopping street much in the style of Getreidegasse. From under the stone arch on the right side of Linzerg. 14, a tiny stone staircase rises up the Kapuzinerberg. At its crest stands the simple **Kapuzinerkloster** (Capuchin Monastery) that Wolf Dietrich built in the late 16th century. The monastery is a sight to behold, but the real draw is the view of the city below. Farther along Linzerg. at the much less crowded #41 is the 18th-century **Sebastianskirche.** Its graveyard contains the gaudy mausoleum of Wolf Dietrich and the tombs of Mozart's wife Constanze and father Leopold. (Open daily 7am-7pm.)

At 17, Mozart moved across the river to Markartpl., and Salzburg's favorite son makes his presence felt on this side of the river. From Linzerg. take Dreifaltigkeitg. leads to **Mozarts Wohnhaus**, Makartpl. 8 (tel. 313; fax 840 693), the composer's residence from 1773 to 1780. The house suffered major damage in World War II air raids, but subsequent renovations allowed the building to reopen on the composer's 240th birthday, January 27, 1996, with expanded displays about Mozart and his family. Visitors with true Mozart mania should head down the street to Salzburg's conservatory for young musicians, the **Mozarteum**, Schwartzstr. 26-28, for the enormous **Mozart Archives.** Inside the grounds stands a tiny wooden shack transplanted from Vienna, the **Zauberflötenhäuschen,** where Wolfgang Amadeus supposedly composed *The Magic Flute* in just five months. The Mozarteum was originally constructed for the Salzburg Academy of Music and the Performing Arts; they now hold regular performances in the concert hall (see **Entertainment,** p. 220).

Mirabellplatz holds the marvelous **Schloß Mirabell.** The supposedly vowed-to-celibacy Archbishop Wolf Dietrich built this rosy-hued wonder in 1606 for his mistress Salome Alt and their 10 children, christening it "Altenau" in her honor. When

---

What about Joe?

Legend has it that the robes of the Kapuzinerkloster's resident monks inspired the world's first cup of cappuccino. A café proprietor with an overactive imagination observed the pious gents on a noonday stroll and *voilà*—the world witnessed the birth of a drink with the rich coffee color of the monk's robes topped by white froth hoods. The country's resident food buffs and cultural authorities, Austrian schoolchildren, will tell you that Italy's cappuccino is no more than a rip-off of the much older *Kapuziner,* still ordered in Viennese cafés today.

successor Markus Sittikus imprisoned Wolf Dietrich for arson, he seized the palace for himself and changed its name. The castle is now the seat of the city government, and many of the mayor's gorgeous offices are usually open for public viewing. (Open Mon.-Fri. 7am-4pm.) The castle also hosts classical concerts in the evening; some fans swear that the *Marmorsaal* (Marble Hall) rivals all other European concert halls. Next to the palace sits the delicately manicured **Mirabellgarten,** which includes extravagant rose beds and labyrinths of groomed shrubs. Students from the nearby Mozarteum often perform here, and Maria and the children made this one of their stops in *The Sound of Music* for a rousing rendition of "do-re-mi." Slightly more adorable than the von Trapp children are the vertically challenged statues in the **Dwarf Garden,** a favorite Mirabellgarten play area for Salzburg toddlers. The statues' grotesque marble faces were modelled on those of Wolf Dietrich's court jesters.

The Sound of Music

In 1964, Julie Andrews, Christopher Plummer, and a gaggle of 20th-Century Fox crew-members arrived in Salzburg to film *The Sound of Music,* based on the true story of the von Trapp family. Salzburg has never been the same. The city voraciously encourages the increased tourism due to the film's popularity, and Salzburg now hosts three official companies that run Sound of Music Tours. These companies are remarkably similar; the best choice is often the one that stops closest to your accommodation—many hostels and pensions work exclusively with one of the firms and offer discounts to guests. **Salzburg Sightseeing Tours** (tel. 881 616; fax 878 776) and **Panorama Tours** (tel. 874 029; fax 871 618; email panorama@alpin.or.at) operate rival kiosks on Mirabellpl. (350AS, with *Let's Go* or student ID 315AS; tours leave from Mirabellpl. daily 9:30am and 2pm). The renegade **Bob's Special Tours,** Kaig. 19 (tel. 849 511; fax 849 512), has no high-profile kiosk, but they do have a minibus. The smaller vehicle enables them to tour more of the *Altstadt*, a location that the big tour buses can't reach (330AS; tours daily in summer 9am and 2pm; in winter 10am). All three companies offer free pick-up from your hotel, and all tours last four hours. The tours are generally worth the money if you're a big *Sound of Music* fan or if you've only got a short time in Salzburg and want an overview of the city and surrounding area—the tours venture into the Salzkammergut lake region as well.

If you have time, however, consider renting a bike and doing the tour on your own. As is generally the case with films based on "real life," the film's writers and producers took a great deal of artistic license with the von Trapp's story—many of the events were fabricated for Tinseltown. Maria was a nun-apprentice in the film, whereas in reality she merely taught at **Nonnberg Abbey,** high above the city near the Festung. In this abbey, the crew filmed the nuns singing "How do you solve a problem like Maria?" and parts of the wedding scene. To reach the abbey, walk out of Kapitelpl. along Kapitelg. and turn right onto Kaig., where stairs lead up to the nunnery. The darling little gazebo where Liesl and Rolf unleashed their youthful passion is on the grounds of **Schloß Hellbrunn** (see **Near Salzburg,** p. 222). The gazebo is disappointingly small but wonderfully photogenic, and the walk back from Hellbrunn to Salzburg's *Altstadt* is glorious on nice summer afternoons. From the Hellbrun parking lot, head down Hellbrunner Allee. You'll pass the yellow castle used for the exterior of the von Trapp home (Maria sang "I Have Confidence" in front of the long yellow wall). The house is now a dorm for music students at the Mozarteum. Continue along Hellbrunner Allee until it turns into Freisaalweg. At the end of Freisaalweg, turn right on Akadamiestr., which ends at Alpenstr. and the river. The river footpath leads all the way back to Mozartsteg and Staatsbrücke (1hr.). The back of the von Trapp house (where Maria and the children fell into the water after romping around the city all day) was filmed at the **Schloß Leopoldskron** behind the Mönchberg, now a center for academic studies. Take bus #55: "Pensionistenheim Nonntal" and turn left on Sunnhubstr. then left again up Leopoldskroner Allee to the castle.

There are several film locations within the *Altstadt*. The von Trapp family hid behind the headstones of the **Petersfriedhof,** the cemetery where Rolf blew the whistle. At the **Festspielhaus** (Opera House), the family sang their final performance while all the Nazis swayed to the melodious "Edelweiss." The opera house is closed to the public, but the stairs leading up to the right sometimes provide a glimpse of the stage—the opera occasionally leaves the top of the house open. The **Mirabellgarten** by Mirabellpl. was a favorite haunt of Maria and the children while they made their forbidden daytrips. Several statues and fountains should look familiar.

The von Trapps were actually married in the church at Nonnberg Abbey, but Hollywood filmed the scene in **Mondsee** instead (see p. 237). The sightseeing tours allow guests to waddle around Mondsee for 45 minutes, but town is really worth a whole daytrip for its beautiful lake and sinful pastry shops. Buses leave the Salzburg train station from the main bus depot (every hr., 45min., 57AS). The hills that are alive with the sound of music, inspiring Maria's rapturous twirling in the opening scene, are along the Salzburg-St. Gilgen route near Fuschl. Any of the hills in the Salzkammergut region, however, could fit the bill. For your own re-creational and recreational purposes, try the Untersberg, just south of Salzburg (see **Near Salzburg,** p. 222).

As if all these sites weren't enough saturation, the Stieglkeller hosts a **Sound of Music Live Dinner Show** (tel. 832 029; fax 832 02 913). Performers sing your favorite film songs while servers ply you with soup, *Schnitzel* with noodles, and crisp apple strudel. (Show daily May-Oct. 8:30pm. 360AS. Dinner at 7:30pm plus the show 520AS. 30% student discount, children under 13 free.)

MUSEUMS

Salzburg's small, specialized museums often get lost in the shadow of the *Festung, The Sound of Music,* and the *Festspiele*. Should you desire to indulge a personal museum-mania, buy a combination ticket (60AS, students 20AS) for the Carolino Augusteum, the Spielzeug, the Domgrabung, and the Hellbrunn Folklore museums. The small private galleries on Sigmund-Haffner-Gasse provide budget art viewing.

Haus der Natur (Museum of Natural History), Museumpl. 5 (tel. 842 653; fax 847 905), across from the Carolino Augusteum. An enormous natural history museum with an eclectic collection—from live alligators to fossils to gems. Get up close and personal (through the glass, of course) with over a dozen giant snakes. Open daily 9am-5pm. 55AS, students 30AS.

Rainer Museum, inside the fortress. Medieval relics, including torture devices. Open daily June-Oct. 10 8am-7pm, Oct. 11-May 8am-6pm. Entrance only with entrance to the castle; museum entrance includes castle tour. 30AS, children 15AS.

Dom Museum (tel. 844 189; fax 840 442). Inside the cathedral's main entrance. Houses an unusual collection called the **Kunst- und Wunderkammer** (Art and Miracles chamber) that includes conch shells, mineral formations, and a 2ft. whale's tooth. The archbishop accumulated all of these curiosities to impress distinguished visitors. The bottom floor always houses a temporary exhibit that attempts to do the same. Open mid-May to mid-Oct. Mon.-Sun. 10am-5pm. 50AS, students and ages 16-18 25AS, ages 6-15 10AS.

Domgrabungsmuseum (tel. 845 295), entrance on Residenzpl. Displays the fascinating excavations of the Roman ruins under the cathedral. You'll feel like an archaeologist clambering around in a dig. Open May-Oct. Wed.-Sun. 9am-5pm. 20AS, students 10AS. English guides available.

Stiegl Brauwelt, Brauhausstr. 1 (tel. 838 73 80; http://www.stiegl.co.at). Bus #1: "Brauhaus" and walk up the street to the giant yellow building. Stiegl: It's Austrian for beer. The *Brauwelt* (Brew World) is Salzburg's own beer museum, attached to the Stiegl brewery just minutes from downtown. Three floors showcase beer-making, the history of brewing, and modern beer culture—including "30 Ways to Open a Beer Bottle," a photo essay featuring Stiegl employees, and the wonder of the *Brauwelt,* a 2-story beer-bottle pyramid constructed of 300 Austrian beers.

Hop on down to the final hands-on exhibit—the tour concludes with 2 complimentary glasses of Stiegl beer, a beer *Brezel* (pretzel), and a souvenir beer glass. You'll barley be able to wipe the smile off your mug. Open Wed.-Sun. 10am-5pm, last entrance 4pm. 75AS, students 50AS, children 40AS.

Museum Carolino Augusteum, Museumpl. 1 (tel. 843 145; fax 841 13 410). Named after Emperor Franz I's widow, Caroline Augusta. The lower floors house Roman and Celtic artifacts, including excellent mosaics and burial remains, preserved compliments of the region's salt. Gothic and Baroque art on the upper floors. Open Wed.-Sun. 9am-5pm, Tues. 9am-8pm. 40AS, students 15AS.

Spielzeug Museum (Toy Museum), Bürgerspitalg. 2 (tel. 847 560), near the Festspielhaus. Three floors of puppets, wooden toys, dolls, and electric trains. Nifty pre-Lego castle blocks from 1921. Puppet show every Tues. and Wed. 3pm. Open Tues.-Sun. 9am-5pm. 30AS, students 10AS.

Rupertinum Gallery, Wiener Philharmonikerg. 9 (tel. 804 22 336; fax 804 22 542), across from the Festspielhaus. The works of Kokoschka, Klimt, and lesser known living artists are housed in an older, gracefully arched building touched up by Hundertwasser. Very interesting temporary exhibits and a small sculpture room. Open mid-July to Sept. Thurs.-Tues. 9am-5pm, Wed. 10am-9pm; Oct. to mid-July Tues.-Sun. 10am-5pm, Wed. 10am-9pm. 50AS, students 35AS, under 16 free.

Residenz Gallery, Residenzpl. 1 (tel. 80 42). Not really known for its permanent collection, the gallery has rotating exhibits of 16th- through 19th-century art with occasional works by Titian, Rubens, and Brueghel. Open April-Sept. daily 10am-5pm; Oct.-March Thurs.-Tues. 10am-5pm. 45AS, students 34AS.

Baroque Museum (tel. 877 432), in the Mirabellgarten's Orangerie. Elaborate tribute to the ornate aesthetic of 17th- and 18th-century Europe. Open Tues.-Sat. 9am-noon and 2-5pm, Sun. 9am-noon. 40AS, students and seniors 20AS, ages 6-14 free.

MUSIC AND ENTERTAINMENT

Max Reinhardt, Richard Strauss, and Hugo von Hofmannsthal founded the renowned **Salzburger Festspiele** (Festivals) in 1920. Every year since, Salzburg has become a musical mecca from late July to the beginning of September. A few weeks before the festival, visitors strolling along Getreideg. often bump into world-class stars taking a break from rehearsal. On the eve of the festival's opening, over 100 dancers don regional costumes, accessorize with torches, and perform a *Fackeltanz* (torch-dance) on Residenzpl. During the festivities themselves, operas, plays, films, concerts, and tourists overrun almost every available public space. Information and tickets for Festspiele events are available through the **Festspiele Kartenbüro** (ticket office) and **Tageskasse** (daily box office) in Karajanpl., against the mountain and next to the tunnel. (Ticket office open Mon.-Fri. 9:30am-noon and 3-5pm. Box office open Mon.-Sat. 9:30am-5pm.) The festival prints a complete program of events that lists all crucial concert locations and dates one year in advance. The booklet is available at any tourist office (10AS). Music fans snap up the best seats months in advance. To order tickets, contact **Kartenbüro der Salzburger Festspiele,** Postfach 140, A-5010 Salzburg (tel. 844 501; fax 846 682; email info@salzb-fest.co.at; http://www.salzb-fest.co.at/salzb-fest), no later than the beginning of January. After the early January deadline, the office publishes a list of remaining seats, which generally include some cheap tickets to the operas (around 300AS), concerts (around 100AS), and plays (around 100AS), as well as some standing room places for other events (50-100AS). These tickets, however, are often gobbled up quickly by subscribers or student groups, leaving very expensive tickets (upwards of 1000AS) and seats at avant-garde modern-music concerts (often as little as 200AS). Middle-man ticket distributors sell marked-up cheap tickets, a legal form of scalping—try American Express or Panorama Tours. Those 26 or younger can try for cheap subscription tickets (2-4 tickets for 200-300AS each) by writing about eight months in advance to Direktion der Salzburger Festspiele, attn: Carl-Philip von Maldeghem, Hofstallg. 1, A-5020 Salzburg.

The powers that be have discontinued hawking last-minute tickets for dress rehearsals to the general public—nowadays, you've got to know somebody to get your hands on one of these cheap tickets ("Oh, sure, Placido and I go *way* back!"). Those without the foresight to be hit by an international opera star while walking across the street should take advantage of the **Fest zur Eröffungsfest** (Opening Day Festival), when concerts, shows, and films are either very cheap or very free. Folksingers perform at 8 and 10pm, and dancers perform the traditional *Fackeltanz* around the horse fountain, aerobically lighting up the area and kicking off the festivities. Tickets for all these events are available on a first-come, first-served basis during the festival's opening week at the box office in the Großes Festspielhaus on Hofstallg. The only other event visitors can always attend without advance tickets is **Jedermann.** The city stages Hugo von Hofmannsthal's modern morality play by every year on a stage in front of the cathedral. At the end, people placed in strategic locations throughout the city cry out the eerie word "Jedermann," which then echoes all over town. Shouting contests determine which locals win the opportunity to be one of the ghostly criers. Standing-room places for the current night's show are available at the Festspielhaus or a ticketing agency (60AS).

Even when the Festspiele are not in full force, many other concerts and events brighten the city. The popular **Mozarteum** (Music School) performs a number of concerts on a rotating schedule, available at the tourist office. The school often dedicate one cycle of concerts to students and reduces the ticket price to 80AS. For tickets to any of the Mozarteum concerts, contact Kartenbüro Mozarteum, Postfach 345, Schwarzstr. 36, 1st Fl., A-5024 Salzburg (tel. 873 154; fax 872 996; open Mon.-Thurs. 9am-2pm, Fri. 9am-4pm). For a bit more money but a lot more fun, check out the evening **Mozart Serenaden** (Mozart's Serenades) at Hellbrunn July through August. Musicians in traditional garb (knickers, white hair, etc.) perform Mozart favorites; an intermission buffet is included. Afterward, guests have the option of touring the *Wasserspiele* (water fountains). In winter these concerts move to Mirabellplatz. For information and tickets, contact Konzertdirektion Nerat, A-5020 Salzburg, Lieferinger Hauptstr. 136 (tel. 436 870; fax 436 970). Tickets are 300AS, with the *Wasserspiele* 350AS, at the Schloß Hellbrunn ticket window. (Open on concert days only 10:30am-12:30pm and after 4pm.)

For a particularly enchanting (and expensive) evening, attend a **Festungskonzert** (Fortress Concert) in the fortress's ornate *Fürstenzimmer* (Prince's chamber) and *Goldener Saal* (Golden Hall). Concerts occur every night from May to October. (Tickets 270AS, available 1hr. before the concert). For more information, contact Festungskonzerte, Anton-Adlgasserweg 22, A-5020 Salzburg (tel. 825 858; fax 825 859; open daily 9am-9pm). A less tourist-oriented concert activity is the year-round **Salzburger Schloßkonzerte** in Schloß Mirabell or the Residenz. Mozart is still the most-performed composer, but at least he doesn't hold a monopoly. Tickets for the classy concerts are 350-380AS, students 250AS. In July and August, **outdoor opera** occasionally rings out from the historical hedge-theater of Mirabellgarten (300AS, students 150AS, standing room 120AS). Tickets for both series are available from the box office in Schloß Mirabell (tel. 848 586; fax 844 747; open daily 7am-4pm).

The **Dom** also has an extensive concert program. The church's organ has four separate pipe sections, creating a dramatic "surround sound" effect during its concerts Thursday and Friday at 11:15am. Tickets are available at the door (100AS, students 70AS, children free). The church has periodic evening concerts—check the door for upcoming programs (280AS, students 180AS, standing room 100AS, children free). Other churches throughout Salzburg perform wonderful music during their services and post information on other concerts, particularly around Easter and Christmas.

From May through August various **outdoor performances,** including concerts, folk-singing, and dancing, dot the Mirabellgarten. The tourist office has a few leaflets on scheduled events, but an evening stroll through the park might prove just as enlightening. Mozartplatz and Kapitelplatz are also popular stops for talented street musicians and touring school bands, and the well-postered Aicher Passage next to Mirabellpl. is great source of information for other upcoming musical events.

At the **Salzburger Marionettentheater** (tel. 872 406; fax 882 141), handmade marionettes perform to recorded Festspiele opera. The theater is small in order to accommodate the diminutive size of the actors. For more information, contact Marionettentheater, Schwarzstr. 24, A-5020 Salzburg. (Box office open on performance days Mon.-Sat. 9am-1pm and 2hr. before curtain. 250-400AS, students 200AS. Visa, MC, AmEx.) Track down English-language **movies** with the film program in the **Das Kino** newspaper. Cinemas rotate a few films each month and often offer films in English with German subtitles.

■ Near Salzburg: Lustschloß Hellbrunn and Untersberg

Just south of Salzburg lies the unforgettable **Lustschloß Hellbrunn** (tel. 820 372; fax 820 37 231), a one-time pleasure dome for Wolf Dietrich's nephew, the Archbishop Markus Sittikus. The sprawling estate includes fish ponds, trimmed hedge gardens, the "I am sixteen, going on seventeen" gazebo, and tree-lined footpaths through open grassy fields perfect for picnicking or a round of ultimate frisbee. The neighboring **Wasserspiele** (water fountains) are perennial favorites—Archbishop Markus amused himself with elaborate water-powered figurines and a booby-trapped table that could spout water on his drunken guests. Prepare yourself for an afternoon of wet surprises. (Open daily July-Aug. 9am-10pm; May-June and Sept. 9am-5pm; April and Oct. 9am-4:30pm. Castle tour 30AS, students 20AS. Wasserspiele tour 70AS, 35AS. Tours of both 90AS, 45AS.) The **Steintheater** on the palace grounds is the oldest natural theater north of the Alps. On the hill above the manicured grounds sits the tiny hunting lodge **Monats-schlößchen** (Little Month-Castle), so named because someone bet the archbishop that he couldn't build a castle in a month. As one of the archbishop's many weaknesses was gambling, he accepted the challenge and began spending the church's money on architects, engineers, and laborers who toiled around the clock. He won. The castle now houses the **Folklore and Local History Museum** (tel. 820 37 221), with three floors of surprising exhibits, including animals made out of bread, a papier-mâché-and-glitter diorama of St. George slaying the dragon, and several *Salzburger Schönperchten*—bizarre 5ft. hats worn in a traditional Austrian ceremony intended to scare away the demons of winter. (Open daily mid-April to mid-Oct. 9am-5pm. 20AS, students 10AS.) Near the castle lies the **Hellbrunn Zoo** (tel. 820 176; fax 820 17 66). Plan about two hours to wander through the lions and tigers and bears...oh my, that's Oz. (Open daily 8:30am-4pm; extended summer hours. 70AS, students 50AS.) To reach Hellbrun, take bus #55 (dir: Anif): "Schloß Hellbrunn" from the train station, Mirabellpl., or Mozartsteg, or bike 40 minutes down beautiful, tree-lined Hellbrunner Allee.

Bus #55: "Untersberg" runs south to the **Untersberg peak,** where Charlemagne supposedly rests and prepares to return and reign over Europe once again. A **cable car** (tel. (06246) 871 217 or 724 77) glides over Salzburg to the summit. (July-Sept. daily 8:30am-5:30pm; March-June and Oct. 9am-5pm; Dec.-Feb. 10am-4pm. Ascent 115AS, descent 100AS, round-trip 190AS; children 60AS, 45AS, 90AS.)

■ Munich (München)

Only 120km from its Baroque Austrian sister, Munich provides a quick escape into Germany and a great starting point for further Euro-hopping. As Germany's Second City, Munich's sensual air of merriment—most obvious during the wild *Fasching* and the legendary *Oktoberfest*—contrasts with Berlin's starker, more cutting-edge energy. But despite the brilliance of Munich's postwar economic glory, the modern city emerges from a troubled history. The Bavarian Golden Age of the 18th and 19th centuries, characterized by the wildly extravagant castles of Ludwig II, ended abruptly with Germany's defeat in World War I, and Munich was home to Adolf Hitler's squashed Beer Hall Putsch in 1923. After Chamberlain's Munich Agreement sold the Sudetenland to Hitler but failed to buy "peace in our time," the second World War shattered the city, leaving less than three percent of the city center intact. Efforts to redeem Munich's reputation by hosting the 1972 Olympics failed after Palestinian terrorists attacked Israeli athletes during the Games. Munich has become a sprawling, relatively liberal metropolis in the midst of solidly conservative southern Germany, but beneath the good spirits lurk memories of darker times.

ORIENTATION AND PRACTICAL INFORMATION

A map of Munich's center looks like a skewed circle quartered by one horizontal and one vertical line. The circle is the main traffic **Ring**, encircling the lion's share of Munich's sights. The east-west and north-south thoroughfares cross at Munich's epicenter, **Marienplatz** (home to the **Neues Rathaus**), and meet the traffic ring at **Karlsplatz** in the west, **Isartorplatz** in the east, **Odeonsplatz** in the north, and **Sendlinger Tor** in the south. The **Hauptbahnhof** is just beyond Karlspl. outside the Ring in the west. To get to Marienpl. from the train station, go straight on Schützenstr. to Karlspl., then continue through Karlstor to Neuhauserstr., which becomes Kaufingerstr. before it reaches Marienpl. (15-20min.). Or take S-Bahn 1-8 two stops from the main train station to "Marienpl."

At **Odeonspl.**, the Residenz palace sprawls; **Ludwigstraße** stretches north from there toward the university district. **Leopoldstraße**, the continuation of Ludwigstr., reaches farther toward **Schwabing**. This district, also known as "Schwabylon," is student country. To the west is the **Olympiazentrum**, constructed for the 1972 games. Further west sits the posh **Nymphenburg**, built around the **Nymphenburg Palace**. Southwest of Marienplatz, **Sendlingerstraße** leads past shops to the Sendlinger Tor. From there, Lindwurmstr. proceeds to Goethepl., from which Mozartstr. leads to **Theresienwiese**, the site of the *Oktoberfest*—the annual beer extravaganza.

Tourist Offices: Fremdenverkehrsamt (tel. 23 33 02 56 or 23 33 02 57; fax 23 33 02 33; email Munich-Tourist-Office@compuserve.com; http://www.munich-tourist.de) is located on the east side of the main train station. Books rooms for a DM5 per room fee (plus DM3-9 deposit), sells accommodations lists (DM0.50), and gives out excellent free city maps. *München Infopool* (DM1) is aimed at young tourists. Open Mon.-Fri. 10am-1pm. A **branch office** (tel. 97 59 28 15), at the airport in the *Zentralgebäude*, provides general information but no room bookings. Open Mon.-Sat. 8:30am-10pm, Sun. 1-9pm. **EurAide in English** (tel. 59 38 89; fax 550 39 65; http://www.cube.net/kmu/euraide.html), along Track 11 (room 3) of the *Hauptbahnhof*, is particularly good for transportation needs. Room reservation DM6. Open from June-*Oktoberfest* daily 7:45am-noon and 1-6pm; Oct.-April Mon.-Fri. 7:45am-noon and 1-4pm, Sat. 7:45am-noon; May daily 7:45am-noon and 1:4:30pm.

Tours: Mike's Bike Tours (tel. 651 42 75) gives 4-6hr. tours that leave (rain or shine) 1-4 times daily March-Oct. from the *Altes Rathaus*. DM29-45. **Munich Walks** (tel. (0177) 72 27 59 01) gives 2½hr. guided tours that give a historical overview (1-2 times daily) or emphasize Nazi history (2-4 times weekly). DM10-15.

Budget Travel: Council Travel, Adalbertstr. 32 (tel. 39 50 22; fax 39 70 04), near the university, sells ISICs. Open Mon.-Fri. 10am-1pm and 2-6:30pm.

Consulates: Australians contact the consulate in Bonn (Godesberger Allee 105-107; tel. (0228) 81 30). **Canada,** Tal 29 (tel. 219 95 70). Open Mon.-Thurs. 9am-noon and 2-5pm, Fri. 9am-noon and 2-3:30pm. **Ireland,** Mauerkircherstr. 1a (tel. 98 57 23). Open Mon.-Thurs. 9am-noon and 2-4pm, Fri. 9am-noon. **New Zealanders** head to the consulate in Bonn (Bundeskanzlerpl. 2-10; tel. (0228) 22 80 70). **South Africa,** Sendlinger-Tor-Pl. 5 (tel. 231 16 30). Open Mon.-Fri. 9am-noon. **U.K.,** Bürkleinstr. 10, 4th Fl. (tel. 21 10 90). Consular section open Mon.-Fri. 8:45-11:30am and 1-3:15pm. **U.S.,** Königinstr. 5 (tel. 288 80). Open Mon.-Fri. 8-11am.

224 ■ MUNICH (MÜNCHEN)

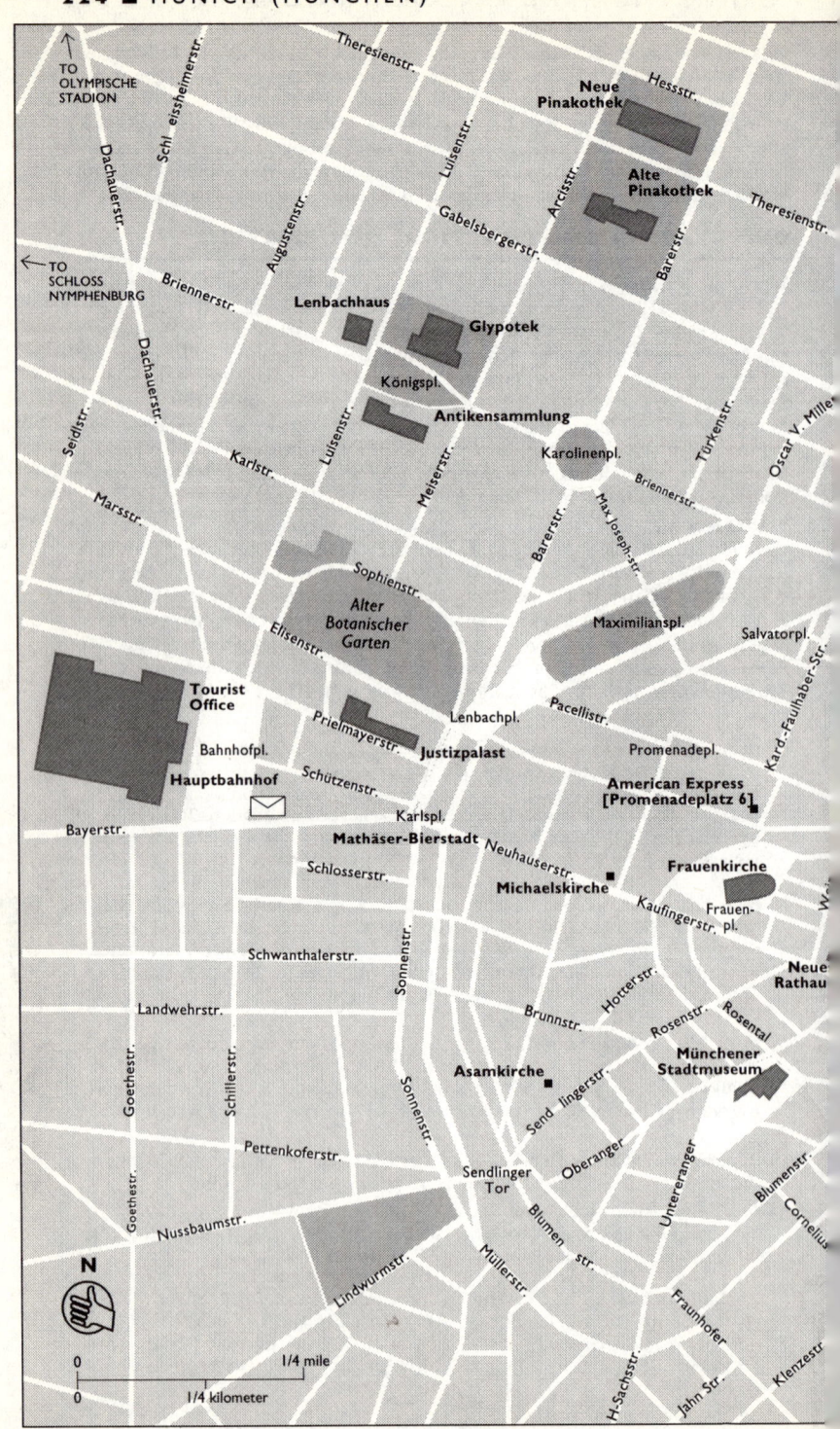

ORIENTATION AND PRACTICAL INFORMATION ■ 225

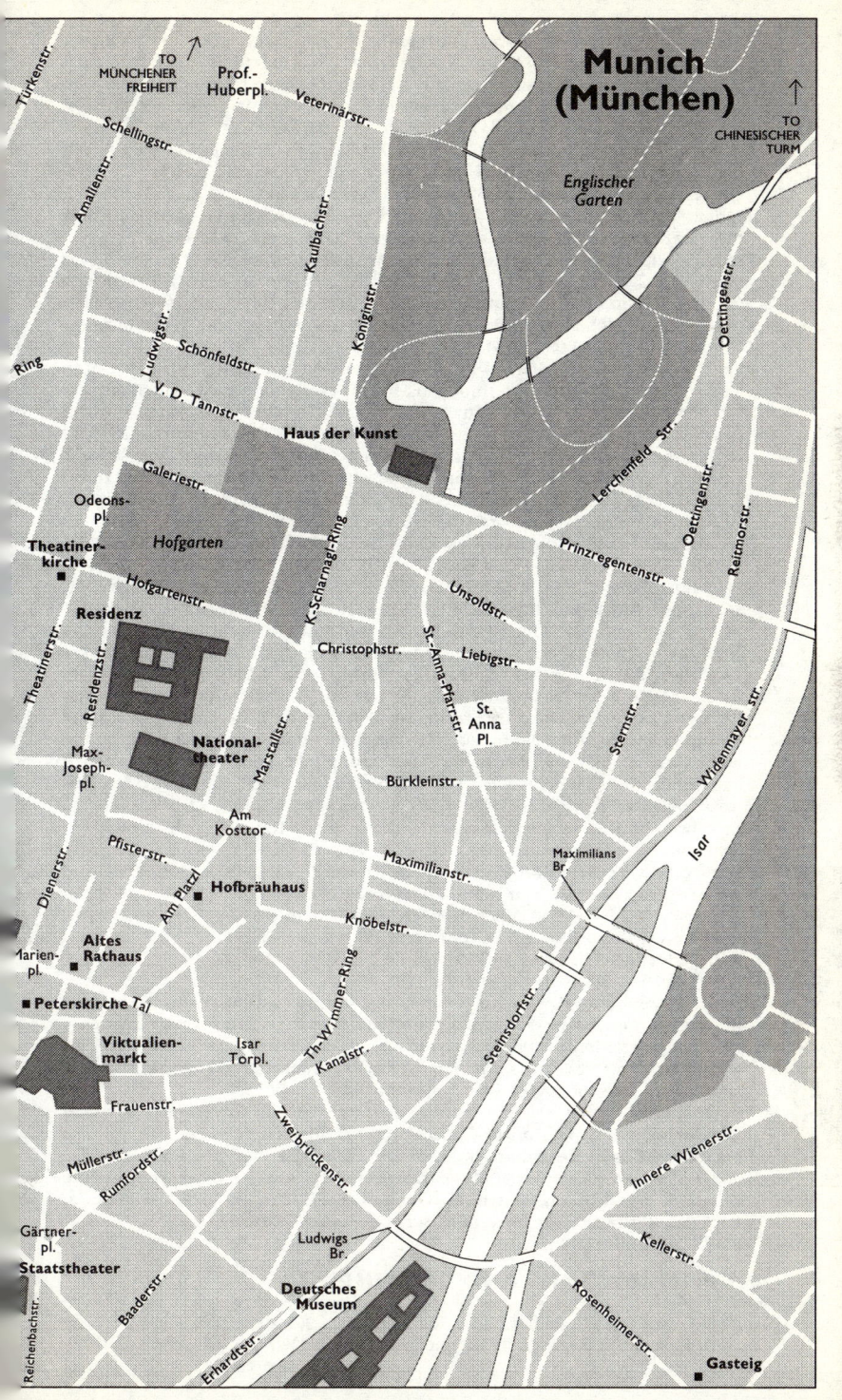

MUNICH (MÜNCHEN)

Currency Exchange: American Express has the best rates; otherwise, pick up a copy of EurAide's free publication *Inside Track* and take it to the Reise Bank for a 50% discount on commission (regularly DM3-10) if cashing US$50 or more in U.S. traveler's checks. At the **main station** in front of the main entrance on Bahnhofpl. (open daily 6am-11pm) and at track 11 (open Mon.-Sat. 7:30am-7pm).

American Express: Promenadepl. 6 (tel. 29 09 00, 24hr. hotline (0130) 85 31 00; fax 29 09 01 18), in the Hotel Bayerischer Hof. Holds mail, cashes traveler's checks. Open Mon.-Fri. 9am-5:30pm, Sat. 9:30am-12:30pm.

Flights: For information, call 97 52 13 13. **Flughafen München** is accessible from the train station by S-8, which runs daily every 20min. 3:22am-12:42am.

Trains: Hauptbahnhof (tel. 22 33 12 56). The transportation hub of southern Germany. To: **Zurich** (4-5hr.), **Prague** (6-7½hr.), **Vienna** (4-5hr.), **Frankfurt** (3½hr.), **Berlin** (7½hr.), **Hamburg** (6hr.), **Paris** (9½-10hr.), and **Amsterdam** (9hr.). Call for schedules and fare information (tel. 194 19) and reservations (in German only; tel. 13 08 23 33).

Public Transportation: The **MVV** system runs Mon.-Fri. 5am-12:30am, Sat.-Sun. 5am-1:30am. A few lines run through the night every hour. Eurail, InterRail, and German railpasses are valid on any S-bahn (commuter rail) but *not* on the U-bahn (subway), *Straßenbahn*, or buses. Single-ride tickets (with transfers) are DM3.40 within the *Innenraum* (city center). A *Streifenkarte* (11-strip ticket; strike 2 strips per person) costs DM15. One-day tickets give one person unlimited travel (city center DM8). Stamp your ticket in the boxes marked with an "E" *before* you go to the platform (or on board a bus). If you cheat, the fine is DM60.

Bike Rental: Radius Touristik (tel. 59 61 13), in the rear of the *Hauptbahnhof*, near tracks 30-31. DM10-15 for 2hr., DM30-45 for 24hr. DM100-200 deposit. 10% discounts for students and Eurailpass holders. Open daily April to early Oct. 10am-6pm. **Aktiv-Rad**, Hans-Sachs-Str. 7 (tel. 26 65 06). DM18 per day. U-bahn 1 or 2: "Frauenhoferstr." Open Mon.-Fri. 9am-1pm and 2-6:30pm, Sat. 9am-1pm.

Hitchhiking: Those offering rides post information in the **Mensa**, on Leopoldstr. 13. Otherwise, hitchers try Autobahn on-ramps. To reach these on-ramps, hitchers heading toward Salzburg-Vienna-Italy, take U-1: "Karl-Preis-Pl." For Stuttgart or France, they take U-1: "Rotkreuzpl.," then tram 12: "Amalienburgstr." Those aiming north to Berlin take U-6: "Studentenstadt" and walk 500m to the Frankfurter Ring. A safer bet is **McShare Treffpunkt Zentrale**, Klenzestr. 57b and Lämmerstr. 4 (tel. 59 45 61; DM54 to Berlin; open daily 8am-8pm). **Frauenmitfahrzentrale**, Klenzestr. 57b, is for women only. U-1 or 2: "Fraunhoferstr.," then walk up Fraunhoferstr. away from the river and turn right. Open Mon.-Fri. 8am-8pm.

Laundromat: Waschsalon Prinz, Paul-Heyse-Str. 21, near the station. Wash and soap DM7. Open daily 6am-10pm. **Münz Waschsalon**, Amalienstr. 61, near the university. Wash DM5.20. Open Mon.-Fri. 8am-6:30pm, Sat. 8am-1pm.

Crisis Lines: Rape Crisis, Frauennotruf München, Güllstr. 3 (tel. 76 37 37). **AIDS Hotline**, tel. 520 73 87 or 520 74 12 (Mon.-Thurs. 8am-3pm, Fri. 8am-noon) or 194 11 (Mon.-Sat. 7-10pm).

Pharmacy: Bahnhof Apotheke, Bahnhofpl. 2 (tel. 59 41 19 or 59 81 19), outside the station. Open Mon.-Fri. 8am-6:30pm, Sat. 8am-2pm. 24hr. service rotates—call 59 44 75 for information in German or get a schedule at the tourist office.

Medical Assistance: Clinic across the river on Ismaningerstr. U.S. and British consulates carry a list of English-speaking doctors.

Emergencies: Police, tel. 110. **Ambulance,** tel. 192 22. **Emergency Medical Service,** tel. 55 77 55. **Poison Control,** tel. 192 40. **Fire,** tel. 112.

Post Office: Post/Telegrafenamt, Arnulfstr. 32. (tel. 54 54 23 36). *Poste Restante* and money exchange. Go out of the train station and turn left onto Arnulfstr.; the post office will be on your right. Open Mon.-Fri. 8am-8pm, Sat. 8am-noon. EurAide offers a message-forwarding service. **Postal Code:** 80074.

Telephone Code: 089.

ACCOMMODATIONS AND CAMPING

Munich accommodations fall into one of three categories: seedy, expensive, or booked. Reserve in advance in summer and during *Oktoberfest*, when all three

ACCOMMODATIONS AND CAMPING ■ 227

often apply. Sleeping in the *Englischer Garten* or train station is unsafe and illegal. Augsburg's hostel (40min. by train) is an option, but mind the 1am curfew. HI hostels are not supposed to accept solo travelers over 26, although families may book rooms.

Hostels and Camping

Jugendherberge München (HI), Wendl-Dietrich-Str. 20. (tel. 13 11 56). U-1: "Rotkreuzpl." then cross Rotkreuzpl. toward the Kaufhof store. Reception 24hr. Check-in begins at 10:30am, but lines start before 9. Dorms DM23-25.50. Breakfast and sheets included. Key deposit DM20. Safes with DM50 deposit.

Jugendlager Kapuzinerhölzl ("The Tent"), In den Kirschen 30 (tel. 141 43 00). From the station, tram 17 (dir: Amalienburgstr.): "Botanischer Garten," go straight on Franz-Schrank-Str., and then turn left. Sleep with 400 others on a foam pad under a circus tent. Reception 5pm-9am. DM13 with breakfast. Under 24 only (under 27 if there's room). Actual "beds" DM17. Lockers provided; bring a lock. Reservations for groups only. Open mid-June to early Sept.

Jugendherberge Pullach Burg Schwaneck (HI), Burgweg 4-6 (tel. 793 06 43; fax 793 79 22). S-7 (dir: Wolfratshausen): "Pullach." Romantic, but swarming with schoolchildren. Reception 4-11pm. Curfew 11:30pm. Dorms DM18.50-22.50. Breakfast included. Sheets DM5. Try to make reservations 7:30-10am.

Jugendgästehaus Thalkirchen, Miesingstr. 4 (tel. 723 65 50). U-1 or 2: "Sendlinger Tor" then U-3 (dir: Fürstenrieder West): "Thalkirchen." Follow Schäftlarnstr. in the direction of Innsbruck and bear right along Frauenbergstr., then turn left on Münchnerstr. Reception 7am-1am. Curfew 1am. Dorms DM27.50; singles DM35.50; doubles DM63; triples DM88.50; quads DM117. Sheets and breakfast included.

4 you münchen (Ökologisches Jugendgästehaus), Hirtenstr. 18 (tel. 552 16 60; fax 55 21 66 66), 200m from the *Hauptbahnhof*. Beautiful and ecological. Guests over 27 pay 15% surcharge. Dorms DM24-29; singles DM54; doubles DM76. Sheets DM5. Key deposit DM20. Breakfast DM7.50. In adjoining hotel: singles DM69; doubles DM99; breakfast included. Reception daily 7am-noon, 3-7pm, and 7:30-10pm.

Jugendhotel Marienberge, Goethestr. 9 (tel. 55 58 05), less than a block south of the train station. Staffed by jolly nuns. Reception 8am-midnight. Curfew midnight. Open only to **women under 26.** 6-bed dorms DM30; singles DM40; doubles DM70; triples DM105. Showers and breakfast included. Kitchen and laundry facilities. Wash DM2, dry DM2.

CVJM (YMCA) Jugendgästehaus, Landwehrstr. 13 (tel. 552 14 10; fax 550 42 82; email muenchen@cvjm.org). Take the Bayerstr. exit from the station, and go straight down Goethestr. Spic 'n' span rooms. Reception 8am-12:30am. Curfew 12:30am. Singles DM50; doubles DM86. Coed rooms for married couples only. Over 27 add 15%. Breakfast included. Closed at Easter and Dec. 20-Jan. 7.

Haus International, Elisabethstr. 87 (tel. 12 00 60). U-2 (dir: Feldmoching): "Hohenzollernpl.," then tram 12 (dir: Romanpl.) or bus 33 (dir: Aidenbachstr.): "Barbarastr." It's the 5-story beige building behind the BP gas station. Reception 24hr. Singles DM55-85; doubles DM104-144; larger rooms DM138-200.

Camping: Campingplatz Thalkirchen, Zentralländstr. 49 (tel. 723 17 07; fax 724 31 77). U-1 or 2: "Sendlinger Tor," then 3: "Thalkirchen" and change to bus 57. Laundry facilities and a restaurant (meals DM3-8). Curfew 11pm. DM7.80; tents DM5.50-7. Showers DM2. Open mid-March to late Oct.

Hotels and Pensions

When the city is full, finding clean singles under DM55-65 and doubles under DM80-100 in a safe area is nearly impossible. Reserving weeks ahead is particularly important during *Oktoberfest*. The tourist office and EurAide find rooms for a DM5-6 fee.

Hotel Kurpfalz, Schwanthalerstr. 121 (tel. 540 98 60; fax 54 09 88 11; email hotel-kurpfalz@munich-online.de). Exit the station onto Bayerstr., turn right down Bayerstr., and veer left onto Holzapfelstr. Singles DM59-69; doubles DM85-119, with extra cot DM120-135. Breakfast included. Free **Internet access.**

Hotel Helvetia, Schillerstr. 6 (tel. 55 47 45; fax 55 02 381), to the right as you exit the station. Recently renovated. Singles DM53-62. Doubles DM68-115. Triples DM99-120. Showers and breakfast included. Hostel-like dorms DM19-24. Shower included. Breakfast DM7. Sheets DM4. Laundry service DM8.50.

Pension Locarno, Bahnhofpl. 5 (tel. 55 51 64; fax 59 50 45), right outside the train station. Plain rooms with TVs. Reception daily 7:30am-midnight. Singles DM55-75; doubles DM90; triples DM135; quads DM160. Hall showers and breakfast included.

Hotel Central, Bayerstr. 55 (tel. 453 98 46; fax 543 98 470), 5min. to the right from the Bayerstr. exit of the train station. Spacious, plain rooms. Singles DM50-60; doubles DM85-95, with bath DM100-120.

Pension Frank, Schellingstr. 24 (tel. 28 14 51; fax 280 09 10). Take U-4 or 5: "Odeonspl.," then U-3 or 6: "Universität." Reception daily 7:30am-10pm. Dorms DM35; singles DM55-65; doubles DM78-85. *Oktoberfest* surcharge DM5. Shower and breakfast included.

Pension am Kaiserplatz, Kaiserpl. 12 (tel. 34 91 90), close to the nightlife. U-3 or 6: "Münchener Freiheit." Exit onto Herzogstr., turn left onto Viktoriastr. and walk to the end. Elegantly decorated rooms. Reception daily 7am-9pm. Singles DM49-59; doubles DM82-89; larger rooms DM30-35 per person. Breakfast included.

Hotel-Pension am Markt, Heiliggeiststr. 6 (tel. 22 50 14; fax 22 40 17), right in the city center. S-Bahn 1-8: "Marienpl.," walk through the *Altes Rathaus,* and turn right. Singles DM62-110; doubles DM110-160; triples DM165-205. Breakfast and showers included. Reserve rooms at least 3-4 weeks in advance.

FOOD

Munich's gastronomic center is the vibrant **Viktualienmarkt,** two minutes south of Marienpl., with a rainbow of bread, fruit, meat, pastry, cheese, wine, vegetable, and sandwich shops. (Generally open Mon.-Fri. 9am-6:30pm, Sat. 9am-2pm.) Otherwise, look for cheap meals in the **university district** off Ludwigstr. **Tengelmann,** Schützenstr. 7, near the train station, satisfies grocery needs quickly and conveniently. (Open Mon.-Wed. and Fri. 8:30am-6:30pm, Thurs. 8:30am-8:30pm, Sat. 9am-2pm.)

Türkenhof, Türkenstr. 78. Smoky and buzzing at night. Entrees (*Schnitzel*, omelettes, soups) DM7-14. Open Sun.-Thurs. 11am-1am, Fri.-Sat. 11am-3am.

Café Puck, Türkenstr. 33. Spacious café/bar with a young and energetic attitude. Breakfast DM5-16. Veggie specials DM11-16. Open daily 9am-1am.

La Bohème, Türkenstr. 79. Pastas DM7-11; pizzas DM7-11; salads DM5-13. At dinner add DM1. 0.4L beer DM3.50.

News Bar, Amalienstr. 55, at the corner of Schellingstr. Bustling, trendy, and youthful new café. Crepes DM6-11. Sandwiches DM7-11. Open daily 7:30am-2am.

Shoya, Orlandostr. 5, across from the Hofbräuhaus. The most reasonable Japanese restaurant/take-out joint in town. Rice dishes DM13-19; *teriyaki* DM8-16; sushi DM5-30. Other meat and veggie dishes DM4-16. Open daily 10:30am-midnight.

buxs, Frauenstr. 9, on the Viktualienmarkt. Vegetarian café/restaurant with salads (DM3 per 100g) and tasty pastas. Open Mon.-Fri. 11am-8:30pm, Sat. 11am-3:30pm.

Beim Sendlmayr, Westenriederstr. 6, off the Viktualienmarkt. A slice of Little Bavaria. Specials DM7-25. Beer DM5.30 for 0.5L. Open daily 11am-11pm.

Internet-Café, Nymphenburgerstr. 145 (http://www.icafe.spacenet.de). U-1: "Rotkreuzpl." Unlimited free **Internet access** with an order of pasta (DM9.50), pizza (DM7.50-10), or beer (DM4.90 for 0.5L). Open daily 11am-4am.

SIGHTS

Marienplatz serves as an interchange for major S-bahn and U-bahn lines as well as the social nexus of the city. On the square, the onion-domed towers of the 15th-century **Frauenkirche** have long been one of Munich's most notable landmarks. (Towers open April-Oct. Mon.-Sat. 10am-5pm. DM4, students DM2.) At the neo-Gothic

SIGHTS ■ 229

Neues Rathaus, the **Glockenspiel** marks the hour at 11am, noon, 5, and 9pm with jousting knights and dancing barrel-makers. At 9pm, a mechanical watchman marches out and a Guardian Angel escorts the *Münchner Kindl* ("Munich Child," the city's symbol) to bed. (Tower open Mon.-Fri. 9am-7pm, Sat.-Sun. 10am-7pm. DM3.)

The 11th-century **Peterskirche** is at Rindermarkt and Peterspl. Locals have christened its saintly tower *Alter Peter*. (Open Mon.-Sat. 9am-6pm, Sun. 10am-6pm. DM2.50, students DM1.50.) Nearby, Ludwig II of Bavaria rests in peace in a crypt of the 16th-century Jesuit **Michaelskirche,** on Neuhauserstr. (DM0.50). A Bavarian Rococo masterpiece, the **Asamkirche,** Sendlingerstr. 32, is named after brothers Cosmas and Egid, who vowed to build it if they survived a shipwreck. The magnificent **Residenz,** Max-Joseph-Pl. 3, boasts rich rooms built with the wealth of the Wittelsbachs, Bavaria's ruling family from the 12th to the early 20th century. The grounds now house several museums, and the **Schatzkammer** (treasury) contains jewels and swords from as early as the 10th century. (Treasury open Tues.-Sun. 10am-4:30pm. DM5, students DM2.50.) To reach the *Residenz*, take U-3, 4, 5, or 6: "Odeonspl."

Ludwig I's summer residence, **Schloß Nymphenburg,** is worth the trip northwest of town on tram 17 (dir: Amalienburgstr.). A Baroque wonder set in a winsome park, the palace hides such treasures as a two-story granite marble hall seasoned with stucco, frescoes, and a Chinese lacquer cabinet. Check out Ludwig's "Gallery of Beauties"—whenever a woman caught his fancy, he would have her portrait painted. (*Schloß* open April-Sept. Tues.-Sun. 9am-noon and 1-5pm; Oct.-March 10am-12:30pm and 1:30-4pm. Main palace DM6, students DM4; entire complex DM8, DM5. Grounds free.) Next door is the immense **Botanischer Garten,** where greenhouses shelter rare flora from around the world. (Garden open daily 9am-7pm. Greenhouses open daily 9-11:45am and 1-6:30pm. DM3, students DM1.50.) Abutting the city center is the **Englischer Garten,** one of Europe's oldest landscaped parks.

Museums Munich is a supreme museum city. Take a break from Monet *et al* at the **Deutsches Museum,** on the *Museumsinsel* (Museum Island) in the Isar River (S-1-8: "Isartor"), one of the world's largest, most exciting museums of science and technology. Particularly interesting are the mining exhibit, which winds through a labyrinth of re-created subterranean tunnels, the planetarium (DM3), and the daily electrical show. (Open daily 9am-5pm. DM10, students DM4.) The **Neue Pinakothek,** Barerstr. 29, exhibits the work of such 18th- to 20th-century masters as Van Gogh and Klimt. (Open Tues. and Thurs. 10am-8pm, Wed. and Fri.-Sun. 10am-5pm. DM7, students DM4.) **Lenbachhaus,** Luisenstr. 33, houses Munich cityscapes, along with works by Kandinsky, Klee, and the *Blaue Reiter* school, which forged the modernist modernist abstract aesthetic. (Open Tues.-Sun. 10am-6pm. DM8, students DM4.) Between them, **Glyptohek,** Königspl. 3, and **Antikensammlung,** Königspl. 1, hold Munich's finest collection of ancient art. (Glyptohek open Tues.-Wed. and Fri.-Sun. 10am-5pm, Thurs. 10am-8pm. Antikensammlung open Tues. and Thurs.-Sun. 10am-5pm, Wed. 10am-8pm. Joint admission DM10, students DM5.) **Staatsgalerie moderner Kunst,** Prinzregentenstr. 1, in the Haus der Kunst, has a sterling 20th-century collection that includes Klee, Picasso, and Dalí. The Haus der Kunst was built by Nazis and opened with a famous exhibit on "degenerate art." (Open Tues.-Wed. and Fri.-Sun. 10am-5pm, Thurs. 10am-8pm. DM6, students DM3.50.) The **ZAM: Zentrum für Außergewöhnliche Museen** (Center for Unusual Museums), Westenriederstr. 26, includes favorites like the Corkscrew Museum, Museum of Easter Rabbits, and the Chamberpot Museum. (Open daily 10am-6pm. DM8, students DM5.) If you're looking for something kinky rather than quirky, try the **Museum für erotische Kunst** (Museum of Erotic Art), Odeonspl. 8 (U-3-6: "Odeonspl." or bus #53).

ENTERTAINMENT

Munich's streets erupt with bawdy beer halls, rowdy discos, and cliquey cafés every night. Pick up *Munich Found* (DM4), *in münchen* (free), or the hip and hefty *Prinz* (DM5) at any newsstand to find out what's up.

Beer To most visitors, Munich means beer. The six great city labels are *Augustiner, Hacker-Pschorr, Hofbräu, Löwenbräu, Paulaner-Thomasbräu,* and *Spaten-Franzinskaner;* each brand supplies its own beer halls. Beer is served by the *Maß* (about a liter, DM8-11). The biggest keg party in the world, Munich's **Oktoberfest** (Sept. 19-Oct. 4 in 1998; http://www.munich-tourist.de), features speeches, a parade of horse-drawn beer wagons, and the mayor tapping the first ceremonial barrel. The Hofbräu tent is the rowdiest. Most *Müncheners* claim that **Augustiner Keller,** Arnulfstr. 52 (S-1-8: "Hackerbrücke"), is the finest beer garden in town, with lush grounds and 100-year-old chestnut trees. (*Maß* DM9-10. Open daily 10am-1am; beer garden open 10:30am-midnight. Food served until 10pm.) The world-famous **Hofbräuhaus,** Am Platzl 9, two blocks from Marienpl., has been tapping barrels for the commoners since 1897 and now seems reserved for drunken tourists. About 15,000 to 30,000L of beer are sold each day. (*Maß* DM10.40. 2 *Weißwurst* sausages DM7.50. Open daily 10am-midnight.) The new **Augustiner Bräustuben,** Landsbergerstr. 19 (S-1-8: "Hackerbrücke"), in the Augustiner Brewery's former horse stalls, offers delicious Bavarian food for DM6-20. (Open daily until 11pm.) The largest beer garden in Europe, **Hirschgarten,** Hirschgartenallee 1 (U-1: "Rotkreuzpl." then tram 12: "Romanpl."), is boisterous and verdant. (*Maß* DM8.60. Open daily 11am-11pm. Restaurant open Nov.-Feb. Tues.-Sun. same hours.) **Chinesischer Turm,** in the *Englischer Garten* next to the pagoda (U-3 or 6: "Giselastr."), is a fair-weather tourist favorite with lots of kids. (*Maß* DM9.50; salads DM7-13.50. Open daily in good weather 10:30am-11pm.)

Theater, Music, and Nightlife Stages sprinkled throughout the city span styles and tastes from dramatic classics at the **Residenztheater** and **Volkstheater** to comic opera at the **Staatstheater am Gärtnerplatz** to experimental works at the **Theater im Marstall** in Nymphenburg. The tourist office's *Monatsprogramm* (DM2.50) lists schedules for all Munich's stages. Leftover tickets sell for about DM10. Munich's **Opera Festival** (in July) is held in the **Bayerische Staatsoper** (tel. 21 85 19 20), accompanied by a concert series in the Nymphenburg and Schleissheim palaces. (Regular season standing-room and student tickets DM15-20. Box office open Mon.-Fri. 10am-6pm, Sat. 10am-1pm.) **Gasteig,** Rosenheimerstr. 5 (tel. 48 09 80, box office 54 89 89), hosts diverse musical performances on the former site of the *Bürgerbräukeller* where Adolf Hitler launched his abortive Beer Hall Putsch. (Box office open Mon.-Fri. 10:30am-2pm and 3-6pm, Sat. 10:30am-2pm, and 1hr. before curtain.) The **Muffathalle,** Zellerstr. 4 (tel. 45 87 50 00), in Haidhausen, a former power plant, still generates energy with techno, hip-hop, jazz, and dance performances (DM30).

Munich's nightlife is a curious mix of Bavarian *Gemütlichkeit* (traditional living) and trendy cliquishness, so dress well. **Münchener Freiheit** is the most famous and touristy bar/café district. More low-key is the southwestern section of **Schwabing,** directly behind the university on Amalienstr. The center of Munich's gay scene lies within the **Golden Triangle** defined by Sendlinger Tor, the Viktualienmarkt/Gärtnerpl. area, and Isartor.

Mingle with an English-speaking crowd at **Günther Murphy's,** Nikolaistr. 9a. (Guinness DM6. Open Mon.-Fri. 5pm-1am, Sat.-Sun. 11am-1am.) **Reitschule,** Konigstr. 34, is more relaxed (*Weißbier* DM6). Live music at **Shamrock,** Trautenwolfstr. 6, runs the gamut from blues and soul to Irish fiddling to rock. (Guinness DM6.20. Open Mon.-Thurs. 5pm-1am, Fri.-Sat. 5pm-3am, Sun. 2pm-1am.) Things get rolling late at **Nachtcafé,** Maximilianspl. 5, with live jazz, funk, soul, and blues until the wee hours (beer DM8 for 0.3L). Dance clubs include the huge complex **Kunstpark**

Ost, Grafingerstr. 6 (hours, cover, and themes vary—call 49 00 29 28 for information and tickets); and **Nachtwerk and Club,** Landesbergerstr. 185, twin clubs spinning mainstream dance tunes for sweaty crowds. (Beer DM6. Cover DM10. Open daily 10pm-4am.) **Club Morizz,** Klenzestr. 43, reminiscent of *Casablanca,* is frequented by gay men and lesbians. (Open Sun.-Thurs. 7pm-2am, Fri.-Sat. 7pm-3am.)

■ Near Munich

DACHAU

"Once they burn books, they'll end up burning people," wrote the 19th-century German poet Heinrich Heine. This eerily prophetic statement is posted at **Konzentrationslager-Gedenkstätte,** the concentration camp at Dachau, next to a photograph of one of Hitler's book burnings. Though most of the buildings had fallen apart by 1962, the walls, gates, and crematoria were restored. The terrifying legacy of Dachau lives on in the several memorials and chapels on the grounds and in photographs and letters housed in the Dachau **museum.** Take S-2 (dir: Petershausen): "Dachau," then catch bus 724 (dir: Kräutgarten) or 726 (dir: Kopernikusstr.; either one DM2) in front of the station to "KZ Gedenkstätte," a 20-minute ride. (Grounds open Tues.-Sun. 9am-5pm.) The state offers free two-hour tours in English that leave the museum daily at 12:30pm. Call (08131) 17 41 for more information.

THE CHIEMSEE

For almost 2000 years, artists and musicians have marveled at the picturesque islands, mountains, and forests of the Chiemsee region. The main attractions of the area are the two inhabited islands on Lake Chiem, the largest lake in Bavaria. Ferries ply the waters from the port in Prien to the **Herreninsel** (Gentlemen's Island), the **Fraueninsel** (Ladies' Island), and towns on the other side of the lake (DM10-14). On Herreninsel, the architecture of **Königsschloß Herrenchiemsee,** King Ludwig II's third and last "fairy-tale castle," is fabulously overwrought. Candlelit concerts are given in the **Hall of Mirrors** throughout the summer. (Open daily April-Sept. 9am-5pm; Oct.-March 10am-4pm. Obligatory guided tour DM7, students DM4.) Frauensel offers subtler pleasures. Its miniature world has no room for cars; only footpaths wander through this village of fishermen and nuns. The **abbey** dates back to at least 866. Various artifacts, including the impressive 8th-century Merovingian **Cross of Bischofhofen,** are on display in the room above the Torhalle, the oldest surviving part of the cloister. (Open mid-June to Sept. daily 11am-6pm; Oct. to mid-June Mon.-Sat. 11am-6pm. DM4, students DM1.50.)

The town of **Prien** works well as a base for exploring the lake. The **tourist office,** Alte Rathaus 11 (tel. (08051) 690 50 or 69 05 55), offers free maps and brochures and finds rooms in private houses (DM20-40) for no fee. (Open Mon.-Fri. 8:30am-6pm, Sat. 9am-noon.) The cheapest beds in town are at the raucous **Jugendherberge (HI),** Carl-Braun-Str. 66 (tel. (08051) 687 70; fax 68 77 15), a 10-minute walk from the lake. (Reception daily 8-9am, 5-7pm, and 9:30-10pm. Curfew 10pm. Dorms DM22.80. Sheets DM5.50. Open Jan.-Oct.) **Campingplatz Hofbauer** is at Bernauer Str. 110 (tel. (08051) 41 36; fax 626 57). To reach the site, walk right from the station, turn left at Seestr., then left again at the next intersection and follow Bernauerstr. out of town. (DM8.20; tent DM9. Open late March-Oct.) You can much on a hearty meal for 9-20DM at **Scherer SB Restaurant,** Alte Rathausstr. 1 (open Mon.-Fri. 8am-8pm, Sat. 8am-3pm), or grab prepackaged goods from **HL Markt,** Seestr. 11 (open Mon.-Fri. 8am-6pm, Sat. 8am-4pm).

■ The Bavarian Alps (Bayerische Alpen)

South of Munich, the land buckles into dramatic peaks and valleys that stretch through Austria and into Italy. Mountain villages, glacial lakes, icy waterfalls, and ski resorts dot the landscape, but rail lines are scarce. Buses fill in the gaps. For regional information, contact the **Fremdenverkehrsverband Oberbayern,** Bodenseestr. 113 (tel. (089) 829 21 80), in Munich. (Open Mon.-Fri. 9am-4:30pm, Sat. 9am-noon.)

BERCHTESGADEN

At the easternmost point of the Bavarian Alps, Berchtesgaden profits from a sinister and over-touristed attraction—Hitler's **Kehlsteinhaus,** a mountaintop retreat christened "Eagle's Nest" by occupying American troops and now a restaurant. The best reason to visit the Kehlsteinhaus is for the stunning view from the 1834m mountain peak. On your way back down, inspect the remains of the **Berghof;** here in 1938 Hitler browbeat Austrian Chancellor Kurt von Schuschnigg into relinquishing control of the Austrian police, paving the way for the *Anschluß*. The Berchtesgaden **Schloß,** a monastic priory until Bavarian rulers appropriated the property, now houses a mixture of art and weaponry. (Open Sun.-Fri. 10am-1pm and 2-5pm; Oct.-Easter closed Sun. Last admission 4pm. DM7, students DM3.50.)

The **tourist office,** Kurdirektion (tel. (08652) 96 70), opposite the train station on Königsseerstr., sells hiking passes (DM5) with trail information. (Open June-Oct. Mon.-Fri. 8am-6pm, Sat. 9am-5pm, Sun. 9am-3pm; Nov.-May Mon.-Fri. 8am-5pm, Sat. 9am-noon.) Hourly **trains** (tel. (08652) 50 74) run to Munich (2½hr.) and Salzburg (1hr.); change at Freilassing for both. The **Jugendherberge (HI)** is at Gebirgsjägerstr. 52 (tel. (08652) 943 70; fax 94 37 37); from the station, take bus #9539 (dir: Strub Kaserne): "Jugendherberge." (Reception daily 8am-noon and 5-7pm; check-in until 10pm. Dorms DM23. Sheets DM5.50. Breakfast and tax included. Open Dec. 27-Oct.) Pick up a *Wurst* from vendors or groceries at **Edeka Markt,** Dr.-Imhof-Str. near Griesstätterstr. (Open Mon.-Fri. 8am-12:30pm and 1:30-6pm, Sat. 8am-2pm.)

■ The German Danube

The Danube Valley, with Baroque Passau and Gothic Regensburg, is every bit as inviting as the Engadin Valley. Northeast of Munich, the valley's rolling hills and lovely riverscapes attract Germans and international tourists year-round.

REGENSBURG AND THE BAVARIAN FOREST

Regensburg was once the capital of Bavaria, later became the administrative seat of the Holy Roman Empire, and then established itself as the site of the first German parliament. The (Holy Roman) Imperial Parliament met in the **Reichstags Museum,** housed in the Gothic **Altes Rathaus.** The different heights of the chairs reflect the political hierarchy of the legislators. (English tours May-Sept. Mon.-Sat. 3:15pm. German tours daily year-round. DM5, students DM2.50.) The splendid high-Gothic **St. Peter's Cathedral** towers over the city. (Open April-Oct. daily 6:30am-6pm; Nov.-March 6:30am-4pm. DM4, students DM2.)

The **tourist office,** Altes Rathaus on Rathauspl. (tel. (0941) 507 44 10; fax 507 44 19), finds rooms (DM1.50) and provides a free map. From the train station, walk down Maximilianstr. to Grasg. and take a left. Stay on the road as it turns into Obermünsterstr., then turn right at the end to Obere Bachg. and walk straight to Rathauspl. **Trains** chug to Munich via Landshut (1½hr.), Nuremberg (1hr.), and Passau (1-1½hr.). The **Jugendherberge (HI),** Wöhrdstr. 60 (tel. (0941) 574 02), offers pleasant but sterile rooms. (Reception daily 7am-11:30pm. Dorms DM20. Under 27 only. Partial wheelchair access. Closed mid-Nov. to mid-Jan.) Campers should head for the **Campingplatz,** Am Weinweg 40 (tel. (0941) 27 00 25); from Albertstr., take bus #11 (dir: West bad): "Westheim." (DM10; tent DM7). Eat at **Goldene Ente,** Badstr. 32, a beer garden with steaks, spare-ribs, *Würstchen*, and *Schnitzel* for wallet-friendly prices. (Open Mon.-Sat. 11am-2pm and 5pm-1am, Sun. 10am-1am.) A store, **Tengelmann** grocery store is on Ernst-Reuter-Pl. off Maximilianstr. (Open Mon.-Fri. 8:30am-6:30pm, Sat. 7:30am-2pm.)

Northeast of Regensburg and Passau along the Austrian and Czech borders, the **Bavarian Forest** *(Bayerischer Wald)* is Central Europe's largest range of wooded mountains. The **Bavarian Forest National Park** is strictly protected from any activities that may alter the forest ecosystem. Clearly marked trails lace 20,000 acres of woods. You can hoof it alone or sign up for guided walking, botanical, and natural history tours. For information and schedules, contact the **Nationalparkverwaltung Bayerischer Wald,** Freyunstr. 94481 Grafenau (tel. (08552) 427 43; fax 46 90). The **Tourismusverbad Ostbayern,** Luitpoldstr. (tel. (0941) 58 53 90; fax 585 39 39), in Regensburg, gives news of the rest of the forest. The park's thick woods hide palaces and 17 **HI youth hostels;** Regensburg's tourist office has an omniscient brochure.

PASSAU

Poised on two peninsulas forged by the confluence of the Danube, Inn, and Ilz Rivers, **Passau** embodies the ideal Old World European city. The city's Baroque architecture reaches its apex in the sublime **Stephansdom** (St. Stephen's Cathedral). Hundreds of cherubs are sprawled across the ceiling, and the world's largest **church organ** looms above the choir. (Open Mon.-Sat. 8-11am and 12:30-6pm. Free. Organ concerts May-Oct. Mon.-Sat. noon, DM4, students DM2; Thurs. 7:30pm, DM10, DM5.) The **Domschatz** (cathedral treasury), within the **Residenz** behind the cathedral, houses an extravagant collection of gold and tapestries. (Open May-Oct., Mon.-Fri. 10am-4pm. DM2.) Nearby is the gilded **St. Michael,** built by the Jesuits. (Open April-Oct. Tues.-Sun. 9am-5pm; Nov.-Jan. and March 10am-4pm. DM3, students DM1.50.) The 13th-century **Rathaus** is less opulent but still stunning. (Open May 16-Sept. daily 10am-5pm; Easter-May 15 10am-4pm; Oct. Mon.-Fri. 10am-4pm. DM2, students DM1.)

The **tourist office,** Rathauspl. 3 (tel. (0851) 95 59 80), has free maps and reserves rooms for a DM5 fee. (Open April-Oct. Mon.-Fri. 8:30am-6pm, Sat.-Sun. 10am-2pm; Nov.-March Mon.-Thurs. 8:30am-5pm, Fri. 8:30am-4pm.) The **train station** (tel. (0851) 194 19), west of downtown on Bahnhofstr., serves Regensburg (1-2hr.), Nuremburg (2hr.), Munich (2hr.), and Vienna (3¼hr.). **Rotel Inn** (tel. (0851) 951 60; fax 951 61 00) has wide beds in tiny rooms overlooking the Danube. To get there, go through the tunnel in front of the station toward the blue head of this hotel—it's built in the shape of a sleeping man. (Reception 24hr. Singles DM30; doubles DM50.) **Pension Rößner,** Bräug. 19 (tel. (0851) 93 13 50; fax 931 35 55), has homey rooms on the Danube. (Singles DM60-85; doubles DM80-100. Breakfast included.) The **Jugendherberge (HI),** Veste Oberhaus 125 (tel. (0851) 413 51; fax 437 09), is a long walk for adequate facilities. (Reception 7-11:30am and 4-11:30pm; new arrivals after 6pm only. Curfew 11:30. Dorms DM16.50. Breakfast included. Sheets DM5.50.)

The **Mensa,** Innstr. 29, offers cafeteria meals for DM2.40-4.50; any student ID will do. From Ludwigspl., follow Nikolastr. and turn right. (Open July-Aug. Mon.-Thurs. 8am-3:30pm, Fri. 8am-3pm; Sept.-June Mon.-Thurs. 8am-4pm, Fri. 8am-3pm.) **Innsteg,** Innstr. 13, one block from Nikolastr. is popular from morning till night (menu DM5-21; open daily 10am-1am). **Ratskeller,** Rathauspl. 2, a bustling restaurant in the back of the *Rathaus* overlooking the Danube, serves salads (DM4) and daily "local cuisine" specials (DM8-17; open daily 10am-11pm).

THE SALZKAMMERGUT

East of Salzburg, the landscape swells into towering mountains interspersed with unfathomably deep lakes. Corny as it sounds, this area is Austria's primary honeymoon destination—really. Like everything else in the area, the Salzkammergut takes its name from salt mines that, in their glory days, underwrote Salzburg's architectural treasures. The region is remarkably accessible, with 2000km of footpaths, 12 cable cars and chairlifts, and dozens of hostels. Winter brings mounds of snow to the valleys and downhill skiing to the slopes.

Hostels abound, but you can often find far superior rooms in private homes and *Pensionen* at just-above-hostel prices. *"Zimmer Frei"* signs peek out from virtually every house. **Campgrounds** dot the region, but many are trailer-oriented. Away from large towns, many travelers camp discreetly almost anywhere usually without trouble. Hikers can capitalize on dozens of **cable cars** in the area to gain altitude before setting out on their own, and almost every community has a local trail map available. At higher elevations there are **Alpine huts**—check carefully at the tourist office for their opening hours. These huts are leased through the **Österreichischer Alpenverein** (Austrian Alpine Club), which supplies mountains of information. The central office of the ÖAV is in Innsbruck (tel. (0512) 594 47), and there's a branch in Linz (tel. (0732) 773 22 95); locally experienced volunteers staff regional branches.

Within the region, there is a dense network of **buses**. Most routes run 4 to 12 times per day, and since the mountainous area is barren of rail tracks, buses are the most efficient and reliable method of travel into and through the lake region. Check at the Bad Ischl kiosk (tel. (06132) 231 13) or any other Salzkammergut town bus station for leaflets detailing bus-and-hike routes, especially the biggie *Postbus: Salzkammergut*.

Hitchers from Salzburg usually take bus #29 to Gnigl and come into the Salzkammergut at Bad Ischl. The lake district is one of the rare, refreshing Austrian regions in which hitchhikers can make good time. Two-wheeled transport is much more entertaining, but only with a good **bike**—some mountain passes top 1000m. Pedaling the narrow, winding roads on the lake banks is far less strenuous and equally scenic. Reasonably priced **ferries** serve each of the larger lakes, with railpass discounts on the **Wolfgangsee** line and the private **Attersee** and **Traunsee** lines.

While much of the Salzkammergut is technically in the province of Upper Austria, the region culturally aligns itself with Salzburgerland and Tirol. Every February brings **Carnival**, called *Fasnacht* in Western Austria and *Fasching* elsewhere else. Carnival commences with the January ball season. In the countrified areas, traditional processions of masked figures are the season headliners, featuring *Schiache* (ugly masks supposed to be evil). All this celebration requires months of preparation, with only men allowed. At the **Ausseer Fasching**, the carnival at Bad Aussee, *Trommelweiber* (women with drums, i.e. men in white nighties and night-caps) march through town. The Carnival near Ebensee culminates in the **Fetzenfasching** (carnival of rags): the people sing in falsetto, imitate spooky voices, and wave old umbrellas.

On January 5, the **running of the figures with special caps** (*Glöcklerlaufen*) takes place after dark in the Salzkammergut. These *Glöckler* derive their name from the custom of knocking at the door (*glocken* means "to knock") and not from the bells attached to their belts (*Glocke* mean "bell"). These caps, reminiscent of stained-glass windows, have an electric light inside. In return for their Happy New Year wish, runners are rewarded with a special doughnut, the *Glöcklerkrapfen*. Although the satisfaction of legions of stained-glass-hat fetishists seems enough, the masked figures also get money and refreshments from the citizenry, which indicates a little about their origin—a long, long time ago, seasonal workers needed such handouts to survive.

On the Sunday after November 25, about 30 bird-catcher clubs in the Salzkammergut region organize a **bird exhibition**. The birds squawk away the winter in people's living rooms and are then released. A **Christmas passion play** is performed every fourth year (next in 1998) at Bad Ischl.

■ Bad Ischl

For centuries, Bad Ischl (population 15,000) was a mere salt-mining town, until a certain Dr. Franz Wirer arrived in 1821 to study the potentially curative properties of the heated brine baths. Pleased with his findings, he began to prescribe brine bath vacations in Bad Ischl for his patients as early as 1822. Real fame descended on the resort only when the brine's healing powers kept the Habsburgs from sputtering into extinction. Archduke Francis Charles and Archduchess Sophia journeyed to Bad Ischl seeking a cure for their state of childlessness. The magical, mystical, almost fairy-tale results were three sons, the so-called **Salt Princes**. When the first Salt Prince, Franz Joseph I, ascended the throne in 1848, he proceeded to make Bad Ischl his annual summer residence, vacationing here for 40 years. Bad Ischl quickly became an imperial city, attracting noblemen, aristocrats, and stressed-out composers like Brahms, Bruckner, and Lehár. Bad Ischl is one of the few towns in the region not on a lake, which eliminates half the fun of visiting the Salzkammergut, but German vacationers (including German Chancellor Helmut Kohl) flock to the town anyway.

Orientation and Practical Information Bad Ischl lies at the junction of the **Traun** and **Ischl** rivers, which form a horseshoe around the city. The Ischl runs from the Wolfgangsee to the Traun on the way to the Danube. Bad Ischl is within splashing distance of seven Salzkammergut oases: the Hallstättersee, Gosausee, Wolfgangsee, Mondsee, Attersee, Traunsee, Grundlsee, and the Altausee.

By car, Bad Ischl lies on Rte. 158 and 145. From **Vienna,** take the A-1 West Autobahn to Rte. 145 at the town of Regau. From **Innsbruck** or **Munich,** take the A-1 East past Salzburg and exit onto Rte. 158 near Thalgau. From **Salzburg** proper, the best way is to take Rte. 158 straight, through the beautiful towns of St. Gilgen and Fuschl. One **train** comes through the station, running from Attnang-Puchheim in the north (68AS) through Hallstatt (34AS) and Bad Aussee (64AS). Indirect trains go to **Vienna** (376AS), **Linz** (147AS), and **Zell am See** (296AS). **Buses** leave from Salzburg to Bad Ischl every two hours (95AS), making stops in Fuschl and St. Gilgen.

The **train station** (tel. 244 070) has **bike rental** (150AS per day, 90AS with train ticket; open daily 7am-8pm). There are small **lockers** (20AS) and **luggage storage** (30AS per piece per day; open daily 7am-7:30pm). Bad Ischl's **bus station** (tel. 231 13) is right next to the train station. The **tourist office** (tel. 277 570 or 235 200; fax 277 5777) is straight out of the train station and two minutes down the road, across from the huge yellow Kaiser Therme building at Bahnhofstr. 6. The office has extensive lists of *Pensionen* and *Privatzimmer,* will help find a room, and has a 24-hour **electronic accommodations board.** A free basic English brochure is available. (Open June-Sept. Mon.-Fri. 8am-6pm, Sat. 9am-4pm, Sun. 9-11:30am; Oct.-May Mon.-Fri. 8am-noon and 2-5pm, Sat. 9am-noon.) The **post office** is two minutes farther down Bahnhofstr., on the corner of Auböckpl. (Open June-Sept. Mon.-Fri. 8am-8pm, Sat. 9am-noon; Oct.-May Mon.-Fri. 8am-7pm, Sat. 9-11am; **currency exchange** Mon.-Fri. until 5pm.) The **postal code** is A-4820. The **telephone code** is 06132.

Accommodations and Food Every guest who stays the night must register with his or her individual hotel or pension and pay a *Kurtax,* a tax levied by the local government (June to mid-Sept. 14-19AS per person per night depending on proximity to the city center; Oct.-May 12-13AS). In return, the local **guest card** gives discounts on museums, mountain cable cars, and other treats. Bad Ischl's **Jugendherberge (HI),** Am Rechenstag 5 (tel. 265 77; fax 265 77 57), is minutes from the Kaiser's summer residence. From the tourist office, walk left on Bahnhofstr., turn right on Kaiser-Franz-Josef-Str., bear right at the fork, and watch for the *Jugendherberge* sign to the left, near the bus parking lot across from the swimming pool. The hostel offers many comfortable one- to five-bed rooms off long corridors. Since it often fills with groups, call in advance. (Reception daily 8-9am and 5-7pm. Quiet hour 10pm; keys available. Dorms 130AS, plus the *Kurtax.* Sheets, showers, and breakfast included.) If the hostel is full, try **Haus Stadt Prag,** Eglmoosg. 9 (tel. 236 16), where large and airy rooms await your tired bones. From the train station, walk left on Bahnhofstr., turn right on Kaiser-Franz-Josef-Str., and bear left at the fork. Continue down Salzburgerstr., and bear left again on Stiegeng. at the *Goldschmied* sign. Continue along Stiegeng. and go up the steps—Haus Stadt Prag is the pink, balconied building on your right. (Singles 250AS, with shower and toilet 320AS; doubles 500AS, 600AS; triples with shower and toilet 850AS. Breakfast included.)

Restaurants are tucked into every possible spot along Schulgasse and the other streets of the pedestrian zone. When Bad Ischlers make a run for the border, they head to **Amigos Tex-Mex Restaurant,** Auböckpl. 9 (tel. 213 17), across from the Konsum market. This restaurant's tongue-in-cheek slogan, "Warm beer, lousy food, shitty service," obviously goes ignored by the thick crowd of devotees who tumble in for the quesadillas (60-82AS). Burgers run 68-78AS, enchiladas 75-85AS. Nearly all entrees are under 100AS. (Open Mon. and Wed.-Fri. 11:30am-2pm and 5:30-11:30pm, Sat.-Sun. 5-11:30pm; take-out available.) Almost as famous as the Kaiser himself is the **Konditorei Zauner,** Pfarrg. 7 (tel. 235 22). Established in 1832, this place has a reputation for heavenly sweets and tortes. Zauner also operates a riverside restaurant-café on the Esplanade. It's probably out of the question to actually eat at either, but it's lovely to have an ice cream (8AS) to go or a cup of coffee (from 22AS) at a riverside table along the Esplanade. The **Konsum grocery store** is conveniently located at Auböckpl. 12. (Open Mon.-Fri. 8am-6:30pm, Sat. 8am-12:30pm.) There is an **open air market** every Friday from 7am to noon in Salinenpl.

Sights and Entertainment Other than the baths, Bad Ischl's main attraction is what the Habsburgs left behind. Walking tours leave the tourist office 8:30am on Tuesday mornings in summer (30AS, free with guest card; register by the day before. Austria's last emperor, Franz Josef, received as a wedding gift a house at the edge of town, which quickly became known as the **Kaiservilla** (tel. 232 41). The emperor made it his summer getaway palace and crammed it with expensive hunter kitsch. The interior motif is strictly dead-animal-Ma-where-should-I-put-it; the villa's foyer displays a pantheon of horns and antlers, big and small, each with the date and place of the animal's demise at Franz's hands. Entrance to the Kaiservilla is only possible through a guided tour in German, but it's worth it. Look for the old red armchair where he napped every afternoon (note the area where the chair is worn and indented—his snuggliest napping position), and the desk where he signed the declaration of war against Serbia in 1914 that led to WWI. (Tours May to mid-Oct. daily 9-11:45am and 1-4:45pm. Open weekends in April. 100AS, with guest card 90AS, students 65AS, children 40AS.) You can wander through the verdant 14-hectare **Villapark,** where the regal couple spent several cool summer afternoons (35AS, children 25AS). At the rear of the grounds lies the empress's **Marmorschlößl** (tel. 244 22), which houses a **Photo Museum.** The emperor commissioned this very marble palace so that the empress could sleep solo. Head left from the tourist office onto Bahnhofstr., and turn right on Franz-Josef-Str. to the villa's entrance. (Open April-Oct. daily 9:30am-5pm. 15AS, with guest card 12AS; children 10AS, plus entrance to the park.) An unfairly overlooked city monument is the **Stadtpfarrkirche** (city parish church), on Kaiser-Franz-Josef-Str., dedicated to St. Nikolaus (*not* Santa Claus). With its tiled floor and broad, arched ceiling beautifully painted with Biblical scenes, this church stands out from the pack. The church is most renowned for its magnificent **Kaiserjubiläumsorgel** (Emperor's Jubilee Organ). Played by the likes of organ virtuoso and composer Anton Bruckner, the organ is regarded as one of the best in the world.

A tour through Bad Ischl's **Salzbergwerke** salt mines (tel. 239 48) gives a didactic but amusing glimpse of the trade that brought wealth and fame to the Salzkammergut. The mines are outside of the city in Perneck and are best reached by car via Grazerstr. to Pernechstr. City bus #8096 also travels to Perneck and leaves from the Bahnhof two to five times daily (16AS, day pass 25AS). The last bus from Perneck is at 4:15pm. (Mines open daily July-Aug. 10am-4:45pm, May 6-June and Sept. 1-22 9am-3:45pm. 135AS, with guest card 120AS; children 65AS.)

Whether or not the **salt baths** really contain curative powers, something must be said for the town's relaxed atmosphere. The bath facilities are mostly in the **Kaiser Therme,** a resort across from the tourist office on Bahnhofstr. 1 (tel. 233 24; fax 233

24 44). Splash around in the heated salt baths with whirlpool (3hr. for 105AS, students 78AS, children 55AS; open Mon.-Sat. 9am-9pm, Sun. 1:30-9pm, last entrance 8pm), or relax in the spacious **sauna** (3hr. including pool entrance 145 AS, children 77AS; open Tues.-Sun. 1:30-9pm, Thurs. women only, Tues. men only). Confront your inner effete with a **full-body massage** (270AS for 25min.). Mud baths, acupuncture, and other more exotic experiences generally require a doctor's prescription.

For the low-down around town, pick up the brochure *Bad Ischl Events* from the tourist office. Free outdoor **Kurkonzerte** take place on Tuesdays at the Kurpark, the voluptuous green garden outside the Kurhaus along Wirerstr. The exact program of pieces performed by the 20-piece Kurorchestra is posted weekly on kiosks, in the hotels, and at the Kurhaus itself. Every year in mid-August, the **Bad Ischler Stadtfest** brings a weekend of music—classical, pop, jazz, boogie-woogie, oom-pah-pah, etc. Just before the Stadtfest on August 15th, the Bad Ischlers celebrate Franz Josef's birthday with live music late into the night on the Esplanade—their little way of commemorating bacchanalian Kaiser-era bashes. In late summer, the **Bad Ischl Operetten Festspiele** celebrates the musical talent of the composer Franz Lehár, the Lawrence Welk of opera, who lived in Bad Ischl for 30 years. (Festival July-Aug. Wed.-Fri.) Tickets are 140-500AS, available from Büro der Operettengemeinde Bad Ischl, Wiesengerstr. 7, A-4820 Bad Ischl (tel. 238 39; fax 233 84; open Mon.-Fri. 8am-noon). After June 30, purchase tickets from the Bad Ischl Kurhaus (tel. 237 66; fax 233 84; open Mon.-Fri. 9am-noon and 3-6pm). The genius who created *Gypsy Love, The Merry Widow,* and *The Land of Smiles* resided at the **Lehár Villa.** (Open May-Sept. daily 9am-noon and 2-5pm. Obligatory tour 50AS, with guest card 45AS; students and children 25AS.)

Hiking paths around the town are shown on a 93AS map available at the tourist office. **Bikers** can invest in a 35AS trail map, as well. In winter, the town valiantly battles against neighboring ski resorts. Beside an excellent network of **cross-country skiing** trails (free maps at the tourist office), Bad Ischl offers all sorts of Yule festivities, including a **Christkindlmarkt** (Christmas market), Advent caroling in the Kurhaus, tours of elaborate **Weihnachtskrippen** (nativity scenes) in the area, and horse-drawn sleigh rides *(Pferdeschliffen)* through the snow. In both summer and winter, the **Katrinseilbahn** (tel. 237 88) runs to the summit of nearby Mt. Katrin (1544m), a peak laced with fine hiking trails. Get to the cable car by taking a city bus (dir: Kutrinseilbahn) from the train station or Schröpferpl. The last bus runs back at 6:25 on weekdays and noon on Saturday. (Cable car runs mid-May to Oct. and Dec. 7 to Easter daily 9am-4pm. Ascent 139AS, descent 109AS, round-trip 160AS; with guest card 79AS, 104AS, 140AS; children round-trip 110AS.) From April to October, a **flea market** comes the Esplanade the first Saturday of the month.

▨ Mondsee

The Salzkammergut's warmest lake, the **Mondsee** (Moon Lake), gets its romantic name from its crescent shape. Although privately owned, the lake is available for general use. The town of Mondsee (pop. 2000) lies at the northern tip of the crescent, close to Autobahn A1. For a more scenic drive, take Rte. 158 from Salzburg to St. Gilgen and then Rte. 154 along the edges of the lake to downtown Mondsee. The town has no train station but is accessible by **bus** #3010 from Salzburg (every hr., 50min., last one at 8:20pm, 57AS). Buses also run six times a day to **St. Gilgen** on the Wolfgangsee (25min., 29AS). The closest lake resort to Salzburg, Mondsee is also one of the least touristed, perhaps because the town is not directly on the beach itself but 200m away—light-years by Salzkammergut standards. Still, air-conditioned tour buses rumble through the town several times daily to see the local **Pfarrkirche,** a Gothic church redesigned with a bright yellow Baroque exterior; the towers dominate the town skyline. A Benedictine monastery as early as AD748, the parish church made its big-screen debut in *The Sound of Music*'s wedding scene. Next door is the **Museum Mondsee,** which houses some beautifully illuminated manuscripts. (Open May-Sept. Tues.-Sun. 9am-6pm; first 2 weeks of Oct. Tues.-Sun. 9am-

5pm, last 2 weeks Sat.-Sun. 9am-6pm. 30AS, seniors 25AS, students 15AS.) The open-air **Freilichtmuseum,** on Hilfbergstr. (behind the church and up the hill to the right), features a 500-year-old smokehouse. Common in this area and in parts of Bavaria, the smokehouses have no chimneys—smoke wafted straight through the roof. This design served the practical purpose of drying the *Getreide* (cereal or grain) that hung from the ceiling and asphyxiating all humans who dared enter prematurely. (Open May-Sept. Tues.-Sun. 9am-6pm, first 2 weeks of Oct. Tues.-Sun. 9am-5pm, April and last 2 weeks of Oct. Sat.-Sun. and holidays 9am-6pm. Same prices as Museum Mendsee.)

The **tourist office** (*Tourismusverband*), Dr.-Franz-Müllerstr. 3 (tel. 22 70; fax 44 70; email robert.hanh@ris.telecom.at), is a five-minute walk from the bus station, halfway between the church and the lake. From the bus stop, head up the road past the post office, turn right on Rainerstr., and continue to the end. Turn right again, and the office is on the left. The English-speaking staff gladly gives out every brochure they have and finds accommodations for free. The free sightseeing pamphlet suggests three solid tours: the shortest (1-2hr.) covers just the town highlights; the longest (6-7hr.) requires a car. (Open July-Aug. Mon.-Fri. 8am-7pm, Sat. 9am-7pm, Sun. 9am-1pm; Sept.-June Mon.-Fri. 8am-noon and 1-5pm.) Up the street toward the church from the tourist office, the *Tabak* sells daily **English newspapers** and some **magazines**. The **post office,** on Franz-Kreuzbergerstr. across from the bus station, is the most convenient place for **currency exchange.** (Open Mon.-Fri. 8am-noon and 2-6pm, Sat. 8-10am. Exchange closes at 5pm.) There are **ATMs** at the Volksbank by the tourist office and at the Ruffeisenbank on Rainerstr. **Public restrooms** are under the *Rathaus* in Marktpl. The **postal code** is A-5310. The **telephone code** is 06232.

Mondsee is brimming with *Pensionen, Privatzimmer,* and hotels. The **Jugendgästehaus (HI),** Krankenhausstr. 9 (tel. 24 18; fax 241 875), offers doubles and quads with private showers, as well as one 10-bed dorm. From the bus station, walk up Kreuzbergerstr. toward the post office, turn right on Rainerstr., walk up the hill, and then go left on Steinbachstr. At the first intersection, go left 10m and then right up narrow little Krankenhausstr. Follow the signs to the hostel, hidden off a driveway to the left. The main entrance is below the brown balcony. Tread on brown carpets reminiscent of your grandmother's hide-the-stain approach. Bunkbeds are tucked into every possible nook, making the rooms a little snug. It's normally filled with groups; call first. (Reception daily 8am-1pm and 5-10pm. Curfew 10pm; key available. Members only. Dorms 140AS; doubles 340-440AS. Breakfast included; lunch and dinner available in the restaurant below.)

Pizzeria Nudelini, Marktpl. 5 (tel. 41 93), upstairs from Café Mexico in the blue building just down from the church, spins cheap 'n' tasty pizzas (68-105AS) and noodle dishes. (Open Sun.-Wed. noon-2pm and 5:30-11pm, Fri.-Sat. 5:30-11pm.) For delicious coffee and cake at better prices than the flamboyant cafés in front of the church, head to **Café Übleis,** by the tourist office at Badg. 6 (tel. 24 33). They specialize in homemade *Mozartkugeln* and yummy ice cream for 8AS. (Open daily July-Aug. 9am-11pm; Sept.-June 9am-9pm.) **China Restaurant,** Rainerstr. 13 (tel. 44 68), near the bus stop, is one of the few Austrian-Chinese restaurants to feature seafood, including squid (115-145AS) and prawn (160-190AS). They also have a lunch *menu* that includes soup and an entree for 62-69AS. (Open daily 11:30am-2:30pm and 6-11pm. Visa, MC.) The grocery-filled **SPAR Markt** has branches on Steinbachstr. just past the main square on the way up to the hostel and on Rainerstr. by Marktpl. (Both open Mon.-Fri. 7:30am-6:30pm, Sat. 7:30am-1pm.)

Mondsee's baby grand is the **lake.** In summer, the waters buzz with activity; in winter, though, everyone seems to hibernate. **Alpenseebad,** the public beach (tel. 22 91), is fine for swimming, but jumping in at undesignated areas along the shore is forbidden by the lake's wildlife conservation laws. (Open in fair weather May-Sept. daily 8:30am-7pm. 30AS, children 12AS; after 1:30pm 18AS, 6AS.) If you want to go on (not in) the lake, rent a **boat** from **Peter Herretsberger** (tel. 49 34) on the shore by the playground, down the street from the tourist office. (Rowboats 75-90AS per hr., paddleboats 100AS, electric boats 130-150AS.) Herretsberger also offers boat

1998
TRAVEL CATALOG

EURAIL PASSES
TRAVEL
guides gear accessories ID and more

1-800-5-LETSGO
http://www.hsa.net/travel/letsgo.htm

LET'S GO TRAVEL GEAR

PACKS

World Journey
Equipped with Eagle Creek Comfort Zone Carry System which includes Hydrofil nylon knit on backpanel and shoulder straps, molded torso adjustments, and spinal and lumbar pads. Parallel internal frame. Easy packing panel load design with internal cinch straps. Lockable zippers. Detachable daypack. Converts into suitcase. 26x15x9" 4700 cu. in. Black, Evergreen, or Blue. $20 discount with rail pass. $205

Continental Journey
Carry-on size pack with internal frame suspension. Detachable front pack. Comfort zone padded shoulder straps and hip belt. Leather hand grip. Easy packing panel load design with internal cinch straps. Lockable zippers. Converts into suitcase. 21x15x9" 3900 cu. in. Black, Evergreen, or Blue. $10 discount with rail pass. $160

Security Items

Undercover Neckpouch
Ripstop nylon with a soft Cambrelle back. Three pockets. 5 1/4" x 6 1/2". Lifetime guarantee. Black or Tan. $10.50

Undercover Waistpouch
Ripstop nylon with a soft Cambrelle back. Two pockets. 4 3/4" x 12" with adjustable waistband. Lifetime guarantee. Black or Tan. $10.50

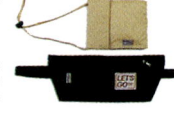

Travel Lock
Great for locking up your World or Continental Journey. Two-dial combination lock. $5.25

Hostelling Essentials

1997-8 Hostelling Membership
Cardholders receive priority and discounts at most domestic and international hostels.
Adult (ages 18-55) $25.00
Youth (under 18) $10.00
Senior (over 55) $15.00
Family (parent(s) with children under 16) $35.00

Sleepsack
Required at many hostels. Washable polyester/cotton. Durable and compact. $14.95

International Youth Hostel Guide
IYHG offers essential information concerning over 2500 European hostels. $10.95

Discounted Airfares

Discounted international and domestic fares for students, teachers, and travelers under 26. Purchase your 1997 International ID card and call 1-800-5-LETSGO for price quotes and reservations.

1998 International ID Cards

Provides discounts on airfares, tourist attractions and more. Includes basic accident and medical insurance.
International Student ID Card (ISIC) $20
International Teacher ID Card (ITIC) $20
International Youth ID Card (GO25) $20

When ordering an International ID Card, please include:
1. Proof of birthdate (copy of passport, birth certificate, or driver's license).
2. One picture (1.5" x 2") signed on the reverse side.
3. (ISIC/ITIC only) Proof of student/teacher status (letter from registrar or administrator, proof of tuition, or copy of student/faculty ID card. FULL-TIME only).

Publications and More

Let's Go Travel Guides—The Bible of the Budget Traveler
- USA, Europe, India and Nepal, Southeast Asia................$19.99
- Eastern Europe, France, Italy, Spain & Portugal $18.99
- Alaska & The Pacific Northwest, Australia, Britain & Ireland, California, Germany, Greece & Turkey, Israel & Egypt, Mexico, New Zealand $17.99
- Central America, Ecuador & The Galapagos Islands, Ireland, Austria & Switzerland $16.99
- London, New York, Paris, Rome, Washington, D.C. $14.99

Let's Go Map Guides
Fold out maps and up to 40 pages of text
Berlin, Boston, Chicago, London, Los Angeles, Madrid, New Orleans, New York, Paris, Rome, San Francisco, Washington D.C. $7.95

Michelin Maps
Know the country inside out! Great to accompany your Eurail pass—get 25% off with any Eurail purchase.
Europe, Poland, Czech/Slovak Republics, Greece, Germany, Scandinavia & Finland, Great Britain and Ireland, Germany/Austria/Benelux, Italy, France, Spain and Portugal $10.00

1-800-5-LETSGO
http://www.hsa.net/travel/letsgo.html

EURAIL PASSES 1998
WHY GO WITH LET'S GO?

- Get a Let's Go Travel Guide of your choice for $5.00 with the purchase of a Eurail pass.
- Free shipping—no handling fees!
- Discounted travel gear with every pass—$10.00 off the Continental Journey backpack or $20.00 off the World Journey backpack.
- We will find the best price available for your particular travel plans!

We Sell:

Eurailpass • Eurail Youthpass • Eurail Saverpass • Eurail Flexipass • Eurail Youth Flexipass • Eurail Saver Flexipass • Europass • Europass Youth • Euraildrive Pass • Europass Drive • European East Pass • Eurostar–the Channel Tunnel Train • Artesia amd Thalys High Speed Trains • Austrian Railpass • Benelux Tourrail Pass • Britrail Pass • Bulgarian Flexipass • Czech Flexipass • Finnrail Pass • France Railpass • France Rail 'n' Drive Pass • France Rail 'n' Fly Pass • France Fly Rail 'n' Drive Pass • Paris Visite Pass Exchange Voucher • German Railpass • Greek Flexi Rail 'n' Fly Pass • Hungarian Flexipass • Holland Railpass • Norwegian Railpass • Norwegian Fjord Excursion • Portuguese Railpass • Romanian Pass • Scanrail Pass • Scanrail 55+ Pass • Scanrail 'n' Drive • Spain Flexipass • Spain Rail 'n' Drive • Sweden Railpass • Swiss Pass • Swiss Flexipass • Swiss Pass • UKFrance Sampler • Best Western, IBIS, Mercure Hotels • Sofitel • Wunderhotels–Danubechecks

1998 EURAIL Prices*

Eurailpass: Unlimited travel in and between all 17 countries: Austria, Belgium, Denmark, Finland, France, Germany, Greece, Holland, Hungary, Italy, Luxembourg, Norway, Portugal, Republic of Ireland, Spain, Sweden and Switzerland.

Eurail Pass (First Class)
15 days $538
21 days $698
1 month $864
2 months $1224
3 months $1512

Eurail Saverpass (First Class, 2 or more people)
15 days $458
21 days $594
1 month $734
2 months $1040
3 months $1286

Eurail Youthpass (Second Class, passengers under 26)
15 days $376
21 days $489
1 month $605
2 months $857
3 months $1059

Eurail Flexipass: Travel by train on 10 or 15 days within 2 months in all 17 Eurail countries.

Eurail Flexipass (First Class)
10 days in 2 months $634
15 days in 2 months $836

Eurail Youth Flexipass (Second Class, passengers under 26)
10 days in 2 months $444
15 days in 2 months $585

Europass: Travel in the five Europass countries: France, Germany, Italy, Spain and Switzerland. Associate countries (Austria and Hungary, Benelux, Greece, Portugal) and extra rail days (up to 10) may be added.

Europass (First Class, one passenger)
Any 5 days in 2 months (base fare) $316
Any 5 days in 2 months with 1 associate country (base fare) $376
Any 5 days in 2 months with 2 associate countries (base fare) $406
Any 5 days in 2 months with 3 associate countries (base fare) $426
Any 5 days in 2 months with 4 associate countries (base fare) $436
Each additional rail day (Max: 10; added to above base fares) $42

Europass (First Class, two passengers)
Any 5 days in 2 months (base fare) $253
Any 5 days in 2 months with 1 associate country (base fare) $301
Any 5 days in 2 months with 2 associate countries (base fare) $325
Any 5 days in 2 months with 3 associate countries (base fare) $341
Any 5 days in 2 months with 4 associate countries (base fare) $349
Each additional rail day (Max: 10; added to above base fares) $33.50

Europass Youth (Second Class, passengers under 26)
Any 5 days in 2 months (base fare) $210
Any 5 days in 2 months with 1 associate country (base fare) $255
Any 5 days in 2 months with 2 associate countries (base fare) $280
Any 5 days in 2 months with 3 associate countries (base fare) $295
Any 5 days in 2 months with 4 associate countries (base fare) $303
Each additional rail day (Max: 10; added to above base fares) $29

Pass Protection:
For an additional $10, insure any railpass against theft or loss.

Call for more information on the many other Eurail products.

*Rail prices are subject to change. Please call to verify price before ordering.

1-800-5-LETSGO
http://www.hsa.net/travel/letsgo.html

LET'S GO ORDER FORM

Last Name _____ First Name _____ Date of Birth _____

Street _____ *We cannot ship to Post Office Boxes*

City _____ State _____ Zip Code _____

Phone (very important) _____ Citizenship (Country) _____

School/College _____ Date of Travel _____

Description, Size	Color	Quantity	Unit Price	Total Price

Shipping and Handling

Eurail Passes do not factor into merchandise value.

Domestic 2-3 Weeks
Merchandise value under $30 ....$4
Merchandise value $30-$100 ....$6
Merchandise value over $100 ....$8

Domestic 2-3 Days
Merchandise value under $30 ....$14
Merchandise value $30-$100 ....$16
Merchandise value over $100 ....$18

Domestic Overnight
Merchandise value under $30 ....$24
Merchandise value $30-$100 ....$26
Merchandise value over $100 ....$28

All international shipping $30

Total Purchase Price _____
Shipping and Handling _____
MA Residents add 5% sales tax on gear and books _____
TOTAL _____

From which Let's Go Guide are you ordering? ☐ Europe ☐ USA ☐ Other _____

☐ **Mastercard**   ☐ **Visa**

Cardholder name: _____
Card number: _____
Expiration date: _____

Make check or money order payable to:
Let's Go Travel
17 Holyoke Street
Cambridge MA, 02138
(617) 495-9649

1-800-5-LETSGO
http://www.hsa.net/travel/letsgo.html

rides around the lake (*Serundfahrten;* 40min. ride 63AS, 60min. 90AS; children half-price). Water skiing, with **Sportland Mondsee,** Prielhofstr. 4 (tel. 40 77), costs 100AS per circuit, 80AS for two tries at the slalom course.

In the world of dry entertainment, Mondsee holds the **Musiktage,** an annual classical music festival in early September. (Tickets 200-450AS; for ticket information write by July 12 to Postfach 3, A-5310 Mondsee, call 22 70, or fax 35 44.) Every year Hugo von Hofmannsthal's 1922 morality play, **Jedermann,** is performed (in German) at the open-air **Freilichtbühne** theater every Saturday from mid-July to August. (Tickets 120-160AS; available at the Salzburger Sparkasse in Marktpl.)

■ St. Wolfgang

More than a thousand years ago, Wolfgang, the world-weary bishop of Regensburg, left the big city and set out for greener pastures in the Salzkammergut, finally stopping on the pacific shores of the Wolfgangsee (Abersee at the time). After performing several miracles, Wolfgang was canonized, and soon thereafter up to 70,000 disciples made pilgrimages to visit St. Wolfgang each year. The numbers haven't dropped since: the formerly hermetic village, St. Wolfgang (pop. 3000) is today arguably the most touristed lake resort in the Salzkammergut. Most visitors come for the legendary **Pilgrimage Church** on the Wolfgangsee, home of the famous Michael Pacher altar. Others see the **Schafberg,** a mountain peak offering the best vista of the lake region. They stay, however, for the idyllic landscape, the swimming, the hiking, and just plain good living. In winter, St. Wolfgang all but shuts down, getting some much-needed rest before the next onslaught of tourists arrives with the first bloom.

Orientation and Practical Information St. Wolfgang rests lazily on the shore of the Wolfgangsee, across the water from St. Gilgen. Access to St. Wolfgang is easiest **by car.** From **Vienna,** take Autobahn A1 west to Mondsee and then head south through St. Lorenz and Scharfling and on to St. Wolfgang. From **Salzburg,** take Rte. 158 east through Hof, Fuschl, and St. Gilgen. St. Wolfgang has no train station, but **buses** run every hour to **Bad Ischl** (46AS) and **Salzburg** (96AS; change at Strobl). A breezy option is the Wolfgangsee **ferry** (tel. 223 20), which runs to nearby St. Gilgen (40min., 52AS) and Strobe (20min., 38AS) and between St. Wolfgang's two ferry landings at St. Wolfgang Markt and the Schatbergbahnhof. (Runs mid-June to mid-Sept. 17 times per day, May to mid-June and mid-Sept. to Oct. 9 times per day, 8:15am-6:15pm. Day and week passes also available. Children half-price. Eurail passes valid.)

St. Wolfgang's main drag is its only drag—Pilgerstraße and Michael-Pacher-Straße collide and form a quasi-**pedestrian zone.** Automobiles are strictly prohibited from this thoroughfare most of the day—park in one of the lots at either end, or, to bypass the town, take the tunnel that cuts around downtown St. Wolfgang. The **bus** stop is at the end of the west tunnel entrance, outside the post office. To get to the **tourist office,** Pilgerstr. 28 (tel. 22 39; fax 22 39 81; email info@stwolfgang.gv.at; http://www.salzkammergut.at/wolfgangsee), make a left and walk a bit down Pilgerstr. Watch for the poorly marked green building on the left, labeled *Marktgemeindeamt.* The helpful, mutilingual office hands out oodles of information and reserves rooms for free. There's also a full-service **information kiosk** down the block by Hotel Peter, with a 24-hour **electric accommodations board.** (Main office open July-Aug. Mon.-Fri. 8am-6pm, Sat. 8am-noon; Sept.-Oct. Mon.-Fri. 8am-noon and 2-6pm, Sat. 8am-noon; Nov.-April Mon.-Fri. 8am-noon and 2-5pm, Sat. 9am-noon; May-June Mon.-Fri. 8am-noon and 1-6pm, Sat. 8am-noon. Kiosk open Mon.-Sat. 10am-9pm, Sun. 2-7pm.) **Currency exchange** is available at the kiosk (Mon.-Sat. 9am-7pm, Sun. 10am-7pm) and at Rieger Bank, Marktpl. 87 (tel. 28 07; open daily in summer 9am-8pm, in winter 9am-7pm) at hefty rates. There is an **ATM** at the Sparkasse in Marktpl. The **post office** at the bus station (tel. 22 01) will also change money.

(Open Mon.-Fri. 8am-noon and 2-6pm, Sat. 8-11am. Exchange open Mon.-Fri. 8am-5pm.) The **postal code** is A-5360. The **telephone code** is 06138.

Accommodations and Food Almost 2000 tourists troop through St. Wolfgang every sunny summer day. The tourist office's brochure features a canonical list of hotels, *Pensionen*, and private rooms. St. Wolfgang has no youth hostel, but **Haus am See**, Michael-Pacher-Str. 98 (tel. 22 24), offers 50 beds in a rambling old house, right on the lake, at hostel prices. From the tourist office, simply continue down the main road away from the post office (7min.) until you reach the east entrance of the tunnel; the happy Herr Brosch's Haus is just beyond, on the right. Look for a *Zimmer frei* banner. The sheets might not all match, but the gorgeous view and swimmable-shore access more than compensate. (Singles 150-280AS; doubles 360-550AS; 2-room quads 800-1000AS. Prices depend on balcony and view. Hall showers and toilets. Breakfast included. Parking available. Open May-Oct.) The best deal might be Haus Am See's renovated **boathouse**, with 10 beds in singles and doubles starting at 150AS. The rooms are primitive, but the balcony is literally over the lake and the boathouse has a large, well-kept grass area for sunning, picnicking, or barbecues. Herr Brosch will even let guests borrow his paddleboat and rowboat. Also check out **Gästehaus Raudaschl**, Deschbühel 41 (tel. 25 61), on the way to the major hiking paths. From the tourist office, continue down the main road, and turn left at Hotel Peter. Climb up the small hill, and the pension is on the left (5min.). This smaller *Pension* offers a private shower and private balcony in each of its seven well-furnished rooms. Watch for the stuffed animals that adorn the staircases. (Singles 250AS first night, then 210AS; doubles from 380-420AS. Breakfast included. Open May-Oct.)

Most of St. Wolfgang's restaurants and *Imbiße* price their wares very competitively. Try any of the snack shacks lining the main road, where almost nothing is above 45AS. *Konditoreien* also serve up a local specialty—*Schafbergkugeln* (23AS), named after the mountain. A variant of the *Mozartkugel*, the *Schafbergkugel* is a supersweet treat, but unlike the tiny *Mozartkugel*, this yummy-bomb is about the size of your fist. It probably tastes better, too, unless *your* hands are made from nuts and marzipan dipped in creamy milk chocolate. Pick one up at **Bäckerei Gandl,** Im Stöckl 84 (tel. 23 66; open daily 7am-7pm). Cheap pizzas roll out of **Pizzeria Julio,** Au 36 (tel. 31 57), on the hill above the east tunnel entrance near Haus am See. Pies range from 69AS for a cheese to 110AS for a seafood pizza. Pastas are 71 to 94AS. (Open daily 11am-11pm.) **Hauer's Imbißstube,** a self-service restaurant, lies near the kiosk on the main road and serves up Austrian standards for under 90AS (most entrees 50-70AS) inside or out. (Open daily 9am-5:30pm.)

Sights and Entertainment For St. Wolfgang's top attraction, follow the throngs to the **Wallfahrtskirche** (Pilgrimage Church) in the center of town. While the tiny chapel St. Wolfgang built here went up in smoke in the Great Fire of 1429, the present church honors Wolfie's sense of humility, with a single tower and arched arcades looking out onto the tranquil lake. Inside the church, however, the meek are swiftly disinherited: look no further than **Michael Pacher's altarpiece** for a taste of ecclesiastical grandeur and luxury. Completed by Pacher in 1480, the altarpiece has two pairs of altar wings—originally, the inner shrine was revealed only on Easter and Christmas. Fully closed, the altar displays scenes of a humble pilgrim's life. When the outer wings are opened, eight scenes in the life of Christ are revealed. The final pair of wings displays the Coronation of Mary, with Christ blessing his mother. Pacher's altar is almost overshadowed by the **Schwanthaler Altar,** in the middle of the church behind wrought-iron gates. Installed in 1676, the frenetic, high Baroque altar was originally made to replace Pacher's "obsolete" one, but the sculptor Thomas Schwanthaler bravely persuaded the abbot to leave Pacher's masterpiece alone. Together the two altars almost overwhelm the church—try not to miss the smaller treasures, like Schwanthaler's **Rosenkranzaltar** (Rose Garland Altar) in the Maria Chapel.

St. Wolfgang's other big sight is the **Schafbergbahn** (tel. 22 320), a romantic steam engine that laboriously ascends to the 1732m summit of Schafberg. The railway was built in 1892, and in 1964 Hollywood found it precious enough to deserve a cameo in *The Sound of Music*, with the children waving from the windows. From the top, dozens of trails unravel down the mountain, leading to several nearby towns, including St. Gilgen, Ried, and Falkenstein. Train tickets for the 40-minute ride run as steep as the mountain (ascent 140AS, halfway 110AS, round-trip 250AS), but luckily, Eurailpasses are valid. (Train runs May-Oct., every hr. 7:15am-6:40pm. Round-trip tickets discounted at 7:15 and 8:10am. Children half-price.) If you must pay full price, you might as well take advantage of the special deal offered by the **Berghotel Schafbergspitze** (tel. 22 32 18), a lovely mountain inn peeking over the Schafberg's steepest face. For 500AS per person, you get a round-trip ticket on the railway, a night's lodging, and breakfast. Reserve in advance.

Nature-lovers can love their momma here, too—the **lake** provides plenty of water-sport activities. If you like swimming, you can go off the deep end at **Strandbad Ried** (tel. 25 87; 40AS, children 20AS). Water skiing is available through **Stadler** (tel. (0663) 917 97 53), on the Seepromenade. One round costs 120AS; daredevils can try the water-ski jump. Rent **boats** at the beach on Robert-Stolz-Str. across from the tennis courts or in town at the landing near Marktpl. (Motor boats 30min. 90AS, 1hr. 150AS. Pedal boats 50AS, 90AS. Open in the summer daily 8am-7pm.)

Hiking the mountains at the lake's edge is another possibility. All trails are marked clearly and described in detail in the free, English *Info* brochure from the tourist office, which also sponsors guides. (July to mid-Sept. Thurs. at 9:30am. Hike free, return boat trip 52AS. Meet at the office. No registration necessary.)

▓ Hallstatt

Perched on the banks of the **Hallstätter See** in a valley surrounded on all sides by the sheer rocky cliffs of the Dachstein mountains, Hallstatt is—without the slightest exaggeration—**the most beautiful lakeside village in the world.** The tiny village of 1100 inhabitants seems to defy gravity, with medieval buildings clinging to the face of a stony slope. Over four millennia ago, a highly advanced Celtic culture thrived in Hallstatt, but they didn't come for the view—Hallstatt was a world-famous settlement back when Rome was still a village, thanks to its "white gold." The salt also helped to guarantee the preservation of Hallstatt's archaeological remains, so extensive that the pre-historical era in Celtic studies (800-400BC) is dubbed the "Hallstatt period." You may have to brave a bunch of tourists, but this place is well worth it.

Orientation and Practical Information Hallstatt stands poised on the Hallstätter See, a pristine emerald oasis at the southern tip of the Salzkammergut. The place's charm lies in its isolation and the fact that it hangs off a cliff—two things that make it a royal pain in the rear to access. If **driving** from Salzburg or the Salzkammergut towns, take Rte. 158 to Bad Ischl and then Rte. 145 toward Bad Aussee. After Bad Goisern, it's approximately 5km to the narrow road leading along the Hallstätter See into Hallstatt (watch for the signs). From Salzburg, the **bus** is the easiest and fastest option (148AS; via Bad Ischl). The main bus stop in Hallstatt is "Hallstatt-Lahrs" at the edge of downtown on Seestr., where you can catch a bus to nearby **Obertraun.** Hallstatt's main byway, **Seestraße,** hugs the lakeshore all through town.

Hallstatt's **train station** lies on the opposite bank of the lake from downtown and has no staffed office. All trains come from Attnang-Puchheim in the north or Stanach-Irnding in the south, so connections to major cities go through one of these two towns. Trains run to Attnang-Puchheim (110AS), to Bad Ischl (34AS), and Salzburg via Attnang-Puchheim (262 AS). After every train, there is a **ferry** across to town that waits for all the passengers from the train (20AS; last ferry 6:45pm). If you do happen to arrive later, stay on the train to the next stop (Obertraun) and take a taxi (170AS) or walk (5km) to downtown Hallstatt. After a brief, spectacular trip across the lake, the ferry terminates at Landungspl.; it leaves again, half an hour before the train departs. In town, there are strict limits on the number of cars. Ample day **parking** lots are available by the tunnels leading into town (free for those staying in Hallstatt). If you want to drive through Hallstatt on the narrow road deluged with pedestrians, beware that two electronic gates pose further obstacles daily 10am to 6pm. A gate pass (available only to those staying in town) is required to open the gates. You can park your car at the lot outside of the gate, walk into town to your *Pension* or hotel, obtain a pass, and fetch your car later.

The **tourist office** *(Tourismusbüro)*, in the Kultur- und Kongresshaus at Seestr. 169 (tel. 82 08; fax 83 52), finds vacancies among the plentiful, cheap rooms for no fee. While the office sells a map for 10AS, you can pick up a free one at many souvenir kiosks. (Open July-Aug. Mon.-Fri. 8:30am-6pm, Sat. 10am-6pm, Sun. 10am-2pm; Sept.-June Mon.-Fri. 9am-noon and 1-5pm.) The **post office**, Seestr. 160, below the tourist office, offers the best **currency exchange** rates. (Open June 15-Sept. 15 Mon.-Fri. 8am-noon and 2-6pm, Sat. 8-10am; Sept. 16-June 14 Mon.-Fri. 8am-noon and 2-6pm. Exchange open Mon.-Fri. 8am-noon and 2-5pm.) There is an **ATM** next to the post office. The **telephone code** is 06134.

Accommodations and Food *Privatzimmer* at just-above-hostel prices speckle the town, and the tourist office will help you locate one for free. Wherever you tuck yourself in, don't forget to ask your host or hostess for Hallstatt's free **guest card**, which offers discounts on mountain lifts and sporting facilities in Hallstatt, Gosau, Obertraun, and Bad Goisern. Establishments may not always automatically give guests the guest card, but all provide it on request. The largest youth hostel is limited to groups, but **Gästehaus Zur Mühle**, Kirchenweg 36 (tel. 83 18), is a quasi-hostel with three- to 18-bed dorm rooms and lots of English-speaking backpackers. It's also close to the city center. From the tourist office, walk a few steps up the hill as if heading toward the Heimatmuseum, and swing right at the end of Platz. The hotel is through the little tunnel on the left, by the cascading waterfall. (Reception daily 8am-2pm and 4-10pm. Dorms 100AS. Showers and lockers included. Sheets 35AS. Breakfast 35AS. Lunch and dinner available at the restaurant downstairs.) **Frühstückspension Sarstein**, Gosaumühlstr. 13 (tel. 82 17), offers the prettiest accommodations in town, luring visitors with homey rooms, wonderful vistas of the lake and village, and a beachside lawn for sunning and swimming. Diving from your balcony, though tempting, is forbidden. From the tourist office, head toward the ferry dock and continue along the road nearest the lake (7-8min.), past the Pfarrkircher steps. (Dorms 190-210AS, with private bathroom and shower 250-300AS. Hall showers 10AS for 10min. Breakfast included.) Frau Sarstein's sister **Franziska Zimmerman** (tel. 83 09) lives up the block toward town on the other side of the street at #69 and offers similar (but fewer) accommodations. (Dorms 190-200AS. Showers 10AS. Breakfast included. Call ahead.) **Frühstückspension Seethaler**, Dr.-F.-Mortonweg 22 (tel. 84 21), sits on the hill near the tourist office. Head uphill, bear left, and follow the signs. All rooms have balconies with lake views. The breakfast room is adorned with innumerable antlers and furs. (Dorms 195-215AS, with private bathroom 280AS.) **Camping Klausner-Höll**, Lahnstr. 201 (tel. 83 22), is three blocks past the bus stop on Seestr., one street from the public beach. (Check-out noon; gate closed daily noon-2:30pm and 10pm-7am. 45AS plus 10AS tax, children under 14 25AS plus 5AS; tents 40AS; cars 30AS. Breakfast 100AS. Showers included. Laundry 60AS.)

Hallstatt has so many attractive restaurants that it can be difficult to decide among them. Many of them, however, will bore a hole through your wallet—be forewarned that at lakeside establishments you pay double for the view. **Gästehaus zur Mühle**, below the hostel, offers one of the best deals in town. Pizza (68-94AS) and pasta (68-88AS) are the specialties, although there is also a wide range of salads (54AS and up). Three kinds of canneloni (one vegetarian) are 88AS each. (Open daily 10am-2pm and 4-10pm.) Another local favorite is the **Gästehaus zum Weißen Lamm** (tel. 83 11), across from the Heimatmuseum. This restaurant has a "mountain man's cellar" with a mining motif. They offer two daily *menus* (90 and 120AS) for lunch and dinner, all with appetizer, main course, and dessert. (Open daily 11am-3pm and 5-10pm.) The recently opened **Amigos Tex-Mex Take-Away Restaurant,** Seestr. 156 (tel. 83 54), near the main bus stop at the edge of town, is a pit-stop for the guacamole-starved. Tuck away or take away tasty Tex-Mex treats like chicken quesadillas (70AS) and veggie cheeseburgers (42AS). Close your eyes, sip your margarita, and the Hallstättersee *may* start to resemble the Gulf of Mexico (if you have a *very* active imagination and *very* many margaritas). It's also Hallstatt's only late-night scene for the under-25 crowd. (Open daily 10am-2am.) For do-it-yourself meals, try Hallstatt's one grocery store, the **Konsum Market,** right by the main bus stop at the edge of town. (Open Mon.-Fri. 7:30am-12:30pm and 3-6:30pm, Sat. 7:30am-12:30pm and 2-5pm.)

Sights and Entertainment Hallstatt packs some heavy punches for tourists, despite its lean frame. The tourist office sells a 30AS English cultural guide, but you don't really need it—exploring the narrow, crooked streets is entertainment in itself. Depending on one's point of view, a visit to St. Michael's Chapel at the **Pfarrkirche** is macabre, poignant, or intrusive. Next to the chapel is the parish charnel house, filled with sundry skeletons. Walking into the creepy crypt is like stumbling onto an Indiana Jones set. Bones from the surrounding cemeteries are transferred here after 10 to 20 years because the graveyard is too small to accommodate all those who wish to rest there. (They're buried vertically as it is.) Each neatly placed skull is decorated with a flower (for females) or ivy (for males) and inscribed with the name of the deceased and the date of death. (Open May-Sept. daily 10am-6pm. In winter, call the Catholic church (tel. 82 79) for an appointment. 10AS.)

In the mid-19th century, Hallstatt was the site of an immense, incredibly well-preserved Iron Age archaeological find: a plethora of artifacts, a pauper's grave, and the well-maintained crypts of the ruling class—all circa 1000-500BC. The **Prähistorisches Museum** (Prehistoric Museum), across from the tourist office, exhibits some of these finds, as well as artifacts from the famous excavation site on Hallstatt's *Salzberg* (salt mountain) that give scientific proof of prehistoric salt-mining activity. Extensive salt-trading brought bronze ornaments from Northern Italy and amber from the east coast to this remote valley. (Open May-Sept. daily 10am-6pm, Oct.-April Thurs.-Tues. 10am-4pm, Wed. 2-4pm; 40AS, with guest card 35AS, students 20AS.) The price of admission also covers entrance to the **Heimatmuseum,** around the corner, with exhibits on the artifacts of daily living, such as clothes, kitchen utilities, and mining tools. It also maps the work of Dr. Franz Morton, who studied the development of local fauna. (Open May-Sept. daily 10am-6pm; Oct.-April 10am-4pm.)

The 2500-year-old **Salzbergwerke** is the oldest saltworks in the world, though these days tourists have replaced miners in the tunnels. The guided tours (1½hr., in English and German) lead you down a mining slide on a burlap sack and to an eerie lake deep inside the mountain. (Open June to mid-Sept. 9:30am-4:30pm; April-May and mid-Sept. to Oct. 9:30am-3pm. 135AS, with guest card 120AS; students 60AS; children under six 35AS.) To reach the salt mines, wander up the steep path near the Pfarrkirche to the top (1hr.) or take the **Salzbergbahn** at the southern edge of town (follow the black signs with the yellow eyes to the bottom of the train station). If walking from the tourist office, head away from the ferry dock along the lake, and turn right at the large bus circle. (June to mid-Sept. 9am-6pm; April-May and mid-Sept. to Oct. 9am-4:30pm. Last train runs 30min. before the last tour. 55AS, with guest card 45AS; round-trip 97AS, 85AS; children 65AS.)

Hallstatt offers some of the most spectacular day hikes in the Salzkammergut. The tourist office offers a 70AS English Dachstein hiking guide, detailing 38 hikes in the area, as well as a 35AS mountain bike trail map. Beyond the Salzbergwerk is the **Echental,** a valley carved out millennia ago by glaciers and now blazed with trails leading deep into the valley. Hardy (or foolhardy) hikers can attempt the **Gangsteig,** a slippery, nefarious primitive stairway carved onto the side of the cliff that makes up the valley's right wall—for experienced hikers only. Those without the gumption or experience to delve so deep into the forest can visit the **Waldbachstub waterfall** or the **Glacier Gardens** in the valley. These beautiful hills, nooks, and crannies are the scars left in the glacier's wake. The melting glacier water ("glacier-milk") was filled with so much sand and silt and rushed past at such a high velocity that it had the same effect as a sand-blaster, permanently scouring the rocks. To reach the Echental, head toward the Salzbergwerk and continue on either Malerweg or Echenweg; about 20 minutes later, a sign will post the area's layout. Gangstieg is about one hour up on the right, and the glacier gardens are about 40 minutes up on the left side, right before the mountain tunnel. Up above the town lies the 700-year old **Rudolfsturm** (Rudolph's tower). Perched on a mountain 855m above the village, the lonely tower guards the entrance to the Salzburg Valley.

For a view of the mountains from below rather than above, try the scenic boat trips around the lake (*Schiffrundfarten;* tel. 82 28), departing from either ferry landing (late June to mid-Sept. daily 10:30am-4:45pm. 50min. ride 70AS, 1½hr. 90AS). Winter visitors with guest cards can take advantage of Hallstatt's free **ski bus** (tel. 231 13), which runs to the Krippenstein and Dachstein-West Ski areas, leaving Hallstatt at 9:30, 10:55am, and 12:55pm; the last bus goes back at 4:05pm. The tourist office can provide a map for area skiing.

■ Near Hallstatt: Obertraun

At the end of the lake in Obertraun, the prodigious **Dachstein Ice Caves** (tel. (06131) 362) eloquently testifies to the geological hyperactivity that forged the region's natural beauty. (Open May to mid-Oct. daily 9am-5pm. Admission to either Giant Ice Cave or Mammoth Cave 85AS, children 40AS; combined "Gargantuan Experience" 125AS, 60AS.) To reach the caves from Hallstatt, catch the bus (25AS) at the stop near the lake, six minutes from the tourist office in the direction away from the ferry dock. Obertraun is also accessible by boat or train, but the bus runs most frequently and drops you right at the **Dachstein cable car** station. Ride the cable car up 1350m to "Schönbergalm." (Open daily 9am-5pm. Round-trip 165AS, children 105AS.) The **tourist office** stands in the Gemeindeamt, Obertraun 180 (tel. (06131) 351; open Mon.-Fri. 8am-noon and 2-6pm; in summer also Sat. 9am-noon). Obertraun's sparkling **Jugendherberge (HI)**, Winkl 26 (tel. (06131) 360), is a refuge for summer hikers and winter skiers alike. (Reception daily 8-9am and 5-7:30pm. Flexible 10pm curfew. Dorms 167AS first night, then 157AS; under 19 110AS. Breakfast 50AS.)

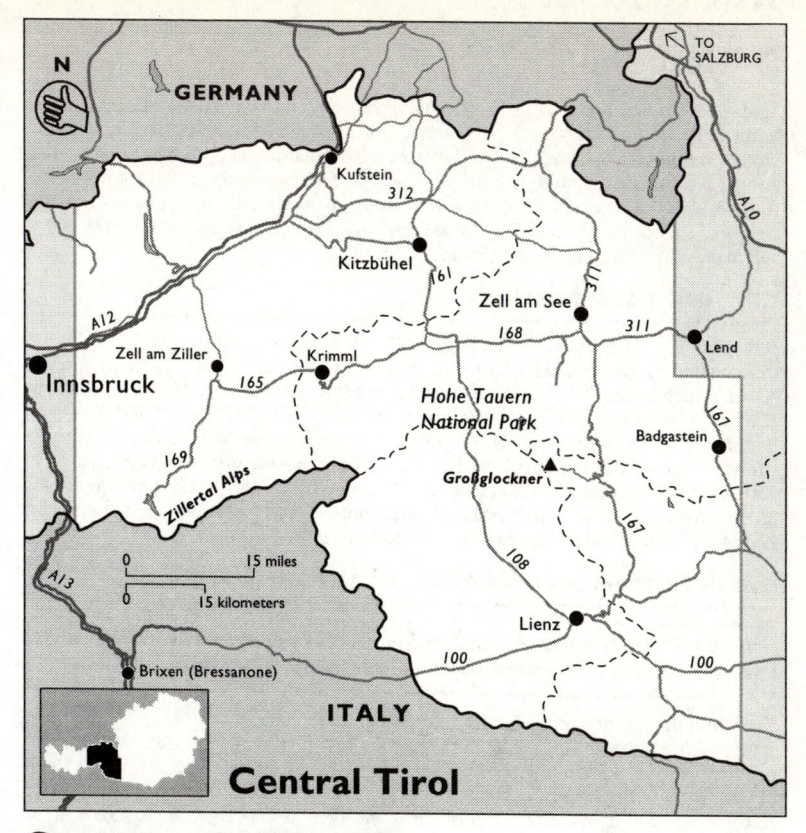

Central Tirol

The Central Tirol region is a curious amalgam—parts of Tirol, Salzburg, Carinthia, and East Tirol, wedged between Italy and Germany, have established a unique flavor defined by Alpine terrain, not provincial boundaries. Central Tirol enthralls visitors with breathtaking vistas of rugged mountains and sweeping valleys. The Zillertal Alps overwhelm with their enormity and grandeur; the sight of mountaintop rock and *névé* (partially compacted granular snow) is, simply stated, unforgettable. Jagged contours in the Kaisergebirge above St. Johann and Kufstein in the northwest fade slightly to the rounded shapes of the Kitzbühel Alps to the south, but the peaks rise again above the beautiful blue-green **Zeller See** at Zell am See. Mountainous crags create two of the most spectacular natural wonders in all of Europe; if you're within hours of Central Tirol, take a detour to the **Krimmler Wasserfälle** or the **Großglockner Straße** in the **Hohe Tauern National Park**—words don't do them justice.

East Tirol is the geopolitical oddity of the region, technically a semi-autonomous, wholly-owned subsidiary of the province of Tirol. The two provinces, however, share no common border. In the chaos following World War I, Italy stealthily snatched South Tirol, the connecting portion, away, leaving the province awkwardly divided by an Italian sliver. Although East Tirol resembles its mother province culturally and topographically, Easterners retain a powerful independent streak.

Kitzbühel

Since 1928, when Kitzbühel's first downhill run was built on the towering **Hahnenkamm** (1960m), the town has been a mecca for skiing pilgrims. Its "Ski Circus" consists of six different peaks, making it Austria's largest and most popular ski area. The annual international Hahnenkamm race (see p. 248) boasts the toughest course in the world and thus manages to attract amateurs, professionals, and spectators alike. Despite its popularity, Kitzbühel hasn't expanded much geographically—the town still makes do with only two traffic lights.

GETTING TO KITZBÜHEL

Kitzbühel lies on Rte. 161 north/south and at the east terminus of Rte. 170. By **car** from Salzburg, take Rte. 21 south to 312 west; at St. Johann in Tirol, switch to 161 south, which leads straight to Kitzbühel. From Innsbruck, take Autobahn A12 east; at Kramsach, switch to Rte. 171 north and then take Route 170 east to Kitzbühel. Several major rail lines converge on the town. The routes from Munich and Innsbruck funnel through Wörgl and into Kitzbühel before running on to Zell am See. Kitzbühel has two **train stations**, one at each side of the "U" formed by the tracks. From Salzburg, you arrive first at the **Hauptbahnhof;** from Innsbruck or Wörgl, at the **Hahnenkamm Bahnhof. Buses** stop next to both train stations.

ORIENTATION AND PRACTICAL INFORMATION

> In fall 1997, most telephone numbers in Kitzbühel will add a 6 to the beginning of the local number. If a listed number doesn't work, try starting it with a 6.

Kitzbühel sits prettily on the banks of the Kitzbüheler Ache River. Nearby, the warm, mud-bearing Schwarzsee proffers its luscious and mythically curative waters. The town cowers under a number of impressive peaks, including the Kitzbüheler Horn (1996m) and the Steinbergkogel (1971m). In the center of town, Kitzbühel's *Fußgängerzone* hosts multitudes of cafés and benches where the paparazzi lie in wait for strolling celebrities. To reach the *Fußgängerzone* from the main train station, head straight out the front door down Bahnhofstr. and turn left at the main road. At the traffic light, turn right and follow the road uphill to the cobblestone *Fußgängerzone*. The city center is a maze of twisting streets; if you get confused, look for the *Zentrum* (center) signs to point you back to the middle of town.

Tourist Office: Hinterstadt 18 (tel. 21 55 or 22 72; fax 23 07), near the Rathaus in the *Fußgängerzone*. Free room reservation service; after hours, try the free telephone at the **electronic accommodations board** (operates daily 6am-10pm). Maps and English brochures are also available at the board. A small **bank** in the office exchanges money during the high season. Free 1hr. **city tours** in English start at the office in summer daily at 8:45am. From mid-July to mid-Aug. there's also a cultural tour Fri. at 9:15am. Open July-Sept. and mid-Dec. to late April Mon.-Fri. 8:30am-6:30pm, Sat. 8:30am-noon and 4-6pm, Sun. 10am-noon and 4-6pm; Oct. to mid-Dec. and late April to June Mon.-Fri. 8:30am-12:30pm and 2:30-6pm.

Budget Travel: Reisebüro Eurotours (tel. 606; fax 60 66), across from the tourist office. Provides discounts on package tours and makes local room reservations for free. Exchanges currency at so-so rates. Open Mon.-Fri. 8:30am-noon and 3-6:30pm, Sat. 8:30am-noon and 4:30-6:30pm, Sun. 10am-noon.

Currency Exchange: All banks, travel agencies, and the post office. The post office and most banks have **ATMs** outside.

Trains: Hauptbahnhof (tel. 405 53 85) and **Hahnenkamm Bahnhof**. To: **Innsbruck** (10 per day, 1hr., 125AS), **Salzburg** (every hr., 3hr., 228AS), **Vienna** (7 per day, 6hr., 560AS), and **Zell am See** (every 30min., 1hr., 94AS).

Taxis: In front of the *Hauptbahnhof*, or call 661 50, 69 69, or 23 83.

ACCOMMODATIONS AND CAMPING ■ 247

Car Rental: Hertz, Josef-Pirchlstr. 24 (tel. 48 00; fax 721 44), at the traffic lights on the way into town from the main station. Open Mon.-Fri. 8am-noon and 2-6pm, Sat. 9am-noon. 20% discount with valid guest card. Visa, MC, AmEx.
Bike Rental: At the main train station. 150AS per day, with train ticket for that day 90AS. Mountain bikes 200AS, 160AS.
Parking: There are four lots in Kitzbühel: **Griesgasse, Pfarrau, Hahnenkamm,** and **Kitzbühlerhorn.** The latter 2 are next to the 2 major ski lifts. In winter a free park-and-ride service operates between the 4. Free parking at the Fleckalmbahn for the cable car (open 8am-6pm). Winter parking at Hahnekamm is 50AS per day.
Luggage Storage: At both stations. Open daily 6:30am-10:30pm. 30AS.
Emergencies: Police, tel. 133. **Fire,** tel. 122. **Red Cross Ambulance Service,** Wagnerstr. 18 (tel. 40 11). **Medical,** tel. 144.
Ski Conditions: tel. 181 (German) or 182 (English).
Post Office: Josef-Pirchlstr. 11 (tel. 27 12), between the stoplight and the *Fußgängerzone*. Bus schedules, fax, and an expensive self-serve copier inside. Open Mon.-Fri. 8am-noon and 2-6pm, Sat. 8-11am. **Currency exchange** open Mon.-Fri. 8am-noon and 4-5pm. **Postal code:** A-6370.
Telephone Code: 05356.

ACCOMMODATIONS AND CAMPING

Kitzbühel has almost as many guest beds (7445) as inhabitants (8000), but the only youth hostel is far from town and restricted to groups. Pricey hotels with fancy pastel facades dominate the town center. They offer enticing views, but the prices will also take your breath away. Austrians claim that in Kitzbühel, you pay German prices for German comfort (read: twice the price, half the comfort). Rooms during the summer generally run 200 to 300AS per person; expect to shell out an extra 100AS during the winter. The Hahnenkamm Ski Competition in January creates a bed shortage so great that most residents are willing to vacate their homes and rent them to visitors. Wherever you stay, be sure to ask for your **guest card** upon registration—it entitles you to discounts on all sorts of town facilities and local attractions.

Hotel Kaiser, Bahnhofstr. 2 (tel. 47 08 or 47 09), down the street from the main station. The native English-speaking owner and staff, all former backpackers, are happy to greet road-weary travelers. Terrace and an inexpensive bar. Singles with bathroom 250AS; doubles with bathroom 400AS. Nov.-Dec. brings a special deal for backpackers looking for work in the area: 120AS per person for a 4-bed dorm, plus free career advice from those who've done it before. Laundry facilities 50AS (wash and dry). Parking available. Visa, MC, AmEx, DC.

Pension Hörl, Josef-Pirchlstr. 60 (tel. 631 34). From the main station, take a left after Hotel Kaiser; Pension Hörl will be on the left. Quiet and unassuming, with simple rooms and reasonable rates. If they don't have a free bed, they'll try to put you up at their nearby **Gästehaus Hörl** (Bahnhofstr. 8). 180-220AS per person, with private shower 190-260AS. Add 40AS in winter. Breakfast included. English spoken.

Pension Neuhaus "Motorbike," Franz-Reichstr. 23 (tel. 22 00). Facing the tourist office, walk through the archway to the left and follow Franz-Reichstr. on the right (look for Wienerwald). The *Pension* is on the left, enticingly close to the chairlift. Its name is not capriciously chosen—the English-speaking proprietors here *really* like motorcycles, as the interior of the relaxed bar attests. Sporting chic Kawasakis, the chopper crowd is more hubris than Harley. Rooms house up to 6 people. 200-300AS per person. Winter 300-400AS. Breakfast included.

Camping Schwarzsee, Reitherstr. 24 (tel. 28 06; fax 44 79 30). Train: "Schwarzsee" (one stop past "Hahnenkamm" coming from the main train station) and walk toward the lake. If you're up for the walk, turn right at the tourist office and pass under the archway. Bear right at the Wienerwald up Franz-Reischstr., which becomes Schwarzseestr. and leads to the lake, or follow the signs from Franz-Reichstr. to the *Waldweg zum See* (forest path to the lake) for a more scenic route. 85AS, ages 2-12 65AS, under 2 free; guest tax 6AS; tents 92AS; caravans 90-100AS; dogs 40AS. Aug. 16-June 76AS per person, all other prices the same.

CENTRAL TIROL

FOOD

Although many of Kitzbühel's restaurants prepare gourmet gastronomy at astronomic prices, more affordable establishments pepper the *Fußgängerzone* and surrounding area. Check the prices before you sit down to eat.

- **Huberbräu-Stüberl,** Vorderstadt 18 (tel. 56 77). Located smack in the center of town, Huberbräu offers high-quality traditional cuisine at comparably low prices, making it a local hangout. Besides their *Wiener Schnitzel* (98AS) or *pizza margherita* (65AS), check out the incredibly filling *prix fixe* menu—soup, entree, potato, and dessert for 90AS. Open daily 8am-midnight.
- **Café-Restaurant Prima,** Bichlstr. 22 (tel. 38 85), on the second floor. Inexpensive meals on a sunny patio with an eye-boggling vista of the mountains. This self-serve eatery chain has a wide selection of food, including spaghetti (60AS), *Wiener Schnitzel* (75AS), and salad. Open daily 9am-10pm.
- **La Fonda,** Hinterstadt 13 (tel. 736 73). A Tex-Mex joint deep in the heart of Kitzbühel, down the road from the tourist office. Serves cheap, snack-style meals like hamburgers, nachos, Texas spare ribs, and potato skins. The Tirol-Mex tacos don't taste quite like the ones they make in Texas, but you can afford to try them anyway—nothing on the menu is over 80AS. Open daily noon-11pm.

Markets

- **SPAR Markt,** Bichlstr. 22 (tel. 50 91), on the corner of Ehreng. and Bichlstr. Open Mon.-Fri. 8am-6:30pm, Sat. 7:30am-1pm.
- **Billa Markt,** Hammerschmiedstr. 3 (tel. 42 54), next to Hotel Hummer. Open Mon.-Wed. 8am-7pm, Thurs. 7:30am-7pm, Fri. 7:30am-7:30pm, Sat. 7:30am-5pm.

SKIING, SIGHTS, AND ENTERTAINMENT

Few visitors to Kitzbühel remain at ground level for long. The Kitzbühel **ski area,** jovially dubbed "Ski Circus," is simply one of the best in the world. Site of the first ski championships in 1894, the range challenges skiers and hikers with an ever-ascending network of lifts, runs, and trails. These very mountains honed the childhood skills of Olympic great Toni Sailer; bow before you ascend. Since 1931, Kitzbühel has hosted the true *crème de la crème* during the **Hahnenkamm Ski Competition,** part of the annual World Cup. The competition turns the town into an electric 24-hour party for seven days straight. Entry tickets are available at the gate.

Amateurs, however, can also partake of Kitzbühel's skiing. The best deal is the new **Kitzbüheler Alpen SkiPass,** which gives access to 260 lifts in 22 villages (1990AS, children 995AS; good for any 6 days of the ski season). A one-day ski pass (385-410AS, children 205-330AS) grants you free passage on 64 lifts and the shuttle buses that connect them. Lift ticket prices drop after the first day. You can purchase passes at any of the lifts or at the Kurhaus Aquarena (pool, sauna, solarium). You can **rent skis** at the Hahnenkamm lift or from virtually any sports shop in the area. Try **Kitzsport Schlechter,** Jochbergerstr. 7 (tel. 22 04 11; open Mon.-Fri. 8:30am-noon and 2:30-6pm, Sat. 8:30am-12:30pm). Downhill equipment rental runs 180-350AS per day; lessons cost 500AS per day, snowboards 270-380AS per day. Ask at the tourist office about prefabricated **ski packages:** one week of lodging, ski passes, and instruction (available right before Christmas and after Easter). The rock-bottom rate for a week-long package without instruction is 3900AS.

For summer visitors, an extensive network of 70 **hiking trails** snakes up the mountains surrounding Kitzbühel. The tourist office provides maps with suggestions in English, but some of the best views are from the Kampenweg and Hochetzkogel trails. Most are accessible by Bichalm bus (26AS, with guest card 20AS), which leaves from the Hahnenkamm parking lot (every hr. 8am-5:10pm) or the Hahnenkammbahn (8am-5:30pm, 160AS up or round-trip, with guest card 140AS, children 80AS; half-price to go down only). You might also consider climbing up yourself (about 2hr. of varying terrain). At the top are two cafeteria-style restaurants and the free **Bergbahn Museum Hahnenkamm.** Historical information on the cable car pales in

SKIING, SIGHTS, AND ENTERTAINMENT ■ 249

comparison to video clips of past Hahnenkamm races and a larger-than-life skier into which you insert 10AS and climb inside. Assume the tuck position, look through the viewer, and experience three minutes of a breathtaking virtual run down the Hahnenkamm. The **Kitzbüheler Hornbahn lift** ascends to the **Alpenblumengarten**, where more than 120 different types of Alpine flowers blossom each spring. (Open late-May to mid-Oct.; cable car 80AS per section; gondola 120AS, with guest card 105AS, children 80AS.) The smaller **Gaisberg, Resterhöhe**, and **Streiteck** lifts also run in the summer. A three-day **summer holiday pass** is valid for unlimited use of all cable cars, free Bichalm bus service, and Aquarena pool entrance (340AS, children 170AS; for local buses as well 450AS, 225AS). Guest card holders can take advantage of the tourist office's *wunderbar* **mountain-hiking program**. The guided hikes (3-5hr.) cover over 100 routes. Each day guides Pepi, Klaus, and Madeleine lead an easy hike and a moderate hike. (Mid-May to mid-Oct. Mon.-Fri. at 8:45am from the tourist office; call ahead for weekend hikes (min. 5 people). Free, but you pay for any cable car rides.) Former Olympic ski champion Ernst Hinterseer (tel. 629 20) leads hikes down the Streif downhill course by request. **Mountain bike trails** also abound; rent a bike from **Stanger Radsport**, Josef-Pirchlstr. 42 (tel. 25 49), for 250AS per day. (Open Mon.-Fri. 8am-noon and 1-6pm, Sat. 9am-noon.) A booklet detailing bike paths through the Kitzbüheler and other Alps is available at the tourist office (54AS).

Back down at lake level, the **Schwarzsee** (Black Lake), 2.5km northwest of Kitzbühel, is famed for its healing mud packs. Float in the deep blue water and look at the snow-capped mountains high above. (Open daily 7am-8pm. 45AS, with guest card 40AS, children 12AS; discounts after 1pm; more discounts after 5pm. Electric boats 80AS for 30min., 150AS for 1hr.; rowboats 45AS, 85AS.) To get to the Schwarzsee, follow the directions to Camping Schwarzsee above.

Kitzbühel's stark and somber church steeples dominate the town's diminutive skyline. The **Pfarrkirche** and the **Liebfrauenkirche** (Church of Our Lady) lie in an ivy-enclosed courtyard on the holy hill, surrounded by a beautiful cemetery. Between the churches stands the **Ölberg Chapel**, dating from 1450, with frescoes from the late 1500s. The town built its **fountain** in the Hinterstadt to mark its 700th anniversary in 1971. The local **Heimatmuseum**, Hinterstadt 34, stocks its wares in Kitzbühel's oldest house, which dates from the 12th century. Its three floors house instruments both rustic and rusty, including prehistoric European mining equipment and the first metal bobsled. (Open Mon.-Sat. 9am-noon. 30AS, with guest card 25AS, children 5AS.)

Eclecticism reigns at the *gratis* music concerts during July and August; the repertoire runs the gamut from local folk harpists to brass Sousa bands. Check for signs posted around town, or call the tourist office for the identity of the day's performers. (Every Fri. at 8:30pm, weather permitting, in the center of town.) **Casino Kitzbühel** is near the tourist office. Go on, raise the stakes—you've got to finance that lift ticket for tomorrow. (Open daily July-Sept. 7pm-late. Mon. ladies' night: free glass of champagne; Tues. men's night: free glass of beer. No cover. 18 or older. Semi-formal.) At the end of July, the **Austrian Open** Men's Tennis Championships come to town, frequently drawing such athletes as Michael Stich and Goran Ivanesivic to the Kitzbühel Tennis Club. Call 33 25 or fax 661 25 for ticket information.

THE ZILLERTAL ALPS

The Zillertal (Ziller River Valley) Alps are a popular destination for Austrians seeking a weekend escape from camera-clicking foreign hordes. Keeping international tourism to a minimum, the Zillertal's residents have defiantly crafted a mountainside paradise for locals to relish. Transportation in the region is simple and convenient, thanks to the **Zillertalbahn** (better known by its nickname, the **Z-bahn**), an efficient network of private buses and trains connecting all the villages (tel. (052) 244 606; railpasses not valid). This line would make the Swiss proud; it arrives late *at most* twice per year. The starting point is **Jenbach**, and the route's southern terminus is

Mayrhofen (round-trip 118AS). You can reach Jenbach from Innsbruck (30min., 60AS, Eurailpass valid). The Z-bahn has two types of trains, the **Dampfzug** and the **Triebwagen**. The Dampfzug is an old, red steam train, targeted at tourists; it costs twice as much and moves half as fast. Less romantic is the Z-bahn's bus line, which runs through the towns. The Triebwagen and the Z-bahn Autobus have the same rates, and one or the other leaves daily every hour from 6am to 8pm.

In the Zillertal, skiing reigns supreme. If you plan to ski in the area for more than three days, the most economical choice is the **Zillertal Super Skipass** (tel. 716 50), available at any valley lift station and valid on all of the area's 151 lifts (4 days 1210AS, 7 days 1860AS, 10 days 2450AS, discounts for children). The cost of the lift ticket includes unlimited use of the Zillertalbahn transportation network. The Zillertal Alps also have some of the most glorious **hiking** in western Austria—the region claims more footpaths than roads and more Alpine guides than police officers. The popular four-out-of-six-day **Z-Hiking Ticket** is valid on all lift stations in the Zillertal, including Zell am Ziller, Fügen, Mayrhofen, Gerlos, and Hintertux (360AS, children ride free with the purchase of 2 regular tickets; 590AS for unlimited local transportation as well). Procure passes at any lift or at the railway stations in Zell am Ziller and Mayrhofen. When strolling around the mountain paths, be especially careful where you place your feet—don't dislodge any stones into the **Wetter See** (Weather Lake), under the shadow of Mount Gerlos. According to local lore, anyone who throws a rock into its waters will be pummeled by torrential thunderstorms, hail, and winds.

■ Zell am Ziller

Twenty kilometers south of Jenbach and deep in the Ziller valley rests the quiet resort town of Zell am Ziller. Billing itself as the "second smallest community in Tirol," it features neither gilt palaces nor Golden Arches and is in many ways just another of the Zillertal's many ski villages—a few restaurants, some quaint cottages, and a cable car or two. However, thanks to the *Gauderfest* and the Paragliding World Championships, Zell am Ziller packs a bit more heat than your average Alpine village. Founded by monks in the second half of the 8th century, Zell soon fell to materialism in the 1600s when it became a flourishing gold-mining town. Its current riches, however, are its untarnished natural beauty and quiet elegance.

Orientation and Practical Information Zell stands at the south end of the Zillertal, between Jenbach and Mayrhofen. Those traveling by train should get off at Jenbach and switch to the **Zillertalbahn (Z-bahn)** train or bus (tel. 22 11; Jenbach to Zell am Ziller 51AS; see **The Zillertal Alps** above for more information), which leaves from the front of the train station. Z-bahn trains and buses leave every hour for Jenbach or Mayrhofen. Most railpasses are not valid in this region. Zell am Ziller basically has one main street. To reach it, head right out of the train station onto Bahnhofstr. and continue until the street ends at Dorfpl. at the center of town. The intersecting street is Zell's main drag, called Gerlosstr. to the right and Unterdorfstr. to the left. The town **tourist office** is at Dorfpl. 3a (tel. 22 81; fax 22 81 80; email tourist.info.zell@netway.at; http://www.tiscover.com/zell). From the rail station, head right along Bahnhofstr. and turn right at the end. The office is on your left, just before the rail tracks. Pick up a town map, skiing information, and a *Frühstückspension* list if you want to track down a room on your own, although the staff will make reservations for free. (Open May-Nov. Mon.-Fri. 8:30am-12:30pm and 2:30-6pm, Sat. 9am-noon and 4-6pm; Dec.-April Mon.-Fri. 8am-noon and 2-6pm, Sat. 9am-noon and 4-6pm.) **Christophorus Reisen**, Bahnhofstr. 2 (tel. 25 20), handles all **budget travel** concerns. Banks offer the best rates for **currency exchange** (open Mon.-Fri. 8am-noon and 2-5pm), and most have 24-hour **ATMs**. For a **taxi**, call 26 25, 23 45, or 22 55. **Rent bikes** and **store luggage** (30AS) at the train station. In an **emergency**, call 22 12. The **post office** (tel. 23 33) is at Unterdorf 2. (Open July-Sept. Mon.-Fri. 8am-noon and 2-6pm, Sat. 9-11am; mid-Dec. to mid-March Mon.-Fri. 8am-noon and 2-6pm.) The **postal code** is A-6280. The **telephone code** is 05282.

Accommodations and Food With two guest beds available for every resident, Zell has no shortage of lodgings. To reach **Haus Huditz,** Karl-Platzer-Weg 1 (tel. 22 28), cross the rail tracks by the tourist office and continue onto Gerlosstr.; bear left onto Gauderg. (at the *Mode Journal* building) and look for Karl-Platzer-Weg on the left (10min.). The owner provides beverages, conversation *(auf Deutsch)*, and luscious down comforters. Spread out in the huge terraced rooms. (Reception daily 8am-noon and 1-10pm. 190AS per person first night, then 170AS. Winter 200AS. 7-min. shower tokens 15AS. Breakfast included.) **Camping Hofer,** Gerlosstr. 33 (tel. 22 48), sports hot showers, laundry machines, a market across the street, evening barbecues, and free bike tours and weekly hikes for campers. (Summer high season 50-55AS per person; in winter 55-60AS. 60-80AS per campsite. Off season: 1200-1300AS for 2 people for 1 week. Guest tax 12AS.)

When you stop for a bite to eat, savor some of the local specialties. **Gasthof Kirchenwirt,** Dorfpl. 18 (tel. 22 80) serves up *Zillertaler Kasrahmspätzln*, doughy noodles cooked with onions and garnished with cheese, for 80AS. (Open daily 8am-2pm and 6-9pm.) A traditional summer dish is the *Scheiterhaufen*, a monstrous mixture of rolls, apples, eggs, milk, lemon, cinnamon, sugar, butter, and raisins, drizzled with rum. *Zillertaler Krapfen* are sweet, heavy doughnuts, available in every bakery. All sorts of red meat outlets flank **Dorfplatz.** Check out the **SB Restaurant Zeller Stuben,** Unterdorf 12 (tel. 22 71), for cheap food, including self-service half-chickens (80AS) and *gulaschsuppe* (35AS). The sit-down restaurant upstairs features five daily *menus* including soup, entree, and dessert for 105-160AS. Children's and vegetarian menus are available. (Open daily 11am-9pm.) Cap off dinner with a decadent visit to **Café-Konditorei Gredler,** Unterdorf 14 (tel. 24 89), where 1995 Confectioner of the Year Tobias Gredler whips up gorgeous desserts for patrons to enjoy on the riverside patio (strawberry torte 30AS). The local **SPAR Markt** is around the corner from the tourist office and across from the brewery. (Open Mon.-Fri. 7:30am-12:30pm and 2-6:30pm, Sat. 7:30am-1pm and 2-5pm.)

Skiing and Entertainment Zeller skiing comes in two packages: **day passes** for shorter visits, valid on the Kreuzjoch-Rosenalm and Gerlosstein-Sonnalm slopes (1 day 380AS, children 210AS; 2 days 650AS, 390AS; 3 days 915AS, 550AS); and **Super Skipasses** for longer visits (see **The Zillertal Alps,** p. 249). Single tickets are also available for non-skiers who tag along to watch. Obtain passes at the bottom of the **Kreuzjoch** (tel. 716 50), **Gerlosstein** (tel. 22 75), or **Ramsberg** (tel. 27 20) cable cars. The lifts are all open daily from 8:30am to 5pm. **Rent skis** at any of Zell's sporting goods stores. Try **Pendl Sport,** Gerlosstr. 3 (tel. 22 87; open Mon.-Fri. 8:30am-noon and 2:30-6pm, Sat. 8:30am-noon; Visa, MC) or **Ski School Lechner,** Gerlosstr. 7 (tel. 31 64; open Mon.-Fri. 8am-noon and 3-6pm, Sat. 9am-noon; Visa, MC). Skis cost 150-250AS per day and 750-1150AS per week, snowboards 250AS, 1250AS. **Summer skiing** is possible at the **Hintertux Glacier,** 15km south of Zell am Ziller and accessible by Z-bahn and BundesBus (1-day lift tickets 390AS, youth 330AS, children 260AS).

Register in any town hotel or *Pension* to get a **guest card,** which among other benefits snags you a free **hike** led by the tourist office (June-Sept.; register one day in advance at the office). Two of the three ski lifts in Zell's vicinity also offer **Alpine hiking:** the **Kreuzjochbahn** (tel. 71 65; open daily 8:30am-12:15pm and 1-4:45pm; round-trip 150AS, to mid-station 100AS) and the **Gerlossteinbahn** (tel. 227 511; open daily 8:30am-12:20pm and 1-5:10pm; round-trip 100AS). The cheapest **bike rentals** are at **Sb-Markt Hofer,** Gerlosstr. 30 (tel. 22 20), across from the campground (1 day 100AS, 3 days 120AS; mountain bike 170AS, 410AS). The **Paragliding World Championships** glide into Zell during the last week of June, when many a modern-day Icarus fills the skies. You can try too—tandem flights cost 700-1250AS. The term "take-out" will develop a whole new meaning when you trust your life to the gliding guides at **Pizza-Air,** Zelbergeben 4 (tel. 22 89; fax 228 94).

For a glimpse of Zell am Ziller's history, take a tour of the nearby **gold mine** (tel. 230 10; fax 230 14; open daily 9am-6pm; 130AS, children 65AS). For liquid gold, visit the town on the first Sunday in May for the **Gauderfest,** when the whole town gets sauced in a three-day celebration of cold, frothy beverages. The name is not derived from the German word *"Gaudi"* (fun) but from the farmer's estate that owns the local private brewery. The *Bräumeister's* vats, Tirol's oldest, concoct the beloved and rather potent Gauderbock for the occasion. The festival even has its own jingle: *"Gauderwürst und G'selchts mit Kraut, / hei, wia taut dösmunden, / und 10 Halbe Bockbier drauf, / mehr braucht's nit zum G'sundsein!"* ("Gauder sausage and smoked pork with sauerkraut, / Hey, how good it tastes, / and 10 pints of beer to go with it, / what more could you need for your health!") The rhyme is in near-incomprehensible Austrian dialect, but fear not—pronunciation deteriorates as the festivities wear on, so by midnight you'll blend in perfectly. The festival's highlight is the **Ranggeln,** traditional wrestling for the title of "Hogmoar." There are also animal fights (attended by a veterinary surgeon) and customary activities like the **Grasausläuten** (ringing bells in order to wake the grass up and make it grow). Revelry continues into the night with Tirolean folk singing and dancing. By June, at least half of the residents are sober enough to court the tourist trade.

THE HOHE TAUERN NATIONAL PARK

The enormous **Hohe Tauern range** is part of the Austrian Central Alps, comprising parts of Carinthia, Salzburg, and Tirol. This range, spanning about 10 towns across the south of Austria, boasts 246 glaciers and 304 mountains over 3000m. Expanses of ice, mountain pasture land with Alpine heaths of grass, and forested bulwarks partition the Ice-Age valleys. The region of rock and ice at the very heart of this Alpine landscape remains largely unspoiled, prompting conservationists to lobby early this century for the creation of a **national park.** In Salzburg and Carinthia, between 1958 and 1964, large tracts of mountain land were declared preserves, and on October 21, 1971, the provincial government leaders of Carinthia, Salzburg, and Tirol signed an agreement at Heiligenblut to "conserve for present and future generations the Hohe Tauern as a particularly impressive and varied region of the Austrian Alps." Thus designated, the Hohe Tauern National Park became the largest national park in all of Europe, officially enclosing 29 towns with a total of 60,000 residents. The Glocknergruppe, in the heart of the park, boasts the highest of the Hohe Tauern peaks and dazzling glaciers. A number of lakes crowd together amid the Glocknergruppe, including the Weißsee, the Tauernmoos See, and the Stausee. The spectacular **Großglockner Straße** runs north to south through this region, and the **Krimmler Wasserfälle** is in the far west.

The Hohe Tauern are accessible by **car, bus,** and, in certain parts, **train.** Schnellstr. 167 runs north to south, intersecting Schnellstr. 168, which runs west to Krimml. If you drive, make sure your brakes work, as there are multiple blind spots. Any imperfection could cause a premature ending to your Austrian holiday. Shift your car to low gear, drive slowly, brake occasionally, and *never* pass anyone, even a turtle-paced coal truck. The federal **BundesBus** travels the main arteries flowing through the Hohe Tauern. Bus #3230 (162AS) runs from Böckstein to Badgastein roughly once an hour, and bus #4094 (round-trip 116AS) runs from Zell am Ziller to Krimml five times each day. Buses also run from Zell am See to Krimml (12 per day, round-trip 190AS) and to Kaiser-Franz-Josefs-Höhe on the Großglockner Str. (2 per day July to early Sept; 1 per day mid-June to July and Sept. to mid-Oct.; round-trip 226AS). A rail line from Zell am See terminates at Krimml; **trains** run nine times per day in each direction (190AS round-trip). Another line runs south from Salzburg through Badgastein to Spittal an der Drau, with trains approximately every two hours. For general information about the park, contact Nationalparkverwaltung Hohe Tauern, 5741 Neukirchen Nr. 306, Austria (tel. (06565) 655 80; fax 65 58 18).

GROßGLOCKNER STRAßE ■ 253

Ess-terminate with Ess-treme Prejudice!

The story of the *ess-tsett* (ß) begins hundreds of years ago with the Goths, who devised a letter that efficiently did the work of a cumbersome double S with only one stroke, freeing more time for rape and plunder. As time passed, the letter gained fame and renown, featuring prominently in the works of such greats as Goethe and Schiller. But once a lovable "letter" as *echt*-ly Germanic as *Gemütlichkeit*, *Lederhosen*, and morbid obesity, the ß may soon be a fugitive in its own lands. It's the most visible victim of a recent series of language and spelling reforms concocted by representatives of all the German-speaking lands in Europe as a "systematic dismantling of anomalies" to be legally implemented in 1998. Thus far, opposition in Germany has been most vocal, with legal challenges cropping up from Weimar to Wiesbaden, and it is increasingly unlikely that the reforms will become law. In Austria and Switzerland, however, all systems appear set for go, and *Kinder* are already learning to spell ketchup *"Ketshup"* (other reforms standardize the spelling of assimilated foreign and eclectically spelled words). But don't panic! Austrian border guards will not be stripping this book from your pack and issuing fines for smuggling renegade "esses" just yet—the old spellings will be acceptable at least until 2005. Indeed, tourists in German-speaking lands will notice little difference—though the controversial standardization has apparently made Teutonic children better spellers (they now make 40% fewer mistakes on dictation tests), it has yet to make them less irritating to share hostels with.

■ Großglockner Straße

More than a million visitors annually brave the nausea-inducing trek to gaze and gawk at the stunningly beautiful **Großglockner Straße,** one of Austria's most popular attractions. Skirting the country's loftiest mountains, Bundesstraße 107 (its less catchy moniker) winds for 50km amid silent Alpine valleys, meadows of edelweiss, tumbling waterfalls, and a staggering glacier. Conjure up all the superlatives you know—they won't begin to do the road justice. Many of the high-mountain-sweeping-panorama-hairpin-turn-sports-car commercials (you thought German words were long) are filmed here. Switzerland and France used the Großglockner as an example when engineering their own mountain highways. Consider the Austrian work ethic that made it possible: in only five years (1930-35), during a global economic crisis, over 3000 workers constructed the mother-Bahn.

The trip up to Kaiser-Franz-Josefs-Höhe (the midway point of the Großglockner Straße) and Edelweißspitze (the highest point) takes you from the flora and fauna of Austria into Arctic-like environments. Although tours generally run from **Zell am See** or **Lienz** to the park, the highway is officially only the 6.4km stretch from **Bruck an der Großglockner** to **Heiligenblut.** Coming from Zell am See, you'll pass the **Alpine Nature Exhibit** (2300m) on the way up to Kaiser-Franz-Josefs-Höhe. Well-designed nature exhibits, a 25-minute movie (in German), and souvenirs less expensive than those at either of the other stops on the Großglockner Straße are some of the attractions. If you take the early bus up here in the summer, you'll have an hour to roam through the exhibits before catching the next bus. (Open daily 9am-5pm. Free. English headphones 20AS.) Once you reach Kaiser-Franz-Josefs-Höhe, you can gaze on Austria's highest peak, the **Großglockner** (3797m), and ride the **Gletscherbahn** funicular (tel. 25 02 or 22 88) to Austria's longest glacier, the **Pasterze.** (Funicular runs daily mid-May to Oct. every hr. 9:30am-5pm. Round-trip 95AS, children 50AS.) The **Gamsgrube Nature Trail** is a spectacular path (1½hr.) along the glacier, culminating in the roaring, pouring **Wasserfallwinkel** (2548m). Beware of patches of quicksand, unique to this part of the Alps.

The Großglockner Straße snakes through the **Hohe Tauern National Park.** The park was created to safeguard indigenous flora and fauna, including the stone pine, ibex, grouse, and the ubiquitous marmot. Before starting out on a hike, check with park officials. Many regions pose special problems, and some of the areas are strictly off-limits. Contact the **Regional Großglockner Association** (tel. (04824) 200 121) in Heiligenblut or the **Carinthian Park Center** (tel. (04825) 61 61) in little Dollach, 10km from Heiligenblut. (Offices open Mon.-Fri. 9am-5pm.) You can also hire a guide for hiking, rock and ice climbing, or ski touring. Pick up the brochures *Bergführer und Bergsteigerschulen* at any area tourist office. For information on sleeping in the regional Alpine huts that operate from mid-June to September, check out **Edelweißhütte's** roadside information kiosk, by the Edelweißspitze.

TRANSPORT ON THE GROßGLOCKNER

Total transport time on the Großglockner (with scenic rest stops in between) will take five hours of intense self-discipline as you attempt to resist the urge to snap blurry photos through moving bus windows. Many visitors come here for weeks and find that they're much happier dividing these five hours over several days. If you only have one day, resist the urge to disembark at any of the cutesy villages along the way; buses come so infrequently that you'll be stuck in Nöwheresdorf for hours. Your time is better spent at the magnificent Kaiser-Franz-Josefs-Höhe. Try to choose a clear day for your excursion—there's no need to pay the park entrance fee on a day when viewing conditions are utterly horrid.

Many visitors traverse the Großglockner Straße in a **tour bus** or **rental car,** neither of which are recommended for those with light pocketbooks or weak stomachs. The hairpin curves along the narrow roads are simply dizzying, and driving through the mountains incurs a hefty 350AS toll (a 400AS day pass grants access to the entire Hohe Tauern and includes return fare). Parking areas are strategically situated at lookout points along the road. The warmer weather from June to September creates the best driving conditions; be aware that the park forbids traffic from 10pm to 5am. Snowfalls, sometimes dumping up to 18m of heavy snow on the road, force the Großglockner to close entirely from November to April. For information on the road's condition (in German) call the information office (tel. (04824) 26 06), or the Heiligenblut (tel. (04824) 22 12) or Ferleiten toll booths (tel. (06546) 517).

Wise budget travelers choose **BundesBus.** Cashing in on the incredible demand for a cheap means of traveling the Großglockner Straße, the federally owned postal bus offers daily return trips from Zell am See or Lienz to Kaiser-Franz-Josefs-Höhe. The trips are sometimes accompanied by a pleasant narration, compliments of the bus driver. Watch in disbelief (and horror) as the driver dispenses educational facts about the Hohe Tauern (in German) and delivers and picks up mail along the road, all the while nonchalantly navigating the harrowing loops of the road. From the **north,** bus #3064 leaves for Kaiser-Franz-Josefs-Höhe from **Zell am See's** main bus station behind the post office, swinging by the stop directly across from the train station (round-trip 226AS). From the **south,** the odyssey begins in **Lienz** (185AS). Bus schedules shift often—buses run every morning and afternoon at least two to four times a day. Inquire at town bus stations for the latest schedules.

Travel to and from Lienz is even cheaper with the new 24-hour **Verkehrs Verbund Kärnten** card (80AS), which provides for unlimited **train** travel in one region of Carinthia and for discounts on buses. This bus discount will save you a bundle on the Großglockner, although you still have to pay the road entrance fee. Buy the red and yellow card at the Lienz train station (drivers can only give you the regular rate). Look also for discounts on travel to the valley village of Heiligenblut, a great base for exploring the Hohe Tauern. The round-trip ride from Heiligenblut to Franz-Josefs-Höhe generally runs about 74AS (Zell am See to Heiligenblut round-trip 135AS; Lienz to Heiligenblut 116AS).

For anyone planning a lengthy stay in the area, BundesBus also offers a **National Park Ticket,** good for 10 days of unlimited travel between Lienz, Heiligenblut, Hochtor, and other stops in the region and reduced fares on cable cars and other sights. The bus to the Krimmler Wasserfälle (see p. 258), the Gletscherbahn in Kaprun, and the Schmittenhöhebahnen in Zell am See (see p. 257) are all fare game (mid-June to mid-Oct.; 590AS, children 295AS). For further details, check the brochure *Der*

BundesBus ist WanderFreundlich (available at the bus stations in Lienz and Zell am See and the tourist offices in Lienz and Heiligenblut), which contains a schedule of bus departure times, destinations, maps, hiking paths, and other general information.

Zell am See

Surrounded by a ring of snow-capped mountains that collapse into a broad, pale turquoise lake, Zell am See (TSELL am ZAY) is one of Europe's most beautiful small towns. Zell am See's horizon is dominated by 30 "three-thousanders," that is, 30 peaks over 3000m tall, part of the Hohe Tauern National Park. Indeed, Zell is a fine base for exploring the park—buses and trains leave frequently for the Krimmler Wasserfälle and Kaiser-Franz-Josef Höhe on the breathtaking Großglockner Straße. For *Wanderlust*-filled tourists, the Alpine terrain around Zell offers numerous hiking and skiing challenges, while the cool blue lake calls to those who desire summer rest and relaxation. While making merry in the water, raise your eyes to the splendor of the Schmittenhöhe mountain just above or the 3203m Kitzsteinhorn to its southwest.

Real, Live People

In addition to Alpine ibex, chamois, and snow voles, the Hohe Tauern National Park is home to... people. The hilltop meadows and pastures that form the Alpine cultural landscape—the stone dikes, cattle paths, and farmsteads—are now considered integral components of the national park conservation areas. The golden vulture, once extinct in the Alps, is presently in recovery, but time continues to threaten the park's human traditions. How long the practice of *hoagaschten*—sitting together, telling stories—can remain unrushed by worldly concerns is anyone's guess.

GETTING TO ZELL AM SEE

Zell am See lies at the intersection of Rte. 311 from the north and Rte. 168 from the west. It's also accessible by Rte. 107 from the south, which runs into Rte. 311 north. From Salzburg, take Rte. 21 south to 312 south; at Lofer, switch to 311 south to Zell. The **train station** is at the intersection of Bahnhofstr. and Salzmannstr. on the waterfront. There are direct connections to most major Austrian cities. **BundesBuses** travel to nearby cities, to Krimml, and along the Großglockner Straße.

ORIENTATION AND PRACTICAL INFORMATION

Zell am See's relative proximity to the German border makes it a prime destination for international tourists. The town's accessibility to Salzburg and Innsbruck and its magnificent mountain slopes make it popular among Austrians, too. Go to the right and up the hill from the train station to reach the *Fußgängerzone*.

Tourist Office: Brucker Bundesstr. 1 (tel. 770; fax 720 34; email zell@gdd.at; http://zell.gold.at), within walking distance of the train station. From the station, take a right and follow the green "i" sign by the stairs on the left. A nifty computer prints information in German or English on accommodations, events, and services (machine operates daily 8am-midnight). The staff can't make reservations, but they will ferret out vacancies and bury you with brochures. Open July to mid-Sept. and mid-Dec. to March Mon.-Fri. 8am-6pm, Sat. 8am-noon and 4-6pm, Sun. 10am-noon; April-June and Sept. to mid-Dec. Mon.-Fri. 8am-noon and 2-6pm, Sat. 8am-noon.

Currency Exchange: At banks or the post office. **ATMs** at almost every bank.

Trains: The **train station** (tel. 73 21 43 57) is at the intersection of Bahnhofstr. and Salzmannstr. To: **Salzburg** (133AS), **Innsbruck** (8 per day, 1½-2hr., 228AS), **Vienna** (6 per day, 4¼hr., 500AS), and **Kitzbühel** (15 per day, 1hr., 94AS). Make international connections in Innsbruck or Salzburg.

THE HOHE TAUERN NATIONAL PARK

Buses: BundesBus station on Postpl., behind the post office and facing Gartenstr. Buy tickets from the driver.
Taxis: At the train station, or call 731 71, 733 59, or 575 51.
Car Rental: Hertz, Postpl. 3 (tel. 473 77), through the Eurotours Travel Agency.
Auto Repairs: ÖAMTC (Austrian Automobile and Touring Club), Loferer Bundesstr. (tel. 741 32). In case of a breakdown, dial 120.
Parking: Parking garage at the Kurcenter sport center past the post office.
Bike Rental: At the train station. 150AS per day, with Eurailpass 90AS.
Luggage Storage: At the train station. 30AS per piece. High-tech, 24hr. electronic lockers 30AS, with accommodations for both bags and skis.
AIDS Hotline: AIDS-Hilfe Außenberatungsstelle Zell am See, Saalfenderstr. 14 (tel. 20 10). Hotline open Thurs. 5-7pm.
Mountain Rescue: Bergrettung Zell am See (tel. 140).
Police: Bruckner Bundesstr. (tel. 737 01).
Post Office: Postpl. 4 (tel. 37 91). Open early July to mid-Sept. and late Dec. to March Mon.-Fri. 7:30am-6:30pm, Sat. 7:30-11am; mid-Sept. to late Dec. and April to early July Mon.-Fri. 7:30am-6:30pm, Sat. 7:30-10am. **Postal Code:** A-5700.
Telephone Code: 06542.

ACCOMMODATIONS AND CAMPING

Zell am See has more than its share of four-star hotels (and prices), but it has not forgotten the budget traveler. Many affordable accommodations roll out the red carpet for cost-conscious travelers. Ask for a **guest card,** which provides numerous discounts on activities throughout the city.

Haus der Jugend (HI), Seespitzstr. 13 (tel. 551 71 or 571 85; fax 571 854). Exit the back of the train station, turn right, and walk along the well-lit footpath beside the lake; at the end of the footpath, take a left onto Seespitzstr. (15min.). An amazing hostel on the lakefront. Large, immaculate rooms with showers, toilets, and lakeside terraces. Other goodies include a TV room with VCR, a pinball machine, and a snack shop in the reception area. Screaming school groups sometimes descend, so reserve ahead. 106 beds divided into doubles, quads, and 6-bed rooms. Throw down some plush carpet, hang a picture or two, and you'd be paying triple the price. Reception daily 7-9am and 4-10pm. Check-out 9am. Lockout noon-4pm. Curfew 10pm. Dorms 170AS first night, then 145AS. Tax for guests over 25 in summer 9.50AS, in winter 10.50AS. Breakfast and sheets included. Lunch and dinner each 60AS. 10AS refundable deposit for lockers. Key deposit 200AS. Open Dec.-Oct.

Pensione Sinilill (Andi's Inn), Thumersbacherstr. 65 (tel. 735 23). BundesBus (dir: Thumersbach Ort): "Krankenhaus" (19AS, last bus 7:14pm). Turn left upon exiting, walk about 200m, and look for a *Zimmer Frei* sign on the left side of the street. If you call ahead, Andi will pick you up. On the north shore of the lake. You'll think you died and went to heaven—paradise for backpackers and road-weary travelers. Andi's swimming trophies and stories, Joy's culinary and karaoke prowess, and the friendliest hound this side of the Großglockner make for an eminently homey atmosphere. 160-200AS per person. Camping in the front yard 50AS. Hall shower. Huge breakfast and late-night conversation over beer or hot tea included.

Camping Seecamp, Thumersbacherstr. 34 (tel. 21 15, fax 21 15 15), in Zell am See/Prielau, just down the road from Pension Sinilill. This campground is the Ritz-Carlton of sites. Situated on the lakefront, it offers phones, a restaurant, a café with terrace, and even a small shopping market. Reception 7am-noon and 2-10pm. Check-out 11am. 87AS per person, ages 2-15 45AS; tents 50AS; cars 30AS; trailers 100-120AS. Guest tax 9AS. Showers included. Visa, MC, AmEx.

FOOD

Here in the Pinzgau region, food is prepared to sustain the farmers during their strenuous labors. Try the *Brezensuppe* (a clear soup with cheese cubes) as an appetizer and then *Pinzgauer Kasnocken* (homemade noodles and cheese, topped with fried

ZELL AM SEE: SIGHTS AND ENTERTAINMENT ■ 257

onions and chives). Top it all off with *Lebkuchen Parfait* (spice cake parfait). *Blattlkrapfen* (deep-fried stuffed pancakes) and *Germnudeln* (noodles served with poppy seeds, butter, and sugar) have also survived generations of finicky eaters.

Ristorante Pizzeria Giuseppe, Kirchg. (tel. 23 73), in the *Fußgängerzone*. From the station walk past the church and continue straight. Plenty of vegetarian options. English menu. Pasta dishes 78-115AS; pizza 50-125AS; salads 55-89AS. Open Thurs.-Sun. 11:30am-2:30pm and 5-11pm. Visa, MC, AmEx, DC.

Fischrestaurant "Moby Dick," Kreuzg. 16 (tel. 33 20). The great white hope—with fries. Staggering double fishburger with potatoes and salad for only 85AS. Single fishburger 25AS. A few entrees feature fish straight from the lake. Most dishes 85-160AS. English menu available. Open Mon.-Fri. 9am-6pm, Sat. 8am-1pm.

Pizza Mann, Bruckner Bundesstr. 9 (tel. 473 57). Cheese out with the Mann's pies (85-102AS). Hang out with Zell's teenage population. May-June Thurs. and Fri. are a bargain traveler's dream: all-you-can-eat pizza for 85AS (starting at 7pm). Pasta 69-75AS; salads 30-70AS. Open daily 11am-midnight.

Crazy Daisy Restaurant, Bruckner Bundesstr. 10-12 (tel. 25 16 58). Mexican and American food very popular with young, English-speaking tourists. Jalapeño peppers 65AS; hamburgers 95AS; burritos 120AS; salads 40-60AS; "breath-killer garlic bread" 30AS. Children's portions available. Open daily 7pm-midnight.

Markets

SPAR Markt, Brucker Bundesstr. 4. Open Mon.-Fri. 8am-6:30pm, Sat. 7:30am-1pm.

Billa Markt, on Schulstr. near the Mozartstr. intersection. Open Mon.-Wed. 8am-7pm, Thurs. 7:30am-7pm, Fri. 7:30am-7:30pm, Sat. 7:30am-5pm.

SIGHTS AND ENTERTAINMENT

Zell's buildings are clustered in the valley of the broad, beautiful, blue **Zeller See.** Stroll around the lake on the well-kept path, or get your feet wet at one of the beaches: **Strandbad Zell am See,** near the center of town (walk toward the lake down Franz-Josef-Str.), complete with platform diving and a waterslide; **Strandbad Seespitz,** by the Haus der Jugend; or **Thumersbacher Strandbad** on the eastern shore. (All open late May to early Sept. daily 9am-7pm; 30-64AS, generally half-price after 5pm and free after 6pm.) **Boat tours** around the lake depart from and return to the Zell Esplanade, off Salzmannstr. along the river (9 per day 10am-5:30pm, 40min., 77AS, ages 6-14 40AS). One-way trips leave every half-hour (May to mid-Oct. 9am-6:45pm, 22AS, round-trip 38AS.) Purchase tickets on the boat. From the lake, the land rises swiftly into verdant peaks crowned with snow. You can conquer these local mountains on one of the town's five **cable-cars.** The BundesBus (dir.: Schmittenhöhebahn/Sonnenalmbahn Talstation) goes to the **Schmittenhöhebahn,** about two km north of town on Schmittenstr. (Mid-May to late-Oct. daily 8:30am-5pm. Ascent 175AS, children 90AS; round-trip 220AS, with guest card 200AS, children 110AS.) The **Sonnenalmbahn,** which travels half the height, is adjacent to the Schmittenhöhebahn. It connects to the **Sonnkogelbahn,** which rises to 1834m. (Early June to early Oct. daily 9am-5pm. Ascent 95AS for each lift, with guest card 85AS, children 50AS; round-trip 120AS, 110AS, 60AS.) The **Zeller Bergbahn** (780-1335m) is right in the center of town at the intersection of Schmittenstr. and Gartenstr. (Early June to late Sept. daily 9am-5pm. Ascent 105AS, with guest card 95AS, children 55AS. Round-trip 135AS, 125AS, 70AS.) In Kaprun, one town over and accessible by bus, the **Kitzsteinhorn** mountain (3203m) and its glacier offer **year-round skiing.** Get there as early as possible to avoid skiing in slush. Between June 10 and October 18, a day pass costs 330AS, children 210AS. Skis, boots, and poles run 215AS per day and snowboards 180AS per half-day; all are available at **Intersport Brundl** on the glacier (tel. (06547) 862 13 60). Skiing, of course, is not only limited to the summer. Every winter Zell am See transmogrifies into an Alpine ski resort. The new **Zell/Kaprun Ski Pass** covers both Zell am See and nearby Kaprun, and a free bus runs between the two every 20 to 30 minutes. (2 days 710-780AS, students 640-700AS, children 435-470AS.) One-day passes are available for Zell's Schmittenhöhe lift run (370-410AS, children 220-250AS). For a report in German of the ski conditions in the Schmittenhöhe area call 36 94; for the Kitzsteinhorn-Kaprun area call (06547) 84 44.

The Zell area provides many opportunities to work those expensive hiking boots. The Schmittenhöhe lift provides five brochures (with English translations) detailing **hikes** ranging from a leisurely stroll to masochistic torture. In the former category, the Erlebnisweg Höhenpromenade connects the top stations of the Schmittenhöhe and Sonnkogel lifts. Seventeen displays on history, nature, and ecology along the way exercise your mind. The brochure *Three Panorama Round Trips of the Schmittenhöhe,* available at any cable-car station, suggests other light hikes. Free guided hikes leave from the lower stations (July-Oct. Mon.-Fri.). Contact the **Schmittenhöhebahn Aktiengesellschaft** (tel. 36 91) or the lower station for details. For longer hikes, pick up a *Wanderplan* or consider the *Pinzgauer Spaziergang,* a leisurely but very long 10-hour hike. The trail begins at the upper terminal of the Schmittenhöhebahn and is marked as *"Alpenvereinsweg"* #19 or 719. A brochure is available. For **rafting** (480AS), **canyoning** (520AS), **paragliding** (800AS), **climbing** (420AS), or **mountain bike** information, contact **Adventure Service,** Steinerg. 9 (tel. 35 25; fax 42 80).

Finally, no visit to Zell would be complete without a glimpse of the toilet Franz Josef used when he visited the Schmittenhöhe. This artifact and four floors of equally eclectic exhibits (the largest pike ever caught in the lake, old gingerbread-making utensils, and hundreds of minerals) join the erstwhile royal throne in the entertaining **Heimatmuseum** within the Vogtturm (tower), Kreuzg. 2. The tower itself is more than 1000 years old, and its walls have cracked from the vibrations caused by cannon fire through the roof hatches. Zell's enemies of old, however, were probably unphased by the shots: the cannons were fired at oncoming thunderstorms, a practice believed to disperse the clouds. This process continued until the science of meteorology reached Zell sometime in the mid-19th century. (Open Mon.-Fri. 1-5pm, rainy days 11am-5pm, Sat. 10am-1pm. 20AS, ages 6-18 10AS. English guide available.)

NIGHTLIFE

If all the mountain exercise isn't enough, cut some serious rug at Zell's clubs. Those who want to get really hammered check out the local bar game **Nageln,** in which drinkers compete to see who can drive a nail into a tree stump first—with the *sharp* end of a hammer.

- **Bierstad'l,** Kircheng. 1 (tel. 470 90). 33 different brews in stock; you'll be on the floor by number 9. Dark beer enthusiasts must try the EKU 28, billed as the strongest beer in the world (0.3L 83AS). Open daily 8:30pm-3am.
- **Crazy Daisy's Bar,** Brucker Bundesstr. 10-12 (tel. 25 16 58). A predominantly English-speaking crowd floods into that crazy Daisy's every day during happy hour for their 2-for-1 beer deal. Open in summer daily 8pm-1am; in winter 4pm-1am. Happy hour in summer 8-10pm; in winter 4-6pm.
- **Pinzgauer Diele,** Kircheng. 3 (tel. 21 64). Two bars and a small dance area guaranteed to get you moving. A mostly under-25 crowd. Mixed drinks 50-95AS, beer 60-75AS. Cover 85AS. Open Wed.-Mon. 10pm-3am.

■ Near Zell am See: Krimml

Amid the splendor of Alpine crags in the Höhe Tauern National Park, Mother Nature cuts a truly extraordinary **waterfall** near Krimml in southwest Austria. This superlative cascade, the Krimm de la Krimm of falls, doesn't unleash the monstrous energy of Niagara or match the sheer height of Angel Falls—nevertheless, with three spectacular 140m cascades, the **Krimmler Wasserfälle** are the highest in Europe.

You can reach Krimml, the waterfall's base town, by bus or train. **Buses** are most convenient, since they drop you at the start of the path to the falls. Many run from **Zell am See** (12 per day, 1½hr., 190AS round-trip) and **Zell am Ziller** (5 per day,

1hr., 116AS round-trip). **Trains** come only from the east, through **Zell am See** (9 per day, 1½hr., 190AS round-trip, railpasses valid). The train station is 3km from the waterfall—either cross the street to catch the bus (19AS) to the falls or hike on the foot path. Stay on the left side of the brook and beware of stray cattle. Don't forget a raincoat and camera bag; the mist is very wet. In fact, to avoid hordes of tourists, come on a drizzly day—you'll get wet even if the sun is out, and the falls are spectacular in any weather. The lowest major cascade is visible a few meters past the entrance booth and to the left, but the well-maintained path will guide you through the scenic forest and its views. The highest point is 1½ hours up. (15AS, children 5AS.) For English brochures and pamphlets about the falls, try the Österreichischer Alpenverein's **tourist information booth** (tel. (06564) 72 12; fax 721 24) located along the path to the falls. This organization first built the path in 1900-1901 and currently provides mounds of hiking information and maintains the path's benches. (Open May-Oct. Mon.-Sat. 11am-4pm.) Munchies are available at the myriad **food stands** on the path, but prices are inflated. Stock up at the **Nah und Frisch** market down the main road in Krimml. The only significant attraction in Krimml is the waterfall, rendering the tourist office largely unnecessary. But if you insist, Krimml's main **tourist office** (tel. (06564) 239) is a short walk from the "Mautstelle Ort" bus stop. Head toward the church spire; the office is directly behind the church, adjacent to the post office. (Open Mon.-Fri. 9am-noon and 2:30-5pm.)

■ Lienz

Visitors to Lienz find themselves with nowhere to go but up—the bald, angry peaks of the Dolomites and the gentle, snow-capped summits of the Hohe Tauern mountains surround the town. Although the Alpine vista and the pink and yellow low-slung houses betray an Austrian heritage, the dusty cobblestone roads, hazy summer heat, and authentic pizzerias impart an Italian flair. Even the weather cooperates—the valley around Lienz registers about 2000 sunshine hours per year. Perhaps Lienz has been so doubly blessed because of its pervading religious ethos—residents leave flowers and burn candles in front of the crucifixes at traffic intersections, and niches in building facades hold statues of the Virgin Mary.

GETTING TO LIENZ

> Lienz is distinct from Linz, an industrial city in northeast Austria. Lienz is pronounced "LEE-ints"; Linz is known as Linz an der Donau. Make the distinction before boarding any trains.

Lienz lies at the conjunction of several highways: Rte. 108 from the northwest, 106 and 107 from the northeast, 100 from the west, and E66 from the east. By **car** from Salzburg, take Autobahn A-10 south to 311, and just before Zell am See switch to 107 south to Lienz. From Innsbruck, take Autobahn A-12 east to 169 south. At Zell am Ziller, switch to 165 east, and at Mittersill take 108 south to Lienz. The more direct route from Innsbruck passes through Italy. **Trains** arrive at the **Hauptbahnhof**, at Bahnhofpl. and connect directly to points all over Austria and indirectly to points elsewhere. **Buses** leave from the station in front of the *Hauptbahnhof* for destinations all over the region and throughout Austria. (Ticket window (tel. 670 67) open Mon.-Fri. 7:45-10am and 4-6:30pm, Sat. 7:45-10am.)

ORIENTATION AND PRACTICAL INFORMATION

Bordered on the south by the jagged Dolomites (the mountain range shared with Italy and Slovenia) and cut off from the rest of Tirol by the Alps, Lienz is the unofficial capital of **East Tirol** (Osttirol). The city is about three hours by train from Innsbruck or Salzburg but just 40 kilometers from the Italian border. The **Isel River**, which feeds into the Drau, splits the town.

Tourist Office: Tourismusverband, Europapl. (tel. 652 65; fax 652 652). From the train station, turn left onto Tirolerstr. and right onto Europapl. at the SPAR Markt. Courteous staff showers you with brochures (mostly in English) including a list of private accommodations, *Lienzer Dolomiten Preisliste.* The booklet *Information für unsere Gäste* lists area restaurants, hotels, emergency and service numbers, museum hours, and schedules for local cultural events. An electronic accommodations board works outside after hours. Free **city tours** (in German) leave the office Mon. and Fri. at 10am. National park tours are offered in summer Wed.-Thurs. Open July-Aug. and mid-Dec. to March Mon.-Fri. 8am-7pm, Sat. 9am-noon and 5-7pm, Sun. 10am-noon and 5-7pm; April-June and Sept. to mid-Dec. Mon.-Fri. 8am-noon and 2-6pm, Sat. 9am-noon. **Alpine Information,** Alpenvereinhaus, Franz-von-Defregger-Str. 11 (tel. 721 05). Open Fri. 8:30-11:30am and 3-6pm.

Currency Exchange: Best rates are in the **post office.** Exchange desk open Mon.-Fri. 8am-noon and 2-5pm. Also at the train station and banks. Try **Lienzer Sparkasse,** Johannespl. Open Mon.-Fri. 8am-noon and 2-4pm.

Trains: Hauptbahnhof, Bahnhofpl. (tel. 660 60). To: **Klagenfurt** (3 per day, 1¾hr., 216AS), **Innsbruck** (4 per day, 3-3½hr., 332AS), and the **Vienna Südbahnhof** (2 per day, 6hr., 560AS). Indirect connections (most through Innsbruck, Vienna, or the regional hub of Spittal-Millsätersee) to **Graz** (456AS), **Salzburg** (296AS), and **Zell am See** (186AS). Open daily 5am-11pm.

Taxi: tel. 640 64.

Parking: Free at Europapl. and in lots on Tinderstr. across from the train station.

Automobile Association: ÖAMTC, Tirolerstr. (tel. 633 32).

Bike Rental: At the train station. 150AS per day, with train ticket or Eurailpass 90AS. Mountain bike 200AS.

Luggage Storage: At the train station. 30AS per piece per day. Lockers 30AS.

Hospital: Emanuel-von-Hibler-Str. (tel. 606).

Emergencies: Police, Hauptpl. 5 (tel. 631 550, 626 00, or 133). **Fire,** tel. 122. **Mountain Rescue,** tel. 140. **Ambulance,** tel. 144 (also for water rescue).

Post Office: Boznerpl. 1 (tel. 66 88), on the corner of Hauptpl. across from the train station. Open Mon.-Fri. 8am-8pm, Sat. 8-11am. **Postal Code:** A-9900.

Telephone Code: 04852.

ACCOMMODATIONS AND CAMPING

Although the Lienz Youth Hostel closed in 1993, the town still offers affordable accommodations, most just beyond Hauptplatz and the town center. Most *Pensionen* and *Privatzimmer* have rooms that cost between 250 and 300AS per person.

Frühstückpension Gretl, Schweizerg. 32 (tel. 621 064; fax 619 79). From the train station, cross Tirolstr., bear left into Hauptpl., walk through the square, and veer right onto Mucharg., through Neuerpl. when Mucharg. becomes Schweizerg. The *Pension* will be on your right behind large unmarked glass doors (10min.). Reception to the right. Traditional rooms with private toilet and shower. Lovely geraniums in summer. Reception 8am-8pm. 250AS per person. Ample breakfast included.

Egger, Alleestr. 33 (tel. 720 98). From the station, Stadtbus: "Hochsteinbahn" and walk 2 blocks, or walk through Hauptpl., bear left on Roseng., and then bear right at the Il Gelato ice cream shop onto tree-lined residential Alleestr. Walk about 10min. down Alleestr. The pension is the white house on your left (20min.). Large, well-lit rooms and a great vegetable garden. The owner greets guests with open arms. 160-170AS per person. 10AS surcharge for stays of less than 3 nights. Showers and big breakfast included.

Bauernhof in the Siechenhaus, Kartnerstr. 39 (tel. 621 88). From the station, turn right onto Tirolerstr., follow it across the Isel, and take the first left then an immediate right at the first junction. Walk 1 block to Kartnerstr. and turn left. The hotel, with its ancient frescoes of Lazarus, is on the right. A real farmhouse that served as a home for the sick in the Middle Ages (often against their will). Large, pleasant rooms. 160-180AS per person. 40AS surcharge for stays less than 3 nights.

LIENZ: FOOD ■ 261

Camping Falken, Eichholz 7 (tel. 640 22; fax 640 226), across the Drau River near the foot of the Dolomites. From the station, turn left onto Tirolerstr. and left at the Sport Hotel, pass through the tunnel and over the Drau, and go straight when the road splits. Follow the road as it curves left and, after passing the soccer and track facilities, head left down the small paved footpath through the field. The campsite is just beyond the *Gasthof* of the same name. 60AS, under 15 45AS; site 105AS. Off-season: 45-50AS; 30-35AS; 90-95AS. People over 15 pay 7AS tax per night. Showers, laundry facilities, and a small store. Gate closed daily 10pm-7am. Reservations strongly recommended July-Aug. Open July-Aug. and mid-Dec. to March.

FOOD

Calorie-laden delis, bakeries, butcher stores, and cafés lie in wait in **Hauptplatz** and along **Schweizergasse.**

- **Imbiße Köstl,** Kreuzg. 4 (tel. 620 12). Mother-daughter dynamic duo prepares the cheapest eats in town (19-49AS) in this diner-style restaurant. Chow down on the *Wienerschnitzel* (49AS), curry *Würstl* (27AS), or pastries (8-17AS). Eat in or take out. Open Mon.-Thurs. 7:30am-8pm, Fri. 7:30am-10pm, Sat. 7:30am-noon.
- **Pizzeria-Spaghetteria "Da Franco,"** Agydius Peggerstr. (tel. 650 51). Head through Hauptpl. to Johannespl., turn left at Zwergerstr., and continue down the small alley. Captained by Franco, a native Italian who decided to try to make it big up north. Watch through the window as he conjures up the best gnocchi you've ever tasted. Pizza and pasta 50-110AS; salad 40-105AS. Open in summer daily 11:30am-2:30pm and 6pm-midnight; in winter Mon.-Sat. 11:30am-2pm and 5:30pm-midnight. Visa, MC, AmEx.
- **China Restaurant Szechuan,** Beda-Weberg. 13 (tel. 651 22). Cross the bridge adjoining Neuerpl., bear right in the gardens, and turn left onto Marcherstr. The restaurant is on the left. Tasty entrees (75-85AS) and a 55AS lunch special with soup or spring roll (11 entree choices) reward those willing to cross the Isel. Beautiful porcelain soup spoons. Open daily 11:30am-2:30pm and 5:30-11:30pm.
- **Café Wha,** Schweizerg. 3. Wha? You heard me! Young, body-pierced, alternative crowd rocks and rolls way past the midnight hour. Peer through the smoke at the bizarre art hanging on the walls or venture into the back room for a game of pool. Beer 24-35AS; wine 21-25AS. Open daily 6pm-1am.

Markets

- **SPAR Markt,** across Europapl. from the tourist office. Open Mon.-Fri. 7:30am-6:30pm, Sat. 7:30am-5pm.
- **ADEG Aktiv Markt,** Südtirolerpl; next to the tall pink Hotel Traube; and in Hauptpl. Open Mon.-Fri. 8am-6pm, Sat. 8am-noon.
- **Bauernmarkt** (farmer's market), Marktpl. Local produce. Sat. 8am-noon.

SIGHTS AND ENTERTAINMENT

Above Lienz, the **Schloß Bruck,** home of the **East Tirolean Regional Museum** (BundesBus: "Lienz Schloß Bruck Heimatmuseum" or city bus: "Schloßg.") houses everything the town didn't have the heart to throw away, from Roman remains to carved Christmas crèches. This lonely castle was once the mighty fortress of the fearless counts of Gorz (circa 16th century) before it fell to the even more fearless Habsburgs. Inside the fortress, the **Kapelle zur Alterheiligsten Dreifaltigkeit** boasts beautifully preserved 15th-century frescoes. Count Leonhard of Görz and his wife Paola of Gonzaga sought immortality as well as divine protection by having themselves painted into the chapel mural *Death of the Virgin*. The **Rittersaal** (Knights' Hall) houses an unbelievable 34 sq. m tapestry comprised of 42 different squares illustrating the life and death of Christ. The fine-art collection also features the works of renowned local turn-of-the-century painter **Albin Egger-Lienz**—over 75 works track his development from traditional portrait painting to a personal, robust expressionism. (Castle open mid-June to mid-Sept. daily 10am-6pm; mid-Sept. to Oct. and April to mid-June Tues.-Sun. 10am-5pm. 50AS, students and seniors 25AS.)

The **Hochsteinbahnen** chairlift, which runs from the base station near the castle at the intersection of Iseltaler-Str. and Schloß., rises 1500m up to the Alpine wonderland of **Sternalm** (runs late June to mid-Sept. Wed.-Sun. 8:45am-11:45pm and 1-5:15pm; round-trip 100AS, children 50AS; family pass 200AS). At the top, the unforgiving Dolomites to the south and the gently rounded Hohe Tauern to the north appear in spectacular confrontation. A "Fairy Tale Hike" (1½hr.) leads past limestone peaks to a peek at the Großglockner Strasse (details at the tourist office or chairlift station). Also at the summit of the chairlift is the **Moosalm Children's Zoo,** with a menagerie of rabbits, goats, and ducks available for your petting pleasure. (Open daily 10am-5:30pm. Free.) The **Dolomiten-Wanderbus** delivers nature lovers to another challenging hiking base, the **Lienzer Dolomitenhütte** (1620m). Over 40 trails of varying difficulty spiral off from this Alpine hut. (Buses leave from the left side of the train station mid-June to late Sept. 8am, 1:10, and 4:30pm. 75AS, round-trip 120AS.) Seventeen other huts dot the area—for more mountain hiking information, contact Lienz's chapter of the **Österreichischer Alpenverein,** Franz-von-Defreggerstr. 11 (tel. 489 32; open Mon., Wed., and Fri. 9am-noon).

Aquaphiles also venture on the 5km hike to the **Tristacher See,** a sparkling blue lake hugging the base of the Rauchkofel mountain. The tourist office has the brochures *Wandertips* and *Radtouren in der Ferienregion Lienzer Dolomiten* (Bike Tours in the Linzer Dolomites). Couch potatoes can enjoy the lake's facilities (25AS) by riding the free **Bäder- und Freizeitbus** (Bath- and Leisure-Bus) in front of the train station to the terminus: "Parkhotel Tristachersee" (runs daily July to early Sept.).

Lienz serves as an excellent base to attack the ski trails comprising the **Lienzer Dolomiten Complex.** (One-day ski pass 290AS, seniors and youths 230AS, under 15 145AS. Half-day tickets 230AS, 185AS, 115AS. Off-season: one-day 275AS, 220AS, 145AS. Half-day 220AS, 175AS, 115AS.) The **Skischule Lienzer Dolomiten** (tel. 656 90; fax 710 80) at the Zettersfeld lift offers hour-long private lessons at 410AS for one person, 190AS for each additional person. Four-hour lessons costs 440AS. Private snowboard lessons are also available. **Hans Moser und Sohn** (tel. 691 80 or 681 66), at the apex of the Zettersfeld lift, supplies **ski or snowboard rental.** A complete set of downhill equipment, here or elsewhere, runs 210AS per day, children half-price.

During the second weekend of August, the sounds of alcohol-induced merriment reverberate off the daintily painted facades of Lienz's town buildings in celebration of the **Stadtfest** (admission to town center 50AS). The summer months also welcome the reaffirmation of Tirolean culture and heritage in a series of **Platzkonzerte.** Watch grandfathers dust off their old lederhosen and perform the acclaimed shoe-slapping dance (free; consult *Informationen für unsere Gäste*). On the third Sunday of January, the world's greatest male cross-country skiers gather in Lienz to compete in the 60km **Dolomitenlauf.** All year, disco-lovers dance the night away at **Stadtkeller-disco,** Tirolerstr. 30, near Europapl. (Open daily 9pm-4am.)

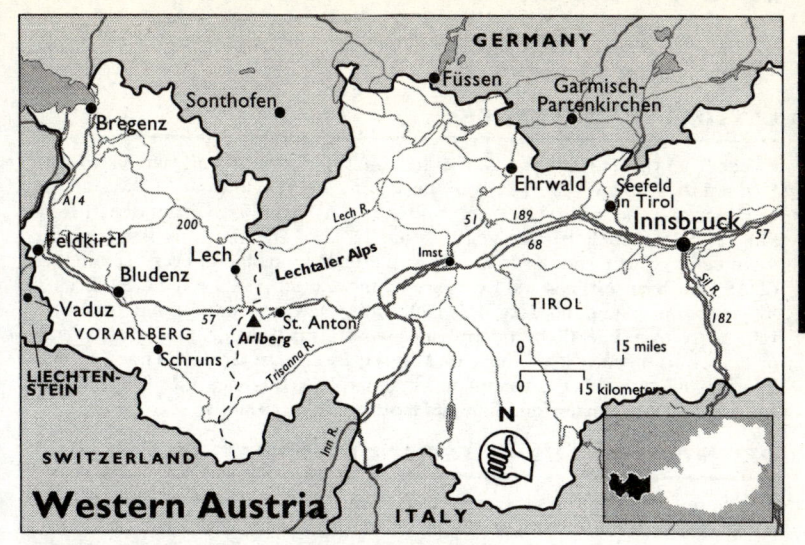

Western Austria

The western provinces of Tirol and Vorarlberg are to Austria as Bavaria is to Germany: a haven of iconic images of the "real" country. Visitors relax in mountain chalets, listening to old folks in *Lederhosen* yodelling. Patriotic and particularist almost to a fault, **Tirol** (12,648 sq. km; pop. 630,358) is the most traditional and beautiful of Austria's federal states. Only 13% of the territory is inhabited, concentrated mainly in the Inn valley. You can identify tourists by their craned necks—while the locals nonchalantly carry on with daily life, visitors can't stop gawking at the spectacular, snow-capped mountains, which in many Tirolean towns form a 2000m horizon on all sides. Tirol counts almost 600 peaks over 3000m as well as 169 ski schools to coax skiers down them. Five glacier regions also offer skiing opportunities.

Perched on the intersection of three nations, the residents of the **Vorarlberg** (1004 sq. mi.; pop. 322,551), Austria's westernmost province, speak like the Swiss, eat like the Germans, and deem their land a world unto itself. From the tranquil Bodensee in the west, the country juts increasingly upward with each easterly move; at the boundary with Tirol, the Arlberg Alps form an obstacle passable only through the 10km Arlberg Tunnel. The unforgiving terrain that characterizes West Austria isn't hospitable to agriculture or manufacturing (except chocolate), so tourism is by far the leading industry. In fact, Tirol earns more foreign currency from tourism than any other province. The skiing in the region is perhaps the best in the world—we only say "perhaps" because we don't want to offend the Swiss.

■ Innsbruck

Innsbruck takes much pride in preserving its Baroque buildings, architectural reminders of a cultural past once graced by the Habsburgs. Despite its imperial artifacts housed behind historic gates, however, Innsbruck attracts visitors mainly because of its mountains. These white-haired, primordial giants rise above the town's intricate facades and quiet cobblestones, conveniently shield the town from northerly winds, and contribute to the mild climate. They also help, along with over 150 cable cars and chairlifts and an extensive network of mountain paths, to garner Innsbruck enthusiastic thumbs up from passers-through. Many travelers and inhabitants regard Innsbruck as the third member of the triumvirate formed with Salzburg and Vienna, the provincial counterpart to Vienna's cultural and political dominance and Salzburg's musical notoriety.

GETTING TO INNSBRUCK

By **car** from the east or west take Autobahn A12. From Vienna take A1 west to Salzburg then A8 west to A12. From the south, take A13 north to A12 west. From Germany and the north, take A95 to Rte. 2 east. **Flights** arrive and depart from **Flughafen Innsbruck,** Fürstenweg 180 (tel. 225 25). The airport is 4km from the town center. Bus F shuttles to and from the main train station every 15 minutes (21AS). **Austrian Airlines** and **Swissair,** Adamg. 7a (tel. 58 29 85), have offices in Innsbruck. Austrian Airlines has daily flights from New York or Boston to Innsbruck via Vienna (from US$800 round-trip), and Swissair has daily flights from New York or Boston to Innsbruck via Zurich. (Also see **Essentials: Getting There,** p. 30.) **Trains** arrive at the **Hauptbahnhof** on Südtirolerpl., on bus lines A, D, E, F, J, K, R, S, and #3; the **Westbahnhof** and **Bahnhof Hötting** are cargo stops.

ORIENTATION AND PRACTICAL INFORMATION

Most of Innsbruck lies on the eastern bank of the **Inn River.** Because of Innsbruck's compact size, nearly any two points lie within easy walking distance of each other, making public transportation largely unnecessary. **Maria-Theresien-Straße,** the main thoroughfare, runs north to south. The street is open only to taxis, buses, and trams, but tourists and open-air cafés crowd its sides. To reach the *Altstadt* from the main train station, take tram #3 or 6 or bus A, F, or K: "Maria-Theresien-Str.," or turn right and walk to Museumstr. then turn left and walk for about 10 minutes. Small maps of the city are available at the train station information booth, the *Jugendwarteraum,* or any tourist office. Continue down Museumstr. and toward the river (curving left onto Burggraben, across Maria-Theresien-Str., and onto Marktgraben) to reach the **University district,** near Innrain. The university itself is to the left down Innrain.

Tourist Offices

Step one in experiencing Innsbruck is the new **Innsbruck Card,** available at the tourist offices. The card gives holders access to all attractions and free travel on the city's public transportation. Innsbruck's myriad tourist offices offer comparable services with equal competence and friendliness. A two-hour **bus tour,** including a walk through the *Altstadt* and visit to the ski jump, leaves from the train station. (In summer noon and 2pm; in winter noon. 160AS.)

Innsbruck-Information, Burggraben 3 (tel. 53 56; fax 53 56 14), on the edge of the *Altstadt* just off the end of Museumstr. Huge and high-tech, with hundreds of brochures. A private, profit-maximizing consortium of local hotels oversees the offices, so arrange tours and concert tickets but don't expect to reserve budget accommodations. Open Mon.-Sat. 8am-7pm, Sun. and holidays 9am-6pm. **Branches** at the train station and major motor exits.

Jugendwarteraum (tel. 58 63 62), in the *Hauptbahnhof* near the lockers. Gives directions, suggests hostels, and hands out free maps and skiing information. English spoken. Open Mon.-Fri. 11am-7pm, Sat. 10am-1pm. Closed July-Aug.

Österreichischer Alpenverein, Wilhelm-Greil-Str. 15 (tel. 595 47; fax 57 55 28). The Austrian Alpine Club's main office. Provides mountains of Alpine hiking information and discounts on Alpine huts and hiking insurance. Services available to members only. Club membership 530AS, ages 18-25 and over 60 390AS, under 18 180AS. Open Mon.-Fri. 9am-1pm and 2-5pm.

Tirol Information Office, Maria-Theresien-Str. 55 (tel. 512 72 72; fax 512 72 727; email tirol@tis.co.at; http://www.tis.co.at/tirol), on the second floor. Dispenses excellent information on all of Tirol. Open Mon.-Fri. 8am-6pm.

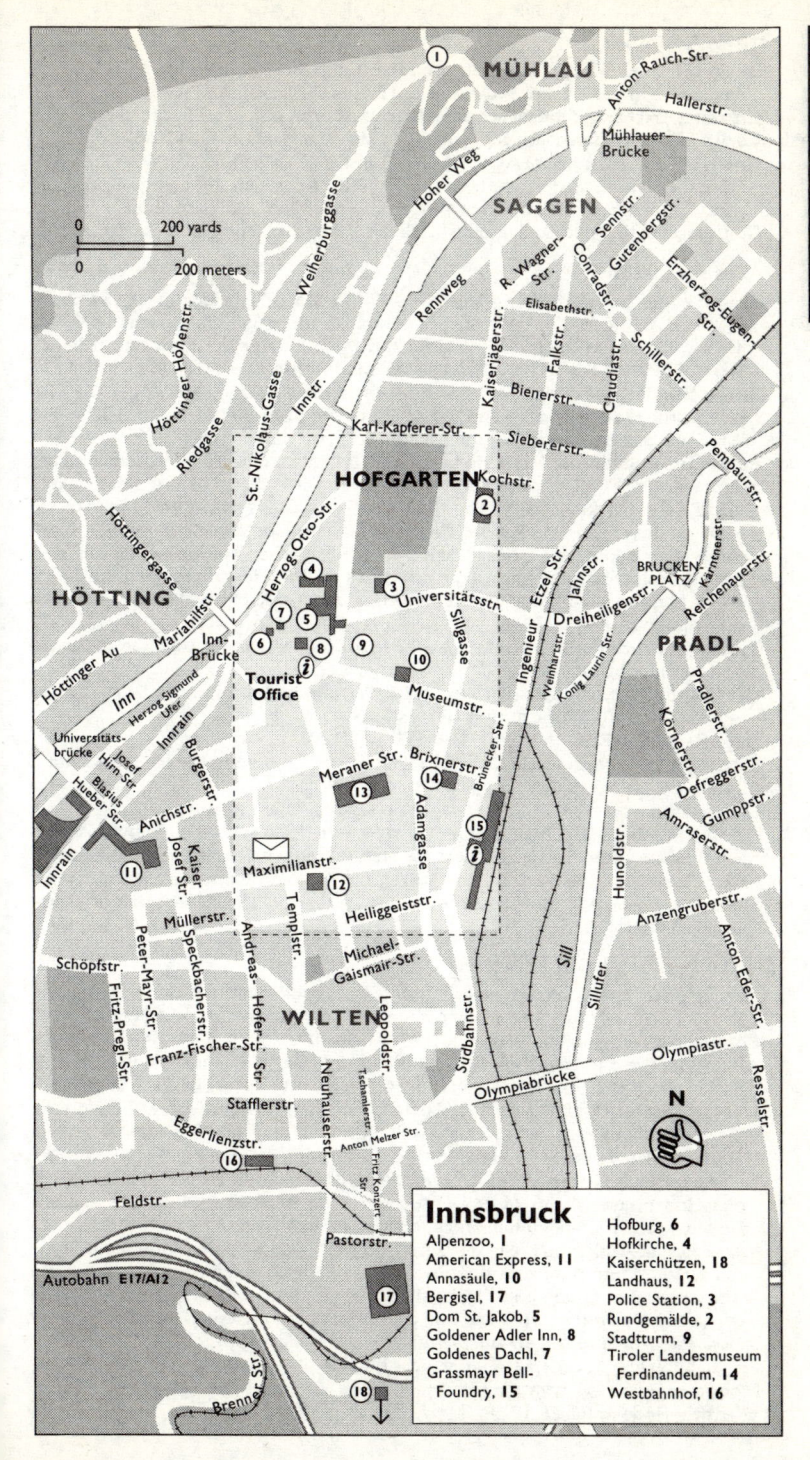

ORIENTATION AND PRACTICAL INFORMATION ■ 265

Innsbruck

- Alpenzoo, 1
- American Express, 11
- Annasäule, 10
- Bergisel, 17
- Dom St. Jakob, 5
- Goldener Adler Inn, 8
- Goldenes Dachl, 7
- Grassmayr Bell-Foundry, 15
- Hofburg, 6
- Hofkirche, 4
- Kaiserschützen, 18
- Landhaus, 12
- Police Station, 3
- Rundgemälde, 2
- Stadtturm, 9
- Tiroler Landesmuseum Ferdinandeum, 14
- Westbahnhof, 16

Other Agencies

Budget Travel: Tiroler Landesreisebüro (tel. 598 85) on Wilhelm-Greil-Str. at Boznerpl. Open Mon.-Fri. 9am-noon and 2-6pm. Visa, MC, AmEx.
Currency Exchange: Innsbruck Information tourist office, on Burggraben. Open daily 8am-7pm. **Banks** are generally open Mon.-Fri. 8am-noon and 2:30-4pm.
American Express: Brixnerstr. 3, A-6020 Innsbruck (tel. 58 24 91; fax 57 33 85). From the station, take a right then the first left. Holds mail. No commission on its checks; small fee for cash. Open Mon.-Fri. 9am-5:30pm, Sat. 9am-noon.
Consulate: U.K., Matthias-Schmidtstr. 12 (tel. 58 83 20). Open Mon.-Fri. 9am-noon.

Transportation

Trains: Hauptbahnhof, Südtirolerpl. (tel. 17 17). Open 7:30am-9pm. To: **Salzburg** (14 per day, 3hr., 376AS); **Vienna** (14 per day, 5½hr., 1650AS); **Zurich** (3 per day, 3¾hr., 533AS); **Munich** (18 per day, 2hr., 338AS); **Berlin** (2 per day, 12½hr., 1564AS); **Paris** (2 per day, 11hr., 1306AS); and **Rome** (2 per day, 9hr., 520AS).
Buses: Bundesbuses (tel. 58 51 55) leave from the station on Sterzingerstr., adjacent to the *Hauptbahnhof* and to the left of the main entrance. Open Mon.-Fri. 7am-5pm, Sat. 8am-noon. For information on Sun., call 35 11 93.
Public Transportation: The main bus station is in front of the main entrance to the train station. You can purchase single-ride 1-zone tickets (21AS), 1-day tickets (45AS), 4-ride tickets (58AS), and week-long bus passes (valid Mon.-Mon., 105AS) from the driver or at any *Tabak*. The 4-ride ticket can be used by more than 1 person (e.g., 4 people for 1 ride). Punch your ticket when you board the bus, and push the white button to signal the driver to stop. Push it again to open the doors. To enter, push the flashing green button on either side of the doors. Most buses stop running 10:30-11:30pm, but check each line for specifics.
Taxis: Innsbruck Funktaxi (tel. 53 11, 17 18, or 455 00). About 100AS from the airport to the *Altstadt,* dig?
Car Rental: Avis, Salurnerstr. 15 (tel. 57 17 54). **Budget,** Leopoldstr. 54 (tel. 58 84 68; fax 58 45 80); or the airport (tel. 28 71 81).
Auto Repairs: ARBÖ (tel. 123). **ÖAMTC** (tel. 120).
Hitchhiking: Hitchers usually take bus K: "Geyrstr." and go to the Shell gas station by the DEZ store off Geyrstr.
Bike Rental: (tel. 503 53 95), at the train station. Open April to early Nov. 150-200AS per day, with Eurailpass or that day's train ticket 90-160AS. **Sport Neuner,** Salurnerstr. 5 (tel. 56 15 01), near the station, rents mountain bikes. 220AS per day.
Ski Rental: Skischule Innsbruck, Leopoldstr. 4 (tel. 58 23 10). Skis, boots, poles, and insurance 250AS.

Other Practical Information

Luggage Storage: Luggage watch and **lockers** (both 30AS) at the train station. Watch open daily July-Aug. 6:30am-midnight; Sept.-June 6:30am-10:30pm.
Bookstores: Wagner'she, Museumstr. 4 (tel. 59 50 50; fax 595 05 38). Open Mon.-Fri. 9am-6pm, Sat. 9am-1pm. **Buchhandlung Tyrolia,** Maria-Theresien-Str. 15 (tel. 596 11; fax 58 20 50). Travel literature. Open Mon.-Fri. 9am-6pm, Sat. 9am-5pm.
Library: Innsbruck Universität Bibliothek, Innrain 50, near the intersection with Blasius-Heuber-Str. Take bus O, R, or F: "Klinik." Open July-Aug. Mon.-Fri. 8am-8pm, Sat. 8am-noon; Sept.-June Mon.-Fri. 8am-10pm, Sat. 8am-6pm.
Bi-Gay-Lesbian Organizations: Homosexuelle Initiative Tirol, Innrain 100, A-6020 Innsbruck (tel. 56 24 03). **Frauenzentrum Innsbruck** (Women's Center), Liebeneggstr. 15, A-6020 Innsbruck (tel. 58 08 25).
Laundromat: Waltraud Hell, Amraserstr. 15 (tel. 34 13 67). Take a right out of the train station, turn right after the post office, and head under the train tracks onto Amraserstr. Turn right, go over the river, and continue for another 2 blocks. The laundromat is on the left. Wash and dry 150AS, soap included. Open in summer Mon.-Fri. 8am-2pm and 4-7pm; in winter Mon.-Fri. 8am-6pm.
Public Showers: At the train station, near the rest rooms. 30AS.
Mountain Guide Information Office: tel. 532 01 78. Open Mon.-Fri. 9am-noon.
Weather Report: tel. 28 17 38. **Snow report:** tel. 532 01 70.

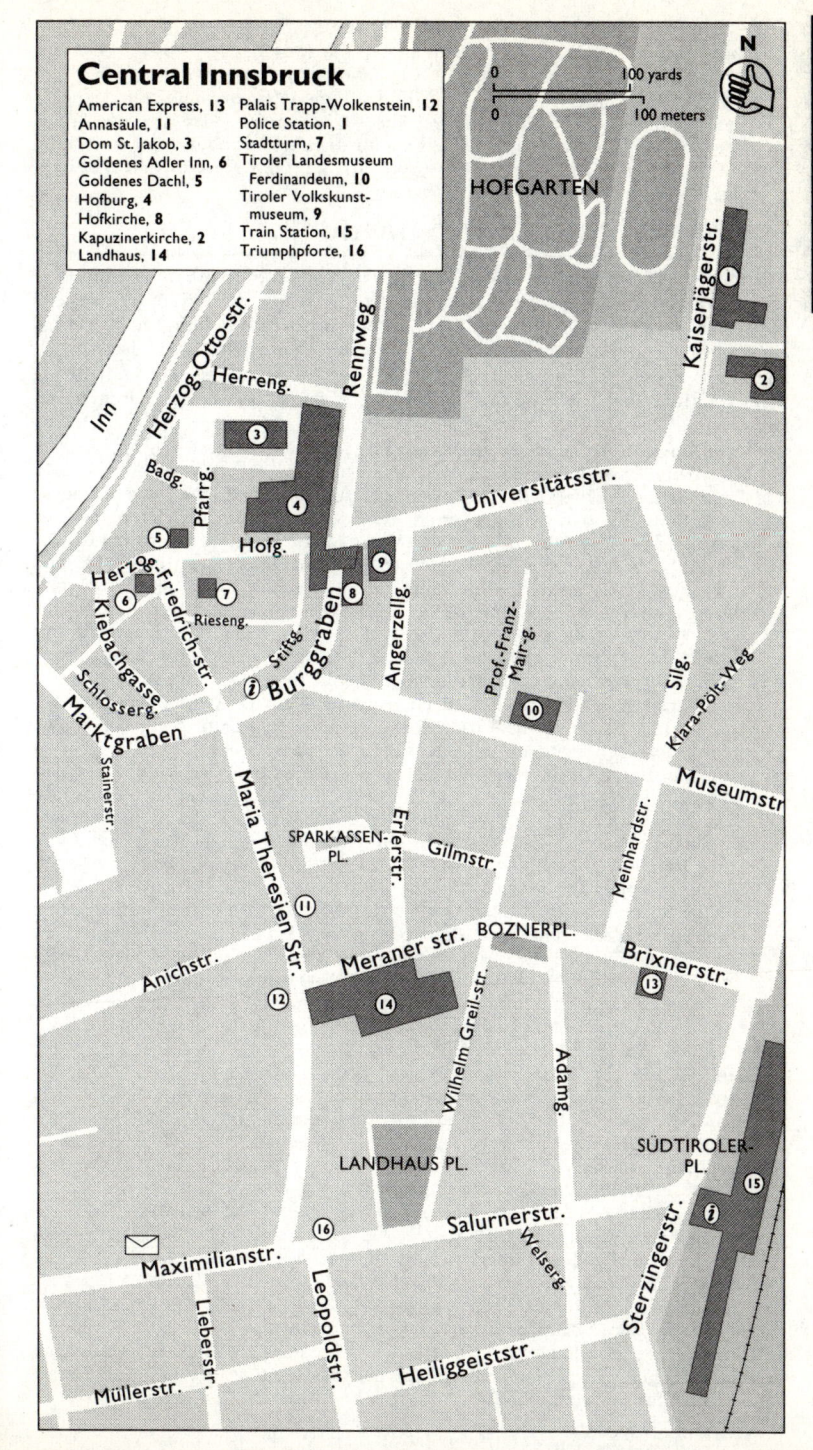

ORIENTATION AND PRACTICAL INFORMATION ■ 267

Central Innsbruck

- American Express, 13
- Annasäule, 11
- Dom St. Jakob, 3
- Goldenes Adler Inn, 6
- Goldenes Dachl, 5
- Hofburg, 4
- Hofkirche, 8
- Kapuzinerkirche, 2
- Landhaus, 14
- Palais Trapp-Wolkenstein, 12
- Police Station, 1
- Stadtturm, 7
- Tiroler Landesmuseum Ferdinandeum, 10
- Tiroler Volkskunstmuseum, 9
- Train Station, 15
- Triumphpforte, 16

Medical Assistance: University Hospital, Anichstr. 35 (tel. 50 40).
Emergencies: Police, tel. 133. Headquarters at Kaiserjägerstr. 8 (tel. 590 00). **Ambulance,** tel. 144 or 2. **Fire,** tel. 122. **Mountain Rescue,** tel. 140.
Post Office: Maximilianstr. 2 (tel. 500), down from the *Triumphpforte* and straight ahead from the station. Open 24hr. Address *Poste Restante:* Postlagernde Briefe, Hauptpostamt, Maximilianstr. 2, A-6020 Innsbruck. **Branch** next to the station (tel. 500 74 09). Open Mon.-Fri. 7am-8pm, Sat. 8am-6pm. **Postal Code:** A-6020. **Telephone Code:** 0512.

ACCOMMODATIONS AND CAMPING

Although 9000 beds are available in Innsbruck and suburban Igls, inexpensive accommodations are scarce in June when only two hostels are open. Book in advance if possible. Visitors should join **Club Innsbruck** by registering at any central Innsbruck accommodation for one or more nights. Membership gives discounts on museums, skiing, ski buses (Dec. 21-April 5), bike tours, and the club's fine hiking program (June-Sept.). Ask the tourist office staff if your accommodation is included.

Hostel Torsten Arneus-Schwedenhaus (HI), Rennweg 17b (tel. 585 814; fax 585 81 44; email youth.hostel@idk.netwing.at; http://www.goli.org/youth-hostel). From the station, bus C: "Handelsakademie" and continue to the end and straight across Rennweg to the river, or turn right from the station, make a left onto Museumstr., turn right at the end of the street onto Burggraben, and follow it under the arch and onto Rennweg (20min.). This 95-bed hostel offers a convenient location and a front-yard view of the Inn River. Reception daily 7-10am and 5-10:30pm. During the week in the summer, you can store your luggage at the front desk any time. Lockout 10am-5pm. Curfew 10:30pm; keys on request. 3- to 4-bed dorms 120AS. Private shower included. Breakfast 7-8:30am (45AS). Dinner 65AS. Sheets 20AS. Reservations recommended, honored until 7pm. Open July-Aug.

Jugendherberge Innsbruck (HI), Reichenauer Str. 147 (tel. 34 61 79 or 34 61 80; fax 34 61 79 12; email yhibk@tirol.com). Bus R: "König-Laurin Str." then bus O: "Jugendherberge." Or, turn right from the main train station, turn right again on Museumstr., and take the first left fork after the train tracks on König-Laurin-Str. When the street ends, make a right onto Dreiheiligenstr., which merges into Reichenauer Str. (40min.). With tinted octagonal windows and an efficient and knowledgeable staff, this 178-bed hostel resembles a high-power corporation. Three large lounges with hot plates, TV, and a small (German) library. Large turquoise lockers in the rooms offset the flowered quilts the Partridge family left behind. Reception daily 7-10am and 5-10pm. Lockout 10am-5pm. Curfew 11pm; key available. Quiet time from 10pm. 6-bed dorms 145AS first night, then 115AS; 4-bed dorms 175AS, 145AS. Showers and sheets included. July-Aug. singles with showers 350AS; doubles with shower 500AS. Non-members add 40AS. Breakfast 7-8:30am; dinner 6-8pm. Laundry facilities 45AS, but you must notify the desk by 5pm if you intend to do laundry (bring your own soap). They'll honor phone reservations until 5pm. Open July 15-Aug. 31.

Haus Wolf, Dorfstr. 48 (tel. 54 86 73), in Mutters. Stubaitalbahn tram: "Birchfeld" then walk down Dorfstr. in the same direction. (The Stubaitalbahn stop is on the 3rd traffic island in front of the train station's main entrance. 25AS, week-long ticket 85AS. Last train 10:30pm. Tickets available from driver.) Unload your pack, take in the amazing view, bask in the maternal comfort, and eat, eat, eat. The tram ride up is 30min. of scenic bliss; the beds are at least 8hr. of heaven. Singles 190AS; doubles 380AS; triples 570AS. Breakfast and shower included.

Pension Paula, Weiherburgg. 15 (tel./fax 292 262). Bus K: "St. Nikolaus" then walk uphill. Satisfied guests frequently return to this inn-like home down the hill from the Alpenzoo. Fantastic views of the river and city center. Singles 320AS, with shower 420AS; doubles 520AS, with shower 600AS, with shower and toilet 640AS. Breakfast included. Reservations recommended.

Technikerhaus, Fischnalerstr. 26 (tel. 282 110; fax 282 11 017). Bus R: "Unterbergerstr./Technikerhaus." Or, walk straight out from the train station onto Salurnerstr. Take the first right onto Maria-Theresien-Str. then the first left onto Anichstr.

Cross the bridge on Blasius-Hueber-Str., turn left on Fürstenweg, and turn left onto Fischnalerstr. Though a bit far from the station, this recently renovated student housing complex is conveniently near the university district and the *Altstadt*. Restaurant and TV room. Breakfast room straight from a Disney animator's sketchbook. Reception 24hr. Singles 235AS; doubles 470AS; triples 705AS. Showers included. Breakfast 40AS. Reservations recommended. Open mid-July to Aug.

Internationales Studentenhaus, Recheng. 7 (tel. 501 592 or 594 770; fax 501 15). Bus O, R, or F: "Klinik" on Innrain then turn right on Recheng.; or bus C: "Studentenheim." To walk from the station, go straight out onto Salurnerstr., turn right on Maria-Theresien-Str., take the first left onto Anichstr., and then turn left onto Innrain. Pass the main university complex and turn right on Recheng. A modern 560-bed dormitory with English-speaking staff. Parking available a short distance away on Innrain. Reception 24hr., but call in advance. Singles 260AS, with shower 350AS; with student ID 210AS, 300AS. Doubles 440AS, with shower 600AS. All-you-can-eat American buffet breakfast 70AS. Laundry facilities. Open July-Aug.

Haus Rimml, Harterhofweg 82 (tel. 28 47 26). From Boznerpl., bus LK: "Klammstr." (20min.), or bus F, R, or O: "Klinik" and switch to the LK there. From the stop, walk downhill and turn left. Buses run infrequently, so prepare to rest awhile in this consummately comfortable hotel. Singles 270AS, with shower 300AS. Breakfast included. Call ahead. Open Dec.-Oct.

Camping Innsbruck Kranebitten, Kranebitter Allee 214 (tel. 284 180). Bus LK: "Klammstr." (20min.), or bus F, R, or O: "Klinik" and switch to the LK. Reception July-Aug. 7am-9pm; April-June and Sept.-Oct. 7am-noon. If reception is closed, find a site and check in the next morning. 60AS, children under 15 45AS; tents 40AS; cars 45AS. Tax 6AS. Showers included. Washing machines available.

FOOD

Most tourists first glimpse cosmopolitan Innsbruck from the glamour of Maria-Theresien-Str. Gawking at the overpriced delis and *Konditoreien* won't fill your stomach, so escape the *Altstadt* and its profiteers by crossing the river to Innstr. in the university district where you'll uncover ethnic restaurants, *Schnitzel Stuben*, and grocers.

Al Dente, Meranestr. 7 (tel. 58 49 47). Snug place with stylish wood, candlelight, salad bar, and delicious pasta. After finishing your entree (82-142AS), try the delicious *tiramisú* (46AS). Plenty of vegetarian options. English menu. Open Mon.-Sat. 7am-11pm, Sun. and holidays 11am-11pm. Visa, MC, AmEx, DC.

Philippine Vegetarische Küche, Müllerstr. 9 (tel. 58 91 57), at Lieberstr. one block from the post office. A vegetarian rest stop on a highway of meat, this whimsically decorated restaurant serves some of the best food in carnivorous Innsbruck. Entrees from zucchini cream soup to tortellini run 82-168AS. Daily special 45-98AS. Midday *menu* with soup and entree 75AS. Open Mon.-Sat. 10am-11pm. Visa, MC.

Churrasco la Mamma, Innrain 2 (tel. 58 63 98). Outdoor seating next to the river—watch the moon rise, and fall in love over a plate of spaghetti. Pasta 84-116AS. Brick-oven pizza 68-118AS. Open daily 9am-midnight. Visa, MC, AmEx, DC.

Crocodiles, Maria-Theresien-Str. 49 (tel. 58 88 56). This tiny restaurant on the right of Intersport Okay serves 33 different brick-oven pizzas, including 8 vegetarian options. English menus and a "croco-crew" of waiters available to help you decide. Large pizzas 55-85AS. Open Mon.-Fri. 10am-10pm, Sat. 10am-2pm.

Baguette, Maria-Theresien-Str. 57, in front of the *Triumphpforte* and down from the post office. This air-conditioned corner café offers fresh bread, pizza, and cheese-covered baguettes. Exotic drinks 18-36AS. Small salads 15AS. Sandwiches 25-35AS. Open Mon.-Fri. 7am-6:30pm, Sat. 9am-12:30pm. Branch at Innrain 30a.

Gasthof Weißes Lamm, Mariahilfstr. 12 (tel. 28 31 56). Home-style, Tirolean restaurant popular with the local crowd. 100AS can go a long way with their heaping portions and special *menus* (soup, entree, and salad 80-115AS). Other entrees 100-200AS. Open Mon.-Wed. and Fri.-Sun. 11:30am-2pm and 6-10pm.

Salute Pizzeria, Innrain 35 (tel. 58 58 18). Popular student hangout near the university. Pizza 35-100AS; pasta 55-90AS. Open daily 11am-midnight.

University Mensa, Herzog-Siegmund-Ufer 15 (tel. 58 43 75), on the second floor of the university at Blasius-Hueber-Str. near the bridge. Student cafeteria open to the public. Meals 35-65AS. Open Mon.-Thurs. 11am-2pm, Fri. 11am-1:30pm.

Markets

M-Preis Supermarket has the lowest prices around. Branches on the corner of Reichenauerstr. and Andechstr; on Maximilianstr. by the arch; and at Innrain 15. Open Mon.-Fri. 7:30am-6:30pm, Sat. 7:30am-1pm.

Indoor Farmer's Market, in the Markthalle next to the river at the intersection of Innrain and Marktgraben (look for the giant apple). Stands sell the 4 food groups, gorgeous flowers, and more. Open Mon.-Fri. 7am-6:30pm, Sat. 7am-1pm.

SIGHTS

For discounts on all of Innsbruck's sights, register for Club Innsbruck (see p. 264). Failing that, visit the Maximilianeum Museum first, as the ticket includes admission to the Tiroler Landesmuseum and Zeughaus. The museum is behind the **Goldenes Dachl** (Little Golden Roof), on Herzog Friedrichstr. This balcony serves as the city's center and is its most potent symbol, built to commemorate the marriage of the Habsburg couple Maximilian I and Bianca, the great-great-great-great-great-great grandparents of Maria Theresa. Beneath the 2657 shimmery gold shingles, Maxi and his wife kept watch over their crew of jousters and dancers in the square below. Today, images of the roof grace postcards, parking signs, and even lingerie displays. Inside the building, the new **Maximilianeum Museum** commemorates Innsbruck's favorite pug-nosed ruler. Nifty headphones explain the exhibits in multiple languages and offer anecdotes about Maxi's personal life and exploits. (Open May-Sept. daily 10am-6pm; Oct.-April Tues.-Sun. 10am-12:30pm and 2-5pm. 60AS, students 30AS, seniors 50AS, family pass 120AS.) Many of the buildings surrounding the Goldenes Dachl are splendid 15th- and 16th-century structures. To the left, the facade of the **Helblinghaus,** a 15th-century Gothic town residence, is flushed salmon pink and blanketed with 18th-century Baroque floral stucco. Climb the 168 narrow stairs of the 15th-century **Stadtturm** (city tower), across from the Helblinghaus, to soak in the panoramic view. Look up before you climb—on a clear, sunny day, space in the tower can be tighter than a pair of Jordache jeans and even harder to move in. (Open daily July-Aug. 10am-6pm; Sept.-Oct. and April-June 10am-5pm; Nov.-March 10am-4pm. 22AS, students and children 11AS.) The 15th-century **Goldener Adler Inn** (Golden Eagle Inn) is a few buildings to the left of the Goldenes Dachl. Goethe, Heine, Sartre, Mozart, Wagner, Camus, and even Maximilian I ate, drank, and made merry here. A block behind the Goldenes Dachl rise the twin towers of the Baroque **Dom St. Jakob** (built 1717-1724). The church houses a superb *trompe l'oeil* ceiling by C. D. Asam depicting the life of St. James and an altar decorated with Lukas Cranach's *Intercession of the Virgin.* A 1944 air raid destroyed much of the church, but renovations through 1993 restored the finely molded stucco to its original lovely light pink. (Open daily April-Sept. 8am-7:30pm; Oct.-March 8am-6:30pm. Free.)

The Habsburgs' influence is obvious at the intersection of Rennweg and Hofg., where the grand Hofburg (Imperial Palace), Hofkirche (Imperial Church), and Hofgarten (Imperial Garden) converge. Built between the 16th and 18th centuries, the **Hofburg** brims with the trappings of the old dynasty. Empress Maria Theresa plumply rules over nearly every room, and a portrait of Maria's youngest daughter, Marie Antoinette (with head), shines over the palace's main banquet hall. Enjoy the delicate furniture and grand rooms on your rococo wanderings. In 1998, the Gothic Cellar, a kitchen in Maximilian's time, will open to visitors. (Open daily 9am-5pm. Last entrance 4:30pm. 55AS, students 35AS, children 10AS. English guidebook

25AS, indispensable if you want any historical details, since the palace has no descriptions posted. Prices may rise in 1998 when more of the palace opens to visitors.) The **Hofkirche** holds an intricate sarcophagus, decorated with scenes from Maximilian I's life, and the *Kaisergrab*, 28 larger-than-life bronze statues standing guard lest anyone try to "grab" the Kaiser. Dürer designed the statues of King Arthur, Theodoric the Ostrogoth, and Count Albrecht of Habsburg. Maxi resides elsewhere, however—the monument was never completed to his specifications, so he was buried outside Vienna. The elegant Silver Chapel does hold Emperor Ferdinand II. (Open daily July-Aug. 9am-5:30pm; Sept.-June 9am-5pm. 20AS, students 14AS, children 10AS.) A 50AS combination ticket will admit you to the **Tiroler Volkskunstmuseum** (Tirolean Handicrafts Museum) in the same building. Built between 1553 and 1563 as the "New Abbey," the building was converted into a school in 1785 and has served as a museum since 1929. The exhaustive collection of dusty implements, peasant costumes, and furnished period rooms provides a thorough introduction to Tirolean culture. Learn how the Tiroleans worked, dressed, fell asleep, moved dirt, and carried things. (Open July-Aug. Mon.-Tues. and Thurs.-Sat. 9am-5:30pm, Wed. 9am-9pm; Sept.-June Mon.-Sat. 9am-5pm. Museum alone 40AS, students 25AS, children 15AS.) The **Hofgarten** across the street is a beautifully groomed, shaded picnic spot, complete with ponds, gorgeous flowers, and a concert pavilion. The knee-high chess set in the middle of the park adds a physical dimension to the usually cerebral game.

The collection of the **Tiroler Landesmuseum Ferdinandeum**, Museumstr. 15 (tel. 594 89), several blocks from the *Hauptbahnhof*, includes exquisitely colored, delicately etched stained-glass windows, some outstanding medieval altars and paintings, and works by several eminent Tiroleans and others (Schiele, Klimt, and Rembrandt). The Zeughaus extension (across town) has a weapons collection. (Open May-Sept. Mon.-Wed. and Fri.-Sun. 10am-5pm, Thurs. 10am-5pm and 7-9pm; Oct.-April Tues.-Sat. 10am-noon and 2-5pm, Sun. 10am-1pm. 50AS, students 30AS.)

Near the Schwedenhaus youth hostel and across the covered bridge, signs point to the **Alpenzoo** (tel. 29 23 23), the loftiest zoo in Europe, with every vertebrate species indigenous to the Alps. When you've had your fill of high-altitude baby ibex, descend on the network of scenic trails that weave across the hillside. (Open daily in summer 9am-6pm; in winter 9am-5pm. 70AS, students and children 30AS.) Tram #1 or 4 or bus C, D, or E: "Hungerbergbahn" drops you at the summit's cable car.

In town, the Baroque grandeur of **Maria-Theresien-Straße** gives a clear view of the snow-capped *Nordkette* mountains. At the beginning of the street stands the **Triumphpforte** (Triumphal Arch) built in 1765 to commemorate the betrothal of Emperor Leopold II. Down the street, the **Annasäule** (Anna Column), erected between 1704 and 1706 by the provincial legislature, commemorates the Tiroleans' victory after an unsuccessful Bavarian invasion during the War of Spanish Succession.

Farther from the city center, the **Grassmayr Bell-Foundry** (tel. 594 16 37) runs under the supervision of the Grassmayr family, who have been crafting bells for 14 generations. Church bells take two months, but they'll make small ones for tourists. (Open Mon.-Fri. 9am-6pm, Sat. 9am-noon. 40AS, children 25AS.) The Rococo **Basilika Wilten** and the Baroque **Stiftskirche Wilten** await down the street. Other museums in the area, including the **Kaiserschützen** and the **Bergisel**, exhibit enough old military equipment to fend off legions of tourists. Continue in the same direction or take tram #1 or 6: "Bergisel" to reach the **Olympische Skischanze** (Olympic Ski Jump) on the hill overlooking the city. From their vantage point, the Olympians looked out over Innsbruck and a graveyard right under the hill from the stadium—it was clear where a bad landing would lead. Spanning the Sil River on the *Brennerautobahn* (motorway) is Europe's tallest bridge, the 2330ft **Europabrücke**.

Outside the city, Archduke Ferdinand of Tirol left a stash of 16th-century armor and artwork (including pieces by Velazquez and Titian) at **Schloß Ambras**. The medieval castle was a royal hunting lodge, but Ferdinand transformed the structure into one of the most beautiful Renaissance castles and gardens in Austria. A portrait gallery with detailed historical accounts depicts European dynasties from the 14th to the 19th centuries. The collection also includes armor displays and a 16th-century bathroom. To reach the palace, take tram #6 (dir: Igls): "Schloß Ambras," and follow the signs. Walk only if you have a hiking map, as the trail is poorly marked. (Open daily 10am-5pm. 60AS, children and students 30AS; with tour 85AS, 55AS.)

OUTDOORS INNSBRUCK

A **Club Innsbruck** membership (see **Accommodations,** p. 268) lets you in on one of the best deals in all Austria. The club's excellent mountain **hiking** program provides guides, transportation, and equipment (including boots) absolutely free to hikers of all ages and experience levels. Participants assemble in front of the Congress Center (June-Sept. daily at 8:30am), board a 9am bus, and return from the mountain ranges by 5pm. The hike is not strenuous, but the views are phenomenal and the guides are qualified and friendly. Free lantern hikes also leave every Tuesday at 7:45pm for Gasthof Heiligwasser, just above Igls; enjoy an Alpine hut party once there. If you wish to attack the Alps alone, pick up a free guidebook at any of the tourist offices.

The Club Innsbruck membership also significantly simplifies winter **ski** excursions; just hop on the complimentary club ski shuttle (schedules at the tourist office) to any suburban cable car (Dec. 21-April 5). Membership also provides discounts on ski passes. **Innsbruck Gletscher Ski Pass** (available at all cable cars and at Innsbruck-Information offices) is a comprehensive ticket valid for all 52 lifts in the region (3 days 1180AS, 6 days 2140AS; with Club Innsbruck card 980AS, 1780AS). The tourist office also rents equipment on the mountain. (Alpine approximately 270AS per day; cross-country 160AS; bobsled 300AS per person per ride.) The summer bus to **Stubaier Gletscherbahn** (for glacier skiing) leaves at 7:20 and 8:30am. Take the earlier bus—summer snow is often slushy by noon. There are also buses at 9:45, 11am, and 5pm in the winter (1½hr., round-trip 150AS). The last bus back leaves at 4:30pm, when the lifts close. One day of winter glacier skiing costs 420AS; summer passes cost 330AS after 8am, 275AS after 11am, and 170AS after 1pm. You can rent skis for approximately 270AS at the glacier. Innsbruck-Information and its train station branch offer the most reliable daily glacier ski packages: in summer 660AS, including bus, lift, and rental; in winter 540AS.

For a one-minute thrill, summer and winter **bobsled** rides are available at the Olympic bobsled run in Igls (tel. 33 83 80; fax 33 83 89), 5km from Innsbruck. Summer rides, however, are akin to spruced-up *Cool Runnings* carts with wheels. Professionals pilot the four-person sleds. Reservations are necessary. (In summer Thurs.-Sat. 4:30-6pm; in winter Tues. at 10am, and Thurs. from 7pm on. 360AS.) For a calmer ride, try the **Hafelekar Cable Car** (daily; 264AS with Club Innsbruck card).

ENTERTAINMENT

When you descend from Alpine peaks, peruse the posters plastered on the university kiosks or the monthly cultural brochures available at the tourist office for comprehensive listings of exhibitions, films, and concerts. In August, Innsbruck hosts the **Festival of Early Music,** featuring concerts by some of the world's leading soloists on period instruments at the Schloß Ambras, Congress Center, and Hofkirche. (For tickets, call 535 621 or fax 535 643.) Several of the festival's performances occur at the **Tiroler Landestheater** (tel. 520 744) across from the Hofburg on Rennweg. (Tickets available Mon.-Sat. 8:30am-8:30pm, Sun. 6:30-8:30pm or 7-8pm at the door before the performance; 40-540AS). The theater also presents top-notch plays, operas, and dance most nights throughout the year (65-440AS; student rush tickets 80AS, available 30min. before the show to anyone under 21 and students under 27).

The **Tiroler Symphony Orchestra of Innsbruck** (tel. 58 00 23) plays in the Congress Center, across from the Landestheater, between October and May (tickets 280-440AS; 30% discount for children and students). **Chamber music concerts** cost 160-260AS and the same discounts apply. Many Tuesday nights in summer, the Spanish mall at Schloß Ambras holds **classical music concerts** (140-380AS). Late

June and mid-July bring the **International Dance Summer**. Chestnuts in the Altstadt, cribs in the folklore museum, and caroling at the congress center are all components of the annual **Christmas market** (Nov. 22-Dec. 23).

NIGHTLIFE

Most visitors collapse into bed after a full day of Alpine adventure, but Innsbruck provides enough action to keep a few party-goers from their pillows. Much of the lively nightlife revolves around the students, making the **university quarter** a mecca for late-night revelry. The **Viaduktbogen**, a cluster of bars and music joints along Ingenieur Etzel Str., can also rock the house.

Treibhaus, Angerzellg. 8 (tel. 586 874), in an alley to the right of China Restaurant. Innsbruck's favorite student hangout. Colorful plastic squiggles on the ceiling and a brightly lit tent outside. Extensive Volksgarten series includes free concerts on Sat. evenings, while jazz reigns supreme on Sun. Jazz and blues festivals throughout the summer. Food 50-95AS. Open Mon.-Fri. 9am-1am, Sat.-Sun. 10am-1am.

Hofgarten Café (tel. 588 871), inside the Hofgarten park. Follow Burggrabenstr. around under the archway and past Universitätstr., enter the park after passing the Landestheater through the small gateway, and follow the path—you'll hear the crowd gathering. The elegantly lit garden and white tented splendor resemble a party Jay Gatsby would be proud to host. The crowd starts gathering around 8pm, and by 10pm hundreds of students and professionals fill the outdoor tents and tables. Note: the park closes at 10pm; use the back entrance to get to the café. Snack food 50-100AS, beer 28-48AS, wine spritzers 31AS. Open in summer daily 10am-1am, in winter Mon.-Sat. 5pm-1am, Sun. 10am-6pm.

Krah Vogel, Anichstr. 12 (tel. 580 149), off Maria-Theresien-Str. Amber walls and sleek black railings line this hip bar packed with people. Check out the "black box room," a sensory walk through the jungle—pitch black. Big screen TV, outdoor tables, and a garden out back. Ice cream 38-56AS; beer 29-37AS; food 38-146AS. Open Mon.-Sat. 9:30am-1am, Sun. 10am-1am.

Jimmy's, Wilhelm-Greilstr. 17 (tel. 570 473), by Landhauspl. The front end of an old-fashioned yellow Opel sticks out of the bar. *Happy Days* meets Hard Rock; they elope and head for the Tirol. Packed with students who revere the Italian, Mexican, and American food, especially the "Go to Hell" (a heavenly pasta, 50-105AS). Open Mon.-Fri. 11am-1am, Sat.-Sun. 7pm-1am. Visa, MC, AmEx.

Bet Your Bottom Thaler

American currency has its foundations in the small town of Hall, a few miles downriver from Innsbruck. Here, in the 16th century, Duke Sigmund (a Habsburg) coined the silver *Joachimsthaler* coin. Over the next century, this currency, shortened to *Thaler*, gained acceptance through Europe. When a bunch of upstarts in the American colonies got fed up with paying taxes and declared their independence from Britain, they adopted this name for their new currency, the dollar. Hall has yet to see any royalties.

■ Seefeld in Tirol

With the '64 and '76 Olympiads padding its resumé, ritzy Seefeld in Tirol lays a serious claim to winter-sports mecca status. Innsbruck twice used Seefeld's terrain for nordic skiing events (although disappointing snowfall in '64 required an appalling 20,000 metric tons of imported snow). Skiing is the cash cow here, but lush meadows and breathtaking Alpine scenery invite travelers in all seasons. Seefeld is the picture-perfect Austrian village. Feast your senses on towering peaks and bubbling fountains and hear the clip-clop of Haflinger mountain horses pulling Tirolean wagons on the narrow cobblestone streets (1hr. tour 400AS). In winter, the clip-clop becomes a swoosh-swoosh as sleighs replace the wagons, and the stream of tourists headed to Seefeld quickens. Be sure to make reservations at least a month in advance.

Orientation and Practical Information

Seefeld in Tirol perches on a broad plateau 1180m above sea level, surrounded by the **Hohe Munde, Wetterstein,** and **Karwendel** mountain ranges. Innsbruck, 26km away, runs 19 trains to Seefeld each day (40min., 48AS). Sit on the right as the train approaches Seefeld for the best view of the valleys. If you can tear your eyes away from the windows on the world once the train comes to a stop, head straight down the street in front of the train station, Bahnhofstrasse, to the *Fußgängerzone* and the center of town. Seefeld's main square, Dorfplatz, will appear on your left at the first major intersection. Bahnhofstr. becomes Klosterstr. beyond Dorfpl., and the cross-street (the other main arm of the *Fußgängerzone*) is Münchenstr. to the right of the plaza and Innsbruckstr. to the left.

Seefeld's **tourist office,** Klosterstr. 43 (tel. 23 13; fax 33 55; email info@seefeld.tirol.at; http://tiscover.com/seefeld), is equipped to handle the town's celebrity status. The helpful and knowledgeable staff gives away plenty of information in English, Italian, French, *und natürlich,* German. From the station, walk straight up Bahnhofstr. The office is on the right just past Dorfpl. (Open mid-June to mid-Sept. and mid-Dec. to March Mon.-Sat. 8:30am-6:30pm; mid-Sept. to mid-Dec. and March to mid-June Mon.-Sat. 8:30am-12:15pm and 3-6pm.) You can **exchange money** at banks (open Mon.-Fri. 8am-12:30pm and 2-4pm) and at the post office until 5pm. Walk straight out of the train station to find an **ATM** at the Sparkasse across the street. You can find **taxis** in front of the train station or by calling 26 30, 22 21, or 42 42. You can **store luggage** (30AS) and **rent bikes** (150-200AS per day) at the station. If all the station bikes are rented, try **Sport Sailer** (tel. 25 30) in Dorfpl. A mountain bike costs 220AS for a full day, 350AS for a weekend. (Open July to mid-Sept. Mon.-Fri. 9am-6pm, Sat. 9am-noon; mid-Sept. to Dec. and April-June Mon.-Fri. 9am-noon and 3-6pm, Sat. 9am-noon.) The **Tip-Top Laundromat,** Andreas-Hofer-Str. 292 (tel. 20 44), is behind and to the right of the station. (Open Mon.-Tues. and Thurs. 8am-12:30pm and 2:30-6pm, Wed. 8am-12:30pm, Sat. 9am-noon.) For a **snow report,** call 37 90. The **post office** (tel. 23 47; fax 38 73) is right down the road from the tourist office. (Open Mon.-Fri. 8am-noon and 2-6pm; Dec. 16-April 15 and July-Sept. also open Sat. 9am-noon.) The **postal code** is A-6100. and the **telephone code** is 05212.

Accommodations and Food

Seefeld boasts seven five-star hotels (that's *thirty-five* stars!), but no hostel. This proliferation of constellations means the price of a hotel bed runs 500 to 1200AS, depending on the season. *Pensionen* or *Privatzimmer* are the best budget option. Prices for these rooms average 200-300AS per night in the summer; slap on about 100AS more in winter. Make reservations well in advance, particularly if you're traveling alone, since singles are few and far between. The tourist office has a list of all accommodations; call ahead and the staff will help you find a room. Wherever you stay, inquire about a **guest card** *(Kurkarte)* for 10-20% discounts off skiing, swimming, concerts, and local attractions.

Several *Pensionen* cluster along Kirchwaldstr. To get there, walk straight out of the train station onto Bahnhofstr. as it becomes Klosterstr. Take Klosterstr. past the sports center until the road descends into Mosererstr. Kirchwaldstr. is the narrow, uphill road with a guard rail on its left-hand side. One of the best guest houses here is **Haus Felseneck,** Kirchwaldstr. 309 (tel. 25 40), the third house on the right. Bask in luxurious bed chambers boasting balconies, TV, lace lampshades, and a view you'll wish you could write a quick message on the back of, stamp, and send home. The friendly owners like to practice their English. All the rooms have double beds. (In summer singles and doubles 260AS; in winter 360AS. Breakfast and private shower included.) Another *Pension*-filled area (with less spectacular views) lies on the other side of town. Exit left from the station and then turn left onto Reitherspitzstr., crossing the tracks. **Haus Carinthia,** Hocheggstr. 432 (tel. 29 55), on the left after a short walk, was revamped in June '97, but antlers still hang on the wall in typical Tirolean style. (Singles 260AS. Winter 360AS. Toilet, shower, and breakfast included. Call ahead.) **Bozherhof,** Hocheggstr. 355 (tel. 29 41), offers guests the use

SKIING, SIGHTS, AND ENTERTAINMENT ■ 275

of a kitchen and enough breakfast to satisfy you until dinner. (Singles 250AS; doubles 270AS. Winter: 300AS; 320AS. Shower and breakfast included.)

Finding inexpensive food in Seefeld is less arduous than hunting down a cheap room. The entire *Fußgängerzone* is stocked with rows of restaurants, outdoor cafés, and bars. **Luigi and Lois,** Innsbruckstr. 12 (tel. 22 58 67), offers a double-header: Italian fare on the Luigi side and Tirolean fare *chez* Lois. Move from an Adriatic villa to a rustic mountain farm simply by crossing the hall. They serve masterpieces in ice cream and chocolate (35-68AS), equally expressive pasta and pizza (79-130AS), and Tirolean munchies (89-220AS). (Kitchen open daily 10:30am-11pm, bar open till 1am. Visa, MC, AmEx.) Locals recommend *Wiener Schnitzel al fresco* at the **Tiroler Weinstube,** Dorfpl. 130 (tel. 22 08), next to the tourist office. Most dishes are 80-155AS, specials from the grill cost 135-250AS, and desserts run 30-95AS. There are few vegetarian offerings. (Open daily 9am-midnight. Visa, MC.) The **Albrecht Hat's supermarket,** Innsbruckstr. 24 (tel. 22 29), is located across from Sport Sailer just off Dorfpl. (Open Mon.-Fri. 8:30am-noon and 3-6pm, Sat. 8am-noon.)

Knee-Deep in Church

In 1384, Oswald Milser put Seefeld on the map. Although dutifully attending Easter Mass like a good little knight, Oswald one day fancied himself as being better than the masses. Rejecting the small host usually given to laypeople, he demanded the consecrated wafer reserved for the clergy, and the timid priest complied. When Oswald took the host in his mouth, he suddenly began to sink into the ground, deeper and deeper, until the priest pulled the now blood-red wafer from his mouth. Hailed as an acute example of the proverb "pride goeth before a fall," the instructive miracle turned Seefeld into a pilgrimage site. The devout come to see the 1½-foot hole in the ground (now covered by a protective grate) and the deep hand-print on the altar where the sinking Oswald had attempted to support himself.

Skiing, Sights, and Entertainment The tourist office prints *Seefeld A-Z*, an unbelievably detailed listing of summer and winter activities. The luxurious **Olympia Sport Center** (tel. 32 20; fax 32 28 83) is a popular attraction year-round, featuring an **indoor pool** with decorative boulders and greenhouse windows and a massive **sauna** complex, ready to soothe those battered by a tough day of hiking or skiing the slopes. (Pool open daily in summer and winter 9:30am-10pm; in fall and spring 1-10pm. 88AS with guest card, children 44AS. Sauna open daily in spring, summer, and fall 2-10pm; in winter 1-10pm. Sauna and pool 155AS with guest card, children 115AS.) The Center screens **movies** nightly during the high skiing and hiking seasons (80AS).

Summer in Seefeld brings a multitude of outdoor activities. The tourist office and the **Tirol Alpine School** run an excellent summer **hiking** program that will satiate even the most accomplished veteran's *Wanderlust*. The four- to six-hour hikes wind among local sky-scraping peaks, including the **Pleisenspitze** (2569m) and the **Gehrenspitze** (2367m). The tourist office schedules hiking trips for every Tuesday at 9am and Friday at 8am from mid-June to mid-September. (Register by 3pm the day before the hike. All hikes leave from the tourist office. 150AS plus transportation fees.) The **Kneipp Hiking Society** invites visitors to join its free weekly four- to five-hour outings, which depart from the train station Thursday at 12:30pm. The **Bergbahn Rosshütte** (tel. (05242) 241 60) offers "four hours of mountain adventure" with its "Cable Car Experience." For 205AS participants ride a tram, a cable car, and the *Jochbahn* railway to Alpine heights of 2000m and up, followed by selected jaunts on several short trails and a delectable "Austrian coffee break" at the Rosshütte restaurant.

If not overwhelmed by Seefeld's immense sporting machinery, the Renaissance jock can plunge into the full program of cultural events designed to introduce visitors to the true Tirolean way. For the summer, the tourist office prints a pamphlet of events and a children's program that includes nature adventure days, music, sports, and farm animals. When the day is done, gussy up and head to the **Tirolean Evenings** on Tuesday at Ferienhotel or Thursday at Hotel Tirol (June-Sept. 9pm). In summer the Parish Church holds **chamber music concerts** Fridays at 8:30pm, and **brass band concerts** occur in the Music Pavilion on Thursdays at 8:30pm. The rustic **Bauerntheater** performs almost every week at the Olympic Center on Wednesday evenings.

When the blanket of snow falls in winter, skiers aplenty from around the globe descend upon the town. Seefeld offers two money-saving ski passes. The **Seefelder Card** provides access to slopes at Seefeld, Reith, Mösern, and Neuleutasch (1-day pass 340AS, ages 5-15 210AS, ages 16-17 305AS). The other option is the comprehensive **Happy Ski Pass,** valid for skiing at (take a deep breath) Seefeld, Reith, Neuleutasch, Mittenwald, Garmisch-Partenkirchen, Ehrwald, Lermoos, Biberwier, Bichbach, Berwang, and Heiterwant (whew!). This pass is available for 3-20 days and requires a photograph. Three days of happy skiing costs 975AS, ages 5-15 620AS, ages 16-17 895AS. Ten different **sports equipment rental shops** lease alpine and cross-country skis, snowboards, and toboggans—all at standardized prices. Downhill skis with poles and boots cost 140-250AS, children 80-130AS; snowboard 200-300AS. The *Seefeld A-Z* pamphlet will guide you to the nearest rental store and includes a schedule for the **ski bus,** free with the Seefeld guest card. The ski shuttle runs every 15 minutes daily from 9:15am to 5pm between the train station and the Rosshütte and Gschwandtkopf ski areas. For those who prefer their skiing on the level, choose from the 100km of *langlaufen* (cross-country skiing) trails surrounding Seefeld. The tourist office has a trail map. *Seefeld A-Z* and the tourist office's winter calendar of events cover other winter activities, from skating to tobogganing to snow hiking.

THE LECHTALER ALPS

The Lechtaler Alps, a region of 3000m peaks and lake-speckled valleys, hugs the German border in northwestern Tirol. Friendly to mountain beasts and mythical dwarves—but not to rear-wheel-drive cars—the alpine terrain is four-fifths uninhabitable. As a result, guest beds are concentrated in large resort areas, and cheap lodgings are few and far between. Portions of the Lechtal do offer alternative accommodations; the Innsbruck branch of the Tirol Information Service, Adamg. 3-7, A-6020 Innsbruck (tel. 56 18 82), prints *Urlaub am Bauernhof* ("Vacation on the Farm").

The best time to visit the Lechtal is when the mountains are your only companions; consider a trip in the off season, April to June or October to November. Carry your passport at all times, since you may pop over a border or two in the course of travel. The **Inn River,** the primary waterway of the valley, runs southwest to northeast from the Swiss frontier at Finstermünz through Innsbruck to the German border by Kufstein. Cutting a swath of land through Innsbruck, Imst, and Landeck before heading south to Switzerland, the Inn has served as a pivotal transport route for two millennia. Parallel to and north of the Inn, the **Lech River** has eroded its own wide valley. Between the lowlands of the Inn and Lech, the mountains are virtually people-free.

The Lechtaler Alps offer some of the best skiing in Austria and the world. For a 24-hour **weather report,** call (0512) 15 66. Swimming, skiing, hiking—all of this hearty cardiovascular activity is going to make you hungry. Try the *Tiroler Speckknödel* (bacon-fat dumplings), served either *zu Wasser* (in broth) or *zu Lande* (dry, with salad or sauerkraut); or *Gröstel* (a combination of potatoes, meat, bacon, and eggs).

Ehrwald

Of his hometown Ehrwald, poet Ludwig Ganghofer once importuned God, "If You love me, please let me live here forever." Though at last report his request went unheeded (he died in 1920 and was buried near Munich), some divine power has certainly smiled on the city. Other than a few damaged buildings, the World Wars spared the hamlet, and to date nothing has blemished Ehrwald's prized attraction, the majestic **Zugspitze** (2962m, Germany's highest). The mountain straddles the German-Austrian border and brings 400,000 tourists a year to Ehrwald (pop. 2500), though many visitors flock like lemmings to the peak's more congested German resort **Garmisch-Partenkirchen**. Plucky Ehrwald responds with the motto "Ehrwald—on the *sunny* side of the Zugspitze." While no meteorologist has confirmed this oddity, Ehrwald *is* more pleasant than its German counterpart in many ways: it's quieter, it boasts a faster cable car (the **Tiroler Zugspitzbahn**), and it's cheaper (rooms run 50-100AS less). Compare for yourself; trains cross between the countries nine times per day.

Orientation and Practical Information Autobahn A12 follows the Inn from Innsbruck to Imst, the old market town. Bundesstr. 314 runs north from Imst to Ehrwald, close to Germany and Garmisch-Partenkirchen. Bundesstr. 198 runs along the Lech River. Ehrwald lies in a cul-de-sac of the Austrian Alpine railroad: all trains to and from major cities must pass through Garmisch-Partenkirchen in Germany, where Ehrwald-bound travelers must switch onto a two-car train. The little Ehrwald **train station** (tel. 22 01 34) offers **luggage storage** (30AS, open daily 6am-9pm). **Trains** go to **Garmisch-Partenkirchen** (48AS), **Innsbruck** (142AS), **Munich** (245AS), and **Salzburg** (456AS). Ehrwald has few street signs, but street names are often listed under house numbers on buildings, and ubiquitous signs direct visitors to *Pensionen* and ski slopes. In the central town square, all buildings have Kirchplatz addresses instead of street addresses. To reach the town center from the train station, turn left out of the station onto Bahnhofstr. and go straight ahead into Hauptstr. After about 20 minutes, Kirchpl. will appear when Hauptstr. curves around to the left. The **tourist office**, Kirchpl. 1 (tel. 23 95; fax 33 14; email ehrwald@zugspitze.tirol.at; http://www.tiscover.at/tirol/ehrwald) lies on Hauptstr. beyond the church. The staff is eager to help, and various brochures are on hand. (Open Mon.-Fri. 8:30am-noon and 1:30-6pm; mid-June to Sept. and mid-Dec. to Feb. also open Sat.) **Currency exchange** is available at banks (open Mon.-Fri. 8am-noon and 2-4:30pm) and the post office (open Mon.-Fri. 8am-5pm). A 24-hour **ATM** at BTV, Kirchpl. 21a (tel. 29 14), accepts only Visa. For a **taxi**, call 22 68 or 23 25. **Rent bikes** at **Zweirad Zirknitzer**, Zugspitzstr. 16 (tel. 32 19), across the tracks and up the hill. (70AS per ½-day, 90AS per day. Mountain bikes 50AS per hr., 100-150AS per ½-day, 200AS per day, 350AS per weekend. Lower rates for children's bikes.) The **post office**, Hauptstr. 5 (tel. 33 66; fax 31 40), is on the right about 100m before the town center as you walk from the train station. (Open Mon.-Fri. 8am-noon and 2-6pm; July to mid-Sept. and mid-Dec. to Aug. also open Sat. 8-10am.) Ehrwald's **postal code** is A-6632, and its **telephone code** is 05673.

Accommodations, Camping, and Food Ehrwald is filled with relatively inexpensive guest houses. The tourist office has a complete listing of prices and locations, but wherever you stay, be sure to pick up a **guest card** for tourist discounts. **Gästehaus Konrad**, Kirweg 10 (tel. 72 71), is only a few minutes down Hauptstr. from the station toward the town center. After you pass the post office and SPAR supermarket, take the first right onto Kirweg. Konrad is on your right, down a private driveway. Each room has a painted Alpine scene, but you can open the curtains and step out onto the balcony for the real thing: a phenomenal view of green fields and small villages, with breathtaking mountains in all directions. You may never want to go back into the room. (Singles with shower 240AS, 3 nights or more 210AS. Winter: singles with shower 470AS, without shower or for stays of 3 nights or more 440AS. Breakfast included.) Camping is available—if you're willing to walk about 25 minutes uphill—at **Comfort Camping** (tel. 26 66). Head left out of the train station and immediately turn left up the hill. Take the right-hand fork past Zweirad Zirknitzer and continue uphill (ignore the "Leaving Ehrwald" sign). As the road curves left at the Thörleweg intersection, the well-marked campground soon appears on your right. (Open daily 2pm-midnight. Telephones, restaurant, and washing machines on site. 70AS; tent and car 194.50AS; town tax 9.50AS.) As for eats, the town center is filled with cafés and restaurants serving Tirolean specialties as well as pizza and *gelato*. If you are planning a picnic on the summit of the Zugspitze, try the local **SPAR supermarket,** Hauptstr. 1 (tel. 27 40), next to the post office. (Open Mon.-Thurs. 8am-7pm, Fri. 8am-7:30pm, Sat. 7:30am-1pm; July to mid-Sept. and mid-Dec. to March extended Sat. hours 7:30am-6pm.)

Sights and Entertainment The **Tiroler Zugspitzbahn** (tel. 23 09) is Ehrwald's leading tourist attraction and greatest engineering feat to date. This cable car climbs 2950m to the summit of the Zugspitze in a hold-your-breath (for some, hold-your-lunch) seven minutes and 12 seconds. The outdoor platforms of the crowded restaurant (open mid-May to mid-Oct.) at the ride's end have what some deem the most breathtaking view on the entire continent: on a clear day, visibility extends from Salzburg to Stuttgart. Be sure to bring a sweater, since snow may still be on the ground. (Late May to late October and late November to mid-April daily 8:40am-4:40pm. Round-trip 410AS with guest card, ages 16-17 290AS, children 250AS.) The **Ehrwalder Almbahn** (tel. 24 68) doesn't climb quite so high ("only" 1510m), but the prices aren't so steep either. (Daily May-Oct. 9am-4:30pm; Dec.-April 9am-4pm. 120AS with guest card, children 65AS.) To reach either cable car, hop on a Summerrund bus at the town green, at the tracks across from the train station, or at any of the orange "H" signs scattered throughout the city. (Schedules are at the stops. Day tickets 34AS.) In summer the Ehrwald tourist office organizes free **mountain bike tours** every Friday, leaving from the office at 8:30am, as well as daily guided mountain tours. Registration for both is open until Thursday at 5pm at the tourist office. The tourist office also provides information on hiking, fishing, swimming, billiards, boats, skating, climbing, paragliding, horseback riding, squash, tennis, kayaking, and rafting in Ehrwald and neighboring areas. Visitors can **swim** outdoors at **Hotel Spielmann,** Wetterstr. 4 (tel. 22 55), or indoors at the **Familienbad Ehrwald,** Hauptstr. 21 (tel. 27 18), a short distance before the town center (look for the Sport Center sign). A children's **playground** sits next to the Sports Center.

For winter guests Ehrwald offers the charmingly dubbed **Happy Ski Pass.** The cheerful little card gives access to 128 lifts, 244km of alpine ski runs, 100km of cross-country trails, and several other winter time sports arenas. (For more information and prices see **Seefeld** listing above.) You can rent **skis** at **Intersport Leitner,** Kirchpl. 13 (tel./fax 23 71) for 230-360AS per day for downhill skis or snowboards, 190AS for cross-country skis. (Open Mon.-Thurs. 8:30am-noon and 2:30-6pm.)

THE ARLBERG

Looming halfway between the Bodensee and Innsbruck, the jagged peaks of the Arlberg mountains make for an extreme Alpine experience. Since the first descent into the valley by Lech's parish priest in 1895, incomparable conditions have catapulted the area to glory. Where once only knickerbockered spitfires dared tread, Spandex-clad pedal pushers and stooped aristocrats now cavort. In summer, streams pour down each steep mountainside in almost-continuous waterfalls, creating gorgeous **hiking** prospects. Most lifts operate in summer for high-altitude hikes, but **skiing** remains the area's main draw. With hundreds of miles of ski runs ranging in altitude from 1000 to 3000m, the Arlberg offers unparalleled terrain December through April. Dauntingly long cross-country trails (up to 42km) link the various villages throughout the valleys. All resorts have ski schools in German and English for children and beginners as well as proficient skiers. In fact, the world's first ski instructor still makes his home in Oberlech. The comprehensive **Arlberg Ski Pass** gives access to some of Austria's most coveted slopes, including the famed **Valluga** summit. The pass is valid for over 88 mountain railways and ski lifts in St. Anton, St. Jakob, St. Christoph, Lech, Zürs, Klösterle, and Stuben, amounting to more than 192km of prime snow-draped terrain. Locally, the Galzigbahn lift tends to attract the longest morning lines, because of its central location just outside St. Anton's *Fußgängerzone*, while the Rendl ski area remains largely pristine. You must purchase passes at the Galzig, Vallugagrat, Vallugipfel, Gampen, and Kapall cable car stations from 8am to 4:30pm on the day prior to use. (1 day 465AS, 2 day 890AS, 1 week 2610AS, 2 week 4230AS. 100AS senior discount, 40% discount for children under 15; 50% discount April 21-Nov.)

On the eastern side of the Arlberg tunnel, in the province of Tirol, you'll find the hub of the region, **St. Anton,** and its distinctly less cosmopolitan cousin, **St. Jakob.** The western Arlberg is home to the classy resorts **Lech, Zürs,** and **St. Christoph,** each pricier than the last. In high season, book rooms six to eight weeks in advance; in off season, two weeks is sufficient. **Buses** link the Arlberg towns together, and trains connect St. Anton to the rest of Austria. Bus #4235 runs from Landeck to St. Anton every hour; #4248 runs from St. Anton to St. Christoph, Zürs, and Lech five times per day and returns four times per day.

■ St. Anton am Arlberg

France has St. Tropez, Switzerland has St. Moritz, and Austria has St. Anton am Arlberg. Don't be fooled by the pious name, the hillside farms, or the cherubic schoolchildren. As soon as the first winter snowflake arrives, St. Anton (non-tourist pop. 2300) awakens with a vengeance as an international playground brimming with playboys, partygoers, and plenty of physical activity (including skiing, skating, and snow-shoeing). Downhill skiing was born here at the turn of the century when some Austrians barreled down the mountain with boards on their feet, and the town has definitely retained its daredevil panache. To escape the tabloid reporters in St. Moritz, many members of the Euro jet set (including Prince Edward of England) winter here. St. Anton *loves* its flock of traveling socialites; establishments accept all major credit cards, and salespeople have a healthy knowledge of English. Whether calculated for tourists or just standard practice, the many traditional touches—lederhosen-clad marching bands, colorful festivals, and early evening cattle drives through the *Fußgängerzone*—round out the Tirolean experience. Be warned that this posh ski town doesn't emerge from spring hibernation until mid-July, and the sleep is so deep that restaurants and museums often close for a late spring cleaning. If you visit in May or June, you may feel like you're at Disneyland after hours—the city has all the tourist machinery in place but no one to run it. Nonetheless, summer in St. Anton offers beautiful, isolated hiking trails and quiet, affordable accommodations. Only then does the town reveal its roots as a small, unpretentious mountain village.

Orientation and Practical Information St. Anton is lies along major rail and bus routes. Typical of the town's celebrity status, even the **Orient Express** stops here. More than 40 **trains** come and go daily, with destinations including **Innsbruck** (13 per day, 1½hr., 131AS), **Munich** (3¾hr., 472AS), and **Zurich** (5 per day, 3½hr., 410AS). The St. Anton **train station** (tel. 240 23 85) will **store luggage** for 30AS. During the high seasons (late June to Sept. and Dec.-April) **buses** run almost every hour between St. Anton and the neighboring Arlberg villages, including **Lech** (24AS) and **St. Christoph** (10AS). Year-round buses run frequently to **Landeck** (6am-7pm, 46AS). A *Tageskarte* allows unlimited bus travel between the towns (80AS). The bus station is across the street from the tourist office, under Sport Pangratz.

Though St. Anton has few street signs, there's really only one main road, which runs the length of the *Fußgängerzone*. From the train station, walk down the hill to the right (or straight ahead if you're coming from the tunnel beneath the platform). Within seconds you'll find yourself on St. Anton's main drag, with the *Fußgängerzone* to the left. To reach the **tourist office** (tel. 226 90; fax 25 32; email st.anton@netway.at; http://www.stantonamarlberg.com), turn right on the main road as you come out of the station. The tourist office is off a small square on the left just before the railroad crossing. The office is as chic as the town—luxurious leather chairs, mahogany reception stands, and no fewer than six full-size English brochures. The foyer, with brochures in multiple languages, is open 24 hours. (Open July to mid-Sept. Mon.-Fri. 8am-noon and 2-6pm, Sat.-Sun. 10am-noon; May to early June and mid-Sept. to Dec. Mon.-Fri. 8am-noon and 2-6pm; Dec.-April Mon.-Fri. 8am-6pm, Sat. 9am-noon and 1-7pm, Sun. 10am-noon and 3-6pm.) The **Tiroler Landesreisebüro** (tel. 22 22; fax 22 21), near the tourist office and directly opposite the railway crossing, is a well-equipped regional **travel agency** offering **currency exchange**, plane and train reservations, and **car rental**. (Open only during the high seasons: in summer Mon.-Fri. 8:30am-noon and 2:45-6pm, Sat. 8:30am-noon; in winter Mon.-Sat. 9am-noon and 2:30-6pm.) You can also **exchange currency** (at exorbitant rates) at any of the 24-hour ATM machines around town or at the three local banks, all in the *Fußgängerzone*. (Banking hours are Mon.-Fri. 8am-noon and 2-4:30pm.) **Biking** in the Arlberg is arduous but extraordinarily rewarding. The folks at **Sporthaus Schneider,** in the pedestrian zone, will be glad to rent you a bike and dispense maps and trail advice. (Full day rental 250AS, morning or afternoon 130AS, weekend 440AS. Open daily July-Sept. 8am-6:30pm; Dec.-April 8am-7pm.) Call 25 65 for 24-hour updated **ski conditions;** for **weather reports,** 226 90. To **report accidents,** 235 20. For the **police,** call 23 62 13. In an **emergency,** call 22 37. To find the **post office** (tel. 33 80; fax 35 30), turn left on the main road from the station and walk to the end of the *Fußgängerzone,* and then follow the yellow Post P.S.K. signs. (Open in summer Mon.-Fri. 8:30am-noon and 2-6pm; in winter Mon.-Fri. 8:30am-7pm, Sat. 9-11am.) The **postal code** is A-6580. St. Anton's **telephone code** is 05446.

Accommodations and Food In the summer, affordable accommodations are relatively easy to find. During the ski season, however, prices generally double. If you book far enough in advance (about 2 months), you *may* find relatively cheap housing. Since street anonymity makes directions unclear, the best bet is to ask for precise directions at the tourist office or when you make a reservation. An invaluable resource is the **24-hour electronic accommodation board** outside the tourist office that lists all *Pensionen,* hotels, and prices and has a free telephone to call for reservations. **Pension Pepi Eiter** (tel. 25 50; fax 36 57) sits to the right on the hill behind the train station. Turn right on the main road when you exit the station and continue past the tourist office, across the railroad tracks, and up the hill. After a few minutes, the hotel will appear on your right; turn around and head up the hill. At the end of the short road, the *Pension* will magically appear. The gracious owner will let you in the entrance at the back of the garage. Pepi Eiter provides luscious beds, hearty repasts, light pine rooms, and a chocolate every night on your pillow. (Singles 170-220AS; doubles 360AS. Winter: 420-480AS; 800AS. Add 20AS in summer and 50AS in winter for stays shorter than 3 nights. Breakfast and private bathroom included.) **Pension Elisabeth** (tel. 24 96; fax 292 54) is one of the town's least expensive three-star B&Bs. Follow the directions to Pension Pepi Eiter, but stop when you reach Haus Schollberg. Pension Elisabeth is right next door (enter up the stairs). The friendly young owner speaks perfect English. (230-250AS per person. Winter: 410-530AS, depending on ski conditions. Add 20AS for stays of less than 3 nights. Bath, TV, radio, breakfast, and parking included.) To find **Pension Klöpfer** (tel. 28 00), start at the train station, turn left down the narrow, paved path directly in front of the station, and then go left up the larger road. Continue across the railroad tracks and follow the road as it curves right up the hill. At the top, walk straight ahead along the gravel path, following the sign. Pension Klöpfer is on the left at #419. (Singles 250AS. Winter: 400-600AS, depending on ski conditions. Private bathrooms, breakfast, and parking included.)

The *Fußgängerzone* is riddled with such restaurants as **SportCafé Schneider** (tel. 25 48), which serves up soups and sandwiches for 35-55AS and ice cream desserts for 35-80AS. (Open daily 9am-midnight.) To combat St. Anton's generally high prices, the local supermarkets may be your best bet for a meal. The **Nah und Frisch Supermarket** (tel. 35 81) beckons from the *Fußgängerzone*. (Open in summer Mon.-Fri. 7am-noon and 2-6pm, Sat. 7am-noon; in winter Mon.-Sat. 7am-noon and 2-6:30pm.) The local **Spar Markt** lies farther down the main road, just past the *Fußgängerzone*. (Open Mon.-Fri. 7am-noon and 2-6pm, Sat. 7am-12:30pm.)

The Arlberg Channel

St. Anton's economy (like its full name) depends on that pretty old hunk of rock, the Arlberg. Understandably, the town really likes its pet peak. A lot. How much? The town has set up a TV station that provides nothing but live footage of the mountain—hour after hour of trees, rocks, some more rocks, and snow. All Arlberg, all the time. Showing up-to-the-minute weather, the channel is ostensibly a service for skiers, but anyone in town can tell you the real reason for it: St. Anton is simply paying high-tech homage to its provider. Twenty-four-hour surveillance replaces burnt offerings—and, anyway, you never know when the mountain might pack up and leave if no one kept an eye on it. Right?

Sights and Entertainment St. Anton in the summer is a quiet haven for mountain hikers and sport-lovers. On summer Sundays, the local **hikers** hit the **Wanderwege** in full Tirolean hiking gear—join them for some spectacular mountain views and beautiful hikes along rushing streams. For starters, try the **Mühltobelweg,** a shady trail that runs up the mountain alongside a thundering stream, complete with a misty 20-foot waterfall. To reach the trail head, go up the hill toward Pension Pepi Eiter but turn right at the red Museum Café sign and follow the signs to the café. The trail starts along the right side of the mini-golf course. (1hr. round-trip, including several stops for open-mouthed gawking at the scenery.) Once a week, the tourist office sponsors wildflower hikes for flora-lovers. Daredevil cyclists might try for the **Arlberg Mountainbike Trophy,** bestowed every August upon the winner of a treacherous 20.5km race with steep climbs and dangerously rapid downhill sections. Any psychotic velocipedist eager to undertake the journey may enter for a 200AS registration fee—it's a great way to pace yourself against Olympic and professional cyclists. Otherwise, 60km of marked mountain bike paths await you, including the popular Ferwall Valley and Moostal trails. Swimming in St. Anton's **outdoor pool,** with a 36m twisty red slide, is also available, along with golfing, tennis, fishing, and concerts. Children can enjoy a special week-long program, free for families with guest cards.

In the winter, the world-famous Alpine slopes of St. Anton await, but you must pay for the fame and glamour. St. Anton's resorts boast a list of clientele that reads like the December special issue of *People* magazine. European royalty, public figures, and Hollywood stars stay incognito in bulky ski-wear and extra-terrestrial goggles. Prince Edward, JFK Jr., Clint Eastwood, Charles Schulz, and Paul Anka have all graced the slopes at St. Anton. To follow in their ski tracks may be costly, but if you stay in St. Anton and ski for more than three days, you become eligible for a minor reduction in price (about 100AS off your Arlberg Ski Pass). If Demi Moore has crowded you out of the lift line, you might want to turn to St. Anton's winter spectator sports. In December, the town offers a professional **tennis tournament,** the Isospeed Trophy, which features some moderately famous European players, like Goran Ivanisevic, Henri Leconte, and Javier Sanchez. Also in December, the **Kandahar Ski Race** (men's or women's, depending on the year) on the World Cup circuit attracts the sport's best. Or watch the **Synchro Ski World Cup,** where two skiers tackle the mountain simultaneously and are judged not only on speed but also on how closely they mirror each other's form with Germanic precision. In 2001, St. Anton will host the Alpine Skiing World Championships. Start planning soon if you want to attend.

Near St. Anton: Lech

In 1300 the call went out: "There's gold in them thar hills," and the settlers came, leading their cattle from the Valais region of western Switzerland to Lech. As others found, however, the real gold here is powdery and white. The ski resort industry saw a seminal event here, when some lost Tirolean daredevil skiers happened upon the Swiss dairy men in their little valley between the Rüflikopf (2362m), Karhorn (2416m), and Braunarspitze (2648m) peaks. Gasping in awe at the mountains, they took a quick swig of schnapps, checked their bindings, and immediately shooshed to the nearest bank. They promptly mortgaged all they had to bring the sport of skiing (and its wealthy practitioners) to the valley. The skiing was so good that people couldn't head up the hill quickly enough; 1939 saw the first T-bar lift. From these humble beginnings sprung a giant among resorts; no fewer than four Olympic gold medalist skiers call Lech home. If you think the mountains are steep, you should check out the prices—you can go for broke on the slopes, but you'll just go broke at the bars. Lech is farther up the mountain than its neighbor St. Anton—above the tree line, in fact—which makes for amazing, panoramic views but also means Lech is even slower to awaken from the post-ski-season slumber. In the summer, the shiny peaks looming above the town beckon those ready to lace up their boots and exercise as Mother Nature intended, before Stairmaster took over. **Hike** through Lech's peaks or swim laps in the shadow of the mountains at the 1200 square meters outdoor, heated swimming pool, the **Waldbad,** down the road to Zug. In an effort to convince summer visitors to come all the way up the mountain, Lech now offers free access to all cable cars and swimming facilities to visitors with Lech guest cards.

Guest beds outnumber permanent Lech residents five to one, but when the snowflakes fall the beds fill up and the prices rise. Luckily, there is a **youth hostel** in Lech kept discreetly at a distance. From the bus stop, head down the main road into town, cross over the river when the road cuts left, and continue along this road. Don't panic when you reach the *auf wiedersehen* sign, but turn right when the road splits, down the hill and back over the river. Continue for about 15 minutes, and when the road curves back toward Lech, bear right at the tiny white chapel, head up hill to the left of *Haus Tristeller,* and climb one more hill. **Jugendheim Stubenbach(HI)** (tel. 24 19; fax 24 194) is at the top of that hill, decorated by a large mural of a prophet right in the middle of a revelation. (180AS per person, stays of 2 nights or more 160AS. Winter: 280AS, 260AS. Breakfast included. Open July-late April.) To get to **Pension Brunelle** (tel. 29 76), follow the main road downhill past the church and over the river. Take the third right, and Pension Brunelle will be on your right at #220. (Singles 190-220AS. Winter: 310-350AS. Open late June-early Sept. and Dec.-April. Breakfast included.) The ski mavens who brought hordes of people to the valley were quick to learn that in order to ski, you have to fuel up. **Pizza Charly** (tel. 23 39) does the job. Down the main road past the church and just after the bridge, Pizza Charly sits underneath the cables of the *Schloßkopfbahn* (where they hang their tablecloths in the summer). The place serves up pizza (80-195AS) and pasta (68-115AS) and gives free yodeling lessons with coffee. (Open July to late April daily 11am-2pm and 4:30-11pm. Take-out available.) **S'Caserol Bistro** (tel. 37 41) lies beyond the church on the right beneath the Volksbank sign and serves tasty baguettes and pasta with numerous vegetarian options for 105-150AS. (Open only during high seasons.)

During the off season (May-July and Oct.-Dec.), Lech is almost inaccessible by public transportation, with only a few buses each day from nearby Langen. In the high skiing and hiking seasons (Dec.-April and July-Sept.), several **buses** run daily to **St. Anton, Zürs, Langen,** and **Bludenz** (44AS one way, day pass 80AS). The **tourist office** (tel. 21 61; fax 31 55; email lech-info@lech.at; http://www.lech.at), a model of efficiency, is just down the road from the bus stop, on the right. The **24-hour electronic accommodations board** in the foyer has a free phone to make reservations, and there's a **travel agency** in the office. (Open late June to mid-Sept. Mon.-Sat. 8am-

1pm and 2-6pm, Sun. 9am-noon and 3-5pm; mid-Sept. to Nov. Mon.-Fri. 8am-noon and 2-6pm, Sat. 9am-noon; Dec.-April Mon.-Sat. 9am-6pm, Sun. 10am-noon and 3-5pm; May to late June Mon.-Fri. 9am-noon and 2-5pm.) The banks are also a step away and are generally open 8:30am to noon and 2 to 4pm. **Raiffeisenbank,** opposite the church and next to the post office, has a **24-hour ATM. Free parking** is available in the Esso garage under the church. For **weather reports,** dial 18 in Lech. To **report accidents,** dial 28 55. Walk past the church and down the hill to find the **post office** (tel. 22 40; fax 22 50) on your left. (Open Mon.-Fri. 8am-noon and 2-6pm.) The **postal code** is A-6764, and the **telephone code** is 05583.

VORARLBERG

On Austria's panhandle, Vorarlberg (2600 sq. km, pop. 340,000) is the westernmost province (and the smallest, barring Vienna). Here, at the crossroads of four nations, carry your passport at all times; foreign borders are never more than two hours away, and a little daytrip may become an international excursion. The area's dialect, Allemannian, combines tones from Swiss-German and German Swabia, and Vorarlberg's culinary specialty, *Käsespätzle,* mixes Switzerland's cheese addiction and Austria's carbohydrate-heavy noodle passion. **Feldkirch,** on the Ill River, lies just off Liechtenstein's border. **Bregenz,** on the banks of the Bodensee (Lake Constance), would be German but for half a dozen kilometers. The area between the Bodensee and the Arlberg massif contains a variety of sumptuous scenery, from the soft-edged contours of the lake's shoreline to the plains of the glacial upper Rhine Valley. Snow conditions are dependably *wunderbar* from December to April, with trails as high as 2600m. Further, over 1610km of marked hiking paths ranging in altitude from 400 to 3350m crisscross Vorarlberg, and mountain railways carry hikers to the summit quickly and conveniently. Alpine associations maintain dozens of huts that provide hikers with accommodations and refreshments from May to October; opening times depend on the altitude, so contact the local tourist offices. Vorarlberg's 161km network of cycling paths ranges from leisurely strolls through the Bodensee and Rhine plain to challenging mountain-bike routes in the Alps. The 125km Bodensee circuit circumnavigates the lake. Cycling maps are available at bookstores and tourist offices.

■ Feldkirch

Since the 13th century, Feldkirch has healed and rejuvenated road-weary wanderers and the city's 27,000 residents. Feldkirch is an excellent base for international expeditions; the city is on the banks of the Ill River just minutes from the Swiss and Liechtensteinian borders and handles all trains to Bregenz and the German Bodensee. Feldkirch is small enough to be tourist-friendly but large enough to have a vibrant life of its own. Students from a nearby *Hauptschule* flood the Fußgängerzone during their midday break and in the evenings, while the many specialty groceries and kebap restaurants are evidence of the city's Turkish community. The narrow streets, with their carefully restored buildings, are functional and fashionable reminders of the Middle Ages. Walking through Feldkirch's city center, between ancient towers and carefully restored edifices, you may feel like you've entered a medieval city temporarily occupied by 20th-century inhabitants.

Orientation and Practical Information Eleven generations of city planners have left their marks on Feldkirch, confounding any navigation. Free maps are available outside the **tourist office,** Herreng. 12 (tel. 734 67; fax 798 67). Walk from the train station to the end of the road, turn left onto Bahnhofstr., and cross the pedestrian underpass at the first major intersection. Head toward the *Zentrum,* and walk through the open doors of the *Bezirkhauptmannschaft* building. The office is about 100m ahead on the right. The office helps with reservations and hands out historic walking-tour maps and information about cultural events. (Open mid-June to mid-Sept. Mon.-Fri. 9am-6pm, Sat. 9am-noon; mid-Sept. to mid-June Mon.-Fri. 8:30am-noon and 1:30-6pm, Sat. 9am-noon.) Feldkirch is easily accessible by **train** from major Austrian cities: **Bregenz** (45min., 56AS); **Innsbruck** (2hr., 228AS); and **Salzburg** (4hr., 550AS). **Swiss PTT buses** travel from the train station to Liechtenstein and to Buchs and Sargans in Switzerland. **Bundesbuses** leave from the train station and go to nearby Austrian towns. **City buses** (*Stadtbus*) connect Feldkirch's various subdivisions (12AS, day pass 24AS). Hop in a **taxi** outside the station, or call 17 18 or 17 12. **Currency exchange,** an **ATM**, **bicycle rental** (150AS, with train ticket 90AS), and **lockers** (20-30AS) are available at the train station. Feldkirch's **post office** is on Bahnhofstr. across from the train station. (Open Mon.-Fri. 7am-7pm, Sat. 7am-noon.) The **postal code** is A-6800. The **telephone code** is 05522.

Accommodations and Food Feldkirch's youth hostel, **Jugendherberge "Altes Siechenhaus,"** Reichstr. 111 (tel. 731 81; fax 793 99), might be the highlight of your visit. Buses #1, 2, and 60: "Jugendherberge" run to the hostel from the station (5min.), or you can walk straight out of the station to the end of the road, then turn right on Bahnhofstr. (which becomes Reichstr.) and walk for 15 to 20 minutes. Buses to and from the city center run every 10 to 15 minutes until 7pm and at least twice an hour until midnight Monday through Saturday. The hostel is an ancient white brick-and-wood building on the right of the street, next to a small stone church. This 600-year-old structure served as an infirmary during the Black Plague and several other epidemics. Later it was a poor house and then a grammar school after a fire in 1697. Today, all the lepers, paupers, and displaced schoolchildren are gone, replaced by a friendly proprietor and a spotless, modern house with thick wooden beams, white stucco walls, and a decidedly medieval feel. The garden lets guests laze the day away or strike up a game of ping pong. (Reception Mon.-Sat. 7am-11pm, Sun. 7-10am and 5-11pm. Key deposit 12AS. Dorms 130AS. Breakfast 30AS. Candy, soft drinks, wine, and beer sold at the desk. Wheelchair accessible.) Bus #2 or 3: "Burgweg" leads to **Gasthof Löwen** (tel. 728 68), in Tosters-Feldkirch. From the stop, walk a half-block toward the tall pink and white building on Egelseestr., from where you can see the green shutters of the Gasthof. The hotel offers simple rooms in a quiet neighborhood. (250-400AS per person. Breakfast and showers included.)

A stroll through the *Fußgängerzone* reveals many restaurants and cafés that provide opportunities to sample Feldkirch's *Spezi*, a mixture of Coke and lemonade. A vegetarian's Valhalla, **Pizzeria-Trattoria La Taverna,** Vorstadtstr. 18 (tel. 792 93), offers a cool Mediterranean atmosphere and affordable pizza (55-95AS) and pasta (75-95AS). (Open daily 11:30am-2pm and 5pm-midnight.) For a quick meal, head to vegetarian-friendly **König Kebap,** Kreuzg. 9 (tel. 380 42), down the street from the tourist office. (Open Mon.-Sat. 9am-11pm, Sun. 11am-11pm.) The restaurant inside the huge iron doors of the **Schattenburg Castle** serves enormous portions of *Wiener Schnitzel* (135AS) and *Apfelstrudel* (35AS). (Open Tues.-Sun. 10am-midnight.) In the center of the *Altstadt,* find picnic supplies at **Interspar Markt,** under Hervis Sport Mode at the top of Johanniterg. off Marktg. (Open Mon.-Fri. 9am-7:30pm, Sat. 8am-5pm.) Its smaller cousin, **Spar Markt,** is across from the hostel, one minute toward the city center. (Open Mon.-Fri. 7am-noon and 2:30-6pm, Sat. 7am-12:30pm.) The appropriately named Marktpl. houses an **outdoor market** (Tues. and Sat. mornings).

Sights and Entertainment The tourist office's historic walking-tour map will help you locate the monuments to Feldkirch's 700-year-old past. Begin your voyage to the era of chivalry at the green steeple of the Gothic **Dom,** the St. Nikolaus Kirche, which forms one edge of the *Altstadt.* Mentioned in print as early as 1287, the edifice received a facelift in 1478 after a series of devastating fires and now boasts beautiful stained-glass windows and an elaborately vaulted ceiling. A

Pietà, crafted in 1521 by Wolf Huber (a master of the Danube School), graces the altar on the right. Frescoes of Feldkirch history and the coats of arms of local potentates adorn the 15th-century **Rathaus,** originally a granary, on Schmiedg. On nearby Schloßerg. stands the **Palais Liechtenstein,** completed in 1697. The palace, which once supported the royal seat of the Prince of Liechtenstein, now houses the city archives and the town library. The third-floor **art gallery** hosts frequent exhibitions, often for free. At the edges of the *Altstadt,* three towers remain of the original city wall: the **Katzenturm,** the **Pulverturm,** and the **Wasserturm.** Just outside the *Altstadt* lies the **Kapuzinerkloster** (Capuchin monastery), built in 1605. For a fantastic view of the *Altstadt,* stroll up either the castle staircase or Burgg. to **Schattenburg,** Feldkirch's most impressive structure. From the early 1200s until 1390, the castle was the seat of the Count of Montfort. The town purchased the castle in 1825 to save it from demolition and converted it into the **Feldkirch Heimatmuseum** (tel. 719 82). Check out the museum's impressive medieval furnished rooms to see what castle life was really like. (Open Tues.-Sun. 9am-noon and 1-5pm. 25AS, youth 15AS, child 5AS.)

Feldkirch's annual **Schubertiade** (June 17-29 in 1998) honors one of its most famous residents. Musicians perform works by and inspired by Schubert in Feldkirch's concert halls and manor houses, and painters, sculptors, and performance artists exhibit throughout the city. (For tickets, call 720 91, fax 175 450, or write to Schubertiade Feldkirch GmbH, Postfach 625, Schubertpl. 1, A-6803 Feldkirch. Tickets 100-1300AS, outdoor concerts 100-400AS.) During the second weekend of July (10-12 in 1998), Feldkirch's annual **wine festival** intoxicates all those who venture to Marktpl. The circus comes to town on the first weekend of August, when the annual **Festival of Traveling Entertainers** sweeps jugglers, mimes, and clowns into every cobblestone path. December brings the annual **Christmas bazaar,** with crafts, candy canes, and crèches for sale throughout Advent.

▨ Bregenz

A playground city on the banks of the **Bodensee** (Lake Constance), Vorarlberg's capital city Bregenz approaches tourist nirvana. Thousands of Swiss, Germans, and Austrians come Speedo-clad to bake on the banks of the lake, occasionally exerting themselves to sail or to hike in the nearby mountains. When the Romans conquered Brigantium two millennia ago, they set up a thriving bath and spa center here. Later, Gallus and Columban, two Irish missionaries, were unable to escape Bregenz's magnetism. As they lifted their heads from their medieval beach blankets, they observed the vast shimmering lake ringed by mountains and dubbed the locale "Bregenz" (Golden Bowl). They set up camp on the hill above the lake, where modern tourists hike to soak up some medieval culture along with the sun's rays. Bregenz's less leisurely past manifests itself in the **White Fleet,** an armada of Bodensee ferries that have abandoned aggression and now deliver wealthy vacationers from three different currencies—er, countries—to the city's open ports.

ORIENTATION AND PRACTICAL INFORMATION

With multiple layers of history and architecture, from modern department stores in the *Fußgängerzone* to the medieval Martinsturm in the *Oberstadt,* Bregenz does not have the most intuitive city layout. Pick up a **free map** *(Bregenz At a Glance)* outside the tourist office. Most sights, and the tourist office, lie within the compact *Zentrum.*

> **Tourist Office:** Anton-Schneider-Str. 4A (tel. 433 910; fax 433 91 10; email tourismus@bregenz.vol.at). From the train station, head left along Bahnhofstr. and take the 4th right onto Rathausstr. then the first left onto Anton-Schneider-Str. The office is on the right, set back from the street. Makes hotel reservations (30AS) and dispenses *Privatzimmer* lists, hiking and city maps, and concert information. English spoken. Open Mon.-Fri. 9am-7pm, Sat. 2-7pm, Sun. 4-7pm. In June 1998,

the office will move to the Tourismushaus, Bahnhofstr. 14, the giant building easily visible about a block to the left of the train station.
Consulate: U.K., Bundesstr. 110 (tel. 78 586), in neighboring Lauterach.
Trains: Bahnhofstr. (tel. 675 50). **Trains** every hr. to **Bludenz** and **St. Gallen,** and daily connections to **Zurich, Innsbruck, Vienna,** and **Munich.** The train station has **lockers, luggage storage** (30AS), **bike rental,** an **ATM,** and **public showers.**
Buses: BundesBuses leave from the train station.
Public Transportation: Buses run throughout the city. 12AS, day pass 24AS.
Taxis: tel. 17 18.
Car Rental: Hertz, Immler Schneeweiss, Am Brand 2 (tel. 44 995), at the intersection of Deuringstr. and Belruptstr. **Avis-ARBÖ,** Rheinstr. 86 (tel. 78 100).
Parking: Free parking by the Festspielhaus. **Hypobank parking garage** is in the city center, and there are metered parking lots and spaces throughout the city.
AIDS Information: AIDS-Hilfe Voralberg, Neug. 5, A-6900 Bregenz (tel. 465 26). Hotline open Tues. and Thurs. 4-7pm, Wed. and Fri. 10am-1pm.
Post Office: Seestr. 5 (tel. 490 00), across the street from the harbor. Open Mon.-Sat. 7am-7pm (cashier's desk closes at 5pm), Sun. 9am-noon. **Postal Code:** A-6900.
Telephone Code: 05574.

ACCOMMODATIONS AND CAMPING

Bregenz caters to the wealthy, but budget travelers can get a good night's rest. When the Festspiele comes to town, however, prices soar and reservations are a must.

Jugendherberge (HI), Belrupstr. 16a (tel. 228 67), a quick stroll from the tourist office. Head right on Anton-Schneider-Str., turn right on Bergmannstr. at the Österreichischer Nationalbank building, and then turn left on Belrupstr. A few blocks later, bear right up the hill at the hostel sign to the wood-and-stucco hostel. The elongated barn house has an easy, one-corridor layout. The open lawn is good for a sun bath, ping pong, or Frisbee. Six beds to a room and 6 shower heads to a stall. Reception 5-8pm. Curfew 10pm; key with passport deposit. Dorms 126AS. Breakfast and shower included. Free lockers on request. Sheets 30AS. Open April-Sept.

Pension Sonne, Kaiserstr. 8 (tel. 425 72), off Bahnhofstr. near the station. Quiet rooms and an English-speaking staff in the heart of the *Fußgängerzone*. Singles 330-490AS; doubles 600-940AS. Some rooms with private bath. Breakfast included.

Pension Gunz, Anton-Schneider-Str. 38 (tel. 436 57), the last building on the right straight down from the tourist office. Enter through Café Gunz, around the corner on Schillerstr. Comfy rooms, convenient location, and a downstairs restaurant. 250-270AS per person, with bathroom 280-340AS. Breakfast and shower included.

Seecamping (tel. 718 96 or 718 95). Bus #2 (dir: Achsiedlung Weidach): "Viktoria." Or, take a left from the train station onto Strandweg and walk along the lake. Beautiful lakeside location and sparkling bathrooms. 60AS; tent, car, or caravan 60AS. Showers included. Guest tax 17AS. Open May 15-Sept. 15.

FOOD

Ikaros, Deuringstr. 5. A little taste of the Mediterranean on the Bodensee. Fish nets and wine bottles line the walls of this little café, and baklava (10AS) warms the heart. Gorgeous Greek salads 58AS. Open Mon.-Fri. 10am-midnight, Sat. 9am-4pm.

Zum Goldenen Hirschen, Kirchstr. 8 (tel. 428 15). Look for the old wooden building with the small stained-glass windows and a flying gold reindeer over the door. Dark wooden furniture and an outside patio. Traditional Austrian fare, including *Schnitzel* (105AS). Visa, MC, AmEx.

SPAR Café Restaurant (tel. 422 91, ext. 15) on the first floor of the GWL building at Kaiserstr. and Römerstr. If Austrian food makes you daydream about fresh vegetables, the self-serve salad and fruit/dessert bars (10AS per 100g) are a godsend. Cafeteria-style entrees 56-98AS. Open Mon.-Fri. 8:30am-6pm, Sat. 8:30am-4pm.

SIGHTS AND ENTERTAINMENT

Four hundred years ago, Bregenz's medieval residents snatched up its prime real estate, on the hill overlooking the Bodensee. To reach the center of the historic town, the *Oberstadt* or "high city," walk uphill from the *Fußgängerzone* to St. Martinspl. The **Martinsturm,** Bregenz's landmark, rules the *Oberstadt* and boasts Europe's largest onion dome. The second and third floors of the tower house the **Voralberg Militärmuseum.** (Open May-Sept. Tues.-Sun. 9am-6pm. 10AS, children 7AS.) Although you can see all of the museum in 10 minutes (20 if you can read the German descriptions), the third floor's breathtaking view of the blue Boden expanse and Germany and Switzerland beyond is worth the 10AS entrance fee. Next to the tower is the **Martinskirche,** filled with frescoes dating back to the early 14th century. Particularly noteworthy are the depictions of St. Christopher, the Holy Symbol of Grief, and the 18th-century Stations of the Cross. Across Ehregutapl. (with the fountain) is **Deuring Schloßchen,** a 17th-century castle that now houses a non-budget hotel.

The walk up to the **St. Gallus Pfarrkirche,** at the top of Kirchstr., provides a sweeping view of the *Oberstadt.* The white-stucco sanctuary of the 11th-century church now glows under lavish gold ornamentation and a detailed painted ceiling that dates from 1738. The shepherdess in the altar has the face of Empress Maria Theresa, who donated 1500 guilders to the church in 1740. The imposing **Herz-Jesu Kirche** looms one block from the youth hostel. Built in 1907 and recently renovated in neo-Gothic style, the brick, wood, and sea-green accents in the huge sanctuary complement the abstract stained-glass windows. The **Voralberg Landesmuseum,** Kornmarktpl. 1, examines pre-tourist Bregenz. The museum's collection spans thousands of years, with carefully explained exhibits on the city's inhabitants from the Stone Age to the 18th century. All explanations are in German, but many exhibits are interesting even without the text, particularly in the third-floor Middle Ages rooms. (Open Tues.-Sun. 9am-noon and 2-5pm. Ring the bell if the door's locked. 20AS, students 10AS.)

For many people, Bregenz's main attraction is not its rich history but the Bodensee and its surrounding mountains. All along the waterfront, carefully groomed paths and strategically placed ice-cream stands surround fantastic playgrounds, a mini-golf course, and paddle boat rental agencies. Away from the city center and past the train station lies the **Strandbad** (tel. 442 42), a huge swimming pool, sauna, and sunbathing area. (Open in fair weather mid-May to mid-Sept. Tues.-Fri. 9am-9pm, Sat. 9am-7pm, Sun. 10am-6pm. 34AS, students 28AS, seniors 30AS, children 11AS.) Ferries run to the **Blumeninsel Mainau** (Mainau Flower Isle; tel. (07531) 30 30), which features a Baroque castle, an indoor tropical palm house, a new butterfly house, and gardens rife with orchids, tulips, dahlias, and 1100 kinds of roses. (See p. 453 for more information. 116AS for admission to all sights. Ferries depart Bregenz May-Sept. daily at 11am and leave Mainau at 4pm, returning to Bregenz at 6:45pm. Round-trip 280AS; special family packages available.) The **Drei-Länder-Rundfahrt** (tel. 428 68) runs along the Swiss, German, and Austrian waterfronts. (Departs daily July-Aug. at 2:30pm and returns at 5pm. 140AS, with Eurailpass or Austrian Rail Pass 70AS. Children's discount. Bring your passport on board all boat rides.) All cruises leave from the harbor across from the post office. The **Pfänderbahn** cable car (tel. 421 600; fax 421 604) near the hostel sways up the **Pfänder mountain** (the tallest peak around the Bodensee) for a panorama spanning from the Black Forest to the Swiss Alps. (Every 30min. daily April-Aug. 9am-6pm; Sept.-March 9am-7pm. Closed the 2nd and 3rd weeks in Nov. Ascent 84AS, descent 60AS, round-trip 123AS. Discounts for seniors and children under 19.) At the top of the cable-car ride, wander with native animals in the **Alpen wild park** (free). The many hikes down (45min.-2hr.) are worth every scenic step.

The concrete monstrosity on the edge of the lake is not a ski ramp gone awry but the world's largest **floating stage** and the centerpiece for the annual **Bregenzer Festspiele.** Every year from mid-July to mid-August, the Vienna Symphony Orchestra and other opera, theater, and chamber music groups come to town, bringing some 180,000 tourists with them. The main event is the performance on the floating stage, drawing capacity crowds of 6000. In 1998, the opera will be *Porgy and Bess* in English. Tickets for all events go on sale in October. (150-1350AS. Standing room tickets can only be purchased 1hr. before performance; arrive as early as possible but expect to face a huge line and painful wait.) For more information, write to Postfach 311, A-6901 Bregenz; call 407 223; fax 407 400; email bregenzer@festspiele.vol.at; or check out http://www.vol.at/bregenzerfestspiele. For late-night entertainment, check out **Vive's Bier-Bar** (18 and older; open daily 7pm-1am) or the **Royal Dart Club** (open Tues.-Sun. 5pm-1am), popular student hangouts on Kirchstr.

SWITZERLAND

US$1 = 1.53 Swiss francs (SFr)
CDN$1 = 1.11SFr
UK£ = 2.48SFr
IR£1 = 2.22SFr
AUS$1 = 1.14SFr
NZ$1 = 0.99SFr
SAR1 = 0.33SFr
1AS = 0.12SFr
1DM = 0.84SFr
1kč = 0.04SFr
1Ft = 0.008SFr

1SFr = US$0.66
1SFr = CDN$0.90
1SFr = UK£0.40
1SFr = IR£0.45
1SFr = AUS$0.88
1SFr = NZ$1.01
1SFr = SAR3.01
1SFr = 8.59AS
1SFr = DM1.20
1SFr = 22.38kč
1SFr = 130.56Ft

Country code: 41
International Dialing Prefix: 00

Like the snowy Alps that dominate the landscape, Switzerland *(die Schweiz, la Suisse, la Svizzera, Confederatio Helvetica)* has been around for a while. Comprising 23 cantons and 3 sub-cantons, Switzerland was first conceived in 1291 and slowly accumulated canton after canton through the 19th century. Mere treaties formed for brutally pragmatic reasons of survival united these linguistically and culturally distinct areas. High German is the country's official language, but some two-thirds of the 7.2 million Swiss speak Swiss-German *(Schwyzerdütsch)*, about one-fifth French, 12 percent Italian, and 1 percent Romansch (a Latinate relic). The vast majority speak more than two languages, and the stew of a growing immigrant population accounts for the remaining 5 percent. Switzerland clings tenaciously to its diverse land, uniting inhabitants though a revered democratic tradition. Swiss politics generally have an old-fashioned, "small town" feel: about 3000 local communes retain a great deal of power, and national referenda routinely settle major policy disputes.

While other countries hear the siren's song of imperialism and war, official neutrality since 1815 has spared this postcard-perfect paradise from the devastation suffered by the rest of Europe. Neutrality has also nurtured the growth of trade routes and ultimately big money in the staid banking centers of Geneva and Zurich. Most Swiss, however, are more down to earth and enjoy the pleasures of hiking, skiing, and good food—all specialties of the extensive, experienced Swiss service industry.

The country's varied population conducts its affairs against a universal backdrop of unparalleled natural beauty. Hikers, skiers, bikers, and paragliders from everywhere journey to Switzerland's snow-capped peaks. Mountains cover 58 percent of the country's 41,293 sq. km and extend into four other countries. Surprisingly, the Swiss have put 77 percent of country's area to productive use (46 percent meadowland, 25 percent forest, 6 percent arable land). Victorian scholar John Ruskin dubbed the Alps that comprise the remaining 23 percent of area "the great cathedrals of the earth." You're welcome to worship here if you can spare the cash.

History and Politics

> In Italy for thirty years under the Borgias they had warfare, terror, murder, bloodshed—they produced Michelangelo, Leonardo da Vinci, and the Renaissance. In Switzerland they had brotherly love, 500 years of democracy, and peace. What did that produce? The cuckoo clock.
> —Orson Welles, *The Third Man*

EARLY YEARS (TO AD500)

Switzerland was too cold for regular habitation until 8000BC, when Mesolithic hunter-gatherers first inhabited the area. Two thousand years later Indo-European farmers arrived, civilization progressed, tools changed from stone to bronze to iron, and by 750BC, Switzerland was an important center of **Celtic** culture. The artistic and warlike **Helvetians** were the most influential Swiss-Celtic tribe. Their attempts to invade Roman Italy in 222BC and again as allies of Carthage between 218 and 203BC (when they facilitated Hannibal's famous elephant-assisted crossing of the Alps) gained little territory. Attempts to advance into Gaul in 58BC were halted by Julius Caesar, who (as was his wont) crushed, then colonized, the Helvetians. Romanized between 47BC and AD15, they enjoyed a settled, peaceful, urban civilization for the next two centuries. **Romansch,** more closely related to Latin than any other Romance language, is still spoken in former Roman territories.

After the first barbarian raids in the AD250s, Switzerland militarized itself, metamorphosing from a peaceful farming province into an armed frontier in the face of Eastern European invaders. After Roman influence waned in the 5th century, the barbarians began to form permanent settlements. **Burgundians** settled the west, merging peacefully with the Romanized Celts and absorbing their culture and language. The less communicative **Allemanians** populated the center and northeast, eventually pushing the Burgundians west to the Sarine River, which remains the border between German and French Switzerland.

THE MUDDLED AGES (500-1517)

After Roman influence waned, the country lay in the clutches of pagans and barbarians. The arrival of the Franks in the 530s brought three centuries of foreign influence that aided monastic growth but had little effect elsewhere. Otherwise, landowners gobbled up more and more land, gaining enough power to beat on less-wealthy neighbors (see **Tell-tale,** p. 291). After the break-up of the Carolingian empire in the 9th century, the feudal power of these **lords** grew. They became vassals of the Frankish king, but eventually established themselves as part of the Burgundian dynasty, joining their own area of influence (Helvetica) with an external ruler. The last Burgundian King died in 1032, and his nephew, the King of Germania, incorporated Helvetica into his growing kingdom. Part of Switzerland thus enjoyed a stint in the **Holy Roman Empire,** during which Zurich and Solothurn prospered and Bern and Fribourg were established. During this entire time, the **Houses of Savoy, Habsburg,** and **Zähringen** were still fighting over the territories left after the dissolution of Carolingian rule and the divisions wrought by the 12th-century **Investiture Conflict.** When Berthold V of Zähringen died in 1218 without an heir, the greedy Habsburgs immediately tried to overtake the Zähringen lands. Eventually defeated, the Habsburgs signed a letter of franchise in 1231 guaranteeing freedom to the inhabitants of Zähringen. Worried by all of the power-hungry lords, the three forest cantons of **Uri, Schwyz,** and **Unterwald** signed a secret agreement in 1291 forming the **Ewige Bund (Everlasting League),** obligating the cantons to defend each other from outside attack. (Switzerland therefore celebrated its 700th anniversary in 1991.) After the **Battle of Morgarten** in 1315, in which the imperial

> Uri, Schwyz, and Unterwald signed a secret agreement in 1291 forming the Ewige Bund. Switzerland celebrated its 700th year in 1991.

> ### Tell-tale
> First found in a 15th-century ballad and probably the product of an older oral tradition, the tale of Wilhelm (William) Tell has appeared in wide and varied versions, culimating with with Friedrich Schiller's drama *Wilhelm Tell* in 1804. The tale takes place sometime in the early 1300s, when Tell and his young son visited the town of Altdorf in his native canton of Uri. While in town, Tell disobeyed the order given by the much-loathed Habsburg governor to doff his hat in the presence of Gessler's hat, which had been sycophantically affixed to a pole in the town square. Tell was arrested for his disobedience and made to shoot an apple off his son's head as punishment. As Tell prepared to shoot, Gessler found that Tell had two arrows in his quiver and asked why. Without a second's hesitaiton Tell replied that if the first arrow missed its mark, he would aim the second at Gessler's heart. Tell scored a bull's-eye, but because of his threat to Gessler, he was re-arrested and sent by boat to a prison on the opposite side of Lake Lucerne. As Tell and his captors traversed the lake, a violent storm seized the little boat and allowed Tell to overpower his guards. He returned to shore safely, slew Gessler, and lived happily ever after. The Swiss herald the myth as befitting the country's tenacity in its struggle for freedom.

family tried to crush the confederation, Habsburg leaders agreed to a truce and granted the alliance official recognition .

Though conflict between the League and the emperors continued, the three-canton core of Switzerland gradually expanded through merger and conquest over the next several centuries. Of course, the increasingly diverse population had increasingly complicated problems. Social tensions between the town and country residents threatened to erupt in the 15th century, the peak of the confederation's power, but the leadership of **Niklaus von Flüe** (a.k.a. Brüder Klaus), a mystical hermit-farmer, subdued the conflict. The internal crisis averted, Swiss soldiers became terrifyingly efficient mercenaries, with clients including the pope and the northern Italian city-states. The **Swiss Guard** still defend the Vatican, resplendent in their 16th-century uniforms and armaments. The **Swabian War** with the Habsburgs of 1499-1500 brought virtual independence from the Holy Roman Empire, while now Switzerland entered the fray in 1496 as the French invaded Italy to reclaim Naples from the pope. French military superiority caused Switzerland to rethink its aggression, and in 1516 the two countries signed the **Perpetual Peace** agreement, which made the Swiss mercenaries in French armies and thus prevented much independent action.

REFORMATION TO REVOLUTION (1517-1815)

The **Protestant Reformation** rocked the confederation to its foundations. As Lutheranism swept through Northern Europe, radical theologian **Ulrich Zwingli** of Zurich spearheaded his own brand of reform that advocated a less literal reinterpretation of the symbols and gestures of Catholicism. In 1523, the city government of Zurich sanctioned Zwingli's proposed *Theses* and thus strengthened Zwingli's hold over the local government—the city banned the differently minded **Anabaptists** and imposed harsh disciplines on its inhabitants. **John Calvin,** another leader of the Swiss Reformation, was a priest and a lawyer born in Northern France. His doctrine urged saintly living in order to "prove" one's chosen status. He soon took a theocratic grip of Geneva and instituted puritanical reforms that influenced leaders as far away as England. In 1527, brawls erupted between Roman Catholic and Protestant cantons, culminating in the 1531 defeat of the Protestants at Kappel and Zwingli's death. The confederation finally took action, granting Protestants freedoms but prohibiting them from imposing their faith on others. Divisions didn't disappear overnight, though, and money (from economic ties) remained the only real common interest.

Despite these religious differences, the confederation remained neutral during the Thirty Years War, escaping the devastation wrought on the rest of Central Europe. The 1648 **Peace of Westphalia** recognized the independence and neutrality of the

13 cantons. Independence and periodic inter-religious alignments did little to heal the Catholic-Protestant rift, however, and the next century saw the Catholics ally themselves with France and Spain, as the Protestants fostered hierarchies and social control, expanded banking and literacy, and hunted the witches they believed were plaguing Europe.

Caught up in Revolutionary fervor and perhaps peeved at the Swiss Guard, who loyally defended King Louis XVI and the royal family until their death, French troops invaded Switzerland in 1798 and, by Napoleon's order, established the **Helvetic Republic.** The republic restructured relationships between the cantons and the federal government and granted citizens freedom of religion and equality before the law. The over-achieving Napoleon later added six cantons and redesigned the confederation: he separated church and state, established free trade among the cantons, and emancipated the peasantry. After Napoleon's defeat, the Congress of Vienna recognized **Swiss neutrality** and created a new conservative constitution, under which the old elite lost some of their previous monopoly on wealth and power. The constitution also added 2 cantons and returned Geneva, annexed into France by Napoleon, to Switzerland, bringing the total to 26—today's magic number.

THE NEUTRALITY THING (1815-1945)

A major period of economic growth began after 1815. Agriculture and tourism, especially from England, expanded, but the industrial sector saw the most significant gains. Because a continental blockade excluded Britain from the European market during the Napoleonic Wars, the Swiss were forced to modernize and mechanize their own industry. Unfortunately, this era of material prosperity was not trouble-free. The Mediation Act disappeared with Napoleon, and the **Federal Pact** of 1815 that replaced Napoleon's decrees once again established Switzerland as a confederation of sovereign states united only for common defense and maintaining internal order—forming or executing united foreign policy was still impossible. Because of legal barriers (each canton had its own laws, currency, postal service, weights, measures, and army), the confederation had revoked the right to reside freely in any canton, and the inhabitants of one canton regarded the inhabitants of other cantons as foreigners. Furthermore, civil liberties were almost non-existent and religious tensions re-emerged.

These religious differences led, in 1846, to the formation of a separatist defense league of Catholic cantons known as the **Sonderbund,** comprising Lucerne, Uri, Schwyz, Unterwalden, Zug, Fribourg, and Valais. In July 1847, the **Diet,** representing the other cantons, declared the Sonderbund incompatible with the Federal Pact and demanded its dissolution. In keeping with the fashion of the time, a civil war broke out, lasting only 25 days and resulting in a victory for the federalist forces. The country wrote a **new constitution,** modeled after that of the United States, in 1848 (modified in 1874). Finally balancing the age-old conflict between federal and cantonal power, the constitution guaranteed republican and democratic cantonal constitutions and for the first time set up an executive body. The central government established a unified postal, currency, and railway system and ushered in a free-trade zone among all the cantons. In that same year, a crisis arose over Neuchâtel, formerly the property of the King of Prussia. In the revolutionary spirit of the age, the citizens of Neuchâtel rebelled against the king, who eventually renounced his rights to the territory while retaining the title of Prince of Neuchâtel. The canton thus remained part of Switzerland.

During this time, Switzerland cultivated its reputation for resolving international conflicts (or at least getting its name on anything diplomatic). The **Geneva Convention of 1864** established international laws for the conduct of war and the treatment of prisoners of war. At the same time, the **International Red Cross** set up its headquarters in Geneva. Free of the tangle of alliances that characterized Europe's turn-of-the-century balance of power, Switzerland remained neutral throughout the Franco-Prussian war and **World War I.** You can't blame 'em: since forty percent of the coun-

A Heavy Cross to Bear

After a childhood on the shores of Lake Geneva, Henri Dunant, founder of the Red Cross, packed his bags for Algeria, where he made his fortune as a grain speculator. Subsequent bad luck sent him back to Geneva searching for funds. Though he received the needed capital, extended complications convinced Dunant that French bureaucrats were obstructing his ventures. To rectify the situation, he decided to go straight to the top: Napoleon III himself.

Procuring an audience with Louis-Napoleon did not prove to be an easy task. Dunant wrote a book "definitively" proving that the French leader was the heir to Emperor Augustus and the crown of the Holy Roman Empire. He had just one copy printed and then undertook to deliver it to the emperor. By the time Dunant caught up with Louis-Napoleon, the emperor had battled his way into the Italy and had other things on his mind than his ancestry. Raging around Napoleon was the infamous Battle of Solferino, one of history's most brutal battles—the first day alone saw 33,000 casualties. Though clad in a white suit, Dunant rolled up his shirtsleeves and attempted to save the wounded.

Rejected by Napoleon, Dunant returned to Geneva and recounted the horrors he had witnessed. His piece, *A Souvenir of Solferino*, pleaded for the creation of a neutral organization that would offer aid to victims of battle. The idea won favor among members of in Geneva's public administration, and Dunant toured Europe in search of emotional and monetary support. His actions brought about the first Geneva Convention in 1864.

In the meantime, the investors in his failed Algerian venture began wondering what had become of their money. A bankrupt Dunant fled Geneva, only to return to a semi-incognito life in Appenzell in 1887. One journalist unearthed the founder of the Red Cross, and exposé soon followed exposé. In 1901, Henri Dunant was internationally honored as the joint recipient of the first Nobel Peace Prize. Even the blinding limelight of fame could not obscure his financial debts, however—the majority of the prize money went to his creditors.

try's total consumed food was imported, Switzerland had to maintain the goodwill of its neighbors (and their farmers). Throughout the 20th century, Swiss anxiety grew as German and Italian territories united to form nation-states. In an effort to prepare for possible conflict, Switzerland revised its constitution in 1874 to strengthen federal power over the military. The new constitution also revised labor laws to address rapidly advancing industrial mechanization. Throughout the first half of the century, power increasingly moved to the federal government—in 1912, the cantons yielded their control over civil law and, in 1942, penal law.

In 1920, Geneva welcomed the headquarters of the ill-fated **League of Nations**, becoming *the* place for international diplomacy. **World War II** found Switzerland surrounded by the Axis powers, but trade with both sides and a hard-hitting invasion-contingency plan kept the country neutral. While some Jews and other refugees from Nazi Germany found refuge in Switzerland, the Swiss government, not eager to incur the wrath of the monster that surrounded it, generally impeded passage through its territory and assumed the hiding-tortoise position. Displeased, the Allies complicated Swiss diplomacy after the war. Switzerland has maintained strict neutrality to this day, hosting a branch of the **United Nations** and training some army units for peacekeeping roles with the U.N. but abstaining from participation in the organization.

CURRENT GOVERNMENT

Swiss government is based on a three-tiered system of cantons, communes, and confederation. Each **canton** has extensive self-governing rights, each citizen actively participates in the government, and the entire country realizes that only by recognizing basic human rights will it maintain unity among its diverse citizens.

Over 3000 **communes** (the smallest administrative unit of government) compose the 26 cantons that have existed in Switzerland since the beginning of 1979. Cantons are real states with their own constitutions, legislatures, executives, and judiciaries. Legislative power rests with the people or with a popularly elected parliament. The cantons themselves are incorporated into the **Confederation,** which has a two-chamber legislature, the Federal Assembly. The Assembly consists of the **National Council,** representing the people, and the **Council of States,** composed of canton representatives. The National Council's 200 seats are distributed according to population, with a minimum of one seat per canton. Decisions of the Federal Assembly take effect only with a majority in both chambers.

The executive branch consists of a group a seven members—the **Federal Council**—elected to a four-year term by a joint meeting of both legislative chambers. No canton may have more than one representative in the Federal Council at a time. The Federal Council chooses the **president** from among its ranks. The president holds office for only one year, responsible for his ministerial department. To maintain a system of checks and balances, the Federal Council provides the legislative branch with an annual account of its activities.

Politics play a role in Swiss daily life through **referenda** or **initiatives.** Citizens can bring a constitutional amendment to the fore by an initiative of at least 100,000 votes. A majority of citizens must approve any constitutional change by means of referendum before it becomes law. 50,000 voters or eight cantons can demand approval of a federal law passed by both chambers.

RECENT YEARS

Switzerland's policy of **armed neutrality** persists to the present: there is no standing army, but every adult male faces compulsory military service. With the threat of an east-west conflict fading, a 1989 referendum proposing to disband the army garnered surprising support (see **Semper Paratus**). Switzerland has become increasingly wealthy, liberal, successful, and service-oriented since WWII, but the country is still fiercely independent and wary of entanglements with the rest of Europe. After years of economic stagnation, Swiss citizens continue to feel strongly about the EU issue and a recent vote rejecting the treaty on a **European Economic Area (EEA)** boasted a voter turnout of almost 80 percent. So while Austria accepted EU membership in early 1995, the "No" vote on the EEA indicates that Switzerland will sit another round out. The division between those who opt to resist change in order to retain *Sonderfall Schweig* (the Swiss Way) and those who envision growth and involvement with the EEC reveals a split along linguistic lines: all six Francophone cantons lean towards integration, while the German-speaking cantons and Italian-speaking Ticino fear being swallowed by their neighbors.

The world has recently begun to examine Switzerland's actualy involvement with the Nazis during WWII, as accusations of complicity fly throughout the world press. Switzerland's "blind account" policy, allowing Holocaust victims and Nazi leaders alike to deposit money, has created complex situations. In the summer of 1997, more names of bank accounts from the World War II era were released, even though several Swiss banks had in the past claimed they had released all they could—a sticky P.R. situation, to say the least. A proposed constitutional amendment that would establish a humanitarian fund has pleased international Jewish organizations.

■ Art and Architecture

The country's central location at the juncture of three cultural spheres has often prevented the Swiss from creating a unified and independent art of their own. Yet there does exist a Swiss flavor, despite a government built on pragmatism and consensus in contrast with art's individualist pursuit. The Renaissance produced **Urs Graf,** a swashbuckling soldier-artist-poet excellently suited to court portraiture. **John Henry Füssli** was the most significant Swiss painter of the 19th century, echoing the advent of Romanticism with his emotional works. Their horrifying images of demons and goblins did much to further the popularity of Romanticism in Switzerland. **Ferdinand**

Hodler, an early Symbolist painter, worked with powerful images of Swiss landscapes and characters to convey metaphysical messages.

Twentieth-century artist **Paul Klee** was born near Bern but spent his childhood and early career in Germany, where he produced unique works as a member of *der blaue Reiter* school and of the Bauhaus faculty. He returned to Switzerland just before World War II. The **Zurich School of Concrete Art** between the wars united the Surrealists with the Constructivist ethos absorbed from Russia and from architectural theory. The school also worked with objects and environment as they explored interactions between humans and space. **Max Bill's** Mondrian-derived canvases, focusing on color relationships and the texture and form of the surface itself, are quintessental Concrete paintings. The school includes Paul Klee and **Meret Oppenheim,** a Surrealist famous for her *Fur Cup.* The philosophy guided sculptor **Alberto Giacometti** to play with spatial realities in creating his celebrated works in the 1930s. Later, Giacometti rejected the premise of Surrealism in order to concentrate upon representation, creating small, exaggeratedly slender figures like *Man Pointing.* **Jean Tinguely** created kinetic, mechanized Dada fantasies that celebrated the beauty of motion.

Robert Maillart developed the slab technique for bridge design in 1900, and for the first years of the century produced elegant ferro-concrete bridges that were much more efficient and airy than any previous concrete bridge. The world-acclaimed architect **Le Corbusier** applied the ferro-concrete building technique to domestic and commercial building, inspired by the geometric shapes and rugged textures of his Swiss Jura home. Le Corbusier brought a new, animated spirit to contemporary architecture in Paris, Moscow, Stuttgart, Zurich, and Cambridge, Massachusetts. The house *(la petite maison)* that he built on the edge of the lake at Corseaux-Vevey for his parents in 1924 is now a national monument.

■ Literature

> "We wanderers are very cunning—the love that actually should belong to a woman, we lightly scatter among small towns and mountains, lakes and valleys, children by the side of the road, beggars on the bridge, cows in the pasture, birds, and butterflies."
> —Hermann Hesse (1877-1962), German-born Swiss novelist, *Wandering,* 1920

Jean-Jacques Rousseau, born in Geneva in 1712 and best known for his *Social Contract* that inspired the French Revolution, always proudly recognized his Swiss background—despite the fact that he spent most of his time outside the country and that the Swiss burned his books. **Jacob Burckhardt** promoted a new history of culture and art from his Basel home in the late 19th century. An expert in Renaissance Italian art, his main works include *History of the Italian Renaissance* and *Cicerone: A Guide to the Enjoyment of Italian Art.* **J.J. Bodmer** and **J.J. Breitinger** pioneered modern literarary thought in Switzerland, advocating the supremacy of feeling and imaginative vision central to Romanticism. **Madame de Staël** (Germaine Necker, from the prominent Genevan family) was the primary force behind Romanticism's spread from Germany to France. As a result of her political intrigues and alleged rebuff of Napoleon's advances (she succeeded where Europe failed), de Staël was forced into a miserable exile in Coppet. The theories of **Carl Gustav Jung** arose from his work in Swizerland. He began his psychological career as an acolyte of Freud but had split off by 1915 with his *Symbols of Transformation,* a work directly contradicting Freud's system.

Hermann Hesse moved to Switzerland in 1899 and became a Swiss citizen in 1924. He earned the Nobel Prize for literature in 1946 for his collected oeuvre, which dealt with contradiction of the body and the spirit and thus combined Western and Eastern wisdom. Hesse is only one of several well-known and respected Swiss authors. **Benjamin Constant de Rebecque,** a native of Lausanne, one-time lover of Mme de Staël, and author of the novel *Adolphe,* joined **Léonard de Sismondi** of

Geneva and Mme de Staël in contributing to the French Romantic movement. **Gottfried Keller** was a popular Swiss novelist and poet integral to the rising influence of Poetic Realism in late German Romanticism. **Conrad Ferdinand Meyer,** however, is acknowledged by most authorities as the greatest Swiss poet. His works feature strongly individualistic heroes and were some of the only German works to effectively unite Romanticism and Realism.

Twentieth-century Switzerland has produced two widely respected modern playwrights and a formerly obscure novelist who wrote so tiny as to fit entire works on café bills. Critics laud **Max Frisch** for his Brechtian style and thoughtful treatment of Nazi Germany; his most widely known work is the play *Andorra*. **Friedrich Dürrenmatt** has written a number of excellent plays dealing with individual responsibility and morality, most notably *The Visit of the Old Lady* and *The Physicists*. Both Dürrenmatt and Frisch are critical of their home country, however. The novelist **Robert Walser** has been celebrated for his diffuse, existential works; they were largely ignored until his death in 1956 by an audience expecting clearly defined morals and themes. Posthumously, his novels, poetry, and plays are recognized for their fragile, shady, ironic, and melancholic language.

Switzerland also has a life in the literature of other nations. **Henry James's** Daisy Miller toured here; **Mark Twain** incorporated cuckoo clocks into his revenge fantasies and followed well-touristed paths with his own rough grace, chronicled in *A Tramp Abroad*. The ghosts of geniuses hover in the Alpine countryside surrounding Geneva: Gogol, Dostoyevsky, Hugo, Hemingway, and Fitzgerald.

■ Exiles and Emigrés

Voltaire arrived in Geneva in 1755; since then, a steady stream of intellectuals, artists, and other soon-to-be-famous personalities have called Switzerland home. The notion of Switzerland as a neutral refuge among more quarrelsome nations has held appeal for many since November 20th, 1815, when the Treaty of Paris recognized Switzerland as the eternally impartial next-door neighbor.

George Gordon, otherwise known as the opium-smoking Romantic **Lord Byron**, quit England in 1816 and fled to Switzerland. Here he met **Percy Shelley,** and the two composed some of their greatest works. Byron wrote *Sonnet on Chillon* while brooding on Lake Geneva, while Shelley crafted *Hymn to Beauty* and *Mont Blanc* in the vale of Chamonix. During an especially wet summer in Switzerland, some ghost stories fell into **Mary Wollstonecraft Shelley's** hands; these stories, Switzerland's eternal mist, and the craggy Alps inspired the Gothic elements of *Frankenstein*.

The international onslaught did not end with the Romantics. **Charles Dickens** vacationed in the Lausanne area and wrote *Dombey and Son* on the shores of Lake Geneva. Along the shores of this same lake in the early 20th-century, **T.S. Eliot** languished as he wrote *The Wasteland*. **James Joyce** fled to Zurich during World War I and stayed in the city to write the greater part of his modernist work *Ulysses* between 1915 and 1919; World War II drove him to Zurich once again, where he died in 1941.

From across the borders of Germany, Austria, and Italy flocked other great minds. **Johann Wolfgang von Goethe** caught his first distant view of Italy from the top of St. Gotthard Pass in the Swiss Alps, the clouded path that would serve as an allegory for the rest of his life. **Friedrich Schiller** wrote about the massive church bell in Schaffhausen and then came forth with the play *Wilhelm Tell*. **Rossini** later wrote the opera, whose overture is more commonly known on these shores as the *Lone Ranger* theme song. While on holiday in the Engadin Valley, **Friedrich Nietzsche** went nuts, cooked up some historical and philosophical ramblings, and produced *Thus Spoke Zarathustra*. His complex personal relationship with **Richard Wagner** began here while Nietzsche held a professor's chair at Basel University. Wagner produced most of his major works during his years in Switzerland.

Zurich and Basel served as a wellspring for intellectual revolution in the sciences; **Albert Einstein** studied there and by 1901 was a Swiss citizen. He moved to Bern to work in a patent office, where various applications inspired the foundation for the theory of relativity and the law of equality of matter and energy. This pacifist won the Nobel Prize for physics in 1924. **Karl Jaspers,** the German physician and psychologist of self-fulfillment and self-knowledge, has taught in Basel since 1948, and became a citizen of Basel in 1967.

Switzerland's tolerance and neutrality attracted hordes of talented refugees from the World Wars. Such a congregation of artistic personalities, combined with the increasing trend toward decadence in the early 1900s, produced the **Dada** explosion in Zurich in 1916, led by **Hans Arp** and **Tristan Tzara. Hugo Ball,** Italian playwright, novelist, actor and dramatist, emigrated as an antiwar activist to Switzerland and founded the "Cabaret Voltaire" and "Galerie Dada," centers of Dada activity. After sitting out the war in London and spending time in Prague, Austrian expressionist painter **Oskar Kokoschka** also moved to Switzerland in 1953, settling in Villeneuve. When Kokoschka died in 1980, his widow, Olda, found herself with an embarrassment of pictures and subsequently founded the Foundation Oskar Kokoschka in the Musée Jenisch in Vevey. The two German greats **Thomas Mann** and **Carl Zuckmayer** also found Switzerland a safe haven. Switzerland's recent aquisitions include writers and scientists from the former Eastern bloc, notably Russian author **Alexander Solzhenitsyn.**

■ Food and Drink

Little known to those individuals not among the ranks of chefs or culinary experts, Switzerland has one of the finest culinary traditions in all of Europe—the majority of famous French chefs have undergone some schooling in this mountainous land. The reason behind this seemingly odd fact of Swiss life is once again linked to Swiss neutrality and the endurance of traditional, even peasant cuisine.

While most budget travelers may not be able to enjoy the *crème de la crème* of Swiss cuisine, trickle-down gastronomics operates in full force. Superseding all regional dishes and possible pretensions to four-star cuisine, are Switzerland's culinary masterpieces: **cheese** and **chocolate.** While the words "Swiss cheese" may conjure images of lunch-boxed sandwiches filled with a hard, oily, holey cheese, Switzerland actually has innumerable varieties, each made from a particular type of milk with its own flavor and production. Cheese with holes is usually Emmentaler, from the eponymous northwest region, but nearly every canton and many towns have specialty cheeses. To name a few of the most well-known: *Gruyère* is a stronger and tastier version of *Emmentaler; Appenzeller* is a milder hard cheese from the Appenzell region, sometimes using sheep's milk instead of cow's milk; *tome* is a generic term for a soft, uncooked cheese similar to French *chèvre*. In the Italian regions, look for Southern influences; cheese often resembles the *parmigiano* from Italy more than the cheeses of the north. As far as **chocolate** goes, Switzerland is home to two of the largest producers of chocolate: **Lindt** and **Suchard,** and each town has amazing concoctions at the local confectioner's shelves. With the invention of milk chocolate in 1875, Switzerland was positioned to rule the world (or at least its taste buds).

> **With the invention of milk chocolate in 1875, Switzerland was positioned to rule the world.**

Unsurprisingly, the flavor of regional cooking bends with the contours of Switzerland's linguistic topography. The basic geography is simple and logical: Frenchified in the west, Italianish in the south, Swiss-German everywhere else. Each of these regions is represented, however, in the collective pool of "typical" Swiss dishes. A Swiss national menu might include the Zurich speciality, *Geschnetzeltes* (strips of veal stewed in a thick cream sauce). Other possible contenders are *Luzerner Chugelipastete* (pâté in a pastry shell), *Papet Vaudois* (leeks with sausage from the canton of Vaud), *Churer Fleischtorte* (meat pie originating from Chur), and Bernese salmon.

Three dishes in particular best represent Switzerland. **Rösti,** a patty of hash brown potatoes skilleted and occasionally flavored with bacon or cheese, is as prevalent in the German regions as **fondue** (from the French, *fondre*—to melt) is in the French.

Usually a blend of Emmentaler and Gruyère cheeses, white wine, *kirsch,* and spices, *fondue* is eaten by dunking small cubes of white bread into a *caquelon* (a one-handled pot) kept hot by a small flame. The mother of all cheese dips originated as weay to use up stale bread and cheese shavings. **Raclette** is made by cutting a large cheese in half and heating it until it melts; the melted cheese is then scraped onto a baked potato and garnished with any number of other foodstuffs.

The Swiss are particularly good at baking and **confectionery**. To match each type of local cheese, there is usually a bread specific to the region or town. Ask for it by name (e.g. when in St. Gallen, ask for *St. Galler-brot*). Among the most tempting **cakes** are the *Baseler Leckerli* (a kind of gingerbread), *Schaffhauser Zungen, Zuger Kirschtorte* (Kirsch torte of Zug), Engadin nutcakes, the *bagnolet crème* of the Jura (eaten with raspberries and aniseed biscuits), soda rolls, *rissoles* (pear tarts), nougat and pralines of Geneva, and the *zabaglione* of Ticino. *Vermicelli* (not the Italian pasta but a dessert made of chestnut mousse) is popular all over Switzerland.

The Romans introduced **wine** to the region, but it was not until the 9th century that beer-drinking laity pried it away from the clergy—who used it, of course, for liturgical purposes. By the 19th century production had grown so indiscriminately, and the results so indifferently, that consumers went back to drinking beer. A wine statute in 1953 imposed rigorous quality controls, and since then Swiss wine has regained its reputation. Most wine is produced in the west and the Valais, about three-quarters of it white. The wine produced around Lake Zurich and in the Thurgau and Schaffhausen areas is predominantly *Blauburgunder,* with a small quantity of a *Riesling-Slyvaner* hybrid. Ticino specializes in reds made from the Merlot grape, and most restaurants offer a house wine as *nostrano* (one of ours). These wines are usually home-pressed blends, comparatively cheap, and delicious.

Semper Paratus

Every household holds at least one Swiss Army knife. But as we open wine bottles, cut French bread, and spread pâté all with the same handy gadget, we rarely consider the oxymoronic nature of a Swiss Army. For a nation that has been neutral since its independence and the global icon of pacifism through the Cold War era, the concept, let alone the reality, is surprising. Behind the sweet-toothed, storybook facade stands one of the most heavily armed populations and most highly trained armies in the world. Mountains bristle with fortifications, pastures conceal airstrips, bridges are mined to self-destruct, and tanks and fighter jets lurk deep within the Alpine rock. Every Swiss male stores a gas mask, a repeating rifle, and a sealed, government-issued box of ammunition. He must participate in 17 weeks of military training and must return for an annual three-week refresher course until the age of 36—after that, and until retirement, the course lasts only two weeks. In 1986, a coalition of pacifists, socialists, and religious leaders dared to ask for what exactly the neutral nation was preparing. They brought the issue to a vote, and for the first time in history a European nation was presented with the option of abolishing its army. The referendum drew a passionate response: 35.6% of the population voted against the army, irked by the $1000 per capita spent annually on defense and the peculiar effects the army training has on the workforce: companies must overhire to compensate for the gaps left by men in training, but many employees work their way up the business ladder through army contacts (especially if they're in the officer corps) and use the refresher courses more as elite alumni meetings than as training. Despite the popular outcry, however, the measure failed, and for now Switzerland's charming landscape continues to hide not-so-charming military might. As the Swiss saying goes, "Switzerland does not have an army; it *is* an army."

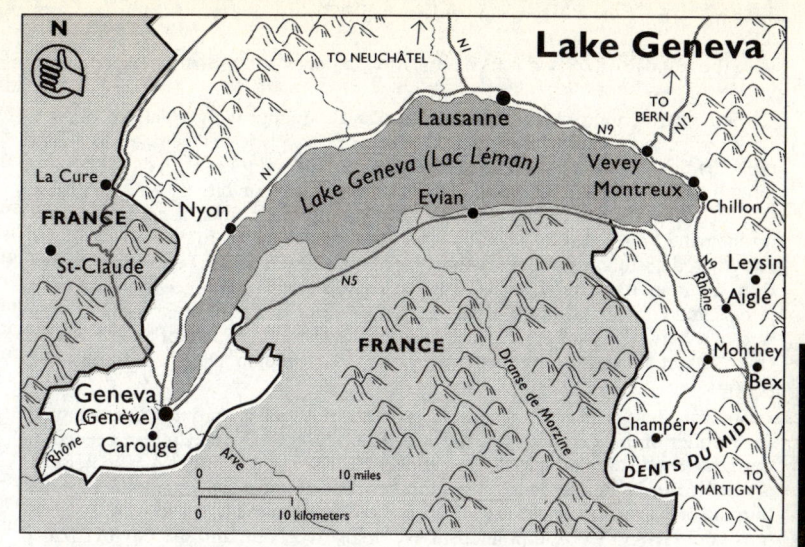

Western Switzerland

LAKE GENEVA (LAC LÉMAN)

A reliable rule of economic geography states that incomes rise exponentially as you approach Lac Léman. Obviously, Switzerland is not the first country that comes to mind when most budget travelers plan their low-to-the-ground itineraries—there is admittedly no lack of high-altitude prices within Lac Léman's main cities of Geneva, Lausanne, and Montreux. But the towns along the lake abound with at least three of Switzerland's cheapest commodities: quiet is just a short stroll along the tree-lined quay or up into the vine-laced hills, chocolate is a yummy pittance nearly everywhere, and the unforgettable views are, as always, free. The landscape of lakes lapping the shore and hills dotted by villas or festooned with the terraced garlands of ever-ripening grapes easily becomes familiar and seemingly settled—that is, until the haze clears and the rough-hewn mountain peaks poke out from behind the gentle, rounded hills. And then the lake momentarily loses its quaint charms and polished urbanity and takes on the energizing promise of unpeopled wildness and wide lonely expanse. For many on the grand tour of Europe, Lac Léman's cities are a brief stop-over. But they can be a gateway for all that beckons beyond the next ridge and the culmination of everything tranquil and beautiful that flows from the rest of Switzerland out into the world in the silent but steady currents of the Rhône River.

■ Geneva (Genève, Genf)

"I detest Geneva," muttered Napoleon Bonaparte shortly before "liberating" the city in 1798, "they know English too well." They still do. Geneva is very much a cosmopolitan city: only one-third of the population are genuine *Genevois;* the other two-thirds are foreign-born internationals or transplants from other cantons. The large concentration of international banks and multinational organizations preserves the intricate melange of the city's voices—quite a contrast to Switzerland's other, mostly homogeneous towns. Indeed, many say that all Geneva holds in common with the rest of Switzerland is its neutral foreign policy and the state religion, banking.

The French Emperor had more than linguistic contempt with which to contend. He knew all too well that Geneva's citizens have a long and belligerent tradition of doing battle to protect their political and religious independence. Medieval Geneva fended off constant attacks, protecting its strategically desirable site on the outflow to Lac Léman. In 1536, however, Geneva openly welcomed a more insidious invader: the Protestant Reformation. The townspeople voted to convert *en masse* and invited an unknown twenty-five-year-old, John Calvin, to their cathedral. His fiery sermons from Geneva's pulpit between 1536 and 1564 brought in waves of persecuted French and Italian refugees to the "Rome of Protestants." Geneva then waged a hard-won battle for freedom from the Catholic House of Savoy, whose Duke sought to crush both Protestantism and Genevan democracy (see **Soup's On**, p. 300).

Unfortunately, however, religious freedom did not spell tolerance. Calvin adopted the manner of the Catholic rule, renamed it the Protestant rule, and proceeded to burn those who didn't think he was running his new church correctly. The Reformists' ardent zeal continued for at least another century and a half, exemplified by the burning of Rousseau's books in a square just blocks from the house in which he was born. But Geneva's cosmopolitanism eventually won out, and the city became a gathering place for literary elites and free thinkers. Voltaire lived and worked in the Geneva area for 23 years, and his compatriot Madame de Staël later held her salons in nearby Coppet. In the early 19th century, such mountain-happy romantics as Shelley and Byron found inspiration in the city's surroundings. Mary Wollstonecraft Shelley created *Frankenstein*'s monster here, and George Eliot resided in Geneva, the city of her hero, Jean-Jacques Rousseau. One of Geneva's most famous political refugees was Lenin, who bided his time here from 1903 to 1905 and again in 1908.

Today's Geneva preserves and memorializes both extremes of its varied history. Street names alternate between rigid reformers and free-thinking artists and intellectuals. As a city that lost its compact identity once its massive fortifications were scrapped to build up the lakefront, Geneva has had no alternative but to absorb every idea and culture and lifestyle that has entered its boundaries. The city now collects, alters, and renews the various identities that flood its streets, protecting inhabitants with its tolerance rather than its military might. There are more McDonald's here than you'll find in the rest of Switzerland, but there are even more "traditional Swiss" restaurants in cubby-hole locations all over this most un-Swiss of Swiss cities.

The city's unique atmosphere attracted more than individuals. Under the inspiration of native Henri Dunant, the **International Committee of the Red Cross** established itself in Geneva in 1864, and nations from around the world signed the First Geneva Convention in the same year. In 1919, Geneva's selection as the site for the League of Nations confirmed the city's reputation as a center for both international organizations and arbitrations. Geneva still retains the European office of the **United Nations** (responsible for economic and humanitarian programs) and dozens of other international bodies ranging from the Center for European Nuclear Research to the World Council of Churches.

Soup's On

Before it became part of the Swiss Confederation, Geneva warded off almost constant attack. One of the most persistent invaders was the House of Savoy. Geneva battled the Savoys sporadically for over 200 years, but the city finally triumphed due to Swiss practicality. On the night of December 11, 1602, Savoyard soldiers attempted to scale the city walls. A lone housewife saw the attack and proceeded to dump a pot of boiling soup on the soldiers' heads, buying enough time to sound the city's alarm. Each year, the **Festival of the Escalade** (climbing) celebrates this event, as costumed citizens reenact the battle and children eat chocolate *marmites* (pots) filled with marzipan vegetables.

GETTING TO GENEVA

Geneva has two rail stations. **Gare Cornavin** is the primary station and departure point for all major Swiss and foreign cities. The second station, the tiny Gare des Eaux-Vives on the eastern edge of the city, connects to France's regional rail lines. Geneva's **Cointrin Airport** is a **Swissair** hub. To reach the city from the arrivals hall, go up a level and turn left to catch bus #10 to town (2.20SFr) or take the train for a shorter trip to Cornavin Station (every 10min., 6min., 4.80SFr). By **car**, Geneva is more accessible from France than from the rest of Switzerland. To drive to Geneva from the west, take A40 or E62 east, which continues on to Lausanne and Montreux. From the south take N201 north. From the north, take E21 from France and E25/62 from Switzerland. From the east, take A40 (E25) west. E62 is also the best way to reach Geneva from Lausanne or Montreux. Don't go crazy looking for the route numbers—they're not all that visible. You'll be better off just following the signs for Geneva posted on all of the auto routes. Hugely popular **ferries (CGN)** connect Geneva to Lausanne and Montreux. A round-trip ticket includes the option of returning to Geneva by train, so sight-seeing itineraries need not depend on the infrequent boat services, which are more recreational than practical anyway.

ORIENTATION AND PRACTICAL INFORMATION

Geneva has more districts than most cities twice its modest size of 200,000 people. In the *vieille ville*, steep cobbled streets and quiet squares surround the Cathédrale de St-Pierre and the university. To the north, banks, bistros, and boutiques form the beautiful line of the Rhône River. The lakeside attempts to assuage the Swiss national yearning for a seaside resort with mixed (mostly concrete) results. On sunny afternoons couples will promenade, ladies of a certain age will walk their poodles, and the ultra-cool will rent a paddle boat (20SFr, by the Jetée de Pâquis). Overlooking the city in a northern suburb, the headquarters of the United Nations, Red Cross, World Trade Organization, and other international bodies enjoy an Alpine panorama from their spacious gardens. Be sure to carry your passport with you at all times; the French border is just a few steps from Annemasse (tram #12), and regional buses frequently cross over it. Local buses provide a maze of swift Swiss service, with major hubs at the Gare Cornavin and pl. Bel Air, near the ponts de l'Ile.

Tourist Offices: Geneva is a well-developed, highly refined tourist town; any town that can turn the random piddly gurgling of turned-off hydraulic pressure taps into an honest-to-God tourist attraction (the Jet d'Eau) knows how to sell itself. All the offices have oodles of information, but the must-haves are: the city map; *Info Jeunes* (filled with budget accommodations and excellent activity and excursion information); and *Genève pratique* (detailed city info). Nice but not necessary is the excellent and reassuring *Guide to the English-Speaking Community in Geneva*. There are least 4 places where you can arm yourself for a full-touristic assault on the now unfortified city. The **main office**, rue du Mont-Blanc 3 (tel. 909 70 00; fax 929 70 11; email info@geneve-tourisme.ch; http://www.gcncvc-tourisme.ch), 5min. to the right of the station. Qualified staff books hotel rooms (5SFr fee), offers **walking tours**, and provides information on sights, excursions, and local events. Ask for anything your heart desires—they can even provide a list of vegetarian or kosher restaurants. The office maintains a **free direct phone line** to Geneva hotels in Gare Cornavin. Open June 15-Sept. 15 Mon.-Fri. 8am-7pm, Sat.-Sun. 9am-6pm; Sept. 16-June 14 Mon.-Sat. 9am-6pm. **Office du Tourisme,** pl. du Molard 4 (tel. 311 98 27; fax 311 80 52), across the river. Same services, friendlier staff. Open Mon. 12:30-6:30pm, Tues.-Fri. 9am-6:30pm, Sat. 10:30am-4:30pm. Budget travelers should head toward the magic bus, the **Centre d'Accueil et de Renseignements (CAR)** (tel. 731 46 47), parked during the summer at the top of rue du Mont Blanc after the pedestrian underpass beneath Gare Cornavin. Geared toward young people, especially backpackers, the office answers all sorts of questions and posts a daily updated list of theater, music, and other performances.

LAKE GENEVA (LAC LÉMAN)

Open June 16-Sept. 6 daily 9:30am-11pm. A last resort is the **Anglo-phone** (tel. 157 50 14), a 24hr. hotline (in English) that answers questions about any aspect of life in Switzerland. Be quick: 2.13SFr per min.

Budget Travel: SSR, rue Vignier 3 (tel. 329 97 34), off av. Henri-Dunant near Plaine de Plainpalais. Very friendly service with special youth and student fares. Open Mon.-Thurs. 9:15am-6:30pm, Fri. 9am-6pm. Visa, MC, AmEx.

Consulates: Australia, rue de Moillebeau 56-58 (tel. 918 29 00). **Canada,** rue du Pré-de-Bichette 1 (tel. 919 92 00). **New Zealand,** chemin du Petit-Saconnex 28a (tel. 734 95 30). **South Africa,** rue de Rhône 65 (tel. 849 54 54). **U.K.,** rue de Vermont 37-39 (tel. 734 38 00). **U.S.,** rue de Pré-Bois 29 (tel. 798 16 05; recorded emergency information 798 16 15). Call each office to schedule appointments.

Currency Exchange: Throughout town. **Gare Cornavin** has good rates and no commission on traveler's checks. Will advance cash on credit cards (minimum 200SFr) and arrange Western Union transfers. Open daily 6:45am-9:30pm.

American Express, rue du Mont-Blanc 7, P.O. Box 1032, CH-1211 Geneva 01 (tel. 731 76 00; fax 732 72 11). Mail held 2-3 months. All banking services; reasonable exchange rates. AmEx **ATM.** Hotel (20SFr) and train (10SFr) reservations and tickets for city tours and excursions. Open in summer Mon.-Fri. 8:30am-6pm, Sat. 9am-noon; in winter Mon.-Fri. 8:30am-5:30pm, Sat. 9am-noon.

Flights: Cointrin Airport (tel. 717 71 11, flight information 799 31 11; fax 798 43 77) is a hub for **Swissair** (tel. (0848) 800 700). Several direct flights per day to New York, Paris, London, Amsterdam, and Rome. **Air France** (tel. 798 05 05) has 7 per day to Paris, and **British Airways** (tel. (0800) 556 969) has 7 per day to London. Bus #10 (2.20SFr) or the train (every 10min. to Gare Cornavin, 6min., 4.80SFr) leads to town from the airport. The **Taxi-Bus** (tel. 331 41 33) will take you from your nearest bus stop to the train station when the local buses aren't working.

Trains: Gare Cornavin, pl. Cornavin. To: **Lausanne** (every 20min., 40min., 19.40SFr), **Bern** (every hr., 1¾hr., 48SFr), **Zurich** (every hr., 3hr., 74SFr), **Basel** (every hr., 2¾hr., 67SFr), **Montreux** (every hr., 1hr., 27SFr), **Interlaken** (every hr., 3hr., 60SFr), **Paris** (5 per day, 3½hr., 77SFr plus reservation fee, under 26 61SFr plus reservation fee), and **Rome** (1 per day, 10hr., 109SFr, under 26 84SFr). To book a seat on any long-distance or international trains, take a number from the machine in Cornavin's reservation and information (open Mon.-Fri. 8:30am-7:40pm, Sat. 8:30am-5:40pm) and settle down for a long wait. Train schedules at http://www.sbb.ch. **Gare des Eaux-Vives** (tel. 736 16 20), on av. de la Gare des Eaux-Vives, connects to France's regional rail lines through **Annecy** (every hr., 1½hr., 14SFr) or **Chamonix** through St. Gervais (every hr., 3¼hr., 24SFr). Be aware that the automatic machine at the station does not return change.

Public Transportation: Geneva has an efficiently integrated bus and tram network. **Transport Publics Genevois** (tel. 308 34 34), next to the tourist office in Gare Cornavin, provides a free but intensely confusing map of the local bus routes called *Le Réseau.* (Open daily 6:15am-8pm.) 2.20SFr buys 1hr. of unlimited travel on any bus; 3 stops or less cost 1.50SFr. Your best bets are a full-day pass for 5SFr; six 1hr. trips for 12SFr; or twelve 1hr. trips for 22SFr. Swisspass valid on all buses; Eurailpass not valid. Buy multi-fare and day tickets at the train station, others at automatic vendors at every stop. Stamp multi-use tickets before boarding or suffer fines if caught. Buses run roughly 5:30am-midnight.

Taxis: Taxi-Phone (tel. 331 41 33). 6.30SFr plus 2.70SFr per km. Taxi from airport to city 25-30SFr, max. 4 passengers (15-20min.).

Car Rental: Avis, rue de Lausanne 44 (tel. 731 90 00). **Budget,** rue de Lausanne 37 (tel. 732 52 52). **Europcar,** rue de Lausanne 37 (tel. 731 51 50; fax 738 46 50), is probably the cheapest: weekly unlimited-mileage rentals start at 104SFr per day. All have offices at Cointrin, but check for airport-supplements (around 11%).

Parking: On-street 0.60SFr per hr., 2hr. max. The garage (tel. 736 66 30) under Cornavin station (enter at pl. Cornavin), is 2SFr for 1hr., 3SFr for 2; 1SFr for 2hr. at night. **Garage Les Alpes,** rue Thalberg, has 350 spaces (2SFr per hr. weekdays, 1SFr per hr. nights and weekends). Strategically positioned digital boards on the highways list each of several car-parks and the number of spaces free.

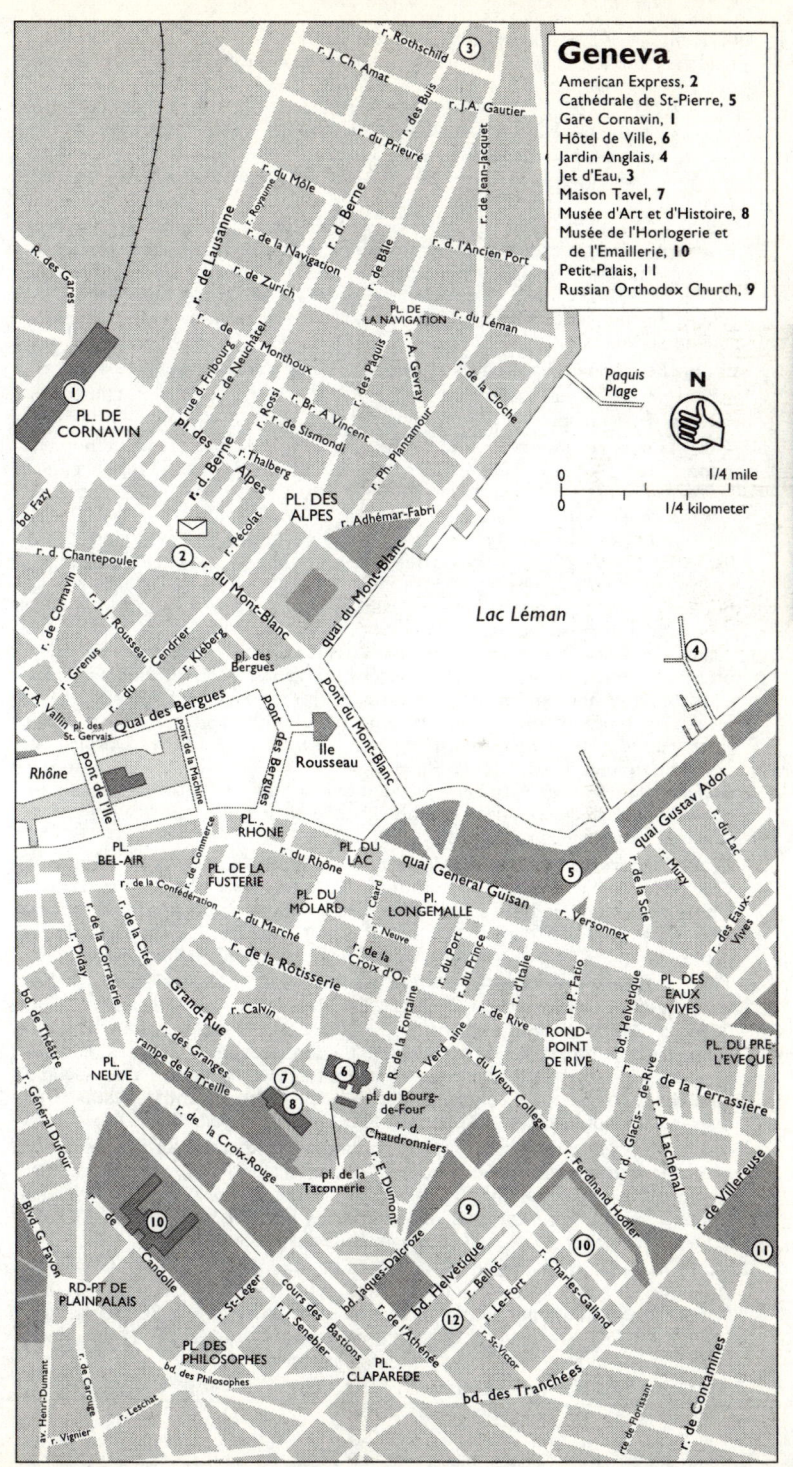

GENEVA: PRACTICAL INFORMATION ■ 303

Geneva

American Express, **2**
Cathédrale de St-Pierre, **5**
Gare Cornavin, **1**
Hôtel de Ville, **6**
Jardin Anglais, **4**
Jet d'Eau, **3**
Maison Tavel, **7**
Musée d'Art et d'Histoire, **8**
Musée de l'Horlogerie et de l'Emaillerie, **10**
Petit-Palais, **11**
Russian Orthodox Church, **9**

WESTERN SWITZERLAND

Bike Rental: Geneva is pedal-happy, with well-marked bike paths and special traffic lights for spoked traffic. For routes, get *Itineraires cyclables* or *Tours de ville avec les vélos de location* from the tourist office. Behind the station, **Veloc,** pl. Montbrillant 17 (tel. 740 13 43), rents bikes cheaply. ½-day 4SFr, 1 day 6SFr. You can also try the baggage check in **Gare Cornavin** (tel. 715 22 20). 22SFr per day, 88SFr per week. Mountain bike 29SFr, 116SFr. Open Mon.-Fri. 6:50am-6:45pm, Sat.-Sun. 7am-12:30pm and 1:30-5:45pm. Visa, MC, AmEx. Reservations recommended.

Hitchhiking: *Let's Go* does not recommend hitchhiking. Hitchers say, however, that Switzerland is one of the safer countries in Europe in which to hail a ride. Those headed to Germany or northern Switzerland take bus #4/44: "Jardin Botanique." Those headed to France take bus #4/44: "Palettes" then line D: "St. Julien." In summer, **Telstop** has a list of available rides in front of the CAR information booth.

Luggage Storage: Gare Cornavin. 3-5SFr per day. Open daily 4:30am-12:45am.

Lost Property: rue des Glacis de Rive 7 (tel. 787 60 00). Open Mon.-Thurs. 8am-4:30pm, Fri. 8am-4pm.

English-Language Bookstores: ELM (English Language and Media) Video and Books, rue Versonnex 5 (tel. 736 09 45; fax 786 14 29), has a quality range of new books in English, a fine selection of *Let's Go* guides, and a book-ordering service. Open Mon.-Fri. 9am-6:30pm, Sat. 10am-5pm. Visa, MC, AmEx, DC. The adjoining video store (tel. 736 02 22) rents videos in English (from 5.50SFr). Open Mon.-Fri. 9am-8pm, Sat. 9am-7pm. **Librairie des Amateurs,** Grand Rue 15 (tel. 732 80 97), in the *vieille ville.* Classy secondhand dealer has a roomful of English-language books in a strange mix of battered leather-bound classics and lurid late-70s romances and mysteries. Open Mon. 2-6:30pm, Tues.-Fri. 10am-6:30pm, Sat. 10am-5pm. **Book Worm,** rue Sismondi 5 (tel. 731 87 65), near the train station off rue de Berne. An American couple runs this genteel store of used books and classic English-language videos (4SFr for 2 days). Tea room serves pots of tea/coffee (2SFr), lunch (noon-2pm, 4.50SFr including drink), and desserts (5.50SFr). Open Tues.-Sat. 10am-8pm, Sun. 10am-5pm. Visa, MC AmEx. **Payot Libraire,** rue de Chantepoulet 5 (tel. 731 89 50; fax 738 48 03), is the biggest bookstore in Geneva, with an English-language section that includes *Let's Go* and occasional 50%-off specials. Open Mon. 1-6:30pm, Tues.-Wed. and Fri. 9am-6:30pm, Thurs. 9am-8pm, Sat. 9am-5pm. Visa, MC, AmEx, DC.

Library: American Library, rue de Monthoux 3 (tel. 732 80 97), at Emmanuel Church. 20,000 titles and a subscription to the *International Herald Tribune.* One-month membership (25SFr) allows you to borrow books (6 max.) for 2 weeks with a 0.50SFr deposit and to rent from a small but eclectic collection of books on tape (2SFr per 2 weeks). Open Tues. and Fri. 12:30-5pm, Wed. 2-8pm, Thurs. 2-5pm, Sat. 10am-4pm, Sun. 11am-12:30pm.

Bi-Gay-Lesbian Organizations: Dialogai, Case Postale 27, av. Wendt 57 (tel. 340 00 00; fax 340 03 98). Bus #3, 9, or 10: "Servette-Ecole." Resource group with programs ranging from couples counseling to outdoor activities. Publishes *Dialogai,* a guide to Switzerland's gay scene. Mostly men, though women are welcome. Phoneline and center are only open Wed. 8-10pm. **Centre Femmes Natalie Barney** (women only), av. Peschier 30, CH-1211, Geneva 25 (tel. 789 26 00).

Travelers with Disabilities: CCIPH (Centre de Coordination et d'Information pour Personnes Handicapées), rte de Chée 54 (tel. 736 38 10). The tourist office also provides a free comprehensive guide to the city for the disabled, called *Guide à l'Usage des Personnes Handicapées,* which lists accessibility of all the main hotels, sights, shops, and transport. Huge map included.

Laundromat: Salon Lavoir, on rue Prader, close to the station off rue Mt. Blanc, is equipped with shiny new machines and helpful English instructions. Wash 3-6.40SFr, dry 0.80 SFr per 15min., detergent 1SFr. **Salon Lavoir St. Gervais,** rue Vallin 9 (tel. 731 26 46), off pl. St. Gervais. Wash 4SFr, dry 1SFr per 12min., detergent 1SFr. Open Mon.-Sat. 7:30am-9pm, Sun. 10am-9pm.

Rape Crisis Hotline: Viol-Secours (tel. 733 63 63). Open Mon. 4-11pm, Tues. 2-6pm, Wed. and Fri. 9am-noon, Thurs. 2-9pm.

GENEVA: ACCOMMODATIONS AND CAMPING ■ 305

Late-Night Pharmacy: Every night 4 pharmacies stay open late (9 or 11pm). Consult *Genève Agenda* for addresses and phone numbers or call 144 or 111 (daily 7pm-8am). The pharmacy at the train station has the longest regular hours.

Medical Assistance: Hôpital Cantonal, rue Micheli-du-Crest 24 (tel. 372 81 20). Bus #1 or 5 or tram #12. Door #3 is outpatient care. Walk-in clinics dot the city; call the **Association des Médecins** (tel. 320 25 11) for further information.

Emergencies: Police, rue Pecolat 5 (tel. 117), next to post office. **Fire,** tel. 118. **Ambulance,** tel. 144. **Lifeline** (tel. (059) 504 23 704), a 24hr. hotline for problems ranging from drug addiction to extreme depression.

Post Office: Poste Centrale, rue de Mont-Blanc 18, a block from Gare Cornavin in the stately Hôtel des Postes. Open Mon.-Fri. 7:30am-6pm, Sat. 8-11am. Address *Poste Restante* to CH-1211, Genève 1 Mont-Blanc. **Postal Code:** CH-1211.

Telephone Code: 022.

ACCOMMODATIONS AND CAMPING

Generally speaking, Geneva is not a budget-hotel kind of a town. It could hardly be otherwise in a city replete with international bankers, diplomats, and luxury-yacht owners. Luckily, the seasonal influx of university students and interns buoys up the cheap long-term bed market. Dorm beds and rooms do exist at relatively reasonable rates in the scattered pensions, small hotels, and university dormitories that crouch behind the five-star hotels with their bellhops and limo services. The indispensable *Info Jeunes* lists about 50 options; we list the highlights below. The tourist office has responded to the demand with a brochure most imaginatively titled *Budget Hotels*, stretching definitions a bit to include rooms at 43-120SFr per person. Even for the shortest stays, reservations are a must. Many university dorms rent attractive rooms in the summer for the best prices in town. For longer stays, check *Tribune de Genève*'s weekly supplement of apartment classifieds or the tourist office's board. Employees of international organizations can contact the **Centre d'Accueil pour les Internationals de Genève,** rue de Varembé 9-11 (tel. 327 17 77; fax 327 17 27) for assistance.

Auberge de Jeunesse (HI), rue Rothschild 28-30 (tel. 732 62 60; fax 738 39 87). Walk 15min. left from the station down rue de Lausanne and then turn right on rue Rothschild. Bus #1 (dir: Wilson) stops right in front of the hostel. Despite its 350 beds spread over 2 buildings, this hostel is a very efficient, modern establishment. The friendly staff speaks enough languages with impressive facility to keep you entertained during the unavoidably long check-in line. Whatever you do, get your hands on an arrival slip and fill it out before you get to the window; otherwise, you'll lose your place and extend an already tedious wait. Do not expect luxury so much as no-frills comfort. Amenities include a sizable lobby, restaurant (dinner 11.50SFr, dessert 1.80SFr), kitchen facilities, TV room with CNN, library, and snack bar. Flexible 3-night max. stay. Reception in summer 6:30-10am and 4pm-midnight; in winter 6:30-10am and 5pm-midnight. Lockout in summer 10am-4pm, in winter 10am-5pm. Curfew midnight. Quiet time from 10:30pm. Singles 23SFr, non-members 28SFr; doubles 70SFr, 80SFr; triples with bath 85SFr, 120SFr. Hall showers, sheets, and breakfast included. Lockers in every dorm (bring your own lock) and in the lobby. Laundry 6SFr. Special facilities for disabled guests.

Centre St-Boniface, av. du Mail 14 (tel. 321 88 44; fax 320 47 94). Bus #1 or 4/44 (dir: Voirets): "Cirque" then continue down av. du Mail. To walk from the station (20min.), head right on bd. Fazy, across pont de La Coulouvrenière and along av. du Mail. This Catholic-run center has rooms just minutes from the *vieille ville*. Reception Mon.-Fri. 9:30-11:30am, 4:30-6:30pm, and 7:30-8:30pm, Sat. 10am-noon. Dorms without sheets 16SFr, with sheets 24SFr; singles (mid-July to late Sept. only) 39SFr, students 34SFr; doubles (mid-July to late Sept. only) 62SFr, 57SFr. Try to get one with shower and balcony. Access to kitchen, TV room, and dining room included. No breakfast, but residents get a discount at the restaurant next door, **La Pleine-Lune,** with a card from the reception. Reservations preferred.

Hôme St-Pierre, cours St-Pierre 4 (tel. 310 37 07; fax 310 71 98). Bus #5: "pl. Neuve." Or walk 15min. from the train station: cross the Rhône at pont du Mont-Blanc then go up rampe de la Treille and take the third right. Mere seconds from the west entrance of the cathedral, this "home" for **women only** features comfy beds, large windows, inexplicably short (but very fluffy) comforters, and a church-bell serenade every 15min. A large kitchen, dining room, and rooftop terrace with spectacular views create a convivial atmosphere for both long- and short-term residents. Reception Mon.-Sat. 8:30am-1pm and 4-8pm, Sun. 9am-1pm. No lockout or curfew. Dorms 22SFr; singles 35SFr; doubles 50SFr. Showers and lockers included. Big breakfast (Mon.-Sat.) 7.50SFr. Popular, so reserve ahead.

Cité Universitaire, av. Miremont 46 (tel. 839 22 11; fax 839 22 23). Bus #3 (dir: Crêts-de-Champel) to the last stop. Find the bus at pl. de 22 Cantons on the far right as you exit the train station. Far from the station on the other side of the *vielle ville.* Institutional college housing in a modern tower block with heaps of facilities: TV rooms, newspapers, restaurant, disco, ping pong (paddles at the reception), tennis courts, internet access. Reception Mon.-Fri. 8am-noon and 2-10pm, Sat.-Sun. 8am-noon and 6-10pm. Lockout 10am-6pm. Curfew 11pm. 4 dorms (July-Sept. only) 15SFr, including very small lockers; singles 43SFr, students 36SFr; doubles 58SFr, 52SFr; studios with kitchenette and bathroom 61SFr. Hall showers included.

Hotel Pension St-Victor, rue François-le-Fort 1 (tel. 346 17 18; fax 346 10 46; email willacuna@mail.span.ch; http://geneva.yop.ch/hotels/smp). Bus #1, 3, or 5: "pl. Claparède." An elegant building with a view of the Russian Church's gilded domes across an expanse of stately trees. Large, clean, distinguished rooms individually decorated with impeccable taste. Homemade jam and eggs fresh from the owner's farm for breakfast. Friendly anglophone atmosphere. Reception Mon.-Fri. 7:30-8pm, Sat.-Sun. 8am-8pm. Singles from 65SFr; doubles from 90SFr; triples from 110SFr. Breakfast included. Reservations are imperative. Visa, MC.

Hôtel de la Cloche, rue de la Cloche 6 (tel. 732 94 81; fax 738 16 12), off quai du Mont-Blanc across from the Noga Hilton. A genteel old hotel, with hallways lined with feet-engulfing oriental carpets and doors hung with heavy drapery. Bright, airy rooms, many of which have balconies and fantastic view of the Jet d'Eau. Reception 8am-midnight. Singles 50SFr; doubles 80SFr; triples 85SFr; quads 130SFr. A few rooms have showers; hall showers 2SFr. Breakfast 5SFr. Only 18 beds, so reserve in advance. Visa, MC, AmEx.

Hôtel Beau-Site, pl. du Cirque 3 (tel. 328 10 08; fax 329 23 64). Bus #1 or 4/44: "Cirque." Or walk from the station: turn right on bd. Fazy, cross the Rhône at pont de la Coulouvrenière, and follow bd. Georges-Favon to pl. du Cirque (20min.). Comfortably quirky, in the middle of a busy square lined with chatty cafés. Paneled rooms with quilt-covered beds and antique furniture—some even have marble fireplaces to accompany the ornamental plaster moldings. Reception with the clever trumpet lamp daily 7am-11pm; call if you'll be arriving later. Singles 57SFr, with shower 63SFr, with bath 75SFr; doubles 79SFr, 83SFr, 102SFr; triples 94SFr, 98SFr, 120SFr; quads 104SFr, 108SFr. All rooms with sink and radio. 6 sinkless rooms, usually occupied by long-term guests, available for 45SFr each. Call ahead for availability. 10% student discount. Breakfast included; coffee and tea in lobby 10am-10pm. Free street parking 7pm-8am. Visa, MC, AmEx.

Hôtel St-Gervais, rue des Corps-Saints 20 (tel./fax 732 45 72). From the train station, cross the street and walk right 3min. down rue de Cornavin. The dark, low-ceilinged rooms provide some (but not much) refuge from the bright tartan carpeting that must have been laid down by deranged or color-blind Scots. Some of the very clean bonny bathrooms even have tartan ceilings to mesmerize droopy early morning eyes. Reception 8am-midnight. Singles 62SFr, with shower 88SFr; doubles 78SFr, 98-105SFr; 1 triple 98SFr. Breakfast included. Visa, MC, AmEx. Only 26 rooms, so reservations are preferred.

Forget-Me-Not, rue Vignier 8 (tel. 320 93 55; fax 781 46 45). Bus #4/44 or tram #12: "Plainpalais" then walk down av. Dunant and turn left on rue Vignier. Cement high-rise on a busy street above a pool hall. The atmosphere of this residence/hotel sparks up the otherwise characterless architecture. The rooms, once the narrow cells of devout nuns, compensate for their spareness with yards of cabinets and bright orange bed covers. Though law students and UN interns stay on for months, backpackers regularly join the ranks who gather in the communal kitchens and lounges on each floor and the wide rooftop terrace. Kitchen, laundry, TV/video room, night guard, telephones, food/drink machines, 2 pianos, free luggage storage, study room, and a partridge in a pear tree. Reception Mon.-Fri. 9:30am-8pm, Sat. 10am-6pm, Sun. 3-6pm; call if you're arriving after 10pm. No curfew. Dorms 25SFr; singles 50SFr; doubles 80SFr. Breakfast and showers included. Slightly more expensive "hotel" rooms, with carpeting, nicer sheets, and a fridge: singles 60SFr; doubles with shower 110SFr.

Sylvabelle, chemin de Conches 10 (tel. 347 06 03). Bus #8: "Conches." Nearest camping site to town. Reception 7-10am and 7-10pm. 6SFr; tent 4SFr; car 3SFr. Shower 2.50SFr. Open Easter-Oct.

Pointe-à-la-Bise (tel. 752 12 96). Bus #9: "Rive" then bus E (north): "Bise" (about 7km). 6SFr; tents 9SFr. Open April to mid-Oct. Consult *Info Jeunes* (at the tourist office) for additional locations.

FOOD

Although it's true that you can find anything from sushi to *paella* in Geneva, you'll need a banker's salary to foot the bill. For a picnic, shop at the ubiquitous supermarkets. Many supermarkets also have cafeterias with some of the best deals available, and *Info Jeunes* lists many university cafeterias that won't tax your wallet.

Boulangeries and *pâtisseries*, however, offer unparalleled opportunities for gourmet food at budget prices—6SFr goes a long way when you combine a fresh loaf of bread with an avocado and cheese from Migros or Co-op. *Pâtisseries* and pasta/pizza parlors permeate **place du Bourg-de-Four,** below Cathédrale de St-Pierre, as do some of the best cafés. By dining in the village of **Carouge** (tram #12: pl. du Marché), you can combine gastronomy with history. Carouge gained a reputation for fun back in Calvin's day, when those who wished to defy their leader's ban on cafés gathered outside the city limits to chat and drink the night into oblivion.

Restaurant Manora, rue de Cornavin 4 (tel. 909 44 10), 3min. from the station on the right in the Placette Dept. Store. Huge, very affordable self-serve restaurant with a fresh, varied, high-quality selection. Salads (big bowl 4SFr), quiche (6.90SFr including salad), fruit tarts (3SFr), fresh fruit juices (3.90SFr), and entrees (from 11SFr). Wheelchair accessible. Open Mon.-Sat. 7am-9:30pm, Sun. 9am-9pm.

Auberge de Saviese, rue du Pâquis 20 (tel. 732 83 30). Bus #1: Monthoux. Even *Genevois* load up on traditional Swiss specialties here. Rustic interior with wood-shingled roofs over the bar and entrance, as well as flat, massive barrels for chandeliers. Share coffee (1.90SFr) with local early-risers hiding behind their newspapers (9am-11am). In addition to a selection of 3 *plats du jour* (13-14SFr), the regular menu features an excellent *fondue au cognac* (19SFr), *raclette* with all the trimmings (28SFr), pasta (13-19SFr), and salads (10-17SFr). Open Mon.-Fri. 8:30am-midnight, Sat. 2:30pm-midnight. Visa, MC, AmEx, DC.

Le Rozzel, Grand-Rue 18 (tel. 311 89 29). Breton-style *crêperie* with outdoor seating amid the cobblestones and inviting antique shops of the most elegant street in the *vieille ville.* Large dinner crepes 7-16SFr; dessert crepes 5-14SFr; cider 4.50SFr. Open Mon.-Thurs. 7:30am-9pm, Fri.-Sun. 7:30am-1am. Visa.

La Crise, rue de Chantepoulet 13 (tel. 738 02 64). From the station, go right on rue de Cornavin and turn left on rue de Chantepoulet. Eat among the talkative locals and watch the chefs cook your food 2ft. away in this restaurant hardly bigger than a kitchen. Can't beat the prices or the portions: a huge meal (large slice of quiche and a plate full of veggies) for a mere 7SFr; a hearty bowl of soup 3.50SFr, vegetable or dessert 6SFr. Open Mon.-Fri. 6am-8pm, Sat. 6am-3pm.

Mañana, rue Chaponnière 3 (tel. 732 21 31). From pl. Cornavin, take the first left down rue du Mont-Blanc. Hopping Tex-Mex joint with jolly Mexican guitarist who strums away in an atmospheric mix of stone arches, ceiling fans, and very green place mats. Typical Mexican entrees 18-20SFr; boot of beer (no joke) 5.30SFr. Vegetarian plates 15-22SFr; nachos 13SFr. Open Mon.-Fri. noon-2pm and

6-11:30pm, Sat.-Sun. noon-11:30pm. Visa, MC, AmEx. Happy hour at the **Cactus Club** downstairs nightly 7-10pm. Live music Wed. and Thurs. nights, DJ other nights.

Navy Club, pl. du Bourg-de-Four 31 (tel. 310 33 98). The *vieille ville* meets *The Love Boat*. The owner obviously followed the cardinal rule for clever Swiss restauranteurs: if you've got a gimmick, run with it. Or sail with it, as with the Navy Club's profusion of marine memorabilia, anchor motif, and unceasing color scheme. Still, it's plenty of fun, especially after dark when the place wakes up for after-hours music and drinking. All aboard! Veal sausage with *Rösti* and salad 14.50SFr; pizza 11-18SFr; pasta 15-21SFr. Open in summer Mon.-Fri. 11am-2:30pm and 5:30pm-1am, Sat. 6pm-2am; in winter Mon.-Fri. 11am-1am, Sat. 6pm-2am. Visa, MC, AmEx.

Les 5 Saveurs, rue du Prieuré 22 (tel. 731 78 70). Seconds from the hostel. A *very* health-conscious restaurant. Amid dire cancer warnings, stock up on super-good-for-you fresh veggies and luscious desserts (made, of course, with no sugar or white flour) at the ever-changing noon-time buffet (400g for 12SFr), or enjoy the *plat du jour* (10-13SFr) or *du soir* (15SFr) in the beaded, very kitcheny atmosphere. Open Mon.-Fri. noon-2pm and 6:30-9pm.

Sunset, rue St-Léger (tel. 320 15 13), off pl. des Philosophes. A vegetarian university hang-out with conical hanging lamps and sleek black furniture. Doubles as a bookstore specializing in Swiss authors. Eat out or sit inside with the tropical fish and haphazard bookstall. *Pita au champignons* (pita with mushrooms, 15SFr), inventive salads (13-17SFr), and gnocchi (15SFr). Open Aug. 19-July 6 Mon.-Fri. 7:30am-7pm; July 7-Aug. 18 Mon.-Fri. 7:30am-4pm. Visa, MC, AmEx.

Les Armures, rue du Puits-St-Pierre 1 (tel. 310 34 42). Read the polished brass plaque next to the door and inform everyone you ate at the same five-star hotel as Bill Clinton and Jimmy Carter. One small step up in price, one giant leap up in atmosphere. Wear clean socks. Clear Plexiglass dividers separate the gorgeous cobblestone terrace from the gawking tourist rabble, but the site still offers a clear (OK, slightly hazy) view of the Hôtel de Ville. Tasty onion soup 9SFr; good-sized fondue 19SFr; pizza 12-15SFr; *Rösti* 34SFr. Open Mon.-Fri. 8am-3pm and 6pm-midnight, Sat.-Sun. noon-midnight. Visa, MC, AmEx.

EPA, pl. de Molard. The department store's third-floor restaurant serves meals for 9-16SFr. Open Mon. 9:30am-6:45pm, Tues.-Wed. and Fri. 8:30am-6:45pm, Thurs. 8:30am-8pm, Sat. 8:30am-5pm.

Markets

Co-op, Migros, Grand Passage, and **Orient Express** branches stand throughout the city. On Sundays, the few options include Gare Cornavin's **Aperto** (open daily 6am-10pm) and scattered neighborhood groceries and bakeries. If you want to spare yourself the trek back to the station or a wild goose chase through empty streets for *pain au chocolat*, do your food shopping Saturday afternoon.

Co-op, corner of rue du Commerce and rue du Rhône. La Marmite on the first floor has a menu from 9.50SFr and salads for 2SFr per 100g. Open Mon. 9am-6:45pm, Tues.-Fri. 8:30am-6:45pm, Sat. 8:30am-5pm.

Migros, av. de Lausanne 18-20, left from Gare Cornavin in the Centre Commercial Les Cygnes. Reasonably priced cafeteria with salad bar. Open Mon. 9am-6:45pm, Tues.-Wed. and Fri. 8am-6:45pm, Thurs. 8am-8pm, Sat. 8am-5:45pm.

Marché des Eaux-Vives, bd. Helvétique, between cours de Rive and rue du Rhône. Huge dairy, vegetable, and flower market. Open Wed. and Sat. 8am-1pm.

Public Market, rue de Coutance, leading down to the river just above the ponts de l'Ile. Fresh fruits and cheese. Open Mon.-Sat. 8am-6pm. Another produce market is located on Plaine de Plainpalais Tues. and Fri. mornings.

SIGHTS

Although Geneva is a small city, over the centuries the *Genevois* have been so adept at digging up and showcasing its points of interest that it's hard to walk down any street without stumbling upon a random plaque and learning that someone famous happened to live in such and such a house for three days, two centuries ago. Fortunately, to prevent the warped view of the city that such haphazard trivia acquisition can inspire, the tourist office (which has thought of everything—and put it in a brochure) offers two-hour **walking tours** during the summer (June 14-Oct. 3 Mon.-Sat., 10SFr). Qualified guides lead tours on all things *Genevois:* the Reformation, internationalism, the Red Cross, the *vieille ville,* and even the city's museums. All tours start at 2:30pm; pick up the tourist office's leaflet for departure points and timetables. If you're not here in summer, don't fret—the tourist office has a special little something to keep you as informed as your summer cohorts. Recordings of the tours are available, and a portable cassette player will enable you to walk through 2000 years of Geneva's history *tout(e) seul(e)* for 10SFr plus a 50SFr deposit.

The *vieille ville's* **Cathédrale de St-Pierre,** the navel of the Protestant world, is as austerely pure as on the day that Calvin stripped the place of its popish baubles. From its altar, he preached to full houses from 1536 to 1564 as diligent listeners recorded 2,300 of his sermons. Two plain rosette windows shed light on the darkness (as all things Protestant are wont to do) of such hopelessly Catholic remnants as the amusingly demonic column capitals and cute walnut misericords. The brightly painted **Maccabean Chapel,** restored in a flamboyant style, gives an idea of how the cathedral walls might have looked pre-Reformation. The 157-step **north tower** provides a commanding view of the old town's winding streets and flower-bedecked homes. (Cathedral open daily June-Sept. 9am-7pm; Oct. and March-May 9am-noon and 2-6pm; Nov.-Feb. 9am-noon and 2-5pm. Tower closes 30min. earlier. Tower 3SFr. June-Sept. bell-ringing Sat. 5pm and free organ recital Sat. 6pm.) The ruins of a Roman sanctuary, a 4th-century basilica, and a 6th-century church rest in an **archaeological site** below the cathedral. (Open Tues.-Sun. 10am-1pm and 2-6pm. 5SFr, students 3SFr.)

Surrounding the cathedral are the town's vintage edifices. One minute from the west end sits **Maison Tavel,** Geneva's oldest private residence, which sports a round tower, mullioned windows, and 10 sculpted human and animal heads. The 14th-century structure now houses a historical municipal museum (see **Museums,** p. 311). Five cannons stand guard on a nearby street corner opposite the **Hôtel de Ville,** whose components date from the 15th through 17th centuries. Inside the courtyard, a ramp goes up the square tower, a unique feature that enabled dignitaries to attend meetings on horseback. Rousseau was exiled here for his radical publications, just a block from his birthplace. On August 22, 1864, world leaders signed the first **Geneva Convention** (governing conduct during war) in the Alabama room, so called because in another international settlement in 1872, the British agreed to compensate America for sinking the Southern ship, the *Alabama,* during the American Civil War. Walk among the **Grand-Rue's** medieval workshops and 18th-century mansions, and pay particular attention to the hastily added third or fourth floors, the makeshift result of the real estate boom following the influx of French Protestant Huguenots after Louis XIV repealed the Edict of Nantes. Plaques commemorating famous residents abound here, including one at number 40 marking the birthplace of philosopher **Jean-Jacques Rousseau.**

The city of Geneva may have overestimated the municipal problem of weary legs when it built the **world's longest bench** (394ft.) below the Hôtel de Ville. Stonily facing the Promenade des Bastions farther down, **Le Mur des Réformateurs** (Reformers' Wall) displays a sprawling collection of bas-relief narrative panels, a dizzying array of multilingual inscriptions, and the towering figures of the Reformers themselves. As the largest "elite 4" (Knox, Beze, Calvin, and Farel) jostle each other sternly for "leader of the Protestant pack" bragging rights, Cromwell and Rhode Island's Roger Williams trail behind. The static groupings imitate the stiff postures of the many rare trees that fill the surrounding wooded campus of Geneva University. As the Reformers look on, lovers lounge, sunbathers soak, and tourists traipse across the grass. Similarly stiff poses and steady stares people the icons in the nearby **Russian Orthodox Church,** rue Toepffer, near the Musée d'Art et d'Histoire. Inside, bearded monks shuffle about, genuflecting before these hauntingly lovely images and murmuring prayers in the lulling, liturgical cadences of Old Church Slavonic. Incense fills the nine gilded domes rising in shining summits above the cathedral. Note that photography and short skirts or shorts are not allowed.

A stroll along the lakefront (5min. from the *vieille ville*) is a rewarding, relaxing, and cost-effective way to enjoy Geneva. One figure gazes perpetually at the water; in 1834, admirers of Jean-Jacques Rousseau finally persuaded the town council to erect a statue in his honor. The council, unwilling to pay too much homage to a radical who had been sent into exile, placed the statue on a tiny island off the pont des Barques and surrounded it on 3 sides by poplar-tree walls and fenced-in swans, making the free-thinking philosopher visible only to those on the lake (or those who eat at the lakefront's conveniently located restaurant). The much more visible **Jet d'Eau,** down quai Gustave-Ardor, spews a spectacular plume of water 140m into the air. At any given time from March to October, the world's highest fountain keeps about seven tons of water aloft. The **floral clock,** in the nearby **Jardin Anglais,** pays homage to Geneva's watch industry and has the world's largest second hand (2.5m). The clock is probably Geneva's most overrated attraction and was once the city's most hazardous. Almost a meter had to be cut away from the clock because tourists, intent on taking the perfect photo, continually backed into unfortunate encounters with oncoming traffic. The rose-lined quays lead to two fun-parks. On the north shore, **Pâquis Plage,** at quai du Mont-Blanc, is laid-back and popular with the *Genevois* (1SFr). Farther from the city center on the south shore, **Genève Plage** offers a giant waterslide, an Olympic-sized pool, volleyball and basketball tournaments, and topless sunbathing (6SFr). The source of these waters, the Rhône, was consecrated by the pope during a particularly bad outbreak of the bubonic plague as a "burial" ground for plague victims. As you frolic in the lake, be reverent or repulsed accordingly.

Ferry tours leave from quai du Mont-Blanc and offer a lovely way to see Geneva. **CGN** (tel. 732 39 16) cruises to lakeside towns, including Lausanne, Montreux, and the stupendous Château de Chillon (round trip 47-57SFr, Eurailpass and Swisspass valid). **Swiss Boat** (tel. 732 47 47) and **Mouettes Genevoises** (tel. 732 29 44; fax 738 79 88) provide shorter winter cruises narrated in English (35min. 8SFr, 1hr. 13SFr, 2hr. 20SFr; fair weather only). Call ahead for reservations and departure times.

Farther up on the *rive droite,* the lakeside gardens become an attractive series of parks with modern bronzes, fountains, and 19th-century imitation Renaissance villas. The **Museum of the History of Science** (see p. 311) lives in one and the **World Trade Organization (WTO)** has its headquarters in another, less-attractive building farther north. Opposite the WTO, the basilica-shaped greenhouses of the **Jardin Botanique** (see p. 312) grow a collection of rare plants whose aroma wafts across rue de Lausanne. On a hill above these parks sits Geneva's international city, a group of multilateral organizations and embassies. Of these organization, the **Red Cross-Red Crescent** headquarters has the most interesting offerings for visitors (see below). Take bus #8, F, or Z, or walk 15 minutes from the station. The guided tour of the **United Nations,** on av. de la Paix, is—like Orson Welles's conception of peace—quite dull, despite art treasures donated by all the countries of the world. The constant traffic of international diplomats, brightly clothed in their native garb, provides more excitement than anything the tour guides have to say. The building was once the Palais de Nations, originally built for the ill-fated League of Nations. A not-so-subtle display of Cold War one-up-manship is the **armillary sphere** depicting the heavens, donated by the U.S. in memory of President Woodrow Wilson. Nearby is the monument dedicated to the **"conquest of space"** donated by the USSR. Don't miss the lovely view of the lake and France's Mont Blanc. (Open July-Aug. daily 9am-6pm; April-June and Sept.-Oct. daily 10am-noon and 2-4pm; Nov.-March Mon.-Fri. 10am-noon and 2-4pm. 8.50SFr, seniors and students 6.50SFr, children 4SFr, children under 6 free. For information, contact the Visitors' Service (tel. 907 45 60; fax 907 00 32), which also conducts 1hr. tours in any of 18 languages when a sizable group requests them.)

MUSEUMS

Geneva is home to a good number of exceptional museums, usually housed in splendid surroundings, whether architectural or natural. Fortunately, many are free; unfortunately, the most alluring aren't. Still, the selection is an exciting grab bag of huge, impressive collections mixed with smaller, more intimately passionate displays. Most museums are open six days a week (generally closed Mon. or Tues.), making weekends the perfect time to do the rounds.

International Red Cross and Red Crescent Museum, av. de la Paix 17 (tel. 734 52 48; fax 734 57 23). Bus #8, F, V or Z: "Appia" or "Ariana." A *Let's Go* pick to ponder. It's not often that a museum can truly affect the way you think and feel, especially if it's one in a long line of "learning experiences." Using the latest multimedia museum science, the curators have brought home in a starkly powerful manner Dostoyevsky's keynote words: "Each of us is responsible to all others for everything." 7 million POW records, including de Gaulle's, from World War I. Displays in English, French, and German. Self-guided audio tours 5SFr. No photography. Open Wed.-Mon. 10am-5pm. 10SFr, students and seniors 5SFr, under 11 free.

Petit-Palais, terrasse St-Victor 2 (tel. 346 14 33; fax 346 53 15), off bd. Helvétique. Bus #1, 3, or 5: "Claparède." This beautiful mansion encompasses the incredibly dynamic period from 1880-1930. Intimate galleries contain works from Renoir to Chagall. The big names, however, only frame and contextualize the stunning diversity of the work of lesser-known artists. Open Mon.-Fri. 10am-noon and 2-6pm, Sat.-Sun. 10am-1pm and 2-5pm. 10SFr, students and seniors 5SFr.

Musée Barbier-Mueller, rue Jean-Calvin 10 (tel. 312 02 70; fax 312 01 90), off Grand Rue in the *vieille ville*. This collection of so-called primitive art encompasses time periods as far-flung as early European and regions as exotic as tribal Africa. Whether marble, metal, or wood, each pieces glows as a work of art and not merely as a cultural artifact. Open daily 11am-5pm. 5SFr, children 3SFr.

Musée d'Art et d'Histoire, rue Charles-Galland 2 (tel. 418 26 00). Bus #1 or 8: "Tranchées." An eclectic collection sprawls over thousands of years. The crown jewel is Konrad Witz's 1444 *Jesus and the Apostles Fishing on Lake Geneva* (not the Sea of Galilee), one of the earliest paintings to use perspective in landscape. Open Tues.-Sun. 10am-5pm. Museum free; temporary exhibition rates vary.

Musée de l'Horlogerie (Museum of Watches and Enameling), rte de Malagnou 15 (tel. 418 64 70; fax 418 64 71). Bus #6 (dir: Malagnou): "Museum." A jewel of a museum that ticks away to the rhythms of its still-functioning antique horological masterpieces. Fingernail-sized wonders, free-standing giants, and enamelled confections of Swiss watchmakers' whimsy compete to be the first to ring before the hour and confuse wrist-watched tourists. Open Wed.-Mon. 10am-5pm. Free.

Musée Ariana, av. de la Paix 10 (tel. 418 54 50; fax 418 54 51). Bus #8, 18, or F: "Appia" or "Ariana." An offshoot of the Musée d'Art et d'Histoire, Ariana surpasses her mother in the setting and comprehensibility of her glass and ceramic collection. The approach along the gravel path may inspire faintness long before you swoon at the marbled hall inside. Open Wed.-Mon. 10am-5pm. Free.

Musée d'Ethnographie, bd. Carl-Vogt 65-67 (tel. 418 45 50; fax 418 45 51; email jerome.ducor@ville-ge.ch; http://www.ville.ge.ch/musinfo/ethg/index.htm). Bus #1, 4, or 44: "Bains." A pleasantly cluttered permanent collection of cultural artifacts and very compelling and challenging temporary exhibitions, none of which are afraid to confront real issues. As usual, the art of Asia and Oceania steals the show with the menacing armor of Japanese samurai and strikingly Mirò-esque monumental sculpture. Open Tues.-Sun. 10am-5pm. 5SFr, students 3SFr, children free.

Musée d'Histoire des Sciences, Villa Bartholoni, rue de Lausanne 128 (tel. 731 69 85; fax 741 13 08), in the park at La Perle de Lac. Bus #4 or 44. This elegant *palazzo* houses esoteric scientific gear. Downstairs starts sensibly enough with sundials, astrolabes, globes, and an orrery or two, but upstairs gets odder and bloodier with amputation saws, trepanning kits, a wax model of a syphilis patient, skull drills, and the gruesomely crude tools of early gynecology and obstetrics. Exhibits in French. Open Wed.-Mon. 1-5pm. Free.

Institut et Musée Voltaire, rue des Délices 25 (tel. 344 71 33). Bus #7 (dir: Lignon): "Délices." The ardent Voltairist might think that this house, where Voltaire lived from 1755 to 1763, is the best of all possible museums. Meaty labels (in French) contrast with Voltaire's generally arch, epigrammatic style, as recorded in scores of letters, manuscripts, and first editions. Particularly diverting are Huber's cartoons of the *philosophe*, Frederick of Prussia's sycophantic letters, and Voltaire's cantankerous replies to Rousseau. Considerably more effort has gone into cultivating the garden. Exhibits in French. Open Mon.-Fri. 2-5pm. Free.

Musée d'Histoire Naturale, rte de Malagnou 1 (tel. 418 63 00; fax 418 63 01). Bus #6 (dir: Malagnon): "Museum." Huge rambling exhibits of stuffed beasties trying hard to look life-like. Unfortunately, only the carnivores snarl and growl in convincing postures; the stubbornly un-dynamic herbivores look blankly on. Transfixed with fear? Nope, just stuffed. Open Tues.-Sun. 9:30am-5pm. Free.

Maison Tavel, rue du Puits-St-Pierre 6 (tel. 310 29 00), next to the Hôtel de Ville. This house stores everything that the city couldn't bear to throw away: the 1799 guillotine from pl. Neuve, a collection of medieval front doors, and a vast zinc and copper model of 1850 Geneva that took 16 years to build. A not-terribly-detailed multilingual guidebook available at the entrance. Open Tues.-Sun. 10am-5pm. Free.

Jardin Botanique, chemin de l'Impératrice 1 (tel. 752 69 69). Bus #4/44: "Jardin Boutique." Flummoxed flamingos ponder relaxing gardens with a deer park, greenhouses, rock gardens, pea hens, and children bearing ice-cream cones like frozen assault weapons. A great place to spend a lazy Sunday afternoon. Open April-Sept. daily 8am-7:30pm; Oct.-March 9:30am-5pm. Free.

Château de Penthes (Museum of the Swiss Abroad), chemin de l'Impératrice 18 (tel. 734 90 21; fax 734 47 40). Bus 2: "Penthes." A cozy chateau cloaked in ivy and girdled by hydrangeas. The museum chronicles the history of Swiss international relations from the Middle Ages to today—"today" meaning the world-famous, flamboyantly dressed, highly obedient Swiss Guard. Stroll through the surrounding parks—Lac Léman will never look quite so languid. Guides in French, English, and German. Open Tues.-Sun. 10am-noon and 2-6pm. 5SFr, students 1.50SFr.

Jean Tua Car and Cycle Museum, rue des Bains 28-30 (tel. 321 36 37). Bus #1, by rue des Grenadiers. Fun collection of 70 cars as well as motorcycles and bicycles, all dating before 1939. Open Wed.-Sun. 2-6pm. 8SFr.

ENTERTAINMENT AND NIGHTLIFE

Genève Agenda and *What's on in Geneva* are available at the tourist office and list events ranging from major festivals to daily movie listings (be warned, a movie runs about 15.50SFr). You would have to live in an box not to find an enjoyable diversion in Geneva. Summer days bring festivals, free open-air concerts, and **organ music** in Cathédrale de St-Pierre. In July and August, the **Cinelac** turns Genève Plage into an open-air cinema that screens mostly American films. Check the listings in *Genève Agenda* for indoor cinemas, and keep in mind that films marked "v.o." are in their original language with French and sometimes German subtitles and "st. ang." means that the film has English subtitles. *The* party in Geneva is **L'Escalade,** commemorating the dramatic repulse from the city walls of the invading Savoyard troops (see **Soup's On,** p. 300). The revelry lasts a full weekend and takes place in early December. Summer festivals include the biggest celebration of **American Independence Day** outside the U.S. on July 4 and the **Fêtes de Genève,** August 7-10, filled with international music and artistic celebration culminating in a spectacular fireworks display. **La Bâtie Festival,** a music festival traditionally held late August to early September, draws Swiss music-lovers down from the hills for a two-week orgy of cabaret, theater, and concerts by experimental rock and folk acts. Many events are free; students pay half-price for the others (regular prices 10-32SFr). For information, call 738 55 77 or email batie@world.com.ch. **Free jazz concerts** take place from July 5 to August 23 on Wednesday and Friday nights at 8:30pm at the Théâtre de Verdure

GENEVA: ENTERTAINMENT AND NIGHTLIFE ■ 313

in Parc de la Grange. Most parks offer similar free concerts; check at the tourist office for information and tickets. **Nyon,** a few minutes by train from Geneva on Lac Léman, holds a big-name rock festival at the end of July (30-35SFr per day).

Budget travelers should limit their shopping in Geneva to the windows, especially on the upscale rue Basses and rue du Rhône. The *vieille ville* contains scads of galleries and antique shops to explore. Those looking for Swiss souvenirs like Swiss Army knives and watches should head to the department stores. **La Placette** in pl. Cornavin is particularly good for the cheap and chintzy. (Open Mon.-Wed. and Fri. 8:30am-6:45pm, Thurs. 8:30am-8pm, Sat. 8am-5pm.) Exquisite Swiss chocolate awaits in any supermarket, but the specialty store *par excellence* is **Chocolats Micheli,** rue Micheli-du-Crest 1 (tel. 329 90 06), which makes 40 different edible gems. The aromas alone inspire lust in the strongest individual. (Open Tues.-Fri. 7am-6:30pm, Sat. 8am-5pm.) Bargain hunters can ogle the goods in a number of markets. Head over to Plainpalais to browse at the huge **flea market.** (Open Wed. and Sat. 8am-6pm.) Smaller markets grace pl. de la Madeleine (Mon.-Sat. 8am-7pm) and pl. du Molard (Mon.-Sat. all day). A **book market** fills the Esplanade de la Madeleine Monday to Saturday from 8am to 7pm. More ephemeral wares bloom at the **flower market,** usually hidden amid the sprawling outdoor cafés in pl. du Molard (Mon.-Sat.). Stock up on bargain melons and strawberries at **Marché des Eaux-Vives,** bd. Helvétique, between cours de Rive and rue du Rhône, the biggest dairy, vegetable, and flower market. (Open Wed. and Sat. 8am-1pm.)

Summer nightlife centers around the lakeside quays and the many cafés, where the city drinks, converses, and flirts. Two popular areas brimming with cafés are **Place du Bourg-de-Four,** below Cathédrale de St-Pierre, and the village of **Carouge** (tram #12: "pl. du Marché"), both of which attract young people, especially on those sultry summer evenings. You can easily deduce where "the places to be" are by listening for the buzz of chatter, audible long before you actually hit the crowds. Those looking for a late night on the town should make friends with a native or bartender to discover the location of the week's **squat bar,** a moving party that attracts a trendy, artsy crowd for some of the cheapest drinks in town.

- **Casting Café,** rue de la Servette 6 (tel. 733 73 00), 2min. behind the station or bus #3, 9, or 10: "Lyon." This theme restaurant/café/bar is one of the city's most popular joints. Neon lights, blaring music, and cigarette smoke attract college students to the Wild West, gas station, and Hollywood bars. The waitstaff dresses up to play the roles of the characters in the latest American movies showing next door at the Cinéma des Grottes. For those brave enough (or totally insomniac), DJs spin house music Sat. and Sun. 4:30-8am. The even-braver try their hand at karaoke. Sat.-Sun. the bar reduces drink prices by 85% for randomly announced 5min. periods. Open Mon.-Fri. 11am-2am, Sat.-Sun. 2pm-2am. Visa, MC, AmEx.

- **La Clémence,** pl. du Bourg-de-Four 20 (tel. 312 24 92). Generations of students have eaten at this famous and traditionally chic bar, named after the big bell atop the Cathédrale de St-Pierre. The tables overflow into the square come nightfall, and the waves of murmured small talk and sometimes forced laughter undulate through the otherwise quiet cobblestone streets. Come for breakfast (croissant 1.20SFr, coffee 2.70SFr), or beer (4-8SFr), or both. Open Mon.-Fri. 7am-1am, Sat.-Sun. 7am-2am.

- **Au Chat Noir,** rue Vautier 13, Carouge (tel. 343 49 98). Tram #12: "pl. du Marché," just off the square. The upside-down red car hanging from the ceiling is a bit of a puzzle, but the sensuously curved old bar and dark red curtains proclaim the place to be an understandably popular venue for jazz, funk, rock, and sax-moaning blues. Open Mon.-Thurs. 6pm-4am, Fri. 6pm-5am, Sat. 9pm-5am, Sun. 9pm-4am.

- **Flanagan's,** rue du Cheval-Blanc 4 (tel. 310 13 14), off Grand Rue in the *vieille ville*. Friendly bartenders pull a good beer in this Irish bar and subdued cellar. Hangout for Anglophones of all nationalities and the occasional francophone Anglophile. Chat merrily away in the mother tongue amid dusty, liquor-inspired memorabilia. Pint o' Guinness 7SFr; lager 6SFr. Happy hours Wed.-Mon. 5-7pm and all day Tues.; live, non-Irish contemporary music Thurs.-Sat. Open daily noon-2am.

Post Café, rue de Berne 7 (tel. 732 96 63), just off rue de Mont-Blanc. Tiny bar draws a big crowd. Inexpensive (for Geneva) drinks and friendly atmosphere amid festooned beer-label garlands and several flashing TVs. Happy hour daily 5-8pm. Mon.-Fri. 6:30am-2am, Sat. 10am-2am, Sun. 4pm-2am.

Lord Nelson, pl. du Molard 9 (tel. 311 11 00). Pseudo-English pub that attracts the young and very young to its outdoor tables. Open Mon.-Thurs. 11:30am-1am, Fri. 11:30am-2am, Sat. 1pm-2am, Sun. 2pm-midnight.

L'Usine, pl. des Volontaires 4 (tel. 781 34 90; fax 781 41 38; http://www.fusions.ch/smart/usine.html). This riverside warehouse is the major center for alternative music, theater, and 3-D "B" films. Most of the theater performances are free (in true starving-artist tradition), but the music and dance events usually charge anywhere from 5 to 16SFr at the doors—which usually open around 10 or 10:30pm. Check the posters splattered all over town for details, or find the monthly schedule near bulletin boards on the university campuses. Beer, sold from a window on the river side of the building, 3-5SFr. Entry varies with the gig. See billboards for times.

■ Lausanne

The story of Lausanne is really a tale of two cities. The *vieille ville* is cosmopolitan and businesslike; the lakefront at Ouchy lazy and more than a bit decadent. On warm evenings locals, loners, and loungers converge at Ouchy's fountains and restaurants to listen to one of the city's many free concerts, play open-air chess, or melt into each other's arms amid the sonorous lull of the waves. Lausanne has drawn many to its lakeside— T.S. Eliot wrote *The Wasteland* beside Lake Léman, and nearly a century earlier Dickens wrote *Dombey and Son* here. The city has much to offer, and whether your budget is on the boot-strap or matched-luggage level, Lausanne will welcome you with its marvelous parks, museums, and views.

ORIENTATION AND PRACTICAL INFORMATION

Lausanne was built on steep hills, and the train station sits on a brief plateau between two demanding slopes—one leading up to the *vielle ville* and the other down to the lakefront. The efficient public transportation system, however, will help you avoid an undignified collapse while climbing uphill. The Métro Ouchy and bus lines #1, 3, and 5 serve the station. Most buses are routed to pl. St. François, a vital reference point in the center of the city and the location of several banks and the main post office.

Tourist Office: Branch office (tel. 613 73 91; general information tel. 617 73 73; email information@lausanne-tourisme.ch; http://www.lausanne.tourisme.ch) in the main hall of the train station. Open Mon.-Fri. 9am-8pm (Oct.-March 9am-7pm), Sat. 10am-7pm, Sun. 10am-2pm and 3-7pm. Vastly larger **head office,** av. de Rhodanie 2 (tel. 613 73 21; fax 616 86 47). Take the Métro Ouchy: "Ouchy" or bus #2 (dir: Bourdonnette): "Ouchy" and walk 1.6km down av. d'Ouchy. Pick up the staggeringly comprehensive collection of literature they produce—*Useful Information* and *Plan Officiel* (a map and guide to public transportation) are excellent—and their lists of private rooms for rent (generally cheaper than hotels). Museum passports (see p. 318). Hotel reservation service 4-6SFr. Wheelchair accessible. Open April-Sept. Mon.-Fri. 8am-7pm, Sat. 9am-6pm, Sun. 9am-1pm and 2-6pm; Oct.-March Mon.-Fri. 8am-6pm, Sat. 9am-1pm and 2-6pm.

Budget Travel: SSR Voyages, bd. de Grancy 20 (tel. 617 56 27; fax 614 60 45), 2 streets downhill from the station past the overpass. Sells and books student tickets and organizes group travel. Open Mon.-Fri. 9:15am-6pm.

Currency Exchange: (tel. 312 38 24), at the station. Competitive rates. No commission on traveler's checks. Western Union transfers. Cash advances with Visa, MC, AmEx, DC. Open daily Nov.-March 6:20am-7:30pm; April-Oct. 6:20am-8:30pm.

American Express: av. Mon Répos 14 (tel. 310 19 00; fax 310 19 19), across from parking garage. Cashes traveler's checks, sells airline tickets, and holds mail.

Travel services open Mon.-Fri. 8:30am-5:30pm; financial office open 8:30am-12:45pm and 2-5:30pm.

Trains: pl. de la Gare 9 (tel. 157 22 22; 1.19SFr per min.) To: **Montreux** (every hr., 20min., 8.40SFr); **Geneva** (every 20min., 40min., 19.40SFr); **Basel** (every hr., 2½hr., 57SFr); **Zurich** (every hr., 2½hr., 62SFr); **Rome** (1 per day, 11hr., 73SFr); and **Barcelona** (1 per day, 12hr., 95SFr); **Paris** (4 per day, 4hr., 76SFr, 13SFr reservation required). Open daily 7am-9pm.

Public Transportation: The 5-stop **Métro Ouchy,** which runs from the *vieille ville* to the Ouchy waterfront, is useful for climbing the city's steep streets. The **Métro Ouest** runs from the center of town west to the University of Lausanne and the Federal Institute of Technology. The Métro runs Mon.-Sat. 5:30am-12:15am, Sun. 6:15am-12:15am. Buses cross the city and run roughly 6am-midnight (check bus stops for specific lines). 3-Stop ticket 1.30SFr; 60min. pass 2.20SFr; 24-hr. pass 6.50SFr. Métro free with Swisspass or Museum Passport, but not with Eurailpass.

Ferries: CGN, av. de Rhodanie 17 (tel. 617 06 66; fax 617 04 65). To: **Montreux** (6 per day, 1½hr., last ferry 6:05pm, 18SFr one-way, 31SFr round-trip); **Geneva** (4 per day, 3½hr., last ferry 5:15pm, 30SFr one-way, 47SFr round-trip). Buy tickets at the dock. Eurailpass and Swisspass valid. Open daily June-Sept. 8am-7:30pm; Oct.-May 8:30am-12:30pm and 1:30-5:15pm.

Taxis: Available at rue Madeline 1 (tel. 331 41 33), pl. St. François, and in front of the station. For late night or early morning service, call the taxibus (tel. 312 20 00).

Car Rental: Budget, av. Ruchonnet 2 (tel. 323 91 52). **Avis,** av. de la Gare 50 (tel. 320 66 81; fax 320 05 76). **Hertz,** pl. du Tunnel 17 (tel. 312 53 11). **Europcar,** pl. de la Riponne 12 (tel. 323 71 42).

Parking: Parking Simplon-Gare, rue du Simplon 2 (tel. 617 67 44), behind the station, has spots for 2SFr per hr. during the day, 0.50SFr per hr. at night, and 22SFr per day. On city streets, white zones indicate unlimited parking, red zones allow parking for 15hr., and blue zones for 1½hr. To park on the street, pick up a parking disc from the tourist office. Dial up the present time and the maximum stay time, and leave the disc prominently displayed on the dash.

Bike Rental: (tel. (0512) 24 21 62), at the baggage check in the station. Rentals 21SFr per day, 17SFr per ½day. Return bikes at another station for an additional 6SFr. Open daily 6:40am-7:50pm.

Luggage Storage: At the train station. Lockers 3SFr and 5SFr per day. Open 24hr.

Lost Property: pl. Chauderon 7 (tel. 319 60 58). Open Mon.-Fri. 8am-noon and 1:45-5:45pm, Sat. 8am-11:45pm.

Bookstore: Payot Libraire, pl. Pépinet 4 (tel. 341 31 31; fax 341 33 45). Impressive English section has contemporary fiction as well as the greats. Open Mon. 1-6:30pm, Tues.-Fri. 8:30am-6:30pm, Sat. 8am-5pm.

Library: Cantonal and University Palais de Rumine, pl. de la Riponne 6 (tel. 312 88 31). Open for general borrowing Mon.-Fri. 8am-6pm, Sat. 8am-noon. Reading room open Mon.-Fri. 8am-6pm, Sat. 8am-5pm.

Laundromat: Quick Wash, bd. de Grancy 44, 2 streets behind the train station toward the lake. Wash and dry around 10SFr. Open Mon. and Wed.-Sat. 8:30am-8:30pm, Tues. noon-8:30pm, Sun. 9am-8:30pm. Last wash 1hr. before closing.

24-hr. Pharmacy: Dial 111 to find out which pharmacy is open all night; they rotate weekly. **24-hr. medical service:** (tel. 314 11 11), at the hospital.

Emergencies: Police: tel. 117. **Fire:** tel. 118. **Ambulance:** tel. 144. **Intoxication:** tel. 01 251 51 51.

Post Office: Centre Postal, av. de la Gare 43bis (tel. 344 35 14), on the right as you exit the station. Address *Poste Restante* to: 1000 Lausanne 1 dépot. Open Mon.-Fri. 7:30am-noon and 1:30-6:30pm, Sat. 8-11am. Express mail Mon.-Fri. 6:30am-10pm, Sat. 6:30am-8pm, Sun. 9am-noon and 6-10pm. To dispatch your postcard from the site where Edward Gibbon wrote his *Decline and Fall of the Roman Empire,* visit **Poste St. Françoise,** 15 pl. St.-François (tel. 344 38 31). Open Mon.-Fri. 7:30am-6:30pm, Sat. 8-11am. **Postal Code:** CH-1002

Telephone Code: 021.

LAKE GENEVA (LAC LÉMAN)

ACCOMMODATIONS AND CAMPING

As the home of the world's oldest hotel school, Lausanne has a well-deserved reputation for service-industry excellence. The city offers a huge range of accommodations, from *fin-de-siècle* palaces to lakeside tent plots. Lausanne's budget accommodations rarely fill completely, but you may need to pick up the tourist office's list of cheap hotels, private boarding houses, and family *pensions* in July and August, when innumerable festivals, conferences, and congresses take place. The owners of these establishments generally prefer stays of at least three nights and often as long as a month. Since Lausanne is also a university town, many hoteliers and private citizens cater to those on a student-type budget. Travelers looking for apartments to rent for longer stays can turn to the local paper *24 Heures,* which carries regular listings, or even to the notice boards of big department stores.

Jeunotel, Chemin du Bois-de-vaux 36 (tel. 626 02 22; fax 626 02 26). Bus #2 (dir: Bourdonnette): "Bois-de-Vaux." Cross the street, and follow the signs. The hotel is down a long concrete driveway on your right just past the Musée romain de Lausanne-Vidy. A barracks-like complex 2.5km from town, Jeunotel replaced the recently closed Auberge de Jeunesse as Lausanne's official youth hostel. Its 300 rooms feature ultra-modern decor with generous amenities, but the gargantuan entrance door may clue you in: the place is a better deal for groups than for singles. Clean, institutional architecture will bring back your fondest childhood hospital memories. 24-hr. reception. Dorms 26SFr; singles 65SFr, with shower 75SFr; doubles 74SFr, with shower 92SFr; triples 78SFr; quads 104SFr. Monthly rentals available. Buffet breakfast 3SFr. Lunch 10.90SFr. Dinner 13.50SFr. Laundry 1.20SFr. Wheelchair accessible. Visa, MC.

Pension Bienvenue, rue du Simplon 2 (tel. 616 29 86), 5min. from the train station. Turn right along av. de la Gare, right onto av. d'Ouchy, and right after the bridge. **Women only.** Peace pervades this 25-room *pension*, broken only by phone calls and passing trains. Shared bathrooms and showers demonstrate courteous communal living at its best. Reception Mon.-Fri. 8-11am and 5-8pm, Sat.-Sun. 8:30-11am. Call if arriving later. Singles 25-41SFr; doubles 47-73SFr. Breakfast included. Access to kitchen, laundry facilities, and TV room.

Hotel "Le Chalet," av. d'Ouchy 49 (tel. 616 52 06). Métro Ouchy (dir: Ouchy): "Jordils" or bus #2 (dir: Bourdonnette): "Jordils." An elegant, pleasant matron reigns in this 19th-century chalet and its evergreen-cloaked garden, which shields her domain from the sight of the busy roads outside. Above the dining-room clutter of flowered pots, pillow-backed chairs, and the odd Russian samovar, the 5 rooms, all with private balcony, are pleasingly unadorned. Singles 62SFr; doubles 87SFr. Four smaller singles (no view) in the annex 48SFr. Hall showers. Breakfast 8SFr.

Camping: Camping de Vidy, chemin du Camping 3 (tel. 624 20 31). Bus #2 (dir: Bourdonnette): "Bois-de-Vaux." Cross the street and go down chemin du Bois-de-Vaux, past Jeunotel and underneath the overpass. The reception office is straight ahead across rte. de Vidy. Separated from the lake by a footpath, the site boasts lush shade and the lullaby hum of Lac Léman's waves. Restaurant, supermarket, and playground nearby. Reception daily 8am-8pm. 6.50SFr, students 6SFr; tents 7-11SFr; 1- to 2-person bungalow 54SFr; 3- to 4-person bungalow 86SFr. City tax 1.20SFr per person, 2.50SFr per car. Showers included. Wheelchair accessible.

FOOD

Lausanne's specialty is Lac Léman's perch and salmon, and the city's links to the nearby countryside produce marvelous cheese fondue. Restaurants, cafés, and bars line pl. St.-François, while similar eateries hike up their prices as you hike down the hills to the Ouchy waterfront. *Boulangeries,* where local businessmen on the run buy their sandwiches (3.50-8SFr), appear on every street. Numerous groceries and frequent markets make for affordable picnics to enjoy in any of Lausanne's parks.

Café du Vieil-Ouchy, pl. du Port 3 (tel. 616 21 94), 30sec. from the Métro or bus #2 stop "Ouchy." Popular with both locals and tourists, the café invokes a neighborhood feel despite its prime location along the ultra-trendy lake front. Specialties include *croûte au fromage* (13.50SFr), *Rösti* (9.50-20SFr), and fondue (20SFr). Open Thurs.-Tues. 11am-11pm. English/French menus. Visa, MC.

Crêperie d'Ouchy, pl. du Port 7 (tel. 616 26 07). Sandwiched between 2 upscale restaurants staffed by waiters in white shirts and vests, this restaurant has jean- and sneaker-clad waitresses weaving between white iron lawn furniture as leather-draped bikers compete with noisy families for their attention. Crepes 4-17SFr. Try the seasonal specialty garnishes, like fresh fruit and ice cream in the summer. Open daily in summer 9am-midnight; in winter 10am-11pm (barring rain).

Crêperie "La Chandeleur," rue Mercerie 9 (tel. 312 84 19), just below the cathedral. From the lace-veiled windows to the light pine furniture inside, this restaurant aims for homey-ness and succeeds. Crepes prepared to your tastes, whether traditional (with butter, sugar, or honey 4-9SFr), sugar-deprived (with ice cream 8-9SFr), or gourmet (*flambées* with your choice of liqueur 12-18SFr). Open Tues.-Thurs. 11am-10pm, Fri.-Sat. 11am-11:30pm. Visa, MC, DC.

Manora, pl. St-François 17 (tel. 320 92 93). Manora's salad, fruit, sandwich, pasta, and dessert bars smother you with innumerable choices and a strange sense of urgency. *Menus du jour* run 7-14SFr—one of the best values in town. Open Mon.-Sat. 7am-10:30pm, Sun. 9am-10:30pm. Hot food served 11am-10pm.

Au Couscous, rue Enning 2 (tel. 311 86 87), at the top of rue de Bourg. Walk upstairs—a hanging carpet marks the door to the restaurant proper. Inside, a North African theme prevails with ornamentally hinged menus, red tablecloths, mosaic-tiled floor, and sequined pillows. Extensive, vegetarian-friendly menu (15-22SFr). Not surprisingly, couscous is the real specialty (23-24SFr). Special lunch plates (14.50SFr) served 11:30am-2:30pm weekdays. At night the restaurant reopens for dinner, Sun.-Thurs. 6pm-12:30am, Fri.-Sat. 6pm-midnight. AmEx, DC.

Markets

Co-op, rue du Petit Chêne. From the train station, head toward the town center. Bring your own bag or you'll have to pay 0.10SFr for one the size of an envelope. Open Mon.-Fri. 8am-12:15pm and 1:30-7pm. Branch at bd. de Grancy.

Migros, av. d'Ouchy. Down av. de la Gare from the train station and right on av. d'Ouchy. You will see it immediately after you walk under the overpass. Open Mon. 9am-6:45pm, Tues.-Fri. 8am-6:45pm, Sat. 7:30am-5pm.

Produce markets, April to mid-Oct. at Ouchy Sun. 8am-8pm; on rue de Bourg behind the Eglise St.-François Wed. and Sat. mornings; on bd. de Grancy Mon. and Thurs. mornings; and on rue du Petit-Chêne off pl. St.-François on Fri. mornings. If you are here at the end of Aug. check out the flower and honey market 8am-11pm, Derrière-Bourg in the *vieille ville*.

SIGHTS

Lausanne is built on three hills, the highest of which supports the Gothic **Cathédrale,** consecrated in 1275 under the auspices of Holy Roman Emperor Rudolph and Pope Gregory X. Bus #16: "Cathédrale" or a series of medieval covered stairs take you to the top of the hill, where the cathedral's huge wooden doors open up into the dimmed, hushed, and stark interior—the iconoclastic days of the Protestant Reformation ensured the demise of most of the cathedral's ornamentation. Fortunately, the rose window in the south transept was spared. One hundred and five windows (78 of them original) depict the zodiac, the elements, the winds, and other mystical groupings, all arranged into a geometrical scheme; the non-religious nature of the depictions may explain why the window survives. During the window's restoration, officially scheduled for completion in 1998, the most stunning visuals await from the top of the 200-step **tower** where the view of the city, lake, and mountains is unparalleled. Lausanne is one of the last towns in Switzerland to retain a night watchman, and from the airy heights of the tower he cries the hour between 10pm and 2am. (Cathedral open July to mid-Sept. daily 7am-7pm; mid-Sept. to June

7am-5pm. Free guided tours (tel. 323 84 34) daily July-Sept. at 10:30, 11:15am, 3, and 3:45pm. Tower open 8:30-11:30am and 1:30-5:30pm. 2SFr, children 1SFr.) Bronze dragons spread their wings atop the **Hôtel de Ville** (tel. 323 84 34). The Renaissance building now houses temporary exhibitions and is the meeting point for the guided walking tours of the city. (Tours Mon.-Sat. 10am and 3pm. 1-2hr. Available in English. 10SFr, students and children free, seniors 5SFr.) Also in the square, at no. 23, an ornamental clock depicts the history of the canton on the hour from 9am to 7pm.

Despite the charms of the *vieille ville*, a large number of visitors prefer to sun themselves on the Ouchy waterfront or in one of the city's many parks. The local conceit is that Lausanne's women have the best-looking legs in Switzerland, the hard-won prize of a life spent hiking the city's hills. The claim is debatable, but short skirts and trendy 3-inch stacked heels that would be suicide in the *vieille ville* make frequent appearances along the lake; outdoor café patrons are in the best position to judge Lausanne's claim to fame. Ouchy's main promenades, the **quai de Belgique** and **place de la Navigation,** permit more discreet investigation of the evidence.

Any other curiosity concerning the relative beauty of Lausanne's inhabitants can find satisfaction at the **Bellerive Complex** (bus #2: "Bellerive"), a beach park where locals set their children loose on spotless, activity-filled lawns while they remove their tops and take in the sun to a serenade of soothing waves. (Open mid-May to Aug. daily from 9:30am until dark or rain. 4.50SFr, students and seniors 3SFr, under 17 2SFr. 0.50SFr discount after 5pm.) The Bellerive Beach is just one of the many places one can sun and be seen in Lausanne. In the center of town, the **Derrière-Bourg Promenade** uses flowers to depict events from the canton's history. Nearby **Mon-Repos** is a green oasis featuring venerable trees, aviaries, an orangery, and a small circular temple. Farther down the #2 bus route from Bellerive lies the **Plaines de Vidy,** a huge sports and leisure complex, and the **Vallée de la Jeunesse Rosegarden,** which blooms with a spectacular collection of 10,000 rosebushes.

MUSEUMS

Lausanne's museums are like glowing pieces of stained glass held together by the delicate lead lines of the city's parks and promenades. The verdant areas surrounding these museums make negotiating Lausanne's bus system worthwhile. To simplify the process, the tourist office provides museum passports, entitling visitors to free museum entry, public transportation, and one film at the **Cinémathèque Suisse,** allée E. Ansemet 3 (tel. 331 01 00). A three-day pass is 26SFr, students and seniors 20SFr.

> **Musée Olympique,** quai d'Ouchy 1 (tel. 621 65 11; fax 621 65 12). Take bus #2 or Métro to "Ouchy," and the museum is a short walk along the quay. Escalators nestled in terraced grounds speed tourists up the hillside amid countless fountains and a forest of finely formed statues. The latter serve as idols to the temple at the summit, where sport is the religion and athletes are the gods. Inside, the green profusion gives way to theatrically dim modernity. If the sleek exhibits of the Games' greatest moments, figures, and mementos do not inspire you, a walk out onto the sun-filled terrace will. The view deserves a gold. Fully bilingual English/French. Wheelchair accessible, via av. de l'Elysée. Open May-Sept. Mon.-Wed. and Fri.-Sun. 10am-7pm, Thurs. 10am-8pm; Oct.-April Tues.-Wed. and Fri.-Sun. 10am-6pm, Thurs. 10am-8pm. 14SFr, students and seniors 9SFr, ages 10-18 6SFr. Visa, MC.
>
> **Collection de l'Art Brut,** av. Bergières 11 (tel. 647 54 35; fax 648 55 21). Bus #2 or 3 to "Jomini." An art gallery founded by postwar Primitivist painter Jean Dubuffet, who despised the pretentious avant-garde art scene so much he filled his gallery with the works of "non-artists"—the criminally insane, the institutionalized, and children. Housed in the outbuilding of the grand 18th-century Chateau de Beaulieu, Art Brut is art on the fringe, if not totally over the edge. The gallery is aptly dark and attic-like to show off the painstakingly intricate, mind-bogglingly huge, or downright creepy works to gruesome perfection. Sporadically bilingual

English/French. Open Tues.-Sun. 11am-1pm and 2-6pm. 6SFr, students and seniors 4SFr.

Musée de l'Elysée, av. de l'Elysée 18 (tel. 617 48 21; fax 617 07 83; email dgirardin@ping.ch or waewing@swissonline.ch). Take bus #2: "Croix-d'Ouchy" and make a left on av. de l'Elysée. The 18th-century mansion houses a stunning collection and photography archive. From the 1820 prints to the most contemporary artistic endeavors in film, the series of collections within the white-washed galleries engage the eye and mind. The basement's resonant tile and hushed atmosphere make the images even more haunting. Open Tues.-Wed. and Fri.-Sun. 10am-6pm, Thurs. 10am-9pm. Archives open Thurs. by appointment. 5SFr, students 2.50SFr.

Hermitage, rte. du Signal 2 (tel. 320 50 01; general information tel. 312 50 13; fax 320 50 71), north of the *vieille ville.* Bus #16: "Hermitage" stops infrequently out front. Magnificent house given over to temporary exhibitions that vary from single artists and special themes to individual public and private collections. Call ahead for a schedule, since the museum closes between shows. The magnificent grounds offer some of the most panoramic views in Lausanne. Open Tues.-Wed. and Fri.-Sun. 10am-6pm, Thurs. 10am-10pm. 13SFr, students 5SFr, under 19 2.50SFr, seniors 10SFr. Tours in English Thurs. 6:30pm, Sun. 3pm. Visa, MC, AmEx.

Museum of Pipes and Tobacco, rue de l'Académie 7 (tel. 323 43 23), behind the cathedral. Go up rue Cité-devant and turn right on a street marked "La Rue des Antiquaries." Behind 26 glass cases, 2500 pipes await both the meerschaum maven and the simply curious. Once you enter, you'll know Magritte was wrong—*ceci est une pipe.* Also the meeting place of the ultra-exclusive Pipe Club of Lausanne. Open June 15-Aug. Mon. 10am-noon and 3-6pm, Wed. and Fri. 3-6pm; Sept. Mon. 3-6pm; Oct.-Feb. Mon. 2-5pm; March-June 14 Mon. 3-6pm. Daily guided tours by appointment. Bilingual English/French. 3.50SFr.

Botanical Garden of Lausanne, av. de Cour 14 bis (tel. 616 24 09; fax 616 46 65). A lovely terraced garden in one section of pl. de Milan-Montriond Park, down the road from the bus #1 stop "Beauregard." Everything from towering pines to flowers so delicate that they stand in pots the size of espresso cups. Outstanding views of the lake below and the town above. Open daily May-Sept. 10am-noon and 1:30-6:30pm; March-April and Oct. 10am-noon and 1:30-5:30pm.

ENTERTAINMENT AND NIGHTLIFE

For every exhibit in Lausanne's museums, there are several performances already in progress on stage and screen: the **Béjart Ballet, Lausanne Chamber Orchestra, Cinémathèque Suisse, Municipal Theatre, Opera House,** and **Theatre of Vidy** reflect Lausanne's thriving cultural life. The tourist office publishes *Momento,* a monthly update and schedule of the most significant events, and posters on the streets and in *tabacs* should clue you in on everything else. For information, reservations, and tickets, call Billetel (tel. 617 18 50). During the first two weeks of July, the **Festival de la Cité** brings the *vieille ville* to life with many free theater and dance events. Swiss craftwork fills the **Marché des Artisans** in pl. de la Palud from 10am to 7pm on the first Friday of every month from March to December. As for nightlife, you can't heave a brick in the pl. St.-François without putting it through the window of a café/bar or hitting the bouncer of a night-club. *Lausannois* party-goers inhabit the bars until 1am (2am on weekends) and dance at the clubs till 4 in the morning. The seriously hardcore then head over to the bar in the train station, which opens at 5am.

Dolce Vita, rue César Roux 30 (tel. 323 09 43). From pont Bessières, head up rue Caroline past the large crossroads. A funky and pungent room with frequent live shows of rap, indie, world music, and blistering acid jazz. The pillar of Lausanne's nightlife—the volume and variety of groups that congregate here are testimony to its success. Beer 4-5SFr. Happy hours Wed.-Thurs. and Sun. 10pm-midnight (beer 2SFr). Open Sun. and Wed. 10pm-2am, Fri.-Sat. 10pm-4am; in summer also Thurs. 10pm-3am. Weekend cover 5-25SFr depending on the act.

Le Lapin Vert, ruelle du Lapin Vert (tel. 312 13 17), off rue de l'Académie behind the cathedral. An ancient pub filled with rock music and young students. Look for the green rabbit hanging outside. Beer 4SFr. Particularly busy during the July Festival when it features jazz acts on a stage set up in the otherwise quiet road outside. Open Sun.-Thurs. 8pm-1am, Fri.-Sat. 8pm-2am.

Bleu Lézard, rue Enning 10 (tel. 312 71 90), at rue de Langaliereie. An artsy crowd fills this bistro, gushing over sinful desserts (5.50SFr) and beer from 9 countries (4.50-6SFr). Vegetarian dishes 17SFr. Window sculptures, re-designed by local artists every 2 months, are *absolutely fabulous*, sweetie darling. Open Mon.-Thurs. 6am-1am, Fri. 6am-2am, Sat. 9am-2am, Sun. 9:30am-1am. Hot food served Mon.-Sat. 11:30am-2pm and 6:30-10:30pm, Sun. 10am-5pm and 6:30-10:30pm.

Le Barbare, Escaliers du Marché 27 (tel. 312 21 32). Perched by the wooden steps up to the cathedral, this traditional bar has red leather seats, a half-timbered ceiling, and button-mushroom barstools. Devastating hot chocolate in regular, *Viennoise*, and *Liégeoise* (4-6SFr). Snacks like *croques monsieur* (toast with cheese and ham) 5-6SFr. Open Mon.-Thurs. 8:30am-11:30pm, Fri.-Sat. 8:30am-midnight.

Ouchy White Horse Pub, av. d'Ouchy 66 (tel. 616 75 75). Perfect for a quiet evening, enclosed in your own private, white-picket paddock steps from the lakefront. Inside, the equestrian theme gives way to lush carpets and dark wood, which combine oddly with the bright plaster moldings and scattered neon-filled jars. Beer on tap 5-7SFr per pint, 0.50SFr cheaper at the bar. *Tapas* 4.50-8SFr; hamburgers, fries, and a soda 10SFr. Open Sun.-Thurs. 7am-1am, Fri.-Sat. 7am-2am. Kitchen closes 12:30am. Visa, MC, AmEx, DC.

■ Montreux

Although it's terribly gauche to drop names, Montreux can't seem to avoid it. Byron, Stravinsky, Coward, Hemingway, and Nabokov are a few bandied about on street signs and in tourist-office publications. While locals describe their home as somewhat staid, outsiders who pop in for the **Montreux Jazz Festival** in early July find a hip, artsy town bustling with endless concerts and countless crowds. Once *le jazz* has come and gone, Montreux settles back into its self-satisfied groove, hosting smaller music festivals throughout the year. But Montreux's flower-lined quay, shaded lakeside promenade, and numerous grand resorts speak for themselves: this is postcard Switzerland at its swanky, but genteel, best. The clear mirror of Lac Léman makes it obvious that the crowds will come, if not for the verve, then for the view.

ORIENTATION AND PRACTICAL INFORMATION

The train station is only a short stroll from the city's sights. Hiking up rue du Marché brings you into the older parts of town. Among its steep hills, Montreux reveals amazing views that not even the quay can match.

Tourist Office: pl. du Débarcadère (tel. 962 84 84; fax 963 78 95; email tourism@montreux.ch; http://www.montreux.ch). Descend the stairs opposite the station and head left on Grand Rue. The office is set back on the right. Fun-loving staff shares the office with desks for festival tickets and bus and train information. Free hotel reservation service within Montreux. Neither the free photocopied map nor the 1SFr map has all of Montreux's street names. Instead, grab the excellent free map from **Union de Banques Suisses,** av. de Casino 26. Tourist office open daily June-Aug. 9am-7pm; Sept.-May 9am-noon and 1:30-6pm.

Budget Travel: SSR Voyages, av. des Alpes 25 (tel. 961 23 00; fax 961 23 06). Open Mon.-Fri. 9am-12:30pm and 1:30-6:30pm.

Currency Exchange: Good rates and no commission at the station. Western Union transfers and credit card advances. Open daily 6:40am-9:30pm. Banks in Montreux are generally open Mon.-Fri. 8:30am-12:30pm and 1:30-4:30pm. Rates for traveler's checks are better at banks than at the station.

Trains: (tel. 963 45 15) on av. des Alpes. To: **Geneva** (every hr., 1hr., 27SFr); **Lausanne** (every 30min., 20min., 8.40SFr) and **Bern** (every hr., 1½hr., 37SFr). Direct trains also go to **Martigny, Aigle, Sion,** and **Brig** and through (literally) the mountains to **Gstaad.**

Public Transportation: Buy tickets at the back of each bus. A map divides the area into several zones; your fare will depend on the number of zones you cross to reach your destination. 1 zone 1.70SFr, juniors 1.20SFr; 2 zones 2.40SFr, 1.60SFr; 3 zones 3SFr, 2SFr; 4 zones 3.60SFr, 2.40SFr. Swisspass valid. The tourist office offers a 5.50SFr day-pass April-Oct. Special late-night buses run during the Jazz Festival.

Ferries: CGN, quai du Débarcadère, next to the tourist office. To: **Lausanne** (1½hr., 18SFr); **Geneva** (5hr., 35SFr); **Vevey** (25min., 7SFr). Even shorter rides to Villeneuve, which is near the hostel, and Château de Chillon. Buy tickets at the quay, the tourist office, or on board. Eurail and Swisspass valid.

Bike Rental: At the baggage check in the train station. 21SFr per day, 17SFr per ½day; mountain bikes 33SFr per day, 27SFr per ½day. 6SFr charge to return bikes to other stations (including Martigny, Aigle, and Sion) by prior arrangement. Open daily 5:40am-9:30pm. Visa, MC, AmEx.

Luggage Storage: At the station. Lockers 2SFr and 5SFr. Luggage watch 5SFr per bag. Open daily 5:40am-8:45pm.

Bookstore: Payot Libraire, av. du Casino 42 (tel. 963 06 07). Open Mon. 10:30am-12:30pm and 1:30-6:30pm, Tues.-Fri. 8:30am-12:30pm and 1:30-6:30pm, Sat. 9am-5pm. Visa, MC, AmEx, DC.

Laundromat: Salon-Lavoir, rue Industrielle 30. Open Mon.-Fri. 7am-6:45pm. Also at the **hostel** (8SFr).

Jazz Hotline: tel. 983 82 82.

Late-Night Pharmacy: tel. 962 77 00.

Emergencies: Police: tel. 117. **Fire:** tel. 118. **Ambulance:** tel. 144. **Hospital:** tel. 966 66 66.

Post Office: Main Office, av. des Alpes 70, left as you exit the station. A surfeit of employees to keep things running smoothly. Address *Poste Restante* to: CH-1820 Montreux 1. Open Mon.-Fri. 7:30am-6pm, Sat. 8-11am. **Postal Code:** CH-1820.

Telephone Code: 021.

ACCOMMODATIONS AND CAMPING

Cheap rooms are scarce in Montreux and almost non-existent during the jazz festival. Proprietors start accepting reservations for rooms a year before the festivities, and hotels and hostels are often fully booked by May. Revelers frequently stash their bags in the train station lockers and crash on the lakefront, but be aware that the police will move lake-loungers out at 7am. When Montreux seems packed, ask the tourist office for the list *Pensions et Petits Hôtels*. If you still can't find a room, take bus #1 to "Villeneuve," 5km away, where there are a handful of budget hotels, or consider commuting from Lausanne, Martigny, or Vevey.

Auberge de Jeunesse Montreux (HI), passage de l'Auberge 8 (tel. 963 49 34; fax 969 27 29). Pick up bus #1 on Grand Rue (dir: Villeneuve) to "Territet." Continue up the street, take the first right (rue du Bocherex), and go down the stairs (passage de l'Auberge). Or, walk 20min. along the lake past the Montreux Tennis Club. The hostel is behind a small underpass in a fine lakefront location. Cheery, rainbow-bright dorms have double-paned windows that help muffle the noise of trains rumbling overhead. 112 beds in rooms of 4, 6, or 8 beds. Clean and private hall showers and bathrooms. Friendly, multilingual staff (English, French, German, Spanish). Call several weeks in advance April-Oct., when school groups, jazz fans, and tourists pack the hostel, some making reservations 6 months in advance. Reception April-Sept. 7:30-10am and 5-11pm; Oct.-March 7:30-9:30am and 5-11pm. Lockout 10am-5pm. Checkout 9:30am. Curfew midnight, but groups and families can request a key with a passport deposit. Members: singles 27SFr first night, then 24.50SFr; doubles (5 available) 72SFr, then 67SFr. Non-members add 5SFr per night. Breakfast and linens included. Wheelchair accessible. Two rooms have bathrooms for disabled visitors at dorm price. Tasty dinner with salad and dessert 11SFr. Lockers 2SFr deposit. Laundry 8SFr, including detergent. TV room. Free non-affiliated bike- and car-parking nearby. Visa, MC, AmEx, DC.

Hôtel Pension Wilhelm, rue du Marché 13-15 (tel. 963 14 31; fax 963 32 85). From the station, walk left 3min. up av. des Alpes and turn left onto rue du Marché, up the hill and past the police station. The Wilhelm family has kept this hotel in business since 1870. Sunny, brightly furnished, comfortable rooms and convenient hallway showers. Reception all day and at night by prior notice. All rooms have sink. In summer: 37SFr per person, with shower 60SFr; breakfast included. Off-season: 32SFr, 55SFr; no breakfast. Closed Dec.

Hôtel du Pont, rue du Pont 12 (tel./fax 963 22 49), at the top of the *vieille ville*. From the station, turn left 800m from the station onto av. des Alpes (3min.) and then take a right up rue du Marché. Continue up the hill until it becomes rue du Pont at an intersection with a fountain; the hotel is down the road on the left. Plain but clean rooms overlook quiet streets but find themselves close to an irrepressibly noisy waterfall. All rooms have bathrooms and TVs. The café downstairs is also part of this family-run establishment, with evening meals for 13.80SFr. Reception Mon.-Sat. 7am-midnight, Sun. 8:30am-midnight. Singles 60SFr; doubles 110-120SFr; triples 140-150SFr. Breakfast included. Visa, MC, AmEx.

Camping: Les Horizons Bleues (tel. 960 15 47). Take bus #1: "Villeneuve." From the bus stop, follow the lake to the left (5min.) to this supreme lakeside site. Reception 8am-10pm. 7SFr per person; 4.50-11SFr per tent; municipal tax 1SFr. Free showers. 10% discount in winter.

FOOD

Montreux doesn't offer gastronomic adventure at reasonable rates—prices match the country-club atmosphere. If you must dine lakeside, pack a picnic. The tourist office publishes a catalog listing establishments by cuisine, but it omits price ranges.

Babette's, Grand Rue 60 (tel. 963 77 96; fax 961 15 10), down the stairs from the station and to the left. An order-out *pâtisserie* in front gives way to a plush, artsy restaurant inside. Settle into the velvet cushions and mull over the menu as jazz plays softly among the booths. Crepes of all types for lunch (10-14SFr) and dessert (6-9SFr). Sandwiches to go at the outside counter 5-10SFr. Open daily 7am-7pm.

La Locanda, av. du Casino 44 (tel. 963 29 33). A hidden, romantic restaurant filled with regulars, and a pleasant break from people-watching by the lake. Large pizzas 12-19SFr; healthy portions of pasta from 11SFr; *gnocchi* 14.50-16SFr; *risotto* 16-17SFr. Open Mon.-Sat. 11am-2pm and 5:30pm-midnight. Visa, MC, AmEx.

Caveau des Vignerons, rue Industrielle 30bis (tel. 963 25 70), at the corner of rue du Marché. Swiss dishes are served in this cave of whitewashed walls and candlelight. The intimate atmosphere of this former wine cellar attracts mostly neighborhood regulars with fine stocks of meat (including Argentine beef and American horse) and local wines (35-40SFr a bottle). Cheese fondue 20SFr; *raclette* 5.50SFr per portion, 25SFr entire meal; *assiette du jour* 14SFr. Open Mon.-Fri. 7am-midnight, Sat. 3pm-midnight. Closed late July to mid-Aug. Visa, MC, AmEx.

The White Horse, 28 Grand Rue (tel. 963 15 92), opposite the covered market. Montreux's oldest bar strives gamely for a dark, English pub atmosphere. Except for its Francophone staff, the place pretty much succeeds. The result: un-Swiss food at un-Swiss prices. Sandwiches 5-7SFr; salads 6-8SFr; spaghetti 11SFr; fish and chips or chicken nuggets 12.50SFr; steak with fries and salad 18SFr. Beer 5.50SFr per pint. Pinball, darts, füßball, and arcade games in back to keep you occupied. Open Mon.-Sat. 11am-1am (flexible), Sun. 3pm-midnight. Food served until 11pm.

Restaurant Le Palais "Hoggar," quai du Casino 14 (tel. 963 12 71). Blue-tiled decor and authentic Middle Eastern cuisine are an ideal backdrop for people-watching. *Harira*, a Moroccan soup, 9SFr; chicken curry 22SFr. Twenty different ice creams. Open April-Nov. daily 11am-10:30pm. Visa, AmEx, DC.

Markets

Marché de Montreux, place du Marché. Covered outdoor market of fresh fruits, vegetables, meats, cheeses, breads, and pastries along both quai de la Rouvenaz and quai Jaccoud. Every Fri. 7am-3pm. Also look for the **flea market** at this site.

Migros, av. du Casino. Restaurant next door. Open Mon. 9am-7pm, Tues.-Thurs. 8am-7pm, Fri. 8am-9pm, Sat. 7:30am-5pm.

Jelmoli, rue du Théâtre, next to the Migros. Open in summer Mon.-Fri. 8:30am-6:30pm, Thurs. 8:30am-8pm, Sat. 8am-5pm, Sun. 2-6pm; in winter closed Sun.

Co-op, Grand Rue 80. Open Mon.-Fri. 8am-12:15pm and 2-6:30pm, Sat. 8am-5pm.

SIGHTS

The Montreux-Vevey **museum passport** (15SFr), available at the tourist office, covers entry to ten museums, including Montreux's main attraction, the **Château de Chillon** (tel. 963 39 12; fax 963 85 81), 20 minutes past the hostel. Built on an island, Chillon is a perfect 13th-century fortress with all the comforts of home: prison cells, a torture chamber, an armory, and enough loopholes to fend off attackers who got past the moat. The chateau inspired narratives by Rousseau, Victor Hugo, and Alexandre Dumas, as well as Lord Byron's *The Prisoner of Chillon,* which tells the tale of a priest manacled to a pillar for four years. The souvenir shop sells copies, and you can see where Byron scratched his name into a dungeon pillar. A brochure leads you through a tour of 28 chilly and chilling rooms. (Open daily July-Aug. 9am-6:15pm; April-June and Sept. 9am-5:45pm; Oct. 10am-4:45pm; Nov.-Feb. 10am-noon and 1:30-4pm; March 10am-noon and 1:30-4:45pm. 6.50SFr, students 5.50SFr, ages 6-16 3SFr.) A lot less interesting than the castle, the **Musée du Vieux-Montreux,** rue de la Gare 40 (tel. 963 13 53), on the outskirts of the *vieille ville,* describes the history of Montreux through municipal bric-à-brac, with an emphasis on wood-working and weights and measures. (Open April-Oct. 10am-noon and 2-5pm. 6SFr, students and seniors 4SFr.)

When the weather isn't too hazy, **Rochers-de-Naye** (2045m) offers views as far as Mont Blanc and the Matterhorn. An expensive cog railway chugs up Montreux's stately Alps, and you can purchase tickets at the station or the tourist office. (Round-trip 50SFr, one-way 30.80SFr; with Swisspass 31.50SFr, 15.80SFr; with Eurailpass 28.30SFr, 15.40SFr. Tourist office ticket counter open April-Oct. Mon.-Fri. 9am-noon and 1:30-5:30pm.) To shave a few francs off the price, take the train to Caux (11.80SFr) and walk up from there. The round-trip back to Montreux, following the crest of the ridge, will take about seven hours.

THE MUSIC FESTIVALS

The **Montreux Jazz Festival,** a world-famous magnet for exceptional musical talent and one of the biggest parties in Europe, pushes everything aside for 15 days starting the first Friday in July. The 1998 lineup will be made public at Christmas 1997; the 1997 headliners included Van Morrison, Eric Clapton, David Sanborn, B.B. King, Sheryl Crow, and Ray Charles. Demand has sent ticket prices rocketing into the stratosphere: individual tickets range from 49 to 129SFr; a festival pass sells for 1300SFr. Standing room tickets range from 29 to 69SFr. Write to the tourist office well in advance for information and tickets. The **booking desk** (tel. 623 45 67; http://www.grolier.fr/festival/montreux) is open Monday through Friday 9am to noon and 1:30 to 6pm off-season and non-stop during the festival. From mid-March the **jazz hotline** in Montreux is active (tel. 983 82 82). The **postal address** for ticket orders is rue du Théâtre 5, CH-1820 Montreux. You can also get tickets from Société de Banque Suisse ticket counters in major Swiss cities; from the Swiss National Tourist offices, 608 Fifth Ave., New York, NY 10020 (212-757-5944); or from Swiss Court, London W1V 8EE (tel. (0171) 734 19 21). Most events sell out before July, some do so as early as January. If you can find a room but no tickets, come anyway for the **Jazz Off,** 500 hours of free, open-air concerts by new bands and established musicians.

From late August to early October, the **Montreux-Vevey Classical Music Festival** takes over with philharmonics from Moscow to Memphis. Tickets to concerts in Montreux and neighboring Vevey, Martigny, St. Maurice, and Chillon range from 20 to 140SFr. Contact the Office of the Classical Music Festival at rue du Théâtre 5, 1st Floor, Case Postale 162, CH-1820 Montreux 2 (tel. 963 54 50; fax 963 25 06).

> ### The Passing of a Giant
> On July 8, 1991, at the Montreux Jazz Festival, the great jazz trumpeter Miles Davis played his last live performance. An historic concert, the performance marked the first time Davis had returned to the musical style with which he began his career. Davis contributed much to jazz, including the "fusion" of jazz and rock and the invention, with Gil Evans, of "cool" jazz. In their pioneering collaboration, Davis and Evans broke away from the frenetic scale structure of be-bop improvization. Davis's smooth, modal improvisations, heard on such albums as *Kind of Blue* and over the rich orchestral settings of the Gil Evans Orchestra on *Sketches of Spain*, influenced a whole generation of artists, including John Coltrane and Bill Evans. Although other artists expanded and developed modal jazz, Davis moved on and never looked back, abandoning some of his most-loved works for over 20 years until Quincy Jones stepped in. Jones had long wanted to do a concert with Davis and revive Davis' earlier material. When Davis finally agreed, the two performed together at Montreux, with the Gil Evans Orchestra (then under the direction of Evans's son, Miles) and the Charles Grundtz Concert Jazz Orchestra, playing songs that hadn't been performed live for a generation. Jones has said that he had never seen Davis as pleased and as connected with the audience in any other concert. Several weeks later, Davis fell ill. He died of pneumonia on September 28, 1991.

NIGHTLIFE

Montreux caters to all tastes and personalities, and its vibrant nightlife centers around the polished atmosphere of the bar- and club-lined quays.

- **Casino de Montreux,** rue du Théâtre 9 (tel. 962 83 83). From av. du Casino, turn on rue Igor Stravinsky toward the lake. Montreux's fun-focus has no entry fee, but finds other ways to munch your money. 200 slot machines (daily 5pm-3am; 21 and over); *boule*, a roulette variant (8:30pm-1am); **Western Saloon** country music club (Thurs.-Sat. 8pm-3am); **Le Cabaret** nightclub (Mon.-Sat. 10pm-4am); **Platinum,** an underground disco; a piano bar; billiards; and a pool (7SFr; 8:45am-2am).
- **Café Rock,** rue de l'Auberge 5 (tel. 963 88 88; fax 961 26 27), just up the stairs from the youth hostel. The youth hostel's own little Hard Rock—loud music, young crowd, billiard room, video games, darts, and pinball. Beer 6SFr per pint; choose among bottles from 8 countries. Open Mon. 4pm-midnight, Tues.-Thurs. 8:30pm-midnight, Fri.-Sat. 8:30am-2am, Sun. 2pm-midnight. Visa, AmEx, DC.
- **Duke's Jazz Bar,** Grand Rue 97 (tel. 963 51 31), 50m down Grand Rue toward Vevey past the Auditorium Stravinski. Enter through the posh Royal Plaza Inter-Continental Hotel; the swooshing doors open to reveal a sweeping view of the lake. As one of the venues of the Montreux Jazz Festival, this high-class establishment bursts at the seams for 2½ weeks in July. After performing, artists often arrive to hang out with the crowd. Celebrate with 295SFr champagne or stick to the impressive 6-7.50SFr range of beers. Sun.-Thurs. open until 1am, Fri.-Sat. until 3am, during Jazz Festival until 6am. Happy hour 6-8pm.

■ Near Montreux

VEVEY

Flanked by the better-known resorts of Lausanne and Montreux, Vevey occupies an often overlooked site along the Vaud Riviera. Perhaps the Nestlé factory headquarters deters tourists, but Jean-Jacques Rousseau, Victor Hugo, Fyodor Dostoyevsky, Henry James, Charlie Chaplin, le Corbusier, and Graham Greene have all worked within the borders of this quirky, lakeside town. As you follow the tourist office's walking tour through all the famous "guess who slept here" spots, you'll see why handsome, serene Vevey drew so many great minds to its shores.

Orientation and Practical Information There are three ways to reach Vevey from Montreux: train (every 30min., 5min., 2.80SFr); bus #1 to "Vevey" (every 10min., 20min., 2.40SFr); and cruise (5 per day, 25min., 7SFr). The **tourist office** is at Grand-Place 29 (tel. 922 20 20; fax 922 20 24; email veveytourism@vevey.ch; http://www.vevey.ch). To get there from the station, cross pl. de la Gare, go past av. de la Gare, and turn left on av. Paul Cérésole. At the end of the road, cut across the parking lot toward the columned arcade; the office is inside. (Open June 15-Sept. 15 daily 8:30am-7pm; Sept. 16-June 14 Mon.-Fri. 8:30am-noon and 1:30-6pm, Sat. 8:30am-noon.) **Lockers** (3SFr) and **bike rental** are available at the station. In an **emergency,** call 117. The **post office** is across pl. de la Gare. (Open Mon.-Fri. 7:30am-6pm, Sat. 8-11am.) The **postal code** is CH-1800; the **telephone code** is 021.

Accommodations and Food Great views abound from the **Riviera Lodge,** pl. du Marché 5 (tel. 923 80 40; fax 923 80 41), a newly opened budget hostel that overlooks Grand-Place through handsome mauve shutters. Sixty bright, shiny, newly renovated rooms offer comfortable beds and lavish facilities. The entrance foyer has lockers and an activities/dining room. On the fifth floor, the reception desk shares the space with a terrace, a spotless kitchen, laundry facilities, several common rooms, and the engaging manager, François. (Reception daily 7:30-10am and 4:30-6:30pm. Call if arriving later. 4-, 6-, or 8-bed dorms 20SFr. Doubles 70SFr. Sheets 5SFr. Co-ed showers (with separate, lockable stalls) and shared bathrooms on each floor. Breakfast 7SFr.) Many family homes also house travelers; try **Pension Bürgle,** rue Louis Meyer 16 (tel. 921 40 23), just off Grand-Place. Herr Bürgle usually requires a check for the first night as a reservation, so book in advance. (38SFr. Breakfast included. Dinner 12SFr.) Ask at the tourist office for other housing options.

For nourishment, check out the **produce and flea market** at the Grand-Place (pl. du Marché) on Tuesday and Saturday mornings from 8:30am to noon. The ubiquitous **Migros** (open Mon. 9am-6:30pm, Tues.-Wed. 8am-6:30pm, Thurs. 8am-8pm, Fri. 8am-6:30pm, Sat. 7:30am-5:30pm) and **Coop** (same hours) glower at one another across av. Paul Cérésole off Grand-Place. Café-restaurants line Grand-Place, but food is cheaper away from the lakefront. Next to the train station entrance stands an **Apisto convenience store.** (Open daily 6am-9:30pm.) For a more interesting location, cross the square from the station to the post office and follow the underpass (passage St. Antoine) across the tracks. At the top of the stairs, in Vevey's industrial area, hang signs for **Les Temps Modernes,** rue des Deux Gares 6bis (tel. 922 34 39). A factory turned café, record store, and dance studio that (although it still looks and smells like a factory) has become the cultural junction for local artists. Thursdays and Saturdays bring jazz and contemporary rock to the central stage area, which is swathed in red, furnished with plush chairs, and directly across an old air vent. (Salads 5-14SFr. *Plats du jour* 13-16SFr. Drinks 1SFr more Thurs. and Sat. Open Mon.-Thurs. 11am-midnight, Fri. 11am-2am, Sat. 5pm-2am. Occasional extended hours Fri.-Sat.)

Sights and Entertainment At the end of July, Vevey's **International Comedy Film Festival,** dedicated to former resident Charlie Chaplin, features official competitions during the day and more relaxed, open cinema every night at pl. Scanavia (tickets 13SFr). Hordes come out for a cartoon and pasta party that crowns the festival's last evening. From August to September, Vevey teams up with its big sister Montreux to present the **International Festival of Music,** a classical music celebration that hosts several renowned international orchestras as well as noted soloists for a series of concerts and master classes. Venues lie in both Montreux and Vevey, but the Theatre of Vevey, rue de Théâtre 4 (tel. 923 60 55), provides information and handles reservations and ticket sales for Vevey. As the capital of the Lavaux wine region, Vevey eagerly awaits the **Fête des Vignerons** (Vevey Wine-Growers Festival), an event that occurs approximately every 25 years. This festival is the most lavish in Europe, and farmers and wine-growers from the surrounding regions begin practicing their dances and preparing their traditional costumes years in advance. The last celebration, in 1977, lured nearly 200,000 spectators and 4000 participants; the next will occur in all its splendor from late July to mid-August 1999. Make hotel reservations in 1997! The festival will end in mid-August with a raucous display honoring Bacchus, the ancient Roman god of wine. On a less spectacular scale, the **Folklore Market** (in pl. du Marché, mid-July to Aug. Sat. 9am-noon) allows you to sample all the local wine you can hold for only 5SFr. The **Winetrain** winds its way through 13km of villages and vineyards in Lavaux (every hr. from Vevey station, round-trip up to 9.60SFr, Swisspass and Eurailpass valid). The tourist office has a list of tasting venues; a map with directions to the two wine centers, Chexbres and Puidox; and a guide to six hiking tours of the region.

One of these hikes is really a stroll, passing a number of interesting museums, along the quay to the neighboring town of Tour-de-Peilz. For an excellent deal, pick up a Montreux-Vevey Museum Passport (15SFr), which grants free entrance to 10 museums in the cities, including the **Musée Jenisch**, av. de la Gare 2 (tel. 921 29 50; fax 921 62 92). A collection of engravings and etchings by masters like Dürer, Rembrandt, and Corot graces the first floor, while upstairs more contemporary Swiss artists display works that all but melt into the soft cream and eggshell hues of the gallery walls. (Open Tues.-Sun. March-Oct. 10:30am-noon and 2-5:30pm; Nov.-Feb. 2-5:30pm. 10SFr, students 4SFr. Guided tours 14SFr.) Near the tourist office, signs point across the square to the **Swiss Camera Museum**, ruelle des Anciens-Fossés 6 (tel. 921 94 60). The museum covers three floors—one blue, one red, one yellow—with cameras from the early days of daguerreotypes and World War I spy cameras to the present, as well as an upstairs gallery. (Open Tues.-Sun. April-Oct. 11am-5:30pm; Nov.-March 2-5:30pm. 5SFr, students 4SFr, children free. Guided tours 3SFr.) From the museum, you can either turn left onto rue du Lac and stroll through Vevey's many-fountained *vieille ville* or head straight for the flower-lined quay. A few minutes either way will bring you to the **Alimentarium/Food Museum** (tel. 924 41 11), on the corner of rue du Léman and quai Perdonnet. This highly didactic and interactive museum tells the story of food from its production in cows to its processing in the human body. Check out the curious blend of food processing machinery, ethnographic recreations, Nestlé commercials, and the inexplicable top-floor, permanent exhibit on Chinese food. (Open Tues.-Sun. April-Oct. 10am-5pm, Nov.-March 10am-noon and 2-5pm. Bilingual French/German. 6SFr, students and seniors 4SFr, school groups free.) A short walk farther along the quay, the **Swiss Museum of Games** (tel. 944 40 50; fax 944 10 79), is housed in the ivy-clad, 13th-century Château de la Tour-de-Peilz. The mountain of neon-colored knapsacks at the entrance and the squeals of delight from the board-games room instantly identify the museum's target audience. (Open Tues.-Sun. 2-6pm. Exhibits in French, German, English, and Italian. 6SFr, students 3SFr, under 17 free. Guided tours an additional 2.50SFr.)

GSTAAD AND SAANEN

Lying at the juncture of four alpine valleys, Gstaad is in the heart of ski country. As far as small alpine villages go, however, Gstaad is an anomaly. While neighboring Saanen, has a goat for a mascot, Gstaad's emblems are glitzy five-star hotels and designer boutiques. In Saanen's main street, farmers prominently display tractors for potential buyers, while low-set convertibles hum down Gstaad's main drag. As Gstaad moves into the most rarefied realms of 20th-century tourism, Saanen seems content to stay its own small self. Both offer visitors slices of small-town, alpine life,

NEAR MONTREUX: GSTAAD AND SAANEN

but one bursts at the seams and the other continues to follow the same, age-old pattern.

A study in contrasts, these towns nevertheless share a superlative sports scene. **White-water rafting** starts at 85SFr for four hours in Gstaad (Eurotrek: tel. (01) 462 02 03) and 99SFr for three hours in Saanen (Swissraft: tel. 744 50 80). In summer Swissraft also goes **canyoning** (80SFr for approx. 3hr.). You can try **ballooning** with either CAST Balloonfahrten (tel. 744 62 59; 390-500SFr for 2hr.) or Hans Büker (tel. (026) 924 54 85; fax 924 76 42; 485SFr for 1½-2hr.). If you prefer the ocean blue to the wild blue yonder, **paragliding** (tel. 744 03 72; email parasport@spectraweb.ch; http://www.beo.ch/gstaad/paragliding) is an option at 130SFr for four to six hours. To see the countryside with at least your horses' feet planted firmly on the ground, try **horse-trekking** (tel. 744 24 60; 30SFr per lesson) or riding in a **horse-drawn cart** (tel. 744 24 60; 30min. ride 40SFr per person in a group of at least 5). Rounding out your options are 150km of hard-core **mountain-bike trails**; the tourist office publishes a very helpful map and guide describing distances and difficulty levels. Within the city, covered tennis courts, saunas, and swimming pools wait on nearly every corner. For the **indoor public pool** (tel. 744 44 16), turn right on the main road out of the station and take the first right after the river. (Open Mon. 2-9pm, Tues. and Thurs. 10am-9pm, Wed. and Fri. 10am-10pm, Sat.-Sun. 10am-7pm. 9SFr, with visitor's card 8SFr.) In July, the annual **Swiss Open Tennis Tournament** (tel. 748 83 83; fax 748 83 50; http://www.gstaad.ch/swiss.open) attracts players who decided to skip Wimbledon and 40,000 spectators who each made a similar decision. (Tickets 20-100SFr.)

Once rested and sufficiently inspired to retackle the mountains, try a rugged panoramic hike up the **Giferspitz horseshoe**. Turn right on the main road from Gstaad station and head left on the main road just before the river, and then take the second big road on the right over the river (with signs to "Bissen"; the turn is 1km from Gstaad). Follow the yellow *Wanderweg* signs for Wasserngrat and power up the steep hill flank to the top cable car station (1936m). The very fit and adventurous can continue up to the **Lauenehorn** (2477m) and, after a rocky scramble, even farther to the **Giferspitz** (2541m), Gstaad's tallest peak. The path circles down to Bissen again, but a bus eases the descent (1800m of ascent; perfect weather only; allow

---

Gstaar-Struck

If the chateau walls of Gstaad could whisper, disciples of highbrow culture would perk up their ears. Namedropping can be a rather casual activity in Gstaad. Elizabeth Taylor, Jackie Kennedy, Audrey Hepburn, Bill Buckley, and other elite of Hollywood and politics have spent their winters here skiing, drinking, and showering their glamour on the town. Such calibre of company merited no ordinary treatment, even in gentle Gstaad: David Niven, a prominent British actor of the 50s and 60s known for *Around the World in 80 Days* and other flicks, was not allowed on the slopes without a trained ski teacher lest he break a limb.

The greats were first drawn to Gstaad in the 40s and 50s by the quality of its international schools. Prince Ranier of Morocco spent his boyhood at the city's Le Rosey school; he later returned to show off the town to his wife, Grace Kelly—and to show her off to the town. In fine Fitzgeraldian fashion, Gstaad filled with affluent British and Americans, who established an informal literary and artistic clique. Audrey Hepburn made frequent visits, and Elizabeth Taylor relaxed here with her two-time husband Robert Burton (maybe dreams of Taylor's Swiss chateau convinced Burton to try again). Not far down the hill, American economist John Kenneth Galbraith spent peaceful and prolific winters in the third floor of a chateau. Bill Buckley, Galbraith's political archrival, did the same, and the two engaged in good-natured competition to fill Gstaad's bookstore with more of their respective books. Just something to ponder while dodging screaming *Schulkinder* at the Saanen *Jugendherberge*.

one whole day. The tourist office offers a map for this trail (#5009, 24.50SFr) and others.

In winter, Gstaad turns to **skiing**. With 250km of runs and 69 lifts, the town generally has something open from mid-December through April. Expert skiers will find little to challenge them, but middling ones will be spoiled. The **Top Card ski pass** (tel. 748 82 82; fax 748 82 60; email ski.gstaad@gstaad.ch) is 50SFr for one day on all sectors; more limited passes are slightly cheaper. A week of skiing will run about 263SFr, depending on your age. For the dedicated, a **season ski pass** (890SFr) from the Gstaad region gives its holder the right to ski in Oberengadin/St. Moritz, Kitzbühel/Tirol, Adelboden-Lenk, Alpes Vaudoises, Ordino-Arcalis, and Pal Arinsal (Andorra). Consult the tourist office for details on **heliskiing, snowboarding, curling,** and **skating**.

Gstaad proper has few hotels with fewer than three stars, but the tourist office publishes a list of budget options. Most of these establishments lie outside of Gstaad, and reaching them can be quite taxing by foot or bothersome by bus. The **Jugendherberge** (tel. (033) 744 13 43), 2mi. away in Saanen, is a godsend. From Gstaad station, take the train (every hr., 5-7min., 2.40SFr) or post bus (every hr., 10min., 2.40SFr). Or turn left on Gstaad's main street and hike along the road for 25 to 30 minutes, past the Saanen station and post office, and then turn right on the main street and go straight at the crossroads, following the "Spital" signs (40min.). This slightly chilly rural hostel has an exceptionally warm welcome and is full of family flavor—everyone chips in to wash the dishes. The hostel offers doubles, triples, and quads with balconies for couples and families, and 6- and 8-bed dorms. (Reception 7:30-9am and 5-10pm. Curfew 11pm. Dorms 25.30SFr first night, then 22.80SFr; doubles 37.50SFr, 34.80SFr. Children ages 2-6 half price; children under 2 stay free. Breakfast, sheets, and showers included. Three-course dinner 11SFr. Closed Nov. and May. Phone ahead in winter.) **Camping Bellerive** (tel. 744 63 30) rests between Gstaad and Saanen. (Arrive any time. Check-in 9-10am and 6-7pm. 6.40SFr, children 2.20SFr. Winter: 7.50SFr, 2.20SFr. Tent 5.30SFr.) Farther along the same river, Saanen has a **summer-only camping site** (tel. 74 46 19) on the edge of town at the end of Campingstr. (Arrive any time. Check-in 6-7pm. 6.40SFr; tent 5.30SFr; caravan 8.50SFr. Visa, MC.)

Back in Gstaad, budget diners should take advantage of the **Co-op**, left on the main street from the train station. (Restaurant open Mon.-Fri. 7:30am-6:30pm, Sat. 7:30am-4:30pm. Supermarket open Mon.-Fri. 8am-12:15pm and 1:30-6:30pm, Sat. 8am-4pm.) In front of the train station, the **Hotel Bernerhof café** (tel. 748 88 44) serves up a reasonably priced *menu du midi* (15-17SFr) and a healthy selection of vegetarian dishes (15-18SFr), with a nice view of the endearing train station and the mountains beyond. For a change of atmosphere, slide into soft leather chairs and have a burger and fries with a beer (14-18SFr) at **Richi's Pub** (tel. 744 57 87), just after the church on the main street to the right of the station. (Open daily noon-12:30am.)

Gstaad's very friendly, well-organized **tourist office** (tel. 748 81 81, for direct reservations for hotels, apartments, and package deals 748 81 84; fax 748 81 31; email tvsl@gstaad.ch; http://www.gstaad.ch) is just past the railway bridge on the main road to the right of the station. (Open July-Aug. Mon.-Sat. 9am-6pm; Sept.-June Mon.-Fri. 8:30am-noon and 2-6pm, Sat. 9am-noon, occasional Sun. in June.) Saanen's main street also has a tourist office. (Open Mon.-Fri., same hours.) By **train,** get to Gstaad from **Montreux** (every hr., 1½hr., 19.40SFr, round-trip 34SFr) or **Interlaken** (every hr., 2hr., 21SFr, change trains at Zweisimmen). Catch a **bus** to **Les Diablerets** (1hr., 11.40SFr). For **taxis** try 744 80 80. The train station in Gstaad has 5SFr, 4SFr, and 3SFr **lockers** plus **bike rental, currency exchange,** and a **ski rack.** Gstaad's **post office** is next to the train station. (Open Mon.-Fri. 7:45am-noon and 2-6pm, Sat. 7:45-11am.) In an **emergency,** call 117. The **postal code** is CH-3780, and the **telephone code** is 033.

LEYSIN

Rumor has it—not confirmed, of course—that some of Leysin's residents are Swiss. In this laid-back town where people show up to work in sweats or flannels, the locals are not quite so local. A clutch of American and Japanese colleges and international schools have increased Leysin's population for a couple of generations. Many visitors come to study; some never leave. Maybe they stay for Leysin's myriad activities, more than would be expected in a town its size. Or maybe they stay for the placid hills and winding streets that invite and beguile. Perhaps they just stay for the peace. Leysin offers long views of the mountain-girded Rhône Valley and the distant shores of Lac Léman, but the town is far removed from the tourist frenzy engulfing those areas.

The only way to reach Leysin by transport is the **cog railway** from Aigle. Aigle lies on the high-speed train line from **Lausanne** (2 per hr., 30min., 12.20SFr) and **Montreux** (2 per hr., 10min., 4.80SFr). From Aigle, the railway leisurely chugs passengers to the top of the steep climb in 30 minutes (every hr. 6am-10pm; Swisspass valid). There are four stops, Leysin-Village (7.80SFr), Versmont, Feydey (9SFr), and Grand-Hôtel (9.60SFr). The staff of the **tourist office** (tel. 494 29 21 or 494 22 44; fax 494 13 64; email o.t.leysin@pingnet.ch; http://www.leysin.ch) waits behind sleek metal and glass counters at the New Sporting Club just down from pl. du Marché. (Open Mon.-Fri. 8am-9pm, Sat.-Sun. 9am-8pm.) For an **ambulance,** call 494 27 37. For the **police,** call 494 25 41. In an **emergency,** dial 117. In a **fire,** call 118. There are two **post offices,** one next to the Feydey station (tel. 494 11 05) and one down the hill in Leysin-Village on rue du Village (tel. 494 12 05). (Both open Mon.-Fri. 8-11:30am and 2:30-6pm, Sat. 8:30-11am.) The Feydey office serves as the town's post bus station. The **postal code** is CH-1854, and the **telephone code** is 025.

The two sports centers in the village offer amenities at rather not-so-friendly rates. The pools and Turkish bath, however, in the **New Sporting Club** (tel. 494 29 21; email o.t.leysin@pingnet.ch; http://www.leysin.ch), are only 5SFr and 3SFr with a **Leysin holiday card.** You receive the card, valid for 10-50% discounts at any of Leysin's sports centers, slopes, cable cars, and ski lifts, after your first night's stay at any hotel. The New Sporting Club also contains squash and tennis courts and a (brand new) climbing wall—as well as guides and lessons for all three. (Open 9am-9pm; pools have slightly shorter hours.) Down the hill near the campsite, the **Centre des Sports** (tel. 494 24 42; fax 494 13 55) offers **ice skating.** (Open daily 8am-10pm.) Skiers can rent equipment from **Hefti Sports** (tel. 494 16 77; fax 494 26 61), two minutes from the New Sporting Club on pl. du Marché, then head off into the unknown reaches of the skies and slopes (skis or snowboard plus boots 43SFr). One-day ski passes are approximately 38SFr, children 23SFr; weekly passes 212SFr, 128SFr. The holiday card also grants discounts on these passes and the cable car that bobs up to the nearby summit of Berneuse (daily June-Oct. and mid-Dec. to mid-April; 13.50SFr, round-trip 18SFr; Visa, MC, AmEx). Another car rises to Mayen beneath the craggy **Tour d'Aï** (2331m; same dates and prices). At the end of January, the pros appear for the **World PRO Tour Snowboarding Championships** held in Leysin every year, a week that shatters the general calm and expands the pocket of activity (usually centered around the American College) into the lower terraces of the town.

Winter is unquestionably Leysin's high season, so reserve rooms in advance. For cheap accommodations, the recently opened **Hiking Sheep Guesthouse,** Villa La Joux (tel./fax 494 35 35, portable (79) 416 37 82) warrants your attention. Curiosity may be enough to sustain you on the hike up, but what killed the cat will lead you to astoundingly vibrant sheep-sponsored lodgings. Shining wooden bunks, ready to be sheathed in fluffy IKEA sheets and comforters, await those tired legs. Cheeky sheep floor mats lead to other wonders: a convivial log-fire-heated dining room, two breathtaking balconies (with hammocks!), a pristine kitchen open for use, and a TV and game room stocked with enough books and childhood parlor games to lure you from your pillow. Best of all is the unique atmosphere, in which sharing stories, whether lived or imagined, is an impulse no one can resist. (Check-out 10:30am. No curfew; door never locked, but try to be quiet by 10pm. Dorms 23SFr, after 3 nights 20SFr; doubles 53SFr, then 50SFr. Only 2 showers, so keep it short. Buffet breakfast 6SFr, English breakfast 8SFr; request either the night before. Laundry 10SFr. Visa, MC.) Down the road to the right is **Club Vagabond,** rte des Quatre Chalets (tel. 494 13 21; fax 494 13 22), slightly past its glory days but still revered among Leysin's under-30 English speakers for its soap-and-trash-bag parties, live music, Sunday evening barbecues (in summer at 6pm; bring your own meat; 5SFr for bread and salad buffet), and occasional art exhibitions. The floors have new carpeting, the walls fresh paint, and the bunk beds firm mattresses. Leather armchairs and an English library look out across Leysin's slopes. The free-entrance discotheque in the cellar, "The Ice Cave," has, like Gloria Gaynor, survived with 70s style still intact, and the late-night bar serves beer (5SFr). As "the home of mountain sports," Club Vagabond even offers its own rock climbing and mountain biking packages. (Reception Tues.-Sun. 8am-5pm; after hours head to the bar, open till 3am. Dorms 25SFr; singles 36SFr; doubles 50SFr. Sheets and towels 6SFr. Breakfast 6SFr.) **Hotel de la Paix** (tel./fax 494 13 75), on av. Rollier, is opposite the "Versmont" train stop. Narrow hallways choking on oriental carpeting connect old-fashioned rooms with fading prints of *belle epoque* Leysin. In the outside garden, red-and-white-striped deck chairs swallow up the older clients. (Reception daily 8am-8pm. 44-63SFr per person. Breakfast included. Lunch or dinner 22SFr, both 36SFr. 10% student discount.) **Camping Semiramis** (tel. 494 11 48; fax 494 20 29) is a 4-star site beside the Centre des Sports. From Leysin-Village station, walk left on rue de Village then turn right onto rte du Suchet just past the post office. (5.20-6.20SFr, children 3.70-4.60SFr; tents 4.10SFr. Visa, MC, AmEx, DC.)

A **Co-op** supermarket is just off the big bend in rue Favez, below pl. du Marché and the New Sporting Club. (Open Mon.-Fri. 8am-noon and 2-6:30pm, Sat. 8am-noon and 2pm-7pm.) A stroll uphill to the Feydey district and **La Grotta** (tel. 494 15 32) promises the added attraction of the owner's gold-club member Swatch collection—a dazzling expo of all the editions since 1983, including special music alarm, beeper, and ski-pass versions. Slightly cheaper food awaits at **Forest Hill** (tel. 494 19 90), above the New Sporting Club. Eat heaping plates of spaghetti and salad (10-15SFr) on a rooftop terrace. (Open daily noon-1pm and 6-10pm.) Locals recommend any of several mountain restaurants for real atmosphere and non-canned local charm. Hikers will relish the good meal that awaits at the top of a challenging slope, but all others should take a car or risk road-side collapse. The revolving **Kuklos restaurant** (tel. 494 31 41) is very touristy, but **l'Horizon** (tel. 494 15 05) comes highly recommended, and **La Prafandaz** (tel. 494 26 26) has a breathtaking belvedere overlooking Lac Léman and a soulful St. Bernard in addition to a fine list of traditional dishes. These restaurants keep irregular hours according to demand, but they usually post their daily status on road signs well before you encounter darkened buildings and an empty parking lot.

LES DIABLERETS

As one of the few Swiss towns that can claim two high seasons, Les Diablerets' little devils frolic year-long among its creaky chalets and down its glacial slopes. These pan-piping little mascots lure the snow-starved Swiss from Geneva and Bern to this nearby unglittery resort every weekend. There may be only five lifts open on Diablerets' glacier in July and August, but the snow is 100% guaranteed. Come winter, the town is an intimate alternative to its snootier local rivals: Gstaad, Crans-Montana, and Verbier. Snowboarders will appreciate the respect they receive, and hikers can putter about peacefully on the surprisingly varied terrain.

Only two public transport services connect Les Diablerets to the rest of Switzerland. The hourly **train** down to **Aigle** takes one hour (9.60SFr), and the **post bus** over the mountains to **Gstaad** (11.40SFr) via the Col du Pillon leaves about five times per day depending on the season. In summer this bus is the only way to reach the Diablerets glacier cable cars at the Col. The first bus leaves at 9:39am and the last returns at 4:40pm, so plan accordingly or prepare yourself for a 45-minute walk back to town. The helpful and all-knowing **tourist office,** rue de la Gare (tel. 492 33 58; fax 492 23 48), basks in a chalet to the right of the train station and publishes a devilishly impressive range of literature. It also keeps a list of weekly activities and annual events like the **Adventura Sports Weekend** (25 sports over two days, June 21-22), the giant **Rösti Festival** at Isenau (July 14-Aug. 10), the **Crossing-roads Country Music Festival** (early Aug.), and the **International Alpine Film Festival** (late Sept.). (Open July-Aug. Mon.-Sat. 8am-noon and 2-6pm, Sun. 9am-noon and 3-6pm; mid-Dec. to mid-April Mon.-Sat. 8:30am-12:30pm and 2-6pm, Sun. 9am-noon and 3-6pm; Sept.-June Mon.-Fri. 8am-noon and 2-6pm, Sat.-Sun. 9am-noon.) For **taxis,** call (079) 205 05 55. The **pharmacy** is just before the bend in rue de la Gare. (Open Mon.-Fri. 8am-12:30pm and 3-6:30pm, Sat. 8am-12:30pm and 3-6pm, Sun. 10am-noon and 5-6pm; call 492 32 83 in an emergency.) For an **ambulance,** call 494 37 27. For the **police,** call 492 24 88. Turn right out of the train station for the **post office.** (Open Mon.-Fri. 8am-noon and 2:30-6pm, Sat. 7:45-10:45am.) The **postal code** is CH-1865, and the **telephone code** is 024.

The cheapest accommodations are unfortunately on the outskirts of town. **Les Diablotins,** rte du Pillon (tel. 492 36 33; fax 492 23 55), is a big modern block popular with young snowboarding groups. From the station, turn right, bend around the hairpin at the pharmacy, and turn right along rte du Pillon at the top of the hill. Avoid the ensuing 20-minute walk by calling from the station; the hostel will send a mini-bus. Two- to four-bed rooms are in good shape (all have private sinks and most have balconies) in spite of the thousands of school groups that have tramped and trounced their way through the halls and the shared showers. This large establishment features four dining halls, several lounges, and a bar and disco—all segregated by age and noise-tolerance levels. (Reception 8am-noon and 2-6pm. Ready for the price scheme? Here goes. Jan. and April-Christmas: 31SFr, after 4 days 28SFr; youths under 18 26SFr, then 23. Christmas-New Year's and mid-Feb. to mid-March: 44SFr, 40SFr; youths 37SFr, 34SFr. March-April: 40SFr, 36SFr; youths 34SFr, 30SFr. Breakfast included. Evening *menu* 15SFr. Reserve ahead in winter. Visa, MC, AmEx, DC.) Left from the station and down the road toward Vers-l'Eglise, slightly older and hipper snowboarders call **Hotel Mon Abri** (tel. 492 34 81; fax 492 34 82) their home away from the slopes. Piled-up gear makes the cozy double rooms seem smaller than they really are. The hotel's nightlife centers around the B'bar and its satellite Bar'B, whose mutilated Barbie dolls rock along with the main disco from 10pm to 4am. Activities from pinball to petanque offer the chance to blow off steam. (Reception 5-7pm. Doubles 35 SFr. Showers and breakfast included. Closed May. Visa, MC.) Farther down the road in Vers-l'Eglise stands **Hotel Mon Séjour** (tel./fax 492 30 13). Take the train one stop, wander up the hill past the post office and church, and turn right over the river to get to this family-run chalet near the river. Pack into the large, intimate dorm (30SFr) or a less cramped room (39SFr; reservations preferred). Hall showers and breakfast are included. The hotel is immediately above **Camping La Murée** (tel. 492 21 99), an attractive, flat site next to the river. (6.50SFr; tents 9SFr.)

Hikers, bikers, and snowboarders load up packed lunches from one of the three supermarkets. Right from the station along rue de la Gare, **Pam Super Discount** stares down at its competitor. (Open Mon. 7:30am-noon, Tues.-Fri. 7:30am-noon and 2-6:30pm, Sat. 7:30am-noon and 2-5pm.) The **Co-op** awaits on rue de la Gare, left of the station. (Open Mon.-Fri. 8am-12:15pm and 2:15-6:30pm, Sat. 8am-12:30pm and 2-5pm.) The terrace of **Le Muguet** (tel. 492 26 42), opposite the tourist office, puts the glacier center stage. Try a cheese and bacon *galette* (8SFr) or a dessert crepe (5-10SFr) with *cidre* (2.50SFr). Alternatively, cross the channel for their sandwiches (7SFr) and the all-important pot of tea. (Open daily 6:30am-7pm.) Just around the big bend by the pharmacy, **Locanda Livia** (tel. 492 32 80) is a family Italian restaurant. Navigate your way through a crustacean creation—pasta drowning in mussels, scampi, and prawns. They also serve a scrumptious four-cheese pizza with a conspicuous Swiss addition (*gruyères* cheese) and the cute name of *rêve de* *souris* (mouse's dream; pasta and pizza 12-18SFr; open Thurs.-Tues. 11:30am-6:30pm).

The **summer skiing cable car** leaves from the **Col du Pillon** above the village to the glacier (day pass 49SFr, children 29SFr; round-trip 45SFr, 22.50SFr). For multiple day excursions you must buy a pass for the whole Diablerets-Villars region (6 days 210SFr, students 178SFr, children 126SFr) and provide a photo. The slightly more expensive **Alpes Vaudoises pass** entitles its holder to all forms of transport (cable cars, trains, and post buses) as well as access to the Gstaad Super Ski Region and Lenk/Adelboden (6 days 233SFr, students 203SFr, children 140SFr). There are special deals for groups, families, and seniors. Through the **Swiss Village Club**, many hotels offer special three-day/four-night weekend or six-day/seven-night weekly deals that include half-board ski passes, a fondue evening, tobogganing, curling, skating, and even babysitting services—ski or eat a nice dinner while the hotel keeps the kiddies occupied. The tourist office can offer suggestions, but you must book directly with the hotel. You can rent skis, boards, and boots (25SFr) at the top of the glacier, but in winter you must acquire your equipment before ascending. **Jacky Sports** (tel. 492 32 18; fax 492 31 64; http://www.swissrentasport.cn), opposite the tourist office, rents equipment in the Swiss Rent-a-Sport system. (Skis or snowboard 28SFr per day; 6 days 105SFr. Boots 15SFr, 52SFr. Open Sun.-Tues. and Thurs.-Fri. 9am-noon and 2-6pm. Visa, MC, AmEx, DC.) The **ski/snowboard school** (tel. 492 20 02; fax 492 23 48), in the Maison du Tourisme, offers lessons (6 days 125SFr, children 117SFr). If no one's there, the tourist office can help you contact the ski instructor of your choice via the portable phones—an apparent must for the area's busy outdoorsy types.

Other sports are a lot easier to arrange. Jacky Sports rents **mountain bikes** for 35SFr per day (6 days 125 SFr). A circuit, also possible on foot, leaves the village from the tourist office. Head around the hairpin turn at the junction with the Col du Pillon road, go straight over, and climb upwards to La Ville and its long view of the Diablerets glacier spilling over the edge high above the village. Turn right along the valley wall to Métraille and La Crua, and then begin a long descent to the crag-cradled Lac Retaud and Col du Pillon before free-wheeling back to Les Diablerets. (Full day, with good weather.) If the hike above doesn't tempt, head deeper into the mountains by turning right over the river at the pharmacy, and then right again so that you are facing the **Sommet des Diablerets** (3209m) and the glacier. The valley sides close in as you continue the level riverside walk, depositing you onto the stage of a rugged 200m-high amphitheater at **Creux de Champ** (1320m, 160m ascent., 1hr., very easy). The path starts to climb steeply up the sides to the refuge de Pierredar at 2278m (1110m ascent, 3hr. above Les Diablerets). The agile can then push on up the scrambly new track (ladders) to **Scex Rouge** (2971m), the cable car terminus on the glacier, which affords an unforgettable alpine panorama (full day hike, high summer and perfect weather only). Once-in-a-lifetime thrills have their outlets too. **Mountain Evasion** (tel./fax 492 32 32) is anything but; they organize **canyoning** (70-120SFr), **glacier bivouacs** (140SFr), **rappelling** (80SFr), and guided **hiking** and **mountain biking** (40-120SFr). (Office at the Parc des Sports across the river. Open daily Dec.-Oct. 5:30-6:30pm.) Left from the train station and past the post office along rue de la Gare, **Centre ParAdventure** (tel. 492 23 82; fax 492 26 28; email cevic@bluewin.ch) offers **paragliding** (60-150SFr), more **canyoning** (80SFr), and the all-new **mudbike** that lacks pedals and a motor but features giant wheels. (Open daily 9-9:30am and 5:30-6:30pm or call (079) 435 25 82 anytime). Snowboarders may be happy to know that the **New Devil School of snowboarding** (tel. (079) 212 24 72) has entered its bid for the town's corniest name pun. A one-hour initiation into snowboard devilry costs 55SFr, while a more comprehensive day-long course costs 200SFr.

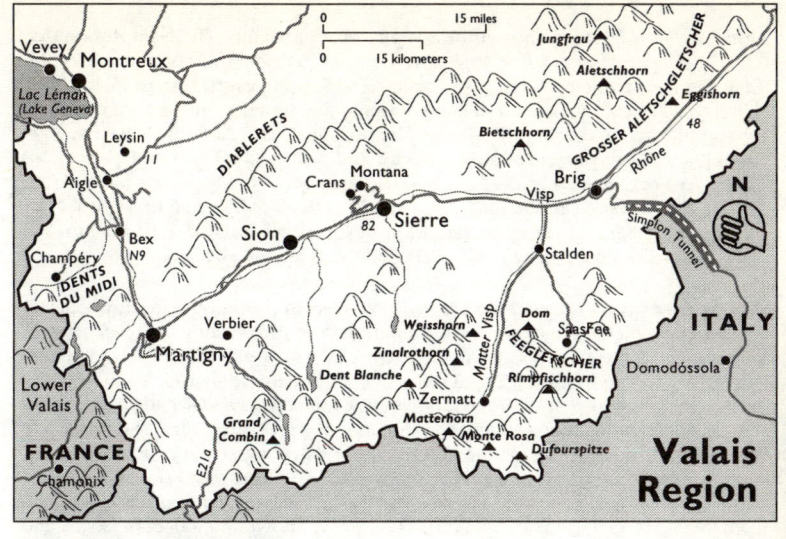

VALAIS (WALLIS)

The territory bounded by Canton Valais sits snugly in the catchment area of the Rhône valley, mainly in the deep, wide glacier cleft shaved by the river. In the west, Martigny and Sion are French-speaking; upriver in Brig, Swiss-German dominates. On the right bank rise the southern slopes of the Berner Oberland peaks; on the left bank along the Italian border jut the Valais Alps and their mighty Matterhorn. Switzerland stereotypes the Wallisers as dour folk with independent minds. In reality, the region's inhabitants have a vibrant and riotous community life still untouched by the tourism that has engulfed the high mountain villages.

■ Martigny

Martigny is a small town with a big town feel—a busy concrete aluminum-processing break from all those creaky wooden chalets. As the gateway for the **St. Bernard Pass,** the town has always had special strategic significance for emperors wishing to control any crawl space between Switzerland and Italy. You can visit unearthed portions of the fort built by the Roman emperor Claudius, the first town in the Valais, and the medieval castle that replaced it. Also of note is a 20th-century addition, the Fondation Gianadda, a leading center for modern art and classical music. While other towns adopt such stand-by Swiss mascots as bears or cows, Martigny has mournful St. Bernards, their slack postures mirroring the valley's trees, beaten into tilted poses by the winds. Strong breezes buffet man and dog alike in Martigny's wide streets and whip long-enduring flags about with Valaisian gusto. Locals maintain that the winds lighten their spirits and invigorate their bodies.

Orientation and Practical Information Frequent trains run west to **Lausanne** (every 30min., 1hr., 21SFr); **Montreux** (every 30min., 30min., 13.20SFr); and **Aigle** (9SFr); and east to **Sion** (every 30min., 15min., 8.40SFr). Two tiny private lines leave for **Orsières,** where you can change for **Aosta** in Italy via the St. Bernard Pass (30SFr); and for **Châtelard** where you can change for **Chamonix** in France (every hr., 1¾hr., 28SFr). Martigny's **tourist office,** pl. Centrale 9 (tel. 721 22 20; fax 721 22 24), is straight down av. de la Gare at the far corner of pl. Centrale. (Open July-Aug. Mon.-Fri. 9am-6pm, Sat. 9am-noon and 2-6pm, Sun. 10am-noon and 4-6pm;

Sept.-June Mon.-Fri. 9am-noon and 1:30-6pm, Sat. 9am-noon.) The **train station** (tel. 723 33 30; open Mon.-Sat. 5:45am-8:45pm, Sun. 6:15am-8:45pm) provides all of the usual services: **currency exchange, lockers** (3-5SFr), **luggage storage** (5SFr), **bike rental** (22SFr per day), and a **rail information** office (open Mon.-Fri. 8am-noon and 1:30-6pm, Sat. 9am-noon and 2-4pm). The **hospital** (tel. 722 53 01) has a switchboard that can tell you the late-night doctor and pharmacy. For an **ambulance,** call 722 01 76. For the **police,** call 722 01 76. The large **post office,** av. de la Gare 32 (tel. 722 26 72), sits between the train station and the tourist office and has a public fax awaiting your next P.R. coup. (Open Mon.-Fri. 7:30am-noon and 1:30-6:30pm, Sat. 7:30-11am.) The **postal code** is CH-1920, and the **telephone code** is 027.

Accommodations and Food Since travelers in Martigny are mainly business types, budget pickings are meager. Commuting from the recently built **Auberge de Jeunesse** in **Sion** (see p. 336) is an excellent idea, especially if you have a railpass. Otherwise, try the **Hôtel du Stand,** av. du Grand-St-Bernard 41 (tel. 722 15 06; fax 722 95 06), straight past the tourist office near the Fondation Gianadda. This unassuming family hotel comes highly recommended by Swiss regulars. The rooms are spacious and spotless, despite the hotel's unprepossessing cream concrete exterior and the puce deep-pile carpet on the lobby walls. The restaurant downstairs has a *plat du jour* (16SFr) and three-course *menus* (22SFr). (Reception daily 7am-midnight. Singles 65SFr; doubles 94SFr; triples 120SFr. Shower included. Breakfast and parking included. Sauna 5SFr. The hotel hosts many autocar groups; reserve ahead July-Sept. Visa, MC.) **Camping Les Neuvilles,** rue du Levant 68 (tel. 722 45 44), packs its shaded plot with motor homes. From the station, head straight on av. de la Gare, take the second left on av. des Neuvilles, and turn right onto rue du Levant after the soccer field. The site's three-star amenities include playgrounds, a store, laundry machines, a sauna, a solarium, giant chess sets, and names for every "street." (Reception Mon.-Sat. 8am-noon and 1:30-10pm, Sun. 3-9pm. July-Aug.: 5.80SFr; tents 6SFr; 4-person bungalow 60SFr. Sept.-June: 4.80SFr; 7.50SFr; 85SFr. Children 6-16 half-price. Shower included.)

Cafés crowd Martigny's tree-lined pl. Centrale, some with *menus* in the 15-20SFr range. For cheaper fare, **Lords' Sandwiches,** av. du Grand-St-Bernard 15 (tel. 723 35 98), serves 36 sorts of sandwiches (4-11SFr), including a bacon burger with fries, and the Zeus, an overflowing roast beef sandwich—hey, easy on the ambrosia. (Open daily 7am-midnight.) **Le Rustique,** av. de la Gare 44 (tel. 722 88 33), has fashionably rustic mats around a terrace, behind which you can enjoy crispy savory crepes (9-13SFr) and sweet ones, too (5-10SFr). Wash them down with a mug of cider (3.50SFr). (Open daily 11:30am-10:30pm.) For straightforward Italian food, locals recommend **Le Grotto,** rue du Rhône 3 (tel. 722 02 46), just off pl. Centrale on the left as you walk toward the station. (Open Wed.-Mon. 8:30am-midnight. Visa, MC.) The immense **Migros** supermarket at pl. du Manoir 5, just off pl. Centrale, has 18 different boutiques and moving sidewalks. (Open Mon.-Thurs. 8:15am-6:30pm, Fri. 8:15am-8pm, Sat. 8am-5pm.) Down rue de la Poste, a **Co-op** is (not surprisingly) open the same hours with the same services. Stroll down av. de la Gare on Thursday mornings to buy goods both edible and wearable at the **public market.** (Open 7:30am-noon.)

Sights and Festivals The tourist office runs 1½-hour **guided tours** of Martigny at 10am and 2pm in July and August (12SFr, students 5SFr, family ticket 25SFr; includes admission to the Fondation Gianadda). Martigny's most engaging attraction is the **Fondation Pierre Gianadda,** rue du Forum 59 (tel. 722 39 78; fax 722 52 85; http://www.gianadda.ch). Local engineer Léonard Gianadda discovered the vestiges of a Gallo-Roman temple here in 1976, and, when his brother died in a plane crash two months later, he set up a foundation to preserve his beloved brother's memory. Around and above the ancient temple he constructed an oddly shaped cultural center to bear his brother's name—think landing pod meets pineapple warehouse. More eclectic randomness awaits inside. The first floor **Gallo-Roman**

Museum showcases classical works like the Octoduran bronzes discovered in Martigny, while the central courtyard below hosts blockbuster **international traveling exhibitions.** The provenance lines are a joy for knowledgable museum-goers to compare; there are enough well-known lenders like the Centre Pompidou mixed in with mysterious "private collections" to impress upon viewers the once in a lifetime nature of these assemblages. A peek into the always busy museum shop reveals that Picasso, Goya, Chagall, Braque, Dufy, and Miró were recent features. The foundation celebrates its 20th anniversary year (Nov. 18, 1997 to Jan. 18, 1998) with an exhibition of Russian icons from the famed Tretiakov Gallery in Moscow, and a ceremonial concert of Orthodox Liturgical chants sung by the Choir of the Patriarchate of Moscow. (Open daily 10am-6pm.) More retrospectives of the most impressive sort will follow: Diego Rivera and Gauguin. Descend the stairs to the **Automobile Museum** to scan more than 50 vintage cars—Bugattis, gleaming early Peugots, and a Rolls Royce Silver Ghost—built between 1897 and 1939, most in working condition and all unique. The surrounding garden successfully blends unearthed Roman remains with modern sculptures, including some excellent ones by Brancusi, Miró, and Rodin. The foundation regularly hosts quality **classical music concerts,** many in conjunction with the **Festival Tibor Varga** and the **Montreux-Vevey Classical Music Festival.** Call ahead for tickets (20-80SFr, students half-price). (Fondation hours vary; call ahead. 12SFr, students 5SFr, family ticket 25SFr. Tickets include admission to the Gallo-Roman and Automobile Museums, the temporary exhibitions, and the Sculpture Gardens. Free guided tours Wed. at 8pm or by prior arrangement. Wheelchair accessible.)

Martigny also has a handful of ruins that are worth a short ramble. Most of the Roman settlement is not marked so well; the Mithraic temple ruins huddle inconspicuously beneath an apartment block 50m from the Fondation. The grassy 4th-century **Amphithéâtre Romain,** however, is well worth the short detour over the railway tracks from the Fondation Gianadda gardens (follow the brown signs; free). Re-opened in 1991 after two decades of excavation work, the structure is the spectacular setting for the final contest of the Valais **cow fighting** season at the start of October. Farther out from the center down av. du Grand-St-Bernard, the **Semblanet Mill** (tel. 722 51 98) restored its four water wheels, 18th-century threshers, and giant millstones to working condition as recently as 1994. One of the oldest industrial mills in Switzerland, Semblanet offers the added attraction of an on-site restaurant serving Valaisian specialties alongside local wine, honey, and bread from the mill. (Open Tues.-Sun. 10am-10pm. 5SFr, children 2SFr. Guided tours 30SFr.) **Le Château de la Bâtiaz,** the ruins of a 13th-century castle that once belonged to the bishops of Sion, crouches on a hill overlooking Martigny. From the station, head along av. de la Gare, and turn right at pl. Centrale along rue Marc-Morand. Climb the massive stone tower extending over an outcrop of bare rock for a bird's-eye perspective of the flat Rhône floodplain. (Open daily mid-July to mid-Aug. 10am-6pm. Free.) Now an apartment building, the 17th-century **Grand Maison,** rue Marc Morand 7, near pl. Centrale, was once a hostel-stop for 18th- and 19th-century literati on their grand tours. Rousseau (1754), Goethe (1779), Stendhal (1800), Byron (1816), and Michelet (1830) all rested their weary heads here. Equally elegant, **Maison Supersaxo,** rue des Alpes 1, behind the tourist office, is Martigny's oldest building (1440). Within its walls, Valais bigwig Georges Supersaxo plotted his attack on the Château Bâtiaz. His 1518 siege ended in a ruinous fire, leaving only an old woman and her three goats in residence.

Each year in the beginning of October the town hosts the **Foire du Valais,** the regional trade fair of the Valais canton, in the blue and yellow CERU convention center. Local businesses and farmers offer their best, from shoes to marble sculptures. (Oct. 3-12 10am-9pm. 8SFr, children 4SFr.) The final Sunday brings all-day cow-fighting; the knock-'em-all-down finale decides the reigning queen of all Valaisian cows. The event is a must-see if you are in southern Switzerland. The **Foire du Lard** (Bacon Fair) has overtaken the pl. Centrale every first Monday in December since the Middle Ages. Traditionally, Valais mountain folk descended on Martigny to stock up on pork products for the winter, but now the festival has expanded to a large open-air market—though the theme is still "pig." Martigny also sponsors film, theater, and music festivals throughout the year, notably the **International Folklore Festival** every two years. The city is also an important venue for the annual **Tibor Varga Classical Music Season,** which brings big-league European orchestras and performers like Alfred Brendel and Vladmir Ashkenazy to town every July and August. Tickets are available through the Fondation Gianadda (20-80SFr; for more info, see http://www.nouvelliste.ch/varga/tvarga.htm).

■ Sion

Schizophrenic Sion has a noisy, heavy industrial tangle of towering blocks bordering the Rhône, while the quiet, churchy old town cowers beneath two rocky bluffs topped with castle ruins. Sion's three castles sharpen the flat valley skyline and provide focal points for many local landscape painters. The moody town inspired writers and poets like Goethe, Rousseau, and Rilke. At times you may feel like you're walking through Gauguin's Brittany, so intentionally quaint and traditional is everything, but Sion has proven itself as forward-looking as it is adept in canned culture. The city lost its bid for the 1972 Winter Olympics to Sapporo and just recently for the 2002 Games to Salt Lake City, Utah. Nevertheless, it has enthusiastically announced its application for the 2006 Winter Games. Red and white flags flutter in the valley winds and the tourist shops are already glutted with pre-Olympic paraphernalia.

Practical Information As a conspicuous addition to its Olympic candidacy profile, Sion now boasts an aspiring international **airport** (tel. 322 24 80; fax 322 29 68) just outside the town. At the moment, it's only a regional hub with daily flights to Zurich, charter flights of glacier aviation, and an Aviation School. **Trains** pass every 30 minutes in each direction along the Rhône Valley, going west to **Martigny** (15min., 8.40SFr), **Aigle** (25min., 16.60SFr), **Montreux** (50min., 21SFr), and **Lausanne** (1¼hr., 27SFr); and east to **Sierre** (10min., 5.40SFr) and **Brig** (30min., 16.60SFr), where you connect to **Zermatt** (48SFr) and **Saas Fee** (28SFr). The **train station** (tel. 157 22 22; open daily 6am-8:45pm) provides **currency exchange** (open daily 6am-8:30pm), **lockers** (3-5SFr), **luggage storage** (5SFr for 24hr.; open 6am-8:45pm), **bike rental** (22SFr), and a **rail information** office (open Mon.-Fri. 8:30am-noon and 1:30-6:30pm, Sat. 8am-12:30pm and 1:45-5pm). Just outside, Switzerland's largest post bus station congests the square with a blur of yellow buses, going near and far (mostly near). To get to the **tourist office,** pl. de la Planta (tel. 322 85 86; fax 322 18 82), from the train station, walk directly up av. de la Gare, and turn right on rue de Lausanne. The office provides free room reservations, a Billetel desk (tel. 322 85 93) for tickets to any event from Sion to Geneva, and two-hour guided tours. (July-Aug. Tues. and Thurs. 2pm; additional group tours on request; 8SFr, children and students 5SFr. Open July 15-Aug. 15 Mon.-Fri. 8am-6pm, Sat. 10am-4pm; Aug. 16-July 14 Mon.-Fri. 8:30am-noon and 2-5:30pm, Sat 9am-noon.) Across pl. de la Gare to the right, **American Express** resides within **Valais Incoming,** in Lathion Voyages la Gare 4, av. de Tourbillon 3, P.O. Box 579, CH-1951 (tel. 329 24 23; fax 329 24 29; open Mon.-Fri. 8am-noon and 1:30-6pm, Sat. 8am-noon). For a **taxi,** call 322 33 33. For the **police,** call 117. In a **fire,** call 118. For an **ambulance,** call 323 33 33. The **post office,** pl. de la Gare, is left of the train station. (Open Mon.-Fri. 7:30am-noon and 1:30-6:15pm, Sat. 8:15-11am). The **postal code** is CH-1950, and the **telephone code** is 027.

Accommodations Built in 1991, the **Auberge de Jeunesse (HI),** av. de l'Industrie 2 (tel. 323 74 70; fax 323 74 38), maintains clean bathrooms, skinny semicircular balconies, and lockers in every room. Leaving the train station, walk left and descend the ramp to rue de la Blancherie; continue left underneath the train tracks. Look for the crazy colorful artwork in front. The reception desk overlooks an airy dining room that in turn leads onto a patio with table tennis. Although a large establishment, the hostel can often be fully booked by marauding school groups in July and August. The closest HI hostel is in Montreux (ack!), so call ahead. (Reception 7:30-9:30am and 5-10pm. Curfew 10pm; keys on request. Lockout 9:30am-5pm. 4-bed dorms 25.80SFr first night, then 23.30SFr; 3-bed dorms 29.80SFr, 27.30SFr; 2-bed dorms 32.80SFr, 30.30SFr. Breakfast included. Dinner 11SFr if you reserve it. Kitchen facilities 2SFr.) Staying anywhere else will give you a painful sting. The cheapest hotel rooms are at the smartly renovated **Hôtel Elite,** av. du Midi 6 (tel. 322 03 27; fax 322 23 61), on the edge of the *vieille ville* and surrounded by stores and cafés. From the station, head up av. de la Gare and turn right. Pristine rooms with TV, phone, private bathroom, and extravagant mountain views. (Reception 6:30am-midnight. Singles 70SFr; doubles 120SFr. Breakfast included. Visa, MC, AmEx.) Enterprising (or desperate) travelers seeking a cheap bed can try some of the villages outside Sion. The tourist office's imaginatively titled booklet *Sion* gives details. (In Pont-de-la-Morge singles run 35-40SFr, doubles 68-80SFr; in Saint-Léonard 50-70SFr, 70-90SFr.) Post buses run to both towns. **Camping Les Iles,** rte d'Aproz (tel. 346 43 47; fax 346 68 47), is a riverside five-star site. Take a very short bus ride past the aerodome to Aproz. (6.80SFr; tents 9SFr. Low season: 5.40SFr; 6.50SFr. Open Jan.-Oct.)

Food and Wine The stone streets of the *vieille ville* are flanked by cafés and restaurants, most with white-washed terraces where patrons sip glasses of *Valais Fendant* or *Johannisberg-Tavillon,* the leading labels in town. Consult the tourist office for organized **wine-tasting excursions** and a list of local cellars. A long-distance path through the vineyards, *le chemin du vignoble,* passes close to Sion and through tasting territory. Always ring before you arrive at a *cave,* and try to rustle up a group if you want the proprietor to be more welcoming and forthcoming. One *centre de dégustation* is the **Varone vineyard,** av. Grand-Champsec 30 (tel. 203 56 83), just across the river. (Open Mon. 2-6:30pm, Tues.-Fri. 10am-noon and 2-6:30pm, Sat. 10am-noon and 2-5pm.) Picnics for hiking await immediate assembly at **Co-op City,** pl. du Midi, right off av. de la Gare along av. du Midi. (Open Mon. 1-6:30pm, Tues.-Thurs. 8:30am-6:30pm, Fri. 8:30am-8pm, Sat. 8am-5pm.) Not bigger or better or noticeably different (same hours even), the **Migros Centre** has 19 different stores as well as a supermarket and restaurant (main courses 8-15SFr) on av. de France one block left from the station. **Manora,** at the corner of av. du Midi and rue de la Dent-Blanche, on the ground floor of the Placette department store and supermarket, leads the pack of the buffet self-serve restaurants (entrees 5-13SFr). (Open Mon.-Thurs. 8am-7pm, Fri. 8am-7:30pm, Sat.-Sun. 8am-6pm.) Huddle amid dark old wood in the **Restaurant la Bergère,** av. de la Gare 30 (tel. 22 14 81), which specializes in pizza and pasta (10-17SFr) and sandwiches (5-7SFr). (Open Mon.-Fri. 7am-1am, Sat. 10:30am-1am, Sun. 5pm-1am. Closed Sun. in July. Visa, MC, Amex, DC.)

Sights It's an age-old problem: how to keep the peace between a bossy bishop, a grumpy chapter, and a fractious town. Sion's solution was to build the bishop's house, the now-towering Château de Tourbillon, on one hill; the chapter's seat, the Château de Valère, on another; and the municipal powerhouse, the Château de la Majorie, down in the town. (A laser beams around this power triangle Thurs.-Sat. nightfall-1am.) The first two castles stare each other down from across the hilltops and offer panoramas of the entire Valais valley, the Rhône, the Alps, and the city itself. From the station, proceed up av. de la Gare opposite and turn right on rue de Lausanne, left on rue du Grand-Pont, then right up the narrow rue des Châteaux just past the bright orange town hall. To the left on the way up is the Château de la Majorie, home to the **Musée des Beaux-Arts** (Fine Arts Museum), pl. de la Majorie 15-19 (tel. 606 46 90). Devotees of Valais art will be thrilled, but even the uninitiated will enjoy the 8-piece metal sculpture suspended from the ceiling of the stark Jesuit chapel—from the right viewpoint, the sculpture resolves into a seamless replica of the building's interior. See becastled landscapes and dour-looking Valais matrons galore. (Open Tues.-Sun. 10am-noon and 2-6pm. 5SFr, students 2.50SFr.) Up the Château de Valère's hill, the shabby but intriguing **Basilique Notre Dame de Valère** boasts the oldest working organ in the world (c. 1390-1430) and presents its annual festival of ancient organ music in July and August every Saturday at 4pm (20SFr, students 10SFr; call the tourist office or 323 57 67 for details). The Château also houses the **Cantonal Museum of History and Ethnology.** (Open Tues.-Sun. 10am-6pm. Cathedral free. Museum 5SFr, students 2.50SFr.) The more challenging lefthand hill projects higher with the imposing ruins of the **Château de Tourbillon**. Once the summer residence of the bishop, it is now the seasonal nest of mice and the odd sparrow. Although endowed with typical ruin fare of crumbling walls and ambiguous architecture, the payoff for the grueling hike is definitely the view. (Open Tues.-Sun. 10am-6pm. Free.)

Sion's most amusing museum is the **Natural History Museum,** 42 av. de la Gare (tel. 606 47 30), up the road from pl. de la Planta and the tourist office. Swiss museum buffs who realize that Swiss natural history means stuffed armadillos will not be disappointed by the "Honey, guess what I shot last night" hodge-podge of local relics. There is the contorted body of a chamois pulled out of a glacier in 1920 after centuries on ice, dinosaur footprints from Emossons, and the scrappy Last Bear in the Valais, who required the efforts of an entire Valaisian posse before giving up the ghost. (Open Tues.-Sun. 2-6pm. 3SFr, students 1.5SFr, children free.)

The *vielle ville*, with its medieval churches and colorfully painted buildings, hosts yearly music festivals. The open-air **Jazz Festival** takes over the streets at 11pm on Friday from May through November. (20SFr, festival passes 150SFr; tickets available at tourist office or at the gate.) Most summer evenings bring **free concerts** of classical music at the **Academie de Musique** (tel. 322 66 52). From July to September there are also major orchestral events during the **Tibor Varga Festival** (tel. 323 43 17; fax 326 46 62; email festivalvargasion@vtx.ch; http://www.nouvelliste.ch/varga/tvarga.htm; tickets 20-80SFr, available through Billetel).

■ Brig (Brigue)

A junction town at the base of the Simplon, Furka, and Grimsel passes, Brig grew up as a place to change your horses and trade your wares, and even now the town is mainly a place to go through rather than go to. Nonetheless, Brig burgeons with slender-spired churches, narrow houses, and slate-gray squares. Along the Rhône Valley, trains go to **Sierre** (every 30min., 30min., 12.20SFr); **Sion** (every 30min., 40min., 16.60SFr); **Lausanne** (every hr., 2hr., 43SFr); and **Geneva** (every hr., 2¾hr., 55SFr). Through the Lötschberg tunnel, trains head to **Bern** (every hr., 1¾hr., 46SFr) and **Interlaken** (every hr., 1½hr., 39SFr). The Simplon tunnel trains lead to **Domodossola** in Italy (every hr., 30min., 12.20SFr) and **Locarno** (every hr., 2½hr., 48SFr, change at Domodossola). A mass of bus lines spread their tentacles through the surrounding hillsides from Bahnhofpl. The most important leaves every hour for **Saas Fee** (1¼hr., 17.40SFr) from just left of the station exit. The hyper-helpful, cyber-friendly office in the station library helps bewildered travelers sort all of this out. (Open Mon.-Fri. 8am-6:30pm, Sat. 8am-5pm.) If you insist on exploring, get information at the **tourist office** (tel. 923 19 01; fax 924 31 44), up the yellow stairs on the first floor of the train station. They have piles of hotel info, but beware—they tend to clam up if you ask them about anything outside of Brig. (Open mid-June to mid-Oct. Mon.-Fri. 8:30am-noon and 1:30-6pm, Sat. 8:30am-noon and 2-5:30pm; mid-Oct. to mid-June Mon.-Fri. 8:30am-noon and 1:30-6pm, Sat. 8:30am-noon.) The station has **currency exchange** (tel. 922 24 24; open Mon.-Sat. 6:15am-7:30pm, Sun. 8-11:30am and 2-6pm); **lockers** (3-5SFr); **luggage storage** (open daily 7am-7pm); and a free phone line to all hotels. A **Migros** stands on Belalpstr., on your left as you leave the station. (Open Mon.-Fri. 8:15am-6:30pm, Sat. 7:45am-4pm.) The **post office** is directly opposite the train station, Bahnhofstr. 1 (tel. 923 66 56; open Mon.-Fri. 7:30am-noon and 1:30-6:15pm, Sat. 7:30-11am). The **postal code** is CH-3900, and the **telephone code** is 027.

Zermatt and the Matterhorn

A trick of the valley blocks out the great Alpine summits ringing Zermatt, allowing the Matterhorn (4478m) to rise alone above the town. Instantly recognizable and stamped on everything from scarves to pencils by Zermatt's merchants of kitsch, the peak still causes an intake of breath whenever one looks up. At dawn it blazes bright orange; some days—some weeks—it is swathed in clouds, completely hidden from view. Zermatt itself is mostly a missable mix of tourists and rock jocks. The main road, Bahnhofstraße, is often populated by hikers with knee-pants and tandem walking sticks, snowboarders crucified on neon boards slung across their shoulders, and skiers with their unmistakable snow struts and unnatural tans. Unfortunately, Zermatt's tourism tends to be so slick that at "random" moments, officials traipse herds of photogenic goats through town to lend a (rather pungent) air of "authentic traditional Swiss charm" to this largely un-Swiss village. But while tourists shoot "candid" photos of their kids being tormented by ornery goats, you could escape it all with a short hike or cable car ride to lonely Alpine meadows and splintered icefalls—feasts for the eye and the real reason to visit Zermatt.

PRACTICAL INFORMATION

To preserve the Alpine air from exhaust fumes, Zermatt has outlawed cars and buses; locals in their electrical buggies alternately dodge and target pedestrians. The road head at Täsch has a covered **parking lot** for 6SFr per day; you can leave your car in an uncovered lot for 3-5SFr per day. The only way to Zermatt is by the hourly **BVZ (Brig-Visp-Zermatt) rail** line. The main street, Bahnhofstraße, runs in front of the station and houses many of the town's hotels and restaurants.

Tourist Office: Bahnhofpl. (tel. 967 01 81; fax 967 01 85; email zermatt@wallis.ch; http://www.zermatt.ch), in the station complex. All the hard facts you could possibly need on Zermatt are contained in the chunky free booklet *Prato Borni* and the glossy *Zermatt*. Both appear in summer and winter editions. Panorama plans with suggested hikes 1.60SFr. To navigate on a hike, however, you will need a real map, available here or at kiosks and bookstores along Bahnhofstr. Open mid-June to mid-Oct. Mon.-Fri. 8:30am-6pm, Sat. 8:30am-7pm, Sun. 9:30am-noon and 4-7pm; mid-Oct. to mid-June Mon.-Fri. 8:30am-noon and 1:30-6pm, Sat. 8:30am-noon.

Mountaineering (Bergführerbüro; tel. 966 24 60; fax 966 24 69) and **Ski School Office** (Skischulbüro; tel. 967 24 66), both on Bahnhofstr. From the train station, turn right on Bahnhofstr. and walk 5min. past the post office. Posts detailed weather forecasts every morning for the next 4 days and coordinates guided private and group climbing expeditions. In summer, groups go daily up to the Breithorn (120SFr), Pollux (230SFr), and Castor (240SFr). The Matterhorn is 670SFr but requires technical experience and at least a week's prior training. Prices do not include equipment, hut accommodations, or lifts to the departure points. Whatever you do, get insured (30SFr) or be prepared to risk a 4-figure helicopter rescue bill from Air Zermatt (tel. 967 34 87; fax 967 40 04). Open July-Sept. Mon.-Fri. 8:30am-noon and 4-7pm, Sat. 4-7pm, Sun. 10am-noon and 4-7pm.

Trains: Bahnhofpl. (tel. 967 22 07). The only way into or out of Zermatt is the hourly BVZ (Brig-Visp-Zermatt) rail line. Join at **Brig** (1½hr., 37SFr, round-trip 63SFr); **Visp** (if coming from Lausanne or Sion; 34SFr, round-trip 58SFr); **Stalden-Saas** (if coming from Saas Fee; 1hr., 30SFr, round-trip 51SFr); or **Täsch** (every 20min., 7.20SFr). The station has a free direct phone line to all of Zermatt's hotels, as well as **lockers** (2-8SFr) and **hotel taxis** waiting to round up guests after each train arrives.

Currency Exchange: Zermatt Tours, next to the tourist office. No commission. Open Mon.-Fri. 8:30am-noon and 2-6pm, Sat. 8:30am-noon and 2-7pm, Sun. 9am-noon and 3-6pm. **Banks** are open Mon.-Fri. 8:30am-noon and 2:30-6pm.

Bike and Ski Rental: Roc Sport (tel. 967 39 27) on Kirchstr. (left at the church) or its outlet **Sulen Sport** on Hoffmattstr. Mountain bikes 35SFr per day. 10% discount on bikes and skis for youth hostelers. Open Mon.-Sat. 8-10am and 4-6pm. Visa, MC, AmEx, DC. Also try **Slalom Sport** (tel. 966 23 66) on Kirchstr. Open Mon.-Sat. 8am-noon and 2-7pm, Sun. 8am-noon and 4-6:30pm.

English-Language Library: In the English Church behind the post office. Small collection of battered novels loaned on the honor system. Be honorable!

Weather Conditions: Call 162 or check the window of the Bergführerbüro. **Winter Avalanche Information,** tel. 187.

Emergencies: Police, tel. 117. **Fire,** tel. 118. **Ambulance,** tel. 67 12 12. **24hr. Alpine Rescue,** tel. 967 20 00.

Post Office: Bahnhofstr., in Arcade Mont-Cervin 5min. to the right of the station. Open Mon.-Fri. 8am-noon and 1:30-6pm, Sat. 8:30-11am. **Postal Code:** CH-3920.

Telephone Code: 027.

ACCOMMODATIONS

Climbers, hikers, and snowboarders buoy up the demand for budget beds in Zermatt. A healthy supply generally provides adequate accommodations, but finding a dorm bed on the spot can be a squeeze July through August, Christmas and New Year's, and mid-February through mid-March. Many hotels in winter and all chalets in summer only accept bookings for a week at a time. In desperation, some campers are tempted to park their bodies illegally in the wide-open spaces above town—this practice can incur fines between 50 and 100SFr.

Jugendherberge (HI), Winkelmatten (tel. 967 23 20; fax 967 53 06), is a 15min. walk from the station. Turn right along Bahnhofstr. and left at the church. Cross the river, take the second street to the right (at the Jugendherberge sign), and select the left fork in front of Hotel Rhodania. The hostel's on the mountain side of town, so that you get a full frontal view of the Matterhorn from your bedroom window (which makes up for the slight overcrowding). Friendly staff, a convivial terrace where folks sit around and tell hiking tales, and 2 yummy meals are all included in the higher-than-normal hostel price. Reception in summer 7:30-9am and 4pm-midnight; in winter 6:30-9am and 3pm-midnight. No lockout. Curfew 11:30pm. Dorms 40SFr first night, then 37.50SFr; one double 108SFr, 96SFr. Breakfast, sleepsack, showers, and dinner (kosher and vegetarian available) included. Laundry 8-16SFr. Closed May and late Oct. to mid-Dec. Visa, MC, AmEx, DC.

Hotel Bahnhof, Bahnhofstr. (tel. 967 24 06; fax 967 72 16). 1min. from the station—turn left and pass the Gornergratbahn. A charming older woman keeps a wood-paneled hotel popular with climbers and clean communal-types seeking a peaceful break. Dorms 26-28SFr; 4- to 6-bed dorms 32SFr; singles 40-50SFr; doubles 71-79SFr. Dorms do not have sheets. No breakfast, but kitchen and large dining room in the basement. Open mid-Dec. to mid-Oct.

Hotel Weisshorn, Bahnhofstr. (tel. 967 11 12; fax 967 38 39). From the train station, turn right along Bahnhofstr. The hotel is 30m past the church. Low, paneled ceilings and winding staircases draw guests into this hotel. The beds bulge with cushy comforters while the bathrooms sparkle, resplendent with very pink towels. Reception daily 7am-10pm. Singles 46-55SFr, with shower, TV, and phone 63-78SFr; doubles 94-106SFr, 110-142SFr; triples 114-150SFr. Breakfast included. Reservations necessary in winter high season, up to one week in advance. Visa, MC.

Hotel Garni Tannenhof (tel. 967 31 88; fax 967 12 64). From the station, turn right on Bahnhofstr., walk 300m, take the second left after the bank, then turn right. The hotel serves up comfortable rooms and a generous breakfast buffet. Rustic furniture, rich rugs, and copious sunlight make this hotel as welcoming as the affable couple that runs it. Reception daily 7am-7pm. Singles 45-48SFr, with shower 60-70SFr; doubles 90-96SFr, 110-116SFr; triples 105-120SFr. Reserve at least 1 month in advance in winter, 2-3 weeks in summer. Closed Oct.-Dec. 15. Visa, AmEx, DC.

Hotel Cima Garni (tel. 967 23 37; fax 967 55 39), 250m from the station. This charming bed-and-breakfast blends a standard Swiss exterior (red shutters on brown building) with a remarkably modern interior of subdued grays and very shiny pine paneling—you can almost smell the Pledge. Oriental rugs line the stairs to the 25 rooms, all in a spotless state of Swiss serenity and almost all with balcony. The prices can be scary, but the comfort is well worth it. Singles 37-70SFr, with shower 50-100SFr; doubles 74-140SFr, 100-200SFr. Breakfast included. Visa.

Camping Alphubel (tel. 967 36 35) in Täsch. What with Zermatt car-free and all, caravanners and motorists can park their vehicles and stay here. 5.50SFr; tent 5SFr; car 4SFr; caravan 6SFr. Open May to mid-Oct.

Camping Matterhorn Zermatt, Bahnhofstr. (tel. 967 39 21), 5min. to the left of the train station. Perhaps Zermatt's only unscenic spot. The spotty, grass-covered area looks onto train tracks and landing paragliders. Reception May-Sept. daily 8:30-10am and 5:20-7pm. Showers included. 8SFr, children 5.50SFr.

Mountain Huts: The tourist office has a list of private huts in the Zermatt area. For 23SFr a night, they offer a good deal for bona fide climbers, but others will find them too high for a proper night's sleep. **Schönbiel** (tel. 967 13 54; 2694m); **Rothorn** (tel. 967 20 43; 3198m), the crowded **Gandegg** (tel. 967 21 96; 3029m); **Hörnli** (tel. 967 27 69; 3260m); and **Monte Rosa** (tel. 967 21 15; 2795m; crampons and guide advised) are all open July-Sept. and accessible to walkers if there's no snow. All are about full day's hike from Zermatt.

FOOD AND NIGHTLIFE

Rather than charge the usual inflated Alpine prices, a surprising number of the cafés along Bahnhofstr. leave both your wallet and your stomach pretty full. Several supermarkets provide picnic supplies for day hikes.

Restaurants and Bars

Walliser Kanne, Bahnhofstr. (tel. 967 22 98), next to the post office. At street level, this establishment offers inventive Swiss food on a 4-language menu with such dishes as *Käsespätzli* (16.50SFr), *Rösti Walliserkanne* (17SFr), deer steaks and dumplings (20SFr), and *Apfelstrudel* with vanilla sauce (6SFr), as well as the usual pizza and pasta (13-19SFr). Open daily 10am-midnight. Visa, MC, AmEx, DC. This sedate people-watching outpost hides the somewhat rowdy **Dance Garage "Harley"** bar and disco downstairs. Beer of the week 4SFr; cider 6SFr. Nachos 5SFr. Open daily 7pm-3am; happy hour until 10:30pm.

The North Wall Bar (tel. 967 28 63). Head over the river on Kirchstr. and take the second right. *En route* to the youth hostel. No frills, 100%-English-speaking climbers' haunt where skiing and mountaineering videos play every evening alongside the less dynamic (but still potentially dangerous) dart games. The place to scrounge a job in Zermatt. The kitchen will serve you anything you like, as long as it's pizza (10SFr, plus 1SFr for fancy topping like mussels, corn, broccoli, or egg). At 4.50Sfr for 0.5liter, the beer is probably the cheapest in town. Open mid-June to Sept. and mid-Dec. to April daily 6:30pm-midnight.

Café du Pont, Bahnhofstr. (tel. 967 43 43), 7min. from the station at the top of Bahnhofstr. and next to Hotel Weisshorn. Zermatt's oldest restaurant still maintains its romantic atmosphere with subdued lighting and soothing music. Browse through the large menus, burnt into slabs of wood, as you listen to the river. Then try to decide between stick-to-your-ribs Swiss dishes like *raclette* (7SFr), *Rösti* (14SFr), and *fondue du Pont* (22SFr). Sandwiches 6.50SFr. Open June-Oct. and Dec.-April daily 9am-midnight; food served 11am-3pm and 5-10pm.

Swiss Rock Café, Bahnhofstr. (tel. 967 68 80). Sleek new restaurant and bar with a blue waterfall and a line of stuffed parrots. Neon lights and wood and metal decor—a very trendy shade of blue, mind you. Serves never-ending bratwurst with baked potatoes (15SFr), corn on the cob (5SFr), and *enchiladas* (18SFr). Open 10:30am-12:30am. Piano bar downstairs has beer at 5.20SFr for 0.5L. 2-for-1 drinks 6-7pm. Open daily until 2am. Closed May and mid-Oct. to Nov.

Grampi's Pub, Bahnhofstr. (tel. 966 77 88). Central bar welcomes serious drinkers by day and thumps with dance music by night. Draft beer 3.50SFr for 0.25L; bottled beer 4.50-7SFr. Nightly DJ 8:30pm-2am. Open daily 9am-2am.

342 ■ VALAIS (WALLIS)

Markets

Co-op Center, across from the station. Open Mon.-Sat. 8:15am-12:15pm and 1:45-6:30pm, Sun. 4-6:30pm.

Migros, Hofmattstr., down from Bahnhofstr. between the station and the church. Open Mon.-Fri. 8:30am-12:15pm and 2-6:30pm, Sat. 8:30am-12:15pm and 2-6pm, Sun. 4-6:30pm.

SKIING, SPORTS, AND ENTERTAINMENT

Seventy-three lifts, 14,200m of combined elevation, and 245km of prepared runs make Zermatt one of the world's best-equipped ski centers. Where it really outshines its rivals, however, is in its ski-mountaineering and high-level ski-touring potential. The town also has more **summer ski trails** than any other Alpine ski resort—36 sq. km of year-round runs between 2900 and 3900m. In the summer, the **ski school** (tel. 967 24 66) offers group classes for skiing and snowboarding (either activity: 1 day 60SFr, 6 days 130SFr). **Ski and boot rental** is standard throughout the area—43SFr for one day, 157SFr for six—but youth hostel residents secure an additional 10% discount at Roc Sport (see p. 339). Sports stores flood Zermatt, and finding a reliable dealer is not a problem. Note that most shops are open daily 8am to noon and 2 to 7pm and that renting equipment the evening before will maximize your time on the slopes. Zermatt's **ski passes** operate on a regional system. You can buy passes for any combination of days and regions (Matterhorn complex, Gornergrat complex, and Sunnegga complex). For example, the Matterhorn region costs 58SFr for one day, 240SFr for six days; all three regions combined cost 60SFr, 292SFr. The Klein Matterhorn/Trockener Steg sub-region is open in summer only, and you cannot use passes to ascend after 1pm (1 day 58SFr, 6 days 204SFr, 3 days within a 6-day period 150SFr).

Zermatt is at least three hours from any worthwhile indoor attraction; when it rains you will quickly wish you had scheduled your trip to North Dakota instead. The posher hotels have **swimming pools,** with **Hotel Christiania** (tel. 967 19 07) offering the biggest. Follow the right bank of the river past the Rothorn/Sunnegga cable railway station. (10SFr, children 6SFr. Open Mon., Wed., and Fri.-Sat. 8am-8pm, Tues. 2-8pm, Thurs. 8am-10pm.) For an additional 10SFr, you can work up a sweat in the sauna or go off to another hotel to find a massage. Less self-indulgently sensual pursuits await at the **Cinema Vernissage** (tel. 967 66 36), at the Centre Culturel on Hofmattstr., which has two or three screenings nightly Monday to Saturday of nearly new releases, usually in English (15SFr, hostelers 13SFr; Visa, MC, AmEx, DC). Another rainy day refuge is the **Alpine Museum** (tel. 967 41 00), near the post office. If you enjoy learning the gory details of climbing expeditions gone horribly wrong and poring over the frayed ropes and mangled shoes that remain, this museum is for you. Of special note is the room marked "14th of July 1865," a collection of pictures, letters, and records commemorating the tragic first ascent of the Matterhorn. See the haunting photograph of the young Lord Francis Douglas, whose mortal remains were never found. In the graveyard next to the church, the bodies of those who never descended alive lie next to victims of sad tales as of yet untold. (Open July-Sept. daily 10am-noon and 4-6pm; Oct.-June Mon.-Fri. and Sun. 4:30-6:30pm. 3SFr, children 1SFr. Guide in English 1SFr.)

The town celebrates with festivities throughout August. During the **Alpine Folklore Parade,** locals take a break from their mountain chores mid-month and dust off their alphorns and frilly costumes. The Roman Catholic church sporadically hosts **classical music concerts** (20-25SFr) throughout the month, and at the end of August, thighs burn through the **Matterhornlauf,** a fun-run that climbs 1001m from Zermatt to the Schwarzsee at the foot of the Matterhorn.

OUTDOORS AROUND ZERMATT

Outstanding walks into the world of glaciers and high mountains spread from Zermatt in every direction. Although these paths are well-made and well-marked, a

ZERMATT AND THE MATTERHORN ■ 343

proper non-panoramic map is essential for safety and adds to your appreciation of the mountains. Lifts and railways to the south and east are also valuable hiking tools; they can save you difficult climbs and precious energy. Swisspasses will win you a 25% discount on many of these lifts, but Eurailpasses are generally not valid. Prudent walkers should come prepared (see **Health,** p. 15). Zermatt is particularly prone to sudden electrical storms, and you may need to dive for cover. The *Bergführerbüro* posts a conservative pictoral weather forecast in its window on Bahnhofstr. To rent hiking boots, try **Skihaus Matterhorn,** Bahnhofstr. (tel. 967 29 56), or **Glacier Sport,** Bahnhofstr. (tel. 967 21 67). One-day rentals are 14SFr; seven days 52SFr; fourteen days 80SFr. Both stores are open daily 8am to noon and 2 to 7pm.

West and Northwest

West of Zermatt, the mountains are savage, spiky pinnacles. The **Zinalrothorn** (4221m), **Ober Gabelhorn** (4063m), and **Dent Blanche** (4357m) are some of the toughest climbs around the town. An easier, though long, walk to **Zmutt** (1936m, 1hr.) and the **Schönbielhütte** (2694m, 4hr.), leads along the base of these magnificent peaks and offers the most dramatic encounter with the Matterhorn's north face. The path is wide, clear, and well-marked, and the views get exponentially better as you rise. From Zermatt, follow Bahnhofstr. past the church and to the river. Walk 100m past the bank and then follow the sign to the right. A steady gradient pulls you up through Arolla pines to the weathered chalets of the minuscule hamlet of Zmutt. The path then continues through the meadows above a small reservoir, granting views of the Hörnli ridge and the Matterhorn. As you go on, the Matterhorn's north wall, which drops 200m with an average gradient well over 45°, comes breathtakingly into view. The hike becomes more difficult as it ascends by lakes and waterfalls at the outlet of the rock-strewn Zmuttgletscher and follows the lateral ridge to the **Schönbielhütte,** an ideal spot for lunchtime carbo-loading of pasta or *Rösti* while you examine the icefalls rising from three sides. On the return journey, the valley frames the **Rimpfischhorn** (4199m) and **Strahlhorn** (4190m) The full-day hike is 25km, with 1050m of gentle, beautiful elevation.

Southwest

No visit to Zermatt is emotionally complete without struggling up to the **Hörnlihütte,** the base camp for the normal route up the Matterhorn and a good platform for watching brightly colored dots claw their way upward along the ridge. A legend in the history and literature of the Matterhorn, the 1600m ascent is for the fit and well-booted only; a cable car to the Schwarzsee saves you 900m of elevation (18.50SFr; round-trip 29.50SFr). Leave Zermatt along the left bank of the Matter Vispa, as for the Zmutt/Schönbielhütte hike. A mile or so from Zermatt, after a few minutes of climbing, a wide track marked "Zum See, Schwarzsee und Hörnlihütte" heads down left across the river. Follow the three-hour path as it zigzags steeply up to the tiny lake, the **Schwarzsee** (2552m), admiring the monstrous Gorner gorges on the left. A group of climbers caught in a snowstorm built the chapel on the lake in an act of piety when their prayers to Mary were answered and the clouds miraculously lifted. The path becomes rockier and wilder as it joins the true northeast ridge of the Matterhorn, climbing gently at first but ending in a merciless, exposed arête (sharp ridge) by the buildings at Hörnli. Rest at the finish and know that casual hikers *cannot* continue above the hut. More than 500 people have died in the mile above this point, as a sobering walk around Zermatt's cemeteries will prove. A guide, perfect physical condition, a 4am start, and extensive rock climbing experience (at least PD+) are essential requirements for proceeding past the hut. To descend a different way, bear right at the Schwarzsee to the Furgg cable car terminus and follow the path down to the beck. The path traverses a steep cliff but is stable underfoot and has even closer views of the gorges carved by the Gornergletscher.

South

South from Zermatt the Matterhorn changes its clothes again, this time parading the pyramidal west face. This direction is the way to wilderness—steep icefalls peel off the **Breithorn** (4164m), and below the icefalls are the glacier-scoured, sun-bleached boulder fields. The highest **cable car** in Europe alights on the **Klein Matterhorn**, 6km from the Matterhorn. (Operates high season daily 7am-6pm; 55SFr.) A track leads out from the tunnel below the viewing platform to **Gobba di Rollin** (3899m), following the T-bar all the way, but the hike requires good weather, caution, and a tortoise pace due to the altitude. From the Trockner Steg cable-car station (2939m), however, you can walk back to Zermatt: leave the complex on the Monte Rosa side away from the Matterhorn and follow the path to the left along the gully in front of you (2½hr.).

Southeast and East

Southeast from Zermatt are the **Monte Rosa** (4634m) and the **Liskamm** (4527m), squat blocks that are the highest and the third highest mountains in Switzerland, respectively. Leonardo da Vinci, incidentally, thought the Monte Rosa was the highest mountain on Earth. Among its unlikely conquerors have been Pope Pius XI, who pioneered a new route to the Grenzsattel in 1889, and a youthful Winston Churchill, who climbed the monster in 1894. From the southeast, framed by woods and reflected in lakes, the Matterhorn takes on its best-known angle, reproduced on everything from tea towels to cookie tins. A rack railway winds up to the best viewpoint, the **Gornergrat** (3090m; 37SFr, round-trip 63SFr) by way of **Riffelalp** (2211m; 16.60SFr, round-trip 32SFr). Other stops include **Riffelberg** (2582m; 26SFr, round-trip 45SF) and **Rotenboden** (2815m; 32SFr, round-trip 55SFr). The train departs opposite Zermatt's main station (daily 7am-7pm). The train's main path from Zermatt follows the right bank of the river upstream, stopping at all the stations. Since the round-trip hike to Gornergrat demands a great deal of stamina, grabbing a lift for part of the ascent will preserve your strength for clambering around the top or taking a more interesting path down. From the top, tracks lead down to the wide, flat Gornergletscher and along the ridge toward the **Stockhorn** (3532m). A cable car also runs to this point (12SFr). Each destination provides a closer encounter with the ice but loses a fraction of the panorama that makes the Gornergrat so special. You can also descend after the Riffelalp station by following the contour around to the Grüensee, facing the snout of the Findelngletscher, then crossing the river and returning to Zermatt by way of the **Moosjesee** and the **Leisee**, two small pools that provide a beautiful foreground to the majestic Matterhorn.

Northeast and Northwest

Compared to the well-trodden highways south of Zermatt, the hikes to the north are unsung. Rockier and steeper, these difficult paths lead to proper summits rather than huts or viewpoints. A **northeast hike** starts from the Zermatt station. Head down to the river beside the Gornergratbahn, cross it, turn left, then hop on the Sunnegga-Rothorn railway and lift as far as **Blauherd** (2560m; 24SFr, round-trip 32.40SFr). A wide path gently circles the Unterrothorn's right flank to a mountain pass at 2981m. Take the blistering series of zigzags on the right (some offering fixed handrails) up to the **Oberrothorn** (3415m), a satisfying rocky fang. A **northwest hike** begins midway between the church and post office and opposite Hotel de la Poste on Bahnhofstr. The path initially climbs steeply up toward **Alterhaupt** (1961m) and **Trift** (2337m) but then levels off. The little-known glacier cirque beneath the icefalls of the **Ober Gabelhorn** and **Zinalrothorn** provides a turn-around point, but supermen and women will bear right up to the **Metterhorn** (3406m), accessible to agile walkers and a popular endurance-training hike for those about to try the Matterhorn.

■ Saas Fee

Nicknamed "the pearl of the Alps," Saas Fee (1800m) occupies one of Switzerland's most glorious sites. Situated in a hanging valley above the Saastal, the city snuggles among 13 grand 4000m peaks, including the **Dom** (4545m), the second highest mountain in Switzerland. The ice of the Feegletscher comes so low that you can visit the primordial giant on a 20-minute evening stroll. To protect all this Alpine glory, the entire resort town is closed to cars, giving electrically powered mini-vans and trucks free run of the rambling, gossipy streets. As the chatty chalet roofs of the village crowd in toward each other, brightly-clad tourists shuttle from souvenir store to sun terrace in search of instant memories. Others go farther (and higher) afield. As in Zermatt, the abundance of red knee-highs and sleek neon suits set against the low serenading hum of electric motors proves that Saas Fee's main draw is the outdoor scene. Town officials prohibit disturbing "the fairy-like charm of Saas Fee" after 10pm (noisemakers receive a 200SFr fine), but most guests are so exhausted from a full day's skiing, climbing, or hiking that few are likely to have energy for late-night carousing.

The **tourist office** (tel. 957 14 57, direct reservations 997 51 20; fax 957 18 60; email to@saas-fee.ch; http://www.saas-fee.ch), across from the bus station, is small and usually packed. The staff dispenses seasonal information, hiking advice, guides, and reasonably useful town maps with more hotels than street names. The room reservation service may cost as much as 5SFr; try the free phone board outside for do-it-yourself arrangements. Long-term visitors should pick up the list of available chalets. (Open July-Sept. and Dec.-April Mon. and Wed.-Fri. 8:30am-noon and 2-6:30pm, Tues. 8:30am-noon and 3-6:30pm, Sat. 8am-7pm, Sun. 9am-noon and 3-6pm; May-June and Oct.-Nov. Mon. and Wed.-Fri. 8:30am-noon and 2-6:30pm, Tues. 8:30am-noon and 3-6:30pm, Sat. 8am-noon and 3-7pm, Sun. 10am-noon and 4-6pm.) A **post bus** runs every hour to **Brig** (1¼hr., 17.40SFr, round-trip 33SFr); **Visp** (1hr., 13.20SFr), which connects to Lausanne, Sion, and the Valais; **Stalden Saas** (35min., 10.40SFr), which connects to Zermatt for another 30SFr; and **Saas Grund** (10min., 2.80SFr). You must reserve a place on all buses starting at Saas Fee at least two hours before departure. Call 957 19 45 or drop by the bus station. (Open Mon.-Fri. 7:20am-12:35pm and 1:15-6:35pm, Sat. 7:20am-6:35pm, Sun. 7:20am-12:35pm and 2:15-6:35pm.) Drivers can **park** at the lower end of the village with a guest card from their hotel (1 day 13SFr, in summer 11SFr; with guest card after 2nd day 9SFr, 7.50SFr; after 8th day 7SFr, 6SFr). For a **taxi**, call 957 33 44. The pharmacy, **Alpen Apotheke** (tel. 957 26 18), sits on the main street down the road to your right as you leave the tourist office. (Open Mon.-Fri. 8:30am-noon and 2-6:30pm, Sat. 8:30am-noon and 2-5pm.) In an after-hours emergency, call the pharmacist at 957 44 17 or (079) 417 67 18. In an **emergency,** call 117. The bus depot has small **lockers** (2SFr) and houses the **post office** with its public fax. (Open Mon.-Fri. 8:30am-noon and 2-6pm, Sat. 8:30-11am.) The **postal code** is CH-3906. The **telephone code** is 027.

While spine-tingling mountain exploits are Saas Fee's main draw, the town also demands a different brand of courage—this resort is definitely not for the financially faint at heart. The town's unofficial mascot, the merry marmot, may not be quite so chipper when he receives his hotel bill. To complicate housing further, from May 3 to June 13 much of Saas Fee's infrastructure and more than a few hotels are closed—keep this fact in mind when planning your visit. **Hotel Feehof Garni** (tel. 957 23 08; fax 957 23 09) attempts to fill the budget gap without sacrificing any elegance. From the bus station, head down to the main street left of the tourist office, turn left, and pass the church and the mountaineering school's office. Feehof is on the right opposite Hotel Imseng, which often has a large **public alphorn** outside. Warm, wooden, and wonderful, nearly all of the creaky pine rooms have balconies and the beds are deliciously soft. The overly metallic showers, however, require an odd little ritual with a vacuum pump. Ah, the quaint idiosyncracies of Alpine charm. (49-63SFr per person. In winter 53-69SFr. Showers and breakfast included.) One of the town's better values is **Pension Garni Mascotte** and its two sister chalets, **Alba** and **Albana** (tel. 957 27 24; fax 957 12 16). With your back to the station, head down the road opposite you just left of the tourist office. At the main street, turn right and continue up the hill for 200m; Mascotte is on the left. (Alba dorms 27-30SFr. Albana 5-bed dorms 28-32SF; 4-bed dorms 30-35SFr; 2-bed dorms 38-45SFr. Albana's rooms have shower and toilet. Smarter rooms in Mascotte 45-55SFr. All prices include breakfast. Add 10SFr for half-pension. Laundry facilities, ski storage, and TV lounge. Open mid-Dec. to April and July-Sept.) Right behind Hotel Feehof Garni, **Hotel Berghof** (tel. 957 24 84; fax 957 46 72) has expensive dorms in the basement of the three-star hotel. The clean, clinical 48-bed dorm provides fresh insight into Swiss order. Store your bags in the new, unforgettably pink lockers. (Dorms 35-40SFr. Bring your own sheets. Closed in May.) A bit farther up on the price (and comfort) scale, **Hotel Bergfreude** (tel. 957 21 31) offers surprisingly bright, low-ceilinged rooms amid highly polished pine paneling. Try to get a room with a balcony view of the glacier—the blinding snow will invigorate you more than a jolt of caffeine and is definitely worth the extra price. (Singles 45-65SFr; doubles 100-170SFr. Includes breakfast in the comfy lounge or out on an inertia-inducing sun terrace.) If you're not burdened by luggage of the unwieldy, matched variety, a spunky alternative to staying in Saas Fee proper is a night in a **mountain hut**. From July to September, the **Mischabelhütte** (3329m; tel. 957 11 17; 26SFr) above Saas Fee, **Hoh-saas** (3098m; tel. 957 17 13; 22SFr), and **Weissmieshütte** (2726m; tel. 957 25 54; 25SFr) above Saas Grund are all accessible. All three huts serve breakfast and dinner to compensate for the tough hike up. The Saas Fee tourist office has further details.

Three supermarkets compete for hungry shoppers in small Saas Fee, and all three have the same hours (Mon.-Fri. 8:30am-12:15pm and 2:15-6:30pm, Sat. 8:30am-12:15pm and 2:15-7pm). Nearest the tourist office and Pension Mascotte is the **Supermarkt**, right next to the pharmacy on the main street. A small **Konsum Center** stands next to the ski school across from the Alpine guide picture board. The pick of the lot, though, is the super-duper new **Migros**, just down the hill from the church. Saas Fee manages to support a few restaurants as well. **Spaghetteria da Rasso** (tel. 571 526), two minutes to the left of the pharmacy under the flower-strewn Hotel Britania, has 14 variations on spaghetti (13-20SFr; double portion with 4 different sauces 24SFr). Pizza (15-19SFr), salads (6-9SFr), and garlic bread (3.50SFr) also make an appearance. The shady terrace, grotesque wooden face, and occasional accordionists attract quite a crowd. (Open Dec.-April and July-Oct. daily 11:30am-10:30pm. Visa, MC, AmEx.) A few steps toward the pharmacy, local favorite **Restaurant la Ferme** (tel. 957 14 61) serves outstanding Valais specialties. This chalet has the best mountain view on the street, and the occasional cowbell clang drifts in to remind diners to look out the window and enjoy. The chefs conjure excellent *Käseknöpfli* (16SFr), *Sennerrösti* (17SFr), *raclette* (8SFr), fondue (24SFr), and vegetarian dishes (13-15SFr) for your dining enjoyment. (Open daily 10:30am-10pm.)

Once properly nourished, visitors turn their attention to the mountains. A cable car to **Felskinn** (3000m) and a discreet underground funicular, the "Metro Alpin," to Mittelallanin (3500m) enable summer **skiers** to enjoy 20km of runs and a stupendous Alpine view. (Round-trip to Mittelallanin 56SFr, to Felskinn 30SFr; 1-day summer ski-pass 56SFr, children 32SFr. No skiing May 12-June 13.) In winter, an immense network of lifts opens to the delight of impatient skiers everywhere (day ski passes 56SFr, children 32SFr; 6 days 260SFr, 150SFr; 13 days 465SFr, 265SFr). For those as-of-yet disinclined toward inclines, the **Ski School** (tel. 957 23 48; fax 957 23 66) offers a week of group skiing or snowboarding lessons (skiing 163SFr, snowboarding 150SFr; 15SFr reductions available in late Jan.). Renting equipment is fairly simple due to the impressive number of sports stores in the village—trust us, in Saas Fee, if it doesn't sell stuffed marmots, it rents skis. Stores in the **Swiss Rentasport System** (look for the black and red logo) offer good rates (skis or snowboard and boots 43SFr per day, 6 days 157SFr). The *über*-organized can call ahead of time and have equipment set aside for their arrival; call or fax the main Swiss Rentasport outlet in town, **Anthamatten Sport Mode** (tel. 958 19 18; fax 957 42 10).

In summer, Saas Fee is among the three or four best places to enjoy **Alpinism**. The **Alpine Guide's office** (tel. 957 44 64) by the church has a selection of climbs to 4000m summits like the Allalinhorn for both amateurs and experts. (Open Mon.-Sat. 9:30am-noon and 3-6pm.) Day tours can run anywhere from 130 to 370SFr per person. If the office is closed, you can choose and contact a guide from the display of photographs and phone numbers on the side of the building—note that questionable ties, but not mustaches, are standard uniform for the job. Regular **hikers** have 280km of marked trails from which to choose, but the whole mountain-town thing tends to create rather steep paths. A lovely half-day walk begins with a cable-car ride to **Plattien** (2570m). The cable-car runs from the end of Saas Fee's main street (roundtrip 22SFr, children 11SFr). From the cable-car stop and its picture-perfect views of the Dom and Lezspitze, a path leads to the right and zigzags left after five minutes. From the top it descends for a quarter of an hour and then heads left around the cirque, spiralling slowly down below the Feegletscher. The view opens up to the other high peaks as you drop down to the Gletschersee (1910m) at the glacier snout, and the path then gently follows the left bank of the outlet stream back to Saas Fee. For a hard, steep, brutal, blunt walk, hike up to the **Mischabelhütte** (3329m), which has the single best panorama of the Saas Fee cirque accessible to walkers. Coming from the pharmacy along the main street, turn right after the church and take the right fork 100m farther on. The track heads straight up the spur of the Lenzspitze, and the views improve monumentally with each step. Check for snow cover before you leave, however—the last part of the hike is rocky and highly unpleasant with any hint of snow or ice (1550m ascent, full-day, June-Sept. only). A **Saas Valley Hiking Pass** (149SFr, family rate 299SFr) provides access for a week to all cable cars and post buses in the valley and entrance to the ice pavilion at Mittelallanin, the **Bielen Recreation Center,** and the Saas and Bakery museums. The pass is available at the tourist office or any cable car station. Note, however, that most lifts close May to early June and mid-October to mid-December and that bad weather renders much of Saas Fee inaccessible. On those inevitable rainy days, you can amuse yourself at the Bielen Recreation Center (tel. 957 24 75), next to the bus station. The complex has an expensive but excellent **swimming pool** and **jacuzzi**. (Open daily June 14-Sept. 7 10am-8pm; June 15-July 13 and Sept. 8-Oct. 1: 1:30-8pm. 14SFr, with guest card 12SFr; children 8SFr, 7SFr.)

LAKE NEUCHÂTEL REGION

■ Neuchâtel

In a candid moment, Alexandre Dumas once likened Neuchâtel to a city carved out of a block of butter. Although probably referring to the unique yellow stone that makes up a large part of the city's architecture, Dumas could easily be mistaken as an overly appreciative fan of the calorie-laden treats in the local *pâtisseries*. Even after the visual novelty has worn off, the town possesses pockets of remarkably intact medieval beauty, focused in the graceful **Eglise Collégiale** and the commanding **chateau**. *Neuchâteloise* cuisine boasts quality as distinctive as the city's trademark hue, especially in its fondue, sausages, and the fresh fish from the lake and nearby rivers.

Orientation and Practical Information Neuchâtel regally presides over the longest lake entirely in Swiss territory, and the Jura mountains rise from the lake's northeast corner. From pl. Pury, the center of town, face the lake and walk two blocks to the left to find the **tourist office,** Hôtel des Postes (tel. 889 68 90; fax 889 62 96; email neuchatel@tourisme.ch; http://www.etatne.ch). Look for the large building with the names of countries inscribed all along its facade. The office dispenses several attractive brochures (in various languages), including a practical guide, hotel and restaurant listings, lists of seasonal events, a regional biking guide (22SFr), and a nightlife guide. They also offer *La Route du Vignoble Neuchâteloise*, which lists all the vineyards in the local towns. (Open July-Aug. Mon.-Sat. 9am-7pm, Sun. 4-7pm; Sept.-June Mon.-Fri. 9am-noon and 1:30-5:30pm, Sat. 9am-noon.) The train station houses a tourist office geared toward rail travel. (Open Mon.-Fri. 8:30am-noon and 1:30-6pm, Sat 8:30am-noon.) **Trains** connect Neuchâtel to **Basel** (every hr., 1¾hr., 35SFr); **Bern** (every hr., 40min., 16.60SFr); **Interlaken** (every hr., 2hr., 39SFr); **Geneva** (every hr., 1½hr., 41SFr); and **Fribourg** (every hr., 1hr. via Ins, 18.20SFr). Train station **lockers**, accessible until midnight, are 2SFr per day. A series of stairs leads down to the shore from the station, and bus #6 goes to pl. Pury, the central **bus stop**. **Ferries** provide service to **Murten** (15SFr) and **Biel** (22SFr). The **post office** is down pl. des Armes. (Open Mon.-Fri. 7:30am-6:30pm, Sat. 8-11am.) For the **police**, call 725 10 17; for the **hospital**, 722 91 11. The **postal code** is CH-2001. The **telephone code** is 032.

Accommodations and Food The **Oasis Neuchâtel**, rue de Suchiez 35 (tel. 731 31 90; fax 730 37 09), is a long way from the center of town but boasts a friendly, multilingual management and a fine view of the lake from its immaculate dining room and numerous terraces. From the station, take bus #6: "pl. Pury," then bus #1 (dir: Cormondrèche): "Vauseyon." From there head uphill and follow the pedestrian signs up a flight of stairs. Turn right and the hostel will be up the road and to your left, well marked by yellow happy faces. The chronic cheeriness continues inside with plastic magnolias lining the stairs and pictures of animals decorating the bathroom. (Reception 8-9am and 5-9pm. Curfew 10:30pm; 20SFr key deposit. 4- to 6-bed dorms 22.50SFr the first night, then 20SFr; doubles 51SFr, 46SFr. 2- to 4-person garden teepee in summer 20SFr per person, then 17.50SFr. Breakfast, shower, and sheets included. Stay for free on your birthday!) Closer to town is **Hotel Terminus** (tel. 723 19 19), across from the station. (Reception 7:30am-10pm. Singles 50SFr, with shower 90SFr; doubles 90SFr, 120SFr. Breakfast 7.50SFr.) The *Hôtel Restaurant* guide lists inexpensive options in nearby towns. The closest **campground** is in Columbier: **Paradise Plage** (tel. 841 24 46), on the lakefront, boasts a four-star rating. (10SFr; single tent 14.50SFr; double tent 20SFr. July-Aug. 15 add 2SFr. Open March-Oct.)

With its barrage of university students, Neuchâtel offers good, inexpensive meals—a lunchtime *menu* for 15SFr featuring fresh fish is not uncommon. Budget cafés and restaurants abound near the university; bus #1 (dir: Marin) stops right in front of the campus 50m from the university toward pl. Pury. The student hang-out **creperie Bach et Buck**, av. du Premier-Mars 22 (tel. 725 63 53), is especially satisfying if, and only if, you like crepes, since that's all they serve. Though limited, their menu goes around the world, from the Hawaiian crepe back to the ubiquitous Swiss cheese option. The restaurant offers a very green interior and serene courtyard with complete meals for under 10SFr. (Open Mon.-Thurs. 7:30am-10:30pm, Fri. 7:30am-midnight, Sat. 11am-midnight, Sun. 5-10:30pm.) If pretty pastries are more your thing, head for **A.R. Knect Boulangerie, Pâtisserie**, pl. des Halles (tel. 725 13 21). Locals crowd the terrace on the edge of the Maison des Halles in pl. du Marché to devour meaty sandwiches and flaky pastries for a pittance. A croissant piled with ham can be yours for only 1.70SFr, or choose from an endless variety of lacy fruit tarts (3.10SFr). Past the Halles des Maisons along rue Moulins sits the unassuming bistro **Chauffrage Compris** (tel. 721 43 96). Tucked into the street wall, this bar-restaurant serves up a well-endowed *plat du jour* consisting of meat or fish, vegetables, and some form of starch. (Open Mon.-Thurs. 6am-1am, Fri.-Sat. 6am-2am, Sun. 2-8pm.) As a bonus, the bar connects to the **Centre d'Art Neuchâtel (CAN)** (tel. 724 01 60), a gallery for starving artists that focuses on the interface of "society and art," and, the hungry artists hope, "food and art" as well. (Open Wed. and Fri.-Sat. 2-7pm, Thurs. 2-9pm, Sun. 2-5pm. 4SFr, students 2SFr.) In the center of town, **Migros**, rue de l'Hôpital 12, is a good place for groceries and prepared meals. (Open Mon. 1:15-6:30pm, Tues.-Wed. 8am-6:30pm, Thurs. 8am-10pm, Fri. 7:30am-6:30pm, Sat. 7:30am-5pm.) A **Co-op** sits down the hill and across the main road from the hostel.

Lake Neuchâtel Region

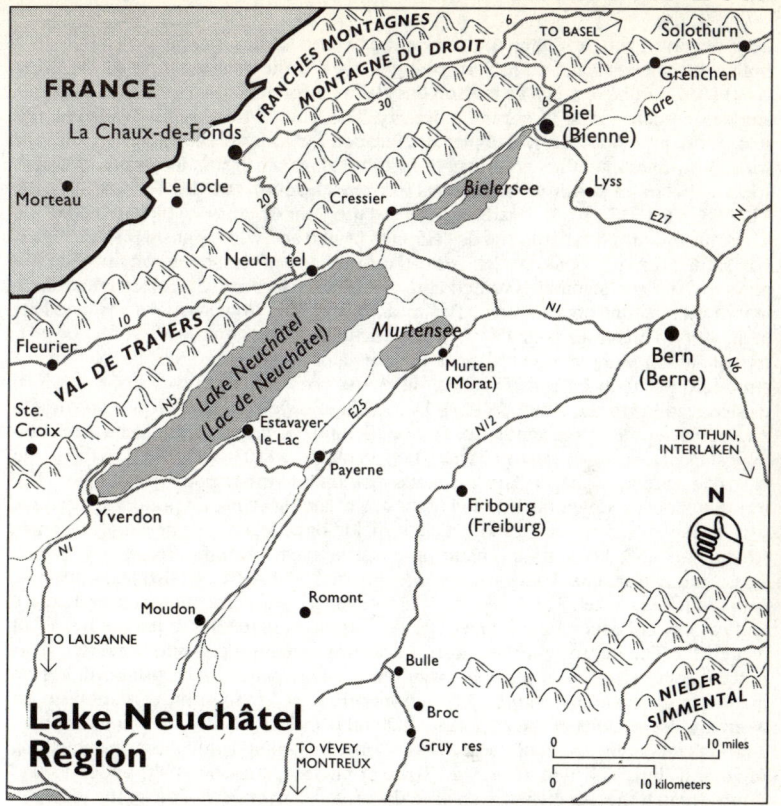

Sights and Entertainment Not surprisingly, the chateau for which the city is named and its neighboring church dominate the town from their crenulated hilltop perches. The medieval ramparts enclosing these connected monuments are open to the public and provide wonderful views of the town's closely huddled buildings. The 12th-century **chateau** served as the seat of the Count of Neuchâtel during the Middle Ages, but today only the bureaucrats of the cantonal government sit behind the striped shutters and flower boxes. Free guided tours of the complex (in English) meet at door #1. (Tours April-Sept. Mon.-Fri. every hr. on the hr. 10am-4pm, Sat. 10-11am and 2-3pm, Sun. 2-4pm.) A small cloister garden connects the chateau to the **Eglise Collégiale.** Inside, the church mixes Romanesque and Gothic architecture: massive walls, punctured by narrow windows, arch heavenward to a dramatic vaulted ceiling painted blue and decorated with gold stars. The church's true claim to fame is the gaudy **Cenotaph** (from 1372), a sculptural composition of the successive nobility of Neuchâtel. The stiff Counts of Neuchâtel barely escaped destruction during the Reformation; the weepers at the base of the monument, mistaken for saints, were not so lucky. Plywood currently encloses the entire arrangement, but guided tours occur the next-to-last Friday of every month at 5:30pm. Each following Friday, the church hosts a **free concert.** (Church open daily 8am-6pm.) Down the steps from the churchyard, the **Tour des Prisons** on rue Jehanne-de-Hochberg is worth every centime of the 0.50SFr entry fee; just plunk your loose change into the automatic turnstile. The town used the two wooden dungeons inside until 1848, but their unfortunate residents could not enjoy the magnificent view that tourists now climb up to see. (Open April-Sept.) As Rue Jehanne-de-Hochberg becomes rue de Château, the rarefied heights of monuments to Neuchâtel's political, ecclesiastical, and judicial past give way to the daily rhythms of the living city. Pl. du Marché features **La Maison des Halles,** a 16th-century covered market that lends uncommon style to common activity. The fanciful turrets and cream-colored stonework provide locals with a pleasant location for window shopping or a lunch of *saucisson neuchâteloise* and crusty French bread. You can find locals of a different species locked in poses at the **Natural History Museum,** rue des Terreaux 14 (tel. 717 79 60; fax 717 79 69). Head back toward the Tour de Piesse, which marks rue de Château, and turn right onto rue de l'Hôpital. Brown and white signs will signal when you should turn left onto rue des Terreaux. At the top of the street, the museum displays Switzerland's animals, stuffed and mounted in surprisingly entertaining dioramas of their natural environment. This means everything from swans by a lake to bats in an attic to rats in garbage cans. (Open Tues.-Sun. 10am-5pm. 6SFr, students 3SFr, free on Wed.) Along rue de l'Hôpital, elegant gates and two exotic sphinxes invite a stroll into place du Peyrou. The clean lines and crunchy gravel walks of the formal garden lead up to the Hôtel du Peyrou, the home of Jean-Jacques Rousseau's friend and publisher, Pierre-Alexandre du Peyrou. Behind the mansion, the small **Archaeological Museum,** av. du Peyrou 7 (tel. (038) 33 69 10; fax (038) 39 62 86), is the home base of a passionate, expanding local investigation into the region's remote past. The museum houses some of the results of these continuing activities: pottery shards give way to increasingly recognizable artifacts, including an entire 7th-century (BC) grave (rocks, soil, and skeleton) and handsome marble busts from the Roman era. (Open Tues.-Sun. 2-5pm. Free.) Toward the lake, the **Musée d'Art et d'Histoire,** esplanade Léopold-Robert 1 (tel. 717 79 20; fax 717 79 29), houses a dizzyingly comprehensive and eclectic collection of paintings, coins, weapons, and textiles to tell the history of Neuchâtel. The uncanny 18th-century automatons are a special sideshow; two barefoot boys in velvet coats scribble away while a lady plays the harpsichord. Performances are on the first Sunday of each month at 2, 3, and 4pm. Upstairs, the Art Nouveau decorations of the cupola include oil paintings, stained glass, and sculpted angels that literally fly out of the walls—making the jumbled art collection something of an anti-climax. (Open Tues.-Sun. 10am-5pm. 7SFr, students 4SFr, under 17 and Thurs. free.) If the museums haven't sated you, get an overview of the entire city with a guided tour. (Thurs. at 9:30am from the Tour de Piesse. 8SFr, children 3SFr.)

The university makes the nightlife predictably lively; the city is famous among regional club-goers for its techno DJs. Across the street from Crêperie Bach et Buck, the **Casino de la Rolande,** fbg. du Lac 14 (tel. 724 48 48), has enveloped several smaller bars and turned them into a massive arena of disco worship. During the day, an arm of the Casino, **Café-Restaurant Premier Mars,** serves American-style pizzas from 12SFr. (Open Mon.-Fri. 8am-7pm.) On weekends, the building transforms itself into a dance complex, with occasional bands, plenty of dancing, and cabarets. (Beers 3-5SFr. Admission 10SFr and up depending on the event. Open Mon.-Sat. 10pm-4am.) The popular **Shakespeare Pub,** rue des Terreaux 7, across from the Musée d'Histoire, turns into a dance cave as the night progresses (or disintegrates), with three levels of leisure-suited pleasure. (Open Tues.-Sun. 10:30pm-4am.) Those looking for a more sedate evening should explore one of the nearby wine-producing villages (see **Cressier** below) for dinner and a sampling of the local wine.

■ Near Neuchâtel

CRESSIER

The grape vine swag that almost obscures Cressier's train station sign, along with the rambunctious ranks of thistles and daisies that have been allowed to conquer the far side of the tracks, suggest a few things about Cressier. Wine is the local and regional obsession, but Cressier's semi-landlocked position makes it fairly unattractive to most tourists, and the weeds therefore replace the regimented vegetation of the scrubbed and manicured quays in neighboring areas. Built around a tiny chateau, the medieval village packs no less than seven **caves** (wine cellars) where one can participate in *la dégustation,* or sampling wines poured by the sunburnt hands that tend the grapes. To enter one of the rich and musty barrel-stacked cellars, ring the doorbell and ask: *"Deguster du vin, s'il vous plaît?"* Choose from *chasselas, pinot noir,* or *l'oeil-de-perdrix,* or leave it to the expert *("Votre choix"),* and you'll be poured a glass of Cressier wine, straight out of the vineyard's barrels. Many *caves* line the one and only main street. Of note are the particularly traditional and congenial *caves* of **Jean-Paul Ruedin,** rte. de Troub 4 (tel. (032) 757 11 51; fax 757 06 05), and the **Lauriers** family, rue de Château 6 (tel. (032) 757 11 62). Though sampling is encouraged, it is considered impolite not to buy. The cheapest bottles run around 10SFr.

Once slightly tipsy on young wine, many find that Cressier is perfect rambling ground. The town itself is not so much sleepy as narcoleptic—midday breaks regularly push the 2:30-3pm mark—but the streets overflow with enough architectural curiosities and enormous rosebushes to make an afternoon stroll pleasant. To reach the vineyards and breathtaking views of the valley and chateau, follow rue de Château and the signs for *tourisme pédestre.* By evening, the combined effects of sun and wine should dull any keenness for escape to more lively locales. Cressier's restaurants tend to be pricey, but the size and quality of their fresh, traditional meals are well worth the extra charge. **La Croix Blanche,** rue de Neuchâtel 12 (tel. (032) 757 11 66; fax 757 32 15), serves delicious fresh trout (16SFr) and a massive fondue for two (50-60SFr). (Open Thurs.-Tues. 11:30am-2pm and 6-10pm.) Weighted down by the sumptuous meal, you may find physical movement well-nigh impossible. Indulge your lethargy and spend a night upstairs in the restaurant's hotel. (Singles 60SFr; doubles 90SFr. Shower, TV, and breakfast included.) The **Hôtel de la Couronne,** rue de Neuchâtel 2 (tel. (032) 757 14 58; fax 757 32 01), is an inexpensive, friendly establishment a bit farther down the road. Their restaurant serves 20 varieties of fresh fish (20-28SFr) and a rival fondue (25SFr). Upstairs, the attic rooms feature half-timbered walls. (Reception at the bar. Singles 40SFr, with shower 60SFr; doubles 60SFr, 90SFr. Restaurant open Tues.-Thurs. 8am-11:30pm, Fri. 8am-12:30am, Sat. 9am-12:30am, Sun. 9am-5:30pm.) You can get a loaf of bread to go with your wine at the **Co-op** next to the church on rue Gustave Jeanneret. (Open Mon.-Tues. and Thurs.-Fri. 7:45am-12:15pm and 2-6:30pm, Wed. 7:45-12:15pm, Sat. 7:45am-12:15pm and 1:30-4pm.) **Trains** run every hour to Cressier from **Neuchâtel** (3.60SFr).

LA CHAUX-DE-FONDS

Forty minutes by train from Neuchâtel (9.60SFr), La Chaux-de-Fonds attracts tourists with a lot of time on their hands. A major watchmaking center, the town showcases a museum exploring "man and time," the center of the city's attractions. The streets' checkerboard organization makes navigation easy, and the tourist office has a map of self-guided walking tours, marked by blue and yellow walking eyes.

The **Musée International d'Horlogie,** rue des Musées 29 (tel. (032) 967 68 61; fax 967 68 89), not content merely to display examples of the Swiss watch industry, chronicles humanity's quest to measure and use the great continuum, from Stonehenge to the atomic clock. The vast and the minuscule unite in two of the museums's finest pieces. Dardi's astrarium and Ducommun's planetarium illustrate the rigidly timed dance of the planets in the Ptolemian and Copernican systems. In this underground museum, sleek cylindrical and spherical display cases rise from the floors and hang from the ceiling like space-age stalagmites and stalactites. Dominating one corner of the museum's park outside, the **carillon,** an artistic conglomeration of steel pipes and colored slats, measures time to the hundredth of a second and emits acoustically precise musical ditties in synch with carefully orchestrated panel movements every 15 minutes. (Open June-Sept. Tues.-Sun. 10am-5pm; Oct.-May 10am-noon and 2-5pm. 8SFr, students 4SFr; free Sun. 10am-noon.) Nearby, the gaudily painted exterior and mosaic-covered foyer of the **Musée des Beaux-Arts,** rue des Musées 33 (tel. (032) 913 04 44; fax 913 61 93), contrast sharply with the blindingly white gallery walls. Hung with mostly 20th-century Swiss art on the

> ### Man and Machine
>
> Born Charles Edouard Jeanneret-Gris in 1887, **Le Corbusier**, architect, city planner, and painter, has a monumental presence in 20th-century art. This son of a La-Chaux-de-Fonds watchmaker rebelled against the monumental tendencies of 19th-century nationalism and historicism, seeking pure, precise forms motivated by function rather than cultural reference. He therefore designed in glass and reinforced concrete, a revolutionary choice of material that was to be repeated by countless others throughout the 20th century. He was also infatuated with iconic machines of modernity, like the automobile and the airplane, and believed that houses and cities should be designed and organized like a machine, with regard to economy of structure and efficient use. As he said in his seminal work *Toward a New Architecture*, "the house is a machine for living."

ground floor, including works by Charles-Edouard Jeanneret-Gris (a.k.a. **Le Corbusier**), the mood softens slightly once you climb the metal and glass staircase. An eclectic arrangement of minor works by major artists awaits. (Open Tues. and Thurs.-Sun. 10am-noon and 2-5pm. 6SFr, students 3SFr.) To reach both museums, turn right as you exit the station onto rue Jacquet-Droz and then follow the *musées* signs. Bus #3 (dir: Les Foulets): "Polyexpo" back toward the station deposits you in front of the **Musée Paysan et Artisanal,** Eplatures-Grise 5 (tel. (032) 926 71 89). This authentic 16th-century farmhouse, where logs still burn in the cavernous fireplace and slippers lie unattended at the bedside, reconstructs the home, workshop, and general lifestyle of a rural artisan. (Open May-Oct. Sat.-Thurs. 2-5pm; Nov.-April Wed. and Sat.-Sun. 2-5pm. 3SFr, students 2SFr.)

Outdoorsy types will drool at the variety of alpine activity in the area. **Tête de Ran** (1422m), in nearby **Les Hauts-Geneveys** (tel. (032) 853 11 51), offers downhill and cross-country **skiing** (15SFr per day, 13SFr per ½day). Reach Les Hauts-Geneveys by regional rail. A bus runs from the La Chaux-de-Fonds train station to **La-Vue-Des-Alpes** (tel. (032) 853 30 18), which offers both night skiing and group and private downhill and cross-country lessons. (1-day lift ticket 16SFr, ½-day 13SFr. Buses run 3-4 times Wed. and Sat.-Sun. Reservations (tel. (039) 26 12 75) required.) In summer, **bikers and hikers** will enjoy the miles of well-marked trails that lace the region. (Bikes at the station, but ask the tourist office for trail maps and bike rental information.)

The **tourist office** (tel. (032) 919 68 95; fax 919 62 97; email montagnes@tourisme.etatne.ch; http://www.etatne.ch) is at Espacité 1. From the station, walk one block straight ahead, then turn right onto av. Léopold-Robert and look for the red and silver tubular tower—*Swiss Family Robinson* meets *Star Trek*. Take the free elevator ride to the 14th floor for a panoramic view of La Chaux-de-Fonds and the surrounding area. (Open May-Oct. Mon. 2-6:30pm, Tues.-Fri. 9am-6:30pm, Sat. 9am-12:15pm and 2-5pm; Nov.-April Mon.-Fri. 9am-12:15pm and 2-6:30pm, Sat. 9am-12:15pm and 2-5pm.) The dim but spotless **Auberge de Jeunesse,** rue du Doubs 34 (tel. (032) 968 43 15; fax 968 25 18), sits at the corner of rue du Stand behind a wrought-iron gate; take bus #4 (dir: L'Hôpital). Tell the driver you are going to *"l'Auberge"* for door-to-door service. The dark, wide hallways resemble the subdued streets of the quiet neighborhood outside. (Reception daily 7:30-9:30am and 5-10pm. No curfew. 23SFr first night, then 20.50SFr; doubles 30SFr, 27.50SFr. Non-members add 5SFr. Breakfast and sheets included. Laundry 6SFr. Wheelchair accessible. Visa, MC, AmEx, DC.)

While the **nightlife** may be limited, it does have its hot spots. The **Bikini Test,** La Joux-Perret 3 (tel. (032) 968 06 66), off rue Fritz-Courvoisier on the edge of town, could easily have fit into Wolfe's *Electric Kool-Aid Acid Test,* with tripped-out murals on the outside and such oddities as a red, furry, enclosed cab for intimate *tête-à-têtes* on the inside. **Le P'tit Paris,** rue du Progrès 4 (tel. (032) 928 65 33), a café two blocks from the hostel, offers live music on the milder side, including jazz, reggae, and blues. (Beers 2.60SFr. Admission around 12SFr. Open Mon-Thurs. 8am-midnight, Fri.-Sat. 8am-2am.) For food, **La Pinte Neuchâteloise,** rue du Grenier 8 (tel. (032) 913 38 64), just past the fountain, offers authentic Swiss cuisine. Try their specialities: *Rösti* (5SFr), *croûte de fromage* (15SFr), or an excellent fondue (15SFr). For portable, do-it-yourself eats look no further than the **Co-op Super Centre** on rue du Modulor off av. Léopold-Robert. (Open Mon. 1-6:30pm, Tues.-Wed. and Fri. 8am-6:30pm, Thurs. 8am-8pm, Sat. 8am-5pm.)

■ Solothurn

Snugly sandwiched between the Jura Mountains and the Aare River, Solothurn boasts one of the best hostels in Switzerland and eleven of everything else. Solothurn was the eleventh canton to join the Swiss Confederation (in 1481), and the city is home to eleven churches and chapels, eleven historic fountains, and eleven towers. **St. Ursen Kathedrale,** fashioned from pale marble, has eleven bells, and the staircase down from the main door is organized into flights of eleven steps.

Orientation and Practical Information Trains run to Solothurn from **Basel** (every hr., 1hr., 24SFr), **Neuchâtel** (every hr., 40min., 17.40SFr), and **Bern** (every 30min., 40min., 13SFr). For hiking tips, a map of Solothurn, or free room reservations, head to the **tourist office,** Hauptg. 69 (tel. 622 15 15; fax 623 16 32). From the Solothurn train station, walk through the underpass toward the *Zentrum* and follow Hauptbahnhofstr. across Kreuzackerbrücke up Hauptg. The office is to the left of the cathedral. (Open Mon.-Fri. 8:30am-noon and 1:30-6pm, Sat. 9am-noon.) **Exchange currency** or **rent bikes** (22SFr per day) at the **train station.** (Both counters open daily 5am-8:50pm.) For **taxis,** call 622 66 66 or 622 22 22. **Lockers** and **luggage storage** (3-5SFr) are at the station, as is an **Aperto grocery.** (Open daily 6am-10pm.) For the **police,** call 117; in a **fire,** 118; for the **hospital,** 627 31 21. The **post office** (tel. 625 29 29) is past the hostel on Postpl., a left off Kreuzackerbrücke and onto Landhausquai. (Open Mon.-Fri. 7:30am-noon and 1:30-6pm, Sat. 8-11am.) The **postal code** is CH-4500, and the **telephone code** is 032.

Accommodations and Food Perched on the river in the *Altstadt,* the **Jugendherberge "Am Land" (HI),** Landhausquai 23 (tel. 623 17 06; fax 623 16 39), is easy to find—if you don't mistake it for an art gallery. Walk five minutes from the train station over Kreuzackerbrücke and take the first left onto Landhausquai. A wrought-iron staircase connects the four white-walled, wood-floored stories, but you can also ride in the stately elevator. Giant picture windows overlooking the river and modern chrome track lighting keep this *El Dorado* of hostels well lit day and night. Soothe your aching bones under the high-pressure water of the showers in the sparkling white bathrooms. Drop your wearied carcass onto a firm bed, rest your head on a soft pillow, and snuggle up under soft sheets (no starchy white sleepsacks here) and a fluffy white comforter. Enjoy the myriad amenities: pool table, roof terrace, music room, and conference room. Sleep in if you wish (there's no lockout), but you'll miss the unlimited supply of cheese, bread, yogurt, and other treats that await you every day from 8 to 10am in the Art Deco dining room. (Reception 7:30am-10:30pm. Singles 24.50SFr, with shower 35.50SFr. Additional nights 22SFr, 33SFr. Breakfast included. Dinner 11SFr.) The **Hotel Kreuz,** Kreuzg. 4 (tel. 622 20 20; fax 621 52 32), is the only other budget option. (Singles 43SFr; doubles 77SFr. Showers included.)

Cafés and restaurants line the streets of the *Altstadt,* but the **Taverna Amphorea,** Hauptg. 51 (tel. 623 67 63), outshines almost all others with large portions of vegetarian-friendly Greek and Middle Eastern specialties under 20SFr. (Open Tues. and Thurs. 11am-11:30pm, Wed. 9am-11:30pm, Fri. 11am-12:30am, Sat. 9am-12:30am.) Stock up on foodstuffs at the **Manora** grocery store and restaurant on Gurzelng. (open Mon.-Wed. and Fri. 9am-6:30pm, Thurs. 8:30am-9pm, Sat. 8am-5pm), or try the **farmer's market** at Marktplatz (Wed. and Sat. 8am-noon). Outside the old city walls, the **Co-op** and **Migros** stand near the post office. (Both open Mon.-Wed. and Fri. 8am-6:30pm, Thurs. 8am-9pm, Sat. 7:30am-5pm.)

Sights and Entertainment Solothurn's unique charm gets downright quirky in its numerous festivals and museums. **Chesslete,** a procession with bizarre masks and festivities intended to drive away winter, marks the beginning of Carnival. In this celebration, citizens re-name their town "Honolulu," since the tropical city is directly opposite Solothurn on the other side of the world. In the heart of the *Altstadt,* the **Museum Altes Zeughaus,** Zeughauspl. 1 (tel. 62 33 528), hoards one of Europe's largest collections of weapons and armor, with over 400 suits standing guard. True to the building's origins as an arsenal, the weapons hang in massive stockpiles, with bayonets still attached and swords unsheathed—ready to be grabbed off the wall at a moment's notice. (Open May-Oct. Tues.-Sun. 10am-noon and 2-5pm; Nov.-April Tues.-Fri. 2-5pm, Sat.-Sun. 10am-noon and 2-5pm. 6SFr, students 4SFr.) The **Naturmuseum,** Klosterpl. 2, within the town walls and to your right as you cross Kreuzackerbrücke, lets kids poke and prod animals and minerals. (Open Tues.-Wed. and Fri.-Sat. 2-5pm, Thurs. 2-9pm, Sun. 10am-noon and 2-5pm. Free.) On the fringes of town, the **Kunstmuseum,** Werkhofstr. 30 (tel. 622 23 07), houses a small collection of Swiss works, though a Van Gogh and a few token Impressionists spruce up the walls. The best galleries are upstairs, where luminous medieval Madonnas sit in strawberry patches and sinuous Klimt women writhe in multicolored fabrics. (Open Tues.-Sat. 10am-noon and 2-5pm, Thurs. 10am-noon and 2-9pm, Sun. 10am-5pm. Free.) Take bus #4: "St. Niklaus" and walk 10 minutes up Riedholzstr., or take the Solothurn-Niederbipp train: "Feldbrunnen," to the stately **Schloß Waldegg,** surrounded by wheat fields and tree-lined walks like any proper country estate. The castle preserves its aristocratic life and houses the **Ambassadorial Museum,** detailing the history of the French embassy in Solothurn. Revel in the view from the balcony onto gardens so formal that even common daisies look elegant. (Open Apr. 15-Oct. Tues.-Thurs. and Sat. 2-5pm, Sun. 10am-noon and 2-5pm; Nov.-Dec. 20 and Feb.-April 14 Sat. 2-5pm, Sun. 10am-noon and 2-5pm. Wheelchair accessible. Parking available. 6SFr, students 4SFr.)

The Jura mountains watch lovingly over Solothurn, and their many trails beckon fans of Mother Nature to get up close and personal. Stock up on tourist-office information and maps of marked **hiking and biking trails** through the Jura, then hike to nearby Altreu (2hr.) to see the oldest and best-known stork colony in Switzerland (perhaps one of them carried you to your expectant parents). The trek to the Weissenstein Alpine center is more challenging and rewarding (2hr., trail head at the corner of Wengisteinstr. and Verenawegstr.; follow the yellow signs to Weissenstein). Take the chairlift down from Weissenstein and hop on a train (4.20SFr) in Oberdorf to return to Solothurn. **Boat tours** leave Solothurn for Biel and from there to Murten or Neuchâtel. In the winter, **skiing** dominates the sports scene. Weissenstein (1280m) has 7km of cross-country trails and two chairlifts for downhill skiing.

When the tiny shops and boutiques of the *Altstadt* close their doors, people flood the village's many pubs, cinemas, and other hot spots. Ask the friendly hostel receptionist for tips. **Löwen,** Löweng. 15 (tel. 62 25 055), serves up good beer, cheap Italian food (pasta and pizza for under 15SFr), and a mix of world music (funk, jazz, reggae, and, mercifully, no techno). For funky dance music, spin over to **Kofmehl Fabrik,** Gibelinstr. (tel. 623 50 60), on the outskirts of town. Just off the railroad tracks, this old metal factory is now decked out in trippy graffiti art. Kofmehl holds occasional movie nights, but for more regular fare, try **The Cinema Palace,** Hauptg. 57 (622 25 15), showing recently released, subtitled American films (13-15SFr).

▪ Biel (Bienne)

In 1765 Rousseau spent what he claimed to be the happiest moments of his life in Biel. The charms of this bilingual town, engulfed by mountains and an alpine lake, evidently were enough to cheer the heart of this generally miserable man. Biel's *Altstadt* retains some of this charm, but the rest of the city has become thoroughly modern. Once considered the Detroit of watch manufacturing, Biel still houses the Rolex and Omega factories. Perhaps Biel's best features lie outside the town proper. **Lake**

BIEL (BIENNE) ■ 355

Biel provides an admirable quay and serves as an excellent starting point for moderate hikes in the mountains that surround the town.

The two best **hikes** surrounding Biel pass through magnificent gorges: the walk to Twannbachschlucht leads to open mountaintop fields ripe for picnics, and the jaunt to Taubenloch threads through a rugged canyon and its canopy forest. To get to **Twannbachschlucht**, take the rail car from Biel to Maggligen (every 30min; 4.20SFr, Swisspass and Swiss Card valid.) From this vantage point, signs point to Twannberg, which leads to Twannbachschlucht. The trail follows a ridge perched above Lake Biel and alternately passes through dense forest and flower-filled meadows. The journey from Biel to the lakeside town of **Twann** at the bottom of the gorge lasts about three hours. Return to Biel by train or by lake ferry (6SFr, Eurailpass not valid), or move on to Neuchâtel. **Taubenloch** is a less ambitious hike, though perhaps a bit more rewarding. Bus #1 runs to the conjunction of Bozingenstr. and Herman Lienhard-Str., where you can enter the canyon through the Zum Wilden Mann Restaurant's garden (2SFr suggested donation). The gorge walls shoot upwards over 30m, and a mountain stream gurgles over rocks and fallen trees. Bridges allow views of the forest canopy and the magnificent waterfalls hung with moss and sheets of mist. Most hikers turn back once they reach the water treatment plant (35-40min.), but those who press on and follow the signs to Frinvillier will find the **Hotel de la Truite** (tel. 358 11 42). A *tulipe* of the local **Schafiser** or **Twanner** wine complements the fresh trout (14SFr) perfectly. (Open Mon. 8:30am-1:30pm, Tues. 8:30am-2pm, Thurs. 8:30am-4pm, Fri.-Sat. 8:30am-12:30pm, Sun. 9am-1:30pm.) The well-marked walk back from Frinvillier to Biel takes about an hour. Many vineyards line the lake, and a self-guided walking tour (1-4hr., map at tourist office) or rented bike will take you through them.

A **boat tour** of the lake or soaking up rays on the Strandboden provides a more leisurely introduction to the city. To reach the harbor and the beach from the train station, take a left onto Veresiusstr. and then a left onto quai du Bas. Walk straight ahead and follow the signs. Boat tours range from 12SFr (Biel-Twann, 25min.) to 46SFr (Biel-Murten with a change at Neuchâtel, 4hr.) round-trip. In early July, an **open-air cinema** runs recent releases and classic films in **Schloßpark Nidau**. (Tickets at the tourist office or Hello Yellow (157 18 18). Information at http://www.post.ch.)

Since few budget accommodations bless Biel, consider making it a daytrip from Solothurn (20min., 8.40SFr), Neuchâtel (20min., 9.60SFr), or Bern (30min., 10.40SFr). **The Hostel**, Solothurnerstr. 137 (tel. 341 29 65), is reminiscent of Camp Hiawatha and features commune-style management, no lockout, no curfew, and free luggage storage. Don't think about walking; hop on trolleybus #1: "Zollhaus," and then walk away from the town for approximately ten minutes. (Reception open until 10pm; call if arriving later. Dorms 22SFr; doubles 30SFr. Hall showers. Breakfast, sheets, and tea included. Kitchen and backyard grill available.) For picnic supplies, trust **Migros**, Spitalstr. or Freierstr. 3 (open Mon. 9am-6:30pm, Tues.-Wed. and Fri. 8am-6:30pm, Thurs. 8am-9pm, Sat. 7:30am-4pm), or the **Co-op**, Rechbergerstr. 1 (open Mon-Fri. 8am-12:30pm and 2-6:30pm, Sat. 7:30am-4pm).

The Biel **tourist office** (tel. 322 75 75; fax 323 77 57) is just outside the **train station** at Bahnhofpl. (Open May-Oct. Mon.-Fri. 8am-12:30pm and 1:30-6pm, Sat. 9am-noon and 2-5pm; Nov.-April Mon.-Fri. 8am-12:30pm and 1:30-6pm). The train station **exchanges currency** (Mon.-Fri. 6am-8pm, Sat.-Sun. 6am-7pm), **rents bikes** (22SFr, ½-day 17SFr; mountain bike 30SFr, 24SFr), and rents **lockers** and **stores luggage** (3 and 5SFr; open 5am-12:30am). You can call a **taxi** at 322 11 111. **Buch und Presse Center** on Bahnhofstr. sells English-language books and magazines. (Open Mon. 1:30-6:30pm, Tues.-Wed. and Fri. 7am-6:30pm, Thurs. 7am-9pm, Sat. 7am-4pm). For the **police**, call 32 12 385; for the **hospital**, 322 93 93. The **telephone code** is 032.

WESTERN SWITZERLAND

Fribourg (Freiburg)

Fribourg, Bern's sister city to the southwest, lies in a deep wooden gorge and straddles the sharp linguistic border between French- and German-speaking Switzerland. The river that divides the town, looping around a low-lying medieval *vieille ville*, is known as the Sarine from the west bank and the Saane from the east. The upper town is the newer part of Fribourg and the scene of most of its official and daily operations, leaving the *vieille ville* so quiet that the swollen, slow-moving river dictates the tempo. Fortunately, even in the new town, tourism takes third place behind the university and Catholicism as the focus of the city's energy. Evidence of Fribourg's century-old position as the last redoubt against encroaching Protestantism is everywhere. Religious foundations sit on every corner, and even the local brew, Cardinal beer, celebrates the career development of a 19th-century bishop.

Orientation and Practical Information Fribourg sits on the main train line between Zurich and Geneva. Connections leave nearly every 30 minutes to **Bern** (25min., 10.40SFr) and **Lausanne** (45 min., 21SFr). Other connections include **Neuchâtel** (every hr., 1hr., 18.20SFr); **Interlaken** (every hr., 1½hr., 32SFr); and **Basel** (every hr., 1¾hr., 43SFr). Fribourg's friendly **tourist office**, av. de la Gare 1 (tel. 321 31 75; fax 322 35 27), is 100m to the right of the station door. (Open Mon.-Fri. 9am-12:30pm and 1:30-6pm, Sat. 9am-12:30pm and 1:30-4pm.) You can make hotel reservations through the tourist office (3SFr fee) or at the station. **Currency exchange** is at the train station (open daily 6am-8:30pm) or at one of the many banks lining rue du Romont. **GMT buses** for Bulle and the Schwarzsee (13.20SFr each) leave from the station. **Lockers** (small 3SFr; large 5SFr); **luggage watch** (open Mon.-Sat. 6am-8:55pm, Sun. 7am-8:55pm; 5SFr per item); and **bike rental** (22SFr per day, ID deposit) are all available at the station. Call 117 for the **police** and 323 12 12 for **medical assistance**. The **post office**, av. de Tivoli, is the unmissable skyscraper left of the train station. The **postal code** is CH-1701; the **telephone code** is 026.

Accommodations and Food The **Auberge de Jeunesse** stands at rue de l'Hôpital 2 (tel. 323 19 16). Hang a left out of the train station and walk past the houses, across av. de Tivoli, past the post office, and onto the narrow rue du Criblet. Turn left at the playground and walk up the path to the hostel. The piped-in elevator music (played constantly until the reception closes) spoils the peace in this otherwise quiet converted hospital. (Reception Mon.-Fri. 7:30-9:30am and 5-10pm, Sat.-Sun. 7:30-9:30am and 6-10pm. Curfew 10pm; key deposit 50SFr. Dorms 23SFr first night, then 20.50SFr; doubles 37SFr, 34.50SFr. Non-members add 5SFr. Breakfast, sheets, and showers included. Lunch 11SFr. Lockers, laundry, and kitchen facilities available. Open Feb.-Nov. Reservations strongly recommended.) **Hotel du Musée**, rue Pierre Aeby 11 (tel./fax 322 32 09), above a Chinese restaurant, is tucked in a quiet street one block from the cathedral. Rooms are large and well furnished, despite the building's unassuming appearance. (Singles 40SFr, with shower 50SFr; doubles 80-90SFr, 90-100SFr. Breakfast 5SFr. Visa, MC, AmEx. Reservations preferred.) From the station, campers can catch a GFM bus: "Marly," where **Camping La Follaz** (tel. 436 30 60) offers lakeside plots. (Reception 9am-10pm. 4SFr. Open April-Oct.)

Small cafés selling quasi-Italian or German Swiss food line rue de Romont and rue de Lausanne, a major shopping district. The options are endless, but two deserve specific mention. **Café du Midi**, rue de Romont 25 (tel. 322 31 33), buzzes with locals devouring specialty *schöni* fondue (22SFr) and *tranche de porc* (18SFr) under white umbrellas outside or surrounded by pine and terra-cotta inside. The fondue (with truffles, 26SFr) is available until 11pm. The *menu du jour* (15.50SFr) awaits the hungry starting at noon. (Open Mon.-Sat. 7:30am-11:30pm, Sun. 4pm-midnight.) **Bindella Ristorante Bar,** rue de Lausanne 38 (tel. 322 49 05), cooks inventive, high-quality pasta and pizza dishes, like spaghetti with mussels and clams (19SFr). Leather sofas line the spacious interior, just the right atmosphere for jazz on the last Thursday of every month at 8:30pm. (Cover 8SFr. Open Mon.-Sat. 9am-11:30pm.)

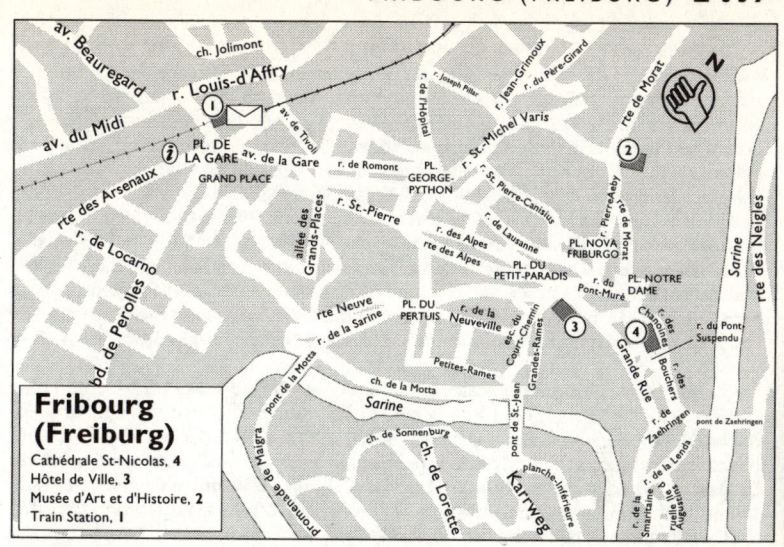

Fribourg (Freiburg)

- Cathédrale St-Nicolas, **4**
- Hôtel de Ville, **3**
- Musée d'Art et d'Histoire, **2**
- Train Station, **1**

Better deals and unusual food lie hidden deeper in the city. Workers and locals pack the bar and restaurant of **Les Tanneurs**, pl. du Petit-St.-Jean (tel. 322 34 17), filling its outdoor tables on the pleasant old town square. Plates are piled high with steak and fries (15SFr), and the beer is cheap (2.60SFr). A **produce market** stands in pl. Georges Python between rue de Romont and rue de Lausanne on Wednesdays 7am to 1pm or in pl. Hôtel de Ville on Saturdays 7am to 1pm. The virtually inseparable supermarket twins, **Co-op** and **Migros,** share the same street (6a and 2 rue St-Pierre) and the same hours (Mon.-Fri. 8am-6:30pm, Sat. 8am-5pm). There is a **supermarket** in the basement of La Placette Shopping Mall (the first building on rue de Romont) and a **Manora** self-service restaurant on the 6th floor.

Sights and Entertainment A walking tour around town provides a taste of Fribourg's many churches, monasteries, and convents. From the station, head down rue de Romont, past pl. Georges Python, and along rue de Lausanne and its open-air, pedestrian shopping galleries. Rue de Lausanne empties into pl. Nova-Friburgo, a busy intersection with a fine view of the **Hôtel de Ville** and its whimsical clock tower. As the Renaissance automatons regularly chime in the hours, the fountain of St. George dominates the courtyard below. When the wind picks up, both visitors and the commemorative **Morat Linden Tree** receive unexpected showers.

From pl. Nova-Friburgo, rue Pierre Aeby leads to the **Musée d'Art et d'Histoire** (tel. (037) 22 85 71; fax (037) 23 16 72). Numerous rooms display religious art scavenged from local churches and monasteries. Run-of-the-mill 18th-century portraiture shares space with the truly macabre products of monastic artists. The medieval statuary recovered from the cities' fountains and the porch of Cathédrale St-Nicolas stare silently as modern artist Jean Tinguely's noisy chains and motored cogs power huge sculptures bristling with metal and bone. (Open Tues.-Wed. and Fri.-Sun. 10am-5pm, Thurs. 10am-5pm and 8-10pm. Free; special exhibits 8SFr, students 5SFr.) From the museum, rte. de Morat leads to the stolidly impressive **Franciscan Monastery** on the left. Inside, the walls rise to a beautifully scrolled ceiling, and an intricate altar awaits in the star-topped, arched darkness. (Open daily April-Sept. 7:30am-7pm; Oct.-March 7:30am-6pm.) Farther down the road is the **Basilique de Notre-Dame**, whose dim, incense-laden atmosphere contrasts sharply with the stark, clean lines of the Franciscan church. Across pl. Notre-Dame rises the bell tower of the **Cathédrale St-Nicolas,** the focal point of Fribourg. The 368-step tower offers dizzying views of the town, but the art inside induces speechlessness. (Cathedral open Mon.-Fri. 6:15am-7pm, Sat. 7:45am-7pm, Sun. 9am-9:30pm. Free. Tower open June-Aug. Mon.-Sat. 10am-12:15pm and 2-5pm. 3SFr, students 2SFr.)

Across the river is the *vieille ville*'s knot of medieval architecture. Rue des Augustins passes the **Eglise des Augustins** (Augustinian Monastery) and its church. A huge wooden retable altarpiece, painted and gilded to resemble marble, awaits appreciation inside. Just off pl. du Petit-St-Jean is an odd little museum worthy of a visit. The **Musée Suisse de la Marionette,** rue Derrière-les-Jardins (tel. 322 85 13), houses hundreds of puppets from all over the world. (Open July-Aug. Fri.-Sun. 2-5pm; Feb.-June and Sept.-Dec. Sun. 2-5pm; 4SFr, students 3SFr.) Across the stone bridge (pont du Milieu), several panoramic vistas await; the view from the bridge itself is oft-photographed. Planche-Supérieur leads up the hillside, depositing climbers next to the postage-stamp-sized **Chapelle de St. Jost**, placed there by the Capuchin convent, **Montorge,** across the street. Farther uphill is the statue-encrusted **Chapelle de Lorette.** Situated in a commanding position atop the cliff overlooking the gorge, the tiny chapel houses a magnificently illuminated statue of the Virgin Mary, flanked by wooden angels swinging a silver rosary in front of her.

At night, most *Fribourgeois* sleep, but **Café des Grand Places,** 12 Grand Places (tel. 322 26 58), plays live funk, blues, salsa, industrial hardcore, and karaoke, depending on the night. The restaurant upstairs has *menus* at 13.50SFr and 15.50SFr. Its terrace overlooks the intriguing Jean Tinguely fountain on Grand Places, a favorite hangout in good weather. (Open Mon.-Tues. 11am-11:30pm, Wed. 11am-1:30am, Thurs. 11am-2am, Fri. 11am-3am, Sat.-Sun. 5pm-3am. Music starts at 9pm. Visa, MC, AmEx.) On the right from the station, **Rock Café,** bd. de Pérolles 1 (tel. 322 24 14; fax 322 24 24), has mid-air motorbikes and fenders on the wall, resembling the Hard Rock Café without offending it too much. The **Garage Bar** and **Le Sélect** nightclub downstairs try desperately to fit that worldwide derivative-biker mode. (Vegetarian dishes 16SFr, *menus* from 14SFr. Open till 3am on weekends.)

■ Near Fribourg

GRUYÈRES

Tiny Gruyères carries a weighty reputation that can be summed up in six letters: cheese. The **Cheese Dairy,** near the train station at Pringy, can deal with all your urgent cheese questions and curiosities. This working dairy churns 77lb. wheels of cheese for visitors daily at 12:30 and 3pm. A multilingual presentation details the particulars of production as visitors watch the cheesemakers in action from an observation booth reminiscent of instructional surgery sessions. Later, samples are at hand in the specialty shop. (Open daily 8am-7pm. Tours in English. Free.)

With the obligatory cheese-history lesson under your belt, you can lay siege to the steep hill fully armed. The **tourist office** (tel. (026) 921 10 30; fax 921 38 50) lies at the top of the stairs leading to the *vieille ville* from the **parking lot.** (Tourist office open mid-May to Oct. Mon.-Sun. 8am-noon and 1:30-5pm; Oct. to mid-May Mon.-Fri. 8am-noon and 1:30-5pm.) From this vantage point, the main street of the town opens up in a surprisingly vast expanse, dipping down to the fountain but rising once more to follow the lines of the castle. A few other roads branch off, splitting Gruyères into bits and pieces. It'll take some time to ramble over the ramparts, scramble over gravel walks, and crawl into watchtower niches. With cow bells echoing dolorously in the valley below, one beautiful vista follows another as the geranium-lined main street leads to the **Château de Gruyères** (tel. (026) 921 21 02; fax 921 38 02). Built for the counts of Gruyères, the castle features countless cranes—*grue* is French for "crane"—that fly off its ramparts and serve as a living adornment. The castle's unique museum, the **International Center of Fantastic Art,** constantly surprises visitors with odd combinations of medieval, Renaissance, 18th-century, 19th-century, and modern art. The rooms are sequentially numbered to guide even the most befuddled visitor. (Open daily June-Sept. 9am-6pm, March-May and Oct. 9am-noon and 1-5pm; Nov.-Feb. 9am-noon and 1-4:30pm. 5SFr, children and students 2SFr, guide 0.50SFr.)

To get to Gruyères from **Fribourg,** take the **GFM bus** or **train** to Bulle then the train to Gruyères (35-40min., 15.80SFr). A GFM-TF-FRI-Pass (available at any train station on the line) permits unlimited use of the entire bus and train network in the Fribourg area for one day (valid June-Oct., 25SFr, children 12.50SFr). Trains pass through Gruyères every hour in each direction, but the last train from Gruyères to Bulle leaves at 8:17pm and the last bus from Bulle to Fribourg departs at 9:35pm.

MURTEN (MORAT)

In the linguistic give and take of the area, German can count at least one success: Murten, or "Morat," as the 12% French-speaking minority insists on calling the town. Murten/Morat, surrounded by its medieval ringmauer/ramparts, overlooks the calm Murtensee/Lac de Morat—despite the orthographic schizophrenia, Murtern is a surprisingly unified town, self-contained and easy to explore on foot.

As Bahnhofstr. curves uphill, it leads to the crowd of swaying lindens that mark the entrance to the town. Following the road past the impressive chateau (rather, *schloß*) and to the right brings you to the main street, Hauptstr., and its arcades, crowded with the odd jumble of vendors' wares and the intimate knots of a dozen cafés. Flower boxes overflow with geraniums, the crimson spilling onto the fountains below. A climb up onto the **ramparts** quickly brings fairyland back to earth. At the end of Hauptg., turn right onto Franz Kirchg. and past the church at the end of the alley. Behind the church are the stairs to mount the ramparts, which afford backyard views of the red-clay-tiled roofs below and the lake beyond. On the other side of the ivy-covered walls is the Staatgraben—garden allotments rife with riotous roses, carpets of fragrant pink honeysuckle, and skyscraper cities of multicolored lupins.

The Staatgraben path descends the ramparts and ends at the linden tree park. Following Lausannestr. in the opposite direction and obeying the signs brings you to the town's old mill, now the **Murten Historisches Museum** (tel. 670 31 00). The water wheel still churns outside, and inside this eclectic little museum houses ancient coins, leather fire buckets, Morat's famously deadly absinthe ("Poison Vert"), weapons and armor from the Battle of Murten, and even the cannonball used to kill the American circus elephant that went wild in the city streets in 1866. (Open May-Sept. Tues.-Sun. 10am-noon and 2-5pm; Oct.-Dec. and March-April Tues.-Sun. 2-5pm; Jan.-Feb. Sat.-Sun. 2-5pm. 4SFr, students 2SFr, children 6-16 1SFr.) **Ferries** leave regularly for Neuchâtel (every 2hr., 2hr., 15SFr), as well as for tours of the lake (1 per day in July at 3:45pm, 2 per day in Aug. at 3:45 and 4:45pm; 1hr.; 13SFr). For more information concerning special tours and evening cruises, call LNM (tel. (032) 725 40 12).

The **train station** (tel. 670 26 46) shares its tiny square with the post office. Murten lies on the low-speed train line to Fribourg (every hr., 26min., 9.60SFr); Neuchâtel (every hr., 30min. via Ins, 10.40SFr); and Bern (every hr., 50min. via Lyss, 18.20SFr).

Death, the Maiden, and a Linden Tree

Once upon a time (April, 1476) in a land far, far away (Fribourg), there lived an old man named Nicholas who declared that he would give his daughter Beatrice's hand to the man who proved himself most valiant on the battlefield. As the knights went off to battle Charles the Bold in Morat, Beatrice waved a linden branch at Rudolphe, her childhood love. Determined to win her hand, Rudolphe proved himself the bravest knight on the battlefield—at the cost of a mortal wound. Undaunted, he ran back to Fribourg, waving a linden branch and shouting "Victory!" When he finally reached Beatrice's balcony in pl. Hôtel de Ville, he collapsed. Beatrice ran to her love, who could say only "Homeland! Love! To Heaven!" before dying in her arms. The town planted the linden branch as a relic of the victory in the square. In 1984, a traffic accident uprooted the tree, but the town salvaged a shoot and replanted it in the tree's original spot, where it flourishes today. In memory of the battle and of Rudolphe's plight, runners from Morat and Fribourg race between the two cities every October.

Basel (Bâle)

Perched on the Rhine and buffered by France and Germany, Basel (rhymes with nozzle) exemplifies the cultural dimorphism of Northern Switzerland. Basel feigns a medieval image, subtly masking the vibrancy of a modern university town. The students at the university (Switzerland's oldest and perhaps most prestigious) create a nightlife centered around the gray-stoned **Barfüsserplatz,** which rages until morning with outdoor cafés, smoky bars, and live music. The biggest party of them all, *Fasnacht,* allegedly rivals Mardi Gras; residents chase away winter and let it all hang out after Ash Wednesday. All the partying hides Basel's industrial side—Switzerland's second largest city is home to pharmaceutical giants Roche, Sandoz, and Ciba-Geigy.

Even without such nocturnal debauchery, Basel is compelling. Majestic and enticing, the city sights include café-lined squares, serene churches, and world-class museums. The Münster presides over the *Altstadt* in a towering conglomeration of red sandstone, stained glass, and sprouting spires. Farther along the river, the elegant St. Alban district houses 30 carefully orchestrated museums in its hilly, winding streets. You can see art from Roman times to the 20th century in one stroll, as the green waters of the serpentine Rhine drift slowly through the city on their way to Germany. This intimate, surprisingly rich city makes a perfect weekend destination.

GETTING TO BASEL

Basel stands at the international crossroads of Switzerland, France, and Germany. If **driving** from France, take A35, E25, or E60; from Germany, E35 or A5. If traveling within Switzerland, take Rte. 2 north. The **Euroairport** (tel. 325 31 11) serves continental Europe; all trans-continental flights are routed through Zurich. There are flights several times per day to both Geneva and Zurich. Shuttle buses run passengers between the airport and the SBB train station every 20-30 minutes from 5am until the last plane arrives. The city has three **train stations:** the French SNCF station is next door to the Swiss SBB station in Centralbahnpl. near the *Altstadt,* and trains from Germany arrive at the DB station, across the Rhine down Riehenstr. City buses to the town center depart from the SBB every 6-7½ minutes during the day and every 15 minutes toward evening. **Buses** to Swiss, French, and German cities depart from their respective train stations. Carry your passport with you for international crossings.

ORIENTATION AND PRACTICAL INFORMATION

Basel sits in the northwest corner of Switzerland, so close to France that the *Tour de France* annually bikes through the city. The *Gross-Basel* portion of town, where most sights are located, lies on the left bank of the Rhine on two hills separated by the Birsig valley. *Klein-Basel* lies on the right bank. Be sure to pick up a city map (0.50SFr) and other useful publications at either of the two tourist offices.

Tourist Office: Schifflände 5 (tel. 268 68 68; fax 268 68 70; email office@basel.tourismus.ch). From the SBB station, tram #1: "Schifflände." The office is on the river, near Mittlerebrücke. Lists of hotels, restaurants, museums, cultural events, and tours and excursions in Basel and the surrounding area. A **bus tour** of the city leaves from the SBB station. (May-Oct. daily at 10am. 20SFr, students 10SFr.) Open Mon.-Fri. 8:30am-6pm, Sat. 10am-4pm. The **branch office** (tel. 271 36 84; fax 272 93 42; email hotel@messebasel.ch) at the SBB station also makes hotel reservations (10SFr). Open June-Sept. Mon.-Fri. 8:30am-7pm, Sat. 8:30am-12:30pm and 1:30-6pm, Sun 10am-2pm; Oct.-May Mon.-Fri. 8:30am-6pm, Sat. 8:30am-noon.

Currency Exchange: At any bank or the SBB station bureau (open daily 6am-9pm).

American Express: Reise Müller, Steinenvorstadt 33, CH-4002 (tel. 281 33 80). Tram #1: "Barfüsserpl."; the office is 1 block from the square. Checks cashed, mail held. Open Mon.-Fri. 9am-6:30pm, Sat. 10am-4pm.

Trains: SNCF station (tel. 333 63 535 36), on Centralbahnpl. **SBB station** (tel. 157 22 22; 1.19SFr per min.), on Centralbahnpl. **DB station** (tel. 690 11 11), across the Rhine down Riehenstr. To: **Zurich** (every 15-30min., 1hr., 30SFr); **Geneva** (every

BASEL (BÂLE) ■ 361

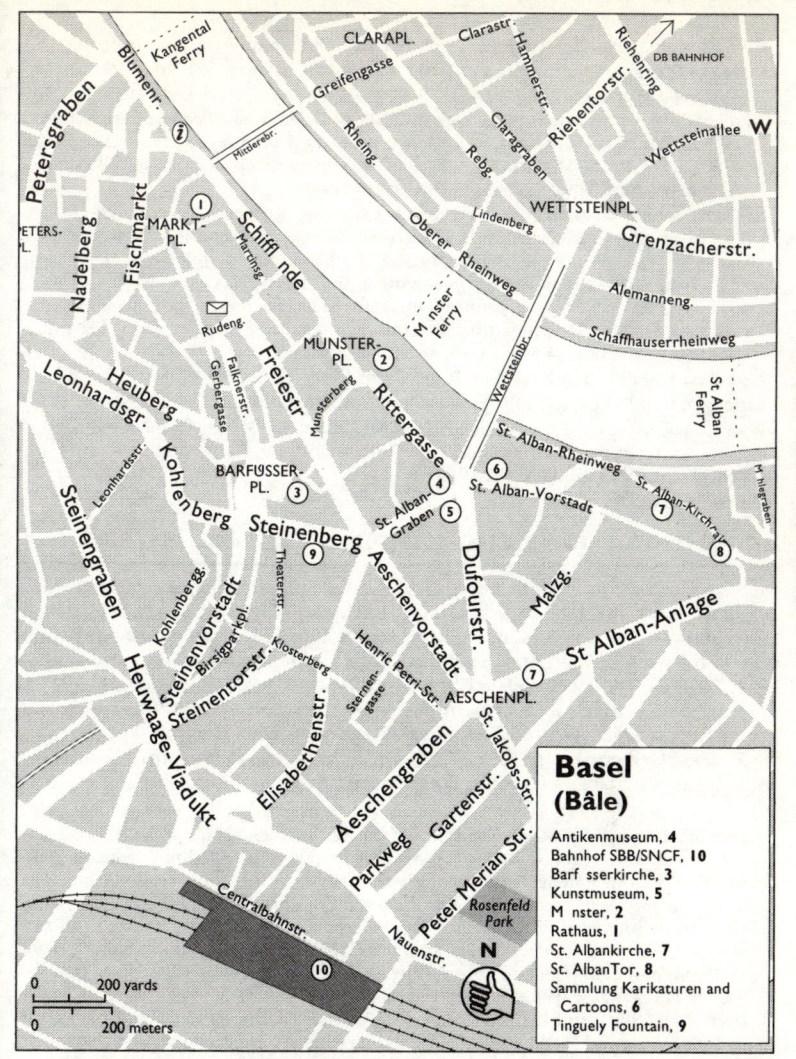

Basel (Bâle)

Antikenmuseum, 4
Bahnhof SBB/SNCF, 10
Barfüsserkirche, 3
Kunstmuseum, 5
Münster, 2
Rathaus, 1
St. Albankirche, 7
St. AlbanTor, 8
Sammlung Karikaturen and Cartoons, 6
Tinguely Fountain, 9

hr., 3hr., 67SFr); **Lausanne** (every hr., 2½hr., 57SFr); **Bern** (every hr., 1hr., 34SFr); **Salzburg** (2 per day, 7hr., 124SFr); **Vienna** (2 per day, 10hr., 154SFr); **Paris** (9 per day, 5-6hr., 675SFr); and **Rome** (2 per day, 7hr., 1195SFr). Make international connections at the French (SNCF) or German (DB) stations.

Public Transportation: Trams and buses run daily 5:45am-11:45pm. Most sights are within a single zone (#10). One-zone tickets 2.60SFr, day ticket 7.40SFr. Automatic vendors at all stops sell tram tickets. Maps at the tourist office or the train station.

Ferries: Ferries cross the Rhine whenever someone, generally a commuter, jumps in the boat. 1.20SFr. Boats run daily in summer 9am-7pm; in winter 11am-5pm. Rhine cruises depart daily from the *Schiffstation* (tel. 639 95 00; fax 639 95 06) next to the tourist office. 4 per day May-Oct. 13. Round-trip to Rheinfelden 42SFr, to Waldhaus 18SFr. Tickets available 30min. before departure.

Taxis: In front of the train station, or call 271 11 11, 633 33 33, or 271 22 22.

Parking: Throughout the city, including at the SBB station. 2.50SFr per hr.

Bike Rental: At the train stations. 22SFr per day. Open Mon.-Sun. 7am-9pm.
Luggage Storage: At all stations. 5-10SFr. Open daily 5:30am-12:15am.
Bookstores: Buchhandlung Tanner, Streitg. 5 (tel. 272 45 47; fax 281 09 88), off Freiestr., is Basel's English-language bookshop. Open Mon.-Wed. and Fri. 8:15am-6:30pm, Thurs. 8:15am-8pm, Sat. 8:15am-5pm. **Jäggi Bücher,** Freiestr. 32 (tel. 261 52 00; fax 261 52 05), carries English-language paperbacks. Open Mon.-Wed. and Fri. 9am-6:30pm, Thurs. 9am-8pm, Sat. 9am-5pm.
Bi-Gay-Lesbian Organizations: Arcados (gay center), Rheing. 69 (tel. 681 31 32; fax 681 66 56), in Klein Basel, has videos (4-8SFr per day) and information. Open June-Aug. Tues.-Fri. noon-3:30pm and 4:45-7pm, Sat. 11am-5pm; Sept.-May Tues.-Fri. 1-7pm. **Schlez** (gay and lesbian center), Gartenstr. 55, Case postale 640, CH-4010 (tel. 631 55 88), off Centralbahnhofpl. There's also a Jugendgruppe (for young gays) and **HUK** (for Christian gays). Ask for the "Schwules Basel" brochure for a listing of groups, bars, discos, saunas, and shops.
Hotlines: Helping Hand, tel. 143. **Rape Crisis Line,** tel. 261 89 89.
Emergencies: Police, tel. 117. **Medical,** tel. 144. **Hospital,** tel. 265 25 25.
Post Office: Freiestr. 12, at Rudeng. Tram #1, 8, or 15: "Marktpl." then 1 block up Gerberg. to Rudeng. Open Mon.-Fri. 7:30am-noon and 1:30-6pm, Sat. 8-11am.
Postal Codes: CH-4000 to CH-4060.
Telephone Code: 061.

ACCOMMODATIONS AND CAMPING

Basel is a vibrant town with an atmospheric *Altstadt*, superb museums, and a raucous nightlife—don't miss it because you didn't call ahead. There is but one overpacked hostel and very few hotels even remotely approaching budget status. Just one phone call—you have time right now. Stop reading this sentence and make a reservation. Now. Trust us. The tourist office has information on a new service (tel./fax 702 21 51) that books private rooms in metropolitan Basel for 20SFr. (Open 10am-noon and 2-6pm. Rooms generally 50-60SFr, but run as high as 100SFr.) The truly desperate can try **Stadhof,** Gerberg. 84 (tel. 261 87 11), which has showerless rooms in extremely limited numbers. (Singles 60-70SFr; doubles 110-120SFr.)

Jugendherberge (HI), St. Alban-Kirchrain 10 (tel. 272 05 72; fax 272 08 33). Tram #1: "Aeschenpl." then tram #3: "St. Alban-Tor." Or walk 10-15min. from the SBB station down Aeschengraben to St. Alban Anlage. At the tower, follow the signs down the hill. Near a calm stretch of the river, this curious old building offers large windows with views of the gorgeous St. Alban district. The efficient institutional set-up has lockers for every bunk and wheelchair access. Reception daily 7-10am and 2pm-midnight. Check-in 6pm. Check-out 10am. Lockout 10am-3pm, but the lounge is open all day. Curfew midnight; no keys. Dorms 26.80SFr the first night, then 24.30SFr; doubles 37.80SFr, 35.30SFr. Showers, sheets, and breakfast included. Dinner 11SFr. Laundry 8SFr. Reservations recommended. Visa, MC.

Hotel-Pension Steinenschanze, Steinengraben 69 (tel. 272 53 53; fax 272 45 73). From the SBB station, turn left on Centralbahnstr. and continue toward Heuwage-Viadukt. Three-star advantages abound: private rooms with telephone, radio, and TV; thick mattresses and feather-light comforters; private bathrooms with showers spouting hot, high-pressure water; balconies over the hotel garden or the street; breakfast with unlimited bread, milk, juice, *müesli*, yogurt, and espresso. No curfew. Singles from 100SFr, under 25 with ISIC 50SFr; doubles with shower from 150SFr, 100SFr. 3-night max. stay. Daytime luggage storage. Visa, MC, AmEx, DC.

Hecht am Rhein, Rheing. 8 (tel. 691 22 20; fax 681 07 88). Cross Mittlerebrücke next to the tourist office and turn right onto Rheing. As the bubbly, patched carpets change from room to room, so does the general decor and quality. Uniformly welcoming bedspreads, but sub-par showers. Women on their own may not feel comfortable in the neighborhood. Reception 7am-6pm. Single 70SFr, with river view 80SFr; doubles 120SFr, 130SFr. Breakfast included. Visa, MC, AmEx, DC.

Camping: Camp Waldhort, Heideweg 16 (tel. 711 64 29), in Reinach. Tram #1: "Aeschenplatz" (one stop), then tram #11: "Landhof." Backtrack 200m toward

Basel, cross the main street, and follow the signs. Reception daily 8am-12:15pm and 2:30-10pm. 6.50SFr; tents 4SFr. Open March-Oct.

FOOD

With all the students about, relatively cheap eateries are numerous, even in the heart of the city. Marktplatz and the *Altstadt* are especially laden with restaurants.

Hirscheneck, Lindenberg 23 (tel. 692 73 33). Cross Wettsteinbrücke and take the first left. An unabashedly left-of-center restaurant-bar where dreadlocks, piercings, and the hammer and sickle prevail. Features at least 2 vegetarian and organically grown dishes every day. *Menu* 13SFr. Open Mon. 5pm-midnight, Tues.-Thurs. 8am-midnight, Fri. 8am-1am, Sat. 2pm-1am, Sun. 10am-midnight.

Zum Schnabel, Trillengässlein 2 (tel. 261 49 09). Tram #1 or 8: "Marktpl."; walk one block on Hutg. to Spalenberg., and then take a left onto Schnabelg. In this corner terrace, Italian-speaking servers present well-prepared German dishes. 12.80SFr buys bratwurst with caramelized onions, *Rösti*, and a salad. Pasta 14-22SFr. Open Mon.-Sun. 8am-midnight. Visa, MC, AmEx, DC.

Topas Kosher Restaurant, Leimenstr. 24 (tel. 271 8700), next to the Basel Synagogue and down the street from the Marcel Hess (self-proclaimed "kosher sausage king") kosher deli. Entrees 19-28SFr. Open Sun.-Tues. and Thurs. 11:30am-2pm and 6:30-9pm, Fri. 11:30am-2pm. Fri. dinner and Sat. lunch by reservation only.

Markets

Migros, Steinenvorstadt; Clarapl.; or Sterneng. 17. Open Mon.-Wed. and Fri. 8am-6:30pm, Thurs. 8am-8pm, Sat. 8am-5pm.
Co-op, on Centralbahnpl. Open Mon.-Sat. 6am-10pm, Sun. 9am-10pm.
Public market, on Marktpl. Fresh fruits, vegetables, and baked goods are offered every weekday morning. Open until 6:30pm on Mon., Wed., and Fri.

Lizard Lunacy

In 1529, Basel's residents enthusiastically joined the Reformation and threw out the bishop, but they kept his *crozier* (staff) as the town's emblem. The staff shares this honor with the basilisk, a creature part bat, part dragon, and part rooster, which spawned what may have been the world's first and only public trial and execution of a chicken. In 1474, a hen allegedly laid an egg on a dung heap under a full moon, an action sure to hatch a basilisk. The bird was tried, found guilty, and beheaded, and the egg was ceremonially burnt. Despite this anti-basilisk fervor, replicas of Basel's namesake appear throughout the city. The more innocuous *crozier*, however, remains Basel's primary symbol.

SIGHTS

The **Münster,** Basel's medieval jewel, stands on the site of an ancient Celtic town and a Roman fort, a fact catalogued by the archaeological excavation in the crypt beneath the apse. Stained glass, delicate carvings, and hanging lamps adorn the lofty church, but the red sandstone facade steals the show, with hundreds of figures in various acts of pedantic piety ranging from trumpet-playing to dragon-slaying. Behind the altar, gilt Latin inscriptions memorialize the life of Erasmus, the renowned scholar and staunch Catholic who remained loyal to his faith even after his beloved Basel joined the Reformation. When he died, the city set aside its dogma and gave him a proper Catholic burial in its Protestant cathedral. Bernoulli, the mathematician who discovered the math behind the spiral and several laws concerning flight, also rests in the cloister. (Bernoulli's Principle explains why a piece of paper rises when you blow on its edge.) The **tower** boasts the city's best view of the Rhine, *Klein Basel*, and Black Forest tower. (Open in summer Mon.-Fri. 10am-5pm, Sat. 10am-noon and 2-5pm, Sun. 1-5pm; in winter Mon.-Sat. 11am-4pm, Sun. 2-4pm. Free. Tower 2SFr; due to recent suicides, you can't go up alone.) For a contrasting aesthetic, walk toward Barfüsserpl. onto Steinenberg, where the **Jean Tinguely**

Fountain memorializes modern chaos. Iron sculptures maniacally spew water as they parody human foibles.

Petersgraben leads to the University and Peterspl. The park forms a *de facto* quadrangle and bicycle parking lot for the university and is ideal for frisbee, picnicking, napping, reading Kant, or any other collegiate endeavor. Bargain-hunters flock here every Saturday morning for the **flea market,** which starts at 9am and goes until early afternoon. Potential souvenirs like old coins and beer steins lurk among the flotsam, but the friendly students unloading and accruing junk are the best finds. Strike up a conversation while browsing, and you may wind up with a new-found guide.

Basel's oh-so-friendly and easy-to-use pedestrian tourist signs point the way back to Freiestr., the main shopping avenue, and to Marktpl. The very red **Rathaus,** erected in the early 1500s to celebrate Basel's entry into the Confederation, brightens Marktpl. with a blinding facade adorned with gold and green statues. In an attempt to gain influence in state affairs, Basel's then-powerful guilds locked the government inside the Rathaus in 1691. While the politicians starved inside, the guilds partied outside, feasting on ale and sweets in an uprising later dubbed the "Cookie Rebellion." Freiestr. #25 and 34 exemplify guild-hall architecture. Off Marktpl., Sattlegasse (Saddler's Lane) marks the beginning of the **artisan's district,** with such street names as Schneidergasse (Tailor's Lane). St. Ursula's pilgrimage of girls to the Holy Land during the Children's Crusade passed through the **Elftausendjungfern-Gässlein** (Lane of 11,000 Virgins). The medieval practice of gaining indulgences by walking this lane is now defunct, but people still stagger down here after overindulging at nearby clubs. A colorful Gothic fountain spices up the nearby **Fischmarket,** while a more refined, pastel-and-eggshell theme dominates the St. Alban district, home of many established Basel families. By the hostel, on a calm stretch of the Rhine, **St. Alban-Tor** is one of the old city wall's three remaining towers. Play with the passing dogs who walk their owners back and forth in the park, or head down St. Alban-Vorstadt to the *Altstadt.*

The **Zoologischer Garten** (tel. 295 35 35; fax 281 00 05), one of the best zoos in Europe, is located on Binningerstr., 10 minutes down Steinenvorstadt from the *Altstadt.* The zoo is most famous for successfully breeding several endangered species, and the gardens are as much of an attraction as the animals. Restaurants, picnic areas, and ice cream vendors abound. (Open daily May-Aug. 8am-6:30pm; Sept.-Oct. and March-April 8am-6pm; Nov.-Feb. 8am-5:30pm. 10SFr, students 8SFr.)

MUSEUMS

Basel's 30 museums may seem overwhelming, but they warrant more than a casual glance. The **Kunstmuseum** is deservedly the most famous, but many esoteric galleries are also fascinating. Subjects range from medieval medicine to musical mechanisms to Monteverdi motorcars. Pick up the comprehensive museum guide at the tourist office, or check out Basel's museum website at http://www.unibas.ch/museum. If you're visiting several museums, it may make sense to buy a **three-day Basel museum pass,** sold and honored at nearly all the local museums and in nearby **Augst** (23SFr, students 16SFr). The pass becomes valid with entry to the first museum visited. A full-year pass is also available (60SFr, students 40SFr). Many museums are free on the first Sunday morning of each month.

Kunstmuseum (Museum of Fine Arts), St. Alban-Graben 16 (tel. 271 08 28; fax 271 08 45). Tram #2. In 1661, the culturally minded city bought and displayed a private collection as the first public gallery not derived from previous royal acquisitions. The collection focuses on 13th-, 14th-, and 15th-century art, with works from Mathias, Witz, and the Holbeins. The 19th and 20th centuries appear with Matisse and Van Gogh, excellent groupings of Dalí, Miro, and Klee, and enough Chagalls and Kandinskys to send your senses swimming and stumbling into the excellent collection of Picassos next door. The museum acquired these works when they had an opportunity to buy 2 Picassos but could not raise the money. Basel granted the money through a resoundingly affirmative referendum, and the aged Picasso was so touched that he donated 4 additional paintings. Open Tues.-Sun. 10am-5pm,

Wed. 10am-9pm. 7SFr, students 5SFr. Free on Sunday. Special rates for exhibitions.

Museum für Gegenwartskunst (Museum of Contemporary Art), St. Alban-Rheinweg 60 (tel. 272 81 83), by the youth hostel. Clever art from the 1960s onward displayed in galleries swathed in a stark, sophisticated pretention. Unlike most modern-art museums, however, this museum makes the art approachable—and dynamically so. Fascinating explanatory notes in English and German guide one through the well-chosen collection of recent works and important pieces by Beuys, Stella, and Trockel. Open Tues.-Sun. 11am-5pm. 7SFr, students 5SFr.

Antikenmuseum (Museum of Ancient Art), St. Alban-Graben 5 (tel. 271 22 02; fax 272 18 61), near the Kunstmuseum. A jewel of a museum that employs ultra-modern, sleek display cases to house a treasure trove of antiquities in 2 elegant, Neoclassical mansions. Greek and Roman works predominate, but the Egyptian and Etruscan collections are compelling. Open March-July Tues. and Thurs.-Sun. 10am-5pm, Wed. 10am-9pm. 5SFr, students 3SFr.

Museum der Kulturen Basel (Museum of Ethnology) and **Naturhistorisches Museum** (Natural History Museum), Augusting. 2 (tel. 266 55 00; fax 266 56 05), off Munsterpl. The Museum of Ethnology's mansion is topped by Neoclassical friezes but contains an off-beat gathering of exotic, non-Western art. Dizzying variety of art and artifacts from the South Seas, South America, and Central/Western Africa. Everything is well labeled, contextualized, and accessible. The human exhibits share the building with the animals and minerals of the Natural History Museum. Expert taxonomists have created engaging exhibits of woolly mammoths and inventive display cases in which the model animals interact with their own skeletal mirror images. Open March-Aug. Tues. and Thurs.-Sun. 10am-5pm, Wed. 10am-9pm; Sept.-April Tues. and Thurs.-Sun. 10am-5pm. 6SFr, students 4SFr.

Barfüsserkirche (Historical Museum), Steinenberg 4 (tel. 271 05 05; fax 271 05 42), on Barfüsserpl. Only here will you see the king of Basel stick his tongue out at you. Originally set on a gate facing *Klein Basel* in the 17th century, the *Lälle-Koenig* (king with tongue) is a clock with a protruding tongue that gestures at onlookers every other second. The museum is inside an old church, an exhibit in itself with glorious pink stone columns and huge windows veiled in transparent linen. The downstairs rooms contain original medieval and Renaissance furniture. Open Mon. and Wed.-Sun. 10am-5pm. 5SFr, students 3SFr, first of the month free.

Papiermühle (Paper Mill), St. Alban-Tal 37 (tel. 272 96 52; fax 272 09 93), a quick float down the river from the hostel. Everything you wanted to know about the art of papermaking but were afraid to ask. A restored medieval mill with a noisy water wheel that continues to mash rags so that visitors can make their own paper (a great rainy day activity for kids). Sprawling exhibits upstairs on the history of paper, writing, and printing. Try your hand at writing with a quill or typesetting a souvenir. Open Tues.-Sun. 2-5pm. 9SFr, students 6SFr.

Sammlung Karikaturen and Cartoons (Cartoon and Caricature Collection), St. Alban-Vorstadt 28 (tel. 271 12 88; fax 271 12 71). All the carefully mounted cartoons are in German, but the humor is universal, if the visitors' constant stifled chuckles are anything to judge by. Hilarious 20th-century works, including *Snoopy* and *Calvin and Hobbes*. Much of the humor leans toward *New Yorker* sneers rather than outright guffaws, but there are picture books for the kids to titter at. Open Wed. and Sat. 2-5:30pm, Sun. 10am-5:30pm. 6SFr, students 3SFr.

Jüdisches Museum der Schweiz (Jewish Museum of Switzerland), Kornhausg. 8 (tel. 261 95 14). Tram #37: "Lyss." Small but well-done exhibits with many rare items. The 3 sections include the law, the Jewish year, and Jewish life. Open Mon. and Wed. 2-5pm, Sun. 11am-5pm. Free.

ENTERTAINMENT AND NIGHTLIFE

While parties abound year-round, the carnival, or **Fasnacht,** blows the rest away. At 4am on the Monday after Ash Wednesday (February 30 in 1998), the festivities commence with the *Morgenstreich,* the morning parade. The 621-year-old festival features colorful processions, fife and drum music, and traditional lampooning of the year's local and regional scandals. Revelers hide behind brilliant masks in an attempt to scare away winter. Though *Fasnacht* is *the* party in Basel, the town hardly slumbers the rest of the year. Basel's many cultural offerings include an accomplished ballet and several theaters. Music is especially popular here; one rewarding event is the free weekly **organ recital** at St. Leonard's Church (Wed. at 6:15pm). The best sources of information are tourist office pamphlets, which have lists in English of concerts, plays, gallery exhibits, fairs, and other happenings for a three-month period.

A university town through and through, Basel's varied nightlife presents an entertaining change of pace from the surrounding bucolic and historical offerings. Start bar-hopping at **Barfüsserplatz**, where students and adults sit at outdoor tables and drink wine on the steps of the Barfüsserkirche. The two most popular local beers are **Warwick** and **Cardinal**. When the bars close, revelers often head for the hipper-than-thou clubs—don't worry, all you need is that thousand-watt smile and some clean jeans. Most places have a 21 and older policy, but the crowds get younger on weekends. Talk to students at the Petersplatz flea market to find the hot spots.

- **Atlantis,** Klosterburg 13. Big. Hot. Smoky. Loud. Fun. A large bar that sways to all grooves, including reggae, jazz, and funk. Bands play every night the Italian soccer team does not. Cover 5-7SFr. Open Sun.-Thurs. 10am-midnight, Fri.-Sat. 10am-1am.
- **Brauerei Fischerstube,** Rheing. 45 (tel. 692 66 35). Cross Mittlerebrücke and take the first right. Nary a beer sign in sight, but this bar happens to be Basel's smallest brewery, crafting 4 of the best beers in town. At this old-school *biergarten*, the delectably sharp *Hell Spezial* goes well with the homemade pretzels on each table. Open Mon.-Thurs. 10-midnight, Fri.-Sat. 10pm-1am, Sun. 5pm-midnight. Visa, MC.
- **Pickwick Pub,** Steinenvorstadt 13 (tel. 281 66 87), 100m from Barfüsserpl. This English-style pub, draped in football memorabilia, hosts students and adults alike. Happy-go-lucky bartenders prepared to go the distance, even if it's shot for shot. Open Mon.-Thurs. 11am-midnight, Fri.-Sat. 11am-3am, Sun. 2pm-midnight.
- **Caveau Mövenpick Wine Pub,** Grünpfahlg. 4 (tel. 261 22 12), by the post office. A sophisticated change from the bar scene. Fine regional wine selection, particularly Alsatian, but prices are steep. Glasses 6-10SFr. Open Mon.-Sat. 11am-midnight.
- **Fifty-fifty,** Leonardsburg 1 (tel. 261 33 22). 50s Americana on the walls and wine, beer, and "energy drinks" for under 5SFr on the menu. *Happy Days* diner motif throughout. Beers 2.50SFr during Happy Hour (Mon.-Sat. 5-7pm). "Gourmet" burgers (14-19SFr) and "Famous Wings" (30 pieces for 42SFr). Open Mon.-Thurs. and Sun. 6:30pm-2am, Fri.-Sat. 6:30pm-4am.
- **Campari Bar,** near the Tinguely fountain. On warm summer nights, head to this elegant outdoor bar surrounded by shady trees. One of the meeting places of the Basel art scene. Open Sun.-Thurs. 5pm-midnight, Fri.-Sat. 5pm-1am.
- **Babalabar,** Gerbelg. 74, next to Fifty-fifty. Dark, modern dance club for the beautiful people. Techno the night away among the disco bars and mirrors. Cover about 10SFr, depending on the night. Open in summer Sun.-Thurs. 10pm-1:30am, Fri.-Sat. 10pm-2:30am; in winter Sun.-Thurs. 8pm-midnight, Fri.-Sat. 8pm-whenever.

■ Near Basel

AUGUSTA RAURICA

The twin villages of **Augst** and **Kaiseraugst** will take you farther back than Basel's merely medieval remnants. Founded in 43 BC, **Augusta Raurica** is the oldest Roman colony on the Rhine. By the 2nd century AD, it had grown into an opulent trading center with a population of 20,000. After its destruction at the hands of the Alemanni in the late 3rd century, the Romans built a fortress adjacent to the old colony. Ongoing excavations continue to uncover temples, baths, and workshops. A helpful multilingual guidebook lists walking tours. If time is short, skip the smallish **Roman Museum** for a ramble through the fields to the **Roman Farm Animal Park,** where selfish donkeys, bullying pigs, and token peacocks are sure to amuse even the most blasé roamin' tourist. (Sites, museum, and park open March-Oct. Mon. 1-5pm, Tues.-Sat. 10am-5pm, Sun. 10am-6pm; Nov.-Feb. Tues.-Sat. 10am-noon and 1-4pm, Sun. 10am-noon and 1-5pm, Mon. 1-4pm. Museum 5SFr, students 3SFr; parks free.)

If you're stuck for cash on your travels, don't panic. Western Union can transfer money in minutes. We've 37,000 outlets in over 140 countries. And our record of safety and reliability is second to none. Call Western Union: wherever you are, you're never far from home.

WESTERN UNION | MONEY TRANSFER®

The fastest way to send money worldwide.

Austria 0660 8066 Canada 1 800 235 0000* Czech 2422 9524 France (01) 43 54 46 12 or (01) 45 35 60 60 Germany 0130 7890 or (0180) 522 5822 Greece (01) 927 1010 Ireland 1 800 395 395* Italy 167 22 00 55* or 167 464 464* Netherlands 0800 0566* Poland (022) 636 5688 Russia 095 119 82 50 Spain 900 633 633* or (91) 559 0253 Sweden 020 741 742 Switzerland 0512 22 33 58 UK 0800 833 833* USA 1 800 325 6000*.
*Toll free telephone No.

Get the MCI Card.
The Smart and Easy Card.

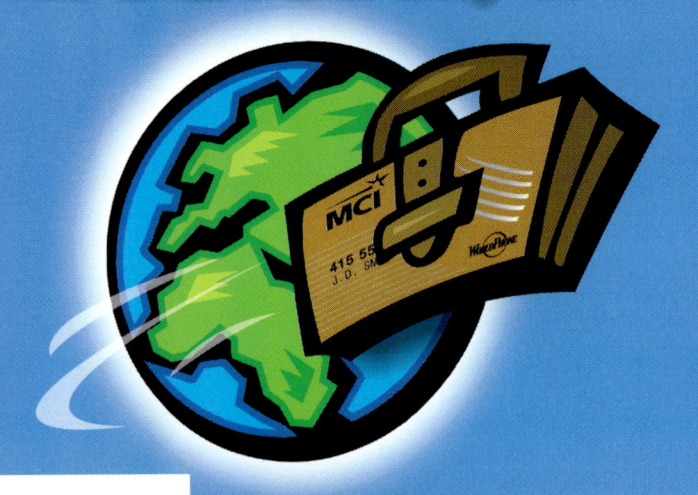

The MCI Card with WorldPhone Service is designed specifically to keep you in touch with people that matter the most to you. We make international calling as easy as possible.

The MCI Card with WorldPhone Service....
- Provides access to the US from over 125 countries and places worldwide.
- Country to country calling from over 70 countries
- Gives you customer service 24 hours a day
- Connects you to operators who speak your language
- Provides you with MCI's low rates with no sign-up or monthly fees
- Even if you don't have an MCI Card, you can still reach a WorldPhone Operator and place collect calls to the U.S. Simply dial the access code of the country you are calling from and hold for a WorldPhone operator.

For more information or to apply for a Card call:
1-800-444-1616

Outside the U.S., call MCI collect (reverse charge) at:
1-916-567-5151

© 1997, MCI Telecommunications Corporation. MCI, its logo, as well as the names of MCI's other products and services referred to herein are proprietary marks of MCI Communications Corporation.

Pick Up The Phone.
Pick Up The Miles.

You earn frequent flyer miles when you travel internationally, why not when you call internationally? Callers can earn frequent flyer miles with one of MCI's airline partners:

- American Airlines
- Continental Airlines
- Delta Airlines
- Hawaiian Airlines
- Midwest Express Airlines
- Northwest Airlines
- Southwest Airlines

Please cut out and save this reference guide for convenient U.S. and worldwide calling with the MCI Card with WorldPhone Service.

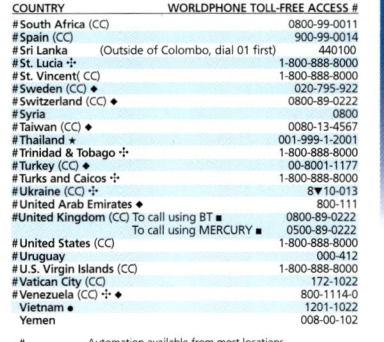

Your MCI Worldphone Access Numbers

COUNTRY	WORLDPHONE TOLL-FREE ACCESS #
# South Africa (CC)	0800-99-0011
# Spain (CC)	900-99-0014
# Sri Lanka (Outside of Colombo, dial 01 first)	440100
# St. Lucia ⁑	1-800-888-8000
# St. Vincent (CC)	1-800-888-8000
# Sweden (CC) ◆	020-795-922
# Switzerland (CC) ◆	0800-89-0222
# Syria	0800
# Taiwan (CC) ◆	0080-13-4567
# Thailand ★	001-999-1-2001
# Trinidad & Tobago ⁑	1-800-888-8000
# Turkey (CC) ◆	00-8001-1177
# Turks and Caicos ⁑	1-800-888-8000
# Ukraine (CC) ⁑	8▼10-013
# United Arab Emirates ◆	800-111
# United Kingdom (CC) To call using BT ■	0800-89-0222
To call using MERCURY ■	0500-89-0222
# United States (CC)	1-800-888-8000
# Uruguay	000-412
# U.S. Virgin Islands (CC)	1-800-888-8000
# Vatican City (CC)	172-1022
# Venezuela (CC) ⁑ ◆	800-1114-0
Vietnam ●	1201-1022
Yemen	008-00-102

\# Automation available from most locations.
(CC) Country-to-country calling available to/from most international locations.
⁑ Limited availability.
▶ Wait for second dial tone.
◆ When calling from public phones, use phones marked LADATEL.
■ International communications carrier.
● Not available from public pay phones.
★ Public phones may require deposit of coin or phone card for dial tone.
▲ Local service fee in U.S. currency required to complete call.
● Regulation does not permit intra-Japan calls.
● Available from most major cities

And, it's simple to call home.

1. Dial the WorldPhone toll-free access number of the country you're calling from (listed inside).
2. Follow the voice instructions in your language of choice or hold for a WorldPhone operator.
   - Enter or give the operator your MCI Card number or call collect.
3. Enter or give the WorldPhone operator your home number.
4. Share your adventures with your family!

The MCI Card with WorldPhone Service... The easy way to call when traveling worldwide.

MCI Calling Card
415 555 1234 2244
J.D. SMITH

For more information or to apply for a Card call:
1-800-444-1616

Outside the U.S., call MCI collect (reverse charge) at:
1-916-567-5151

Please cut out and save this reference guide for convenient U.S. and worldwide calling with the MCI Card with WorldPhone Service.

COUNTRY	WORLDPHONE TOLL-FREE ACCESS #
#American Samoa	633-2MCI (633-2624)
#Antigua (Available from public card phones only)	#2
#Argentina (CC)	0800-5-1002
#Aruba ✦	800-888-8
#Australia (CC) ◆	
To call using OPTUS ■	1-800-551-111
To call using TELSTRA ■	1-800-881-100
#Austria (CC) ◆	022-903-012
#Bahamas	1-800-888-8000
#Bahrain	800-002
#Barbados	1-800-888-8000
#Belarus (CC) From Brest, Vitebsk, Grodno, Minsk	8-800-103
From Gomel and Mogilev regions	8-10-800-103
#Belgium (CC) ◆	0800-10012
#Belize	
From Hotels	557
From Payphones	815
#Bermuda ÷	1-800-888-8000
#Bolivia ◆	0-800-2222
#Brazil (CC)	000-8012
#British Virgin Islands ÷	1-800-888-8000
#Brunei	800-011
#Bulgaria	00800-0001
#Canada (CC)	1-800-888-8000
#Cayman Islands	1-800-888-8000
#Chile (CC)	
To call using CTC ■	800-207-300
To call using ENTEL ■	800-360-180
#China ✦	
(Available from most major cities)	108-12
for a Mandarin-speaking Operator	108-17
#Colombia (CC)	980-16-0001
Colombia IIIC Access in Spanish	980-16-1000
#Costa Rica ÷	0800-012-2222
#Cote D'Ivoire	1001
#Croatia (CC) ✶	0800-22-0112
#Cyprus ◆	080-90000
#Czech Republic (CC) ◆	00-42-000112
#Denmark (CC) ◆	8001-0022
#Dominica	1-800-888-8000
Dominican Republic (CC) ÷	1-800-888-8000
Dominican Republic IIIC Access in Spanish	1121
#Ecuador (CC) ÷	999-170
#Egypt ◆	
(Outside of Cairo, dial 02 first)	355-5770
El Salvador ◆	800-1767
#Federated States of Micronesia	624

COUNTRY	WORLDPHONE TOLL-FREE ACCESS #
#Fiji	004-890-1002
#Finland (CC) ◆	08001-102-80
#France (CC) ◆	0800-99-0019
#French Antilles (CC) (includes Martinique, Guadeloupe)	0800-99-0019
French Guiana (CC)	0-800-99-0019
#Gabon	00-005
#Gambia ✦	00-1-99
#Germany (CC)	0130-0012
#Greece (CC) ◆	00-800-1211
#Grenada ÷	1-800-888-8000
#Guam (CC)	950-1022
#Guatemala (CC) ◆	99-99-189
#Guyana	177
#Haiti ÷	
Haiti IIIC Access in French/Creole	190
#Honduras ÷	8000-122
#Hong Kong (CC)	800-96-1121
#Hungary (CC) ◆	00▼800-01411
#Iceland (CC) ◆	800-9002
#India (CC)	000-127
(Available from most major cities)	
#Indonesia (CC) ◆	001-801-11
#Iran ÷	(SPECIAL PHONES ONLY)
#Ireland (CC)	1-800-55-1001
#Israel (CC)	177-150-2727
#Italy (CC) ◆	172-1022
#Jamaica ÷	1-800-888-8000
(from Special Hotels only)	873
Jamaica IIIC Access	#2 from public phone
#Japan (CC) ◆	
To call using KDD ■	0039-121
To call using IDC ■	0066-55-121
To call using ITJ ■	0044-11-121
#Jordan	18-800-001
#Kazakhstan (CC)	8-800-131-4321
#Kenya ✦	
(Available from most major cities)	080011
To call using KT ■	00309-12
#Korea (CC)	
To call using DACOM ■	00309-14
Phone Booths÷	
Military Bases	Press red button, 03, then ∗
#Kuwait	800-MCI (800-624)
#Lebanon ÷	600-MCI (600-624)
#Liechtenstein (CC) ◆	0800-89-0222
#Luxembourg	0800-0112

COUNTRY	WORLDPHONE TOLL-FREE ACCESS #
#Macao	0800-131
#Macedonia (CC) ◆	99800-4036
#Malaysia (CC) ◆	800-0012
#Malta	0800-89-0120
#Marshall Islands	1-800-888-8000
#Mexico	
Avantel (CC)	95-800-674-7000
Telmex ▲	91-800-021-1000
#Micronesia	624
#Monaco (CC) ◆	800-99-019
#Montserrat	1-800-888-8000
#Morocco	00-211-0012
#Netherlands (CC) ◆	0800-022-9122
#Netherlands Antilles (CC) ÷	001-800-888-8000
#New Zealand (CC)	000-912
Nicaragua (CC)	166
Nicaragua IIIC Access in Spanish	∗2 from any public payphone
#Norway (CC) ◆	800-19912
#Pakistan	00-800-12-001
#Panama	108
#Papua New Guinea (CC)	2810-108
#Paraguay ÷	05-07-19140
#Peru	008-112-800
#Philippines (CC) ◆	0800-500-01
To call using PLDT ■	105-14
To call using PHILCOM ■	1026-14
Philippines (Outside of Manila, dial 02 first)	105-15
Philippines IIIC Access via PLDT in Tagalog	105-14
Philippines IIIC via PhilCom in Tagalog	1026-15
#Poland (CC) ÷	00-800-111-21-22
#Portugal (CC) ÷	05-017-1234
#Puerto Rico (CC)	1-800-888-8000
#Qatar ∗	0800-012-77
Romania (CC) ÷	01-800-1800
#Russia (CC) ÷	
To call using ROSTELCOM ■	747-3322
(For Russian speaking operator)	747-3320
To call using SOVINTEL ■	960-2222
#Saipan (CC) ◆	950-1022
#San Marino (CC) ◆	172-1022
#Saudi Arabia (CC)	1-800-11
#Singapore	8000-112-112
#Slovak Republic (CC)	00421-00112
#Slovenia	080-8808

MCI

NEAR BASEL: BLACK FOREST (SCHWARZWALD) ■ 367

To get to the ruins from Basel, take the hourly regional train three stops to **Kaiseraugst** (4.60SFr). A ferry (tel. 639 95 06) runs from Schifflände, by the Basel tourist office, to Kaiseraugst (4 per day, 2¼hr., 16SFr, round-trip 29SFr). Ignore the tourist information stand at the train station and follow the signs to Augusta Raurica. Bring a full picnic to the temples or the amphitheater; the only nearby restaurant with reasonable prices is **Ristorante Römerhof Pizzeria** (tel. 811 17 67), just past the museum, with pizzas for 12 to 17SFr. (Open Mon.-Sat. 11am-2:30pm and 6pm-midnight, Sun. 11am-midnight. Visa, MC, AmEx, DC.)

■ Black Forest (Schwarzwald)

At Basel's back door spreads the dark majesty of the Black Forest. Throughout its rocky development, the German cultural consciousness has shown a love of the sinister, a craving for the ominous, a collective dream of the dark. Nowhere are such nightmarish desires more at home than in the Black Forest, a tangled expanse of evergreen covering the southeastern corner of the country. The forest owes its foreboding name to the eerie darkness that prevails under its canopy of vegetation, and its depths have inspired the most quintessentially German fairy tales, including the adventures of Hänsel and Gretel, as well as a slew of poetry and folk traditions. Many of these regional quirks are now exploited at the pervasive "cuckoo-clock, *Lederhosen*, bratwurst, key-chain, and ice-cream kiosks, which conspire with the devastation of acid rain to erode the region's authenticity. You can easily avoid the hordes of tourists, however, as the trails that wind through the region lead willing hikers into the dense forest in mere minutes. Skiing is also available here; the longest slope is at Feldberg (near Titisee), and smaller hills smatter the Schwarzwald Hochstraße.

Basel is one of the main entry points into the forest; the German cities of Freiburg, in the center; Baden-Baden to the northwest; and Stuttgart to the east also provide entry. Most visitors cruise around in (or on) their own set of wheels, as public transportation is sparse. Rail lines encircle the perimeter, with only one main **train** actually penetrating the region (from Donaueschingen in the southeast to Offenburg in the northwest). The **bus** service is more thorough, albeit slow and less frequent. The best source of public transportation information is the **Südbaden public transport office** at the Freiburg *Hauptbahnhof* (a copy of the indispensable *Fahrplan* costs DM1). The **Freiburg tourist office,** Rotteckring 14 (tel. (0761) 368 90 90; fax 37 00 37), is the best place to gather information about the Black forest before your trip.

TITISEE AND SCHLUCHSEE

Thirty km east of Freiburg, the touristed town of **Titisee** is set against dark pine-forested ridges and a lake of the same name. Hourly **trains** connect Freiburg to Titisee. The **tourist office** is in the *Kurhaus,* Strandbadstr. 4 (tel. (07651) 980 40; fax 98 04 40). To reach the building, turn right in front of the train station, walk to the first intersection, and turn right before the entrances to the pedestrian zone. The office books rooms (DM3) and sells maps (DM1-15) of the 130km of hiking trails surrounding the lake. (Open May-Oct. Mon.-Fri. 8am-6pm, Sat. 10am-noon and 3-5pm, Sun. 10am-noon; Nov.-April Mon.-Fri. 8am-noon and 1:30-5:30pm.) You can rent **paddleboats** from any one of several vendors along Seestr. (DM11-15 per hr.). Guided **boat tours** of the lake (25min., DM6) depart from the same area. **Jugendherberge Veltishof (HI),** Bruderhalde 27 (tel. (07652) 238; fax 756), is beautifully if inconveniently located at the far end of the lake. From the train station, take Südbaden bus #7300: "Feuerwehrheim" (every 1-3hr., DM3). By foot, the hostel is 30 minutes along the main road from the tourist office. (Reception daily 5-8pm. Curfew 10pm. Members only. DM22, over 26 DM26. Resort tax DM2.10.) Several campgrounds lie along the same road; **Naturcamping Weiherhof,** Bruderholde 26 (tel. (07652) 14 68 or 14 78), has laundry facilities and great, tree-shaded sites to pitch a tent. (DM8; tent DM6.50. Tax DM2.10. Open mid-May to Sept.)

South of Titisee is the comparably picturesque, less-touristed **Schluchsee.** Hourly **trains** make the 30-minute jaunt from Titisee. The **tourist office** (tel. (07656) 77 32; fax 77 59), a block into the pedestrian zone in the *Kurhaus,* sells hiking maps and finds rooms for tourists who didn't call ahead. (Open July-Aug. Mon.-Fri. 8am-6pm, Sat. 10am-noon and 4-6pm, Sun. 10am-noon; Sept.-Oct. and May-June Mon.-Fri. 8am-noon and 2-6pm, Sat. 10am-noon; Nov.-April Mon.-Fri. 8am-noon and 2-6pm.) The **Jugendherberge Schluchsee-Wolfsgrund (HI)** (tel. (07656) 329; fax 92 37) is situated on the shore; from the station, cross the tracks, hop the fence, and then follow the path right, over the bridge parallel to the tracks. (Reception closed daily 2-5pm. Curfew 11pm. Dorms DM22, over 26 DM27.)

ST. PETER, ST. MÄRGEN, AND TRIBERG

North of Titisee and about 15km east of Freiburg, the twin villages of **St. Peter** and **St. Märgen** lie within the High Black Forest. **Bus** #7216 runs occasionally from Freiburg to St. Märgen via St. Peter; the more timely route requires a train ride on the Freiburg-Neustadt line to "Kirchzarten," where bus #7216 stops on the way to St. Peter's. **St. Peter's,** an abbey designed by architect Peter Thumb, appears where a halo of green farmland breaks through the dark crust of pine forests. The interior of the abbey's **Klosterkirche** is aflutter with Baroque angels. (Sporadic tours; call the tourist office for scheduling information.) From the "Zähringer Eck" bus stop, the **tourist office** (tel. (07660) 91 02 24; fax 91 02 44) is about 100m up the street. (Open June-Oct. Mon.-Fri. 8am-noon and 2-5pm, Sat. 11am-1pm; Nov.-May Mon.-Fri. 8am-noon and 2-5pm.) Well-marked **trails** cover the surrounding area; an 8km trail from the abbey leads to St. Märgen.

Nestled in a valley 800m above sea level and about two hours by train from Constance, the touristy whistle stop of **Triberg** has Germany's highest **waterfalls,** a series of white cascades tumbling over mossy rocks for 162 vertical meters (park DM2.50, students DM2). **Hiking trails** abound on the outskirts of town, including a portion of the Pforzheim-Basel *Westweg.* Triberg's **tourist office** (tel. (07722) 95 32 30; fax 95 32 36), on the ground floor of the local *Kurhaus,* dishes out brochures, sells town maps (DM1; not good enough for hiking) and hiking maps (DM5.50), and dispenses a catalog of all accommodations in the region. (Open May-Sept. Mon.-Fri. 9am-5pm, Sat. 10am-noon; Oct.-April Mon.-Fri. 9am-5pm.) The town's sparkling, modern **Jugendherberge (HI),** Rohrbacherstr. 35 (tel. (07722) 41 10; fax 66 62), requires a grueling 30-minute climb up Friedrichstr. (which turns into Rohrbacherstr.) from the tourist office. (Reception 5-7pm and at 9:45pm. Dorms DM22, over 26 DM27. Sheets DM5.50. Call ahead.) For those avoiding the climb, the **Hotel Zum Bären,** Hauptstr. 10 (tel. (07722) 44 93), offers worn-in rooms, most with showers, closer to the town center. The jolly staff has been dealing with American students and other fun-lovers for 25 years. (Singles DM46; doubles DM86.)

Central Switzerland

■ Zurich (Zürich)

Switzerland has one bank for every 1200 people, and half of those banks are in Zurich. The battalions of briefcase-toting, Bally-shoed, Armani-suited executives charging daily through the world's fourth-largest stock exchange and largest gold exchange help pump enough money into the economy to keep the upper-crust boutiques and expense account restaurants thriving. There is, however, more to Zurich than money. The city was once the focal point of the Reformation in German Switzerland, led by the anti-Catholic firebrand Ulrich Zwingli. This Protestant asceticism succumbed to the avant-garde spirit of 1916, a year in which artistic and philosophical radicalism shook the town's calm institutions. During this time, living at Universitätstr. 38, James Joyce toiled away to produce *Ulysses*, the quintessential modernist novel. Nearby at Spiegelg. 14, Russian exile Vladimir Lenin bided his time, read Marx, and watched over this capitalist center, dreaming of revolution and trying to ignore all the brouhaha next door as a group of raucous young artists calling themselves the Dadaists founded the seminal proto-performance art collective, the Cabaret Voltaire. Today's *Altstadt* retains some of this youthful irreverent spirit, with lively cafés and bars sprawling onto the narrow, cobblestoned streets.

GETTING TO ZURICH

Because PTT buses cannot go into Zurich proper, the easiest way into the city is by plane, train, or car. **Kloten Airport** (tel. 816 25 00) is the largest hub for Swissair (tel. 157 10 60) and a layover for many international flights. Zurich has daily connections to Frankfurt, Paris, London, and New York. Trains leave every 10 to 20 minutes from the airport for the Hauptbahnhof in the city center (train operates 5:37am-12:20am; 6SFr; Eurailpass and Swisspass valid). **By car,** N3 east connects to E60, which leads to Zurich from Basel. When approaching Zurich from the south (including Geneva), take N1 northeast, then connect to E4 or E17. From Austria or southeast Switzerland, get onto N3 west. Zurich is a city of **trains**. The *Hauptbahnhof* faces the legendary Bahnhofstrasse on one side and the Limmat River on the other. Zurich has connections to all major European and Swiss cities.

ORIENTATION AND PRACTICAL INFORMATION

Zurich sits smack in the middle of northern Switzerland, not far from the German border and surrounded by numerous Swiss playgrounds: the resort lake Bodensee to the north, the ski resorts in the Engadin Valley to the east, and the hiking bases in the Berner Oberland to the south and west. Zurich lies among the lowest land in Switzerland, quite distant from the mountains and skiers that have made the nation famous. Although the suburbs sprawl for miles, most of the activity within Zurich is confined to a relatively small, walkable area. The **Limmat River** splits the city down the middle on its way to the Zürichsee. Grand bridges, offering an elegant views of the stately old buildings that line the river, bind the two sectors together. The university presides from the hillside of the lively far bank that, like Paris's Left Bank, pulses with crowded bars, hip restaurants, and a student's quarter, all loud and lively into the wee hours of the night. By contrast, Zurich's real Left Bank is rather conservative and very expensive. Bahnhofstrasse overflows with bankers and well-coiffed shoppers by day and falls dead quiet when the shops and banks close around six. Straddling the Limmat, the *Altstadt* fills the space between the pedestrian zones. The **Sihl River** edges the other side of the city, joining the Limmat around the train station. The *Altstadt*'s **Limmatquai** (also known as Uto-Quai and Seefeldquai), across the bridge from the Hauptbahnhof, is a favorite strolling destination for many residents and tourists.

Tourist Offices: Main office in the station at Bahnhofpl. 15 (tel. 211 40 00, hotel reservation service tel. 211 11 31; fax 211 39 81; email zhtourismus@access.ch; http://www.zurichtourism.ch). Exit the station to Bahnhofpl. and walk left behind the taxi stand along the building. Have your questions ready, as lines are long and interviews short. Concert, movie, and bar information in German and English and copies of *Zürich News* and *Zürich Next*, which print restaurant and hotel lists. Decipher the German *ZüriTip*, a free entertainment newspaper, for tips on nightlife and alternative culture. Walking tours (see p. 376). The special reservation desk finds rooms after 10:30am. Open April-Oct. Mon.-Fri. 8:30am-9:30pm, Sat.-Sun. 8:30am-8:30pm; Nov.-March Mon.-Fri. 8:30am-7:30pm, Sat.-Sun. 8:30am-6:30pm. Another office at **airport terminal B** (tel. 816 40 81), with the same services and hotel reservations in all of Switzerland for 10SFr. Open daily 10am-7pm. The **head tourist office** for Switzerland, Bellariastr. 38 (tel. 288 11 11), offers information mainly for convention planners and travel agents. Open Mon.-Fri. 9am-6pm.

Tours: The tourist office leads frequent, expensive tours: the "Stroll through the Old Town" (2hr., 18SFr, May-Oct. Mon.-Fri. 2:30pm, Sat.-Sun. 10am and 2:30pm); a standard tour of major sites (2hr., 29SFr, May-Oct. daily 10am, noon, and 2pm; Nov.-April 10am and 2pm); and the same tour plus a cable car and boat ride (2½hr., 39SFr, May-Oct. daily 9:30am).

Budget Travel: SSR, Bäckerstr. 40 (tel. 297 11 11). Open Mon.-Fri. 9am-6pm. Branch office at Leonhardstr. 10 (tel. 241 12 08). Arranges student package tours and helps with most travel questions. Open Mon.-Fri. 10am-8pm. **Globe-Trotter Travel Service AG,** Rennweg 35 (tel. 211 77 80), specializes in overseas travel. Caters to individual travelers (no package tours) and arranges European transport and accommodations. Open Mon.-Fri. 9am-12:30pm and 1:30-6pm, Sat. 9am-3pm.

Consulates: U.K., Dufourstr. 56 (tel. 261 15 20). Open Mon.-Fri. 9am-noon and 2-4pm. **U.S.,** Zollikerstr. 141 (tel. 422 25 66). Visas available only at the embassy in Geneva (see p. 302). Open Mon.-Tues. and Thurs.-Fri. 9-11am, Wed. 1:30-4:30pm. **Australians, Canadians,** and citizens of **Ireland** should contact their embassies in Bern (see p. 392). **New Zealand's** consulate is in Geneva (see p. 302).

Currency Exchange: Train station rates are competitive. Open daily 6:30am-10:45pm. You could also try **Credit Suisse** or **Swiss Bank** on Bahnhofstr. **ATMs** stand throughout the city, but most take only MasterCard. Swiss Bank honors Visa, with branches in Paradepl., Bahnhofstr. 70, and Bellevuepl.

American Express: Bahnhofstr. 20, P.O. Box 5231, CH-8022 (tel. 211 83 70), just after Paradepl. from the train station. Mail held. Travel services. Checks cashed and exchanged, but limited banking services. ATM. Open May-Sept. Mon.-Fri. 8:30am-6:30pm, Sat. 9am-1pm; Oct.-April Mon.-Fri. 8:30am-5:30pm, Sat. 9am-noon. Traveler's check toll-free **emergency line** (tel. 155 01 00).

Trains: Bahnhofpl. To: **Winterthur** (every 15min., 20min., 12SFr); **Lugano** (1-2 per hr., 3hr., 62SFr); **Lucerne** (1-2 per hr., 1hr., 22SFr); **Geneva** (every hr., 3hr., 77SFr); **Basel** (2-4 per hr., 1hr., 32SFr); and **Bern** (1-2 per hr., 1¼hr., 45SFr).

Public Transportation: Trams criss-cross the city, originating at the Hauptbahnhof. Long rides (more than 5 stops) cost 3.40SFr (press the blue button on automatic ticket machines), and short rides (1hr. or less) cost 2.20SFr (yellow button)—the city is small enough to avoid long rides. Buy a 24hr. *Tageskarte* (7.20SFr) if you plan to ride several times. Purchase a ticket before boarding and validate it by inserting it into the ticket machine. Stern, merciless policeman won't hesitate to fine you (50SFr and up) if you try to ride free. *Tageskarten* are also valid for ferry rides down the Limmat River within the Zurich Zone (check the maps at each stop or the tourist office). They are available at the tourist office, hotels, hostels, the automatic ticket machines, or the **Ticketeria** under the train station in Shop-Ville (open Mon.-Sat. 6:30am-7pm, Sun. 7:30am-9pm). Ticketeria also offers 3- and 7-cards. All public buses, trams, and trolleys run Sun.-Thurs. 5:30am-midnight, Fri.-Sat. 5:30am-2am. Railpasses valid on all S-Bahnen.

Ferries: Boats on the **Zürichsee** leave from Bürklipl. and range from a 90min. jaunt between isolated villages (10.80SFr) to a "grand tour" (4-5hr., 28.40SFr). Ferries also leave from the top of the Bahnhofstr. harbor daily at 11:40am (8SFr).

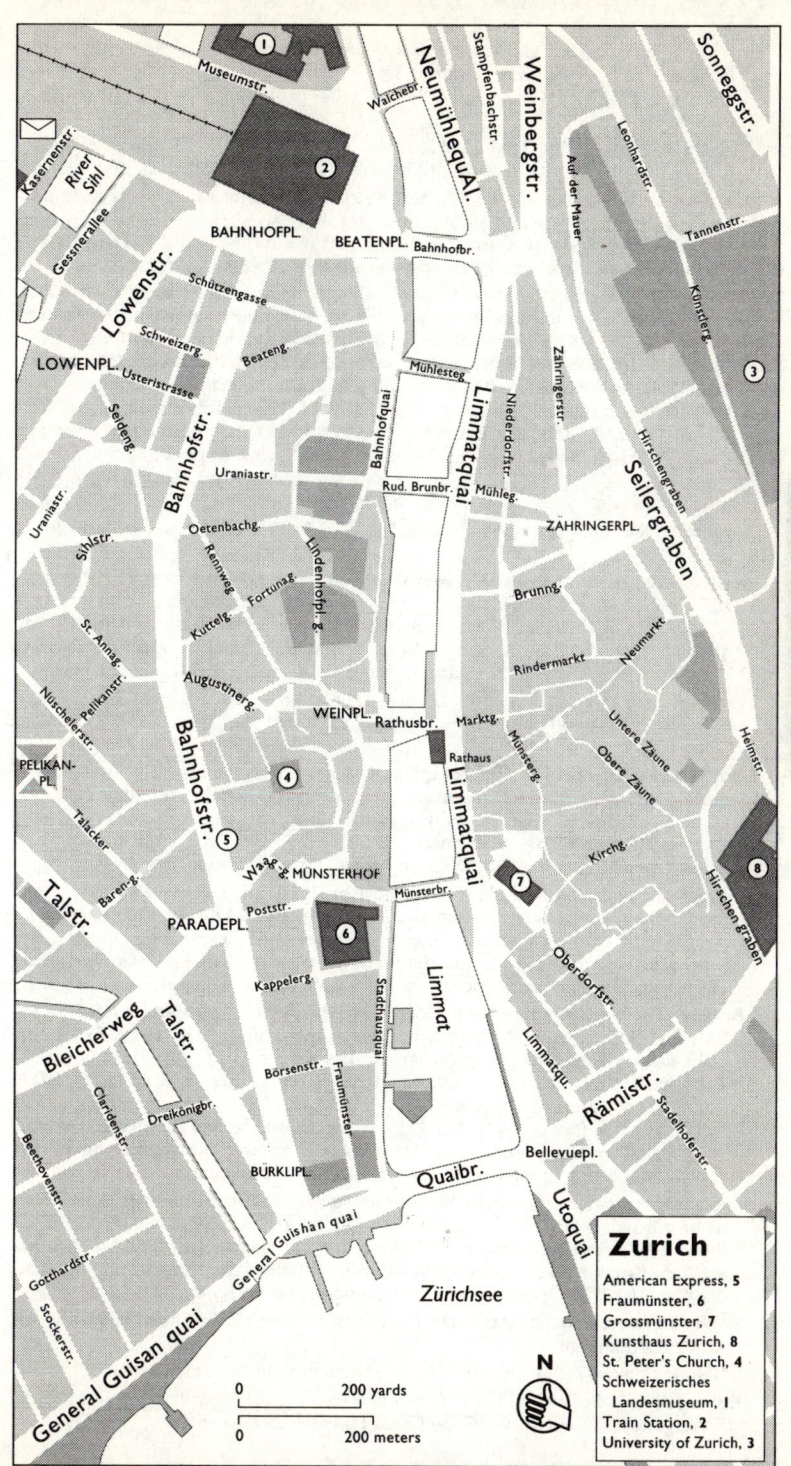

ORIENTATION AND PRACTICAL INFORMATION ■ 371

Zurich

- American Express, **5**
- Fraumünster, **6**
- Grossmünster, **7**
- Kunsthaus Zurich, **8**
- St. Peter's Church, **4**
- Schweizerisches Landesmuseum, **1**
- Train Station, **2**
- University of Zurich, **3**

Enjoy a jump-suited night with the "Swiss Elvises" Wed. at 8pm during July on the Zürichsee (22SFr). For more information, call 482 10 91. On the **Limmat River,** boats run daily April-Oct. (1hr., 6.80SFr). Eurailpass valid; reduced fare for *Tageskarte.*

Taxis: Hail a cab or call **Taxi 2000 Zürich** (tel. 444 44 44), **Taxi Zentrale Zürich** (tel. 155 55 15), or **Taxi for the disabled** (tel. 272 42 42). 6SFr plus 3SFr per km.

Car Rental: Hertz (tel. 814 05 11), at the airport; Morgartenstr. 5 (tel. 242 84 84); Hardturmstr. 319 (tel. 272 50 50). **Avis** (tel. 241 70 70), at the airport. **Budget Airport** (tel. 813 31 31). **Europcar** (tel. 813 20 44), at the airport; Josefstr. 53 (tel. 271 56 56). The airport and train station tourist offices also arrange car rental.

Parking: Metropolitan Zurich has many public parking garages; the Zurich police advise parking in the suburbs and taking a tram or train from there. **Universität Irchel** (tel. 257 43 85), near the large park on Winterthurstr. 18, and **Engi-Märt,** Seestr. 25 (tel. 205 71 11), are both suburban lots. City parking costs 1SFr per hr., 0.50SFr in the suburbs. In the city, try the garages at the major department stores: **Jelmoli,** Steinmühlepl. (tel. 220 49 34), **Migros Limmatplatz,** Limmatstr. 152 (tel. 277 21 11), and **Globus,** at Löwenstr. (tel. 221 33 11). Pick up the free brochure *Guide for Visitors Traveling by Car* at any tourist office or police station.

Bike Rental: At the baggage counter (*Gepäckexpedition Fly-Gepäck*) in the station. 23SFr per day; mountain bike 30SFr. Open daily 6am-7:40pm. **Free bike rental** at Werdmühlepl. and Theaterpl. daily 7:30am-9:30pm. Passport and 20SFr deposit.

Hitchhiking: Hitchers to Basel, Geneva, Paris, or Bonn take streetcar #4: "Werdhölzli" from the station. Those bound for Lucerne, Italy, and Austria take streetcar #9 or 14: "Bahnhof Wiedikon," and walk 1 block down Schimmelstr. to Silhölzli. For Munich, they often take streetcar #14 or 7: "Milchbuck" and walk to Schaffhauserstr. toward St. Gallen and St. Margarethen. Hitchhiking is illegal on the freeway.

Luggage Storage: At the station. Lockers 4SFr and 8SFr. 24hr. access, but you pay extra every time you open the locker. Luggage watch 5SFr at the *Gepäck* counter. Open 6am-10:50pm.

Bookstores: Librairie Payot, Bahnhofstr. 9, has a large selection of original-language English and French literature. Also has travel books, including *Let's Go.* Open Mon. noon-6:30pm, Tues.-Fri. 9am-6:30pm, Sat. 9am-4pm. **Travel Bookshop** and **Travel Maps,** Rindermarkt 20 (tel. 252 38 83), have...travel books and maps. Open Mon. 1-6:30pm, Tues.-Fri. 9am-6:30pm, Sat. 9am-4pm.

Libraries: Zentralbibliothek, Predigerpl. (tel. 261 72 72). Open Mon.-Wed. and Fri.-Sat. 8am-5pm, Thurs. and Sun. 8am-7pm. **Pestalozzi Library,** Zähringerstr. 17 (tel. 261 78 11), has foreign-language magazines and newspapers. Open June-Sept. Mon.-Fri. 10am-7pm, Sat. 10am-2pm; Oct.-May Mon.-Fri. 10am-7pm, Sat. 10am-4pm. Reading room open Mon.-Fri. 9am-8pm, Sat. 9am-5pm.

Bi-Gay-Lesbian Organizations: Homosexuelle Arbeitsgruppe Zürich **(HAZ),** P.O. Box 80232, CH-8023; library and meetings at Sihlquai 67 (tel. 271 22 50). **HAZ-lesben Schwule!** (for lesbians), c/o Urs Bühler, Wildbachstr. 60, CH-8008. **Zart und Heftig** (Gay University Forum Zurich), P.O. Box 7218, CH-8023. **BOA** (for lesbians), Freyastr. 20, CH-8004. **NKCOT** (National Committee for Coming Out Day), Case Postale 7679, CH-8023. **Andershume-Kontiki** (publication), Box 7679, CH-8023. **Gay Bikers,** Box 9313, CH-8036. Ask the tourist office for **Zürich Gay Guide,** listing groups, discos, saunas, bars, and restaurants.

Laundromat: Under the tracks at the train station; ask at the shower desk. Wash 6kg for 8-10SFr. Dry 5SFr per hr. Soap included. Open daily 6am-midnight. **Self-Service Wachari,** Weinbergstr. 37. Wash and dry 5kg for 10.20SFr. Open Mon.-Sat. 7am-10pm, Sun. 10:30am-10pm. **Laundry Mühlegasse,** Mühleg. 11. Wash and dry 5kg for 17SFr. Open Mon.-Fri. 7:30am-noon and 1-6:30pm.

Public Showers and Toilets: At the train station. Toilets 1SFr. Showers 8SFr. Open daily 6am-midnight.

24-Hour Pharmacy: Theaterstr. 14 (tel. 252 56 00), on Bellevuepl.

Emergencies: Police: tel. 117. **Ambulance:** tel. 144; English spoken. **Medical Emergency:** tel. 261 61 00. **Rape Crisis Line:** tel. 291 46 46.

ACCOMMODATIONS AND CAMPING ■ 373

Internet Access: Internet Café, Uraniastr. (tel. 210 33 11), between the observatory and the river, above a parking garage. Access to World Wide Web and email 5SFr per 20min. Open Tues.-Sun. 10am-11pm, Mon. 10am-6pm.

Post Office: Main office, Kasernenstr. 95/97 (tel. 296 21 11). Tram #13, 14, or 31: "Kaserne." Open Mon.-Fri. 7:30am-6:30pm, Sat. 7:30-11am. *Poste Restante* pickup Mon.-Fri. 6:30am-10:30pm, Sat. 6:30am-8pm, Sun. 11am-10:30pm; 1SFr charge for after 6:30pm. Address *Poste Restante* to: Sihlpost, Kasernenstr., Postlagernde Briefe, CH-8021 Zürich. **Branches** throughout the city. **Postal code:** CH-8021. **Telephone Code:** 01.

ACCOMMODATIONS AND CAMPING

There are a few budget accommodations in Zurich, and these bargain basement way stations often emulate the ritzy hotels that made Switzerland famous. Though not five-star hotels, they are clean, comfortable, and easily in reach of Zurich's extensive public transportation system. Hotel rooms in Zurich are sparse for a city of this size, and business-people and rampaging school groups often flood the 100 or so hotels and hostels. Reserve at least a day in advance, especially during the summer.

Jugendherberge Zürich (HI), Mutschellenstr. 114 (tel. 482 35 44; fax 480 17 27). Trains S-1 or S-8: "Bahnhof Wollishofen" (Eurailpass and Swisspass valid). Walk straight up the hill from the station, 3 blocks to Mutschellenstr.; then turn right onto the farthest right (Mutschellenstr.) at the 5-way intersection. The hostel is 2 blocks down Mutschellenstr. You can also take tram #7: "Morgantal" and walk 10min. back toward Zurich along Mutschellenstr. Huge, orderly, and impeccably clean, the hostel's pink stucco structure looms well outside the city center, concealing diverse travelers and fluffy pillows in its depths. The kiosk, lounge, and dining room are perhaps the largest, best-stocked, and most comfortable in Switzerland. Tune in to CNN or watch one of the free nightly laser disc movies. 24hr. reception. Checkout 6-9am. No lockout. 29SFr, non-members 34SFr. Subsequent nights 26.50SFr, non-members 31.50SFr. Doubles 88SFr, non-members 98SFr. All-you–can-eat dinner 11SFr. Showers, sheets, breakfast, and blow-dryers included. Lockers available, but bring your own padlock. Visa, MC.

The City Backpacker-Hotel Biber, Niederdorfstr. 5 (tel. 251 90 15; fax 251 90 24). From the Hauptbahnhof, cross Bahnhofbrücke to the left, make a right at Limmatquai, and then walk to Niederdorfstr. Follow Niederdorfstr. until you reach Weing. at the corner by the Spaghetti Factory. The hotel is down the street on the right. In the heart of the *Altstadt*, Biber boasts a rooftop deck (an ideal spot to picnic or party with fellow travelers) and a prime location with tantalizing bar-hopping possibilities on boisterous Niederdorfstr. Rosenhof courtyard just behind Hotel Biber shakes, rattles, and rolls with laughter and clinking glasses all night and hosts a small market on the weekends. The busy beavers who staff the hotel are incredibly friendly and helpful. Pick up a copy of *Swiss Backpacker News* to supplement your itinerary. Reception daily 8-11am and 3-10pm. 4- to 6-bed dorms 30SFr; singles 65SFr; doubles 85SFr. Winter discounts. Kitchen facilities and showers included. Lockers available. Sheets 3SFr. Laundry 9SFr.

Justinhaus heim Zürich, Freudenberg 146 (tel. 361 38 06; fax 362 29 82). Take tram #9 or 10: "Seilbahn Rigiblick"; then take the hillside tram (by the Migros) up the hill to "Rigiblick." Perched on a hill overlooking Zurich, the recently renovated hotel features freshly painted rooms with huge windows that provide a spectacular view. Reception daily 8am-5pm and 7-8pm. Singles 50-60SFr; doubles 75-90SFr. Breakfast and access to the huge, teal kitchen included.

Hotel Seefeld, Seehofstr. 11 (tel. 252 25 70). Take tram #2 or 4 (dir: Tiefenbrunner): "Opernhaus." This aging, hidden hotel is pleasingly uncrowded. Somber, greenish rooms near the *Altstadt*, one street from the lake. Parking available. Singles 64SFr; doubles 98-128SFr; triples 135SFr. Showers and breakfast included.

Martahaus, Zähringerstr. 36 (tel. 251 45 50; fax 251 45 40). Take a left from the station, cross Balinkofbrücke, and take the second (sharp) right after Limmatquai at the Seilgraben sign. Simple but comfortable, with a pleasant dining room, a

CENTRAL SWITZERLAND

lounge, and a prime river location near the nightlife. Private balconies in many rooms and a roof terrace. Dorms have partitions and curtains. Reception daily 7am-11pm; ring the bell after hours. April-Oct. dorms 34SFr; singles 65SF; doubles 96SFr; triples 114SFr. Nov.-March dorms 33SFr; singles 62SFr; doubles 94SFr; triples 111SFr. Showers and breakfast included. Locker deposit 5SFr. Visa, MC.

Aparthotel, Karlstr. 5 (tel. 422 11 75; fax 383 65 80). Tram #2 or 4 (dir: Tiefenbrunner Bahnhof): "Fröhlichstr." Removed from the city center, this family-run hotel is only a 3min. walk from the beach. The pink-curtained, flowery rooms may clash with the jazzy black-and-white exterior, but they all have cable TV. Jacuzzi/sauna. Reception daily 8am-8pm. Singles 68-78SFr; doubles 98-128SFr. No smoking. Showers included. Breakfast 12SFr, but **Konditorei Kirch,** across Seefeldstr., has freshly baked goods for less (open Mon.-Fri. 6:30am-6:30pm).

Studenthaus, Rötelstr. 100 (tel. 361 23 13). Take tram #11: "Bucheggpl." and walk downhill 5min. on Rötelstr. Student housing turns into a backpacker haven in summer. Youthful feel with funky furniture, a hammock in the yard, and a beautiful view of Zurich and the lake from the rooftop terrace. Singles 45SFr; doubles 60SFr. Kitchen available. Laundry 4SFr. Call ahead. Open July 15-Oct. 15.

Pension St. Josef, Hirschergraben 64/68 (tel. 251 27 57; fax 251 28 08). Hang a left out of the train station, cross Bahnhofbrücke, trot up the steps at the Seilgraben sign, and then head right a few hundred meters to the *Pension* (10min.). Possibly the most comfortable place to stay in Zurich. The 200-year-old green-shuttered exterior encloses elegant, wood-paneled, gracefully silent rooms. Lounge with VCR and cable. Reception Mon.-Sat. 7:30am-7pm, Sun. 7:30am-2pm. Singles 70SFr; doubles 105SFr; triples 145SF; quads 205SFr. Enormous breakfast buffet included.

Foyer Hottingen, Hottingenstr. 31 (tel. 261 93 15; fax 261 93 19). Take tram #3 (dir: Kluspl.): "Hottingerpl." Surrounded by plants and biblical flourishes, the guardian nuns usually admit **women only** (men should try only as a last resort). The number of languages spoken at the front desk (5) far exceeds the number of minutes each guest is allotted for the shower (3). Reception daily 6am-midnight. Curfew midnight (with permission). Dorms 25SFr, with partitions 30SFr; singles 55SFr; doubles 85SFr; triples 105SFr; quads 120SFr. Small breakfast included.

Hotel Splendid, Roseng. 5 (tel. 252 58 50; fax 261 25 59). Small hotel atop a very popular, very loud piano bar. Newly renovated rooms are small and sparsely furnished. Convenient for Niederdorfstr. bar-hopping or hanging out downstairs and listening to lounge music. Singles 58SFr; doubles 96SFr. Showers included. Breakfast 10SFr. Visa, MC, AmEx, DC.

Camping Seebucht, Seestr. 559 (tel. 482 16 12; fax 482 16 60). Take tram #7: "Wollishofen" and walk the remaining 15min. along the shore to the right, or take bus #161 or 165: "Grenzsteig" from Bürgklipl. at the lake end of Bahnhofstr. Somewhat far away, but the scenic lakeside location makes up for it. Shop, terrace, and café on the premises. Tents and caravans available. Reception daily 7:30am-noon and 4-8pm. 6SFr per person; 10SFr per tent. Open early May to late Sept.

FOOD

Zurich boasts over 1300 restaurants, covering every imaginable ethnic, dietary, and religious preference, but few are affordable for budget travelers. The cheapest meals in Zurich are at *Würstli* stands, which sell sausage and bread for 3-4SFr, or at fruit and vegetable stands. For hearty appetites, Zurich prides itself on its *Geschnetzeltes mit Rösti,* slivered veal in cream sauce with hash-browned potatoes. Check out the *Swiss Backpacker News* (available at the tourist office and the Hotel Biber) for more information on budget meals in Zurich. (See also **Food and Drink Sampling,** p. 379.)

Mensa der Universität Zürich, Rämistr. 71. Streetcar #6: "ETH Zentrum" from Bahnhofpl. or take the Polybahn uphill from Central Station. Exquisite cafeteria food in a posh, pastel room with plants and colonnades. Take a look at the bulletin boards in the university buildings for info on rides, apartments, rooms for rent, and cultural events. Hot dishes 6-7SFr with ISIC card, salad buffet 6SFr. Open July 15-Oct. 21 Mon.-Fri. 11am-2pm; Oct. 22-July 14 Mon.-Fri. and alternate Sat. 11am-2:30pm and 5-7:30pm. Self-service cafeteria open Oct. 22-July 14 Mon.-Sat. 8am-4:30pm. **Mensa Polyterrasse** is just down the street at #101. Turn right out of the Polybahn station and follow the crowds of students down the stairs to the terrace on Künsterstr. Same food and prices. Open Mon.-Sat. 11:15am-1:30pm and 5:30-7:15pm. Self-service cafeteria open Oct. 22-July 14 Mon.-Fri. and alternate Sat. 7am-7:30pm, July 15-Oct. 21 Mon.-Fri. 7am-5:30pm. Closed during school vacations.

Zeughauskeller, Bahnhofstr. 28a (tel. 211 26 90), near Paradepl. This *Biergarten* features handsome wooden roof beams and knights in shining armor who stare down hungrily from the walls. Serves Swiss specialties like fondue, *Rösti*, sausage, and bratwurst (all 10-30SFr) on long wooden tables. The outdoor seating permits prime people-watching. Open Mon.-Sat. 11:30am-11pm.

Restaurant Raclette-Stube, Zähringerstr. 16 (tel. 251 41 30), near the Central Library. Swiss fondues are at their richest, largest, and cheapest at this tiny, candle-lit restaurant on the outskirts of the *Altstadt*. The *Rösti* "side-dishes" are meals in themselves. Share fondue for 20SFr per person. *Raclette* 8SFr per person. Open Sat.-Thurs. 6-11:30pm, Fri. 11am-2pm and 6-11:30pm.

Ban Song Thai Restaurant, Kirchg. 6 (tel. 252 33 31), near the Grossmünster. This tiny place in the *Altstadt* bursts with flavor. Specialties include fish, coconut *currigo*, and *pad thai*. Lunch buffet from 15SFr; all-you-can-eat 22SFr. Open Mon. 11:30am-3pm, Tues.-Fri. 11:30am-3pm and 6-11:30pm, Sat. 6:30-11:30pm.

Rheinfelder Bierhalle, Niederdorfstr. 76 (tel. 251 54 64), in the *Altstadt*. At the narrow end of the food pyramid—the Rheinfelders liberally wield the meat cleaver and also serve up *Rösti* in all its variations. A local crowd enjoys the food and the self-proclaimed "cheapest beer in town" (4.10SFr for 0.5liter). Good for people- and party-watching. Entrees 11-30SFr. *Menus* 15-28SFr. Open daily 9am-12:30am.

Hiltl Vegi, Sihlstr. 28 (tel. 221 38 70; fax 221 38 74). Trade carrot sticks with the vegetarian elite at this swanky restaurant, one street toward the Sihl from Bahnhofstr. Huge, scrumptious salad buffet (supposedly the best in Zurich, 10SFr per 0.50kg) and fresh pastas are among the highlights. Entrees 14-25SFr. Open Mon.-Sat. 7am-11pm, Sun. 11am-11pm.

Gleich, Seefeldstr. 9 (tel. 251 32 03), behind the opera house. Herbivore impulses thwarted by industrialization? This completely vegetarian restaurant and bakery may be the oasis of green you need. Although the interior is rather dark, the bright orange terrace glows cheerily beneath orange canopies. Salads 6.40-12SFr. Entrees from 10SFr. *Menus* 21-34SFr. Open Mon.-Fri. 6:30am-9pm, Sat. 8am-4pm.

Rindermart, Rindermarkt 1 (tel. 251 64 15), in the *Altstadt* near Rathausbrücke. Crepes, ravioli, desserts, and creamy milkshakes scream to be eaten. Special vegetarian dishes as well as the usual meat and potatoes. *Menus* from 22SFr. Entrees under 20SFr. Open Mon.-Thurs. 7:30am-11pm, Fri.-Sat. 7:30am-midnight.

Schalom Café Restaurant, Lavaterstr. 33 (tel. 201 14 76), 2 blocks behind Mythenquai. Tram #5, 6, or 7: "Bahnhof Enge" on General Willis; then turn right on Lavaterstr. Don't let the tight security deter you—asking for ID is a necessary precaution due to slight religious tensions, not a cue to leave. Kosher delights from falafel (9.50SFr) to salmon (21SFr). Most items 10-30SFr. Open Mon.-Thurs. 11am-2:30pm and 6-10pm, Fri. 11am-2:30pm, Sat. for groups by reservation only.

Tres Kilos, Dufourstr. 175 (tel. 422 02 35), at Fröhlichstr. Mexican dishes (around 20SFr) served outside beneath a leafy trellis. Avocado salad (12.50SFr), beers (including Corona, 5.50SFr and up), and free chips and salsa set the mood for a gastronomical rhumba. The *chile con carne* (18SFr) gets rave reviews. Open Mon.-Fri. 11:45am-2pm and 6pm-12:30am, Sat.-Sun. 6pm-12:30am.

Cafés

Sprüngli Confiserie Café, Paradepl. (tel. 252 35 06). A Zurich landmark, founded by one of the original Lindt chocolate makers, who sold his shares to his brother. A chocolate heaven, the *Confiserie-Konditorei* lays out exquisite confections, concocting delicious, expensive sundaes (8-12SFr) with homemade ice cream and sherbet. Lunch *menus* 16.50-25SFr. Confectionery open Mon.-Fri. 7:30am-

6:30pm, Sat. 8am-4pm. Café open Mon.-Fri. 6am-midnight, Fri.-Sat. 7:30am-midnight.

Zahringer Café, Zahringerpl. 11 (tel. 252 05 00), across the square from the library. Sip coffee, frappes, and other hyphenated, caffeinated beverages with the young, hip, writerly crowd at this unassuming café. Opens early on weekends so late-night revelers can top off the night with the requisite grease bomb (*Rösti* topped with a fried egg 9SFr). Open Tues.-Fri. 6:30am-midnight, Sat.-Sun. 5am-midnight.

Gran-Café, Limmatquai 66 (tel. 252 35 06). Great views abound at this teddy-beared, people-watching place *par excellence*. Every plate and every patron is meant to be seen. The giant inflated ice-cream cone on the corner lures customers to buy a cone (a steal at 2.50SFr) or a more expensive, artsy sundae. Entrees start at 9SFr, *menus* at 11.80SFr. Open Mon.-Fri. 6am-midnight, Sat.-Sun. 7:30am-midnight.

Infinito Espresso Bar, Sihlstr. 24. Chic, angular bar with a coffee selection broader than Juan Valdez's smile. Espresso starting at 3.30SFr, sandwiches and snacks 3-5SFr. Open Mon.-Wed. and Fri. 7am-6pm, Thurs. 7am-8pm, Sat. 9am-6pm.

Rosika's Rathaus Café, Limmatquai 61 (tel. 262 04 81), across from Gran-Café. Watch passing boats while sipping coffee or a creamy frappe (4-8SFr) at an umbrella-shaded table. Sandwiches 6.50-13SFr. Open daily 7am-midnight.

Markets and Bakeries

Two bakery chains that you can find throughout Zurich, **Kleiner** and **Buchmann,** offer freshly baked bread, sweets (whole apricot pies around 13SFr), and *Kuchen* (*Bürli* rolls 0.50SFr) for reasonable prices (open Mon.-Wed. and Fri. 8:30am-6pm, Thurs. 8:30am-7pm, Sat. 8:30am-4pm). The 24-hour vending machine in the Shop-Ville beneath the train station has pasta, juice, and other staples, but you may feel uncomfortable heading over there alone at night.

Farmer's Market, at Burklipl. Fruit, flowers, and veggies. Tues. and Fri. 7am-noon.

Co-op Super Center. The Co-op to end all Co-ops straddles the Limmat River next to the train station. Watch for free promotional treats. Open Mon.-Fri. 7am-6:30pm, Thurs. 7am-9pm, Sat. 7am-4pm. **Branch** next to the tram stop near the hostel. Open Mon.-Fri. 8am-12:30pm and 1:30-6:30pm, Sat. 7:30am-4pm.

Migros, near the hostel on Mutschellenstr. (open Mon.-Fri. 7am-6:30pm, Sat. 8am-4pm with adjoining café); under the train station in the Shop-Ville (open Mon.-Wed. and Fri. 7am-8pm, Thurs. 7am-9pm, Sat. 8am-8pm); and on Falkenstr. off Seefeldstr. (open Mon.-Fri. 7am-6:30pm, Sat. 7:30am-4pm).

SIGHTS

Start your tour of Zurich on the stately and colorful **Bahnhofstraße,** which runs from the station to the Zürichsee. Shaded by the trees along this causeway of capitalism, shoppers peer into the windows of Cartier, Rolex, Chanel, and Armani. One square meter of the street will run you 250,000SFr; start saving up for that lemonade stand. To avoid the I'll-just-charge-it urge, throw yourself into one of the many more affordable side streets in the *Altstadt*, where antique, curiosity, and second-hand shops dominate. Alternatively, walk through the money depositories themselves—banks only give tours to bankers, but they don't fault anyone for going ga-ga over their lovely interiors. **Bank LEU,** Bahnhofstr. 34, is the fairest of them all with an elegant marble and gold-leafed interior. Halfway down Bahnhofstr. lies **Paradeplatz,** the town center, under which Zurich's banks reputedly keep their gold reserves. You won't spot any open manholes full of precious metal, however, so keep walking. At the Zürichsee end, **Bürkliplatz** hosts a colorful Saturday **market** (May-Oct. 7:30am-3:30pm), with umbrella-hidden vendors hawking everything from vinyl records to elephantine cowbells to Swiss Smurfs. Across Quaibrücke from Bürkliplatz, locals stroll and rollerblade along the tree-lined Uto-Quai, emptying bags of stale bread for the Zürichsee swans and their June cygnets.

Two giant cathedrals stonily face off in the *Altstadt*. To the east loom the brutal twin towers of the **Grossmünster,** built by Charlemagne on the site of a spirited deer chase. The blood-red and cobalt-blue stained-glass windows by **Alberto Giacometti** brighten this otherwise forbidding church, from whose pulpit Zwingli spearheaded the Swiss Reformation. Venture downstairs to the 12th-century crypt to see Charlemagne's statue and seven-foot sword. To the left of the main entrance of the church lies the **Krenzgarg** (Cloisters). (Church open March 14-Oct. daily 9am-6pm; Nov.-March 13 Sun., Tues.-Wed., and Fri.-Sat. 10am-6pm, Mon. and Thurs. 10am-5pm. Cloisters open Mon.-Sat. 9am-4:30pm.) For a stunning view of Zurich, climb the steps of the **Turm.** (Open May-Sept. Mon.-Sat. 9am-noon and 2-6pm; March-April and Oct. daily 10am-noon and 2-5pm; Nov.-Feb. daily 10am-noon and 2-4pm. 2SFr.) Across the river rises the steeple of the 13th-century **Fraumünster,** founded in the 9th century by the daughters of the local sovereign. The church holds one transept window by **Augusto Giacometti** and a stunning series of stained-glass scenes by **Marc Chagall.** Asked to design the windows in 1978 despite his Jewish ancestry, Chagall created these five fanciful panels. Round-nosed crimson horses draw Elijah's chariot in the prophet's window, and, to the right, the cobalt blue of Jacob's window gleams with angels and his eponymous winding ladder. Jerusalem glows gold on the Zion window, and angels with butterfly wings flit about Moses on the Law window. The central panel depicts Mary holding Christ beneath the emerald tree of Jesse. Around the Fraumünster on Fraumünsterstr., a mural decorates the Gothic archway in the courtyard. On the right, angels embrace the three decapitated patron saints of Zurich, who clutch their impossibly placid heads in their hands. The nearby **St. Peter's Church** has the largest clock face in Europe; the second hand reaches nearly 12 feet. Just down Thermeng. from St. Peter's, the recently excavated Roman baths of the original, first-century customs post Turricum lie underneath the iron stairway. Up the steps at the intersection of Strehlg., Rennweg, and Glockeng. is **Lindenhof,** the original site of Turricum and the birthplace of Zurich. Play some giant chess under the trees, then see the Zurich that inspired Nietzsche, Joyce, and Lenin.

Directly opposite Lindenhof, the **University of Zurich** presides over the city. The school was the first in Europe to admit women, and home, at least temporarily, to Einstein and the inventors of the electron microscope. Trams #6, 9, and 10: "ETH" uphill from the university run to the **grave of James Joyce,** in the Fluntern Cemetery. (Open daily May-Aug. 7am-8pm; March-April and Sept.-Oct. 7am-7pm; Nov.-Feb. 8am-5pm. Free.) Next door is the **Zürich Zoo,** Zürichbergstr. 221 (tel. 252 71 00), featuring over 2000 species of land and water animals. Take tram #5 or 6: "Zoo." (Open daily March-Oct. 8am-6pm; Nov.-Feb. 8am-5pm. 12SFr, students and children 6SFr.)

Botanical buffs will want to sniff out Zurich's many gardens and parks. The University's **Botanical Garden,** Zollikerstr. 107 (tel. 385 44 11), houses such oddities as the blue Himalayan poppy and a huge aquarium filled with carnivorous plants. Even the horticulturally challenged will enjoy lounging on the surrounding grassy hills and listening as the hilarious green pond-frogs bubble out their cheeks and ribbit. Take tram #2 or 4: "Höschgasse." (Open March-Sept. Mon.-Fri. 7am-7pm, Sat.-Sun. 8am-6pm; Oct.-Feb. Mon.-Fri. 8am-6pm, Sat.-Sun. 8am-5pm.) Escape from the city on tram #3 to "Hubertus," where you can forage through the jungle courtesy of the **Städtgartneri,** Sackzeig 25-27 (tel. 492 14 23). This greenhouse worthy of Dr. Livingston shelters hundreds of varieties of tropical and sub-tropical plants, including a stunning display of orchids. (Open daily 9-11:30am and 1:30-4:30pm. Free.) The lush, tree-filled, perfect for a picnic **Rieterpark,** overlooking the city, creates a romantic backdrop for the **Museum Rietberg.** Take tram #7: "Museum Rietburg."

Uetliberg, also known as the "top of Zurich," is the king of picnic spots, with a view of Zurich's urban sprawl on one side and of pristine countryside on the other. The flat walk from Uetliberg to Felsenegg is a peaceful escape from the city's hustle and bustle. From Zurich's Hauptbahnhof, take the train to "Uetliberg" (every 30min.), and then follow the yellow signs to Felsenegg (1½hr.). A cable car runs

ZURICH (ZÜRICH)

from Felsenegg to Adliswil, where a train goes back to Zurich. (Buy tickets at any train or cable car station or at most hotels. Free with Eurailpass.)

MUSEUMS

Zurich has channelled much of its banking wealth into its universities and museums, fostering outstanding collections. The larger institutions hold the core of the city's art and historical wealth, but many of the smaller museums are equally spectacular. The specialized schools of the university, scattered throughout the city, open the doors of their museum collections to the public.

Kunsthaus Zürich, Heimpl. 1 (tel. 251 67 65), at Rämistr. Take tram #3, 5, 8, or 9: "Kunsthaus." One of Switzerland's most extensive collections of 15th- and 20th-century art. Grab a map; an inadvertent jump from Dalí to medieval devotionals can be confusing. Monet and Picasso hold their own in the sprawling rooms of modern art. Works by Klee, Chagall, and the Dada artists, as well as an entire loft devoted to Alberto Giacometti, round out the stunning assembly, enhanced by temporary exhibits from around the world. Open Tues.-Thurs. 10am-9pm, Fri.-Sun. 10am-5pm. 4SFr, students 3SFr. Sun. free. Additional charge for special exhibits.

Museum Rietberg, Gablerstr. 15 (tel. 202 45 28). Tram #7: "Museum Rietberg." An exquisite collection of Asian, African, and other non-European art housed in 2 mansions set in the Rieter Park. **Park-Villa Rieter** features an internationally accredited exhibit of Chinese, Japanese, and Indian works. Open Tues.-Sat. 1-5pm, Sun. 10am-5pm. **Villa Wesendonck** stores the bulk of the permanent collection, including an ancient Buddha from Tibet, a multi-armed Shiva from India, and African tribal costumes. Open Tues.-Sun. 10am-5pm. 5SFr, students 3SFr. Main exhibitions and collections, including a grand collection of Indian paintings with love-making and feast-devouring in exquisite, gold-tinted detail, 10SFr, students 5SFr. Combination ticket for Kunsthaus Zürich and Rietberg 20SFr, students 10SFr.

Völkerkundemuseum, Pelikanstr. 40 (tel. 634 90 11). Tram #2 or 9: "Sihlstr." This small museum features stunning photographs, music, and religious artifacts from non-European cultures. Upstairs from the candle-lit Tibetan sanctuary, visitors listen to African, Indian, and Japanese music while laughing over the juxtaposition of African ceremonial marking and present-day Zurich tattoos. Open Tues.-Fri. 10am-1pm and 2-5pm, Sat. 2-5pm, Sun. 11am-5pm. Free.

Museum für Gestaltung (Museum of Design), Ausstellungsstr. 60 (tel. 446 22 11; fax 446 22 33). Tram #4 or 13: "Museum für Gestaltung." Features outstanding photography, architecture, and design exhibitions. Highlights include giant corn, desserts, and steam-shovel art. Open Tues. and Thurs.-Fri. 10am-6pm, Wed. 10am-9pm, Sat.-Sun. 10am-5pm. Special collections by appointment. 6SFr, students 3SFr; permanent collection only 4SFr, 2SFr.

E.G. Bührle Collection, Zollikerstr. 172 (tel. 422 00 86). Tram #2 or 4: "Frölichstr." From Seefeldstr. turn left on Münchaldenstr., walk uphill several blocks, and then turn right on Zollikerstr. The museum is a few yards down on the right. Bührle's mansion overlooking the Zürichsee holds a prestigious collection of French Impressionists, medieval carvings, and a Grecian urn or two. On nice days, breezes from the open windows waft past works by Monet, Van Gogh, Ingrès, Tiepolo, and Gericault. Open Tues. and Fri. 2-5pm, Wed. 5-8pm. 9SFr, students 3SFr.

Schweizerisches Landesmuseum, Museumstr. 2 (tel. 218 65 11; fax 211 29 49). Tram #4, 11, 13, or 14: "Bahnhofquai." Housed in a castle behind the station, the Swiss National Museum may be old news for field-tripping Swiss schoolkids, but visitors gawk happily at exhibits dating from prehistory to the present. Highlights include the intricately wood-panelled, gnome-like rooms from Wiggan castle, a mechanized 16th-century gold astrological globe, and a tiny bejeweled clock, complete with a golden skeleton morbidly pointing to the hour. Open Tues.-Sun. 10am-5pm. Free. Special exhibit admission prices vary (about 8SFr).

Paleontology Museum and the Zoological Museum, Künstlerg. 16 (tel. 257 38 38). Tram #6, 9, or 10: "ETH." Home to a mammoth moose and elephant-sized armadillo (both stuffed), as well as a menagerie of mandibled day-glo bugs (also happily inert), these museums could cast the next Spielberg movie. The museums take a hands-on approach, with interactive computer exhibits and microscope viewing stations. Open Tues.-Fri. 9am-5pm, Sat.-Sun. 10am-4pm. Free.

Museum of Classical Archaeology, Rämistr. 73 (tel. 257 28 20). Tram #6, 9, or 19: "ETH." A tiny museum on the 1st floor of the archeological lecture halls with an extensive collection of Greek vases and coins—use the microscope to peruse both sides—and Mesopotamian and Egyptian artifacts. Temporary exhibits in the basement next to statue storage. Open Tues.-Fri. 1-6pm, Sat.-Sun. 11am-5pm. Free.

Mühlerama Museum, Seefeldstr. 231 (tel. 422 76 60). Tram #2 or 4: "Wildbachstr." Originally a brewery, this fully-operational mill has been processing grain since 1913. Grind wheat on an exercise bike, or see the flour fly and the wooden parts spin as the miller takes you through the art of making *Brot* (bread). Mainly for kiddie food-lovers. Open Tues.-Sat. 2-5pm, Sun. 1:30-6pm. 7SFr, students 5SFr.

Zurich Toy Museum, Fortunag. 15 (tel. 211 93 05; fax 401 20 36), corner of Renweg 26. Zurich's local branch of Santa's factory has puppets, dolls, and other playthings from the 1700s to the present. Open Mon.-Fri. 2-5pm, Sat. 1-4pm. Free.

Food and Drink Sampling

Zurich's many food and beverage industries offer visitors a behind-the-scenes look and a taste of the action. The **Lindt and Sprüngli Chocolate Factory,** Seestr. 204 (tel. 716 22 33), welcomes visitors to its **chocolate museum** with an open box of Lindt chocolate, a free movie about chocolate machines starring many smiling Swiss children gobbling cocoa-based delights, and a carnival game that grabs chocolates with a claw and delivers them to drooling visitors. The chocolate spree ends as visitors leave with free boxes of—what else?—souvenir Lindt chocolate. (Open Wed.-Fri. 10am-noon and 1-4pm. All exhibits in German. Free.) To reach the factory, take the train S-1 or S-8: "Kilchberg" from the Hauptbahnhof (5.40SFr) or take bus #165: "Kilchberg." From the stop, take a right out of the station, a left down the first street, and an immediate right for a three-minute walk straight to the factory. The **Johann Jacobs Museum: Collection on the Cultural History of Coffee,** Seefeldquai 17 (tel. 388 61 51), at Feldeggstr., houses black-box display cases into which visitors peer to see historical and modern coffee pots. At the end of the exhibits, enjoy a delicious caffeine-filled cup in the villa's drawing room. (Open Fri.-Sat. 2-5pm, Sun. 10-5pm. All exhibits in German; summaries in English. Free.) Take tram #2 or 4: "Feldeggstr." and walk two minutes down Feldeggstr. The museum is on the right at the end of the street.

ENTERTAINMENT AND NIGHTLIFE

Bathing areas line the shores of the Zürichsee. **Strandbad Mythenquai** lies along the Western shore. Take tram #7: "Brunaustr." and follow the signs. (Open Mon.-Fri. 9am-8pm, Sat.-Sun. 9am-7:30pm; 5SFr.) Many movie theaters offer **English films** with German and French subtitles (marked E/d/f). For information, check the huge posters that decorate the streets, the cinemas at Bellevuepl. or Hirschenpl., or *Zürich News* and *ZüriTip.* Films generally run about 15SFr, 11SFr on Mondays. After July 18, the open-air cinema at Zürichhorn (tram #4 or 2: "Frölichstr.") attracts huge crowds to its lakefront. To ensure a seat, arrive at least an hour before the 9pm showing (15SFr) or reserve a seat at the open-air ticket counter at the Bellevue tram station. Niederdorfstr. rocks as the epicenter of Zurich's nightlife. Due to the high number of strip clubs, however, women walking alone may feel uncomfortable in this area at night. On Friday and Saturday nights during the summer, Hirschenpl. on Niderhofstr. hosts sword-swallowers and other daredevil street performers from around the world. Other hot spots include Münsterg. and Limmatquai, both lined with cafés and bars that overflow with people well into the wee hours of the morning. Beer in Zurich tends to be extremely expensive (7SFr and up), and establishments often charge double drink prices or a hefty cover charge after midnight, so plan your evening accordingly. **Kaufleuter,** the most posh and popular bar in Zurich charges a 20SFr cover before you even hit the bar. Tourists and locals whose wallets have passed out before they've downed their first beer often buy alcohol at Migros or along Niederhofstr. and head to the benches and fountain of Rosenhofplatz.

Casa Bar, Münsterg. 30, a tiny, crowded pub with first-rate live jazz. Drink prices will hasten bankruptcy (beers from 9.50SFr). No cover. Open daily 7pm-2am.

Oepfelchammer, Rindermarkt 12 (351 23 36). A popular Swiss wine bar (4-5SFr per glass) with low wooden ceilings and crossbeams, all covered with initials and messages. Free glass of wine for any idiot who can climb up and through the rafters—it's harder than it looks. Open Tues.-Sat. 11am-midnight.

Luv, Dufourstr. 43 (tel. 262 40 07), entrance around the corner on Kreuzstr. Take tram #2 or 4: "Kreuzstr." Groove on down to Luv for some musical "psychic entanglement." With its bizarre music (watch for science-fiction jazz night) and dance floor, Luv attracts all types, from spike-heeled to spike-headed. Beer starts at 6SFr. No cover. Open Sun.-Thurs. 10pm-2am, Fri.-Sat. 10pm-4am.

Bar Odeon, Limmatquai 2 (tel. 251 16 50), near Quaibrücke. Thornton Wilder and Vladimir Lenin used to get sloshed in this posh, atmospheric, artsy joint. Great street-side seating. Beers 6SFr and up.

Oliver Twist, Rindermarkt 6 (tel. 252 47 10). Please, sir, could I have some more...Anglophiles? English-speaking crowd enjoys Guinness (7SFr per pint) and British beers in this English pub with an Irish twist. Open Mon.-Fri. 11:30am-midnight, Sat. 3pm-midnight, Sun. 4pm-midnight.

Limmatbar, Limmatquai 82 (tel. 261 65 30). Tiny and candle-lit, this cozy bar attracts crowds of locals on the weekends. If you ask the bouncer a question, you can often avoid the line. No cover. Open Sun.-Thurs. 9pm-2am, Fri.-Sat. 9pm-4am.

Emilio's Bagpiper Bar, Zähringerstr. 11 (tel. 252 05 00). A gay bar serving good drinks, snacks, and occasional male strip shows. (Nice pipes!) Extremely crowded on weekends. Beers 4.30SFr. Open daily 3pm-midnight.

Cinecittà Bar Club, Stadthausquai 13 (tel. 211 57 52). The bar has both a scruffy biker and a young banker feel, while teens and students bump and grind on the dance floor. Watch for the theme nights (Tues. 70s night; Fri.-Sat. disco, Sun. gay night). No cover, but obligatory first drink 5-15SFr, depending on the night.

■ Near Zurich: Einsiedeln

An hour by train from Zwingli's Protestant pulpit in Zurich, the tiny town of Einsiedeln attracts pilgrims from all over Europe to its spectacular cathedral and legendary Black Madonna. A bizarre blend of pious Catholicism and fervent capitalism, the town houses a large monastery and convent just inches from souvenir booths hawking plastic holy-water bottles, giant rosaries, and hologram Jesus postcards. To find the **cathedral,** take a left at the train station onto the main street and walk about 10 minutes. Consecrated in 1735, the cathedral's Milanese exterior with twin lemon-shaped domes dominates the surrounding hills. The Asam brothers dreamed up the interior, its bubbly-Baroque ceiling overflowing with plump, pink cherubs against an overwhelming pastel background of lavender, green, and gold. A single bright orange window illuminates Mary and Jesus in the Christmas dome. Priests welcome pilgrims with services in the Madonna chapel, chanting mass as coins chink in the collection boxes for candle-lighting (1SFr per candle). The three-foot **Black Madonna,** dressed in Royal Spanish attire, is the cathedral's centerpiece. Years of smoky candle-light and underground storage during the French Invasion darkened the figure. An Austrian craftsman once restored her natural color, but locals who regarded her dark shade as a miracle demanded that he undo his damage.

Einsieldeln's other attractions include a monastery with a renowned library and horse stables (tours Sun. at 4pm); a cyclorama of Jesus' crucifixion (3.50SFr); and the largest *crèche* in the world, with 360 carved kings, angels, and camels. The tourist office has a map showing their locations. Einsieldeln's position amid lush hills beside the Sihlsee and its 100km of well-marked trails attract **horseback riders** and

NEAR ZURICH: EINSIEDELN ■ 381

hikers. For more information on trails, riding, and Sihlsee windsurfing, contact the tourist office or Röbi Kälin (tel. 412 87 22) for guided outdoor adventures.

You won't need more than a half-day to see all of Einsiedeln, but rooms abound for sleepy pilgrims who decide to stay the night. The only truly budget accommodation is **Schweizer Jugend und Bildungs Zentrum (SJBZ)** (tel. 412 91 74), about 15 minutes from town. Facing town from the cathedral entrance, turn right and follow the road heading to Ybrig. After about seven minutes, make a soft left by the field of clanking cows and the faded red SJBZ sign. The hotel is just beyond the Lincoln Restaurant sign. Rooms open onto beautiful lake and valley views marred only by the unfortunate 60s architecture. Reservations are a must from June to August due to mega school-group invasions. (Singles 32.20SFr; doubles 43.20SFr. Breakfast 12SFr. Dinner 15SFr.) Across from the cathedral, **Hotel Sonne** (tel. 412 28 21; fax 412 41 45) offers cozy, rustic rooms with forest murals, pine beams, radios, and telephones. (Reception 8:30am-10pm. Singles 70SFr; doubles 120SFr; lower if hotel is empty. Breakfast included. Visa, MC, AmEx.) For the hungry pilgrim, prices at most of Einsiedeln's 180 restaurants are anything but charitable. Near the tourist office on Hauptstr., **Restaurant Glocke** (tel. 412 24 83) blares perky Swiss music onto the street, luring tourists into its snug, bratwurst-happy interior. (*Schnitzel* and salad 12.50SFr. Open Tues. 5-11pm, Wed.-Sat. 11am-11pm, Sun. 11am-4pm.) **Migros** looms huge and shining behind the station, offering reasonably priced groceries and its usual simple fare at the restaurant. (Open Mon.-Thurs. 8am-6:30pm, Fri. 8am-10pm, Sat. 8am-4pm.) Einsiedeln's **tourist office**, Hauptstr. 85 (tel. 418 44 88; fax 418 44 80), distributes hiking maps and cathedral brochures in German. Turn left at the station and walk down the main street for about seven minutes. (Open Mon.-Fri. 9am-noon and 2-5:30pm, Sat. 9am-noon and 2-6pm.) **Change currency** at **Raiffeisbank,** Hauptstr. 19. (Open Mon.-Fri. 8am-noon and 1:30-5:30pm.) The **ATM** outside accepts MasterCard. **Trains** leave Zurich for Wädenswil every 20 minutes, connecting to Einsiedeln five minutes later. The **post office** is in the train station. (Open Mon.-Fri. 7:30am-noon and 1:30-6pm, Sat. 7:45-11am.) The **postal code** is CH-8840; the **telephone code** 055.

■ Winterthur

Once the country home of eastern Switzerland's wealthy industrialists, Winterthur (VIN-ter-tur) continues to profit from the cultural endowment of philanthropy. Overshadowed in all things commercial by omnipotent neighboring Zurich, Winterthur fights anonymity with a brave artistic barrage of 15 museums, a few private galleries, two castles, and a lively street scene—performers strum, pose, trumpet, and yodel to attract audiences in the *Altstadt* along hustly-bustly Marktgasse.

Orientation and Practical Information Winterthur's **tourist office** (tel. 212 00 88; fax 212 00 72) within the train station overflows with pamphlets on museums and excursion ideas. The office's hotel reservation service is 3SFr. (Open Mon.-Fri. 8am-noon and 2-6pm, Sat. 9am-noon and 2-4pm.) Trains run twice per hour to **Zurich** (10.60SFr) and connect there to **Basel** and **Geneva;** trains leave every hour for **St. Gallen** (18.20SFr) and cities in Austria. **Parking** is available at **Parkhaus Theater am Stadtgarten** and **Parkhaus Winterthur,** both off Museumstr., and **Parkhaus SSB** at the station. **Currency exchange** (open daily 5:35am-9:45pm), **bicycle rental** (23SFr per day; open Mon.-Sat. 6:40am-7:50pm, Sun. 8:10am-12:30pm), and **luggage storage** (5SFr, same hours as bike rental) are at the **train station.** The **post office** eagerly awaits your correspondence across from the train station. (Open Mon.-Fri. 7:30am-6:30pm, Sat. 7:30-11am.) The **postal code** is CH-8401. The **telephone code** is 052.

Accommodations and Food After exploring the nooks and crannies of the Schloß Hegi, drop the backpack and call it a day at the **Jugendherberge Hegi (HI),** Hegifeldstr. 125 (tel. 242 38 40), inside the castle. To reach the castle, take the postal bus: "Schlossacker" (2.10SFr); or take the train or bus # 1: "Oberwinterthur Bahnhof" then backtrack a few steps along Frauenfeldstr., turn left on Hegistr., turn left again on Hegifeldstr. after going through the underpass, and then walk 10 minutes farther. Surrounded by marvelous meadows, hedges, and fruit trees and serenaded by clucking hens and turkeys, the hostel offers no-frills, 15th-century living. There are only two dorm rooms, along with a loft generally reserved for groups. The hostel is as convenient to Zurich (Kloten) airport as the Zurich hostel; a direct train to the airport leaves every hour from Oberwinterthur and the S-12 train from Zurich (10.60SFr) makes a bee-line to Oberwinterthur five times per day. (Reception daily 5-10pm. Lockout Mon. and Fri. 10am-5pm, Tues.-Thurs. and Sat.-Sun. 10am-2pm. Dorms 16SFr. No breakfast. Kitchen facilities. Open March-Oct.)

Fruit and vegetable **markets** invade the streets of the *Altstadt* on Tuesdays and Fridays. The shelves of the **Manor** supermarket and café across from the tourist office burst with prepackaged goodness. (Open Mon.-Wed. and Fri. 8am-6:30pm, Thurs. 8am-9pm, Sat. 7:30am-4pm.) The **Hegimart** supermarket sits across from the Schloß Hegi. (Open Mon.-Wed. and Fri. 8:15am-12:15pm and 2:30-6:30pm, Thurs. 8:15am-12:15pm, Sat. 8am-4pm.) Bringing the supermarket tally up to three, a **Co-op** hides behind Manor. (Open Mon.-Fri. 8am-12:15pm and 2:30-6:30pm, Sat. 8am-5pm.) A local favorite, **Pizzeria Pulcinella,** behind Stadtkirche St. Laurentius on Metzg., serves up pizzas (13-17SFr) and Italian specialties, none of which top 21SFr. (Open Mon.-Fri. 11:15am-1:45pm and 5:45-11:30pm, Sat.-Sun. 5:45-10:30pm.)

Sights and Entertainment Unfortunately, the **Oskar Reinhart Collection,** Winterthur's best museum, is in the throes of renovations. The most famous paintings—Manet's *Au Café,* Van Gogh's *L'Hôpital à Arles,* and others—are on display on the top two floors of the Museum am Stadtgarten (see below). In August 1998, the paintings will go into storage until 1999. Winterthur's **Kunstmuseum,** Museumstr. 52 (tel. 267 51 62), holds an extensive collection of 16th- to 20th-century Swiss and French works, including pieces by Maillol, Bonnard, and Léger, as well as German works from the 19th and 20th centuries. In the summer, temporary exhibits of 20th-century art enhance the collection. The museum is up Marktg. from the station, left at Oberer Graben (which becomes Lindstr.) at the second intersection. (Open Tues. 10am-8pm, Wed.-Sun. 10am-5pm. 10SFr, students 7SFr.) Closer to the town proper and to the right of the train station, the **Museum am Stadtgarten,** Stadthausstr. 6 (tel. 267 51 72), balances broad international holdings with 18th- to 20th-century Swiss, Austrian, and German works. (Open Tues.-Sun. 10am-5pm. 10SFr, students 7SFr.) The miniatures of the Dutch "little masters" and timepieces from every corner of the globe shimmer and shine in the early town hall at the **Uhrenmuseum Kellenberger und Museum Jakob Briner,** Marktg. 20 (tel. 267 51 26; open Tues.-Sat. 2-5pm, Sun. 10am-noon and 2-5pm; free).

Painless even for techno-phobes, the **Technorama der Schweiz** (Swiss Technology Museum), Technoramastr. 1 (tel. 243 05 05), lies much farther down Marktg. Bus #5 (dir: Technorama) runs to the museum. The center lets its visitors perform hands-on experiments on everything from textile production to sector physics. The hair-raising experience includes giant bubble production, flying bikes, and a Lilliputian train that chugs around the museum's park. Surf the internet exhibit or land a jumbo jet on the flight simulator. (Open Tues.-Sun. and public holidays 10am-5pm. 14SFr, students 10SFr.) Visitors into bones and stones trek to the **Naturwissenschaftliche Sammlungen** (Museum of Natural Science), Museumstr. 52 (tel. 267 51 66), in the Kunstmuseum. Geological models explain the creation of the Alps and classify the region's flora and fauna. (Open Tues.-Sun. 10am-5pm. Free.)

Winterthur's environs boast two remarkably well-preserved medieval castles. The **Mörsburg** (tel. 337 13 96), former home of the Kyburg family dynasty as early as the 13th century, now holds 17th- to 19th-century fine art and furniture. Take bus #1: "Wallrüti" then follow the yellow signs for a 40-minute hike through the *Schwarzwald.* (Open March-Oct. Tues.-Sun. 10am-noon and 1:30-5pm; Nov.-Feb.

Sun. 10am-noon and 1:30-5pm. Free.) The **Schloß Hegi**, Hegifeldstr. 125 (tel. 242 38 40), maintains its 15th-century grandeur overlooking the meadows of Oberwinterthur. The original heirs to the castle still maintain the creaky staircases, 800-year-old tower, working cannon, and stained glass with medieval glee. Take the train (Eurailpass valid) to Oberwinterthur or bus #1: "Oberwinterthur." (Open March-Oct. Tues.-Thurs. and Sat. 2-5pm, Sun. 10am-noon. Free.) Built in 1180, **Stadtkirche St. Laurentius**, off Marktg., was renovated in the late Gothic style between 1501 and 1515 and now blazes with Alberto Giacometti's stained-glass windows and Paul Zehnder's day-glo 1925 murals of green-haired Jesuses against fluorescent heavens. The church acquired its 1766 organ from the Salem Cloister in 1809. (Open daily 10am-4pm.)

■ Lucerne (Luzern)

Though this northern gateway to the Swiss Alps quietly defends its fold with antique towers, turrets, and ramparts, Lucerne's natural fortifications, the majestic peaks of Mt. Pilatus, tower over such puny human efforts. Pilatus rises 2132m in a tumult of craggy rocks, snow, and ice. The Reuss River flows into the placid Vierwaldstättersee (Lake Lucerne), which separates Pilatus from Rigi Kulm, a gentler peak (1800m) dotted by meadows, picturesque villages, and grazing cows. The breathtaking views of the surrounding peaks have inspired the likes of Twain, Wagner, and Goethe. Although the landscape is hard to beat, the city holds its own with the lovely *Altstadt*, a number of museums covering glaciation and Picasso, and its eerie painted bridges.

ORIENTATION AND PRACTICAL INFORMATION

From Zurich, take N4 south to N14 south to enter the town on Baselstr. (1hr., traffic permitting). The mammoth train station (complete with book store, grocery store, barber shop, two restaurants, and a maze of lockers) owns the junction of the Reuss River and the Vierwaldstättersee. Most of Lucerne's museums and hotels are located near the quays that line the river and the lake, but they're not confined to any specific area or neighborhood. Numerous bridges connect both sides of the town. The largest one, Seebrücke, is also closest to the center of town activity.

- **Tourist Office:** Frankenstr. 1 (tel. 410 71 71; fax 410 73 34). Follow the "i" signs behind the McDonald's to the left of the station. Large selection of maps (free-1SFr) and a hotel reservation service (1-5SFr refundable deposit). **Guided walking tours** of the major monuments. (mid-April to Oct. Mon.-Sat. at 9:30am and 2pm; Nov. 4-April 13 Wed. and Sat. 9:30am and 2pm. 15SFr.) Ask about the Visitor's Card, which, in conjunction with a hotel or hostel stamp, gives discounts at museums, bars, car rental agencies, and more. Open April-Oct. Mon.-Fri. 8:30am-6pm, Sat. 9am-5pm, Sun. 9am-1pm; Nov.-March Mon.-Fri. 8:30am-noon and 2-6pm, Sat. 9am-1pm.
- **Budget Travel: SSR Reisen,** Grabenstr. 8 (tel. 410 86 56). Student travel and discount flights. Open Mon.-Wed. and Fri. 10am-6pm, Thurs. 10am-9pm.
- **Currency Exchange:** At the station. Open Mon.-Fri. 7:30am-8:30pm, Sat.-Sun. 7:30am-7:30pm. The best rates in town, however, are at the **Migros bank,** Seidenhofstr. 6, off Bahnhofstr. Open Mon.-Wed. and Fri. 9am-5:15pm, Thurs. 9am-6:30pm, Sat. 8:15am-noon. **American Express** also exchanges currency.
- **American Express:** Schweizerhofquai 3, P.O. Box 2067, CH-6002 (tel. 410 00 77). Offers all services including ATMs. Travel services open Mon.-Fri. 8:30am-6pm, Sat. 8:30am-noon. Money exchange open Mon.-Fri. 8:30am-5pm, Sat. 8:30am-noon.
- **Trains:** Bahnhofpl. (tel. 157 33 33). To: **Basel** (2 per hr., 1¼hr., 30SFr), **Bern** (1-2 per hr., 1¼hr., 33SFr), **Geneva** (1 per hr., 3¼hr., 65SFr), **Interlaken** (1 per hr., 2hr., 25SFr), **Lausanne** (1 per hr., 1¾hr., 55SFr), **Lugano** (1 per hr., 2¾hr., 55SFr), **Zurich** (1 per hr., 1hr., 22SFr), and **Zurich airport** (1 per hr., 1¼hr., 28SFr).

Public Transportation: VBL buses depart from in front of the station and provide extensive coverage. 1 zone 1.50SFr, 2 zones (to the youth hostel) 2SFr, 3 zones 2.50SFr. *Tageskarte* 10SFr, 2-day pass 15SFr. Swisspass valid.

Taxis: Cabs congregate in front of the train station, at Schwanpl., at Pilatuspl., and in front of the Municipal Theater. You can also call 211 11 11.

Car Rental: Europcar, Horwerstr. 81 (tel. 310 14 33). Special tourist offers. Compact car 35SFr per day plus 0.35SFr per km. **Hertz,** Maihofstr. 101 (tel. 155 12 34).

Parking: Lucerne has 10 parking garages, including **Bahnhof-Parking,** Bahnhofpl. 2, under the train station, and **City Parking,** Zürichstr. 35 (tel. 410 11 51). Parking garages run 25-50SFr per day. Free parking at the **Transport Museum.**

Bike Rental: At the train station. 22SFr per day. Open daily 7am-7:45pm.

Luggage Storage: At the station. Luggage held 5SFr. Open daily 6am-9pm. Small lockers 3SFr, medium 5SF, large 8SFr.

Bookstores: Buchhandlung Josef Stocker, Weinmarkt 8 (tel. 410 49 47). Some English books. Open Mon. 1:30-6:30pm, Tues.-Wed. and Fri. 9am-6:30pm, Thurs. 9am-9pm, Sat. 8am-4pm.

Bi-Gay-Lesbian Organizations: Homosexuelle Arbeitsgruppen Luzern (HALO), Postfach 3112, CH-6002 Luzern, PC-Konto 60-5227-2, publishes a monthly calendar of events available at the tourist office. **Why Not,** Postfach 2304, CH-6002 Luzern, offers Wed. discussion groups for young gays at 8 and 11:30pm at the **Schwullesbisches Zentrum Uferlos,** Geissenteinring 14.

Laundromat: Jet Wasch, Bruchstr. 28 (tel. 240 01 51). Full laundry service. Wash and dry 16SFr; wash, dry, and fold 19SFr. Soap included. English-speaking staff. Open March-Sept. Mon.-Fri. 8:30am-12:30pm and 2:30-6:30pm, Sat. 9am-1pm; Oct.-Feb. Mon.-Fri. 8:30am-12:30pm, Sat. 9am-1pm.

Emergency: Police: tel. 117. **Fire:** tel. 118. **Ambulance:** tel. 144. **Pharmacy or Doctor:** tel. 111.

Post Office: Main branch near the station on the corner of Bahnhofstr. and Bahnhofpl. Address *Poste Restante* to: Hauptpost, CH-6000 Luzern 1. Open Mon.-Fri. 7:30am-6:30pm, Sat. 8-11am. **Postal Code:** CH-6000.

Telephone Code: 041.

ACCOMMODATIONS AND CAMPING

Relatively inexpensive beds are available in limited numbers in Lucerne, so call ahead in order to ensure a roof over your head.

Backpackers, Alpenquai 42 (tel. 360 04 20; fax 360 04 42), 15min. from the station. Facing the lake, turn right, walk along Inseli-Quai, and then cross the concrete bridge to Alpenquai. Backpackers is on the right at the very end of Alpenquai across from a little park. The resort of budget hotels. Brand-new and lovingly decorated, this hostel boasts 2- and 4-bed balconied rooms with lake or mountain views, plus a chic, comfy dining/sitting room with fresh flowers and hundreds of travel books and magazines. Gorgeous lakeside location with a beach just over the little bridge. A bomb-shelter and "survival" kits (8SFr) of pasta, sauce, and wine await in case of Armageddon. The individual rooms don't lock, but huge personal lockers are free. Reception daily 7:30-11am and 4-11pm. No lockout. 2-bed dorms 26.50SFr; 4-bed dorms 21.50SFr. Sheets 2SFr. Breakfast Mon.-Fri. 6SFr. Kitchen facilities. Bike rental 7SFr per day. Tickets sold for Rigi Kulm and Mt. Pilatus.

Jugendherberge (HI), Sedelstr. 12 (tel. 420 88 00; fax 420 56 16). Bus #18: "Gopplismoos." After 7:30pm you must take bus #1: "Schlossberg" and walk 15min. down Friednetalstr. A contemporary, white-concrete building. Some rooms have a beautiful valley view, but you'll have to share with up to 11 fellow travelers. Reception daily 7am-9:30am and 2pm-midnight; bring a book or newspaper for the queue. Lockout 10am-2pm; but the lounge is always open. 12-bed dorms 29.50SFr first night, 27SFr thereafter; doubles 36.50SFr, 34SFr, with shower 42.50SFr, 40SFr. Lockers, sheets, hall shower, and breakfast included. Dinner 11SFr. Laundry 10SFr. Visa, MC, AmEx. Call ahead in summer.

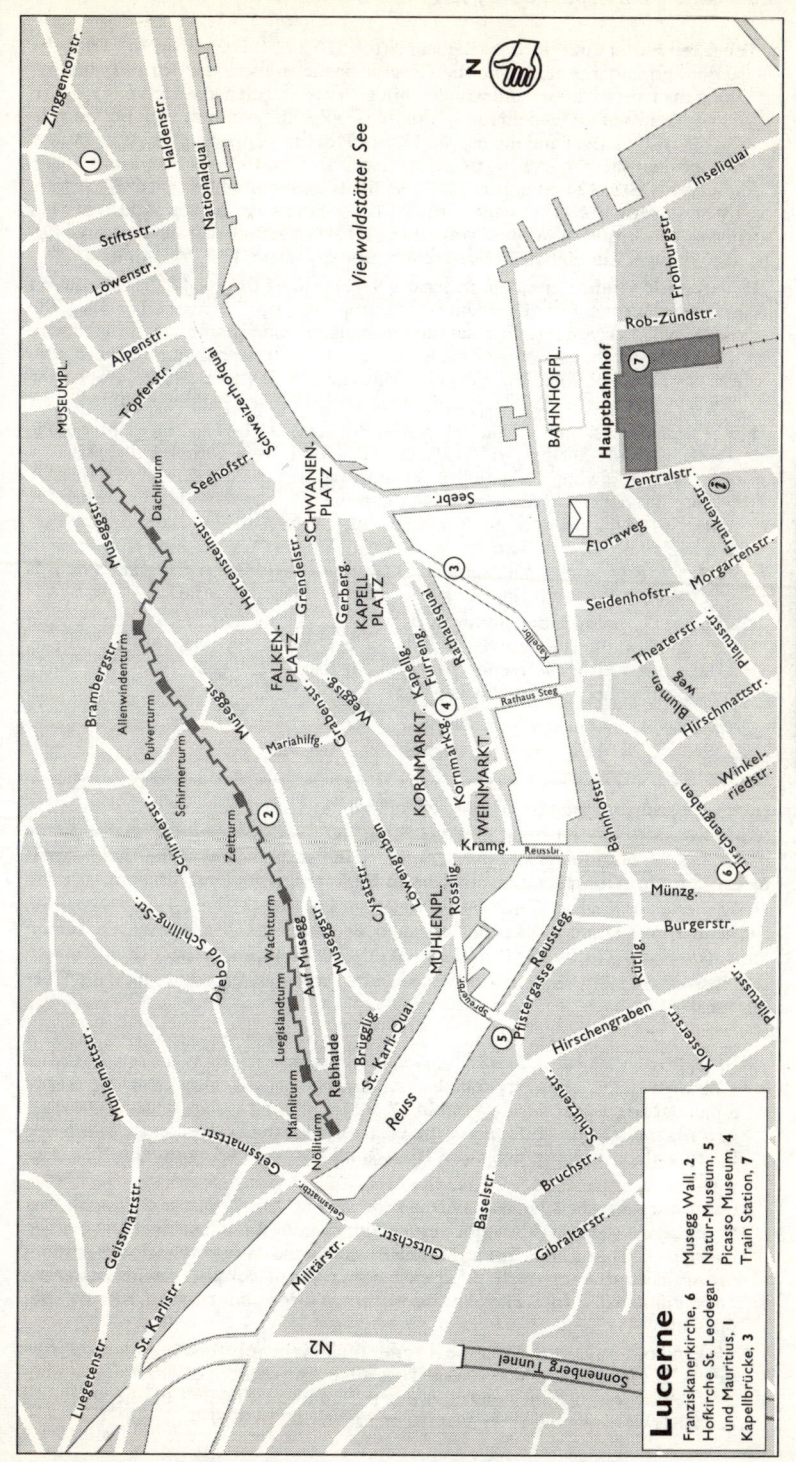

ACCOMMODATIONS AND CAMPING ■ 385

Lucerne

Franziskanerkirche, 6
Hofkirche St. Leodegar und Mauritius, 1
Kapellbrücke, 3
Musegg Wall, 2
Natur-Museum, 5
Picasso-Museum, 4
Train Station, 7

LUCERNE (LUZERN)

Touristen Hotel Luzern, St. Karliquai 12 (tel. 410 24 74; fax 410 84 14). From the station, go underground, take the elevator or the steps to the *Altstadt*, turn left along the river to the second wooden bridge, cross it, and make a left onto St. Karliquai. Train station pick-up for 3 or more people. Big windows with big views—the big rushing river and the big Mt. Pilatus. Pleasant peppermint-stick rooms feel fresher than the hall bathrooms. Reception daily 7am-10pm. 4-bed dorms 36SFr; students 33SFr; 12-bed dorms 31SFr, students 28SFr; doubles 98-108SFr; triples 135SFr; quads 172SFr. In winter, rooms 10-15SFr less per person. Add 10SFr per person for private shower. All-you-can-eat breakfast included in summer. Free luggage storage. Laundry 10SFr. Free scooter for city travel. Visa, MC, AmEx.

Privatpension Panorama, Kapuzinerweg 9 (tel. 420 67 01; fax 420 67 30). Bus #4 or 5 (dir: Wesemlin): "Kapuzinerweg" drops you up the street. For 5SFr, the owner will pick you up at the station. Clean, quiet, comfortable, and on a hill with absolutely gorgeous views of Pilatus or the *Altstadt*. Homey atmosphere with friendly family patrons. No reception; ring the bell or yodel. Singles 45SFr; doubles 70-90SFr; triples 120SFr; quads 140SFr. Breakfast and parking included.

Hotel Alpha/Pension Pro Filia (tel. 240 42 80; fax 240 91 31), at the corner of Pilatusstr. 66 and Zähringerstr. 24. From the station, walk 10min. left down Pilatusstr. This sprawling *Pension* is in a residential area, removed from the *Altstadt*. Despite the funky 70s leather chairs, the rooms are airy, comfy, and remarkably spotless. The hotel was formerly women-only, as the name indicates, but men are now welcome. Reception daily 7am-9:30pm. Singles 70SFr; doubles 98SFr, with shower 128SFr; triples with shower 138SFr; quads with shower 164SFr. Prices 2-3SFr cheaper in winter. Huge breakfast included. Visa, MC, AmEx.

Camping: Camping Lido, Lidostr. 8 (tel. 370 21 46; fax 370 21 45). 30min. from the station on the Lido beach. Cross the Seebrücke and turn right along the quay, or take bus #2 (dir: Würzenbach): "Verkehrshaus." Mini-golf, tennis, and swimming nearby. Reception daily 8am-6pm. 6.50SFr; tent 3SFr; car 5SFr. Open Mar. 15-Oct.

FOOD

Lucerne's gastronomic taste is overwhelmingly Swiss; ethnic specialties are quite expensive. Saturday morning markets along the river purvey inexpensive picnic goods, but the restaurants in supermarkets and department stores offer the cheapest meals in town. The restaurant upstairs in **EPA,** at Rösslig. and Mühlenpl., has 8-14SFr *menus* in English. (Open Mon.-Wed. and Fri. 8am-6:30pm, Thurs. 8am-9pm, Sat. 8am-4pm.) There is a **kosher butcher,** Bruchstr. 26, near Jet Wasch. (Open Mon.-Tues. and Thurs.-Fri. 9am-noon, Wed. 2:30-5:30pm.) **Hotel Drei Könige,** Bruchstr. 35 (tel. 240 88 33; fax 240 88 52), also serves heated kosher food for 45SFr per meal.

Krone, Rösslig. 15 (tel. 419 44 90). Good food with cafeteria-style service. Create your own sandwich, or try the chicken nuggets, kebabs, burgers, or ice cream. Super-deluxe burger with everything 7.50SFr. All sandwiches under 8SFr. Daily specials include an 11SFr *menu*. Be creative with the colored chalk and blackboard walls. Kitchen open daily 10am-9pm; bar open till midnight. Visa, MC, AmEx.

Restaurant Kapellbrücke, Bahnhofstr. 7 (tel. 210 80 20). A short walk from the station, Kapellbrücke has outdoor seating across from the Reuss river and leather-backed, cushioned seats inside. Mountain murals and day-glo animal scenes adorn the walls of this relatively inexpensive Swiss spot. Spaghetti with parmesan cheese and salad for 12.50SFr and full *menus* for under 15SFr. Banana split 6.80SFr.

Café Emilio, Grendelstr. 12. In the *Altstadt* off Shwanenpl., this elegant caffeinated den boasts surprisingly good deals. Locals munch yogurt and *muesli* while tourists head for the 2 mini-pizza and salad combo (8.80SFr) or the tortellini (10.20SFr). Open Mon.-Fri. 6:30am-8pm, Sat. 7am-6pm, Sun. 9am-6pm.

Markets
Migros, Hertensteinstr. 44, has a wonderful self-serve restaurant and a vast supply of groceries. Open Mon.-Wed. and Fri. 8am-6:30pm, Thurs. 8am-9pm, Sat. 8am-4pm.
Reformhaus Müller, Wienmarkt 1. Sells tofu, lentils, and scrumptious, organic, whole-grain bread. Open Mon.-Fri. 7:45am-6:30pm, Sat. 7:45am-4pm.

SIGHTS AND ENTERTAINMENT

Much of Lucerne's tourist drawing power comes from the Vierwaldstättersee and the streets of the *Altstadt*, which cobblestone both sides of the rapidly and ruthlessly raging Reuss River. The *Altstadt* is famous for its frescoed houses and *oriel* windows, especially the colorful scenes of the Hirschenplatz. Swiss historical scenes adorn the 660-year-old **Kapellbrücke,** a wooden-roofed bridge originally built as part of the city's fortification. Though a barge accidentally set the bridge aflame in 1993, Lucerne successfully restored it to its former glory. Down the river, confront your mortality as you cross the covered **Spreuerbrücke,** adorned with Kaspar Meglinger's eerie *Totentanz* (Dance of Death) paintings, in which skeletons lurk like gremlins. On the hills above the river, the ramparts of the medieval city still tower. Climb 124 grassy steps past the bell-ringing cows and then scale 124 claustrophobia-inducing steps up the tower for panoramic bliss. The **clock tower,** with its ancient clock mechanism and view of the valleys surrounding Lucerne, provides another excellent opportunity for panoptic pleasure. To find it, walk along St. Karliquai, make a right uphill, and follow the brown castle signs. (Open daily 8am-7pm.)

The city mascot, the dying **Lion of Lucerne,** carved out of a cliff on Denkmalstr., throws its pained eyes over a small reflecting pool. World-traveler Mark Twain described the lion as "the saddest and most moving piece of rock in the world." The nine-meter monument honors the Swiss Guard who died while unsuccessfully defending Marie Antoinette in Revolution-era Paris. Next door is the **Glacier Garden,** with its lunar landscape of smooth rocks curved and pot-holed into massive, other-worldly sculptures. Tickets (7SFr, with visitors card 5.50SFr, students 5SFr) include admission to the **Glacier Garden Museum** with its carefully designed glaciation models and portrayal of prehistoric humans. Roam among woolly mammoths for a while, but don't miss the *Spiegellabyrinth* (mirror maze)—be careful not to lose yourself or your mind. (Open daily May-Oct. 15 8am-6pm; March-April and Oct. 16-Nov. 15 9am-5pm; Nov. 16-Feb. Tues.-Sun. 10:30am-4:30pm.) Wexstrasse leads to the **Hofkirche St. Leodegar und Mauritius,** at the end of Schweizerhofquai. An 8th-century Romanesque basilica, the church was refurbished in the 14th century in the Gothic style. A spectrum of saints greets you as you walk through the oak doors, though the gaudy gilded statues and altars seem almost sinful in their ornamentation.

A cruise on the **Vierwaldstättersee** (see **Near Lucerne,** p. 389) takes visitors past the beautiful countryside and then deposits them in one of the many tiny villages that dot the lake. Glass-blowing demonstrations lie in wait at **Hergiswil,** while a quick and scenic hike lurks at **Bürgenstock,** where you can climb to ex-U.S. president Jimmy Carter's top choice in Swiss resorts. For an easier walk along the lake, alight at **Weggis.** To return to Lucerne, simply jump on board again. The length of the journey determines the fare (Eurailpass, Swisspass, and Swiss Card valid). Consult the Lucerne tourist office for specifics on each town and the boat routes. For a free lakeside dip, turn right from the station walk about 15 minutes along the lake to the **Seepark.**

From mid-August to mid-September, Lucerne will host its **International Festival of Music.** The festival celebrates both classical and contemporary music, sometimes with irreverent, tongue-in-cheek interpretations. Outdoor serenades, cruise concerts, and broadcasts at the Lion of Lucerne are annual highlights. For tickets or further information, contact: Internationale Musikfestwochen Luzern, Postfach/Hirschmattstr. 13, CH-6002 Luzern (tel. 210 35 62; fax 210 77 84). On June 28, Lucerne celebrates its **anniversary** with fireworks and parties throughout the *Altstadt*.

388 ■ LUCERNE (LUZERN)

Every summer, elite crews from all over the world snake their way to Lucerne for the **National and International Rowing Regattas** on the Rotsee by the hostel. Usually held on back-to-back weekends, the 1998 *Internationale Ruderregatta* will take place in mid-July (10SFr entry fee). On Saturdays from 8am to noon, catch the **flea market** along Burgerstr. and Reussteg.

MUSEUMS

Since Lucerne is sometimes called the "laundry" or "washing machine" of Switzerland for its frequent precipitation, the city has more than ample entertainment ready for rainy days. If you plan to visit several museums, purchase a 25SFr **museum pass**, good for one month and available at most museums and the tourist office.

Verkehrshaus der Schweiz (Transport Museum), Lidostr. 5 (tel. 370 44 44; fax 370 61 68), near Camping Lido, is the Disney World of transportation. If you can drive, fly, steer, float, or roll it, it's here. Climb into big-rigs and jet planes or go for a ride in the virtual reality exhibit. Planetarium and 3 Imax shows every day. Open daily April 4-Oct. 9am-6pm; Nov.-March 10am-5pm. 16SFr, students 14SFr. Imax 12SFr. Both 25SFr, students 23SFr. Discounts with Eurailpass or guest card.

Picasso Museum, Am Rhyn Haus, Furreng. 21 (tel. 410 35 33), presents a slice of Picasso's life through photographs taken by a close friend. Though the lithograph collection of Picasso's later work is average, the photographs of Picasso pirouetting, painting, and chomping on fish are unforgettable. Open daily April-Oct. 10am-6pm; Nov.-March 11am-1pm and 2-4pm. 6SFr, with guest card 5SFr, students 3SFr.

Natur-Museum, Kasernenpl. 6 (tel. 228 54 11). Hands-on exhibits, including live animals, distinguish this 1987 "European Museum of the Year." Extensive butterfly, fossil, and stuffed fauna collections. All exhibits in German; English summaries available. Open Tues.-Sat. 10am-noon and 2-5pm, Sun. 10am-5pm. 4SFr, students 3SFr. Add 1SFr for special exhibits.

Richard Wagner Museum, Wagnerweg 27. Bus #6 or 8: "Wartegg," or turn right from the station and walk 25min. along the lake. In Wagner's secluded former lakeside home, where he wrote *Siegfried* and *Die Meistersänger*, the museum displays the composer's original letters, scores, and instruments as well as a collection of historic instruments from around the globe. The luxurious green lawn extends from the house to the lake and makes for an ideal picnic spot. Open April 15-Oct. Tues.-Sun. 10am-noon and 2-5pm; Feb.-April 14 Tues., Thurs., and Sat.-Sun. 10am-noon and 2-5pm. 5SFr, students and guest card holders 4SFr.

NIGHTLIFE

While concentrated in the crowded corridors of the *Altstadt*, Lucerne's nightlife also sprawls into more distant reaches of town. On the river, **Mr. Pickwick's Pub**, Rathausquai 6 (tel. 410 59 27), has a British feel and friendly bartenders who pump out brews (from 4.50SFr) and music. (Open Mon.-Sat. 11am-12:30am, Sun. 4pm-12:30am.) Up the river, **Hexenkessel**, Haldenstr. 21 (tel. 410 92 44), resembles a witch's haunt. Replete with broomsticks, it boils Lucerne's twentysomethings in a two-story cauldron of loud music and DJs. (Obligatory beer 7SFr; no cover. Open daily 9pm-2:30am.) Across the street is the bright yellow **Kursaal** (Casino), Haldenstr. 6. **Cucaracha**, Pilatusstr. 15 (tel. 210 55 77), offers a spicy night of Coronas (7.50SFr) and nachos. (Open daily 5pm-midnight.) Wind up the night dancing at **Piranha** in Bundespl. Try not to get bitten—unless that's what you want. (Doors open at 10pm.) Dance, eat, and thrill to Swiss folklore from May to September on **Night Boats** (tel. 319 01 78), which leave at 8:45pm from piers 5 and 6. (40SFr, with Eurailpass 33SFr. Reservation, ride, entertainment, and one drink 50SFr, with Eurailpass 43SFr.)

Near Lucerne

ENGELBERG AND THE VIERWALDSTÄTTERSEE

Lucerne's position in the heart of Switzerland makes it a daytrip departure point *par excellence*. Boats from the train station cruise the Vierwaldstättersee; get a list of destinations from the tourist office (day pass for unlimited boat travel 39SFr, free with Eurailpass or Swisspass). The hour-long train ride (14.20SFr) to **Engelberg** is well suited for outdoors people and sightseers alike. Ride the world's first revolving cable car (tel. 639 50 50; email titlis@titlis.ch) to the top of **Mount Titlis** (3020m), the highest outlook in central Switzerland, in a dizzying 45 minutes. The gondola gives magnificent views of the crevasses below and peaks above. A illuminated ice grotto, observation deck, and restaurants conclude the trip. (Departs daily from Engelberg at noon. 73SFr, with Eurailpass 58.40SFr, with Swisspass 54.80SFr, with Engelberg guest card 20% discount. Guided tours from Lucerne including round-trip rail and Titlis fares only 85SFr, same discounts.) The glorious glacier lake, **Trübsee**, awaits your ogling halfway up Mt. Titlis (round-trip 24SFr, same discounts).

Engelberg also attracts **hikers** to its many trails, including an exceptional route from Engelberg to Herrenrüti along the valley floor next to the cliffs of Titlis (4hr. round-trip, easy terrain). Ask the tourist office for maps of other hikes and guided jaunts. The faint of heart may prefer a sedate yet rewarding trip to the local **Benedictine Monastery.** Over 850 years old, the monastery boasts some impressive Biblical wood inlay and Switzerland's largest organ. Tours every day at 4pm are free, but donations are appreciated. Enter through the door marked "Kloster Monastery." When winter rolls around, the skiers roll in. (Daypass Mon.-Fri. 47SFr, Sat.-Sun. and holidays 54SFr. 10% off with guest card.)

The quintessential Swiss ski chalet, otherwise known as the **Jugendherberge Berghaus (HI),** Dorfstr. 80 (tel. (041) 637 12 92), is a 10-minute walk out of town. Turn left off Bahnhofstr. onto Dorfstr., and keep walking. (Reception daily 8-11am and 5-10:30pm. Lockout 9am-5pm, but the lounge is always open. Dorms 25.50SFr first night, then 23SFr; doubles 31.50SFr, 29SFr. Non-members add 5SFr. Breakfast and sheets included. Key available on request.) Dinner at the hostel (18.50SFr), like meals everywhere else in Engelberg, is expensive, so make it an instant-soup night.

Engelberg's **tourist office,** Klosterstr. 3 (tel. 637 37 37; fax 637 41 56), is a left on Bahnhofstr. from the train station, a right onto Dorfstr., and another right onto Klosterstr. It hosts daily activities like hikes on the Brunni trail or across Gross-Titlis glacier (both Tues. 9am, each 15SFr, with guest card 10SFr). For those who prefer water in raging liquid form, Thursday features river rafting (9am and 1pm, 60SFr, with guest card 45SFr; office open June 23-Oct. 19 Mon.-Sat. 8am-6:30pm, Sun. 4-7pm; Oct. 20-Dec. 15 Mon.-Fri. 8am-12:15pm and 2-6:30pm, Sat. 8am-6:30pm; Dec. 16-April 13 Mon.-Sat. 8am-6:30pm, Sun. 9am-6pm; April 14-June 21 Mon.-Fri. 8am-12:15pm and 2-6pm, Sat. 8am-6:30pm).

MOUNT PILATUS AND THE RIGI KULM

> We could not speak. We could hardly breathe. We could only gaze in drunken ecstasy and drink it in.
>
> —Mark Twain

Soaring 2132 meters into the sky, the peak of Mt. Pilatus provides views that stretch all the way to Italy. Legend has it the devil threw St. Pilatus up here during the Ascension, but *Let's Go* does not recommend the Evil One as a safe mode of transportation—the cable cars are much more reliable. Catch a boat to Alpnachstad and ascend by the **steepest cogwheel train in the world** (48° gradient). Tourist-watch and capitalize on your photo-opportunities, then return by cable car to Kriens and bus to Lucerne (round-trip 75.40SFr, with Eurailpass 40SFr, half price with Swiss Half-Fare Card). From July to September 15, the **Pilatus railway** (tel. (041) 329 11 11) offers special half-price evening fares after 4:30pm from Alpnach and Krienz. If it's cloudy, don't waste your money—visibility is next to nothing. Though the Swiss banned the practice until the 17th century for fear of angry ghosts, climbing Pilatus by foot is now legal. The trails require sturdy hiking boots and at least five hours. Meeting the cable car at one of its two stops on the way up the mountain shortens the hike. The descent to Kriens takes about 4½ hours. For a **weather report** in German, call 162.

Across the sea from Pilatus soars the **Rigi Kulm.** Sunrise on the summit is a Lucerne must, though sunsets get pretty good reviews too. In his 1879 travelogue *A Tramp Abroad,* Mark Twain chronicles the ritualistic sunrises on the "Queen of the Mountains." Staying at **Massenlager Rigi Kulm** (tel. (041) 855 03 03) on the summit makes early morning viewing possible. Part of Hotel Rigi Kulm, this dormitory has 28 simple bunks (25SFr). Trips to Rigi begin with a ferry ride to Vitznau and a cogwheel railroad ride on the mountain railway to the top. Return the same way, or hike down to **Rigi Kaltbad** (1hr.), take a cable car to **Weggis,** and return to Lucerne by boat (round-trip 78SFr, with Eurailpass 40.60, with Swiss Half-Fare Card 39SFr).

■ Bern (Berne)

The Duke of Zähringen founded Bern in 1191, naming it for his mascot, the bear, and the city has been Switzerland's capital since 1848. Don't imagine fast tracks, power politics, or screeching motorcades—Bern would rather focus attention on its Toblerone chocolate and beautiful flowers. Situated in a bend of the winding Aare River, Bern has high bridges with tree-filled panoramas of the Bernese countryside. Cobblestone streets of the medieval *Altstadt* twist around brightly painted fountains and the 15th-century arcades. Rebuilt in 1405 after a devastating fire, Bern's sandstone and mahogany buildings lend the city an endearing compactness and architectural unity.

GETTING TO BERN

If **driving** from Basel or the north, take N2 south to N1 south. From Lucerne or the east, take 10 west. From Geneva or Lausanne, take E62 east to E27/N12 north. From Thun or the southeast, take N6 north. The **Bern-Belp Airport** (tel. 961 34 11) is 20 minutes from central Bern and is served by Swissair, Crossair, and Air Engadina. Direct flights go daily to Basel, Amsterdam, London, Lugano, Frankfurt, Munich, Paris, Prague, and Vienna. Fifty minutes before each flight, an airport bus that guarantees you'll make your flight runs from the station (10min., 14SFr). Bern's main **train station,** in front of the tourist office, is a stressful tangle of essential services and extraneous shops. Check-in, information, buses, luggage watch, bike rental, and a pharmacy are upstairs; tickets, lockers, police, and currency exchange are downstairs.

ORIENTATION AND PRACTICAL INFORMATION

Stately Bern resides in a diplomatic location, tangential to the French- and German-speaking areas of the country. Most of medieval Bern lies in front of the train station and nestled along the Aare River. **Warning:** Like many cities, Bern has a nocturnal drug community that occasionally settles in the area around the Parliament park and terraces. Bundesgasse bypasses the area.

Tourist Office: Verkehrsbüro (tel. 311 66 11; fax 312 12 33; email info@bernetourism.ch; http://www.bernetourism.ch), on the street level of the station. Distributes maps and *Bern Aktuell* (This Week in Bern). Room reservations 3SFr. The 24hr. board outside the office has a direct phone line to hotels, computerized receipts, and directions in German, French, and English. **City tours** by bus (2pm; June daily; April-May and Oct. Mon.-Sat.; Nov.-March Sat.; 2hr., 22SFr); foot (May-Oct. at 11:15am; 1¾hr., 12SFr); and raft (May-Oct. at 5:30pm; 2hr., 35SFr). Open June-Sept. daily 9am-8:30pm; Oct.-May Mon.-Sat. 9am-6:30pm, Sun. 10am-5pm.

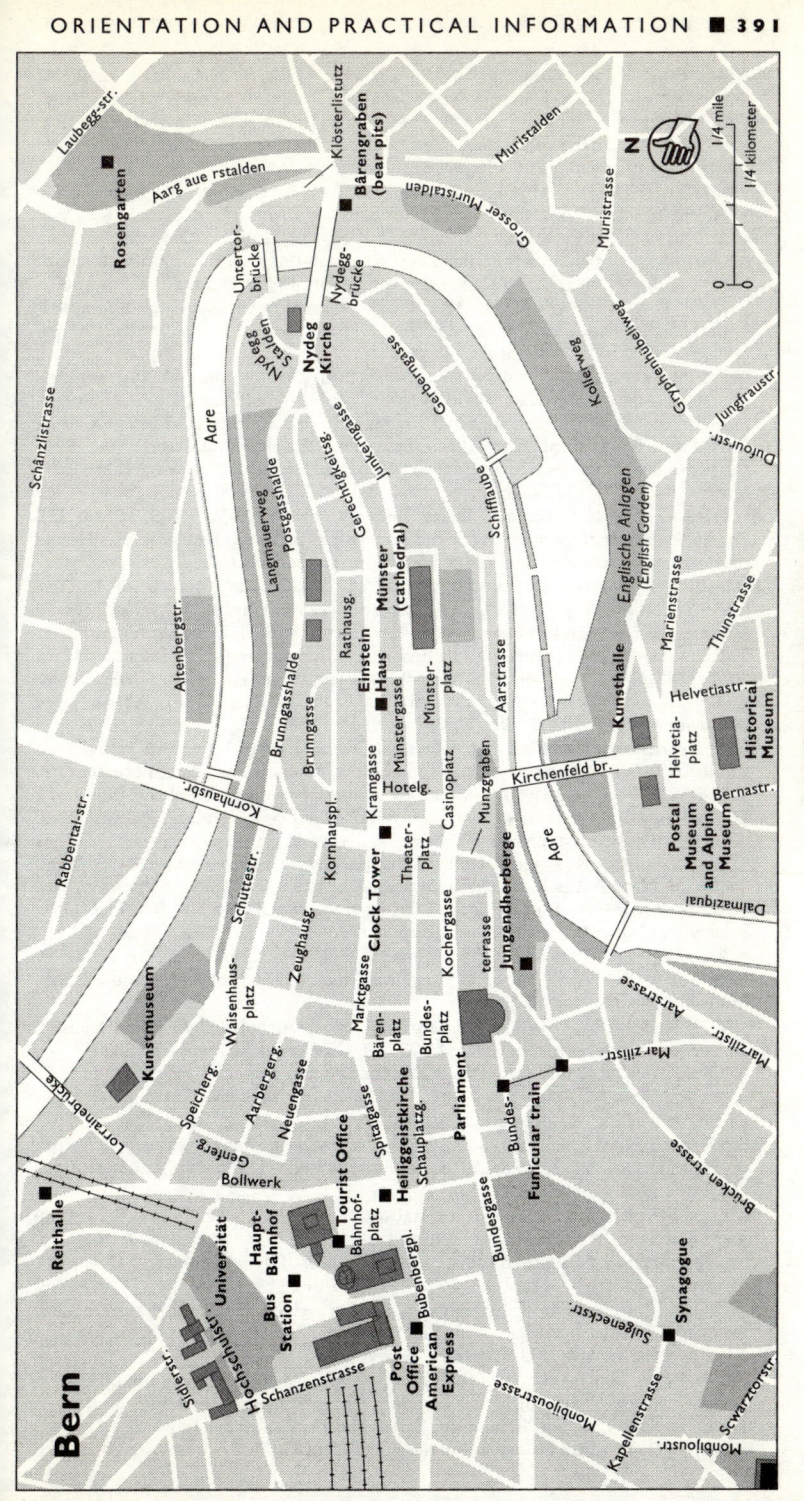

ORIENTATION AND PRACTICAL INFORMATION ■ 391

Budget Travel: SSR, Rathausg. 64 (tel. 312 07 24). Bus #12: "Rathaus." Sells BIJ tickets. Open Mon.-Wed. and Fri. 9:30am-6pm, Thurs. 9:30am-8pm, Sat. 10am-1pm. **Wasteels,** Spitalg. 4 (tel. 311 93 93; fax 311 90 10), has BIJ and plane tickets. Open Mon. 2-6:15pm, Tues.-Wed. and Fri. 9am-12:15pm and 1:45-6:15pm, Thurs. 9am-12:15pm and 1:45-7pm, Sat. 9am-noon.

Embassies: Australia, Alpenstr. 29 (tel. 351 01 43). Open Mon.-Thurs. 10am-12:30pm and 1:30-3pm, Fri. 10am-12:30pm. To get to the Canadian, U.K., Irish, and Australian embassies, take tram #3 (dir: Saali): "Thunpl." **Canada,** Kirchenfeldstr. 88 (tel. 352 63 81). Open Mon.-Fri. 8am-noon and 1-4:30pm. **Ireland,** Kirchenfeldstr. 68 (tel. 352 14 42). Open Mon.-Fri. 9:15am-12:30pm and 2-5:30pm. **U.K.,** Thunstr. 50 (tel. 352 50 21). Open Mon.-Fri. 9am-12:30pm and 2-6pm. **U.S.,** Jubiläumsstr. 93 (tel. 357 70 11). Bus #19 (dir: Elfenau): "Ka-We-De." Open Mon.-Fri. 9-11:30am and 2:30-4pm.

Currency Exchange: Downstairs in the station. No commission on traveler's checks. Credit card advances and Western Union transfers. Open daily June to mid-Oct. 6:15am-9:45pm; mid-Oct. to May 6:15am-8:45pm. **ATMs** at **Credit Suisse** and **Swiss Bank Corp.** Visa advances at **Bank Finalba** and Swiss Bank Corp. Banks are generally open Mon.-Wed. and Fri. 8am-4:30pm, Thurs. 8am-6pm.

American Express: In **Kehrli & Oeler,** Bubenbergpl. 9, CH-3001 (tel. 311 00 22). From the train station, walk to the bus area across Bahnhofpl. Mail held. All banking services. Open Mon.-Fri. 8:30am-6:15pm, Sat. 9am-noon.

Trains: Bahnhofpl. For rail information, call 157 22 22 (6am-10pm daily). The **rail information office** is open Mon.-Fri. 8am-7pm, Sat. 8am-5pm. To: **Geneva** (every 30min., 2hr., 48SFr); **Lucerne** (23 per day, 1½hr., 31SFr); **Interlaken** (every hr., 1hr., 24SFr); **Zurich** (every hr., 1½hr., 42SFr); **Lausanne** (every 30min., 1¼hr., 30SFr); **Basel** (every 30min., 1¼hr., 34SFr); **Paris** (3 per day, 4½hr., 76SFr); **Prague** (1 per day, 12½hr., 163SFr); **Munich** (1 per day, 5¾hr., 115SFr); **Rome** (1 per day, 13hr., 74SFr); and **Berlin** (1 per day, 9¼hr., 238SFr).

Public Transportation: SVB (tel. 321 88 88; fax 321 88 66). A visitor's card from the ticket offices downstairs in the station or at the Jurahaus office, Bubenbergpl. 5 (tel. 321 86 31), entitles the holder to unlimited travel on all SVB routes and a 10% discount on city tours. 24hr. pass 6SFr; 48hr. 9SFr; 72hr. 12SFr. Automatic vendors dispense daypasses (7.50SFr) and simple one-way tickets (1-6 stops 1.50SFr; 7 or more stops 2.40SFr; Swisspass valid.) Buses run daily 5:45am-11:45pm. **Nightbuses** leave the train station at 12:40, 1:40, and 3:15am Fri.-Sat., covering major bus and tram lines (5SFr; no passes valid). Both SVB offices in the train station distribute maps and detailed timetables. Open Mon.-Wed. and Fri. 6:30am-7:30pm, Thurs. 6:30am-9:30pm, Sat. 6:30am-6:30pm.

Taxis: Bären-Taxi (tel. 371 11 11) or **NovaTaxi** (tel. 301 11 11). Stands at Bahnhofpl., Bollwerk, and Casinopl.

Parking: Bahnhof (tel. 311 22 52), entrance at Schanzenbrücke or Stadtbachstr. **Bellevue Garage,** Kocherg. (tel. 311 77 76). **City West,** Belpstr. (tel. 381 93 04), is 2.80SFr per hr., 25SFr for 24hr., 12SFr for 2nd and 3rd day.

Car Rental: Avis AG, Wabernstr. 41 (tel. 372 13 13). **Hertz AG,** Kasinopl. (tel. 318 21 60). **Europcar,** Laupenstr. 22 (tel. 381 75 55).

Bike Rental: Fly-Gepäck (tel. 680 34 61) at the station. 22SFr per day, 88SFr per week; mountain bikes 30SFr, 120SF; children's bikes 15SFr, 60SFr. Reservations recommended. Open daily 6:15am-11:45pm.

Luggage Storage: Downstairs in the train station. 24hr. lockers 4 and 8SFr. **Luggage watch** at the Fly-Gepäck counter upstairs 5SFr. Open daily 7am-9pm.

Lost Property: Downstairs in the station. Open Mon.-Fri. 8am-noon and 2-6pm.

Bookstore: Stauffacher, Neueng. 25 (tel. 311 24 11). From Bubenbergpl., turn left on Genferg. to Neueng. Large English-language selection. Open Mon.-Wed. and Fri. 9am-6:30pm, Thurs. 9am-9pm, Sat. 8am-4pm. **Branch** at the train station.

Libraries: Municipal and University Library, Münsterg. 61 (tel. 320 32 11), stacks books for the central library of the University of Bern and the city's public library. Lending library open Mon.-Fri. 10am-6pm, Sat. 10am-noon. Reading room open Mon.-Fri. 8am-9pm, Sat. 8am-noon. **Swiss National Library,** Hallwylstr. 15 (tel. 332 89 11). Lending library and catalog room open Mon.-Tues. and Thurs.-Fri.

9am-6pm, Wed. 9am-8pm, Sat. 9am-2pm. Reading room open Mon.-Tues. and Thurs.-Fri. 9am-6pm, Wed. 9am-8pm, Sat. 9am-4pm.

Bi-Gay-Lesbian Organizations: Homosexuelle Arbeitsgruppe die Schweiz-HACH (Gay Association of Switzerland), c/o Anderland, Mühlepl. 11, CH-3011. The headquarters of Switzerland's largest gay organizations. **Homosexuelle Arbeitsgruppe Bern (HAB),** Mühlepl. 11, Case Postale 312, CH-3000 Bern 13 (tel. 311 63 53). **Schlub** (Gay Students Organization), c/o Studentinnenschaft, Lercheweg 32, CH-3000 Bern 9 (tel. 381 18 05).

Information: General information tel. 111.

Pharmacy: In the station. Open daily 6:30am-8pm. **Bären Apotheke,** at the foot of the clock tower. Open Mon. 1:45-6:30pm, Tues.-Wed. and Fri. 7:45am-6:30pm, Thurs. 7:45am-9pm, Sat. 7:45am-4pm. For a 24hr. pharmacy, call 311 22 11.

Emergencies: Police, tel. 117. **Ambulance,** tel. 144. **Doctor,** tel. 311 22 11. **Rape Crisis Hotline,** tel. 332 14 14.

Post Office: Schanzenpost 1, next to the train station. Address *Poste Restante* to Schanzenpost 3000, Bern 1. Open Mon.-Fri. 7:30am-6:30pm, Sat. 7:30-11am.

Postal codes: CH-3000 to CH-3030.

Telephone Code: 031.

ACCOMMODATIONS AND CAMPING

Bern's shortage of inexpensive hotels thwarts budget travelers. Even outside the city itself, cheap accommodations are rare. Consider staying in Fribourg (30min. by train).

Jugendherberge (HI), Weiherg. 4 (tel. 311 63 16; fax 312 52 40). From the station, walk across Bubenbergpl., past the tram lines toward your left, and then onto Christoffelg. Turn left on Bundesg. and follow it as it turns into Kocherg. and empties into Casinopl. Münzrain leads down the slope and signs guide the rest of the way. The hostel's location on the banks of the Aare make for a peaceful stay. The majority of the 186 beds are in 8-bed arrangements, but services are efficient and the facilities accommodating. You can buy candy and city excursion tickets at the office. 3-night max. stay. Reception daily June-Sept. 7-9:30am and 3pm-midnight; Oct.-May daily 7-9:30am and 5pm-midnight. Check-out 7-9am. Lockout June-Sept. 9:30am-3pm, Oct.-May 9:30am-5pm, but the dining room/lounge is always open. Curfew midnight. 20SFr fine for disturbing guests during quiet hours (10:30pm-7am). Dorms 18SFr; mattress on the floor 10SFr. Hall showers. Breakfast 6SFr. Lunch or dinner 11SFr. Laundry 6SFr. Parking available. Swiss cash only.

Pension Marthahaus, Wyttenbachstr. 22a (tel. 332 41 35; fax 333 33 86). Bus #20: "Gewerbeschule," and then the first right. Or walk from the station: turn left onto Bollwerk, cross Lorrainebrücke on the right, bear right onto Victoriarain, and then take the first left onto Wyttenbachstr. Matronly hostess maintains a comfortable *Pension* in a quiet suburb. Its one-star status offers a few small luxuries, including privacy amid fluffy white blankets, shiny private sinks, and elegant sitting rooms. Even the hall showers are invitingly homey. Reception daily 7am-9pm, but a porter accommodates latecomers. Singles 55SFr, with shower 85-90SFr; doubles 85-95SFr, 110-120SFr; triples 110-120SFr, 140-150SFr. 10SFr discount in winter; special rates for large groups. Breakfast included. Laundry 5SFr, dry 2SFr. Limited parking available. Reservations recommended in summer. Visa, MC.

Hotel National, Hirschengraben 24 (tel. 381 19 88; fax 381 68 78). Left off Bubenbergpl. English-speaking staff and beautiful rooms with Oriental rugs. The restaurant downstairs has a 16SFr *menu*. Singles 60-75SFr, with shower 85-110SFr; doubles 100-120SFr, 120-150SFr; 3- to 5-person family room 170-260SFr. Breakfast included. Reservations recommended in summer. Visa, MC, AmEx, DC.

Hotel Goldener Schlüssel, Rathausg. 72 (tel. 311 02 16; fax 311 56 88). Tram #9 or 12: "Zytglogge." A newly renovated, central hotel, with a popular restaurant-café downstairs. The cheaper showerless rooms are all in low-ceilinged attic space, and the hall showers are basically closets. Downstairs rooms are much brighter and larger. Every room is comfortably equipped with soft beds, sinks, TVs, and

394 ■ BERN (BERNE)

telephones. Reception daily 7am-midnight. Singles 75SFr, with shower 95SFr; doubles 110SFr, 135SFr. Breakfast included. Reserve ahead May-Oct. Visa, MC.

Camping: Camping Eichholz, Strandweg 49 (tel. 961 26 02). Take tram #9: "Wabern," backtrack 50m, and take the first right. Verdant riverside location across from the zoo, with occasional sightings of snuffling wild boars, drooling bison, and bounding mountain goats. 5.50SFr, students 4.30SFr, children 2.90SFr; small tent 4.30SFr; large tent 8.60SFr. 2-bed rooms 13SFr plus 5.50SFr per person. Showers 15SFr; electricity 3SFr; laundry 5SFr. Restaurant. Reserve ahead. Open May-Sept.

FOOD

The **Bärenplatz** is a lively square overflowing with cafés and restaurants, most with *menus* and lighter fare in the 9-17SFr range. The sidewalk arcades that line Bern's main drags are a treasure trove of potential culinary curiosities, including Bern's specialties: **Gschnätzltes** (fried veal, beef, or pork) and **sur chabis** (a sauerkraut). Sweet teeth will enjoy an airy **meringue** or the world-renowned **Toblerone chocolate.**

Manora, Bubenbergpl. 5A (tel. 311 37 55), over the tramlines from the station. As usual, this self-service chain tends to be overheated and crowded but serves big platefuls that are indisputably nutritious and reasonably priced. The regulars hover over the yummy fruit tarts and freshly squeezed orange juice. Salad bar 5-10SFr; pasta 8-10SFr; veggie burger plate 9SFr. Open Mon.-Sat. 7am-10:45pm, Sun. 9am-10:45pm. Hot food served until 10:30pm.

Zähringerhof, Hallerstr. 19 (tel. 301 08 60), at Gesellschaftstr. This neighborhood joint cooks up great Swiss dishes, with 6 *menus* (17-19SFr). Bushes and vines shield the raised outdoor terrace from the street. Open daily 9am-midnight.

Café des Pyrenées, Kornhauspl. (tel. 311 60 44). A buzzing bistro-café complete with a super-small sidewalk terrace and toy sheep and plastic tulips in the front picture window. The equally tiny menu has inventive sandwiches (calamari, 6.50SFr), but conservative spaghettis (10-11SFr). The spirits list looks extravagant, with 6 types of Spanish brandy. Open Mon.-Fri. 9am-12:30am, Sat. 8am-5pm.

Schoog-Dee, Bollwerk 4 (tel. 311 37 08). Bus #20: "Bollwerk" or a short walk from the station. The Thai and Chinese specialties are one of Bern's best deals, served in a dining room filled to "exotic" capacity with ambitious tropical greenery and loads of random bric-a-brac. *Dim sum* (13.50SFr), chow mein (10-11SFr), and enticing papaya salad (10SFr). Open Mon.-Fri. 11am-2pm and 5-11:30pm, Sat.-Sun. 5-11:30pm. June-Aug. closed Sun. Visa, MC, AmEx, DC.

Pizza Lamarque, Kramg. 42 (tel. 311 70 51). Red geraniums on the terrace give way to a dining room that sports blood-red brick and rippled plaster walls—an appropriately oven-like setting for a pizzeria. Humming with local life. While staring, try some pizza (11-19SFr), pasta (11-20SFr), or beer (4SFr). Open Mon. 9am-11:30pm, Tues.-Thurs. 9am-1:30am, Fri.-Sat. 9am-2:30am, Sun. 11am-10pm.

Markets

Migros, Marktg. 46. Open Mon. 9am-6:30pm, Tues.-Wed. and Fri. 8am-6:30pm, Thurs. 8am-9pm, Sat. 7am-4pm.

Reformhaus M. Siegrist, Marktg.-Passage, is a popular health food market. Open Mon. 2-6:30pm, Tues.-Fri. 8am-12:15pm and 1:30-6:30pm, Sat. 7:45-11am.

Fruit and vegetable markets sprawl fresh produce daily over Bärenpl. (May-Oct. 8am-6pm) and every Tues. and Sat. over Bundepl. (all year). The **onion market** on the fourth Mon. of Nov. is probably Bern's single best known festival.

SIGHTS

Church and state combat for control of the Bernese skyline. The massive **Bundeshaus** dominates the Aare river and hides its politicians in the **Parlamentsgebäude** (45min. tour every hr. 9am-noon and 2-4pm, free; watch the parliament in session from the galleries). From the state house, Kockerg. and Herreng. lead to the 15th-century Protestant **Münster.** The imagination of the late-Gothic period runs riot in the portal sculpture of the Last Judgment. The white-robed pious stand smugly on the left, while the naked damned shuffle off unhappily to the fiery furnaces on the right. Climb the highest spire in Switzerland for a fantastic view, or wander out onto the terrace behind the church, poised between the river below and the mountains beyond. From the convenient shade of chestnuts, watch amateurs and experts pull out measuring sticks to settle *bocci* disputes on the gravel walks. (Open Easter-Oct. Tues.-Sat. 10am-5pm, Sun. 11am-5pm; Nov.-Easter Tues.-Fri. 10am-noon and 2-4pm, Sat. 10am-noon and 2-5pm, Sun. 11am-2pm. Tower closes 30min. before the church. 3SFr.)

Head down Münsterg. and take a right and then the first left to find the 13th-century **Zytglogge** (clock tower). Join the crowd four minutes before the hour to watch bears dance, jesters drum, and a squeaky rooster announce the hour. (Tours of the interior May-Oct. daily at 4:30pm. 6SFr.) The similarly gaudy, colorful fountains were the whimsical notion of Hans Gieng, who loyally carved them on Bernese themes between 1539 and 1546. Even Bern's brown bears turn up in gummy-bear red.

The slender copper spire of the **Nydegg Kirche** peeks down Kramg. and Gerechtigkeitsg. The church stands on the remains of the Nydegg imperial fortress that was destroyed in the mid-13th century. Bärengrabenbrücke leads to the **Bärengraben** (bear pits). The structure dates back to the 15th century; imagine generations of sullen bears enduring tossed carrots and screaming children and you'll understand the current occupants' lethargy. One gets the distinct feeling that these omnivorous creatures would like nothing more than the occasional juicy toddler to supplement their diets. On Easter, newborn cubs emerge for their first public display. (Open April-Sept. daily 8am-6pm; Oct.-March 9am-4pm. 3SFr to feed the bears—carrots, not kids.) The path snaking up the hill to the left leads to the **Rosengarten;** sit among the blooms and admire one of the best views of Bern's *Altstadt.*

The **Botanical Gardens** of the University of Bern, Altergrain 21 (tel./fax 631 49 11), sprawl down the river at Lorrainebrücke. Exotic plants from Asia, Africa, and the Americas thrive cheek to leaf with native Alpine greenery. (Park open March-Sept. Mon.-Fri. 7am-6pm, Sat.-Sun. 8am-5pm. Greenhouse open 8-11:30am and 2-5pm. Free.) A walk south along the Aare (or bus #19: "Tierpark") leads to the **Dählhölzli Städtischer Tierpark** (Zoo), Tierparkweg 1 (tel. 357 15 15; fax 357 15 10). The vivarium echoes the greenhouse at the Botanical Gardens, as the occasional animal lurks far behind and underneath lush swags of vegetation and murky, green pools. Outside among marvelously tall trees, a wide range of cute and fierce creatures roam behind fences. The zoo relegates its less crowd-pleasing inhabitants—spitting bison, noisy wild boars, bashful badgers, and ugly vultures—to out-of-the-way riverfront pens. (Open daily in summer 8am-6pm, in winter 9am-4:30pm. 6SFr, students 4SFr, children 3SFr. Parking available.) Farther down the river is the entrance to the **Stadtgärtnerei Elfenau** (tel. 352 07 13), a nature reserve that was once an 18th-century country estate. The English-style landscaping offers belvederes, greenhouses, and concerts in the orangery. (Open Mon.-Sat. 8am-5pm, Sun. 8am-5:30pm. Free.)

MUSEUMS

Several of Bern's museums huddle in a compact ring around **Helvetiaplatz,** across Kirchenfeldbrücke (tram #3 or 5). Consider purchasing a **day ticket** *(Tageskarte)*—the 7SFr ticket (students 5SFr) grants admission to the Historical Museum, Natural History Museum, Swiss Alpine Museum, Kunsthalle, PTT Museum, and Rifle Museum. Other tiny museums lurk throughout the *Altstadt,* and compact curiosities await in the most unexpected places.

Kunstmuseum, Hodlerstr. 8-12 (tel. 311 09 44; fax 311 72 63), near Lorrainebrücke. This mostly modern Swiss collection sprawls over 3 floors and a couple of buildings, top-heavy with the world's largest Paul Klee collection. 2500 works, from his school exercise-books to his largest canvases, along with some works by his chums Kandinsky and Feininger, culminate in 2 breathless rooms of classic

Klee. Upstairs holds a smattering of the century's big names: lots of Braque, some Picasso, many Pablo wannabes, more Kandinsky, some surprising Matisse, and the odd Delacroix. The basement is mainly Swiss with some grotesquely conceived Bernese canvases, but an unexpected room of the Italian *trecento* will soothe your hell-wracked nerves. The museum also holds a chic café and screens art films. Open Tues. 10am-9pm, Wed.-Sun. 10am-5pm. 6SFr, students and seniors 4SFr.

Bernisches Historische Museum, Helvetiapl. 5 (tel. 351 18 11; fax 351 06 63), in the downtown museum district. So big you won't know where to begin. Luckily, multilingual explanatory notes await in almost every room in the museum's 7 jam-packed levels. Chuckle in time to the hilarious Dance of Death or humble yourself beneath the original figures of the Last Judgment from the cathedral's front portal; wander through the lavishly appointed apartments of the *Ancien Regime;* puzzle over the astonishing Islamic collection; decipher the life of Caesar in monumental medieval tapestries; trace the odd "Changes in Daily Life" through the random yard-sale collection of Bern's backyard history. Or just climb up to the heights of antique elegance and onto the belvedere, which offers a cunning view of the climbers on the Munsterspire looking back at you. Open Tues.-Sun. 10am-5pm. 5SFr, students 3SFr, under 17 and school groups free. Tours on request. Additional charge for special exhibitions. Free on Sat.

Museum of Natural History, Bernastr. 15 (tel. 350 71 11), off Helvetiapl. Most people come to see "Barry," the now-stuffed St. Bernard who saved over 40 people in his lifetime. The other dioramas, however, are so convincing you might think yourself in a zoo—a zoo where hyenas pick at zebra corpses while cheetahs wait in ambush, or weasels steal out of a hen house eggs in mouth, or the more dynamic cousins of the Bärengraben bears dispute a recently downed moose. Open Mon. 2-5pm, Tues.-Sat. 9am-5pm, Sun. 10am-5pm. 3SFr, students 1.50SFr, free on Sun.

Swiss Alpine Museum, Helvetiapl. 4 (tel. 351 04 34; fax 351 07 51). Vast, spellbindingly intricate models of Switzerland's most popular mountains and the story of Switzerland's beautiful maps. Interactive computer terminals tell you that all is not sunny on the summits of Switzerland: The Alps are an endangered treasure, threatened by none other than you—the tourist—pressing the buttons! Despite the guilt trip, the museum is a mountain- or map-lover's must-see. Open mid-May to mid-Oct. Mon. 2-5pm, Tues.-Sun. 10am-5pm; mid-Oct. to mid-May Mon. 2-5pm, Tues.-Sun. 10am-noon and 2-5pm. 5SFr, students and seniors 3SFr.

Albert Einstein's House, Kramg. 49 (tel. 312 00 91). This small apartment where the theory of general relativity was born in 1905 is now filled with photos, a few of Einstein's letters, resonating brain waves, and not much else. The museum dedicates itself to emphasizing that Albert loved Bern and Bern loves Albert. Open Feb.-Nov. Tues.-Fri. 10am-5pm, Sat. 10am-4pm. 3SFr, students and children 2SFr.

Kunsthalle, Helvetiapl. 1 (tel. 351 00 31). Temporary exhibits of contemporary art, often by unknowns, so it's potluck. As its pamphlet says, the museum is "ready to take risks." Open Tues. 10am-9pm, Wed.-Sun. 10am-5pm. 6SFr, students 3SFr.

ENTERTAINMENT AND NIGHTLIFE

Artsy Bern has symphonies, concerts, and theater performances galore. Productions at the **Stadttheater** (tel. 311 07 77) range from operas to ballets. Tickets are 6-115SFr, and students receive a 50% discount. For more information, contact Theaterkasse, Kornhauspl. 18, CH-3000 Bern 7. (Open Mon.-Fri. 10am-6:30pm, Sat. 10am-6pm, Sun. 10am-12:30pm.) The theater season ends in June, but the **Berner Altstadtsommer** picks up the slack in July and August with free dance and music concerts, ranging from tango to jazz to funk to choral, in the squares of the *Altstadt*. Bern's **Symphony Orchestra** plays in the fall and winter at the Konservatorium für Musik at Kramg. 36. For tickets, call 311 62 21. July's **Gurten Festival** has attracted such luminaries as Bob Dylan, Elvis Costello, and Björk to its stage. For ticket information, contact the Bern Tourist Office (tel. 311 66 11), check http://www.gurten-festival.ch, or write to Gurten Festival, Billett-Versand, Postfach, 3000 Bern 13. Tickets are about 55SFr per day. Jazz lovers arrive in early May for the **International**

The Berner Oberland

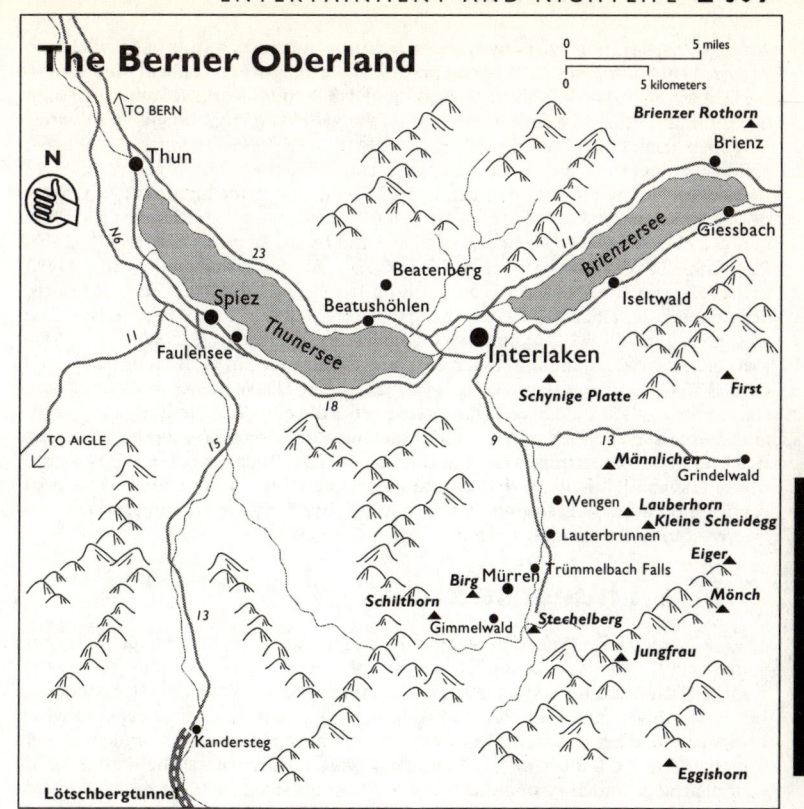

Jazz Festival. For tickets, go to the ticket counter at any Bankverein Swiss Bank branch.

Bars and late-night cafés line Bärenplatz, but venture farther into the *Altstadt* for a Bern tradition: the **Klötzlikeller Weine Stube,** Gerechtigkeitsg. 62 (tel. 311 74 56). Bern's oldest wine cellar resides in a brick-roofed cavern that resonates with the patrons' singing from within. (Open Tues.-Sat. 4pm-12:30am.) Just one block away, the **Art Café,** Gurteng. 3 (tel. 311 42 64), is a café by day and a bar for the cigarette-smoking, hand-waving set at night. The black and white decor and 18 vast Donald Ducks *après* Warhol create a *Der Stijl* meets Disney feel. Drinks run 6-7SFr. (Open Mon.-Thurs. 7am-12:30pm, Fri.-Sat. 7am-7pm and 8pm-2:30am, Sun. 6pm-12:30am.)

THE BERNER OBERLAND

Pristine and savage, the hulking peaks and isolated lodges of the Berner Oberland are at the geographic and emotional heart of Switzerland. When World War II threatened to engulf the country, the Swiss army resolved to defend this area, *le réduit*, to the last. A young, international, and rowdy crowd migrates here every summer to get its fill of crisp Alpine air and clear, starry nights. Opportunities for paragliding, mountaineering, and whitewater rafting here are virtually unparalleled and bewitch not only rubber-boned physical types, but also romantics searching for a lasting memory

You have to be iron-willed to stick to a budget in the Oberland. The heartiest adventures can cost three-figure sums, and transportation is obscenely expensive.

Avoid transportation costs by using a town or village as a hub from which to explore. The Thun-Interlaken-Brienz rail link is a standard Swiss railway, but the various cable cars to the breathtaking peaks and the Berner Oberland Bahn (the string of mountain trains that link Interlaken to the valleys) charge high-altitude fares. Eurailpass sometimes ekes out only a 25% discount, and even the magic Swisspass, valid on trains to Grindelwald, Wengen, Lauterbrunnen, and Mürren, loses its power here—it barely scrapes together a 25% reduction to the higher peaks. Drivers hoping to save a buck should be aware that certain towns, notably Mürren and Wengen, are closed to cars. Of uncertain value is the 15-day **Berner Oberland Regional Pass** (190SFr, with Swisspass or Half-Fare Card 155SFr; Eurailpass not valid), which gives free travel for five days on many railways and cable cars (e.g. Rothorn, Schynige Platte, First, Niesen) and half-price travel on the remaining 10 days. The pass gives only a 25% discount on the Schilthorn and Kleine Scheidegg-Jungfraujoch. A seven-day variation is also available with three free days and four half-priced days (150SFr, with Swisspass or Half-Fare Card 120SFr). Both are available at train stations or any tourist office. Train service generally ends at midnight. Eurailpasses and Swisspasses are valid on the useful **Thunersee** or **Brienzersee ferries.** These ferries lead to hidden surprises like the **Giessbach Falls** (Brienzersee) or the **Beatushöhlen Caves** (Thunersee) that would be inaccessible without them. The boat service, however, ends around 7pm in summer and 5pm in the spring and fall, and winter hours are extremely limited.

■ The Thunersee

Two jade-green lakes framed by steep wooded mountainsides and the distant snowy summits of the Jungfrau sandwich the town of Interlaken. The westerly **Thunersee** is more settled and the mountains less stark than around its twin, the **Brienzersee,** but its northwestern shores are sprinkled or saturated with castles, depending on how many you get to see and your general tolerance for repetitive opulence. Visitors to Fribourg complain of "church crash," which usually hits at the sixth magnificent altarpiece and after one too many of the city's steep hills. Those who return from large cities like Lausanne, Basel, or Bern later slip into a form of "museum madness" that results in a grumbling resentment of even the most reasonable admission prices and an increasing dislike for the brown and white museum signs infesting the motorways. In the Thunersee, "crippling castle syndrome" joins the "momentous mountain disease" to turn most holiday seekers into quivering, fatigued masses of the optically oversaturated and economically emaciated. The area around the Thunersee is bursting with activities, sights, and excursions, but the views are timeless—and free. Stop often and smell the ubiquitous roses. Take note of the mist stretching like vast silken sheets over the lake and mountains before continuing on your whirlwind tour.

Luckily, travel around the Thunersee is surprisingly stress-free. Its three significant towns, **Thun, Spiez,** and **Interlaken,** all lie on the main rail line from Bern to Interlaken to Lucerne. **Boats** putter to the smaller villages between the Thun and Interlaken West railway stations (every hr. daily June-Sept. 8am-8pm; special evening cruises available; 1 per day Nov.-March; Eurailpass, Swisspass, and Berner Oberland pass valid). The whole trip from Thun to Interlaken takes two hours. A ferry daypass plus train and bus travel along the regional lines costs 32SFr in June and September, 42SFr in July and August. Point-to-point tickets may be cheaper depending on how much ground you wish to cover in one day. For current information, consult the BLS shipping company (tel. 334 52 11; http://www.thunersee.ch).

THUN

Thun straddles the Aare River as it leaves the Thunersee on its way to Bern. The station is on the south bank, while the main street, the tree-lined boulevard Bälliz, runs along an island in the river. The oldest squares and the castle (with its flag-impaled

THE THUNERSEE: THUN ■ 399

tower) lie on Aare's north bank. Thun's **tourist office,** Seestr. 2 (tel. 222 83 23), is outside and to the left of the station. Ask about housing and pick up a free map. (Open July-Aug. Mon.-Fri. 9am-7pm, Sat. 9am-noon and 1-4pm; Sept.-June Mon.-Fri. 9am-noon and 1-6pm, Sat. 9am-noon.) **Trains** leave every hour for **Interlaken East** (14SFr) and **Interlaken West** (12.20SFr) and every half hour for **Spiez** (6SFr) and **Bern** (11.40SFr). The rail **information desk** can provide any information you might need to get out of the tiny town. (Open Mon.-Fri. 8am-7:30pm, Sat. 8am-5pm.) The **boat landing** (tel. 223 53 80) is just to the right of the station. Boats depart for **Interlaken West** (15.60SFr), **Spiez** (7.80SFr), **Faulensee** (8.60SFr), **Hilterfingen** (4.40SFr), and **Oberhofen** (5SFr). The train station has **currency exchange** (open daily 5:50am-8:30pm), **bike rental** (22SFr per day; open Mon.-Sat. 7am-7:50pm, Sun. 8:20am-noon and 2-7:50pm), and **lockers** (3-5SFr). **Taxis** are usually waiting outside the train station, or call 222 22 22. **Park** at the Parkhaus Aarestr. on Aarestr. (1.30SFr per hr., 15SFr per day). The **post office** is at Bälliz 60, opposite Mühlebrücke. (Open Mon.-Fri. 7:30am-6pm, Sat. 7:30-11am.) The **postal code** is CH-3600. The **telephone code** is 033.

Accommodations in Thun are not cheap. For private rooms and apartments for longer stays, try the regional reservations office in Spiez (tel. 654 72 56; fax 654 72 49), which makes reservations all year for more than 100 apartments throughout the Berner Oberland. In Thun, your best bet is probably **Hotel Metzgern,** Untere Hauptg. 2 (tel. 222 21 41; fax 222 21 82), which sits in the heart of town on Rathauspl. Carpeted hallways lead to sunny rooms, attractively furnished and equipped with sinks. The hall showers are admirably well-kept. (Reception Tues.-Sun. 7:30am-midnight. Singles 55SFr first night, then 50SFr; doubles 110SFr, 100SFr; triples 165SFr, 150SFr. Breakfast included. Visa.) Other options lie farther away from town, toward Gwatt. Take the bus toward Interlaken to "Schandausdal" and take the first right. **Gasthof Rössli Dürrenast** (tel. 336 80 60; fax 335 28 66) offers six recently renovated doubles. Four have private showers and bathrooms (108SFr); the other two share hallway facilities (94SFr). Single travelers can use the rooms for 53SFr, with shower 60SFr, and groups of three pay 120SFr, with shower 141SFr. (Reception daily 8am-11:30pm. Breakfast included. Reservations recommended, especially in summer. Visa, MC.) Camp at **Bettlereiche** (tel. 336 40 67); take bus #1: "Bettlerrreniche" or turn right from the station and walk 45 minutes. (8.80SFr; tent 6.30-16SFr. Open April-Sept.)

Unlike hotel rooms, food in Thun is surprisingly cheap. Affordable restaurants line Bahnhofstr., and both **Migros** and **Co-op** have markets and restaurants on Allmendstr. straddling the Kuhbrücke. (Both open Mon.-Wed. and Fri. 8am-6:30pm, Thurs. 8am-9pm, Sat. 7am-4pm.) At the open-air market in the *Altstadt* across the river from the train station, vendors hawk souvenirs, clothes, and food. (Open Sat. 8am-9pm.) A food market takes over Bälliz on the island all day on Wednesdays. On the 2nd floor of the *Aare-Zentrum* building is **Le Pavillon,** a self-service restaurant featuring spicy, Asian specialties as well as Swiss staples. (Open Tues.-Wed. and Fri. 7:45am-6:30pm, Thurs. 7:45am-9pm, Sat. 7:30am-4pm.) For delectable pastries and sandwiches in a comfy corner tea room, try **Konditorei Steinmann,** Bälliz 37 (tel. 222 20 47). Enjoy tarts for 2.40SFr or a mouth-watering strawberry custard for 3.50SFr. (Open Mon. 1:30-6:30pm, Tues.-Fri. 6:45am-6:30pm, Sat. 6:45am-4pm.)

To get to the **Schloß Thun** (tel. 223 20 01) from the station, bear left down Bahnhofstr. and go over two bridges, right on Obere Hauptg., left up the stone steps (Risgässli), and left again at the top. Inside the castle, the **Turm Zähringer** houses a historical museum whose inexplicable upper floors juxtapose a collection of vicious weaponry with a selection of antiquated musical instruments. The tower was the site of a gruesome fratricide in 1322, when Eberhard of Kyburg unsportingly defenestrated his brother Hartmann. The Romanesque square tower with four corner turrets looks especially imposing with the Alps as a backdrop. The views from the attic's turrets are impressive, but slightly dangerous—the windows are so deep that you can sit in them and fall out quite easily. Downstairs in the Rittersaal, the castle hosts summer classical music concerts (call 223 35 30 or contact the tourist office; tickets 30-50SFr). (Castle open daily June-Sept. 9am-6pm; April-May and Oct. 10am-5pm. 5SFr, students 2SFr, children 1SFr.) Turning left on Hauptg. at the bottom of the Risgässli steps leads to the **Kunstmuseum,** Hofstettenstr. 14 (tel. 225 84 20; fax 225 82 63; bus #6: "Thunerhof"), which exhibits contemporary art, usually from its collections of Swiss pop art and prints. Call ahead to learn which rooms will be open; exhibits change monthly and the staff is always preparing the next behind braided ropes. (Open Tues. and Thurs.-Sun. 10am-5pm, Wed. 10am-9pm. 3SFr, students 2SFr, children free.)

The popular local walk up **Heilingenschwendi,** the hillside above Thun on the lake's north shore, provides a view of the distant Jungfrau mountains. Past the casino and the village of Seematten (where the lake proper starts), turn left, cross the river, and head up through the wooded ridge to Heilingenschwendi (1152m). From the village of Schwendi near the top, you can head back to Oberhofen on the right, keeping the castle on the right (600m ascent, ½-day). At Oberhofen, the 13th-century **Schloß Oberhofen** (tel. 243 12 35; fax 243 35 61) attracts visitors with its wild and riotous gardens, but its interior does not disappoint. The owner, an enterprising American lawyer, bought the castle in 1926 and, leaving the exterior intact, completely renovated the building, decorating each room in a different historical style. Bern museum veterans may recognize pieces of the History Museum's Islamic collection in the lavishly languid decor of the Turkish smoking room. (Open May to mid-Oct. daily 10am-noon and 2-5pm. 5SFr, children 1SFr. Garden open 9:30am-6pm. 1SFr.) Ferries and buses run back to Thun, but you can also continue down the road to the **Schloß Hünegg** (tel. 243 19 82), on a cliff above the boat landing at **Hilterfingen.** The most elaborate of the Thunersee castles, its excessively Victorian rooms are beyond beautiful. The main bedroom so defies description that you'll have to step onto the balcony to catch your breath, only to faint at the tree-framed view of the lake. (Open mid-May to mid-Oct. Mon.-Sat. 2-5pm, Sun. 10am-noon and 2-5pm. 5SFr, 1SFr group discount.)

Back in pedestrian, plebeian Thun, a 15-minute walk to the right of the station brings up the pink **Schloß Schadau,** Seestr. 45 (tel. 223 14 32), in the Walter Hansen Schadaupark. This Victorian folly in a tree-lined, waterfront garden hosts long-running temporary exhibitions. From June 1997 to Easter 1998, the castle will be taken over by toys from all over the world. The fun begins with a ramble through the park, where signs explain old children's games suitable for the wide-grass lawns. (Open daily July-Aug. 10am-6pm; May-Nov. 10am-5pm. 4SFr, students 3SFr, under 17 free.)

SPIEZ

Spiez is happy to forgo the proud grandeur of prim chalets or imposing monuments. Quiet and understated, the town fills its tiny harbor with bobbing boats and surveys the **Thunersee** from its gentle hills. Spiez's **tourist office,** Bahnhofstr. 12A (tel. 654 21 38; fax 654 21 92), left as you exit the train station, sells hiking maps and helps find inexpensive rooms. (Open July-Aug. and Oct. Mon.-Fri. 8am-noon and 2-6pm, Sat. 9am-noon and 2-5pm; May-June and Sept. Mon.-Fri. 8am-noon and 2-6pm, Sat. 9am-noon; Nov.-April Mon.-Fri. 9am-noon and 2-5pm.) **Trains** leave every 30 minutes and connect the town with **Bern** (15.80SFr), **Thun** (6SFr), and **Interlaken West** (8.40SFr). **Boats** float to Thun (17.80SFr) and Interlaken (10.60SFr). The **Migros** market and restaurant is across the train station parking lot to the right. (Open Mon.-Thurs. 8am-6:30pm, Fri. 8am-9pm, Sat. 7:30am-4pm.) Seestr. leads to Oberlandstr. and its banks and **Co-op.** (Open Mon.-Thurs. 7:30am-12:15pm and 1:30-6:30pm, Fri. 7:30am-12:15pm and 1:30-9pm, Sat. 7:30am-4pm.) The **post office** is to the left of the station. (Open Mon.-Fri. 7:30am-noon and 1:45-6pm, Sat. 8:30-11am.) The **postal code** is CH-3700, and the **telephone code** is 033.

Budget accommodations are almost non-existent in Spiez itself. **Hotel Krone,** Oberlandstr. 28 (tel. 654 41 31; fax 654 94 31), has smallish, plain, but very clean rooms, some affording great views. Passing traffic makes the rooms on the lake noisier than those facing the mountains, but if the ear does not take offense, the eye is sure to feast. (Reception Tues.-Thurs. 8:30am-11:30pm, Fri.-Sat. 8:30am-midnight,

Sun. 9am-noon. Singles 45-50SFr; doubles 80-95SFr. Hall showers and toilets. Open May-March. Visa, MC, AmEx.) Better options exist in surrounding villages. A bus to "Rossli" or a 20-minute hike to Spiezailer leads to **Hotel Rössli**, Frutigenstr. (tel. 654 34 34; fax 654 56 35). The hotel offers dorms for 20SFr, breakfast included. These cellar bunks and showers have a definite meat-locker atmosphere, so bring your own sleepsack or your toes may develop serious chilblains. The upstairs attic rooms are somewhat pricey but much cleaner (and warmer!). (Reception Mon.-Thurs. 7:30am-11:30pm, Fri.-Sat. 7:30am-midnight. Singles 58SFr; doubles 102SFr. Off-season: 54SFr; 90SFr. Visa, MC, AmEx, DC.) **Camp** at **Panorama Rossern,** Aeschi (tel. 654 43 77 or 223 36 15; fax 223 36 65). To find the campsite, catch the bus to Mustermattli (2SFr), and then follow the signs. (6.40SFr; tent 6-7SFr. Open May-Sept.)

Spiez's castle, the **Schloß Spiez** (tel. 654 15 06), was a medieval fortress that became a residential castle for Oberlander bigwigs like the Bubenbergs and Erlachs. The castle is next to the dock; from the station, go down the ramp to Hotel Krone, and cross over onto Seestr., following it to the right before heading left on Schlossstr. A stone tower with unconventional spiral shutters leads to a quiet grassy courtyard, a 10th-century churchyard, and a rose garden. Inside the fortress is a historical museum with a mesmerizing tower view, but the highlight of the visit is the fabulous woodwork that graces nearly all the rooms. (Open July-Aug. Mon. 2-6pm, Tues.-Sun. 10am-6pm; April-June and Sept.-Oct. Mon. 2-5pm, Tues.-Sun. 10am-5pm. 4SFr, students 1SFr.) Around the corner, the **Wine-Making Museum,** Spiezbergstr. 48, has rustically decorated rooms, a cask-maker's workshop, and a pressing shed. (Open May-Oct. Wed. and Sat.-Sun. 2-5pm. Guided tours available. Free.) The mountain piercing the sky is the **Niesenberg** (2363m). Hikes on the mountain, while not for beginners, are not remotely as spine-tingling as they look. Pick up hiking maps at tourist offices in Interlaken, Thun, or Spiez. Hiking all the way up or down the mountain is prohibited, but a funicular chugs to the top, and the Lötschberg train from Spiez (every hr., 7.20SFr round-trip) connects with the funicular at Mülenen (May-Oct.; 23SFr, 38SFr round-trip, 12SFr one-way to Schwandegg). A 3-stop funicular ticket is 31SFr. The funicular's builders pushed the frontiers of human achievement by building steps alongside the track, which thereby became the **longest flight of steps in the world.** Unfortunately, only the company's maintenance teams or the thunder-thighed locals who pound all 11,674 of them in the annual **Niesen Steps Race** are allowed to walk on them. Hiking routes head down from the summit to **Mülenen** (3hr.) and **Wimmis** (3½hr.). For more scenic bliss, hike to Schwandegg (1¼hr.) and take the train again through the woods to Mülenen. To spend a night in an unspoiled, friendly *Berggästehaus,* visit the **mountain guest-house** (tel. 676 11 13) on the summit. The hotel has seven guest rooms with 15 beds, a roomy dining area, and a large terrace and wine cellar hewn into the rock-face. (38SFr per person. Breakfast 14SFr. The "Sunset-Sunrise" package offers dinner, breakfast, and round-trip transportation for 110SFr.)

BEATENBERG AND THE CAVES

Little more than a sprinkling of chalets stretched over a 7km strip of hillside, Beatenberg is known as the sun-terrace of the Berner Oberland. Perched 600m above the Thunersee, the town offers hiking for all levels. Bus #21 from Interlaken to Thun stops in the village, where the **tourist office** waits (tel. (033) 841 18 18; fax 841 18 08; open Mon.-Fri. 8am-noon and 2-6pm, Sat. 9am-noon; July-Sept. also Sat. 3-5pm).

The superb **Güggisgrat ridge** rewards a short climb with long views. Yellow signs from the village center point the almost-vertical way up the Niederhom (1950m; 830m ascent; 2½hr.). Four miles of airy ridgeway then lead northwest to the Gemmenalhorn (2061m) at an easy gradient. Dozens of paths loop back to civilization; the tourist office's topographical map will untangle them. **Gondolas** also climb the Niederhom (20SFr, 30SFr round-trip; with Eurailpass or Swisspass 15SFr, 22.60SFr; closed 2 weeks in Nov. and 2 weeks in April). Routes start at the eastern (Interlaken) end of the village. The **restaurant** (tel. (033) 841 11 97) at the top has **dorm beds** (30SFr; breakfast included), singles (45SFr), and doubles (90SFr).

Down from Beatenberg village, **Beatushöhlen** (St. Beatus' Caves) riddle the hillside for over 14km. You can spelunk through the first 100m of glistening stalactites, waterfalls, and grottoes. At the cave entrance, visit a plastic replica of the 6th-century hermit Beatus, who sits reading a bible next door to his prehistoric plaster cavemates. Legend has it that the Augustinian monk had to fight off a dragon in the caves before he could preach the gospels in peace. In one of the grottoes, an iguana-sized, stained-glass critter glows as a monument to the fight. Even on hot summer days, the interior of the caves stays a cool 8-10 degrees Celsius. Half-hour tours leave every 30 minutes from the cave entrance. To get there, walk 15 minutes up the hill from the Beatushöhlen dock, take a half-hour boat ride from Interlaken, or take bus #21, which runs between Thun and Interlaken (8.20SFr round-trip from Interlaken). You can also walk from Interlaken (2hr.) or Beatenberg (1hr. on a steep path downhill through woods and farmland). The admission fee includes entry to the **Caving Museum** (tel. (033) 841 16 43), five minutes down the hill. This tiny room chronicles the discovery and mapping of Swiss grottoes. (Caves open April-Oct. daily 9:30am-5pm. Museum open April-Oct. Tues.-Sun. 10:30am-5pm. 12SFr, students 10SFr, children 5.50SFr.)

■ The Brienzersee

The more rugged of the sister lakes, the Brienzersee lies still, clear, and cold beneath sharply jutting cliffs, frothy waterfalls, and dense forests. Cruises on the lake depart from Interlaken's *Ostbahnhof*. (June-Sept. one per hr. 9am-5pm; April-May and Oct. five per day. Eurailpass and Swisspass valid.) Brienz, at the eastern end of the lake, is the Brienzersee's only town. The south shoreline, having escaped human attention save for the hamlet of Iseltwald, makes a great hike.

BRIENZ AND THE ROTHORN

Occupying the thin strip of level land between brilliant tourmaline water and deep green hillside, Brienz overflows with Alpine flowers, wooden figurine shops, and intricately carved houses with wood-scalloped walls. The station, dock, and Rothorn rack railway terminus occupy the center of town, flanked on Hauptstr. by the post office, banks, and a supermarket. At the west end of town is Brienz-Dorf wharf; at the eastern end lie the hostel and two campsites. Twenty minutes by train or 1¼ hours by boat (10.60SFr) from Interlaken, Brienz makes a peaceful daytrip.

Brienz's **tourist office,** Hauptstr. 143 (tel. 952 80 80; fax 952 80 88), across and left from the train station, suggests trails for hikers of all levels. Ask here about *Privatzimmer* or the week's events, such as guided hikes, tours of the wood-carving school (10AS), "carve your own cow" fests, and other fab happenings. (Open July-Aug. Mon.-Fri. 8am-6:30pm, Sat. 9am-noon and 4-6pm; Sept.-June Mon.-Fri. 8am-noon and 2-6pm, Sat. 8am-noon.) The **train station** rents **bicycles** (21SFr per day), **exchanges currency,** and offers small **lockers** (2SFr). The **post office** (tel. 951 25 05) is also nearby. (Open Mon.-Fri. 7:45am-noon and 1:45-6pm, Sat. 8:30-11am.) The **postal code** is CH-3855, and the **telephone code** is 033.

For lodgings, cross the tracks at the station, face the lake, and walk left on the shore path (15min.) to find the **Brienz Jugendherberge (HI),** Strandweg 10 (tel. 951 11 52; fax 951 22 60). The lakeside hostel rents bicycles (1 day 10SFr, 2 days 15SFr) to its mountain-hungry guests. (Reception daily 8-10am and 5-10pm. Dorms 23SFr the first night, then 20.50SFr; doubles 28SFr, 25.50SFr. Guest tax 2.10SFr. Dinner 11SFr. Kitchen facilities. Open May-Oct.) The cheapest hotel in town is **Hotel Sternen am See,** Hauptstr. 92 (tel. 951 35 45), left from the station, with a winning lakeside terrace. (Reception 8am-8pm. Singles 50-60SFr; doubles 80SFr, with shower 120SFr; triples 110SFr, 150SFr; quads with shower 180SFr. Breakfast included. Visa, MC.) Continue past the hostel to hit two waterfront campgrounds: **Camping Seegärtli** (tel. 951 13 51; 7SFr, tents 5-7SFr, cars 3SFr; open April-Oct.) and **Camping Aaregg** (tel. 951 18 43; fax 951 43 24; reception 7am-noon and 2-

8pm; 9SFr, tents 16SFr; open April-Oct.). A **Co-op** nests on Hauptg. across from the station. (Open Mon.-Thurs. 7:45am-6:30pm, Fri. 7:45am-8:30pm, Sat. 7:45am-4pm. Visa, MC.) **Restaurant Adler,** Hauptstr. 131 (tel. 951 41 00), has a terrace with a spectacular view of the Brienzersee and the Axalphorn. Main dishes are 15 to 19SFr. (Open June-Oct. daily 7:30am-11:30pm; Nov.-May Tues.-Sun. 7:30am-11:30pm.) **Steinbock Restaurant** (tel. 951 40 55), farther along Hauptstr., has outside tables and a low-ceilinged, wooden interior with subdued lighting. Main courses start at 11SFr. (Open daily 11am-11pm.)

The campy **Ballenberg Swiss Open-Air Museum,** on the outskirts of town along Lauenenstr. (tel. 951 11 23; fax 951 18 21), is a 50-hectare country park displaying traditional rural dwellings, big-bellied cows, happy muddy pigs, and Swiss artisans toiling away. The park is about an hour's walk from the Brienz train station, but an hourly bus (round-trip 5.60SFr) connects the two, and the local train from Brienz to Meiringen and Lucerne stops in Brienzwiler opposite the museum. (Open mid-April to Oct. daily 10am-5pm. 12SFr, with visitor's card 10.80SFr; students 10SFr.) At the other end of town stands the **Wood-Carving Museum** (tel. 951 17 51) on Schleeg., 15 minutes down the main road and to the right. (Open Mon.-Fri. 8-11am and 2-5pm. Free.) The **Violin-Making School** (tel. 951 18 61) is just around the corner on Oberdorfstr. Home to 10 students ages 15 to 30, the school houses a collection of antique instruments, a showroom of gleaming finished violins (approx. 5000SFr each), and a workroom where the shy, humble craftspeople carve, sand, and varnish their instruments with loving precision. (Open Sept.-June Wed. 2-4pm. Free.) Many local wood-carvers also let you watch them work; contact the tourist office for a map.

For even more of authentic Switzerland, you can ascend the **Rothorn** (2350m) for an outstanding view of the Brienzersee and the Berner Oberland mountain chain, well beyond the familiar Eiger, Mönch, and Jungfrau. From June to October, the **Brienz Rothorn Bahn** (tel. 951 44 00) huffs and puffs its way up every hour. Over 100 years old, this small open train is the only steam rail line left in Switzerland. The one-hour trip is pricey (40SFr, round-trip 62SFr; with regional pass free, 31SFr; with Swisspass 30SFr, 47SFr), but as you ascend 1800m, your feet will bless you. A trip to **Planalp** in a hanging valley at 1341m leaves you 2½ hours from the top (26SFr). The view on the way down is breathtaking; fortunately, the pace isn't. Either follow the railway, turning left below Planalp through Baalen and Schwanden (3½hr.), or leave the summit to the east toward the lake and turn right at the Eiseesaltel, continuing down to Hofstetten, Schwanden, and Brienz (4hr.). The tourist office publishes a leaflet, *Wanderberg,* with these options clearly marked. After a long day of hiking, you can spend the night on Rothorn's peak at the *Berggasthaus* (tel. 951 12 32; fax 951 37 95; dorms 32SFr; singles 70SFr; doubles 140SFr; no showers; breakfast included).

THE SOUTH SHORE

Boat service gives easy access to the wild, romantic south shore of the lovely Brienzersee. Float 10 minutes from Brienz or one hour from Interlaken to **Giessbach Falls,** and climb along its 14 frothy cascades. You can walk up the hill in 15 minutes (turn left at the tiny dock) or take the funicular (open May to mid-Oct. 3SFr, round-trip 5.50SFr; students and Regional Pass holders 2.50SFr, 3SFr). The hotel provides a classic view, and the path that criss-crosses and passes behind the falls provides a deafening, dampening experience. Trails (1½hr.) stretch around the lake from the falls to **Iseltwald,** a small village whose only tourist attraction is professional fishing. Postal buses and steamers serve the gloriously sleepy village. Iseltwald's campground, **Camping du Lac** (tel. (033) 845 11 48), has many conveniences, from water sport facilities to a seafood restaurant. (10SFr; tents 5-10SFr. Open May-Sept.)

To reach a satisfying little peak, the **Axalphorn** (2321m), you can take a bus from Brienz station to Axalp (8.40SFr) and head up either the east or west ridge (800m, ½ day). Get a map (check the tourist office at Brienz) and some navigational skills, since both paths are indistinct in places.

MEIRINGEN AND REICHENBACH FALLS

Meiringen is seven miles from the Brienzersee, but its famous gorge and waterfall make it a great daytrip from Brienz (10min. away) or Interlaken (30min.). The spooky **Gorge of the Aare** is 200m deep but only 1m wide at its narrowest point. Direct sunlight hardly ever reaches the bottom—home to the legendary fork-tongued **Tatzelworm**. To reach the gorge, follow signs from Meiringen's main street (2km). On Wednesday and Friday July to August, the gorge shines under floodlights after 9pm. (Open April-Oct. 5SFr, students 3.50SFr.)

More famous but less spectacular, the **Reichenbach Falls** hurl their glacier water into the Aare River at Meiringen. Sherlock Holmes and Professor Moriarty tumbled together into the falls on May 4, 1891, apparently ending the greatest struggle between good and evil in the history of the detective novel. To reach the falls, walk down Meiringen's main street and turn right over the river to Reichenbach. From there, take the **funicular** (open mid-May to Sept; 4.40SFr, 6.50SFr round-trip) or walk up. Continue onwards and you will soon reach the deserted, high-alpine pastures of the Rosenlaui valley, the icefall of the Rosenlaui glacier, and the shapely Wellhorn peak (600m ascent, ½-day). The **Sherlock Holmes Museum** (tel. 971 42 21) is in the old Anglican church in Meiringen and replicates 221B Baker Street. (Open May-Sept. daily 10am-6pm; Oct.-April Wed.-Sun. 3-6pm. 3.80SFr.) If you don't find a Tatzelworm at the gorge, you can look in Meiringen's bakeries, which specialize in *Tatzel-würmli* cakes (6in.-2ft.), éclair-like pastries with almond eyes, chocolate coats, cream bellies, and scary, strawberry-candy teeth. For details on local accommodations and other excursions, see the **tourist office** (tel. 972 50 50) near the station.

■ Interlaken

In 1130 two ruthlessly literal-minded Augustinian monks named the land between the Thunersee and the Brienzersee "Interlaken." Most of its visitors, however, come not for the lakes but for the giant mountains to the south: the Eiger, Mönch, and Jungfrau. Although the sight of the Jungfrau rising 4158m above the gardens lining Höheweg is entrancing, realize that Interlaken is a way-station for the villages to the south and not really a destination in itself—which doesn't stop the hordes of English- and Japanese-speaking tourists who have virtually eliminated Swiss-German from menus and street signs. Each year, swarms of thrill-seekers descend on the town in search of canyoning, rafting, and bungee-jumping. Without the painted wooden cows and distant mountains, tourists might forget they were in Switzerland.

One of the eeriest and most fascinating sights in the Berner Oberland is the face in the **Harder Mountain**, called the **Harder Mann**. No human hand sculpted him, but there he is, looking out over Interlaken with his brooding gaze. On a clear day he is easy to see, a pale triangular face resting against a pillow of trees on one side and a wedge of naked rock on the other. His black moustache has a certain despondent droop, and his deep-socketed eyes have a melancholic, hunted look. To see him, stand on Höheweg across from Buddy's and look up through the buildings. There are many legends about the Harder Mann, some of them dark: a man, guilty of murder or rape, fled to the mountains and was turned to stone, his face left behind for all eternity. For the children of Interlaken, there is a brighter story: every year the Harder Mann comes down from the mountains to fight off winter. On January 2, they celebrate this fight with wooden Harder Mann masks and a large carnival. Hikers may hike this landmark, but they should not leave the marked paths. Deaths occur every summer when people attempt to master roped-off areas.

ORIENTATION AND PRACTICAL INFORMATION

Interlaken lies south on N6, west on N8, and north on Route 11, and the city has two train stations. The Westbahnhof stands in the center of town bordering the

INTERLAKEN: ACCOMMODATIONS AND CAMPING ■ 405

Thunersee, near most shops and hotels; trains from Bern, Basel, and other western towns stop here first. The Ostbahnhof, on the Brienzersee, is 10 minutes away from the town center by foot or bus (2.20SFr) but is near the youth hostel. Both stations have hotel prices posted and direct free phones for reservations.

Tourist Office: Höheweg 37 (tel. 822 21 21), in the Hotel Metropole. From the Westbahnhof, turn left on Bahnhofpl. and right on Bahnhofstr., which becomes Höheweg. From the Ostbahnhof, turn left and keep going. Free maps and schedules, tickets to the Jungfraujoch, and a TV link to all cable cars and railway stations. Open July-Aug. Mon.-Fri. 8am-noon and 1:30-6:30pm, Sat. 8am-noon and 1:30-5pm, Sun. 5-7pm; Sept.-June Mon.-Fri. 8am-noon and 2-6pm, Sat. 8am-noon.

Currency Exchange: Good rates at the **train station** (though you might do 1% better in town). No commission on traveler's checks. Credit card advances and Western Union transfers. Open daily 8am-noon and 2-6pm.

Trains: The **Westbahnhof** (tel. 826 47 50) and **Ostbahnhof** (tel. 822 27 92) have trains to: **Bern** (24SFr), **Basel** (54SFr), **Zurich** (60SFr), **Geneva** (60SFr), **Lucerne** (25SFr), and **Lugano** (69SFr), among others. Trains to the mountains leave every 30min. from the Ostbahnhof to: **Wengen** (11.40SFr), **Grindelwald** (18SFr), **Mürren** (28.20SFr, change at Lauterbrunnen), **Lauterbrunnen** (6SFr), **Kleine Scheidegg** (59.20SFr), and the **Jungfraujoch** (153.20SFr round-trip; see **The Jungfraujoch**, p. 412). Swisspass valid for Wengen, Grindelwald, and Mürren, 25% discount at higher stops. Eurailpass 25% discount on mountain trains. Computers on the platforms at both stations spew information in English, German, and French.

Taxis: City Taxi (tel. 823 33 33).

Parking: Lots at the train stations, behind the casino, and on Centralstr.

Bike Rental: At either **train station**, 22SFr per day, mountain bikes 30SFr. Open daily 5am-10pm. At **Zumbrunn Velo**, Postg. 4 (tel. 822 22 35), 8SFr per day, mountain bikes 18SFr.

Bookstore: Buchhandlweg Haupt, Höheweg 11 (tel. 822 35 16). English-language books, German and French dictionaries, and *Let's Go.* Open Mon.-Fri. 10am-6:30pm, Sat. 8:30am-4pm.

Library: Marktpl. 4 (tel. 822 02 12). German, French, and English books. Open Mon.-Tues. and Thurs.-Fri. 4-6pm, Wed. 9-11am and 3-7pm, Sat. 10am-noon.

Laundromat: See **Balmer's Herberge** below.

Snow and Weather Info: For the Jungfrau, call 855 10 22.

Late-Night Pharmacy: Call 111. **Grosse Apotheke,** Bahnhofstr. 5A, is open Mon.-Fri. 7:30am-12:15pm and 1:15-6:30pm, Sat. 7:30am-5pm. Visa, MC, AmEx.

Emergencies: Police: tel. 117. **Hospital:** tel. 826 26 26. **Doctor:** tel. 823 23 23.

Internet Access: Buddy's, Höheweg 33. 15SFr. for 15min. (See p. 409).

Post Office: Marktg. 1 (tel. 824 89 50). From the Westbahnhof go left on Bahnhofpl., right on Bahnhofstr., and left on Marktg.. Open May-Sept. Mon.-Fri. 7:45am-6:30pm, Sat. 8:30am-4pm; Oct.-April Mon.-Sat. 7:45am-noon and 1:30-6:15pm, Sat. 8:30-11am. **Postal Code:** CH-3800.

Telephone Code: 033.

ACCOMMODATIONS AND CAMPING

Hotels in the mountains are going through a lean patch, and Interlaken is seriously over-bedded. Finding a place to sleep is easy. The tourist office has a list of self-catering chalets for rent, but in high season these accommodations are often unavailable.

Balmer's Herberge, Hauptstr. 23-25 (tel. 822 19 61; fax 823 32 61), in the nearby village of Matten. Bus #5: "Hotel Sonne" (2.20SFr) and then backtrack 1min., or walk 15-20min. from either station. From the Westbahnhof, take a left on Bahnhofpl., a right on Bahnhofstr., and a right on Centralstr. After the post office, Centralstr. becomes Jungfraustr.; at the end, dodge right off Gasthof Hirschen and Balmer's is on the left. From June to Aug., Balmer's runs a shuttle bus from both stations approx. every hr. Sign in, drop off your pack, and return at 5pm when beds are assigned (no reservations). When you see Americans in Interlaken, it's not hard to guess where they're staying. A back-to-the-mother-tongue break for linguistically challenged Anglophones, Balmer's is the country's oldest private hostel (since 1945) and a legend on the international hostelers' circuit. During U.S. college vacations, it takes on a distinctive frat-party, summer-camp atmosphere, replete with fast-flowing beer and numerous lounges. "Uncle Erich" provides tons of services for his guests, including mountain bike rental (30SFr per day), nightly movies, TV with CNN and MTV, book exchange and reading room, email, kitchen facilities (1SFr per 20min.), laundry (8SFr per load), a mini-department store (open daily until 10pm), safety deposit boxes (1SFr for the entire stay), and oodles of information. A newly-built **club-room** with **jukebox,** live music by staff members, a **game-recreation room,** and summer **bonfires** in the nearby forest (shuttle bus free) all entertain Balmer's guests into the wee hours of morning. Partake of the entertainment with caution—wake-up music starts at 7:30am to get half-conscious guests out by 9:30am. The staff makes a real effort to get guests out on the trails and slopes (see **Outdoors Near Interlaken,** p. 407). In the winter there are free sleds and a 20% discount on ski and snowboard rental. Many of those in the dorms or Balmer's tent (a huge white circus tent with no insulation) value comradeship above comfort. Reception daily in summer 6:30am-noon and 4:30-11pm; in winter 6:30-9am and 4:30-11pm. Dorms and tent 17-19SFr; singles 40SFr; doubles 56SFr; triples 72SFr; quads 96SFr. If beds are full, crash on a mattress (13SFr). Showers 1SFr per 5min. of hot water. Breakfast included. No one gets turned away, but it's best to show up early. Visa, MC, AmEx with a 50SFr minimum and a 5% surcharge.

Jugendherberge Bönigen (HI), Aareweg 21 (tel. 822 43 53; fax 823 20 58). Bus #1 (dir: Bönigen): "Lütschinenbrücke" (2 stops). Follow the signs on the left for 2min. From the Ostbahnhof, turn left and left again on the main road (20min.). Catering to a more international crowd, the *jugi* is the ying to Balmer's yang. The lake laps at the doorstep while gnomes frolic in the garden. The 6-bed dorms are quieter than the 25-bed behemoths on the top floor. Reception daily 6-10am and 4-11pm. No lockout. Six- and 25-bed dorms 18.30SFr first night, then 15.80SFr; 4-bed dorms 22.30SFr, 19.80SFr; doubles 62.60SFr. Showers, sheets, and lockers included. Breakfast 7SFr. Dinner 10.50SFr. Kitchen facilities 0.50SFr. Laundry around 8SFr. Bike rental 10SFr. Reserve at least 2 days in advance June-Aug. Open Feb.-Oct.

Heidi's Garni-Hotel Beyeler, Bernastr. 37 (tel./fax 822 90 30). From the Westbahnhof, turn right, then bear left on Bernastr. (behind the Migros), and walk straight for about 3min. A friendly, family-run hotel in a rambling old house decorated with sleds, bells, old photographs, and carousel horses. Wood-beamed TV room with CNN and lots of information on things to do. A very bouncy dog named Pedro keeps watch over the guests. Cheap, livable rooms have showers and bathrooms, some have balconies, views, and flowery Swiss furniture. More expensive modern doubles (80-90SFr) across the street in an apartment with kitchen, phone, balcony, and TV room. Doubles 75SFr; triples 93SFr; quads 124SFr. Free lollipops. Visa, MC.

Alp Lodge, Marktg. 59 (tel. 822 47 48; fax 822 92 50). Take a left from Westbahnhof, bear right on Bahnhofstr. and left down Marktg. at the post office. The hotel is down an alley by the pink Hotel Bellevue, opposite Mr. Hong's. Jazzy primary colors in the halls and funky, home-painted safari animals in the rooms. The staff are a gas and the rooms sparkle, though the stairwell carpet may get a bit frayed. Reception 7am-9pm. 27-29SFr per person, with shower 37-39SFr. Breakfast included. Open mid.-Dec. to Oct.

Happy Inn Lodge, Rosenstr. 17 (tel. 822 32 25; fax 822 32 68). Turn left as you exit the Westbahnhof, make a right on Bahnhofstr., go past the post office, and then make a right onto Rosenstr. Look for the yellow happy face. Hostel-type dorms with exceptionally fluffy pillows and quads and doubles with a less institutional feel. Thin walls do little to block out the occasional bands playing downstairs at the restaurant/bar, **Brasserie 17.** 6-bed dorms 19SFr, with breakfast 26SFr; doubles 70SFr, 82SFr; quads 108SFr, 136SFr. MC, AmEx.

INTERLAKEN: FOOD ■ 407

Camping

Camping Sackgut (tel. 822 44 34) is closest to town, just across the river from the Ostbahnhof. Head toward town, but take a right across the first bridge and another right on the other side. 7.60SFr; tent 6.50-14SFr. Open May-Sept.

Camping Jungfraublick (tel. 822 44 14; fax 822 16 19). Bus #5 from the Westbahnhof, 5min. past Balmer's on Gsteigstr. Peaceful location with splendid views. 12SFr; off-season 7SFr. Open May.-Sept.

Five other sites are clustered together near the Lombach River and the Thunersee in Unterseen. From the Westbahnhof, cross the Aare River on Bahnhofstr. and follow the signs down Seestr. 5.60-11SFr.

FOOD

Interlaken's restaurants, unlike its accommodations, are as expensive as the rest of Switzerland. Along Höheweg, restaurants are exorbitant and overwhelmingly touristy. Head across the river to old Interlaken (from Höheweg turn onto Marktg. and cross the bridge) for cheaper meals, a better atmosphere, and menus that are actually in German. Generally, the Balmer's crowd eats at Balmer's (fondue, bratwurst, and burgers all under 10SFr), and the hostel crowd eats at the *Jugendherberge* (11SFr).

Pizpaz, Bahnhofstr. 1 (tel. 822 25 33), is a buzzing, central Italian restaurant with pinkish outdoor tables. "Farinaceous dishes" (presumably pasta) 9.50-16.50SFr, pizza 10.50-17SFr, shrimp and gorganzola risotto 17.50SFr. Open July-Aug. daily 11am-midnight; Sept.-June Tues.-Sun. 11am-midnight. Visa, MC, AmEx.

Café Restaurant Spatz, Spielmatte 49 (tel. 822 97 22), 5min. from Höheweg. Turn onto Marktg. and cross the first bridge. This café serves up fondue (16.50SFr); a platter of chicken, potatoes, and veggies (11SFr); and *Apfelstrüdel* with whipped cream (4.50SFr) on a terrace overlooking the river. Open Mon.-Sat. 8:30am-11pm.

Chalet Oberland, Postg. (tel. 821 62 21). A romantic, rustic wooden chalet interior for up-market traditional Swiss food. Turkey Schnitzel with mushroom sauce 16SFr, Bernese bratwurst and *Rösti* 15SFr. Big salad buffet 13SFr. Open Sun.-Thurs. 11am-11:30pm, Fri.-Sat. 11am-1am. Visa, MC, AmEx.

Confiserie Rieder, Marktg. 14 (tel. 822 36 73). Truffle pyramids, tarts (4.50SFr), sweet-smelling strudel, and meringues heaped with ice cream. Open Tues.-Fri. 8:30am-6:30pm, Sat.-Sun. 8:30am-6pm.

Mr. Wong's Chinese Take-Out, Marktg. 48 (tel. 823 55 44). For evenings too beautiful to eat inside, Mr. Wong cooks up a huge variety of stir-fries to go. Chomp on mixed veggies (10SFr), sweet and sour chicken (13SFr), or pork fried rice (11SFr) on a bench by the nearby river. Open April-Oct. Mon.-Sun. 11:45am-10pm.

Markets

Migros, across from the Westbahnhof, also houses a restaurant with giant prancing cows on the ceiling. Market and restaurant open Mon-Thurs. 7:30am-6:30pm, Fri. 7:30am-9pm, Sat. 7:30am-4pm; restaurant also open Sun. 9am-5pm.

Co-op, on Bahnhofstr. on the right after you cross into Unterseen. Market open Mon.-Thurs. 7:30am-6:30pm, Fri. 7:30am-9pm, Sat. 7:30am-4pm. Restaurant open Mon.-Thurs. 8am-6:30pm, Fri. 8am-9:30pm, Sat. 8am-5:30pm, Sun. 9am-5:30pm.

OUTDOORS NEAR INTERLAKEN

Interlaken is the base for many outdoor excursions, boasting such nausea-inducing, pants-wetting, heart-attack-producing activities as bungee jumping, parachuting, glacier climbing, canyoning, kayaking, and paragliding. Guests at Balmer's can sign up near the reception desk for activities run by **Adventure World,** Kirchg. 18 (tel. 826 77 11; fax 826 77 15), Interlaken's main "adventure coordinator." Thrill-seekers flock to a host of daredevil pursuits. On the water, there's **river rafting** (½-day 85SFr) and **canyoning,** the most popular Alpine adrenaline rush—wet-suited, harnessed future stunt doubles rappel and swim down a waterfall (½-day 85-125SFr).

On land, struggle up and rappel down the alps on your **rock-climbing** adventure (½-day 75SFr). In the air, enjoy the graceful, peaceful beauty of **tandem paragliding** (½-day 140-200SFr, depending on altitude) or experience the free-fall rush of **bungee jumping** from the Schilthorn (100m, 129SFr; 180m, 259SFr, prerequisite of one previous jump). Adventure World also offers combination packages (150-350SFr).

Interlaken's *Flugschule*, **Ikarus,** offers intensive and expensive classes in **parachuting** and **paragliding,** as well as a one-day program of **tandem paragliding** (from 100SFr; 1 week 890SFr). Contact Claudia or Hanspeter Michel, Brunng. 68, CH-3800 Matten (tel. 822 04 28). **Alpin Raft,** another Interlaken-based group, also offers **rafting** (50-108SFr), **canyoning** (75-112SFr), **kayaking** (35SFr), and **horseback riding** (75SFr for 2hr.). Student discounts are available. Contact Heinz Looshi, Postfach CH-3800, Matten (tel. 823 41 00; fax 823 41 01).

Minutes from Interlaken on the Brienzersee, Alpin Raft's **sea-kayaking** provides a strenuous day in the sun and on the water (54-70SFr). **Euro-trek** leads guided **boat trips** on the Vierwaldstättersee near Lucerne and on the Brienzersee (from 71SFr). Contact Euro-trek Abenteuerreisen, Malzstr. 17-221, CH-8026 Zürich (tel. (01) 462 02 03). For those who want to get really cold and wet, **Alpine Guides,** Hano Tschabold, Bergführer, CH-3852 Ringgenberg (tel. 22 05 69), offers **glacier climbing** (June-Oct., 120SFr), one-day **rock-climbing courses** (95SFr), and one-day **glacier walks** (100SFr) daily in summer. Interlaken's winter activities include skiing, snowboarding, ice canyoning, snow rafting, and glacier skiing. Contact **Verkehrsverein Interlaken,** Höheweg 37 (tel. 822 21 21; fax 822 52 21) or Adventure World for information.

With all these activities, the situation is very fluid; companies tend to come and go as individual guides and instructors move into and out of Interlaken. Shop around, and watch the fine print for insurance coverage and travel costs to the starting point.

HIKES FROM INTERLAKEN

Interlaken is in a deep valley, so picture-perfect views require that you sweat. A gentle lakeside path rings the Brienzersee, and the south shore provides a scenic walk or bike ride from Böningen or the youth hostel garden. The half-day climb up the **Harderkulm** (1322m) brings you touchably close to the white wall of the Jungfrau, Eiger, and Mönch peaks, towering 3700m above Interlaken's rooftops. The hike zigzags through dense, dull woods, but the view from the top is extraordinary. From the Ostbahnhof, head toward town and take the first road bridge right across the river. On the other side, the path has yellow signs (destination: "Harderkulm") that later give way to white-red-white *bergweg* flashes on the rocks. A house in a clearing stands halfway from Interlaken West; from here, turn left and left again across the river on Bahnhofstr., later called Scheidgasse. After seven minutes the path intersects with Beatenburgstr. at the edge of town and then rises at the junction across the road. Bus #21: "Beatenberg" also stops at the trailhead (2 per hr. from both stations). The path is not very difficult, but rain can make it gloopy (750m ascent, 2hr. up, 1½hr. down). A **restaurant** at the top serves spaghetti for 11.50SFr and *Rösti* with fried eggs for 11.80SFr, but try to carry liquids to protect your bank balance. To facilitate your ascent, a **funicular** climbs up from the start of the Interlaken Ost path (roughly May-Oct.; 12.40SFr, 20SFr round-trip; 25% discount with Eurailpass and Swisspass). After the ascent, the path extends across the ridge's crest where the views improve, the gradient lessens, and you start to lose the accursed trees. Paths on the right dive down to Ringgenberg and Niederried, where buses run back to Interlaken.

A gruesome hike for a hot, clear day is the climb up **Schynige Platte** (2070m). Though the path is very long and very steep, the panoramic view is one of the best in the Jungfrau region. Take bus #5 south of Interlaken (or any of the mountain trains from Interlaken Ost) to the village of Wilderswil across the river; the path heads up (and up and up) from the back of the churchyard (1500m of ascent, full day, steep in places). In May and early June check for snow before heading out.

From roughly June to mid-October, a train leaves from Wilderswil (30.80SFr, 50.60SFr round-trip; 25% discount with Eurailpass and Swisspass). If you are considering taking the railway up and walking down, bear in mind that the descent is out of sight of the Jungfrau massif and that walking off Schynige Platte northwards to Zweilütschinen, while possible, is extremely steep and only for the experienced.

NIGHTLIFE

Interlaken's nightlife heats up during high season but never gets quite red-hot. Most Americans head to **Balmer's** (see p. 405) for the cheapest beer in town (3SFr) and outdoor hammocks. When the staff clears the patio at 11pm so that guests can sleep, many revelers head to **Buddy's**, Höheweg 33, a small, crowded English pub where the beer is cheap (3.20-5.30SFr) and the email exorbitant (15SFr for 15min.; bar open daily 10am-12:30am). The drunken herds then migrate to Interlaken's oldest disco, **Johnny's Dancing Club**, Höheweg 92, downstairs in the Hotel Carlton. (Drinks from 5.50SFr. Sat. cover 7SFr. Open Dec.-Oct. Tues.-Sun. 9:30pm-2:30am.)

Interlaken is a good place to cleanse yourself of that nagging desire to see leather-clad Swiss men slap their thighs, toot their alpenhorns, ring their cowbells, and yodel a bit. The **Swiss Folklore Show** (tel. 827 61 00) at the casino will fill these gaps in your life for only 16SFr. (Shows at 8:30pm daily July-Aug., sporadically May-Oct.) At 6:30pm the theater serves fondue and ice cream for an additional 23.50SFr. The other apex of Interlaken's cultural life is the summer production of Friedrich Schiller's **Wilhelm Tell** (in German; English synopsis 2SFr). 250 local men with bushy beards and heavy rouge and local lasses with flowing locks ham the tale of Swiss escape from the thumbscrew of Austrian rule. The showmanship is superb—20 horses gallop by in every scene, and a magnificent mock-village amphitheater around the corner from Balmer's allows the cast to make real bonfires. A cunning distraction leaves you pondering whether they actually shoot the apple off the wee lad's head, however. The audience stamps their feet with delight—or possibly just to keep them warm. (Shows late June to mid-July Thurs. 8pm; mid-July to early Sept. Thurs. and Sat. 8pm.) Tickets (12-32SFr) are available at Tellbüro, Bahnhofstr. 5A (tel. (036) 822 37 23; open May-Sept. Mon.-Fri. 8:30-11:30am and 2-5pm; Oct.-April Tues. 8-11am and 2-5pm), or at the theater on the night of the show. Children under 7 are not admitted.

■ The Jungfrau Region

A few miles south of Interlaken, the hitherto middling mountains rear up and become hulking white monsters. Welcome to the Jungfrau, home to Europe's largest glacier and many of its steepest crags and highest waterfalls. The Jungfrau region's list of firsts reflects its irresistible appeal to sportsmen: the first Alpine mountaineering, the first skiing, and the first part of Switzerland opened to tourists. In summer, the Jungfrau region's hundreds of kilometers of hiking blast the senses with spectacular mountain views, wildflower meadows, roaring waterfalls, and pristine forests. In winter, skiing is divine—almost literally, thanks to Emperor Hirohito's visit here to learn the rudiments. The three most famous peaks in the Oberland are the **Jungfrau**, the **Eiger**, and the **Mönch**. In English, that's the Maiden, the Ogre, and Monk. Natives say that the monk protects the maiden by standing between her and the ogre. Actually, the Jungfrau is 4158m high, so she'd probably kick the Eiger's puny little 3970m butt.

Commitment to tourism is thorough: some villages have gone car free, with most locals scooting around in electric buggies, sneaking up silently behind visitors. The quietest periods are November and April to May, and hordes descend and prices rise during the ski season. Keeping to a strict budget in these villages is even trickier than elsewhere in the Oberland. Fortunately, every village has dorm beds and most have supermarkets. The budget-killers are the buses, trains, and cable cars. Many tourists opt to hitchhike between mountain towns and are more often than not picked up by other tourists. Since the Jungfrau and Schilthorn trains don't stop for hitchhikers, those peaks may be off-limits to truly budget travelers. If you do decide to shell out cash for a ticket for the Jungfraujoch or Schilthorn, pick a cloudless day. To maximize time in the mountains and minimize transportation costs, *Let's Go* strongly recommends using a village as a base for day hikes, as most villages are really only service stations to springboard visitors into the hills and not worth a full tour.

> **Tourist Transgressions, or Of Free-Range Goats and Fungi**
> Out on the hiking trails, it's always the little rules that count as you uproot the stationary wildlife or tiptoe through the pastures. First off, don't put endangered wildflowers in your bouquets. When gathering toppings for your hostel spaghetti, be aware that local by-laws forbid picking wild mushrooms until the 8th of each month and each person is allowed only 1kg (remember that some mushrooms can be dangerous). If the mushrooms don't get you, the mysterious alpine gates might. They appear out of nowhere, tricky to open and surrounded by menacing barbed wire. Has your hiking trail led you inadvertently to a top-secret Swiss military bunker? No, you've simply reached a farmer's cow pasture—breakfast, lunch, and dinner for the area's belled bovines. The gates may not be padlocked or laser-rigged, but don't take them lightly. Just ask a group of American backpackers who last year forgot to shut a gate behind them near Obersteinberg. When they arrived in Gimmelwald three hours later, they noticed a large herd of goats merrily clopping along behind them. The tourists laughed, but they soon realized they had nowhere to put their hungry friends. Eventually, a small group of local farmers coerced the herd back up the trail in the middle of the night to prevent the herd's owner from panicking and to protect Gimmerwald's gardens and window boxes from ravenous goat gourmands.

GRINDELWALD

The town of Grindelwald, beneath the north face of the **Eiger,** is a skier's and climber's dream. The lush green valley ringed with blue glaciers glinting in the sun is Switzerland distilled to its purest and most stunning. Although it only has two important streets, Grindelwald is the most developed part of the Oberland's two major valleys, dotted with isolated chalets for several miles. The Berner-Oberlander-Bahn runs from **Interlaken's** *Ostbahnhof* (9SFr; sit in the rear half of the train). Trains to Kleine Scheidegg (26SFr, 45SFr round-trip, Eurailpass 25% discount, Swisspass 30%) and the Jungfraujoch (round-trip 137SFr, with "Good Morning" ticket 99SFr, same discounts) start from the station. There is also a bus from Balmer's (round-trip 15SFr).

The **tourist office** (Verkehrsbüro; tel. 854 12 12; fax 854 12 10), located in the Sport-Zentrum in the middle of town, provides hiking maps (9SFr), chairlift information, and a list of free guided excursions. Turn right from the train station, ignoring the "i" sign that points down the hill. The office also find rooms in private homes (25-50SFr; usually 3-night min. stay). (Open July-Aug. Mon.-Fri. 8am-7pm, Sat. 8am-5pm, Sun. 9-11am and 3-5pm; Sept.-June Mon.-Fri. 8am-noon and 2-6pm, Sat. 8am-noon and 2-5pm.) There is a **post office** opposite the station. (Open Mon.-Fri. 8am-noon and 1:45-6pm, Sat. 8-11am.) The **postal code** is CH-3818, and the **telephone code** is 036.

Grindelwald's hotel prices push most budget travelers into dorms, which fortunately are thick on the ground to cater to the hiking and skiing crowd. Two superb hostels deserve stars for comfort and views. The **Jugendherberge (HI)** (tel. 853 10 09; fax 853 50 29) is a ranking contender for the title of World's Best Youth Hostel. To get there, head left from the station (5-7min.) then cut up the hill to the right (8min.) by the minuscule brown sign. Turn left at the fork by the blue SJH sign. The living rooms with fireplaces and dorms still smell of freshly cut pine. The surprisingly private dorms have state-of-the-art bar code locks and balconies facing the

THE JUNGFRAU REGION: GRINDELWALD ■ 411

Eiger. Comparable views at a hotel would cost about 400SFr. (Reception Mon.-Sat. 6:30-9:30am and 3-11pm, Sun. 6:30-9:30am and 5-11pm. No lockout. Dorms 29.50SFr first night, then 27SFr; quad or double with sink 34.50SFr, 32SFr; double with shower 45SFr, 42.50SFr. Giant dinner 11SFr. Huge, free lockers and proper bed linen (not sleeping sacks) included. Laundry 2SFr.) Its rival is the bright blue **Mountain Hostel** (tel. 853 39 00; fax 853 47 30) at the Grund station next to the river. Turn right out of the train station, and then turn right down the hill just after the bus station. At Hotel Glacier, bear right, and head past the station. Renovated in 1996, the hostel has gleaming four- and six-bed dorms and a plush reception area with TVs, ping-pong, and pool. (Dorms 29-34SFr; doubles 78-88SFr. Buffet breakfast included. Outside cooking facilities 0.50SFr; teeter-totters free. Laundry 8SFr.) To see two glaciers from your bedroom, stay at the friendly **Mounty's/Alpenpub** (tel. 853 11 05; fax 853 44 84). Follow the main street right from the station for 20 minutes, passing the church on the right. (Reception until 12:30am. Dorms 34SFr; singles 60SFr; doubles 100SFr. Oct.-Nov. and April-June: doubles 80-90SFr. Hot egg-and-bacon breakfast 12SFr. Visa, MC, AmEx. Reserve in winter high season.) One hour from town (see below) but a step from the Upper Glacier, **Hotel Wetterhorn** (tel. 853 12 18) has dorms for 42.50SFr, including breakfast. The Grosse Scheidegg bus (5.40SFr) stops at the door. *Zimmer frei* (room for rent) notices are also posted on the information board at the bus station, though most rooms require a one-week minimum stay. **Gletscherdorf** (tel. 853 14 29; fax 853 31 29) is the nearest of all Grindelwald's **campgrounds**. From the station, take a right, then the first right after the tourist office, and then the third left. The small grounds have clean facilities and a phenomenal view of the mountains. (9SFr; tents 4-9SFr.) **Camping Eigernordwand** (tel. 853 42 27) is across the river and to the left of the Grund station. (9.50SFr; tents 7-8SFr.)

Frugal gourmets shop at the **Co-op** across from the tourist office. (Open Mon.-Thurs. 8am-6:30pm, Fri. 8am-9pm, Sat. 8am-5pm.) A **Migros** is farther along the main street away from the station. (Open Mon.-Thurs. 8am-noon and 1:30-6:30pm, Fri. 8am-noon and 1:30-9pm, Sat. 8am-5pm.) For huge plates of *Rösti,* omelettes, salads, and fresh-baked desserts, hit the **Tea Room Riggenburg** (tel. 853 10 59) on the main street past the tourist office away from the station. Drink a huge hot cocoa (3SFr) on the heated terrace as sparrows dive-bomb for crumbs. Main courses run 12 to16SFr, and more extravagant frozen desserts are 9 to 20SFr.

Outdoor Activities near Grindelwald

Only Zermatt could challenge Grindelwald's claim as Switzerland's premier hiking hot spot. The town has nearly everything: easy valley walks, high-altitude level walks, accessible glaciers, and peaks to stretch even top climbers. The terrain varies in every direction, and a competent network of railways, cable cars, and buses makes the most exciting areas accessible without hours of uphill toil. Ride **Europe's longest chairlift** to the top of the **First Mountain** for awesome scenery, marmots, icebergs, lakes, rare flowers, and good access to the Faulhorn and Schwarzhorn peaks. (27SFr, round-trip 43SFr, discounts with Swisspass and Regional pass.) The First Mountain (Firstbahn and buses tel. 853 36 36) provides oodles of spectacular hiking, unlike the less inviting Jungfrau and Schilthorn. Other transport links north and east are the buses to **Bussalp** (1807m, 8 per day, 14SFr, half-price with Swisspass and Eurailpass) and to **Grosse Scheidegg** (1926m, 11 per day, 7.80SFr, same discounts). Budget combinations for non-circular hikes are possible. In the south and west, the **Männlichen** (2230m) separates the Grindelwald and Lauterbrunnen valleys. The summit affords a glorious vista of the Eiger, Mönch, and Jungfrau. The **Grindelwald-Männlichen gondola** (tel. 853 38 29) transports passengers there from the Grindelwald-Grund station (27SFr, round-trip 43SFr, Eurail 50% discount, Swisspass 25%). Take the railway up to Kleine Scheidegg, enjoy the stroll to Männlichen, and ride the cable car down for 50SFr. The **Kleine Scheidegg railway** (tel. 828 71 11) costs 26SFr, round-trip 43SFr, and the tiny **Pfingstegg cable car** on the path to the Lower Glacier costs 9.20SFr, round-trip 14SFr. Show your railpass at all trains and lifts. Past the tourist office from the station stands the joint **Bergführerbüro** (Mountain Guides Office) and **Ski School** (tel. 853 52 00; fax 853 12 22). The office sells maps for hiking and coordinates rugged activities like glacier walks, ice climbing, and mountaineering. (Open June-Oct. Mon.-Sat. 9am-noon and 3-6pm, Sun. 4-6pm. One-day activities about 395SFr. Reserve ahead for multi-day expeditions.)

A classic, level mountaintop walk is from **Männlichen** to **Kleine Scheidegg** (1hr.) with airy panoramas and a close-up view of the Eiger. Every September, a marathon beginning in Interlaken finishes on this ridge, 2061m above the starting line. Descending from either end to Grindelwald-Grund station takes 3-4 hours at a gentle pace through trees and forests. Another fine level walk is from **First** to **Schynige Platte** (1 day) past high hidden alpine valleys and the lovely Bachsee (2265m), up to the Faulhorn peak (2680m). (Path generally closed until late June or mid-July because of snow.) A compact version of the First-Schynige Platte hike is to take the cable car to First, hike up the Faulhorn (the path crosses large and slippery snowbanks), descend to Bussalp, and catch the bus back to Grindelwald. This captures the long views and marmot-filled glens of the longer walk but is cheaper and more manageable. You can even walk down from First or Grosse Scheidigg back to Grindelwald, a 2- to 3-hour downhill stroll through shrubs, fields, and pastures.

Some people, however, aren't happy unless they get to the *top* of something. The **Schwarzhorn** (2928m) offers a simple but challenging alternative to the smaller Faulhorn. From Grosse Scheidegg or First, go up through the high valley of Chrinnenboden. The finish is steep and treacherous when covered in snow, but the panorama from the top covers a dozen 4000m peaks. Allow three to four hours for the ascent; buses and cable cars quicken the descent. **Mountaineers** should contact the Mountain Guides Office (see above) for excursions, but should note that even the first train to Jungfraujoch is too late for the high peaks, requiring an overnight stay at the Mönchsjochhütte. Guides lead big climbs most summer days. For two people the Eiger is 890SFr, Mönch 560SFr, and Jungfrau 900SFr. They also give skills training for a day, weekend, or week. Always reserve at least three days in advance.

Many mountaintops have places to spend the night, and nothing is more beautiful than waking up to a still dawn over the mountains. At Kleine Scheidegg (2061m), dorm beds go for 32 to 35SFr at **Grindelwaldblick** (tel. 855 13 74) and 28 to 50SFr at **Bahnhofbuffet** (tel. 855 11 51). At Männlichen, a bunk is 35SFr (tel. 853 10 68; 2227m), and on the Faulhorn, dorms are 33SFr (tel. 853 27 13; 2681m). **Berggasthaus First** (tel. 853 12 84) at the cable car terminus has a **touristenlager** (tourist camp) for 38-40SFr including breakfast; dinner is 20SFr.

After a long hike, cool off with some **glaciers.** Take Grindelwald's main street right from the station past the church, turn right just after Mounty's (yellow sign: "Hotel Wetterhorn"), and then follow signs from Hotel Wetterhorn (1½hr. ascent, easy grade). Paths go up both sides of the **Upper Glacier** via Restaurant Milchbach or the Schreckhomhütte, but both are tricky, exposed, and linked with terrifying ladders. The **Lower Glacier** is much more approachable. Turn right just after the church, cross the river, and zigzag up to Pfingstegg. On the way, there's a detour to the **Glacier Gorge**. At Pfingstegg (1392m) turn right to the glacier and follow the edge as far up as you please (1½-3hr. up, 45min.-2hr. down).

Winter **skiing** is phenomenal. Ski passes are 100SFr for two days, 254SFr for a week, and 400SFr for two weeks (ages 16-20 80SFr, 204SFr, 320SFr; under 16 50SFr, 127SFr, 200SFr). Eagle-eyed rental companies watch one another's prices, so there isn't much choice. Or for 5-10SFr you can rent a **sled** from a ski rental store and rocket down 2000m of mountainside. For winter hikes, some mountain paths like Faulhorn even get cleared. All year, **Adventure World** (tel. 826 77 11) coordinates high adrenaline activities: **paragliding** (120-200SFr), **rock-climbing** (75SFr), **canyoning** (85SFr), and **rafting** (85SFr). Write to Adventure World, 3800 Interlaken.

THE JUNGFRAUJOCH

The area's most arresting ascent is up the **Jungfraujoch**, a head-spinning, breath-shortening, 3454m adventure on Europe's highest railway. Chiseled into solid rock, the track tunnels right through the Eiger and Mönch mountains. The construction of the railway was one of the greatest engineering feats of all time, taking 16 years and a work force of 300 men. The line was to have gone even higher to the Jungfrau summit itself (4158m), but by 1912, the project was so over budget that the final 700m were left to the gods and to hard-core mountaineers. Thanks to the rarefied air's lack of pollution, the top now shelters Europe's highest manned meteorology station and the **Sphinx laboratory** for the study of cosmic radiation. The half-million visitors a year can also explore the **Ice Palace** (free), a super-smooth maze with cutesy sculptures cut into ice. Beware of skidding children and temporary blindness caused by trainloads of tourists taking flash photos of the gargantuan ice sumo wrestler. Siberian huskies scoot lazy mountaineers across the snow on sleds for 10SFr. Budget sportsmen opt for free "snow-hurtling" i.e. sledding down bunny-level slopes on garbage bags (30SFr; bring your own bag). Gaze down the 24km **Aletschgletscher,** Europe's longest, and, at 900m, thickest glacier. If the weather is perfect, try the 30-minute, snowy trek to the **Mönchsjoch** climbing hut.

Trains start at Interlaken's *Ostbahnhof* and travel to Grindelwald and Lauterbrunnen, continuing to **Kleine Scheidegg** and finally to the peak itself. The entire trip costs a scary 153SFr, but the earliest trains from Interlaken's *Ostbahnhof*, the Lauterbrunnen, and Grindelwald cost only 115SFr (the "Good Morning" ticket; see each town's listings). All tickets are round-trip, and there is no way down from the top except by train, so you must leave the top by noon. (With Eurail 116SFr, with Swisspass 105SFr; morning ticket 101SFr, 90SFr.) Call 855 10 22 for a **weather forecast,** and use the cable TV broadcast live from the Jungfraujoch and other mile-high spots (in all tourist offices and big hotels). Let's Go hint: A snow-white or gray TV screen indicates not a broken mountain-cam but a viewless peak. Bring winter clothing and food—it can be 10°C (50°F) on a July day, and in winter alcohol thermometers crack and car antifreeze freezes. Beware of overwhelming crowds on clear summer days.

WENGEN

Tiny Wengen occupies the only ledge along the cliff-curtained *Lauterbrunnental*. The village offers the best of two worlds: the raw grandeur of craggy waterfalls and gentle, local slopes for quality hiking and skiing. Though car-free, Wengen is easily accessible on hourly trains from **Interlaken** (11.40SFr) and **Lauterbrunnen** (5.40SFr) to **Kleine Scheidegg** (19.60SFr) and the **Jungfraujoch** (126SFr, morning ticket 88SFr). Leave cars in the Lauterbrunnen parking garage (9SFr per day).

To reach the **tourist office** (tel. 855 14 14; fax 855 30 60), turn right from the station and then take an immediate left. The office issues competent hiking details and will find you a tennis partner. (Open mid-June to mid-Oct. and mid-Dec. to March Mon.-Fri. 8am-noon and 2-6pm, Sat. 8:30-11:30am and 4-6pm, Sun. 4-6pm; mid-Oct. to mid-Dec. and April to mid-June Mon.-Fri. 8am-noon and 2-6pm, Sat. 8:30-11:30am.) At the **train station** you can **exchange currency,** book hotel rooms, and watch the cable car TV channel. The **pharmacy** (tel. 855 12 46), left out of the station, is two minutes past the tourist office. (Open Mon.-Fri. 8am-noon and 2-6:30pm, Sat. 8am-noon and 2-5pm.) A public **laundry** hides under the Hotel Silberhorn between the station and the tourist office. (Open daily 7am-9:30pm.) For a **doctor,** call 856 28 28; for the **hospital,** 826 26 26. The **post office** is next to the tourist office. (Open Mon.-Fri. 8am-noon and 1:45-6pm, Sat. 8-11am.) The **postal code** is CH-3823. The **telephone code** is 033.

Ski passes for the Wengen-Kleine-Scheidegg-Männlichen area start at 52SFr for one day, 95SFr for two; for longer periods, purchase a Jungfrau regional pass. (Ages 6-16 50% discount, ages 16-20 20%.) Ski rentals should be 28SFr per day, 115SFr per week. Boots are 19SFr, 85SFr. The **Swiss Ski School** (tel./fax 855 20 22), by the Coop one minute right of the station, is the cheaper of the town's two schools. (Open late-Dec. to early April Sun.-Fri. 8:30am-noon, 1-2:30pm, and 3:30-6pm, Sat. 9-11am and 4:30-6:30pm.) For **snow information,** call 855 10 22. For a **weather report,** call 157 45 06. As you watch golf carts schlepping lazy tourists around, you may find it hard to believe that Wengen attracts the athletically intense to its slopes and trails twice a year. Every January, Wengen hosts the (skiing) World Cup's longest and most dangerous downhill race, the **Laubehorn.** In early September Wengen marks the 30km point to the **Jungfrau marathon.** Beginning in Interlaken, hundreds of runners (the type of people who refuse anesthesia) huff and puff their way to Kleine Scheidegg, a tortuous 1424m ascent. Hotels generally won't allow you to book rooms until about two weeks in advance so that they can guarantee all the racers and support crews a place to sleep. The downhill course starts 2315m above Kleine Scheidegg, curls around Wegenalp, and ends at Ziel (1287m) at the eastern end of the village, a drop of nearly 3500 feet in 2½ minutes.

The funkiest place to eat, sleep, drink, and groove is **Hot Chili Peppers** (tel. 855 50 20), smack dab in the center of town. Turn left from the station and head past the tourist office. The decor of this Tex-Mex eatery turned hostel is decidedly freaky-styley. The newly renovated dorms are 24-26SFr; a small breakfast is 5SFr, and a hot breakfast is 12.50SFr. Jalapeño keys complement day-glo comforters. Smart, freshly painted singles are 38 to 48SFr and doubles are 76 to 96SFr including breakfast. (Tacos and burritos 5-9SFr; chips and salsa 5SFr. Sangria 5SFr; beer 5-6SFr.) Much closer to what you might expect budget accommodations in Wengen to look like, **Eddy's Hostel** (tel. 855 16 34; fax 855 39 50) has three-story bunks and 20 beds to a room, annexed to Hotel Eden. (Dorms 26SFr. In winter: 30SFr.) **Eddy's Corner** has beer (4.50SFr a pint) and main courses like bratwurst and spaghetti (from 7.50SFr). Jam on your accordion at the informal folklore evenings on Fridays. Simple rooms with back-to-the-70s orange hall showers await you at **Hotel Bären** (tel. 855 14 19; fax 855 15 25). From the station, turn right under the railway and walk for two minutes. (6-bed dorms 35SFr; singles 50SFr; doubles 100SFr. Breakfast included. Open Dec.-Oct. Visa, MC, AmEx.)

Anywhere else, Wengen is expensive. Opposite the station, the **Co-op** is cooperatively central (open Mon.-Fri. 8am-12:15pm and 1:30-6:30pm, Sat. 8am-6pm), while fancier fodder awaits at the **Victoria Lauberhorn** just past the tourist office. Wolf down some berry and ice cream crepes (11.50SFr). Pasta, *raclette,* and other vegetarian options range from 9 to 20SFr. (Open daily 9:30am-11:30am.)

Hikes from Wengen

Wengen snoozes beneath the steep flanks of the **Lauberhorn** (2472m) and **Männlichen** (2343m) peaks. The ultimate view of the Eiger Norwand and a superb panorama make the climb worthwhile. Since hiking down the sharp gradients is more comfortable than hiking up, make use of the **Männlichen cable car** (19.60SFr, round-trip 32SFr; with Swisspass 14.70SFr, 24SFr; closed briefly in Nov. and May) and the railway to Kleine Scheidegg (same rates). For the best ascent, turn right just after Eddy's Hotel and follow the yellow signs and train tracks that snake around the Lauberhorn to Wengeneralp and Kleine Scheidegg. From here, the view unfolds eastward to the Eiger and Wetterhorn north faces. Turn left up the Lauberhorn across the level track to Männlichen, and slither abruptly back to Wengen from the pass between Männlichen and the Lauberhorn. (1350m, a leisurely full day.) You can buy a combination ticket lifting you up to Kleine Scheidegg and down from Männlichen, which turns the excursion into a half-day outing (39.60SFr, with Swisspass 30SFr). For mountaintop sleeping, see **Grindelwald,** p. 410. For a perfect view of the Lauterbrunnen valley, turn right out of the station under the tracks to the Ziel chair lift. The easy walk skirts the valley wall and drops into the secluded cove above the Trümmelbach Falls (1hr. round-trip). Descend steeply to the valley base and walk 30 minutes to reach Lauterbrunnen, where a 5.40SFr train ride returns you to Wengen (half day through spectacular landscapes).

LAUTERBRUNNEN VALLEY

The "pure springs" that give Lauterbrunnen its name are the 72 waterfalls that plummet down the sheer walls of the narrow, glacier-cut valley. Stark but beautiful Lauterbrunnen is reminiscent of a time when valleys were valleys. The small

THE JUNGFRAU REGION: LAUTERBRUNNEN VALLEY ■ 415

Lauterbrunnen tourist office (tel. 855 19 55; fax 855 36 04) is 200m to the left of the train station on the main street. (Open Mon.-Fri. 8am-noon and 2-6pm, July-Aug. also Sat.-Sun. 10am-noon and 2-5pm.) **Trains** connect every 30 minutes with **Interlaken East** (6SFr), **Wengen** (5.40SFr), **Kleine Scheidegg** (25SFr), **Jungfraujoch** (round-trip 136.80SFr), and **Mürren** (8.40SFr). The station has **lockers** (2SFr) and **currency exchange.** The **post office** is between the train station and the tourist office. (Open Mon.-Fri. 7:45-11:45am and 1:45-6pm, Sat. 7:45-11am.) The **telephone code** is 033.

Lauterbrunnen has a wide range of shops and services plus an array of cheap, basic beds. By the post office lies a small but satisfactory **Co-op.** (Open Mon.-Fri. 8am-noon and 2-6:30pm, Sat. 8am-noon and 1:30-5pm.) **Matratzenlager Stocki** (tel. 855 17 54), a farmhouse-hostel, offers a full kitchen stacked with spices and a mellow atmosphere. Leave the train station's rear exit, descend the steps, cross the river, turn right, and walk 200m. The sign on the house on your right will read *"Massenlager."* (Check-in before 6pm. 10SFr. Open Jan.-Oct. Reserve ahead.) More central, **Chalet im Rohr** (tel. 855 21 82), on the main street near the church, has 40 beds in comfortably lived-in rooms with balconies and thousand-dollar views. (Dorms 24-26SFr. Kitchen facilities 0.50SFr. Parking available.) Lauterbrunnen also has two souped-up campsites with cheap eats. **Camping Jungfrau** (tel. 856 20 10; fax 856 20 20), up the main street from the station toward the large Staubachfall, provides cheap beds, kitchens, showers, lounges, and a grocery store. (Reception 8am-noon and 2:30-6:30pm. 8-10SFr; tents 6-15SFr; dorms 18SFr. Restaurant *menus* 10-11SFr. Laundry 5SFr. Visa, MC, AmEx.) **Camping Schützenbach** (tel. 855 12 68; fax 855 12 75) is on the way toward Trümmelbach from the station (15min.; follow the signs). Take a left on the main road and a left over the river by the church. The communal bathrooms whisper "summer camp." (Reception 7am-noon and 2-7pm. 4.60SFr; tents 11SFr; dorms 14-16SFr; doubles with sink 46-56SFr; 4-bed "tourist rooms" in barracks-like huts 18-20SFr per person. Shower 0.50SFr. Kitchen facilities 1SFr. Laundry 5SFr.)

At the bottom of a trough, Lauterbrunnen's **hikes** are either very steep or very flat. An easy 40-minute hike or a quick postal bus ride from the main street (every hr., 3.20SFr) are the fabulous **Trümmelbach Falls,** 10 glacier-bed chutes that gush up to 20,000 liters of water per second and generate mighty winds and a roaring din. Explore tunnels, footbridges, and an underground funicular (12AS, with visitor's card 10AS). (Open July-Aug. 8am-6pm; April-June and Sept.-Nov. 9am-5pm.) The best flat walk is a **waterfall** tour. From the western side, follow the main road past the church. In succession the Staubbachfall, Spissbachfall, Agertenbachfall, and Mümenbachfall crash from overhead, leaving dark cones on the rock where the wind has blown the spray. Crossing the river by the Stechelberg power station (5-7km) brings you face to face with the Staldenbachfall and Mattenbachfall. The return leg with gorgeous views of the Lauthorn passes the Trümmelbachfälle and the Hasenbachfall. (3hr. with virtually no climbing; the best walk in the area during a prolonged wet spell.) Follow the signs along the river to **Stechelberg,** a scattered, three-horse town with a **Co-op** (open Mon. and Wed.-Fri. 8am-noon and 2:30-6pm, Tues. 8am-noon, Sat. 8am-noon and 2-4pm); the **Breithorn campground** (tel. 855 12 25; 6-7SFr); and the **Schilthorn Bahn cable car** leading to **Gimmelwald** (7.20SFr), **Mürren** (14SFr), **Birg** (32.20SFr), and the **Schilthorn** (46SFr). All rides 25% off with Swisspass. Since Gimmelwald and Mürren are carless, leave your car at the parking lot near the cable car (day 5SFr, week 21SFr, month 30SFr) or back at Lauterbrunnen by the train station.

Imboden Bike Adventures (tel. 855 21 14), on the main street, rents out mountain bikes at 25SFr per day and bursts with suggestions about where to go with them. A favorite is the **Mürren Loop,** where you take your bike for free on the funicular to Grütschalp (6.60SFr), pedal along to Mürren and Gimmelwald, and freewheel it down to Stechelberg and Lauterbrunnen. Imboden lets you leave the bike at Central Sport in Wengen opposite the tourist office or the sports center in Mürren for no extra charge. (Open Tues.-Sun. 9am-noon and 2-6:30pm.)

MÜRREN AND THE SCHILTHORN

The cogwheel train from Lauterbrunnen (8.40SFr), the cable car from Stechelberg (14SFr) or Gimmelwald (7.20SFr), or a brisk hike from Gimmelwald will take you to **Mürren,** a car-free skiing and sport resort. Brits muddle around Mürren as they have done since George Bernard Shaw came for Fabian fresh air and Field Marshal Montgomery for mushrooms. More of a paved cow path than a main street, "downtown" Mürren features spectacular gnome gardens, gingerbread houses with chamois antlers on the walls, and lovely cow and mountain views. The all-knowing **tourist office** (tel. 856 86 86; fax 856 86 96) in the sports center is five minutes from the train station, off the right fork. Ask at the tourist office for *Privatzimmer,* hiking trails, and skiing prices. Check the chalkboard for dorms (30-35SFr), or get the list of cheap sleeps in Mürren. (Open Mon.-Fri. 8:30am-noon and 1:30-5:30pm, Sat. 8:30am-noon and 1:30-4pm.) The **pharmacy** is on the upper street near the tourist office. (Open Mon.-Sat. 8:30am-noon and 4-6pm.) For **medical assistance,** call 855 17 10. For the **police,** call 855 28 17. For the **Alpine rescue service,** call 855 45 55. The **post office** is on the station side of the main street. (Open Mon.-Fri. 8am-noon and 2-5pm, Sat. 8-10:15am.) The **postal code** is CH-3825, and the **telephone code** is 033.

To rest your weary body after a long day of hiking, seek shelter at the central **Chalet Fontana** (tel. 855 26 86). Its seven lovely, distinctive rooms are run by a bubbly English woman, who opens the reception whenever she's in—the best time to catch her is in the morning. (35-45SFr per person, breakfast included. Mid-Sept. to mid-Dec. 30SFr per person, no breakfast. Reservations recommended.) **Hotel Belmont** (tel. 855 35 35; fax 855 35 31) is right next to the train station and has bunk beds in bright, newly decorated rooms. (27SFr or 35SFr; doubles 90SFr, with shower 130SFr. Breakfast included. Visa, MC, AmEx.) There is a **Co-op** on the town's main walkway (open Mon.-Fri. 8am-noon and 1:45-6:30pm, Sat. 8am-4pm), but eating out in Mürren is unexpectedly cheap. Next door to the Co-op is **Restaurant Stägerstübli** (tel. 855 13 16), a family joint with a tiny wooden interior featuring many portraits of men smoking pipes. The creamy, scrumptious, delicious, and rich *raclette* (12.50SFr) melts in your mouth. Entrees are 11 to 20SFr. (Open Wed.-Sun. 8:30am-11:30pm.)

The 2970m **Schilthorn,** made famous by the Alpine exploits of James Bond in *On Her Majesty's Secret Service,* is a short (albeit expensive) cable car trip from Mürren (32SFr, round-trip 55SFr; morning ticket discounts). The four-hour ascent, one of the rockiest and snowiest around, requires perfect hiking boots. At its apex spins the immoderately priced **Piz Gloria Restaurant.** Daily menus run 16 to 17SFr. Warm up (summer or winter) with *Glühwein* (mulled wine, 7SFr), or take in the astounding 360° Alpine panorama from the Schilthorn station's deck. The staff at the Mürren stop courteously remind you that there is very little to do at the top when it's cloudy. At the Schilthorn cable car stops (Birg, Mürren, Gimmelwald), beautiful rocky paths lace the mountains. Hiking uphill from Mürren leads to wildflower fields straight out of Oz and cows demurely munching the hillside. In snowy early summer, consider the one-way trip down to **Birg** (18.20SFr). Check with the tourist office for maps before embarking on any of these trips, however, and get a weather forecast via the live TV link at the cable car station. From the train station take either road to the other end of the village (10min.). Mürren pioneered two graceful ways of enjoying the mountains. In 1910 the first Alpine balloon crossing was made from the village, a fact now celebrated annually in September with an **international ballooning week** that fills the skies with big colorful bulbs. The other sport, **skiing,** took off with even more panache. Mürren was the stage for the first major ski race (1922), the first ski school (1930), and the first World Championship (1931). **Ski passes** for the Mürren-Schilthorn area are 50SFr for one day and 254SFr for a regional week pass; children aged 6-16 receive a 50% reduction, teenagers 16-20 20%. The **ski school** (tel. 855 12 47) has a comprehensive spread of classes for downhill, slalom, and snowboarding. Six half-days of group lessons cost 123SFr. The

THE JUNGFRAU REGION: GIMMELWALD ■ 417

calf-killing **Inferno Run** seeks volunteers every year to race from Lauterbrunnen to the top of the Schilthorn, a 2150m climb that only sinewy superstars finish.

GIMMELWALD

A tiny speck on the massive valley wall, Gimmelwald is accessible only by foot or the Schilthorn cable car (6.80SFr) from Stechelberg or Mürren. There is something indescribably beautiful about this place, something that puts the "wild" back in wildflower, that enchants daytrippers into staying for months, surrounded by silences deepened by the jingle of cowbells and the distant rush of waterfalls. A steep, scenic trail leads from Stechelberg, after the left fork at the road's end. Most visitors walk 30 minutes down from Mürren, take the left fork after the post office, and follow the yellow signs. Gimmelwald has a **post office** (open Mon.-Fri. 8:30-10:15am and 4-5pm, Sat. 8:30-10:15am), and its **postal code** is CH-382. The **telephone code** is 033.

Accommodations in Gimmelwald are definitely back to basics, but wonderfully so. Although some local barns offer haystack accommodations for a ridiculous 17SFr, more civilized bungalows are nicer, cheaper, and equipped with real beds. Next door to the cable car station awaits the hiker's mecca, the **Mountain Hostel** (tel. 55 17 04), not to be confused with the Grindelwald hostel of the same name. Run by a laid-back couple, Petra and Walter, the hostel exudes friendliness and communalism, and hostel regulars happily do limited chores. There's a kitchen and life's essentials—bread (2.50SFr), milk (2SFr), and chocolate (2SFr). You can reserve a bed, but only after 10am on the day you plan to arrive. Arrive early, as beds fill very fast. (Dorms 15SFr. Showers 1SFr. Sheets and sleds included.) Pension Gimmelwald is temptingly close to the Mountain Hostel, but *Let's Go* believes that the Mountain Hostel is a much better choice than its neighbor. At **Hotel Mittaghorn** (tel. 55 16 58), up the hill toward Mürren, sample some *Glühwein* (mulled wine) or Heidi cocoa (hot chocolate spiked with peppermint *schnapps*) made by the owner, Walter. Often seen sporting Edelweiss suspenders, Walter cooks a three-course dinner for his guests for only 15SFr. (Dorms 25SFr; doubles 60SFr; triples 85SFr; quads 105SFr. Order meals in advance. Open May-Nov.) Be forewarned that Gimmelwald lacks a market, so stock up on food at the **Co-op** in Lauterbrunnen or Stechelberg.

The descent to Stechelberg—down the hill by the Mountain Hostel, over the river, and through the woods—gives a great long view of the sheer rock slabs lining the Lauterbrunnen valley. It's a grand approach to the **Trümmelbach Falls** (1½hr.), with a return facilitated by the cable car. The hikes from Gimmelwald radiate in other directions. Five minutes after the river crossing on the Stechelberg path, you can fork right and climb along the flank of the unsettled Lauterbrunnen valley head. At the top lies the tiny Oberhornsee (2065m), a lilliputian lake fringed by a gargantuan glaciers. The climb up the oft-snowcapped Schilthorn (2970m), zigzagging straight up the hill, is for *Übermenschen* only (1600m ascent). Lauterbrunnen-lovers who don't intend to leave anytime soon should buy *Exploring the Lauterbrunnen Valley*, a thick pamphlet bursting with detailed trail information (7SFr; available at Hotel Mittaghorn).

Eastern Switzerland

ITALIAN SWITZERLAND (TICINO)

The Swiss took Ticino from Italy in 1512 and never gave it back. Ever since, the Italian-speaking canton of Ticino (Tessin, in German and French) has been renowned for its refreshing mix of Swiss efficiency and Italian *dolce vita*. The language is not the only thing that sets the region apart from the rest of Switzerland. The white and charred-wood chalets of the Graubünden and Berner Oberland fade away, replaced by jasmine-laced villas the bright colors of Italian *gelato*. Lush, almost Mediterranean vegetation, emerald lakes, and shaded castles render Ticino's hilly countryside as romantic as its famed resorts, Lugano and Locarno. Pastel church facades front ancient sanctuaries, where gawking tourists are more of a nuisance than a welcome industry. A **Ticino Card** is available for use on cable cars, museums, and other attractions (valid for any 3 days, 70SFr, children ages 6-16 and students under 21 45SFr).

■ Lugano

Arcaded passageways explode with blood-red geraniums, and orange tiles are scattered up and down the hills that make up this hybrid Swiss town. Lugano, Switzerland's third-largest banking center, hides from German Switzerland in the dramatic crevassed bay between San Salvatore and Monte Brè. With Italian language, food, and architecture, Lugano holds onto its Swiss identity by a fingernail. Never fear, though—trains, buses, and services are all extraordinarily efficient. A striking contrast from the rugged, frostbitten Alpine areas that surround it, this sun-drenched oasis is the retirement fantasy of Switzerland's northern residents and draws many elderly tourists to the relaxing shores of Lago di Lugano. Younger crowds now come by the busload, spicing up the BluesFest with impromptu performances, peppering the sky with paragliders, and filling Lugano's gardens and pools with relaxed laughter.

GETTING TO LUGANO

From **Geneva** in the west, trains run to Lugano through **Domodossola, Italy** (52SFr from Domodossola, Swisspass valid). From **Chur** and **St. Moritz** in the east, postal buses go to **Bellinzona,** where you can catch a train to Lugano (3½hr., 3 daily, 60SFr plus 5SFr reservation fee; Swisspass valid). For info call 807 85 20. To reach Lugano **by car,** take Rte. N2/E35 (or just follow the signs). The small **Lugano-Agno Airport** services Crossair flights from Basel, Bern, Geneva, London, Nice, Rome, and Zurich. Trains go to the Lugano train station from Agno Airport (every 20min., 4.20SFr).

ORIENTATION AND PRACTICAL INFORMATION

Cobblestone *piazze* dots Lugano's large pedestrian zone, bounded by the ridge on which the train station sits, Corso Pestalozzi, and the Fiume Cassorate. At the center of all the *piazze* sits the arcaded and café-inundated **Piazza della Riforma.** Northwest of this lies the **Piazza Cioccaro,** home to the **funicular** (ascending cable car) that carries passengers from Lugano's center on the waterfront to the train station (0.80SFr, Swisspass valid). The town boasts an extensive public transportation system. Buses run from the neighboring towns into the center and criss-cross the city (0.90-1.70SFr per ride, 24hr. "Carta Giorno" 4.40SFr, Swisspass valid). If you can navigate the winding roads, the uphill journey from town to the station takes only 15 minutes.

> **Tourist Office:** (tel. 921 46 64; fax 922 76 53) in the Palazzo Civico, Riva Albertolli, at the corner of P. Rezzonico. From the station, cross the footbridge labeled "Centro," and proceed down via Cattedrale straight through P. Cioccaro as it turns into

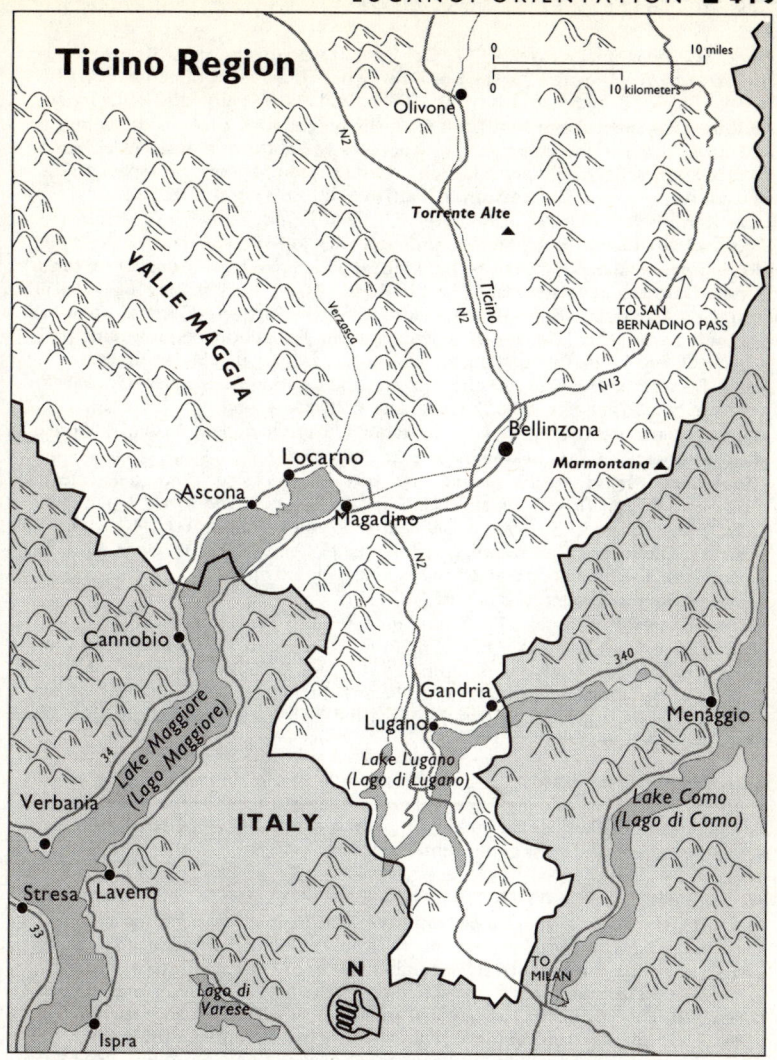

via Pessina. Then take a left on via del Pesci, and left on Riva via Vela, which becomes Riva Giocondo Albertolli. The office is just past the fountain on the left, across the street from the ferry launch. Pick up maps or make hotel reservations (4SFr). The tourist office also offers a free guided city walk April-Oct. at 9:45am, starting at Chiesa degli Angioli and a wide range of other guided excursions (from 15SFr per person), such as a walk up Monte San Salvatore. Open April-Oct. Mon.-Fri. 9am-6:30pm, Sat. 9am-12:30pm and 1:30-5pm, Sun. 10am-2pm; Nov.-March Mon.-Fri. 9am-12:30pm and 1:30-5pm, Sat. 9am-12:30pm and 1:30-5pm.

Consulates: U.K., 19 via Motta/32 via Nassa (tel. 923 86 06).

Currency Exchange: Good rates in the train station. Open Mon.-Sat. 7:10am-7:45pm, Sun. 8am-7:45pm.

American Express: In **VIP Travels,** 10 via al Forte, P.O. Box 3530, CH-6901 (tel. 923 85 45; fax 922 02 66). Standard services, mail held, but traveler's checks cannot be cashed. Open Mon.-Fri. 8:30am-noon and 2-6pm, Sat. 9am-noon.

Trains: P. della Stazione (tel. 157 22 22). To: **Locarno** (every ½hr., 1hr., 15.80SFr); **Basel** (every hr., 4½hr., 77SFr); **Bern** (every hr., 5hr., 74SFr); **Lucerne** (every hr., 3hr., 55SFr); **Zurich** (every hr., 3hr., 59SFr); and **Milan** (every hr., 1½hr., 14SFr).

Public Transportation: Buses run from the neighboring town to the center of Lugano and also traverse the city. Schedules and automatic ticket machines at each stop (0.90-1.70SFr per ride, 24hr. "Carta Giorno" 4.40SFr; Swisspass valid).

Taxis: Associazone Concessionari Taxi (tel. 922 88 33 or 922 02 22).

Car Rental: Avis, 8 via C. Maraini (tel. 922 62 56). **Budget,** 14 via C. Maraini (tel. 964 17 19). **Hertz,** 13 via San Gottardo (tel. 923 46 75).

Parking: Several parking garages, but little long-term parking (*"Autosilo"*). **Comunale Balestra,** on via Pioda, offers hourly rate (1SFr), daily ticket (10hr. 15SFr), and a ½-day ticket (5hr., 10SFr). Open 7am-7pm. **Autosilo Central Park** has hourly rates (1SFr, 12hr. max.). Open 7am-7pm. For information regarding parking, call 800 71 76. City parking meters scattered about are 1SFr per hour.

Bike Rental: At the baggage check in the train station (21SFr per day, 6SFr to return bike to another station). Open daily 5:20am-8:45pm.

Luggage Storage: Lockers at the train station (5SFr). Open daily 5:20am-8:45pm.

Lost Property: 206 via Beltramina 206 (tel. 800 80 65).

Bookstore: Melisa, 4 via Vegezzi (tel. 923 83 41), stocks such intriguing titles as *The Self Shiatsu Handbook* and V.S. Naipaul's *A Way in the World.* Open Mon.-Fri. 8am-noon and 1:30-6:30pm, Sat. 8am-noon and 1:30-5pm. Visa, MC, AmEx.

Library: Biblioteca Cantonale, 6 viale Cattaner (tel. 923 25 61). Open Mon.-Fri. 9am-7pm, Sat. 9am-noon and 2-5pm; July-Aug. closed on Sat.

Medical Services: Doctor or dentist (tel. 111).

Emergencies: Police: tel. 117. **Ambulance:** tel. 144. **Fire:** tel. 118.

Post Office: via della Posta, 2 blocks up from the lake near via al Forte. Open Mon.-Fri. 7:30am-noon and 1:15-6:30pm, Sat. 8-11am. Telephones, telegraphs, and faxes at the Via Magatti entrance to the PTT building. Open Mon.-Fri. 7:30am-8pm, Sat. 9am-7pm, Sun. 9:30am-12:30pm and 2:30-7pm. **Postal code:** CH-6900.

Telephone code: 091.

ACCOMMODATIONS

Though Lugano's lakesides are lined with five-star hotels and restaurants, surprising bargains can be found even in the center of town.

Ostello della Gioventù (HI), Lugano-Savosa, 13 via Cantonale (tel. 966 27 28; fax 928 23 63). Note: there are 2 via Cantonales, one in downtown Lugano and one in Savosa, where the hostel is. Take bus #5 (from the left of the station, go down the second ramp, cross the street, and uphill 100m) to "Crocifisso" (6th stop), then backtrack a bit and turn left up via Cantonale. Friendly and helpful English-speaking staff. This place feels like home, if your home is a lush villa with stunning gardens and various tropical flora. Jasmine and wisteria climbing the walls, a full-sized pool with waterslide out back, and a peaceful neighborhood. Reception 7am-noon and 3-10pm. No lockout. Strict curfew at 10pm. Dorms 17SFr; singles 32SFr, with kitchenette 42SFr, after 3 nights 28SFr, 38SFr; doubles 46SFr, with kitchenette 60SFr, after 3 nights 40SFr, 50SFr. Breakfast 6SFr. 1SFr for kitchen use after 7:30pm only. Sheets 2SFr. Key available. Apartments available for families (7-day min. stay; 70-100SFr per day). Reserve ahead. Open mid-March to Oct.

Hotel Montarina, 1 via Montarina (tel. 966 72 72; fax 966 12 13), just behind the train station. Walk 200m to the right from the station, cross the tracks, and hike up the hill. Newly renovated with skylights, romantic doubles, and a gorgeous chandeliered reading room-with-a-view, Montarina welcome tourists with big smiles, good, cheap coffee, and joke books, plus tons of information and suggestions about what to do. The lush grounds look like a friendly Disney jungle with stone caverns, jasmine, beach volleyball, ping pong, and a huge pool and slide. Shuttles to discos and the nearby mountains. The adventure company ASBEST is located in the adjoining Hotel Continental. Reception daily 8am-10pm. Dorms 20SFr; singles 45SFr; doubles 70SFr. Buffet breakfast 15SFr. Sheets 4SFr. Open March-Dec.

Lugano

- Autosilo (Parking), 13
- Bagno Publico, 17
- Basilica del Sacro Cuore, 15
- Cathedral San Lorenzo, 5
- Chiesa Loreto, 2
- Chiesa San Rocco, 8
- Chiesa Santa Maria degli Angioli, 3
- Museo Cantonale d'Arte, 7
- Palazzo dei Congressi, 11
- Parco Civico, 12
- Parco Tassino, 16
- PTT Centro (Post Office), 6
- Stazione F.F.S. (Train Station), 4
- Tourist Office, 9
- Villa Ciani, 10
- Villa Malpensata, Museo d'Arte Moderna, 1
- Villa Saroli, 14

Casa della Giovane, 34 corso Elvezia (tel. 922 95 53), 3 blocks from the hospital and across the street from Basilica Sacro Cuore. A 20min. walk from the station, left on P. della Stazione, right on via San Gottardo, and a sharp right on via Cantonale. Follow via Cantonale as it becomes corso Pestalozzi, and make a left on corso Elvezia; look for a blue and brick building about four blocks on your right. Or take bus #9 (leaves opposite train station) to "Corso Elvezia." For **women only.** Crayola-covered furniture fills big, bright, immaculate rooms. Colorful cafeteria nostalgic of nursery school. Beautiful rooftop terrace with views of lake and mountains allows serious tanning. Some vacationers may not like the pious atmosphere. Candle-lit sanctuaries are downstairs from the TV room. Reception 7am-10pm. Under age 18, curfew 9:30pm; ages 18 and up 11:15pm weekdays, 2am weekends. Dorms 20SFr. In summer: doubles with bathrooms with breakfast and one meal 35SFr, with all three meals 40SFr. Breakfast 4.50SFr. Lunch or dinner 12SFr. Lockable armoires in rooms. Laundry 3SFr. During the school year, make reservations.

Hotel Pestalozzi, 9 P. Indipendenza (tel. 921 46 46; fax 923 20 45). Live it up for a night by staying in this upscale version of a budget hotel. A smattering of affordable singles and doubles with huge, fluffy white pillows and floral wallpaper. Turkish rugs. 24hr. reception. Singles 54-92SFr; doubles 96-148SFr; triples 135-250SFr. Breakfast included. Reserve ahead. Visa.

Pensione Selva, 36 via Tesserete (tel. 923 60 17; fax 943 47 81). Bus #9: "Sassa." Walk 20 min. from the station, then along via Gottardo for 250m, then right on via Tesserete. Romantic rooms spruced up by paintings. Outdoor pool and grapevine-draped lattice greets you as you enter. Singles 46-72SFr; doubles 108-130SFr.

Hotel Zurigo, 13 corso Pestalozzi (tel. 923 43 43; fax 923 92 68). Just down the street from the Pestlozzi, and across the AmEx office. Clean and spacious. All rooms have telephones and yellow walls. Rooms with showers also have TV. 24hr.

reception. Singles 55SFr, with shower 85SFr; doubles with shower 90SFr, with shower and toilet 120SFr; triples with shower 160SFr. Breakfast and parking included. Closed in Dec.

Camping: There are 5 campsites nearby, all in **Agno.** Take the Ferrovia-Lugano-Ponte-Tresa (FLP) train to Agno (4.20SFr). From the train, turn left, and turn left again on Via Molinazzo for **La Palma** (tel. 605 25 21) and **Eurocampo** (tel. 605 21 14; fax 605 31 87). 7.50SFr; tents 4-15SFr. All sites are open April-Oct.

FOOD

As the central city in the Ticino, Lugano knows the way to visitors' hearts. Serving up plates of *penne* and *gnocchi* and freshly twirled pizzas, Lugano's many outdoor restaurants and cafés pay homage to the canton's Italian heritage. It doesn't take a genius to realize that Lugano's specialty is sausage. *Spätzle* steps aside here in deference to spaghetti. For a simple meal, your might try **Ristorante Inova**, on the third flood of the department store Inovazione in piazza Dante. They have the same old self-serve goodies: salad bar (4-10SFr), grand pasta bar (7-10SFr per plate), and other warm entrees-of-the-day (8-13SFr). (Open Mon.-Sat. 7:30am-10pm, Sun. 10am-10pm.) For some quick *al fresco* shopping and eating, **via Pessina** livens up at midday with outdoor sandwich and fruit shops. Try the Salumeria at 12 via Pessina for quick sandwiches to go (3-6SFr). The snack shop **DiGustibus** (see Migros below) on the ground floor of Migros saves the close-to-penniless with huge slices of tomato, eggplant, and zucchini pizza (3.90SFr), and ice-cream cones (1.60SFr).

- **La Tinèra,** 2 via dei Gorini (tel. 923 52 19). Tucked away in a tiny alley off a quiet cobblestone road, this low-lit, romantic, underground restaurant is full of Ticinese ambience and not to be missed. You can't go wrong with the daily specials (10-15SFr). The *pollo alla compagnola* (13.50SFr) looks particularly scrumptious. Open Mon.-Sat. 11am-2:30pm and 6-10pm. Visa, MC, AmEx.
- **Pestalozzi,** 9 P. Indipendenza (tel. 921 46 46), in the hotel. Simple, non-alcoholic restaurant offers ten veggie dishes (from 10.50SFr), including tofu burgers. *Lasagne bolognese* and mixed salad 8.50SFr. Open daily 11am-10pm.
- **Ristorante Cantinone,** P. Cioccaro (tel. 923 10 68). Friendly pizzeria serves lunch and dinner throngs the usual pasta and pizza (11-17SFr) as well as some more unusual goodies like Tuscan pizza with apples and nuts (14SFr). Large salads 16SFr and up. Open daily 9am-midnight. Visa, MC, AmEx.
- **Ristorante Sayonara,** 10 via Soave (tel. 922 01 70), in P. Cloccaro across from Cantinone. You can't miss the fluorescent orange chairs that clash with the light green tablecloths. A huge lunchtime crowd comes for the homemade pasta (12-17SFr) and pizza (from 11.50SFr). Open daily 8am-midnight. Visa, MC, AmEx.
- **Bistro Tango,** P. della Riforma (tel. 922 27 01). Take a break from pizza and head for the border. Central and South American food in a lively tango atmosphere. Tacos and burritos 15SFr. Open daily 11:30am-1am. Visa, MC, AmEx.

Markets

- **Migros,** 15 via Pretoria, in the center of town, offers freshly made pasta and delicious Italian *ciabatta,* as well as the usual fare. **Branch** around the corner from the hostel. Open Mon.-Fri. 8am-6:30pm, Sat. 7:30am-5pm.
- **Public Market,** P. della Riforma. Displays the seafood and produce of the region and yummy veggie sandwiches (4SFr). Open Tues. and Fri. 7am-noon.
- **Reformhaus Müller** in the Quartiere Maghetti (next to Chiesa San Rocco) for vitamins, muscle powders, and about 100 varieties of "guaranteed" diets. Open Mon.-Fri. 8am-6:30pm, Sat. 8am-5pm.

SIGHTS AND ENTERTAINMENT

The leafy frescoes of the 16th-century **Cattedrale San Lorenzo,** just below the train station, gleam through centuries of dust, scarred with grooves and tiny, teenaged lovers' initials. In the vaults, brilliant red and blue suns explode with snake-like rays, more like images out of hell than out of heaven's pastoral serenity. To soak in the

LUGANO: SIGHTS AND ENTERTAINMENT ■ 423

spectacular contrast of the blue Lago di Lugano and the sienna Ticinese rooftops, cross the street and follow the curved path down the hill. The **Chiesa San Rocco,** on via Canova, dating from 1349, houses an ornate Madonna altarpiece and Passion frescoes by Discopoli. The national monument **Basilica Sacro Cuore,** on corso Elevezia and across from the Casa della Giovane, features Swiss hikers walking alongside the disciples in the altarpiece fresco. A tribute to the combination of church and state, the Swiss flag is tucked into nouveau Biblical scenes. The most spectacular frescoes are Bernardino Luini's gargantuan *Crucifixion* and *Last Supper* in the **Chiesa Santa Maria degli Angioli,** on P. B. Luini. They throb with loud, crowded color, denying their centuries of age. These precursors to neon could keep even the most sinful dozer awake. (Open daily 8-11:45am and 3-5:45pm.)

Lugano lost one of its largest assets in a rush of art-world intrigue. The **Thyssen-Bornemisza Gallery,** in Villa Favorita, Castagnola (tel. 962 17 41), has a fascinating international history and a rather lackluster permanent collection of modern art. (See **Art for Art's Sake** p. 423. Open April 4-Nov. 3 Fri.-Sun. 10am-5pm. 10SFr, students 6SFr.) The **Museo d'Arte Moderna,** Villa Malpensata, 5 riva Caccia (tel. 944 43 70), has a more impressive collection of 20th-century art, European and American, as well as yearly retrospectives and special exhibitions. (Open only for special exhibitions. Contact the tourist office for information.) The **Museo Cantonale d'Arte,** 10 Via Canova (tel. 910 47 80), features 19th- and 20th-century works, including Swiss artists such as Klee, Vela, Ciseri, and Franzoni, and foreign artists such as Nicholson, Morandi, Degas, and Renoir. Temporary exhibits focus on modern art. (Open Tues. 2-5pm, Wed.-Sun. 10am-5pm. Special exhibits 10SFr, students 5SFr; permanent collection 7SFr, students 5SFr.) The Brignoni family heirlooms at the **Museo delle Culture Extraeuropee,** 324 Via Cortivo (tel. 971 73 53), on the footpath to Gandria in the Villa Heleneum, does not include cuckoo clocks or Swiss army knives. If, however, cuckoo clocks were made in Samoa and Papa New Guinea, they might resemble this museum's collection of outrageous wooden artifacts—masks, statues, and totems grin at passersby. (Open March 5-Oct. 31 Tues.-Sun. 10-5pm. 5SFr, students 3SFr.)

Lugano's waterfront park are an ideal place for a few hours' introspection. The **Belvedere,** a sculpture garden on quai riva Caccia, stretches along the lakeside promenade in the direction of Paradiso. Lugano is chock full o' summer **festivals**. At the end of June, the **Tour de Suisse** comes to a dramatic finish in Lugano, and from the end of June to early August, **Cinema al Lago** shows international films on the lakeside beach. A huge screen is installed at water level on the lake, with 1000 seats available for viewers. In early July, Lugano's **Jazz Festival** heats up at no charge. Previous performers include Miles Davis and Bobby McFerrin. The looser **Blues to Bop Festival** celebrates R&B, blues, and gospel at the end of August, hosting international singers as well as local amateurs. The festive season wraps up with the **Wine Harvest Festival** in late September and early October, boozing away summer's fresh memories.

Art for Art's Sake? Whatever.

The **Thyssen-Bornemisza Gallery,** in Villa Favorita, once housed one of the most outstanding private collections in Europe, until the owner (a fantastically rich, old Baron) and his young Spanish wife (a former beauty queen) started looking around for a permanent home for all of those Rembrandts, Dürers, Van Goghs, and Kandinskys. In the international bidding war that ensued, the collection first moved into the hands of the Spanish government for a while to up the ante. When Spain became attached to the paintings, he talked them into building a museum and paying him a cool US$350 million for the stash. Spain wins, Switzerland loses, end of story. The Villa is still maintained by the very piqued Swiss and open to the public with some leftovers and pleasure-dome architecture. Learn a lesson in Swiss tact by asking the guides—with the best look of open innocence you can muster—where all of the paintings have gone.

Though the tops of the Ticinese mountains are littered with tourists, the dizzying views stretch into Italy. The tourist office and hostel both have topographic maps and trail guides (the tourist office sells them; the hostel lends them). The bay's guard towers, **Monte Bré** (933m) and **Monté San Salvatore** (912m), scream out a leisurely hike. With a 13th-century church perched on top, San Salvatore is the more striking of the two, craggy cliffs extending to the water. The trail head is just past the funicular station at Paradiso (about a 15-minute walk from the tourist office, to the right along the shore). After studying the lake, Lugano, and the Alps, follow the signs to Carona, a small village halfway up the mountain that has an Olympic-sized pool with high dive (1SFr). Continue walking to Morcote, on the shore, where you can catch a ferry back to Lugano (14SFr, Swisspass valid). The walk from the summit takes about three and a half hours. Both mountains have funiculars (12SFr, 18SFr round-trip, students 16-18 6SFr, 9SFr round-trip). For more information contact the San Salvatore Funicular office (tel. 994 13 52) or the Monte Bré office (tel. 971 31 71). More rugged hikers should ask at Hotel Montarina for information on hiking **Monte Boglio**.

The arcades of the *città vecchia* come alive at night as people meander through the *piazze* and along the lake. The outdoor cafés of P. della Riforma are especially lively. The slot machines spin at **Casinò Kursaal di Lugano** (tel. 923 32 81), near the tourist office. (Casino open daily 9pm-2am for game tables, noon-midnight for slots. Pants and collared shirts required after 8pm.) The **Pave Pub,** riva Albertolli 1 (tel. 922 07 70), is a self-proclaimed *museo de birra* (beer museum), offering 50 different beers and an English pub atmosphere with a great lakeside view of the lit fountains. (Beers start at 4-5SFr. Open daily 11am-1am.) **B-52,** 4 via al Forte (tel. 923 96 58), draws a young crowd that loves to mix and mingle. (Open Tues.-Sun. 10pm-3am.) The Latin American **Mango Club**, 8 P. Dante (tel. 922 94 38), gets nice and spicy. (Opens at 11pm and goes until last person leaves.)

Travelers jumpy from too much lounging in the Lugano sun should call on the **ASBEST Adventure Company,** via Basilea 28, CH-6900 Lugano (tel. 966 11 14; fax 966 12 13; http://www.tourism.ticino.ch/text/asbest.html), for adrenaline-intensive relief. Based in the Hotel Continental, the ebullient ASBEST Alpine guides offer dozens of spinning, splashing, diving, and snow-shoeing quests. In the winter, snow-shoe and ski (full-day 89SFr) and paraglide (150SFr), returning in the evening to ever-flowery Lugano. Canyoning (89SFr) and river-diving are especially nice in Ticino because the water isn't as cold as the numbing mountain Alpine glacier streams. Or choose from rock-climbing (89SFr), mountain biking (guided 1-day trip 89SFr), and the insane Rap-jump, a kind of spinning bungee that's a bit slower (89SFr).

■ Near Lugano: Gandria

From Lago di Lugano, Gandria looks like a collection of antique dominoes ready at any moment to topple over into the lake. Alas, Gandria isn't half that exciting, specializing in ice cream, twisty streets, and oodles of souvenir shops. Advertised as a "small fishing village" and a former smuggling port for pirates, Gandria now relegates its poles and pirates to shop windows, although nooks in the cliff wall seem perfect for hidden treasure. A picturesque walk from Lugano along the lakeshore, through overgrown vegetation just above the lapping waters (1hr.), leads to the almost absurdly cute village. Boats also travel from Lugano (every 30min. 8:30am-10:15pm, 30min., 10SFr, round-trip 16SFr, Swisspass valid). Gandria's winding streets escape the ravages of modern design—city ordinances forbid construction and prohibit cars—but not modern tourists. When there's not much to do, a slow afternoon of eating ice cream while looking over the lake is always pleasant. Naughty pirates head to **Chiesa Parrochiale San Vigilio** for confession, lured by a huge gold crown over the altar. The church is a cool spot to beat the heat and view some lovely sculpture and interior architecture. A short boat ride from Gandria's town center to **Gandria-Cantine** (boat stop "Museo delle Dogane") leads to the

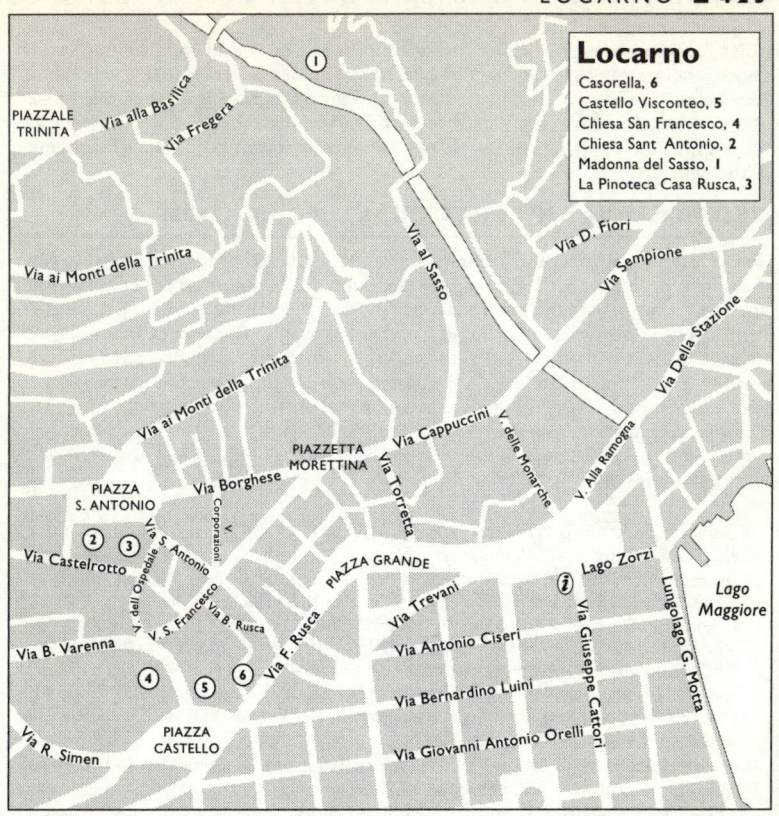

Swiss Customs Museum. The museum glorifies those brave men and women who keep gold pure and smugglers on the lookout. Several hands-on exhibits show the intricacies of detecting fake IDs and searching cars; another covers the life of a turn-of-the-century border policeman. (Open daily 1:30-5:30pm. Free. Exhibits in Italian and German, with some introductory notes in English and French.) If you need a place to rest after an exhausting day of lounging by the lake, stroll over to **Hotel Miralago** (tel. (091) 971 43 61). The hotel offers tropical rooms with Tarzan jungle scenes, floral everything, and a leafy lakeside breakfast terrace. (38SFr per person. Breakfast included.)

Locarno

On the shores of **Lago Maggiore,** which straddles Italy and Switzerland, Locarno basks in warm near-Mediterranean breezes and bright Italian sun. Luxuriant palm trees replace the stark Alps and jar with the rest of Switzerland. More serene than even its Italian cousin to the south, Locarno offers balmy evenings and *al fresco* lounging to its visitors. For much of the inter-war era, hopes for peace were symbolized by "the Spirit of Locarno"—a futile attempt in 1925 by England, France, and Italy to appease Germany after World War I. History records that Locarno was chosen over other Swiss cities because the mistress of one of the representatives insisted that the conference be held on the Maggiore. Perhaps the *bella donna* needed some work on her tan. Sun-worshippers flock to pay homage to the UV deities in this relatively unspoiled resort town that gets over 2200 hours of sunlight per year—the most in all of Switzerland. Nestled in the Ticinese foothills, Locarno is also an excellent starting point for mountain hikes along the pristine **Verzasca** and **Maggia** valleys, or for regional skiing. James Joyce loitered around Maggiore's waters in 1917, waiting for Ezra Pound to return a critique of *Ulysses*. Locarno's arcades brim with live music and kinetic cafés. The town blends an Swiss orderliness and efficiency with Italian food, spirit, and exuberance. People talk loudly with Italian hands, yet stay on time with Swiss watches.

ORIENTATION AND PRACTICAL INFORMATION

By car, Locarno is accessible from motorway N2, which extends from Basel to Chiasso (exit: Bellinzona-süd). **Piazza Grande,** home of the International Film Festival, anchors Locarno, with the town's cultural and commercial life gravitating around its century-old Lombardian arcades. Just above P. Grande, **Città Vecchia** in the old town is blessed with 16th- and 17th-century architecture, as well as extravagantly economical accommodations. **Via Ramogna** connects the Piazza to the train station and ferries groups of gawking tourists to the Madonna del Sasso via the funicular. **Via Rusca,** extending from the other side of the Piazza, winds up at the Castello Visconti. South of the Piazza lies the residential district, in a traditional grid plan. The vacation homes of many Swiss are here.

- **Tourist office:** Largo Zorzi (tel. 751 03 33), on P. Grande. From the main exit of the train station, walk diagonally to the right, and cross via della Stazione; continue through the pedestrian walkway (via alla Ramogna). As you come out, cross Largo Zorzi to your left; the tourist office is in the same building as the *Kursaal* (casino). Hotel reservations for 5SFr deposit, deducted from the hotel room price. The office also organizes **bus excursions** around Lago Maggiore and beyond. City tours in English leave the tourist office March 25-Oct. Tues. at 9:45am. Pick up a map of Locarno and browse the many brochures. Open March-Oct. Mon.-Fri. 8:30am-7pm, Sat.-Sun. 9am-5pm, Sun. 9am-noon; Nov.-Feb. Mon.-Fri. 8am-noon and 2-6pm.
- **Currency exchange:** Try any one of the banks lining P. Grande. Good rates are also at the train station. Open daily 5:45am-9pm.
- **Trains:** P. Stazione (tel. 157 22 22). To: **Bellinzona** (every 30min., 20min., 6.60SFr), connecting every hour north to **Lucerne** (2¾hrs., 54SFr) and **Zurich** (3hrs., 57SFr) and south to **Lugano** (15.80SFr) and **Milan** (2½hrs., 22SFr). For **Zermatt** (85SFr), **Montreux** (69SFr), or **Geneva** (5½hrs., 84SFr), change trains in **Domodossola,** Italy.
- **Buses: Buses** depart from the train station or from the lakeside of Piazza Grande to Locarno and to nearby towns such as Ascona (#31) and Minusio. Buses also run regularly through the **San Bernadino Pass** to Eastern Switzerland.
- **Ferries: Navigazione Lago Maggiore,** 1 Largo Zorzi (tel. 751 18 65; fax 751 30 24), presents tours of the entire lake, all the way into Italy. A full day on the Swiss side of the lake costs 10SFr. Trips to Ascona (7 per day, 10min., round-trip 10SFr) and especially the Island of Brissago (6 per day, 20min. round-trip 19SFr), an island famous for its gardens and cigars, are well worth the visit.
- **Car rental: Europcar,** 5a Viaggi Verbano (tel. 791 43 24).
- **Taxi:** tel. 743 11 33.
- **Parking:** Metered public parking found on via della Posta and major streets (1SFr per hr.). Also, the 24-hr. parking garage, **Autosilo Largo SA** (tel. 751 96 13), awaits beneath the *Kursaal,* and is accessible by via Cattori.
- **Bike Rental:** At the train station. 21SFr per day, 84SF per week; mountain bike 29SFr per day. To return a bike to another station 6SFr (open daily 5:45am-9pm).
- **Luggage Storage:** At the train station. 5SFr. Open daily 5:45am-9pm. **Lockers** 5SFr.
- **Bookstore: Fantasia Cartoleria Libreria,** 32 P. Grande. English books, travel books, and maps (open Mon.-Fri. 8am-6:30pm, Sat. 8am-5pm).
- **Emergencies: Police:** 117. **Fire:** 118. **Road rescue:** 163. **Weather:** 162. **Medical Assistance:** 111. **Ambulance:** 144.

Post Office: Across the street from the train station. Open Mon.-Fri. 7:30am-6:30pm, Sat. 8-11am. **Postal Code:** CH-6600. **Telephone Code:** 091.

ACCOMMODATIONS

Pensione Città Vecchia, 13 via Toretta (tel./fax 751 45 54). From P. Grande, turn right on via Toretta (*not* vigola Toretta; look for a brown sign with the *pensiones* on it) and continue to the top. A gorgeous 300-year-old fresco clashes charmingly with freshly painted walls and a brand-new, bright pink facade. With a great price and a location to match, it's no small wonder that it's always full. Reception daily 8am-9pm. Check-in 1-6pm; reservation required if you come between 6-9pm. No curfew. 22SFr per person; monkish singles 33SFr. Sheets 4.50SFr. Small breakfast 4.50SFr. Reserve ahead. Open March-Oct.

Reginetta, 8 via della Motta (tel./fax 752 35 53). Walk along the arcades to the end of P. Grande, and make a right onto via della Motta. Run by the world-traveled Miss Bertolutti (the currency-postered walls are proof), this traveler's haven provides bright, spacious and impeccably clean rooms. Ruined by fire while the owner was vacationing in Australia in March '97, the restored hostel opened in September. The friendly owner offers good advice on local sights; check the chalkboard for local events of interest. Reception daily 8am-9pm. 39SFr per person, 45SFr with breakfast. Showers included. Open March-Oct. only. Visa, MC, AmEx.

Ostello Giaciglio, 7 via Rusca (tel. 751 30 64; fax 752 38 37). Walk to the end of the P. Grande, make a right onto via della Motta, and take the left fork in the road onto via Rusca. Sunshiny, black-and-white-checked dorms for 4, 6, or 8 people. Kitchen facilities available, along with a sauna (20SFr) and tanning salon (10SFr) in case a cloud invades Locarno's air space. Book rooms early since rowdy high-school groups take over July-Aug. 30SFr per person, no breakfast. If the hostel is full, cross the street to **Hotel Garni Sempione** to find the hostel's supervisor. Visa, MC, AmEx.

Delta Camping, 7 via Respini (tel. 751 60 81; fax 751 22 43). A 20min. walk along the lakeside from the tourist office brings you to these campstyles of the rich and famous; a reservation fee of 100SFr, which is not deducted from the bill, is recommended for July and August. Offers a rock beach nearby and an enticing view of the lake. No dogs allowed. Reception open daily 8am-noon and 2-9pm. 24SFr, kids 2-14 7SFr. Site 70-80SFr; lake site 30-40SFr. Open March 1-Oct. 31.

Rivabella (tel. (091) 745 22 13; fax 745 66 38). in nearby **Tenero,** is much more affordable and is accessible by boat or a 45min. walk along the water in the opposite direction of Delta Camping. 11SFr; tents 20SFr.

FOOD

Panini and pasta reign supreme in Locarno, as gruyère cheese gives way to Gorgonzola. While the majority of restaurants lean toward the expensive side, most offer pasta and pizza in the 10-20SFr range.

Casa de Popolo, P. del Corporazioni (tel. 751 12 08). Specializes in pizza (10-16SFr) and fresh pasta (12-18SFr), with wine-racks, red and white picnic-table cloths, courteous Italian waiters, and a gurgling fountain in front of the outdoor seating. Open Mon.-Sat. 7am-midnight, Sun. 5pm-midnight. Visa, MC, AmEx.

Inova, 1 via della Stazione (tel. 743 76 76), left as you exit the station. Huge self-serve restaurant. Wooden food bars bring otherwise financially inaccessible luxuries such as fruits and vegetable to your fingertips: fruit bar (4-7SFr), salad bar (4-11SFr), grand pasta buffet (9.60SFr). Also a tantalizing host of desserts. Open Mon.-Fri. 8:30am-6:30pm, Sat. 8am-5pm.

Contrada, 26 P. Grande (tel. 751 48 15), offers outdoor dining ideal for people-watching. Pizzas and pasta (10.50-15SFr). Ask for the list of daily specials (14SFr). Open Mon.-Sat. 8am-6:30pm. Visa, MC.

Gelatina Primavera, 4 via all'Ospedale (tel. 31 77 36), across from the Chiesa San Francesco. Feel like those 2200 hours of sun are hitting you all at once? Grab a delicious store-made ice cream cone and cool off. Sandwiches from 5.50SFr and brick oven pizza from 11SFr. Open Wed.-Mon. 8am-midnight, Sat.-Sun. 10am-midnight.

- **Al Böcc,** 14 P. Grande (tel. 751 49 39), opposite the lake side of Piazza Grande. Busy little sandwich shop on the piazza. Sandwiches 3-6SFr. Serves warm *focaccia* bread (4.50-6.50 SFr) and cold pizza (3-6SFr). Open daily 6:30am-midnight. Visa, MC.

SIGHTS AND ENTERTAINMENT

A 20-minute walk up shaded, streamside stairway of via al Sasso, by a mountain stream, leads to the shocking orange and magenta church of **Madonna del Sasso** (Madonna of the Rock). A popular pilgrimage destination, the church was under construction longer than it has been a site: three centuries to build, but only a 200th birthday in 1992. The interior overwhelms with its breathtaking frescoes, ornate carvings, and brilliant painting, while the outdoor terrace pacifies with its tranquil view of Locarno and the lake. Almost close enough to touch, the low-lying ceiling frescoes dazzle the eye with brightly colored, gilded figures and brilliant cobalt heavens. Velvet-cased silver hearts gleam from the walls. Freestanding, life-sized scenes of the *Pietà, The Last Supper,* and *Lamentation* hide mysteriously in shady niches on the church grounds. The lady of the house herself, the **Madonna,** is tucked away in the museum next door, as are masterpieces by Ciseri and Raphael. (Grounds open daily 7am-10pm, Nov.-Feb. 7am-9pm. Museum open April-Oct. Mon.-Fri. 2-5pm, Sun. 10am-noon and 2-5pm. 2.50SFr, students 1.50SFr.) The museum next door, well worth the minuscule admission fee, houses a curious collection of delicate bone relics, ancient pilgrimage souvenirs, and bizarre paintings of the Madonna appearing in the clouds over macabre catastrophes. Although the paintings depict tragedies, each is actually more an ex-voto to the Madonna, thanking her for her miraculous and timely intervention. The museum also houses an all-too-hasty thank-you to the Madonna for the hoped-for success of the pact of Locarno.

Closer to sea level the cavernous **Chiesa Sant' Antonio** presides over the outskirts of the *città vecchia.* Built between 1668 and 1674 it features vaulted ceilings and an immense and colorful fresco depicting Christ being taken off the cross. Founded by the brethren of St. Francis of Assisi shortly after his death, the **Chiesa San Francesco** unassumingly sits on the Piazza San Francesco. The church's current architecture, mellowed by old cobblestones and fading frescoes, is a melange of styles starting from the 13th century. Downhill from Chiesa San Francesco along via Ripacanova, the **Castello Visconteo** gazes on Locarno. After learning about the spirit of Locarno in the room where the pact was signed, wander through dungeons and up towers where soldiers many have poured boiling oil on attackers in the truly peace-loving spirit of the Middle Ages. The medieval castle, constructed between the 13th and 15th centuries, now houses the **Museo Civico e Archeologico,** which exhibits Roman glassware, pottery, and coins. Each room's function in medieval times is explained. (Open April-Oct. Tues.-Sun. 10am-noon and 2-5pm. 5SFr, students 3SFr.)

As the sun sets and the temperature drops, gamble at the **Kursaal** (casino) next to the tourist office, more a video arcade than a casino. (Open Sun.-Thurs. noon-2am, Fri.-Sat. noon-4am. Must be over 19. Proper attire required.) Catch a movie at the **Cinema Rex** on via Bossi, or nurse a long drink at one of the numerous cafés along P. Grande. The **Record Rock Café,** via Trevani 3 (tel. 751 4433), a Hard Rock look-a-like, pumps out American and English rock along with contemporary hits. The sign over the bar reads "All you need is love," but you'll still need 10SFr for the cover, and an additional 6SFr for any beer. Live bands play from September to June. (Open July-Aug. Tues.-Sun. 5pm-1am; Sept.-June Tues.-Sun. 4pm-1am. Cover 10SFr.)

Locarno is the ideal starting/stopping/break point for outdoor enthusiasts. For the faint of heart or short of breath, ride to up to **Cimetta,** which hangs over Locarno at a lofty 1671m by taking the Madonna Funicular to the Cardada Cable Car, which, in turn, takes you to the Cimetta chair lift. (Round-trip 33SFr; funicular only round-trip 6SFr, with Swisspass 4.50SFr; Locarno-Cardada 28SFr round-trip. Cable cars depart twice per hour, funicular every 15 min.) To escape the city, head out on Postal Bus 630-55 to **Sonogo** (1hr., 15.80SFr, Swisspass valid) and bask amid the extraordinarily rugged peaks at the end of **Val Verzasca** (Verzasca valley). From the bus stop, make your first left and follow the yellow signs to Lavertezzo. Pass through cool, shady glens and rocky riverbeds as you follow the Verzasca river through the pristine valley. Peaks rise on either side as you walk (primarily downhill) by deserted villages and cascading waterfall. Close to **Lavertezzo,** the river eases its rapid, crashing pace and offers the soul-cleansing cold of its refreshing pools to hikers, thermally overloaded or otherwise. Pick your swimming hole carefully, however, as current can be fast and colder than you think. Climb the **Ponte dei Salti,** a vaulted stone bridge built at the end of the Middle Ages, and gaze into the clear green ponds. The walk from Sonogroto Lavertezzo take about 3½hr., but you can rest anytime by meeting the postal bus at stops along the valley. The trail is marked by yellow signs with direction and town names and also by painted red stripes sandwiched by two white stripes.

The Locarno Film Festival

Every August, Locarno hosts an **International Film Festival** which has perhaps the most widely-attended world premieres of movies anywhere. In 1997 the festival hits Locarno August 7-17. Unlike Cannes, no snooty invitations are required. Thousands of big-screen enthusiasts squeeze themselves like sardines in a film cannister into the Piazza Grande and watch the night's spectacle on the 800ft. movie screen—Europe's largest. More than 100,000 spectators definitively make it Switzerland's biggest party. In past years Woody Allen, Milos Forman, Stanley Kubrick, Spike Lee, and Bernardo Bertolucci have all screened films here. Officially, Locarno's festival focuses on the promotion of young filmmakers and new film movements.

During the festival, accommodations are gone with the wind. Reserve at least six months in advance. For festival information, as well as information about student discounts, contact International Film Festival, via della Posta 6, CH-6600 Locarno (tel. 751 02 32; fax 751 74 65). Tickets go for one screening 15SFr, 2 screenings 25SFr, whole day (3 screenings) 30SFr. For information in the U.S. on the East coast, contact Norman Wang and Sophie Gluck, New York (tel. (212) 226-3269; fax 941-1425); on the West Coast, contact Bill Krohn, Los Angeles (tel./fax (213) 883-0078).

■ Near Locarno: Ascona

Queen of the Lago Maggiore, Ascona rules with a languorous hand. Ascona has welcomed many diverse groups to her shores. In the Renaissance, a small bunch of sculptors and artists established their studios in Ascona. Their legacy is emblazoned in the facades that grace the **Casa Serodine.** More recently, a group of vegetarian hippies "colonized" **Monte Verità,** Ascona's beautiful mountain, seeking a return to truth through natural living. Their efforts are immortalized in the **Museo Casa Anatta** (tel. 791 01 81), at the summit of Monte Verità, a 20-minute walk up a stairway (scallinata della Ruga) from the town center. (Open April-June and Sept.-Oct. Tues.-Sun. 2:30-6pm, July-Aug. Tues.-Sun. 3-7pm. 5SFr, students 3SFr.) Take bus #33 from the post office, as it winds its way to the top. With the utopian, heavily sedated ascetics taking the high road, the burghers colonized the lower *città vecchia* as a bastion of good taste and expensive delicacies. Jewellers, *haute couture* boutiques, and exclusive art galleries line the narrow winding streets. Ascona tries to go incognito as the quaint fishing town of yore. Don't believe the hype; in reality it is an *über*-resort, with many plentifully starred hotels as yet untouched by the *hoi polloi*. But what it lacks in humble charm it makes up for in almost disconcerting picturesqueness. Each jasmine-draped nook seems to have framed itself for the tourists' clicking cameras.

Down the road from the bus stop to the right is the **Collegio Pontificio Papio.** Founded in the 16th century, the private school brilliantly displays the coat of arms of the Papio family of Ascona. Faded islands of 16th-century frescoes float mystically on the newly whitewashed walls of the **Chiesa Santa Maria della Misericordia,** built in 1399. The church's dim, incense-laden interior clashes ancient stained glass with a brand-new, puritanically simple organ. The church now presides over the school, reminding students to be pious, but the jazz and blues CDs in the music shop on the church grounds sing of love, sing, and loss. **The Chiesa S.S. Pietro e Paolo,** in the heart of the pedestrian sector of Ascona, was constructed in the 16th century, but Baroque restoration coated the church's interior walls with colorful frescoes. Ascona's **Museo Comunale d'Arte Moderna,** 34 via Borgo (tel. 791 67 57), displays an extensive permanent collection including such artists as Klee, Utrillo, Amiet, and Jawlensky, as well as a collection of caricatures done both in color and black and white. (Open March-Dec. Tues.-Sat. 10am-noon and 3-5pm, Sun. 10am-noon. 5SFr, students and seniors 3SFr.) Private galleries line the winding streets, promoting such artists as Niki de St. Phalle, Chagall, and Braque. A testimony to Ascona's incorporation of history and capitalism is the **Castello dei Ghiriglioni** at the far end of Piazza Motta. Touted as a site of historical interest, the lone remaining tower of the 13th-century castle is now a hotel and restaurant. The **Museo Epper,** 14 via Albarelle (tel. 791 19 42), beyond the Castello, presents temporary exhibits and retrospectives of 20th-century artists. (Open March-June, Sept.-Oct. Tues.-Fri. 10am-noon and 4-6pm, Sun. 4-6pm; July-Aug. Tues.-Fri. 10am-noon and 8-10pm, Sat.-Sun. 8-10pm. Free.)

In late June and early July, Ascona sets up the bandstands and claps its hands to the beat of the **Festa New Orleans Music.** Local cafés and the waterfront host musicians who bring the night to life with jazz, gospel, soul, blues, and even zydeco. This ain't your mama's sippin' jazz—it's the real thing with acts from jazz hotspots the world over. The festival takes place in late June; entrance is 5SFr per night, 30SFr for the whole festival. If you're planning a trip, other events include an international horse jumping competition at the end of July, an international music festival (late Aug.-mid-Oct.), and an international puppet festival (Sept. 5-15). Locarno's younger crowd flocks to Ascona's subterranean dance club, **Cincilla,** via Moscia 6. (Open Wed.-Thurs. and Sun. 11pm-3am, Fri.-Sat. 11pm-4am.) The club is a little heavy on the zebra motif, but heavy on the groove also, located beneath mysterious arcades beside Lago Maggiore.

A village of only 4500 inhabitants, Ascona with its neighboring twin, Losone, boasts over 3000 hotel beds. Unfortunately, close to none fall into a budget price range. Try the rooms above the **Ristorante Verbano** (tel. 791 12 74) on via Borgo near the museum (44SFr per person, breakfast included), or ask the tourist office for a list of **camere private** (private rooms), which run 24-65SFr per person. Grab a bite to eat at **Otello** on via Papio 8 (tel. 791 33 07), just down the street to the right from the bus stop. Their specialty is *crêpes* (8.50SFr and up), but they also have an expensive Chinese and cheap Italian kitchen. During the jazz festival and on other random occasions, you can hear original New Orleans jazz in the bandstand on the terrace in back. (Open Sun.-Thurs. 7am-midnight; Fri.-Sat. 7am-1am; Visa, MC.) **Restaurante il Torre,** via de Motta 61 (tel. 791 54 55), makes pasta like your mother's, if your mother cooks fresh pasta on a lakeside terrace across the street from a jazz bandstand in Ascona. Pastas and pizza starts at 11SFr, sandwiches at 6SFr. (Open daily 9am-midnight. Visa, AmEx.) And then there is always the **Co-op.** You can't miss the orange sign from the bus stop. (Open Mon.-Fri. 8am-6:30pm, Sat. 8am-5pm.)

Ascona's **tourist office** (tel. 791 00 90; fax 792 10 08) is in the Casa Serodine, just behind the Chiesa S.S. Pietro e Paolo with its sumptuous Baroque facade. (Open March 20-Oct. 20 Mon.-Fri. 9am-6:30pm, Sat. 9am-6pm, Sun. 9am-2pm; Oct. 21-March 19 Mon.-Fri. 9am-12:30pm and 2-6pm.) **Guided tours** of Ascona leave the tourist office from March-Nov. on Tues. and Fri. at 10am (5SFr, approx. 1½hr.). The tourist office **exchanges currency,** but the train station in Locarno offers better rates and hours. **Buses** run from Ascona to Locarno (#31, every 15min., 2.40SFr). **Parking** in Ascona shouldn't be too difficult, though cars cannot enter the center of town. Try the **Autosilo** at the corner of via Papio and via Buonamno. The **post office** is at the corner to the left of the bus stop, on via della Posta (open Mon.-Fri. 7:30am-noon and 1:45-6pm, Sat. 8-11am). The **postal code** is CH-6612. The **telephone code** is 091.

Bellinzona

The capital of Ticino, *"citta dei castelli"* (city of castles), "gateway to the Alps"— Bellinzona boasts many monikers. Though primarily a crossroads linking the sojourner to the Ticinese pearls of Lugano and Locarno, Ticino appeals to the medieval buff in all of us who longs to linger happily beneath ancient city walls and castles holding Switzerland's best collection of military architecture from the Dark Ages.

Orientation and Practical Information Bellinzona's **tourist office,** 2 Via Camminata (tel. 825 21 31; fax 825 38 17), adjacent to the city hall, makes free hotel reservations. From the train station, walk left 10 minutes straight along Viale Stazione, past P. Collegiata, and along Via Nosetto, and you'll hit a big blue "i" sign at P. Nosetto. (Open April-Oct. Mon.-Fri. 8am-6:30pm, Sat. 9am-5pm; Nov.-March Mon.-Fri. 8am-noon and 1:30-6:30pm, Sat. 8-11am.) The easiest way to Bellinzona is by **train.** There are direct connections to **Basel** (every hr., 4hr., 70SFr), **Lugano** (3 per hr., 30min., 10.40SFr), **Locarno** (2 per hr., 20min., 6.60SFr), **Lucerne** (2¼hr., 50SFr), **Zurich** (every hr., 2½hr., 54SFr), **Milan** (every hr., 2hr., 23SFr), **Rome** (3 per day, 7hr., 65SFr), and **Venice** (1 per day, 5hr., 41SFr). Trains to and from **Geneva** require a change in Domodossola, Italy (10 per day, 5½hr., 87SFr). Call 157 22 22 for train information. **Post buses** leave from the station for **Chur** (5 per day, 2½hr., 50SFr) and points in eastern Switzerland. **Motorists** arrive from the north on N2/E35 or N13/E43; from Lugano or the south, on N2/E35 north; from Locarno or the west, on Rte. 13 east. The train station has **currency exchange, luggage storage** (5SFr at baggage check), **lockers** (3SFr), and **bike rental** (22SFr per day at baggage check; open daily 6am-9pm). **Public parking** is available at the train station or in the Collectivo at P. del Sole (1SFr per hr.; open daily 8am-7pm). The ultra-new **post office** on Viale Stazione is a block left from the station. (Open Mon.-Fri. 6:30am-noon and 1-7pm, Sat. 6:30-11:50am.) The **postal code** is CH-6500. The **telephone code** is 091.

Accommodations and Food Bellinzona has yet to build a youth hostel, even though any one of those castles would be perfect for one (hint, hint). **Hotel Moderno Garni,** 17b Viale Stazione (tel. 825 13 76), left from the station, gives you a two-star hotel at one-star prices. For the reception, turn right on Via Claudio Pelladini and take another immediate right on Via Cancelliere Molo. The pleasant rooms have flowery sheets and the occasional balcony. (Reception in the hotel's café daily 6:30am-midnight. Singles 55SFr; doubles 90SFr; triples 120SFr; quads 160SFr. Shower and breakfast included. Visa, MC.) **Hotel San Giovanni,** 7 Via San Giovanni (tel. 825 19 19), provides clean, smallish rooms with big breezy windows above a popular restaurant. From the station, go left on Viale Stazione and turn right down Scalinata Dionigi Resinelli; continue straight for 100m. (Reception daily 6:30am-midnight. Singles 60SFr; doubles 90SFr. Breakfast included. Parking available. Visa, MC, AmEx.) Postal bus #2: "Arbedo Posta Vecchia" leads to **Camping Bosco de Molinazzo** (tel. 829 11 18; fax 829 23 55) and sleeping fitfully under the stars. (5-6SFr, children half-price; tent 5.20SFr; car 16SFr. Open April 3-Oct. 6.)

Aromas from the restaurant in Castelgrande waft over the campgrounds, but, alas, the five-star eatery is for dukes and duchesses only. Those nobles in spirit but peasant in pocket head to **Ristorante Inova,** Viale Stazione 5, in the Inovazione. There's no version of nightingale tongue here, but there's sometimes sautéed salmon. (Entrees 10-13SFr, salads 5-10SFr. Open Mon.-Fri. 8:30am-6:30pm, Sat. 8am-5pm.) A wannabe comedian waiter serves cappuccino (3SFr), *panini* (5SFr), and chocolate and pecan bugs (2SFr) at **Peverelli Panetteria Tea Room Pasticceria** in P. Collegiata off Viale Stazione. (Open Mon.-Fri. 7am-7pm, Sat. 7am-6pm.) Rustle up your own grub at **Migros** on P. del Sole, across from the Castelgrande entrance. (Open Mon.-Fri. 7am-6:30pm, Sat. 7am-5pm.) **Bio Casa,** near the tourist office, stocks organically grown fruits and veggies, tofu burgers, and vitamins. (Open Mon.-Fri. 8:30am-6:30pm, Sat. 8am-5pm.) The huge **outdoor market** along Via Stazione lays out everything from typical fruits and breads to incense and rugs. (Open Sat. 8am-noon.)

Sights and Entertainment The **Castelgrande** looms menacingly over Bellinzona, retaining illusions of grandeur by pretending the surrounding hills and trees hide thousands of armed troops within their Trojan interiors. Above the castle rise the *bianca* (white) and *nera* (black) towers, both 28m high. The Duke of Milan built up the castle in 1487, but, like some marriages, subsequent years saw destruction and dilapidation. The recently restored interior sports a chic new **museum** with hundreds of red and blue frescoes from the ceiling of a 15th-century Bellinzona house. On these panels, rabbits frolic, knights glare, and lovers chase each other in their underwear. The Castelgrande is accessible by the elevator near P. del Sole or by the winding paths up the hill from P. Collegieta and P. Nosetto. (Open in summer Tues.-Sun. 10am-12:30pm and 1:30-5:30pm; in winter Tues.-Sun. 9am-noon and 2-5pm. 4SFr, students 2SFr.) Across from Castelgrande, the **Castello di Montebello** stirs the imagination with medieval gadgets. Once past the two working drawbridges, visitors scramble along ramparts and explore spooky underground dungeons. The castle's mildly amusing eight-floor museum displays chunky ancient jewelry, vases galore, and a large collection from the stash of Bellinzona's medieval Tooth Fairy. To invade the castle, walk up the slippery, mossy steps of Via Motta. Battering rams, fiery arrows, and boiling oil are optional. (Open in summer Tues.-Sun. 9am-noon and 2-6pm; in winter Tues.-Sun. 9am-noon and 2-5pm. Museum 2SFr, students 1SFr.) Worth a look but not the walk, the **Castello di Sasso Corbaro** (230m above city level), the smallest of Bellinzona's three castles, surveys the Ticinese mountains. The Duke of Milan had the place slapped together in six months after the battle of Giornico. Available at the castles and the tourist office, a **"3 Castelli" ticket** grants entry to all three castle museums (8SFr, students 4SFr).

A fire charred the interior of the beloved 15th-century **Chiesa Santa Maria della Grazie,** but the nearby **Chiesa di San Biagio** flaunts a gigantic 16th-century painting of St. Christopher and a flock of saints on its columned interior. From the train station, walk 15 minutes to the left or take bus #4: "Cimiterio." The **Ticino River,** all the way down to Lago di Maggiore, is perfect for idle strollers out for mountain air and scenery. For a 45-minute hike with grand views of Sasso Corbaro and the valley, first take a short postal bus ride to Monti di Ravecchia. The trail begins at the hospital parking lot and follows an ancient mule path, leading to now-deserted Prada, an ancient trading post possibly dating to pre-Roman times.

The annual **Blues Festival** draws crowds from throughout Switzerland in late June. Previous performers include Luther Allison and Joe Louis Walker. Free concerts occur in the piazzas. Contact the tourist office for more information. Near Bellinzona, **Alcatraz** (tel. 859 31 34), the biggest dance club in Ticino, brings in disco tykes and tycoons. Take the train to nearby Riazzino, but hurry, Cinderella—the club closes at 3am, but the last train runs at midnight. Taxis are available but exorbitant.

■ Near Bellinzona: San Bernardino Pass

A short bus ride from Bellinzona, the San Bernardino Pass leads into the heart of the Alps, tunneling through rock, twisting around horn-honking curves, and crossing deep river gorges. San Bernardino village is practically bite-sized, a tiny collection of lichen-roofed houses and minuscule churches. Though slightly marred by ugly modern ski chalets, the surrounding hills and craggy peaks give a taste of the beauty to come. The weather-beaten, snow-capped peaks conjure images of age-old struggles—one pictures long rope-trains of hikers with their wool hats and leather straps, or one grabs for an old copy of Hemingway, a Baedeker, and a swig of whisky. Hiking and biking through this romantic playland reveal vistas and natural wonders that will put a swing in anyone's stride. Several hikes lead up to the village of **Ospizio** and the **San Bernardino Pass** (2065m). The easiest route is along the road past the Capanna Genziana for 1½ hours. The trails through the taiga and Alpine trees are only sporadically marked by white and red paint marks or posts, so maps are a must. The shores of the pure Alpine **Lago Moesola,** a congregation point for cyclists and hikers, await, as do commanding views of the valley. A small restaurant marks the village of Ospizio, where you can refuel and exchange stories with other hikers. A postal bus travels on to **Thusis** (22SFr); from there, catch a train to **Chur** (12.20SFr). Or keep on truckin'—the valley seems to go on forever.

The San Bernardino **tourist office** (tel. (091) 832 12 14) has maps and information on hiking and skiing. (Open Mon.-Fri. 8:30am-noon and 2-5pm, Sat.-Sun. 8:30am-noon.) From the bus stop, walk straight 10m, take the first left, and walk straight on this road (there are no street names) for 200m. The tourist office is on the left. Grab a pizza (12SFr) at **Ristorante Pizzeria Postiglione** (tel. 832 12 14) at the bus stop (open Tues.-Sun. 9:30am-10pm), or stock up on trail mix at the **Satellite Denner.** Go right from the bus stop—in the opposite direction from the tourist office—and the Satellite supermarket is 100m away on your left. (Open Mon.-Fri. 8:30am-noon and 3-6:30pm, Sat. 8:30am-noon and 2-5:30pm.) Bushed after a long climb from Bellinzona? The Alpine hut **Capanna Genziana** (tel. (091) 832 12 04) has Spartan rooms with bunk beds. To reach the hut, continue past Denner over a small stream and bear left, then bear right at the next intersection and follow the signs to the San Bernardino Pass. The hut is on your right. (Dorms 25SFr, half-pension 35SFr.)

GRAUBÜNDEN (GRISONS)

The largest, least populous, and most Alpine of the Swiss cantons, Graubünden's remote valleys and snow-clad peaks are bound to bring out the wild-hearted, lusting-for-life yodeler in everyone. Deep, rugged gorges, forests of larch and fir, and eddying rivers imbue the region with a wildness seldom found in ultra-civilized Switzerland. The area is also a microcosm of Swiss cultural heterogeneity—from valley to valley the language changes from German to Romansch to Italian, with a wide range of dialects in between. Though only 1-2% of the country converses in the ancient Romansch tongue, it is a fiercely preserved subject in schools and books—especially hymnals—and is recognized as an official language, whereas Swiss-German is not.

Once a summer visiting spot, the region was changed forever by the St. Moritz hotel pioneer Johannes Badrutt in 1864. The innkeeper made a bet with four British summer visitors: if they came back in the winter and didn't like it, he would pay their travel costs from London and back. If they did like it, he'd let them stay as long as they wanted, *for free*. Alas, that was the last of cheap housing in Graubünden. This region may be the Switzerland of Heidi, but it is now also a point of mountain pilgrimage for Hollywood celebrities and royal families. Yet the environs retain their original untamed nature—once you step off the beaten (gilded?) track.

Travel around the Graubünden is made easier with the **Graubünden Regional Pass,** which allows 5 days of unlimited travel in a 15-day period and a 50% discount on the other days (140SFr, children 16 and under 70SFr), or three days of unlimited travel in a seven-day period and a 50% discount on the other days (110SFr, children 55SFr). The Regional Pass is issued only in Switzerland from May through October. The ubiquitous **Swisspass** is valid as well. Visitors should plan excursions carefully in this part of the country—high season, when reservations are absolutely required, runs December to mid-April and peaks again in July and August. In May and early June, virtually everything shuts down as locals take their own vacations.

Chur

The capital of Graubünden, Chur is perhaps Switzerland's oldest settlement. Chur was a thriving religious and commercial center as early as AD 400 when the Romans established the town as a key checkpoint on the north-south passageway. Today the city is important as a transportation hub, shuffling visitors on to other points.

From the Ticino, **postal buses** run between Chur and **Bellinzona** (5 per day, 2½hr., 50SFr plus 5SFr reservation fee). Chur connects to the rest of Switzerland by rail through **Zurich** (every 30min., 1½hr., 37SFr), and direct trains also link Chur with **Basel** (every hr., 2½hr., 59SFr), **Disentis** (for the **Furka-Oberalp line;** every hr., 2½hr., 25SFr), **Arosa** (every hr., 1hr., 11.40SFr), **St. Gallen** (every hr., 1½hr., 32SFr), and **St. Moritz** (every hr., 2hr., 39SFr). The **train station** provides **currency exchange** (open daily 5:40am-9:15pm), **luggage storage** (5SFr), and **bike rental** (22SFr at the baggage check; open daily 5:40am-9:15pm), and **lockers** (2SFr). Chur's **tourist office,** Grabenstr. 5 (tel. 252 18 18; fax 252 90 76), finds rooms for a 2SFr fee. From the train station, walk to the left and up Bahnhofstr.; at the second intersection (Postpl.), turn left on Grabenstr. (Open Mon.-Tues. 1:30-6pm, Wed.-Fri. 8:30am-noon and 1:30-6pm, Sat. 9am-noon.) Graubünden's **regional tourist office,** Alexanderstr. 24 (tel. 254 24 24; fax 254 24 00), is located in Chur and brims with brochures for every city in the canton. From the station, go down Bahnhofstr. and turn left on Alexanderstr. (Open Mon.-Fri. 8am-noon and 1:30-5:30pm.) **English-language books** await at F. Schuler, Gäuggelistr. (Open Mon. 1-6:30pm, Tues.-Thurs. 8:30am-6:30pm, Fri. 8:30am-9pm, Sat. 8:30am-4pm.) In an **emergency,** dial 117. **Check email** at Millennium on Untereg. (5SFr per 15min.). Chur's **postal code** is CH-7000. Its **telephone code** is 081.

Few tourists spend any amount of time in Chur, so budget accommodations are few and far between. The *Jugendherberge* has fled in hopes of a better life in youth hostel heaven. On the outskirts of the old town, high-altitude **Hotel Rosenhügel,** Malixerstr. 32 (tel./fax 252 23 88), offers warm beds and panoramic views. From the train station (15min.), head right, and then take Engadinstr. (even as it becomes Grabenstr.) to the intersection. Continue on Malizerstr. (the inclined road), and the hotel is five minutes away on your right. (Reception 8am-midnight. Singles 45-50SFr; doubles 90SFr, with shower 100SFr, with shower and toilet 120SFr. Breakfast and parking included. Visa, MC, AmEx.) If you've got a tent buried somewhere in your backpack, try **Camp Au Chur,** Felsenaustr. (tel. 284 22 83). The riverside site features a large sports complex featuring tennis and swimming. Take bus #2: "Obere Au" then walk past the sports complex cash registers, and hang a left on the gravel path; the campsite is a five-minute walk from there. (12.40SFr; 2 people 15.70SFr. You must have your own tent.) The **Co-op Center** market, at the corner of Alexanderstr. and Quaderstr. off Bahnfhofstr., mimics fine dining with a café of its own. (Open Mon.-Thurs. 8am-6:30pm, Fri. 8am-9pm, Sat. 8am-5pm.) Cross-town rival **Migros,** at the corner of Gäuggelistr. and Gürtelstr., off Engadinstr., offers much of the same. (Open Mon.-Thurs. 8am-6:30pm, Fri. 8am-9pm, Sat. 8am-5pm.) Hit the alternative scene at **Shoarma-Grill,** Untereg. 5 (tel. 252 73 22), packed with twenty-somethings, painted sheets, world music, and alternative beats. (Kebabs 8SFr; falafel with veggies 7SFr; beers from 3.50SFr. Open Mon.-Fri. 11:45am-2pm and 5pm-midnight, Sat. 11:45am-midnight, Sun. 11:45am-10pm.) For all Chur's lack of flavor, a surprisingly lively young crowd takes over the town by night.

If your train's delayed for an hour or two, wander into the town center; Chur's sights are all within walking distance of the town's center. The highlight, a 12th-century Romanesque **cathedral** at the top of the old town, boasts eight altarpieces in addition to the **Hochaltar,** a flamboyant 15th-century masterpiece of gold and wood. The security alarm seems rather ridiculous, since only a determined elephant could lift the thing. Paradisiacal flora adorn the nave ceiling while gruesome infernal beasts gnaw on wide-eyed sinners on the columns. When services end, tour groups invade. The crypts, where the Capuchin martyr St. Fidelis is buried, also house the **Dom-museum** (tel. 252 92 50), replete with relics. (Open Tues.-Sat. 10am-noon and

2-4pm. You must request the key at Hofstr. 2.) The **Martinskirche** downstairs counters the cathedral's grandiose flair with understated simplicity: the church's sole decorations are three stained-glass windows by Augusto Giacometti. The eerie panels depict the birth of an oddly beefy Christ. Clad in blood-red instead of her usual blue, Mary stares with wide, alien eyes beside her thoroughly befuddled husband. Chur's **Bündner Kunstmuseum** (tel. 257 28 68), at the corner of Bahnhofstr. and Grabenstr., gathers the canton's treasures, including an impressive collection drawn from the three Giacomettis: Giovanni, Alberto, and Augusto. (Open Tues.-Wed. and Fri.-Sun. 10am-noon and 2-5pm, Thurs. 10am-noon and 2-8pm. 10SFr, students 7SFr.)

■ Arosa

Once a simple farming village, Arosa was transformed by a certain Dr. Herwig's "discovery" of the area's salutary climate in 1888. Since then, Arosa has metamorphosed twice: first into a spa for the treatment of tuberculosis and then into a skiing and hiking mecca. Just below craggy peaks and granite slopes at the end of an Alpine valley, the town has outstanding views and clean air. Arosa's mountain peaks barely dip under 2000m, and the tallest, the **Weisshorn,** towers 2653m above sea level. Hiking the landscape, skiing the slopes, lolling in the sun next to a mountain stream, and sipping cappuccino on an outdoor terrace are all acceptable activities in this mile-high village. For those affected by vertigo, Arosa's 25km of cross-country ski trails, ice rinks, indoor tennis courts, and swimming pools are perfect winter treats. Best of all, Arosa is a little less glitzy and glamorous than its sister resorts in the Engadin Valley.

Orientation and Practical Information Arosa's pink **tourist office**, Poststr. (tel. 377 51 51; fax 377 31 35), in front of the truly weird moving-eyeball fountain, can help arrange ski lessons and hiking trips and makes free hotel reservations. Head right from the station and then take the first right onto Poststr. A free bus shuttles visitors from the newsstand to the tourist office two stops away at "Kursaal." (Open Dec. 7-April 13 Mon.-Fri. 9am-6pm, Sat. 9am-5:30pm, Sun. 10am-noon and 4-5:30pm; April 14-Dec. 6 Mon.-Fri. 8am-noon and 2-6pm, Sat. 8am-1pm; June 29-Aug. 17 also open Sat. 2-4pm.) Secluded Arosa is accessible by **train** only by way of a scenic route from **Chur** (every hr., 1hr., 11.40SFr). **Parking** is free in the summer at the **Parking Garage Obersee,** but the rates are steep during ski season. Beware—a strict traffic ban has been imposed from midnight to 6am every night. Climb on board the **free public bus,** which stops at the Hörnli and Prätschli ski lifts, the Untersee, the train station, and everywhere in between. The **train station** provides **currency exchange** (Mon.-Sat. 5:30am-8:05pm, Sun. 6:30am-8:05pm), **lockers** (2SFr), and **bike rental** (22SFr). In an **emergency**, dial 117. The **post office** is in Arosa's main square, to the right of the train station. (Open Mon.-Fri. 7:45am-noon and 1:45-6:30pm, Sat. 8-11am.) The **postal code** is CH-7050, and the **telephone code** is 081.

Accommodations and Food Arosa's hotels tend to demand high prices for "Bliss at 1800 Meters," but there are a number of budget options. Arriving in town without reservations is a big no-no. Most places, including the ones listed below, set arbitrary opening dates, so it's impossible to foretell what's open when. **Reserve up to a year in advance for prime ski-season vacation spots.** The **Jugendherberge (HI),** Seewaldstr. (tel./fax 377 13 97), has a friendly, multilingual staff. Walk right from the station, take the first right onto Poststr., go past the tourist office, and bear left down the hill (you'll see a sign). Or take the free bus from the newsstand, get off two stops later at "Kursaal," continue past the tourist office, and bear left down the hill. The pale yellow building has uncanny automatic lighting and 100 cozy beds in six-bed honeymoon suites. Be sure to stock up on 0.50SFr coins for the shower. (Reception daily 7-10am and 5-10pm. No lockout. Curfew 10pm; key available. Dorms 24SFr; doubles 58SFr; triples 87SFr; quads 116SFr. High season (Dec. 26-Jan. 10, Feb. to mid-March, and Easter week): 36SFr; 92SFr; 138SFr; 184SFr. Sheets and hearty breakfast included. Bag lunch 7.50SFr; dinner 12SFr. Open mid-June to mid-Oct. and mid-Dec. to mid-April.) Hidden up in the woods, **Pension Suveran** (tel. 377 19 69; fax 377 19 75) is the quiet, homey, wood-paneled chalet that you came to Switzerland to find. To the right of the Co-op, head up the small walkway to the left. At the top, turn right and follow the sign up the gravel path. (Singles 47SFr; doubles 84SFr. Winter: 58SFr; 106SFr. Add 5SFr in summer and 10SFr in winter for stays of less than 3 nights. Breakfast included.) **Hotel Garni Haus Am Wald** (tel./fax 377 31 38), behind the train station and 150m to the left of the Weisshornbahn, offers clean, bright rooms and a small café downstairs. Call ahead to verify that they're accepting guests. (Singles 45-55SFr, doubles 90-104SFr. Winter: 70-80SFr; 120-140SFr.) **Camping Arosa** (tel. 377 17 45; fax 377 30 05) is open year-round in a brook-babbling valley and offers showers and cooking facilities. (7.30-8.30SFr plus tax, children 4-4.50SFr; tents 4.50SFr.) For a tasty and scenic meal, head to **Orelli's Restaurant,** Poststr. (tel. 377 12 08), after the post office and before the tourist office. Hikers young and old chomp happily in this panoramic family restaurant decorated with Mickey Mouse and stained glass. Thriftmeisters can eat soup and four slices of bread for only 4.50SFr. A special vegetarian *menu* (14-17SFr), salad buffet (6-14SFr), and warm entrees (10-16SFr) round out your options. (Open daily 7:30am-9pm. Closed May and Nov. Visa, MC.) **Café/Restaurant Oasis** (tel. 377 22 20), diagonally across the street from Orelli's, has an outdoor deck just over Poststr., good for people-watching and mountain-gazing. Entrees include spaghetti *bolognese* with parmesan for 11SFr, spaghetti and tomato sauce with parmesan 11SFr, or chicken *cordon bleu* with fries for 15SFr. (Open daily 8:30am-11pm; May-June and Sept.-Nov. closed Sun.) Get groceries at the **Co-op,** before the tourist office on Poststr. (open Mon.-Fri. 8am-12:30pm and 2-6:30pm, Sat. 8am-4pm), or **Denner**

Superdiscount in the main square (open Mon.-Wed. and Fri. 8:30am-12:15pm and 2:30-6:30pm, Sat. 8:30am-12:15pm and 1:15-4pm).

Skiing, Hiking, and Entertainment Fourteen **ski lifts and cableways** hoist skiers to the 70km network of slopes in the Arosa-Tschuggen ski area. Ticket offices in Arosa seem to love making **passes** (day passes, morning passes, afternoon passes, 1½-day passes, "choose-your-day" passes, etc.). The town offers passes for all 14 lifts and cableways (49SFr per day, 239SFr for 1 week, and 362SFr for 2); for those with small children in need of a little practice, the smaller Tschuggen-sector day pass is 30SFr. Children under 15 ski for half-price; young people 16-19 get a 15% discount.

When the snow melts, spring brings golf courses and flower-covered **hiking** paths, with over 200km available for rambling and prancing. An Alpine guide leads seven- and nine-hour hikes at beginning, intermediate, and advanced levels for only 10SFr. (Mid-June to mid-Oct. Tues.-Thurs. Contact the tourist office for details.) For a mellow hike below treeline, start at the hill right of the Co-op and cruise along the ridge overlooking the Obersee to the small town of Maran, where you can catch a bus back to Arosa (1hr.). The comprehensive system of **cable cars** test the valley's upper reaches. The **Weisserhornbahn** cable-car departs behind the train station and whisks travelers to the top of the Weisserhorn (every 15min., 9SFr, round-trip 30SFr, 30% off with Swisspass). From the 2653m summit, you can gaze upon all of the Engadin, even back to San Bernardino. Several splendid trails (usually 2-2½hr.) lead down to Arosa. For more snow-capped peaks than you can shake a walking stick at, follow the yellow signs down along the ridge to the **Hörnli-Express** (1½hr., 24SFr, round-trip 30SFr, 30% reduction with Swisspass, free to Arosa with Weisshornbahn ticket).

For the more sedentary, the fish of the Obersee and local rivers bite friskily. (Permits at the tourist office; day 25SFr, week 65SFr, 2 weeks 100SFr, month 125SFr.) The Untersee's **free beach** welcomes swimmers and sunbathers. The **1997 International Jazz Festival** grooves in late July with free admission to various local venues. The festival features New Orleans jazz played by American, Swiss, Australian, and English bands. Previous performers include Tuba Fats and Jambalaya.

▩ Davos

A famed vacation venue, Davos challenges St. Moritz's title as the ski and spa capital of Graubünden. Settled in 1289 by the Wallisers, Davos emerged as a health resort in the 19th century and quickly became a finely tuned ski center. Now, while most ski resorts feel as remote as their host mountains, Alpine Davos maintains a cosmopolitan atmosphere while maintaining a pleasing blend of town and country.

Orientation and Practical Information Davos is easily accessible from the rest of Switzerland by **train** through **Chur** via Landquart (every hr., 1½hr., 26SFr) or **Klosters** (8.40SFr) on the Rhätischebahn lines. The town is divided into two areas, **Davos-Dorf** and **Davos-Platz**, each with its own train station and linked by the long **Promenade**. Davos-Dorf is closer to most hotels and the Bergbahn, while Davos-Platz holds the tourist office and the main post office. An intra-city **bus** (2SFr, with Swisspass 1SFr) runs between the two train stations and stops near major hotels and the hostel on the Davosersee. Drivers to Davos can find many **parking lots** along the Promenade and Talstr. but should be aware the Promenade traffic is one-way west (parking generally 1SFr per hr.; free at Kongresszentrum). The high-tech **main tourist office,** Promenade 67 (tel. 415 21 21; fax 415 21 00), in Davos-Platz, plans skiing and hiking packages and helps find rooms. Walk up the hill to the right of the Davos-Platz train station and then right along the Promenade for five minutes. The tourist office is on the left. A smaller **branch** office, across from the Davos-Dorf train station, also offers information and calls hotels. (Both offices open June 22-Sept. 28 and Dec.-April 15 Mon.-Fri. 8:30am-6pm, Sat. 8:30am-4pm; April 16-June 21 Mon.-Fri. 8:30am-12:30pm and 1:45-6pm, Sat. 8:30am-12:30pm;

Sept. 30-Dec. 1 Mon.-Fri. 8:30am-12:30pm and 1:45-6pm, Sat. 8:30am-12:30pm and 1:45-4pm.) Both train stations **exchange currency** (open daily 7am-8pm), **store luggage** (5SFr; at Platz Mon.-Sat. 4:30am-8pm, Sun. 5:30am-8pm; at Dorf daily 6:50am-9pm), and rent **lockers** (2SFr). Rent **bikes** at the Davos-Dorf station (23SFr per day) or the hostel (see below). The main **post office** is in Davos-Platz at Promenade 43. (Open Mon.-Fri. 7:45am-6pm, Sat. 8:30am-11pm.) The **postal code** is CH-7270. The **telephone code** is 081.

Accommodations and Food Wherever you stay, ask for the Davos **visitor's card,** which grants unlimited travel on the city's buses and reduced tickets for plays, concerts, ice rinks, swimming pools, and golf courses. The **Jugendherberge Höhwald (HI)** (tel. 416 14 84; fax 416 50 55) in Davos-Wolfgang has seen its share of ski seasons. Take the bus (dir: Davos-Wolfgang): "Hochgebirgsklinik," backtrack 100m, and turn left; or head right from the Davos-Dorf train station and walk 30 minutes along the Davosersee. The old house sits directly on the Davosersee and has a large front porch and swimming dock. The gorgeous bamboo and green wood dining room looks far too elegant for a hostel—but don't worry! Fourteen sardine-like beds in each dorm room reassure with the sweet smell of roommates. (Reception 8-11am and 5-9pm. No lockout. No curfew. Quiet time from 10:30pm. Dorms 22.70SFr first night, then 20.20SFr; doubles 56.40SFr, 51.40SFr. Winter: 23.10SFr, 20.60SFr; 57.40SFr, 52.20SFr. Family rooms available. Sheets, showers, and breakfast included. Kitchen facilities 2SFr. Bag lunch or dinner 11SFr. Bike rental 12SFr per day. Closed April 22-June 7 and Oct. 24-Dec. 13.) Spic-'n'-span lodgings beckon from **Hotel Edelweiss,** Rosswiedstr. 9 (tel. 416 10 33; fax 416 11 30), in Davos-Dorf. Head left on Bahnhofstrassedorf, turn right on Mühlestr., turn left on Dorfstr., walk 10 minutes, then turn right on Bohbahnstr. and left on Rossweidstr. This huge old house pampers skiers and hikers with a big-screen TV, a heart-filled dining room, and pretty wallpapered bedrooms. (Reception daily 7am-10pm. Singles 45-87SFr; doubles 80-170SFr. Winter: 50-105SFr; 96-170SF. Breakfast included. Visa, MC, AmEx. Closed April-June 15.) The **Sportzentrum Davos,** Talstr. 41 (tel. 415 36 36; fax 415 36 37), just opened a large, spotless, locker-roomish dormitory with shocking color schemes (brown, chartreuse, blue, and orange) and airy balconies overlooking the tracks. (Reception daily 7am-midnight. If no one's at the desk, check in at the restaurant downstairs. Dorms 42SFr; doubles 100SFr. Breakfast included. Guests skate free at the ice rink.) **Camping Färich** (tel. 416 10 43) in Davos-Dorf is a four-star facility relatively close to the ski lifts and attractions of the town. Take bus #1 (dir: Pischa): "Stilli." (5-7SFr, children half-price; tents 6SFr. Open May 18-Sept. 29.)

Haven't had your *Rösti* fix for the day yet? Shame on you. Visit **Röstizzeria,** Promenade 128 (tel. 416 33 23), and satisfy your craving for 14.50SFr and up in a dining room decorated with carved wood and Japanese fans. (Open Mon.-Sat. 5pm-midnight, Sun. 11am-2pm and 5pm-midnight.) The bright, flowery, locally beloved **Café-Konditorei Weber,** Promenade 148 (tel. 410 11 22), in Davos-Dorf, offers colorful and friendly service to match. Choose from the daily *menu,* which includes at least one vegetarian dish (10-18SFr), or order à la carte (from 11SFr). (Open daily 6:30am-7pm.) Grab a Bud and a bar stool—American style—at **Café Carlo's,** Promenade 58 (tel. 413 17 22), in Davos-Platz across from the tourist office. The café offers a daily *menu* (13-16SFr), salad (6-14SFr), sandwiches (10-14SFr), and pasta (13-18SFr) under the gaze of a Mona Lisa in the corner. (Open daily 8am-midnight. Visa, MC, AmEx.) For a local hole in the wall, try **Restaurant Helvetia,** Talstr. 12 (tel. 413 56 44), a 10-minute walk out of the train station and to the right. Adorned with sports memorabilia and oddities (look for the New Hampshire "Davos" vanity plate), the restaurant serves up spaghetti (9.50SFr) and *Kalbswurst* with *Rösti* (14SFr). (Open Mon.-Sat. 10am-2pm and 5pm-midnight.) For hiking snacks, stop by **Migros** on the Promenade in both Davos-Dorf (open Mon.-Fri. 8:30am-12:30pm and 1:30-6:30pm, Sat. 8am-4pm) and Davos-Platz (open Mon.-Fri. 8:30am-6:30pm, Sat. 8am-4pm). A brand-spankin'-new **Co-op** with a restaurant should open by 1998 to the

Luge Much?

Before the advent of spandex uni-suits and titanium, flying down mountains was a very simple affair. As early as 1883, the natives of Arosa increasingly found their rustic sleds missing and the hills outside the town sprinkled with very bored and very insane recovering English invalids. These dashing chaps officially brought the sport of tobogganing to Switzerland in 1883 when they started the Davos Tobogganing club and inaugurated the famed Cresta Run. Among the many innovations tested on the Arosa hills were iron runners and the head-first plunge technique. A quote from *The Bystander* in 1905 perhaps summed it up best: "Tobogganing itself is absurd. It glories in being absurd."

right of the train station on Bahnhofpl.—if not, blame the construction company and leave us out of it.

Sights and Entertainment Davos provides direct access to three mountains—the **Parsenn, Schatzalp,** and **Jakobshorn**—and five **skiing areas,** covering every degree of difficulty. **Day passes** start at 25SFr for the Schatzalp and go all the way to 46SFr for the Jakobshorn. **Regional ski passes** are available for the Davos-Klosters area, including unlimited travel on most transport facilities (2 days 113SFr, 1 week 259SFr). Comprehensive information and maps are available at the tourist office. (Jakobshorn ascent 23SFr, descent 20SFr, round-trip 27SFr. Schatzalp 10SFr, 8SFr, 12SFr.) In addition to downhill runs, Davos boasts 75km of **cross-country trails** throughout the valley, including a trail flood-lit at night and a trail on which dogs are allowed. **The Swiss Ski School of Davos,** Promenade 157 (tel. 416 24 54; fax 416 59 51 for information and booking), offers lessons, starting at 30SFr for a half-day downhill lesson and at 55SFr for a half-day snowboard lesson. Europe's largest natural **ice rink** (22,000 sq. m; tel. 415 36 00) reserves space for figure skating, ice dancing, hockey, speed skating, and curling (5SFr; skate rental at the rink).

Davos does not wilt when the snow melts. In the summer the town offers indoor/outdoor **swimming pools** with sauna and solarium (6.50SFr, students 4.50SFr), and of course, the **Davosersee,** in which you can swim and fish and on which you can sail and windsurf. The tourist office handles fishing permits (day 73SFr, week 211SFr, month 447SFr). Davos's snowless slopes uncover a web of over 450km of **hiking** trails. The exquisite mountains engulfing the area provide views deep into the Dolomites and all along the valley. One possible day hike begins at the top of Jakobshorn (2590m) and traverses a ridge over Jatzhorn (2682m) to Tällifurgga (2568m). Or meander down the velvety green ski slopes to the village of Sertig Dörfli. The hike from the summit to Sertig Dörfli takes three hours, and the walk from there, down the Sertigal valley, to Davos-Platz is another two and a half hours. The last Saturday in July brings the **Swiss Alpine Marathon,** a grueling 67km mountain race.

A hike (or funicular ride) up to the Schatzalp reveals the **Alpine Garden** with 800 different species of plants. (Open mid-May to Sept. daily 9am-5pm. 3SFr. Guided tours in German every Mon. at 2pm—other languages by arrangement.) Once you've finished exercising your muscles, exercise your eyes at the **Davos Kirchner Museum** (tel. 413 22 02), the frosted glass structure across from the grand Hotel Belvedere on the Promenade, which houses an extensive collection of Ernst Ludwig Kirchner's artwork. This avatar of early 20th-century German Expressionism lived in Davos for nearly 20 years before his death, and is buried in the Davos cemetery. (Museum open July 15-Sept. Tues.-Sun. 10am-noon. 7SFr, students 4SFr. Exhibitions open Tues.-Sun. 10am-noon and 2-6pm. 9SFr, 6SFr.) Davos's **Heimatmuseum** (tel. 416 17 82), on Museumstr. behind the train station in Davos-Dorf, displays a collection of centuries-old furniture and crafts of the Graubünden region. (Open June to mid-Oct. and Jan. to mid-April Wed., Fri., and Sun. 4-6pm, or by appointment.)

■ Klosters

Across the Gotschna and Parsenn mountains lies Davos's sister ski resort, Klosters. Though a smaller, more subdued town, Klosters doesn't suffer in Davos' shadow. The charming and surprisingly mellow town draws just as many skiers and, as a four-star resort, its share of royals. But while Davos makes an extra effort to be a city, Klosters keeps a low profile—even its upper-crust hotels look like unassuming Swiss chalets. Aromas from five-star restaurants mingle with the sweet smell of hay from barns just down the road. Mercedes roll down the street next to tractors.

Like Davos, Klosters is divided into **Klosters-Platz** and **Klosters-Dorf,** connected by a 20-minute walk, a 5-minute bus ride, or a 3-minute train ride. There are **tourist offices** in both Platz and Dorf, but the **main tourist office** is in Klosters-Platz (tel. 410 20 20; fax 410 20 10). From the train station, walk to the right, make a right at the Co-op, and cross the street to the building with the "i." The friendly staff can help locate lodgings, suggest hikes, and **exchange currency.** They also plan ski packages with the ski school and offer the **Klosters guest card** (also available at hotels), valid for bargain tickets to events and reduced admission to local facilities. (Open May-Nov. Mon.-Fri. 8:30am-noon and 2:30-6:30pm, Sat. 8am-noon and 2:30-5pm; Dec.-April Mon.-Fri. 8am-noon and 2-6pm, Sat. 8:30am-noon and 2-6pm, Sun. 9:30am-noon and 2:30-6:30pm.) **Trains** arrive in Klosters-Platz and Klosters-Dorf, from **Chur** through Landquart (every hr., 1hr., 18.20SFr) and **St. Moritz** (every hr., 2hr., 32SFr). The local **bus** runs between Dorf and Platz and the major ski lifts (1-6 stops 1SFr, 7-10 2SFr, more than 10 3SFr; free with guest card). **Parking** is free in summer; in winter, get a public parking card (8 days 20SFr, 16 days 40SFr, 1 month 80SFr) from the tourist office or the local **police** (tel. 422 35 33). The Klosters-Platz **train station** provides **currency exchange** (open daily 6am-8:30pm), **lockers** (2SFr), and **luggage storage** (open daily 6am-7pm; 3SFr). The **postal code** is CH-7250. The **telephone code** is 081.

Like everything else in Klosters, the **Jugendherberge Soldanella (HI),** Talstr. 73 (tel. 422 13 16; fax 422 52 09), is quietly elegant, laid back, and unassuming. Head right from the Klosters-Platz train station, bear left at the rotary, turn right on Talstr., and hike 10 minutes uphill. Run by a friendly and knowledgeable family, this massive renovated chalet with wood paneling and a flagstone terrace treats guests to a view of the Madrisa and distant glaciers. (Reception daily 7-9:30am and 5-10pm. No lockout, no curfew. Quiet time from 10pm. Dorms 25.50SFr first night, then 23SFr; doubles 36.50SFr, 34SFr. Family rooms available. Add 1.90SFr tax per day in summer; in winter 2.20SFr. Sheets, shower, and breakfast included. Dinner 11SFr. Closed May to mid-June and Nov. to mid-Dec. Visa, MC, AmEx.) **Gasthaus Casanna,** Landstr. 171 (tel. 422 12 29; fax 422 62 78), offers pink-flowered comforters that clash with the brown carpeting and lamps, and a smoky restaurant that serves diverse fondues (20-30SFr). (Singles 45SFr; doubles 60SFr. Winter: 60SFr, 120SFr. Breakfast included.) Better yet, choose from the list of **private rooms** starting at 15SFr (list at the tourist office).

Pretend you aren't a budget backpacker for a few hours at **Chesa Grischuna,** Bahnhofstr. 12 (tel. 422 22 22), to the right of the Klosters-Platz train station. They serve some pricey meat dishes, but if you stick to the cheeses and salads, you can still leave sated and financially solvent: cheese plate 8SFr, salads 9-16SFr, soups and sandwiches 9-12SFr, vegetarian plate 18.50SFr. Make reservations during winter—even the celebrities who come here have to phone in advance. (Open daily 7am-11pm, or until the last person leaves; hot meals served 11:30am-9:30pm. Visa, MC, AmEx. Closed May and Nov.) **À Porta,** Bahnhofstr. 22 (tel. 422 14 96), at Landstr., is a 70-year-old, family-run restaurant and bakery that serves fresh pizzas (from 12SFr) and *Rösti* with ham and onions (14.50SFr). **Tasty bakery** serves sugary treats and fresh bread. (Open daily 7:30am-10:30pm; Nov. and May-June closed Mon.-Tues. Bakery open daily 10:30am-6:30pm.) If all this non-budget food will require several nights on lovely park-bench accommodations, visit the **Co-op,** halfway to the train station, for sustenance. Get cheap groceries, or chow down at the restaurant upstairs on *spaghetti Napoli* for 8SFr. (Open Mon.-Fri. 8am-12:30pm and 2-6:30pm, Sat. 8am-4pm.)

One words sums up entertainment in Klosters: plastics. Er... **skiing.** Klosters has some of the best skiing in Switzerland, with 315km of trails stretching from the city into the neighboring Davos mountains. **Ski passes** for the Klosters-Davos region run 113SFr for two days and 288SFr for one week (includes public transportation). For the Klosters area, a Grotschna-Parsenn-Strela/Schatzalp-Madrisa one-day ticket goes for 52SFr, one week 246SFr. The **ski school** in Klosters, conveniently located in the tourist office, offers ski and snowboard lessons for children and adults. (Class instruction from 40-50SFr per day; call 410 20 28 the day before to book private lessons.) All this skiing combines with 40km of **cross-country trails,** an **ice rink,** and **sled runs** to make Klosters a winter *Wunderland*. From early July to early October, the **mountain cable car** to the **Madrisa** provides a means to explore the peaks all the way into Austria. (Ascent 15SFr, descent 10SFr, round-trip 18SFr.)

Klosters offers plenty of bang for your shoe leather, even for the less ambitious. In the summer, the tourist office has an extensive list of **hiking** suggestions, with exact directions, elevation levels, anticipated times, and a trail map. To start, the **Gotschna-bahn** cable car whisks you up to Gotschnagrat (2285m) for incredible views of the Silvrettagletscher, Klosters, and the quintessentially Swiss valley embracing the village. Take a leisurely three-hour walk down to Klosters, crossing the ski runs just below the striking, jagged peak (Casanna Alp). Drop below treeline and follow the signs to Serneuser Schwendi and Klosters. Got vertigo? Stay closer to the luscious green valley floor and make a large loop, going from the Klosters Protestant church up-valley on Monbielstr. to Monbiel. Loop again around toward the left and follow the signs to Pt. 487 and Monbieler Wald. The trail ends at the Alpenrösli restaurant, from where you can grab Talstr. back to the hostel. **Guided tours** (tel. 422 23 23) include accommodations, breakfast, and dinner and start at 55SFr for one and a half days and 80SFr for two days. (Hikes typically 4-5hr. per day; bring your passport. Advance booking recommended.) The **Klosters Adventure Program** offers guided hikes and mountain tours, canyonning, horseback riding, river rafting, glacier walks, canoeing, mountain-bike tours, paragliding, and more every weekday mid-June to mid-October. Most events are free or discounted for Adventure hotel guests; the Adventure hotels include Jugendherberge Soldanella (see below). (Guided hikes 15SFr with guest card, free for Adventure hotel guests. River rafting 135SFr, 130SFr. Canoeing 145SFr, 140SFr. Mountain bike tours 15SFr, free.)

Engadin Valley

Swiss downhill-skiing connoisseurs often rate the Engadin Valley behind the Jungfrau and Matterhorn regions—still a glowing compliment, since Switzerland's skiing outranks almost everything anywhere else. But not so fast—hiking here will make you swoon, too. The trails lead you away from the valley's resort facade and into the Swiss wilderness. Whether you're out for a stroll along a babbling brook or scaling ancient glaciers, the Engadin delivers beauty and adventure. Most local tourist offices provide excellent hiking tips and maps. Perched proudly at the center of Upper Engadin, glitzy and glamorous St. Moritz is the hub of the Valley. Either St. Moritz or Maloja, the only two villages with youth hostels, make good bases for day-tripping to the other villages in the valley. The regional culinary specialties please many a visiting tummy. *Capuns,* ham and potato wrapped in leaves, runs from 9 to 18SFr. Famous throughout Switzerland (and deservedly so) is the **Engadin torte,** a variation on the simple nutcake found only in a lone Pontresina bakery (see p. 448). Candied almonds and raisins top multiple layers of cream and nut puree. Yum.

Three hundred and fifty kilometers of **ski trails** and 60 **ski lifts** lace the lower Graubünden, and thousands of ski bunnies gather here each year. Unlike Zermatt and the Jungfrau regions, where Japanese and American tourists abound, the Engadin valley attracts mostly German and Swiss visitors to its trails, making it not-as-kitschy but also not-as-convenient, since information in English is often difficult to get in smaller towns. Ski rental is standard throughout the region (downhill 35-45SFr per day, cross-country 25SFr). Novices should head for **Zuoz** or **Corviglia,** experts for **Diavolezza, Corvatsch, Piz Nair,** or **Piz Lagalb** (for more information, call (081) 833 88 88 or fax 833 76 68). Anyone hoping to catch a glimpse of Hollywood should head for **St. Moritz.** Passes covering transport and T-bars for the entire area run 48SFr per day (available in St. Moritz only), 286SFr per week, 442SFr for two weeks, and 900SFr for the season (all lifts and access to indoor swimming pools). Cross-country fanatics should glide to **Pontresina,** where hundreds train for the cruel and unusual **Engadin Ski Marathon,** stretching from Maloja to Zuoz. The race takes place every year on the second Sunday in March (call (081) 842 65 73 or fax 842 65 25 for application/registration; entry fee 70SFr). **Ski schools** in just about every village offer private lessons.

MALOJA

Crown of the Upper Engadin, the village of Maloja (pop. 230; 1815m) rests on the source of the Inn River and precariously atop the 360m precipice that separates the Engadin and Bregaglia Valleys. Thirty-two kilometers from the Italian border, Maloja has Italian as its official language, and both Catholic and Protestant churches have a following here. The **tourist office** (tel. 824 31 88; fax 824 36 37) sits just beyond the youth hostel. The staff does not speak English, but you can pick up information on hikes here. (Open Mon.-Fri. 8:30am-noon and 2-6pm, Sat. 9-11am and 3-5pm; closed Sat. during low season.) **Postal buses** run between Maloja and **St. Moritz** (7am-7pm every 30min., 40min., 9SFr). The **postal code** is CH-7516. The **telephone code** is 081.

Maloja is blessed with its own **Jugendherberge (HI)** (tel. 824 32 58; fax 824 35 71), but unless you can round up a group of 10 fellow backpackers, you'll have to sleep in a tent. Walk 200m to the right from the post office. The dark wood walls and quiet yard of this former farmhouse camouflage the building—spoiled only by the big blue "Hostelling International" sign. (Reception daily 8-9am, 5-6pm, and 8-9pm. No lockout. No curfew. Quiet time starts at 10pm. Dorms 23.70SFr first night, then 21.20SFr. Non-members add 5SFr. Sheets, showers, and breakfast included. Kitchen facilities 2.50SFr. Laundry 10SFr. Open July-Oct. and Dec.-May.) **Camping TCS** (tel. 824 31 81), surprisingly close to the town center (15min.), also doubles as a windsurfing landing and beach. Cross the street from the bus stop and walk to the right. Take a left on the small street after Hotel Schweizerhaus that leads past the candy-cane church to the lake and bear left at the fork. (4.60-5.40SFr, children half-price; tents 4.20-5.30SFr. Guest tax 2SFr. Open June-Sept.) The **Alimentari** across from the post office peddles groceries. The **restaurant** at the Schweizhaus (tel. 824 34 55) churns out yummy *Capuns*. (Open daily 8am-9pm.)

On most mornings and late afternoons, the **Malojaschlange,** a stream of confused clouds, creeps over the pass and, unable to adjust to the altitude change quickly enough, occasionally takes the form of an enormous twisted snake. During most of the day, though, artist Giovanni Giacometti found he could not remember "a sun so bright and clear as shines upon the plateau of Maloja." This brightness ensnared Italian Expressionist painter Giovanni Segantini, who spent the last 15 years of his life in Maloja and was buried in the village's idyllic mountain cemetery in 1899. Private pictures, sketches, documents, and personal memorabilia are on display in the artist's refurbished studio, **Atelier Segantini.** (Open July 7-Oct. 12 Tues.-Sun. 3-5pm. 2SFr.) Construction of the **Belvedere Tower,** a 15-minute walk from the post office, began in 112 (no, that's not a typo). Today it houses various exhibits on the Engadin and Bregaglia Valleys. The observation tower provides a phenomenal panoramic view extending across the border into Italy. Here the *Malojaschlange* ruffles your hair as it blows over the valley floor. (Open daily 9am-5pm. Free.) Fauna, flora, and *Gletschermühlen* (massive glaciated potholes, some 4.6m wide and 5.5m deep) in the protected nature reserve surround the tower. The tiny reflective pools at the bottom of the *Gletschermühlen* resemble enchanted wishing wells.

ENGADIN VALLEY: ST. MORITZ ■ 443

Hiking in this region is glorious. A challenging guided walk (in German) of the **Septimer Pass** to **Juf,** the highest village in Europe, takes place every other Tuesday at 6:45am (rise and shine!), starting from the PTT station (June 25-Oct. 1; 50SFr). A guided **historical tour** leaves the Maloja tourist office for the heart of the **Bregaglia Valley** (June 20-Oct. 3 Thurs. 8am; 12SFr). In the opposite direction, a seven-hour trek over the hills to the northeast will take you through **Grevasalvas,** the village where *Heidi* was filmed, all the way to **Signal,** where you will find Heidi's hut. From there, a cable car departs for **St. Moritz.** The hike to Grevasalvas begins to the left of Aparthotel Interhomeutoring; follow the signs to Signal Cable Car. To cut this journey down to Heidi size, you can take the postal bus from Maloja (dir: St. Moritz): "Plaun da Lej" and begin there. Don't forget your dainty blonde braids.

One final, lovely hike is a bit more complicated. On the Italian frontier, 22km down the valley from Maloja, lies **Soglio,** a matchbox Swiss-Italian village with narrow, crooked streets. Soglio lies on the legendary **Panorama Highway,** a footpath that begins at **Casaccia,** just south of Maloja. The natives call the trail "the beauty of the Graubünden" with good reason. The gorgeous route follows the Bregaglia valley downstream, meandering past waterfalls, bright Alpine blossoms, and deserted Roman ruins. Views of the needlepoint peaks towering overhead alternate with tree-covered patches on the trail. You can reach Casaccia by foot (the path starts 200m to the right of the post office, across from the youth hostel) or catch the **postal bus** (every 30min., 3.60SFr). The bus goes on to Soglio (1hr., 11.40SFr; change in Promontogno). If you decide to sojourn in Soglio, **Casa Giovanoli** has rooms for the sleeping. (48SFr per person. Breakfast included. Closed Nov.-May.) At the hotel **restaurant,** mountain gourmands splurge on the magically delicious *Kartoffelkhehlein mit Steinpilzrajout* (cakes made from regional chestnut and potato flours with a mushroom cream sauce, 24SFr) or slurp spaghetti. (Open daily 6am-midnight; kitchen open daily 11:45am-10pm.)

ST. MORITZ

> *In St. Moritz are the hangers-on of the rich...the jewel thieves, the professional backgammon players and general layabouts, as well as the high-class ladies of doubtful virtue (if such a thing still exists)...*
> —Peter Viertel

St. Moritz (1856m) is one of the most famous ski resorts in the world. Chic, elegant, and exclusive, it caters to the filthy rich that Robin Leach used to crow about. This "Resort at the Top of the World" will convert almost anyone into a window-shopper, tamed by the likes of Armani, Versace, and Calvin Klein (each, incidentally, possessing his own *Wanderweg* sign). St. Moritz hosted the Olympic Games in 1928 and again in 1948, and nowadays the town offers every winter sport imaginable from world-class skiing and bobsledding to golf, polo, greyhound racing, cricket tournaments on the frozen lake, and *skikjöring*—a sport similar to water skiing in which the water is replaced by ice and the motorboat is replaced by a galloping horse.

The resort's huge **tourist office** *(Kurverein),* Via Maistra 12 (tel. 837 33 33; fax 837 33 77), beats in the heart of town. From the train station, cross the street, climb Truoch Serlas, and take Via Serla to the left past the post office. As you pass the Badrutt Palace Hotel on your left, make a right up the Réduit Passage. Emerge from the shopping arcade onto Via Maistra; the tourist office is on the right. The office provides free hotel reservations, skiing information, and advice on hiking in the smaller towns of the Engadin Valley. (Open July to mid-Sept. and mid-Dec. to mid-April Mon.-Sat. 9am-6pm; May-June and Nov. Mon-Fri. 8am-noon and 2-6pm.) From the Matterhorn to the Engadin Valley, the legendary **Glacier Express** covers the 270km to **Zermatt** in a leisurely eight-hour chug (1 per day, 142SFr, Swisspass valid), affording ample time to take in the magnificent Alpine landscapes while crossing 291 bridges and going through 91 tunnels. If you can't sit still for that long, the **Bernina Express** makes the excursion to **Tirano, Italy** (every hr., 2½hr., 27SFr, Swisspass valid). It's the only Swiss train that crosses the Alps without entering a single tunnel. Trains also run every hour to **Chur** (2hr., 39SFr), **Celerina** (5min., 2.40SFr), **Pontresina** (15min., 4.20SFr), and **Zuoz** (30min., 8.40SFr). Yellow **postal buses** (*not* the local blue buses) cover almost all the same routes as the trains. They're also your only access from the southwest tip of the Upper Engadin Valley, since St. Moritz is the railway terminus. Buses run twice every hour to **Silvaplana** (15min., 3.60SFr), **Sils** (20min., 6SFr), and **Maloja** (40min., 9SFr), departing from the left of the train station. The **train station** provides **currency exchange** (open daily 6:50am-8:10pm), **luggage storage** (5SFr; open daily 7:30am-6:15pm), **bike rental** (22SFr per day; open daily 7:30am-6:15pm), and **lockers** (2SFr). In an **emergency**, call 111. The **post office** is located on Via Serla. (Open Mon.-Fri. 7:45am-noon and 1:45-6:15pm, Sat. 8-11am.) The **postal code** is CH-7500. The **telephone code** is 081.

You can rest your ski-weary bones at **Jugendherberge Still (HI)**, Via Sur Punt 60 (tel. 833 39 69; fax 833 80 46). Follow the signs around the lake to the left of the station (30min.), or take the postal bus (dir: Maloja): "Hotel Sonne" (2.40SFr) and then go left on Via Sur Punt for 10 minutes. The hostel is run more like a Republican convention than a youth hostel—carpeted lobby, impersonal staff, spotless rooms, and terse intercom announcements reminding everyone that there are only 30 minutes remaining for breakfast. Finding the reception is an adventure in this enormous modern building; follow the red signs. (Reception daily 7-9am and 4-10pm. No lockout. Curfew midnight; keys available. Quiet hours start at 10pm. Dorms 41.50SFr first night, then 39SFr; doubles 108SFr, 103SFr, with shower 130SFr, 125SFr. Nonmembers add 5SFr. Sheets, showers, lockers, breakfast, and dinner included—show up before 7:15pm for dinner. Laundry 4SFr. Visa, MC, AmEx.) You might opt instead to take the "See" exit at the train station and drop all your belongings at **Hotel Bellaval,** Via Gravass 55 (tel. 833 32 45; fax 833 04 06). With its prime location on the lake and behind the train station, this hotel is the diamond in the rough of St. Moritz. (Reception daily 7:30am-10pm. Singles 55-62SFr; doubles 111-158Fr. Huge delicious breakfast included. Closed Oct.-Dec. and Easter-May. Visa, MC, AmEx.) For camping, catch the postal bus to **St. Moritz-Bad Signal** (tel. 833 40 90). From the stop, walk along the foot path across the street to the right (away from the lake) for 10 minutes. (4.20-6SFr, children half-price; tent 5-6SFr. Open May 18-Sept. 29.)

Living the four-star lifestyle of St. Moritz is expensive. Unfortunately, *looking* as though you're living it is almost as pricey. An outdoor lunch at the **Giardino Café,** Via dal Bagn 54 (tel. 837 07 07), on the flower- and gnome-ridden terrace of the Hotel Schweizerhof, is a prime spot for glitterati-gazing. Try the salad buffet (7-9SFr), daily special (16-18.50SFr), or something grilled (12-21SFr; open 10am-6pm if it's not raining). The red-checked **Restaurant Engadinia,** P. da Scoula (tel. 833 32 65) serves up classic Swiss favorites including bratwurst with fries (16SFr), fondue for two (25SFr), or the more Italian spaghetti *bolognese* (16.50SFr; open Mon.-Sat. 8:30am-11pm). It never hurts to forage for groceries at the **Co-op Center,** one square up from the tourist office or at Via dal Bagn 20, en route to the youth hostel. (Open Mon.-Fri. 8am-12:15pm and 2-6:30pm, Sat. 8am-12:15pm and 2-5pm.) If you're here in late January, try the culinary delights of the annual week-long **St. Moritz Gourmet Festival.**

The **Engadiner Museum,** Via dal Bagn 39 (tel. 833 43 33), down from the tourist office, gives tourists a sneak-peek at the unbelievably intricate wood-lace interior of those unassuming white houses. The house, built in 1905 by an obsessed collector, features tiny gnomish doorways, beautiful and unpronounceable *chuchichästlis* (cupboards), and a four-poster bed from the plague era, decorated with skeletons. (Open June-Oct. Mon.-Fri. 9:30am-noon and 2-5pm, Sun. 10am-noon; Dec.-April Mon.-Fri. 10am-noon and 2-5pm, Sun. 10am-noon. 5SFr, students 4SFr, children 2.50SFr.) One street up from the Engadiner Museum sits the domed tower of the **Segantini Museum,** Via Somplaz 30 (tel. 833 44 54), dedicated to the Italian Expressionist painter. Housed in a stone basilica, the museum features some of Segantini's

ENGADIN VALLEY: SILVAPLANA ■ 445

well-known wall-sized, speckly Alpine landscapes with floating wood nymphs. Note: the museum will be closed September '98 to spring '99. (Open June-Oct. Tues.-Sat. 9am-12:30pm and 2:30-5pm, Sun. 10:30am-12:30pm and 2:30-4:30pm; Dec.-April Tues.-Sat. 10am-12:30pm and 3-5pm, Sun. 3-5pm. 7SFr, students 5SFr, children 2SFr. Joint pass for Engadiner and Segantini museums 10SFr, students 8SFr.) The **Mili Weber House,** Via Dim Lej 35 (tel. 833 33 09, 833 31 86, or 833 42 95), features a huge collection of Alpine paintings by Mili, a tiny red-headed legend in St. Moritz. (To visit, call for an appointment.) The leaning tower at the top of the village is all that is left of the 13th-century **St. Mauritius Church,** pulled down in 1890.

A roundabout **day hike** from St. Moritz to Pontresina takes you past the Olympic Ski Jump and towering glaciers and through narrow Alpine valleys. From St. Moritz-Bad, at the junction of Via Mezdi and Via Teglatscha, walk to the **Hahnensee,** an Alpine lake. From there, follow the signs to Fuorcla-Surlej. The trail then snakes along to the Ova da Roseg and the Roseg valley downstream to **Pontresina** (6hr. total). To scout out the slopes on foot before the ski season begins, ride from St. Moritz up to **Corviglia** (18SFr, round-trip 32SFr) and pick your line down (about 2hr.). From the top of Corviglia another lift glides up to **Piz Nair** (3075m; 18SFr, round-trip 32SFr). After admiring the rooftop view of the Engadin, you can hike down to Survetta Lake (2580m). Picnics at **Survetta Lake,** underneath the majestic **Piz Julier** (3380m), are a must. Follow the Ova da Survetta back down to the Signal-bahn or St. Moritz (3hr.).

You've probably heard of St. Moritz's reputation for world-class skiing (call 837 33 99 for ski packages; week packages start at 550SFr). Surprisingly, a larger number of guests travel to St. Moritz in the summer than in the winter. **Windsurfing** is one draw (tel. 833 44 49; 2hr. rental 30-40SFr, private lessons 50SFr per hr. 10 lessons 240SFr). **River rafting** is certainly another (with Eurotrek (tel. (01) 462 02 03), ½-day 80SFr, day 140SFr; with Swissraft (tel. (081) 911 52 50), ½-day 60SFr, day 143SFr). **Horseback riding** (tel. 833 57 33; 45SFr per hr., 80SFr for 2hr.), and **skeet shooting** (tel. 828 81 88; 15SFr) also add to the annual tourist flow.

SILVAPLANA

At the foot of the Julier mountain pass, Silvaplana (1815m) is situated amid the magnificent Upper Engadin lake country and, not unexpectedly, the town's main attraction is its **See** (lake). Silvaplana's beaches beckon sun-worshipers, campers, sailors, and hikers eager to soak their aching feet. The "Gorge" of Switzerland, the See hosts a bevy of wetsuited windsurfers, and from afar the lake appears to be populated by gargantuan freshwater sharks with neon fins. Silvaplana's hyperactive winds also frolic with kites, the fancy loop-de-looping variety, christened at the town's annual **kite festival** in September. Rent **sailboards** (tel. 828 92 29) next to the campground. (1hr. 20-25SFr, with wetsuit 25-30SFr; 2hr. 30-40SFr, 40-50SFr; 1 day 50-60SFr, 60-80SFr. Group lessons start at 50SFr per hr. Longer lessons advised for novices: 9hr. 240SFr, 18hr. 380SFr. Open June 15-Sept. 15 daily 9am-7pm.) While the lake is free for all to enjoy, windsurfing, sailing, and fishing fees reflect the lake's prime location and southern winds. Go **fish** after buying a day ticket (28SFr), weekend ticket (66SFr), or monthly permit (132SFr) at the tourist office. In August, Silvaplana hosts the **Nitro-Cup** (International Slalom Windsurfing Competition), and in July the **Swiss National Sailing and Windsurfing Championships** come to town.

Unfortunately, due to rising temperatures, the Corvatsch glacier is no longer large enough for summer skiing. Not to worry; snow is guaranteed in the winter. A cable car (tel. 828 82 42) ascends from **Surlej** (on the other side of the lake) high up into the **Piz Corvatsch** peak region (21SFr, round-trip 30SFr). The intermediate station of **Murtèl** (17SFr, round-trip 24SFr) is the center of an extended and varied ski region with links to Sils' Furtschellas runs and the downhill run past the Hahnensee Lake to St. Moritz (day pass 54SFr, children 42SFr; half-day 45SFr, 30SFr; with Graubünden pass and Swiss Card 50% off, with Swisspass 25%). From the Corvatsch cable car station, yodel your way up the rest of the glacier to **Piz Corvatsch**

(3451m) and you'll see the entire glacier and the striking surrounding peaks. Resist the urge to jump into what appears to be a large bowl of Ben and Jerry's glacial vanilla. The trip up takes 1-1½hr.; the trip down is approximately 20 minutes of hiking and 10 minutes of world-class glissading. The **Wanderbillet** takes you from Surlej up to Corvatsch and then halfway down to Murtèl (25SFr, children 16 and under 13SFr). For a hike below the glaciers, walk from the mid-station to Fuorcla Surlej (2755m) and down to Pontresina, crossing the mountain range along the Roseg valley (about 4hr.). For flatlandlubbers, Silvaplana's **Sportszentrum Mulets** (tel. 828 93 62) offers tennis (18SFr per hr.), volleyball (2hr. 20SFr), and soccer (2hr. 60SFr). In winter, soccer gives way to ice-skating, hockey, and that esoteric and bizarre European pastime, curling.

This village of 870 residents offers several very expensive hotels. Stay instead at the youth hostel in St. Moritz (see p. 444) or Maloja (see p. 442) or sleep on the beach at **Camping Silvaplana** (tel. 828 84 92; 7.60SFr; tent 5-7SFr; open mid-May to mid-Oct.). Grab food at the **Volg supermarket,** to the left of the tourist office. (Open Mon.-Fri. 8am-noon and 2-6:30pm, Sat. 8am-noon and 2-4pm.) Silvaplana and its lake are a mere one-hour hike or 10-minute bus ride from **St. Moritz** (every 30min. 7am-8pm, 3.60SFr). The **tourist office** (tel. 838 60 00; fax 838 60 09) at the corner of Via Maistra and Via dal Farrer can help plan hikes, arrange wind-surfing lessons, or reserve a room. Walk two blocks left from the post office. (Open Mon.-Fri. 8:30am-6:30pm, Sat. 9am-noon and 4-6pm.) The **postal code** is CH-7513. The **telephone code** is 081.

SILS (SEGL)

More than a century ago, **Friedrich Nietzsche** praised Sils as "the loveliest corner of the Earth." This comment contributed greatly to the town's present fame, but Sils has managed to preserve its quiet winding streets and placid, bovine-filled meadows that mask any sign of a vacation resort. A **traffic ban** has been imposed on all visiting cars (Sils has generously built a parking garage to make up for the inconvenience). A short bus ride from St. Moritz (a **postal bus** leaves every 30min. 7am-8:30pm; 6SFr), Sils is the perfect antidote to the kitsch of many Swiss ski resorts. The town is divided into two areas: **Sils Baselgia,** a small cluster of homes near the **Silsersee,** and **Sils Maria,** the town center. After a morning hike, stop by the **Nietzsche House** (halfway between the post office and the tourist office along Sils' main road), where the philosopher lived during summers 1887-88 and drifted into syphilitic madness. German-speakers pore over letters, histories, and quotables (all in German), getting chills up and down their spines from Nietzsche's mouthless, demonically mustachioed death mask. Non-German speakers look at the pictures and twiddle their thumbs. A tiny exhibit on wide-eyed Anne Frank and her lovingly written diary contrasts with Nietzsche's stern looks. (Open Tues.-Sun. 3-6pm. 4SFr, students 2SFr.)

Sils' side valleys, untamed and teeming with flora and fauna, are accessible only by foot and horse. The path of choice through **Val Fex** to **Curtins** begins just in front of the tourist office and winds its way beneath glaciers and 3000m peaks. If the hiker in you is dormant, **horse-driven omnibuses** make the round trip in 2 hours (20SFr). Grab your team in front of Hotel Maria, just to the right of the post office. Those who wish to commune with nature on a higher level may ascend the **Furtschellas** cable car (tel. 826 54 46) for a fascinating view of the entire Upper Engadin Valley (ascent 12SFr, descent 10SFr, round-trip 18SFr). The Furtschellas cable car is a 10-minute walk to the right of the post office (the opposite direction from the tourist office). From the summit, hike north over rocky hills and through green fields to **Murtèl,** where you can catch the cable car back to **Surlej** (12SFr). For a mellow afternoon beneath snowy peaks and along breezy shores, walk along the Silersee to **Maloja** (2hr.) and return by boat (tel. 826 53 43; 4 per day both ways; 12SFr, round-trip 18SFr). From December to April, Furtschellas and its 14 downhill runs offer **skiing** the way it's meant to be—without waiting (day pass 47SFr, children 34SFr; half-day 39SFr, 29SFr). For private or group skiing lessons, contact the tourist office.

The town's studied tranquility doesn't come cheaply. Sils' housing choices are limited, with few hotels in the budget range. **Pension Schulze** (tel. 826 52 13), up the street behind the tourist office, houses you in large rooms with puffy blankets and delicious scents wafting in from the downstairs bakery/café. (Reception daily 7:30am-noon and 2-6:30pm. Singles 60SFr, with shower 70SFr; doubles 120SFr, 140SFr. Breakfast included.) The bakery specializes in huge chocolate marzipan balls (3SFr), supposedly akin to the legendary larch-needle-wrapped food little friendly goblins floated to Sils during a bad flood and famine. Eat one of these fairy-tale delights and die happy. To carbo-load for the hikes ahead, dash to **Volg**, just left of the post office. (Open Mon.-Fri. 8am-noon and 2-6:30pm, Sat. 8am-noon and 2-4pm.) The **tourist office** (tel. 838 50 50; fax 838 50 59), down the street to the left from the post office, provides maps for hiking and skiing and can call hotels for vacancies. (Open Mon.-Fri. 8:30am-noon and 2-6pm, Sat. 9am-noon and 4-6pm; April-June and Oct.-Dec. closed Sat.) The Sils Maria **post office** stands just at the "Sils/Segl Maria" bus stop. The **postal code** is CH-7514, and the **telephone code** is 081.

CELERINA

Celerina possesses all the merits of the more famous Engadin towns—skiing, hiking, biking, and fonduing—yet resides just outside the resort veneer created by the likes of St. Moritz. The proudest moments in Celerina's history came when St. Moritz hosted the Winter Olympics in 1928 and 1948. Visitors can see the remains of the games in the **Bob-run** and **Cresta-run**, both of which came to a dramatic, revelry-filled finish in Celerina. Each run is re-built every year around the end of November by 14 specialized laborers from the village of **Naturns, Italy**. They use 5000 cubic meters of snow and 4000 cubic meter liters of water to make a mush that is used like cement to form each canal. The exclusive band of crazed thrill seekers, better known as the **St. Moritz Tobogganing Club** (tel. 833 41 10), presides over the runs and offers nonmembers a chance to ride on most mornings for a stiff fee. Bob runs will run you 190SFr, includes one run, one photo, one drink, and one certificate. The **Cresta Run** (tel. 833 31 17) is a modified, head-first toboggan ride down the icy course (first 5 rides with lessons costs 450SFr, subsequent rides 44SFr). Besides these runs, Celerina offers...well...hmmm...hiking and skiing away from the large crowds. The **Celerina gondola** and **Marguns chairlift** bring you to the midst of 80km of hiking trails in the summer. (Celerina-Marguns 17SFr, round-trip 26SFr; Marguns-Corviglia 8SFr, 12SFr.) In the winter, it's all snow, baby (tel. 833 80 15; daily ticket 50SFr, half-day 42SFr, children 35SFr). A moderate hike from Marguns (the top of the Gondola), the Chna Saluvan sits just below the mighty peak of the same name. Traverse the valley, head down to Alp Clavadatsch, and back to Celerina—the hike will take you from the rocky Alpine ski area down through the green, open fields rising above Celerina (total time approx. 4hr.). For additional suggestions, contact the friendly **tourist office** (tel. 830 00 11; fax 830 00 19) in the middle of town. From the Cresta Run train station, turn right; from the bus stop, turn left. The staff is a solid resource for hiking and skiing information, but hotel bookings are not their forte. (Open Mon.-Fri. 8:30am-noon and 2-6pm, Sat. 10am-noon and 4-6pm.) Unfortunately, super-cheap housing has been run out of town by valley competition. The friendly family at the **Hotel Trais Fluors-Garni** (tel. 833 88 85; fax 832 10 01) can put you up in spacious, clean, 300-year-old rooms with old-fashioned floral wallpaper and wood cabinets. The place feels like home but smells like a bakery—sweets and breads abound in the in-house bakery downstairs. (Singles 48-63SFr; doubles 92-98SFr, with shower 110-140SFr. Dec.-April: 52-61SFr; 98-106SFr, 116-144SFr. Breakfast included. Closed May and Nov.) Across from the tourist office is a **Volg** supermarket. (Open Mon-Fri. 8am-noon and 2-6:30pm, Sat. 8am-noon and 2-4pm.) Down the street from the tourist office lurks a **Co-op**. (Open Mon.-Fri. 8am-12:15pm and 2-6:30pm, Sat. 8am-12:15pm and 2-5pm.) If the Co-op or Volg aren't going to cut it, head for the elegant pueblo-style interior of **Restaurant La Court** (tel. 837 01 01), directly in front of Hotel Trais Fluors and right on the river. Eat

448 ■ GRAUBÜNDEN (GRISONS)

under the restaurant's huge skylight or outside by the river. (Salad buffet 7.70SFr, homemade lasagna 13.50SFr, *Capuns* 18SFr. Open daily noon-10pm.) The **Church of San Gian** proudly stands on a knoll just outside of town. In the center of the valley, the crumbling spire and ancient graveyard add a sense of history to the modern ski lifts and hotels. From anywhere in town, follow the yellow church signs to the Church of San Gian, 10 minutes from the town center. Occupying its own tiny tree-filled knoll (perfect for bird-watching), the church hides beautiful ancient frescoes beneath its crumbling spire. Infrequent opening hours are subject to change. (Generally open Mon. 2-4:30pm, Wed. 4-6:30pm, Fri. 10:30am-noon.) The closest town north of **St. Moritz,** Celerina is easily accessible by foot (45min.), **train** (2.40SFr), or **postal bus** (2.80SFr). The **postal code** is CH-7505. The **telephone code** is 081.

PONTRESINA

Pontresina lies in one of the highest wind-sheltered valleys of the Upper Engadin, along a mountainside terrace facing southwest. Surrounded by candy-bright Alpine meadows and fragrant woods, the city is a popular starting and stopping point for outdoorsy people. Rather than the credit cards and love-you-dahlings of St. Moritz, ice axes and crampons abound. This rugged *Burg* is internationally acclaimed thanks to the skiers' paradise of **Diavolezza,** the only glacier in the Engadin Valley that still offers summer skiing on its eternal snow. (All the other glaciers have melted due to rising temperatures and are no longer large enough for summer skiing.)

Pontresina's **tourist office** (tel. 838 83 00; fax 838 83 10), in the center of town, plans free excursions (see below), gives hiking advice, and finds hotel vacancies. From the train station, head right and follow Via de la Stazium to its end. (Open mid-April to mid-Oct. Mon.-Fri. 8:30am-noon and 2-6pm, Sat. 8:30am-noon and 3-6pm, Sun. 4-6pm; mid-Oct. to mid-Dec. and mid-April to mid-June Mon.-Fri. 8:30am-noon and 2-6pm, Sat. 8:30am-noon; late Dec. to mid-April Mon.-Fri. 8:30am-noon and 4-6pm.) **Postal buses** connect Pontresina to the villages of the Upper Engadin Valley all the way to **Maloja.** Trains run to Pontresina from **St. Moritz** (every 30min., 10min., 4.20SFr) and **Chur** through Samdan (every hr., 2hr., 39SFr). The train station provides **currency exchange** (daily 6:40am-7pm), **luggage storage** (5SFr), **lockers** (2SFr), and **bike rental** (22SFr at baggage check; open daily 6:40am-7pm). The **postal code** is CH-7504. The **telephone code** is 081.

The **Jugendherberge Tolais (HI)** (tel. 842 72 23; fax 842 70 31), in the modern, salmon-pink building directly across from the train station, is quite convenient for early-morning ski ventures and connections throughout the Engadin Valley. The hostel boasts a full-fledged restaurant, ping pong, swings, a soccer field, and friendly service that blows St. Moritz away. Inside the hostel, yellow *Wanderweg* signs tell you the hostel's elevation and where everything is, from the toilets to the dining facilities. (Reception daily in summer 6:45-9am, 4-6:30pm, and 7:30-9pm; in winter 7:30-9am, 4-6:30pm, and 7:30-9pm. No lockout. Quiet time from 10pm. Curfew 11pm; key available. Dorms 30.25SFr first night, then 27.75SFr; doubles 110.50SFr, 105.50SFr; quads 161SFr, 151SFr. Lockers, sheets, and breakfast included. Lunch 11SFr. Huge dinner of bread, salad, soup, entree, and dessert at 6:30pm 11SFr; mandatory July-Aug. and Feb.-March 15. Laundry 5SFr. Open June 16-Oct. 20 and Dec. 15-April 7. Call ahead for quads and doubles. Visa, MC, AmEx.) **Hotel-Pension Hauser,** Cruscheda 165 (tel. 842 63 26; fax 842 65 41), is another option. Head left from the tourist office uphill along Cruscheda. You'll feel right at home in this residential neighborhood, and once you've slept in the inviting beds you might never want to get up and hit the slopes—well, maybe only to escape the 70s color scheme in each balconied room. (Reception daily 7:30am-midnight. Singles 55-65SFr, with shower 65-75SFr; doubles 110-130SFr, with shower and toilet 150-180SFr. Parking and buffet breakfast included. Open mid-Dec.to mid-April and mid-June to mid-Oct.) Right in the heart of town, **Pension Valtellina** (tel. 842 63 63) features a boisterous Italian staff, pink bathrooms, and traditional rooms with outrageously fluffy down blankets. (Singles 46-54SFr; doubles 92-104SFr. Breakfast included. Closed June.) The tourist office also has an extensive list of **private rooms** starting at 30SFr per person. Beautiful **Camping Plauns** (tel. 842 62 85) offers all the amenities a tent-dweller could hope for (including clotheslines!). From the train station, walk 3km towards the Bernina Pass to Morteratsch; the trail is clearly marked. (7.50SFr; tents 9SFr. Open June to mid-Oct.) Pontresina's dining choices are more limited. If the alluring perfume of chlorine triggers your appetite, try **Bistro im Hallenbad,** in the swimming complex across from the tourist office and 50m up the hill. The restaurant offers a hearty daily *menu* and a daily vegetarian dish that should suit you fine. They also have a chlorine-free outdoor patio. (Open Mon.-Fri. 9am-8pm, Sat.-Sun. 10am-6pm.) The **Co-op** resides at the corner of Via Maistra and Via da Mulin. (Open Mon.-Fri. 8am-noon and 3-6pm, Sat. 8am-5pm.) The only bakery (tel. 838 60 40) that sells **Engadiner Torte** (3.50SFr per slice, 22SFr for a small cake) is right next to the Pontresina post office. (Open daily June-Oct. and Dec.-April 7:30am-6:30pm.)

If the idea of perpetual snow amazes and astounds you, then you'll probably want to ski on it. The Diavolezza **summer ski lift** (tel. 842 64 19) operates in June and July daily from 8:30am to noon. (Day pass 35SFr, children 16 and under 25SFr. Winter: 44SFr, ½day 36SFr; children 31SFr, 26SFr.) When the ski lift closes, trade your ski boots for **hiking** boots and explore the nearby valleys and vales. The tourist office has extensive hiking maps (14.50SFr) and suggestions. One nearby hike takes you along a green ridge, just below the mighty 3157m **Piz Muragl.** From Pontresina, walk or take the postal bus: "Punt Muragl." From there a funicular whisks hikers away to **Mouttas Muragl** (2456m; every 30min. 8am-11pm; 16SFr, round-trip 25SFr). Follow the yellow signs to **Alp Languard** (2330m; 2½hrs), hike down to Pontresina (1hr.), or take the chairlift back (13SFr, round-trip 19SFr; open 8:30am-5:30pm). To see global warming in action, hike to the receding **Morteratsch Glacier.** From the train station, walk toward town on Via de la Stazium and hang a right at the trail sign just before the second bridge. Walk for two hours along the valley floor through pine groves and tall grassy meadows. Or you can take the train (every hr., 3.60SFr) to Morteratsch. From the train station, bear right and follow the signs to the glacier (approx. 45min.). Follow the signs marking the glacier's recession since the turn of the century along the gushing river created by the melting waters. Though disappearing, the glacier is still a massive wall of ice and snow, seemingly arrested in motion as it crawls through the rugged valley. **The Mountaineering School Pontresina** (tel. 838 83 33) offers daily guided hikes over the Diavolezza and Pers glaciers and down through the Morteratsch glacier and valley. No technical equipment or experience is necessary, but a raincoat, warm clothes, and rubber-soled hiking boots are a must. (20SFr, children 7-16 10SFr; approx. 4hr.) The school also leads easier hikes daily through regional valleys (30SFr). If you're tired of physical exertion, horse-drawn carriages and winter sleighs offer (at least) four legs and a good time (call 842 60 57 for booking).

Guests of Pontresina—that's you—are entitled to a number of **free sports, tours,** and **excursions,** including free trout fishing in Lej Nair and Lej Pitschen, free botanical excursions, free mushroom picking with a local expert, free guided hiking tours into the **National Park** (see below), and free excursions to experience an unforgettable sunrise on Piz Lagalb. **Museum Alpin,** Chesa Delnon (tel. 842 72 73), up the street from the tourist office on your left, presents life in the Engadin as it used to be: void of wimpy polypropylene and high-tech hikers and full of hundreds of birds and flowers now kaput. Photos of bearded, pipe-smoking, wool-clad mountaineering men with picks and ropes adorn the walls of the mountaineering room, while birds in the adjoining bird room twitter to psychedelic mountain music. Don't miss the impressive blend of music and picture in the slide-show thriller *Mountain Experience* from 4:30 to 5:15pm. (Open mid-June to mid-Oct. Mon.-Sat. 4-6pm. 5SFr, children 2SFr.)

THE SWISS NATIONAL PARK

Switzerland's only national park is flanked by **Zernez** (the official park town) and **S-chanf.** Wildflowers scarce elsewhere, like the bearberry and the yellow alpine poppy, abound; **ibex, red deer,** and **chamois** roam free; and fluorescent butterflies flit about in this naturalist's nirvana. The park spearheads many re-introduction programs for such nearly extinct animals as the much underrated bearded vulture, and, as a result, forbids fires, dogs, straying from the well-marked trails, or picking mushrooms. Zernez is accessible by rail from **St. Moritz** (every hr., 1hr., 15.80SFr) or **Chur** (every hr., 2¾hr., 46SFr, change at Samedan). **Zernez's tourist office** (tel. (081) 856 13 00; fax 856 11 55) has information about the park, but the **National Park House** (tel. (081) 856 13 78) in Zernez might be a better bet. The house displays the park's highlights and relevant scientific information and is a good starting point for hikes. Walk past the bus stop in front of the train station and make a left, then walk past the **Co-op** (open Mon.-Fri. 8am-noon and 2-6:30pm, Sat. 8am-noon and 2-4pm) and turn right at the intersection. The building is 200m on the right. (Open June-Oct. Tues. 8:30am-10pm, Wed.-Mon. 8:30am-6pm. 4SFr, students 3SFr. Park admission free.)

Only one road penetrates the park. **PTT buses** depart from the train station and take hikers and strollers to the nine stops within the park. This road provides access to the park's limited hiking potential; flora, fauna, and footpaths are all within easy reach. To see the quest to save the endangered bearded vulture, take the bus to stop #7 and climb through **Val dal Botsch** to **Margunet** (2328m), where the birds are being re-introduced. If the vultures don't grab you, the views certainly will. Hike back down over the Stabelchod pass (1958m) to stops #8 or 9 (round-trip approx. 3hr.).

If you feel a bus ride would interfere with your enjoyment of your natural surroundings, hike directly from the Park House to the Chamana Cluozza, an Alpine hut and one of the few places to sleep in the park proper. From the Park House, head to the right, and cross the covered bridge 200m to the right. Signs to Cluozza will soon appear. The trail starts out as a weedy access road but soon becomes a soft pine-needle-cushioned walk leading up the foothills facing Zernez, ultimately to 2329m. A 15-minute detour to **Bellavista,** near the summit, yields spectacular views of the mountain, the valley, and Zernez. From Bellavista, signs again lead the way to Cluozza through the Alpine forest and out onto the rocky ridge traversing Val Cluozza. The **Chamana Cluozza** (tel. (081) 856 12 35) lies 100m up from the river on the other side of the valley. Recharge with pasta from 11SFr. (Accessible by foot only. 3hr. from Zernez, 2½hr. back. Dorms 25SFr. Breakfast included. Open June to mid-Oct.) You can rest here before scaling **Spi Murter** (2545m), a majestic peak presiding over the valley. From here, exit the park down **Plan dals Poms** to bus stop #3 (3½hr.).

Shelter outside the park in Zernez is expensive, but camping is cheap and pleasant at riverside **Camping Cul** (tel. 856 14 62). Take a right out of the train station and follow the tent signs for five minutes, passing behind the lumber yard. (6.50SFr; tents 4SFr; cars 2.50SFr. Guest tax 0.90SFr. Open May-Oct. 15.) Across the park from Zernez, S-chanf can also serve as base camp for hiking in the park or Engadin Valley skiing. Downhill from the S-chanf train station and left from the church lies **Gasthaus Sternen,** Via Maistra (tel. (081) 854 12 63). Though dwarfed by the vibrant Parc-Hotel Aurora next door, the *Gasthaus* allows sufficient beauty sleep for the next day's hike. (45SFr per person, with shower 55SFr. Add 10SFr in winter. Breakfast included.) **S-chanf's tourist office** (tel. (081) 854 13 48) in the Banca Raiffeisen can offer more information about lodgings. (Open Mon.-Tues. and Fri. 8:30-11am and 4-5:30pm, Wed. 8:30-11am, Thurs. 8:30-11am and 4-6:30pm.)

ZUOZ

Burnt to the ground by residents in 1499 to keep it from the Austrians, Zuoz rebuilt itself in the early 16th century and is today the best preserved medieval village in the Upper Engadin. Ibexes, pinwheels, and flowers float on the whitewashed walls of patrician houses, and a big carved bear defends the fountains from bloodthirsty Austrians. In town you can also catch the sounds of Switzerland's leftover Latinate dialect, Romansch. Zuoz is not for the thrill-seeker, but the town has a few ancient customs that may baffle the accidental tourist. On March 1, the **Chalandamarz** engulfs all of Engadin as young boys wander from house to house, ring huge bells, and sing songs to drive off evil spirits and welcome the spring. Originally a pagan fertility rite, the more peculiar **San Gian's Day** commemorates John the Baptist on July 24, when village boys spritz girls with water from Zuoz's many fountains. The defenseless Swiss maidens then flee to their houses and pour huge buckets of water over the boys' heads. Perhaps there's some Italian blood in this region yet.

The **tourist office** (tel. 854 15 10; fax 854 33 34), on Via Maistra, provides keys for the church and tower and suggests hikes in the area. From the station walk up La Passarella, directly across from and perpendicular to the station. At the top of the pedestrian walkway, turn right on the main street, and the tourist office will be past the main square on your right. (Open July-Aug. and Dec.-April Mon.-Fri. 9-11am and 2-6pm, Sat. 9-11am; May-June and Oct.-Nov. Mon.-Fri. 9am-11am and 3-5pm.) Zuoz is a short **train** ride from **St. Moritz** (every hr., 30min., 10SFr) on the way to the Swiss National Park. The **train station** provides **luggage storage** (5SFr), **bike rental** (22SFr), and **currency exchange**. The **postal code** is CH-7524. The **telephone code** is 081.

The 400-year-old **Chesa Walther** (tel. 854 13 64), before the tourist office, offers rooms that look decorated by the Swiss Family Robinson after the whole island thing. Zebra, cougar, and other critter skins adorn the ivy-tangled walls, competing for space with gold-fringed mirrors and antique Graubünden stoves. (Dorms 35-38SFr. Kitchen facilities 5SFr.) **Restaurant Dorta** (tel. 854 20 40) is around the corner from the train station. This elegantly ancient establishment serves such regional specialities as *Rösti* (9SFr), *raclette* (9.50SFr), and fondue (23SFr) on tables made from antique sleighs and horse-carts. (Open Tues.-Sun. 6pm-1am. Visa, MC, AmEx.) Food begs to be bought at the **Co-op** opposite the station (open Mon.-Fri. 8am-12:15pm and 2-6:30pm, Sat. 8am-12:15pm and 2-5pm) or at the **Volg** supermarket next to the tourist office (open Mon.-Fri. 8am-noon and 2-6:30pm, Sat. 8am-noon and 2-4pm).

The small **Church San Luzius** on Via Maistra has sweet-smelling pine pews and hymnals in Romansch. Next door is the **prison tower,** filled with spiky, blood-curdling, gut-wrenching implements of torture (ask the tourist office for the key). The *graffito* carvings in Zuoz are eye-catching in their detail—look up at **Crusch Alva** in the main square. The town also woos **bikers** with 37km of marked trails, and **hikers** can use the Inn River as a starting point for many delightful jaunts. The path to **Punt Muragl** (4hr.) follows the river along the Engadin's green valley floor. To put a bit of altitude into your walk, follow the trail from Zuoz to **Madulain** (2hr.) along the ridge overlooking the valley floor. The trail crosses others leading to alpine huts, including the Chamana d'Es-cha (a full day's hike away), and to the terraced farms and vineyards of the other valley villages. To find the trail, start uphill from Zuoz's main square and head 300m up Somvih street. For a more rugged afternoon, follow the **Ova d'Arpiglia** to a crashing 20m waterfall. From the other side of the train tracks and the highway at the Resgia Parking lot past the Restaurant Dorta, signs lead the way to **Sagl d'Arpiglia** along a magnificent rock-strewn gorge. That's the view of the falls from below—now climb the **"Stairway to Heaven."** Tickling the skies, this steep, green meadow to the right of the falls burgeons with purple wildflowers and prehistoric-looking leaves and fronds. At the top of the stairway, chase butterflies to you heart's content and hum your favorite Led Zeppelin riff in the valley's swath of green. Signs point the way from this perfect picnic-haven back to Zuoz (round-trip 1½hr.).

THE BODENSEE

The third largest lake in Europe, the Bodensee forms a graceful border at the conjunction of Austria, Switzerland, and Germany. Ancient castles, manicured islands, and endless opportunities to achieve a melanomic crisp draw residents of all three countries (and then some) to the lake throughout the summer.

■ Constance (Konstanz)

Spanning the Rhine's juncture with the Bodensee is the elegant university city of Constance. Though technically in Germany, the city extends into Switzerland, which spared it the bombing that leveled many Germany cities of similar size in WWII. This German/Swiss mix, Austrian rule until 1805, and the city's large student population create an open, international feel. Locals and students crowd the old resort beaches on the edge of town, and the *Altstadt*'s narrow streets wind around beautifully painted Baroque and Renaissance facades crowned with a tangle of ancient tiles, stork nests, and TV antennae. Along the river promenades, gabled and turreted 19th-century houses gleam with undeniable gentility. Be aware that Constance's currency is the Deutschmark, the phones are on the German system, and border controls are in effect—you will need to show your passport to walk into Constance from the Swiss hostel, and border guards occasionally search bags.

Orientation and Practical Information The **tourist office** (tel. 133 030; fax 133 060), in the arcade to the right of the train station, provides an excellent walking map and lots of area information. The office will find rooms for a three-night minimum stay in private homes (DM5). The free self-guided walking tour brochure includes a map, suggested routes, and a brief explanation of the many sites. (Open May-Sept. Mon.-Fri. 9am-6:30pm, Sat. 9am-1pm; Oct. and April Mon.-Fri. 9am-noon and 2-6pm, Sat. 9am-1pm; Nov.-March Mon.-Fri. 9am-noon and 2-6pm.) **Trains** connect Constance every hour to **Stein am Rhein** (30min., 9SFr) and **Schaffhausen** (1hr., 15SFr). Travelers looking for ride-sharing options can contact **Mitfahrzentrale,** Münzg. 22 (tel. 214 44; open Mon.-Fri. 9:30am-1pm and 2-6pm, Sat. 9:30am-2pm), or the university **ride board.** You can buy a six-ride ticket (DM11) for the Meersburg-Constance **ferry** from any machine. Ships depart about once every hour from behind the Constance train station to all ports on the Bodensee. One ferry stops at various points in Germany (June to late Sept. daily). For more information and schedules independent of the tourist office, contact the **Weiße Bodenseeflotte** counter (tel. 281 389), in the harbor behind the train station. (Open Sun.-Fri. 7:40am-6:10pm, Sat. 7:40am-8:15pm. Trips on the lake half-price with Eurailpass; Eurailpass valid on trips west of Constance.) **Private boats** run every hour from behind the train station to the **Freizeitbad** and the **Freibad Horn** (June-Aug. daily 10:30am-5:30pm; May and Sept. Sun. 10:30-5:30pm; 2.50-3SFr). **City buses** in Constance cost DM2.40 per ride. **Paddleboat** and **rowboat** rentals are available at **Am Gondelhafen** (tel. 218 81) for about DM14 per hour from 9am to dusk. For the **police,** call 110. The **postal code** is D-78462. The **German telephone code** is 0049, and the city's **telephone code** is 07531.

Accommodations and Food Far and away the nicer of Constance's two youth hostels is the clean, comfortable **Jugendherberge Kreuzlingen (HI),** Promenadenstr. 7 (tel. (071) 688 26 63; fax 688 47 61; use the Swiss access code), resting in an old manor house on the water in Kreuzlingen, Switzerland (but actually the closer hostel to downtown Constance). From the Constance *Bahnhof,* cross the tracks on the left and walk 20 minutes on the trail that hugs the water. From the park path—shortly after the caged sheep—take a right into the castle-like villa grounds, walk a bit, and then take a soft right onto a tree-lined path that leads straight to the hotel. (Reception daily 5-9pm. Dorms 21.20SFr first night, then 18.70SFr. March-April and Oct.-Nov.: 18.70SFr; 16.20SFr. Breakfast and sheets included. Dinner 11SFr. Kayak rental 30SFr per day. Closed Dec.-Feb.) **Jugendherberge Otto-Moericke-Turm (HI),** Zur Allmannshöhe 18 (tel. 322 60; fax 311 63), is probably the world's only hostel housed in a former water tower. Take bus #4:

NEAR CONSTANCE: MAINAU ■ 453

"Jugendherberge." (Reception daily 4:30-5:30pm. Curfew 10pm. DM20, non-members DM26. Breakfast included. Sheets DM7. Open March-Oct. Call ahead.) **Jugendwohnheim Don Bosco,** Salesianerweg 5 (tel. 622 52; fax 606 88), is an excellent alternative to the hostels. From the station, take bus #1: "Salzberg" then walk two minutes, following the main road around the corner, and turn at the yellow Bosco sign into the gargantuan yellow Bosco house. The building is the Swiss youth hostel's version of Pinnochio's sin city: a huge game room with foosball, chess, pinball, and board games; long linoleum hallways echoing with screaming school groups; and a TV in the dayroom that crackles with 39 channels, including MTV. (Curfew 12:30am; key available. 4- to 8-bed dorms DM25; a few singles DM35; doubles DM60. Sheets DM5. Call ahead.) **Campingplatz Konstanz-Bruderhofer,** Fohrenbühlweg 50 (tel. 330 57), offers a cheaper alternative. Take bus #1: "Staad"; the campground is along the water. Definitely make reservations. (DM6; tent DM5-8. Open April 15-Sept.).

Compared to the rest of Switzerland, German Constance has refreshingly low prices. The **University Mensa** dishes out Constance's cheapest food—lunches, including dessert and a view of the lake, cost DM3-4 (DM1 discount with student ID). Take bus #9, 9a, or 9b from the station. (Open July 15-Oct. 8 Mon.-Thurs. 8am-5pm, Fri. 8am-3pm; Oct. 9-July 14 Mon.-Thurs. 8am-6:30pm.) The area around Rheingasse, the oldest part of Constance and now the center of a vibrant alternative scene, overflows with health-food stores, left-wing graffiti, student cafés, and bars. **Sedir,** Hofhaldestr. 11, serves big bowls of vegetarian noodles for DM10. (Open Mon.-Fri. 11am-2pm and 6pm-midnight, Sat.-Sun. 6pm-2am.) A fun *Biergarten* atmosphere reigns at **Seekuh,** Kouzilstr. 1 (tel. 272 32). Diners devour cheap pizza (from DM10) outside under a hanging garden or inside in the all-wood bar. (Open Sun.-Thurs. 6pm-1am, Fri.-Sat. 6pm-2am.) At **Mamma Mia,** St. Johanng. 9 (tel. 270 07), the incredibly fast and polite waitstaff serves more traditional pizza (DM9-14) and pasta (from DM11) to those starved for Italian Switzerland. (Open daily 11:30am-2pm and 5pm-midnight.)

Sights and Entertainment The city abounds with picturesque sights. The **Münster,** built over the course of 600 years, features a soaring Gothic spire, 17th-century vaulting, and a beautiful corner sanctuary with blue mosaic-like windows. (Open mid-April to mid-Oct. Mon.-Sat. 8am-5:30pm. Tower DM1, students DM0.50.) The elaborate frescoes on the 14th-century **Rathaus** depict Constance's history, and the inner courtyard titillates visitors with intimate greenery. **Seestraße,** near the yacht harbor on the lake, and **Rheinsteig,** along the Rhine, offer picture-perfect Constance water views. The tree-filled **Stadtgarten** next to Constance's main harbor provides a peaceful, unbroken view down the length of the Bodensee. A voluptuous revolving statue guards the Gondelhafen harbor.

Constance boasts a number of grass and pebble **public beaches;** all are free and open from May to September. **Strandbad Horn,** the largest and most crowded, sports a section for nude sunbathing. In inclement weather, thwarted sunbathers head next door to **Freizeitbad Jakob,** Wilhelm-von-Scholz-Weg 2 (tel. 661 63), an ultra-modern indoor-outdoor pool complex with thermal baths and *faux*-summer sun lamps. To reach both complexes, walk 30 minutes along the waterfront from the train station, or take bus #5. (Both open daily 9am-9pm. DM8, students DM5.)

The **Bodensee-Festival,** featuring concerts by the Bodensee Symphony Orchestra, occurs in nearby Meersburg May 14-21. Constance shoots fireworks over the Bodensee every August 2—find a good spot and enjoy the rockets' red glare.

■ Near Constance

MAINAU

The rich and magnificently manicured garden covering the German island of Mainau is the result of the horticultural prowess of generations of Baden princes and the Swedish royal family. An arboretum, greenhouses, and **huge animals made of flowers** surround the Baroque palace built by the Knights of the Teutonic Order, who lived here from the 13th to the 18th century. Now thousands of happy little tourists scamper across the foot bridge from Constance to pose with the blooming elephants and ooh at the 30 different varieties of butterflies fluttering about the tropical-climate greenhouse. Truly amazing are the dozens of fully grown palm trees planted around the palace, able to survive year-round due to the lake's moderating effect on the climate and the magic green fingers of the island's massive gardening army. To reach the island, take a romantic boat trip from behind the Constance train station (one-way DM5.40, round-trip DM9). Bus #1: "Staad" also runs to the island. (Park open 7am-8pm; DM16.50, students DM9, seniors DM13, children DM5.50; Nov. to mid-March 9am-5pm; DM5, children free.) For more information call (49 07531) 30 30 or fax 30 32 48.

LINDAU IM BODENSEE

Connected to the lake shore by a narrow causeway, the romantic medieval city of **Lindau im Bodensee, Germany** looks out across the Bodensee, where the aquamarine waters and the small but oh-so-significant detachment from the mainland contribute to the city's resort ambience. The central part of town around **Maximilianstraße** features captivating half-timbered houses, and the view of the Alps is almost the same as the one you see on good chocolates. The **Städtische Kunstsammlung** (town art museum) is located in **Cavazzen-Haus,** an ornate Baroque mansion. (Open April-Oct. Tues.-Sun. 10am-noon and 2-5pm. DM4, students DM1.) The harbor is framed by a rather imposing 19th-century **Bavarian Lion** and the **New Lighthouse,** the latter offering an illuminating overview of the neighborhood. (Open daily 10am-7pm. DM2, students DM1.) The **Rathaus,** halfway along Maximilianstr., is a fruity blend of frescoes. A walk down the less touristed equivalent of Maximilianstr.—In der Grube (In the Pit)—will lead you to the **Diebstahl Turm** (robbery tower). Covered with ivy and newly renovated, the color-speckled tin-roofed turret looks more like Rapunzel's tower than a former prison. For those over 21 and possessing a coat and tie or a formal dress, the **casino** on the island (one of four in Bayern) is an entertaining option. The bet ceiling is DM12,000, so don't worry about losing too much money. (Open 3pm-2am. Admission DM5 and a passport—and please, daaahling, no jeans.)

The **tourist office,** Am Hauptbahnhof (tel. 26 00 30; fax 26 00 26), across from the station, finds rooms for a DM5 fee. (Open Mon.-Sat. 9am-1pm and 2-7pm.) **Tours** leave from the office at 10am (Tues. and Fri. in German, Mon. in English; DM5, students and overnight guests DM3). **Ferries** link Lindau with Constance, stopping at Meersburg, Mainau, and Friedrichshafen (5-7 per day, 3hr., one-way DM18). The **train** takes two hours (DM13). Crazy kids can rent **boats** (tel. 55 14) 50m to the left of the casino, right next to the bridge. (Open mid.-March to mid.-Sept. daily 9am-9pm. Paddleboats DM12-15 per hr. for up to 5 people. Power boat DM45.) One-hour excursions (tel. 781 94) on a small boat leave from the dock behind the casino at 11:30am, 1, 2:30, and 6pm (DM12, children DM6). **Rent bikes** at the train station (tel. 212 61) for DM15. (Open Mon.-Fri. 9am-noon and 2:30-6pm, Sat. 9:30am-noon.) The **post office,** 88101 Lindau im Bodensee (tel. 277 70), is 50m right from the train station. (Open Mon.-Fri. 8am-6pm, Sat. 8:30am-noon.) The **telephone code** is 08382.

The spectacular **Jugendherberge,** Herbergsweg 11 (tel. 967 10), lies across the Seebrücke off Bregenzerstr. Sleekly modern interior sports a staff that is just as hip. The *only* downside of this place is their policy for single travelers—they don't hold beds for same-day arrivals. Call as soon as you know that you will arrive. (Reception 9am-midnight. Curfew midnight. Under 27 and families with small children only. Dorms DM27.50. Breakfast, sheets, and tax included.) You could eat off the floor in the fine rooms at **Gästehaus Holdereggen,** Näherweg 4 (tel. 65 74). Follow the railroad tracks across the causeway to the mainland (after the bridge, the path continues to the left of the tracks); turn right onto Holdereggeng. and left onto

Jungfernburgstr. Näherweg is on the left (20min.). (Singles DM38; doubles DM70. Add DM3 extra per person for one-night stands. Showers DM2.) **Campingplatz Lindau-Zech,** Frauenhoferstr. 20 (tel. 722 36), 3km south of the island on the mainland. It's within spitting range of the Austrian border and a beach. From the station, take bus #1 or 2: "Anheggerstr.," then bus #3 (dir: "Zech") to finish the journey. (DM9.50; tent DM4. Tax DM1.50. Showers included. Open April-Oct.)

Lindau has three beaches. (All open June to mid-Aug. and weekends year round daily 10am-8pm; other times 10:30am-7:30pm. Last entrance 1hr. before closing.) **Römerbad** is the smallest and most familial, located left of the harbor on the island (DM5, students DM3). To reach the quieter **Lindenhofbad,** take bus #1 or 2: "Anheggerstr." and then bus #4: "Alwind" (DM4, students DM3). Lindau's biggest beach is **Eichwald,** about a 30-minute walk to the right facing the harbor along Uferweg. Alternatively, take bus #1 or 2: "Anheggerstr.," then bus #3: "Karmelbuckel" (DM5, students DM3). Sit down for Greek at **Taverna Pita Gyros,** Paradiespl. 16 (tel. 237 02), which offers big platters (DM6-15) on the sidewalk or inside. (Open daily 10am-9pm.) There is a **Plus grocery store** in the basement of the department store at the conjunction of In der Grub and Cramerg. (Open Mon.-Fri. 8:30am-6:30pm, Sat. 8am-1pm.)

■ St. Gallen

Once upon a time in the 7th century, St. Gall, an Irish missionary, attempted a whirlwind tour of the pagan regions near the Alps. When he reached a small town near the Bodensee, he stumbled into a bier. Interpreting this miraculous occurrence as a sign from God, St. Gall set up camp on the spot, with the help of a friendly local bear who moonlighted as a carpenter. Combine this questionable heritage with the rather sing-songy Gallenese accent and you'll understand why St. Gallen is the butt of many a Swiss joke. Actually, the rest of the country is probably just jealous. In 1983, UNESCO named the city library a world heritage treasure. Today St. Gallen fuses the likes of the monastery's stupendous Baroque library and the city's magnificent cathedral with a modern university and lively cafés and bars. The youthful crowd that fills the streets makes this medieval city of learning and piety come alive, and though a compelling city in itself, St. Gallen's proximity to the Bodensee, Zurich, Germany, Austria, and smaller mountain villages makes it even more of a regional hotspot.

ORIENTATION AND PRACTICAL INFORMATION

St. Gallen's sights and services are centered around the *Altstadt* near the *Kloster,* but the city's tentacles also spread far into the surrounding hills.

Tourist Office: Bahnhofpl. 1a (tel. 227 37 37; fax 227 37 67). From the train station, cross straight through the bus stop and pass the fountain on the left; the tourist office is on the right. The English-speaking staff makes free hotel reservations within St. Gallen. Maps, brochures, and a **city tour** are also available. (Tour June 12-Sept. Mon., Wed., and Fri. 2:30pm. 15SFr, museum admissions included.) Office open Mon.-Fri. 9am-noon and 1-6pm, Sat. 9am-noon.

Currency Exchange: Union Bank of Switzerland, Bahnhofpl., is convenient. Open Mon.-Wed. and Fri. 8:30am-4:30pm, Thurs. 8:30am-6:30pm.

Trains: Bahnhofpl. To: **Zurich** (1hr., 26SFr), **Geneva** (4½hr., 87SFr), **Bern** (2½hr., 59SFr), **Lugano** (4hr., 74SFr), and **Munich** (3hr., 60SFr, under 26 49SFr).

Buses: Convenient buses cross the hills and valleys of the St. Gallen region. Single fare 2SFr, *Tageskarte* (day card) 7.20SFr, 12 rides 20SFr. Buy tickets at each stop; multi-fares and *Tageskarten* available at large kiosks or the **VBSG Transit Authority** across from the train station.

Taxis: Sprenger AG, Rohrschacherstr. 281 (tel. 222 23 33).

Car Rental: Herold Autovermietung AG, Molkenstr. 7 (tel. 220 20 30; fax 223 88 31). 72SFr per day, 3 days 151SFr. **Budget Rent-A-Car,** City Garage AG, St.

Leonhardstr. 35 (tel. 222 11 14; fax 222 01 57). 118SFr per day, weekend package Fri.-Mon. 201SFr.

Parking: Neumarkt Parking Garage (tel. 222 11 14). 5am-9pm 2SFr per hr.; 9pm-5am 1SFr per hr. Open Mon.-Sat. 5am-12:40am. **Rathaus Parking Garage** (tel. 223 11 25). 7am-10pm 1.80SFr per hr.; 10pm-7am 0.50SFr per hr. Open 24hr. Or park in one of the city's **blue zones** for 5.50SFr per day.

Luggage Storage: At the train station. Lockers 2SFr. Luggage watch 5SFr. Open Mon.-Fri. 7:30am-7:45pm, Sat.-Sun. 7:30am-noon and 2-6pm.

Laundromat: Quick Wash, Rohrschacherstr. 59 (tel. 245 31 73). Soap 1.50-5SFr, wash 4-7SFr, dry 1.80-3.80SFr. Open Mon.-Sat. 8am-10pm.

Internet Access: Media Lounge, Marktpl. (tel. 22 50 01). Blue-carpeted lounge offers amazingly cheap access to your neglected email account. 2SFr for 10min., 12SFr for 1hr. Open Mon. 11:30am-9pm, Tues.-Fri. 10am-9pm, Sun. 9:30am-9pm.

Post Office: St. Leonhardstr. 7, across the street and to the right of the train station exit. Open Mon.-Fri. 7:30am-6:30pm, Sat. 7:30-11am. **Postal Code:** CH-9000.

Telephone Code: 071.

ACCOMMODATIONS

Jugendherberge St. Gallen (HI), Jüchstr. 25 (tel. 245 47 77; fax 245 49 83). From the train station, take the *Trogenerbahn* (Orange Train) from the smaller Appenzeller/Trogener station to the right. From Marktpl. take the train (dir: Speicher-Trogen): "Schülerhaus," walk up the hill on the right, make a left across the train tracks at the sign, and walk downhill 2min. Perched on a hill overlooking St. Gallen, the hostel is filled with bright murals and posters. Clean, quiet, with breakfast room, terrace, barbecue pit, grassy lawn, juke box, library, English-speaking staff, and board games. Fall asleep counting the baas of nearby sheep. Reception Mon.-Sat. 5-10:30pm, Sun. 6-10:30pm. Check-out 9am (9:30am in winter). Lockout 10am-5pm, but lounge is open. Dorms 23SFr first night, then 20.50SFr; singles 57SFr, 54.50SFr; doubles 64SFr, 59SFr. Parking available. Closed Dec. 15-March 7.

Hotel Elite, Metzgerg. 9-11 (tel. 222 12 36; fax 222 21 77). Simple, airy rooms with chocolates on the pillows. The owner's black and orange boxer, Penny, looks scary but isn't. Rooms without showers smell fresher than those with, but there aren't any hall showers. Singles 54-100SFr; doubles 108-150SFr. Breakfast included.

Hotel Weisses Kreuz, Engelg. 9 (tel. 223 28 43; fax 223 28 77), one block from Hotel Elite and atop a lively bar. Shabby stairs lead up through storage spaces to plain, tired rooms. But the beds are cozy and the location's great for delving into the *Altstadt's* nightlife. Reception daily 5am-midnight. Singles 40-60SFr; doubles 70-100SFr. 5% student discount. Breakfast and hall showers included.

FOOD

Restaurant Spitalkeller, Spitalg. 10 (tel. 222 50 91). From Marktpl., head down Marktg. and turn left on Spitalg. Unidentifiable plastic fruit hangs from this smoky wooden-raftered joint. Hearty Alpine food for mountain folks taking a break from the wilderness. Local sausage specialties stay the appetite of any flannel-clad lumberjack (or jill). Appenzeller macaroni with sausage or Ticino *Rösti* (with tomatoes and cheese) 11.50SFr. Daily *menus* from 13SFr. Open Tues.-Sat. 8am-midnight.

Christina's, Weberg. 9 (tel. 238 808). A sleek, new-age, indigo-tinted bar/café/restaurant. Exotic vegetarian specialties. Bring your sunglasses and prepare to ooze new-age sophistication. Sleek decor will get even sleeker after current renovations end. Veggie dishes from 16SFr. Fish and meat dishes from 19SFr. Open Tues.-Thurs. 9:30am-11:30pm, Fri.- Sat. 9:30am-12:30am, Sun.-Mon. 3-11:30pm.

Pizzeria Boccalino, Burggraben 20 (tel. 222 96 66), left off Spiserg. Italian-speaking waiters (who understand English and German) serve pasta and pizza. Flowers encircle the tables and red balcony. Homesick Vikings snarf "pizza Nordica" (with salmon lox, 17SFr). Pizza Margherita 11SFr. Open Mon.-Sat. 10:30am-11pm.

Markets

Migros, St. Leonhardstr., two blocks up from the train station. Open Mon.-Wed. and Fri. 8am-6:30pm, Thurs. 8am-9pm, Sat. 7:30am-5pm. Buffet-equipped restaurant open Mon.-Wed. and Fri. 6:30am-6:30pm, Thurs. 6:30am-9pm, Sat. 6:30am-5pm.

Reformhaus Müller, Spiserg. 13, sells organically grown goodies and health foods. Open Mon.-Fri. 8am-6:30pm, Sat. 8am-5pm.

Birreria, Brühlg. 45. Over 700 types of beer let you take a barley trip around the globe without moving your lazy gut. Open Mon. 11:30am-7pm, Tues.-Wed. 10:30am-7pm, Thurs.-Fri. 10:30am-12:30am, Sat. 9am-12:30am.

Public market, on Marktpl. Fresh produce, bread, and meat daily 9am-7pm.

SIGHTS AND ENTERTAINMENT

Anyone who loves books will gasp at the sight of St. Gallen's main attraction, the **Stiftsbibliotek** (Abbey Library; tel. 227 34 15) and the Abbey that houses it. Awestruck visitors shuffle across the dazzling parquet floors in huge gray slippers, which the library provides to protect the floors. The library maintains a collection of 140,000 volumes and 2000 manuscripts, 500 of which date back to the 13th century. Although the appearance of the resident death-blackened mummy might indicate otherwise, the Stiftsbibliotek is a living, lending library serving scholars the globe over. Umberto Eco was seen sniffing around here to get inspiration for *The Name of the Rose*. However, the ancient manuscripts on display and the books that line the main reading room are over-shadowed by the breathtaking **Baroque reading room.** The room was built between 1758 and 1767 and has never required restoration. The parquet floors and the ceiling paintings are among the most exquisite examples of the period in Switzerland. (Open June-Aug. Mon.-Sat. 9am-noon and 1:30-5pm, Sun. 10:30am-noon and 1:30-4pm; May and Sept.-Oct. Mon.-Sat. 9am-noon and 1:30-5pm, Sun. 10:30am-noon; Dec.-March Tues.-Sat. 9am-noon and 1:30-4pm; April Mon.-Sat. 9am-noon and 1:30-5pm. 7SFr, students and children 5SFr.) The **Kathedrale St. Gallen** (tel. 227 33 88), part of the Abbey, was founded in the 8th century but took its present form in the mid-18th century. Though technically Neoclassical and Baroque, with high white columns and windows, the cathedral exudes a gothic spookiness. Dark, forbidding ceiling frescoes culminate in the main cupola, where bleak, gruesome gray clouds spiral upward like inverted tornadoes. Pale green stucco branches tangle and poke around frescoes like the trees that attacked Snow White. Last but not least are the 16 confessionals constructed of tangled wood and manned by blank-eyed angels. The brighter abbey courtyard is a great place for a picnic or a sunbath. Near the Catholic abbey, the **Evangelical Church of St. Lawrence,** founded in the 9th century, sports castle-like organs, Easter-egg wall patterns, and a geometric, blue ceiling. (Open Mon.-Fri. 9:30-11:30am and 2-4pm.) Across the train tracks to the left and uphill (a bit of a walk from the center of town), the **Peter and Paul Wildpark** (tel. 222 67 92), on Rosenberg in Romonton, is where the ibex was saved from near extinction. The animals now roam the grounds freely. (Open 24hr. Free.) Explore the campus of the **St. Gallen University** by taking bus #5 (dir: Rotmonten): "Hochschule." The huge park donated to the city of St. Gallen in 1963 provides a magnificent view of the city and the Bodensee.

St. Gallen's celebration of music and general debauchery takes over the fields surrounding the town at the end of June. The **Open Air St. Gallen Music Festival** features over 20 live bands; past headliners have included Red Hot Chili Peppers, Cypress Hill, the legendary B.B. King, and the Godfather of Soul, James Brown. You must buy a ticket for all three days. Tickets run a steep 135SFr, but housing is included if you bring a tent and camp out (showers and toilets available). Or stay in St. Gallen and take the free shuttle bus from the train station to the concert grounds. For information about tickets and bands, call 223 41 01 or write to Open Air St. Gallen, Bahnhofstr. 6, CH-9000, St. Gallen, Switzerland. The **Stadttheater,** Museumstr. 24 (tel. 242 06 66), hosts over 200 concerts and dramatic works annually (Sept.-June). There are several **movie theaters** at Marktplatz (movie info tel. 122).

MUSEUMS

St. Gallen's aptly named Museumstraße holds four museums. One ticket grants admission to all four.

- **Historical Museum,** Museumstr. 50 (tel. 244 78 32). The local half of the museum displays linen processing, ancient kitchens, a random barber shop, and spiky weapons a tad more formidable than the modern Swiss army knife. The ethnological half brims with pierced African mannequins, masks, and a Native American with a scalp-decorated spear and vest embroidered with the "Bad Pianu Chicken." Indeed. Open Tues.-Sat. 10am-noon and 2-5pm, Sun. 10am-5pm. 6SFr, students 2SFr.
- **Natural History Museum,** Museumstr. 32 (tel. 245 22 44). Examples of almost everything Mother Nature has birthed in the last four billion years reside here. The **Kunstmuseum** in the same building juxtaposes modern art on the top floor with works by more traditional 19th- and 20th- century artists like Monet and Giacometti. The moving-eyeball television on the chandelier is just plain weird. Both open Tues.-Sat. 10am-noon and 2-5pm, Sun. 10am-5pm. 6SFr, students 2SFr.
- **Kirchofer House Museum,** Museumstr. 27 (tel. 244 75 21). Modest art collection but an impressive array of coins, Russian imperial silver, and the Appenzeller cave bear skeletons, all in the house of one of St. Gallen's first families. A rare painting depicts 3 sets of 18th-century St. Gallen twins, who bear a striking resemblance to the cave bear. Open Tues.-Sat. 10am-noon and 2-5pm. 6SFr, students 2SFr.

NIGHTLIFE

For a small city, St. Gallen is surprisingly perky—the *Altstadt* pulses with techno beats and clinking glasses. The cafés and bars in Marktpl. are popular but money-hungry. Head instead for the streets radiating out from Marktpl., which are packed with cheaper, hole-in-the-wall bars with tattooed, chained, and bejewelled clientele.

- **Filou,** Schwertg. (tel. 244 74 54). Smoky bar pumps 80s rock for a twentysomething crowd. Beer-guzzlers overflow into the camp-like picnic tables outside. Good luck finding space to dance on the weekend. Open Mon.-Sat. 5pm-midnight. No cover.
- **Goliath,** Goliathstr. 27, is a dark, local joint with red velvet walls, a crooked wooden bar, and a diverse crowd. Open Sun.-Fri. 7pm-midnight, Sat. 7pm-12:30am.
- **Ozon,** Goliathg. 28 (tel. 244 81 24). Non-stop chrome and mirrors lend the illusion of size to this compact club. If the flashing lights and smoke don't blind you, the prices will (beer from 9SFr). DJ spins different wax each night (techno Thurs.). Cover usually 10SFr. Open Sun. and Tues.-Thurs. 10pm-2am, Fri.-Sat. 10pm-3am.
- **Dancing,** Brühlg. 18 (tel. 226 09 00). Dance-floor action is projected onto a field of screens. Local bands, karaoke, and other theme nights (foxtrot, anyone?). Mon. is taxi-drivers' night. Are you talkin' to me? Sun.-Wed. no cover; Thurs.-Sat. 7-17SFr. Open July-Aug. Thurs.-Tues. 10pm-5:30am; Sept.-June 9pm to whenever.

■ Near St. Gallen: Appenzell

The jewel of Appenzellerland, Appenzell can't help but flaunt its beautiful location in the foothills and its well-preserved *Altstadt*. A stroll along Appenzell's streets reveals a remarkable number of centuries-old buildings, all of which—the tourist office will remind you—support the town's claim to be one of the most "authentic" Swiss villages. The Rathaus, which houses the museum, town hall, cantonal library, and tourist office, is itself remarkable, especially the **Großratssaal,** with intricately carved wood-paneled walls and 16th-century frescoes. The Rathaus was built in

1563 and escaped any Baroque intrusion on its heavy wooden beams and parquet floors.

The Appenzell **tourist office** (tel. 788 96 41; fax 788 96 49) is in the Rathaus. From the train station, walk down Bahnhofstr., bearing right as the road curves and intersects Hauptg. The tourist office is to the left of the church. They provide detailed hiking maps and specific dates for all of Appenzell's intriguing festivals, like the early October **Viehschau (cattle show)** or the pulse-pounding **goat show** the next day. You'll have to wait till November for the sheep show. There are different activities every day, from a tour of the Appenzeller Alpenbitter factory (Wed. 10am, meet at Weissbadstr. 27; free) to a course in woodcarving (Thurs. 2pm, make your own butter dish 20SFr; register before 5pm the previous day). They also make hotel reservations (free if you call in; 20SFr deposit required if you show up in person) and book cable car excursions (round-trip 21-28.50SFr). (Open June-Oct. Mon.-Fri. 9am-noon and 2-6pm, Sat. 9am-noon and 2-4pm; Nov.-May Mon.-Fri. 9am-noon and 2-5pm, Sat. 9am-noon.) **Buses** connect Appenzell to the smaller towns of the canton, and the **Appenzellerbahn** chugs to St. Gallen every hour (1hr., 10.20SFr). **Parking lots** are across from the Co-op and along the Sitter river across the bridge from the St. Mauritius Church. Appenzell's **telephone code** is 071.

Particularly picturesque lodgings await at **Haus Lydia,** Eggerstrandenstr. 53 (tel. 787 42 33). A staff member will pick you up at the train station if you call ahead. Otherwise walk 20 minutes from the station and turn right on Gringelstr., left on Weissbadstr., right on Gaiserstr., and right onto Eggerstrandenstr. Run by a friendly, English-speaking family, the house offers large rooms with great pastoral views and a kitchen for guest use. (37.50SFr per person. Breakfast included. Reservations required.) The **Gasthaus Hof** (tel. 787 22 10; fax 787 58 83), near the center of the *Altstadt*, is a bustling family-run restaurant with guest-rooms upstairs. (Dorms 25SFr; doubles with TV 65SFr. Breakfast included. Restaurant open daily 8am-midnight.) Many hiking trails anticipate hikers with **Gasthöfe** (guest houses), gorgeous old farmhouses and restaurants for the road-weary along the way. One of the nicest farmhouses is **Berggasthaus Seealpsee** (tel. 799 11 40; fax 799 18 20), with sweet-smelling wood rooms and a pristine location on the edge of the Seealpsee. From Wasserauen, take the Eberalp cable car up to the top and hike one hour to the Seealpsee. (Dorms 22SFr; doubles 80SFr. Breakfast included.) **Gasthof Freidenberg** (tel. 87 12 40) provides gorgeous, oh-so-Swiss painted beds and wardrobes and Appenzell's best panoramic view of the Alpstein from its hilltop locale. From the rear exit of the train station walk about 12 minutes, mostly uphill, and follow the signs, eventually taking the gravel footpath up the hill past the pet rabbits to the guest house. (Reception and restaurant open Thurs.-Tues. Singles 58SFr; doubles 98-116SFr. Breakfast included.) The **restaurant** downstairs offers huge portions, and all prices are under 27SFr (even the steak). For more Swiss specialties—with a cheesy twist—try some of the Appenzeller specialties at **Restaurant Traube,** Marktg. 7 (tel. 787 14 07). The candle-lit restaurant has cheesy *Chäsdorfli*, an Appenzeller specialty of cheese, potatoes, and noodles. (Open March-Jan. 9am-midnight.) For hiking sustenance, try the **Co-op,** Marktg. 14. Walk along Rathauspl. to Marktg. on the left, and look for the orange sign behind Marktpl. (Open Mon. 1-6:30pm, Tues.-Fri. 8am-12:15pm and 2-6:30pm, Sat. 8am-4pm.)

In the heart of the *Alpstein*, or foothills of the Alps, Appenzell is ideal for **hiking** without the temperature extremes of Zermatt or the Ticino region. The area has an extensive networks of marked trails connecting the small towns of the canton to the larger urban areas of St. Gallen and Winterthur. Ask at the tourist office for *Wandervorschläge: Appenzellerland*, which has a detailed map with timed distances. For an easy walk through the green pastures whose product eventually become the renowned Appenzeller cheese, walk along the Sitter River to Weissbad by exiting the tourist office, turning left on Hauptg., and following the signs to Weissbad at the river (about 1hr.). You can then take the Appenzellerbahn back (Eurailpass valid). For phenomenal views above the treeline, take the train to Jakobsbad and then a cable car to the top of **Mt. Kronberg** (1663m; round-trip 21SFr; with Eurailpass

14SFr). Follow the trail through remote villages all the way back to Appenzell (about 3hr.).

Tucked inside the **Rathaus** and the adjoining Haus Buherre Hanisefs, the **Museum Appenzell,** Hauptg. 4 (tel. 787 9631), holds a six-floor collection of Swiss crafts, costumes, and culture. Mannequins stand, blank-faced, frozen mercilessly in the acts of cheese- and lace-making. One visit will give you a lifetime dose of Swiss culture. (Open April-Oct. daily 10am-noon and 2-5pm; Nov.-March Tues.-Sun. 2-4pm. 5SFr, students 3SFr.) On Wednesday mornings, visit **Herr Fässler,** an honest-to-goodness Swiss farmer and cheesemaker in Grosshütter who loves talking about cheese—for free! Contact the tourist office for details.

Schaffhausen

Surrounded by Germany on three sides, Schaffhausen understandably retains a rather Teutonic language and look. *Oriel* (bay) windows, gilded shopkeepers' signs, and fountains fill the pedestrian Marktplatz and *Altstadt*. Schaffhausen is proud of its history and architecture; after the U.S. mistakenly bombed many of its buildings during WWII, citizens painstakingly rebuilt each structure in the same fashion as the original. The **Munot Fortress** stands tall and proud above the city. Built in the 1500s to protect the citizens, the fortress proved rather unnecessary—no one ever attacked.

Orientation and Practical Information The local **tourist office** (tel. 625 51 41; fax 625 51 43) looks out onto the lively Fronwagpl. From the train station, head down Schwertstr., the narrow street to the right, and walk until you reach the main square and fountain; the tourist office is on the right at the back of the square. The office has maps, hotel listings, and hiking information, and gives city tours in German, French, or English. (Open April-Sept. Mon.-Fri. 10am-noon and 2-5pm, Sat.-Sun. 10am-noon; Oct.-March Mon.-Fri. 2-5pm. Tours April-Oct. Mon., Wed., and Fri. 2:15pm; 1½hr; 10SFr, children 5SFr.) Schaffhausen is accessible by train, bus, and boat. A **Tageskarte** (26SFr) allows one day of unlimited travel on Bodensee area railways, waterways, and roadways, including those belonging to Schaffhausen, Stein am Rein, Constance, and St. Gallen. **Trains** arrive every hour from **Zurich** (15.80SFr), **St. Gallen** (26SFr), and **Winterthur** (9.60SFr). PTT **buses** connect Schaffhausen to the smaller towns in St. Gallerland (2SFr). Numerous **ferries** traverse the Bodensee, departing from Schaffhausen to **Stein Am Rein** (3 per day, 13.80SFr) and **Constance** (3 per day, 26SFr). **Parking** is available in the parking garage off of Rheinstr., in the lots near the cathedral, off Moeratz, and behind the train station. The train station **exchanges currency** (daily 5:30am-8:10pm), **rents bikes** (23SFr per day), and **stores luggage** (5SFr; both open Mon.-Fri. 6am-8pm, Sat.-Sun. 8am-8pm). The **postal code** is CH-8200. The **telephone code** is 053.

Accommodations and Food Schaffhausen's **Jugendherberge (HI),** Randenstr. 65 (tel. 625 88 00; fax 624 59 54), is in the newer—i.e. early 19th-century—section of town. Once a villa, the building now houses the mammoth youth hostel within its high garden walls. (Reception 5:30-10pm. Check-out 9am. Curfew 10pm; keys available. Dorms 21.50SFr first night, then 19SFr; singles 27SFr, 24.50SFr; doubles 54SFr, 49SFr. Members only. Breakfast, sleepsack, and showers included. Kitchen facilities 2SFr per meal.) Brown and pink are the dominant colors of the **Hotel Steinbock,** Weberg. 47 (tel. 625 42 60), above a lively painted-window bar in the *Altstadt*. Walk from the tourist office along the Vorstadt and turn left on Weberg. (Reception 2pm-midnight. Singles 46SFr; doubles 75SFr; triples 95SFr. Showers included. No breakfast. Closed Sun.) **Camping Rheinwiesen** (tel. 659 33 00) stands at the edge of the Rhine, 3km from Schaffhausen. Take the bus to "Langswiesen" or the train to Stein am Rein. (6.20SFr; tents 6.30SFr. Sept.-June: 4.20SFr; 5.30SFr.)

The Fronwagpl. comes alive during the day with outdoor cafés, restaurants, and live entertainment ranging from mimes to fire-breathers. Schaffhausen's modern **Migros,** Vorstadt 39, puts up a good medieval front, blending harmoniously with the rest of the Vorstadt. (Open Mon.-Wed. and Fri. 8:15am-6:30pm, Thurs. 8:15am-9pm, Sat. 7:30am-4pm.) Stock up on fresh produce at the **farmer's market** at Johannkirche. (Tues. and Sat. 7am-noon.) **Restaurant Falken,** Vorstadt 5 (tel. 625 32 21), has been a Schaffhausen landmark for years. The former Falken brewery is still home to many beer-drinking traditions and clubs and sports an inexpensive but hearty Swiss menu. Create your own *Rösti* for 8SFr and up. The owner of **Restaurant Tiergarten,** across from the Allerheiligen Monastery, adds atmospheric spice by serving a different national cuisine each year and decorating to extremes. Past influences include the Caribbean, Greece, and Mexico. Find out where he's off to next, or dig into one of the seasonal specialties, such as longhorn sheep in winter. *Bratwurst* and *Rösti* for 14.50SFr are among the permanent Swiss classics. (Open daily 9am-11pm.)

Sights and Entertainment At the corner of Vorstadt and Löwengässchen in the *Altstadt*, the gilded *oriel* windows on the medieval **Goldener Ochsen** shine in the sun. Throughout the *Altstadt*, colorful frescoes and fountains and intricate clocks and carvings embarrass the wandering dullard commonfolk with their shimmering finery. Of particular note is the **Knight's House,** Vordenstr. 65, covered by brilliantly colored frescoes portraying scenes from Greek and Roman mythology in high Renaissance style. On the other side of town, the 16th-century **Munot Fortress** spooks even the most brazen, with cavernous ground floors, dimly lit interiors, and narrow, winding staircases. Medieval skylights cast glowing circles of light on the cool, dark interior, conjuring visions of townsfolk huddling around fires to the sounds of cannonballs. (Open daily May-Sept. 8am-8pm; Oct.-April 9am-5pm.) On the outskirts of the *Altstadt*, the **Münsterkirche** maintains a peaceful oasis amid the buzz and whir of the nearby power plants. The Reformation stripped the 11th-century church of ornamentation, leaving the holy confines stark and majestic. The adjoining monastery, **Kloster Allerheiligen,** is a labyrinth of porticoes and courtyards and houses a music school, museum, and the enormous **Schiller Bell,** the inspiration for Schiller's famous poem. The poet, however, never actually saw the bell—his chum Goethe described it to him. The monastery also shelters well-tended herb gardens still used for medicinal purposes (or so they claim). The **Museum Zu Allerheiligen** holds the **Natural History Museum** (tel. 625 43 77; fax 625 43 70) and the **Kunstverein Schaffhausen.** The huge museum complex juxtaposes stuffed boars, modern Schaffhausener art, and antler-bedecked monastic dining halls. The highlight is the onyx, a bedazzling hunk of gold jewels and a cameo so priceless you have to ask at the desk for a staff member to unlock its room. (Open Tues.-Sun. 10am-noon and 2-5pm. Free.)

A short bus ride from the train station to **Neuhausen** (bus #1 or 9: "Rheinfalls") leads to the **Rheinfalls,** a waterfall so huge that Goethe thought it was the source of the ocean. A path leads along the river's edge, and a bridge offers a closer look at the massive column of water (1SFr). **Rhein Travel,** Schlauchbootfahrten, 8455 Rüdlingen (tel. (01) 867 06 38), has information about river rafting. Boats float downstream with **Rhyfall Mändli** (tel. 672 48 11), departing approximately every 45 minutes from Schloß Laufen (June-Aug. 11am-6pm, May-Sept. 11am-5pm; 5.50SFr, children 3SFr). The rushing river lulls backpackers to sleep at **Jugendherberge Dachsen (HI)** (tel. 659 61 52; fax 659 60 39). Take the train: "Schloß Laufen am Rheinfall," two stops from Schaffhausen, and then walk up the stairs to the castle and follow the signs for the hostel. The hostel fills up quickly; reserve in advance. (Reception 7-10am and 5-10pm. Dorms 22SFr first night, then 19.50SFr; one triple 72SFr, 64.50SFr; one quad 96SFr, 86SFr. Members only. Breakfast included for dorms. Kitchen facilities 2SFr.) The **Bannerstube** (tel. 659 67 67) in the castle serves a few reasonably priced dishes and has a fantastic view of the falls. (Soups 6-8SFr.

Pasta from 14SFr. Children's menu available. Open daily March-Dec. 11:30am-2pm and 6:30-9:30pm.)

■ Stein am Rhein

Stein am Rhein (not to be confused with Stein) is roughly the Swiss equivalent of America's Plymouth or Williamsburg—the entire hamlet a proud showcase of Switzerland's modest origins, displayed in museums, reconstructions, and reenactments. A port of call for the tourist-packed ferries that cruise the lake, Stein am Rhein has seen fit to merge its medieval architecture and docile streets with the rather profitable Bodensee tourist trade. Although postcard shops outnumber the sights two-to-one, mellow paint-lovers amble gleefully along cobblestone streets, old fountains, and pretty medieval facades.

Orientation and Practical Information The *Altstadt* lies down Bahnhofstr. and across the bridge from the train station. Stein am Rhein's **tourist office** (tel. 741 28 35; fax 741 51 46) lies on the Oberstadt to the left of the *Rathaus*. The staff can recommend hotels, provide maps, and give cruise information. (Open Mon.-Fri. 9-11am and 2-5pm.) **Trains** connect Stein am Rhein to **Schaffhausen** (6.60SFr), **St. Gallen** (23SFr), **Winterthur** (11.40SFr), and **Constance** (9SFr). **Buses** connect the city to the string of small towns in the area and to Germany. **Boats** depart three times each day (once on Sun.) for Schaffhausen (1¼hr.; 13.80SFr), Constance (2¼hr.; 16.60SFr), and other Bodensee towns. **Parking** is available along Hemihoferstr., off Untertor (lot open 10am-6pm). The train station has **currency exchange** and **bike rental** (23SFr; open Mon.-Fri. 5am-11pm, Sat.-Sun. 5:55am-11pm). The **post office** is carefully hidden off the main street on Brodlaubeg. From the *Rathaus*, walk down Rathauspl. and turn right onto Brodlaubeg. The post office is straight ahead on the right. (Open Mon.-Fri. 7:30am-noon and 1:45-6pm, Sat. 8-11am.) Stein am Rhein's **postal code** is CH-8260. The city's **telephone code** is 054.

Accommodations and Food The suburban **Jugendherberge (HI)** stands at Hemihoferstr. 711 (tel. 741 12 55; fax 741 51 40). From the train station, take the bus: "Strandbad," cross the street, and walk along the gravel path to the end. You'll see the flags in front of the hostel across the street. An English-speaking staff maintains this clean hostel. Many rooms overlook the Rhine. (Reception 7:30-9am and 5:30-10pm. Curfew 10:30pm; keys available. Dorms 21.50SFr first night, then 19SFr; doubles 27SFr, 24.50SFr. Non-members add 5SFr. Breakfast, sheets, and showers included. Open March-Oct.) Picnickers fill up their baskets at the **Co-op** at the corner of Rathauspl. and Schwarzhorng. (Open Mon.-Fri. 8:15am-12:15pm and 2-6:30pm, Sat. 7:30am-4:50pm.) Rathausplatz's many outdoor restaurants and cafés provide great people-watching venues. **The Spaghetteria,** Schifflände (tel. 741 22 36), sits directly on the Rhine and serves cheap but tasty Italian fare, with pasta dishes from 11SFr and beers at 4.20SFr for 0.50L. The restaurant houses the world's longest piece of spaghetti at 188.8m. (Open March 15-Oct. daily 9am-midnight. Free beer with lunch if you show your *Let's Go*.) **Restaurant Roten Ochsen,** Rathauspl. 9 (tel. 741 23 28), cooks up Swiss dishes (9-29SFr) and tosses a mean salad (11-17SFr) beneath a grapevine ceiling fresco. (Open Tues.-Thurs. and Sun. 9:30am-11:30pm, Fri.-Sat. 9:30am-12:30am.)

Sights and Entertainment Stein am Rhein first came into prominence in the 12th century with the establishment of the **Kloster St. George** (tel. 741 21 24), a Benedictine monastery. Perhaps the best preserved in the German-speaking world, the monks' rooms have remained unaltered since the 16th century. Intricate frescoes and wood carvings line the paneled walls. (Open March-Nov. Tues.-Sun. 10am-noon and 1:30-5pm. 3SFr, students 1.50SFr.) To the right of the monastery, the stately **Rathaus** surveys Stein am Rhein's main thoroughfare. The exterior's mythological frescoes depict everything from men in barrels to suicidal storks. The third floor holds a to-die-for collection of his-and-her armor (for the lady, may we suggest a nice hauberk, and for the gentleman, why not some smart chain-mail stockings?). Call for a viewing (tel. 741 54 25). On Untertor, the **Wohnmuseum Lindwurm,** Understadt 33 (tel. 741 25 12; fax 741 45 82), reconstructs domestic life in the 19th century. Despite the scary stuffed cat and St. Bernard dog run, this worthwhile museum welcomes visitors with authentic kitchens, nurseries, and barns with real chickens. Not-so-evil stepmothers send the kids to the "servants' room" where they can try on old Swiss clothing and jump in a straw bed. Near the Rhine, on the quiet Schwarzhorngasse (a left off the main street from the monastery), the **Puppenmuseum,** Schwarzhorng. 136 (tel. 741 39 66), displays every kind of doll imaginable, from ancient, balding babies to recent facsimiles of Swiss girls at play. (Open mid-April to mid-Oct. Tues.-Sun. 11am-5pm. 5SFr, students 4SFr.)

The exterior of **Alpen Rock** (tel. 816 60 50) is deceiving. This cute li'l Alpine cottage houses a quintessentially Swiss nightclub—even blond-braided Heidi needs a break from yodelling. Twenty- and thirtysomething locals crowd this booming hangout, head-banging on the dance floor or hiding away for a romantic *Rösti* for two in a little hut in the corner. The club is only accessible by car from Zurich, but many travelers with early morning flights buy a beer instead of a hotel room, party till their flight, and call a cab. (Cover 6SFr, which includes a 0.50SFr contribution to mountain preservation. Open Tues.-Wed. 10pm-2am, Thurs.-Sat. 10:30pm-4am.)

LIECHTENSTEIN

Liechtenstein's minute size (160 sq. km, about the same as Manhattan) and population (30,629 people) render it a favorite among sadistic geography teachers. Famous chiefly for its wines, royal family, and postage stamps, the principality itself is more of a tourist attraction than any individual sight it contains. Brochures entreat visitors to "go *to* Liechtenstein, not through it," but most travelers breeze right through, pausing only long enough to buy the official *"Hurra! Ich bin da"* (hurray, I'm here!) postage stamp or hastily record the visit in a passport.

The only German-speaking monarchy in the world, Liechtenstein remains one of the last vestiges of the former Holy Roman Empire. It has been an independent country since 1719, but its last standing army was an 80-man force in 1868 that patrolled the Italian border and saw no action other than the occasional blizzard on the Stelvio Pass. German is the official language, but many inhabitants also speak English and French. The flatter areas of this green kingdom provide outstanding **biking,** and an efficient and cheap **postal bus** system links all 11 villages (most trips 2.40SFr; Swisspass valid). A one month bus ticket (20SFr) covers all of Liechtenstein and includes buses to such Swiss and Austrian border towns as Feldkirch and Buchs. If you plan to stay more than three days (a sojourn that may tax the imagination), it's a great buy. To enter the principality, catch a postal bus from Sargans or Buchs in Switzerland or Feldkirch in Austria (3.60SFr each). For the **police,** call 117. In a **fire,** call 118. In a **medical emergency,** dial 144. The principality has used the Swiss franc as its currency since 1924 and has adopted the Swiss postal and telephone systems. The **postal code** is FL-9490, and the **telephone code** is 075. Liechtenstein uses the Swiss **country code** (041) and **international dialing prefix** (00).

■ Vaduz

More hamlet than national capital, Vaduz is Liechtenstein's tourist center—and not a budget-friendly place. Tour buses deposit their loads directly in front of the dozens of souvenir shops on the main streets, under the greedy eyes of restauranteurs and their inflated menu prices. Liechtenstein's **national tourist office,** Städtle 37 (tel. 392 11 11 or 232 14 43; fax 392 16 18; email touristinfo@lie-net.li), one block up the hill from the Vaduz postal bus stop, stamps passports (2SFr), locates rooms free of charge, makes hotel reservations at any of the country's 46 hotels and guest houses (2SFr), and distributes free maps and advice on hiking, cycling, and skiing in the area. (Open June-Oct. Mon.-Fri. 8am-noon and 1:30-5:30pm, Sat. 9am-noon and 1-4pm, Sun. 10am-noon and 1-4pm; Nov.-May Mon.-Fri. 8am-noon and 1:30-5:30pm. English spoken.) If the tourist office is closed and you are in desperate need of a passport stamp, head to the postage museum. For **currency exchange** at acceptable rates, go to Switzerland. No kidding. Liechtenstein's banks charge exorbitant rates, so use a credit card whenever you can. **Bicyclists** can rent trusty steeds (20SFr per day) at the train station in Buchs or Sargans with an ID deposit. The tourist office sells bike maps for 2.50SFr. **Swimmers** bathe at **Muhlehölz,** Schaanerstr. 60, just down the street from the youth hostel. The complex boasts two high dives and a wading pool. Walk down the hostel's driveway and then continue straight ahead on the path directly opposite. (Open June-Aug. Mon. 10am-8pm, Tues.-Sun. 9am-8pm; May and Sept. Mon 10am-7pm, Tues.-Sun. 9am-7pm. 4.50SFr, children 2SFr. Lock deposit 10SFr.) The main **post office** (tel. 232 21 55) is near the tourist office and has an amazing selection of—surprise!—postage stamps. (Open Mon.-Fri. 7:45am-6pm, Sat. 8-11am.)

Liechtenstein's lone **Jugendherberge (HI),** Untere Rütig. 6 (tel. 232 50 22; fax 232 58 56), is in **Schaan,** one town over from Vaduz. From the Vaduz bus stand, take the bus (dir: Schaan): "Mühleholz," walk toward the intersection with the traffic lights, and turn down Marianumstr. Walk 4 to 5 minutes and follow the signs to this newly renovated and spotless pink hostel, set on the edge of a farm. The hostel is an arcade junkie's paradise, with foosball, pinball, air hockey, video games, and ping-pong tables. (Reception Mon.-Sat. 5-10pm, Sun. 6-10pm. Lockout 9:30am-5pm. Curfew 10pm. Members only. Dorms 26.30SFr; doubles 64.60SFr; family quads 113.20SFr. Showers and breakfast included. Dinner 12SFr. Leave your bags in the basement lockers for a 2SFr deposit any time. Laundry facilities. Open March-Nov. 15.) Walking 10 minutes back up the road toward Vaduz or taking the bus (dir: Schaan): "Falknis" leads to **Hotel Falknis,** Landstr. 92 (tel. 232 63 77), another budget option. (Singles 50SFr; doubles 100SFr. Breakfast and showers included. Closed Dec. 24-Jan. 15.) Eating out cheaply in expensive Liechtenstein is extremely hard. Shop at **Denner Superdiscount,** Aulestr. 20, across from the tour bus parking lot, for an inexpensive picnic. (Open Mon.-Fri. 8:30am-1pm and 1:30-6:30pm, Sat. 8am-4pm.) In the same shopping complex, **Azzuro Pizza** (tel. 232 48 18) has pizzas for take-out (6-12SFr). (Open Mon.-Fri. 8am-8pm, Sat. 8am-5pm, Sun. 10am-5pm.) For a mechanized treat, pop 2SFr in the **ice-cream machine** just opposite the post office. Pull out the cone and watch the ice cream automatically swirl in, no hands necessary.

Above the town sits the 12th-century **Schloß Vaduz,** regal home to Hans-Adam II, Prince of Liechtenstein. Although the interior of the ruler's residence is off-limits to the bourgeois masses, you can hike up to the castle for a closer look and a phenomenal view of the whole country. (The numerous "Castle this way: No visit" signs, seemingly designed to tease tourists, are only meant to stop the commoners from knocking on the royal front door and inviting themselves inside.) Along with *Seine Durchlaucht* (His Highness), the castle houses an excellent art collection, primarily Dutch and Flemish, gathered by the royal family over the last 400 years. Much of the art makes its way to the **Staatliche Kunstsammlung,** Städtle 37, next to the tourist office. (Open daily April-Oct. 10am-noon and 1:30-5:30pm; Nov.-March 10am-noon and 1:30-5pm. 5SFr, students 3SFr, children 2.50SFr.) Reproductions of the Prince's art almost inevitably end up on postage stamps and thus in the one-room **Briefmarkenmuseum** (Stamp Museum) on the other side of the tourist office. The museum features rare postage from around the globe as well as one of Liechtenstein's staples—nearly one-fourth of the country's income comes from its stamps. (Open daily April-Oct. 10am-noon and 1:30-5:30pm; Nov.-March 10am-noon and 1:30-5pm. Free.) Groups of 10 or more can arrange to visit the **Hofkellerei des Regierenden Fürsten von Liechtenstein** (Wine Cellars of the Ruling Prince of Liechtenstein) and taste wines from the Prince's private vineyards. For the necessary reservations, call 232 10 18, fax 233 11 45, or write to Feldstr. 4, FL-9490 Vaduz. Smaller groups (up to 3) can try knocking on the door of the wine cellars. If the cellar has an open bottle, they'll often let you sample it. If the idea of seeing 300 types of skis and 180 pairs of boots thrills you, check out the **Ski Museum,** Bangarten 10 (tel. 232 15 02), up the road to Schaan and on the left. (Open Mon. and Fri. 2-6pm or by appointment. 5SFr.)

Upper Liechtenstein

It seems impossible that a country so small could have regions, but the cluster of villages in the upper country do have a character of their own. The "upper" in Upper Liechtenstein does not refer to a northern position but to the elevation. High above the frantic town of Vaduz, one is surrounded by clouds, cows, and gorgeous views of the **Rhine Valley.** Buses run to all these towns from Vaduz in under 40 minutes, and the trips are well worth the price even if you're only spending one day in the country.

A group of Swiss immigrants known as the Walsers founded **Triesenberg,** the principal town, in the 13th century. Overpopulation, oppression, and natural disaster drove them from Valais to present-day Liechtenstein, where they chose the highest arable mountain as the site for their village. The **Walser Heimatmuseum** chronicles the Walsers' religious customs, hut construction, cattle trade, and crafts. Watch the slide show (in English) for a panoramic view of the upper country in all seasons, an introduction to its history, and a glimpse at Liechtensteiner life when the tourists aren't around. The ground floor houses wooden sculptures by folk artist Rudolf Schädles. (Open Tues.-Fri. 1:30-5:30pm, Sat. 1:30-5pm, Sun. 2-5pm; Sept.-May closed Sun. 2SFr, children 1SFr.) The **tourist office** (tel. 262 19 26; fax 262 19 22) is in the same building as the museum and has the same hours. **Pension Alpenblick,** Neudorf 383 (tel. 262 35 77), offers beds in spacious rooms 10 minutes (downhill) from the tourist office. Walk down the main road, take the second right, and follow the street as it loops back (the tourist office has a detailed map). (Singles 40SFr; doubles 70SFr; triples 105SFr. After 3 nights: 35SFr, 60SFr, 90SFr. Shower 3SFr. Breakfast included.) Liechtenstein's two **campgrounds,** peaceful almost to a fault, are easily accessible by postal bus. **Bendern** (tel. 373 12 11) is on the Schellenberg line. (3SFr; tent 2-4SFr.) **Camping Mittagspitze** (tel. 392 36 77 or 392 26 86) is between Triesen and Balzers on the road to Sargans. (Reception 7am-noon and 2-10pm. 8SF; tent 5SFr.)

On the other side of the mountain, **Malbun,** dubbed "the undiscovered St. Moritz," offers secluded and affordable ski slopes and has served as a training ground for many an Olympian. The highlights are two chairlifts, four T-bars, two ski schools, and a dearth of other skiers. (Daypass 33SFr; weekly pass 142SFr, off-season 129SFr.) **Malbun A.G.** (tel. 263 97 70 or 262 19 15) offers one-day classes (50SFr), three-day classes (120SFr), and even private snowboard lessons (1 day 200SFr). **Malbun Sport** (tel. 263 37 55) on Berosestr. rents skis. (Open Mon.-Fri. 8am-6pm, Sat. 8am-5pm, Sun. 9am-5pm. Visa, MC, AmEx.) The **Fun Factory** (tel./fax 263 26 36) across the street rents snowboards (35SFr, shoes 12SFr). The Valüna valley, 2km from Malbun, offers four-track, lighted cross-country trails. The superb chalet duo of **Hotel Alpen** and **Hotel Galina** (tel. 263 11 81; fax 263 96 46) are the best accommodation options in Malbun. Family-run, with wood paneling and a heated swimming pool, these hotels are perfect for *après*-ski unwinding. (Reception in Hotel Alpen for both. Singles 40-65SFr, with shower 70-100SFr; doubles 80-130SFr, 140-200SFr. Breakfast and pool included. Open mid-May to Oct. and Dec. 15-April 15.) Malbun's **tourist office** (tel. 263 65 77) stands ready to give advice. (Open June-Oct. and mid-Dec. to mid-April Mon.-Wed. and Fri. 9am-noon and 1:30-5pm, Sat. 9am-noon and 1:30-4pm.)

As two-thirds of the country is undeveloped mountains, **hiking** in Upper Liechtenstein offers breathtaking views from forested trails. The upper country has 150km of trails, clearly marked with yellow *Wanderweg* signs. The tourist offices in Vaduz, Triesenberg, and Malbun offer a free booklet of short hike suggestions; detailed maps cost 15.50SFr at any bookstore or the tourist offices. The top pick is the round-trip hike from Gnalp to Masescha (roughly 3hr.). Other popular power-hikes to prominent peaks include the **Pfälzer-Hütte** (2108m, 4-5hr. through Augustenberg to Bettlerjoch), **Schönberg** (2104m, 4-5hr.), and **Galinakopf** (2198m, 6-7hr.). **Alpine guides** offer group and individual climbing courses in Liechtenstein as well as in neighboring Austria and Switzerland. Contact Michael Bargetze, pat. Bergführer, Lavidina 755, FL-9497 Triesenberg (tel. 268 10 05). A guided tour isn't always necessary; less challenging do-it-yourself hikes start from the Triesenberg church (postal bus: "Philosophenweg") and run from **Masescha** and back (2-3hr.) or from the parking lot at Malbun near the postal bus stop "Sass" to **Kirchli** and down (1-2hr.). The **Liechtenstein Alpine Association** offers guided full- and half-day hikes every Thursday in summer. The Saturday newspaper publishes routes and contact numbers, and the tourist office also has information. If hiking seems too pedestrian, try **paragliding** with **Hang Loose AG Fly and Fun World** (tel. 230 07 07; fax 230 07 06).

APPENDIX

CLIMATE

The climate in the **mountainous areas** of Austria and Switzerland (northern and western Austria and central and northeastern Switzerland) resembles chilly New York City weather throughout the year. Temperatures depend largely on altitude; as a rule, they decrease an average of 1.7°C (3°F) for each additional 1000ft. feet of elevation. Unless you're on a mountain, the countries don't normally get brutally cold, even in the dead of winter. Summer temperatures can reach 38°C (100°F) for brief periods, although summer evenings are usually cool. Warm sweaters are the rule September to May; add a parka, hat, and gloves in winter. Winter snow cover lasts from late December to March in the valleys, from November to May at about 6000ft., and stays year-round above 8500ft. Switzerland's **lake areas,** in the temperate swath of plain that extends across from Lake Constance in the northeast through Zurich and Bern down to Geneva, draw as much rain from the sky as from the lakes. Summertime brings very frequent rains in both countries—almost every other day in Salzburg—suitable rain gear is a must. Switzerland's Italian-speaking canton of **Ticino** lies in a fairly low plateau and boasts a pseudo-tropical clime. The following chart gives the average high and low temperatures in degrees centigrade (Celsius) and the average yearly rainfall in centimeters during four months of the year.

Temp.(C)/ Rain(cm)	January Temp.	Rain	April Temp.	Rain	July Temp.	Rain	October Temp.	Rain
Basel	4/-3	5.3	16/4	6.4	26/13	8.0	15/6	5.2
Bern	2/-4	19	14/4	12	22/13	11	13/5	6
Budapest	1/-4	3.7	17/7	4.5	28/16	5.6	16/7	5.7
Geneva	4/-2	6.3	15/5	5.1	25/15	6.4	14/7	7.2
Graz	1/-5	2.5	15/5	5.0	25/14	12.5	14/6	7.5
Innsbruck	1/-7	5.4	16/4	5.2	25/13	13.4	15/5	6.7
Linz	1/-4	3.9	12/5	4.5	24/14	8.4	14/5	5.6
Lucerne	2/-3	7.4	14/4	7.6	25/14	13.6	14/6	7.7
Lugano	6/-2	6.3	17/7	14.8	27/16	18.5	16/8	17.3
Prague	0/-5	1.8	12/3	2.7	23/13	6.8	12/5	3.3
Salzburg	2/-5	6.5	12/3	8.5	23/13	19.5	14/4	8.0
Vienna	1/-4	3.9	15/6	4.5	25/15	8.4	14/7	5.6
Zermatt	-7/-11	20.2	-2/-6	16.6	8/3	30.2	2/-3	18.3
Zurich	2/-3	7.4	15/4	7.6	25/14	13.6	14/6	7.7

To convert from °C to °F, multiply by 1.8 and add 32. For an approximation, double the Celsius and add 25. To convert from °F to °C, subtract 32 and multiply by 0.55.

°C	-5	0	5	10	15	20	25	30	35	40
°F	23	32	41	50	59	68	77	86	95	104

HOLIDAYS AND FESTIVALS

The *International Herald-Tribune* lists national holidays in each daily edition. If you plan your itinerary around these dates, you can encounter the festivals that entice you and circumvent the crowds visiting the ones that don't. This information is also valuable when determining when to arrive where—many services shut down on holidays and could leave you currency- or foodless in the event of an ill-timed arrival. Note also that in Austria, the first Saturday of every month is *Langer Samstag* (long Saturday); most stores stay open until 5pm. In small towns, stores are often closed from noon Saturday until 8am Monday—important to remember when stocking up on food for weekends. Check the individual town listings for information on the festivals below.

Date	Festival	Region
		Austria
January 6	Epiphany	National
January	Hahnenkamm World Cup Ski Races	Kitzbühel
April 17-24	Easter Festival	Salzburg
May 1	Labor Day	National
Mid-May to Mid-June	Wiener Festwochen	Vienna
May 11	Ascension Day	National
May 22	Whit Monday	National
June 2	Corpus Christi Day	National
June 6-7	Procession of Samson	Tamsweg
End of July	Salzburg Festival	Salzburg
Late July to Mid-August	Music Festival	Bregenz
Late July to Late August	Salzburg Music Festival	Salzburg
August 1	Folklore fair	Villach
August 3-4	Fröhlichgasse	Graz
August 14	Eve of the First Feast of the Assumption	Wörther See
August 15	Feast of the Assumption	National
October 26	Flag Day	National
November 1	All Saints' Day	National
November 11	St. Martin's Day	Regional
November 29	Kathreinsonntag	Regional
December 8	Feast of the Immaculate Conception	National
		Switzerland
January 6	Epiphany	National
March 1-3	Fasnacht (Carnival)	Basel
April 22-29	European Watch, Clock, and Jewelry Fair	Basel
May	International Jazz Festival	Bern
May 1	Labor Day	Regional
May 11	Ascension	National
May 22	Whit Monday	National

TELEPHONE CODES ■ 469

June	*International June Festival: classical music, theater, art*	Zurich
June 2	*Corpus Christi*	Regional
June 15-20	*International 20th-century art festival*	Basel
July 2-17	*International Jazz Festival*	Montreux
August 1	*Swiss National Day*	National
August 24-27	*Folklore Festival*	Fribourg
September 12-13	*Knabenschiessen*	Zurich
October 22-November 6	*Autumn Fair*	Basel
November 21	*Traditional Onion Market*	Bern
December 11-12	*Escalade (Historic Festival)*	Geneva

TELEPHONE CODES

Basel	061
Bern	031
Bregenz	05574
Budapest	1
Geneva	022
Graz	0316

Interlaken	036
Innsbruck	0512
Lausanne	021
Liechtenstein	075
Linz	0732
Lucerne	041

Lugano	091
Munich	089
Prague	02
Salzburg	0662
Vienna	01
Zurich	01

Country Codes

Australia	61
Austria	43
Canada	1
Czech Republic	42

Germany	49
Hungary	36
Ireland	353
New Zealand	64

South Africa	27
Switzerland	41
U.K.	44
U.S.	1

TIME ZONES

Switzerland, Austria, Prague, and Budapest all use Central European time (abbreviated MEZ in German). Add six hours to Eastern Standard Time and one hour to Greenwich Mean Time. Subtract nine hours from Eastern Australia Time and 11 hours from New Zealand Time. Austria and Switzerland use the 24-hour clock for all official purposes: 8pm equals 20.00.

MEASUREMENTS

While the metric system is the rule in Austria and Switzerland, the British system of weights and measures prevails in the U.S. Conversions are provided below; odd traditional units for measuring wine or beer are explained in the text when necessary.

1 inch = 25 millimeter (mm)	1mm = 0.04 inch (in.)
1 foot = 0.30 meter (m)	1m = 3.33 foot (ft.)
1 yard = 0.91m	1m = 1.1 yard (yd.)
1 mile = 1.61 kilometer (km)	1km = 0.62 mile (mi.)
1 ounce = 25 gram (g)	1g = 0.04 ounce (oz.)
1 pound = 0.45 kilogram (kg)	1kg = 2.22 pound (lb.)
1 quart = 0.94 liter (L)	1 liter = 1.06 quart (qt.)

Comparative Values of Measurement

1 foot	= 12 inches
1 yard	= 3 feet
1 mile	= 5280 feet
1 pound	= 16 ounces (weight)
1 cup	= 8 ounces (volume)
1 pint	= 2 cups
1 quart	= 2 pints
1 gallon	= 4 quarts

It should be noted that gallons in the U.S. are not identical to those across the Atlantic; one U.S. gallon equals 0.83 Imperial gallons.

Electrical Current

Most European outlets are 220 volts, which will melt most 110-volt North American appliances. If you absolutely cannot live without your hair-dryer or lava lamp, bring an adaptor and a converter. See **Packing**, p. 28, for more information.

MILEAGE

	Vienna	Salzburg	Innsbruck	Graz	Linz
Vienna		295	481	195	181
Salzburg	295		180	264	130
Innsbruck	481	180		432	316
Graz	195	264	432		227
Linz	181	130	316	227	

	Bern	Geneva	Zurich	Lugano	Interlaken
Bern		171	125	279	57
Geneva	171		292	446	230
Zurich	125	292		221	177
Lugano	279	446	221		221
Interlaken	57	230	177	221	

LANGUAGE

Used widely throughout the Eastern parts of Europe, German is nevertheless a difficult language for many English speakers to learn, with three genders, four cases, and five ways of saying "the." Fortunately, most Austrian and Swiss residents speak at least a smattering of English—usually much more—and quite a few speak it better than the typical American college student. (The situation is considerably different in isolated villages of the Alps, where proprietors are considered proficient if they can regurgitate "hello," "good-bye," and "dollars." In these cases, you might have the tourist office call ahead for help.) All schoolchildren in Austria are required to take English, and most are quite anxious to practice. Don't, however, assume that all Austrians or Swiss speak English, especially outside the major cities. Always preface your questions with a polite *"Sprechen Sie Englisch?"* or *"Parlez-vous anglais?"* or *"Parla inglese?"* in the appropriate regions.

Don't ever be afraid to attempt a bit of German or French. Locals will generally appreciate your effort to acknowledge their culture and will usually be significantly more helpful once they've heard a bit of their native language. If you maintain a formal, polite tone, native speakers will often forgive your linguistic foibles. Always address a German-speaking acquaintance with *Herr* (Mr.) or *Frau* (Ms.) and his or her surname; a French-speaking acquaintance as *Monsieur* (Mr.) or *Madame* (Mrs.). While you can use *Mademoiselle* to refer to any younger Francophone woman, use *Fräulein* to address only a younger German-speaking waitress or stewardess. Always use the formal pronoun (*Sie* in German, *vous* in French) with the plural form of the verb. The transition from formal to informal is occasion for a major ceremony; never assume that you are on informal terms—you will be told. German speakers with post-collegiate degrees or civic positions should be addressed with "Herr" or "Frau" plus their secondary title, e.g. Frau Doktor Puka or Herr Bürgermeister Zabusky.

Pronunciation

Once you learn the few rules of **German** pronunciation, you should be able to tackle even the longest compound noun. All consonant sounds are the same as in English, with the exception of C (pronounced K); F (pronounced V); J (pronounced Y); K (always pronounced, even before N); P (always pronounced, even before F); QU (pronounced KV); S (pronounced Z at the beginning of a word); V (pronounced F); W (pronounced V); Z (pronounced TS). CH, in Austrian and Swiss German, sounds like K. The ß, or *ess-tsett*, is simply a double S. Pronounce SCH as SH. Vowels are as follows: A as in "father"; E as the A in "hay"; I as the ee in "creep"; O as in "oh"; U as in "fondue"; Y as the oo in "boot"; AU as in "sauerkraut"; EU as the oi in "boil." With EI and IE, always pronounce the last letter as a long English vowel—*heisse* is HY-ssuh; *viele* is FEEL-uh.

French pronunciation is more difficult, as many of the letters in a word are silent. Do not pronounce any final consonants except L, F, or C; an E on the end of the word, however, means that you should pronounce the final consonant sound, e.g., *muet* is mew-AY but *muette* is mew-ET. This rule also applies to plural nouns—don't pronounce the final S. J is like the S in "pleasure." To pronounce a French R, arch your tongue and rest the tip behind your bottom teeth, then force air through the constricted space in the back of your throat. C sounds like a K before A, O, and U; like an S before E and I. A ç always sounds like an S. Vowels are short and precise: A as the O in "mom"; E as in "help" (é becomes the a in "hay"); I as the ee in "creep"; O as in "oh." UI sounds like the word "whee." U is a short, clipped oo sound; hold your lips as if you were about to say "ooh," but say ee instead. OU is a straight OO sound. With very few exceptions, all syllables receive equal emphasis in French.

PHRASEBOOK

No.	German	French	No.	German	French
					Numbers
0	null	zéro	17	siebzehn	dix-sept
1	eins	un	18	achtzehn	dix-huit
2	zwei or zwoh	deux	19	neunzehn	dix-neuf
3	drei	trois	20	zwanzig	vingt
4	vier	quatre	21	einund-zwanzig	vingt et un
5	fünf	cinq	30	dreißig	trente
6	sechs	six	40	vierzig	quarante
7	sieben	sept	50	fünfzig	cinquante
8	acht	huit	60	sechzig	soixante
9	neun	neuf	70	siebzig	soixante-dix
10	zehn	dix	80	achtzig	quatre-vingt
11	elf	onze	90	neunzig	quatre-vingt-dix
12	zwölf	douze	100	(ein)hundert	cent
13	dreizehn	treize	101	hunderteins	cent-et-un
14	vierzehn	quatorze	200	zweihundert	deux-cent
15	fünfzehn	quinze	1000	(ein)tausend	mille
16	sechzehn	seize	2000	zweitausend	deux-mille

English	German	Pronunc.	French	Pronunc.
				Time
At what time	Um wieviel Uhr…?	oom VEE-feel oohr…?	A quelle heure…?	ah kell err…?
What time is it?	Wie spät ist es?	vee SPAYT ist ess?	Quelle heure est-il?	kell er ay-teel?
What's the date?	Der wievielte ist heute?	dayr vee-FEEL-tuh ist hoy-tuh?	Quelle est la date?	kell ay lah daht?
June 1st	ersten Juni	AYR-sten YOO-nee	le premier Juin	luh preh-MYAY zhoo-weh
quarter past seven	viertel acht	FEER-tell ackt	sept heures et quart	set err ay kar
half past seven	halb acht	halp ackt	sept heures et demi	set err ay deh-mee
quarter to eight	dreiviertel acht	dry-FEER-tell ahkt	huit heures moins le quart	weet err myah luh kar
morning	Morgen	MOR-ghen	matin	MA-teh
noon	Mittag	MIT-ahk	midi	mee-dee
afternoon	Nachmittag	NACK-mit-ahk	après-midi	ah-PRAY-mee-dee
evening	Abend	AH-bent	le soir	luh swahr
night	Nacht	nahkt	la nuit	lah nwee
midnight	Mitternacht	MIT-er-nahkt	minuit	min-WEE
day	Tag	tahk	jour	zhoor

PHRASEBOOK ■ 473

week	Woche	VOH-kuh	semaine	suh-MEN
month	Monat	MON-aht	mois	mwah
year	Jahr	yahr	an	ahn
now	jetzt	yetst	maintenant	mehnt-noh
yesterday	Gestern	GUEST-urn	hier	ee-ayr
today	Heute	HOY-tuh	aujourd'hui	oh-zhord-WEE
tomorrow	Morgen	MOR-ghen	demain	duh-meh

Directions

direction	die Richtung	dee RIK-toong	la direction	lah dee-rek-see-yon
left	links	linx	à gauche	ah gohsh
right	rechts	rekts	à droite	ah dwaht
straight ahead	geradeaus	ger-AHD-uh-ows	tout droit	too dwaht
here	hier	eer	ici	ee-see
there	da	dah	là-bas	lah-bah
far	fern	fayrn	loin	loo-wahn
near	nah	nah	près	pray

Phrases

hospital	das Krankenhaus	das KRANK-en-hows	l'hôpital	loh-pee-TAHL
pharmacy	die Apotheke	dee a-POH-ta-kuh	la pharmacie	lah farm-ah-SEE
sick	krank	krahnk	malade	mah-LAHD
doctor	der Arzt	dayr artst	le médecin	luh mayd-SEH
police	die Polizei	dee poh-lee-TSY	la police	lah POH-lees
Help!	Hilfe!	HILL-fuh!	Au secours!	oh suh-KOOR!
Caution!	Achtung!/Vorsicht!	ack-TOONG!/for-SICKT!	Avertissement!	ah-VAYR-tees-moh!
Danger!	Gefahr!	geh-FAHR!	Danger!	dahn-ZHAY!
Fire!	Feuer!	FOY-ehr!	Feu!	Fuh!
Stop!	Halt!	Halt!	Arrêt!	ah-RAY!
Ouch!	Autsch!	OWCH!	Aïe!	AH-EE!
consulate	das Konsulat	das KON-soo-laht	le consulat	luh coh-soo-lah
English (language)	Englisch	AYN-glish	Anglais	an-GLAY
German (language)	Deutsch	doytsh	Allemand	ah-luh-moh
French (language)	Französisch	frahn-TSER-zish	Français	frahn-SAY
Hello	Hallo	hah-LO	Bonjour	bohn-ZHOOR
Good morning	Guten Morgen	GOOT-en MORG-en	Bonjour	bohn-ZHOOR
Good day	Servus/Grüß Gott/Guten Tag	sayr-VOOS/groos got/GOOT-en tak/	Bonjour	If you haven't figured it out by now, seeing it again isn't going to help
Good evening	Guten Abend	GOOT-en AH-bent	Bonsoir	bohn-SWHAR
Good night	Gute Nacht	GOOT-uh nakt	Bonne nuit	bun nwee
Goodbye	Tschüß/Auf Wiedersehen/Auf Wiederschauen	choos/owf FEED-er-zayn/owf FEED-er-SHOW-en	Au revoir	oh ruh-VWAHR
How are you?	Wie geht's?	vee GAYTS?	Comment allez-vous?	kohm-mahn tah-lay voo?

APPENDIX

Fine, thanks.	Ganz gut, danke.	gahnts GOOT, dahn-kuh	Bien, merci.	byehn, mer-SEE
Please	Bitte	BIT-uh	S'il vous plait	sih voo play
Thank you	Danke	DUNK-uh	Merci	mayr-see
You're welcome	Bitte	BIT-uh	De rien	duh ree-yen
Excuse me	Entschuldigung	ent-SHUL-dee-gung	Pardon	pahr-DOHN
Yes	Ja	ya	Oui	wee
No	Nein	niyn	Non	noh
I don't know.	Ich weiß nicht.	ick VICE nickt	Je ne sais pas.	zhuhn uh say pah
Sir	Herr	hayr	Monsieur	mi-syer
Madam	Frau	frow	Madame	muh-dahm
I'm sorry.	Es tut mir leid.	ess toot meer liyt	Je suis desolé(e); pardon	zhu swee deh-sol-ay; pahr-doh
I don't speak...	Ich spreche kein...	ick shprek-uh kiyn	Je ne parle pas...	zhu ne parl pah
Do you speak English?	Sprechen Sie Englisch?	SHPREK-en zee AYN-glish?	Parlez-vous anglais?	PARL-ay voo ahn-GLAY?
Can you help me?	Könnten Sie mir helfen?	KERN-ten zee meer HELF-en?	Pourriez-vous m'aider?	POOR-ee-ay voos med-ay?
I don't understand.	Ich verstehe nicht.	ick fer-SHTAY-uh nikt	Je ne comprends pas.	zhu nuh com-proh pah
Do you understand?	Verstehen Sie?	fer-SHTAY-en zee?	Comprenez-vous?	Kom-PREN-ay voo?
Please speak slowly.	Sprechen Sie langsam.	SHPREK-en zee LANG-sum	Parlez lentement.	PARL-ay LOHNT-mohn
How do you say...in...	Wie sagt man...auf...?	vee zakt mahn...owf...?	Comment dit-on ...en...?	koh-MOHN deet ohn...ehn...?
What did you say?	Wie, bitte?	vee, BIT-uh?	Qu'avez-vous dit?	KAH-vay voo dee?
I would like...	Ich möchte...	ikh MERK-tuh	Je voudrais...	zhu VOO-dray
How much does...cost?	Wieviel kostet...?	VEE-feel kost-et...?	Combien coûte...	kohm-BYEN koot...
I'd like to pay.	Zahlen, bitte.	TSAH-len, BIT-uh	Je voudrais payer.	zhu voo-DRAY pay-ay
Where is...?	Wo ist...?	voh ist...?	Où est...?	oo ay...?
When is...?	Wann ist...?	vahn ist...?	Quand est...?	kahn day...?
Why?	Warum?	vah-rum?	Pourquoi?	poor-KWAH?
Non-smoking	Nichtraucher	nikt-RAU-ker	Non-fumeur	noh-foom-ER
Smoking	Raucher	RAU-ker	Fumeur	foom-ER

Reservations

Phone greeting	Servus!	sayr-VOOS!	Allo	ah-loh
Do you speak English?	Sprechen Sie Englisch?	SHPRECK-en zee AYN-glish?	Parlez-vous anglais?	PAR-lay-voo ahn-GLAY?
Do you have a room (single, double) free...	Haben Sie ein Zimmer (Einzelzimmer, Doppelzimmer) frei...	HAH-ben zee iyn TSIM-er (IYN-tsel-tsim-er, DOP-el-tsim-er) fry...	Avez-vous une chambre (simple, pour deux) libre?	AH-vay-voo oon shahm-bruh (sehm-pluh, poor doo) lee-bruh?
for tonight?	für heute abend?	fer HOY-tuh AH-bent?	pour ce soir?	poor suh swahr?
for tomorrow?	für morgen?	fer MORG-en?	pour demain?	poor duh-MEH?
for a day/for two days?	für einen Tag/zwei Tage?	fer IYN-en tak/tsvy TAK-uh?	pour un jour? pour deux jours?	poor uh zhoor? poor doo zhoor?
from the fourth of July...	vom vierten Juli...	fum FEER-ten YU-lee...	de la quatrième Juillet...	duh lah kat-ree-em zhwee-ay...

English	German	German pronunciation	French	French pronunciation
until the sixth of July?	bis zum sechsten Juli?	bis tsoom SEK-sten YU-lee?	à la sixième Juillet?	ah la see-zee-em zhwee-ay?
with bathroom/ shower?	mit W.C./Dusche?	mit vay-tsay/ DOO-shuh?	avec toilettes/ une douche?	ah-VEK TWAH-let/ oon doosh?
with breakfast?	mit Frühstuck?	mit FROO-shtook?	avec le petit déjeuner?	ah-VEK luh puh-TEE day-zhoon-AY?
How much does it cost?	Wieviel kostet es?	VEE-feel KOST-et es?	Combien?	kohm-bwehn?
What's your name?	Wie heißen Sie?	vee HIGH-sehn zee?	Comment appellez-vous?	kohm-mehn tah-play voo?
My name is...	Ich heiße...	ikh HY-suh	Je m'appelle	zhuh mah-PEL
I'm coming immediately.	Ich komme gleich.	ikh KOM-uh glyk	Je viens tout de suite.	zhuh vee-YEN toot sweet
I'm coming at eight in the morning/evening.	Ich komme um acht Uhr am Morgen/Abend.	ick KOM-uh oom akt oor am MORG-en/AH-bent	Je viens à huit heures du matin/ du soir.	zhuh vee-YEN ah wheet err doo mah-TEHN/ doo swahr
No, we're booked/full.	Nein, es ist alles besetzt/voll.	nyn, es ist ALL-us be-SETZT/fol	Non, c'est complet.	noh, say COHM-play
Sorry.	Es tut mir leid.	es toot meer lyt	Je suis desolé(e).	zhuh swee DAY-zol-ay
We don't take reservations by phone.	Wir machen keine Vorbestellungen/ Reservierungen am Telephon.	veer MAK-en KYN-uh for-BEST-el-oong-en/ ray-sayr-FEER-oong-en am TAY-lay-fone	Nous ne pouvons pas reserver une chambre au téléphone.	noo ne poo-voh pah ray-sayr-vay oon shahm-bruh oh tay-lay-fohn
You have to arrive before two o'clock.	Sie müssen vor zwei Uhr ankommen.	zee MOOS-en for tsvy oor an-kom-en	Vous devez arriver avant que deux heures.	voo duh-VAY AH-reev-ay ah-VAHN kuh duhz err

Accommodations

English	German	German pronunciation	French	French pronunciation
toilet	die Toilette/ das WC	twah-LET-uh/ vay-tsay	les toilettes	twah-let
shower	die Dusche	DOOSH-uh	une douche	doosh
key	der Schlüssel	SHLOOS-uhl	une clé	klay
house	das Haus	hows	une maison	may-zon
youth hostel	Jugendherberge	YOONG-ent-hayr-bayr-guh	Auberge de jeunesse	oh-bayrzh duh zhoon-ess
campground	der Campingplatz	comp-eeng-PLATZ	un terrain de camping	tayr-ehduh cahmp-eenk
guest-house	die Pension	PAHN-zee-ohn	une maison d'hôtes	may-zon doht
hotel	das Hotel	HO-tel	un hôtel	oh-tel
inn	das Gästehaus	gahs-hows	une auberge	oh-bayrzh
private apartment	das Privatzimmer	PRY-vaht-tsim-er	appartement privé	ah-pahr-tuh-mohn pree-VAY
bed	das Bett	bet	un lit	lee
single	das Einzelzimmer	IYN-tsel-tsim-er	une chambre pour une personne	shahm-bruh poor oon payr-sun
double	das Doppelzimmer	DOP-el-tsim-er	une chambre pour deux personnes	shahm-bruh poor doo payr-sun
I'm tired.	Ich bin müde.	ick bin MOO-deh	Je suis fatigué(e).	zhuh swee fah-tee-gay

476 ■ PHRASEBOOK

There's an enormous cat in my room.	Es gibt einen riesengroßen Katz in meinem Zimmer.	ess gipt iyn-en REEZ-en-GROSS-en kahts-en in miyn-em tsim-ehr	Il y a un chat très énorme dans ma chambre.	eel ee ah uhn shah TRAYZ ay-norm donh mah shahm-bruh

Travel

travel ticket	die Fahrkarte	dee FAHR-kar-tuh	un billet	uh bee-yay
reservation	die Reservierung	dee RAY-sayr-VEER-oong	une réservation	oon ray-sayr-vah-see-yon
one-way	einfache Fahrt	IYN-fak-uh fahrt	billet simple	bee-yay sehm-pluh
round-trip	Hin- und Rückfahrt	hin-oont-REK-fahrt	aller-retour	al-lay-ruh-toor
arrival	die Ankunft	dee AHNK-unft	l'arrivée	lah-ree-VAY
departure	die Abfahrt	dee AHB-fahrt	le départ	luh DAY-pahr
schedule	der Fahrplan	dayr FAHR-plahn	les horaires	layz or-are
baggage	das Gepäck	dahs guh-PEK	les bagages	lay bah-gazh
airplane	das Flugzeug	dahs FLOOK-zoyk	un avion	uhn ah-vyon
airport	der Flughafen	dayr FLOOK-hah-fen	un aéroport	uhn air-o-por
customs	der Zoll	dayr tsol	la douane	lah doo-wahn
train	der Zug	dayr tsuk	le train	luh treh
train station	der Bahnhof	dayr BAHN-hof	la gare	lah gahr
main train station	der Hauptbahnhof	dayr HOPT-bahn-hof	la gare centrale	lah gahr sahn-tral
(train) track	das Gleis	dahs glys	les rails	lay rehl
train platform	der Bahnsteig	dayr BAHN-styk	le quai	luh kay
express train	der Eilzug	dayr IYL-tsuk	un train exprès/direct	uh trehn ex-pray/deer-ekt
railway	die Bahn	dee bahn	le chemin de fer	luh shuh-meh duh fuh
subway	die U-Bahn	dee OO-bahn	le métro	luh may-troh
subway stop	die Haltestelle	dee hahl-tuh-shtel-uh	un arrêt de métro	uhn ah-RAY duh may-troh
tram, trolley	die Straßenbahn	dee SHTRAHS-en-bahn	le tramway	luh trahm-vay
urban railway	die S-Bahn	dee ESS-bahn		
ferry	die Fähre	dee FEH-ruh	le passage	luh pahs-ahj
bus	der Bus	dayr boos	l'autobus	loh-toh-boos
bus station	der Busbahnhof	dayr BOOS-bahn-hof	la gare routière	lah gahr roo-tee-yare
bus stop	die Bushaltestelle	dee BOOS-halt-uh-shtel-uh	l'arrêt d'autobus	lah-RAY doh-toh-boos
car	das Auto	dahs OW-toh	la voiture	lah vwah-tyoor
no stopping	Halten verboten	hahl-ten fer-BOHT-en	interdit d'arrêter	ehn-tayr-dee dah-ret-ay
parking	parken	PARK-en	parking	pahr-KEENG
no parking	parken verboten	PARK-en fer-BOHT-en	interdit de stationner	ehn-tayr-dee duh stah-shun-ay
parking spot	Parkplatz	PARK-plahtz	place de stationnement	plahs duh stah-shun-uh-moh
short-term parking	Kurzfristzone	kurz-FRIST-tsohn	une stalle	oon stahl
speed limit	Geschwindigkeitsbegrenzung	guh-SHVIND-ik-kyts-bug-RAYN-tsoonk	limite de vitesse	lee-MEET duh vee-tess

APPENDIX

do not enter	*Eintritt verbotten*	IYN-trit fer-BOHT-en	*passage interdit*	pah-sahj ehn-tayr-dee
expressway/highway	*die Autobahn*	dee OW-toh-bahn	*l'autoroute*	loh-toh-root
federal highway	*die Bundesstraße*	dee BOON-duhs-stras-uh	*l'autoroute*	loh-toh-root
one-way street	*die Ein-bahnstraße*	dee IYN-bahn-strahs-uh	*rue à sens unique*	roo ah sahn zoon-eek
dead-end street	*die Sackgasse*	dee ZAHK-gahs-uh	*une impasse/cul de sac*	oon ehm-pahs/cool duh sahk
old part of town	*die Altstadt*	dee AHLT-shtatt	*la vieille ville*	lah vee-ay vill
bicycle	*das Fahrrad*	dahs FAR-ahd	*la bicyclette*	lah bee-see-klet
moped	*das Moped*	dahs MOH-ped	*la mobylette*	lah moh-bee-let
motorcycle	*das Motorrad*	dahs MOH-toh-rahd	*la moto*	lah moh-toh

Food and Drink

hors-d'oeuvres	*gemischte Vorspeise*	guh-MISH-tuh FOR-spy-zuh	*les hors-d'oeuvres*	ohr doov-ruh
vegetables	*das Gemüse*	guh-mew-zuh	*les légumes*	lay-goom
beans	*die Bohnen*	BOHN-en	*les haricots*	ayr-ee-koh
mushrooms	*die Champignons*	shahm-pin-yon	*les champignons*	shahm-peen-yoh
potato	*die Kartoffeln/Erdäpfel*	kar-TOF-eln/ary-DEP-fel	*les pommes de terre*	pum duh tayr
cabbage	*das Kraut/der Kohl*	krowt/kohl	*le chou*	shoo
french fries	*die pommes frites*	pum freet	*les pommes frites*	pum freet
green salad	*der grüne Salat*	grew-nuh SAH-laht	*la salade verte*	sah-lahd vayrt
tomatoes	*die Tomaten*	toh-MAH-ten	*les tomates*	toh-maht
onions	*die Zwiebeln*	TSVEE-beln	*les oignons*	oh-nyoh
pepper	*der Paprika*	PAH-preek-a	*le poivre*	pwah-vruh
fruits	*das Obst*	ohbst	*les fruits*	fwee
cheese	*der Käse/Käsekrainer*	KEZ-uh/KEZ-uh-krayn-er	*le fromage*	froh-mazh
milk	*die Milch*	meelk	*le lait*	lay
bread	*das Brot*	broht	*le pain*	peh
roll	*das Brötchen/die Semmel*	BROHT-shen/SEM-el	*un petit pain*	puh-tee peh
egg	*das Ei*	IY	*un oeuf*	uhf
ham	*der Schinken*	SHINK-en	*le jambon*	zhahm-boh
bacon	*der Speck*	speck	*le bacon/le lard*	bay-koh/lahr
sausage	*die Wurst*	vurst	*le saucisse*	soh-sees
poultry	*das Geflügel*	guh-FLEW-gul	*la volaille*	voh-lay-yuh
duck	*die Ente*	EN-tuh	*le canard*	kuh-nahr
goose	*die Gans*	ganz	*l'oie*	(l)oy
chicken	*das Huhn/Hendl*	hoon/hen-duhl	*le poulet*	pool-ay
pasta	*die Teigwaren*	TYK-var-en	*les pâtes*	paht
beer	*das Bier*	BEE-uh	*la bière*	bee-ayr
chocolate	*die Schokolade*	shock-oh-LAH-deh	*le chocolat*	shoh-kuh-lah
beer hall	*die Bierstube*	BEE-uh-stoob-uh		
wine	*der Wein*	viyn	*le vin*	veh
wine hall	*die Weinstube*	VIYN-stoob-uh	*la cave*	kahv
coffee	*der Kaffee*	KAH-fay	*le café*	kah-fay

478 ■ PHRASEBOOK

coffee and cream	Kaffee mit Sahne	KAH-fay mit SAH-nuh	le café au lait/ café crème	kah-fay oh lay/ kah-fay krem
tea	der Tee	tay	le thé	tay
fruit juice	der Fruchtsaft	FROOKT-zahft	le jus de fruits	zhoo duh fwee
mineral water	das Mineralwasser	MIN-er-ahl-VASS-er	l'eau minéral	(l)oh mee-nayr-ahl
soda	das Soda	ZOH-dah	la soda	soh-dah
water	das Wasser	VASS-er	l'eau	(l)oh

Dining

diabetic	der Diabetiker	DEE-ah-BET-ik-er	un(e) diabétique	dee-ah-bayt-eek
vegetarian	der Vegetarier	vayj-ay-tah-reer	un(e) végétarien(ne)	vay-zhay-tah-ree-yeh/yen
I'm hungry.	Ich habe Hunger.	ick HAH-buh HOONG-er	J'ai faim.	zhay feh
I'm thirsty.	Ich habe Durst.	ick HAH-buh DOO-uhst	J'ai soif.	zhay swahf
meal	das Essen	ESS-en	le repas	ruh-pah
dessert	der Nachtisch	NAHK-tish	le dessert	deh-sayr
lounge, café	die Kneipe	Kuh-NY-puh	le café	ca-fay
pastry shop	die Konditorei	kon-di-TOHR-eye	la pâtisserie	pah-tees-ayr-ee
restaurant	die Gaststätte	GAHST-stet-uh	un restaurant	ray-stayr-ahn
Waiter!	Kellner!	KELL-ner	Monsieur!	miss-yer
Waitress!	Kellnerin!	KELL-ner-in	Madame!	muh-dahm
bill, check	die Rechnung	REK-noong	l'addition	(l)ah-dees-yoh
Check, please	Zahlen, bitte	TSAH-len BIT-uh	L'addition, s'il vous plait	lah-dees-yoh sih voo play
breakfast	das Frühstück	frew-shtewk	le petit déjeuner	puh-tee day-zhoon-ay
lunch	das Mittagessen	MIT-ak-ess-en	le déjeuner	day-zhoon-ay
dinner	das Mittagessen	MIT-ak-ess-en	le dîner	dee-nay
supper	das Abendessen	AH-bent-ess-en	le souper	soop-ay
fork	die Gabel	GAH-buhl	la fourchette	foor-shet
knife	das Messer	MESS-er	le couteau	koot-oh
spoon	der Löffel	LERF-el	la cuillère	kwee-yayr

The Post Office

post office	die Post	pohst	la poste/ le bureau de poste	pohst/byoor-oh duh pohst
main post office	der Hauptpostamt	HOWPT-pohst-ahmt	le bureau de poste principal	byoor-oh duh pohst preen-see-pahl
address	die Adresse	ah-DRES-uh	l'adresse	(l)uh-dres
express	der Eilbote	IYL-boht-uh	exprès	ex-press
air mail	die Luftpost	LOOFT-pohst	par avion	pahr ah-vyon
letter	der Brief	breef	la lettre	let-truh
parcel	das Paket	PAH-ket	le paquet	pah-kay
postcard	die Postkarte	POHST-kar-tuh	la carte postale	kart poh-stahl
Poste Restante	Postlagernde Briefe	POHST-lah-gayrn-duh BREEF-uh	Poste Restante	pohst ruh-stahnt
stamp	die Briefmarke	BREEF-mark-uh	le timbre	tehn-bruh
telegram	das Telegramm	tay-lay-GRAHM	le télégramme	tay-lay-grahm
telephone	das Telefon	tay-lay-FOHN	le téléphone	tay-lay-fohn

telephone number	*die Telefonnummer*	tay-lay-fohn-NOOM-er	*le numero de téléphone*	nu-mayr-oh duh tay-lay-foh
to exchange	*wechseln*	VEK-sayln	*échanger de l'argent*	ay-shahn-zhay duh lahr-zhahn
money	*das Geld*	gelt	*l'argent*	(l)ahr-zhahn

Index

A

A.E.I.O.U. 62, 200
Aare Gorge 404
abbey gales 176
Admont 178-179
AIDS 16
air travel 31-36
 charter flights 35
 courier flights 36
 stand-by flights 35
Air Travel Advisory Bureau 41
airlines 32, 41
 Austrian Airlines 33, 84, 204, 264
 Continental Airlines 33
 Delta 33
 Swissair 33, 204, 264, 301, 302
 USAir 33
airports
 Basel 360
 Bern 390
 Budapest 140
 Geneva 302
 Graz 194, 196
 Innsbruck 264
 Klagenfurt 182
 Munich 226
 Prague 126
 Salzburg 204
 Vienna 84, 85
 Zurich 369
alcohol 14
alliteration alert 177
Alps, Bavarian 231
Alt, Salome 217
alternatives to tourism, see tourism alternatives
altitudes, high 16
American Diabetes Association 15
American Express 10, 12, 56
 Basel 360
 Bern 392
 Budapest 140
 Geneva 302
 Graz 196
 Innsbruck 266
 Lausanne 314
 Linz 172
 Lucerne 383
 Lugano 419
 Munich 226
 Prague 126
 Salzburg 206
 Traveler's Cheques 10
 Vienna 87
 Zurich 370
American Field Service (AFS) 19
American Red Cross 15
Andrew's dream tour 181
Andrews, Julie 204, 218
angry salad 462
anonymous 146
Anschluß 66, 232
Appenzell 458
architecture
 Austrian 71-73
 Baroque 71
 Ringstraße 71
 Swiss 294-295
Arlberg mountains 263, 278-283
Arosa 435-437
art
 Austrian 71-73
 Swiss 294-295
Ascona 429-431
AT&T, see telephones
ATM cards 11
Augst 366
Augusta Raurica 366
Augustiner Bräu, Salzburg 214
Aurelius, Marcus 60
Austria
 architecture 71-73
 art 71-73
 Central Tirol 245-262
 government 66
 history 59-67
 literature 74-75
 Lower Austria 149-170
 music 67-71
 Northwest 171-181
 Salzburger Land 203-244
 Southeast 182-202
 Western 263-288
Austria, Northwest 171-181
Austria, Southeast 182-202
Austria, Western 263-288
Austrian Airlines, see airlines
Austrian Automobile, Motorcycle, and Touring Club, see ÖAMTC
Austrian embassies 4
Austrian National Tourist Office 1
Austrian Rail Pass 39
Austro-Hungarian Empire 64, 65
automatic ice-cream machine 465

B

Babenbergs 59, 61, 100
backpacks 51
Bad Goisern 242
Bad Ischl 234-237
Baden bei Wien 154-157
balls
 Imperial 117
 Vienna *(Wiener Opernball)* 98, 117
Balmer's Herberge, Interlaken 405
Basel
 accommodations 362
 daytrips 366
 homosexual organizations 362
 museums 364
 nightlife 365
 practical information 360
 restaurants 363
 sights 363-365
 transporation 360
Basel (Bâle) 360-367
baths
 Bad Ischl 236
 Baden Bei Wien 156
 Roman Military 146
Battle of Morgarten 290
Bavarian Alps (Bayerische Alpen) 231
Bavarian Forest 232
Beatenberg 401
Beatushölen (St. Beatus' Caves) 402
beer
 Austrian 76
 Budvar 135
 Budweiser, USA 136
 Freistädter 179
 Gösser brewery, Leoben 192
 Munich 230
 Salzburg 214
Beethoven, Ludwig van 68, 70, 72, 103, 108, 154, 156
Bellavista 450
Bellinzona 431-432
Belvedere Palace, Vienna 107
bench, world's longest 309
Berchtesgaden, Germany 66, 232
Bermuda Triangles
 Graz 202
 Linz 175
 Vienna 117
Bern 390-397
 accommodations 393-394
 embassies 392
 homosexual organizations 393

482 ■ INDEX

museums 395
nightlife 396-397
practical information 390-393
restaurants 394
sights 394-396
transportation 390
Berner Oberland 397-417
sports 407
Bernoulli 363
best-looking legs in Switzerland 318
Bezalel, Rabbi Loew ben 131
Biel (Bienne) 354-355
biking 43-44
Tour de Suisse 423
Vienna 98
Billets Internationals de Jeunesse 40
bisexual, see homosexual and bisexual travelers
Bismarck, Otto von 64
Black Forest (Schwarzwald) 367
Black Lake, see Schwarzsee
Bob-run 447
Bodensee 263, 285, 451-463
Bond, James 416
Bregenz 285-288
accommodations 286
embassies 286
practical information 285
restaurants 286
sights 287
Brienz 402
Brienzersee 402-404
South Shore 403
Bruck an der Großglockner 253
Bruckner Organ 176
Bruckner, Anton 175, 176, 236
Brueghel 111, 199, 220
Budapest 136-147
accommodations 141
Buda 145
cafés 144
Castle District 145
daytrips 147
embassies 140
entertainment 146
Pest 146
practical information 136
restaurants 144
sights 145
synagogue 146
budget travel agencies 30-31
Budweiser Brewery 135
BundesBus 41
Bundesnetzkarte 39

bungee-jumping
Interlaken 408
Burckhardt, Jacob 295
Burgenland 154-159, 182
bus travel 40-41
BundesBus 41
Eurobus 40
Eurolines 40
PTT postal bus 41
Bussalp 411
Byron, Lord 296, 300, 320, 323

C

Caesar, Julius 290
café culture 76, 95
calling cards 56
Calvin, John 291
camping 49-53
equipment 51
RVs 52
safety 52
Campus Travel 30
canyoning
Grindelwald 412
Gstaad 327
Interlaken 407
Zell am See 258
Carinthia 182, 245
cars 41-43
renting 41-42
Carter, Jimmy 387
Casaccia 443
cash cards 11
casinos
Baden 156
Lindau 454
Lugano 424
Neuchâtel 350
Castle District, Budapest 145
castles
Aggstein-Gastein 165
Ambras, Innsbruck 271
Babenberg, Vienna 120
Batiaz, Martigny 335
Castelgrande, Bellinzona 432
Chillon, Montreux 323
Eggenberg, Graz 201
Esterházy, Eisenstadt 158
Ghiriglioni, Ascona 430
Gruyères 358
Hegi, Winterthur 383
Hellbrunn, Salzburg 218, 222
Herrenchiemsee, Chiemsee 231
Lamberg 177
Leopoldskron, Salzburg 218
Liechtenstein, Vienna 120
Mirabell, Salzburg 217

Montebello, Bellinzona 432
Mörsburg, Winterthur 382
Munot, Schaffhausen 460
Nymphenburg, Munich 229
Pottenbrunn, St. Pölten 151
Prague 132
Riegersburg 192
Röthelstein 178
Sasso Corbaro, Bellinzona 432
Schallaburg, Melk 170
Schattenburg, Feldkirch 285
Schwarzenberg, Vienna 107
Spiez, Spiez 401
Thun, Thun 399
Tourbillon, Sion 337
Vaduz 465
Valère, Sion 337
Visconti, Locarno 428
Waldegg, Solothurn 354
catacombs 101
Celerina 447-448
Celts 60, 290
Central Tirol 245-262
České Budějovice 135
Český Krumlov 135
Chagall, Marc 377
Chaplin, Charlie 325
Charlemagne 60, 100, 194, 222
Charles II 63
charter flights 33, 35
Château de Chillon 323
cheese 297, 460
cheese dairy, Gruyères 358
Chiemsee, Germany 231
children, traveling with 27
chocolate 297
Lindt Factory 379
Toblerone 394
Christian Socialists 65, 66
Chur 434-435
Cimetta 428
Cirrus network 11
Clemenceau, Premier Georges 65
clothing and footwear 29
Club Innsbruck 268, 272
concentration camps 134, 176, 231
Congress of Vienna 64
Constance 452-453
daytrips 453
consulates, see embassies and consulates
contact lenses 29
contraception 16
Cookie Rebellion 364

INDEX ■ 483

Le Corbusier 295, 325, 352
Corviglia 445
Council 30
Council on International Education Exchange (CIEE) 19
Council on International Educational Exchange (CIEE) 2, 20
Council Travel 30
courier flights and freighters 36
Coward, Noel 320
cows
 bell-ringing beef 387
 carving festival 402
 cattle show 459
 fighting 335
 spotted 215
Cranach, Lukas 270
credit cards 11
Cressier 350
Cresta-run 447
currency exchange 9
Curtins 446
customs
 Australia 6, 7
 Canada 7
 Ireland 7
 New Zealand 7
 South Africa 7
 U.K. 7
 U.S. 7

D

Dachau, Germany 231
Dachstein Ice Caves, Obertraun 244
Dadaism 297, 369
Dampfzug 250
Danube 164–170
Danube Bend (Dunakanyar), Hungary 147
Danube River 59, 109
Danube, German 232
Davis, Miles 324
Davos 437–439
day-glo
 animal scenes 386
 bugs 379
 comforters 414
 murals 383
DDSG 84, 164
de Staël, Madame 295, 300
death wish 157
Decline and Fall of the Roman Empire 315
Defenestration of Prague 132
Derek's favorite word 132, 399
diabetes 15
Dialogai 25
Dickens, Charles 296, 314

dietary concerns 26
Directions Unlimited 25
disabled travelers 24–25
 Geneva 304
Disco Bus 187
Dollach 254
Dollfuss, Engelbert 65
Dolomites (Dolomiten) 259
Donner, George Raphael 71, 99, 100
dormitories 47
Dostoyevsky, Fyodor 325
Drautal 188–190
driving 41–43
 insurance 9
 permits 8
drugs 14
Dumas, Alexandre 323, 347
Dürrenmatt, Friedrich 296
duty tax 6

E

East Tirol 182, 245, 259
Eco, Umberto 457
Educational Travel Centre (ETC) 30
Edward, Prince 279
Ehrwald 277–278
Einsiedeln 380
Einstein, Albert 296, 377, 396
Eisenstadt 157–159
electronic banking 11
electronic mail, see email
Eliot, George 300
Eliot, T.S. 296, 314
Elisabeth, Empress 103, 110
Elvis impersonators 164
email 58
embassies and consulates 4–5
 see also individual cities
emergency telephone numbers 12
Engadin Valley 441–451
Engelberg 389
entrance requirements 6
Erasmus 363
Erlach, Fischer von 71
Erste Donau Dampfschiffahrts-Gesellschaft, see DDSG
Esterházys 157
Esztergom 148
Eugene of Savoy, Prince 107
Eurailpass 38
Eurobus 40
Eurolines 40
Europass 38
Everlasting League (Ewige Bund) 290
Expressionism 73

F

Fackeltanz (torchdance) 221
fairy-tale castles 231
Falco 70, 96, 154
faxes 58
Federation of International Youth Travel Organizations (FIYTO) 2
Feldkirch 283–285
Ferdinand I 64
Ferdinand II 62
festivals 468
 bacon, Martigny 335
 Bad Ischl Operetten Festspiele 237
 La Bâtie Festival, Geneva 312
 Beethoven, Baden 156
 Blues, Bellinzona 432
 Bodensee-Festival 453
 Bregenzer Festspiele, Bregenz 288
 Bruckner, Linz 175
 Budapest Arts Weeks 147
 Budapest Spring Festival 147
 Chalandamarz, Zuoz 450
 classical music, Vevey 325
 comedy film, Vevey 325
 cow-carving, Brienz 402
 dance, Vienna 115
 Donaufestival, Krems 167
 Early Music, Innsbruck 272
 Escalade, Geneva 300
 Fasching, Vienna 117
 Fasnacht, Basel 365
 Fasnacht, Western Austria 234
 Festspiele, Salzburg 220
 Festwochen, Vienna 93
 Gauderfest, Zell am Ziller 252
 Glöcklerlaufen, Salzkammergut 234
 Grape Cure Week, Baden 156
 Gurten Festival, Bern 396
 International Film, Locarno 429
 International Folklore, Martigny 336
 International Music, Lucerne 387
 jazz, Bern 397
 jazz, Lugano 423
 jazz, Montreux 323
 jazz, Sion 338
 Jazzfest Wien, Vienna 115
 Kirchtag, Villach 188
 kite, Silvaplana 445

Montreux-Vevey Classical Music 324
music, Krems 167
music, Montreux 323
music, St. Pölten 151
Musiktage, Mondsee 239
New Orleans Music, Ascona 430
Open Air St. Gallen Music 457
Prague Spring Festival 133
San Gian's Day, Zuoz 451
Schubertiade, Feldkirch 285
Styriarte, Graz 202
Tibor Varga Classical Music, Martigny 336
Traveling Entertainers, Feldkirch 285
Vienna Festival 115
Wine Harvest, Lugano 423
wine, Eisenstadt 159
wine, Feldkrich 285
Fête des Vignerons, Vevey 326
Fêtes de Genève 312
film 29
firsts
 fire-fighting museum in Austria 159
 revolving cable car 389
 ski instructor 279
 skier 279
 university in Europe to admit women 377
Fischer von Erlach, Johann Bernard 201, 216
flower
 clock, Baden 156
 clock, Geneva 310
 huge animals made of 454
 Provincial Competition winner 190
Flying Wheels Travel 25
fondue 297
food and drink
 Austrian 75–76
 Swiss 297–298
forests
 Black 367
 Bohemian 149
 Dunkelsteiner 149
Franz Ferdinand, Archduke 65, 107
Franz II, Emperor 64, 110, 154
Franz Josef, Emperor 64, 65, 72, 103, 104, 105, 110, 186
Freedom Movement 66
Freistadt 179–181
Freud, Sigmund 74, 75, 96, 112

Fribourg (Freiburg) 356–359
Friedrich III 61, 194, 200
Friedrich the Great 63
Frisch, Max 296
frostbite 16
Fux, Johann Joseph 70

G

Gandria 424
Ganghofer, Ludwig 277
Garmisch-Partenkirchen 277
Gatsby, Jay 273
Gauguin, Paul 105
gay, see homosexual
Geneva
 accommodations 305–307
 disabled travelers 304
 embassies 302
 guided tours 308
 homosexual organizations 304
 museums 311
 nightlife 312 314
 practical information 301–305
 restaurants 307–308
 sights 308–312
 transportation 301
Geneva (Genève) 299–314
Geneva Convention 292, 300, 309
Gerlos 250
Giacometti, Alberto 295, 377, 383
Giacometti, Augusto 377
Giacometti, Giovanni 442
Giessbach Falls 403
Gimmelwald 417
glaciers
 Aletschgletscher, Europe's longest 413
 Diavolezza 448
 Grindelwald 412
 Hintertux 251
 Kitzsteinhorn 257
 Morteratsch 449
GO25 Card (International Youth Discount Travel Card) 8
Goebbels, Josef 66
Goethe, Johann Wolfgang von 69, 296
golem 131
government
 Austrian 66
 Swiss 293
Graubünden 433–451
Graz 194–202
 accommodations 197–198
 embassies 196

entertainment 201–202
homosexual organizations 197
nightlife 202
practical information 196–197
restaurants 198–199
sights 199–201
transportation 194
Greene, Graham 325
Grindelwald 410
 Glacier Gorge 412
Grisons, see Graubünden
Großglockner 253
Großglockner Straße 245, 252, 253–254
grottoes
 Beatushölen 402
grottos
 Pöstlingberg 175
Gruyères 358
Gstaad 326–328
Gurten Festival, Bern 396

H

Habsburgs 59, 61–65, 273, 290
Hagar the Horrible 155
Hagenbund 97
Hahnenkamm Ski Competition 247, 248
Hallstatt 241–244
handicaps, see disabled travelers
Hänsel and Gretel 367
Havel, Václav 129
Hawelka, Josephine and Leopold 96
Haydn Hall 158
Haydn, Josef 63, 67, 68, 69, 99, 157, 158
health 15–17
 AIDS 16
 contraception 16
 sexually transmitted diseases (STDs) 16
Heidi 433, 443
Heiligenblut 253
Helvetians 290
Hemingway, Ernest 320
Hercules 186
Hermes Villa 110
Hesse, Hermann 295
Heurigen 115, 120, 165
high-mountain-sweeping-panorama-hairpin-turn-sports-car commercials 253
hiking 53–55
 Appenzell 459
 Arosa 437
 backpacks 51
 Celerina 447
 Davos 439

INDEX ■ 485

equipment 51
Grindelwald 411
Innsbruck 272
Interlaken 408
Kitzbühel 248
Klosters 441
Lauterbrunnen 415
Liechtenstein 466
Maloja 443
Saas Fee 347
safety 52
St. Anton am Arlberg 281
Spiez 401
St. Moritz 445
Swiss National Park 450
Wengen 414
Zell am See 258
Zell am Ziller 251
Zermatt 343
Zillertal Alps 250
Zuoz 451
Hildebrandt, Lukas von 71
Hilterfingen 400
Hintertux 250
history
　Austrian 59-67
　Swiss 290-297
hitching 44
Hitler, Adolf 64, 72, 174, 201, 232
Hofburg, Vienna 101
Hoffmann, Joseph 72
Hofmannsthal, Hugo von 74
Hohe Tauern National Park 252
holidays 468
Hollein, Hans 73
Holy Roman Empire 61, 121, 290, 464
　end of 64
homosexual and bisexual travelers 25
homosexual organizations 25, 208
　Basel 362
　Bern 393
　Geneva 304
　Graz 197
　Innsbruck 266
　Klagenfurt 183
　Linz 173
　Lucerne 384
　Vienna 88
　Zurich 372
Homosexuelle Arbeitsgruppe 25
Homosexuelle Initiative (HOSI) 25
hostel in a castle 178
Hostelling International-American Youth Hostels (HI-AYH) 47
Hostelling International-Canada (HI-C) 47

hostels 45-47
　membership 45-47
Hotel Sacher, Vienna 97, 99
hotels 47
Hugo, Victor 323, 325
Hundertwasser Haus 106
Hundertwasser, Friedensreich 73, 106, 112
Hungary 64
Huns 60
hypothermia 53

I

Igls 272
Inferno Run 417
Innsbruck 263-273
　accommodations 268-269
　Club Innsbruck 272
　embassies 266
　entertainment 272-273
　Goldenes Dachl 270
　homosexual organizations 266
　nightlife 273
　outdoors 272
　practical information 264-268
　restaurants 269-270
　sights 270-272
　transportation 264
Innviertel 171
insurance 17
　car 9
　homeowners' 17
　medical 17
Interlaken 404-409
　accommodations 405-407
　Balmer's Herberge 405
　nightlife 409
　outdoors 407-409
　practical information 404-405
　restaurants 407
International Driving Permit (IDP) 8
International Reply Coupons (IRCs) 56
International Student Identity Card (ISIC) 8
International Student Travel Confederation 2
International Teacher Identity Card (ITIC) 8
International Youth Discount Travel Card (GO25 Card) 8
Internet resources 3-4
InterRail Pass 39
Investiture Conflict 61, 290
Iseltwald 403
ISIC (International Student Identity Card) 8

Italian Switzerland (Ticino) 418-433
ITIC (International Teacher Identity Card) 8

J

James, Henry 296, 325
Jasmine 418, 420, 429
Jedermann 221, 239
Jewish Ghetto, Vienna 99
Jewish Museum, Eisenstadt 159
Jewish neighborhood, Prague 131
Josef II, Emperor 63, 70, 109, 113, 116
Josefov, Prague 131
Joyce, James 296, 369, 377, 426
Jugendstil 72
Jung, Carl Gustav 295
Jungfrau Region 409-417
Jungfraujoch 412

K

Kafka, Franz 75, 93, 131
Kaiseraugst 366
Kaiser-Franz-Josefs-Höhe 254
Karl VI, Emperor 63, 169
Karlštejn 134
Keller, Gottfried 296
Kepler, Johannes 174, 194
Kimberlin, kinda sounds like 223
The Kiss 111
Kitzbühel 246-249
　accommodations 247
　hiking 248
　practical information 246
　restaurants 248
　skiing 248
　transportation 246
Klagenfurt 182-187
　accommodations 184
　homosexual organizations 183
　practical information 182-184
　restaurants 185
　sights 185-187
　transportation 182
Klee, Paul 73, 295, 395
Klestil, Thomas 67
Klimt, Gustav 72, 104, 105, 111
Klosterneuburg 121
Klosters 440-441
Kohl, Helmut Chancellor 235
Kokoschka, Oskar 73, 297
Königer, Veit 199
Konrad von Passau, Bishop 151

Konstanz, see Constance
kosher restaurants
  Kosher Butcher, Lucerne 386
  Schalom Café Restaurant, Zurich 375
  Topas Kosher Restaurant, Basel 363
kosher travelers 26
Kraus, Karl 74, 77, 96
Krems and Stein 165–167
Kremsmünster 176
Kremsmünster Abbey 176
Krimml 258
Krimmler Wasserfälle 245, 254, 258
Kristallnacht 99
Kunst Haus Wien 112
Kutná Hora 134

L

La Chaux-de-Fonds 351
Lac Léman, see Lake Geneva
Lake Constance, see Bodensee
Lake Geneva (Lac Léman) 299–332
Lake Neuchâtel Region 347–355
lakes
  Bodensee 263, 285
  Brienzersee 398, 402–404
  Chiemsee 231
  Erlaufsee 154
  Geneva (Léman) 299
  Hallstätter See 241
  Mondsee 237
  Neuchâtel 347
  Neusiedler See 159
  Schwarzsee 249, 343
  Silsersee 446
  Stausee 252
  Tauernmoos See 252
  Thunersee 398–402
  Trübsee 389
  Vierwaldstättersee 387, 389
  Weißsee 252
  Wetter See 250
  Zeller See 257
  Zurich 370, 379
largest
  onion dome in Europe 287
  organ in Switzerland 389
Lausanne 314–320
  accommodations 316
  museums 318
  nightlife 319
  practical information 314
  restaurants 316
  sights 317
Lauterbrunnen Valley 414–415

Lavertezzo 429
League of Nations 293, 300
Lech 282
Lechtaler Alps 276–278
Lenin, Vladimir 96, 300, 369
Leoben 190–192
Leopold I 161
Leopold II, Margrave 167
Leopold III 61
Leopold of Babenburg 61
Leopold V 61
Les Diablerets 330–332
lesbian, see homosexual
Lessing, Ephraim 100
Leysin 329–330
Liechtenstein 285, 464–466
Lienz 254, 259–262
  accommodations 260
  practical information 259
  restaurants 261
  sights 261
  transportation 259
Lindau im Bodensee, Germany 454
Lindt chocolate factory 379
Lindwurm 186
Linz 172–178
  accommodations 173
  practical information 172
  restaurants 174
  sights 174
  transportation 172
Linzer Torte 76, 174
Lipizzaner stallions 102, 110
Lisa's smiling face 438
literature
  Austrian 74–75
  Swiss 295
Locarno 425–429
  accommodations 427
  International Film Festival 429
  practical information 426–427
  restaurants 427–428
  sights 428–429
longest
  chairlift in Europe 411
  flight of steps in the world 401
long-term stays 49
Loos, Adolf 73, 95, 100
Looshaus 100
Louis XIV 63
Louis-Napoleon 293
Lower Austria 149–170
Lucerne 383–390
  accommodations 384–386
  daytrips 389
  homosexual organizations 384

International Rowing Regatta 388
Lion of Lucerne 387
Mt. Pilatus 389
museums 388
nightlife 388
practical information 383–384
restaurants 386–387
sights 387–388
Vierwaldstättersee 387
Lueger, Karl 64
Lugano 418–425
  accommodations 420–422
  daytrips 424
  embassies 419
  practical information 418–420
  restaurants 422
  sights 422–424
  transportation 418

M

Madonna del Sasso (Madonna of the Rock), Locarno 428
Madonna, Black 380
Mahler, Gustav 69
mail 55–56
Mainau, Germany 287, 453
Malbun 466
Maloja 442–443
Malojaschlange 442
Maria Enzersdorf 120
Maria Gail 190
Maria Theresa, Empress 63, 99, 102, 104, 154, 169, 186, 199, 270
Mariazell 151–154
Marie Antoinette 64, 270
Marriage Woods *(Heiratswald)*, Melk 170
Martigny 333–336
MasterCard 11
Matterhorn 339–344
Matterhornlauf 342
Mauthausen 176
Maximilian I, Emperor 71, 74, 105, 200
Mayrhofen 250
MCI, see telephones
Medic Alert 15
medication 15
Meiringen 404
Melk 167–170
Metternich, Clemens von 64
Meyer, Conrad Ferdinand 296
Minimundus Park, Klagenfurt 186
minority travelers 27
Model Mugging 13
Mödling 120–121

Mogersdorf, Battle of 192
Mönchsberg 215
Mondsee 237–239
money 9–12
  ATM cards 11
  currency exchange 9
  sending from home 12
  tipping 12
  traveler's checks 10
Montezuma 112
Montreux 320–324
  accommodations 321
  nightlife 324
  practical information 320
  restaurants 322
  sights 323
Montreux Jazz Festival 323
Moore, Henry 106
Morat Linden tree 357
Morat, see Murten 359
Mörbisch 163–164
Moser, Hans 165
most beautiful lakeside village in the world 241
mountains
  Axalphorn 403
  Braunarspitze 282
  Dom 345
  Eiger 409, 410
  Erzberg 190
  First 411
  Gerlosstein 251
  Giferspitz 327
  Grosse Scheidegg 411
  Großglockner 253
  Güggisgrat 401
  Harder 404
  Hohe Munde 274
  Jungfrau 409
  Jungfraujoch 412
  Karhorn 282
  Karwendel 274
  Kleine Scheidegg 411, 413
  Lauenehorn 327
  Leopoldsberg 100
  Männlichen 414, 411
  Matterhorn 339–344
  Mischabelhütte 347
  Mönch 409
  Mt. Pilatus 389
  Mount Titlis 389
  Mülenen 401
  Niedere Tauern 190
  Niesenberg 401
  Pfänder 287
  Piz Corvatsch 445
  Piz Julier 445
  Piz Muragl 449
  Piz Nair 445
  Pöstlingberg 175
  Ramsberg 251
  Rigi Kulm 389
  Rosaliengebirge 154
  Rothorn 402
  Rüflikopf 282
  Schafberg 239
  Schilthorn 416
  Schloßberg 194
  Schwarzhorn 412
  Schynige Platte 408
  Sternalm 262
  Valluga 279
  Weisshorn 435
  Wetterstein 274
  Wimmis 401
  Zeller 257
  Zugspitze 277
Mozart Serenaden (Mozart's Serenades) 221
Mozart, Constanze 217
Mozart, Leopold 68, 217
Mozart, Nannerl 68
Mozart, Wolfgang Amadeus 63, 67, 68, 69, 71, 103, 108, 110, 114, 133, 154, 216
Mozart's baby hair 216
Mozartkugeln 212
Mühlviertel 179–181
Mühlviertel Weberstraße 179
Munich 222–231
  accommodations 226–228
  beer 230
  daytrips 231
  embassies 223
  museums 229
  nightlife 230–231
  Oktoberfest 230
  practical information 223–226
  restaurants 228
  sights 228–229
Mürren 416
Murtal 190–202
Murten (Morat) 359
Mushroom Tower 192
music
  Austrian 67–71
  classical 68–69
  festivals, see festivals
  modern 70
  opera 68–71
  romantic 69–70
Mussolini 201

N

Naarn 164
Nabokov, Vladimir 320
Napoleon Bonaparte 64, 169, 190, 192, 194, 200, 299
national parks
  Hohe Tauern 252
  Swiss 449
national tourist offices, see tourist offices, national
Naturns, Italy 447
Nazis 66, 204
Neuchâtel 292, 347–353
Neuhausen 461
Neusiedl am See 160–161
Neusiedler See 159–164
neutrality 292
Nibelungenlied 61
Nic's favorite German word 412
Niedere Tauern mountains 190
Niederösterreich, see Lower Austria
Niesen Steps Race 401
Nietzsche, Friedrich 296, 446
Nonnberg Abbey 218
Nyon 313

O

ÖAMTC 43
Oberndorf 203
Oberösterreich, see Upper Austria
Obertraun 242, 244
Oktoberfest, Munich 230
Olbrich, Joseph Maria 72
older travelers 23
oldest stork colony in Switzerland 354
onion domes 287, 309
opera 70
Opera ball, Vienna 98
Österreichische Bundesbahn (ÖBB) 37
Österreichischer Alpenverein 54, 234, 259, 262, 264
Otto I 61
Ottokar II 61, 116
outdoors 49–55

P

Pacher, Michael 240
packing 28–30
  backpack 28
  clothing and footwear 29
  luggage 28
palaces
  Augarten, Vienna 109
  Belvedere, Vienna 107
  Budavári Palota, Budapest 145
  Herberstein, Graz 199
  Hofburg, Innsbruck 270
  Hofburg, Vienna 101, 104
  Hünegg, Thun 400
  Klosterneuberg 121
  Liechtenstein, Feldkirch 285
  Oberhofen, Thun 400
  Schaudau, Thun 400

INDEX

Schönbrunn, Vienna 107
Schwarzenberg, Vienna 107
see also castles
Panorama Highway 443
paragliding
   Gstaad 327
   Interlaken 408
   Liechtenstein 466
   Zell am See 258
   Zell am Ziller 251
Paragliding World Championships, Zell am Ziller 250
Passau, Germany 233
passports 5–6
   Canada 5
   Ireland 5
   New Zealand 6
   South Africa 6
   U.K. 6
   U.S. 6
Peace of Westphalia 62, 291
Peasants' Wars 62
pensions (Pensionen) 47
permits, work and study 18
Personal Identification Number (PIN) 11
Pferdeisenbahn 179
pharmacies 15
Picasso, Pablo 388
Pilgram, Anton 101
Pirates' Battle 203
plagues
   Black 284
   Bubonic 310
Planned Parenthood Federation 16
Plummer, Christopher 218
PLUS network 11
Polgar, Alfred 96
Pontresina 448–449
Poste Restante 56
Pragmatic Sanction 63
Prague 121–136
   accommodations 127
   cafés 130
   daytrips 134
   entertainment 133
   practical information 124
   sights 130
   Wenceslas Square 130
Prandtauer, Johann 71
Pressburg 68
Prien, Germany 231
Prince Eugene of Savoy 62
Prinzip, Gavrillo 65
private rooms (Privatzimmer) 47
Protestant Reformation 291
PTT postal bus 41
publications, travel 2
pun, requisite composer 108, 158
Pyhrn-Eisenwurz 171

R

Racial Purity Laws 66
raclette 298
Rail Europe Inc. 31
railpasses 38–39
   Austrian 23, 39
   international 38
   Swiss 23, 39
Recreational Equipment, Inc. (REI) 50
Red Cross 292, 293, 300
Regensburg, Germany 232
Reichenbach Falls 404
Reinhardt, Max 220
Reinhardt, Oskar 382
Rembrandt 111
Republic, First 65
Republic, Greater German 65
Republic, Helvetic 292
Republic, Second 60, 66
Rheinfalls 461
Richard the Lionheart 61
Riegersburg 192–194
Rigi Kulm 389
Rilke, Rainer Maria 75
Ringstraße 70, 71, 72, 86, 104
rivers
   Aare 390
   Danube 109, 164–170, 232
   Enns 177
   Inn 276
   Isel 259
   Lech 276
   Limmat 369
   Mur 190, 196
   Rhein 465
   Salzach 204
   Sihl 369
   Steyr 177
   Ticino 432
   Wien 109
rock-climbing
   Interlaken 408
Roman ruins
   Augusta Raurica 366
Romans 60, 290
Romansch 290
Rossini 296
Rothorn 402
Rottmayr 217
Rousseau, Jean-Jacques 295, 300, 309, 323, 325, 354
Rowing Regatta, Lucerne 388
Rubens, Peter Paul 111, 220
Rust 161–163

S

Saanen 326–328
Saas Fee 345–347
Sacher Torte 76, 97

safety and security 12–14
   outdoors 52
Sailer, Toni 248
Sailing and Windsurfing Championships, Swiss National 445
St. Anton am Arlberg 279–281
St. Barbara 203
St. Bernard Pass 333
St. Florian Abbey 176
St. Gallen 455–460
   practical information 455
   accommodations 456
   practical information 455–456
   restaurants 456
   sights 457–458
St. Gilgen 237
St. Märgen, Germany 368
St. Moritz 443–445
St. Moritz Tobogganing Club 447
St. Peter, Germany 368
St. Pölten 150–151
St. Wolfgang 239–241
salt 60, 203
Salt Princes 235
Salzburg 60, 204–222, 245
   accommodations 209–212
   beer gardens 214
   cafés 213
   daytrips 222
   embassies 206
   Glockenspiel 216
   Hohensalzburg (fortress) 215
   homosexual organizations 208
   Mönchsburg 215
   Mozart's birthplace 216
   Mozart's house 217
   museums 219
   music and entertainment 220–222
   music festival 220
   practical information 204–209
   restaurants 212–215
   Schloß Mirabell 217
   sights 215–220
   transportation 204
   University Church 216
   Wasserspiele (water fountains) 221
Salzburger Land 203–244
Salzkammergut 233–244
San Bernardino Pass 432
Schaffhausen 460–462
S-chanf 449, 450
Schiele, Egon 73
Schiller Bell 461

Schiller, Friedrich 69, 296, 409
Schilthorn 416
Schluchsee, Germany 367
Schnitzler, Arthur 74
Schönberg, Arnold 70, 120
Schönbrunn Palace, Vienna 107
Schubert House, St. Pölten 151
Schubert, Franz 67, 69, 71, 154
Schuschnigg, Kurt von 232
Schwarzenberg Palace, Vienna 107
Schwarzenegger, Arnold 75, 103, 194
Schwarzhorn 412
Schwarzsee 249, 343
Secession movement 72, 112
Seefeld in Tirol 273-276
Segantini, Giovanni 442, 444
Segl, see Sils
self-defense courses 13
senior citizens, see older travelers
Serbia 65
sexually transmitted diseases (STDs) 16
Shaw, George Bernard 416
Shelley, Mary 296
Shelley, Percy 296
Sherlock Holmes 404
Sils (Segl) 446-447
Silvaplana 445-446
Sion 336-338
Sittikus, Archbishop Markus 217, 218, 222
skiing 55
 Arlberg 279
 Arosa 437
 Celerina 447
 Davos 439
 Engadin Valley 441
 Gstaad 328
 Happy Ski Pass 276
 Innsbruck 272
 Interlaken 408
 Jungfrau 412
 Kitzbühel 248
 Klosters 441
 Les Diablerets 332
 Lienz 262
 Mürren 416
 Pontresina 449
 St. Anton 281
 Seefeld 276
 Seefeld in Tirol 276
 Wengen 413
 Zell am See 257
 Zell am Ziller 251
 Zermatt 342

Zillertal Alps 250
skikjöring 443
Snow White 457
Social Democrats 65, 66, 73
Soglio 443
Solari, Santino 217
solo traveling 28
Solothurn 353-355
Sonogo 429
The Sound of Music 216, 218-219
 children waving from the train 241
 "Do-re-mi" 218
 "Edelweiss" 219
 hiding behind the headstones 219
 the hills are alive with 219
 "How do you solve a problem like Maria?" 218
 "I Have Confidence" 218
 Liesl's kiss 218
 Live Dinner Show 219
 Maria's forbidden daytrips 219
 tours 218
 von Trapp home 218
 wedding scene 218, 219, 237
Spiez 400
St. Gallen
 museums 458
 nightlife 458
STA Travel 30, 31
Stairway to Heaven 451
stand-by flights 35
State Opera House, Vienna 70, 98, 113
Stechelberg 415
Stein am Rhein 462-463
Stein, see Krems and Stein
Steirische Eisenstraße (Styrian Iron Road) 190
Stephansdom 99
Steyr 177
storks 162, 354
Stowasser, Friedrich, see Hundertwasser, Friedensreich
Strauss, Johann 69, 154, 164
Strauss, Johann the Elder 69
Strauss, Richard 70, 108, 220
Stravinsky, Igor Fedorovitch 320
student discounts 8
study abroad 18
Styria 178, 182, 203
Styrian Iron Road *(Steirische Eisenstraße)* 190
Surlej 445

Swiss Alpine Club 55
Swiss Alpine Marathon 439
Swiss Card 39
Swiss embassies 5
Swiss Flexipass 39
Swiss Guard 291, 312
Swiss National Park 449
Swiss National Tourist Office 2
Swiss Touring Club 43
Swissair, see airlines
Swisspass 39
Switzerland 289-463
 art and architecture 294
 Central 369-417
 Eastern 418-463
 food and drink 297
 government 293
 history 290
 literature 295
 neutrality 292
 Western 299-368
Switzerland, Italian see Italian Switzerland
Szentendre 148

T

tallest
 bridge in Europe 271
Tassilo III, Duke 60
Tatzelworm 404
Taubenloch 355
teacher discounts 8
telegrams 57
telephones 56-57
Tell, William 291, 409
tennis, Austrian Open 249
tents 51
Terezín 134
Tessin, see Italian Switzerland
The Third Man 77, 109
Thirty Years War 62, 100
Thomas Cook 10
Thun 398
Thunersee 398-402
Ticino, see Italian Switzerland
ticket consolidators 33
ticks 16
Tinguely fountain 363
Tinguely, Jean 295, 357
tipping 12
Tirol 245, 263
Titisee, Germany 367
Titian 111, 220
tobogganing 439
Torte
 Linzer 76, 174
 Sacher 76, 97
Tour de Suisse 423
tourism alternatives 18-21
 study abroad 18
 volunteering 21

490 ■ INDEX

tourist offices, national 1, 37
Town Sign War 182
train travel 37-39
   Austrian passes 39
   Austrian Rail Pass 39
   Bundesnetzkarte 39
   CFF 38
   Eurailpass 38
   Europass 38
   international passes 38
   InterRail Pass 39
   Österreichische Bundesbahn (ÖBB) 37
   railpasses 38, 39
   SBB 38
   Swiss Card 39
   Swiss Flexipass 39
   Swisspass 39
   Winetrain 326
Trakl, Georg 74
Travel CUTS 31
travel organizations 2
traveler's checks 10
Treaty of Campo Formio 64
Treaty of Utrecht 63
Triberg, Germany 368
Triebwagen 250
Triesenberg 465
Triple Alliance 65
Triple Entente 65
Trotsky, Leon 96
Trzesniewski 93
Twain, Mark 296, 390
Twann 355
Twannbachschlucht 355
Tyrol, see Tirol

U

U.S. Citizens Emergency Service 12
United Nations 293, 300
United Nations European headquarters, Geneva 310
universities
   Basel 364
   Innsbruck 264
   Salzburg 216
   St. Gallen 457
   Vienna 105
   Zurich 377
Upper Austria 171, 203
Upper Liechtenstein 465-466
Urban Modernism 72
Urban Socialism 73
USIT 31

V

Vaduz 464-465
Valais (Wallis) 333-347
van Gogh, Vincent 105
vegetarian restaurants
   Gleich, Zurich 375
   Hiltl Vegi, Zurich 375
   Philippine Vegetarische Küche, Innsbruck 269
   Rote Lasche, Klagenfurt 185
   Vegy, Salzburg 213
vegetarian travelers 26
Velazquez, Diego 111
Venus of Willendorf 113, 170
Verzasca valley 429
Vevey 324-326
Vienna 77-120
   accommodations 89-92
   art museums 111
   Augarten 109
   bars 118
   Belvedere Palace 107
   buses 84
   camping 92
   Central Cemetery 108
   coffeehouses 95
   daytrips 120
   discos 119
   driving 84
   embassies 87
   entertainment 113-117
   ferries 84
   ferris wheel 109
   festivals 115
   gay clubs 120
   Haas Haus 99
   Hermes Villa 110
   Hofburg (Imperial Palace) 101, 104
   homosexual organizations 88
   hostels and dormitories 89
   Hotel Sacher 99
   hotels & pensions 91
   Hundertwasser Haus 106
   hydrofoils 84
   Jewish Cemetery 108
   Jewish Ghetto 99
   Jewish Museum 113
   Karl-Marx-Hof 106
   Kärntner Str. 86, 99
   Kunsthistorisches Museum 111
   museums 111-113
   music 113
   nightlife 117-120
   Opera ball 98
   orientation 86
   Philharmonic Orchestra 114
   practical information 86-89
   Prater 109
   public transportation 85
   restaurants 93
   Ringstraße 86
   Schönbrunn Palace 107
   Schwarzenberg Palace 107
   Secession Building 105
   sights 97-113
   State Opera House 98, 113
   Stephansdom 99, 100
   theater and cinema 114
   transportation 84-86
   university dorms 90
   weekend excursions 121
   wine gardens *(Heurigen)* 115
   winter festivities 117
Vienna Boys' Choir 71, 103, 109
Villach 188-190
Visa 10, 11
visas 18
Voltaire 296, 312
volunteering 21
von Trapp, Liesl 216
von Trapps 204, 218
von Wald, Scheck 165
Vorarlberg 263, 283-288
Vuillard 105

W

Wachau 149
Wagner, Otto 72, 106
Wagner, Richard 70, 72, 74, 296, 388
Waldheim, Kurt 67
Waldviertel 149
Wallis, see Valais
War of Austrian Succession 63
War of Spanish Succession 63, 271
Wasserspiele (water fountains), Salzburg 222
Wasteels 31
waterfalls
   Giessbach Falls 403
   Krimmler Wasserfälle 245, 254, 258
   Reichenbach Falls 404
   Rheinfalls 461
   Trümmelbach 415
Weggis 387
Weisshorn 435
Wenceslas Square 130
Wengen 413
Western Switzerland 299-368
Western Union 12
White Fleet 285
Wien, see Vienna
Wiener Sängerknabenchor, see Vienna Boys' Choir
Wiener Schnitzel 76
Wienerwald 111, 120, 154, 156

wine 477
  academy, Rust 163
  Ausbruch 161
  Austrian 76
  Cressier 351
  festival, Feldkirch 285
  Schafiser 355
  Sion 337
  tasting 155, 163
  Twanner 355
  Winetrain 326
Winterthur 381-383
Witch Museum, Riegersburg 193
Wolf Dietrich, Archbishop 216, 217, 222
Wolf, Hugo 69
women and travel 22
women-only accommodations
  Casa della Giovane, Lugano 421
  Foyer Hottingen, Zurich 374
  Hôme St-Pierre, Geneva 306
  Jugendhotel Marienberge, Munich 227
  Pension Bienvenue, Lausanne 316
work-abroad programs 20-21
World Cup Skiing 248
World Trade Organization (WTO) 310
World War I 65, 292
World War II 66, 293
World Wide Web 3
World Wildlife Federation 163

Y

youth discounts 8

Z

Zell am See 254, 255-258
  accommodations 256
  nightlife 258
  practical information 255
  restaurants 256
  sights 257
  transportation 255
  Zeller See 257
Zell am Ziller 250-252
Zermatt 339-344
  accommodations 340
  nightlife 341
  practical information 339
  restaurants 341
  skiing 342
Zernez 449
Zillertal Alps 249-252
zoos
  Alpenzoo, Innsbruck 271
  Schönbrunn, Vienna 108
  Zoologischer Garten, Basel 364
  Zurich 377
Zsinagóga, Budapest 146
Zugspitze 277
Zuoz 450-451
Zurich 369-381
  accommodations 373-374
  daytrips 380
  embassies 370
  homosexual organizations 372
  museums 378
  nightlife 379-380
  practical information 369-373
  restaurants 374-376
  sights 376-379
  transportation 369
  University of 377
Zwingli, Ulrich 291, 369

★Let's Go 1998 Reader Questionnaire★

Please fill this out and return it to **Let's Go, St. Martin's Press,** 175 Fifth Ave., New York, NY 10010-7848. All respondents will receive a free subscription to *The Yellowjacket,* the Let's Go Newsletter.

Name: _____
Address: _____
City: _____ **State:** _____ **Zip/Postal Code:** _____
Email: _____ **Which book(s) did you use?** _____
How old are you? under 19   19-24   25-34   35-44   45-54   55 or over
Are you (circle one)   in high school   in college   in graduate school   employed   retired   between jobs
Have you used Let's Go before? yes   no   **Would you use it again?** yes   no
How did you first hear about Let's Go? friend   store clerk   television   bookstore display   advertisement/promotion   review   other
Why did you choose Let's Go (circle up to two)? reputation   budget focus   price   writing style   annual updating   other: _____
Which other guides have you used, if any? Frommer's $-a-day   Fodor's   Rough Guides   Lonely Planet   Berkeley   Rick Steves   other: _____
Is Let's Go the best guidebook? yes   no
If not, which do you prefer? _____
Please rank each of the following parts of Let's Go 1 to 5 (1=needs improvement, 5=perfect). packaging/cover   practical information   accommodations   food   cultural introduction   sights   practical introduction ("Essentials")   directions   entertainment   gay/lesbian information   maps   other: _____
How would you like to see the books improved? (continue on separate page, if necessary) _____
_____
How long was your trip? one week   two weeks   three weeks   one month   two months or more
Which countries did you visit? _____
What was your average daily budget, not including flights? _____
Have you traveled extensively before? yes   no
Do you buy a separate map when you visit a foreign city? yes   no
Have you seen the Let's Go Map Guides? yes   no
Have you used a Let's Go Map Guide? yes   no
If you have, would you recommend them to others? yes   no
Did you use the Internet to plan your trip? yes   no
Would you use a Let's Go: recreational (e.g. skiing) guide   gay/lesbian guide   adventure/trekking guide   phrasebook   general travel information guide
Which of the following destinations do you hope to visit in the next three to five years (circle one)? South Africa   China   South America   Russia   Caribbean   Scandinavia   other: _____
Where did you buy your guidebook? Internet   chain bookstore   independent bookstore   college bookstore   travel store   other: _____